For Reference

Not to be taken from this room

THE
BOOK
OF THE
STATES

2011 EDITION
VOLUME 43

ISBN 978-0-87292-772-8

The Council of State Governments
Lexington, Kentucky

Headquarters: (859) 244-8000
Fax: (859) 244-8001
Internet: www.csg.org

Sharing capitol ideas.

Headquarters:
David Adkins, Executive Director/CEO
2760 Research Park Drive, P.O. Box 11910
Lexington, KY 40578-1910
Phone: (859) 244-8000
Internet: www.csg.org

Southern:
Colleen Cousineau, Director
P.O. Box 98129
Atlanta, GA 30359
Phone: (404) 633-1866
Internet: www.slcatlanta.org

Eastern:
Wendell M. Hannaford, Director
100 Wall Street, 20th Floor
New York, NY 10005
Phone: (212) 482-2320
Internet: www.csgeast.org

Western:
Kent Briggs, Director
1107 9th Street, Suite 730
Sacramento, CA 95814
Phone: (916) 553-4423
Internet: www.csgwest.org

Midwestern:
Michael H. McCabe, Director
701 E. 22nd Street, Suite 110
Lombard, IL 60148
Phone: (630) 925-1922
Internet: www.csgmidwest.org

Washington, D.C.:
Christopher Whatley, Director
444 N. Capitol Street, NW, Suite 401
Washington, D.C. 20001
Phone: (202) 624-5460
Internet: www.csg.org

Foreword

Dear Friends,

Since 1933, The Council of State Governments has served as a resource for state leaders and a catalyst for innovation and excellence in state governance. Deeply embedded in the DNA of CSG is a calling to use sound knowledge to accelerate the development and implementation of sound public policy. While we do that in many ways, our tradition of "sharing capitol ideas" is perhaps best embodied by the work you hold in your hands — *The Book of the States*.

Launched in 1935, *The Book of the States* has been a reference tool of choice, providing relevant, accurate and timely information, answers and comparisons for all 56 states, commonwealths and territories of the United States. Published on a biennial basis for 65 years, in 2002 CSG began releasing the text annually to better capture the pace of change and policy enactments of state governments. In 2010, CSG took this format shift to the next evolutionary level by making *The Book of the States* available online through CSG's Knowledge Center.

CSG's new *The Book of the States* online Web tool, found at *www.csg.org/bookofthestates*, provides immediate access to all of the data in the current edition. This site will soon house all the previous editions of the publication as well. As the Web tool grows, users will be able to view charts and tables in more than 50 different categories and create custom reports based on their queries. This new tool will enable unprecedented access to 76 years of historical state information available only from The Council of State Governments.

We have always believed information can only create knowledge if it is used. That is why we have worked hard to make certain today's generation of state leaders have the resources contained in *The Book of the States* at their fingertips.

The compilation of this book is a labor of love for CSG. This volume includes 200 in-depth tables, charts and figures illustrating how state government operates. We also have included more than 30 articles from state leaders, innovative thinkers, noted scholars and CSG's in-house policy experts that analyze and report on the transformations taking place in state government. We mine more than 500 sources to obtain the information shared here.

We are grateful for the collaborations from our friends and partners at the National Association of State Budget Officers, the National Association of State Treasurers, the National Lieutenant Governors Association, the National Center for State Courts, the National Conference of State Legislatures, the National Association of Secretaries of State, the National Association of Attorneys General, the National Association of State Auditors, Comptrollers and Treasurers, the National Association of State Chief Administrators, the National Emergency Management Association and the Federation of Tax Administrators. Additionally, the Bureau of Justice Statistics, the Bureau of Labor Statistics, the U.S. Department of Education and the Federal Highway Administration were essential to the success of this volume. We also could not do this work without the valued partnership CSG enjoys with the U.S. Census Bureau.

A large team of CSG professionals and contributors make this publication possible, but I want to make special mention of Managing Editor Audrey Wall. She works tirelessly to guide the development of this book. I appreciate all she does to help CSG fulfill its mission. She is ably assisted by many CSG colleagues, including our policy and creative services team. The contributions of Heather Perkins, a member of our membership services team, are also essential to the success of this work.

Finally, we dedicate this volume to our friend and CSG colleague, Kathy Shanklin. For more than 20 years she served as a member of CSG's headquarters team. She passed away in January 2011 after a courageous battle with cancer. Throughout her career, she served our members with dedication and the highest standard of professionalism. Her legacy lives on in all of us who remember her so fondly.

May 2011

David Adkins
Executive Director/CEO
The Council of State Governments

The Council of State Governments is our nation's only organization serving all three branches of state government. CSG is a region-based forum that fosters the exchange of insights and ideas to help state officials shape public policy. This offers unparalleled regional, national and international opportunities to network, develop leaders, collaborate and create problem-solving partnerships.

Staff Acknowledgements

The staff wishes to thank the authors who shared their expertise and insights, the hundreds of individuals in the states who responded to surveys conducted by The Council of State Governments, national organizations of state officials, federal agencies and think tank organizations who made their most recent data and information available for this volume.

The Book of the States 2011

Managing Editor .... Audrey S. Wall

Associate Editor .... Heather M. Perkins

Graphic Designer ...... Chris Pryor

Copy Editors .... Mary Branham
                               Jennifer Ginn

Other CSG Staff
Contributors .... Jennifer Burnett
                               Ericka Harney
                               Jennifer Horne
                               Debra Miller
                               Tim Weldon
                               Paige Anderson
                               Kasey D. Cooke
                               Carol Kaulig
                               Sean Slone
                               Nathan Dickerson
                               Crady DeGolian
                               John Mountjoy
                               Pam Goins
                               Bill Voit
                               Nancy Vickers

Table of Contents

Chapter Three
STATE LEGISLATIVE BRANCH 71

ARTICLES
2010 Legislative Elections

Legislative Options to Achieve Public Retirement Plan Reforms

TABLES
State Legislatures

Chapter Four
STATE EXECUTIVE BRANCH 115

ARTICLES
The State of the States: Governors Aggressively Chip Away

Gubernatorial Elections, Campaign Costs and Powers

TABLES
Governors

Executive Branch

ARTICLES
The Constant Evolution of the Office of Lieutenant Governor

CONTENTS

Chapter Five
STATE JUDICIAL BRANCH 191

Chapter Six
ELECTIONS 225

CONTENTS

Chapter Seven

STATE FINANCE

CONTENTS

Chapter Nine
SELECTED STATE POLICIES AND PROGRAMS 353

CONTENTS

Chapter One

STATE CONSTITUTIONS

State Constitutional Developments in 2010

By John Dinan

None of the 116 constitutional amendments enacted in 2010 attracted as much attention as California's 2008 same-sex marriage ban or other high-profile amendments in recent years. Nevertheless, some notable amendments were adopted. Voters approved rights amendments regarding health care, union organizing, affirmative action, guns and voting. Institutional design amendments were enacted regarding legislative redistricting, party primaries, legislative sessions and the gubernatorial recall. Policy amendments dealt with budgeting, rainy day funds, taxation, debt, education and veterans' benefits, among other issues.

State constitutional amendment activity was brisk in 2010, especially in comparison with recent years. Voters considered amendments regarding controversial issues such as health care, union organizing, affirmative action and abortion. Other amendments targeted the design of governing institutions on topics including redistricting, party primaries, legislative sessions and the gubernatorial recall. Policy amendments dealt with budgeting, rainy day funds, taxes, debt, education and veterans' benefits. Meanwhile, four of the 14 states that require periodic submission of a constitutional convention referendum held referendums in 2010 and all were defeated.

Constitutional Amendment and Revision Methods

Constitutional amendments appeared on the ballot in 2010 in 37 states, which is higher than the 30 states voting on amendments in the last even-year election in 2008 and slightly higher than the 34 states voting on amendments in the last midterm election in 2006. One hundred sixty-five amendments appeared on the ballot in 2010 and 116 were approved. These numbers exceed the data for 2008, when 140 amendments were proposed and 87 were approved, and are comparable to 2006, when 166 amendments were proposed and 125 were approved.

Legislative Proposals and Constitutional Initiatives

All the amendments on the ballot in 2010 were proposed by legislatures or through the initiative process. One hundred forty-eight amendments were proposed by legislatures, and 106 were approved by voters, for a passage rate of 71.6 percent. This is comparable to the approval rate for legislature-referred amendments in other years. Seventeen amendments were proposed via the

Table A: State Constitutional Changes by Method of Initiation: 2006–07, 2008–09 and 2010

Method of initiation	Number of states involved 2006–2007	Number of states involved 2008–2009	Number of states involved 2010	Total proposals (a) 2006–2007	Total proposals (a) 2008–2009	Total proposals (a) 2010	Total adopted (b) 2006–2007	Total adopted (b) 2008–2009	Total adopted (b) 2010	Percentage adopted (c) 2006–2007	Percentage adopted (c) 2008–2009	Percentage adopted (c) 2010
All methods...............	37	32	37	200 (d)	161 (e)	165	158 (d)	104 (e)	116 (f)	78.0	64.6	69.7
Legislative proposal...	36	31	35	167 (d)	127 (e)	148	147 (d)	88 (e)	107 (f)	86.8	69.3	71.6
Constitutional initiative..................	12	10	7	33	30	17	11	13	9	33.3	43.3	52.9
convention	...	...	...	...	...	...	...	...	...	...	...	...
commission.............	...	1	...	...	4	...	...	3	...	...	75.0	...

Source: John Dinan and The Council of State Governments, February 2011.

Key:
(a) Excludes Delaware, where proposals are not submitted to voters.
(b) Includes Delaware.
(c) In calculating the percentages, the amendments adopted in Delaware (where proposals are not submitted to voters) are excluded (two amendments were adopted in 2007 and one in 2010).
(d) Excludes one Alabama amendment that was proposed by the legislature and appeared on the ballot but was determined by the governor's office prior to the vote not to have received enough votes in the legislature to properly appear on the ballot, and thus even though the amendment was approved by voters in November 2006 and the vote totals were certified by the state canvassing board, the governor did not proclaim the results for the amendment and so it has not received an official amendment number.
(e) Excludes one New Mexico amendment approved by voters in November 2008 but declared invalid by the state supreme court on single-subject grounds in December 2008.
(f) Excludes one Alabama local amendment approved by voters in November 2010 but not certified pursuant to a court order.

initiative process and nine were approved, for a passage rate of 52.9 percent, which is slightly higher than the typical passage rate for initiated amendments. Additionally, one amendment was enacted in Delaware, which is unique among the states in that amendments there are approved by a two-thirds vote of the legislature in successive sessions without a popular referendum.

Alabama alone accounted for 47 proposed and 27 enacted amendments. The vast majority of these Alabama amendments were local amendments proposed by the legislature but only voted on by residents of the affected county.[1] The inclusion of these local amendments in the Alabama Constitution accounts, in part, for the reason Alabama has the longest constitution in the world.

Constitutional Commissions

The Utah Constitutional Revision Commission was the only constitutional commission active in 2010. Utah's commission is the only one in the country with an ongoing charge to propose constitutional amendments to the legislature for consideration and possible submission to voters. The commission also gives advice to legislators on amendments under consideration. The main item on the commission's agenda in 2010 was an amendment to prohibit racial preferences in government hiring and contracting and in university admissions. The commission held several meetings featuring remarks by supporters and critics, but commission members decided to delay issuing a recommendation until the measure is formally re-introduced in the legislature.

Constitutional Conventions

2010 brought important developments regarding constitutional conventions in two U.S. territories. The U.S. Virgin Islands is one of two territories — along with Guam — that do not have a constitution. A convention was held from 2007 to 2009 to draft an inaugural U.S. Virgin Islands constitution. The 30 convention delegates completed their work in May 2009, but Gov. John DeJongh Jr. determined the proposed constitution was inconsistent with various guarantees in the U.S. Constitution and should not be submitted to the president and Congress, who are required to give their approval before it can be voted on by residents of the territory.

Although that seemed to be the end of the process, in December 2009 the U.S. District Court for the U.S. Virgin Islands ordered the governor to submit the draft constitution to the president, who then forwarded it to Congress. House and Senate committees held hearings and in June 2010, Congress approved a resolution identifying a number of problems with the proposed constitution and urging the territorial convention to reconvene and consider changes to address these concerns. Failure of the convention to reconvene — and no steps have been taken toward this end — would bring an end to the fifth effort to draft a U.S. Virgin Islands constitution.

American Samoa is one of three territories — along with Puerto Rico and the Northern Mariana Islands — that have constitutions. In June 2010, American Samoa Gov. Togiola Tulafono called a convention to consider revisions to the territory's 1967 constitution. One hundred forty-five delegates participated in a two-week convention that concluded in July 2010 by agreeing to 34 recommended changes. These changes were submitted to voters in a single up-or-down vote. During the November 2010 election, voters rejected the package by a vote of 7,660 to 3,257.[2]

Four of the 14 states that require automatic submission of a convention referendum at regular intervals held referendums in 2010: Iowa, which requires a referendum every 10 years; Michigan, which requires a referendum every 16 years; and Montana and Maryland, which require a convention referendum every 20 years. All were defeated. In contrast with the 2008 election — when mandatory convention referendum campaigns in Connecticut, Hawaii and Illinois attracted significant attention and funding, especially from convention critics — the 2010 convention referendums did not generate much in the way of supporting or opposing campaigns.

Iowa's referendum attracted the most attention, with some critics of the Iowa Supreme Court's 2009 decision legalizing same-sex marriage viewing a convention as a vehicle for reversing the decision. The Iowa Catholic Conference endorsed the convention referendum for that reason. However, conservative critics of the state court ruling were divided on the merits of a convention, with some expressing concern about the unpredictable nature of a convention and the difficulty of confining the proceedings to selected issues. Iowa voters rejected the convention referendum by a 67 to 33 percent margin.

Michigan voters also rejected a convention referendum by a 67 to 33 percent margin. Outgoing Democratic Gov. Jennifer Granholm supported a convention out of a general desire to modernize the state constitution. However, the two main gubernatorial candidates to replace Granholm opposed a convention on the grounds that it would delay and hinder efforts to boost the state economy. Groups from across the political spectrum joined them in opposition, including the state Chamber of Commerce and AFL-CIO.

In Montana, voters rejected a convention referendum by a 58 to 42 percent margin. Adopted in 1972, the Montana Constitution is one of the most recent state constitutions, so there was little call for modernization of the document. Rather, convention supporters focused primarily on the benefits of revisiting privacy and environmental rights provisions that first appeared in the 1972 document and generated several controversial state court rulings. However, no organized campaigns came out for or against a convention, although many of the surviving delegates from the 100-member convention of 1971–72 opposed calling a convention.

In Maryland, the absence of a galvanizing issue or organized campaign suggested to many observers that the referendum would have no more success than the other three state convention referendums in 2010. The only meaningful support came from J.H. Snider, the president of a democracy-focused policy institute, who wrote newspaper editorials touting the benefits of a convention. Additionally, at a radio debate held on Oct. 21, 2010, between incumbent Democratic Gov. Martin O'Malley and Republican challenger Robert Ehrlich, both candidates responded to a reporter's question by expressing support in some fashion for the referendum. But neither campaigned on the issue and no groups put forth concerted efforts to rally support for or against a convention. It was quite a surprise, then, when 54 percent of voters who cast votes on the referendum supported it. However, Maryland requires a convention referendum to obtain the support of a majority of voters in the entire election, and because a number of voters left the referendum question blank, the measure obtained support from only 48.5 percent of voters and was rejected. Maryland's narrow rejection is the closest a mandatory convention referendum has come to passage since a New Hampshire referendum in 2002 attracted 49 percent of the vote. The last time a mandatory convention referendum was approved was in Rhode Island in 1984.[3]

Efforts to call conventions continued in several other states in 2010 but did not come close to generating convention referendums. In California, a lack of funding led the group Repair California to suspend its campaign to qualify two measures for the November 2010 ballot that would have enabled voters to call a convention via the initiative process. In Alabama, where the group Alabama Citizens for Constitutional Reform has been working for the better part of the past decade to obtain legislative support for a convention, legislators in the state house and senate introduced bills to call a convention referendum, but they were not brought to a vote in either chamber.

Constitutional Changes

Voters in 2010 considered rights-related amendments on topics including health care, union organizing, affirmative action, abortion, guns and voting. Voters also passed judgment on institutional reform amendments regarding redistricting, the frequency of legislative sessions, the gubernatorial recall and judicial selection. Policy-related amendments dealt with rainy day funds, taxation, debt, education and veterans' benefits, among other issues.

Individual Rights

Voters in two states in 2010 approved amendments prohibiting enforcement of any law requiring individuals to purchase health insurance or otherwise participate in a health care system. Arizona was the first state to vote on such an amendment in 2008, when voters narrowly defeated an initiated amendment intended to prevent the state legislature from enacting an individual mandate of the sort included in a 2006 Massachusetts health care law. The amendments proposed in 2010, however, were intended to target a provision in the recently enacted federal Patient Protection and Affordable Care Act that requires nearly all individuals to purchase health insurance or pay a financial penalty. Voters in Colorado rejected an initiated amendment along these lines, and the Florida Supreme Court ordered a legislature-referred amendment to be removed from the ballot on the grounds that the ballot language was ambiguous and misleading. However, voters in Arizona and Oklahoma approved legislature-referred "health freedom" amendments. Because these amendments—and the similar statutes adopted in six states in

Table B: Substantive Changes in State Constitutions: Proposed and Adopted: 2006–07, 2008–09 and 2010

Subject matter	Total proposed (a)			Total adopted (b)			Percentage adopted (c)		
	2006–2007	2008–2009	2010	2006–2007	2008–2009	2010	2006–2007	2008–2009	2010
Proposals of statewide applicability	172	123 (d)	122	134	77 (d)	89	76.7	62.6	72.1
Bill of Rights..............................	30 (e)	16	19	26 (e)	12	15	86.7	75.0	78.9
Suffrage & elections	7	11	15	4	6	12	57.1	54.5	80.0
Legislative branch......................	12	13	6	7	8	5	58.3	61.5	83.3
Executive branch	1	5	5	1	4	3	100.0	80.0	60.0
Judicial branch	8	1	6	6	0	5	50.0	0.0	66.7
Local government	1	3	5	0	0	2	0.0	0.0	40.0
Finance & taxation	65	37	33	51	18	25	78.5	48.6	75.8
State & local debt	10	6	12	9	6	11	90.0	100.0	91.7
State functions...........................	5	4	9	4	3	3	80.0	75.0	33.3
Amendment & revision.............	1	0	0	1	0	0	100.0	0.0	0.0
General revision proposals	0	0	0	0	0	0	0.0	0.0	0.0
Miscellaneous proposals............	32	27	12	25	20	8	78.1	74.1	66.7
Local amendments........................	28 (f)	38	43	24 (f)	27	27 (g)	85.7	71.1	62.8

Source: John Dinan and The Council of State Governments, February 2011.

Key:

(a) Excludes Delaware, where amendments do not require popular approval.

(b) Includes Delaware.

(c) In calculating the percentages, the amendments adopted in Delaware (where proposals are not submitted to voters) are excluded (two amendments were adopted in 2007 and one in 2010).

(d) Excludes one New Mexico amendment approved in November 2008 but declared invalid by the state supreme court in December 2008.

(e) Includes amendments restricting the use of eminent domain, regardless of whether these protections were actually inserted in the bill of rights or in other articles.

(f) Excludes one Alabama amendment that was proposed by the legislature and appeared on the ballot but was determined by the governor's office prior to the vote not to have received enough votes in the legislature to properly appear on the ballot, and thus even though the amendment was approved by voters in November 2006 and the vote totals were certified by the state canvassing board, the governor did not proclaim the results for the amendment and so it has not received an official amendment number.

(g) Excludes one Alabama local amendment approved by voters in November 2010 but not certified pursuant to a court order.

2010—conflict with the Affordable Care Act, they are not viewed as having legal effect. Their main purpose, aside from expressing popular disapproval of the federal law, is to create a conflict between state and federal law and thereby boost the prospects that federal lawsuits filed by state attorneys general challenging the constitutionality of the federal law will be deemed justiciable prior to the individual mandate actually taking effect in 2014.

Four states approved amendments targeting a proposed federal Employee Free Choice Act, which would limit secret balloting in union organizing campaigns and rely more often on a "card check" procedure for determining union representation. Voters in Arizona, South Carolina, South Dakota and Utah approved legislature-referred amendments guaranteeing individuals the right to a secret ballot not only in political elections, but also in any workplace election to determine union representation. The 111th Congress did not pass the Employee Free Choice Act, so it is unclear whether these state constitutional amendments have any effect or even if they would have had any effect if the act

had been enacted, given that these state amendments are seemingly pre-empted by federal labor relations statutes. Their primary purpose was to highlight an unpopular aspect of the Employee Free Choice Act as a way of preventing its passage or, failing that, to assist in legal challenges to its legitimacy.

Arizona became the fourth state to approve a constitutional amendment banning racial preferences in hiring, contracting and university admissions. In previous years, voters in California (1996), Michigan (2006) and Nebraska (2008) approved initiated amendments of this kind, and voters in Washington approved an initiated statute in 1998. Voters in Arizona were the first to approve a *legislature*-referred amendment seeking to limit affirmative action.

Although no amendments dealing explicitly with abortion appeared on the ballot in 2010, Colorado voters defeated an initiated amendment defining a "person" as any "human being from the beginning of the biological development of that human being." Colorado voters in 2008 defeated a similarly motivated but differently worded amendment defining personhood

Table C: State Constitutional Changes by Legislative and Initiative Proposal: 2010

State	Legislative proposal			Constitutional initiative		
	Number proposed	Number adopted	Percentage adopted	Number proposed	Number adopted	Percentage adopted
Alabama	47	27 (a)	57.4%			
Alaska	1	0	0.0			
Arizona	8	4	50.0			
Arkansas	3	3	100.0			
California	2	2	100.0	6	4	66.7
Colorado	3	1	33.3	4	0	0.0
Delaware	(b)	1	(b)			
Florida	3	1	33.3	3	2	66.7
Georgia	5	3	60.0			
Hawaii	2	2	100.0			
Idaho	4	4	100.0			
Illinois	1	1	100.0			
Indiana	1	1	100.0			
Iowa	1	1	100.0			
Kansas	2	2	100.0			
Louisiana	12	10	83.3			
Maryland	2	2	100.0			
Michigan	1	1	100.0			
Missouri	2	2	100.0	1	1	100.0
Montana				1	1	100.0
Nebraska	3	2	66.7			
Nevada	3	0	0.0			
New Jersey	1	1	100.0			
New Mexico	5	3	60.0			
North Carolina	1	1	100.0			
North Dakota	1	1	100.0			
Ohio	2	2	100.0			
Oklahoma	9	8	88.9	1	0	0.0
Oregon	5	5	100.0	1	1	100.0
Rhode Island	1	0	0.0			
South Carolina	4	4	100.0			
South Dakota	2	1	50.0			
Tennessee	1	1	100.0			
Utah	4	4	100.0			
Vermont	1	1	100.0			
Virginia	3	3	100.0			
Washington	2	2	100.0			
Totals	148	107	71.6 (c)	17	9	52.9

Source: John Dinan and The Council of State Governments, February 2011.
Key:
(a) Excludes one local amendment approved by voters in November 2010 but not certified pursuant to a court order.
(b) Delaware does not provide for submission of amendments to the people.
(c) Excludes Delaware's legislature-approved amendment.

as beginning "from the moment of fertilization." The intent of these amendments—a similar amendment has qualified for the 2011 Mississippi ballot—is presumably to create a conflict between state law and the U.S. Supreme Court's abortion jurisprudence and thereby provide a vehicle for the court to reconsider its precedents in this area.

Three states approved amendments dealing with gun rights in some fashion. Kansas voters approved an amendment making clear that individuals' right to bear arms is not tethered solely to "their defense and security." The amendment declares that: "A person has the right to keep and bear arms for the defense of self, family, home and state, for lawful hunting and recreational use, and for any other lawful purpose." Meanwhile, Arkansas and Tennessee voters approved amendments recognizing an individual's right to hunt and fish, while Arizona voters defeated a similar amendment.

Three states enacted amendments expanding the suffrage. A Vermont amendment permits 17-year-olds to vote in primary elections as long as they will turn 18 by the day of the general election. A Kansas amendment eliminated vague and sweeping language authorizing the legislature to disenfranchise individuals because of "mental illness." A New Mexico amendment eliminated outdated language disfranchising "idiots" and "insane persons" and instead provided for disqualification of individuals due to "mental incapacity," as indicated by an inability to mark a ballot or communicate a voting preference. This amendment also eliminated outdated age and residency requirements that had long been superseded by federal law.

Several other proposed or enacted rights amendments are also worthy of note. In response to the 2009 killing of four police officers by a man recently released on parole from another state, Washington voters approved an amendment permitting the denial of bail for certain offenses, "upon a showing by clear and convincing evidence of a propensity for violence that creates a substantial likelihood of danger to the community or any persons." Nevada voters, meanwhile, rejected a legislature-referred amendment that would have relaxed several restrictions on the eminent domain process that had been established through an initiated amendment approved in 2008.

Governing Institutions

The most important institutional design amendments approved in 2010 dealt with the redistricting process. A California amendment assigns the task of drawing congressional district lines to an independent commission created by a 2008 amendment and originally entrusted with the task of drawing state legislative district lines. As a result of this 2010 amendment—and the defeat of an initiated amendment that sought to effectively repeal the 2008 amendment—the 14-member commission will be responsible for redistricting both congressional and state legislative seats.

Meanwhile, an Oklahoma amendment changes the size and composition of that state's redistricting commission. Instead of a three-member commission comprised of the attorney general, treasurer and superintendent of public instruction, the 2010 amendment establishes a commission of seven members comprised of the lieutenant governor and two appointees each from the governor and the leaders of the house and senate. Florida voters approved two amendments that take a different approach to regulating the redistricting process. Rather than assigning the task of redistricting to an independent commission, two initiated amendments in Florida establish criteria the legislature must follow in drawing congressional and state legislative districts. Most important, districts and districting plans cannot be drawn to favor or disfavor an incumbent or political party.

California voters approved an amendment making an important change in the electoral system by instituting a top-two primary. Similar to a recently adopted system in Washington—and slightly different from the longstanding nonpartisan "Cajun" primary in Louisiana—the top-two primary requires all candidates for an office to run in a single primary. The top two candidates advance to the general election, regardless of their party affiliation.

Several states adopted amendments altering the qualifications for officeholders or the process

for removing officials. A North Carolina amendment prohibits convicted felons from running for county sheriff. A Michigan amendment prevents individuals from holding state or local elected office or certain non-elected positions for 20 years after their conviction for a felony involving dishonesty, deceit, fraud or breach of the public trust. Illinois became the 19th state to permit voters to recall public officials, albeit limited to the governor and pursuant to an unusual procedure whereby a certain number of state legislators from each party must first give their approval for a recall petition. Oklahoma voters approved an amendment imposing an eight-year lifetime limit on service in the governor's office and other statewide offices.

Several amendments dealt with the legislative branch. Most important, Oregon voters approved an amendment making Oregon the 46th state with annual legislative sessions. Louisiana voters approved an amendment moving up by several weeks the starting and ending dates of legislative sessions. Utah voters approved an amendment creating an independent legislative ethics commission. Voters in Alaska defeated an amendment that would have increased slightly the number of members in the house and senate.

Voters considered a number of amendments regarding the judiciary. Despite the strong backing of retired U.S. Supreme Court Justice Sandra O'Connor, Nevada voters rejected an amendment that would have replaced judicial elections with the Missouri Plan of judicial selection, where open seats are filled through gubernatorial appointment from a list of nominees identified by a merit commission and judges are subject to retention elections at periodic intervals. Nevada voters also rejected an amendment to create an intermediate appellate court. Oklahoma voters approved two judiciary-related amendments. One Oklahoma amendment changes the size and composition of the judicial nominating commission. Another Oklahoma amendment, which attracted significant attention and was enjoined from taking effect by a U.S. district judge ruling on Nov. 29, 2010, prohibits state judges from relying on international or Sharia law.

As has been the norm in recent years, legislatures proposed several amendments to change initiative and referendum processes. Arizona voters defeated an amendment to make it more difficult to use the initiative process by requiring initiative backers to gather signatures on petitions and submit them two months earlier than currently required. But Oklahoma voters approved an amendment that facilitates use of the initiative process by changing the method of calculating how many signatures initiative-backers must obtain in order to qualify a measure for the ballot.

Voters considered assorted other amendments regarding governing institutions. Hawaii voters approved an amendment replacing the current elected state school board with a board made up of gubernatorial appointees. Voters in Louisiana approved an amendment similar to the 27th Amendment to the U.S. Constitution, in that it prohibits pay raises for legislators and other officials from taking effect until an election has been held after the legislative vote on the pay increase. Colorado voters approved an amendment authorizing the temporary removal of the seat of government from Denver in case of a disaster emergency. Nebraska voters, meanwhile, declined to approve an amendment eliminating the state treasurer position.

Policy
The most important policy amendment in 2010 was a California amendment repealing the requirement that two-thirds of the legislature must approve the state budget. Voter approval of this initiated amendment means that only two states—Arkansas and Rhode Island—retain supermajority requirements for passing a budget. However, in the same election, California voters approved an initiated amendment extending an existing two-thirds requirement for increasing taxes by applying this rule to the imposition of new fees as well.

Voters in several states approved amendments increasing taxes or dedicating taxes or other revenues to certain purposes. An Arizona amendment in May 2010 increases the sales tax by 1 cent for a three-year period. Iowa voters approved a complicated amendment that does not increase the sales tax, but rather provides that if the legislature decides to increase the sales tax, three-eighths of the increase must be dedicated to a Natural Resources and Outdoor Recreation Trust Fund. An Oregon initiated amendment permanently dedicates 15 percent of annual lottery revenue to parks and natural resources.

On the other hand, voters approved several tax-limitation amendments. An Indiana amend-ment limits property taxes to a percentage of the assessed value of the property. Meanwhile, voters in Missouri and Montana, two of the 13 states that do not currently impose real estate transfer taxes, approved initiated amendments prohibiting imposition of such a tax. Colorado voters rejected an amendment that would have imposed stringent limits on local taxes, even beyond the limits contained in the Colorado Taxpayers Bill of Rights.

A number of amendments require or permit property tax exemptions for certain groups, such as veterans in Louisiana, disabled veterans in Virginia, veterans' organizations in New Mexico, disabled prisoners of war in Missouri, and active-duty military deployed overseas in Florida. Virginia voters also approved an amendment making it easier for senior citizens or disabled people to qualify for property tax exemptions.

Other amendments dealt with state rainy day funds, by requiring or permitting more funds to be deposited in reserve funds. Voters in Virginia and Hawaii approved amendments allowing the legislature to increase the rainy day fund, whether by increasing the maximum size of the fund, as in Virginia, or authorizing the legislature to deposit excess revenue into the rainy day fund rather than having to refund or credit such revenue to taxpayers, as in Hawaii. Meanwhile, South Carolina and Oklahoma amendments required more funds to be deposited each year into the rainy day fund. A North Dakota amendment requires certain oil and gas revenues to be deposited into a newly created legacy fund.

A number of amendments dealt with state and local borrowing. Colorado voters rejected an amendment that attracted significant national attention. It would have prohibited all state borrowing and imposed significant restrictions on local borrowing. On the other hand, voters approved amendments facilitating the issuance of general obligation bonds for various purposes (economic development in Arkansas and Ohio and education in Oregon), authorizing additional uses of revenue bonds (in Nebraska) and enabling various entities to incur multi-year debt without a referendum (in Idaho). Voters in Washington approved an amendment making it easier for the state to qualify for the federal Build America Bonds program created in the 2009 federal stimulus package.

Several notable education amendments went down in defeat. A legislature-referred amendment in Florida would have relaxed various caps on K–12 class sizes imposed via a 2002 initiated amendment. Although this amendment received 54 percent of the vote, Florida has required, since 2006, that all constitutional changes surpass a 60 percent popular vote threshold, and so it was defeated. Oklahoma voters rejected a highly unusual initiated amendment mandating that the state's per-pupil education spending meet or surpass the average per-pupil spending of all of the states surrounding Oklahoma. Meanwhile, voters in Idaho approved an amendment authorizing the University of Idaho to charge tuition; previously, the University of Idaho had only been allowed to charge fees.

Several states approved amendments granting benefits to veterans. In addition to various amendments exempting veterans from property taxes, a New Mexico amendment allows veterans to pay in-state university tuition and an Oregon amendment increases veterans' eligibility for low-interest home loans.

Voters also considered assorted other policy amendments. Oklahoma voters approved an amendment requiring official state actions to be in English, unless federal law requires the use of other languages. Rhode Island voters soundly defeated an amendment that would have changed the state name from "The State of Rhode Island and Providence Plantations" to simply "Rhode Island." Florida voters rejected an initiated amendment that would have required any changes in local land-use plans to be approved by popular referendum.

Conclusion

Several trends emerge from a review of state constitutional developments in 2010. During the past decade, state constitutional amendment processes have come to serve in various ways as vehicles for exceeding or challenging federal standards, and this continued in 2010. Earlier in the decade, two states enacted amendments—others proceeded on a statutory basis—legalizing medicinal marijuana in the face of a contrary congressional statute. Four states enacted amendments—others again proceeded on a statutory basis—establishing a higher minimum wage than is guaranteed by federal law. And nine states adopted major amendments containing tighter restrictions on the eminent domain power than the U.S. Supreme Court was willing to require in the 2005 *Kelo* decision. In 2010, the principal tar-

gets of state constitutional amendment activity were the recently enacted federal health care law and a proposed union organizing bill. Arizona and Oklahoma enacted amendments expressing opposition and facilitating challenges to the federal health care law, and similar amendments have been circulated in other states for placement on the 2011 and 2012 ballots. Meanwhile, Arizona, South Carolina, South Dakota and Utah approved amendments seeking to achieve similar ends regarding the proposed union organizing bill.[4]

Second, groups continue to turn to the constitutional initiative process to achieve goals that proved unattainable through ordinary political processes. In previous years, initiated amendments have been used to adopt legislative term limits and tax and expenditure limitations, among other institutional and policy changes. In 2010, the constitutional initiative process was the vehicle for adopting several reforms that otherwise would not have found favor with legislators. Voters approved initiated amendments imposing significant restrictions on the redistricting process, as in Florida, and assigned the task of congressional redistricting to an independent commission, as in California. Meanwhile, California voters approved an amendment eliminating the requirement that budgets be passed by a two-thirds legislative vote.

Third, constitutional amendments are frequently a product of contemporary issues and concerns. This was particularly evident in 2010 in the numerous amendments making provision for larger rainy day funds in response to the economic downturn and associated budget shortfalls.

Finally, for the past quarter century, voters have been reluctant to call constitutional conventions. This was evident in 2010 in the rejection of mandatory convention referendums in Iowa, Maryland, Michigan and Montana. However, voters came close to approving the Maryland referendum, and in fact a majority of voters who cast ballots on the convention referendum in that state supported the measure. Three more mandatory convention referendums will be held in 2012 in Alaska, New Hampshire and Ohio and will provide additional opportunities to gauge public support for calling constitutional conventions.

Notes

[1] In fact, one local amendment was approved in November 2010 by a majority of the voters in Blount County but was not certified as a result of an order by a Blount County circuit court that the amendment had been incorrectly placed on the ballot as a local amendment. Therefore, this amendment is not included in the number of amendments approved in Alabama in 2010.

[2] Associated Press, "Faleomavaega wins 12th election to Congress," Nov. 4, 2010, *http://www.kpua.net/news.php?id=21505*.

[3] John Dinan, "The Political Dynamics of Mandatory State Constitutional Convention Referendums: Lessons from the 2000s Regarding Obstacles and Pathways to their Passage," *Montana Law Review* 71 (Summer 2010): 395–432.

[4] On this phenomenon, see John Dinan, "State Constitutional Amendment Processes and the Safeguards of American Federalism," *Penn State Law Review* (forthcoming).

Acknowledgements

The Council of State Governments and the author would like to thank the following individuals for their contribution.

Alabama	Nancy Ekberg
Alaska	Jerry McBeath
Arizona	Toni McClory
Arkansas	Art English
Colorado	Richard B. Collins
Florida	Rebecca Mae Salokar
Hawaii	Anne Feder Lee
Illinois	Ann Lousin
	Victor Salas
Louisiana	Warren M. Billings
Michigan	Robert Allen Sedler
Montana	Fritz Snyder
Nebraska	Anthony B. Schutz
Nevada	Eric Herzik
New Jersey	Robert F. Williams
New Mexico	K. Seckler
New York	Robert N. Wells
North Carolina	John Dinan
North Dakota	Dana Michael Harsell
Ohio	Steven H. Steinglass
Rhode Island	Mel A. Topf
South Dakota	Michael Card
Utah	Robert H. Rees
Virginia	John Dinan
Washington	Hugh D. Spitzer

About the Author

John Dinan is associate professor of political science at Wake Forest University in North Carolina. He is the author of *The American State Constitutional Tradition* and various articles on state constitutionalism.

Table 1.1
GENERAL INFORMATION ON STATE CONSTITUTIONS
(As of January 1, 2011)

State or other jurisdiction	Number of constitutions*	Dates of adoption	Effective date of present constitution	Estimated length (number of words)	Number of amendments Submitted to voters	Adopted
Alabama	6	1819, 1861, 1865, 1868, 1875, 1901	Nov. 28, 1901	367,000 (a)(b)	1,179	854 (c)
Alaska	1	1956	Jan. 3, 1959	13,479	42	29
Arizona	1	1911	Feb. 14, 1912	47,306	266	147
Arkansas	5	1836, 1861, 1864, 1868, 1874	Oct. 30, 1874	59,120	196	98 (d)
California	2	1849, 1879	July 4, 1879	67,048	891	525
Colorado	1	1876	Aug. 1, 1876	66,140	336	155
Connecticut	4	1818 (f), 1965	Dec. 30, 1965	16,401	31	30
Delaware	4	1776, 1792, 1831, 1897	June 10, 1897	25,445	(e)	141
Florida	6	1839, 1861, 1865, 1868, 1886, 1968	Jan. 7, 1969	56,705	154	118
Georgia	10	1777, 1789, 1798, 1861, 1865, 1868, 1877, 1945, 1976, 1982	July 1, 1983	41,684	94 (g)	71 (g)
Hawaii	1 (h)	1950	Aug. 21, 1959	21,498	131	110
Idaho	1	1889	July 3, 1890	24,626	210	123
Illinois	4	1818, 1848, 1870, 1970	July 1, 1971	16,401	18	12
Indiana	2	1816, 1851	Nov. 1, 1851	11,476	79	47
Iowa	2	1846, 1857	Sept. 3, 1857	11,089	59	54 (i)
Kansas	1	1859	Jan. 29, 1861	14,097	125	95 (i)
Kentucky	4	1792, 1799, 1850, 1891	Sept. 28, 1891	27,234	75	41
Louisiana	11	1812, 1845, 1852, 1861, 1864, 1868, 1879, 1898, 1913, 1921, 1974	Jan. 1, 1975	69,876	233	164
Maine	1	1819	March 15, 1820	16,313	204	171 (j)
Maryland	4	1776, 1851, 1864, 1867	Oct. 5, 1867	43,198	261	225 (k)
Massachusetts	1	1780	Oct. 25, 1780	45,283 (l)	148	120
Michigan	4	1835, 1850, 1908, 1963	Jan. 1, 1964	31,010	68	30
Minnesota	1	1857	May 11, 1858	11,734	215	120
Mississippi	4	1817, 1832, 1869, 1890	Nov. 1, 1890	26,229	158	123
Missouri	4	1820, 1865, 1875, 1945	March 30, 1945	69,394	175	114
Montana	2	1889, 1972	July 1, 1973	12,790	56	31
Nebraska	2	1866, 1875	Oct. 12, 1875	34,934	350 (m)	228 (m)
Nevada	1	1864	Oct. 31, 1864	37,418	232	136 (i)
New Hampshire	2	1776, 1784	June 2, 1784	13,060	287 (n)	145
New Jersey	3	1776, 1844, 1947	Jan. 1, 1948	26,360	79	44
New Mexico	1	1911	Jan. 6, 1912	33,198	293 (y)	160 (y)
New York	4	1777, 1822, 1846, 1894	Jan. 1, 1895	44,397	295	220
North Carolina	3	1776, 1868, 1970	July 1, 1971	17,177	43	35
North Dakota	1	1889	Nov. 2, 1889	18,746	265	150 (o)
Ohio	2	1802, 1851	Sept. 1, 1851	52,995	284	171
Oklahoma	1	1907	Nov. 16, 1907	81,666	354 (p)	187 (p)
Oregon	1	1857	Feb. 14, 1859	49,016	490 (q)	249 (q)
Pennsylvania	5	1776, 1790, 1838, 1873, 1968 (r)	1968 (r)	26,078	36 (r)	30 (r)
Rhode Island	3	1842 (f), 1986 (s)	Dec. 4, 1986	11,407	12 (s)	10 (s)
South Carolina	7	1776, 1778, 1790, 1861, 1865, 1868, 1895	Jan. 1, 1896	27,421	686 (t)	497 (t)
South Dakota	1	1889	Nov. 2, 1889	27,774	229	215
Tennessee	3	1796, 1835, 1870	Feb. 23, 1870	13,960	62	39
Texas	5 (u)	1845, 1861, 1866, 1869, 1876	Feb. 15, 1876	86,936	642 (v)	467
Utah	1	1895	Jan. 4, 1896	17,849	167	115
Vermont	3	1777, 1786, 1793	July 9, 1793	8,565	212	54
Virginia	6	1776, 1830, 1851, 1869, 1902, 1970	July 1, 1971	21,899	54	46
Washington	1	1889	Nov. 11, 1889	32,578	176	103
West Virginia	2	1863, 1872	April 9, 1872	33,324	121	71
Wisconsin	1	1848	May 29, 1848	15,102	194	145 (i)
Wyoming	1	1889	July 10, 1890	26,349	125	98
American Samoa	2	1960, 1967	July 1, 1967	6,000	15	7
No. Mariana Islands	1	1977	Jan. 9, 1978	11,000	60	56 (w)(x)
Puerto Rico	1	1952	July 25, 1952	9,281	6	6

See footnotes at end of table.

GENERAL INFORMATION ON STATE CONSTITUTIONS — Continued
(As of January 1, 2011)

Source: John Dinan and The Council of State Governments, February 2011, with research assistance from Bradley Harper.

*The constitutions referred to in this table include those Civil War documents customarily listed by the individual states.

Key:

(a) The Alabama constitution includes numerous local amendments that apply to only one county. An estimated 70 percent of all amendments are local. A 1982 amendment provides that after proposal by the legislature to which special procedures apply, only a local vote (with exceptions) is necessary to add them to the constitution.

(b) An estimate based on prior word counts and recent amendments.

(c) The total number of Alabama amendments includes one that is commonly overlooked.

(d) Eight of the approved amendments have been superseded and are not printed in the current edition of the constitution. The total adopted does not include five amendments proposed and adopted since statehood.

(e) Proposed amendments are not submitted to the voters in Delaware.

(f) Colonial charters with some alterations served as the first constitutions in Connecticut (1638, 1662) and in Rhode Island (1663).

(g) The Georgia constitution requires amendments to be of "general and uniform application throughout the state," thus eliminating local amendments that accounted for most of the amendments before 1982.

(h) As a kingdom and republic, Hawaii had five constitutions.

(i) The figure includes amendments approved by the voters and later nullified by the state supreme court in Iowa (three), Kansas (one), Nevada (six) and Wisconsin (two).

(j) The figure does not include one amendment approved by the voters in 1967 that is inoperative until implemented by legislation.

(k) Two sets of identical amendments were on the ballot and adopted in the 1992 Maryland election. The four amendments are counted as two in the table.

(l) The printed constitution includes many provisions that have been annulled.

(m) The 1998 and 2000 Nebraska ballots allowed the voters to vote separately on "parts" of propositions. In 1998, 10 of 18 separate propositions were adopted; in 2000, 6 of 9.

(n) The constitution of 1784 was extensively revised in 1792. Figure shows proposals and adoptions since the constitution was adopted in 1784.

(o) The figures do not include submission and approval of the constitution of 1889 itself and of Article XX; these are constitutional questions included in some counts of constitutional amendments and would add two to the figure in each column.

(p) The figures include five amendments submitted to and approved by the voters which were, by decisions of the Oklahoma or U.S. Supreme Courts, rendered inoperative or ruled invalid, unconstitutional, or illegally submitted.

(q) One Oregon amendment on the 2000 ballot was not counted as approved because canvassing was enjoined by the courts.

(r) Certain sections of the constitution were revised by the limited convention of 1967–68. Amendments proposed and adopted are since 1968.

(s) Following approval of the eight amendments and a "rewrite" of the Rhode Island Constitution in 1986, the constitution has been called the 1986 Constitution. Amendments since 1986 total twelve proposed and ten adopted. Otherwise, the total is 110 proposals and 62 adopted.

(t) In 1981 approximately two-thirds of 626 proposed and four-fifths of the adopted amendments were local. Since then the amendments have been statewide propositions.

(u) The Constitution of the Republic of Texas preceded five state constitutions.

(v) The number of proposed amendments to the Texas Constitution excludes three proposed by the legislature but not placed on the ballot.

(w) By 1992, 49 amendments had been proposed and 47 adopted. Since then, one was proposed but rejected in 1994, all three proposals were ratified in 1996 and in 1998, of two proposals one was adopted.

(x) The total excludes one amendment ruled void by a federal district court.

(y) The total excludes one amendment approved by voters in November 2008 but later declared invalid on single subject grounds by the state supreme court.

Table 1.2
CONSTITUTIONAL AMENDMENT PROCEDURE: BY THE LEGISLATURE
Constitutional Provisions

State or other jurisdiction	Legislative vote required for proposal (a)	Consideration by two sessions required	Vote required for ratification	Limitation on the number of amendments submitted at one election
Alabama	3/5	No	Majority vote on amendment	None
Alaska	2/3	No	Majority vote on amendment	None
Arizona	Majority	No	Majority vote on amendment	None
Arkansas	Majority	No	Majority vote on amendment	3
California	2/3	No	Majority vote on amendment	None
Colorado	2/3	No	Majority vote on amendment	None (b)
Connecticut	(c)	(c)	Majority vote on amendment	None
Delaware	2/3	Yes	Not required	No referendum
Florida	3/5	No	3/5 vote on amendment (d)	None
Georgia	2/3	No	Majority vote on amendment	None
Hawaii	(e)	(e)	Majority vote on amendment (f)	None
Idaho	2/3	No	Majority vote on amendment	None
Illinois	3/5	No	(g)	3 articles
Indiana	Majority	Yes	Majority vote on amendment	None
Iowa	Majority	Yes	Majority vote on amendment	None
Kansas	2/3	No	Majority vote on amendment	5
Kentucky	3/5	No	Majority vote on amendment	4
Louisiana	2/3	No	Majority vote on amendment (h)	None
Maine	2/3 (i)	No	Majority vote on amendment	None
Maryland	3/5	No	Majority vote on amendment	None
Massachusetts	Majority (j)	Yes	Majority vote on amendment	None
Michigan	2/3	No	Majority vote on amendment	None
Minnesota	Majority	No	Majority vote in election	None
Mississippi	2/3 (k)	No	Majority vote on amendment	None
Missouri	Majority	No	Majority vote on amendment	None
Montana	2/3 (i)	No	Majority vote on amendment	None
Nebraska	3/5	No	Majority vote on amendment (f)	None
Nevada	Majority	Yes	Majority vote on amendment	None
New Hampshire	3/5	No	2/3 vote on amendment	None
New Jersey	(l)	(l)	Majority vote on amendment	None (m)
New Mexico	Majority (n)	No	Majority vote on amendment (n)	None
New York	Majority	Yes	Majority vote on amendment	None
North Carolina	3/5	No	Majority vote on amendment	None
North Dakota	Majority	No	Majority vote on amendment	None
Ohio	3/5	No	Majority vote on amendment	None
Oklahoma	Majority	No	Majority vote on amendment	None
Oregon	(o)	No	Majority vote on amendment (p)	None
Pennsylvania	Majority (p)	Yes (p)	Majority vote on amendment	None
Rhode Island	Majority	No	Majority vote on amendment	None
South Carolina	2/3 (q)	Yes (q)	Majority vote on amendment	None
South Dakota	Majority	No	Majority vote on amendment	None
Tennessee	(r)	Yes (r)	Majority vote in election (s)	None
Texas	2/3	No	Majority vote on amendment	None
Utah	2/3	No	Majority vote on amendment	None
Vermont	(t)	Yes	Majority vote on amendment	None
Virginia	Majority	Yes	Majority vote on amendment	None
Washington	2/3	No	Majority vote on amendment	None
West Virginia	2/3	No	Majority vote on amendment	None
Wisconsin	Majority	Yes	Majority vote on amendment	None
Wyoming	2/3	No	Majority vote in election	None
American Samoa	2/3	No	Majority vote on amendment (u)	None
No. Mariana Islands	3/4	No	Majority vote on amendment	None
Puerto Rico	2/3 (v)	No	Majority vote on amendment	3

See footnotes at end of table.

CONSTITUTIONAL AMENDMENT PROCEDURE: BY THE LEGISLATURE — Continued
Constitutional Provisions

Source: John Dinan and The Council of State Governments, February 2011.

Key:

(a) In all states not otherwise noted, the figure shown in the column refers to the proportion of elected members in each house required for approval of proposed constitutional amendments.

(b) Legislature may not propose amendments to more than six articles of the constitution in the same legislative session.

(c) Three-fourths vote in each house at one session, or majority vote in each house in two sessions between which an election has intervened.

(d) Three-fifths vote on amendment, except amendment for "new state tax or fee" not in effect on Nov. 7, 1994 requires two-thirds of voters in the election.

(e) Two-thirds vote in each house at one session, or majority vote in each house in two sessions.

(f) Majority vote on amendment must be at least 50 percent of the total votes cast at the election (at least 35 percent in Nebraska); or, at a special election, a majority of the votes tallied which must be at least 30 percent of the total number of registered voters.

(g) Majority voting in election or three-fifths voting on amendment.

(h) If five or fewer political subdivisions of the state are affected, majority in state as a whole (and also in affected subdivisions) is required.

(i) Two-thirds of both houses.

(j) Majority of members elected sitting in joint session.

(k) The two-thirds must include not less than a majority elected to each house.

(l) Three-fifths of all members of each house at one session, or majority of all members of each house for two successive sessions.

(m) If a proposed amendment is not approved at the election when submitted, neither the same amendment nor one which would make substantially the same change for the constitution may be again submitted to the people before the third general election thereafter.

(n) Amendments concerning certain elective franchise and education matters require three-fourths vote of members elected and approval by three-fourths of electors voting in state and two-thirds of those voting in each county.

(o) Majority vote to amend constitution, two-thirds to revise ("revise" includes all or a part of the constitution).

(p) Emergency amendments may be passed by two-thirds vote of each house, followed by ratification by majority vote of electors in election held at least one month after legislative approval. There is an exception for an amendment containing a supermajority voting requirement, which must be ratified by an equal supermajority.

(q) Two-thirds of members of each house, first passage; majority of members of each house after popular ratification.

(r) Majority of members elected to both houses, first passage; two-thirds of members elected to both houses, second passage.

(s) Majority of all citizens voting for governor.

(t) Two-thirds vote senate, majority vote house, first passage; majority both houses, second passage. As of 1974, amendments may be submitted only every four years.

(u) Within 30 days after voter approval, governor must submit amendment(s) to U.S. Secretary of the Interior for approval.

(v) If approved by two-thirds of members of each house, amendment(s) submitted to voters at special referendum; if approved by not less than three-fourths of total members of each house, referendum may be held at next general election.

Table 1.3
CONSTITUTIONAL AMENDMENT PROCEDURE: BY INITIATIVE
Constitutional Provisions

State or other jurisdiction	Number of signatures required on initiative petition	Distribution of signatures	Referendum vote
Arizona	15% of total votes cast for all candidates for governor at last election.	None specified.	Majority vote on amendment.
Arkansas	10% of voters for governor at last election.	Must include 5% of voters for governor in each of 15 counties.	Majority vote on amendment.
California	8% of total voters for all candidates for governor at last election.	None specified.	Majority vote on amendment.
Colorado	5% of total legal votes for all candidates for secretary of state at last general election.	None specified.	Majority vote on amendment.
Florida	8% of total votes cast in the state in the last election for presidential electors.	8% of total votes cast in each of 1/2 of the congressional districts.	Three-fifths vote on amendment except amendment for "new state tax or fee" not in effect Nov. 7, 1994 requires 2/3 of voters voting in election.
Illinois (a)	8% of total votes cast for candidates for governor at last election.	None specified.	Majority voting in election or 3/5 voting on amendment.
Massachusetts (b)	3% of total votes cast for governor at preceding biennial state election (not less than 25,000 qualified voters).	No more than 1/4 from any one county.	Majority vote on amendment which must be 30% of total ballots cast at election.
Michigan	10% of total voters for all candidates at last gubernatorial election.	None specified.	Majority vote on amendment.
Mississippi (c)	12% of total votes for all candidates for governor in last election.	No more than 20% from any one congressional district.	Majority vote on amendment and not less than 40% of total vote cast at election.
Missouri	8% of legal voters for all candidates for governor at last election.	The 8% must be in each of 2/3 of the congressional districts in the state.	Majority vote on amendment.
Montana	10% of qualified electors, the number of qualified voters to be determined by number of votes cast for governor in preceding election in each county and in the state.	The 10% to include at least 10% of qualified voters in 1/2 of the counties.	Majority vote on amendment.
Nebraska	10% of registered voters.	The 10% must include 5% in each of 2/5 of the counties.	Majority vote on amendment which must be at least 35% of total vote at the election.
Nevada	10% of voters who voted in entire state in last general election.	None in effect after a U.S. District Court ruling in 2004 invalidated the requirement.	Majority vote on amendment in two consecutive general elections.
North Dakota	4% of population of the state.	None specified.	Majority vote on amendment.
Ohio	10% of total number of electors who voted for governor in last election.	At least 5% of qualified electors in each of 1/2 of counties in the state.	Majority vote on amendment.
Oklahoma	15% of legal voters for state office receiving highest number of voters at last general state election.	None specified.	Majority vote on amendment.
Oregon	8% of total votes for all candidates for governor at last election at which governor was elected for four-year term.	None specified.	Majority vote on amendment except for supermajority equal to supermajority voting requirement contained in proposed amendment.
South Dakota	10% of total votes for governor in last election.	None specified.	Majority vote on amendment.
No. Mariana Islands	50% of qualified voters of commonwealth.	In addition, 25% of qualified voters in each senatorial district.	Majority vote on amendment if legislature approved it by majority vote; if not, at least 2/3 vote in each of two senatorial districts in addition to a majority vote.

Source: John Dinan and The Council of State Governments, February 2011.
Key:
(a) Only Article IV, the Legislature Article, may be amended by initiative petition.
(b) Before being submitted to the electorate for ratification, initiative measures must be approved at two sessions of a successively elected legislature by not less than one-fourth of all members elected, sitting in joint session.
(c) Before being submitted to the electorate, initiated measures are sent to the legislature, which has the option of submitting an amended or alternative measure alongside of the original measure.

Table 1.4
PROCEDURES FOR CALLING CONSTITUTIONAL CONVENTIONS
Constitutional Provisions

State or other jurisdiction	Provision for convention	Legislative vote for submission of convention question (a)	Popular vote to authorize convention	Periodic submission of convention question required (b)	Popular vote required for ratification of convention proposals
Alabama	Yes	Majority	ME	No	Not specified
Alaska	Yes	No provision (c)(d)	(c)	10 years; 2002 (c)	Not specified (c)
Arizona	Yes	Majority	(e)	No	MP
Arkansas	No	No			
California	Yes	2/3	MP	No	MP
Colorado	Yes	2/3	MP	No	ME
Connecticut	Yes	2/3	MP	20 years; 2008 (f)	MP
Delaware	Yes	2/3	MP	No	No provision
Florida	Yes	(g)	MP	No	3/5 voting on proposal
Georgia	Yes	(d)	No	No	MP
Hawaii	Yes	Not specified	MP	9 years; 2008	MP (h)
Idaho	Yes	2/3	MP	No	Not specified
Illinois	Yes	3/5	(i)	20 years; 2008	MP
Indiana	No	No			
Iowa	Yes	Majority	MP	10 years; 2010	MP
Kansas	Yes	2/3	MP	No	MP
Kentucky	Yes	Majority (j)	MP (k)	No	No provision
Louisiana	Yes	(d)	No	No	MP
Maine	Yes	(d)	No	No	No provision
Maryland	Yes	Majority	ME	20 years; 2010	MP
Massachusetts	No	No			
Michigan	Yes	Majority	MP	16 years; 2010	MP
Minnesota	Yes	2/3	ME	No	3/5 voting on proposal
Mississippi	No	No			
Missouri	Yes	Majority	MP	20 years; 2002	Not specified (l)
Montana	Yes (m)	2/3	MP	20 years; 2010	MP
Nebraska	Yes	3/5	MP (o)	No	MP
Nevada	Yes	2/3	ME	No	No provision
New Hampshire	Yes	Majority	MP	10 years; 2002	2/3 voting on proposal
New Jersey	No	No			
New Mexico	Yes	2/3	MP	No	Not specified
New York	Yes	Majority	MP	20 years; 1997	MP
North Carolina	Yes	2/3	MP	No	MP
North Dakota	No	No			
Ohio	Yes	2/3	MP	20 years; 1992	MP
Oklahoma	Yes	Majority	(e)	20 years; 1970	MP
Oregon	Yes	Majority	(e)	No	No provision
Pennsylvania	No	No			
Rhode Island	Yes	Majority	MP	10 years; 2004	MP
South Carolina	Yes	(d)	ME	No	No provision
South Dakota	Yes	(d)	(d)	No	(p)
Tennessee	Yes (q)	Majority	MP	No	MP
Texas	No	No			
Utah	Yes	2/3	ME	No	ME
Vermont	No	No			
Virginia	Yes	(d)	No	No	MP
Washington	Yes	2/3	ME	No	Not specified
West Virginia	Yes	Majority	MP	No	Not specified
Wisconsin	Yes	Majority	MP	No	No provision
Wyoming	Yes	2/3	ME	No	Not specified
American Samoa	Yes	(r)	No	No	ME (s)
No. Mariana Islands	Yes	Majority (t)	2/3	10 years	MP and at least 2/3 in each of 2 senatorial districts
Puerto Rico	Yes	2/3	MP	No	MP

See footnotes at end of table.

PROCEDURES FOR CALLING CONSTITUTIONAL CONVENTIONS — Continued
Constitutional Provisions

Source: John Dinan and The Council of State Governments, February 2011.

Key:

MP — Majority voting on the proposal.

ME — Majority voting in the election.

(a) In all states not otherwise noted, the entries in this column refer to the proportion of members elected to each house required to submit to the electorate the question of calling a constitutional convention.

(b) The number listed is the interval between required submissions on the question of calling a constitutional convention; where given, the date is that of the most recent submission of the mandatory convention referendum.

(c) Unless provided otherwise by law, convention calls are to conform as nearly as possible to the act calling the 1955 convention, which provided for a legislative vote of a majority of members elected to each house and ratification by a majority vote on the proposals. The legislature may call a constitutional convention at any time.

(d) In these states, the legislature may call a convention without submitting the question to the people. The legislative vote required is two-thirds of the members elected to each house in Georgia, Louisiana, South Carolina and Virginia; two-thirds concurrent vote of both branches in Maine; three-fourths of all members of each house in South Dakota; and not specified in Alaska, but bills require majority vote of membership in each house. In South Dakota, the question of calling a convention may be initiated by the people in the same manner as an amendment to the constitution (see Table 1.3) and requires a majority vote on the question for approval.

(e) The law calling a convention must be approved by the people.

(f) The legislature shall submit the question 20 years after the last convention, or 20 years after the last vote on the question of calling a convention, whichever date is last.

(g) The power to call a convention is reserved to the people by petition.

(h) The majority must be 50 percent of the total votes cast at a general election or at a special election, a majority of the votes tallied which must be at least 30 percent of the total number of registered voters.

(i) Majority voting in the election, or three-fifths voting on the question.

(j) Must be approved during two legislative sessions.

(k) Majority must equal one-fourth of qualified voters at last general election.

(l) Majority of those voting on the proposal is assumed.

(m) The question of calling a constitutional convention may be submitted either by the legislature or by initiative petition to the secretary of state in the same manner as provided for initiated amendments (see Table 1.3).

(n) Two-thirds of all members of the legislature.

(o) Majority must be 35 percent of total votes cast at the election.

(p) Convention proposals are submitted to the electorate at a special election in a manner to be determined by the convention. Ratification by a majority of votes cast.

(q) Conventions may not be held more often than once in six years.

(r) Five years after effective date of constitutions, governor shall call a constitutional convention to consider changes proposed by a constitutional committee appointed by the governor. Delegates to the convention are to be elected by their county councils. A convention was held in 1972.

(s) If proposed amendments are approved by the voters, they must be submitted to the U.S. Secretary of the Interior for approval.

(t) The initiative may also be used to place a referendum convention call on the ballot. The petition must be signed by 25 percent of the qualified voters or at least 75 percent in a senatorial district.

Chapter Two

FEDERALISM AND INTERGOVERNMENTAL RELATIONS

State-Federal Relations: Civil War Redux?

By John Kincaid

The 2010 elections exacerbated party polarization and, along with it, a polarization of state-federal relations, which is produced when one party controls most of the federal government and another party controls most of the states. The 2010 federal health care law aggravated this polarization and, because of its impacts on the states, produced an unprecedented challenge to its constitutionality by more than half the states. The 2010 federal financial regulation law and the U.S. Supreme Court's application of the Second Amendment to the states also presage further federal incursions into state and local governance at a time when federal budget cutbacks and rising social welfare costs will heighten state and local fiscal stress.

Ironically, in the year marking the 150th anniversary of the start of the Civil War in 1861, more than half the states are challenging a major federal law as violating state sovereignty. Some states also enacted or are considering resolutions to nullify federal laws, and some are debating a proposed constitutional amendment to allow states to repeal federal laws.[1] About 24 states have rejected the federal REAL ID Act; several states are considering bills to deny U.S. citizenship to children born to illegal immigrants; and three states have spurned federal funds to construct high-speed railways. Another 17 states are seeking to block federal regulation of carbon emissions; Gulf Coast states are resisting a presidential moratorium on offshore oil drilling; 11 legislatures are considering bills requesting more proof that President Barack Obama was born in the United States; and most states are pushing back against the federal government on Medicaid and other major matters. The governor of Texas has declared that "states must band together to fight against the intrusion of a federal government that seems to know no limit to its own wisdom,"[2] and a 2010 poll found 63.4 percent of Americans agreeing that "the federal government interferes in states' decision-making."[3]

At the same time, the federal government has blocked key sections of Arizona's immigration law in court while several other states are pondering similar legislation; the Democratic president intervened rhetorically to support state-local public employee unions in Wisconsin against their Republican governor and legislative majority; and the U.S. Environmental Protection Agency has made an unprecedented move to cancel the authority of a state (i.e., Texas) to issue permits to large power and manufacturing facilities under the Clean Air Act.

State-federal conflict has reached an unprecedented level. The only thing missing from the landscape is Fort Sumter itself. This conflict, however, is not a war between the states, but between the states and the federal government over the limits of federal power and the prerogatives of the states. This conflict is driven mainly by the polarized character of American politics today.

Party Polarization and Federalism

Partisan polarization is a leading feature of contemporary political life. Congress was more polarized between liberal Democrats and conservative Republicans in 2010 than at any time since 1982, when *National Journal* first compiled its polarization data.[4] Congressional polarization has risen steadily and dramatically since 1978.[5] Polarization has infected virtually all political institutions, many media sources and many voters too. The incivility of public discourse—so much commented upon after the tragic shooting of U.S. Congresswoman Gabrielle Giffords and others on Jan. 8, 2011, in Tucson, Ariz.—is one manifestation of this polarization as many Americans hold increasingly intense and self-righteous political views.

Polarization has had two notable impacts on the federal system. First, it has contributed significantly to centralization and coercive federalism because control of Congress, the White House and a majority of the state legislatures and governorships by one party (which might be called unified federalism) smoothes the way for expansive federal policymaking. State partisan allies of the party in power in Washington, D.C., tend to embrace policies emanating from their federal counterparts. Second, polarization contributes significantly to state-federal conflict when the party in power in Washington, D.C., faces a majority of states controlled by the other party (which might be called divided federalism).

The 2010 elections produced such a standoff. Republicans captured the U.S. House of Representatives (241 Republicans, 193 Democrats) while Democrats maintained control of the U.S. Senate (53 Democrats, 47 Republicans) and White House. Republicans gained control of 29 governorships (with Democrats controlling 20 and an independent, but former Republican, in office in Rhode Island) and 26 state legislatures. Another seven legislatures were split between the two parties, and 16 were held by Democrats.[6] Republicans held control of both the legislature and the governorship in 21 states and Democrats held control in 11 states, although Democrats retained control of 26 attorney generalships.

Constitutional Challenges to the Federal Health Law

The most dramatic and confrontational example of this polarization is the constitutional challenge mounted by Republican governors or attorneys general of 28 states against President Obama's chief legislative achievement, the Patient Protection and Affordable Care Act. This law was a major overhaul of the country's health care system. It requires all individuals to purchase health insurance beginning in 2014; authorizes states to sell federally approved health insurance products through state-operated exchanges with a government subsidy for low-income people; expands Medicaid eligibility up to 133 percent of the poverty level; prohibits denial of health insurance for pre-existing conditions; eliminates lifetime coverage limits; and allows young people to remain on their parents' insurance to age 26.

The challengers' principal contention is that the federal health care reform violates state sovereignty. Specifically, they challenge the legislation's individual mandate, saying it exceeds Congress's commerce power. This mandate requires every uninsured citizen and legal resident to purchase federally approved health insurance by 2014 unless they are exempt (e.g., for religious reasons). Those who do not buy insurance will have to pay to the U.S. Treasury an annual penalty of $750 or 2 percent of their annual income (whichever is higher) by 2016. When Congress debated this mandate, the president said the penalty was "absolutely not" a tax or tax increase. In response to states' challenges, the U.S. Department of Justice defended the mandate as a proper exercise of Congress' "power to lay and collect taxes."[7]

The key issues are whether "activity" is required for Congress to employ its interstate commerce power and whether the individual mandate is "activity" or "inactivity." The challengers contend the individual mandate regulates inactivity—because not buying insurance is "inactivity"—and that compelling individuals to purchase insurance would remove all conceivable limits on Congress's commerce power and nullify the concept of federalism that is embedded in the principle of limited federal power. The defenders of health care reform contend that activity is not needed to trigger Congress's commerce power, but that even if it is required, not purchasing insurance is "activity." They also argue the individual mandate can be upheld because it is an appropriate exercise of Congress's power "to make all Laws necessary and proper" to regulate interstate commerce.

Another challenge to the health care reform law is that it violates the 10th Amendment because it commandeers the states to enforce federal law. This ground might be tenuous, though, because the legislation allows states to implement their own provisions or let the federal government do so instead. Some states contend the law also violates the Constitution's spending clause, as well as the Ninth and 10th amendments because it unilaterally increases state Medicaid costs. In addition, Virginia's attorney general filed a separate lawsuit contending that his state's law nullifying the health care reform legislation pre-empts federal law.

As of February 2011, three federal district court judges (all appointed by Democratic presidents) had upheld health care reform, while two federal district court judges (both appointed by Republican presidents) had struck down all or parts of it. Some 29 state legislatures are considering state constitutional amendments to nullify sections of the health care reform law, while more than half have rejected such nullification proposals. Consistent with party polarization, the majority of Democratic governors and legislatures support health care reform, while the majority of Republican governors and legislatures oppose it. Nevertheless, nearly all the states are proceeding with its implementation.

Selected Contours of Coercive Federalism

Does this revolt of the states presage the demise of coercive federalism and a rebalancing of state-federal power? Probably not. The revolt is a product of policy disagreements drawn along polarized party lines; it is not a bipartisan revolt based on federalism principles. When either party controls the federal government, it wields federal power on behalf of its national policy preferences regardless of the preferences of the majority of state officials. The current revolt might curb expansions of federal power in certain policy fields, but will not likely reverse the long-term historical trend of coercive federalism associated with centralization because future elections will produce unified federalism, both Democratic and Republican.

Federal Grants-in-Aid

Federal aid to state and local governments is expected to decrease from $625.2 billion in 2011 to $584.2 billion in 2012 and $567.5 billion in 2013, Federal aid is expected to begin rising again to $622.9 billion in 2014, $660.9 billion in 2015, and $703.2 billion in 2016. Aid is expected to decline from 17.6 percent of federal outlays in 2010 to 15.7 percent in 2016 and from 4.2 percent of GDP in 2010 to 3.6 percent in 2016. Consequently, fiscally stressed state and local governments cannot expect federal funds to alleviate their distress over the next several years.

More importantly, federal aid has shifted dramatically from places to persons since 1978.[8] In 1978, an historic high point in federal aid, only 31.8 percent of aid was dedicated to payments for individuals (i.e., Medicaid and other social welfare). In 2011, 62.8 percent of aid was dedicated to payments for individuals. In 2016, an astounding 78.2 percent of aid will go to payments for individuals according to the president's Office of Management and Budget.

This shift in the composition of federal aid has had six major consequences for state and local governments. For one, it has reduced aid for place-based functions, such as economic development, infrastructure, criminal justice, environmental protection and government administration. Medicaid alone now accounts for nearly half of all federal aid. Because of Medicaid especially, "other federal grants—including those for education, highways, weatherization, housing, and other programs—are projected to decline as a percentage of GDP after 2010," reported the Government Accountability Office (GAO).[9] A long-term impact of this shift is likely to be reduced state and local spending on infrastructure, higher education and other core "place" functions that provide public goods beneficial to all citizens. States now engage in many redistributive functions that transfer wealth from the young to the old and, to a lesser extent, the wealthy to the poor.

Second, this shift has hooked state budgets to social-welfare programs susceptible to escalating federal regulation, cost-shifting, and matching state —and sometimes local—costs, with Medicaid being the gorilla in state budgets. By 2020, states also will pay a portion of the costs arising from the 2010 health care reform law. Because of the aging population, the long-term care portion of Medicaid will become especially costly.

Third, the shift has heightened the role of states as administrative agents for the federal government, whereby they deliver services to individuals on behalf of the federal government under federal rules.

Fourth, the shift of aid from places to persons is the major factor in the decline of federal aid for local governments since the mid-1970s. States are the primary recipients of federal aid for social welfare. Local governments will likely experience further aid reductions, with municipal governments being affected most acutely because they perform the fewest social welfare functions. Spring 2011 negotiations over the federal government's 2012 fiscal year budget pointed toward cuts in such locally important programs as the Community Development Block Grant, Brownfields Economic Development Initiative and the Low-Income Home Energy Assistance Program. In turn, states will have less revenue to send to local governments.

Fifth, the growing scarcity of federal aid for non-social welfare functions will increase competition among all the public and private entities that now receive aid. This competition also will inhibit efforts to consolidate the federal government's 1,122 grants[10] into block grants, because interest groups will defend programs that benefit them.

Sixth, this shift partly explains why, despite the huge increase in federal aid since 1987, federal aid has not significantly alleviated long-term state-local fiscal stress and why the infusion of $87 billion for Medicaid through the American Recovery and Reinvestment Act of 2009 still left most states with large budget shortfalls even after the 2009 end of the recession.

Another coercive aid characteristic is the increased use of crosscutting and crossover conditions (i.e., rules and regulations) attached to federal aid since the mid-1960s. These conditions advance federal policy objectives, some of which fall outside of Congress' constitutional powers, and also extract state and local spending for those objectives.

One category of conditional aid that has been increasing is congressional earmarking. Earmarks in appropriations bills increased from 1,439 in 1995 to 9,129 in 2010, costing $16.5 billion.[11] Congress is reining in overt earmarks because many voters now view them as wasteful, but earmarks are likely to quietly continue (e.g., telephone earmarking).

Escalating Fiscal Crisis

Overall, state-federal relations will be shaped increasingly by fiscal austerity, which will further weaken state and local powers. Austerity will be driven mostly by rising social welfare spending that will siphon funds from critical state and local government functions, such as infrastructure, criminal justice, education and economic development, and also will constrain economic growth. In turn, reduced economic growth will increase social welfare needs and reduce revenues. State and local governments will have less room to raise taxes because the federal government will be the stronger tax competitor. The federal government will limit state and local authority to tax activities deemed important for interstate and global commerce. Citizens will restrain state and local taxes more readily than federal taxes because state constitutional amendments and other tools of democracy—such as the initiative, referendum and recall—are more accessible than are federal officials and the U.S. Constitution.

The GAO estimates that without policy changes, the federal government faces unsustainable debt growth.[12] The 2007–09 recession exacerbated the problem. The GAO concluded, "debt held by the public as a share of GDP could exceed the historical high reached in the aftermath of World War II by 2020."[13] Debt could grow to 85 percent of GDP by 2018 and exceed 100 percent by 2022.[14]

If Congress wishes to prevent debt over the next 75 years from exceeding its 2010 level (53 percent of GDP), it will have to increase revenue by 50 percent or reduce noninterest spending by 34 percent. Under current policies, demographic changes (mostly a growing population of senior citizens), rising health care costs and deficit spending will require the federal government to spend 93 cents of every dollar of federal revenue by 2030 on its major entitlement programs and net interest payments.[15] The Urban Institute[16] and the National Research Council and National Academy of Public Administration[17] issued equally dismal analyses, attributing the causes mostly to an aging population and rising Social Security, Medicare and Medicaid costs.

The GAO also projects fiscal decline for state and local governments through 2060 and expects revenue growth as a percentage of GDP to remain flat.[18] In order to stem this decline, state and local governments will have to reduce spending by about 12.3 percent annually for the next 50 years or increase revenues by a comparable level. The principal driver of state fiscal decline is health care costs, mostly Medicaid and health insurance for state and local government employees and retirees. The health care reform law, moreover, which increases Medicaid eligibility to 133 percent above the poverty line, will likely increase Medicaid enrollment by about 25 percent (18 million more enrollees) by 2014. In addition, state and local governments face huge pension liabilities, along with other social welfare costs for such programs as the Children's Health Insurance Program, Temporary Assistance for Needy Families and unemployment insurance.

Federal Mandates on State and Local Governments

Federal mandates are legal requirements that state or local officials perform functions under pain of civil or criminal penalties. Congress enacted one major mandate in 1931, one in 1940, none during 1941–63, nine during 1964–69, 25 during the 1970s, and 27 in the 1980s. After considerable state and local pressure, however, Congress enacted the Unfunded Mandates Reform Act in 1995. This law is one of the few restraints on coercive federalism. The reform act cut unfunded mandate enactments, though it did not eliminate existing mandates. Only 11 intergovernmental mandates with costs above the reform act's cost threshold were enacted between 1995 and 2010.[19]

However, the Unfunded Mandates Reform Act covers only some of the federal actions imposing costs on states and localities. It does not include conditions of aid, pre-emptions and some other policies. Overall, the National Conference of State Legislatures estimates that up to 10 percent of a state's general fund budget goes to filling in gaps in federal unfunded mandates.[20] During 2002–08, moreover, the federal government promulgated an average of 527 rules per year regulating state governments and 343 regulating local governments, the costs of which are not known.[21]

An unknown question is the extent to which health care reform will become a *de facto* unfunded mandate for the states. A report from the Senate Finance Committee and House Energy and Commerce Committee estimated states will have to spend $118 billion during 2017–23 to cover the legislation's expansion of Medicaid. Previously, the

Kaiser Commission estimated new state spending on Medicaid at $43.2 billion through 2019, and the Congressional Budget Office estimated such new state spending at $60 billion through 2021.[22] The health care reform law does give states the opportunity to withdraw from the Medicaid program if it becomes too costly, although, as a practical matter, withdrawal seems impossible.

Federal Pre-emptions of State Powers and Financial-Reform Legislation

Another major characteristic of coercive federalism is federal pre-emption (i.e., displacement of state law). From 1970 to 2004, Congress enacted some 320 explicit pre-emptions compared to about 200 explicit pre-emptions enacted from 1789 to 1969.[23] That is, 62 percent of all explicit pre-emptions in U.S. history have been enacted since 1969. In addition, a vast but uncounted field of implied pre-emption is embedded in federal agency regulations and federal court rulings, and recent presidents have used executive rule-making to advance pre-emption when Congress drags its feet. Although some pre-emptions benefit the states,[24] the unprecedented leap in pre-emption since 1969 has irrevocably established the federal government as the King Kong-sized partner in the federal system.

Pre-emption will still reign during upcoming years, but its pace could slow, depending on partisan control of Congress, the White House and the Supreme Court. Generally, Republicans prefer total pre-emption of a wide range of state powers pertaining to the economy, consumer affairs, product liability and environmental protection. As U.S. Rep. Henry Waxman (D-Calif.) reported in June 2006, Congress had voted at least 57 times to pre-empt state laws over the previous five years. Those votes yielded 27 statutes, including 39 pre-emptions.[25] Business, too, often prefers total pre-emption because it prefers regulation by one 500-pound gorilla in Washington, D.C., than the 50 states. The pace and number of pre-emptions will likely increase under Republicans.

Democrats are less eager to pre-empt state powers pertaining to the economy, consumer affairs, product liability and environmental protection. When they do so, they often endorse partial pre-emption, whereby federal law establishes a national minimum standard that can be exceeded by states or delineates policy fields subject to state action. In 2009, for example, President Obama signed the Family Smoking Prevention and Tobacco Control Act, which allowed the U.S. Food

and Drug Administration to regulate most tobacco products. The act specifically preserves state product-liability laws.

In the Dodd–Frank Wall Street Reform and Consumer Protection Act of 2010, a major reform of financial regulation, the Democratic majority in Congress, with Obama's support, both pre-empted and strengthened state powers. The law protected most existing state regulatory authority in consumer protection and banking, and reversed some Bush-era pre-emptions. The law allows states to enforce some federal consumer-protection laws on national and state banks, and the new federal Consumer Financial Protection Bureau can examine state banks only jointly with state bank supervisors. A majority of states can petition the new federal consumer bureau to issue new protection rules. The law often treats federal consumer law as a floor, not a ceiling, and does not explicitly pre-empt exclusive state regulation of insurance. State insurance regulators will still oversee equity-indexed annuities, which the law exempts from regulation by the federal Securities and Exchange Commission. The law created a new Office on Insurance in the U.S. Department of the Treasury, but it will not regulate state-regulated insurance or securities. "The act did, however, establish federal authority to create new national standards governing how states regulate the reinsurance market and how states collect taxes for highly specialized and unique risks, known as 'surplus lines.'"[26] Hedge funds and other investment advisers handling less than $100 million will be regulated by the states, not the SEC. The previous threshold was $25 million. "The SEC estimates about 4,000 investment advisors will switch to the states."[27]

In other policy fields, especially civil rights, Democrats more willingly support pre-emption, including total pre-emption. During his 2008 campaign, Obama told Planned Parenthood, "The first thing I'd do as president is sign the Freedom of Choice Act"[28] that would pre-empt virtually all state and local laws deemed to be barriers to abortion. He also has expressed his support for the federal government to take over the establishment and enforcement of safety standards for mass-transit systems and to increase federal regulation of insurance.

Conservatives on the Supreme Court support pre-emption more often than liberal justices. The prospect of a liberal majority appearing on the court in the near future is probably about equal to that of a conservative majority. The average age of the court's liberals is 65; the conservatives' average age is 64. The swing justice, Anthony Kennedy, is 75. Even with a liberal majority, though, the court would be a speed bump, not a barrier, on the freeway of pre-emption.

A major, unknown factor is whether the court will uphold the health care reform legislation. This law contains mandates as well as a blockbuster *de facto* pre-emption, namely, authority for the federal government to enter a state to establish an exchange to sell federally approved health insurance to residents when the elected officials of that state refuse to operate such an exchange. However, the act explicitly pre-empts only state laws that block the application of health care reform. Other state statutes, such as insurance regulation, will still be in force.

This will be a revolutionary federal displacement of traditional state power. Although there is ample judicial precedent for the federal government to enforce its laws within recalcitrant states, the magnitude of enforcing the individual mandate through federal operation of exchanges in unwilling states might be said to violate the Constitution's republican guarantee clause.

Federal Restrictions on State and Local Tax and Borrowing Powers

Federal incursions into the tax and borrowing powers of state and local governments also characterize coercive federalism and will continue to constrain state and local revenue generation. Prominent limits are the Supreme Court's restriction on state sales taxation of out-of-state mail-order sales,[29] which cost the states about $8.6 billion in lost revenue in 2010,[30] and the Internet Tax Freedom Act Amendment Act of 2007, a seven-year extension of an already 10-year-old moratorium on state-local taxation of Internet access.

In response to the Supreme Court's ruling, some states have joined the Streamlined Sales and Use Tax Agreement, a collective interstate effort to set up an enforceable mail-order sales tax system. Congress has not approved the agreement. Some states have devised ways to collect sales taxes on some out-of-state mail-order sales, especially by arguing that in-state marketing affiliates of big online retailers should collect the state sales tax. Some states have retreated in the face of threats from online retailers to drop affiliates in their states and, thus, cause the states to lose businesses and jobs. Whether this tax strategy will withstand judicial scrutiny is unknown.

Another important issue is whether the federal government will increase taxes significantly during the upcoming years or enact a federal sales tax or value-added tax. This would place downward political pressure on state and local sales tax rates, reduce state and local sales tax collections, and especially hurt states such as Florida, Tennessee and Washington, which rely heavily on sales taxes for revenue. The national governments of most federal countries levy a value-added tax and share some of its revenues with their constituent governments. It is unlikely Congress would do the same.

Nationalization of Criminal Law

In the Kentucky Resolutions of 1789, Thomas Jefferson wrote that the U.S. Constitution "delegated to Congress a power to punish" four sets of crimes "and no other crimes whatever." Today, about 4,500 federal criminal laws, including about 50 capital offenses, and 300,000 federal regulations can be enforced by criminal penalties. By one estimate, Congress creates about 56 new crimes each year.[31] Only recently have critics, both left and right, challenged this nationalization,[32] which is another feature of coercive federalism.

One recent proposal for stemming this tide of federal criminalization would be to require both Congress and the executive branch to report regularly on the nature and extent of this nationalization of criminal law. It also would require Congress to analyze whether proposed federal crimes "are consistent with constitutional and prudential considerations of federalism" and compare proposed penalties "with the penalties under existing federal and state laws for comparable conduct."[33]

Demise of Intergovernmental Institutions

Coercive federalism also produced the demise of executive, congressional and independent intergovernmental institutions established during the era of cooperative federalism. Most notable was the death of the U.S. Advisory Commission on Intergovernmental Relations (ACIR) in 1996 after 37 years of operation.[34] Many state advisory commissions have disappeared as well.[35] Congress no longer has important committees on federalism and intergovernmental relations, and federal departments either have no intergovernmental office or a highly political one. President Reagan dismantled the intergovernmental unit in the Office of Management and Budget in 1983, and the GAO's intergovernmental unit was phased out in the early 1990s. The White House Intergovernmental Relations office, now called Intergovernmental Affairs and Public Engagement, is an important political and favor-dispensing office but not a vital node for intergovernmental policymaking.

At a time of fiscal austerity and further interlocking of the federal and state governments as reflected in health care reform, no dedicated institutions address fundamental and systemic intergovernmental structures and processes.[36] There have been occasional calls to revive the Advisory Commission on Intergovernmental Relations, for example, but no such institution is likely to come back into existence.[37]

Federal Judicial Intervention and Gun Rights

Coercive federalism also has included unprecedented numbers of federal court orders requiring state and local governments to undertake policy actions. Although federal court orders dictating major and costly changes in such institutions as schools, prisons and mental health facilities have declined since the early 1990s, state and local governments are still subject to high levels of litigation in federal courts. Judicial consent decrees, some of which last for decades, are another restraint on state and local officials. Decrees are a major way to guarantee state or local government compliance with federal rules in many intergovernmental policy areas, such as education, environmental protection and Medicaid. The U.S. Supreme Court resurrected the 11th Amendment in the 1990s to restrain some types of litigation, but the reach of the court's decisions has been quite limited.

The major U.S. Supreme Court decision affecting state and local governments in 2010 was *McDonald v. City of Chicago*.[38] In this 5-4 ruling, the court opined that the Second Amendment to the U.S. Constitution guarantees individuals the right to bear arms and that the Second Amendment, like most other provisions of the U.S. Bill of Rights, must be applied to the states under the 14th Amendment (1868). The ruling reversed a longheld view that the Second Amendment referred to organized state militias, not individual rights.

The last time the Supreme Court incorporated a provision of the U.S. Bill of Rights into the 14th Amendment was 1969.[39] Indeed, 55 percent of all such incorporations occurred during the 1960s. Incorporation, strongly supported by liberals, produced a flood of citizen litigation against state and local governments. Many conservatives and gun-rights organizations such as the National Rifle Association, however, had long advocated the

incorporation ruling in *McDonald*. This ruling has already spawned many lawsuits challenging state and local gun regulations and will keep the federal courts enmeshed in this state-local policy field for decades. Litigation may be especially prolonged because the Supreme Court set forth no criteria for determining when state laws or local ordinances might violate the Second Amendment. The court did not even rule on the constitutionality of the two gun-control laws from Chicago and Oak Park, Ill., that were at issue in this case. Instead, the Supreme Court remanded the cases to the lower courts to decide whether the ordinances are consistent with the Second Amendment.

Conclusion

The broad and coercive reach of federal power with respect to the states and their local governments shows no signs of abating. Many states are pushing back against federal power, but this revolt is motivated substantially by partisan polarization and will not likely be successful in the long run. One possible exception would be a U.S. Supreme Court ruling striking down portions of the health care reform law, especially the individual mandate, as being an unconstitutional exercise of Congress's commerce power.

Notes

[1] This proposal is very similar to the National Reconsideration Amendment proposed by the States' Federalism Summit in 1995. See The Council of State Governments, *Restoring Balance in the American Federal System* (Lexington, KY: CSG, 1996).

[2] Rick Perry, *FED UP! Our Fight to Save America from Washington* (New York: Little Brown, 2010), 177.

[3] Unpublished 2010 data from Jack Jedwab, Association for Canadian Studies, Montreal, Canada.

[4] Ronald Brownstein, "Pulling Apart," *National Journal* 43 (February 26, 2011): 19.

[5] Nolan McCarthy, Keith T. Poole, and Howard Rosenthal, *Polarized America, http://polarizedamerica.com/* accessed Feb. 16, 2011.

[6] Nebraska has an officially nonpartisan unicameral legislature.

[7] J. Kenneth Blackwell and Kenneth A. Klukowski, "Why the ObamaCare Tax Penalty Is Unconstitutional," *Wall Street Journal*, July 22, 2010, A19.

[8] John Kincaid, "The State of U.S. Federalism, 2000–2001: Continuity in Crisis," *Publius: The Journal of Federalism* 31 (Summer 2001): 1–69.

[9] U.S. Government Accountability Office, *State and Local Governments' Fiscal Outlook: March 2010 Update*. GAO-10-358 (Washington, D.C.: GAO, 2010), 6.

[10] Chris Edwards, "Federal Air-to-State Programs Top

1,100," *Tax & Budget Bulletin* (Cato Institute) No. 63 (February 2011): 1.

[11] Citizens Against Government Waste, *2010 Congressional Pig Book* (Washington, D.C.: CAGW, 2010).

[12] U.S. Government Accountability Office, *The Federal Government's Long-Term Fiscal Outlook: January 2010 Update*. GAO-10-468SP (Washington, D.C.: GAO, 2010), 1.

[13] Ibid.

[14] The Peterson-Pew Commission on Budget Reform, *Red Ink Rising* (Washington, D.C.: Commission, 2009).

[15] U.S. Government Accountability Office, *The Federal Government's Long-Term Fiscal Outlook: January 2010 Update*, 6.

[16] John L. Palmer and Rudolph G. Penner, *Have Recent Budget Policies Contributed to Long-Run Fiscal Stability?* (Washington, D.C.: Urban Institute, 2010).

[17] National Research Council and National Academy of Public Administration, *Choosing the Nation's Fiscal Future* (Washington, D.C.: National Academics Press, 2010).

[18] U.S. Government Accountability Office, *State and Local Governments' Fiscal Outlook: March 2010 Update*.

[19] U.S. Congressional Budget Office, *A Review of CBO's Activities in 2009 Under the Unfunded Mandates Reform Act* (Washington, D.C.: CBO, March 2010).

[20] National Conference of State Legislatures, "Unfunded Mandates Letter" (November 16, 2010) at *http://www.ncsl.org/default.aspx?tabid=21723*, accessed January 28, 2011.

[21] Clyde Wayne Crews, *Ten Thousand Commandments* (Washington, D.C.: Competitive Enterprise Institute, 2009).

[22] U.S. Senate Finance Committee and U.S. House Energy and Commerce Committee, *Medicaid Expansion in the New Health Law: Costs to the States* (Washington, D.C.: U.S. Congress, March 1, 2011), 1.

[23] National Academy of Public Administration, *Beyond Pre-emption: Intergovernmental Partnerships to Enhance the New Economy* (Washington, D.C.: NAPA, 2006).

[24] Joseph F. Zimmerman, *Congress: Facilitator of State Action* (Albany: SUNY Press, 2010).

[25] OMB Watch, "States Losing Ability to Protect Public Due to Federal Preemptions," June 13, 2006 at *http://www.ombwatch.org/node/2957*, accessed Dec. 19, 2010.

[26] Timothy J. Conlan and Paul Posner, "Inflection Point? Federalism and the Obama Administration." Paper presented at the Annual Meeting of the American Political Science Association. Washington, D.C. Sept. 2, 2010, pp. 29–30.

[27] Kara Scannell, "States Will be Hedge-Fund Police," *Wall Street Journal*, August 19, 2010, C3.

[28] YouTube, "Barack Obama Promises to Sign FOCA," July 17, 2007 at *http://www.youtube.com/watch?v=pf0XIRZSTt8*, accessed November 19, 2010.

[29] *Quill Corp. v. North Dakota*, 504 U.S. 298 (1992).

[30] Ana Campoy, "Amazon's Exit Spurs Tax Fight In Texas," *Wall Street Journal*, Feb. 17, 2010, A5.

[31] Brian W. Walsh, "The Criminal Intent Report: Congress Must Justify New Criminalization," *WebMemo* (Heritage Foundation) No. 2933 (June 9, 2010): 1.

[32] Adam Liptak, "Right and Left Join to Take On U.S. in Criminal Justices Cases." *New York Times*. November 24, 2009, A1, A22, and Harvey A. Silverglate, *Three Felonies*

a Day: How the Feds Target the Innocent (New York: Encounter Books, 2009).

[33] Walsh, "The Criminal Intent Report," 2.

[34] John Kincaid, "The U.S. Advisory Commission on Intergovernmental Relations: Unique Artifact of a Bygone Era," *Public Administration Review* 71 (March/April 2011): 181–89.

[35] Richard L Cole, "The Current Status and Roles of State Advisory Commissions on Intergovernmental Relations in the U.S. Federal System," *Public Administration Review* 71 (March/April): 190–95.

[36] John Kincaid and Carl W. Stenberg, "'Big Questions' about Intergovernmental Relations and Management: Who Will Address Them?" *Public Administration Review* 71 (March/April): 196–202.

[37] John Kincaid, "Reviving the ACIR Would Be Wonderful—But It's Unlikely," *State Tax Notes* 20 (Jan. 29, 2001): 369.

[38] 561 U.S. ___, 130 S.Ct. 3020 (2010).

[39] *Benton v. Maryland*, 395 U.S. 784 (1969).

About the Author

John Kincaid is the Robert B. and Helen S. Meyner professor of government and public service and director of the Meyner Center for the Study of State and Local Government, Lafayette College, Easton, Penn. He is former editor of *Publius: The Journal of Federalism*; former executive director of the U.S. Advisory Commission on Intergovernmental Relations; co-editor of *Constitutional Origins, Structure, and Change in Federal Countries* (2005), *Interaction in Federal Systems* (2008), and *Local Government in Federal Systems* (2008) and editor of *Federalism* (4 vols., 2011).

Interstate Relations Trends

By Joseph F. Zimmerman

This article reviews interstate relations developments since 2007 pertaining to uniform state laws, interstate compacts and administrative agreements, same-sex marriage, civil unions and other pertinent legal matters.

An *Imperium in Imperio* (an empire within an empire) is an apt descriptor of a federal system, as sovereign political powers are divided between a national government and constituent state governments. This power division in the United States automatically produces interstate relations characterized by competition, cooperation and/or controversies.

Uniform State Laws

Nonharmonious state laws, particularly regulatory ones, create problems for citizens and businesses operating on a multistate basis. Such laws led to the establishment in 1892 of the National Conference of Commissioners on Uniform State Laws, which drafts uniform laws on a wide variety of subjects and urges state legislatures to enact them.

The commissioners promulgated four uniform laws in 2007, six in 2008, five in 2009 and nine in 2010. Examples include the Uniform Collaborative Law Act (2009), and the Model State Administrative Procedures Act (2010). There were 198 introductions of uniform and model acts and 93 of them were enacted in 2010. In general, Midwestern and Northwestern states have the highest propensity to enact uniform laws, and Southern states have the least propensity to so enact. Various associations—the Multistate Tax Commission, interest groups and citizens—also draft model laws.

Interstate Compacts

The U.S. Constitution (art.I,§10) authorizes states to enter into compacts with sister states with congressional consent. The U.S. Supreme Court, however, opined in 1893 that consent was required only for compacts encroaching upon the powers of the federal government (148 U.S. 503 at 520). The 2004 Insurance Product Regulation Compact is exempt from the consent requirement because in 1945, Congress transferred the authority to regulate the business of insurance to the states. This compact, as of 2010, had been enacted by the legislature in 36 states and Puerto Rico, and represents more than one-half of the premium volume nationwide. A member state may opt out of a compact standard, and Indiana in 2010 became the first state to use the provision by opting out of the Long-Term Care Standard.

Congress in 2007 granted consent (121 Stat. 730) to the Great Plains Wildland Fire Protection Compact enacted by the state legislatures in Colorado, Kansas, North Dakota, South Dakota and Wyoming. Congress in the same year granted consent (121 Stat. 2467) to the International Emergency Management Assistance Memorandum of Understanding entered into by Connecticut, Maine, Massachusetts, New Hampshire, Rhode Island, Vermont, New Brunswick, Newfoundland, Prince Edward Island and Québec. The revised Interstate Compact for Juveniles became effective in 2008 with its enactment by Illinois and Tennessee, and currently has 41 member states. In 2010, Congress granted its consent (124 Stat. 1124) for a minor amendment to the Washington Area Metropolitan Transit Regulation Compact pertaining to the appointment of commission members.

The Interstate Agreement for the Popular Election of the President of the United States is an innovative interstate compact based on section 10 of article I authorizing states to enter into interstate agreements or compacts and section 1 of article II of the U.S. Constitution directing state legislatures to appoint presidential-vice presidential electors. Consent is not required for the agreement since it does not encroach upon federal powers. The California legislature for the second time enacted the agreement, but it was again vetoed by Gov. Arnold Schwarzenegger, who wrote: "Such a significant change should be voted on by the people." Proponents lacked the required two-thirds vote in each house to override the veto. Six state legislatures and the District of Columbia Council, which combined have 76 electoral votes, have enacted the agreement and both houses in four additional states have approved it.

The Interstate Nurse Licensure Compact, enacted by 24 states as of 2010, allows a nurse licensed by a state to work in other compact states. The national shortage of nurses resulted in hospitals relying more heavily on traveling nurses. Pro Publica in 2010 investigated the compact and reported its officers do not keep records on nurses sanctioned by their respective primary states for misconduct elsewhere in the U.S.

Interstate Administrative Agreements

State legislatures enacted numerous laws granting authority to heads of state departments and agencies to enter into administrative agreements with their counterpart in other states. The agreements may be formal contracts, informal written contracts or verbal agreements. The consent requirement is not applicable to the agreements since they are not enacted into law.

The National Governors Association and the National Conference of State Legislatures drafted the Streamlined Sales and Use Tax Agreement, and 19 states launched it, with the cooperation of sellers, in 2005. The agreement simplifies the collection of sales taxes by establishing uniform standards facilitating collection of uncollected sales and use tax revenues on the products sold by electronic commercial transactions. Twenty states were full members and three states were associate members in 2010.

State attorneys general continued to file joint class-action lawsuits resulting in a number of favorable decisions in 2008, 2009 and 2010. There were four 2008 decisions, including: (1) a suit filed by 18 states against a South Carolina company that claimed to help delinquent taxpayers reduce their debt, (2) a suit filed by 14 states and the Federal Trade Commission against businesses taking advantage of the economic downturn to defraud consumers, (3) a suit filed by nine states against the U.S. Environmental Protection Agency for its rule exempting the discharge of pollutants in "transfer waters" from permitting requirements, and (4) a suit by 33 states against Eli Lilly for improperly marketing Zyprexa to patients who did not have schizophrenia or bipolar disorder. Thirty-five states and the Federal Trade Commission won their suit in 2010 against Lifelock, which claimed it could protect any person against identity theft.

In 2010, the 50 attorneys general investigated bank foreclosures of mortgages, and 38 state and the District of Columbia attorneys general examined the unauthorized collection of personal data from wireless computer networks by Google's street view vehicles. Google admitted it collected and stored payload data from unencrypted networks, but not from encrypted networks.

The National Governors Association Center for Best Practices and the Council of Chief School Officers in April 2010 issued Common Core State Standards in English language arts and mathematics designed to improve the quality, cost effectiveness and comparability of state assessments of student progress. Proficiency standards currently vary from one state to another. Twenty-seven states adopted the standards within two months of their issue. Only Alaska, Texas, and Virginia announced they would not adopt the standards. States that adopt the standards may opt for additional standards.

The Western States Contracting Alliance, composed of state purchasing directors of 15 states, continues to promote cooperative multistate purchasing. The Eastern Regional Conference of The Council of State Governments in 1989 organized the Northeast Recycling Council through a memorandum of agreement with 10 states. The council seeks to minimize the amount of materials requiring disposal, and organized the State Electronic Challenge to reduce the adverse environmental impact of computers by purchasing green computers to lower energy consumption, and to recycle them when they become outmoded. Nine states and 27 local governments were members of the challenge as of 2010.

The Western States Climate Initiative, composed of 11 states and Canadian provinces, in 2010 was developing a cap-and-trade initiative to reduce greenhouse gas emissions by 15 percent by 2020. The initiative will trade an estimated $21 billion worth of allowances annually.

Double taxation can be a problem in a federal system. Fifteen states and the District of Columbia have reciprocal state tax agreements with other states providing taxpayers with credit for income taxes paid to sister states, political subdivisions, the District of Columbia and Canadian provinces.

In 2010, Maine, New Hampshire and Vermont pest control officers were engaged in a cooperative program to stop the spread of the hemlock wooly adelgid, first detected in Vermont in 2007, by using a fungi and a natural predator beetle. New York and Vermont signed an administrative agreement to replace a new bridge over Lake Champlain closed for safety reasons; and Massachusetts Gov. Deval Patrick and Rhode Island Gov. Don Carcieri signed an administrative agreement to coordinate proposed wind power projects in a designated 400 square miles of federal waters 12 miles southwest of Martha's Vineyard and 20 miles within Rhode Island Sound.

Utah in 1995 modified its concealed firearm permits rules by waiving residency and other requirements, thereby permitting holders of a Utah permit to carry weapons in 32 sister states that recognize Utah permits or are party to reciprocity agreements with Utah. The U.S. Supreme Court's ruling in 2010 holding the Second Amendment to the U.S. Constitution guarantees the right of an individual to bear arms applies to state and local laws made holding a Utah license attractive to numerous gun owners. Approximately one-half of the 241,811 Utah permits by midyear were held by nonresidents.

The Merrimack River Anadromous Fish Restoration program is a cooperative effort by Massachusetts, New Hampshire and the U.S. government to restore salmon, eels, herring and shad to the river. The agreement in 2010 had very limited success in restoring salmon, but has considerable success with shad.

The Chesapeake Bay Program is a federal-state partnership of six states, the District of Columbia and concerned federal agencies to improve water quality. President Barack Obama expressed his unhappiness with the program and issued Executive Order 13508 on May 12, 2009. It established a federal leadership committee, chaired by the administrator of the U.S. Environmental Protection Agency, to develop strategies and program plans for the watershed and ecosystem of the bay.

The National Governors Association in 2010 selected Colorado, Hawaii, Massachusetts, North Carolina, Utah and Wisconsin to participate jointly in its policy academy on state building efficiency retrofit programs that include such measures as air sealing, appliance replacement, insulation, lighting upgrades, replacement of heating or hot water systems, and window replacements.

Full Faith and Credit

Section 1 of article IV of the U.S. Constitution requires each state to accord full faith and credit to "the public acts, records, and judicial proceedings of every other state." Congress is authorized to prescribe the manner in which documents are to be proved "and the effect thereof."

Same-Sex Marriage

In 1996, Congress responded to the 1994 decision of the Hawaiian Supreme Court opining same-sex couples had the right to marry by enacting the *Defense of Marriage Act of 1996* defining a marriage as a union of one man and one woman, and thereby allowing each state to decline to extend full faith and credit to a same-sex couple who married in another state. The constitutionality of this act was challenged in court in 2010.

The 2003 decision of the Massachusetts Supreme Judicial Court authorizing same-sex marriages reopened the controversy. In 2008, the Connecticut Supreme Court issued a similar decision, and the Iowa Supreme Court invalidated a 1998 law defining a marriage as between one man and one woman.

The California Supreme Court in 2008 struck down Proposition 22 of 2000, approved by 61 percent of the voters, banning same-sex marriages. Proponents of the ban placed Proposition 8 restoring the ban on the Nov. 4, 2008, ballot and voters approved the proposition. The California Supreme Court in 2009 rejected a challenge to the proposition, but opined the 16,000 same-sex couples who married prior to its decision are legally married. Wisconsin voters in 2006 approved a constitutional amendment banning same-sex marriage and its constitutionality was upheld by the state supreme court in 2010.

In 2008, voters in Arizona and Florida also approved constitutional amendments prohibiting same-sex marriages. Arkansas voters in the same year ratified a proposition banning the adoption of children by same-sex couples. New York Gov. David A. Paterson in 2009 issued an executive order directing state departments and agencies to recognize same-sex marriages performed in sister states.

The 2009 Vermont General Assembly, by a one-vote margin, overrode Gov. James Douglas's veto of a bill allowing same-sex marriage, and became the first state legislature to authorize this type of marriage. The Maine State Legislature one month later enacted a same-sex marriage law and Gov. John Baldacci signed it. The New Hampshire General Court in 2009 enacted a same-sex marriage law after amending the first version of the bill, at the insistence of Gov. John Lynch, to exempt religious organizations and their employees from having to participate in such a marriage. Maine voters in November 2009 employed the protest referendum to repeal the same-sex marriage act.

The District of Columbia City Council in 2009 approved an ordinance recognizing same-sex marriages performed in sister states and foreign nations. Congress failed to act on the ordinance during the 30 days it had to review it. In contrast, the New

York Senate in 2009 and the New Jersey Senate in 2010 each rejected a same-sex marriage bill.

Judge Joseph L. Tauro of the U.S. District Court for the District of Massachusetts in 2010 invalidated as unconstitutional a section of the *Defense of Marriage Act of 1996* that forbids the federal government to recognize same-sex marriages because the act forces Massachusetts to discriminate against same-sex couples in order to receive certain federal grants. The judge opined the section violated the *Tenth Amendment* that reserves powers to the states.

Civil Union

In 2000, the Vermont General Assembly authorized civil unions of same-sex couples, and its lead has been followed the state legislature in Connecticut, New Hampshire and New Jersey. Hawaii Gov. Linda Lingle in 2010 vetoed a bill authorizing same-sex civil unions on the ground such a union "is essentially same-sex marriage by another name."

A civil union entered into in one state can create a legal morass if the same-sex couple seeks a divorce in a state with no legal provision for such a divorce. In 2006, a Vermont court dissolved the first civil union in the state, and in 2007 the family court dissolved the civil union of two Virginia women who traveled to Vermont to enter into a union and who subsequently were engaged in a four-year legal battle over custody of the child conceived by one of the woman through in-vitro fertilization. Their civil union was terminated by a Vermont court in 2007.

Another same-sex couple traveled to Vermont in 2003 to enter into a civil union. The couple separated and one travelled to Vermont to have the union annulled, but was informed she must reside in the state for one year prior to applying for an annulment. She returned to New York and sought an annulment in the state supreme court (a trial court) and the judge ruled there was no legal authority to dissolve such a union. She appealed to the Appellate Division of the Supreme Court, which overturned the lower court judgment in 2010.

Wisconsin Attorney General J.B. Van Hollen in 2009 announced he would not defend a law granting same-sex couples spousal benefits, including hospital visits and inheritance, on the ground the legislature acted against voters' decision not to extend the privileges. He noted the state constitution prohibits a same-sex couple to have a legal status "substantially similar" to marriage. In 2010, the Appellate Division of the New York Court of Appeals ruled New York has the authority to annual a civil union entered into in a sister state.

Other Developments

Nonharmonious state regulatory and tax statutes create problems for individuals and businesses operating on a multistate basis.

Michigan has a refundable 10 cent deposit on beer, soft drink and other beverage containers, while other states with such a deposit set it at 5 cents. Michigan in 2008 discovered that many persons who purchased soft drinks in Indiana, Ohio and Wisconsin redeemed the containers in Michigan, thereby resulting in a revenue loss of at least $10 million.

In 2009, Judge Paul A. Magnuson of the U.S. District Court in Jacksonville, Fla., issued a ruling to resolve a dispute involving Alabama, Florida and Georgia by requiring Atlanta to stop withdrawing water from Lake Lanier, a large federal reservoir, within three years unless Atlanta obtains the approval of Congress. The dispute involved a 2003 water-sharing agreement with the U.S. Army Corps of Engineers allowing Georgia to take more water from the lake for drinking purposes. Alabama and Florida maintained the lake had been built for hydropower and providing water to Georgia was not authorized. The judge specifically ruled the corps abused its discretion in authorizing the withdrawal of additional water from the lake, and noted the lake was not constructed for water supply purposes and Georgia's withdrawals were illegal. He did not order an immediate halt of water withdrawal because the lake is the main source of Atlanta's water.

A Massachusetts judge ruled in 2007 that electronic highway tolls systems, such as E-Z Pass, which grant a discount only to state residents, does not violate the interstate commerce clause. Massachusetts Superior Court Judge Allan van Gestet rejected Carol Suprenant's claim that discounted tolls by Massachusetts Turnpike Authority and Massachusetts Port Authority for residents of one Boston area relative to one toll bridge and two tunnels violated the clause because only a minimal burden is placed on the right to interstate travel.

Surprenant, the plaintiff and a Rhode Island resident, responded by filing a suit in the U.S. District Court for the District of Massachusetts alleging violation of her rights guaranteed by the U.S. Constitution's privileges and immunities clause and the dormant interstate commerce clause. The court in 2010 (2010 WL 786306) allowed the defen-

dants' motion to dismiss as to the plaintiff's privileges and immunities claim because she failed to
prove her right to travel is a fundamental one. The
court denied the defendants' motion to dismiss
the dormant commerce clause claim by observing,
based on the record, "the court cannot say that
she has failed to plead a violation of the dormant
Commerce Clause." The court allowed 90 days for
discovery and the filing of additional briefs by the
parties to address the issues raised by the court.

The New York Department of Law and the
Pennsylvania Department of Environmental Protection in 2010 filed suit against Edison Mission,
the owner of a massive coal-fired power plant in
Homer City, Pa., for violating the federal *Clean
Air Act of 1970* by annually producing in excess of
100,000 tons of sulfur dioxide, nitrogen oxides and
particulates.

New Hampshire Gov. John Lynch in 2010 signed
Bill 5 into law, relieving New Hampshire businesses of having to question their customers relative to whether they reside in another state or plan
to use an item purchased in a state with a sales and
use tax. The law was prompted by recent efforts of
the Massachusetts revenue commissioner to collect taxes for sales made to state residents doing
business in New Hampshire.

Summary and Conclusions

Interstate relations generally continue to be cooperative despite the occasional filing by a state of
a petition seeking to invoke the U.S. Supreme
Court's original jurisdiction to resolve an interstate
controversy. Such petitions may become more
common, especially in arid areas, with respect to
river water allocation. Furthermore, disharmoni-
ous state regulatory laws will continue to encourage Congress to pre-empt state regulatory powers.

About the Author

Joseph F. Zimmerman is a professor of political science
at Rockefeller College of the State University of New York
in Albany, and is the author of numerous books on intergovernmental relations.

Table 2.1
SUMMARY OF STATE INTERGOVERNMENTAL EXPENDITURES: 1944–2009
(In thousands of dollars)

Fiscal year	Total	To Federal government (a)	To local governments Total	For general local government support	Education	Public welfare	Highways	Health	Miscellaneous and combined
1944	$1,842,000	...	$1,842,000	$274,000	$861,000	$368,000	$298,000	...	$41,000
1946	2,092,000	...	2,092,000	357,000	953,000	376,000	339,000	...	67,000
1948	3,283,000	...	3,283,000	428,000	1,554,000	648,000	507,000	...	146,000
1950	4,217,000	...	4,217,000	482,000	2,054,000	792,000	610,000	...	279,000
1952	5,044,000	...	5,044,000	549,000	2,523,000	976,000	728,000	...	268,000
1953	5,384,000	...	5,384,000	592,000	2,737,000	981,000	803,000	...	271,000
1954	5,679,000	...	5,679,000	600,000	2,930,000	1,004,000	871,000	...	274,000
1955	5,986,000	...	5,986,000	591,000	3,150,000	1,046,000	911,000	...	288,000
1956	6,538,000	...	6,538,000	631,000	3,541,000	1,069,000	984,000	...	313,000
1957	7,440,000	...	7,440,000	668,000	4,212,000	1,136,000	1,082,000	...	342,000
1958	8,089,000	...	8,089,000	687,000	4,598,000	1,247,000	1,167,000	...	390,000
1959	8,689,000	...	8,689,000	725,000	4,957,000	1,409,000	1,207,000	...	391,000
1960	9,443,000	...	9,443,000	806,000	5,461,000	1,483,000	1,247,000	...	446,000
1962	10,906,000	...	10,906,000	839,000	6,474,000	1,777,000	1,327,000	...	489,000
1963	11,885,000	...	11,885,000	1,012,000	6,993,000	1,919,000	1,416,000	...	545,000
1964	12,968,000	...	12,968,000	1,053,000	7,664,000	2,108,000	1,524,000	...	619,000
1965	14,174,000	...	14,174,000	1,102,000	8,351,000	2,436,000	1,630,000	...	655,000
1966	16,928,000	...	16,928,000	1,361,000	10,177,000	2,882,000	1,725,000	...	783,000
1967	19,056,000	...	19,056,000	1,585,000	11,845,000	2,897,000	1,861,000	...	868,000
1968	21,950,000	...	21,950,000	1,993,000	13,321,000	3,527,000	2,029,000	...	1,080,000
1969	24,779,000	...	24,779,000	2,135,000	14,858,000	4,402,000	2,109,000	...	1,275,000
1970	28,892,000	...	28,892,000	2,958,000	17,085,000	5,003,000	2,439,000	...	1,407,000
1971	32,640,000	...	32,640,000	3,258,000	19,292,000	5,760,000	2,507,000	...	1,823,000
1972	36,759,246	...	36,759,246	3,752,327	21,195,345	6,943,634	2,633,417	...	2,234,523
1973	40,822,135	...	40,822,135	4,279,646	23,315,651	7,531,738	2,953,424	...	2,741,676
1974	45,941,111	341,194	45,599,917	4,803,875	27,106,812	7,028,750	3,211,455	...	3,449,025
1975	51,978,324	974,780	51,003,544	5,129,333	31,110,237	7,136,104	3,224,861	...	4,403,009
1976	57,858,242	1,179,580	56,678,662	5,673,843	34,083,711	8,307,411	3,240,806	...	5,372,891
1977	62,459,903	1,386,237	61,073,666	6,372,543	36,964,306	8,756,717	3,631,108	...	5,348,992
1978	67,287,260	1,472,378	65,814,882	6,819,438	40,125,488	8,585,558	3,821,135	...	6,463,263
1979	75,962,980	1,493,215	74,469,765	8,224,338	46,195,698	8,675,473	4,148,573	...	7,225,683
1980	84,504,451	1,746,301	82,758,150	8,643,789	52,688,101	9,241,551	4,382,716	...	7,801,993
1981	93,179,549	1,872,980	91,306,569	9,570,248	57,257,373	11,025,445	4,751,449	...	8,702,054
1982	98,742,976	1,793,284	96,949,692	10,044,372	60,683,583	11,965,123	5,028,072	...	9,228,542
1983	100,886,902	1,764,821	99,122,081	10,364,144	63,118,351	10,919,847	5,277,447	...	9,442,292
1984	108,373,188	1,722,115	106,651,073	10,744,740	67,484,926	11,923,430	5,686,834	...	10,811,143
1985	121,571,151	1,963,468	119,607,683	12,319,623	74,936,970	12,673,123	6,019,069	...	13,658,898
1986	131,966,258	2,105,831	129,860,427	13,383,912	81,929,467	14,214,613	6,470,049	...	13,862,386
1987	141,278,672	2,455,362	138,823,310	14,245,089	88,253,298	14,753,727	6,784,699	...	14,786,497
1988	151,661,866	2,652,981	149,008,885	14,896,991	95,390,536	15,032,315	6,949,190	...	16,739,853
1989	165,415,415	2,929,622	162,485,793	15,749,681	104,601,291	16,697,915	7,376,173	...	18,060,733

See footnotes at end of table.

SUMMARY OF STATE INTERGOVERNMENTAL EXPENDITURES: 1944–2009—Continued
(In thousands of dollars)

Fiscal year	Total	To Federal government (a)	To local governments						
			Total	For general local government support	For specified purposes				
					Education	Public welfare	Highways	Health	Miscellaneous and combined
1990	175,027,632	3,243,634	171,783,998	16,565,106	109,438,131	18,403,149	7,784,316	…	19,593,296
1991	186,398,234	3,464,364	182,933,870	16,977,032	116,179,860	20,903,400	8,126,477	…	20,747,101
1992	201,313,434	3,608,911	197,704,523	16,368,139	124,919,686	25,942,234	8,480,871	…	21,993,593
1993	214,094,882	3,625,051	210,469,831	17,690,986	131,179,517	31,339,777	9,298,624	…	20,960,927
1994	225,635,410	3,603,447	222,031,963	18,044,015	135,861,024	30,624,514	9,622,849	…	27,879,561
1995	240,978,128	3,616,831	237,361,297	18,996,435	148,160,436	30,772,525	10,481,616	…	28,926,886
1996	252,079,335	3,896,667	248,182,668	20,019,771	156,954,115	31,180,345	10,707,338	10,790,396	18,530,703
1997	264,207,209	3,839,942	260,367,267	21,808,828	164,147,715	35,754,024	11,431,270	11,772,189	15,453,241
1998	278,853,409	3,515,734	275,337,675	22,693,158	176,250,998	32,327,325	11,648,853	12,379,498	20,037,843
1999	308,734,917	3,801,667	304,933,250	25,495,396	192,416,987	35,161,151	12,075,195	13,611,228	26,173,293
2000	327,069,829	4,021,471	323,048,358	27,475,363	208,135,537	40,206,513	12,473,052	15,067,156	19,690,737
2001	350,326,546	4,290,764	346,035,782	31,693,016	222,092,587	41,926,990	12,350,136	16,518,461	21,454,592
2002	364,789,480	4,370,330	360,419,150	28,927,053	227,336,087	47,112,496	12,949,850	20,816,777	23,276,887
2003	382,781,397	4,391,095	378,390,302	30,766,480	240,788,692	49,302,737	13,337,114	20,241,742	23,953,537
2004	388,559,152	4,627,356	383,931,796	29,718,225	249,256,844	42,636,305	14,008,581	19,959,396	28,352,445
2005	405,925,287	4,620,167	401,305,120	28,320,648	263,625,820	48,370,718	14,500,232	17,515,138	28,972,564
2006	432,265,206	6,502,059	425,763,147	30,486,739	280,090,982	48,409,237	15,495,306	18,144,795	33,136,088
2007	459,604,786	4,670,648	454,934,138	31,662,734	300,279,257	52,555,324	14,868,267	19,553,128	36,015,428
2008	478,223,762	4,761,135	473,462,627	32,373,446	314,612,137	53,371,645	16,545,920	19,772,605	36,786,874
2009	491,321,871	4,819,716	486,502,155	30,334,682	324,495,673	54,427,880	16,453,767	20,433,750	40,356,403

Source: U.S. Census Bureau, 2009 Annual Survey of State Government Finances. For information on sampling and nonsampling errors and definitions, see *http://www.census.gov/gov/state/how_data_collected. html.* Data users who create their own estimates from this table should cite the U.S. Census Bureau as the source of the original data only.

Note: Detail may not add to total due to rounding.

Key:
… — Not available.
(a) Represents primarily state reimbursements for the supplemental security July income program. This column also duplicates some funds listed under "Public welfare" and "All other" columns.

Table 2.2

STATE INTERGOVERNMENTAL EXPENDITURES, BY STATE: 2000–2009

(In thousands of dollars)

State	2009	2008	2007	2006	2005	2004	2003	2002	2001	2000
United States	491,321,871	478,223,762	459,604,786	432,265,206	405,925,287	388,559,152	382,781,397	364,789,480	350,326,546	327,069,829
Alabama	6,535,634	6,720,814	6,088,940	5,759,949	5,281,804	4,164,719	4,074,005	4,095,562	3,892,653	3,908,350
Alaska	1,616,689	1,487,649	1,365,793	1,217,110	1,145,032	1,049,706	1,091,391	1,055,596	986,921	1,026,962
Arizona	9,618,970	10,241,927	10,341,643	9,063,746	8,028,519	7,556,518	6,936,753	6,968,635	6,439,144	5,940,651
Arkansas	4,698,889	4,392,340	4,300,048	4,039,533	3,886,756	3,212,815	3,210,582	3,071,214	2,941,918	2,725,242
California	94,909,240	93,643,800	92,415,603	88,317,088	80,948,431	80,132,150	84,468,847	74,687,370	69,747,365	65,389,054
Colorado	6,845,674	6,233,384	6,000,582	5,621,254	5,187,797	4,860,577	4,666,350	4,295,239	3,909,362	3,702,849
Connecticut	4,351,337	4,231,032	3,831,974	3,727,280	3,534,857	3,313,737	3,030,485	3,734,962	3,252,917	3,362,551
Delaware	1,205,247	1,172,083	1,157,652	1,129,736	983,773	922,710	903,476	822,544	788,160	856,008
Florida	17,677,928	19,703,095	19,680,891	19,402,818	17,475,959	15,285,893	14,460,722	14,053,858	15,010,631	14,073,445
Georgia	10,816,572	10,415,395	10,515,856	9,991,603	9,548,675	9,331,174	9,016,458	8,644,827	8,383,261	7,179,698
Hawaii	159,452	137,771	138,054	157,863	147,201	134,452	125,434	130,387	124,448	157,902
Idaho	2,077,028	2,037,507	1,931,829	1,606,232	1,519,654	1,496,785	1,449,076	1,407,058	1,363,445	1,277,688
Illinois	15,235,221	14,749,988	14,259,666	13,946,155	14,212,820	13,303,609	13,369,662	13,090,976	12,770,065	12,050,100
Indiana	8,204,196	7,969,434	8,178,674	7,817,176	7,876,764	7,963,397	6,760,945	6,556,774	7,052,415	6,735,704
Iowa	4,660,802	4,142,960	3,892,136	3,881,967	3,642,335	3,529,971	3,442,552	3,326,499	3,284,057	3,211,878
Kansas	4,314,940	4,214,475	3,869,984	3,594,505	3,281,217	3,123,152	2,925,220	2,971,413	2,953,527	2,853,333
Kentucky	4,769,871	4,700,971	4,526,996	4,384,427	3,915,278	3,963,425	3,693,634	3,559,660	3,620,278	3,280,144
Louisiana	6,505,389	6,022,791	6,175,010	5,654,409	4,588,748	4,410,251	4,329,053	4,168,290	3,800,785	3,721,576
Maine	1,325,723	1,335,469	1,272,764	1,217,377	1,093,027	1,049,160	1,051,164	1,009,582	976,233	912,376
Maryland	8,654,935	8,509,003	7,568,283	6,916,136	5,679,626	5,632,520	5,358,342	5,235,506	5,003,670	4,355,724
Massachusetts	8,890,500	9,251,815	9,364,678	7,231,774	7,271,036	5,393,684	6,435,841	6,283,972	6,886,054	6,240,692
Michigan	19,629,569	19,512,603	19,395,333	19,409,591	19,307,932	19,035,055	19,851,778	19,067,058	18,145,167	17,201,031
Minnesota	11,199,230	11,188,797	10,686,237	10,867,738	10,108,813	9,638,153	9,618,471	8,271,462	8,196,532	7,610,072
Mississippi	5,156,650	5,111,703	5,086,220	4,826,721	4,005,786	3,880,446	3,665,580	3,456,588	3,354,226	3,248,019
Missouri	5,888,392	5,638,642	5,500,811	5,386,306	5,489,120	5,260,101	5,159,094	5,073,185	4,802,371	4,528,746
Montana	1,276,112	1,318,649	1,175,674	1,088,009	1,005,091	955,378	938,000	910,845	863,553	760,511
Nebraska	2,064,173	1,981,940	1,793,817	1,721,265	1,659,130	1,695,613	1,784,749	1,820,137	1,684,159	1,585,847
Nevada	3,864,223	3,860,236	3,826,539	3,667,299	3,272,860	2,948,274	2,648,660	2,432,909	2,271,654	2,250,330
New Hampshire	1,278,589	1,451,976	1,408,445	1,385,014	1,224,831	1,278,988	1,283,091	1,178,642	1,040,566	1,053,267
New Jersey	11,135,809	10,927,571	10,671,445	11,060,423	10,642,426	10,565,755	8,997,417	9,320,357	9,081,634	8,639,491
New Mexico	4,740,669	4,348,451	4,144,807	3,745,089	3,617,407	3,234,697	2,951,328	2,768,420	2,561,979	2,447,354
New York	55,107,082	52,820,634	50,527,547	45,615,561	43,731,212	44,112,115	40,874,514	38,982,253	34,712,602	31,273,000
North Carolina	13,562,079	13,364,918	12,646,039	11,721,637	11,637,674	10,226,422	10,356,152	9,450,766	9,309,537	9,301,095
North Dakota	933,974	805,351	741,535	735,705	701,125	613,513	1,190,923	585,521	569,034	589,807
Ohio	18,988,114	18,105,626	18,042,563	17,347,300	16,368,355	15,730,201	15,249,395	15,052,078	14,594,220	12,932,081
Oklahoma	4,506,456	4,391,706	4,014,883	3,871,758	3,711,117	3,669,052	3,395,494	3,377,045	3,486,043	3,089,257
Oregon	5,703,775	5,640,993	5,047,346	4,947,578	4,764,615	4,637,052	4,071,501	4,212,673	4,027,505	3,919,771
Pennsylvania	19,110,552	17,801,247	17,009,062	13,650,400	13,307,866	12,061,035	11,943,470	12,787,590	13,120,752	11,369,795
Rhode Island	963,902	1,053,782	1,063,067	998,505	908,479	865,956	828,198	749,034	711,439	677,552
South Carolina	5,520,979	5,719,235	4,870,680	4,699,299	4,245,394	4,159,942	4,155,920	4,241,010	4,168,449	3,806,116

See footnotes at end of table.

STATE INTERGOVERNMENTAL EXPENDITURES, BY STATE: 2000–2009— Continued

State	2009	2008	2007	2006	2005	2004	2003	2002	2001	2000
South Dakota............	707,862	679,868	652,117	633,891	608,209	566,853	514,949	506,347	480,960	448,131
Tennessee.................	6,797,935	6,516,598	6,034,661	5,910,319	5,705,768	5,301,665	4,952,923	4,477,936	4,582,883	4,364,404
Texas........................	29,252,364	26,089,474	21,919,511	19,785,626	17,489,900	17,032,016	17,332,957	16,680,780	17,204,468	16,231,378
Utah..........................	3,120,527	3,050,173	2,601,367	2,384,402	2,189,527	2,112,921	2,165,151	2,170,884	2,100,657	1,977,703
Vermont....................	1,532,766	1,340,755	1,415,922	1,357,660	1,266,715	981,307	938,085	918,858	919,865	931,604
Virginia....................	11,810,753	11,052,058	10,458,913	10,019,166	9,720,411	8,820,012	8,352,635	8,369,313	7,869,121	7,132,350
Washington..............	10,043,789	9,143,766	8,602,204	7,820,778	7,443,361	6,911,826	6,785,341	6,806,350	6,576,757	6,370,710
West Virginia............	2,232,558	2,131,100	2,074,429	2,067,829	2,004,862	1,942,069	1,544,758	1,453,707	988,322	1,359,668
Wisconsin.................	10,199,520	10,093,198	9,747,672	9,560,976	9,200,766	9,285,137	9,478,166	9,523,191	8,895,941	8,170,504
Wyoming..................	1,919,231	1,769,009	1,568,884	1,301,223	1,337,226	1,207,193	952,705	974,608	818,841	838,308

Source: U.S. Census Bureau, 2009 Annual Survey of State Government Finances. For information on sampling and nonsampling errors and definitions, see *http://www.census.gov/govs/state/how_data_collected.html*. Data users who create their own estimates from this table should cite the U.S. Census Bureau as the source of the original data only.

Note: Includes payments to the federal government, primarily state reimbursements for the supplemental security income program.

Table 2.3
STATE INTERGOVERNMENTAL EXPENDITURES, BY FUNCTION AND BY STATE: 2009
(In thousands of dollars)

State	Total	General local government support	Education	Public welfare	Highways	Health	Miscellaneous and combined
				Specified functions			
United States	491,321,871	30,334,682	324,495,673	59,183,863	16,453,767	21,019,353	39,834,533
Alabama........................	6,535,634	217,230	5,047,794	66,417	209,944	34,056	960,193
Alaska...........................	1,616,689	41,434	904,344	68,534	3,482	170,491	428,404
Arizona.........................	9,618,970	2,268,279	5,233,462	1,052,176	722,386	69,341	273,326
Arkansas.......................	4,698,889	321,757	3,893,915	0	159,578	1,496	322,143
California	94,909,240	706,873	48,670,381	27,358,723	3,733,254	8,415,795	6,024,214
Colorado.......................	6,845,674	107,572	4,202,979	1,369,948	302,532	93,856	768,787
Connecticut..................	4,351,337	124,737	2,979,139	558,695	2,092	299,389	387,285
Delaware	1,205,247	0	1,077,944	8,394	8,947	16,072	93,890
Florida	17,677,928	1,706,529	13,871,594	58,757	602,131	9,234	1,429,683
Georgia.........................	10,816,572	428,291	9,388,449	445,380	0	176,750	377,702
Hawaii..........................	159,452	95,070	0	350	0	32,578	31,454
Idaho............................	2,077,028	194,337	1,707,614	0	123,736	4,189	47,152
Illinois..........................	15,235,221	1,733,189	9,331,034	1,692,677	700,837	158,904	1,618,580
Indiana.........................	8,204,196	1,341,149	6,369,766	164,781	37,422	86,140	204,938
Iowa.............................	4,660,802	137,165	3,198,762	148,584	433,459	116,926	625,906
Kansas	4,314,940	86,396	3,777,856	988	164,204	37,018	248,478
Kentucky	4,769,871	18	3,952,209	104,556	169,695	158,412	384,981
Louisiana......................	6,505,389	211,425	4,557,637	111,295	69,425	227	1,555,380
Maine	1,325,723	120,845	1,108,250	20,797	25,147	0	50,684
Maryland	8,654,935	115,685	6,691,852	2,267	465,144	705,796	674,191
Massachusetts	8,890,500	1,242,158	6,138,648	301,886	217,052	18,230	972,526
Michigan.......................	19,629,569	1,057,392	13,409,035	2,755,784	1,187,691	207,278	1,012,389
Minnesota.....................	11,199,230	1,395,220	7,446,695	616,862	782,015	177,141	781,297
Mississippi	5,156,650	762,977	3,191,777	295,034	229,067	51,471	626,324
Missouri........................	5,888,392	2,466	5,135,358	72,242	305,833	27,861	344,632
Montana	1,276,112	221,316	850,746	34,180	17,693	15,088	137,089
Nebraska	2,064,173	438,765	1,377,820	33,364	8,697	77,683	127,844
Nevada	3,864,223	1,010,974	2,557,420	108,530	104,516	15,189	67,594
New Hampshire	1,278,589	84,148	1,045,531	62,886	37,933	2,823	45,268
New Jersey	11,135,809	1,877,726	7,395,815	916,238	190,411	56,436	699,183
New Mexico	4,740,669	1,597,960	3,045,552	0	57,360	0	39,797
New York......................	55,107,082	1,654,706	30,050,807	11,188,431	9,535	5,503,269	6,700,334
North Carolina.............	13,562,079	170,431	10,621,932	1,730,419	200,988	191,381	646,928
North Dakota...............	933,974	193,409	526,561	14,335	135,694	11,626	52,349
Ohio..............................	18,988,114	1,993,185	12,147,296	1,854,297	733,786	940,803	1,318,747
Oklahoma......................	4,506,456	86,829	3,654,856	49,738	273,925	225,448	215,660
Oregon..........................	5,703,775	156,069	4,004,256	531,116	469,100	116,518	426,716
Pennsylvania	19,110,552	90,947	11,987,278	2,624,008	719,121	1,120,131	2,569,067
Rhode Island.................	963,902	30,192	856,938	75,276	0	0	1,496
South Carolina.............	5,520,979	1,778,224	3,298,814	63,521	98,965	28,710	252,745
South Dakota................	707,862	38,732	566,145	7,374	38,029	4,767	52,815
Tennessee	6,797,935	566,258	4,719,001	612,284	389,784	4,970	505,638
Texas.............................	29,252,364	217,338	25,863,345	687,120	443,623	288,451	1,752,487
Utah..............................	3,120,527	0	2,845,356	26,588	110,453	41,198	96,932
Vermont........................	1,532,766	29,345	1,422,593	76	54,381	3,242	23,129
Virginia.........................	11,810,753	952,821	7,111,935	722,784	454,091	513,412	2,055,710
Washington...................	10,043,789	68,561	7,995,398	35,813	663,812	465,380	814,825
West Virginia...............	2,232,558	111,098	1,899,471	36,087	11,298	53,125	121,479
Wisconsin	10,199,520	2,023,358	6,215,866	494,013	575,475	271,028	619,780
Wyoming	1,919,231	524,096	1,148,447	258	24	24	246,382

Source: U.S. Census Bureau, 2009 Annual Survey of State Government Finances. For information on sampling and nonsampling errors and definitions, see *http://www.census.gov/govs/state/how_data_collected.html.*

Data users who create their own estimates from this table should cite the U.S. Census Bureau as the source of the original data only.
  Note: Detail may not add to total due to rounding.

Table 2.4
STATE INTERGOVERNMENTAL EXPENDITURES, BY TYPE OF RECEIVING GOVERNMENT AND BY STATE: 2009
(In thousands of dollars)

State	Total intergovernmental expenditure	Federal	School districts	Other local governments
United States	491,321,871	4,819,716	262,281,704	224,220,451
Alabama	6,535,634	0	5,024,516	1,511,118
Alaska.................................	1,616,689	0	0	1,616,689
Arizona...............................	9,618,970	0	5,222,617	4,396,353
Arkansas.............................	4,698,889	32	3,893,910	804,947
California	94,909,240	3,610,709	45,719,173	45,579,358
Colorado............................	6,845,674	4,373	4,186,528	2,654,773
Connecticut.......................	4,351,337	0	28,288	4,323,049
Delaware	1,205,247	1,041	1,073,177	131,029
Florida................................	17,677,928	0	13,487,769	4,190,159
Georgia..............................	10,816,572	0	9,388,449	1,428,123
Hawaii................................	159,452	350	0	159,102
Idaho..................................	2,077,028	4	1,707,614	369,410
Illinois................................	15,235,221	99	9,287,285	5,947,837
Indiana...............................	8,204,196	14,975	6,369,762	1,819,459
Iowa	4,660,802	0	3,197,005	1,463,797
Kansas	4,314,940	653	3,773,853	540,434
Kentucky	4,769,871	529	3,952,209	817,133
Louisiana...........................	6,505,389	0	4,549,959	1,955,430
Maine.................................	1,325,723	12,798	0	1,312,925
Maryland	8,654,935	0	0	8,654,935
Massachusetts	8,890,500	201,212	853,507	7,835,781
Michigan............................	19,629,569	0	13,373,264	6,256,305
Minnesota..........................	11,199,230	0	7,429,018	3,770,212
Mississippi	5,156,650	0	3,169,436	1,987,214
Missouri.............................	5,888,392	0	5,135,358	753,034
Montana	1,276,112	168	850,746	425,198
Nebraska	2,064,173	33,364	1,377,820	652,989
Nevada	3,864,223	1,432	2,557,420	1,305,371
New Hampshire	1,278,589	0	406	1,278,183
New Jersey	11,135,809	0	5,408,492	5,727,317
New Mexico	4,740,669	0	3,045,552	1,695,117
New York............................	55,107,082	686,248	15,029,440	39,391,394
North Carolina...................	13,562,079	0	0	13,562,079
North Dakota.....................	933,974	14,749	526,561	407,413
Ohio...................................	18,988,114	14,749	12,147,296	6,826,069
Oklahoma..........................	4,506,456	47,219	3,654,211	805,026
Oregon...............................	5,703,775	0	4,002,466	1,701,309
Pennsylvania	19,110,552	157,316	11,512,602	7,440,634
Rhode Island......................	963,902	25,138	51,416	887,348
South Carolina...................	5,520,979	0	3,274,317	2,246,662
South Dakota.....................	707,862	0	564,088	143,774
Tennessee	6,797,935	0	282,061	6,515,874
Texas	29,252,364	0	25,638,805	3,613,559
Utah...................................	3,120,527	0	2,843,963	276,564
Vermont.............................	1,532,766	76	1,422,593	110,097
Virginia..............................	11,810,753	2,058	16,775	11,791,920
Washington........................	10,043,789	5,129	7,991,696	2,046,964
West Virginia......................	2,232,558	0	1,897,052	335,506
Wisconsin	10,199,520	0	6,215,866	3,983,654
Wyoming	1,919,231	44	1,147,363	771,824

Source: U.S. Census Bureau, 2009 Annual Survey of State Government Finances. For information on sampling and nonsampling errors and definitions, see *http://www.census.gov/govs/state/how_data_collected.html*.

Data users who create their own estimates from this table should cite the U.S. Census Bureau as the source of the original data only.

Note: Detail may not add to total due to rounding.

FEDERAL AID

Table 2.5
STATE INTERGOVERNMENTAL REVENUE FROM FEDERAL AND LOCAL GOVERNMENTS: 2009
(In thousands of dollars)

State	Total intergovernmental revenue	From federal government					From local governments				
		Total	Education	Public welfare	Health & hospitals	Highways	Total	Education	Public welfare	Health & hospitals	Highways
United States	498,278,914	478,241,224	82,425,828	283,319,087	23,460,209	36,529,755	20,037,690	3,293,035	9,166,679	1,154,689	2,192,177
Alabama	8,622,220	8,072,420	1,558,491	4,888,904	230,184	614,662	549,800	14,802	455,530	42,891	21,191
Alaska	2,391,445	2,386,407	284,650	819,317	76,793	356,182	5,038	4,434	0	0	0
Arizona	10,402,074	10,141,747	1,596,089	7,144,006	302,333	601,237	260,327	15,852	80,356	58,035	33,432
Arkansas	4,949,582	4,920,921	743,526	2,850,696	114,931	421,010	28,661	15,959	0	668	0
California	60,516,817	57,647,315	12,478,919	32,525,430	1,980,327	3,041,883	2,869,502	210,485	801,934	3,258	955,725
Colorado	5,576,955	5,490,899	1,245,316	2,361,092	912,610	509,625	86,056	12,740	499	980	28,657
Connecticut	5,518,398	5,504,832	442,413	3,780,167	226,869	507,597	13,566	1,089	0	0	0
Delaware	1,575,270	1,518,574	173,163	880,857	92,458	190,604	56,696	56,696	0	0	0
Florida	21,083,791	20,645,860	3,582,101	11,952,592	1,601,873	1,989,317	437,931	8,402	0	316,916	0
Georgia	12,830,886	12,571,429	2,498,657	6,354,783	1,300,260	1,078,531	259,457	202,023	0	0	17,703
Hawaii	2,225,268	2,219,831	478,076	1,125,845	117,412	188,440	5,437	0	0	0	2
Idaho	2,153,027	2,137,366	359,394	1,121,966	200,112	231,739	15,661	239	8,783	0	6,625
Illinois	17,409,027	16,988,372	4,175,500	9,678,661	610,244	1,280,071	420,655	23,914	308,491	0	65,460
Indiana	9,383,442	9,248,437	2,066,253	5,090,940	266,773	975,466	135,005	11,921	79,959	7,305	2,877
Iowa	5,670,077	5,450,231	995,386	3,017,959	167,954	514,891	219,846	672	177,203	24,170	8,564
Kansas	3,815,931	3,779,181	692,942	1,976,515	124,545	445,776	36,750	8,000	0	0	28,750
Kentucky	7,487,283	7,463,529	1,221,224	4,744,879	237,729	540,869	23,754	15,613	0	0	0
Louisiana	12,521,094	12,448,789	1,447,085	5,612,775	379,958	925,234	72,305	16,326	0	2,966	0
Maine	3,101,082	3,084,903	314,659	2,131,074	82,963	177,083	16,179	226	0	41	15,436
Maryland	8,775,964	8,437,353	1,483,855	4,580,878	853,924	544,803	338,611	37,458	24,766	172,757	31,745
Massachusetts	12,178,164	11,725,229	1,536,101	7,642,710	393,823	892,258	452,935	9,272	0	0	108
Michigan	16,475,729	16,263,761	3,417,833	9,147,380	1,001,896	921,399	211,968	18,636	75,848	50,847	32,219
Minnesota	8,006,629	7,903,210	1,165,188	5,293,354	237,316	645,459	103,419	2,127	39,604	0	49,598
Mississippi	8,209,225	7,993,969	1,049,921	4,591,812	202,023	544,559	215,256	6,371	56,481	12	99,229
Missouri	9,581,085	9,252,249	1,144,810	5,470,847	1,107,693	870,943	328,836	2,864	248,035	19,442	44,075
Montana	2,097,188	2,089,158	304,531	866,021	102,604	435,274	8,030	54	4,208	0	2,593
Nebraska	2,770,131	2,717,648	177,859	1,970,102	71,088	268,017	52,483	25,771	484	5	23,091
Nevada	2,510,358	2,357,013	434,046	1,171,620	102,828	324,305	153,345	24,028	100,613	1,654	20,567
New Hampshire	1,952,361	1,715,443	207,759	876,659	23,047	172,163	236,918	3,245	207,589	124	5,630
New Jersey	12,424,668	11,797,142	1,547,564	7,179,434	429,471	897,524	627,526	244,940	1,185	88,684	137,051
New Mexico	5,072,725	4,940,092	679,232	3,362,840	168,749	397,048	132,633	49,301	0	83,332	0
New York	49,089,065	42,146,116	4,945,217	30,249,149	1,613,681	1,821,291	6,942,949	452,686	5,122,438	0	0
North Carolina	16,092,266	15,581,818	2,092,603	9,954,952	1,326,446	1,084,023	510,448	135,273	309,988	1,684	28,696
North Dakota	1,349,857	1,303,719	248,141	546,581	54,405	236,088	46,138	78	6,750	2,261	28,679
Ohio	19,265,922	18,674,608	2,320,720	13,111,612	620,859	1,082,450	591,314	58,004	222,913	39,553	84,947
Oklahoma	6,553,620	6,413,876	1,093,807	3,167,101	996,880	791,777	139,744	639	3,322	4,099	32,288
Oregon	5,867,264	5,849,212	1,351,586	3,162,329	156,054	388,908	18,052	13,778	0	0	0
Pennsylvania	18,314,112	18,102,178	2,968,755	11,986,050	594,833	1,568,575	211,934	168,632	55	859	27,646
Rhode Island	2,420,320	2,308,253	339,430	1,231,862	236,785	190,522	112,067	4,452	0	0	0
South Carolina	8,195,615	7,718,470	1,305,009	5,162,824	266,993	447,772	477,145	70,291	274,556	7,053	64,099

See footnotes at end of table.

STATE INTERGOVERNMENTAL REVENUE FROM FEDERAL AND LOCAL GOVERNMENTS: 2009 — Continued
(In thousands of dollars)

State	Total intergovernmental revenue	From federal government					From local governments				
		Total	Education	Public welfare	Health & hospitals	Highways	Total	Education	Public welfare	Health & hospitals	Highways
South Dakota	1,542,361	1,516,956	282,186	638,195	109,667	254,684	25,405	8,613	0	5,685	10,689
Tennessee	8,507,222	8,420,749	1,316,825	5,325,513	322,628	760,888	86,473	30,202	0	3,571	41,698
Texas	35,574,008	34,432,850	6,956,344	19,420,006	1,334,349	2,855,865	1,141,158	532,586	508,851	99,455	0
Utah	3,853,815	3,849,281	928,918	1,947,086	142,794	419,887	4,534	4,430	0	0	0
Vermont	1,573,825	1,572,776	233,837	941,464	59,015	165,162	1,049	0	0	0	1,049
Virginia	8,058,669	7,497,291	1,612,599	4,174,574	363,472	775,243	561,378	388,757	0	65,361	87,498
Washington	9,829,012	9,512,449	2,260,455	4,600,842	1,160,478	709,336	316,563	162,253	0	24,573	67,131
West Virginia	3,775,786	3,707,941	524,361	2,235,653	150,138	463,816	67,845	1,577	0	0	0
Wisconsin	8,796,443	8,619,099	1,989,192	4,873,706	153,168	806,984	177,344	17,286	39,603	22,731	73,067
Wyoming	2,331,836	2,100,272	153,300	377,473	76,774	202,515	231,564	200,038	6,635	3,717	14,362

Source: U.S. Census Bureau, 2009 Annual Survey of State Government Finances. For information on sampling and nonsampling errors and definitions, see *http://www.census.gov/govs/state/how_data_collected. html.* Data users who create their own estimates from this table should cite the U.S. Census Bureau as the source of the original data only.

Note: Detail may not add to total due to rounding.
(a) Total includes other types of intergovernmental revenue not shown separately in this table.

Table 2.6
SUMMARY OF FEDERAL GOVERNMENT EXPENDITURE, BY STATE AND OUTLYING AREA:
FISCAL YEAR 2009
(In millions of dollars)

State and outlying area	Total	Retirement and disability	Other direct payments	Grants	Procurement	Salaries and wages
United States	$3,238,360	$881,105	$762,924	$744,115	$550,803	$299,413
Alabama	54,674	17,448	12,119	10,008	10,396	4,704
Alaska..................................	14,215	1,537	875	3,706	4,968	3,128
Arizona................................	63,029	17,862	12,138	14,479	13,932	4,618
Arkansas..............................	27,302	10,066	7,065	6,937	993	2,240
California	345,970	81,796	80,814	90,919	68,979	23,462
Colorado..............................	47,806	12,341	8,644	8,854	11,123	6,845
Connecticut.........................	42,589	9,763	9,226	8,829	13,005	1,766
Delaware	8,137	2,941	1,795	2,125	621	655
Florida.................................	175,684	62,292	50,666	31,979	18,531	12,215
Georgia................................	83,917	25,199	18,197	19,185	7,705	13,631
Hawaii..................................	24,610	4,222	9,155	3,258	1,819	6,156
Idaho...................................	14,898	4,373	2,848	3,099	3,427	1,151
Illinois.................................	116,070	32,570	32,976	31,485	11,510	7,529
Indiana................................	61,149	18,805	17,353	13,346	7,936	3,709
Iowa	29,369	8,905	8,899	7,578	2,323	1,663
Kansas	34,705	8,202	13,775	5,386	3,004	4,339
Kentucky	50,012	14,327	10,655	11,366	6,972	6,692
Louisiana............................	48,357	12,614	12,616	15,249	4,036	3,842
Maine..................................	14,242	4,772	2,883	4,084	1,431	1,073
Maryland.............................	92,155	18,449	14,331	11,805	34,339	13,231
Massachusetts	83,890	17,781	20,570	22,382	18,892	4,266
Michigan..............................	92,003	30,851	26,237	21,120	9,316	4,478
Minnesota............................	45,691	13,654	12,443	11,744	4,776	3,074
Mississippi...........................	32,848	9,468	7,456	8,305	4,988	2,633
Missouri...............................	67,942	18,475	16,212	13,568	13,508	6,179
Montana	10,925	3,244	3,135	2,940	508	1,099
Nebraska	16,526	5,192	4,917	3,656	1,164	1,597
Nevada	18,894	6,967	4,293	3,757	2,065	1,812
New Hampshire	11,844	4,150	2,315	2,612	1,921	847
New Jersey	80,647	23,873	22,745	16,785	12,051	5,193
New Mexico	27,472	6,455	3,806	6,953	7,736	2,523
New York..............................	194,975	51,663	53,965	62,419	14,507	12,422
North Carolina.....................	84,830	28,595	18,450	20,942	5,203	11,640
North Dakota.......................	8,618	1,865	3,065	2,254	474	959
Ohio.....................................	107,975	33,686	33,135	25,414	9,103	6,637
Oklahoma............................	37,516	12,234	8,869	8,554	3,149	4,710
Oregon.................................	33,594	11,629	8,382	8,705	2,469	2,409
Pennsylvania	135,687	41,892	40,010	27,363	18,098	8,324
Rhode Island........................	11,517	3,229	3,079	3,609	689	911
South Carolina.....................	46,904	15,401	10,177	9,249	8,211	3,865
South Dakota.......................	9,499	2,444	3,051	2,467	569	968
Tennessee	68,546	20,389	17,106	17,064	10,425	3,562
Texas....................................	227,108	58,300	49,452	55,671	39,311	24,373
Utah.....................................	20,702	5,796	3,478	4,945	3,636	2,848
Vermont...............................	7,092	1,931	1,346	2,162	1,075	578
Virginia................................	155,554	27,318	15,515	12,670	81,797	18,253
Washington..........................	66,560	19,748	13,108	15,261	9,214	9,229
West Virginia.......................	19,808	7,518	4,676	4,922	822	1,870
Wisconsin	61,280	16,114	13,772	19,219	9,514	2,662
Wyoming	6,278	1,580	1,165	2,604	260	669
Dist. of Columbia	49,889	2,847	4,980	12,022	7,750	22,290
American Samoa	368	59	14	213	2	80
Fed. States of Micronesia ...	272	1	14	255	2	0
Guam	1,396	272	119	387	305	312
Marshall Islands..................	140	0	4	136	1	0
No. Mariana Islands	241	34	18	170	11	9
Palau	24	0	3	21	0	0
Puerto Rico.........................	21,406	7,708	4,412	7,526	572	1,189
U.S. Virgin Islands	876	238	139	373	63	64
Undistributed......................	22,130	20	263	20	19,597	2,231

Source: U.S. Census Bureau, *Consolidated Federal Funds Report for Fiscal Year 2009.* Released August 2010.

Note: All amounts are aggregates from data included in Tables 2.6–2.11. Data are rounded to millions of dollars. Total expenditure does not include data on contingent liabilities (loans and insurance), which are separately listed in Tables 2.12–2.14. For additional information, see the complete report at *http://www.census.gov/govs/cffr/*.

Table 2.7
FEDERAL GOVERNMENT EXPENDITURE FOR DIRECT PAYMENTS FOR INDIVIDUALS FOR RETIREMENT AND DISABILITY, FOR SELECTED PROGRAMS, BY STATE AND OUTLYING AREA: FISCAL YEAR 2009
(In thousands of dollars)

State and outlying area	Total	Social Security payments				Federal retirement and disability benefits		Veterans benefits		Other
		Retirement insurance payments	Survivors insurance payments	Disability insurance payments	Supplemental security income payments	Civilian	Military	Payments for service connected disability	Other benefit payments	
United States	$881,105,040	$419,976,451	$128,410,217	$116,245,927	$44,987,046	$69,523,821	$38,250,604	$35,455,185	$9,102,257	$19,153,532
Alabama	17,447,622	6,709,199	2,526,667	3,002,636	1,000,595	1,695,988	1,043,872	835,769	313,698	319,198
Alaska	1,537,424	556,389	181,957	171,951	56,371	232,910	170,044	136,550	11,787	19,467
Arizona	17,861,846	8,975,168	2,314,378	2,136,229	655,770	1,429,033	1,067,372	785,844	164,958	333,093
Arkansas	10,066,390	4,165,039	1,414,409	1,815,945	615,808	648,128	432,414	584,011	145,051	245,586
California	81,796,321	40,187,465	11,454,343	9,779,649	6,460,442	5,746,392	3,424,531	2,719,506	736,896	1,287,097
Colorado	12,340,929	5,540,184	1,593,454	1,317,632	365,356	1,287,212	1,088,213	672,943	128,368	347,566
Connecticut	9,762,827	5,833,998	1,450,305	1,152,101	349,421	406,387	188,073	218,597	49,613	114,332
Delaware	2,941,322	1,485,953	392,104	391,835	94,463	251,931	147,506	101,910	20,194	55,426
Florida	62,292,180	31,724,751	7,992,263	6,890,588	2,758,832	4,520,934	3,832,665	2,740,727	730,062	1,101,359
Georgia	25,199,047	10,814,423	3,498,097	3,502,276	1,257,139	2,223,950	1,669,607	1,276,404	361,116	596,035
Hawaii	4,221,560	1,992,128	444,474	335,329	141,941	671,849	335,834	188,013	32,261	79,729
Idaho	4,373,079	2,087,025	597,465	534,462	160,271	386,698	230,516	203,966	39,400	133,277
Illinois	32,570,329	16,897,880	5,428,356	4,009,841	1,748,946	1,816,262	640,150	770,511	205,170	1,053,214
Indiana	18,804,675	9,736,953	3,124,133	2,650,039	702,232	947,466	376,272	574,068	139,370	554,142
Iowa	8,905,314	4,853,914	1,497,994	976,979	282,625	543,562	183,072	263,498	82,575	221,095
Kansas	8,202,043	4,023,425	1,231,231	953,765	265,883	651,163	396,523	283,035	77,425	319,594
Kentucky	14,327,085	5,551,393	2,254,950	2,780,711	1,124,174	907,787	441,973	671,463	161,484	433,150
Louisiana	12,614,203	4,867,274	2,550,863	2,019,089	1,036,878	735,539	446,278	548,588	188,839	220,853
Maine	4,771,519	2,122,845	622,098	759,329	208,895	383,526	205,813	333,579	55,001	80,433
Maryland	18,448,992	7,080,795	2,090,781	1,660,001	629,285	4,719,789	1,108,347	584,295	126,124	449,574
Massachusetts	17,780,967	9,096,968	2,508,325	2,691,469	1,051,401	1,132,178	318,991	604,601	146,683	230,351
Michigan	30,851,410	16,267,375	5,156,463	4,621,589	1,547,125	1,153,076	420,042	824,821	253,081	607,839
Minnesota	13,654,482	7,428,936	2,008,071	1,608,654	517,075	730,161	266,908	606,945	114,321	373,410
Mississippi	9,467,671	3,760,717	1,461,837	1,738,504	708,024	688,124	450,197	360,287	130,712	169,269
Missouri	18,475,166	8,725,330	2,776,849	2,761,034	778,142	1,433,434	620,620	669,622	217,575	492,559
Montana	3,243,549	1,478,587	448,700	349,317	96,976	353,813	151,345	189,692	35,697	139,422
Nebraska	5,192,438	2,504,062	763,729	537,878	141,736	347,567	268,083	309,993	54,991	264,400
Nevada	6,966,581	3,399,781	825,669	822,555	242,684	597,730	520,174	330,648	73,668	153,672
New Hampshire	4,149,690	2,125,070	519,186	629,627	97,397	332,020	184,423	169,647	34,600	57,719
New Jersey	23,873,144	13,659,024	3,566,247	2,904,686	924,442	1,447,341	330,784	570,873	127,636	342,112
New Mexico	6,454,670	2,550,367	812,763	801,973	355,022	773,992	422,804	440,975	78,747	218,028
New York	51,663,455	27,641,412	7,552,379	7,321,400	3,823,515	2,451,852	550,551	1,198,544	265,266	858,536
North Carolina	28,595,002	13,444,051	3,625,757	4,368,085	1,230,471	1,993,747	1,605,580	1,565,715	329,379	432,216
North Dakota	1,865,157	889,787	337,598	173,118	44,861	166,801	76,731	89,872	18,868	67,522
Ohio	33,686,447	16,504,524	6,134,314	4,217,997	1,759,169	1,957,236	759,242	977,031	358,763	1,018,172

See footnotes at end of table.

FEDERAL GOVERNMENT EXPENDITURE FOR DIRECT PAYMENTS FOR INDIVIDUALS FOR RETIREMENT AND DISABILITY, FOR SELECTED PROGRAMS, BY STATE AND OUTLYING AREA: FISCAL YEAR 2009—Continued

(In thousands of dollars)

State and outlying area	Total	Social Security payments				Federal retirement and disability benefits		Veterans benefits		Other
		Retirement insurance payments	Survivors insurance payments	Disability insurance payments	Supplemental security income payments	Civilian	Military	Payments for service connected disability	Other benefit payments	
Oklahoma	12,234,307	5,068,189	1,771,258	1,643,551	552,704	1,280,088	585,652	930,547	215,286	187,034
Oregon	11,629,148	5,936,924	1,586,464	1,368,501	436,637	943,319	377,830	608,607	137,478	233,389
Pennsylvania	41,891,769	21,169,653	6,763,840	5,296,178	2,180,625	2,817,799	835,998	1,090,270	389,919	1,347,485
Rhode Island	3,229,381	1,649,805	402,685	479,509	182,732	223,248	114,051	119,904	32,110	25,337
South Carolina	15,401,211	6,944,921	2,009,774	2,354,001	595,356	1,170,711	1,029,172	811,376	216,647	269,253
South Dakota	2,443,994	1,178,109	370,745	230,540	78,221	261,580	122,753	131,673	32,885	37,488
Tennessee	20,388,859	9,094,616	2,970,277	3,178,846	1,012,365	1,590,673	903,263	846,986	262,276	529,557
Texas	58,300,272	24,849,274	9,200,482	7,381,987	3,443,616	4,379,324	3,731,815	3,411,020	798,077	1,104,678
Utah	5,795,773	2,610,010	783,806	587,825	162,486	978,724	281,080	189,205	40,691	161,946
Vermont	1,931,227	1,013,890	270,906	277,488	71,399	119,100	59,846	78,040	14,407	26,151
Virginia	27,318,469	9,988,146	2,974,946	2,851,732	848,149	4,730,643	3,805,785	1,308,109	258,853	552,106
Washington	19,747,678	9,168,592	2,443,820	2,257,193	890,656	1,841,708	1,379,732	1,028,603	199,019	538,355
West Virginia	7,517,674	2,854,893	1,302,101	1,402,241	488,642	480,281	167,207	390,952	91,868	339,491
Wisconsin	16,113,547	8,942,105	2,486,498	2,051,089	612,384	707,369	298,742	604,420	140,008	270,933
Wyoming	1,579,759	745,744	218,573	165,258	32,903	159,208	87,995	76,641	14,885	78,551
Dist. of Columbia	2,846,625	522,005	155,142	159,652	157,846	1,701,301	59,110	44,663	17,403	29,502
American Samoa	58,540	15,937	16,478	14,275	0	1,678	1,742	7,024	1,258	147
Fed. States of Micronesia	598	0	0	0	0	330	0	252	16	0
Guam	272,056	105,058	48,852	24,904	0	58,451	8,266	21,462	4,005	1,058
Marshall Islands	42	0	0	0	0	11	0	15	15	2
No. Mariana Islands	33,569	8,415	6,178	2,128	6,958	7,891	846	993	130	31
Palau	212	0	20	1	0	107	32	32	53	0
Puerto Rico	7,708,010	3,284,800	1,433,867	2,104,968	0	286,791	22,285	341,751	203,204	30,344
Virgin Islands	237,946	143,169	35,298	25,786	0	17,782	1,884	10,099	2,689	1,238
Undistributed	19,835	0	0	0	0	126	0	0	19,700	9

Source: U.S. Census Bureau, *Consolidated Federal Funds Report for Fiscal Year 2009.* Released August 2010.

Note: Reported amounts represent obligations of federal funds during the fiscal year. Detail may not add to total because of rounding. For additional information see the complete report at *http://www.census.gov/govs/cffr/.*

Table 2.8
FEDERAL GOVERNMENT EXPENDITURE FOR DIRECT PAYMENTS OTHER THAN FOR RETIREMENT AND DISABILITY, FOR SELECTED PROGRAMS, BY STATE AND OUTLYING AREA: FISCAL YEAR 2009
(In thousands of dollars)

State and outlying area	Total	Medicare benefits		Medical prescription drug coverage	Excess earned income tax credits	Unemployment compensation
		Hospital insurance	Supplementary medical insurance			
United States	$762,923,570	$235,645,664	$200,113,170	$29,095,026	$44,189,952	$85,779,259
Alabama..............................	12,118,830	4,414,115	3,254,420	104,727	1,109,510	706,537
Alaska.................................	874,762	196,929	139,479	0	54,836	194,978
Arizona...............................	12,138,475	3,401,498	3,252,920	703	892,496	1,031,589
Arkansas.............................	7,064,988	2,354,501	1,832,296	17,359	589,003	651,062
California	80,813,737	25,791,300	24,691,104	182,131	4,594,443	12,172,101
Colorado.............................	8,643,694	2,353,040	2,049,459	33,996	491,031	1,118,876
Connecticut........................	9,225,939	3,417,663	2,855,435	1,394	302,506	1,455,632
Delaware	1,795,151	599,600	510,729	0	116,002	207,974
Florida................................	50,665,923	17,799,472	18,521,434	56,383	3,268,128	3,378,012
Georgia...............................	18,197,444	5,491,251	4,382,378	3,382	2,067,796	1,725,087
Hawaii.................................	9,154,739	697,723	695,473	6,583,149	153,488	393,510
Idaho..................................	2,847,688	678,942	575,626	249,562	203,171	407,996
Illinois................................	32,976,123	10,715,138	8,327,269	546,320	1,711,288	4,857,048
Indiana...............................	17,353,187	4,807,525	3,725,967	196,723	896,144	1,931,630
Iowa...................................	8,899,270	2,071,184	2,006,074	95,683	318,183	788,090
Kansas	13,774,643	2,066,212	1,874,680	6,559,132	335,383	791,474
Kentucky	10,654,565	3,412,503	2,601,071	248,202	681,820	1,150,117
Louisiana............................	12,615,517	5,006,952	3,315,455	1,520	1,099,191	517,241
Maine	2,882,868	982,289	788,006	0	140,608	273,350
Maryland	14,331,429	4,265,022	3,780,098	293	627,105	1,068,773
Massachusetts	20,569,539	7,643,521	5,262,116	161,552	540,287	2,962,072
Michigan.............................	26,237,235	8,433,240	7,793,748	0	1,325,337	4,213,817
Minnesota...........................	12,442,532	3,089,197	2,532,732	426,747	477,715	1,819,709
Mississippi..........................	7,455,819	2,605,275	1,838,800	0	875,405	335,765
Missouri..............................	16,211,519	5,147,467	4,151,448	128,129	877,043	1,161,605
Montana..............................	3,134,723	594,440	515,492	734,816	123,711	208,358
Nebraska.............................	4,917,173	1,080,883	983,256	712	208,219	225,991
Nevada................................	4,292,852	1,109,797	1,043,750	21,771	333,770	1,158,865
New Hampshire	2,314,838	808,335	617,809	0	101,239	270,381
New Jersey	22,745,398	7,836,609	7,022,772	0	898,900	4,255,215
New Mexico	3,805,535	980,687	914,957	0	385,088	380,631
New York............................	53,964,579	18,792,695	16,142,769	532,143	2,683,133	5,521,274
North Carolina....................	18,450,407	5,558,080	4,336,192	12,409	1,627,257	2,913,862
North Dakota......................	3,064,635	472,799	416,556	9	65,201	92,583
Ohio	33,134,565	9,864,127	8,230,214	4,041,181	1,586,156	3,430,253
Oklahoma............................	8,868,728	3,152,020	2,184,095	20,582	598,101	544,913
Oregon................................	8,382,104	2,148,499	1,997,490	339,414	404,503	1,618,892
Pennsylvania	40,010,075	14,768,338	11,928,866	169	1,434,105	5,441,382
Rhode Island.......................	3,078,954	1,069,973	808,117	19,648	129,137	432,270
South Carolina....................	10,177,289	2,716,547	2,249,872	1,025,785	928,997	1,017,517
South Dakota......................	3,051,382	519,504	441,450	0	100,685	58,979
Tennessee	17,105,741	5,441,907	3,519,070	2,463,609	1,146,184	1,155,666
Texas..................................	49,452,380	14,827,249	11,011,848	885,035	4,781,310	4,184,338
Utah....................................	3,478,165	927,101	725,210	0	283,680	496,607
Vermont..............................	1,345,735	420,628	309,095	0	57,060	199,601
Virginia...............................	15,515,293	4,332,935	3,725,767	288	956,223	1,133,097
Washington.........................	13,108,101	3,466,678	3,175,816	170,497	638,035	2,561,303
West Virginia......................	4,676,007	1,840,016	1,458,585	0	260,495	347,458
Wisconsin	13,772,288	3,613,320	3,129,190	1,429,843	569,437	2,080,970
Wyoming	1,164,688	306,740	241,016	0	52,907	162,831
Dist. of Columbia	4,980,252	654,906	571,003	1,798,630	84,253	216,837
American Samoa	14,162	0	0	0	0	0
Fed. States of Micronesia ...	14,362	0	0	0	0	0
Guam..................................	119,291	1,249	1,001	0	0	0
Marshall Islands.................	3,748	0	0	0	0	0
No. Mariana Islands	17,906	0	0	0	0	0
Palau	2,517	0	0	0	0	0
Puerto Rico.........................	4,411,582	876,083	1,635,725	1,398	4,247	334,836
U.S. Virgin Islands..............	139,122	21,962	17,970	0	0	20,304
Undistributed......................	263,378	0	0	0	0	0

See footnotes at end of table.

FEDERAL GOVERNMENT EXPENDITURE FOR DIRECT PAYMENTS OTHER THAN FOR RETIREMENT AND DISABILITY, FOR SELECTED PROGRAMS, BY STATE AND OUTLYING AREA: FISCAL YEAR 2009—Continued
(In thousands of dollars)

State and outlying area	Supplemental Nutrition Assistance Program (SNAP)	Housing assistance	Agricultural assistance	Federal employees life and health insurance	Student financial assistance	Other
United States	$50,485,010	$14,119,658	$23,827,509	$25,248,506	$42,447,039	$11,972,779
Alabama	970,950	333,003	188,133	424,337	483,425	129,673
Alaska	129,628	19,517	7,589	1,446	23,170	107,189
Arizona	1,223,848	93,173	92,692	367,471	1,453,166	328,921
Arkansas	569,989	98,682	374,177	146,433	366,397	65,090
California	4,382,008	1,218,407	640,913	1,918,772	4,461,703	760,856
Colorado	502,659	148,841	528,654	423,107	806,360	187,670
Connecticut	417,159	240,365	31,838	165,507	244,993	93,447
Delaware	129,099	41,758	72,166	60,954	40,920	15,948
Florida	2,968,376	487,736	283,312	1,266,582	1,935,162	701,325
Georgia	1,943,843	418,933	327,165	709,692	804,803	323,115
Hawaii	273,687	43,766	14,038	196,716	52,653	50,535
Idaho	200,940	23,444	226,664	95,522	124,612	61,209
Illinois	2,322,773	675,270	1,551,850	699,981	1,270,037	299,148
Indiana	1,071,250	318,095	1,009,591	342,450	2,908,701	145,111
Iowa	419,859	61,912	2,211,375	208,523	632,489	85,898
Kansas	301,564	91,736	1,332,052	156,436	196,009	69,966
Kentucky	1,002,095	182,837	389,742	255,279	613,860	117,037
Louisiana	1,119,138	146,989	305,538	233,142	360,929	509,423
Maine	292,705	58,448	61,095	113,184	118,094	55,090
Maryland	668,683	338,420	129,008	2,972,743	322,509	158,775
Massachusetts	925,655	844,052	41,502	441,919	1,612,306	134,557
Michigan	2,107,373	324,982	442,135	372,466	1,036,780	187,358
Minnesota	490,747	206,814	1,559,126	338,688	1,319,543	181,515
Mississippi	691,069	113,055	310,826	198,046	382,013	105,565
Missouri	1,135,614	189,801	858,637	1,543,635	846,443	171,697
Montana	134,566	35,165	488,958	107,675	111,806	79,736
Nebraska	179,069	54,565	1,193,920	140,126	794,113	56,319
Nevada	285,776	52,274	20,137	111,340	84,445	70,927
New Hampshire	115,950	67,315	40,413	155,374	102,609	35,412
New Jersey	750,162	632,869	36,543	527,325	632,046	152,957
New Mexico	410,845	39,944	102,593	198,866	226,249	165,674
New York	3,955,033	2,234,982	141,703	893,210	2,749,449	318,188
North Carolina	1,625,498	312,450	495,717	516,096	785,091	267,756
North Dakota	79,565	18,121	1,699,866	59,498	74,828	85,609
Ohio	2,197,365	759,304	936,729	596,723	1,267,927	224,585
Oklahoma	666,448	100,134	590,647	414,357	439,398	158,034
Oregon	864,381	91,678	196,140	300,543	295,146	125,419
Pennsylvania	1,901,289	609,738	165,337	970,662	2,554,407	235,781
Rhode Island	170,464	186,193	10,915	66,871	164,000	21,365
South Carolina	1,001,693	218,595	180,110	261,426	445,016	131,731
South Dakota	111,278	22,137	994,653	35,153	691,464	76,079
Tennessee	1,603,677	315,841	244,070	374,379	679,624	161,714
Texas	4,399,128	539,928	1,890,530	1,466,075	2,574,345	2,892,594
Utah	267,156	38,177	46,322	314,468	324,755	54,690
Vermont	118,398	28,286	26,666	43,246	113,593	29,163
Virginia	922,885	214,789	176,494	1,693,361	2,053,409	306,045
Washington	1,047,244	195,551	383,314	640,204	483,014	346,444
West Virginia	408,462	67,347	22,590	3,506	172,073	95,475
Wisconsin	680,471	137,517	594,161	304,459	1,085,958	146,962
Wyoming	37,077	12,076	61,167	237,070	35,519	18,285
Dist. of Columbia	159,509	67,708	71,199	1,043,126	57,782	255,298
American Samoa	6,183	0	201	0	6,478	1,301
Fed. States of Micronesia	0	0	0	0	14,306	56
Guam	78,836	4,390	141	19,515	10,641	3,518
Marshall Islands	0	0	0	0	3,731	17
No. Mariana Islands	12,189	1,763	0	0	2,053	1,900
Palau	0	0	0	0	2,517	0
Puerto Rico	0	311,880	26,127	99,625	984,727	136,935
U.S. Virgin Islands	33,705	28,908	328	1,192	7,441	7,312
Undistributed	0	0	0	0	0	263,378

Source: U.S. Census Bureau, *Consolidated Federal Funds Report for Fiscal Year 2009.* Released August 2010.

Note: Reported amounts represent obligations of federal funds during the fiscal year. Detail may not add to total because of rounding. For additional information see the complete report at *http://www.census.gov/govs/cffr/*.

Table 2.9
FEDERAL GOVERNMENT EXPENDITURE FOR GRANTS, BY AGENCY, BY STATE AND OUTLYING AREA: FISCAL YEAR 2009 (In thousands of dollars)

State and outlying area	Total	Agency for International Development	Dept. of Agriculture	Appalachian Regional Commission	Dept. of Commerce	Corporation for Nat'l & Community Service	Corporation for Public Broadcasting	Dept. of Defense	Delta Regional Authority
United States	$744,115,459	$8,567,559	$32,408,903	$75,070	$2,132,894	$654,842	$154,828	$4,713,593	$22,169
Alabama	10,007,503	11,790	511,834	5,156	71,141	7,051	2,835	52,910	1,549
Alaska.........................	3,706,319	750	131,670	0	66,871	3,443	1,845	53,062	0
Arizona.......................	14,479,108	15,765	650,414	0	14,103	8,419	4,598	54,780	0
Arkansas......................	6,936,735	52,975	376,481	9	24,509	7,010	1,947	64,769	1,885
California	90,919,113	138,718	3,942,559	0	191,943	54,018	7,138	447,491	0
Colorado.....................	8,853,610	506	358,703	36	116,228	9,368	443	51,444	0
Connecticut	8,829,480	103,464	228,680	0	16,860	4,469	95	42,785	0
Delaware	2,124,946	350	96,745	0	11,327	2,321	0	23,818	0
Florida.......................	31,979,435	26,853	1,500,209	0	107,293	22,182	9,244	204,763	0
Georgia......................	19,185,429	488,506	1,113,507	3,664	25,217	20,846	5,915	58,931	0
Hawaii........................	3,258,123	0	142,275	0	49,733	5,422	0	78,861	0
Idaho.........................	3,099,254	0	180,428	0	10,400	3,550	1,710	55,852	0
Illinois.......................	31,485,137	29,187	1,025,560	0	26,331	18,158	5,948	157,969	1,617
Indiana.......................	13,345,826	83,181	593,029	0	17,148	8,273	3,085	113,539	0
Iowa	7,577,761	0	323,519	0	31,386	9,067	3,820	53,561	0
Kansas	5,385,716	3,699	313,954	0	5,426	6,586	1,508	58,041	0
Kentucky	11,365,809	1,550	515,243	13,235	17,115	9,912	1,944	64,205	1,045
Louisiana....................	15,248,866	3,018	600,642	0	69,342	10,018	771	54,211	5,563
Maine.........................	4,083,602	3,434	158,161	0	32,700	4,722	78	112,804	0
Maryland	11,804,872	843,027	424,784	2,643	82,459	25,376	3,883	345,323	0
Massachusetts	22,381,652	506,726	428,845	274	60,806	35,449	569	234,259	0
Michigan.....................	21,119,714	21,928	901,814	0	40,213	17,712	8,247	59,683	0
Minnesota...................	11,743,549	38,901	519,628	0	10,572	18,914	2,447	65,633	0
Mississippi	8,304,532	8,175	481,535	7,149	72,049	13,044	2,677	18,237	3,132
Missouri......................	13,568,116	889	587,206	0	15,654	9,691	8,426	40,302	2,728
Montana	2,939,607	0	137,000	0	7,221	9,004	1,978	22,065	0
Nebraska.....................	3,656,267	6,117	198,285	0	6,115	4,541	3,285	57,519	0
Nevada.......................	3,757,480	0	192,364	0	2,290	4,110	1,481	34,506	0
New Hampshire	2,612,141	0	91,896	0	26,664	5,119	60	26,945	0
New Jersey	16,784,513	2,700	583,575	0	43,210	11,159	3,352	104,456	0
New Mexico	6,953,245	441	313,123	0	9,661	5,302	3,897	40,432	0
New York....................	62,418,657	706,094	1,904,553	2,564	45,418	48,577	4,957	183,506	0
North Carolina.............	20,941,735	261,863	913,661	2,833	51,357	11,680	6,970	122,225	0
North Dakota...............	2,254,442	0	95,856	0	8,094	2,148	0	31,033	0
Ohio..........................	25,413,778	300	954,926	6,322	20,145	16,253	4,757	160,827	0
Oklahoma....................	8,554,236	2,155	530,628	0	16,528	7,069	2,757	121,741	0
Oregon.......................	8,705,188	118,306	408,366	0	143,097	11,178	1,688	60,814	0
Pennsylvania	27,362,682	25,959	957,185	6,586	28,902	25,836	4,674	229,403	0
Rhode Island...............	3,609,106	8,188	80,595	0	27,702	5,822	35	26,168	0
South Carolina.............	9,249,360	5,500	464,466	3,531	32,003	4,257	3,309	39,242	0
South Dakota...............	2,467,029	0	121,227	0	6,436	1,970	1,409	29,484	0
Tennessee	17,064,313	5,199	614,742	9,100	20,105	10,358	1,291	25,091	4,650
Texas.........................	55,671,489	30,076	2,823,587	0	149,599	27,707	7,209	295,050	0
Utah..........................	4,944,705	298	250,607	0	3,139	7,367	4,970	39,526	0
Vermont......................	2,162,491	10,064	98,493	0	3,519	3,905	0	19,741	0
Virginia......................	12,670,235	589,448	576,179	2,987	79,089	14,395	1,733	138,968	0
Washington.................	15,261,026	334,547	578,051	0	97,486	24,991	4,127	124,215	0
West Virginia..............	4,921,722	1,230	219,453	8,522	16,323	6,988	1,814	42,731	0
Wisconsin	19,218,993	7,891	450,549	0	40,382	18,960	5,001	70,625	0
Wyoming	2,604,345	0	52,741	0	2,968	2,261	1,075	7,277	0
Dist. of Columbia	12,021,979	4,067,592	114,448	459	29,847	20,579	0	67,722	0
American Samoa	212,563	0	11,006	0	1,357	1,445	654	0	0
Fed. States of Micronesia.............	254,972	0	2,351	0	0	0	0	0	0
Guam.........................	387,303	0	40,592	0	4,051	2,081	0	3,009	0
Marshall Islands...........	135,799	0	1,419	0	0	0	0	0	0
No. Mariana Islands	170,367	0	14,128	0	2,319	340	0	13	0
Palau.........................	21,361	0	210	0	0	0	0	0	0
Puerto Rico.................	7,525,739	0	2,482,689	0	13,890	4,156	3,172	22,025	0
U.S. Virgin Islands	372,685	0	22,528	0	7,149	261	0	0	0
Undistributed..............	19,697	0	0	0	0	0	0	0	0

Source: U.S. Census Bureau, *Consolidated Federal Funds Report for Fiscal Year 2009*. Released August 2010.

Note: Grants data in the CFFR generally cover obligations, which may or may not result in actual expenditures. Obligations that do not result in expenditures may become deobligated.

FEDERAL GOVERNMENT EXPENDITURE FOR GRANTS, BY AGENCY, BY STATE AND OUTLYING AREA: FISCAL YEAR 2009 (In thousands of dollars)—Continued

State and outlying area	Dept. of Education (a)	Election Assistance Commission	Dept. of Energy	Environmental Protection Agency	Equal Employment Opportunity Commission	Dept. of Health & Human Services	Dept. of Homeland Security	Dept. of Housing & Urban Development	Institute of Museum & Library Services
United States	$83,166,189	$100,000	$10,330,468	$9,885,101	$25,819	$414,868,605	$11,342,885	$43,906,149	$255,108
Alabama	1,430,068	1,530	259,398	119,565	0	4,949,269	127,340	554,345	2,842
Alaska......................	440,934	500	15,663	106,864	182	1,145,866	34,867	285,649	2,294
Arizona....................	1,831,713	1,731	184,504	155,330	478	8,598,010	74,085	686,203	5,014
Arkansas..................	821,262	925	109,860	81,810	0	3,761,984	246,506	286,519	1,951
California	10,003,097	11,225	615,538	845,156	2,161	55,229,243	483,761	5,797,415	24,494
Colorado..................	1,195,582	1,474	202,047	150,771	279	3,977,987	37,906	458,762	5,893
Connecticut	845,817	1,184	185,166	107,851	702	5,242,979	38,896	613,974	3,638
Delaware	257,446	500	80,195	67,236	247	1,035,985	13,878	111,242	1,063
Florida....................	4,364,347	5,633	297,422	355,173	1,007	17,178,494	277,978	2,074,169	10,324
Georgia....................	2,526,799	2,756	265,267	197,271	76	10,100,974	154,005	1,097,041	7,610
Hawaii......................	436,838	500	29,626	70,834	98	1,506,314	44,590	225,673	3,181
Idaho.......................	399,665	500	84,325	106,029	288	1,459,517	15,141	106,153	1,774
Illinois.....................	3,564,679	4,193	488,610	398,406	1,200	18,585,652	326,240	2,073,566	9,239
Indiana....................	1,680,379	2,069	264,698	185,862	403	6,979,708	229,693	811,702	4,223
Iowa	776,687	1,015	161,683	132,031	601	3,733,350	557,638	446,082	2,394
Kansas	766,720	917	110,437	101,611	299	2,497,509	320,547	211,607	2,249
Kentucky	1,231,391	1,404	50,062	120,147	320	6,795,522	316,405	478,360	3,991
Louisiana.................	1,395,695	1,496	150,646	121,634	47	6,763,403	2,051,352	2,123,058	4,153
Maine	351,558	500	54,059	93,224	199	2,500,461	36,490	188,388	1,449
Maryland	1,406,420	1,811	114,507	211,102	492	5,191,791	74,940	855,599	4,958
Massachusetts	1,734,808	2,225	321,570	303,397	883	14,660,535	146,260	1,454,040	7,588
Michigan..................	2,731,645	3,360	617,308	379,687	881	11,690,381	73,245	1,111,890	6,570
Minnesota................	1,240,615	1,671	106,172	195,887	448	6,906,603	87,914	617,555	3,906
Mississippi	911,449	959	122,797	98,898	0	4,558,384	378,807	337,372	2,870
Missouri...................	1,501,294	1,914	185,841	228,592	729	7,929,316	248,159	617,518	4,502
Montana	375,810	500	70,087	86,519	329	1,070,262	19,677	148,127	2,640
Nebraska	519,786	591	59,653	72,786	534	1,789,350	63,533	182,875	1,815
Nevada.....................	577,148	694	125,479	60,313	388	1,426,427	25,911	310,882	1,938
New Hampshire	330,532	500	63,759	103,912	109	1,242,439	33,740	158,867	1,321
New Jersey	2,175,049	2,897	191,128	295,228	352	8,956,135	124,051	1,194,788	5,460
New Mexico	873,306	614	162,781	78,562	288	3,787,275	46,804	233,360	2,385
New York.................	5,731,265	6,520	839,833	733,990	2,403	40,700,537	711,559	4,211,501	18,554
North Carolina........	2,413,992	2,787	261,188	224,726	62	12,931,463	80,733	833,902	7,832
North Dakota..........	272,876	500	78,142	90,201	177	689,122	51,924	108,013	1,016
Ohio	2,956,037	3,871	496,506	452,168	1,810	14,966,172	126,694	1,585,282	7,379
Oklahoma................	1,096,785	1,182	128,149	134,817	304	4,329,187	59,784	487,134	4,105
Oregon....................	1,048,943	1,189	114,622	137,966	421	4,416,645	66,737	409,596	2,712
Pennsylvania	1,658,468	4,277	390,829	334,506	1,742	17,333,899	149,199	1,712,765	9,255
Rhode Island...........	312,307	500	44,038	72,185	145	2,210,038	21,613	198,346	1,251
South Carolina........	1,376,984	1,384	159,893	112,513	617	5,015,544	33,922	393,004	3,026
South Dakota..........	314,556	500	125,565	67,511	161	833,643	27,953	137,414	1,430
Tennessee	1,640,992	1,971	143,174	131,714	204	11,250,221	64,445	617,495	7,006
Texas	7,012,848	6,829	745,614	572,062	792	30,607,920	2,447,023	3,472,793	15,255
Utah........................	731,648	707	68,613	73,903	269	2,195,299	23,173	168,692	3,486
Vermont...................	207,660	500	56,756	67,437	42	1,151,801	22,168	102,553	1,318
Virginia...................	1,949,982	2,448	85,962	195,704	186	5,701,026	158,013	703,402	5,170
Washington..............	1,604,496	2,011	229,585	215,920	681	8,356,238	185,114	868,643	6,556
West Virginia...........	507,376	657	86,995	124,913	176	2,637,992	52,768	190,161	1,486
Wisconsin	1,495,887	1,836	270,176	235,590	947	13,835,880	93,036	542,310	5,038
Wyoming	212,765	500	26,850	62,276	104	487,184	12,878	58,124	1,301
Dist. of Columbia ...	386,164	500	67,397	86,286	139	2,449,102	160,215	367,370	4,240
American Samoa	14,003	100	19,421	7,546	0	29,429	9	100	171
Fed. States of Micronesia.......	5,569	0	0	0	0	0	2,044	0	42
Guam	25,536	100	20,501	9,366	9	49,936	2,153	45,243	810
Marshall Islands......	1,992	0	0	0	0	0	6	0	42
No. Mariana Islands..	8,531	0	19,649	3,833	0	22,848	3,325	7,276	140
Palau.......................	3,561	0	11	0	0	0	0	0	42
Puerto Rico.............	1,435,805	1,240	68,182	98,798	405	1,385,913	63,762	798,683	2,565
U.S. Virgin Islands ..	40,626	100	32,553	7,480	6	30,439	12,286	33,565	152
Undistributed..........	0	0	0	0	0	0	0	0	0

Deobligations are shown as negative amounts in the data. *http://www. census.gov/govs/cffr/.*
Detail may not add to total because of rounding.

Key:
(a) Data for certain programs come from *Federal Aid to States for Fiscal Year 2009.*

FEDERAL GOVERNMENT EXPENDITURE FOR GRANTS, BY AGENCY, BY STATE AND OUTLYING AREA: FISCAL YEAR 2009 (In thousands of dollars)—Continued

State and outlying area	Dept. of the Interior	Dept. of Justice	Dept. of Labor	NASA	National Archives and Records Admin.	National Endowment for the Arts	National Endowment for the Humanities	National Science Foundation
United States	$5,778,681	$6,812,571	$14,106,008	$932,433	$8,661	$174,731	$128,347	$8,166,482
Alabama	40,229	100,462	158,515	30,372	0	1,758	921	64,696
Alaska.........................	106,953	32,122	69,764	3,568	78	1,277	745	219,142
Arizona.......................	126,486	242,876	210,862	26,324	117	1,690	1,369	163,275
Arkansas.....................	23,709	60,658	150,461	2,712	0	1,242	1,137	21,537
California	371,262	985,335	1,872,464	123,918	533	15,712	8,462	1,120,343
Colorado.....................	294,487	40,325	163,845	53,398	0	4,162	1,684	403,334
Connecticut.................	9,687	67,118	188,172	3,614	319	1,728	2,648	86,583
Delaware	6,999	29,521	35,513	6,337	0	1,256	815	41,792
Florida	44,233	463,621	551,624	19,712	92	3,407	2,051	202,651
Georgia	21,648	224,099	360,202	17,426	123	4,652	2,081	150,338
Hawaii.........................	41,585	29,743	61,087	21,626	0	1,566	1,060	63,781
Idaho..........................	49,308	35,589	70,688	2,598	50	1,439	608	21,851
Illinois........................	24,146	226,683	662,172	15,438	452	5,256	9,206	412,910
Indiana........................	30,998	107,101	284,813	7,765	105	2,153	3,479	168,732
Iowa	25,732	59,502	139,435	8,021	71	1,244	738	61,977
Kansas	24,319	59,581	84,702	4,923	62	1,297	1,599	42,116
Kentucky	61,434	75,489	213,573	2,552	17	1,746	1,255	38,150
Louisiana.....................	95,785	85,776	165,248	5,896	0	2,932	1,115	59,749
Maine..........................	15,531	24,877	65,562	4,070	67	1,723	1,442	29,287
Maryland	26,919	172,049	310,833	132,185	433	5,270	3,097	175,028
Massachusetts	16,912	142,077	291,288	55,529	313	5,986	7,677	565,232
Michigan......................	40,596	187,862	775,066	16,962	311	2,557	2,316	248,209
Minnesota....................	38,197	42,768	228,927	6,669	232	14,325	1,973	108,821
Mississippi	29,346	59,069	157,768	3,993	123	1,351	1,318	31,771
Missouri......................	29,683	135,364	264,939	9,221	65	4,263	1,719	81,222
Montana	205,530	58,770	51,135	6,622	19	1,492	1,015	45,283
Nebraska	29,461	41,493	56,288	3,206	4	1,270	1,482	30,557
Nevada.........................	93,476	73,515	117,304	2,197	20	1,288	630	28,343
New Hampshire	22,747	31,193	71,432	12,507	0	1,367	943	41,918
New Jersey	11,404	168,663	345,833	12,423	426	2,451	3,127	170,107
New Mexico	469,870	61,117	92,980	6,266	120	2,030	797	72,585
New York......................	35,366	378,207	727,231	34,459	793	25,051	16,383	591,757
North Carolina.............	30,862	186,959	432,278	9,188	209	2,480	3,062	189,864
North Dakota...............	223,644	23,846	44,056	7,379	20	1,206	606	18,193
Ohio............................	36,577	227,058	616,461	13,845	127	3,000	2,650	155,093
Oklahoma....................	28,377	68,787	116,434	11,421	97	1,579	1,136	47,057
Oregon........................	176,096	78,304	229,438	5,996	20	1,854	1,637	92,321
Pennsylvania	82,499	217,167	542,589	24,120	0	5,361	6,206	305,907
Rhode Island................	1,586	31,801	67,850	4,433	176	1,474	1,371	62,939
South Carolina.............	16,451	98,984	257,098	4,071	0	1,520	1,484	63,634
South Dakota...............	206,281	53,363	37,944	5,074	13	1,475	629	17,755
Tennessee	32,230	130,159	254,354	6,415	362	1,859	1,855	114,409
Texas...........................	92,563	405,110	815,511	63,498	321	4,094	4,711	341,535
Utah............................	251,383	45,390	96,634	5,154	20	1,782	1,485	52,688
Vermont.......................	10,605	23,071	37,461	4,484	31	1,715	919	15,856
Virginia.......................	71,102	194,772	344,536	52,924	1,012	2,283	5,435	175,118
Washington..................	96,984	172,981	320,899	11,937	151	4,275	1,275	179,021
West Virginia	75,059	50,991	70,138	3,678	0	1,244	625	13,827
Wisconsin	37,895	107,347	265,739	11,694	515	1,740	2,576	155,940
Wyoming	1,110,669	20,336	36,154	1,253	31	1,072	574	16,803
Dist. of Columbia	22,601	100,981	223,495	19,710	610	7,636	3,079	555,134
American Samoa	77,639	4,929	2,483	0	0	312	326	259
Fed. States of Micronesia............	223,547	0	162	0	0	0	0	0
Guam..........................	89,837	10,976	10,306	0	0	314	354	0
Marshall Islands...........	132,228	0	0	0	0	0	0	0
No. Mariana Islands	39,052	3,070	3,252	0	0	25	343	95
Palau...........................	16,077	0	658	0	0	0	0	0
Puerto Rico..................	9,433	44,168	268,382	3,650	0	1,132	761	26,800
U.S. Virgin Islands	116,282	9,398	12,295	0	0	362	359	3,159
Undistributed...............	7,084	0	0	0	0	0	0	0

See additional footnotes on next page.

FEDERAL GOVERNMENT EXPENDITURE FOR GRANTS, BY AGENCY, BY STATE AND OUTLYING AREA: FISCAL YEAR 2009 (In thousands of dollars)—Continued

State and outlying area	Small Business Admin.	Social Security Admin.	Dept. of State	State Justice Institute	Tennessee Valley Authority (b)	Dept. of Transportation	Dept. of the Treasury (c)	Dept. of Veterans Affairs	Other
United States	$510,381	$48,332	$501,112	$2,618	$505,153	$81,581,662	$1,108,415	$824,892	$314,798
Alabama	5,515	634	3,015	2	120,051	1,358,970	422	12,362	956
Alaska........................	1,600	303	312	20	0	977,910	295	510	1,262
Arizona......................	4,480	502	5,497	169	0	1,400,813	1,191	6,822	1,486
Arkansas.....................	4,199	491	2,086	33	0	823,800	262	3,738	269
California	153,763	5,850	50,867	88	0	8,324,583	4,137	51,066	36,774
Colorado....................	5,041	390	6,539	37	0	1,294,622	654	13,896	3,766
Connecticut.................	4,090	398	5,036	0	0	1,010,127	186	10,712	2,500
Delaware	2,058	303	1,745	0	0	290,465	246	4,698	844
Florida.......................	17,431	1,586	10,474	91	0	4,186,257	5,711	27,245	8,156
Georgia......................	6,963	942	9,592	56	7,850	2,288,236	4,151	14,913	3,773
Hawaii.......................	1,770	268	18,243	0	0	421,103	113	1,448	786
Idaho........................	1,162	303	1,994	8	0	480,391	594	6,400	940
Illinois.......................	20,098	1,061	17,907	2	461	3,339,419	5,399	22,341	5,632
Indiana......................	6,932	567	7,805	8	0	1,738,289	1,408	7,041	1,639
Iowa	3,734	379	8,227	10	0	987,121	90	47,452	1,192
Kansas.......................	10,389	352	4,137	4	0	745,071	138	5,647	269
Kentucky	8,972	730	3,668	0	46,398	1,251,240	847	33,711	4,176
Louisiana....................	5,890	604	4,587	30	0	1,444,569	806	17,884	2,944
Maine........................	2,957	326	1,488	0	0	385,069	597	11,876	503
Maryland....................	5,817	489	9,464	212	0	1,331,381	1,518	10,105	30,956
Massachusetts	5,968	8,503	23,792	1	0	1,302,544	996	30,491	26,109
Michigan....................	12,412	3,741	11,185	43	0	2,112,547	5,146	25,162	11,033
Minnesota...................	4,978	461	10,207	129	0	1,419,280	234	26,999	22,483
Mississippi..................	12,391	508	3,139	2	31,676	931,679	145	21,899	817
Missouri.....................	7,755	644	6,067	18	0	1,602,923	426	38,826	2,223
Montana	4,139	376	1,903	38	0	606,143	106	4,225	1,590
Nebraska.....................	2,969	307	3,206	2	0	505,939	59	12,374	864
Nevada.......................	2,846	320	1,925	45	0	664,467	406	5,883	886
New Hampshire	961	303	2,683	3	0	326,170	1,908	11,521	621
New Jersey	10,751	653	7,368	0	0	2,335,310	551	20,823	1,082
New Mexico	5,700	421	2,385	64	0	675,026	75	3,915	1,659
New York....................	20,566	1,951	62,282	77	0	4,609,128	12,790	33,019	17,766
North Carolina.............	10,480	917	8,755	0	2,573	1,913,116	7,273	12,152	4,292
North Dakota...............	3,158	303	1,407	0	0	484,048	33	17,126	315
Ohio	18,403	1,076	11,621	96	0	2,531,529	792	22,171	13,832
Oklahoma...................	6,545	468	3,166	0	0	1,312,714	375	32,850	905
Oregon.......................	3,395	368	6,398	2	0	1,156,034	1,717	6,134	3,194
Pennsylvania	16,179	1,295	16,615	3	0	3,202,497	541	37,209	31,009
Rhode Island...............	3,110	303	1,578	0	0	415,058	154	6,428	1,912
South Carolina.............	5,047	477	3,039	4	0	1,122,211	4,522	16,420	5,205
South Dakota...............	2,137	294	534	3	0	468,053	96	3,387	730
Tennessee	7,559	730	4,280	10	295,198	1,646,563	2,050	11,686	6,837
Texas.........................	15,119	1,660	13,757	0	0	5,635,715	13,391	28,331	21,809
Utah..........................	2,870	303	2,132	2	0	908,048	121	3,996	1,000
Vermont......................	2,616	303	2,100	80	0	309,313	305	6,180	1,499
Virginia......................	13,674	764	10,435	521	946	1,569,378	1,933	16,669	4,042
Washington.................	6,546	576	8,142	34	0	1,790,083	9,117	24,425	1,920
West Virginia...............	12,425	451	1,241	12	0	788,534	334	2,971	607
Wisconsin	6,597	1,959	6,406	3	0	1,514,964	3,305	25,326	2,879
Wyoming....................	1,125	303	927	0	0	485,207	37	1,401	150
Dist. of Columbia	4,166	203	89,238	302	0	2,630,519	536,741	1,682	3,624
American Samoa	725	102	0	0	0	40,545	0	0	0
Fed. States of Micronesia............	0	0	0	0	0	21,583	0	0	0
Guam	1,204	102	107	0	0	70,717	0	0	0
Marshall Islands...........	0	0	0	0	0	124	0	0	0
No. Mariana Islands	0	102	0	0	0	42,026	0	0	0
Palau	0	0	0	0	0	825	0	0	0
Puerto Rico.................	2,191	503	382	2	0	308,885	473,969	3,344	853
U.S. Virgin Islands	815	102	23	0	0	42,747	0	0	0
Undistributed...............	0	0	0	352	0	32	0	0	12,229

(b) Payments in lieu of taxes have been categorized as "grants."
(c) Includes Treasury payments to recipients that are separate from the government of the District of Columbia and Washington Metropolitan Area Transit Authority (WMATA), as well as distributions to state and local governments of seized cash assets and proceeds from the sale of other seized assets.

Table 2.10
FEDERAL GOVERNMENT EXPENDITURE FOR PROCUREMENT CONTRACTS, BY AGENCY, BY STATE AND OUTLYING AREA: FISCAL YEAR 2009
(In thousands of dollars)

State and outlying area	Dept. of Defense and nondefense Total	Department of Defense				
		Total	Army	Navy	Air Force	Other defense
United States	$550,802,722	$354,669,419	$130,791,826	$95,129,940	$67,682,469	$61,065,184
Alabama	10,396,251	8,345,040	4,564,633	1,153,736	470,312	2,156,360
Alaska.......................	4,967,865	3,477,836	1,846,679	564,993	776,142	290,022
Arizona.....................	13,931,971	12,173,785	4,238,346	2,857,051	1,444,119	3,634,269
Arkansas...................	993,466	501,154	295,474	14,268	26,115	165,297
California	68,979,037	46,052,392	8,245,937	12,473,326	16,192,898	9,140,232
Colorado...................	11,123,042	6,447,571	2,386,419	419,096	2,953,896	688,160
Connecticut	13,004,640	12,163,422	3,103,574	6,319,768	1,490,721	1,249,359
Delaware	620,523	373,361	128,943	15,581	13,535	215,301
Florida	18,530,929	14,284,963	6,240,666	2,553,920	3,074,746	2,415,632
Georgia.....................	7,704,527	5,795,066	2,498,524	822,933	1,977,002	496,607
Hawaii.......................	1,818,886	1,608,551	555,100	675,178	101,221	277,053
Idaho........................	3,426,913	437,527	275,670	11,968	89,022	60,867
Illinois......................	11,509,607	6,275,104	2,306,531	1,594,101	940,587	1,433,885
Indiana.....................	7,936,466	6,735,072	3,889,524	872,492	319,159	1,653,897
Iowa	2,323,122	1,581,924	612,803	348,066	498,715	122,340
Kansas	3,004,220	2,447,585	638,585	93,757	1,589,514	125,729
Kentucky	6,972,351	4,832,666	758,908	75,638	52,214	3,945,907
Louisiana..................	4,036,373	3,006,121	2,057,025	461,034	69,465	418,597
Maine........................	1,430,798	1,242,250	175,166	770,653	6,786	289,645
Maryland...................	34,339,154	17,571,696	6,811,850	6,945,178	1,529,091	2,285,578
Massachusetts	18,891,695	15,130,423	5,454,794	4,382,884	4,035,823	1,256,921
Michigan...................	9,316,430	5,896,899	4,809,595	262,995	436,926	387,383
Minnesota.................	4,776,347	2,985,392	1,170,782	1,260,891	188,575	365,144
Mississippi................	4,987,514	4,104,930	1,089,527	2,661,469	146,050	207,884
Missouri....................	13,508,255	11,813,730	5,242,377	3,590,565	1,955,000	1,025,788
Montana	508,474	225,368	141,504	11,634	49,297	22,933
Nebraska	1,163,683	773,434	239,206	38,931	302,696	192,601
Nevada......................	2,065,199	1,343,051	576,122	205,790	531,170	29,969
New Hampshire	1,921,051	1,648,218	819,578	251,104	316,107	261,429
New Jersey	12,051,202	8,719,583	3,885,247	2,117,494	722,959	1,993,883
New Mexico	7,736,211	1,323,344	644,904	164,344	346,619	167,477
New York...................	14,507,042	8,981,573	2,889,366	3,948,204	956,335	1,187,668
North Carolina..........	5,202,501	2,397,480	1,105,437	641,433	169,477	481,134
North Dakota.............	474,202	170,652	69,424	5,633	64,155	31,439
Ohio..........................	9,103,004	6,768,446	2,033,532	807,168	1,936,232	1,991,514
Oklahoma..................	3,148,698	2,333,605	889,010	208,027	720,157	516,411
Oregon......................	2,468,557	1,616,699	1,326,974	173,670	32,222	83,833
Pennsylvania	18,098,425	10,219,976	4,573,060	1,831,631	1,188,310	2,626,975
Rhode Island.............	688,575	528,324	27,294	476,909	3,394	20,727
South Carolina..........	8,211,198	3,281,493	1,538,652	1,114,213	115,204	513,425
South Dakota.............	568,810	386,737	75,230	3,691	20,667	287,149
Tennessee	10,425,083	2,164,760	1,025,749	210,933	668,078	260,000
Texas........................	39,310,590	28,423,090	1,710,012	10,732,370	9,984,014	5,996,694
Utah..........................	3,635,558	2,097,381	681,839	200,392	1,028,466	186,684
Vermont.....................	1,074,681	805,858	639,605	102,842	22,207	41,204
Virginia.....................	81,796,973	51,612,350	23,170,069	15,529,352	5,242,899	7,670,031
Washington................	9,214,407	4,268,773	1,183,860	1,914,178	717,897	452,839
West Virginia.............	822,453	304,213	143,807	114,421	14,921	31,064
Wisconsin	9,513,516	8,075,176	6,851,591	578,893	70,155	574,538
Wyoming	259,817	35,537	17,851	1,521	11,903	4,262
Dist. of Columbia	7,750,207	1,877,674	611,170	747,172	271,274	248,058
American Samoa	2,390	572	566	6	0	0
Fed. States of Micronesia.........	1,855	2	2	0	0	0
Guam	304,880	289,681	1,269	231,223	52,873	4,316
Marshall Islands........	593	99	0	0	0	99
No. Mariana Islands...	10,825	4,600	82	2,432	2,082	4
Palau	25	52	18	33	0	0
Puerto Rico	572,439	365,588	63,599	7,040	17,654	277,296
U.S. Virgin Islands	62,526	38,478	1,217	2	14	37,245
Undistributed (a).......	19,596,687	8,303,090	4,457,547	1,555,715	1,725,399	564,428

See footnotes at end of table.

FEDERAL GOVERNMENT EXPENDITURE FOR PROCUREMENT CONTRACTS, BY AGENCY, BY STATE AND OUTLYING AREA: FISCAL YEAR 2009—Continued
(In thousands of dollars)

State and outlying area	Total	Dept. of Agriculture	Dept. of Commerce	Dept. of Education	Dept. of Energy	Environmental Protection Agency	General Services Admin.	Dept. of Health and Human Services
					Nondefense agencies			
United States	$196,133,303	$5,803,834	$3,295,612	$1,499,567	$31,812,675	$1,791,291	$14,750,072	$20,452,890
Alabama	2,051,211	30,538	3,459	236	5,459	1,177	178,507	241,621
Alaska......................	1,490,029	43,341	70,045	244	103,013	29,643	164,626	140,916
Arizona....................	1,758,186	67,227	4,081	15,592	9,476	1,547	88,582	398,087
Arkansas..................	492,313	167,667	126	224	2,216	52	15,085	39,435
California	22,926,645	511,490	184,709	85,788	4,086,833	112,157	1,036,355	2,062,141
Colorado...................	4,675,470	213,620	102,256	6,560	1,197,749	149,244	261,674	95,531
Connecticut..............	841,218	36,736	34,162	435	1,792	5,201	42,640	136,120
Delaware	247,162	18,788	933	378	155	13,787	21,854	11,194
Florida.....................	4,245,966	59,938	412,231	2,002	207,632	23,674	252,285	256,395
Georgia....................	1,909,462	72,957	7,916	43,436	28,546	22,033	345,432	-14,392
Hawaii......................	210,334	1,065	8,911	4,381	1,451	86	32,826	8,644
Idaho.......................	2,989,386	82,929	562	183	2,235,441	3,746	31,507	4,849
Illinois.....................	5,234,504	415,235	25,769	40,457	1,370,796	78,591	494,746	203,467
Indiana....................	1,201,395	23,298	3,823	13,146	7,418	895	117,727	228,642
Iowa	741,197	18,607	1,069	109,688	37,629	3,814	32,444	106,435
Kansas	556,634	29,124	2,903	839	4,521	29,873	35,152	21,401
Kentucky	2,139,684	40,527	6,116	196	184,652	24,670	48,307	38,367
Louisiana.................	1,030,252	51,884	13,629	110	141,936	9,704	33,179	30,209
Maine......................	188,548	16,066	2,653	213	26	1,015	28,193	4,969
Maryland	16,767,458	189,876	827,230	185,293	634,804	144,724	1,857,922	3,744,410
Massachusetts	3,761,272	19,546	57,286	38,883	15,256	91,667	342,657	391,255
Michigan..................	3,419,531	105,609	13,378	1,110	18,532	30,775	1,687,597	397,942
Minnesota................	1,790,955	414,657	5,361	28,675	8,628	4,809	123,138	99,576
Mississippi	882,585	29,451	4,465	223	407	555	43,092	12,617
Missouri	1,694,526	262,314	12,689	708	187,271	83,241	190,822	47,346
Montana	283,106	68,820	1,361	212	10,555	1,116	15,644	27,785
Nebraska	390,249	39,492	8,427	5,236	1,668	991	39,134	28,995
Nevada....................	722,149	10,304	2,568	194	64,052	4,461	27,800	17,073
New Hampshire	272,833	4,742	15,895	6,567	1,642	23,751	11,395	21,767
New Jersey	3,331,619	35,603	30,681	60,055	101,240	48,704	255,231	548,443
New Mexico	6,412,867	41,484	1,672	231	5,438,978	9,228	30,323	126,413
New York..................	5,525,469	65,813	228,379	71,331	895,348	75,170	959,687	345,168
North Carolina..........	2,805,020	90,684	47,581	39,876	484,861	43,368	121,038	403,929
North Dakota............	303,551	86,640	376	201	1,449	932	13,188	86,720
Ohio........................	2,334,558	94,115	27,852	794	59,952	107,255	209,356	149,821
Oklahoma.................	815,093	47,946	1,346	2,955	14,379	2,607	133,846	55,893
Oregon.....................	851,857	185,272	31,375	5,787	9,498	1,492	102,778	40,534
Pennsylvania	7,878,448	63,210	99,403	47,563	107,045	73,432	255,663	4,810,115
Rhode Island............	160,251	678	2,410	237	62	2,745	11,852	13,452
South Carolina..........	4,929,705	11,401	22,603	197	4,079,871	847	73,792	227,145
South Dakota............	182,073	28,721	104	207	2,589	0	7,585	32,123
Tennessee	8,260,322	71,894	10,681	1,717	3,824,465	3,405	157,167	88,202
Texas......................	10,887,500	374,687	40,331	263,075	1,116,941	35,615	583,865	554,450
Utah	1,538,177	56,425	6,564	282	8,122	2,288	34,655	50,738
Vermont...................	268,823	4,445	221	208	137	2,139	12,655	5,650
Virginia....................	30,184,622	535,455	580,378	289,848	1,636,725	417,599	2,815,017	2,702,984
Washington...............	4,945,634	107,644	60,275	2,693	3,170,794	18,594	125,176	138,904
West Virginia............	518,240	8,478	9,182	247	115,249	493	38,163	49,787
Wisconsin.................	1,438,341	218,389	38,325	5,266	10,038	4,747	65,388	143,422
Wyoming	224,280	11,228	233	228	5,268	49	2,534	1,305
Dist. of Columbia	5,872,533	60,278	78,446	98,497	45,372	15,574	1,008,751	504,104
American Samoa	1,817	0	765	0	0	0	366	15
Fed. States of Micronesia.........	1,854	6	1,522	0	0	0	0	0
Guam	15,199	157	1,075	0	0	0	6,908	45
Marshall Islands........	494	0	494	0	0	0	0	0
No. Mariana Islands...	6,225	0	750	0	0	0	17	15
Palau	-26	0	0	0	0	0	0	0
Puerto Rico..............	206,851	8,232	688	190	5	50	41,984	1,942
U.S. Virgin Islands	24,048	0	1,396	0	0	10	2,705	127
Undistributed (a)......	11,293,597	549,099	136,491	16,672	114,730	27,947	80,060	568,650

See footnotes at end of table.

FEDERAL GOVERNMENT EXPENDITURE FOR PROCUREMENT CONTRACTS, BY AGENCY, BY STATE AND OUTLYING AREA: FISCAL YEAR 2009—Continued
(In thousands of dollars)

State and outlying area	Dept. of Homeland Security	Dept. of Housing and Urban Development	Dept. of the Interior	Dept. of Justice	Dept. of Labor	NASA	National Archives and Records Admin.	National Science Foundation
United States	$14,559,857	$871,939	$4,210,492	$8,387,196	$2,577,111	$15,862,309	$236,868	$495,559
Alabama	25,118	1,856	10,653	97,572	3,069	346,137	2	48
Alaska	294,362	1,500	122,488	51,511	81,202	35,940	153	0
Arizona	151,318	671	125,095	71,578	53,097	147,742	0	4
Arkansas	10,976	546	19,594	27,434	126	3,778	260	0
California	1,224,330	106,586	728,067	312,501	218,932	3,845,404	5,834	3,049
Colorado	173,684	3,510	154,662	26,962	14,208	1,640,981	1,072	42,666
Connecticut	62,951	595	6,168	38,866	1,749	121,306	128	170
Delaware	1,257	68	61,378	925	8,173	8,808	243	8
Florida	506,664	60,851	68,815	374,159	14,723	375,983	353	440
Georgia	235,051	15,128	39,319	63,872	72,659	76,992	16,157	1,090
Hawaii	13,617	0	21,823	4,210	610	21,035	0	6
Idaho	20,712	0	72,378	11,841	14	2,802	623	-67
Illinois	124,610	1,280	42,573	206,620	48,568	31,671	8,743	8,587
Indiana	141,805	1,860	7,570	23,677	1,573	113,803	40	50
Iowa	58,215	74	7,625	10,587	37,691	20,129	282	4
Kansas	24,917	349	18,781	9,592	98	16,440	2,762	0
Kentucky	15,907	470	14,491	76,552	187,427	4,994	94	29
Louisiana	82,535	852	40,188	29,474	6,576	293,474	404	0
Maine	6,609	60	5,948	1,546	6,288	4,266	0	5
Maryland	1,674,926	149,229	331,879	724,704	226,464	2,211,921	64,892	25,946
Massachusetts	465,278	6,577	75,336	157,511	51,836	206,218	10,252	1,954
Michigan	45,520	8,742	28,877	47,939	1,816	26,362	3,465	1,908
Minnesota	73,057	1,747	195,042	53,567	5,679	11,634	2,448	175
Mississippi	99,476	347	5,358	226,906	93,649	64,128	0	0
Missouri	24,746	1,358	27,258	176,220	12,918	19,039	6,135	829
Montana	1,721	0	43,791	6,314	5,018	9,376	0	0
Nebraska	5,372	-5	20,539	12,205	264	3,330	5	0
Nevada	100,796	472	26,635	25,536	124,356	98,451	0	28
New Hampshire	9,704	220	12,669	5,358	98	20,414	11	159
New Jersey	305,808	4,450	22,647	232,195	31,337	41,232	2,010	2,613
New Mexico	206,087	735	112,578	263,145	15,054	48,992	0	10
New York	176,851	57,294	30,639	142,042	152,736	63,738	2,817	2,364
North Carolina	69,678	54	29,669	51,075	638	13,559	447	1,310
North Dakota	2,175	10	18,936	6,565	4	6,850	0	0
Ohio	195,077	8,501	46,603	56,309	27,817	167,552	219	644
Oklahoma	20,905	171	48,695	34,755	11,867	40,575	115	381
Oregon	30,277	-161	107,394	12,098	1,285	9,415	0	20
Pennsylvania	168,965	14,815	73,673	139,272	18,236	72,013	810	693
Rhode Island	6,069	135	6,741	5,681	32	14,441	0	13
South Carolina	98,493	1,725	9,877	19,317	1,921	5,668	25	11
South Dakota	1,373	168	11,555	8,174	5	5,095	-4	0
Tennessee	269,868	381	29,623	750,839	9,277	711,414	4,579	60
Texas	678,091	113,630	147,623	324,462	30,736	3,013,205	8,257	2,500
Utah	6,565	318	92,280	5,838	327,705	669,842	0	61
Vermont	2,121	0	2,751	322	502	5,372	60	0
Virginia	5,162,658	251,688	874,195	2,335,106	509,336	950,594	69,600	284,332
Washington	168,434	93	95,121	9,161	11,289	31,538	982	1,241
West Virginia	23,769	11	4,215	26,271	8,706	22,391	4,228	225
Wisconsin	135,418	601	19,576	116,853	29,820	14,596	1,591	0
Wyoming	96	0	15,164	302	19	1,318	0	0
Dist. of Columbia	616,037	39,400	64,982	250,708	88,267	85,540	9,143	106,687
American Samoa	-62	0	0	0	0	1	0	0
Fed. States of Micronesia	0	0	0	0	0	0	0	0
Guam	1,618	0	1,798	11	0	0	0	0
Marshall Islands	0	0	0	0	0	0	0	0
No. Mariana Islands...	36	0	5,206	2	0	0	0	0
Palau	0	0	0	0	0	0	0	0
Puerto Rico	13,551	15	1,818	7,626	7	3,665	0	0
U.S. Virgin Islands	444	0	1,227	156	0	0	0	0
Undistributed (a)......	524,224	12,961	908	713,175	21,634	81,143	7,631	5,308

See footnotes at end of table.

FEDERAL GOVERNMENT EXPENDITURE FOR PROCUREMENT CONTRACTS, BY AGENCY, BY STATE AND OUTLYING AREA: FISCAL YEAR 2009—Continued
(In thousands of dollars)

State and outlying area	U.S. Postal Service (b)	Small Business Admin.	Social Security Admin.	Dept. of State	Dept. of Transportation	Dept. of the Treasury	Dept. of Veterans Affairs	Other nondefense (c)
United States	$15,550,988	$111,697	$1,325,905	$7,502,781	$5,413,360	$4,857,480	$21,836,659	$12,927,162
Alabama	203,605	0	1,803	389,354	4,348	-107	187,752	319,004
Alaska	37,279	5,242	43,743	153,555	61,922	15,315	32,400	1,588
Arizona	239,255	1	550	183,061	63,715	8,061	124,603	4,845
Arkansas	132,259	74	251	444	380	192	65,735	5,461
California	1,600,560	2,929	34,029	412,715	426,083	1,008,989	4,823,868	93,297
Colorado	259,017	1,448	7,371	9,216	72,715	28,209	138,112	75,003
Connecticut	207,214	59	2,777	15,823	17,870	8,839	72,288	27,328
Delaware	44,607	0	92	729	27,592	151	22,416	3,625
Florida	824,630	238	6,306	62,482	137,708	26,875	510,284	61,297
Georgia	420,391	1,266	12,350	9,691	15,919	25,986	341,208	56,456
Hawaii	56,161	0	2,320	450	4,070	65	26,645	1,957
Idaho	60,452	0	112	4,747	80,719	348,901	26,299	636
Illinois	748,994	611	72,350	349,478	38,407	126,531	713,447	82,973
Indiana	297,507	24	914	8,339	5,688	3,500	176,416	23,681
Iowa	181,994	36	842	4,447	10,137	61,807	31,926	5,716
Kansas	181,004	8	1,489	785	27,585	2,360	138,060	8,592
Kentucky	194,802	0	8,115	6,701	5,843	4,391	83,767	1,193,265
Louisiana	190,665	112	210	10,960	43,403	817	36,977	12,957
Maine	84,417	2	46	233	6,927	-34	17,897	1,202
Maryland	315,024	19,820	376,872	392,280	766,391	471,655	481,765	949,431
Massachusetts	414,230	1,008	7,365	38,591	301,828	226,987	279,850	559,902
Michigan	528,576	1,707	37,260	32,890	18,240	9,067	309,537	62,685
Minnesota	311,019	2,605	728	22,876	23,986	10,522	348,980	42,046
Mississippi	113,796	0	9,740	102,649	23,458	-221	43,100	9,389
Missouri	365,639	47	22,436	7,651	14,366	13,729	202,608	15,155
Montana	52,398	2	179	764	23,741	323	13,563	423
Nebraska	110,099	312	518	23,477	6,439	2,220	69,637	11,895
Nevada	100,152	0	681	513	72,134	902	43,540	1,500
New Hampshire	82,327	61	1,598	1,980	8,156	4,008	29,416	10,896
New Jersey	576,792	2,012	37,906	23,584	316,545	48,001	304,469	300,061
New Mexico	78,013	31	1,402	715	10,132	131	26,642	869
New York	1,111,332	393	29,238	206,349	86,481	408,255	325,467	88,577
North Carolina	439,185	9	3,611	305,784	31,678	8,387	201,012	417,586
North Dakota	42,803	0	45	253	4,487	14,034	17,575	307
Ohio	593,451	459	6,190	49,320	46,980	92,813	365,896	27,583
Oklahoma	169,142	0	227	28,250	145,974	2,325	46,770	5,967
Oregon	162,078	306	196	15,308	46,253	3,529	85,574	1,550
Pennsylvania	728,659	478	18,908	90,308	293,535	40,980	667,870	92,802
Rhode Island	63,665	0	82	21	428	8,655	22,234	618
South Carolina	172,796	0	6,953	67,932	5,319	672	101,514	21,627
South Dakota	49,427	0	41	5	87	2,951	31,276	593
Tennessee	291,785	148	2,505	3,734	50,045	39,678	215,667	1,723,185
Texas	986,488	2,149	51,173	1,549,254	224,354	125,734	551,014	109,865
Utah	126,032	1	1,492	1,232	46,267	3,860	111,128	-13,517
Vermont	42,385	0	138	1,585	1,528	38	21,512	165,055
Virginia	400,365	51,017	299,724	2,550,400	1,258,294	1,324,905	1,148,692	3,735,710
Washington	292,071	590	6,561	3,885	81,103	2,905	324,233	292,347
West Virginia	93,682	0	148	6,743	1,367	5,734	85,014	14,137
Wisconsin	288,594	9	3,276	4,987	12,018	4,089	310,700	10,639
Wyoming	26,034	0	405	31	11,055	3,275	4,994	140,740
Dist. of Columbia	121,498	10,653	118,448	241,698	212,637	190,895	220,832	1,684,084
American Samoa	242	0	0	0	66	0	425	0
Fed. States of Micronesia	0	0	0	326	0	0	0	0
Guam	2,289	0	0	0	121	9	442	726
Marshall Islands	0	0	0	0	0	0	0	0
No. Mariana Islands ...	198	0	0	0	0	0	0	0
Palau	0	0	0	-26	0	0	0	0
Puerto Rico	65,183	409	199	12,355	7,142	209	40,386	1,195
U.S. Virgin Islands	4,225	0	0	0	13,153	17	581	8
Undistributed (a)	264,501	5,424	83,987	91,865	196,542	115,358	7,212,642	462,645

See footnotes at end of table.

FEDERAL GOVERNMENT EXPENDITURE FOR PROCUREMENT CONTRACTS, BY AGENCY, BY STATE AND OUTLYING AREA: FISCAL YEAR 2009 — Continued

Source: U.S. Census Bureau, *Consolidated Federal Funds Report for Fiscal Year 2009*. Released August 2010.

Note: Detail may not add to total because of rounding. Data shown for U.S. Postal Service represent actual outlays for contractual commitments, while all other amounts shown represent the value of contract actions, and do not reflect federal government expenditures. Nonpostal data generally involve only current-year contract actions; however, multiple-year obligations may be reflected for contract actions of less than three years duration. Negative amounts represent the deobligation of prior-year contracts. For additional information, see the complete repoprt at *http://www.census.gov/govs/www/cffr.html*.

Key:

(a) For all agencies, this line includes procurement purchases made using government-issued purchase cards.

(b) Data shown for U.S. Postal Service represent actual outlays for contractual commitments.

(c) Includes Fiscal Year 2000 procurement data for the Tennessee Valley Authority, which did not provide Fiscal Year 2009 procurement data.

Table 2.11
FEDERAL GOVERNMENT EXPENDITURE FOR SALARIES AND WAGES, BY AGENCY, BY STATE AND OUTLYING AREA: FISCAL YEAR 2009
(In thousands of dollars)

State and outlying area	Total	Nondefense civilian (a)	Department of Defense — Total	Other defense civilian	Military services — Total	Active military	Inactive military	Civilian	Army — Total	Army — Active military
United States	$299,413,089	$162,156,942	$137,256,147	$5,025,466	$132,230,681	$84,815,302	$22,965,433	$24,449,946	$89,485,889	$59,293,397
Alabama	4,704,150	1,880,010	2,824,140	155,188	2,668,952	1,254,790	617,055	797,107	2,290,575	1,005,297
Alaska.......................	3,128,341	786,065	2,342,276	11,826	2,330,450	2,077,719	90,592	162,139	1,676,832	1,528,347
Arizona.....................	4,617,594	2,814,144	1,803,450	57,944	1,745,506	1,262,572	180,724	302,210	894,995	599,521
Arkansas...................	2,240,487	1,167,884	1,072,603	4,145	1,068,458	435,036	518,376	115,046	752,906	162,203
California	23,461,850	14,056,479	9,405,371	329,022	9,076,349	5,182,809	1,391,094	2,502,446	2,950,692	1,393,317
Colorado...................	6,844,570	3,099,207	3,745,363	108,240	3,637,123	2,965,503	285,229	386,391	2,728,458	2,357,877
Connecticut	1,765,788	1,300,024	465,764	43,530	422,234	198,163	149,873	74,198	239,090	93,622
Delaware	654,899	300,315	354,584	2,558	352,026	216,219	74,623	61,184	112,540	35,712
Florida	12,215,459	7,352,004	4,863,455	106,530	4,756,925	2,816,465	826,134	1,114,326	1,679,036	788,093
Georgia.....................	13,630,955	4,733,388	8,897,567	120,199	8,777,368	6,668,434	868,244	1,240,690	7,175,809	5,949,994
Hawaii.......................	6,156,311	633,740	5,522,571	38,850	5,483,721	4,529,364	315,642	638,715	3,763,270	3,325,623
Idaho........................	1,150,923	717,497	433,426	2,034	431,392	261,607	116,236	53,549	198,095	62,645
Illinois......................	7,528,963	5,512,589	2,016,374	67,217	1,949,157	738,269	680,329	530,559	1,245,779	319,977
Indiana......................	3,709,304	1,988,181	1,721,123	222,394	1,498,729	350,647	905,556	242,526	1,266,610	325,229
Iowa	1,663,041	1,149,469	513,572	2,841	510,731	140,071	321,928	48,732	460,516	123,522
Kansas	4,338,817	1,319,393	3,019,424	14,403	3,005,021	2,465,253	334,444	205,324	2,778,727	2,296,222
Kentucky...................	6,692,119	1,715,268	4,976,851	38,018	4,938,833	4,339,243	391,231	208,359	4,888,697	4,314,563
Louisiana..................	3,842,193	1,799,290	2,042,903	14,428	2,028,475	1,417,143	410,608	200,724	1,587,676	1,091,376
Maine	1,072,714	590,661	482,053	25,845	456,208	113,348	87,175	255,685	134,809	45,708
Maryland...................	13,230,558	9,094,190	4,136,368	140,028	3,996,340	2,012,820	421,636	1,561,884	2,055,386	1,094,923
Massachusetts	4,266,193	3,308,722	957,471	67,567	889,904	319,863	312,302	257,739	567,981	189,002
Michigan...................	4,477,887	3,409,161	1,068,726	80,611	988,115	263,638	437,538	286,939	882,654	217,686
Minnesota.................	3,074,463	2,222,125	852,338	12,037	840,301	206,036	557,666	76,599	763,702	177,435
Mississippi	2,632,573	1,124,304	1,508,269	11,027	1,497,242	629,352	558,821	309,069	833,299	183,638
Missouri....................	6,179,441	3,292,972	2,886,469	36,425	2,850,044	1,310,799	1,268,807	270,438	2,514,307	1,105,248
Montana	1,099,067	750,108	348,959	1,419	347,540	187,506	110,398	49,636	170,623	49,624
Nebraska...................	1,596,779	819,843	776,936	3,356	773,580	434,949	198,307	140,324	328,452	90,442
Nevada......................	1,811,946	972,087	839,859	5,147	834,712	600,019	151,343	83,350	223,801	70,090
New Hampshire	846,709	654,015	192,694	9,544	183,150	73,429	78,753	30,968	134,038	42,901
New Jersey	5,192,579	3,470,875	1,721,704	43,806	1,677,898	543,053	507,311	627,534	1,174,591	241,934
New Mexico	2,522,522	1,517,044	1,005,478	23,506	981,972	571,288	148,491	262,193	342,394	109,793
New York...................	12,421,591	8,496,262	3,925,329	98,538	3,826,791	2,701,191	782,279	343,321	3,514,269	2,544,984
North Carolina..........	11,640,367	3,223,368	8,416,999	89,175	8,327,824	7,012,462	729,587	585,775	6,765,035	5,807,618
North Dakota.............	959,462	449,437	510,025	2,172	507,853	335,954	110,138	61,761	170,719	49,464
Ohio	6,636,851	4,119,198	2,517,653	487,815	2,029,838	640,496	609,867	779,475	865,665	244,038
Oklahoma..................	4,709,887	1,679,581	3,030,306	58,492	2,971,814	1,678,570	496,151	797,093	1,809,984	1,193,170
Oregon......................	2,408,525	1,853,445	555,080	1,794	553,286	140,868	300,719	111,699	471,150	102,532
Pennsylvania	8,323,616	5,670,980	2,652,636	425,265	2,227,371	574,034	1,011,822	641,515	1,732,900	485,907
Rhode Island.............	911,405	436,853	474,552	4,875	469,677	120,400	117,397	231,880	182,151	69,036
South Carolina...........	3,865,255	1,489,116	2,376,139	27,199	2,348,940	1,530,304	485,464	333,172	1,494,189	928,643
South Dakota............	968,075	610,313	357,762	1,423	356,339	198,438	115,571	42,330	176,612	49,235
Tennessee	3,561,898	2,446,583	1,115,315	36,046	1,079,269	282,250	572,830	224,189	875,335	199,947
Texas........................	24,372,948	10,087,024	14,285,924	181,714	14,104,210	11,128,462	1,520,699	1,455,049	11,378,476	9,190,449
Utah	2,848,103	1,339,939	1,508,164	53,897	1,454,267	431,738	448,935	573,594	705,850	197,371
Vermont....................	578,293	400,152	178,141	2,128	176,013	64,177	92,561	19,275	148,066	49,190
Virginia.....................	18,253,285	6,759,324	11,493,961	1,622,118	9,871,843	6,214,491	603,453	3,053,899	4,621,705	3,127,773
Washington................	9,228,778	3,203,679	6,025,099	37,836	5,987,263	4,407,343	563,322	1,016,598	4,327,654	3,538,766
West Virginia.............	1,869,772	1,483,431	386,341	529	385,812	106,870	216,627	62,315	331,860	85,126
Wisconsin	2,661,967	1,891,830	770,137	5,647	764,490	222,262	470,144	72,084	699,235	192,333
Wyoming...................	669,235	380,587	288,648	1,060	287,588	177,223	70,775	39,590	104,827	28,050
Dist. of Columbia	22,290,071	19,372,025	2,918,046	75,835	2,842,211	1,906,999	124,189	811,023	1,858,755	1,589,609
American Samoa	79,972	6,104	73,868	0	73,868	56,534	17,250	84	73,835	56,501
Fed. States of Micronesia..........	0	0	0	0	0	0	0	0	0	0
Guam	312,466	46,086	266,380	5,667	260,713	114,218	85,938	60,557	74,142	96
Marshall Islands........	0	0	0	0	0	0	0	0	0	0
No. Mariana Islands...	8,811	8,046	765	0	765	753	0	12	680	668
Palau	0	0	0	0	0	0	0	0	0	0
Puerto Rico	1,188,535	863,532	325,003	6,556	318,447	180,989	102,515	34,943	283,103	170,105
U.S. Virgin Islands	64,119	58,386	5,733	0	5,733	2,869	734	2,130	3,352	1,222
Undistributed............	2,230,608	2,230,608	0	0	0	0	0	0	0	0

See footnotes at end of table.

FEDERAL GOVERNMENT EXPENDITURE FOR SALARIES AND WAGES, BY AGENCY, BY STATE AND OUTLYING AREA: FISCAL YEAR 2009 — Continued
(In thousands of dollars)

	Department of Defense—continued									
	Military services—continued									
	Army—continued		Navy				Air Force			
State and outlying area	Inactive military	Civilian	Total	Active military	Inactive military	Civilian	Total	Active military	Inactive military	Civilian
United States	$21,858,493	$8,333,999	$18,605,176	$9,333,659	$560,372	$8,711,145	$24,139,616	$16,188,246	$546,568	$7,404,802
Alabama	604,790	680,488	19,748	10,575	5,435	3,738	358,629	238,918	6,830	112,881
Alaska.........................	70,230	78,255	6,286	4,787	603	896	647,332	544,585	19,759	82,988
Arizona......................	154,284	141,190	98,185	65,449	8,461	24,275	752,326	597,602	17,979	136,745
Arkansas....................	511,793	78,910	2,596	1,789	651	156	312,956	272,182	4,794	35,980
California	1,277,598	279,777	4,475,800	2,718,573	76,928	1,680,299	1,649,857	1,070,919	36,568	542,370
Colorado....................	260,669	109,912	32,433	20,890	8,351	3,192	876,232	586,736	16,209	273,287
Connecticut...............	132,266	13,202	148,824	95,201	3,840	49,783	34,320	9,340	13,767	11,213
Delaware	69,354	7,474	2,139	591	1,292	256	237,347	179,916	3,977	53,454
Florida	763,522	127,421	1,152,542	612,254	40,444	499,844	1,925,347	1,416,118	22,168	487,061
Georgia......................	827,143	398,672	367,597	172,185	16,025	179,387	1,233,962	546,255	25,076	662,631
Hawaii........................	289,163	148,484	1,200,702	799,767	5,532	395,403	519,749	403,974	20,947	94,828
Idaho..........................	112,980	22,470	5,271	886	1,453	2,932	228,026	198,076	1,803	28,147
Illinois.......................	646,376	279,426	173,677	82,268	20,510	70,899	529,701	336,024	13,443	180,234
Indiana......................	888,905	52,476	164,283	5,787	5,564	152,932	67,836	19,631	11,087	37,118
Iowa	310,191	26,803	4,934	3,039	1,689	206	45,281	13,510	10,048	21,723
Kansas	321,208	161,297	4,385	2,644	1,545	196	221,909	166,387	11,691	43,831
Kentucky	386,034	188,100	18,034	4,979	2,808	10,247	32,102	19,701	2,389	10,012
Louisiana	388,226	108,074	87,858	37,379	16,101	34,378	352,941	288,388	6,281	58,272
Maine.........................	80,220	8,881	295,748	57,819	2,449	235,480	25,651	9,821	4,506	11,324
Maryland	410,539	549,924	1,244,378	349,695	5,379	889,304	696,576	568,202	5,718	122,656
Massachusetts	290,846	88,133	35,626	17,719	6,334	11,573	286,297	113,142	15,122	158,033
Michigan....................	421,106	243,862	30,449	17,236	11,908	1,305	75,012	28,716	4,524	41,772
Minnesota..................	545,274	40,993	18,283	11,064	6,355	864	58,316	17,537	6,037	34,742
Mississippi	545,247	104,414	234,904	124,325	4,064	106,515	429,039	321,389	9,510	98,140
Missouri	1,215,502	193,557	96,030	32,961	42,274	20,795	239,707	172,590	11,031	56,086
Montana	105,553	15,446	1,280	191	1,063	26	175,637	137,691	3,782	34,164
Nebraska	191,477	46,533	21,238	17,168	3,330	740	423,890	327,339	3,500	93,051
Nevada	137,731	15,980	34,966	20,482	3,631	10,853	575,945	509,447	9,981	56,517
New Hampshire	74,529	16,608	21,811	18,839	1,941	1,031	27,301	11,689	2,283	13,329
New Jersey	481,212	451,445	132,130	10,401	9,121	112,608	371,177	290,718	16,978	63,481
New Mexico	134,467	98,134	8,693	3,939	2,399	2,355	630,885	457,556	11,625	161,704
New York...................	750,111	219,174	85,626	58,232	20,762	6,632	226,896	97,975	11,406	117,515
North Carolina..........	713,944	243,473	1,098,097	805,153	10,691	282,253	464,692	399,691	4,952	60,049
North Dakota............	107,187	14,068	1,098	296	671	131	336,036	286,194	2,280	47,562
Ohio	578,118	43,509	34,434	17,250	13,792	3,392	1,129,739	379,208	17,957	732,574
Oklahoma..................	473,800	143,014	54,319	45,304	5,463	3,552	1,107,511	440,096	16,888	650,527
Oregon.......................	283,942	84,676	12,272	6,221	5,046	1,005	69,864	32,115	11,731	26,018
Pennsylvania	976,763	270,230	382,359	46,821	17,267	318,271	112,112	41,306	17,792	53,014
Rhode Island.............	106,458	6,657	256,988	35,199	5,217	216,572	30,538	16,165	5,722	8,651
South Carolina..........	472,736	92,810	344,838	171,324	6,441	167,073	509,913	430,337	6,287	73,289
South Dakota............	113,614	13,763	825	25	690	110	178,902	149,178	1,267	28,457
Tennessee	551,116	124,272	105,153	47,331	11,222	46,600	98,781	34,972	10,492	53,317
Texas	1,455,740	732,287	248,521	146,883	47,765	53,873	2,477,213	1,791,130	17,194	668,889
Utah	441,542	66,937	9,802	4,091	3,662	2,049	738,615	230,276	3,731	504,608
Vermont.....................	89,992	8,884	1,726	1,043	598	85	26,221	13,944	1,971	10,306
Virginia......................	553,124	940,808	3,830,526	1,995,965	33,902	1,800,659	1,419,612	1,090,753	16,427	312,432
Washington................	527,641	261,247	1,206,170	516,841	16,233	673,096	453,439	351,736	19,448	82,255
West Virginia.............	211,268	35,466	12,566	7,663	1,745	3,158	41,386	14,081	3,614	23,691
Wisconsin	457,307	49,595	12,186	5,023	5,771	1,392	53,069	24,906	7,066	21,097
Wyoming	67,923	8,854	516	24	492	0	182,245	149,149	2,360	30,736
Dist. of Columbia	91,464	177,682	716,490	100,337	32,034	584,119	266,966	217,053	691	49,222
American Samoa	17,250	84	33	33	0	0	0	0	0	0
Micronesia.................	0	0	0	0	0	0	0	0	0	0
Guam	73,676	370	41,931	0	0	41,931	144,640	114,122	12,262	18,256
Marshall Islands........	0	0	0	0	0	0	0	0	0	0
No. Mariana Islands...	0	12	85	85	0	0	0	0	0	0
Palau.........................	0	0	0	0	0	0	0	0	0	0
Puerto Rico...............	95,342	17,656	7,739	2,725	2,290	2,724	27,605	8,159	4,883	14,563
U.S. Virgin Islands	0	2,130	46	46	0	0	2,335	1,601	734	0
Undistributed............	0	0	0	0	0	0	0	0	0	0

See footnotes at end of table.

FEDERAL GOVERNMENT EXPENDITURE FOR SALARIES AND WAGES, BY AGENCY, BY STATE AND OUTLYING AREA: FISCAL YEAR 2009—Continued
(In thousands of dollars)

State and outlying area	Total (a)	*Nondefense agencies*							
		Dept. of Agriculture	Dept. of Commerce	Dept. of Education	Dept. of Energy	Environmental Protection Agency	Federal Deposit Insurance Corporation	General Services Admin.	Dept. of Health and Human Services
United States	$162,156,942	$6,431,668	$4,191,011	$411,204	$1,577,175	$1,767,795	$657,843	$1,095,081	$5,947,704
Alabama	1,880,010	74,141	10,795	201	0	4,057	3,654	3,184	6,957
Alaska	786,065	53,885	48,303	9	120	2,750	0	2,711	22,034
Arizona	2,814,144	117,130	17,631	97	21,488	438	3,555	4,223	276,018
Arkansas	1,167,884	120,343	4,146	124	4,002	0	2,668	1,423	30,494
California	14,056,479	541,855	121,637	14,710	44,684	92,909	55,588	77,914	124,982
Colorado	3,099,207	247,937	129,096	5,483	63,959	69,383	4,753	31,123	44,479
Connecticut	1,300,024	11,846	7,429	0	0	593	2,903	1,262	4,784
Delaware	300,315	15,830	1,187	11	0	0	1,641	430	1,136
Florida	7,352,004	120,977	84,393	537	148	7,563	10,367	9,628	43,421
Georgia	4,733,388	172,919	32,460	15,263	5,233	104,491	24,137	62,206	694,449
Hawaii	633,740	33,166	31,878	0	116	592	0	3,274	3,594
Idaho	717,497	159,920	10,125	0	31,548	2,554	0	926	4,038
Illinois	5,512,589	114,998	31,119	13,775	30,559	119,779	31,338	64,337	60,189
Indiana	1,988,181	59,989	92,601	124	258	373	3,980	3,290	3,492
Iowa	1,149,469	140,941	6,852	109	1,066	380	7,975	1,290	3,172
Kansas	1,319,393	65,977	13,827	10	0	49,496	3,349	1,304	13,533
Kentucky	1,715,268	72,805	10,516	0	4,165	316	6,077	1,301	2,794
Louisiana	1,799,290	170,505	14,944	0	7,929	547	5,247	3,717	10,738
Maine	590,661	18,694	7,628	10	0	0	0	551	2,859
Maryland	9,094,190	301,092	1,164,770	11	133,415	9,573	3,634	12,333	3,200,792
Massachusetts	3,308,722	28,306	70,482	6,698	0	67,923	22,574	25,175	55,588
Michigan	3,409,161	82,052	31,836	0	0	32,056	4,919	6,708	13,326
Minnesota	2,222,125	132,475	12,116	99	76	7,569	6,342	2,770	31,632
Mississippi	1,124,304	120,863	23,110	0	0	2,657	3,359	1,049	1,581
Missouri	3,292,972	298,391	47,134	7,015	9,336	711	25,718	67,383	33,670
Montana	750,108	183,846	10,546	0	12,225	3,373	1,060	1,174	59,061
Nebraska	819,843	93,559	8,231	0	1,340	83	3,939	1,530	8,277
Nevada	972,087	28,463	9,853	0	33,465	14,625	0	1,641	6,576
New Hampshire	654,015	24,294	3,792	0	160	0	2,941	1,796	1,771
New Jersey	3,470,875	35,764	25,262	0	1,572	21,593	5,502	14,790	14,845
New Mexico	1,517,044	160,206	7,203	0	111,692	0	1,615	2,635	170,914
New York	8,496,262	78,851	47,143	8,729	16,010	70,854	26,517	58,099	82,198
North Carolina	3,223,368	144,629	49,206	10	98	129,341	6,436	3,994	81,068
North Dakota	449,437	59,684	6,038	0	4,786	0	3,195	993	22,106
Ohio	4,119,198	66,377	16,800	2,879	16,349	58,100	3,505	5,990	63,675
Oklahoma	1,679,581	63,827	30,944	0	8,299	4,593	5,657	3,603	82,907
Oregon	1,853,445	262,689	30,485	127	132,686	10,240	2,100	3,329	16,201
Pennsylvania	5,670,980	110,884	29,645	8,056	34,835	83,462	7,676	51,860	78,537
Rhode Island	436,853	3,689	5,148	11	0	6,759	0	896	3,608
South Carolina	1,489,116	60,573	27,900	97	44,000	0	2,578	1,996	5,489
South Dakota	610,313	62,906	8,487	10	15,321	94	3,120	953	69,811
Tennessee	2,446,583	76,173	12,563	0	63,950	707	13,358	2,490	10,545
Texas	10,087,024	257,095	70,428	10,486	20,404	85,533	89,643	85,384	68,453
Utah	1,339,939	111,073	11,689	0	2,029	162	5,315	1,893	5,439
Vermont	400,152	20,463	3,563	0	0	0	0	538	1,081
Virginia	6,759,324	154,265	1,215,984	122	1,704	135,513	1,645	125,382	13,337
Washington	3,203,679	139,631	145,413	5,218	189,524	51,290	5,514	36,072	58,489
West Virginia	1,483,431	52,146	4,222	0	27,591	2,432	1,409	1,826	29,718
Wisconsin	1,891,830	110,249	11,260	10	0	275	7,688	1,392	4,859
Wyoming	380,587	54,763	4,969	0	5,134	0	0	472	6,388
Dist. of Columbia	19,372,025	697,363	359,168	310,529	475,899	507,283	222,246	292,271	283,773
American Samoa	6,104	490	1,020	0	0	0	0	0	0
Micronesia	0	0	0	0	0	0	0	0	0
Guam	46,086	4,364	2,148	0	0	0	0	76	65
Marshall Islands	0	0	0	0	0	0	0	0	0
No. Mariana Islands	8,046	367	0	0	0	104	0	0	0
Palau	0	0	0	0	0	0	0	0	0
Puerto Rico	863,532	35,259	5,886	560	0	4,535	1,406	2,366	8,589
U.S. Virgin Islands	58,386	689	0	74	0	134	0	128	172
Undistributed	2,230,608	0	0	0	0	0	0	0	0

See footnotes at end of table.

FEDERAL GOVERNMENT EXPENDITURE FOR SALARIES AND WAGES, BY AGENCY, BY STATE AND OUTLYING AREA: FISCAL YEAR 2009 — Continued
(In thousands of dollars)

State and outlying area	Dept. of Homeland Security	Dept. of Housing and Urban Development	Dept. of the Interior	Dept. of Justice	Dept. of Labor	NASA	National Archives and Records	National Science Foundation
				Nondefense agencies — continued				
United States	$13,419,858	$929,630	$4,753,034	$9,432,500	$1,533,091	$1,885,501	$183,900	$153,449
Alabama	103,485	6,217	9,201	88,349	11,902	252,377	0	0
Alaska.........................	196,384	2,775	150,448	15,105	1,332	0	339	129
Arizona.......................	451,476	8,875	261,068	173,145	4,874	108	90	0
Arkansas.....................	23,809	4,378	19,530	64,245	3,157	0	1,955	0
California	1,623,123	58,721	472,632	791,282	80,927	213,928	7,816	0
Colorado.....................	125,518	28,734	541,373	161,025	36,822	1,268	1,982	324
Connecticut...............	119,313	6,142	4,314	62,141	5,830	101	105	0
Delaware	6,454	281	2,250	11,458	1,020	0	0	0
Florida........................	991,990	19,662	86,355	477,438	45,411	203,024	93	0
Georgia.......................	332,079	38,717	70,230	205,496	51,679	98	4,962	0
Hawaii.........................	169,998	2,341	34,811	34,040	1,700	0	0	0
Idaho..........................	19,687	893	139,265	20,953	2,908	0	0	0
Illinois........................	258,706	38,855	16,479	270,511	76,580	0	2,959	0
Indiana.......................	66,977	5,534	15,370	95,484	8,242	151	0	0
Iowa	19,384	2,349	9,270	22,551	2,849	0	1,147	0
Kansas	32,403	13,743	25,089	54,678	4,468	0	4,044	0
Kentucky	56,105	4,921	20,611	162,961	39,342	0	0	0
Louisiana...................	225,360	8,084	74,714	143,476	7,041	2,497	0	0
Maine	87,658	399	12,421	11,126	2,130	0	201	0
Maryland	273,487	11,365	54,494	125,668	7,688	306,396	75,550	0
Massachusetts	279,216	18,242	75,851	131,005	44,025	98	5,831	32
Michigan....................	273,629	13,548	26,271	135,706	9,632	128	1,677	0
Minnesota..................	99,129	7,350	54,924	109,289	4,763	135	0	0
Mississippi	83,198	5,358	25,522	67,651	4,362	34,956	0	0
Missouri.....................	117,128	9,448	46,056	138,138	30,772	235	31,431	0
Montana	49,106	738	127,146	16,461	2,137	0	0	0
Nebraska	63,875	3,059	29,972	21,220	2,698	0	0	0
Nevada.......................	77,182	2,524	130,651	41,248	3,162	0	0	0
New Hampshire	32,425	3,264	6,229	13,667	3,437	0	0	0
New Jersey	333,441	12,027	22,439	190,280	16,687	86	0	0
New Mexico	144,518	2,987	278,444	45,068	3,038	6,207	98	0
New York....................	741,670	44,226	63,655	530,622	56,347	3,258	2,704	32
North Carolina..........	217,138	8,480	35,777	155,561	6,251	171	0	0
North Dakota.............	40,953	609	53,382	9,492	1,537	0	0	0
Ohio...........................	122,411	20,652	18,262	133,670	40,866	160,458	3,816	0
Oklahoma..................	35,744	10,420	68,202	92,972	4,679	0	0	0
Oregon.......................	109,840	4,997	207,588	65,579	3,934	117	0	32
Pennsylvania.............	210,538	37,483	73,447	373,608	85,970	0	3,099	0
Rhode Island.............	40,583	2,234	3,550	12,297	2,168	0	0	0
South Carolina..........	95,164	5,760	14,682	122,392	3,040	106	116	0
South Dakota.............	7,135	479	88,705	20,114	1,344	0	0	0
Tennessee	68,913	10,309	40,706	95,662	9,638	128	0	0
Texas..........................	1,520,324	50,165	76,313	714,715	72,566	352,808	7,848	0
Utah...........................	34,944	1,905	121,090	37,221	9,629	1,298	0	0
Vermont......................	126,561	376	5,070	8,335	381	0	0	0
Virginia......................	1,046,945	8,172	330,339	759,495	44,851	204,406	0	152,900
Washington................	338,507	14,969	156,153	93,591	26,775	0	1,705	0
West Virginia.............	37,541	1,864	46,873	310,479	43,720	3,814	207	0
Wisconsin	51,932	5,572	43,788	58,766	9,293	106	0	0
Wyoming	5,360	198	108,716	9,796	1,863	0	0	0
Dist. of Columbia	1,617,958	352,497	336,677	1,853,366	584,848	137,038	24,125	0
American Samoa	1,160	0	955	200	0	0	0	0
Micronesia.................	0	0	0	0	0	0	0	0
Guam	18,116	74	1,486	5,329	147	0	0	0
Marshall Islands........	0	0	0	0	0	0	0	0
No. Mariana Islands...	4,360	0	733	1,124	84	0	0	0
Palau	0	0	0	0	0	0	0	0
Puerto Rico	163,375	6,658	8,437	60,190	2,545	0	0	0
U.S. Virgin Islands	26,440	0	5,018	7,059	0	0	0	0
Undistributed............	0	0	0	0	0	0	0	0

See footnotes at end of table.

FEDERAL GOVERNMENT EXPENDITURE FOR SALARIES AND WAGES, BY AGENCY, BY STATE AND OUTLYING AREA: FISCAL YEAR 2009—Continued
(In thousands of dollars)

State and outlying area	U.S. Postal Service	Small Business Admin.	Social Security Admin.	Dept. of State	Dept. of Transportation	Dept. of the Treasury	Dept. of Veterans Affairs	All other nondefense (a)
					Nondefense agencies—continued			
United States	$56,543,964	$319,755	$4,644,972	$2,995,100	$5,739,892	$7,697,177	$20,033,371	$9,812,267
Alabama....................	753,124	4,082	156,164	0	24,562	37,613	319,907	10,038
Alaska.......................	137,894	710	3,199	216	103,687	5,562	37,213	1,261
Arizona.....................	884,994	1,644	39,429	2,339	51,365	48,516	423,712	21,929
Arkansas...................	489,221	3,288	30,994	2,121	18,152	16,785	322,916	4,132
California	5,920,391	32,098	452,994	29,722	469,491	824,658	1,862,408	142,008
Colorado...................	958,092	10,902	50,513	5,250	146,381	113,655	279,720	41,434
Connecticut	766,474	1,036	28,879	5,987	18,987	50,728	195,465	5,705
Delaware	165,000	621	6,962	0	3,638	10,113	70,813	1,469
Florida......................	3,050,266	6,545	154,990	38,297	274,630	222,893	1,463,006	40,370
Georgia.....................	1,555,007	10,883	122,051	591	282,356	370,785	498,184	79,112
Hawaii.......................	207,736	1,070	6,494	3,335	34,322	9,572	49,663	6,038
Idaho........................	223,609	829	8,186	0	10,636	8,369	72,100	951
Illinois......................	2,770,490	5,201	231,965	18,845	234,821	188,197	762,352	170,534
Indiana.....................	1,100,463	1,392	54,934	89	108,991	59,607	294,780	12,060
Iowa	673,188	1,455	23,099	0	17,717	16,106	194,826	3,744
Kansas	669,525	1,042	20,880	0	92,184	23,420	224,278	6,143
Kentucky	720,563	2,560	50,547	1,718	38,594	249,848	265,444	4,080
Louisiana..................	705,260	3,644	49,365	22,556	30,148	34,376	270,073	9,069
Maine.......................	312,255	1,054	13,470	75	14,076	8,618	96,118	1,317
Maryland...................	1,165,258	1,657	997,668	6,021	55,108	471,534	273,133	443,543
Massachusetts	1,532,215	2,667	86,915	11,594	119,810	212,266	468,954	43,255
Michigan...................	1,955,176	2,541	95,114	2,052	71,744	150,337	483,019	17,691
Minnesota.................	1,150,443	1,564	33,044	417	115,109	62,622	377,358	12,898
Mississippi................	420,926	1,387	41,108	0	14,030	14,154	251,664	7,369
Missouri....................	1,352,481	4,654	165,942	171	91,556	325,591	472,999	17,012
Montana	193,816	745	7,999	509	13,932	7,006	57,211	2,017
Nebraska	407,250	966	12,092	0	13,738	17,415	127,647	2,952
Nevada	370,457	1,224	14,333	0	32,835	24,894	174,847	4,107
New Hampshire	304,522	812	9,914	82,902	90,655	15,466	54,240	1,728
New Jersey	2,133,526	2,277	64,893	2,464	181,608	124,325	253,978	13,516
New Mexico	288,567	1,133	50,480	539	64,117	11,717	159,853	6,013
New York...................	4,110,761	13,904	288,809	50,665	277,719	545,379	1,252,556	125,554
North Carolina..........	1,624,524	2,558	76,932	2,046	51,588	74,348	538,590	14,622
North Dakota............	158,325	1,040	6,030	0	11,590	6,815	62,126	736
Ohio.........................	2,195,146	3,194	106,236	61	141,875	181,648	732,451	24,777
Oklahoma..................	625,650	1,357	34,363	0	296,749	39,738	265,570	4,307
Oregon......................	599,520	1,483	28,045	0	28,355	43,319	299,473	3,306
Pennsylvania	2,695,275	4,553	274,300	11,671	86,537	401,543	869,409	138,592
Rhode Island.............	235,494	785	11,120	0	8,313	12,195	86,552	1,451
South Carolina..........	639,162	1,171	41,377	108,729	23,944	19,244	266,885	4,711
South Dakota............	182,827	786	6,048	0	7,343	6,444	127,813	573
Tennessee	1,079,299	1,315	67,018	73	109,361	210,147	557,029	17,199
Texas........................	3,648,972	65,123	224,174	39,122	453,509	675,766	1,409,246	88,947
Utah.........................	466,185	1,561	12,117	0	69,552	286,833	154,771	5,233
Vermont....................	156,779	848	4,167	0	5,223	4,382	61,686	699
Virginia.....................	1,480,932	15,869	156,831	2,887	231,292	108,647	426,315	141,491
Washington...............	1,080,357	3,556	102,645	16,289	221,646	92,853	403,960	19,522
West Virginia.............	346,525	1,060	28,979	0	13,168	215,167	310,503	4,187
Wisconsin	1,067,495	1,677	44,076	0	25,854	39,297	400,537	7,703
Wyoming...................	96,298	927	2,875	0	5,318	3,871	73,026	614
Dist. of Columbia	449,416	82,126	20,089	2,525,524	812,421	960,344	647,608	5,819,456
American Samoa	895	0	250	0	450	0	672	12
Micronesia.................	0	0	0	0	0	0	0	0
Guam........................	8,466	327	628	0	3,820	0	1,014	26
Marshall Islands........	0	0	0	0	0	0	0	0
No. Mariana Islands...	733	0	214	223	92	0	0	12
Palau........................	0	0	0	0	0	0	0	0
Puerto Rico	241,110	2,717	22,190	0	14,436	32,028	226,825	24,419
U.S. Virgin Islands	15,629	135	842	0	757	421	873	15
Undistributed............	0	0	0	0	0	0	0	2,230,608

Source: U.S. Census Bureau, *Consolidated Federal Funds Report for Fiscal Year 2009*. Released August 2010.

Note: All amounts represent outlays during the federal government's fiscal year. Department of Defense data represent salaries, wages and compensation, such as housing allowances; distributions by state are based on duty station. State detail for all other federal government agencies are estimates, based on place of employment.

Detail may not add to total because of rounding. For additional information, see the complete report at http://www.census.gov/govs/www/cffr.html.

Key:

(a) The "undistributed" amount includes the salaries and wages for the Federal Judiciary that could not be geographically allocated.

Table 2.12

FEDERAL GOVERNMENT DIRECT LOAN PROGRAMS — VOLUME OF ASSISTANCE PROVIDED BY STATE AND OUTLYING AREA: FISCAL YEAR 2009

(In thousands of dollars)

| State and outlying area | Total | Department of Agriculture | | Federal direct student loans | Other direct loans |
		Commodity loans— price supports	Other loans		
United States	$54,351,584	$6,806,481	$5,840,242	$36,700,014	$5,004,847
Alabama...............................	1,224,911	130,482	90,545	999,027	4,857
Alaska..................................	28,040	0	18,296	1,050	8,695
Arizona................................	410,573	2,485	41,144	366,306	637
Arkansas..............................	753,288	410,804	254,784	82,361	5,340
California	5,198,162	613,662	167,410	3,346,605	1,070,485
Colorado..............................	1,299,093	144,041	35,936	1,118,807	310
Connecticut.........................	407,863	20	41,958	365,809	77
Delaware	186,461	1,634	25,864	158,490	473
Florida	2,122,707	227,224	214,555	1,591,955	88,973
Georgia................................	1,944,248	425,349	109,273	1,402,825	6,801
Hawaii..................................	51,032	0	48,566	716	1,750
Idaho...................................	511,337	191,328	69,315	250,667	27
Illinois.................................	2,726,150	227,433	139,375	2,301,922	57,419
Indiana................................	2,067,499	209,913	275,639	1,551,599	30,348
Iowa	1,675,051	443,788	211,412	973,031	46,819
Kansas	697,879	46,740	78,458	570,921	1,761
Kentucky	600,024	36,223	150,638	400,501	12,662
Louisiana.............................	854,287	210,349	406,763	80,527	156,647
Maine	180,347	283	97,660	81,867	537
Maryland	1,603,364	4,275	51,161	943,948	603,981
Massachusetts	1,796,166	966	31,678	1,734,606	28,916
Michigan..............................	2,950,146	256,472	224,742	2,467,155	1,777
Minnesota............................	1,740,754	524,312	116,751	1,092,320	7,371
Mississippi	903,005	599,706	164,080	124,233	14,986
Missouri	1,209,843	82,040	262,799	832,972	32,032
Montana	90,156	27,776	61,838	507	36
Nebraska	436,053	173,489	104,441	155,282	2,841
Nevada................................	178,995	0	24,509	153,461	1,026
New Hampshire	104,309	0	39,817	64,038	454
New Jersey	904,776	1,514	42,219	783,977	77,066
New Mexico	85,807	3,597	76,880	4,036	1,295
New York.............................	3,130,512	25,585	106,542	2,745,081	253,305
North Carolina.....................	827,332	210,022	151,289	462,793	3,228
North Dakota.......................	127,704	68,972	45,407	1,200	12,124
Ohio	1,902,398	101,350	119,172	1,678,275	3,600
Oklahoma............................	272,210	8,544	78,023	182,428	3,215
Oregon.................................	647,843	3,457	90,541	546,026	7,819
Pennsylvania	1,614,897	10,981	143,781	1,454,034	6,101
Rhode Island........................	188,075	0	5,082	169,618	13,375
South Carolina.....................	418,576	25,844	126,464	265,618	650
South Dakota.......................	200,393	104,826	80,334	14,041	1,193
Tennessee	2,508,858	184,878	149,512	536,827	1,637,640
Texas...................................	3,489,727	935,633	192,166	1,801,394	560,534
Utah....................................	124,956	1,227	72,476	51,148	105
Vermont...............................	52,896	0	48,929	3,217	750
Virginia................................	1,047,263	39,992	118,492	877,054	11,725
Washington..........................	831,603	22,033	147,777	571,389	90,404
West Virginia.......................	583,721	609	119,975	458,765	4,372
Wisconsin	656,061	58,476	210,589	374,254	12,742
Wyoming	21,854	8,152	12,601	969	133
Dist. of Columbia	502,707	0	750	427,268	74,690
American Samoa	0	0	0	0	0
Fed. States of Micronesia.................	188	0	188	0	0
Guam	91,310	0	91,056	254	0
Marshall Islands.................	2,023	0	2,023	0	0
No. Mariana Islands	21	0	21	0	0
Palau...................................	913	0	913	0	0
Puerto Rico..........................	125,367	0	45,689	72,842	6,836
U.S. Virgin Islands	9,847	0	1,940	3,999	3,908
Undistributed......................	30,000	0	0	0	30,000

See footnotes at end of table.

FEDERAL GOVERNMENT DIRECT LOAN PROGRAMS — VOLUME OF ASSISTANCE PROVIDED BY STATE AND OUTLYING AREA: FISCAL YEAR 2009 — Continued

Source: U.S. Census Bureau, *Consolidated Federal Funds Report for Fiscal Year 2009.* Released August 2010.

Note: Amounts represent dollar volume of direct loans made during the fiscal year. For additional information see the complete report at *http://www.census.gov/govs/www/cffr.html.* Detail may not add to total because of rounding.

The CFDA defines "Direct Loans" as "Financial assistance provided through the lending of federal monies for a specific period of time, with a reasonable expectation of repayment. Such loans may or may not require the payment of interest." The CFDA defines "Guaranteed/Insured Loans" as "Programs in which the federal government makes an arrangement to indemnify a lender against part or all of any defaults by those responsible for the repayment of loans." Loan program amounts reflect the volume of loan activities. These amounts represent either direct loans made to certain categories of borrowers, or the federal government contingent liability for loans guaranteed. Loan data does not represent actual expenditures associated with the loan programs.

Any actual outlays under these programs, appear in the direct payments categories in the CFFR.

Federal government contingent liability can vary by program, and caution should be used in comparing one federal loan program to another, or in interpreting the data presented to reflect actual federal outlays over time. The following also should be noted:

1. Amounts guaranteed do not necessarily represent future outlays.

2. All amounts reflect the dollar value of loans provided during the fiscal year, and not the cumulative totals of such activity over the life of the program.

3. Direct loans are not reported on a net basis, as in the federal budget, but rather are shown in terms of total amounts loaned.

4. Programs otherwise similar can vary in the share of the total liability that the federal government guarantees or insures. Certain veterans guaranteed loan programs are guaranteed only up to a stated maximum dollar value, for example. In these cases, the federal government contingent liability is less than the total value of the loan or insured policy agreement.

Table 2.13
FEDERAL GOVERNMENT GUARANTEED LOAN PROGRAMS — VOLUME OF COVERAGE PROVIDED BY STATE AND OUTLYING AREA: FISCAL YEAR 2009
(In thousands of dollars)

State and outlying area	Total	Mortgage insurance for homes	Federal Family Education Loan program	Veterans housing guaranteed and insured loans— VA home loans	Mortgage insurance— condominiums	U.S.D.A. guaranteed loans	Small business loans	Other guaranteed loans
United States	$510,034,145	$313,008,223	$76,162,940	$68,200,787	$17,567,934	$21,854,323	$10,889,038	$2,350,899
Alabama	7,489,224	4,604,566	935,252	1,464,588	32,131	334,106	118,582	0
Alaska	2,030,664	852,698	101,624	813,575	113,318	125,290	24,159	0
Arizona	19,898,516	9,228,486	7,277,698	2,404,976	289,583	439,977	257,796	0
Arkansas	3,883,306	2,156,535	668,173	539,305	5,588	412,807	100,899	0
California	57,418,633	38,540,999	5,766,872	6,045,349	3,916,845	653,451	1,738,721	756,396
Colorado	15,644,392	9,994,858	1,361,543	2,912,154	664,080	424,317	277,438	10,000
Connecticut	6,167,626	4,102,986	630,102	276,083	433,669	67,654	99,820	557,313
Delaware	2,039,135	1,521,049	90,190	301,613	28,090	79,157	19,036	0
Florida	22,690,442	12,277,709	4,310,680	3,915,498	553,178	1,025,844	540,018	67,515
Georgia	17,981,990	11,277,422	1,688,265	2,941,784	351,366	1,295,569	427,583	0
Hawaii	1,934,646	463,454	199,681	963,771	167,649	99,944	40,148	0
Idaho	3,154,825	2,080,248	154,243	498,039	10,058	319,291	92,947	0
Illinois	20,617,467	12,064,025	4,893,386	1,234,092	1,424,104	535,852	466,007	0
Indiana	9,380,775	6,573,421	1,509,406	731,006	75,126	281,095	210,721	0
Iowa	5,223,249	2,155,040	2,161,374	295,062	51,005	404,136	156,632	0
Kansas	4,449,981	2,753,000	428,214	625,679	12,021	527,808	103,259	0
Kentucky	6,144,214	3,400,376	975,327	697,957	97,358	901,988	71,208	0
Louisiana	5,551,913	3,113,415	1,063,084	681,243	40,917	541,173	109,282	2,800
Maine	1,654,373	934,985	266,181	179,805	19,193	210,162	44,046	0
Maryland	17,618,285	12,730,833	604,802	2,700,496	1,114,278	311,810	156,067	0
Massachusetts	8,962,563	6,540,653	1,149,727	507,136	511,550	119,483	134,015	0
Michigan	9,711,398	6,444,847	1,334,973	515,625	557,245	607,504	251,205	0
Minnesota	10,316,730	5,949,105	2,365,992	639,093	367,465	610,737	384,339	-3
Mississippi	3,367,900	1,738,653	694,353	392,785	2,741	426,646	112,732	-10
Missouri	12,007,617	7,548,538	2,042,349	1,084,985	181,778	946,733	203,235	0
Montana	1,923,060	972,555	249,713	320,243	22,741	304,628	53,181	0
Nebraska	3,018,662	1,746,922	523,611	508,466	9,984	141,829	87,851	0
Nevada	6,602,673	4,886,866	204,704	1,271,690	86,180	53,106	100,126	0
New Hampshire	2,415,177	1,445,335	426,424	264,008	116,167	119,188	44,055	0
New Jersey	16,533,504	13,512,999	844,040	606,473	1,309,903	116,618	143,472	0
New Mexico	3,493,067	2,110,469	376,520	752,119	22,581	149,865	73,542	-31
New York	18,701,173	11,407,969	4,941,747	633,265	262,939	209,501	646,333	599,419
North Carolina	14,740,590	8,026,564	1,615,845	3,714,372	133,303	981,245	269,263	0
North Dakota	1,709,652	450,157	269,652	147,753	10,063	792,627	39,400	0
Ohio	14,684,933	9,308,200	2,891,843	1,315,314	323,924	538,983	306,668	0
Oklahoma	5,765,872	3,359,870	792,806	939,633	17,767	543,006	104,791	8,000
Oregon	6,932,558	4,468,557	886,298	929,550	131,431	372,691	144,030	0
Pennsylvania	18,341,569	11,048,482	4,948,399	1,199,940	347,986	513,010	283,752	0
Rhode Island	1,880,583	1,280,905	382,667	117,135	45,800	16,037	38,039	0
South Carolina	7,568,648	3,975,850	1,102,145	1,421,020	46,288	943,740	79,603	0
South Dakota	1,505,489	564,964	327,345	219,065	8,229	335,538	50,350	0
Tennessee	10,537,554	6,889,526	1,430,362	1,506,042	136,420	471,154	104,050	0
Texas	29,991,342	18,047,056	4,173,597	5,588,794	244,837	953,907	983,152	0
Utah	10,472,145	7,843,032	817,490	814,949	469,783	285,664	241,227	0
Vermont	812,383	278,300	363,112	57,015	21,385	60,515	32,057	0
Virginia	23,994,867	12,915,397	1,720,903	7,488,098	1,169,135	502,424	179,410	19,500
Washington	16,592,624	10,550,736	802,618	3,706,694	797,756	411,923	322,896	0
West Virginia	1,556,596	828,717	327,059	217,349	1,173	167,452	14,846	0
Wisconsin	7,796,435	4,830,829	1,349,623	591,054	132,541	572,196	320,192	0
Wyoming	1,582,706	846,890	136,955	251,492	2,746	324,061	20,563	0
Dist. of Columbia	2,616,035	767,982	1,210,737	95,567	349,175	0	12,574	180,000
American Samoa	18	0	0	0	0	0	18	0
Fed. States of Micronesia	13,120	0	0	0	0	13,120	0	0
Guam	63,424	323	8,414	37,119	0	13,785	3,782	0
Marshall Islands	18,526	0	0	0	0	18,526	0	0
No. Mariana Islands...	0	0	0	0	0	0	0	0
Palau	0	0	0	0	0	0	0	0
Puerto Rico	2,642,726	1,571,834	364,818	118,958	325,996	212,475	48,645	0
U.S. Virgin Islands	36,573	15,035	0	5,915	1,365	0	1,280	0
Undistributed	150,000	0	0	0	0	0	0	150,000

See footnotes at end of table.

FEDERAL GOVERNMENT GUARANTEED LOAN PROGRAMS — VOLUME OF COVERAGE PROVIDED BY STATE AND OUTLYING AREA: FISCAL YEAR 2009 — Continued

Source: U.S. Census Bureau, *Consolidated Federal Funds Report for Fiscal Year 2009.* Released August 2010.

Note: Amounts represent dollar volume of loans guaranteed during the fiscal year. For additional information see the complete report at *http://www.census.gov/govs/www/cffr.html.* Detail may not add to total because of rounding.

The CFDA defines "Guaranteed/Insured Loans" as "Programs in which the federal government makes an arrangement to indemnify a lender against part or all of any defaults by those responsible for the repayment of loans." Loan and program amounts reflect the volume of loan activities. These amounts represent the federal government contingent liability for loans guaranteed. Loans and insurance data do not represent actual expenditures associated with the loan or insurance programs. Any actual outlays under these programs, such as insurance claims paid by the federal government, appear in the direct payments categories in the CFFR.

Federal government contingent liability can vary by program, and caution should be used in comparing one federal loan or insurance program to another, or in interpreting the data presented to reflect actual federal outlays over time. The following also should be noted:

1. Amounts guaranteed or insured do not necessarily represent future outlays.

2. All amounts reflect the dollar value of loans or insurance coverage provided during the fiscal year, and not the cumulative totals of such activity over the life of the program.

3. Direct loans are not reported on a net basis, as in the federal budget, but rather are shown in terms of total amounts loaned.

4. Programs otherwise similar can vary in the share of the total liability that the federal government guarantees or insures. Certain veterans guaranteed loan programs are guaranteed only up to a stated maximum dollar value, for example. In these cases, the federal government contingent liability is less than the total value of the loan or insured policy agreement.

Table 2.14
FEDERAL GOVERNMENT INSURANCE PROGRAMS — VOLUME OF COVERAGE PROVIDED BY STATE AND OUTLYING AREA: FISCAL YEAR 2009
(In thousands of dollars)

State and outlying area		Insurance programs by volume of coverage provided				
	Total	Flood insurance	Crop insurance	Foreign investment insurance	Life insurance for veterans	Other insurance
United States	$1,291,389,712	$1,198,452,881	$77,846,347	$265,415	$14,437,730	$387,338
Alabama	11,494,138	10,936,412	352,566	0	204,703	457
Alaska	648,339	621,179	630	0	21,006	5,525
Arizona	8,085,039	7,585,430	178,122	0	320,571	916
Arkansas	3,323,634	2,298,355	898,132	0	127,147	0
California	73,186,307	67,155,715	4,524,362	0	1,443,890	62,340
Colorado	5,433,934	4,118,637	1,020,810	0	238,630	55,857
Connecticut	8,694,314	8,246,212	73,731	150,000	223,615	756
Delaware	5,801,379	5,656,415	98,086	0	46,033	846
Florida	472,732,970	468,567,622	2,855,011	0	1,291,834	18,504
Georgia	22,215,661	20,982,229	882,184	0	344,471	6,776
Hawaii	11,491,501	11,260,753	100,319	0	130,378	51
Idaho	2,558,491	1,533,206	956,866	0	65,199	3,220
Illinois	15,980,159	7,716,419	7,667,315	0	591,238	5,187
Indiana	8,674,503	4,760,701	3,693,569	0	219,203	1,030
Iowa	11,569,153	2,263,369	9,125,597	0	179,281	907
Kansas	6,031,711	1,846,257	4,017,614	21,154	138,555	8,132
Kentucky	4,077,770	2,944,719	977,400	0	151,490	4,161
Louisiana	103,806,484	102,946,902	685,354	0	165,500	8,728
Maine	1,931,987	1,775,371	75,526	0	81,090	0
Maryland	14,493,779	13,887,955	268,276	18,775	296,729	22,044
Massachusetts	11,436,914	10,986,569	67,374	0	373,568	9,403
Michigan	5,865,914	4,011,740	1,446,427	7,500	395,831	4,415
Minnesota	8,538,678	2,167,627	6,056,599	0	308,853	5,599
Mississippi	16,398,413	15,510,104	788,074	0	99,907	328
Missouri	5,993,349	3,750,369	1,961,498	0	276,139	5,343
Montana	1,863,644	703,445	1,094,538	0	59,617	6,045
Nebraska	7,253,491	1,718,037	5,425,481	0	109,973	0
Nevada	3,971,012	3,839,727	23,752	0	98,865	8,669
New Hampshire	1,716,862	1,632,714	6,607	0	76,769	772
New Jersey	49,745,080	49,188,712	65,345	0	484,398	6,624
New Mexico	2,960,166	2,715,605	127,284	0	114,164	3,113
New York	37,613,761	36,303,809	345,550	54,450	907,273	2,679
North Carolina	32,268,358	30,452,665	1,407,929	0	407,764	0
North Dakota	6,879,589	2,772,312	4,068,126	0	36,645	2,506
Ohio	9,032,251	6,049,591	2,448,873	0	517,221	16,566
Oklahoma	3,506,692	2,438,337	893,087	0	173,527	1,741
Oregon	7,783,067	6,887,187	701,544	0	188,651	5,685
Pennsylvania	12,595,712	11,465,356	375,115	0	736,939	18,302
Rhode Island	3,619,494	3,559,568	1,095	0	57,957	874
South Carolina	46,784,515	46,192,745	366,620	0	224,816	333
South Dakota	4,086,274	733,463	3,303,484	0	48,699	628
Tennessee	5,845,862	4,843,568	772,408	0	228,173	1,713
Texas	160,347,543	156,155,686	3,298,087	0	872,106	21,664
Utah	1,055,689	914,016	29,340	0	92,805	19,529
Vermont	687,693	629,397	25,784	0	32,512	0
Virginia	25,801,474	24,953,239	412,752	990	421,298	13,194
Washington	11,366,125	9,137,650	1,907,784	0	315,630	5,060
West Virginia	2,546,914	2,440,488	15,913	0	85,948	4,565
Wisconsin	4,706,058	2,547,767	1,830,175	0	318,683	9,433
Wyoming	657,140	502,172	128,234	0	26,314	421
Dist. of Columbia	279,103	234,845	0	12,547	25,013	6,698
American Samoa	0	0	0	0	0	0
Fed. States of Micronesia	0	0	0	0	0	0
Guam	52,114	52,114	0	0	0	0
Marshall Islands	0	0	0	0	0	0
No. Mariana Islands	108	108	0	0	0	0
Palau	0	0	0	0	0	0
Puerto Rico	5,548,230	5,511,705	0	0	36,525	0
U.S. Virgin Islands	350,569	345,985	0	0	4,584	0
Undistributed	600	600	0	0	0	0

See footnotes at end of table.

FEDERAL GOVERNMENT INSURANCE PROGRAMS — VOLUME OF COVERAGE PROVIDED BY STATE AND OUTLYING AREA: FISCAL YEAR 2009 — Continued

Source: U.S. Census Bureau, *Consolidated Federal Funds Report for Fiscal Year 2009*. Released August 2010.

Note: Amounts represent dollar volume of the face value of insurance coverage provided during the fiscal year. Detail may not add to total because of rounding. For additional information see the complete report at *http://www.census.gov/govs/www/cffr.html*.

The CFDA defines "Insurance" as "Financial assistance provided to assure reimbursement for losses sustained under specified conditions. Coverage may be provided directly by the federal government or through private carriers and may or may not involve the payment of premiums."

All data on insurance programs of the federal government, with the exception of data on flood insurance, come from the FAADS. National Flood Insurance data, reflecting insurance in force on September 30, 2008, are from FEMA, Department of Homeland Security.

Insurance program amounts reflect the volume of insurance activities. Insurance data do not represent actual expenditures associated with the loan or insurance programs. Any actual outlays under these programs, such as insurance claims paid by the federal government, appear in the direct payments categories in the CFFR.

Federal government contingent liability can vary by program, and caution should be used in comparing one federal loan or insurance program to another, or in interpreting the data presented to reflect actual federal outlays over time. The following also should be noted:

1. Amounts insured do not necessarily represent future outlays.

2. All amounts reflect the dollar value of insurance coverage provided during the fiscal year, and not the cumulative totals of such activity over the life of the program.

3. Programs otherwise similar can vary in the share of the total liability that the federal government guarantees or insures.

Table 2.15
PER CAPITA AMOUNTS OF FEDERAL GOVERNMENT EXPENDITURE, BY MAJOR OBJECT CATEGORY, BY STATE AND OUTLYING AREA: FISCAL YEAR 2009
(In dollars)

State and outlying area	United States resident population— July 1, 2009 (a)	Total	Retirement and disability	Other direct payments	Grants	Procurement	Salaries and wages
United States totals	$307,006,550	$10,395.56	$2,842.85	$2,468.80	$2,394.13	$1,727.16	$962.61
Alabama..............................	4,708,708	11,611.33	3,705.39	2.573.71	2,125.32	2,207.88	999.03
Alaska.................................	698,473	20,351.13	2,201.12	1,252.39	5,306.32	7,112.47	4,478.83
Arizona...............................	6,595,778	9,555.96	2,708.07	1,840.34	2,195.21	2,112.26	700.08
Arkansas.............................	2,889,450	9,448.88	3,483.84	2,445.10	2,400.71	343.83	775.40
California	36,961,664	9,360.24	2,213.00	2,186.42	2,459.82	1,866.23	634.76
Colorado.............................	5,024,748	9,514.08	2,456.03	1,720.22	1,762.00	2,213.65	1,362.17
Connecticut........................	3,518,288	12,104.94	2,774.88	2,622.28	2,509.60	3,696.30	501.89
Delaware	885,122	9,192.90	3,323.07	2,028.14	2,400.74	701.06	739.90
Florida	18,537,969	9,476.98	3,360.25	2,733.09	1,725.08	999.62	658.94
Georgia...............................	9,829,211	8,537.55	2,563.69	1,851.36	1,951.88	783.84	1,386.78
Hawaii.................................	1,295,178	19,000.95	3,259.44	7,068.32	2,515.58	1,404.35	4,753.25
Idaho..................................	1,545,801	9,637.63	2,829.01	1,842.21	2,004.95	2,216.92	744.55
Illinois...............................	12,910,409	8,990.43	2,522.80	2,554.23	2,438.74	891.50	583.17
Indiana...............................	6,423,113	9,520.22	2,927.66	2,701.68	2,077.78	1,235.61	577.49
Iowa....................................	3,007,856	9,763.93	2,960.69	2,958.68	2,519.32	772.35	552.90
Kansas	2,818,747	12,312.36	2,909.82	4,886.80	1,910.68	1,065.80	1,539.27
Kentucky	4,314,113	11,592.63	3,320.98	2,469.70	2,634.56	1,616.17	1,551.22
Louisiana............................	4,492,076	10,764.99	2,808.10	2,808.39	3,394.61	898.55	855.33
Maine	1,318,301	10,802.92	3,619.45	2,186.81	3,097.63	1,085.33	813.71
Maryland	5,699,478	16,169.03	3,236.96	2,514.52	2,071.22	6,024.96	2,321.36
Massachusetts	6,593,587	12,722.98	2,696.71	3,119.63	3,394.46	2,865.16	647.02
Michigan.............................	9,969,727	9,228.20	3,094.51	2,631.69	2,118.38	934.47	449.15
Minnesota...........................	5,266,214	8,676.32	2,592.85	2,362.71	2,229.98	906.98	583.81
Mississippi.........................	2,951,996	11,127.42	3,207.21	2,525.69	2,813.19	1,689.54	891.79
Missouri..............................	5,987,580	11,347.24	3,085.58	2,707.52	2,266.04	2,256.05	1,032.04
Montana..............................	974,989	11,205.69	3,326.75	3,215.14	3,015.02	521.52	1,127.26
Nebraska.............................	1,796,619	9,198.58	2,890.12	2,736.90	2,035.08	647.71	888.77
Nevada................................	2,643,085	7,148.49	2,635.78	1,624.18	1,421.63	781.36	685.54
New Hampshire	1,324,575	8,942.06	3,132.85	1,747.61	1,972.06	1,450.31	639.23
New Jersey	8,707,739	9,261.51	2,741.60	2,612.09	1,927.54	1,383.96	596.32
New Mexico	2,009,671	13,669.90	3,211.80	1,893.61	3,459.89	3,849.49	1,255.19
New York............................	19,541,453	9,977.52	2,643.79	2,761.54	3,194.17	742.37	635.65
North Carolina....................	9,380,884	9,042.86	3,048.22	1,966.81	2,232.38	554.59	1,240.86
North Dakota.......................	646,844	13,322.99	2,883.44	4,737.83	3,485.30	733.10	1,483.30
Ohio....................................	11,542,645	9,354.41	2,918.43	2,870.62	2,201.73	788.64	574.99
Oklahoma............................	3,687,050	10,175.03	3,318.18	2,405.37	2,320.08	853.99	1,277.41
Oregon................................	3,825,657	8,781.11	3,039.78	2,191.02	2,275.48	645.26	629.57
Pennsylvania	12,604,767	10,764.70	3,323.49	3,174.20	2,170.82	1,435.84	660.35
Rhode Island.......................	1,053,209	10,935.55	3,066.23	2,923.40	3,426.77	653.79	865.36
South Carolina....................	4,561,242	10,283.23	3,376.54	2,231.25	2,027.82	1,800.21	847.41
South Dakota......................	812,383	11,693.12	3,008.43	3,756.09	3,036.78	700.17	1,191.65
Tennessee	6,296,254	10,886.77	3,238.25	2,716.81	2,710.23	1,655.76	565.72
Texas..................................	24,782,302	9,164.11	2,352.50	1,995.47	2,246.42	1,586.24	983.48
Utah....................................	2,784,572	7,434.65	2,081.39	1,249.08	1,775.75	1,305.61	1,022.82
Vermont..............................	621,760	11,407.02	3,106.07	2,164.40	3,478.02	1,728.45	930.09
Virginia..............................	7,882,590	19,733.90	3,465.67	1,968.30	1,607.37	10,376.92	2,315.65
Washington.........................	6,664,195	9,987.70	2,963.25	1,966.94	2,290.00	1,382.67	1,384.83
West Virginia......................	1,819,777	10,884.65	4,131.10	2,569.55	2,704.57	451.95	1,027.47
Wisconsin	5,654,774	10,836.92	2,849.55	2,435.52	3,398.72	1,682.39	470.75
Wyoming	544,270	11,534.43	2,902.53	2,139.91	4,785.02	477.37	1,229.60
Dist. of Columbia	599,657	83,196.12	4,747.09	8,305.17	20,048.09	12,924.40	37,171.37
American Samoa	65,628	5,601.69	892.00	215.80	3,238.91	36.41	1,218.57
Fed. States of Micronesia ...	107,434	2,529.81	5.57	133.68	2,373.29	17.27	0
Guam	178,430	7,823.77	1,524.72	668.56	2,170.62	1,708.68	1,751.20
Marshall Islands.................	64,522	2,172.63	0.66	58.09	2,104.69	9.20	0
No. Mariana Islands	51,484	4,690.33	652.02	347.79	3,309.13	210.26	171.13
Palau	20,796	1,159.66	10.22	121.05	1,027.17	1.22	0
Puerto Rico.........................	3,967,288	5,395.70	1,942.89	1,111.99	1,896.95	144.29	299.58
U.S. Virgin Islands.............	109,825	7,979.95	2,166.59	1,266.76	3,393.44	569.33	583.83
Undistributed......................	0	0	0	0	0	0	0

Source: U.S. Census Bureau, *Consolidated Federal Funds Report for Fiscal Year 2009*. Released August 2010.

Note: Detail may not add to total because of rounding. U.S. total population and per capita figures in the top row include only the 50 states and the District of Columbia; the U.S. Outlying Areas represented at the bottom of the table are excluded from this figure. For additional information see the complete report at http://www.census.gov/govs/www/cffr.html.

Key:
N.A. — Not applicable
(a) All population figures represent resident population as of July 1, 2009.

Table 2.16
PERCENT DISTRIBUTION OF FEDERAL GOVERNMENT EXPENDITURE, BY MAJOR OBJECT CATEGORY, BY STATE AND OUTLYING AREA: FISCAL YEAR 2009
(In dollars)

State and outlying area	Percent distribution of United States resident population— July 1, 2009 (a)	Total	Retirement and disability	Other direct payments	Grants	Procurement	Salaries and wages
United States	100%	100%	100%	100%	100%	100%	100%
Alabama	1.5	1.7	2.0	1.6	1.3	1.9	1.6
Alaska.................................	0.2	0.4	0.2	0.1	0.5	0.9	1.0
Arizona...............................	2.1	1.9	2.0	1.6	1.9	2.5	1.5
Arkansas.............................	0.9	0.8	1.1	0.9	0.9	0.2	0.7
California	11.9	10.7	9.3	10.6	12.2	12.5	7.8
Colorado.............................	1.6	1.5	1.4	1.1	1.2	2.0	2.3
Connecticut	1.1	1.3	1.1	1.2	1.2	2.4	0.6
Delaware	0.3	0.3	0.3	0.2	0.3	0.1	0.2
Florida................................	5.9	5.4	7.1	6.6	4.3	3.4	4.1
Georgia...............................	3.2	2.6	2.9	2.4	2.6	1.4	4.6
Hawaii.................................	0.4	0.8	0.5	1.2	0.4	0.3	2.1
Idaho..................................	0.5	0.5	0.5	0.4	0.4	0.6	0.4
Illinois................................	4.1	3.6	3.7	4.3	4.2	2.1	2.5
Indiana...............................	2.1	1.9	2.1	2.3	1.8	1.4	1.2
Iowa	1.0	0.9	1.0	1.2	1.0	0.4	0.6
Kansas	0.9	1.1	0.9	1.8	0.7	0.5	1.4
Kentucky	1.4	1.5	1.6	1.4	1.5	1.3	2.2
Louisiana............................	1.4	1.5	1.4	1.7	2.0	0.7	1.3
Maine..................................	0.4	0.4	0.5	0.4	0.5	0.3	0.4
Maryland	1.8	2.8	2.1	1.9	1.6	6.2	4.4
Massachusetts	2.1	2.6	2.0	2.7	3.0	3.4	1.4
Michigan.............................	3.2	2.8	3.5	3.4	2.8	1.7	1.5
Minnesota...........................	1.7	1.4	1.5	1.6	1.6	0.9	1.0
Mississippi	0.9	1.0	1.1	1.0	1.1	0.9	0.9
Missouri..............................	1.9	2.1	2.1	2.1	1.8	2.5	2.1
Montana	0.3	0.3	0.4	0.4	0.4	0.1	0.4
Nebraska	0.6	0.5	0.6	0.6	0.5	0.2	0.5
Nevada................................	0.8	0.6	0.8	0.6	0.5	0.4	0.6
New Hampshire	0.4	0.4	0.5	0.3	0.4	0.3	0.3
New Jersey	2.8	2.5	2.7	3.0	2.3	2.2	1.7
New Mexico	0.6	0.8	0.7	0.5	0.9	1.4	0.8
New York.............................	6.3	6.0	5.9	7.1	8.4	2.6	4.1
North Carolina....................	3.0	2.6	3.2	2.4	2.8	0.9	3.9
North Dakota.......................	0.2	0.3	0.2	0.4	0.3	0.1	0.3
Ohio	3.7	3.3	3.8	4.3	3.4	1.7	2.2
Oklahoma............................	1.2	1.2	1.4	1.2	1.1	0.6	1.6
Oregon................................	1.2	1.0	1.3	1.1	1.2	0.4	0.8
Pennsylvania	4.0	4.2	4.8	5.2	3.7	3.3	2.8
Rhode Island.......................	0.3	0.4	0.4	0.4	0.5	0.1	0.3
South Carolina....................	1.5	1.4	1.7	1.3	1.2	1.5	1.3
South Dakota.......................	0.3	0.3	0.3	0.4	0.3	0.1	0.3
Tennessee	2.0	2.1	2.3	2.2	2.3	1.9	1.2
Texas...................................	8.0	7.0	6.6	6.5	7.5	7.1	8.1
Utah....................................	0.9	0.6	0.7	0.5	0.7	0.7	1.0
Vermont..............................	0.2	0.2	0.2	0.2	0.3	0.2	0.2
Virginia...............................	2.5	4.8	3.1	2.0	1.7	14.9	6.1
Washington.........................	2.1	2.1	2.2	1.7	2.1	1.7	3.1
West Virginia......................	0.6	0.6	0.9	0.6	0.7	0.1	0.6
Wisconsin	1.8	1.9	1.8	1.8	2.6	1.7	0.9
Wyoming	0.2	0.2	0.2	0.2	0.3	0.0	0.2
Dist. of Columbia	0.2	1.5	0.3	0.7	1.6	1.4	7.4
American Samoa	0.0	0.0	0.0	0.0	0.0	0.0	0.0
Fed. States of Micronesia...	0.0	0.0	0.0	0.0	0.0	0.0	0.0
Guam	0.1	0.0	0.0	0.0	0.1	0.1	0.1
Marshall Islands.................	0.0	0.0	0.0	0.0	0.0	0.0	0.0
No. Mariana Islands	0.0	0.0	0.0	0.0	0.0	0.0	0.0
Palau	0.0	0.0	0.0	0.0	0.0	0.0	0.0
Puerto Rico.........................	1.3	0.7	0.9	0.6	1.0	0.1	0.4
U.S. Virgin Islands	0.0	0.0	0.0	0.0	0.1	0.0	0.0
Undistributed......................	0.0	0.7	0.0	0.0	0.0	3.6	0.7

Source: U.S. Census Bureau, *Consolidated Federal Funds Report for Fiscal Year 2009.* Released August 2010.

Note: Detail may not add to total because of rounding. Values for the 50 states, the District of Columbia, and the U.S. Outlying Areas were used in calculating these distributions. For additional information see the complete report at *http://www.census.gov/govs/www/cffr.html.*

Key: (a) All population figures represent resident population as of July 1, 2009.

Table 2.17
FEDERAL GOVERNMENT EXPENDITURE FOR DEFENSE DEPARTMENT AND ALL OTHER AGENCIES, BY STATE AND OUTLYING AREA: FISCAL YEAR 2009

State and outlying area	Federal expenditure (millions of dollars)		Per capita federal expenditure (dollars) (a)		Percent distribution of federal expenditure		Exhibit: Dept. of Energy, defense-related activities (millions of dollars) (b)
	Dept. of Defense	All other federal agencies	Dept. of Defense	All other federal agencies	Dept. of Defense	All other federal agencies	
United States	$534,889	$2,703,471	$1,710.56	$8,685.00	100%	100%	$15,893
Alabama	12,266	42,408	2,604.95	9,006.38	2.3	1.6	0
Alaska	6,043	8,171	8,652.04	11,699.08	1.1	0.3	0
Arizona......................	15,099	47,930	2,289.25	7,266.71	2.8	1.8	0
Arkansas....................	2,071	25,231	716.72	8,732.16	0.4	0.9	0
California	59,330	286,640	1,605.17	7,755.07	11.1	10.6	1,151
Colorado.....................	11,333	36,473	2,255.36	7,258.72	2.1	1.3	137
Connecticut	12,860	29,729	3,655.20	8,449.74	2.4	1.1	0
Delaware	899	7,238	1,015.98	8,176.92	0.2	0.3	0
Florida	23,186	152,498	1,250.72	8,226.26	4.3	5.6	8
Georgia......................	16,421	67,497	1,670.62	6,866.93	3.1	2.5	0
Hawaii.......................	7,546	17,064	5,826.09	13,174.87	1.4	0.6	2
Idaho.........................	1,157	13,741	748.69	8,888.94	0.2	0.5	784
Illinois......................	9,090	106,981	704.05	8,286.38	1.7	4.0	88
Indiana......................	8,946	52,203	1,392.78	8,127.44	1.7	1.9	0
Iowa..........................	2,332	27,036	775.35	8,988.59	0.4	1.0	0
Kansas	5,922	28,784	2,100.78	10,211.58	1.1	1.1	0
Kentucky	10,316	39,696	2,391.15	9,201.48	1.9	1.5	21
Louisiana...................	5,550	42,808	1,235.40	9,529.59	1.0	1.6	0
Maine........................	2,043	12,199	1,549.66	9,253.26	0.4	0.5	0
Maryland	23,162	68,993	4,063.83	12,105.19	4.3	2.6	0
Massachusetts	16,641	67,249	2,523.84	10,199.14	3.1	2.5	0
Michigan....................	7,445	84,557	746.80	8,481.41	1.4	3.1	0
Minnesota..................	4,170	41,521	791.89	7,884.43	0.8	1.5	0
Mississippi	6,082	26,766	2,060.18	9,067.25	1.1	1.0	4
Missouri.....................	15,361	52,581	2,565.50	8,781.74	2.9	1.9	457
Montana	748	10,178	766.92	10,438.77	0.1	0.4	0
Nebraska	1,876	14,650	1,044.17	8,154.41	0.4	0.5	0
Nevada	2,738	16,156	1,035.76	6,112.73	0.5	0.6	560
New Hampshire	2,052	9,792	1,549.39	7,392.67	0.4	0.4	0
New Jersey	10,877	69,770	1,249.06	8,012.45	2.0	2.6	0
New Mexico	2,792	24,680	1,389.31	12,280.68	0.5	0.9	3,940
New York....................	13,640	181,335	698.02	9,279.50	2.6	6.7	427
North Carolina...........	12,542	72,288	1,337.00	7,705.85	2.3	2.7	0
North Dakota.............	788	7,829	1,218.90	12,104.09	0.1	0.3	0
Ohio..........................	10,206	97,768	884.21	8,470.20	1.9	3.6	113
Oklahoma..................	6,071	31,445	1,646.66	8,528.38	1.1	1.2	0
Oregon.......................	2,610	30,983	682.35	8,098.77	0.5	1.1	0
Pennsylvania	13,938	121,749	1,105.77	9,658.93	2.6	4.5	433
Rhode Island.............	1,143	10,374	1,085.35	9,850.21	0.2	0.4	0
South Carolina..........	6,726	40,178	1,474.61	8,808.62	1.3	1.5	2,208
South Dakota	897	8,603	1,103.83	10,589.28	0.2	0.3	0
Tennessee	4,208	64,337	668.40	10,218.37	0.8	2.4	1,413
Texas.........................	46,736	180,372	1,885.86	7,278.25	8.7	6.7	530
Utah..........................	3,926	16,776	1,409.97	6,024.68	0.7	0.6	0
Vermont.....................	1,064	6,029	1,710.61	9,696.41	0.2	0.2	0
Virginia......................	67,051	88,503	8,506.18	11,227.72	12.5	3.3	0
Washington................	11,798	54,762	1,770.33	8,217.37	2.2	2.0	2,372
West Virginia.............	900	18,907	494.84	10,389.81	0.2	0.7	13
Wisconsin	9,215	52,066	1,629.54	9,207.38	1.7	1.9	0
Wyoming	419	5,858	770.68	10,763.75	0.1	0.2	12
Dist. of Columbia	4,923	44,967	8,208.95	74,987.17	0.9	1.7	1,224
American Samoa	76	291	1,160.82	4,440.86	0.0	0.0	0
Fed. States of Micronesia.........	0	272	0.02	2,529.79	0.0	0.0	0
Guam	567	829	3,179.60	4,644.17	0.1	0.0	0
Marshall Islands........	0	140	1.53	2,171.10	0.0	0.0	0
No. Mariana Islands...	6	235	120.90	4,569.43	0.0	0.0	0
Palau........................	0	24	2.48	1,157.18	0.0	0.0	0
Puerto Rico	735	20,671	185.24	5,210.46	0.1	0.8	0
U.S. Virgin Islands	46	830	419.71	7,560.24	0.0	0.0	0
Undistributed	8,303	13,827	0.00	0.00	1.6	0.5	0

Source: U.S. Census Bureau, *Consolidated Federal Funds Report for Fiscal Year 2009*. Released August 2010.
Note: Detail may not add to total because of rounding. For additional information see the complete report at http://www.census.gov/govs/www/cffr.html.

Key:
(a) All population figures represent resident population as of July 1, 2009.
(b) These data are presented for illustrative purposes only. They were compiled from preliminary FY 2009 state budget allocation tables that were prepared for submission to Congress and that were found on the Department of Energy website.

Table 2.18
STATE RANKINGS FOR PER CAPITA AMOUNTS
OF FEDERAL GOVERNMENT EXPENDITURE: FISCAL YEAR 2009

State	Total	Retirement and disability	Other direct payments	Grants	Procurement	Salaries and wages
Alabama	11	2	21	35	10	20
Alaska	1	49	49	1	2	2
Arizona	31	39	45	33	11	32
Arkansas	35	4	27	24	50	29
California	36	48	34	21	12	39
Colorado	33	46	47	47	9	10
Connecticut	9	37	19	20	5	48
Delaware	41	10	37	23	41	31
Florida	34	7	14	48	29	35
Georgia	48	44	43	43	36	8
Hawaii	3	13	1	19	22	1
Idaho	30	35	44	41	8	30
Illinois	44	45	23	22	33	43
Indiana	32	28	17	37	26	44
Iowa	29	27	8	18	38	47
Kansas	8	30	2	45	28	6
Kentucky	12	11	26	17	18	5
Louisiana	23	36	11	8	32	26
Maine	22	3	33	11	27	28
Maryland	4	15	25	38	3	3
Massachusetts	7	40	7	9	6	36
Michigan	39	20	18	36	30	50
Minnesota	47	43	30	31	31	42
Mississippi	17	17	24	14	15	23
Missouri	15	21	16	28	7	17
Montana	16	8	5	13	47	16
Nebraska	40	32	13	39	44	24
Nevada	50	42	48	50	37	33
New Hampshire	45	18	46	42	20	37
New Jersey	38	38	20	44	23	41
New Mexico	5	16	42	5	4	12
New York	28	41	12	10	39	38
North Carolina	43	23	41	30	46	13
North Dakota	6	33	3	3	40	7
Ohio	37	29	10	32	35	45
Oklahoma	26	12	29	25	34	11
Oregon	46	24	32	27	45	40
Pennsylvania	24	9	6	34	21	34
Rhode Island	18	22	9	6	43	25
South Carolina	25	6	31	40	13	27
South Dakota	10	25	4	12	42	15
Tennessee	19	14	15	15	17	46
Texas	42	47	38	29	19	21
Utah	49	50	50	46	25	19
Vermont	14	19	35	4	14	22
Virginia	2	5	39	49	1	4
Washington	27	26	40	26	24	9
West Virginia	20	1	22	16	49	18
Wisconsin	21	34	28	7	16	49
Wyoming	13	31	36	2	48	14

Source: U.S. Census Bureau, *Consolidated Federal Funds Report for Fiscal Year 2009.* Released August 2010.

Note: For additional information see the complete report at *http://www.census.gov/govs/www/cffr.html.* States are ranked from largest per capita amount of federal funds (1) to smallest per capita amount of federal funds (50). Rankings are based upon per capita amounts shown in Table 2.10. Federal funds for loans and insurance coverage are excluded from consideration in this table. Also excluded are per capita amounts for the District of Columbia and the U.S. Outlying Areas.

Chapter Three

STATE LEGISLATIVE BRANCH

THE FOLLOWING TABLES ARE AN ONLINE-ONLY FEATURE FOR THE 2011 VOLUME OF *THE BOOK OF THE STATES.*

THESE TABLES CAN BE ACCESSED AT
http://knowledgecenter.csg.org/drupalview-content-type/1219

2010 Legislative Elections

By Tim Storey

The 2010 state legislative elections brought major change to the state partisan landscape with Republicans emerging in the best position they have had in more than 50 years. Voters shifted majority control to the GOP in 20 legislative chambers. By the time the proverbial smoke had cleared in early March of 2011, three more chambers had moved to Republican control due to special elections and party switches by sitting legislators. Republicans emerged with control of 26 state legislatures compared to only 15 held by Democrats, with eight divided between the two parties.

2010 was a banner year for Republicans in state legislative elections. GOP gains far outpaced expectations that focused on whether Republicans could exceed their 1994 success when the party netted more than 500 legislative seats. Their candidates blew past that mark; when the election was over, they had flipped 720 seats from Democratic to Republican.

Historically, state elections held halfway through the term of the president do not go well for the party in the White House, and 2010 was no exception. Since 1900, the president's party has lost ground in legislatures in 26 of the 28 midterm elections. In November 2010, Republican legislative candidates largely ran against President Obama's economic and health care policies, citing dismal state budgets and a national unemployment rate

of 9.8 percent, which was hovering near its highest point in more than 25 years. Democrats were poised for a letdown, having netted seats in the three previous election cycles. Before the election, Democrats held slightly more than 55 percent of the nation's 7,382 state legislative seats, their highest margin since before the 1994 election. Since the 1920s, neither major party has added legislative seats in four consecutive elections.

All historic trends pointed to a Republican surge in 2010, but no one could have predicted the extent of GOP gains. It was an absolute landslide for Republicans. In every region and in the country as a whole, the GOP made huge gains regardless of the metric. They made huge strides in terms of seats, chambers and legislatures, ending up in the most dominant position since the 1950s.

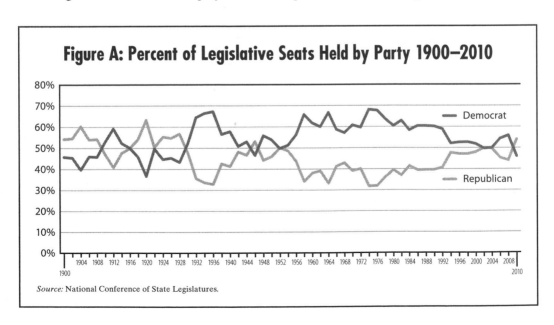

Figure A: Percent of Legislative Seats Held by Party 1900–2010

Source: National Conference of State Legislatures.

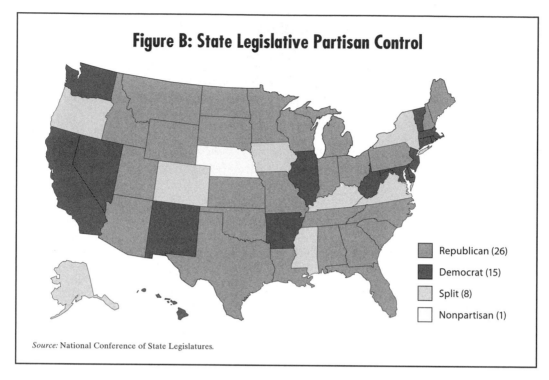

Figure B: State Legislative Partisan Control

- Republican (26)
- Democrat (15)
- Split (8)
- Nonpartisan (1)

Source: National Conference of State Legislatures.

In early 2011, the U.S. Census Bureau delivered detailed census data to states to use in drawing new legislative and congressional districts. The 2010 legislative elections left Republicans in their best position for the decennial task of redistricting since the Supreme Court handed down the historic *Baker vs. Carr* decision in 1962 that marked the beginning of the modern redistricting era.

Final Numbers

In the two-year election cycle from January 2008 to January 2010, Republicans added more than 725 legislative seats to their total. They now control 54 percent of all seats compared to 46 percent in Democratic hands. The shift of 725 seats was the highest since the 1966 election cycle, when Republicans gained 762 seats. Republican legislators occupy 3,948 of the nation's legislative seats, compared to 3,354 held by Democrats. The remaining seats are held by about 25 independent and third-party legislators. The 49 senators in Nebraska's unicameral legislature run in nonpartisan elections and are not included in the tallies. Figure A shows the historic control of all U.S. state legislative seats.

Probably more important than picking up individual districts for Republicans was that they achieved majority status in 20 legislative cham-

bers in 2010, including the Montana House, which was tied prior to the election. And in the Oregon House, Republicans gained enough seats to tie the previously Democrat-held chamber. As if the Nov. 2, 2010, landslide was not bad enough for Democrats, more than two dozen Democratic legislators defected to the Republican party in the months following the election. Those party switches gave Republicans numeric majorities in three additional Southern chambers, the Louisiana House and Senate and the Mississippi Senate.

As 2011 sessions kicked into high gear, Republicans controlled the entire legislature in 26 states. Democrats controlled 15 and eight were divided with neither party having the majority in both chambers. Those top-line partisan control numbers were almost a complete reversal of the Democratic advantage prior to the election. Democrats claimed 27 legislatures compared to only 14 for Republicans before the election. Going into the election, eight states had divided control. Figure B shows the state-by-state partisan control of legislatures.

2011 marked the first time since after the elections of 1952 that the GOP controlled more than half the state legislatures in the U.S. The last time Republicans held as many total seats was in 1928. In terms of chambers, Republicans hold majorities in 59 of the 99 state legislative bodies. Democrats have a majority in 37. The Alaska Senate and Oregon House are both tied. Ties are historically fairly common. The last time that none of the nation's 99 chambers was tied was in 1984.

The sheer change in majorities—all in the direction of the GOP—was also extraordinary in 2010. On average, 13 chambers switch control every two years, but Republicans added 23 in 2010, including the immediate post-election gains in Louisiana and Mississippi. With the Oregon House becoming tied, 24 chambers saw a change in the majority in the election cycle.

The scope of Republican gains was remarkable. Slightly less than 83 percent of all legislative seats were on the 2010 ballot, and 88 chambers held general legislative elections in 2010. The GOP gained seats in all but five. By far, the biggest surge was in the 400-member New Hampshire House, where Republican ranks swelled by more than 25 percent of the chamber's total membership, adding a whopping 122 seats. This was likely the biggest gain in seats in any legislative chamber by one party in American history.

The post-2010 election numbers were certainly grim for Democrats; however, it was perhaps some pre-election data that really pointed to how bad things would get for President Obama's party. About 11,000 candidates ran for the 6,115 state legislative seats up for election in 2010. About 10,000 were either Democratic or Republican. The number of candidates fielded by each party was about even. What was striking about the candidate numbers in 2010 was 49 fewer Democrats were running than in 2008 compared to 820 more Republican candidates than in 2008. Republicans challenged, and won, more districts knowing they had the wind at their backs.

Chamber Switches

Majority control shifts are common in every election cycle, but it is not common for all the changes to go in one direction. But that is exactly what happened in 2010 with all shifts moving to the GOP. As noted, Republican gains in the New Hampshire House were unprecedented and allowed the party to retake the majority in the historically Republican state for the first time since the Democrats won it in 2006. The New Hampshire Senate also switched over to GOP control, going from a 14-10 Democratic edge to 19-5 Republican majority. Only the Wyoming Senate, with four Senate Democrats, has fewer Democratic members.

In Maine, the story was similar to New Hampshire, with Democrats losing control of both chambers. In the Maine House, Republicans took 21 seats. The Maine Senate saw an almost complete reversal ending with a Republican majority of 20-14 with one Independent. Before the election, the Maine Senate had 20 Democrats. Two other Northeastern chambers, the New York Senate and Pennsylvania House, returned to GOP control after only two years in the Democratic column. The 112-91 advantage in the Pennsylvania House was the largest majority either party had held in the competitive chamber since 1976.

Three legislative chambers in the South went for the GOP for the first time since Reconstruction. Until the 2010 election, Republicans had not had a majority of seats in the North Carolina Senate since 1870. They also won back the North Carolina House, which changed party control in five of the past eight elections. In Alabama, Republicans scored solid majorities in both the House and Senate for the first time since the 1870s.

The other Southern legislative bodies to change control were in states that did not have 2010 elections—Louisiana and Mississippi. Party switches by sitting Louisiana House members and senators moved those two chambers to Republican majority status for the first time since 1870. In the Mississippi Senate, Republicans won a vacant Democratic seat district in a special election in February 2011. That switch, combined with a Democratic senator changing parties, left the Republicans with a 27-25 majority, their first since 1875.

Republicans made the most gains in the Midwest, where they won eight chambers in the Great Lakes states. They took back the Ohio House after losing it in 2008. In Indiana, the House switched again with Republicans emerging with a 60-40 majority. The Indiana House has changed hands 20 times since 1900, making it the most competitive House in the country over the past 110 years. Only the Connecticut Senate has changed hands more times; it has gone back and forth 21 times, mostly in the middle decades of the last century. In Michigan, legislative term limits helped Republicans win back the House by seizing 21 seats. Wisconsin has been another very competitive Midwestern state in recent elections, and both chambers went Republican in 2010. Wisconsin was one of two states, along with Maine, where the entire state government switched. In both states, the governorship, House and Senate changed from Democratic to Republican.

Minnesota voters delivered one of the only split decisions in the 2010 election. Both chambers of Minnesota's legislature went to the GOP from Democratic control; however, Democrats retook the governor's office. Gov. Mark Dayton is the first Democrat elected governor in Minnesota since 1986. The switch of one branch of state government to one party and the other branch to the opposite party is very rare. The last time it happened was in 1974, when Democrats won both bodies of the Alaska Legislature but lost the governor's mansion.

With the addition of the Iowa House in 2010, Republicans controlled all but three legislative chambers in the Midwest. The only chambers in the region remaining in Democratic hands were the Iowa Senate, where they clung to a two-vote lead, and both chambers in Illinois.

Republican gains in the West were not as pronounced as in other parts of the country. Only two chambers west of Minnesota changed to the GOP—the Colorado House and the Montana House. In Colorado, Democrats nearly kept control of the House with Republicans winding up with only a one seat majority, 33-32. The opposite was true in the Montana House, where Republicans gained 18 seats and ended up with a supermajority of 68 to 32. Montana's House was tied before the election and ranks as one of the most competitive chambers in the country, having switched control 18 times since 1900.

The only state west of the Rockies to see a legislative control shift was Oregon, where Republicans managed to tie the House at 30-30 after being in the minority for four years. Oregon House members agreed to a power-sharing arrangement, with co-speakers and co-chairs for committees.

Regional Overview

Republicans added seats in every region of the country. One of the most noteworthy outcomes of the 2010 election was the shift in the South, where Republicans added more than 177 legislative seats. For the first time in more than 130 years, a majority of Southern legislators are now Republican. The trend of Republican gains in the South has been steady for decades. Just 20 years ago, prior to the 1990 election, 75 percent of all Southern legislators were Democrats. At that time, Democrats controlled every Southern legislative chamber. As 2011 legislative sessions convened, Republicans held 21 of the 28 Southern legislative bodies—a dramatic reversal in a relatively short span of two decades.

Despite the symbolic tipping point in the South, it is not the strongest region for Republicans. That distinction belongs to the Midwest, where Republicans control more than 62 percent of all seats. It is the best position for Midwestern Republicans in more than 50 years.

The West is home to both the most Republican and the most Democratic legislatures. The Wyoming legislature jumped over Idaho to become the most Republican legislature. Eighty-four percent of Wyoming legislators are Republican. On the opposite end of the spectrum is Hawaii, where 87 percent of legislators are Democrats. Only one Republican is left in the Hawaii Senate, making the Hawaii minority caucus the smallest partisan caucus in the country.

Table A shows the number of seats Republicans netted in each region in the 2010 election cycle. Four states—Louisiana, Mississippi, New Jersey and Virginia—conduct regular legislative elections in odd-numbered years. New Jersey and Virginia held elections in 2009, and those results are included in Table A.

Table A: Seat Changes by Region from 2008 to 2010

Region	Seat changes	Percent of seats held by Republicans in 2011
East	+229 Republicans	47.4%
South	+177 Republicans	54.3%
Midwest	+211 Republicans	62.3%
West	+94 Republicans	54.8%

Source: National Conference of State Legislatures.

Turnover and Term Limits

2010 was a remarkable year for turnover. A new legislator was elected in 24 percent of the seats in states with elections in 2010. Turnover of that magnitude is not unprecedented and is in fact common every 10 years in the election immediately following the redistricting of all legislative districts. After redistricting using 2000 census data, legislative turnover was 24 percent in 2002. Turnover in non-redistricting elections is typically closer to 17 or 18 percent. More than 1,760 new legislators were elected in 2010.

The most dramatic turnover was in the Michigan Senate, where term limits led to 76 percent turnover. Term limits prevented 29 of the 38 incumbent Michigan senators from running in 2010. It was perhaps the highest turnover of any legislative body since before World War II. However, the body will not be without legislative experience since a large number of the new Michigan senators were term-limited House members.

Fifteen states impose term limits on state legislators. The number of legislators ineligible to seek re-election in 2010 was 380, which tied a record set in 2000 when term limits first took effect in many states.

Conclusion

Democrats were hard pressed to find a silver lining in the 2010 election. If ever the word "landslide" was applicable, it was in 2010. Pundits predicted a tough year for Democrats, and the reality was even worse than the direst predictions. After three election cycles where Democrats increased their numbers, the pendulum was almost destined to swing back toward the Republicans, who now find themselves in an historic position of influence at the state level.

In 2012, the story could be completely different. Redistricting is the big wild card for 2012, especially in two large states that substantially changed the process for redistricting in advance of this round of mapmaking—California and Florida. The U.S. Constitution requires states to redraw all state legislative districts prior to the next election once new census data is delivered. In the next legislative election—2011 for Louisiana, Mississippi, New Jersey and Virginia, all legislative candidates will be running in unfamiliar districts that have been redrawn using 2010 census data. The 2012 races will almost certainly bring a great deal of upheaval, and they are likely to be unpredictable and full of surprises.

About the Author

Tim Storey is a senior fellow in the Legislative Management Program of the Denver, Colo.-based National Conference of State Legislatures. He specializes in elections and redistricting, as well as legislative organization and management. He has staffed NCSL's Redistricting and Elections Committee since 1990 and authored numerous articles on the topics of elections and redistricting. Every two years, he leads NCSL's StateVote project to track and analyze legislative election results. He graduated from Mars Hill College in North Carolina and received his master's degree from the University of Colorado's Graduate School of Public Affairs.

Legislative Options to Achieve Public Retirement Plan Reforms

By Girard Miller

State legislatures face mounting pressures to further reform public retirement plans to achieve sustainable, sufficient and competitive levels. A major legal challenge facing many states is their ability to change benefits for current employees. This article reviews both legal and pragmatic issues, and offers specific options, policies and strategies to guide legislative reforms.

Following the stock market swoon of 2008–09 which decimated pension fund investment portfolios and doubled the unfunded liabilities of most public plans, the funding problems of public retirement plans has attracted national attention. With public pension plans now underfunded by about $800 billion using conventional actuarial methods applied to 2010 year-end market values, and public retiree medical benefit plans suffering even deeper deficits of $1.5 to $2 trillion, concerns are mounting over the ability of public employers to meet their obligations. Pension reform has become a rallying cry in many state legislatures, and many states have revised their plans in an effort to address the financial hemorrhages.

The challenge now facing states and localities is that many of the revisions and reforms enacted thus far are still insufficient to align long-term liabilities and costs with the capacity of public employers to pay for these benefits. And for those that have failed to act, the hole keeps getting deeper even though the stock market has rallied handsomely from its 2009 trough. Hence, further rounds of retirement plan reform legislation likely will be necessary in the coming year(s). In some states, taxpayer and watchdog groups are preparing possible ballot initiatives, so the pressure is mounting to take action for both political and economic reasons.

This article will first provide legislators and policy analysts with criteria to consider when revising laws governing public retirement systems. Then it summarizes some of the key legal issues facing legislators seeking to change benefits for retirees and current employees in many states. Finally, in light of these considerations and limitations, it offers suggestions and guidelines for the most efficient forms of pension and retirement benefit plan reform.

Criteria for Retirement Reform

For a public employees' retirement plan or system to operate in the best interests of all stakeholders, including taxpayer-voters as well as the affected employees, it must be affordable, sustainable, sufficient and competitive. Affordable means the employer and the employee must be able to make this year's contributions for proper actuarial funding without extreme sacrifices.

Sustainable means the plan must be designed so that it remains affordable every year into the foreseeable future without reducing public services or employment levels, and each generation pays for the costs associated with the public services it receives. For public employers, this means the total costs to fund the plan actuarially *during the lifetimes of current employees* are within the financial capacity of the sponsoring government. A sustainable plan does not kick the can to future generations to bear the costs of benefits earned by public servants who retired before these younger taxpayers became adults.

Finally, the plan must be sufficient to attract and retain qualified public employees in a competitive labor market in light of their total compensation. When we discuss various options to restructure retirement benefits in order to control costs, we must remain mindful that the benefits must be sufficient to remain competitive in the open labor markets. However, legislative policy should focus on the entire labor markets from which public employees are recruited, and not just the public sector employment categories that are often used in labor arbitration or personnel comparisons. For example, competitive recruitment of firefighters should include an explicit reference to the trades from which such employees are commonly recruited, and not just other fire departments, so that the total compensation of the public employees, including their retirement benefits, do not exceed what similar workers could obtain in competing job markets at the time of recruitment as well as after they have become trained and skilled. Otherwise, competitive compensation standards in the public sector will become a circular exercise that lacks foundation in the real economy. This is a key complaint of public managers who often find their labor costs controlled by state laws that ignore the private sector labor markets and sometimes even use out-of-state public sector comparisons for professions in which employees are never recruited from out-of-state.

How to Change Retirement Benefits Prospectively

Generally, state and federal laws protect the rights of public employees and retirees to receive pensions they were promised to receive for past service. For retirees, this usually means the basic pension they now receive is immutable. Cost-of-living allowances may be subject to revision, depending on state law, but most policy analysts and attorneys would agree retirees are the most protected class under law, since they typically have no way to regain employment status and expand their retirement benefits. In the middle of this spectrum are retiree medical benefits, as many states can declare that such benefits enjoy less protection, if any, should they choose. Texas, for example, has declared retiree medical benefits are a gratuity and employees enjoy no contractual rights to receive such benefits if the employer fails to appropriate funds for such a benefit or declines to enter into a contractual guarantee. At the other extreme, there is near-universal agreement that subject to collective bargaining where applicable, the retirement benefits of future employees can be changed at will by the employer because such employees will accept the new benefits structure as a term of employment when hired. For incumbent employees, however, the laws defining and governing vested rights are heterogeneous and much murkier.

For current employees, there is general agreement that the private-sector standards of the federal Employee Retirement Income Security Act—known as ERISA—which protect the accrued vested rights of employees, should also apply in the public sector. This means employees cannot be forced to accept a retirement benefit of less than what they now are legally entitled to receive for their prior service. What is not so clear, however, is how each state's laws will control the rights of public employees to the continuation of benefits formulas they presently enjoy. This is the "prospective benefits problem" in state and local government. In some states, the state constitution or the courts have established a theory of law that employees—once hired—are entitled to a continuation of benefits formulas in place at the time of hire or plan change, even for service provided in the future. Such employees are not only vested for their past service, they can become immediately vested in the benefits formula that benefits them the most. Herein lies the rub.

Generally, the standard for impairment of contract should be that the actuarial value of previously earned retirement benefits cannot be reduced. No public employee should be forced to work in the future for "negative benefits." But public employees' "entitlement" to continue current benefits formulas will be hotly contested in the legislatures of many states in the coming years. In California, a state legislative advisory commission has formally recommended that state law be changed to permit prospective changes in retirement benefits accruals in order to preserve the overall system.[1] For a complete copy of the Little Hoover Commission report, see *http://www.lhc. ca.gov/studies/204/report204.html.*

At issue are the nature of the constitutional promise, if any, and the contractual rights of public employees even under emergency financial conditions that imperil the financial capacity of the retirement plan to deliver its promised benefits.

Fundamentals of Pension Law

Starting with the state constitutional law issues, the best single source of recent legal research on this topic is the work of Minnesota law professor Amy Monahan, whose 2010 study of state laws regarding vested pension rights is a must-read for any pension reformer and legislator seeking to comprehend this subject.[2] She identifies a dozen states in which the state laws grant incumbent employees some form of protection or at least a claim to continue their current benefits formulas. That said, an emerging body of legal analysis based on case law has found that public employees' contractual rights can be impaired, even under federal law, if (1) the changes in the plan on a prospective basis are necessary to preserve the plan's capacity to pay benefits on a sustainable basis, (2) the benefits reductions do not exceed the minimum amount of change necessary to preserve the plan, and (3) the employer still provides a reasonable retirement benefit (i.e., both sufficient for its intended purpose and competitive in the labor markets).

Saving the System

This "crack in the wall" of contractual rights under federal law is an important development that will ultimately be decided in federal courts. The law here is clearly unsettled and cases are pending in Colorado, South Dakota and Maryland that could ultimately result in new precedents—especially after appeals. Meanwhile, lawyers for taxpayer and watchdog groups are evaluating the concept of emergency suspension of pension accrual rights of incumbent employees. Just what would trigger or signify an emergency is yet to be determined. It could be a legislative declaration based on specific findings of fact, which clearly falls within the authority of most state legislatures, or it could be a constitutional standard imposed by a referendum or ballot initiative.

For example, a pension fund or retiree medical benefits plan—known as OPEB or other post-employment benefits—with an actuarial funding ratio below 79 percent providing benefits to an employer that is failing to make all its actuarially required contributions might be declared to constitute an emergency condition that warrants making prospective benefits formula reductions and raising the retirement age for that employer's workers. Even under such emergency conditions, however, most experts would caution against actions that impair or diminish actuarially the accrued vested benefits of employees and retirees if at all possible, as those would be the benefits most likely to be protected in the courts as well in the theater of public opinion.

Even if the stock market recovers further in the coming years, which would drive the funding ratios of many pension plans above the suggested 79 percent funding threshold, the underfunding problems of OPEB (retiree medical) plans will persist for at least a decade because most of them presently hold no assets. Thus, an employer and its employees could escape emergency restructuring of the pension plan, but still face an emergency requiring plan redesign for the OPEB benefit. In fact, that would be the most likely scenario in many jurisdictions.

In this context, here are the reforms legislatures most likely will consider in an effort to provide authority for public employers to change benefits formulas prospectively for incumbent employees:

1. Raise employee contributions. This is generally the least controversial as a matter of law. Benefits may enjoy protections, but employees' contributions are fair game for legislative reform. A strong argument can be made that employees are more responsible in their views of the benefits when they share in the costs and do not view the retirement benefits as "free money." In some cases, the laws might provide that public employees should pay half the "normal" actuarial cost (for current service) and perhaps also a portion of the cost of unfunded liabilities for benefits they themselves have received—especially if those benefits were increased and awarded retroactively. For retiree medical benefits plans (OPEB), the concept of an employee contribution is relatively new, but will become inevitable in many states because these plans are quite deeply and unsustainably underfunded. Over time, the author expects to see a majority of public employers require their employees to either contribute to the OPEB plan or to opt out into an alternative, lower-cost benefit.

2. Reduce pension multipliers prospectively. Here, the idea is that future service will be rewarded with a lower benefit formula. For example, a state may limit the maximum multiplier for future service to 1.7 percent for general employees and 2.3 percent for public safety employees in the Social Security system, and 2.5 percent for those outside of Social Security. Such benefit levels would be consistent with "sufficient" pension benefits for new hires, and would put senior employees on an equal footing with new employees with respect to their future service. Such reductions, where they apply, will also have a significant impact in reducing employer costs.

3. Raise the retirement age for younger workers. It is not fair to raise retirement ages for workers over age 50 by more than a month or two for each year prior to their planned retirement, but for younger workers, it may be both appropriate and necessary to invoke higher ages ranging from 62 to 67 for civilians and 57 for public safety. Legislatures can consider a variety of transition provisions to provide equitable treatment to in-service employees. As explained previously, a prudent provision for changes of retirement ages would be a provision that any employee whose retirement date has been increased prospectively should not suffer a reduction in the accrued actuarial value of previously earned vested benefits; this adjustment can be made on an individual basis and would optimize the plan transition by giving the plan and the employer the greatest latitude for making changes while still protecting individual rights. For example, a plan now allowing retirement at age 55 could be changed to age 65 as described above, with the caveat that a senior employee with accrued vested rights may retire before age 65 if the result would otherwise be a reduction in the worker's already accrued benefits.

4. Prohibit retroactive pension increases. History has shown that benefits increases awarded retroactively have produced no value to taxpayers, a windfall to the senior incumbents and huge liabilities for the employers.

5. Raise retiree medical benefits (OPEB) eligibility ages. For new hires, age 65 will likely become the new norm for employer-paid retiree medical benefits. For incumbent employees, age 60 for civilians and age 57 for public safety are appropriate and reasonable levels with appropriate transition provisions to protect vested accrued rights. For example, a transition formula could cap the benefits of incumbent employees by a ratio of (a) their years served, divided by (b) either 25 or 30 years as a normal full service career. Again, the rule that accrued vested benefits should not be reduced may apply here if the plan documents and enabling legislation have provided legal claims to full benefits at an early age. Some states and employers are likely to eventually require incumbent employees to contribute at a higher rate if their OPEB benefits begin before age 65.

6. Limit retiree medical benefits to a fixed dollar per month per year of service. A formula allowing $10 or $15 per month per year of service, toward retiree medical expenses, will still be highly competitive in the private labor markets. A Consumer Price Index inflation escalator can be provided, but this will be far less costly than medical inflation.

7. Require employers to make full actuarial contributions by a certain date. In the interim, those presently underfunding must ramp up their contributions. For OPEB plans, this may take five years.

8. Place a dollar cap on pension benefits or pensionable compensation at a level not to exceed two times the state's median household income (presently $50,000 nationally). This would essentially limit public pensions for new hires to five figures on average, and compel those seeking higher retirement income to also participate in a defined contribution (401a, 403b or 457) plan. Illinois set the limit at $106,800 for new hires last year.

9. Require hybrid defined contribution and defined benefit plan for new hires similar to the federal employees' retirement system, or FERS, which provides a pension multiplier of 1 percent and a matched employee savings plan up to 5 percent of salary. Washington state has operated a similar hybrid plan for several years.

10. Limit total compensation to competitive market standards. Some states will likely consider the establishment of statutory limits on total compensation for public employees to prohibit the award of retirement benefits that would exceed private labor market standards when combined with salaries, wages and other benefits. Such a standard would still permit retirement benefits to exceed private sector standards.

11. Other miscellaneous reforms should also be considered, such as "anti-spiking" provisions that eliminate overtime from pension calculations, require a longer average final compensation calculation (e.g., three or five years), elimination of deferred retirement option (DROP) plans, which have rewarded employees for unsustainable early retirements, institution of mandatory or optional defined contribution plans or hybrids for new employees, and governance of the retirement plans to include more, or a majority of, independent disinterested directors.

A key issue in some states will be whether these limits supersede collective bargaining or supplant it. This issue is hotly debated in some states as this article goes to press, and the author makes no definitive recommendation. However, it would seem reasonable for the legislature to set limits by statute that cannot be exceeded in a labor agreement, and permit bargaining within that envelope of restrictions. This assures retirement reform on a universal statewide basis to discourage piecemeal reform efforts, wide and noncompetitive disparities in benefits among public employees, and divide-and-conquer tactics by multiple employee bargaining units.

Conclusion

Legislators are coming to realize that the easiest changes to make—the reduction of benefits or the establishment of a defined contribution plan for new hires—are unlikely to accomplish much in the way of financial savings in the near time, because skyrocketing retirement plan costs will force most public employers to freeze or even reduce their work forces in order to scrape together their required actuarial contributions. So although such reforms are important for both symbolic and long-term reasons, the real challenge in the coming year or two will be the extent to which each leg-

THE LEGISLATORS: NUMBERS, TERMS, AND PARTY AFFILIATIONS: 2011 — Continued

Source: The Council of State Governments, March 2011.

*Note: Senate and combined body (Senate and House/Assembly) totals include Unicameral legislatures.

Key:

... — Does not apply.

(a) The entire Senate comes up for election in every year ending in "2" with districts based on the latest decennial Census. Senate districts are divided into three groups. One group elects senators for terms of four years, four years and two years; the second group for terms of four years, two years and four years; the third group for terms of two years, four years and four years.

(b) Independent.

(c) Unenrolled.

(d) Democratic-Farmer-Labor.

(e) Independence Party.

(f) All 40 Senate terms are on a 10-year cycle which is made up of a 2-year term, followed by two consecutive 4-year terms, beginning after the decennial census.

(g) Independent (3); Progressive (5).

(h) All House seats contested in even-numbered years; In the Senate 17 seats contested in gubernatorial years; 16 seats contested in presidential years.

(i) Council of the District of Columbia.

(j) Senate: senators are not elected by popular vote, but by county council chiefs. House: 21 seats; 20 are elected by popular vote and one appointed, non-voting delegate from Swains Island.

(k) Independent (3); Covenant (1).

(l) Covenant (7); Independent (4).

(m) Popular Democratic Party.

(n) New Progressive Party.

(o) Independent (3); Independent Citizens Movement (2).

(p) Constitutionally, the Senate consists of 27 seats and the House consists of 51 seats. However, extra at-large seats can be granted to the opposition to limit any party's control to two-thirds. After the 2008 election, extra seats for the minority party were added in both the Senate and House.

(q) Carter County Republican.

(r) Progressive Party.

Table 3.4
MEMBERSHIP TURNOVER IN THE LEGISLATURES: 2010

State or other jurisdiction	Senate Total number of members	Senate Number of membership changes	Senate Percentage change of total	House/Assembly Total number of members	House/Assembly Number of membership changes	House/Assembly Percentage change of total
Alabama	35	16	46	105	33	31
Alaska	20	1	5	40	7	18
Arizona	30	20	67	60	33	55
Arkansas	35	13	37	100	46	46
California	40	13	33	80	29	36
Colorado	35	10	29	65	21	32
Connecticut	36	5	14	151	29	19
Delaware	21	1	5	41	7	17
Florida	40	13	33	120	41	34
Georgia	56	13	23	180	35	19
Hawaii	25	7	28	51	8	16
Idaho	35	6	17	70	12	17
Illinois	59	9	15	118	20	17
Indiana	50	6	12	100	19	19
Iowa	50	11	22	100	29	29
Kansas	40	5	13	125	35	28
Kentucky	38	5	13	100	12	12
Louisiana	39	4	10	105	3	3
Maine	35	14	40	151	54	36
Maryland	47	10	21	141	30	21
Massachusetts	40	10	25	160	38	24
Michigan	38	29	76	110	61	55
Minnesota	67	24	36	134	36	27
Mississippi	52	2	4	122	1	1
Missouri	34	12	35	163	78	48
Montana	50	18	36	100	45	45
Nebraska	49	6	12	...Unicameral...		
Nevada	21	11	52	42	20	48
New Hampshire	24	13	54	400	189	47
New Jersey	40	2	5	80	4	5
New Mexico	42	1	2	70	13	19
New York	62	14	23	150	26	17
North Carolina	50	16	32	120	29	24
North Dakota	47	10	21	94	18	19
Ohio	33	13	39	99	37	37
Oklahoma	48	10	21	101	20	20
Oregon	30	3	10	60	9	15
Pennsylvania	50	4	8	203	29	14
Rhode Island	38	7	18	75	23	31
South Carolina	46	0	0	124	21	17
South Dakota	35	18	51	70	27	39
Tennessee	33	4	12	99	23	23
Texas	31	2	6	150	35	23
Utah	29	2	7	75	16	21
Vermont	30	6	20	150	27	18
Virginia	40	1	3	100	3	3
Washington	49	10	20	98	21	21
West Virginia	34	6	18	100	18	18
Wisconsin	33	8	24	99	30	30
Wyoming	30	7	23	60	16	27
Dist. of Columbia	13	1	8	...Unicameral...		
American Samoa	18	0	0	20	7	35
Guam	15	6	40	...Unicameral...		
No. Mariana Islands	9	1	11	18	0	0
Puerto Rico	31	0	0	54	1	2
U.S. Virgin Islands	15	3	20	...Unicameral...		

Source: The Council of State Governments, March 2011.

Table 3.8
METHOD OF SETTING LEGISLATIVE COMPENSATION

State	Method
Alabama	Constitutional Amendment 57
Alaska	Alaska Stat. §24.10.100 , §24.10.101
Arizona	Arizona Revised Statutes 41-1103 and 41-1904—Compensation commission sends to a public vote
Arkansas	Amendment 70, Ark. Stat. Ann. §10-2-212 et seq.
California	Art. IV, §4; Proposition 112; Cal. Gov. Code §8901 et seq.
Colorado	Colorado Stat. 2-2-301(1)
Connecticut	Conn. Gen. Stat. Ann. §2-9a; The General Assembly takes independent action pursuant to recommendations of a Compensation Commission.
Delaware	Del. Code Ann. Title 29, §710 et seq.; §§3301-3304, are implemented automatically if not rejected by resolution.
Florida	§11.13(1), Florida Statutes; Statute provides members same percentage increase as state employees.
Georgia	Ga. Code Ann. §45-7-4 and §28-1-8
Hawaii	Art. III, §9; Commission recommendations take effect unless rejected by concurrent resolution or the governor. Any change in salary that becomes effective does not apply to the legislature to which the recommendation was submitted.
Idaho	Idaho Code 67-406a and 406b; Citizens' Commission
Illinois	25 ILCS 120; Salaries set by Compensation Review Board. 25 ILCS 115; Tied to employment cost index, wages and salaries for state and local government workers.
Indiana	Ind. Code Ann. §2-3-1-1; An amount equal to 18% of the annual salary of a judge under IC 33-38-5-6, as adjusted under IC 33-38-5-8.1.
Iowa	Iowa Code Ann. §2.10; Iowa Code Ann. §2A.1 thru 2A.5
Kansas	Kan. Stat. Ann. §46-137a et seq.; §75-3212
Kentucky	Ky. Rev. Stat. Ann. §6.226-229; the Kentucky committee has not met since 1995. The most recent pay raise was initiated and passed by the General Assembly.
Louisiana	La. Rev. Stat. 24:31 & 31.1
Maine	Maine Constitution Article IV, Part Third, §7 and 3 MRSA, §2 and 2-A; Increase in compensation is presented to the legislature as legislation; the legislature must enact and the governor must sign into law; takes effect only for subsequent legislatures.
Maryland	Art. III, §15; Commission meets before each four-year term of office and presents recommendations to the General Assembly for action. Recommendations may be reduced or rejected.
Massachusetts	Mass. Gen. Laws Ann. ch. 3, §§9,10; In 1998, the voters passed a legislative referendum that starting with the 2001 session, members will receive an automatic increase or decrease according to the median household income for the commonwealth for the preceding 2-year period.
Michigan	Art. IV §12; Compensation Commission recommends, legislature by majority vote must approve or reduce for change to be effective the session immediately following the next general election.
Minnesota	Minn. Stat. Ann §15A.082; Compensation council makes a recommendation. Must be approved by the legislature and governor. Does not go into effect until after next election of the House.
Mississippi	Miss. Code Ann. 5-1-41
Missouri	Art. III, §§16, 34; Mo. Ann. Stat. §21.140; Recommendations are adjusted by legislature or governor if necessary.
Montana	Mont. Laws 5-2-301; Tied to executive broadband pay plan.
Nebraska	Neb. Const. Art. III, §7; Neb. Rev. Stat. 50-123.01
Nevada	§218.210-§218.225
New Hampshire	Art. XV, part second
New Jersey	Statute. NJSA 52:10A-1
New Mexico	Art. IV. §10 ; 2-1-8 NMSA
New York	Art. 3, §6; Consolidated Laws of NY Ann. 32-2-5a
North Carolina	N.C.G.S. 120-3
North Dakota	Statutes 54-03-10 and 54-03-20; Legislative Compensation Commission 54-03-19.1
Ohio	Art. II, §31; Ohio Rev. Code Ann. title 1 ch. 101.27 thru 101.272
Oklahoma	Okla. Stat. Ann. title 74, §291 et seq.; Art V, §21; Title 74, §291.2 et seq.; Legislative Compensation Board
Oregon	Or. Rev. Stat. §171.072
Pennsylvania	Pa. Cons. Stat. Ann. 46 PS §5; 65 PS §366.1 et seq. Legislators receive annual cost of living increase that is tied to the Consumer Price Index.
Rhode Island	Art. VI, §3

See footnotes at end of table.

METHOD OF SETTING LEGISLATIVE COMPENSATION — Continued

State	Method
South Carolina	S.C. Code Ann. 2-3-20 and the annual General Appropriations Act
South Dakota	Art. III, §6 and Art. XXI, §2; S.D. Codified Laws Ann. §20402 et seq.
Tennessee	Art. II, §23; Tenn. Code Ann. §3-1-106 et seq.
Texas	Art. III, §24; In 1991 a constitutional amendment was approved by voters to allow Ethics Commission to recommend the salaries of members. Any recommendations must be approved by voters to be effective. The provision has yet to be used.
Utah	Art. VI, §9; Utah Code Ann. §36-2-2, et seq.
Vermont	Vt. Stat. Ann. title 32, §1051 and §1052
Virginia	Art. IV, §5; Va. Code Ann. §30-19.11 thru §30-19.14
Washington	Art. II, §23; §43.03.060; Wash. Rev. Code Ann. §43.03.028; Salary Commission sets salaries of legislature and other state officials based on market study and input from citizens.
West Virginia	Art. 6, §33; W. Va. Code §4-2A-1 et seq.; Submits by resolution and must be concurred by at least four members of the commission. The Legislature must enact the resolution into law and may reduce, but shall not increase, any item established in such resolution.
Wisconsin	Sections 20.923 and 230.12, Wis. Statutes, created by Chapter 90, Laws of 1973, and amended by 1983 Wis. Act 27 and Wis. Act 33, provide the current procedure for setting salaries of elected state officials. Generally, compensation is determined as part of the state compensation plan for non-represented employees and is approved by vote of the joint committee on employment relations.
Wyoming	Wyo. Stat. §28-5-101 thru §28-5-105

Source: National Conference of State Legislatures, 2010.

Table 3.9
LEGISLATIVE COMPENSATION AND LIVING EXPENSE ALLOWANCES DURING SESSIONS

State	Salaries — Regular sessions			Mileage cents per mile	Session per diem rate
	Per-diem salary	Limit on days	Annual salary		
Alabama	$10 C	...	...	10/mile for a single roundtrip per session. 50.5/mile interim cmte. attendance.	$3,958/month plus $50/day for three days during each week that the legislature actually meets during any session (U).
Alaska	...	...	$50,400	50./mile for approved travel.	$232 or $276/day (depending on the time of year) tied to federal rate. Legislators who reside in the Capitol area receive 75% of the federal rate.
Arizona	...	...	$24,000	44.5/mile on actual miles.	$35/day for the 1st 120 days of regular session and for special session and $10/day thereafter. Members residing outside Maricopa County receive an additional $25/day for the 1st 120 days of reg. session and for special session and an additional $10/day thereafter (V). Set by statute.
Arkansas	...	...	$15,869	50.5/mile.	$136/d (V) plus mileage tied to federal rate.
California	...	...	$95,291	Members are provided a vehicle. Mileage is not reimbursed.	$141.86/day for each day they are in session.
Colorado	...	...	$30,000	46/mile or 48/mile for 4wd. vehicle. Actual miles paid.	$45/day for members living in the Denver metro area. $150/day for members living outside Denver (V). Set by the legislature.
Connecticut	...	...	$28,000	50./mile.	No per diem is paid.
Delaware	...	...	$42,750	40./mile.	$7,334 expense allowance annually.
Florida	...	...	$29,697	44.5/mile for business travel.	$133/day for House and $133 for Senate (V) tied to federal rate. Earned based on the number of days in session. Travel vouchers are filed to substantiate.
Georgia	...	...	$17,342	50¢/mile Ga. Code Ann. §50-19-7 sets rate of reimbursement at the same mileage rate established by the U.S. General Services Administration	$173/d (U) set by the Legislative Services Committee.
Hawaii	...	...	$46,272	...	$150/day for members living outside Oahu during session; $120/day for members living outside Oahu during interim while conducting legislative business; $10/day for members living on Oahu during the interim while conducting official legislative business.
Idaho	...	...	$16,116	One roundtrip per wk. at state rate.	$122/day for members establishing second residence in Boise; $49/day if no second residence is established and up to $25/day travel (V) set by Compensation Commission.
Illinois	...	...	$67,836	50./mile, tied to federal rate.	$132/per session day.
Indiana	...	...	$22,616	55./mile	$152/day (U) tied to federal rate.
Iowa	...	...	$25,000	39/mile	$118/day (U). $88.50/day for Polk County legislators (U) set by the legislature to coincide with federal rate. State mileage rates apply.

See footnotes at end of table.

LEGISLATIVE COMPENSATION AND LIVING EXPENSE ALLOWANCES DURING SESSIONS — Continued

State	Salaries			Mileage cents per mile	Session per diem rate
	Regular sessions				
	Per-diem salary	Limit on days	Annual salary		
Kansas	$88.66 C	…	…	50/mile, set by Dept. of Admin.	$123/d (U) tied to federal rate.
Kentucky	$188.22 C	…	…	50.5¢/mile based on federal mileage rate	$135.30/d (U) tied to federal rate. (110% federal per diem rate).
Louisiana	…	…	$16,800 plus additional $6,000/yr. (U) expense allowance.	50/mile, tied to federal rate.	$152/day (U) tied to federal rate (26 U.S.C. Section 162(h)(1)(B)(ii)).
Maine	…	…	$13,852 for first regular session; $10,082 for second regular session.	44/mile	$38/day housing, or mileage and tolls in lieu of housing (at rate of $0.44/mile up to $38/day) plus $32/day for meals. Per diem limits are set by statute.
Maryland	…	…	$43,500	50¢/mile for authorized events	Lodging $100/day; meals $42/day (V) tied to federal rate and compensation commission. $225/day for out of state travel. Includes meals and lodging.
Massachusetts	…	…	$61,132.99	Between $10 and $100, determined by distance from State House.	From $10/day–$100/day, depending on distance from State House (V) set by the legislature.
Michigan	…	…	$71,685	50/ per mile as of 01-01-2010	$10,800 yearly expense allowance for session and interim (V) set by compensation commission.
Minnesota	…	…	$31,140.90	Reimbursed at federal mileage rate for one trip per week during session (for non-local Members) and for needed business travel during interim.	Senators receive $86/day and Representatives receive $77/legislative day (U) set by the legislature/Rules Committee.
Mississippi	…	…	$10,000	48.5/mile; determined by Federal Register and Legislature.	$109/day (U) tied to federal rate.
Missouri	…	…	$35,915	47/mile	$98.40/d tied to federal rate. Verification of per diem is by roll call.
Montana	$82.64L	…	…	50/mile; Rate is based on IRS rate. Reimbursement for actual mileage traveled in connection with legislative business	$103.69/d (U).
Nebraska	…	…	$12,000	50.5/mile, tied to federal rate.	$109/day outside 50-mile radius from Capitol; $39/day if member resides within 50 miles of Capitol (V) tied to federal rate.
Nevada	$137.90/day max. of 60 days of session for holdover Senators, $146.29/day for all other legislators.	60 days	…	Federal rate, currently 50.5/mile	Federal rate for Capitol area (U). Legislators who live more than 50 miles from the capitol, if require lodging, will be paid at HUD single-room rate for Carson City area for each month of session.

See footnotes at end of table.

Table 3.10
LEGISLATIVE COMPENSATION: OTHER PAYMENTS AND BENEFITS

State	Legislator's compensation for office supplies, district offices and staffing	Phone allowance	Transportation offered to legislators	Insurance benefits				
				Health	Dental	Optical	Disability insurance	Life insurance benefits
Alabama	None, although annual appropriation to certain positions may be so allocated.	Yes (a)	No	S.A., O.P.	S.A., O.P.	N.A.	N.A.	N.A.
Alaska	Senators receive $10,000/y and Representatives receive $8,000/y for postage, stationery and other legislative expenses. Staffing allowance determined by rules and presiding officers, depending on time of year.	Yes (a)	No	S.P.P.	S.P.P.	O.P.; unless included in Health Ins.	Optional; if selected is included in health insurance	Small policy available; additional is optional at legislator's expense.
Arizona	None.	No	(c)	S.A.	S.A.	S.A.	S.A.	State pays 15K policy; additional amount is paid by legislator.
Arkansas	Legislators may receive reimbursement of up to $14,400 annually for legislative expenses incurred. Standing subcommittee chairs and committee chairs may receive additional annual expense reimbursements of up to $1,800 and $3,600, respectively. Legislators who formally decline to receive per diem and mileage reimbursements may receive additional annual expense reimbursements of up to $10,200.	No	No	S.A.	O.P.	O.P.	O.P.	State provides $10,000 coverage with option to purchase greater amount.
California	Based on the size of their districts.	Yes (a)	(d)	S.P.P.	S.P	S.P.	S.P.	S.P.
Colorado	None.	Yes (a)	No	S.P.P.	S.P.P.	N.A.	N.A.	State pays full amount for $12,000 policy; additional is optional at legislator's expense.
Connecticut	Senators receive $5,500 and Representatives receive $4,500 in unvouchered expense allowance.	Yes. (e)	No	S.P.P.	S.P.P.	Some health insurance plans include discounts on eyewear.	O.P.	O.P.
Delaware	Reimbursement provided for office expenses.	Yes (a)	No	S.P.P.—After three months the state pays entire amount for basic plan.	O.P.	O.P.	N.A.	O.P.
Florida	Senate $3,244/month for district office expenses with four staff. House $2,482/month for district office expenses. Speaker $3,408 and Senate President $3,567	No	(f)	S.P.	S.P.	O.P.	S.P.	S.P.

See footnotes at end of table.

LEGISLATIVE COMPENSATION: OTHER PAYMENTS AND BENEFITS — Continued

State	Legislator's compensation for office supplies, district offices and staffing	Phone allowance	Transportation offered to legislators	Health	Dental	Optical	Disability insurance	Life insurance benefits
							Insurance benefits	
Georgia............	$7,000/y reimbursable expense account. If the member requests and provides receipts, the member is reimbursed for personal services, office equipment, rent, supplies, transportation, telecommunications, etc.	No	No	S.A. S.P.P.	O.P.	O.P.	O.P.	O.P.
Hawaii............	There is no set dollar amount for office supplies. All supplies are provided by the House Supply room. Any item not carried in the Supply Room may be purchased with statutory legislative allowance funds which is currently $10,200/year. House members do not have district offices. With the exception of the Speaker's Office and Majority and Minority Leadership offices, the House Finance, Judiciary and Consumer Protection offices, each House Majority and Minority member is allowed 1 permanent full-time Office Manager. During the session each committee chair receives $5,100/month for temporary staff salaries, and all other members receive $4,800 month.	Yes (a)	(g)	S.P.P.	S.P.P.	S.P.P.	S.A.	S.P.P.
Idaho............	$1,700/y for unvouchered constituent expense. No staffing allowance.	Yes (h)	No	S.P.P.	S.P.P.	N.A.	S.P.P.	S.P.P.
Illinois............	Senators receive $83,063/y and Representatives receive $69,409/y for office expenses, including district offices and staffing.	No	No	S.P.P.	S.P.P.	S.P.P.	S.P.	S.P.P.
Indiana............	All of these come out of one main Senate budget. We do not have district offices.	No	No	S.A.	S.A.	S.A.	N.A.	S.A.
Iowa	$300/m to cover district constituency postage, travel, telephone and other expenses. No staffing allowance.	No	No	S.P.P.	S.P.P.	N.A.	S.P.	State pays first $20,000, additional at legislator expense.
Kansas	$7,083/year which is taxable income to the legislators. Staffing allowances vary for leadership who have their own budget. Legislators provided with secretaries during session only.	Yes (i)	No	S.P.P.	S.P., legislator pays dep. portion	O.P.	S.P.	150% of annual salary if part of KPERS. Additional insurance is optional at legislator's expense.
Kentucky	$1,788.51 for district expenses during interim.	No	Yes	S.P., legislator pays dep. portion	O.P.	O.P.	O.P.	State pays $20,000; extra available at legislator's expense.

See footnotes at end of table.

LEGISLATIVE COMPENSATION: OTHER PAYMENTS AND BENEFITS—Continued

State	Legislator's compensation for office supplies, district offices and staffing	Phone allowance	Transportation offered to legislators	Insurance benefits				
				Health	Dental	Optical	Disability insurance	Life insurance benefits
Louisiana	$500/month. Senators and Representatives receive an additional $,1500 supplemental allowance for vouchered office expenses, rent, travel mileage in district. Senators and Representatives staff allowance $2,000/month starting salary up to $3,000 with annual increases.	Yes (j)	No	S.P.P.	S.P.P.—Senators pay 100%	O.P.	O.P.	State pays half; legislator pays half.
Maine	None. However, supplies for staff offices are provided and paid for out of general legislative account.	Yes (k)	No	S.A.	S.A.	O.P.	N.A.	O.P.
Maryland	Each member receives an annual district office allowance. For Fy 2010 the district office allowances are: House members—$39,894 Senate members—$33,395 In addition each Senator is provided with 1 full time administrative aide funded by the Senate. Finally, selected House leadership position holders receive from $845 to $3,471 in additional district office allowance funds annually, and selected Senate leadership position holders receive an additional $1,471 in additional district office allowance funds annually.	No	No	S.A.	S.A., O.P.	Covered under medical plan	N.A.	Term insurance; optional at legislator's expense. $5,000 policy provided; Additional up to 8 times salary at legislator's expense.
Massachusetts	$7,200/y for office expenses.	No	No	S.P.P.	S.P.P.	S.P.P.	O.P.	Offered at different levels as part of cafeteria plan.
Michigan	$51,800 per majority Senator for office budget $51,800 for minority Senator for office budget	Yes (a)	No	Health, vision, life, cancer, prescription offered via cafeteria plan.			N.A.	State pays premium for benefit of $35,000.
Minnesota	No district offices. Supplies provided in State Capitol. In the House, Staffing provided centrally. For Senators, one legislative assistant plus $75/week for interns.	Yes (dd)	(l)	S.A.	State pays—90% single—50% family.	S.A.	O.P.	S.P.P.
Mississippi	A total of $1,500/m out of session.	Yes	No	S.P.—legislator only premiums	O.P.	N.A.	None	S.P.—Additional amounts are optional at legislator's expense.
Missouri	$800/m to cover all reasonable and necessary business expenses.	Yes (m)	No	S.P.P.	O.P.	O.P.	S.P.	State pays $14,000 term policy. Additional at legislator's expense.
Montana	None.	Yes (n)	Limited	S.P.	S.P.	O.P.	N.A.	O.P.

See footnotes at end of table.

LEGISLATIVE COMPENSATION: OTHER PAYMENTS AND BENEFITS — Continued

State	Legislator's compensation for office supplies, district offices and staffing	Phone allowance	Transportation offered to legislators	Insurance benefits				
				Health	Dental	Optical	Disability insurance	Life insurance benefits
Nebraska	No allowance; however, each member is provided with two full-time capitol staff year-round.	Yes (a)	No	O.P.	O.P.	O.P.	O.P.	O.P.
Nevada	None.	$2,800 allowance	(o)	O.P.	O.P.	O.P.	O.P.	N.A.
New Hampshire	None.	No	No	O.P.	O.P.	N.A.	N.A.	Depends on retirement plan enrollment. If State Pension Plan same as all state employees.
New Jersey	$1,250 for office supplies; district office varies by location within state; $110,000 for staffing	None for Assembly	(p)	S.A.	S.A.	S.A.	It depends on the retirement plan they are enrolled in.	
New Mexico	None.	No	No	N.A.	N.A.	N.A.	N.A.	N.A.
New York	Staff allowance set by majority leader for majority members and by minority leader for minority members. Staff allowance covers both district and capitol; geographic location; seniority and leadership responsibilities will cause variations.	Yes (a)	(q)	S.P.P.	S.P.P.	No cost if participating provider used	S.P.	O.P.
North Carolina	Non-leaders receive $6,708/y for any legislative expenses not otherwise provided. Full-time secretarial assistance is provided during session.	Yes (r)	No	S.P.; O.P. family coverage	O.P.	O.P.	O.P.	O.P.
North Dakota	None.	Yes (s)	No	S.P.	O.P.	O.P.	O.P.	State pays for $1,300 term life policy.
Ohio	None.	Yes (a)	No	S.P.P.	S.P.	S.P.	N.A.	Amount equal to salary; premium paid by state. Member may purchase a supplemental policy, which is also offered to state employees.
Oklahoma	$350/y for unvouchered office supplies plus five rolls of stamps.	Yes (t)	No	Allowance ranging from $608.57 for legislator only to $1,596.95 per month for family.	S.A.	S.A.	S.A.	S.A.

See footnotes at end of table.

LEGISLATIVE COMPENSATION: OTHER PAYMENTS AND BENEFITS — Continued

State	Legislator's compensation for office supplies, district offices and staffing	Phone allowance	Transportation offered to legislators	Insurance benefits				
				Health	Dental	Optical	Disability insurance	Life insurance benefits
Oregon........	Session office supplies, ($15.50/d Interim office allowance. ($450–750/d depending on geographic size of district.) Session staffing allowance, $4,858/m; Interim staffing allowance, $3,327/m.	Yes (u)	No	S.A.	S.A.	S.A.	O.P.	O.P.
Pennsylvania........	Staffing is determined by leadership.	No	(v)	Medical/hospital, dental, vision, prescription. State members and employees pay 1% of salary for health benefits.				Equal to salary to maximum of $150,000.
Rhode Island........	None.	No	No	S.A.	S.A.	S.A.	O.P.	O.P.
South Carolina.......	Senate $3,400/y for postage, stationary and telephone. House $1,800/y for telephone and $600/y for postage. Legislators also receive $1,000/m for in district expenses that is treated as income.	Yes (a)	No	S.P.P.	S.P.P.	N.A.	S.P.P.	S.P.P.
South Dakota.......	None.	Yes (w)	No	N.A.	N.A.	N.A.	S.P. for accidental death/dismemberment ins. only	N.A.
Tennessee...........	$1,000/m for expenses in district (U).	Yes (x)	(y)	State pays 80%, legislator pays 20%	O.P.	N.A.	N.A.	State pays $15,000; Legislator pays $7,000.
Texas................	Approved allowance for staff salaries and staff travel. Other expenses such as supplies, stationery, postage, district office rental, telephone expense, etc, provided as needed	No	No	S.P.	O.P.	Included in health coverage	O.P.	O.P.
Utah................	None.	No (z)	No	S.P.P.	S.P.P.	S.P.P.	S.P.	S.P.
Vermont...........	None.	(aa)	No	O.P.	N.A.	N.A.	N.A.	N.A.
Virginia...........	Legislators receive $1,250/m; leadership receives $1,750/m office expense allowance. Legislators receive a staffing allowance of $37,871/y; leadership receives $56,804/y.	Yes	No	S.P.P.	S.P.P.	S.P.P.	S.P.—only permanent disability retirement through retirement system	S.P.P.
Washington...........	Maximum of $7,800/y for legislative expense reimbursement. Legislative staff are paid directly so there is no staffing allowance.	Yes (a)	No	S.P.P.	S.P.	Included in medical	S.P.P.	S.P.P.
West Virginia........	None.	Yes	No	O.P.	O.P.	O.P.	N.A.	O.P.

See footnotes at end of table.

LEGISLATIVE COMPENSATION: OTHER PAYMENTS AND BENEFITS — Continued

State	Legislator's compensation for office supplies, district offices and staffing	Phone allowance	Transportation offered to legislators	Insurance benefits				
				Health	Dental	Optical	Disability insurance	Life insurance benefits
Wisconsin	$12,000 for 2 year session in the Assembly. N/A staffing. DO. $45,000 for two year period for office expenses. In Senate, $55,955 office budget for 2 year session and $204,577 staff salary budget to fund 2 staff persons.	(bb)	No	S.A.	Some HMOs cover	O.P.	O.P.	O.P.
Wyoming	Up to $750 quarter through the constituent service allowance.	(cc)	No	N.A.	N.A.	N.A.	N.A.	N.A.

Source: National Conference of State Legislatures, 2010.

Key:
(U) – Unvouchered.
(V) – Vouchered.
d – day.
m – month.
w – week.
y – year.
N.A. – Not available.
S.P. – State pays full amount.
S.P.P. – State pays portion and legislator pays portion.
S.A. – Same as state employeess
O.P. – Optional at legislator's expense.
(a) Official state business only
(b) Phone cards are allowed for certain districts.
(c) Access to motor pool for legislative trips only.
(d) Members are provided a vehicle, for which they pay a portion of the payment.
(e) Official business only; charges for personal calls are reimbursed by legislator.
(f) Rental cars for official business.
(g) Neighbor Island members are allowed 1 round trip from their home island every week—during session and during the interim. Additional trips are allowed when authorized by the Speaker.
(h) During session only
(i) If monthly bill exceeds $200, leadership is notified
(j) District office line with one extension

(k) Pre-paid phone cards are issued to members of the Senate and the House.
(l) Reimbursement for approved travel.
(m) Phone cards issued but expenditures deducted from monthly expense allowance
(n) Leadership positions only
(o) Motor pool or private; legislative police shuttle to/from Reno airport.
(p) Automobiles for Assembly Speaker, Assembly Majority Leader and Minority Leader.
(q) Top leadership has access to vehicles.
(r) Allowance of $2,275 for postage, stationery and telephone
(s) Only Legislative Council members or chairs of interim cmtes.
(t) Senate members receive phone credit card for state-related business use away from capitol.
(u) State-provided office and district office phone for legislative business only
(v) Business mileage reimbursement or use fleet lease vehicle from Department of General Services.
(w) Telephone allowance: $600/6 m for legislators and $900/6 m for leadership
(x) Phone cards for in-state long distance (only).
(y) In lieu of mileage, members residing greater than 100 miles from the seat of government may be reimbursed for coach class airline fare for attendance at session or committee meetings. Limited to one round trip per week during session.
(z) All members are issued Blackberry phones.
(aa) Leaders for legislative business.
(bb) Members office expenses, including phone expense, are limited to the amount of each legislator's office budget, as established by the committees on Senate and Assembly organization.
(cc) Telephone credit card for official business only with a $2,000 limit during 2 yrs.
(dd) Reimbursed at federal mileage rate for one trip per week during session (for non-local Members) and for needed business travel during interim

Table 3.11
ADDITIONAL COMPENSATION FOR SENATE LEADERS

State	Presiding officer	Majority leader	Minority leader	Other leaders and committee chairs
Alabama	$2/day plus $1,500/mo. expense allowance	None	None	Committee chairs: Senate Finance and Taxation Cmte., $150/mo.
Alaska	$500	None	None	None
Arizona	None	None	None	None
Arkansas	None	None	None	$3,600/yr for committee chairs; $1,800/yr. sub-cmte. chairs.
California	$133,639/yr.	None	None	None
Colorado	$133,639/yr.	$124,923/yr.	$133,639/yr.	None
	All leaders receive $99/day salary during interim when in attendance at committee or leadership meetings.			
Connecticut	$10,689	$8,835	$8,835	Leaders: Dep. min. and maj. ldrs., $6,446/year; asst. maj. and min. ldrs. and maj. and min. whips $4,241/yr. Committee chairs: All cmte. chairs, $4,241.
Delaware	$19,983	$12,376	$12,376	Leaders: Maj. and min. whips $7,794. Committee chairs: Joint Finance Cmte. Chair, $11,459; Capital Improvement Chair and Vice-Chair $4,578; Sunset Cmte. Chair $4,578.
Florida	$11,484	None	None	None
Georgia	None	$200/mo.	$200/mo.	President pro tem, $400/mo; admin. flr. ldr., $200/mo; asst. admin. flr. ldr., $100/mo.
Hawaii	Salary differential for presiding officer is $7,500	None	None	None
Idaho	$4,000	None	None	None
Illinois	$27,477	$20,649	$27,477	Dpty. min. leader $20,649; Asst. maj. and min. ldr., $20,649; maj. and min. caucus chair, $20,649 All cmte. chairs and minority spokesperson $10,327.
Indiana	$7,000	Maj. floor ldr. $5,500; asst. maj. floor ldr. $3,500;	Min. floor ldr. $6,000; min. asst. floor ldr. $5,000; min. ldr. pro tem. emeritus $1,500;	Asst. Pres. Pro Tem. $3,000; Maj. Cauc. Chairman $5,500; Asst. Maj. Cauc. Chair $1,500; Appropriations Comm. Ranking Maj. Mem. $2,000; Tax & Fiscal Policy Ranking Maj. Mem. $2,000; Maj. Whip $4,000; Asst. Maj. Whip $2,000; Min. Cauc. Chair $5,000; Asst. Min. Cauc. Chair $1,000; Appropriations Comm. Ranking Min. Mem. $2,000; Tax & Fiscal Policy Ranking Min. Mem.$2,000; Min. Whip $3,000; Asst. Min. Whip $1,000. Committee Chairs: $1,000
Iowa	$11,593	$11,593	$11,593	Pres. Pro Tem $1,243.
Kansas	$14,039.22/yr	$12,665.64/yr	$12,665.64/yr	Asst. maj., min. ldrs., vice pres., $7,165.34/yr. Committee Chairs: $11,289.98/year for Senate Ways and Means and House Appropriations Committee

See footnotes at end of table.

ADDITIONAL COMPENSATION FOR SENATE LEADERS — Continued

State	Presiding officer	Majority leader	Minority leader	Other leaders and committee chairs
Kentucky	$46.51/day	$36.73/day	$36.73/day	Leaders: Maj. min. caucus chairs and whips, $28.15/day. Committee Chairs: for standing cmtes. only $18.71/day
Louisiana	$32,000	None	None	Pres. Pro Tem $24,500. Joint Budget Cmte. $28,000/yr. for chair and vice-chair.
Maine	150% of base salary	125% of base salary	112.5% of base salary	None
Maryland	$13,000/yr.	None	None	None
Massachusetts	$35,000	$22,500	$22,500	Leaders: asst. maj. and min. ldr., (and 2nd and 3rd assistant), Pres. Pro Tem., each $15,000. Committee Chairs: $7,500–$15,000/yr.
Michigan	$5,513	$26,000	$22,000	Leaders: Maj. flr. ldr., $12,000; min. flr. ldr., $10,000. Committee Chairs: Appropriation Cmte. Chairs $7,000.
Minnesota	None	Additional compensation is 40% of base salary	Additional compensation is 40% of base salary	Assistant Majority Leader—$4,152/year. Tax Committee chair—$4,152/year. Finance Committee chair—$4,152/year. Senate Tax Cmte. and Cmte. on Finance Chair $35,292,
Mississippi	Lt. Gov.—$60,000 total salary; Pres. Pro Tem, $15,000	None	None	None
Missouri	None	None	None	None
Montana	$5/day during session	None	None	None
Nebraska	None	None	None	None
Nevada	$900	$900	$900	Leaders: Pres. Pro Tem, $900. Committee Chairs: Standing cmte. chairs $900.
New Hampshire	$50/two-yr term	None	None	None
New Jersey	1/3 above annual salary	None	None	None
New Mexico	None	None	None	None
New York	$41,500	None	$34,500	Leaders: 22 other leaders with compensation ranging from $13,000 to $34,000. Committee Chairs: between $9,000 and $34,000.
North Carolina	$38,151 and $16,956 expense allowance.	$17,048 and $7,992 expense allowance	$17,048 and $7,992 expense allowance	Dep. pro tem: $21,739 and $10,032 expense allowance
North Dakota	None	$10/day during legislative sessions, $284 ($298 effective 7/1/10) per month during term of office.	$10/day during legislative sessions, $284 ($298 effective 7/1/10) per month during term of office.	Leaders: Asst. ldrs. $5/day during session. Committee Chairs: Substantive standing cmte. chairs $5/day.

See footnotes at end of table.

ADDITIONAL COMPENSATION FOR SENATE LEADERS—Continued

State	Presiding officer	Majority leader	Minority leader	Other leaders and committee chairs
Ohio	President $94,437	President Pro Tem $86,165; Maj Flr Leader $81,163; Asst Maj Flr Leader $76,169; Maj Whip $71,173; Asst Maj Whip $66,175	Minority Leader $86,165; Asst. Min. Ldr 78,668; Min Whip 71,173; Asst Min Whip 63,381	Committee Leaders: $6,500 for all committee chairs except Finance Chair, who receives $10,000. Vice-chairs receive $5,000 with the Vice-Chair of Finance receiving $5,500.
Oklahoma	$17,932	$12,364	$12,364	$12,364 for Appropriations and Budget Committee Chairs
Oregon	President receives additional $21,612/year in salary.	None	None	None
Pennsylvania	$43,939/year	$35,153/year	$35,153/year	Maj. and min. whips, $26,678 maj. and min. caucus chairs, $16,634; maj. and min. caucus secretaries $10,986; maj. and min. policy chairs, $10,986; maj. and min. caucus admin., $10,986; maj. and min. caucus appropriations committee chairs, $26,678
Rhode Island	Senate President receives double the annual rate for Senators	None	None	None
South Carolina	Lt. gov. holds this position	None	None	Leaders: President pro tem, $11,000. Committee Chairs: $600/ interim expense allowance for committee chairs of the Senate.
South Dakota	None	None	None	None
Tennessee	$57,027	None	None	None
Texas	None	None	None	None
Utah	$3,000	$2,000	$2,000	Leaders: Maj. whip, asst. maj. whip, min. whip and asst. min. whip, $2,000. Committee Chairs: $2,000 for Executive Appropriations Chair (Co-chair)
Vermont	Presiding officer is Lt. Governor who is paid an annual salary $60,500.	None	None	None
Virginia	None	$200/d for interim business	$200/d for interim business	President pro tem $200/d for interim business
Washington	Lt. gov. holds this position	$8,000 addition to base salary	$4,000 addition to base salary	None
West Virginia	$150/day during session.	$50/day during session.	$50/day during session.	The Chairman of Finance & Judiciary may receive $150.00/day up to 30 days when the Legislature is not in session or meeting for interims. Up to six add'l people named by presiding officer receive $150 for a maximum of 30 days when the Legislature is not in session or meeting for interims. $150/day (max. 30 days) for Finance and Judiciary chair.
Wisconsin	None	None	None	None
Wyoming	$3/day	4 salary days per month during interim	4 salary days per month during interim	Leaders:None. Committee Chairs:4 salary days per month during interim

Source: National Conference of State Legislatures, 2010.

Table 3.12
ADDITIONAL COMPENSATION FOR HOUSE/ASSEMBLY LEADERS

State	Presiding officer	Majority leader	Minority leader	Other leaders and committee chairs
Alabama	$2/day plus $1,500/mo. expense allowance	None	None	$150/mo. for House Ways and Means and Senate Finance and Taxation chairs
Alaska	$500	None	None	None
Arizona	None	None	None	None
Arkansas	None	None	None	$3,600/yr. for cmte. chairs; $1,800/yr. sub cmte. chairs.
California	$133,639	$124,923	$133,639	2nd ranking min. ldrs. receive $124,923/yr.
Colorado	——— All leaders receive $99/day salary during interim when in attendance at committee or leadership matters.———			
Connecticut	$10,689	$8,835	$8,835	Leaders: Dep. spkr., dep. maj. and min. ldrs., $6,446/yr; asst. maj. and min ldrs.; maj. and min whips, $4,241/yr.Cmte Chairs: $4,241.
Delaware	$19,893	$12,376	$12,376	Leaders: maj. and min. whips, $7,794. Committee Chairs: $11,459 for Joint Finance Committee Chair; $4,578 Capital Improvement Chair and Vice Chair; $4,578 Sunset Committee Chair.
Florida	$11,484	None	None	None
Georgia	$6,812/mo.	$200/mo.	$200/mo.	Governor's flr. ldr., $200/mo; asst. flr. ldr., $100/mo.; spkr. pro tem, $400/mo.
Hawaii	$7,500	None	None	None
Idaho	$4,000	None	None	None
Illinois	$27,477	$23,300	$27,477	Leaders: dpty. maj. and min., $19,791; asst. maj. and asst. min..maj. and min. conference chr. $18,066. Committee Chairs and Minority Spokespersons: $10,327.
Indiana	$6,500	$5,000	$5,500	Leaders: Speaker pro tem, $5,000; maj. caucus chair, $5,000; min. caucus chair, $4,500; asst. min. flr. leader, $3,500; asst. maj. flr. ldr., $1,000; maj. whip, $3,500; min. whip, $1,500. Committee Chairs: $1,000.
Iowa	$11,593	$11,593	$11,593	Speaker pro tem, $1,243
Kansas	$13,696.80/yr.	$12,356.76/yr.	$12,356.76/yr.	Leaders: asst. maj. and min. ldrs., spkr. pro tem, $6,990.62/yr. Committee Chairs: $11,014.64/year for House Appropriations Cmte.
Kentucky	$46.51/day	$36.73/day	$36.73/day	Leaders: maj. and min. caucus chairs & whips, $28.15/day. Committee Chairs: $18.71/day for standing committees only.

See footnotes at end of table.

ADDITIONAL COMPENSATION FOR HOUSE/ASSEMBLY LEADERS — Continued

State	Presiding officer	Majority leader	Minority leader	Other leaders and committee chairs
Louisiana	$32,000 (a)	None	None	Leaders: Speaker pro tem, $24,500 (a). Committee Chairs: $28,000/year for chairman and vice chairman of Joint Budget Cmte.
Maine	150% of base salary	125% of base salary	112.5% of base salary	None
Maryland	$13,000/year	None	None	None
Massachusetts	$35,000	$22,500	$22,500	Leaders: asst. maj. and min. ldr. (and 2nd and 3rd asst.), and spkr. pro tem, $15,000 each. Committee Chairs: $7,500–$15,000/year.
Michigan	$27,000	No position	$22,000	Leaders: Spkr. pro tem, $5,513; min. flr. ldr., $10,000; maj. flr. ldr., $12,000. Committee Chairs: $7,000 for Appropriation Committee chairs.
Minnesota	40% of base salary	40% of base salary	40% of base salary	$35,292 for Committee on Finance.
Mississippi	$60,000 (a)	None	None	Spkr. pro tem, $15,000
Missouri	$208.34/mo.	$125/mo.	$125/mo.	None
Montana	$5/day during session	None	None	None
Nebraska	None	None	None	None
Nevada	$900	$900	$900	Leaders: Speaker pro tem, $900. Committee Chairs: $900/ flat amount for all standing committee chairs.
New Hampshire	$50/two-year term	None	None	None
New Jersey	1/3 above annual base salary	None	None	None
New Mexico	None	None	None	None
New York	$41,500	$34,500	$34,500	Leaders: 31 leaders with compensation ranging from $9,000 to $25,000. Committee Chairs: $9,000 to $34,000 set by statute.
North Carolina	$38,151 (a) and $16,956 expense allowance	$17,048 (a) and $7,992 expense allowance	$17,048 (a) and $7,992 expense allowance	Speaker pro tem, $21,739 and $10,032 expense allowance.
North Dakota	$10/day during legislative session.	$10/day during legislative session, $270/m during term of office.	$10/day during legislative session, $270/m during term of office.	Leaders: Asst. ldrs., $5/day during legislative sessions. Committee Chairs: $5/day for all substantive standing committees
Ohio	$94,437 (a)	Speaker pro tem $86,165; maj flr. leader $81,163; asst. maj. flr. leader $76,169; maj. whip $71,173; asst. maj. whip $66,175	Minority leader $86,165; asst. min. ldr. $78,668; min. whip $71,173; asst. min. whip $63,381	$6,500 for all committee chairs except Finance Chair, who receives $10,000. Vice chairs receive $5,000 with the Vice Chair of Finance receiving $5,500.

See footnotes at end of table.

ADDITIONAL COMPENSATION FOR HOUSE/ASSEMBLY LEADERS — Continued

State	Presiding officer	Majority leader	Minority leader	Other leaders and committee chairs
Oklahoma	$17,932	$12,364	$12,364	Leaders: Speaker pro tem, $12,364. Committee Chairs: $12,364 for Appropriations and Budget Committee Chairs.
Oregon	Speaker receives additional $21,612/year in salary	None	None	None
Pennsylvania	$43,939/year	$35,153/year	$35,153/year	Maj. and min. whips, $25,945; maj. and min. caucus chairs, $16,177; maj. and min. caucus secretaries, $10,683; maj. and min. policy chairs, $10,683; maj. and min. caucus admin., $10,683.
Rhode Island	Speaker of the House receives double annual rate for Representatives.	None	None	None
South Carolina	$11,000/yr	None	None	Leaders: Speaker pro tem, $3,600/yr. Committee Chairs: $600/interim expense allowance for committee chairs of the House
South Dakota	None	None	None	None
Tennessee	$57,027	None	None	None
Texas	None	None	None	None
Utah	$3,000	$2,000	$2,000	Leaders: whips and asst. whips, $2,000. Committee Chairs: $2,000 for Executive Appropriations Chair (Co-chair).
Vermont	$704/week during session plus an additional $10,984 in salary.	None	None	None
Virginia	$8,000 addition to base salary	$4,000 addition to base salary	$4,000 addition to base salary	None
Washington	$49,280, $8,000 additional to (a) base salary	None	$45,280, $4,000 additional to base salary (a)	None
West Virginia	The Speaker may receive $150.00/day. when not in session or interim committees not meeting for attending to legislative business	$50/day during session	$50/day during session	Leaders: The Chairman of Finance & Judiciary may receive $150.00/day up to 30 days when the Legislature is not in session or meeting for interims. Up to six add'l people named by presiding officer receive $150 for a maximum of 30 days when the Legislature is not in session or meeting for interims. Chairs: $150/day (max.30 days) for Finance and Judiciary chairs.
Wisconsin	$25/month	None	None	None
Wyoming	$3/day	$4 salary days per month during interim	$4 salary days per month during interim	$4 salary days per month during interim

Source: National Conference of State Legislatures, 2010.
(a) Total annual salary for this position.

Table 3.13
STATE LEGISLATIVE RETIREMENT BENEFITS

State or other jurisdiction	Participation	Plan name	Requirements for regular retirement	Employee contribution rate	Benefit formula
Alabama	None available.				
Alaska..................	Optional	Public Employees Retirement System	Age 60 with 10 yrs.	Employee 6.75%	2% (first 10 yrs.); or 2.25% (second 10 yrs.); or 2.5% over 20 yrs. x average salary over 5 highest consecutive yrs. x yrs. of service
Arizona................	Mandatory—except that officials subject to term limits may opt out for a term of office.	Elected Officials Retirement System	Age 65, 5+ yrs. service; age 62, 10+ yrs. service; or 20 yrs. service; earlier retirement with an actuarial reduction of benefits. Vesting at 5 yrs.	Employee 7%	4% x years of credited service x highest 3 yr. average in the past 10 yrs. The benefit is capped at 80% of FAS. An elected official may purchase service credit in the plan for service earned in a non-elected position by buying it at an actuarially-determined amount.
Arkansas..............	Optional. Those elected before 7/1/99 may have service covered as a regular state employee but must have 5 years of regular service to do so.	Arkansas Public Employees Retirement System	Age 65, 10 yrs. service; or age 55, 12 yrs. service; or any age, 28 yrs. service; any age if serving in the General Assembly on 7/1/79; any age if in elected office on 7/1/79 with 17 and 1/2 yrs. of service. As a regular employee, age 65, 5 yrs. service, or any age and 28 yrs. Members of the contributory plan established in 2005 must have a minimum of 10 yrs. legislative service if they have only legislative state employment.	Non-contributory plan in effect for those elected before 2006. For those elected then and thereafter, a contributory plan that requires 5% of salary.	For service that began after 7/1/99: 2.07% x FAS x years of service. FAS based on three highest consecutive years or service. For service that began after July 1, 1991, $35 x years of service equals monthly benefit. For contributory plan, 2% x FAS x years of service.
California	Legislators elected after 1990 are not eligible for retirement benefits for legislative service.				
Colorado..............	Mandatory	Either Public Employees' Retirement Association or State Defined Contribution Plan. A choice is not irrevocable.	PERA: age 65, 5 yrs. service; age 50, 30 yrs. service; when age + service equals 80 or more (min. age of 55). DCP: no age requirement & vested immediately	Employee: 8%	PERA: 2.5% x FAS x yrs. of service, capped at 100% of FAS. DCP benefit depends upon contributions and investment returns.
Connecticut..........	Mandatory	State Employees Retirement System Tier IIA	Age 60, 25 yrs. credited service; age 62, 10–25 yrs. credited service; age 62, 5 yrs. actual state service. Reduced benefit available with earlier retirement ages.	2%	(.0133 x avg. annual salary) + (.005 x avg. annual salary in excess of "breakpoint" x credited service up to 35 years. 2003: $36,400 2004: $38,600 2005: $40,900 2006: $43,400 2007: $ 46,000 2008: $48,800 2009: $51,700 After 2009—increase breakpoint by 6% per year rounded to nearest $100.

See footnotes at end of table.

STATE LEGISLATIVE RETIREMENT BENEFITS — Continued

State or other jurisdiction	Participation	Plan name	Requirements for regular retirement	Employee contribution rate	Benefit formula
Delaware	Mandatory	State Employees Pension Plan	Age 60, 5 yrs. credited service	3% of total monthly compensation in excess of $6,000	2% times FAS times years of service before 1997 + 1.85% times FAS times years of service from 1997 on. FAS= average of highest 3 years.
Florida	Optional. Elected officials may opt out and may choose between DB and DC plans.	Florida Retirement System	Vesting in DB plan, 6 years; in DC plan, 1 year. DB plan: Age 62 with 6 years; 30 years at any age. DC plan: any age	No employee contribution. Employer contribution for 2004–2005 for legislators is 12.49% of salary.	DB plan: 3% x years of creditable service x average final compensation (average of highest 5 yrs). DC plan: Dependent upon investment experience.
Georgia	Optional: Choice when first elected.	Georgia Legislative Retirement System	Vested after 8 yrs.; age 62, with 8 yrs. of service; age 60 with reduction for early retirement.	Employee rate 3.75% + $7 month	$36 month for each year of service.
Hawaii	Mandatory	Public Employees Retirement System; elected officials' plan	Age 55 with 5 years of service, any age with 10 years service. Vesting at 5 years.	Main plan is non-contributory; 7.8% for elected officials' plan for annuity.	3.5 x yrs. of service as elected official x highest average salary plus annuity based on contributions as an elected official. Highest average salary = average of 3 highest 12- month periods as elected official.
Idaho	Mandatory		Age 65 with 5 yrs. service; reduced benefit at age 55 with 5 yrs. of service.	6.97%	Avg. monthly salary for highest 42 consecutive months x 2% x months of credited service.
Illinois	Optional	General Assembly Retirement System	Age 55, 8 yrs. service; or age 62, 4 yrs. service	8.5% for retirement; 2% for survivors; 1% for automatic increases; 11.5% total	3% of each of 1st 4 yrs.; 3.5% for each of next 2 yrs.; 4% for each of next 2 yrs.; 4.5% for each of the next 4 yrs.; 5% for each yr. above 12
Indiana	DB plan is optional for those serving on April 30, 1989. Defined contribution plan is optional for those serving on April 30, 1989 and mandatory for those elected or appointed since April 30, 1989.	Legislator's Retirement System and Defined Benefit (DB) Plan and Defined Contribution Plan (DC).	DB plan: Vesting at 10 yrs. with 10 yrs. of legislative service; or if no longer in the legislature, these options apply: at least 10 yrs. service; no state salary; at age 55+ Rule of 85 applies; or age 60 with 15 yrs. of service. Early retirement with reduced benefit. Immediate vesting in the DC plan.	DC plan: 5% employee, 20% state (of taxable income). DB plan and employer contributions funded by appropriation.	DB benefit plan monthly benefit: Lesser of (a) $40 x years of General Assembly service completed before November 8, 1989 or (b) 1/12 of the average of the three highest consecutive years of General Assembly service salary. DC plan: numerous options for withdrawing accumulations in accord with IRS regulations. Loans are available. A participant in both plans may receive a benefit from both plans.
Iowa	Optional	Public Employees Retirement System	Age 65; age 62 with 20 yrs. service Rule of 88; reduced benefit at 55 with at least 4 years of service	3.7% individual	2% times FAS x years of service for first 30 years, + 1% times FAS times years in excess of 30 but no more than 5 in excess of 30. FAS is average of 3 highest years.
Kansas	Optional	Public Employees Retirement System	Age 65, age 62 with 10 yrs. of service or age plus yrs. of service equals 85 pts.	4% of salary, (4% annualized salary for Legislators).	3 highest yrs. x 1.75% x yrs. service divided by 12.

See footnotes at end of table.

STATE LEGISLATIVE RETIREMENT BENEFITS—Continued

State or other jurisdiction	Participation	Plan name	Requirements for regular retirement	Employee contribution rate	Benefit formula
Oklahoma..............	Legislators may retain membership as regular public employees if they have that status when elected; one time option to join Elected Officials' Plan.	Public Employee Retirement System, as regular member or elected official member. [Information here is for the Elected Officials' Plan.]	Elected Officials' Plan: Age 60 with 6 years service vesting at 6 years.	Optional contribution of 4.5%, 6%, 7.5%, 8.5%, 9%, or 10% of total compensation.	Avg. participating salary x length of service x computation factor depending on optional contributions ranging from 1.9% for a 4.5% contribution to 4% for a 10% contribution.
Oregon..............	Optional	Public Employee Retirement System legislator plan	Age 55, 30+ yrs. Service, 5 years vesting.	16.317% of subject wages	1.67% x yrs. service and final avg. monthly salary
Pennsylvania..............	Optional	State Employees' Retirement System	Age 50, 3 yrs. service, any age with 35 years of service; early retirement with reduced benefit.	7.5%	3% x final avg. salary x credited yrs. of service (x withdrawal factor if under regular retirement age - 50 for legislators).
Rhode Island..............	Legislators elected after January 1995 are ineligible for retirement benefits based on legislative service. (a)				
South Carolina..............	Mandatory, but members may opt out six months after being sworn into office.	South Carolina Retirement System	Age 60, 8 yrs. service; 30 yrs. of service regardless of age	10%	4.82% of annual compensation x yrs. service
South Dakota..............	None available.				
Tennessee..............	Optional		Age 55, 4 yrs. service	5.43%	$70 per month x yrs. service with a $1,375 monthly cap
Texas..............	Optional	Employee Retirement System: Elected Class Members	Age 60, 8 yrs. service; age 50, 12 yrs. service. Vesting at 8 years.	8%	2.3% x district judge's salary x length of service, with the monthly benefit capped at a the level of a district judge's salary, and adjusted when such salaries are increased. Various annuity options are available. Military service credit may be purchased to add to elective class service membership. In July 2005, a district judge's salary was set at $125,000, a year.
Utah..............	Mandatory	Governors' and Legislators' Retirement Plan	Age 62 with 10 years and an actuarial reduction; age 65 with 4 years of service for full benefits.	Non-contributory	$24.80/month (as of July 2004) x years of service; adjusted semi-annually according to consumer price index up to a maximum increase of 2%.
Vermont..............	None available. Deferred compensation plan available.				
Virginia..............	Mandatory		Age 50, 30 yrs. service (unreduced); age 55, 5 yrs. service; age 50, 10 yrs. service (reduced)	8.91% of creditable compensation	1.7% of average final compensation x yrs. of service

See footnotes at end of table.

STATE LEGISLATIVE RETIREMENT BENEFITS — Continued

State or other jurisdiction	Participation	Plan name	Requirements for regular retirement	Employee contribution rate	Benefit formula
Washington	Optional. If before an election the legislator belonged to a state public retirement plan, he or she may continue in that by making contributions. Otherwise the new legislator may join PERS Plan 2 or Plan 3.	See column to left. PERS plan 2 is a DB plan. PERS plan 3 is a hybrid DB/DC plan.	PERS plan 2: Age 65 with 5 years of service credit. Plan 3: Age 65 with 10 years of service credit for the DB side of the plan; immediate benefits (subject to federal restrictions) on the DC side of the plan. The member may choose various options for investment of contributions to the DC plan.	PERS plan 2: Employee contribution of 2.43% for 2002. Estimated at 3.33% for 2005–2007. Plan 3: No required member contribution for the DB component. The member may contribute from 5% to 15% of salary to the DC component.	PERS plan 2: 2% x years of service credit x average final compensation. Plan 3: DB is 1% x service credit years x average final compensation. DC benefit depends upon the value of accumulations.
West Virginia	Optional		Age 55, if yrs. of service+age equal 80	4.5% gross income	2% of final avg. salary x yrs. service. Final avg. salary is based on 3 highest yrs. out of last 10 yrs.
Wisconsin	Mandatory		Age 62 normal; age 57 with 30 years of service.	2.6% of salary in 2003, adjusted annually	Higher benefit of formula (2.165% x years of service x salary for service before 2000; 2% x years of service x salary for service 2000 and after) or money-purchase calculation.
Wyoming	None available				
Dist. of Columbia	Mandatory		Age 62, 5 yrs. service; age 55, 30 yrs. service; age 60, 20 yrs. service	Before 10/1/87, 7%; after 10/1/87, 5%	Multiply high 3 yrs. average pay by indicator under applicable yrs. or months of service.
Puerto Rico	Optional	Retirement System of the Employees of the Government of Puerto Rico	After 1990, age 65 with 30 years of service.	8.28%	1.5% of average earnings multiplied by the number of years of accredited service.
Guam	Optional		Age 60, 30 yrs. service; age 55, 15 yrs. service	5% or 8.5%	An amount equal to 2% of avg. annual salary for each of the first 10 yrs. of credited service and 2.5% of avg. annual salary for each yr. or part thereof of credited service over 10 yrs.
U.S. Virgin Islands	Optional		Age 60, 10 yrs. service	8%	At age 60 with at least 10 yrs. of service, at 2.5% for each yr. of service or at any time with at least 30 yrs. service

Source: National Conference of State Legislatures, January 2006 and updated January 2009.

Notes:

This table shows the retirement plans effective for state legislators elected in 2003, 2004 and thereafter.

In general the table does not include information on closed plans, plans that continue in force for some legislators who entered the plans in previous years, but which have been closed to additional members. The information in this table was updated for all states and Puerto Rico in 2004 and updated for 2005 state legislation. Information for the District of Columbia, Guam and the Virgin Islands dates from 2002.

Key:

N.A. — Information not available

None available. — No retirement benefit provided.

(a) Constitution has been amended effective 1/95. Any legislator elected after this date is not eligible to join the State Retirement System, but will be compensated for $10,000/yr. with cost of living increases to be adjusted annually.

Table 3.19
BILL AND RESOLUTION INTRODUCTIONS AND ENACTMENTS:
2010 REGULAR SESSIONS

State	Duration of session**	Introductions		Enactments/Adoptions		Measures vetoed by governor (a)(b)	Length of session
		Bills	Resolutions*	Bills	Resolutions*		
Alabama	Jan. 12 – Apr. 22, 2010	1,425	1,243	296	457	10	105C
Alaska	Jan. 19 – Apr. 19, 2010	739	172	183	91	2	90C
Arizona	Jan. 11 – Apr. 29, 2010	1,233	168	338	33	17	109C
Arkansas	Feb. 8 – Feb. 25, 2010	321	11	297	7	0	25C
California (c)	Jan. 4 – Nov. 30, 2010	1,871	247	1,039	183	296	(f)
Colorado	Jan. 13 – May 13, 2010	783	123	455	98	5	120L
Connecticut	Feb. 3 – May 5, 2010	1,039	192	191	192	13	69L
Delaware	Jan. 12 – Jun. 30, 2010	350	89	261	N.A.	5	52L
Florida	Mar. 2 – Apr. 30, 2010	2,336	252	292	9	18	60C
Georgia	Jan. 11 – Apr. 20, 2010	1,287	3,792	330	1,923	31	40L
Hawaii	Jan. 20 – Apr. 29, 2010	2,112	982	212	222	47	60L
Idaho	Jan. 11 – Mar. 29, 2010	551	69	359 (e)	42	0	88C
Illinois	Jan. 12, 2010 – Jan. 11, 2011	3,697	1,706	686	1,482	5	(f)
Indiana (d)(g)	Jan. 5 – Mar. 12, 2010	420	68	61	43	0	67C
Iowa	Jan. 11 – Mar. 30, 2010	949 (h)	N.A.	196 (h)	N.A.	1	79C
Kansas	Jan. 11 – May 11, 2010	592	27	165 (i)	8	2	89L
Kentucky	Jan. 5 – Apr. 15, 2010	826	637	164	513	1	60L
Louisiana	Mar. 29 – Jun. 21, 2010	2,288	771	1,061	646	14	51L
Maine	Jan. 6 – Apr. 12, 2010	336	30	278	0	0	37L
Maryland	Jan. 13 – Apr. 12, 2010	2,700	20	743	4	67	90C
Massachusetts (j)	Jan. 6 – Dec. 30, 2010	5,363 (k)	N.A.	476	N.A.	1	128L
Michigan	Jan. 13 – Dec. 31, 2010	1,386	35	383	1	0	(f)
Minnesota	Feb. 4 – May 16, 2010	2,721	N.A.	202	4	18	49L
Mississippi	Jan. 5 – May 3, 2010	2,974	504	414	388	4	119C
Missouri	Jan. 6 – May 30, 2010	1,756	83	106 (l)	0	5	72L
Montana	No regular session						
Nebraska (U)	Jan. 6 – Apr. 14, 2010	429	302	197	302 (m)	2	60L
Nevada	No regular session						
New Hampshire (n)	Jan. 6 – Oct. 13, 2010	946	43	378	4	6	22L
New Jersey (o)	Jan. 12 – Apr. 11, 2010	6,131	397	123	6	19	84L
New Mexico	Jan. 19 – Feb. 18, 2010	572	45	125	10	9	30C
New York	Jan. 6, 2010 – Jan. 5, 2011	18,062	N.A.	561 (p)	4,030	148	365C
North Carolina	May 12 – Jul. 10, 2010	704	76	196	31	0	60C
North Dakota	No regular session						
Ohio	Jan. 5 – Dec. 31, 2010 (s)	315	23	41	5	0	(f)
Oklahoma (g)	Feb. 1 – May 28, 2010	1,082	60	226	22	16	68L
Oregon	No regular session						
Pennsylvania	Feb. 5 – Nov. 22, 2010	4,287	1,452	140	N.A.	6	74L
Rhode Island	Jan. 5 – Jun. 10, 2010	2,317	N.A.	429	385	17	(f)
South Carolina	Jan. 14 – Jun. 29, 2010	930	916	190	772	46	(f)
South Dakota	Jan. 12 – Mar. 30, 2010	474	36	247	21	7	39L
Tennessee	Jan. 12 – Jun. 9, 2010	3,157	1,661	583	(q)	1	(f)
Texas	No regular session						
Utah	Jan. 25 – Mar. 11, 2010	626	87	418	62	3	45C
Vermont (j)	Jan. 5 – Jun. 9, 2010	336	N.A.	69	N.A.	1	(f)
Virginia	Jan. 13 – Mar. 14, 2010	2,135	769	871	670	0	61C
Washington	Jan. 11 – Mar. 11, 2010	1,250	50	296	10	4	60C
West Virginia	Jan. 13 – Mar. 20, 2010	2,079	N.A.	207	N.A.	12	67C
Wisconsin (r)	Jan. 5 – Dec. 16, 2010	1,720	264	406	171	6	63L
Wyoming	Feb. 8 – Mar. 5, 2010	202	12	118	3	3	20L

See footnotes at end of table.

BILL AND RESOLUTION INTRODUCTIONS AND ENACTMENTS:
2010 REGULAR SESSIONS — Continued

Source: The Council of State Governments' survey of legislative agencies and state websites, April 2011.

*Includes Joint and Concurrent resolutions.

**Actual adjournment dates are listed regardless of constitutional or statutory limitations. For more information on provisions, see Table 3.2, "Legislative Sessions: Legal Provisions."

Key:

C — Calendar day.

L — Legislative day (in some states, called a session or workday; definition may vary slightly; however, it generally refers to any day on which either chamber of the legislature is in session).

U — Unicameral legislature.

N.A. — Not available.

(a) Line-item or partial vetoes: Alaska — 6; California — 1; Florida — 2; Georgia — 5; Illinois — 17; Iowa — 6; Kansas — 11; Louisiana — 28; Michigan — 9; Minnesota — 5; Missouri — 1; Nebraska — 1; New Mexico — 4; Ohio — 1; South Carolina (Appropriation Act — H. 4657: 107 line-item vetoes); South Dakota — 1; Utah — 1; Washington — 22; Wisconsin — 5; Wyoming — 2.

(b) Number of vetoes overridden: Alabama — 4; Alaska — 1; Connecticut — 6; Hawaii — 11; Illinois — 6; Nebraska — 1; New Hampshire — 1; South Carolina (Appropriation Act — 29, other measures — 36); South Dakota — 3; Tennessee — 1.

(c) Statistics provided are for the second half of the 2009–2010 Regular Session.

(d) The Indiana General Assembly meets for one Organization Day in November (11/17/10) and then does not meet again until it reconvenes in January. This one additional day is included in the number of calendar days noted above.

(e) 354 bills were signed by the governor, with an additional five laws enacted without the governor's signature.

(f) California (125L Assembly; 122L Senate), Illinois (81L House; 72L Senate), Michigan (100L House; 99L Senate), Ohio (111L House; 125L Senate), Rhode Island (58L House; 41L Senate), South Carolina (58L House; 68L Senate), Tennessee (46L House; 48L Senate), Vermont (128C House; 26L Senate).

(g) Senate only.

(h) Includes resolutions.

(i) Includes those carried over from 2009.

(j) House/Assembly only.

(k) Bill introductions 5,363 reflect the total number of measures filed in the House Clerk's office. The high House "bill number" (including committee redrafts) was 5,589.

(l) Includes 15 appropriation bills.

(m) Includes three constitutional amendments passed.

(n) Legislature adjourned to the Call of the Chair on June 6, 2010, and returned on October 13, 2010, to consider veto messages.

(o) Total days in session are combined Assembly and Senate Sessions and Quorum days and Joint sessions (which = 3).

(p) 560 bills signed by the Governor (in regular session), one bill delivered to the Secretary of State (constitutional amendment).

(q) Tennessee does not track the number of resolutions adopted.

(r) The Wisconsin legislature operates on a biennial session schedule that includes the entire two-year period 2009–2010. All figures are for the entire biennium.

(s) Dates given are House only. Senate dates: Jan. 4 – Dec. 27, 2010.

Table 3.20
BILL AND RESOLUTION INTRODUCTIONS AND ENACTMENTS:
2010 SPECIAL SESSIONS

State or other jurisdiction	Duration of session**	Introductions		Enactments/adoptions		Measures vetoed by governor (a)(b)	Length of session
		Bills	Resolutions*	Bills	Resolutions*		
Alabama	Dec. 8 – Dec. 16, 2010	35	76	3	26	0	7L
Alaska	— No special session in 2010 —						
Arizona	Feb. 1 – Feb. 11, 2010	8	3	4	1	0	10C
	Mar. 8 – Mar. 16, 2010	26	4	12	2	0	9C
	Mar. 29 – Mar. 31, 2010	3	2	1	1	0	3C
	Aug. 9 – Aug. 11, 2010	3	2	0	1	0	3C
Arkansas	— No special session in 2010 —						
California (c)	Aug. 31, 2009 – Jan. 11, 2010 (d)	0	1	3	1	0	(e)
	Oct. 26, 2009 – Oct. 8, 2010 (f)	23	2	3	1	0	(e)
	Jan. 8 – Mar. 11, 2010 (g)	113	4	12	1	3	(e)
Colorado	— No special session in 2010 —						
Connecticut	Jun. 21 – Dec. 8, 2010 (h)	2	13	2	13	1	2L
	Jul. 30 – Dec. 8, 2010 (i)	1	4	1	N.A.	0	4L
Delaware	— No special session in 2010 —						
Florida	Jul. 20, 2010	22	11	0	0	0	1C
	Nov. 19, 2010	4	16	2	9	0	1C
Georgia	— No special session in 2010 —						
Hawaii	— No special session in 2010 —						
Idaho	— No special session in 2010 —						
Illinois	— No special session in 2010 —						
Indiana	— No special session in 2010 —						
Iowa	— No special session in 2010 —						
Kansas	— No special session in 2010 —						
Kentucky	May 24 – May 29, 2010	15	76	6	71	0	6L
Louisiana	— No special session in 2010 —						
Maine	— No special session in 2010 —						
Maryland	— No special session in 2010 —						
Massachusetts	— No special session in 2010 —						
Michigan	— No special session in 2010 —						
Minnesota	May 17, 2010	4	N.A.	1	N.A.		1L
	Oct. 18, 2010	13	N.A.	1	N.A.		1L
Mississippi	Apr. 22 – Apr. 23, 2010	2	0	1	0	0	2C
	Aug. 27, 2010	14	34	4	33	0	1C
Missouri	— No special session in 2010 —						
Montana	— No special session in 2010 —						
Nebraska (U)	— No special session in 2010 —						
Nevada	Mar. 23 – Apr. 1, 2010	11	3	10	3	1	6C
New Hampshire	Jun. 9, 2010	3	0	1	0	0	1L
New Jersey	Jul. 1, 2010 (j)	0	0	0	0	0	1L
New Mexico	Mar. 1 – Mar. 4, 2010	24	0	7	0	0	4C
New York	Jul. 28, 2010 (k)(l)	0	N.A.	0	N.A.	0	1L
	Aug. 3, 2010 (k)(l)	1	N.A.	1	N.A.	0	1L
	Jul. 28, 2010 (k)(m)	0	N.A.	0	N.A.	0	1L
	Aug. 3, 2010 (k)(m)	1	N.A.	1	N.A.	0	1L
	Jan. 18 – Jan. 19, 2010 (l)	0	N.A.	0	N.A.	0	1L
	Jun. 27, 2010 (l)	0	N.A.	0	N.A.	0	1L
	Jul. 29, 2010 (l)	0	N.A.	0	N.A.	0	1L
	Nov. 29, 2010 (n)	14	N.A.	6	N.A.	0	1L
	Nov. 30, 2010 (n)	1	N.A.	1	N.A.	0	1L
North Carolina	— No special session in 2010 —						
North Dakota	— No special session in 2010 —						
Ohio	— No special session in 2010 —						
Oklahoma	— No special session in 2010 —						
Oregon	— No special session in 2010 —						
Pennsylvania	May 3 – Nov. 16, 2010	26	1	0	0	0	31L
Rhode Island	— No special session in 2010 —						
South Carolina	— No special session in 2010 —						

See footnotes at end of table.

BILL AND RESOLUTION INTRODUCTIONS AND ENACTMENTS:
2010 SPECIAL SESSIONS — Continued

State or other jurisdiction	Duration of session**	Introductions		Enactments/adoptions		Measures vetoed by governor	Length of session
		Bills	Resolutions*	Bills	Resolutions*		
South Dakota	— No special session in 2010 —						
Tennessee	Jan. 12 – Jan. 25, 2010	42	30	4	(o)	0	8L
Texas	— No special session in 2010 —						
Utah	— No special session in 2010 —						
Vermont	— No special session in 2010 —						
Virginia	— No special session in 2010 —						
Washington	Mar. 15 – Apr. 12, 2010	4	0	4	0	0	29C
	Dec. 11, 2010					0	1C
West Virginia	May 24 – May 26, 2010	N.A.	N.A.	N.A.	N.A.	N.A.	2C
Wisconsin	Dec. 16, 2009 – Mar. 4, 2010 (p)	2	0	0	0	0	23L
Wyoming	— No special session in 2010 —						

Source: The Council of State Governments' survey of state legislative agencies, April 2011.

*Includes Joint and Concurrrent resolutions.

**Actual adjournment dates are listed regardless of constitutional or statutory limitations. For more information on provisions, see Table 3.2, "Legislative Sessions: Legal Provisions."

Key:

N.A.— Not available.

C — Calendar day.

L — Legislative day (in some states, called a session or workday; definition may vary slightly.

U — Unicameral legislature.

(a) Line-item or partial vetoes: Kentucky—26; New Mexico—4.

(b) Number of vetoes overridden: Connecticut—1.

(c) 2009–10 Fifth Extraordinary Session: (4L—Assembly; 4L—Senate), 2009–10 Sixth Extraordinary Session: (31L—Assembly; 44L—Senate), 2009–10 Eighth Extraordinary Session: (25L—Assembly; 26L—Senate). In California's 2009–2010 Fifth Extraordinary Session, no bills were introduced in the calendar year 2010; however, three bills that were introduced in calendar year 2009 were enacted (chaptered) in 2010.

(d) Dates shown are for Assembly only. Senate dates: Aug. 27, 2009 – Jan. 12, 2010.

(e) Statistics are for the second half of the Extraordinary Session.

(f) Dates shown are for Assembly only. Senate dates: Oct. 14, 2009 – Oct. 8, 2010.

(g) Dates shown are for Assembly only. Senate dates: Jan. 11 – Mar. 11, 2010.

(h) Convened 6/21, met one day, officially adjourned 12/8/2010.

(i) Met on 8/30, 8/5 and 8/13. Officially adjourned 12/8/2010.

(j) Governor called for a special session on 7/1/2010—both houses were called into session.

(k) Two extraordinary sessions were held in one day.

(l) House/Assembly only.

(m) Senate only.

(n) House and Senate totals.

(o) Tennessee does not track the number of resolutions adopted.

(p) The special session commenced in 2009, but carried over into 2010.

Chapter Four

STATE EXECUTIVE BRANCH

THE FOLLOWING TABLES ARE AN ONLINE-ONLY FEATURE FOR THE 2011 VOLUME OF *THE BOOK OF THE STATES.*

THESE TABLES CAN BE ACCESSED AT
http://knowledgecenter.csg.org/drupalview-content-type/1219

The State of the States: Governors Aggressively Chip Away

By Katherine Willoughby

The recent economic recession has affected gubernatorial priorities. In the past five years, education has remained the primary focus of governors, but other traditional state functions have slipped off their radar. December 2007 was the official start of the Great Recession. In that year, the four issues most often discussed by governors in their state of state addresses after education, in descending order, were health care, natural resources, jobs and corrections. This year, the four top issues on the minds of governors after education, also in descending order, are jobs, government performance, taxes and health care. In fact, since 2007, corrections and public safety have not been in the top five issues for governors. Natural resources and energy concerns do not appear in the top five for either this year or last year. This research examines the 2011 state of state addresses of U.S. governors to explain their ideas for continuing to manage through the economic recession.[1] Findings indicate a more focused consideration of education reform and job development, sustained attention on cost-cutting and efficiency measures, and continued gubernatorial intransigence regarding "no new taxes."

The Politics

States went decidedly Republican in the November 2010 elections. Considering governors' seats only, a swath of red covers the southwestern and middle U.S. states, runs across the Southeast and includes the states surrounding the Great Lakes, except for Illinois. Democratic blue covers the country's Western border states, California, Oregon and Washington, a vein of states across the mid-Atlantic to middle U.S. states and in the Northeast. Dramatic turnover in gubernatorial seats resulted in 29 Republican governors (58 percent of state chief executives), 20 Democratic governors (40 percent) and one independent governor.

In 2010, 54 percent of state chief executives were Democrats. Twelve states did not have gubernatorial elections in 2010. But in the other states that did hold elections or changed governors,[2] a dozen state gubernatorial seats remained Republican; 11 seats changed from Democratic to Republican; one state—Rhode Island—switched from Republican to Independent (Gov. Lincoln Chafee); nine seats remained Democratic; and in just five states—California, Connecticut, Hawaii, Minnesota and Vermont—the governor's seat changed from Republican to Democratic.

The Republican sweep of state legislatures was equally dramatic in 2010. In 2010, state lower and upper houses were majority Democratic (67 percent and 58 percent, respectively). In 2011, state lower and upper houses are majority Republican (61 percent and 59 percent, respectively). Of the 49 bicameral state legislatures (Nebraska's is unicameral and nonpartisan), 26 are majority Republican, 15 are majority Democratic and eight are split in party affiliation.[3]

Twenty-one states are solidly Republican with a sitting Republican governor and a majority Republican state house and senate, up from just 10 states prior to the 2010 elections. Just three states have Republican governors with majority Democratic legislatures (Nevada, New Mexico and New Jersey). On the other hand, 11 states are majority Democratic, with a Democratic governor and legislature, five states less than last year. Five Democratic governors must work with a majority Republican legislature (Minnesota Gov. Mark Dayton, Montana Gov. Brian Schweitzer, Missouri Gov. Jay Nixon, North Carolina Gov. Bev Perdue and New Hampshire Gov. John Lynch). Chafee of Rhode Island is the lone Independent working with a majority Democratic legislature.

The Money Situation

Collectively, states had budget shortfalls of $191 billion in 2010. Cumulatively, budget shortfalls for 2011 through the 2013 fiscal years are estimated at $317 billion.[4] Many expect the 2012 fiscal year to be the worst year yet for states due to the slow recovery and the discontinuation of federal stimulus money from the American Recovery and

Reinvestment Act of 2009. Just six states are not expecting a deficit in 2012; 43 states have estimated deficits in this next fiscal year totaling $112 billion. Projected deficits as a percent of 2011 spending are estimated to reach 25 percent or more in five states—Nevada (45 percent), New Jersey (37 percent), Texas (32 percent), California (29 percent) and Oregon (25 percent).[5]

State tax revenues are slowly recovering, but have yet to grow quickly enough to advance the nation to pre-recession levels. State sales tax collections in 2011 increased by 4.5 percent from 2010. Personal income taxes increased by 4.7 percent from 2010. Corporate income taxes increased by 8.8 percent from 2010.[6] Still, 2011 total year-end balances as a percent of expenditures are down $3 billion or 0.8 percent from 2010.[7] Unemployment figures are better than those in 2010, but just barely. The nationwide unemployment rate hovers around 9 percent and rates are greater than 10 percent in 10 states—Nevada, California, Florida, Rhode Island, Michigan, South Carolina, Oregon, Kentucky, Georgia and Mississippi.[8]

According to the National Association of State Budget Officers, known as NASBO, the Great Recession has created an "unprecedented fiscal situation" in that state spending from general and some other funds declined in both 2009 and 2010, which had not happened in more than 20 years.[9] State general fund spending is predominantly for education—elementary and secondary education makes up the largest portion—and Medicaid. Together with higher education, these categories make up approximately two-thirds of general fund spending by states. Spending in these and all other major expenditure categories continues to increase—especially as the recession drags on. From 2009 to 2010, only corrections spending realized a drop of 2.8 percent. As NASBO points out, "… State funds comprise approximately 95 percent of total corrections expenditures, and so corrections has not been as supported by the influx of federal stimulus spending."[10]

What's on the Agenda?

Governors presented their agendas to legislators, citizens and the media in a number of interesting ways this year. Some, like Florida Gov. Rick Scott, presented a number of principles, but few details. Michigan Gov. Rick Snyder's transcript of his address is an outline. California Gov. Jerry Brown brought up important state issues, but provided little substance. Recognizing that journalists have

called California a failed state, he urged citizens to actively participate in solving the state's problems by quoting Article 2, Section 1 of the California Constitution: "All political power is inherent in the people. Government is instituted for their protection, security and benefit, and they have the right to alter or reform it when the public good may require."

Other governors did some quoting as well. Connecticut Gov. Dan Malloy's inaugural address, titled "Shared Sacrifice, Shared Prosperity," was peppered with quotes from numerous historical figures, including past Connecticut governors and the writers, Robert Frost and Harriet Beecher Stowe. Iowa Gov. Terry Branstad took a slightly different approach, stating, "At the risk of sounding a bit like the grandfather I am now, I think we need to start with a stern talking to." Perhaps the most novel and comprehensive speech was that of Maryland Gov. Martin O'Malley, who presented a 12-page, single-spaced treatise that included 74 footnotes inclusive of all sorts of measurements, code, descriptions, statistics and explanations of various issues addressed by the governor.

A few other governors included interesting data about their state's fiscal situation to get attention. Montana Gov. Brian Schweitzer explained that his state is, "… one of the few states with cash in the bank. I asked Doctor No, the director of our budget office today, 'David, how much cash do we have in the bank?' And he said, '$330,997,350.84.'" Schweitzer also pointed out that "Wall Street has improved Montana's bond rating for the first time in 30 years, and for the first time in the history of Montana, we now have a double A plus bond rating." Chief executives in a number of states also reminded citizens of their strong credit ratings. Indiana Gov. Mitch Daniels explained that "many states exhausted any reserves they may have had and plunged into the red, but our savings account remains strong and our credit AAA." Delaware Gov. Jack Markell claimed, "Our focus on fiscal responsibility has made Delaware one of only eight states with a AAA rating from all three bond rating agencies." Georgia Gov. Nathan Deal said the same thing, "Georgia is one of only eight states in the nation with a Triple A bond rating by all three major bond rating agencies. I intend to maintain that rating." Missouri Gov. Jay Nixon pointed to fiscal responsibility that has "earned Missouri a Triple-A credit rating—the best you can get—from all three rating agencies. We're one of the few states in the nation that can make that claim."

Table A:
Issues Expressed by Governors in State of the State Addresses, 2007–2011

Issue expressed by governors	2007 percentage of governors mentioning issue (N=43)	2008 percentage of governors mentioning issue (N=42)	2009 percentage of governors mentioning issue (N=44)	2010 percentage of governors mentioning issue (N=42)	2011 percentage of governors mentioning issue (N=47)
Education	100.0%	90.5%	86.4%	90.5%	93.6%
Economic development/jobs	79.5	81.0	79.5	88.1	87.2
Performance/accountability	72.7	42.9	52.3	73.8	83.0
Health care	86.4	83.3	79.5	57.1	72.3
Tax/revenue initiative	84.1	59.5	65.9	83.3	70.2
Transportation/roads/bridges	52.3	59.5	65.9	50.0	46.8
Natural resources/energy	84.1	71.4	79.5	73.8	44.7
Safety/corrections	75.0	59.5	50.0	54.8	38.3
Pensions/OPEBs	36.4	21.4	18.2	19.0	36.2
Surplus/deficit/rainy day funds/reserves	70.5	54.8	45.5	78.6	34.0
Local government	52.3	35.7	20.5	11.9	17.0
Debt reduction	13.6	9.5	4.5	0	8.5
Ethics reform	13.6	11.9	15.9	26.2	8.5
Borders/illegal immigrants	11.4	16.7	6.8	4.8	8.5
Transparency	20.5	14.3	31.8	14.3	2.1

Source: Content analysis of 2007–2008 State of the State Addresses from Table C of Katherine G. Willoughby, 2008, "The State of the States: Governors Keep Agendas Short," *The Book of the States*, Vol. 40 (Lexington, KY: The Council of State Governments): 157–64; Content analysis of 2009 State of State Addresses conducted by Tanya Smilley, MPA candidate and Soyoung Park, Ph.D. candidate, Public Policy, Andrew Young School of Policy Studies, GSU; Content analysis of 2010 State of State Addresses conducted by Soyoung Park, Ph.D. candidate, Public Policy and Scott Allen, MPA candidate, Andrew Young School of Policy Studies, Georgia State University, Atlanta, Georgia; Content analysis of 2011 State of State Addresses conducted by Byungwoo Cho, MPA candidate, Andrew Young School of Policy Studies, Georgia State University, Atlanta, Georgia.

Other governors painted no-growth budgets in a positive light. Arkansas Gov. Mike Beebe put it this way:

"You have before you a list of these challenges facing other states. It's on your desks. It is only a sample of the unenviable dilemmas other state legislatures face this year. That we do not face such bleak crises here is a source of pride. My proposed budget for the coming fiscal year is generally flat. Nearly all agencies and services will remain funded at the same levels as this year. With our state economy recovering, we anticipate a small increase in revenue."

On the other hand, more governors pointed to continuing dark clouds. Compared to Montana's $331 million cash in the bank, Kansas Gov. Sam Brownback pointed to just $876.05 in the bank on the first day of this fiscal year. Kentucky Gov. Steve Beshear said, "Perks like take-home cars are a thing of the past." And Idaho Gov. C.L. "Butch" Otter prepared citizens for impending policy discourse that "could be the kind of legislative session that leaves people wondering why anyone would want to go into politics or public service."

Somewhat uncharacteristic for public officials, Hawaii Gov. Neil Abercrombie claimed "full responsibility for our current situation," which includes an $844 million deficit in the next two years. He warned that the problem is so bad in the state that balancing the budget "will merely be life support for what has become a battered, under-resourced and often dysfunctional democracy."

Table A presents issues mentioned by governors in their state of state addresses for the past five years. In 2011, education remained the top priority of governors, as it has in the past. But jobs and health care are the only other state functions specified by more than half the governors. As national health care reform celebrated its first birthday, governors were 15 percent more likely to talk about their plans for their state to accommodate, or fight, the federal legislation than in 2010.

Also in 2011, governors were more likely to discuss performance improvements, cost-cutting and efficiency measures and accountability efforts than

Table B:
Issues Expressed by at Least Two-Thirds of Governors in Addresses, 2007–2011

2007	2008	2009	2010	2011
Education	Education	Education	Education	Education
Health Care	Health Care	Health Care	Jobs	Jobs
Natural Resources	Jobs	Jobs	Taxes	Performance
Taxes	Natural Resources	Natural Resources	Surplus/Deficit	Health Care
Jobs		Taxes	Natural Resources	Taxes
Public Safety		Transportation	Performance	
Performance				
Surplus/Deficit				

Source: Katherine G. Willoughby.

in 2010. Mention of such measures was up by 9 percent in 2011, while mention of taxes and revenue initiatives was down by 13 percent, although they were still brought up by 70.2 percent of governors. Mentions of natural resources and energy initiatives were down by 29 percent; less than 50 percent of governors mentioned this or a transportation agenda. Talk of public safety and corrections was down by more than 16 percent from 2010.

Of the rest of the issues listed, gubernatorial mention of deficits and the use of reserves or rainy day funds was down the most, by almost 45 percent. This is certainly indicative that states have already raided these funds in the past year. Most of the talk in 2011 around rainy day funds regards efforts to shield or restock them. Governors in Indiana, Texas, Utah and West Virginia talked about protecting their rainy day funds from raids. Others, like Gov. Nathan Deal of Georgia, Lynch of New Hampshire and Haslam of Tennessee talked about restoring, rebuilding and replenishing these funds.

Discussion of state debt (up by 8.5 percent) and state retirement funds (up by 17 percent) increased from 2010. More than one-third of governors brought up employee pensions and other post-employment benefits, explaining their ideas for reducing and controlling these obligations in the future. Not surprisingly, talk of ethics reform and government transparency in these fiscally stressful times was down, by almost 18 percent and 12 percent, respectively. Finally, in their addresses, governors in 2011 were more likely than in 2010 to recognize state-local relationships, though generally by way of pushing more responsibilities onto,

and pulling fiscal support from, local governments. Mentions of the protection of state borders and illegal immigration saw a small uptick as well.

Table B presents the issues addressed by two-thirds or more of governors in their addresses from 2007 to 2011. The items are listed in descending order of popularity in terms of consideration by chief executives. This table provides a clearer trend in gubernatorial focus since the start of the Great Recession in December 2007. That year, 66 percent or more of governors mentioned their vision regarding eight areas, five of which are traditional functions of state government: education, health care, natural resources/energy, economic development/jobs and public safety/corrections. Then, as the Great Recession kicked in, governors focused on education, health care, jobs and natural resources/energy. Public safety and corrections did not find its way into the most popular issues considered by governors after 2007. Transportation replaced public safety in 2009.

Gubernatorial hesitancy about the future of health care is evident in its absence from the list in 2010, as national health care reform was debated. Compared to 2009, 22 percent fewer governors discussed their health care agenda in 2010. But in 2011, health care is back on the docket and the only other state function addressed by more than half the governors, after education and jobs. The next most popular issues mentioned in 2011 were natural resources and transportation, but just under 47 percent of governors addressed each issue.

These results suggest that as the economic recession continued, as slow growing revenues failed to cover increasing expenditures, governors honed in on the most important functions of states—education and jobs. Health and welfare concerns are certainly important, but consideration of the state role has been tempered by federal intervention plans. Continued fiscal pressures pushed governors to question government performance and to consider additional and new cost-cutting and efficiency measures. No doubt, the dramatic influx of Republican governors into the top state seat contributed to a focus on cost-cutting in 2011. That is, the conservative movement to reduce the size of government played into the results presented here.

Education

Governors talked of many things to shore up education in their states; some of their ideas seem like baby steps, others Herculean. Alabama Gov. Robert Bentley spoke of protecting education programs and devoting $5 million of the education budget for teaching supplies. "We expect our teachers to lead our children to succeed and excel in the classroom. By funding classroom supplies, we are giving our teachers the resources they need to meet those expectations," Bentley said. In Alabama, where the Education Trust Fund overshadows the general fund, the governor called for legislation to provide a sustainable funding base for the education fund. In terms of baby steps, Markell of Delaware pointed to his state as "one of a handful to require completion of a world language in order to graduate," and explained that offering a high quality online Chinese language course is important to the educational future of the state.

Many governors pushed funding for prekindergarten programs to advance the state educationally as well as economically. Malloy of Connecticut pressed for pre–K education for every child in the state just as Minnesota Gov. Mark Dayton promoted all-day kindergarten for his state's children. Dayton also wanted to increase state funding for K–12 education, re-establish the Governor's Council on Early Childhood Education and the Children's Cabinet, and continue to expand public-private partnerships that support educational programs.

Kansas's Brownback focused on early childhood learning in his address, calling for $6 million for early childhood centers for the neediest school districts. Hawaii's Abercrombie was seeking to establish a Department of Early Childhood to foster advancements in education programs. Branstad's Iowa budget "proposes a $43 million annual

investment in providing preschool assistance to those families in greatest need."

Farther down the education road, many governors are looking to expand options for students in higher education through community and technical college offerings. Illinois Gov. Pat Quinn asked for increased funding to provide scholarships for qualified, needy students, with a focus on community college students. Maine Gov. Paul LePage promoted community colleges and alternative programs in his budget because "not every student is well served by traditional schools." North Carolina Gov. Bev Purdue talked of rebranding programs in her state's university system by consolidating and more closely linking high schools and community colleges to support greater student affordability. South Dakota Gov. Dennis Daugaard wanted to expand technical education opportunities in his state and offer post-secondary tech schools increased bonding capacity to help the effort.

The words "incentive" and "education" are linked throughout the governors' addresses and ideas about improving performance abound. Governors in Florida, Indiana, Mississippi and New Jersey discussed the expansion of charter schools in their states. And New Jersey Gov. Chris Christie laid out a comprehensive education reform agenda:

"We must empower principals. We must reform poor-performing public schools or close them. We must cut out-of-classroom costs and focus our efforts on teachers and children. I propose that we reward the best teachers, based on merit.... I demand that layoffs, when they occur, be based on a merit system and not merely on seniority. I am committed to improving the measurement and evaluation of teachers.... And, most important, the time for a national conversation on tenure is long past due. The time to eliminate teacher tenure is now."

Arkansas Gov. Mike Beebe asked for a 1 percent increase in spending for higher education and to incentivize funding by linking it to coursework completion and graduation rates. "We can and must double the number of college graduates in Arkansas by 2025 if we are to stay competitive," he said. New York Gov. Andrew Cuomo wanted to establish two competitive funds that reward performance—one for school districts to compete by increasing student performance and one for districts to compete by implementing administrative efficiency measures. Cuomo suggested a $250 million fund for each competition.

North Dakota Gov. Jack Dalrymple supported a strategy "to foster a culture of entrepreneurship where all of our four-year universities operate business incubators that support start-up enterprises of all kinds." In New Hampshire, Lynch stated that, "with this budget, state government is getting out of the financial aid business and redirecting those funds to support our community college and university systems." He wanted to consolidate functions within the Department of Education and restructure an education commission to allow funding the community college and university systems at 95 percent of their current levels. "The Community College System will also receive an additional $2 million a year to create an advanced composite manufacturing program, which will help make possible the expansion of Albany International in New Hampshire and attract additional businesses in this growing field," Lynch said.

Texas Gov. Rick Perry wanted to expand online educational opportunities "that will not only enable students who have dropped out to earn a diploma online, but also give students across the state access to classes their own schools may not offer." He suggested linking school enrollment to getting and keeping a Texas driver's license. Perry also advocated for an incentive program that provides $1,500 to employers for every employee who earns a high school diploma or GED. Employees would have to receive time off with pay to study or go to class.

New Mexico's Gov. Susana Martinez claims her "Kids First, New Mexico Wins" plan will trim education bureaucracy and direct savings to the classroom. Her plan includes grading schools' performance and posting those grades on the Web, targeting immediate help to the lowest-performing students and failing schools, ending social promotions and rewarding the best teachers. Oklahoma Gov. Mary Fallin wants to cut "educational bureaucracy" by sharing resources, encouraging innovation, matching private to state funds for innovative learning programs, eliminating "… trial de novo, a system that makes it nearly impossible to dismiss even the most underperforming teacher," cutting out social promotions, increasing the use of electronic textbooks and reducing remediation rates.

In Kentucky Beshear pressed to improve high school graduation rates by keeping students in school to age 18 and motivated to learn through alternative programming. Mississippi Gov. Haley Barbour supported dual enrollment so that "students can learn more and their parents will save money as college credits are earned while in high school." Nebraska Gov. Dave Heineman supported development of a virtual high school, with support of $8.5 million from lottery funds.

Indiana's Daniels spoke about cleaning up union and collective bargaining of teachers and red tape. "While unions and collective bargaining are the right of those teachers who wish to engage in them," Daniels said, "they go too far when they dictate the color of the teachers' lounge, who can monitor recess or on what days the principal is allowed to hold a staff meeting. We must free our school leaders from all the handcuffs that reduce their ability to meet the higher expectations we now have for student achievement." He also suggested that some students should be able to graduate in 11 years rather than 12.

Governors also mapped out plans for pushing more responsibility to local governments for some educational services. Nevada Gov. Bryan Sandoval called for redirection of property tax receipts among counties to "the support of universities and community colleges in those counties, because property values rise and economic growth occurs where universities contribute to economic development," as well as retooling bonded indebtedness for local school construction. South Dakota's Daugaard suggested that local school boards and school administrators run their own districts "to repeal the 100 student minimum for state aid to school districts, and to remove the cap on school district reserve fund balances." He added, "We must trust local officials to make the best decisions for their districts. And if they fail, we must trust local voters to find new local officials." Connecticut's Malloy suggested that control of state vocational technical schools should be transferred to local districts and regions. Illinois Gov. Pat Quinn promoted consolidation of local school districts to lower "administrative overhead, improve efficiency and save taxpayers $100 million."

Jobs, Jobs, Jobs

The second most discussed topic by governors this year regarded economic development and jobs. Many governors talked about lowering and/or eliminating taxes, exploring and extracting natural resources, advancing tourism and the film industry, infrastructure investments and various organizational changes, such as creating or consolidating offices, public-private partnerships and/or councils. They also talked about cutting red tape, improving workforce training and leveraging relationships with university systems, college student internships and keeping college graduates in the state and employed as ways to expand business opportunities and increase jobs.

Alaska Gov. Sean Parnell provided one of the more detailed plans for economic development, including the suspension of the state's 8 cent per gallon motor fuel tax, completion of various road projects to improve access to resources, and investment in energy generating plants and projects. He also promoted mining untapped rare earth elements, claiming that "today, our Pacific Rim neighbor, China, controls 97 percent of the world market for these rare earth elements. We cannot afford to rely on foreign sources to meet our nation's demand. Alaska is a storehouse of rare earth minerals. Let's explore them." Similarly, Kansas's Brownback discussed how to grow his state's animal agriculture sector.

To incentivize businesses to come into the state, governors also talked about tax changes. Brownback explained his plan, "Enhanced Expensing," will allow businesses in the state to immediately deduct a higher percentage of the cost of an investment. And the Kansas governor's "Rural Opportunity Zones" would waive the state income tax for individuals relocating from out-of-state into a participating county that has experienced a double-digit percentage population decline in the last 10 years. Florida's Scott pushed eliminating that state's corporate income tax. Iowa's Branstad mapped out numerous tax changes: "The small business income tax rate will be cut in half and made a flat 6 percent. Commercial property taxes will be reduced by 40 percent.... New investment will be immediately taxed at 60 percent of its valuation. And existing commercial property tax will be rolled back by 8 percent a year over five years." New Mexico Gov. Susana Martinez wanted to eliminate the tax on locomotive fuel to become more competitive with neighboring states. She also encouraged, "small businesses to hire unemployed workers by covering part of their salaries for the first six months through the unemployment fund."

Pennsylvania Gov. Tom Corbett suggested eliminating the state's capital stock and franchise tax. Also, his budget retains an array of tax credits, such as, film, research and development. Rhode Island's Chafee pointed out that his state's corporate tax code "creates an unfair advantage for multistate companies with operations in Rhode Island by allowing them to send profits out of state to avoid taxes here." He asked for combined reporting to "treat all of our businesses fairly." He also is seeking to phase out other tax credits, lower the corporate minimum tax and reduce the state corporate tax rate to be more competitive with neighboring states.

A number of states are looking at information technology advancements and the expansion of broadband as ways to streamline processes, expand access to opportunities and resources and to grow businesses. Governors in Hawaii, Kansas, Maryland, Missouri, New Hampshire and Nevada discussed such plans specifically. Wyoming Gov. Matthew Mead wants to use state funding to recruit mega data centers. "We have what those centers need," Mead said. "We have the natural advantages: We have a favorable weather climate with a low number of required cooling days; we can produce abundant, relatively inexpensive electricity; we have relative safety from natural catastrophes such as hurricanes, and we have available land."

Delaware's Markell claimed that health care support to businesses can advance economic development. "Too often, small business owners have trouble negotiating and paying for health care coverage for their workforce or attracting the best workers when they don't," Markell said. "We will implement the new federal health care act in a way that most helps our small businesses." Oklahoma's Fallin asked for reform of the state's workers' compensation system so that it "takes care of our injured workers in a more timely fashion, reduces fraud and waste, and puts the brakes on runaway costs that have spiraled upwards each year." Washington's Gov. Christine Gregoire proposed changes to her state's unemployment insurance and compensation rates.

South Dakota's Daugaard provided one of the most comprehensive plans for economic development in his state. In a little more than 1,800 words, this chief executive promoted an economic development fund, a small town focus and microloan program, business attention to the state's agriculture sector and improved tourism. He also asked for reform of the state's large project refund program so that "refunds only be given to those projects that would not otherwise be undertaken, and to give discretion to determine when a project meets that standard. ... I would ask that you would provide this authority so that South Dakota can be protected from unnecessary tax giveaways." He did not forget to mention the Homestake Underground Science Laboratory as well as improvements to the state's aviation industry as ways to grow jobs and state wealth.

Wisconsin Gov. Scott Walker, who kept the newspapers and media outlets working for most of the early spring of 2011 with his effort to cut back union bargaining rights, explained his proposed eight pieces of legislation "to instill in our state an environment that encourages job creation, and to send the message to employers that now is the time to start hiring." Walker said his plan included lower taxes, less regulation, and lower litigation and health care costs, "so that more employers are able to create jobs for our people."

Performance and More

Mentions of government performance, cost-cutting measures and accountability standards made it to third place in 2011 in governors' state of the state addresses. Colorado Gov. John Hickenlooper said, "we are going to undertake a frank analysis of how and where government works—what is the real impact being realized in terms of tax dollars being spent? For those programs and policies that, while undertaken with good intent but have not proven to be effective, we are going to collectively make the decision on how to cut. Our goal is to redefine the role of government to match what the people of this state can afford." He then defined his vision of effective, efficient and elegant public service. "When I say elegant, I'm talking about the delivery of state services in a way that elevates both the state employee and the person receiving state services," Hickenlooper said. "When someone applies for a driver's license or inspection, they shouldn't feel disrespected by the interaction and neither should the state employee. This is the essence of customer service." Other efforts covered accounting rules changes, like Connecticut's Malloy's request to, "... require the state to keep its books according to GAAP principles." His other ideas included reorganizations, consolidation of services and offices, making state buildings more energy efficient, tort reform, cleaning up government regulation, performance awards to state employees and various personnel changes, especially as relates to funding employee benefits.

Wisconsin's Walker's efforts are well known in the employee benefit area. But others, like Florida's Scott, also pressed for such changes. "... We will also modernize our state government," Scott said. "Florida is currently the only state where taxpayers pay for the entire pension of state workers. We need to secure the state's pension system and be fair to the taxpayers of Florida. We will bring Florida's retirement system in line with other states by having government workers contribute towards their own retirement, just like everyone else."

In Maine, LePage includes in his budget "a retirement incentive for state workers. Age-eligible employees who leave the workforce before the end of this calendar year will receive a small cash payment and enter the retirement system before cost-saving adjustments are made to the program." And Pennsylvania's Corbett explained he would be "looking for salary rollbacks and freezes from state employees, as well as asking them to increase their contributions for health care benefits. We also need to start the conversation about the necessary repairs to our public retirement system."

Georgia's Deal promoted downsizing by "eliminating about 14,000 positions." Similarly, Kansas's Brownback noted that "in my FY2012 budget recommendations, I have eliminated over 2,000 unfilled employee positions." Brownback also established an "Office of the Repealer to identify regulations or statutes for repeal that are costly, outdated and ineffective." North Carolina's Perdue talked of consolidating 14 state agencies into eight and "shedding as many as a thousand workers." New Hampshire's Lynch echoed this; his budget "eliminates 1,100 positions, reducing our state employee position count by almost 10 percent." He also explained his consolidation of services and offices, the institution of a new financial management information system and leveraging Internet technology to streamline some state services.

Nevada's Sandoval pointed out that his budget "recommends the consolidation, elimination or centralization of 20 departments and agencies." Tennessee's Haslam also slashed personnel, saying, "there will be 1,180 fewer state positions—almost 90 percent of the reductions come from eliminating unfilled positions and the projects tied to non-recurring state and federal stimulus funds." Haslam also called for "an across-the-board paperwork reduction plan."

Rhode Island's Chafee was one of the few who spoke of direct program cuts to affect performance. "I also propose $20 million in cuts to other departments as a first step in a larger review of their operations and management," Chafee said. South Carolina Gov. Nikki Haley spoke of "commonsense savings, such as physically moving the Department for Alcohol and other Drug Abuse Services from a privately leased space to offices sitting empty in a government-owned building. This simple act will save the people of South Carolina $700,000 over the next four years."

More than half of governors (55.3 percent) mentioned the federal government this year in their addresses and 17 percent mentioned local government. Many of the comments about the federal government regarded national health care reform and its impacts on state functioning. Such comments characterized the health care reform as stifling, limiting, seriously damaging, a takeover, and jeopardizing other state priorities. Alaska Gov. Sean Parnell said his state would "not stand down in the fight to protect the state's sovereignty," while Kentucky Gov. Beshear claimed that "Kentuckians are rightly disgusted by a federal government that defines fiscal management as the speed at which you can print money."

Thoughts about local governments were likely to push more responsibility onto these governments or to promote efficiencies at this level. Indiana's Daniels called for reorganization of local government in that state. "We should join the rest of America in moving to a single, elected county commissioner, working with a strengthened legislative branch, the County Council, to make decision making accountable and implementation swift and efficient," Daniels said. Likewise, New York's Cuomo promoted a consolidation bonus to local governments to share services, suggesting that "50 percent of the bonus money [go] to direct property taxpayer relief for the people of that government."

Conclusion

In the past few years, governors have honed in on the most critical of state functions—education and economic development. In 2011, governors were not shy about presenting their plans for righting the fiscal ship. Idaho's Otter claimed "a new culture of responsible austerity" that seemed to pervade the thoughts of other chief executives around the nation.

Chief executives are holding firm on education, presenting numerous tax relief and other options to draw jobs and business in-state, and requesting a wide variety of cost-cutting initiatives (slashing vacancies, reorganizing state offices, etc.), program changes (highlighting community colleges and on-line education) and evaluations to continue chipping away at state expenditures. In the words of New York's Cuomo, "The economy has retrenched; states now have to recalibrate." And that is what governors are attempting very aggressively in their state of state speeches.

Notes

[1] Chief executives of state governments report annually or biennially to their legislatures regarding the fiscal condition of their state, commonwealth or territory. Governors often use their address to lay out their policy and budget agendas for their upcoming or continuing administration. The 2011 state of the state addresses were accessed from January 1 through March 21, 2011, via *www.nga.org* or *www.stateline.org* or using the state government's home page. This research considers those 47 states with transcripts available at these sites as of March 21, 2011. Speeches not available by this date included Oregon and Vermont. Gov. Jan Brewer's address of Jan. 10, 2011, to the Arizona legislature and state residents is not included in this analysis as she spoke only of the Jan. 8, 2011, shooting of U.S. Rep. Gabrielle Giffords and others in Tucson. Gov. Brewer explained that, "I had intended to deliver a State of the State address to you today—remarks that outline an exciting and solid plan for job creation, education, and tax reform and I will deliver that plan to you. But, not now. Not today." All quotes and data presented here are from the addresses accessed on these websites, unless otherwise noted.

To conduct a content analysis of governors' state of state addresses, as in the past, topics were considered addressed if the chief executive specifically discussed them as relevant to state operations and the budget *going forward*. The governor needed to relay that the function, activity or issue is an important item in next year's—fiscal 2012—budget and policy direction. Just mentioning a state function or policy area like economic development in a speech did not classify the issue as an agenda item addressed by a governor. Further, a review by the governor of past accomplishments alone in any particular issue area did not count in this content analysis.

[2] Includes West Virginia, in which Earl Ray Tomblin, as president of West Virginia's Senate, assumed the governor's seat because of the resignation of Gov. Joe Manchin III, who won the special election in November 2010 to replace U.S. Senator Robert Byrd, who died in office. Both Tomblin and Manchin are Democrats.

[3] National Conference of State Legislatures 2011. State-Vote 2001 State and Legislative Partisan Composition (March 9). Accessed on March 15, 2011 at: *http://www.ncsl.org/documents/statevote/2011_Legis_and_State.pdf*.

[4] McNichol, Elizabeth, Phil Oliff and Nicholas Johnson, 2011. "States continue to feel recession's impact." Washington, D.C.: Center on Budget and Policy Priorities (March 9).

[5] Combs, David, 2011. "State budget gaps: How does your state rank?" Stateline.org (March 15) accessible at: *http://www.stateline.org/live/printable/story?contentId=15158*.

[6] National Association of State Budget Officers 2010. *The Fiscal Survey of the States.* (Washington, D.C.) Fall. Table 19: Comparison of Tax Collections in Fiscal 2009, Fiscal 2010, and Enacted 2011, p. 42.

[7] National Association of State Budget Officers 2010. *The Fiscal Survey of the States.* (Washington, D.C.) Fall. Table 23: Total Year-End Balances, Fiscal 1979 to Fiscal 2011, p. 50.

[8] U.S. Department of Labor, Bureau of Labor Statistics, Local Area Unemployment Statistics: Current Unemployment Rates for States and Historical Highs/Lows accessed on March 15, 2011 at: *http://www.bls.gov/web/laus/lauhsthl.htm*.

[9] National Association of State Budget Officers 2010. State Expenditure Report. (Washington, D.C.) Fall. p. 2.

[10] National Association of State Budget Officers 2010. State Expenditure Report.

About the Author

Katherine Willoughby is professor of public management and policy in the Andrew Young School of Policy Studies at Georgia State University in Atlanta. Her research concentrates on state and local government budgeting and financial management, public policy development and public organization theory. She has conducted extensive research in the area of state budgeting practices, with a concentration on performance measurement applicability at this level of government in the United States.

Gubernatorial Elections, Campaign Costs and Powers

By Thad Beyle

Governors remain in the forefront of activity in the 21st century. While the governorship was not the stepping stone to the presidency for President Barack Obama as it was for our two previous presidents, Democratic Gov. Bill Clinton from Arkansas (1993–2001) and Republican Gov. George W. Bush from Texas (2001–2009), governors continue to be in the middle of addressing the problems facing our country's weak economy. The demands on governors to propose state budgets and then keep them in balance have increased greatly during the current recession. Proposed and adopted budgets have fallen victim to severe revenue shortfalls in the states, which has placed severe limits on the states to address the many growing needs of people trying to live through these very tough times. Politically, this has led to political fallout from unhappy voters as they vent their anger and frustration toward elected leaders on election days.

2010 Gubernatorial Politics

The 2010 state gubernatorial elections were of considerable significance in our political system. There have been 36 gubernatorial races in the even mid-year of a presidential term eight times since 1978. Utah needed to have a special election to let its succeeding Gov. Gary Herbert fill out the remainder of his succession term. Herbert became governor in August 2009 when former Gov. Jon Huntsman was appointed as U.S. ambassador to China. This meant 37 races were held in 2010, the most gubernatorial races ever in a single year.

Twenty-three seats were open; 15 tied to term limits on incumbent governors,[1] while in eight states, incumbents decided not to seek another term, although they were eligible to do so.[2] Incumbent governors sought another term in 14 states; 11 governors won a new term,[3] while those in three states lost their re-election bids.[4]

The party candidates winning in these 37 races were 23 Republicans (62.2 percent),[5] 13 Democrats (35.1 percent),[6] and one Independent (2.7 percent).[7] Democrats won six of the nine races in the Northeast, while Republicans won only two and an Independent only one. Republicans, however, dominated the remaining regions, winning seven in each of them while the Democrats won only one in the South, two in the Midwest, and four in the West.

Victory in the most recent presidential election can have a negative effect on a party's gubernatorial races in the elections in the two following years. After the election of Democrat Barack Obama as president in 2008, Democrats won only 13 of the 39 races in 2009 and 2010 (33.3 percent). This compares to the 28.9 percent Democratic

wins in the two election years following the election of Democrat Bill Clinton in 1992, and the 28.9 percent Democratic wins in the two election years following the re-election of President Clinton in 1996. This also compares to the 42.1 percent Republican wins in the two election years following Republican George W. Bush's re-election win in 2004. However, the initial election of Republican George W. Bush in 2000 did not hurt his party's candidates in the next two years, as they won 57.9 percent of those races.

The political makeup from 2010—with 26 Democratic and 24 Republican governors—shifted in 2011 to 29 Republicans, 20 Democrats and one Independent serving as governors.[8]

These 2010 races ranged from those in which the winner won by 10 or more points—21 states (57 percent), Republicans in 15 states, Democrats in six states;[9] to those in which the winner won by between five and 10 points—six states (16 percent), Republicans in four states, Democrats in two states;[10] to those who won by less than five points—10 states (27 percent), Republicans in four states, Democrats in five states, and an Independent in one state.[11]

Gubernatorial Elections

As seen in Table A, incumbents were eligible to seek another term in 434 of the 572 gubernatorial contests held between 1970 and 2010 (75.9 percent). In those contests, 338 eligible incumbents sought re-election (77.9 percent), and 256 of them succeeded (75.7 percent). Those who were defeated were more likely to lose in the general elec-

Table A: Gubernatorial Elections: 1970–2010

Year	Number of races	Democratic winner		Number of incumbent governors									
				Eligible to run		Actually ran		Won		Lost			
		Number	Percent	Number	Percent	Number	Percent	Number	Percent	Number	Percent	In primary	In general election
1970	35	22	63	29	83	24	83	16	64	8	36	1 (a)	7 (b)
1971	3	3	100	0	...	...	...	...	...	...	...	...	...
1972	18	11	61	15	83	11	73	7	64	4	36	2 (c)	2 (d)
1973	2	1	50	1	50	1	100	...	...	1	100	1 (e)	...
1974	35	27 (f)	77	29	83	22	76	17	77	5	24	1 (g)	4 (h)
1975	3	3	100	2	66	2	100	2	100	...	...	...	...
1976	14	9	64	12	86	8	67	5	63	3	33	1 (i)	2 (j)
1977	2	1	50	1	50	1	100	1	100	...	...	...	...
1978	36	21	58	29	81	23	79	16	73	7	30	2 (k)	5 (l)
1979	3	2	67	0	...	...	...	...	...	...	...	...	...
1980	13	6	46	12	92	12	100	7	58	5	42	2 (m)	3 (n)
1981	2	1	50	0	...	...	...	...	...	...	...	...	...
1982	36	27	75	33	92	25	76	19	76	6	24	1 (o)	5 (p)
1983	3	3	100	1	33	1	100	...	...	1	100	1 (q)	...
1984	13	5	38	9	69	6	67	4	67	2	33	...	2 (r)
1985	2	1	50	1	50	1	100	1	100	...	...	...	...
1986	36	19	53	24	67	18	75	15	83	3	18	1 (s)	2 (t)
1987	3	3	100	2	67	1	50	...	...	1	100	1 (u)	...
1988	12	5	42	9	75	9	100	8	89	1	11	...	1 (v)
1989	2	2	100	0	...	...	...	...	...	...	...	...	...
1990	36	19 (w)	53	33	92	23	70	17	74	6	26	...	6 (x)
1991	3	2	67	2	67	2	100	...	...	2	100	1 (y)	1 (z)
1992	12	8	67	9	75	4	44	4	100	...	...	...	...
1993	2	0	0	1	50	1	100	...	...	1	100	...	1 (aa)
1994	36	11 (bb)	31	30	83	23	77	17	74	6	26	2 (cc)	4 (dd)
1995	3	1	33	2	67	1	50	1	100	...	...	...	...
1996	11	7	64	9	82	7	78	7	100	...	...	...	...
1997	2	0	0	1	50	1	100	1	100	...	...	...	...
1998	36	11 (ee)	31	27	75	25	93	23	92	2	8	...	2 (ff)
1999	3	2	67	2	67	2	100	2	100	...	...	...	...
2000	11	8	73	7	88	6	86	5	83	1	17	...	1 (gg)
2001	2	2	100	0	...	...	...	...	...	...	...	...	...
2002	36	14	39	22	61	16	73	12	75	4	25	...	4 (hh)
2003	4 (ii)	1	25	2	50	2	100	...	...	2	100	...	2 (jj)
2004	11	6	55	11	100	8	73	4	50	4	50	2 (kk)	2 (ll)
2005	2	2	100	1	50	...	...	...	...	...	...	...	...
2006	36	20	56	31	86	27	87	25	93	2	7	1 (mm)	1 (nn)
2007	3	1	33	3	100	2	67	1	50	1	50	...	1 (oo)
2008	11	7	64	9	82	8	89	8	100	...	...	...	...
2009	2	0	0	1	50	1	100	...	...	1	100	...	1 (pp)
2010	37	13	35	22	60	14	64	11	79	3	21	1 (qq)	2 (rr)
Totals:													
Number	572	306		434		338		256		82		21	61
Percent	100	53.5		75.9		77.9		75.7		24.3		25.6	74.4

See footnotes on the next page.

tion than in their own party primary by a 3-to-1 ratio. In the 2010, Gov. Jim Gibbons, R-Nevada, was defeated in his primary, the first such situation for an incumbent seeking re-election since 1994.

Democratic candidates held a winning edge in the 572 elections held between 1970 and 2010 (53.5 percent). In 222 of the races (38.8 percent), the results led to a party shift. But these party shifts have evened out over the years so that neither of the two major parties has an edge in the four decades of gubernatorial elections.

Between 1970 and 1992, Democrats won 200 of the 324 races for governor (62 percent). Then beginning in 1993 to 2003, Republicans leveled the playing field by winning 85 of the 145 races for governor (59 percent). From 2004 to 2010, there has been a virtual tie in which party has won these 102 governor's races as Republicans won 52 races (51 percent), Democrats won 49 races (48 percent), and an Independent won a single race (1 percent).

Another factor in determining how many governors have served in the states is the number of

Table A: Gubernatorial Elections: 1970–2010, Footnotes

Source: The Council of State Governments, *The Book of the States, 2010,* (Lexington, KY: The Council of State Governments, 2010), 170, updated.

Key:
(a) Albert Brewer, D-Ala.
(b) Keith Miller, R-Alaska; Winthrop Rockefeller, R-Ark.; Claude Kirk, R-Fla.; Don Samuelson, R-Idaho; Norbert Tieman, R-Neb.; Dewey Bartlett, R-Okla.; Frank Farrar, R-S.D.
(c) Walter Peterson, R-N.H.; Preston Smith, D-Texas.
(d) Russell Peterson, R-Del.; Richard Ogilvie, R-Ill.
(e) William Cahill, R-N.J.
(f) One independent candidate won: James Longley of Maine.
(g) David Hall, D-Okla.
(h) John Vanderhoof, R-Colo.; Francis Sargent, R-Mass.; Malcolm Wilson, R-N.Y.; John Gilligan, D-Ohio.
(i) Dan Walker, D-Ill.
(j) Sherman Tribbitt, D-Del.; Christopher 'Kit' Bond, R-Mo.
(k) Michael Dukakis, D-Mass.; Dolph Briscoe, D-Texas.
(l) Robert F. Bennett, R-Kan.; Rudolph G. Perpich, D-Minn.; Meldrim Thompson, R-N.H.; Robert Straub, D-Ore.; Martin J. Schreiber, D-Wis.
(m) Thomas L. Judge, D-Mont.; Dixy Lee Ray, D-Wash.
(n) Bill Clinton, D-Ark.; Joseph P. Teasdale, D-Mo.; Arthur A. Link, D-N.D.
(o) Edward J. King, D-Mass.
(p) Frank D. White, R-Ark.; Charles Thone, R-Neb.; Robert F. List, R-Nev.; Hugh J. Gallen, D-N.H.; William P. Clements, R-Texas.
(q) David Treen, R-La.
(r) Allen I. Olson, R-N.D.; John D. Spellman, R-Wash.
(s) Bill Sheffield, D-Alaska.
(t) Mark White, D-Texas; Anthony S. Earl, D-Wis.
(u) Edwin Edwards, D-La.
(v) Arch A. Moore, R-W.Va.

(w) Two Independent candidates won: Walter Hickel (Alaska) and Lowell Weiker (Conn.). Both were former statewide Republican office holders.
(x) Bob Martinez, R-Fla.; Mike Hayden, R-Kan.; James Blanchard, D-Mich.; Rudy Perpich, DFL-Minn.; Kay Orr, R-Neb.; Edward DiPrete, R-R.I.
(y) Buddy Roemer, R-La.
(z) Ray Mabus, D-Miss.
(aa) James Florio, D-N.J.
(bb) One Independent candidate won: Angus King of Maine.
(cc) Bruce Sundlun, D-R.I.; Walter Dean Miller, R-S.D.
(dd) James E. Folsom, Jr., D-Ala.; Bruce King, D-N.M.; Mario Cuomo, D-N.Y.; Ann Richards, D-Texas.
(ee) Two Independent candidates won: Angus King of Maine and Jesse Ventura of Minnesota.
(ff) Fob James, R-Ala.; David Beasley, R-S.C.
(gg) Cecil Underwood, R-W.Va.
(hh) Don Siegelman, D-Ala.; Roy Barnes, D-Ga., Jim Hodges, D-S.C.; and Scott McCallum, R-Wis.
(ii) The California recall election and replacement vote of 2003 is included in the 2003 election totals and as a general election for the last column.
(jj) Gray Davis, D-Calif., Ronnie Musgrove, D-Miss.
(kk) Bob Holden, D-Mo.; Olene Walker, R-Utah, lost in the pre-primary convention.
(ll) Joe Kernan, D-Ind.; Craig Benson, R-N.H.
(mm) Frank Murkowski, R-Alaska.
(nn) Robert Ehrlich, R-Md.
(oo) Ernie Fletcher, R-Ky.
(pp) Jon Corzine, D-N.J.
(qq) Jim Gibbons, R-Nev.
(rr) Chet Culver, D-Iowa; Ted Strickland, D-Ohio.

newly elected governors who are truly new to the office and the number who are returning after complying with constitutional term limits or after holding other positions. Of new governors taking office over a decade, states dropped from a rate of 2.3 new governors per state in the 1950s to 1.9 in the 1970s and to 1.1 in the 1980s. In the 1990s, the rate began to move up a bit to 1.4 new governors per state.

In the first decade of the 21st century, 2000–2009, there were many new faces in the governor's offices. New governors were elected in 61 of the 118 elections held between 2000 and 2009 (51.7 percent). And nine new governors succeeded to office upon the incumbent vacating the office during this period.[12] So during the first few years of the previous decade, 70 new governors were sworn into office, continuing the 1.4 rate per state. In the 2010 elections, the first year of the second decade of the 21st century, 26 new governors were elected in the 37 races, and two other new governors succeeded to the chair upon the resignation of the governor in mid-November as they left to be sworn in as one of the state's new U.S. senators.[13] So, the rate of change in who sits in the governor's chairs

continues to be high as 28 new governors took office in 2011 on the basis of the 2010 elections (56 percent of all state governors).

The New Governors

Over the 2007–2010 set of gubernatorial elections and resignations, new governors took several different routes to office. Twenty-one new governors had previously held an elected statewide office. These include:

- Eight lieutenant governors: Alaska Gov. Sean Parnell, North Dakota Gov. Jack Dalrymple, South Dakota Gov. Dennis Daugaard and Utah Gov. Gary Herbert, all Republicans, and Illinois Gov. Pat Quinn, Kentucky Gov. Steve Beshear, (who served as lieutenant governor from 1983–1987), New York Gov. David Paterson and North Carolina Gov. Beverly Perdue, all Democrats;

- Five attorneys general: California Gov. Jerry Brown (who also previously served as governor from 1975–1983), Missouri Gov. Jay Nixon and New York Gov. Andrew Cuomo, Democrats, and Pennsylvania Gov. Tom Corbett, and Virginia Gov. Robert McDonald, Republicans;

Table C: Cost of Gubernatorial Campaigns, Most Recent Elections, 2005–2009

State	Year	Winner	Point margin	Total campaign expenditures				
				All candidates (2009$)	Cost per vote (2009$)	Winner		
						Spent (2009$)	Percent of all expenditures	Vote percent
Alabama	2006	R★	+15.8	$19,732,443	$15.78	$12,842,382	65.1	57.4
Alaska	2006	R★★	+7.4	5,396,065	22.74	1,412,000	26.2	48.3
Arizona	2006	D★	+27.2	3,947,642	2.57	1,717,098	43.5	62.6
Arkansas	2006	D#	+14.4	10,591,801	14.12	6,888,933	65.0	55.4
California	2006	R★	+16.9	137,305,975	15.82	48,836,830	35.6	55.9
Colorado	2006	D#	+16.8	8,276,021	5.31	4,547,161	54.9	57.0
Connecticut	2006	R★	+27.8	15,182,617	13.51	4,451,470	29.3	63.2
Delaware	2008	D#	+35.5	10,244,478	25.92	7,951,685	77.6	67.5
Florida	2006	R#	+7.1	44,639,532	9.24	21,159,799	47.4	52.2
Georgia	2006	R★	+19.7	30,934,282	14.58	13,779,247	44.5	57.9
Hawaii	2006	R★	+27.1	7,409,497	21.52	6,909,290	93.2	62.5
Idaho	2006	R#	+8.6	3,846,647	8.53	2,077,242	54.0	52.7
Illinois	2006	D★	+10.6	51,570,692	14.79	27,957,849	54.2	49.8
Indiana	2008	R★	+17.8	36,049,543	13.33	27,615,551	76.6	57.8
Iowa	2006	D#	+9.5	17,721,679	16.91	8,038,471	45.4	54.0
Kansas	2006	D★	+17.5	6,826,022	8.03	5,060,386	74.1	57.9
Kentucky	2007	D★★★	+17.4	34,845,590	33.02	9,745,707	28.0	58.7
Louisiana	2007	R#	+36.4	43,612,094	33.60	11,669,041	26.6	53.9
Maine	2006	D★	+7.9	5,307,721	9.64	1,284,487	24.2	38.1
Maryland	2006	D★★★	+6.5	30,796,529	17.25	14,980,160	48.6	52.7
Massachusetts	2006	D#	+20	45,028,958	20.07	9,453,675	21.0	55.6
Michigan	2006	D★	+14	56,205,424	14.79	11,921,950	21.2	56.3
Minnesota	2006	R★	+0.96	9,226,370	4.19	4,182,647	45.3	46.7
Mississippi	2007	R★	+15.8	18,600,309	25.00	13,401,522	72.5	57.9
Missouri	2008	D#	+18.9	1,173,068	0.41	842,492	71.8	58.4
Montana	2008	D★	+33.0	1,522,643	3.13	783,926	51.5	65.5
Nebraska	2006	R★	+48.9	5,540,246	9.36	3,079,985	55.6	73.4
Nevada	2006	R★	+4	15,811,213	27.16	6,042,684	38.2	47.9
New Hampshire	2008	D★	+42.6	1,323,536	1.95	1,206,437	91.2	70.2
New Jersey	2009	R★★★	+3.6	53,293,350	21.99	16,609,064	31.2	48.5
New Mexico	2006	D★	+37.6	8,968,962	16.06	8,298,479	92.5	68.8
New York	2006	D#	+40.9	49,066,665	11.75	35,521,639	72.4	69.0
North Carolina	2008	D#	+3.3	36,150,486	8.47	15,737,308	43.7	50.3
North Dakota	2008	R★	+50.9	2,164,325	6.86	1,825,639	84.4	74.4
Ohio	2006	D#	+23.9	31,237,576	8.18	16,809,413	53.8	60.4
Oklahoma	2006	D★	+33	7,795,569	8.41	4,248,791	54.5	66.5
Oregon	2006	D★	+8	15,078,607	10.96	4,559,052	30.2	50.8
Pennsylvania	2006	D★	+20.8	43,624,089	10.87	32,580,547	74.7	60.4
Rhode Island	2006	R★	+2	4,755,504	12.29	2,434,931	51.2	51.0
South Carolina	2006	R★	+10.0	13,381,055	12.25	7,722,403	57.7	55.1
South Dakota	2006	R★	+25.6	1,378,859	4.11	314,830	22.8	61.7
Tennessee	2006	D★	+38.9	7,492,799	4.14	5,802,862	77.4	68.6
Texas	2006	R★	+9.2	36,764,813	8.36	24,269,719	66.0	39.0
Utah	2008	R★	+58.0	914,338	0.97	822,747	90.0	77.7
Vermont	2008	R★	+31.6	1,609,465	5.30	967,042	60.1	53.4
Virginia	2009	R#	+17.35	53,326,250	26.87	23,786,466	44.6	58.6
Washington	2008	D★	+5.5	25,200,328	8.39	13,613,104	54.0	53.2
West Virginia	2008	D#	+49.1	2,267,686	3.21	2,209,384	97.4	69.8
Wisconsin	2006	D★	+7.4	17,694,396	8.19	9,839,373	55.6	52.8
Wyoming	2006	D★	+39.9	1,473,551	7.60	1,046,283	71.0	69.9

Source: Thad Beyle, www.unc.edu/~beyle.

Note: All dollar figures are in equivalent 2009$. Using the 2009 CPI Index which was 2.14537 of the 1982–84 Index = 1.00, the actual 2006 expenditures were based on a 2.016 index value or .9397 of the 2009$ index, the actual 2007 expenditures were based on a 2.073 index value or .96646 of the 2009$ index, the 2008 expenditures were based on a 2.153 index value or 1.00357 of the 2009$ index, and the 2009 expenditures were the exact dollars spent in that election year. Then the actual expenditures of each state's governor's race were divided by the .9 value for that year to get the equivalent 2009$ value of those expenditures.

Key:
D — Democrat
I — Independent
R — Republican
— Open seat
★ — Incumbent ran and won.
★★ — Incumbent ran and lost in party primary.
★★★ — Incumbent ran and lost in general election.

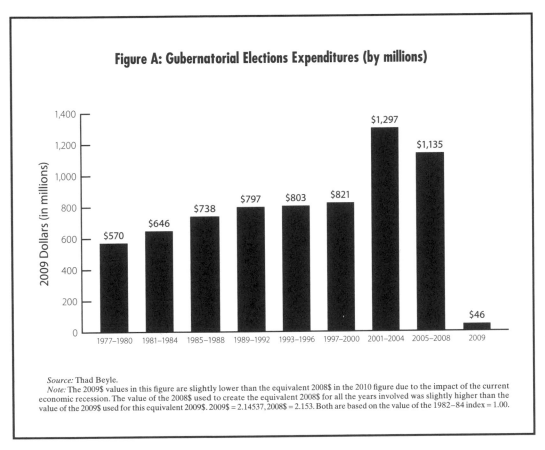

Figure A: Gubernatorial Elections Expenditures (by millions)

Source: Thad Beyle.
Note: The 2009$ values in this figure are slightly lower than the equivalent 2008$ in the 2010 figure due to the impact of the current economic recession. The value of the 2008$ used to create the equivalent 2008$ for all the years involved was slightly higher than the value of the 2009$ used for this equivalent 2009$. 2009$ = 2.14537, 2008$ = 2.153. Both are based on the value of the 1982–84 index = 1.00.

2006 race in California ($137,305,975 in 2009 dollars) to the low-cost 2008 race in Utah ($ 917,000). Both races saw an incumbent Republican governor win re-election—Arnold Schwarzenegger in California and Jon Huntsman Jr. in Utah.

The most money spent by the winning candidates in these elections were in California (just under $49 million in 2009 dollars) by Gov. Arnold Schwarzenegger; in New York ($35.5 million) by newly elected Gov. Eliot Spitzer; in Pennsylvania ($32.6 million) by Gov. Edward Rendell; in Illinois ($29 million) by Gov. Rod Blagojevich; and in Indiana ($27.6 million) by Gov. Mitch Daniels. The least money spent by winning candidates in these elections was in South Dakota ($314,830) by Gov. Michael Rounds; in Montana ($783,926) by Gov. Brian Schweitzer; in Utah ($822,747) by Gov. Jon Huntsman; and in Missouri (842,492) by newly elected Gov. Jay Nixon.

But looking at the amount of money spent by the candidates per general election vote, a slightly different picture evolves. In 2008, the most expen-

sive races per vote occurred in Louisiana at $33.60 per vote and in Kentucky at $33.02 per vote. The Louisiana race was for an open seat, while the Kentucky race saw an incumbent defeated in the general election. The least expensive races per vote were held in 2008 in Missouri at 41 cents per vote and in Utah at 97 cents per vote. The Missouri race was for an open seat, while in the Utah race, an incumbent won his second term.

In Figure A, by converting the actual dollars spent each year into equivalent 2009 dollars, the cost of these elections has increased over time— with a slight decrease in the most recent years. Since 1981, the costs of each four-year cycle of elections can be compared with the previous and subsequent cycles of elections.

In 54 gubernatorial elections held from 1977 to 1980, total expenditures were $570 million in equivalent 2009 dollars. In the 52 elections 2005 to 2008—nearly three decades later— total expenditures were $1.1 billion in 2009 dollars, an increase of 99 percent.

Table F: New Governors Elected Each 4-Year Period, 1970–2010 (a)

Year	Number of gubernatorial elections	New Governors		Incumbents Running			
		Won	Percent	Number	Won	Lost	Percent Lost
1970	35	19	54	24	16	8	36
1971	3	3	100	...	...	...	...
1972	18	11	61	11	7	4	36
1973	2	2	100	1	...	1	100
1974	35	18	51	22	17	5	24
1975	3	1	33	2	2	...	...
1976	14	9	64	8	5	3	33
1977	2	1	50	1	1	...	...
1978	36	20	56	23	16	7	30
1979	3	3	100	...	...	...	...
1980	13	6	46	12	7	5	42
1981	2	2	100	...	...	...	...
1982	36	17	47	25	19	6	24
1983	3	3	100	1	...	1	100
1984	13	9	69	6	4	2	33
1985	2	1	50	1	1	...	...
1986	36	21	58	18	15	3	18
1987	3	3	100	1	...	1	100
1988	12	4	33	9	8	1	11
1989	2	2	100	...	...	...	...
1990	36	19	53	23	17	6	26
1991	3	3	100	2	...	2	100
1992	12	8	67	4	4	...	...
1993	2	1	50	1	...	1	100
1994	36	19	53	23	17	6	26
1995	3	2	67	1	1	...	...
1996	11	4	36	7	7	...	...
1997	2	1	50	1	1	...	...
1998	36	13	36	25	23	2	8
1999	3	1	33	2	2	...	...
2000	11	6	55	6	5	1	17
2001	2	2	100	...	...	...	...
2002	36	24	67	16	12	4	25
2003 (b)	4	4	100	2	...	2	100
2004	11	7	64	8	4	4	50
2005	2	2	100	...	...	...	...
2006	36	9	25	27	25	2	7
2007	3	2	67	2	1	1	50
2008	11	3	24	8	8	...	...
2009	2	2	100	1	...	1	100
2010	37	26	70	14	11	3	21
Totals:	572	315	55	338	256	82	24

Key:
(a) Table A: Gubernatorial Elections: 1970–2009, *The Book of the States, 2010* (Lexington, KY: The Council of State Governments, 2010): 186.

(b) In 2003, there was a recall and replacement election vote in California in which the incumbent Gov. Gray Davis-D was recalled and Republican Arnold Schwarzenegger was elected as his replacement.

Notes

[1] Governors were term limited in AL, CA, GA, HI, ME, MI, NM, OK, OR, PA, RI, SC, SD, TN and WY.

[2] Governors not seeking another term although they were eligible to do so were in CO, CT, FL, KS, MN, NY, VT and WI.

[3] Governors winning another term were in AK, AZ, AR, ID, IL, MD, MA, NE, NH, TX and UT, where the succeeding governor won the ability to serve out that term.

[4] Governors losing their bids for another term were in IA, NV and OH.

[5] Republicans won in AL, AK, AZ, FL, GA, ID, IA, KS, ME, MI, NE, NV, NM, OH, OK, PA, SC, SD, TN, TX, UT, WI and WY.

[6] Democrats won in AR, CA, CO, CT, HI, IL, MD, MA, MN, NH, NY, OR and VT.

[7] An Independent won in RI.

[8] The additional governors serving in 2011 to those listed as winning in the 2010 elections are Republicans currently

serving IN, LA, MS, NJ, ND and VA and Democrats serving currently DE, KY, MO, MT, NC, WA and WV.

[9] State winners by 10 or more points: R—AL, AK, AZ, GA, ID, KS, MI, NE, NV, OK, SD, TN, TX, UT and WY; D—AR, CA, CO, HI, MD and NY.

[10] State winners by between 5 and 10 points: R—IA, NM, PA and WI; D—MA and NH.

[11] State winners by less than 5 points: R—FL, ME, OH and SC; D—CT, IL, MN, OR and VT; I—RI.

[12] Five of these new governors succeeded governors who resigned upon moving on to a new responsibility before the end of their elected terms in Alaska, Arizona, Kansas, Nebraska, Texas; four others succeeded due to problems the incumbents had and were removed from office in California and Illinois, or the incumbent resigned to avoid efforts to remove them due to certain activities they had performed while governor in New Jersey and New York.

[13] In North Dakota, Lt. Gov. Jack Dalrymple (R) succeeded outgoing Gov. John Hoeven (R) who was elected to the U.S. Senate in the 2010 election, and in West Virginia State Senate President Earl Ray Tomlin (D) succeeded outgoing Gov. Joe Manchin (D) who also was elected to the U.S. Senate in the 2010 election.

[14] New Mexico Gov. Susana Martinez (R), Oklahoma Gov. Mary Fallin (R) and South Carolina Gov. Nikki Haley (R).

[15] Arizona Gov. Jan Brewer (R), North Carolina Gov. Beverly Perdue (D) and Washington Gov. Christine Gregoire (D).

[16] In California, Meg Whitman (R), in Florida, Alex Sink (D), in Maine, Libby Mitchell (D), in New Mexico, Diane Denish (D), in Oklahoma, Jari Adkins (D) and in Wyoming, Leslie Petersen (D).

[17] In this four-decade set of election cycles, two states changed the length of their gubernatorial terms from two years to four years. This eliminated the gubernatorial elections being held during presidential election years beginning in 1988 in Arkansas and in 1996 in Rhode Island.

[18] 2011—MS; 2012—IN and MT.

About the Author

Thad Beyle is a professor-emeritus of political science at the University of North Carolina at Chapel Hill. A Syracuse University A.B. and A.M., he received his Ph.D. at the University of Illinois. He spent a year in the North Carolina governor's office in the mid-1960s followed by two years with Terry Sanford's "A Study of American States" project at Duke University, and has worked with the National Governors Association in several capacities on gubernatorial transitions.

Table 4.10
SELECTED STATE ADMINISTRATIVE OFFICIALS: METHODS OF SELECTION

State or other jurisdiction	Governor	Lieutenant governor	Secretary of state	Attorney general	Treasurer	Adjutant general	Administration	Agriculture	Auditor	Banking
Alabama	CE	CE	CE	CE	CE	GS	G	SE	CE	GS
Alaska	CE	CE	(a-1)	GB	AG	GB	GB	AG	L	AG
Arizona	CE	(a-2)	CE	CE	CE	GS	GS	GS	L	AG
Arkansas	CE	CE	CE	CE	CE	AG	AG	AG	CE	GS
California	CE	CE	CE	CE	CE	GS	...	G	GB	GS
Colorado	CE	CE	CE	CE	CE	GS	GS	GS	L	CS
Connecticut	CE	CE	CE	CE	CE	GE	GE	GE	L	GE
Delaware	CE	CE	GS	CE	CE	GS	(c)	GS	CE	GE
Florida	CE	CE	GS	CE	CE (b)	G	GS	CE	L	(b)
Georgia	CE	CE	CE	CE	B	G	G	CE	(d)	G
Hawaii	CE	CE	...	GS	GS	GS	(e)	GS	CL	AG
Idaho	CE	CE	CE	CE	CE	GS	GS	GS	L	AG
Illinois	CE	CE	CE	CE	CE	GS	GS	GS	...	GS
Indiana	CE	CE	CE	SE	CE	G	G	LG	CE	G
Iowa	CE	CE	CE	CE	CE	GS	GS	CE	CE	GS
Kansas	CE	CE	CE	CE	CE	GS	GS	GS	...	GS
Kentucky	CE	CE	CE	CE	CE	G	...	CE	CE	G
Louisiana	CE	CE	CE	CE	CE	GS	CE	CE	G	GLS
Maine	CE	(g)	CL	CL	CL	GLS	GLS	GLS	L	GLS
Maryland	CE	CE	GS	CE	CL	G	GS	GS	N.A.	AG
Massachusetts	CE	CE	CE	CE	CE	G	G	CG	CE	G
Michigan	CE	CE	CE	CE	GS	GS	GS	B	CL	GS
Minnesota	CE	CE	CE	CE	(a-24)	GS	GS	GS	CE	A
Mississippi	CE	CE	CE	CE	CE	GE	GS	SE	CE	GS
Missouri	CE	CE	CE	CE	CE	G	GS	GS	CE	...
Montana	CE	CE	CE	CE	(a-6)	GS	GS	GS	CE	A
Nebraska	CE	CE	CE	CE	CE	GS	GS	GS	CE	GS
Nevada	CE	CE	CE	CE	CE	G	G	BG	...	A
New Hampshire	CE	(g)	CL	GC	CL	GC	GC	GC	...	GC
New Jersey	CE	CE	GS (f)	GS	GS	GS	...	BG	(h)	GS
New Mexico	CE	CE	CE	CE	CE	G	(a-26)	A	CE	N.A.
New York	CE	CE	GS	CE	A	G	...	GS	(a-14)	GS
North Carolina	CE	CE	CE	CE	CE	A	G	CE	CE	G
North Dakota	CE	CE	CE	CE	CE	G	...	CE	CE	GS
Ohio	CE	CE	CE	CE	CE	G	GS	GS	CE	A
Oklahoma	CE	CE	GS	CE	CE	GS	GS	GS	CE	GS
Oregon	CE	(a-2)	CE	SE	CE	G	GS	GS	SS	...
Pennsylvania	CE	CE	GS	CE	CE	GS	G	GS	CE	GS
Rhode Island	SE	SE	CE	SE	SE	GS	GS	GS	LS	GS
South Carolina	CE	CE	CE	CE	CE	CE	B	CE	B	A
South Dakota	CE	CE	CE	CE	CE	GS	GS	GS	L	A
Tennessee	CE	CL (g)	CL	CT	CL	G	G	G	(a-14)	G
Texas	CE	CE	G	CE	(a-14)	G	A	SE	L	B
Utah	CE	CE	(a-1)	CE	CE	GS	GS	GS	CE	GS
Vermont	CE	CE	CE	SE	CE	CL	GS	GS	CE	GS
Virginia	CE	CE	GB	CE	GB	GB	GB	GB	SL	B
Washington	CE	CE	CE	CE	CE	G	G	G	CE	G
West Virginia	CE	(g)	CE	CE	CE	GS	GS	CE	CE	GS
Wisconsin	CE	CE	CE	CE	CE	G	GS	GS	LS	A
Wyoming	CE	(a-2)	CE	G	CE	G	GS	GS	CE	A
American Samoa	CE	CE	(a-1)	GB	GB	N.A.	GB	GB	N.A.	N.A.
Guam	CE	CE	...	CE	CS	GS	GS	GS	CE	GS
No. Mariana Islands	CE	CE	...	GS	CS	...	G	...	GB	C
U.S. Virgin Islands	SE	SE	(a-1)	GS	GS	GS	GS	GS	GS	LG

Sources: The Council of State Governments' survey of state personnel agencies and state websites, April 2011.

Key:
N.A.— Not available.
. . . — No specific chief administrative official or agency in charge of function.
CE — Constitutional, elected by public.
CL — Constitutional, elected by legislature.
SE — Statutory, elected by public.
SL — Statutory, elected by legislature.
L — Selected by legislature or one of its organs.
CT — Constitutional, elected by state court of last resort.
CP — Competitve process.

Appointed by:
G — Governor
GS — Governor
GB — Governor
GE — Governor
GC — Governor
GD — Governor
GLS — Governor

GOC — Governor &
    Council or cabinet
LG — Lieut. Governor
LGS — Lieut. Governor
AT — Attorney General
ATS — Attorney General
SS — Secretary of State

Approved by:
Senate (in Neb., unicameral legislature)
Both houses
Either house
Council
Departmental board
Appropriate legislative committee & Senate

Senate
Senate

SELECTED STATE ADMINISTRATIVE OFFICIALS: METHODS OF SELECTION — Continued

State or other jurisdiction	Budget	Civil rights	Commerce	Community affairs	Comptroller	Consumer affairs	Corrections	Economic development	Education	Election admin.
Alabama	CS	...	G	G	CS	CS	G	(a-13)	B	CS
Alaska	G	GB	GB	(a-12)	AG	(a-12)	GB	(a-12)	GD	AG
Arizona	L	AT	GS	AT	A	AT	GS	GS	CE	(a-2)
Arkansas	A	...	(a-17)	N.A.	A	AT	B	GS	BG	B
California	(a-24)	...	...	GS	CE	G	GS	...	CE	G
Colorado	G	A	...	A	A	AT	GS	G	AB	CS
Connecticut	CS	GE	GE	GE	CE	GE	GE	GE	BG	CS
Delaware	GS	CG	(a-2)	...	CG	AT	GS	GS	GS	GS
Florida	G	AB	G	GS	CE (b)	A	GS	G	GS	A
Georgia	G	G	B	B	CE	G	GD	B	CE	A
Hawaii	GS	B	GS	...	GS	A	GS	GS	B	B
Idaho	GS	B	GS	...	CE	(a-3)	B	GS	CE	CE
Illinois	G	GS	GS	(a-12)	CE	(a-3)	GS	(a-12)	B	B
Indiana	G	G	G	G	(a-8)	AT	G	G	CE	(j)
Iowa	GS	GS	GS	A	...	ATS	GS	GS	GS	SS
Kansas	G	B	GS	C	C	AT	GS	C	B	(a-2)
Kentucky	G	B	G	G	CG	AT	G	GC	B	B
Louisiana	CS	B	GS	G	GS	A	GS	GS	BG	A
Maine	A	B	(a-17)	(a-17)	A	GLS	GLS	GLS	GLS	SS
Maryland	GS	G	GS	...	CE	A	GS	GS	B	B
Massachusetts	CG	G	G	G	G	G	CG	G	B	CE
Michigan	GS	GS	GS	...	CS	...	GS	...	B	(k)
Minnesota	(a-24)	GS	GS	(a-17)	(a-24)	A	GS	GS	GS	(a-2)
Mississippi	GS	...	SE	A	(a-6)	A	GS	GS	BS	A
Missouri	AGS	AGS	GS	A	A	CE	GS	GS	BG	SS
Montana	G	CP	GS	CP	CP	CP	GS	G	CE	SS
Nebraska	A	B	GS	A	A	(a-3)	GS	GS	B	A
Nevada	(a-5)	G	G	...	CE	A	G	GD	B	(l)
New Hampshire	GC	CS	GC	G	AGC	AGC	GC	AGC	B	CL
New Jersey	GS	A	(a-17)	GS	GS	A	GS	G	GS	A
New Mexico	G	N.A.	(a-17)	N.A.	N.A.	AT	GS	GS	GS	CE
New York	G	GS	GS	(a-2)	CE	GS	GS	GS	B	B
North Carolina	(a-24)	A	G	A	G	(i)	G	A	CE	G
North Dakota	A	G	G	...	A	AT	G	N.A.	CE	SS
Ohio	GS	B	GS	A	GS	A	GS	GS	B	(a-2)
Oklahoma	A	B	GS	(i)	A	B	B	GS	CE	L
Oregon	A	A	GS	G	A	GS	GS	GS	SE	A
Pennsylvania	G	B	GS	AG	G	AT	GS	GS	GS	C
Rhode Island	A	B	GS	...	A	(a-3)	GS	GS (m)	B	B
South Carolina	A	B	GS	N.A.	CE	B	GS	(a-12)	CE	B
South Dakota	(a-24)	N.A.	(a-44)	(a-48)	(a-40)	N.A.	GS	GS	GS	SS
Tennessee	A	G	G	G	SL	A	G	G	G	A
Texas	G	B	G	G	CE	(i)	B	G	B	(n)
Utah	G	A	GS	GS	AG	GS	GS	A	B	A
Vermont	CG	AT	GS	CG	CG	AT	CG	CG	BG	CE
Virginia	GB	G	GB	GB	GB	A	GB	B	GB	GB
Washington	G	B	G	(a-12)	(a-10)	CE	G	(a-12)	CE	(a-2)
West Virginia	CS	GS	GS	B	(a-8)	AT	GS	(a-13)	B	(a-2)
Wisconsin	A	A	GS	...	A	A	GS	CS	CE	B
Wyoming	A	A	G	G	(a-8)	G	GS	(a-12)	CE	A
American Samoa	GB	N.A.	GB	(a-12)	(a-4)	(a-3)	A	(a-12)	GB	G
Guam	GS	GS	GS	...	CS	CS	GS	B	GS	GS
No. Mariana Islands	G	A	GS	GS	C	GS	C	C	B	B
U.S. Virgin Islands	GS	GS	GS	GS	(a-24)	GS	GS	GS	GS	B

Appointed by:
C — Cabinet Secretary
CG — Cabinet Secretary
A — Agency head
AB — Agency head
AG — Agency head
AGC — Agency head
AGS — Agency head
ALS — Agency head
ASH — Agency head
B — Board or commission
BG — Board
BGS — Board
BS — Board or commission
BA — Board or commission
CS — Civil Service
LS — Legislative Committee

Approved by:

Governor

Board
Governor
Governor & Council
Senate
Appropriate legislative committee
Senate president & House speaker

Governor
Governor & Senate
Senate
Agency head

Senate

(a) Chief administrative official or agency in charge of function:
(a-1) Lieutenant governor.
(a-2) Secretary of state.
(a-3) Attorney general.
(a-4) Treasurer.
(a-5) Adjutant general.
(a-6) Administration.
(a-7) Agriculture.
(a-8) Auditor.
(a-9) Banking.
(a-10) Budget.
(a-11) Civil rights.
(a-12) Commerce.
(a-13) Community affairs.
(a-14) Comptroller.
(a-15) Consumer affairs.
(a-16) Corrections.

SELECTED STATE ADMINISTRATIVE OFFICIALS: METHODS OF SELECTION — Continued

State or other jurisdiction	Pre-audit	Public library development	Public utility regulation	Purchasing	Revenue	Social services	Solid waste mgmt.	State police	Tourism	Transportation	Welfare
Alabama	(a-14)	B	SE	CS	G	B	CS	G	G	(a-29)	(a-45)
Alaska	...	AG	GB	AG	GB	GB	AG	AG	AG	GB	AG
Arizona	(a-14)	B	B	A	GS	GS	A	GS	GS	GS	GS
Arkansas	N.A.	GS	GA	A	A	GS	N.A.	GS	GS	BS	(a-45)
California	(a-14)	...	GS	(a-26)	BS	GS	G	GS	...	GS	AG
Colorado	(a-14)	BA	CS	CS	GS	GS	CS	A	CS	GS	CS
Connecticut	(a-14)	CS	GB	CS	GE	GE	CS	GE	GE	GE	GE
Delaware	(a-8)	CG	CG	(a-26)	CG	GS (pp)	B	CG	CG	GS	CG
Florida	CE (b)	A	B	A	GOC	GS	A	A	G	GS	A
Georgia	(a-8)	AB	CE	A	GS	GD	A	BG	A	(a-29)	A
Hawaii	CS	B	GS	GS	GS	GS	CS	...	B	GS	CS
Idaho	(a-14)	B	GS	GS	GS	GS	...	GS	A	B	A
Illinois	(a-14)	SS	GS	(a-6)	GS	GS	(a-23)	GS	(a-12)	GS	GS
Indiana	CE	G	G	A	G	G	A	G	LG	G	(a-45)
Iowa	CS	B	GS	CS	GS	GS	CS	GS	CS	GS	(a-45)
Kansas	CS	GS	B	C	GS	GS	C	GS	C	GS	C
Kentucky	...	G	G	G	G	G	AG	G	G	G	(a-45)
Louisiana	CS	BGS	BS	A	GS	GS	GS	GS	LGS	GS	CS
Maine	(a-14)	B	G	CS	A	GLS	CS	A/GLS	(a-17)	GLS	(a-45)
Maryland	A	A	GS	A	A	GS	A	GS	A	GS	(a-45)
Massachusetts	CE	B	G	CG	CG	CG	CG	CG	CG	G	CG
Michigan	...	CL	GS	CS	CS	GS	CS	GS	...	GS	(a-45)
Minnesota	(a-8)	N.A.	G (qq)	A	GS	GS (ii)	GS	A	A	GS	GS (ii)
Mississippi	(a-8)	B	GS	A	GS	GS	A	GS	A	B	GS
Missouri	A	B	GS	A	GS	GS	A	GS	A	B	A
Montana	L	CP	CE	CP	GS	GS	GS	CP	CP	GS	(a-45)
Nebraska	A	B	B	A	GS	GS	A	GS	A	GS	GS
Nevada	...	(rr)	G	A	G	G	...	G	GD	B	(ss)
New Hampshire	(a-14)	AGC	GC	CS	GC	GC	AGC	AGC	AGC	GC	AGC
New Jersey	...	...	GS	GS	A	GS	A	GS	A	GS	A
New Mexico	N.A.	N.A.	G	N.A.	GS	N.A.	N.A.	GS	GS	GS	N.A.
New York	(a-14)	(a-18)	GS	(a-26)	GS	GS	(a-23)	G	(a-17)	GS	(a-45)
North Carolina	(a-8)	A	G	A	G	A	A	A	A	G	A
North Dakota	...	...	CE	A	CE	G	A	G	G	G	G
Ohio	GS	B	BG	A	GS	(tt)	A	GS	LG	A	GS
Oklahoma	(a-14)	B	(uu)	A	GS	GS	A	A	B	B	GS
Oregon	(a-10)	B	GS	A	GS	GS	B	GS	A	GS	GS
Pennsylvania	(a-4)	G	GS	A	GS	GS	A	GS	G	GS	GS
Rhode Island	(a-14)	A	GS	A	GS	GS (vv)	(ww)	G	N.A.	GS	(a-45)
South Carolina	(a-14)	B	B	A	GS	GS	A	GS	GS	G	GS
South Dakota	CE	A	CE	A	GS	GS	A	A	GS	GS	(a-45)
Tennessee	A	A	SE	A	G	A	G	G	G	G	G
Texas	(a-14)	A	B	A	(a-14)	(i)	A	B	A	B	BG
Utah	AG	A	A	A	BS	GS	A	A	A	GS	GS
Vermont	(a-24)	CG	BG	CG	CG	GS	CG	GS	CG	GS	CG
Virginia	(a-14)	B	(xx)	A	GB	GB	(a-23)	GB	G	GB	(a-45)
Washington	(a-4)	(a-2)	(i)	(a-6)	G	G	G	G	N.A.	G	(a-34)
West Virginia	(a-8)	B	GS	CS	GS	C	B	GS	(a-29)	GS	GS
Wisconsin	A	A	GS	A	GS	A	A	A	GS	GS	A
Wyoming	(a-8)	A	G	A	G	GS	A	A	A	(a-29)	(a-45)
American Samoa	(a-4)	(a-18)	N.A.	A	(a-4)	GB	GB	GB	(a-12)	(a-29)	N.A.
Guam	CE	(i)	N.A.	CS	GS	GS	GS	GS	CS	GS	GS
No. Mariana Islands	G	B	B	C	C	C	A	GS	GB	CS	A
U.S. Virgin Islands	GS	GS	G	GS	GS	G	GS	GS	GS	GS	GS

(p) Responsibilities shared between Chancellor of California Community Colleges (B) and California Postsecondary Education Commission (B).

(q) Responsibilities shared between Director of Wildlife, Director of Inland Fisheries and Director of Marine Fisheries (CS).

(r) Responsibilities shared between Director of Budget and Finance (GS) and the Comptroller (GS).

(s) Responsibilities shared between Adjutant General (GS) and Deputy Director (C).

(t) Responsibilities shared between Director (GS), Chief of Fisheries (CS) and Chief of Wildlife (CS).

(u) Responsibilities shared between Administrator, Division of Fisheries, Department of Conservation; Administrator, Division of Wildlife, same department (AB).

(v) Responsibilities shared between State Tax Commissioner, Department of Revenue (GS); Administrator, Budget Division (A) and the Auditor of Public Accounts (CE).

(w) Responsibilities shared between Director, Game and Parks Commission (B), Division Administrator, Wildlife Division, Game and Parks Commission (A).

(x) Responsibilities shared between Director of Health and Human Services (G) and Division Administrator, Health (AG).

(y) Responsibilities shared between Director, Division of Purchase and Property, Department of Treasury (GS), and Director, Division of Property Management and Construction, Department of Treasury (A).

(z) Responsibilities shared between Assistant Director, Office of Budget and Management (A) and Deputy Director, same office (A).

(aa) This employee serves in a dual role as Commissioner of Higher Education and as the President of the Community College of Rhode Island.

(bb) Responsibilities shared between Community and Technical (B) and Higher Education Policy Commissioner (B).

(cc) Responsibilities shared between Director of Mental Health (GS) and Director of Developmental Services (GS).

SELECTED STATE ADMINISTRATIVE OFFICIALS: METHODS OF SELECTION — Continued

(dd) Responsibilities shared between Commissioner of Mental Health (GE) and Commissioner of Retardation (GE).

(ee) Responsibilities shared between Director, Division of Substance Abuse and Mental Health, Department of Health and Social Services (CG); and Director, Division of Developmental Disabilities Services, same department (CG).

(ff) Responsibilities shared between Director of Mental Health (C) and Director of Community Support (C).

(gg) Responsibilities shared between Executive Director, Mental Hygiene Administration (A); and Director, Developmental Disabilities Administration, Department of Health and Mental Hygiene (A).

(hh) Responsibilities shared between Commissioner, Department of Mental Retardation (CG); and Commissioner, Department of Mental Health, Executive Office of Human Services (CG).

(ii) Human/Social Services, Mental Health and Retardation and Welfare are under the Commissioner of Human Services (GS).

(jj) Responsibilities shared between Director of Health and Human Services (G) and Division Administrator, MHDS (G).

(kk) Responsibilities shared between Director, Division of Mental Health Services, Department of Human Services (A) and Director, Division of Developmental Disabilities, Department of Human Services (A).

(ll) Responsibilities shared between Secretary of State (GS) and Commissioner of State Education Department (B).

(mm) Responsibilities shared between Commissioner, Office of Mental Health, and Commissioner, Office of Mental Retardation and Developmental Disabilities, both (GS).

(nn) Responsibilities shared between Director, Department of Mental Retardation and Developmental Disabilities (GS) and Director, Department of Mental Health (GS).

(oo) Responsibilities shared between Director of Disabilities and Special Needs (B) and Director of Mental Health (B).

(pp) Responsibilities shared between Secretary of Health and Social Services (GS); and Secretary , Department of Services of Children, Youth and their Families (GS).

(qq) Responsibilities shared between the five Public Utility Commissioners (G).

(rr) Responsibilities shared between Director, Department of Cultural Affairs (G) and Division Administrator of Library and Archives (A).

(ss) Responsibilities shared between Director of Health and Human Services (G) and Division Administrator, Welfare and Support Services (AG).

(tt) Responsibilities shared between Director, OH Department of Job and Family Services (GS), Superintendent of Department of Education (B), Executive Director of Rehabilitation Services Commission (B), Director of Department of Aging (GS).

(uu) Responsibilities shared between General Administrator Public Utility Division, Corporation Commission (B); and three Commissioners, Corporation Commission (CE).

(vv) This position is filled by two employees: one, Stephen Costantino, is the Commissioner, Office of Health and Human Services; the other, Sandra Powell, serves as the Director of Human Services and reports to the Commissioner, Office of Health and Human Services.

(ww) Solid waste is managed by the Rhode Island Resource Recovery Corporation (RIRRC). Although not a department of the state government, RIRRC is a public corporation and a component of the State of Rhode Island for financial reporting purposes. To be financially self-sufficient, the agency earns revenue through the sale of recyclable products, methane gas royalties and fees for its services.

(xx) No single position. Functions are shared between Communication, Energy Regulation and Utility and Railroad Safety, all (B).

SELECTED STATE ADMINISTRATIVE OFFICIALS: ANNUAL SALARIES — Continued

State or other jurisdiction	Emergency mgmt.	Employment services	Energy	Environ. protection	Finance	Fish & wildlife	General services	Health	Higher education	Highways
Alabama	$80,287	$139,259	$97,751	$134,410	$167,503	$117,439	$95,359	$247,662	$185,952	$102,390
Alaska	113,064	141,012	140,000	135,000	126,264	135,000	(a-43)	135,000	295,000	116,988
Arizona	90,685	110,002	100,000	135,000	(a-14)	160,000	106,982	136,000	300,000	128,700
Arkansas	89,924	136,601	118,580	118,580	(a-6)	118,492	120,019	223,400	188,700	157,430
California	175,000	150,112	132,396	175,000	175,000	150,112	150,112	(v)	(w)	(a-49)
Colorado	131,208	124,500	130,000	144,876	126,540	144,876	130,404	215,000	N.A.	135,840
Connecticut	154,000	132,613	121,146	130,000	163,910	(x)	138,624	162,617	182,126	169,745
Delaware	80,050	93,250	N.A.	(a-35)	143,050	95,650	87,522	165,000	97,316	(a-49)
Florida	140,000	120,000	80,000	140,000	(a-4)	129,430	140,000	N.A.	225,000	128,000
Georgia	122,003	88,455	116,452	155,000	148,000	107,732	N.A.	175,000	425,000	182,504
Hawaii	90,048	83,040 (b)	N.A.	83,040 (b)	(y)	83,040 (b)	(a-14)	N.A.	427,512	83,040 (b)
Idaho	122,865	111,945	101,982	112,340	102,731	129,043	...	141,710	110,011	(a-49)
Illinois	132,300	146,100	(a-42)	136,800	(a-10)	(a-35)	(a-6)	154,200	190,000	(a-49)
Indiana	101,500	105,386	83,132	115,006	(a-10)	77,500	(a-6)	137,500	155,000	(a-49)
Iowa	110,000	140,000	(z)	117,728	117,728	N.A.	117,728	130,000	...	140,400
Kansas	(aa)	(a-32)	72,962	105,019	...	73,320	(a-6)	190,000	197,000	(a-49)
Kentucky (f)	79,537	N.A.	137,865*	N.A.	137,865*	134,352	...	162,504	360,000	113,557
Louisiana	165,000	108,000	122,865	137,197	(a-6)	123,614	(a-6)	236,000	N.A.	(a-49)
Maine	72,800	N.A.	(a-38)	102,689	(a-6)	102,689	N.A.	169,332	N.A.	(a-49)
Maryland	127,500 (b)	116,485 (b)	130,050 (b)	(b)	166,082 (b)	...	(a-6)	166,082 (b)	127,500 (b)	159,858
Massachusetts	130,000	150,000	117,000	130,000	150,000	123,000	98,706	138,216	206,000	125,658
Michigan	130,975	118,470	153,000	140,000	(a-10)	(bb)	...	145,000	...	(a-49)
Minnesota	108,388	102,082	108,388	108,388	108,388	108,367	(a-6)	108,388	360,000	108,388
Mississippi	107,868	122,000	137,996	120,386	(a-6)	120,636	...	200,000	341,250	(a-49)
Missouri	95,004	103,860	...	95,108	100,450	(cc)	95,288	120,000	155,004	(a-49)
Montana	74,202	92,303	88,157	96,967	87,213	96,963	88,951	(a-45)	211,201	(a-49)
Nebraska	84,621	96,527	87,454	114,315	(dd)	(ee)	100,687	142,923	160,865	(a-49)
Nevada	86,757	127,721	99,397	112,275	(a-14)	117,030	...	(ff)	23,660 (gg)	(a-49)
New Hampshire	104,364	104,364	79,774	112,861	(a-10)	98,691	(a-6)	98,691	72,852	(a-49)
New Jersey	132,300	124,020	100,000	141,000	133,507	105,783	(hh)	141,000	86,793	124,110
New Mexico	115,000	95,000	N.A.	105,000	125,000	93,100	105,000	122,500	125,000	N.A.
New York	140,864	127,000	120,800	136,000	151,500	136,000	136,000	136,000	170,165	136,000
North Carolina	97,284	120,363	92,647	113,410	153,000	105,000	120,363	211,251	525,000	154,388
North Dakota	92,100	97,788	108,828	101,592	110,952	107,328	145,500	171,024	213,720	(a-49)
Ohio	100,901	141,981	81,266	125,008	(ii)	98,155	105,123	154,378	186,701	120,016
Oklahoma	75,705	93,190	90,000	105,917	108,000	111,986	90,451	194,244	394,983	(a-49)
Oregon	95,628	150,252	N.A.	136,320	(a-4)	136,320	(a-6)	165,624	219,504	155,760
Pennsylvania (h)	135,003	N.A.	N.A.	142,3210*	149,497	119,257	135,194*	142,310*	116,167	130,602
Rhode Island (i)	98,692	130,152	103,514	108,460	(a-44)	(a-23)	(a-6)	141,724	265,000 (jj)	(a-49)
South Carolina	97,292	N.A.	N.A.	151,942	(a-6)	121,380	120,154	144,746	154,840	143,000
South Dakota	73,181	(a-37)	(a-48)	(a-35)	120,000	104,000	(a-6)	104,000	323,000	(a-47)
Tennessee	90,576	150,000	103,260	150,000	180,000	135,000	150,000	153,540	183,792	(a-49)
Texas	N.A.	140,000	...	145,200	(a-14)	143,000	126,500	183,750	186,300	(a-49)
Utah	69,493	129,688	N.A.	116,938	122,845	116,355	107,266	194,813	129,688	(a-49)
Vermont (l)	80,018	93,995	95,992	92,997	89,669	88,005	89,357	115,606	...	(a-49)
Virginia	114,650	124,741	88,000	150,218	152,793	124,740	141,231	191,906	234,000	189,280
Washington	126,204	141,549	(a-23)	141,549	163,056	141,000	(a-6)	141,549	N.A.	(a-49)
West Virginia	65,000	75,000	95,000	(a-22)	(a-6)	77,772	78,492	95,000	(kk)	92,500
Wisconsin	99,445	104,287	97,501	130,623	122,973	130,623	136,944	123,233	414,593	(a-47)
Wyoming	86,742	128,013	73,042	119,892	(a-8)	138,249	110,047	206,798	129,796	125,417
Guam	68,152	73,020	55,303	60,850	88,915	60,850	65,623	74,096	174,787	88,915
No. Mariana Islands	45,000	40,800 (b)	45,000	58,000	54,000	40,800 (b)	54,000	80,000	80,000	40,800 (b)
U.S. Virgin Islands	71,250	76,500	69,350	76,500	76,500	76,500	76,500	76,500	76,500	65,000

$118,212; Fish and Wildlife, $118,212; Highways, $129,180; Information Systems, $118,212; Parks and Recreation, $118,212; Planning, $125,436; Post Audit, $118,212; Pre-Audit, $118,212; Solid Waste Management, $112,596; Welfare, $118,212.

Maryland: For these positions the salary in the chart is the actual salary and the following are the salary ranges: Adjutant General, $107,196 – $143,270; Administration, $107,196 – $143,270; Agriculture, $107,196 – $143,270; Banking, $73,341 – $117,751; Budget, $124,175 – $166,082; Civil Rights, $86,161 – $115,000; Commerce, $124,175 – $166,082; Consumer Affairs, $78,233 – $125,743; Corrections, $124,175 – $166,082; Economic Development, $124,175 – $166,082; Elections Administration, $86,161 – $115,000; Emergency Management, $99,637 – $133,112; Workforce Development, $92,640 – $123,708; Environmental Protection, $115,356 – $154,235; Finance, $124,175 – $166,082; Health, $124,175 – $166,082; Higher Education, $115,356 – $154,235; Information Services, $124,175 – $166,082; Insurance, $124,175 – $166,082; Labor, $107,196 – $143,270; Licensing, $86,161 – $115,000; Mental Health shared duties, $143,767 – $237,562 (actual, $211,632) and $92,640 – $123,708 (actual, $120,870); Natural Resources, $115,356 – $154,235; Parks and Recreation, $86,161 – $115,000; Personnel, $99,637 – $133,112; Planning, $107,196 – $143,270; Pre-Audit, $92,640 – $123,708; Public Library, $86,161 – $115,000; Purchasing, $80,160 – $106,940; Revenue, $92,460 – $123,708; Social Services, $124,175 – $166,082; Solid Waste Management, $86,161 – $115,000; State Police, $124,175 – $166,082; Tourism, $92,640 – $123,708; Transportation, $124,175 – $166,082; Welfare, $124,175 – $166,082.

Northern Mariana Islands: $49,266 top of range applies to the following positions: Treasurer, Banking, Comptroller, Corrections, Employment Services, Fish and Wildlife, Highways, Insurance, Mental Health and Retardation, Parks and Recreation, Purchasing, Social/Human Services, Transportation.

SELECTED STATE ADMINISTRATIVE OFFICIALS: ANNUAL SALARIES — Continued

State or other jurisdiction	Info. systems	Insurance	Labor	Licensing	Mental health	Natural resources	Parks & recreation	Personnel	Planning	Post audit
Alabama	$165,605	$103,810	$91,014	...	$145,296	$109,206	$104,798	$160,440	(a-13)	$241,695
Alaska	117,300	121,704	135,000	101,400	79,908	135,000	108,960	117,300	...	(a-8)
Arizona	101,970	115,650	126,069	...	94,183	131,500	142,812	117,702	136,150	...
Arkansas	128,542	120,258	117,308	...	106,918	103,611	113,400	102,402	...	157,998
California	175,000	139,189	175,000	150,112	(ll)	175,000	150,112	150,112	...	...
Colorado	156,000	N.A.	146,040	126,516	N.A.	146,040	144,876	119,064	156,468	(a-8)
Connecticut	158,446	143,222	132,613	104,954	(mm)	138,123	138,123	138,624	121,146	(a-8)
Delaware	155,450	105,350	115,550	110,756	(nn)	123,850	96,350	108,957	92,369	(a-8)
Florida	120,000	133,158	120,000	N.A.	125,000	140,000	105,000	100,000	140,000	(a-4)
Georgia	135,000	120,394	121,570	100,000	225,000	141,103	111,420	134,000	(a-10)	(a-8)
Hawaii	83,040 (b)	100,248	103,512	N.A.	N.A.	103,512	83,040 (b)	103,512	88,128 (b)	83,040 (b)
Idaho	78,956	97,323	111,945	74,609	...	112,798	86,320	115,918	...	(a-14)
Illinois	(a-6)	138,600	127,400	(a-9)	(a-45)	136,800	(a-35)	(a-6)	...	(a-8)
Indiana	108,813	86,500	99,180	96,393	105,000	105,000	80,378	111,657	...	98,717
Iowa	129,293	104,533	112,069	...	117,728	128,890	102,294	112,507	...	...
Kansas	N.A.	86,003	102,000	58,938	(oo)	111,490	60,382	N.A.	...	115,296
Kentucky (f)	118,125	100,217	137,865*	...	103,950	95,445	116,655	137,865*	148,719	(a-8)
Louisiana	167,000	115,000	137,000	...	236,000	129,210	115,627	108,160	104,748	N.A.
Maine	102,356	96,553	N.A.	98,737	(a-45)	89,523	(a-35)	90,355	N.A.	N.A.
Maryland	166,082 (b)	(b)	158,974 (b)	100,581 (b)	(b)(pp)	148,778 (b)	115,000 (b)	117,416 (b)	124,848 (b)	N.A.
Massachusetts	125,000	120,000	125,000	100,000	(qq)	150,000	135,000	137,988	150,000	(a-8)
Michigan	140,000	112,199	140,000	123,727	130,978	140,000	117,166	143,948	...	(a-8)
Minnesota	120,000	97,217	108,388	78,571	(a-45)	108,388	108,367	(a-24)	N.A.	(a-8)
Mississippi	160,047	85,500	...	...	164,357	120,386	120,636	111,143	96,303	(a-8)
Missouri	110,000	120,000	120,000	37,500	113,878	120,000	N.A.	95,288	102,000	(a-8)
Montana	111,623	82,420	96,967	89,803	97,309	96,967	77,578	91,502	99,999	119,326
Nebraska	125,387	110,000	118,000	98,810	120,083	107,532	124,097	99,031	96,067	(a-8)
Nevada	123,783	117,030	88,799	...	(rr)	127,721	107,465	97,474	...	...
New Hampshire	106,496	104,364	104,364	104,364	104,364	112,861	90,605	88,933	...	(a-14)
New Jersey	130,380	130,000	141,000	...	(ss)	125,000	102,000	141,000	95,000	...
New Mexico	100,000	100,000	95,000	100,000	...	N.A.	96,396	118,000	73,245	85,000
New York	169,214	127,000	127,000	(tt)	(uu)	136,000	127,000	120,800	120,800	151,500
North Carolina	153,227	123,198	123,198	...	145,000	120,363	106,974	120,363	N.A.	(a-8)
North Dakota	121,260	87,727	84,000	...	95,220	...	87,675	93,288	...	96,600
Ohio	105,123	128,564	87,547	(vv)	(ww)	128,003	100,589	104,998	128,357	(a-8)
Oklahoma	160,000	126,713	105,053	...	133,455	86,310	86,310	80,955	...	...
Oregon	134,220	150,252	72,000	N.A.	140,964	N.A.	136,320	110,556	...	140,964
Pennsylvania (h)	136,998	125,939*	142,310*	N.A.	117,575	135,194*	116,675	127,257	135,003	(a-8)
Rhode Island (i)	133,596	125,676	(a-21)	(xx)	143,206	(a-23)	(a-23)	141,994	112,515	N.A.
South Carolina	137,500	112,407	116,797	116,797	(yy)	121,380	112,504	116,984	N.A.	94,730
South Dakota	107,090	83,015	100,000	N.A.	69,118	100,000	82,995	97,000	N.A.	(a-8)
Tennessee	150,000	150,000	150,000	92,832	150,000	150,000	83,628	150,000	N.A.	(a-14)
Texas	175,000	163,800	140,000	135,000	163,200	145,200	143,000	...	120,000	(a-8)
Utah	129,688	107,266	101,608	98,883	93,662	126,214	110,219	126,214	(a-10)	(a-8)
Vermont (l)	87,776	127,254	93,995	75,005	100,006	115,606	88,005	94,931	...	(a-8)
Virginia	191,906	142,425	125,759	127,124	189,280	152,793	128,004	137,955	(a-10)	(a-8)
Washington	147,000	116,950	139,320	120,579	(a-45)	121,618	120,579	141,549	(a-24)	N.A.
West Virginia	109,999	92,500	70,000	70,000	95,000	75,000	78,636	70,000	(a-17)	91,750
Wisconsin	118,104	117,980	106,031	111,121	109,534	130,623	91,279	104,287	...	(a-8)
Wyoming	194,400	101,567	88,439	72,176	100,200	43,842	100,883	109,824	100,000	(a-8)
Guam	88,915	88,915	73,020	88,915	67,150	60,850	60,850	88,915	75,208	100,000
No. Mariana Islands	45,000	40,800 (b)	45,000	45,360	40,800 (b)	52,000	40,800 (b)	60,000	45,000	80,000
U.S. Virgin Islands	71,250	75,000	76,500	76,500	70,000	76,500	76,500	76,500	76,500	55,000

(c) Responsibilities shared between John C. Geragosian, $144,789 and Robert M. Ward, $144,789.

(d) Florida Gov. Rick Scott does not collect his salary; Michigan Gov. Rick Snyder returns all but $1.00 of his salary; New York Gov. Andrew Cuomo has reduced his salary by 5 percent.

(e) There is no one single agency for Administration. The functions are divided among the Director of Budget and Finance, $108,972; Director of Human Resources Development, vacant; and the Comptroller, $108,972.

(f) Positions with asterisk have taken a 10 percent salary reduction in the reported salary upon request of the Governor in recognition of budget problems.

(g) In Maine, New Hampshire, Tennessee and West Virginia, the presidents (or speakers) of the Senate are next in line of succession to the governorship. In Tennessee and West Virginia, the speaker of the Senate bears the statutory title of lieutenant governor.

(h) The Pennsylvania entries with asterisks denote that 1.7 percent of the officeholders' salary is being repaid as part of the management pay freeze.

(i) A number of the employees receive a stipend for their length of service to the State (known as a longevity payment). This amount can vary significantly among employees and, depending on state turnover, can show dramatic changes in actual salaries from year to year.

(j) Annual salary for duties as presiding officer of the Senate.

(k) Governor Haslam returns his salary to the state.

(l) The officials who have voluntarily taken a five percent reduction in the annual salary set in statue are marked with an *.

(m) Lieutenant Governor receives additional pay when serving as acting governor.

(n) This agency is now a self-directed state agency.

(o) Retired commissioner holding position at reduced salary until

SELECTED STATE ADMINISTRATIVE OFFICIALS: ANNUAL SALARIES — Continued

State or other jurisdiction	Pre-audit	Public library dvpmt.	Public utility reg.	Purchasing	Revenue	Social services	Solid waste mgmt.	State police	Tourism	Trans-portation	Welfare
Alabama	(a-14)	$107,737	$96,609	$131,633	$141,785	$148,899	$113,479	$65,529	$91,014	(a-29)	(a-45)
Alaska	. . .	108,960	105,180	135,912	135,000	(a-27)	121,704	135,000	101,400	135,000	113,064
Arizona	(a-14)	123,352	133,574	103,464	139,971	173,250	96,510	139,549	102,190	130,000	173,250
Arkansas	N.A.	99,886	111,294	100,442	127,959	147,321	N.A.	110,568	88,274	(a-29)	(a-45)
California	(a-14)	. . .	138,528	(a-26)	150,112	165,000	142,968	186,336	. . .	165,000	175,000
Colorado	(a-14)	112,548	114,948	114,948	146,040	150,000	114,948	135,000	100,000	151,840	N.A.
Connecticut	(a-14)	113,525	137,686	124,537	167,169	119,353 (zz)	127,707	155,953	118,450	169,745	119,353 (zz)
Delaware	(a-8)	81,350	103,500	(a-26)	120,950	(aaa)	160,425	140,130	90,005	N.A.	111,650
Florida	(a-4)	95,545	125,000	N.A.	120,000	140,000	95,000	127,500	200,000	N.A.	113,300
Georgia	(a-8)	N.A.	116,452	141,625	158,000	171,600	80,187	132,863	121,048	(a-29)	134,000
Hawaii	83,040 (b)	120,000	90,060	85,524	108,972	103,512	79,104 (b)	. . .	204,576	108,972	83,040 (b)
Idaho	(a-14)	93,808	92,167	78,956	85,447	141,710	. . .	112,008	63,400	165,000	104,400
Illinois	(a-14)	99,516	137,600	(a-6)	146,100	154,200	(a-23)	136,100	(a-12)	154,200	146,100
Indiana	68,772	93,620	109,262	70,750	115,006	130,520	92,712	130,682	85,401	120,000	(a-45)
Iowa	102,294	129,293	125,008	102,294	148,500	150,000	102,294	125,000	93,829	147,909	(a-45)
Kansas	76,960	81,976	91,416	83,640	107,990	112,743	86,965	107,990	82,961	107,990	76,150
Kentucky (f)	. . .	91,947	127,260	90,142	121,632	111,353	79,739	111,352	111,352	137,865*	(a-45)
Louisiana	113,318	107,000	130,000	146,400	124,446	129,995	102,000	134,351	107,000	170,000	87,630
Maine	(a-14)	90,667	112,174	74,297	96,553	109,220	74,297	96,553	(a-17)	102,689	(a-45)
Maryland	110,000 (b)	115,000 (b)	150,000	(b)	120,026 (b)	(b)	114,167 (b)	166,082 (b)	114,444 (b)	166,082 (b)	(a-45)
Massachusetts	(a-8)	104,020	(bbb)	118,671	142,939	136,619	115,000	157,469	108,248	150,000	137,000
Michigan	. . .	. . .	113,612	N.A.	137,523	150,000	130,975	129,842	. . .	140,000	(a-45)
Minnesota	(a-8)	N.A.	(ccc)	104,358	108,388	(a-34)	108,388	108,388	108,388	108,388	(a-34)
Mississippi	(a-8)	108,000	141,505	79,633	108,185	130,000	78,008	138,115	85,748	144,354	130,000
Missouri	95,288	84,072	88,267	95,288	120,000	120,000	72,000	107,184	75,000	164,600	97,300
Montana	119,326	91,962	88,528	88,951	98,421	96,967	96,967	88,400	79,148	96,968	(a-45)
Nebraska	100,000	92,951	118,387	100,687	139,437	155,000	67,059	107,000	59,482	135,000	(a-45)
Nevada	. . .	(ddd)	112,275	88,799	115,847	115,847	(a-23)	115,847	117,030	115,847	(ff)
New Hampshire	(a-14)	90,606	110,036	72,852	116,170	120,095	98,691	104,364	90,606	116,170	90,606
New Jersey	. . .	. . .	141,000	130,000 (eee)	124,765	(fff)	98,299	132,300	90,000	141,000	127,200
New Mexico	79,200	72,253	90,000	N.A.	105,000	105,000	76,841	115,000	N.A.	112,701	N.A.
New York	151,500	170,165	127,000	136,000	127,000	136,000	136,000	121,860	120,800	136,000	136,000
North Carolina	(a-8)	106,787	123,936	101,517	120,363	117,193	110,105	117,406	111,872	120,363	N.A.
North Dakota	. . .	. . .	90,120	72,408	95,212	148,452	80,400	89,436	102,972	128,184	N.A.
Ohio	126,401	N.A.	109,595	105,123	126,401	(ggg)	89,794	128,544	87,984	98,300	141,980
Oklahoma	(a-14)	77,805	(hhh)	95,000	111,933	162,750	98,793	101,030	86,310	133,200	162,750
Oregon	(a-10)	N.A.	N.A.	100,380	150,252	140,964	N.A.	143,064	N.A.	165,276	140,964
Pennsylvania (h)	(a-4)	116,949	137,694	120,001	135,194*	142,310*	111,101	135,194*	116,499	142,310*	142,310*
Rhode Island (i)	(a-14)	120,796	116,002	117,873	156,876	(iii)	(jjj)	148,937	N.A.	130,000	(a-45)
South Carolina	(a-14)	N.A.	160,272	109,323	130,063	144,746	151,942	145,000	112,504	146,000	(a-45)
South Dakota	78,363	70,298	91,390	63,194	95,481	100,000	83,843	84,000	85,000	93,000	(a-45)
Tennessee	105,588	120,000	150,000	70,296	150,000	150,000	86,880	177,996	150,000	150,000	150,000
Texas	(a-14)	104,500	120,000	116,748	(a-14)	168,000	N.A.	162,000	N.A.	192,500	210,000
Utah	(a-24)	110,219	104,395	107,266	N.A.	129,688	107,266	113,235	103,397	160,222	129,688
Vermont (l)	(a-24)	83,990	116,688	89,357	87,818	115,606	92,997	106,912	79,227	115,606	100,006
Virginia	(a-14)	132,890	(kkk)	128,447	136,806	143,450	150,218	145,787	164,000	152,793	143,450
Washington	(a-4)	(a-2)	128,000	(a-6)	141,549	163,056	(a-23)	141,549	N.A.	163,056	(a-45)
West Virginia	(a-8)	72,000	90,000	98,928	92,500	83,652	78,500	85,000	70,000	99,999	95,000
Wisconsin	(a-8)	109,981	113,502	95,426	121,144	121,200	106,887	106,722	108,501	126,412	92,000
Wyoming	(a-8)	97,738	115,712	86,112	116,457	117,144	106,787	112,124	111,266	(a-29)	(a-45)
Guam	88,915	40,788	N.A.	54,475	88,915	74,096	88,915	74,096	55,303	88,915	74,096
No. Mariana Islands	54,000	45,000	80,000	40,800 (b)	45,000	40,800 (b)	54,000	54,000	70,000	40,800 (b)	52,000
U.S. Virgin Islands	76,500	53,350	54,500	76,500	76,500	76,500	76,500	76,500	76,500	65,000	76,500

permanent replacement named. Prior salary as full-time commissioner was $167,496.

(p) Responsibilities shared between Secretary of State, $124,900 and Bureau Director, $118,470.

(q) Responsibilities shared between Secretary of State, $87,982; Deputy Secretary of State for Elections, $97,474 and Chief Deputy Secretary of State, $106,150.

(r) The statutory salary for each of the four members of the Board of Elections is $25,000, including the two co-chairs, Douglas A. Kellner and James A. Walsh.

(s) The Rhode Island Economic Development Corporation is a quasi-public agency.

(t) Responsibilities shared between Secretary of State, $125,880, and Division Director, $112,151.

(u) Responsibilities for St. Thomas, $74,400; St. Croix, $76,500; St. John, $74,400.

(v) Responsibilities shared between Director of Health Care Services, $165,000, and Director, Department of Public Health, $222,000.

(w) Responsibilities shared between Chancellor of California Community Colleges, $198,504, and California Post Secondary Education Commission, $140,000.

(x) Responsibilities shared between Director of Wildlife, $123,973, Director of Inland Fisheries, $127,707, and Director of Marine Fisheries, $121,133.

(y) Responsibilities shared between Director of Budget and Finance, $108,972, and Comptroller, $108,972.

(z) For interim on six months basis $30,000.

SELECTED STATE ADMINISTRATIVE OFFICIALS: ANNUAL SALARIES — Continued

(aa) Responsibilities shared between Adjutant General, $106,394, and deputy director, $72,000.

(bb) Responsibilities shared between Director, Department of Natural Resources, $140,000, and Chief, Fish, $118,470, and Chief, Wildlife, $104,283.

(cc) Responsibilities shared between Administrator, Division of Fisheries, Department of Conservation, $92,688; Administrator, Division of Wildlife, same department, $87,408.

(dd) Responsibilities shared between Auditor of Public Accounts, $85,000, Director of Administration, $128,816, and State Tax Commissioner, $139,437.

(ee) Responsibilities shared between Game and Parks Director, $124,097, and Wildlife Division Administrator, N.A.

(ff) Responsibilities shared between Director, Health and Human Services, $115,847, and Division Administrator, $106,150.

(gg) The Chancellor elected to receive a lower wage than authorized.

(hh) Responsibilities shared between Acting Director, Division of Purchase and Property, Department of the Treasury, $130,000 (acting), and Director, Division of Property Management and Construction, Department of the Treasury, $120,000.

(ii) Responsibilities shared between Assistant Director of Budget and Management, $99,757, and Deputy Director, Accounting, Office of Budget and Management, $113,859.

(jj) Serves a dual role as Commissioner of Higher Education and as the President of the Community College of Rhode Island.

(kk) Responsibilities shared between Community and Technical Policy Commission, $134,000, and Higher Education Policy Commission, $200,000.

(ll) Responsibilities shared between Director of Mental Health, $165,000, and Director of Developmental Services, $165,000.

(mm) Responsibilities shared between Commissioner, Mental Health, $144,999, and Commissioner, Retardation, $167,496.

(nn) Responsibilities shared between Director, Division of Substance Abuse and Mental Health, Department of Health and Social Services, $139,500, and Director, Division of Developmental Disabilities Service, same department, $111,550.

(oo) Responsibilities shared between Director of Mental Health, $79,097, and Director of Community Support, $74,064.

(pp) Responsibilities shared between Executive Director of Mental Hygiene Administration, $211,632, and Director of Developmental Disabilities Administration, $120,870.

(qq) Responsibilities shared between Commissioners Barbara Leadholm, $136,000, and Elin M. Howe, $135,000.

(rr) Responsibilities shared between Director, Health and Human Services, $115,847, and Division Administrator, $112,275.

(ss) Responsibilities shared between Acting Assistant Commissioner Valerie Larosiliere, Division of Mental Health Services, Department of Human Services, $121,432, and position vacant but overseen by Deputy Commissioner Dawn Apgar, Division of Developmental Disabilities, Department of Human Services, $133,000.

(tt) Responsibilities shared between Commissioner, State Education Department, $170,165; Secretary of State, Department of State, $120,800.

(uu) Responsibilities shared between Commissioner of Office of Mental Retardation and Developmental Disabilities, $136,000, and Commissioner of Office of Mental Health, $136,000.

(vv) Numerous licensing boards, no central agency.

(ww) Responsibilities shared between Director of Department of Mental Retardation and Developmental Disabilities, $126,089, and Director, Department of Mental Health, $126,006.

(xx) Varies by department.

(yy) Responsibilities shared between Director for Disabilities and Special Needs, $81,305, and Director of Mental Health, $155,787.

(zz) Retired commissioner holding position at reduced salary until permanent replacement named. Prior salary as full-time commissioner was $159,137.

(aaa) Function split between two cabinet positions: Secretary, Department of Health and Social Services, $143,050 (if incumbent holds a medical license, amount is increased by $12,000; if board-certified physician, a supplement of $3,000 is added), and Secretary, Department of Services for Children, Youth and their Families, $128,850.

(bbb) Responsibilities shared by Chair Ann G. Berwick, $130,000, and Commissioner Geoffrey Why, $116,575.

(ccc) Responsibilities shared between five commissioners with salaries of $88,448 for each.

(ddd) Responsibilities shared between Director, Department of Cultural Affairs, $106,150, and Division Administrator, Library and Archives, $97,474.

(eee) Acting salary.

(fff) Responsibilities shared between Commissioner, Department of Human Services, $141,000, and Commissioner, Department of Children and Families, $141,000.

(ggg) Responsibilities shared between Director, Department of Job and Family Services, $141,980; Superintendent of Department of Education, $194,500; Executive Director of Rehabilitation Services Commission, $120,328; and Director of Department of Aging, $105,684.

(hhh) Responsibilities shared between three Commissioners, $116,713, $114,713 and $109,250 and General Administrator, $96,000.

(iii) Responsibilities shared between Commissioner, Office of Health and Human Services, $141,828, and Director of the Department of Human Services, $129,627, and reports to the Commissioner, Office of Health and Human Services.

(jjj) Solid waste is managed by the Rhode Island Resource Recovery Corporation (RIRRC). Although not a department of the state government, RIRRC is a public corporation and a component of the State of Rhode Island for financial reporting purposes. To be financially self-sufficient, the agency earns revenue through the sale of recyclable products, methane gas royalties and fees for its services.

(kkk) Function split between three agencies: Communications — $142,425; Energy Regulation — $139,762; Utility and Railroad Safety — $128,438.

The Constant Evolution of the Office of Lieutenant Governor

By Julia Hurst

The office of lieutenant governor constantly evolves to offer the greatest service and value to a state. For more than 200 years, states have found no more clear and viable line of gubernatorial succession than the office of lieutenant governor. A lieutenant governor may garner duties and authorities from the constitution, from statute, through gubernatorial appointment, through personal initiative or through a combination of these. This allows the office to evolve to lead on issues of the day or to address unique needs of the state. Electoral provisions, gubernatorial and legislative relationships, assigned duties, office structure and succession law itself impacts the efficiency and effectiveness of the office of lieutenant governor.

Introduction

The rate of lieutenant governors becoming governor appears to be increasing this century and the number of states looking to establish and grow the office of lieutenant governor is also on the rise. As 2011 began, 13 of the sitting governors had once served as lieutenant governor, an increase compared to past years. The rate of gubernatorial successions from 2000 to 2009 increased, too, over the rate of gubernatorial successions since 1900.

On Jan. 6, 2011, West Virginia's acting governor, Earl Ray Tomblin, called for a constitutional amendment creating the office of lieutenant governor. "We need to have some clarity in our constitution" regarding gubernatorial succession, he said. In fact, within the past three years, four of the seven states without a lieutenant governor have examined establishing the office (Arizona, Oregon, Tennessee and West Virginia). The office of lieutenant governor nationally is in a constant state of evolution, which is one of the strengths it gives a state.

Office of Lieutenant Governor

The two most common questions posed about the office of lieutenant governor are why the office should exist and what duties the officeholder should assume. The one shared duty of every lieutenant governor is that of gubernatorial succession. The office of lieutenant governor exists to provide clarity in leadership and continuity in governance should a vacancy in the governor's office occur. Forty-three states maintain an office of lieutenant governor. No state has abolished the office in the modern era, and each of the few states that has abolished the office has re-established it. This demonstrates that for more than 200 years states have found no more clear and viable line of succession than the office of lieutenant governor.

Once established, a lieutenant governor may garner duties and authorities from the constitution, from statute, through gubernatorial appointment, through personal initiative or through a combination of these. These duties may be impacted by state succession law itself, by electoral law on the office of lieutenant governor, by gubernatorial and legislative relationships and by the structure of the office. This allows the office of lieutenant governor to lead on various issues and assume diverse forms depending on each state's perceived or unique needs. A lieutenant governor may be tapped to lead on the pressing issues of the day. Likewise, the office of lieutenant governor may evolve based on the respective expertise of the governor and lieutenant governor. Further, duties of the office may be established to ensure the lieutenant governor is involved in cabinet briefings or budget work to aid in the office's succession duty.

Succession Law

The effectiveness of the office of lieutenant governor in meeting its gubernatorial succession duty often relies on the clarity and thoroughness of a state's succession law. Gubernatorial succession provisions should ensure a sufficiently deep and clearly delineated line of succession; a thorough definition of incapacity; whether the successor becomes the "acting" or "actual" governor; and congruous succession plans in cases of impeachment and recall. The law should be deliberate in addressing the transfer of power from governor to lieutenant governor. Transfer of power may occur when a governor leaves the state, leaves the country or is incapacitated. Incapacitation may occur because a governor is in a war zone, is unconscious, is too physically ill to perform duties, or is unwilling, unable or ill-advised to perform certain required duties. For example, on Dec. 12, 2008, state Attorney General Lisa Madigan petitioned the state supreme court as to whether then Gov. Rod Blagojevich should have been ruled temporarily incapacitated so he could not appoint a U.S. senator after the governor was arrested and under investigation for corruption regarding that appointment. Provisions should address transfer of power for both temporary and permanent incapacitation.

In states where recall or impeachment of the governor is permissible, law regarding these proceedings should be consistent with existing gubernatorial succession law. The 2003 gubernatorial recall election of then-California Gov. Gray Davis brought to light an inconsistency with otherwise established gubernatorial succession. In that state in the event of recall, the state supreme court ruled a new election for governor should be held simultaneous to the recall, negating any succession.

In any case of gubernatorial succession, the law should also be clear on the length of service of the successor. In most states, a successor completes the remaining term of office. Some states, however, require a special election within a specified time period or at the next regularly scheduled statewide election if more than half the term of service remains. Whether a successor completes the term or serves until the next election may determine if s/he is acting governor or actual governor.

The efficiency of gubernatorial succession may be impacted by whether the new governor simultaneously retains his or her power as senate leader (as in New Jersey in periods from 2004 to 2007, or as in West Virginia in 2011), whether the subsequent vacancy in the office of lieutenant governor or first in line of succession is filled and how, and whether transition resources are made available as they often are after an election. In 2009, when New York Gov. David Paterson succeeded to governor, the office of lieutenant governor became vacant. In previous circumstances, the office of lieutenant governor had been left vacant. However, a state senate shutdown was in process. The senate tie-breaking vote of a lieutenant governor could have potentially solved the senate stalemate. Gov. Paterson ultimately decided he had the authority to appoint a new lieutenant governor and did so. The state supreme court upheld that decision. Law in this regard should also be clear as to whether an official succeeding next to governor must be elected or whether he or she may be appointed.

In some states, a new lieutenant governor may be appointed by the governor, but other state statutes mandate that only an elected official may succeed or serve as governor. In that instance, a lieutenant governor may be seated, but should a subsequent gubernatorial succession occur before that lieutenant governor is elected in his/her own right, the next elected official in line of succession would succeed.

Electoral Provisions

The requirements of age and residency, the method of nomination to the office and the ability of the officeholder to raise and hold funds all may impact the form the office of lieutenant governor takes in a state. Twenty-five states elect the governor and lieutenant governor as a team in the general election, while 18 states elect the officials separately. In some states where the officials are elected as a team in the general election, the officials come through the primary elections separately. This may result in an "arranged marriage" of sorts in the general election. State law should also address the ability of a lieutenant governor to raise and hold his or her own funds for campaign or electoral purposes and the duty to file related disclosure reports.

All methods of election for the governor and lieutenant governor have strengths and weaknesses. If the candidates decide to run together, one may presume they have discussed collaborative methods of governance in designing the office of lieutenant governor for its greatest contribution to the state during that administration. Conversely, if candidates are independent of each other, a lieutenant governor may pursue his/her own priorities and may seek to act as a balance to the governor. In any case, the legislature may opt to place permanent or temporary roles with the lieutenant governor via statute. The lieutenant governor may take on a permanent role or office or lead commissions created to tackle specific issues.

Gubernatorial and Legislative Relationships

Whether the governor and lieutenant governor are elected on a ticket together or separately often affects the evolution of the office of lieutenant governor during a term. In more than half the states, though, the office of lieutenant governor is also entwined with the legislature as the only official with specific roles in both the executive and legislative branches. In 27 states, the lieutenant governor (or official first in line of gubernatorial succession) also serves as presiding officer of the state senate.

Lieutenant Governors and the Role of Succession

By Mary Branham

West Virginia Gov. Joe Manchin's election to the U.S. Senate in 2010 set off a series of events the state hadn't seen in 140 years and raised questions about the line of succession to the governor's office. The situation mirrored one in New Jersey in the early 2000s, when several governors left the office and senate presidents took on the role of "acting governor." As in New Jersey, the change sparked debate about the need for the office of lieutenant governor.

When former West Virginia Gov. Joe Manchin was elected to the U.S. Senate in November 2010, he set off a chain of events not seen in the state for 140 years. That's the last time a vacancy occurred in the governor's office and the last time the state had to consider its line of succession.

Under the state's constitution, Senate President Earl Ray Tomblin took over the duties of running the state after Manchin's departure. But the change raised several questions that the West Virginia Supreme Court had to decide. Among those questions, how soon an election must be held to select a permanent replacement to fill out Manchin's unexpired term and whether Tomblin's role as "acting governor" created a conflict under the separation of powers provision in the state constitution as he also served as president of the Senate.

Tomblin said the situation illustrated the need for the office of lieutenant governor to give West Virginia a more distinct line of succession to the governor's office. Tomblin, who's served as senate president—and thus, the next in line for the governor's office—for the past 17 years, thinks the line of succession should be clearer.

"This has only happened one other time in the history of our state, and it was after our first governor was elected to the United States Senate," Tomblin said. "The Senate president at that time served for six days until it was time for the new governor (who had just been elected) to take office."

Two years remained on Manchin's term when he resigned as governor to move to the U.S. Senate. As president of the Senate, Tomblin took over as soon as Manchin's resignation took effect, Nov. 15, 2010. But by virtue of having to hold the office of Senate president to serve as acting governor, Tomblin had to be re-elected to that post in the 2011 legislative session to continue serving in the governor's office. In addition, the succession triggered a legal challenge about when the next election for governor should be held.

The West Virginia Supreme Court ruled in January that an "acting governor" could hold the office for only one year, which means an election to fill Manchin's unexpired term must be held by Nov. 15, 2011.[1] That will leave just one more year on the term. Tomblin is a candidate for the office, as are several other legislative leaders. But Tomblin pushed the idea of amending the state's constitution to include the office of lieutenant governor. In 2000, the state bestowed upon the senate president the title of lieutenant governor, but it didn't have constitutional backing, Tomblin said. And, it still left questions he thought would best be addressed by establishing the office through constitutional amendment.

The legislature didn't see it that way. In fact, a resolution proposing an amendment requiring a statewide vote on creation of the lieutenant governor's post was never introduced in the 2011 legislative session. West Virginia is one of only four states that put a legislator next in line of succession for the top executive branch seat.[2] The line of succession also raised the question of separation of powers as outlined in the state constitution. Tomblin stressed throughout that he would not preside over the Senate while acting as governor. In fact, he said in a statement Dec. 28, 2010, that he was working with colleagues in the Senate to establish the position of acting Senate president to preside while he served as acting governor.

Many in the Senate agreed with Tomblin's assessment. If the Senate president is serving as acting governor, the Senate would need an acting leader, many in the state argued. Sen. Brooks McCabe said in his blog that while some legislators contend the acting governor should also retain his position as Senate president, a majority of lawmakers disagreed. "… One doesn't have to be a constitutional scholar to recognize potential conflicts of interest and possible problems associated with compromising a separation of powers," he wrote Jan. 18.[3] McCabe argued that should the acting governor maintain dual power, the state Supreme Court could nullify any decisions during that tenure, thus creating the need for the position of "acting Senate president."[4]

West Virginia Mirrors New Jersey

The West Virginia situation this year mirrored one in New Jersey several years ago. In 2005, voters approved a constitutional amendment there to establish the office of lieutenant governor and resolve the murkiness surrounding such a situation that occurred in New Jersey, as well as issues it had faced several times in recent years.

Kim Guadagno—who voted against the amendment creating the position in 2005[5]—became New Jersey's first lieutenant governor in 2010. She also serves as secretary of state.

"You really are writing on a clean slate. You have to think of everything—not only with what I'd like to see, but what do you think lieutenant governors are going to want to see or need in the future?" she said in January 2011.[6] Guadagno worked with Gov. Chris Christie to shape the responsibilities of her office. In the combined office, Guadagno has taken over the role of the secretary of state—including overseeing the arts, tourism and cultural programs as well as the Division of Elections—and has taken on a key economic development role in Christie's administration.[7]

The amendment to the New Jersey State Constitution, which took effect Jan. 17, 2006, required a substantial role for the lieutenant governor, who runs on a ticket with the governor. Article V, Section 1, Paragraph 10 says:

"The Governor shall appoint the Lieutenant Governor to serve as the head of a principal department or other executive or administrative agency of State government, or delegate to the Lieutenant Governor duties of the office of Governor, or both. The Governor shall not appoint the Lieutenant Governor to serve as Attorney General. The Lieutenant Governor shall in addition perform such other duties as may be provided by law."[8]

Like West Virginia, the first in line of succession in New Jersey had been the president of the state Senate. But beginning in 2001, New Jersey faced a series of acting governors after the elected governor left office and the Senate president succeeded to the position. Then-Gov. Christine Todd Whitman became head of the U.S. Environmental

Protection Agency in January 2001, and then-Senate President Donald DiFrancesco became acting governor. He served as acting governor until Jan. 8, 2002, when a new legislature was installed. That legislature had equal membership from the Democrat and Republican parties, so co-Senate presidents John O. Bennett and Richard Codey consecutively served as acting governors until Jan. 15, 2002, when Gov. James E. McGreevey was sworn in for a four-year term.[9] Codey again served as acting governor from Nov. 15, 2004, to Jan. 17, 2006, when McGreevey resigned the office.[10] At that time, the governor was the only statewide elected official—nonfederal—in New Jersey.

"I think primarily we wanted to be assured—not withstanding the wonderful job that Gov. DiFrancesco and Gov. Codey did—that constitutionally the anomaly was to have one person serve both as senate president and as governor. Controlling two-thirds of our government is really not what's appropriate and in the best interest of the people," Assemblyman John McKeon told NJN Public Television and Radio in an interview Jan. 19, 2011, explaining the reasoning behind establishing the lieutenant governor's position.[11] Sen. Joseph Kyrillos, in that same interview, said, "It's too much power for one person and it became clear that we were an anomaly in the country."[12]

The Office and Succession

In four states, senate presidents are the first in line of succession to the governor's office. Two of those states—Tennessee and West Virginia—bestow the title of lieutenant governor in recognition of that function.[13] In the other two states—New Hampshire and Maine—the Senate president is first in line of succession but does not carry the title of lieutenant governor.[14] In three other states—Arizona, Oregon and Wyoming—the secretary of states move to the governor's office when there's a vacancy; the remaining 43 states include an office of lieutenant governor.[15]

Arizona voters considered Proposition 111, which would have amended the state constitution to replace the office of secretary of state with the office of lieutenant governor. The proposition, which voters considered in November 2010, would have taken effect in 2014 with the first lieutenant governor taking office in 2015.[16]

The proposal had supporters and detractors, even among those who were running for secretary of state in the 2010 election. Sam Wercinski, a former state real estate commissioner, said having an office of lieutenant governor would make clear the line of succession. "It makes it clear to voters who is next behind the governor. We know that … people are surprised when the secretary of state becomes governor."[17] His opponent, state Rep. Chris Deschene, was concerned about conflict of interest with regard to elections if the lieutenant governor served as secretary of state. "If we look at a race where there's a sitting lieutenant governor and a governor, and they're both part of the same party, now we have the lieutenant governor administering the election for his boss," said Deschene.[18]

Historian Philip VanderMeer, a professor who studies the history of the western United States, told *The Arizona Republic* in October 2010 that the push for a lieutenant governor in Arizona was likely rooted in the state's recent history.[19] Since 1988, three secretaries of state have succeeded to the office of governor, the most recent being Gov. Jan Brewer after Gov. Janet Napolitano was appointed as U.S. Secretary of Homeland Security.[20] "If it happens once every 25 years, people don't notice it too much. When it starts happening more frequently, people say, 'This is a problem,'" VanderMeer said.[21]

Voters rejected the amendment in the general election.

Regardless, the office of lieutenant governor has been shown to be an important one in state governments across the country. Despite varying job responsibilities, they all share one—that of succeeding to the governor's office should a vacancy occur. That clear line of succession can help states avoid problems such as questions regarding one person controlling two branches of government, a lack of checks and balances, the role of an acting governor retaining the role of Senate president, that the governor is not a statewide elected official and related legal challenges such as those that have arisen in the West Virginia case.[22] And, according to Julia Nienaber Hurst, executive director of the National Lieutenant Governors Association, the office is an important training ground for future governors. Nearly one in four governors for the past 100 years have previously served as lieutenant governor, a 2006 study commissioned by NLGA found.[23]

Notes

[1] Phil Kabler, "Supreme Court Orders Election For Governor by Nov. 15," *The Charleston Gazette*, Jan. 18, 2011, *http://wvgazette.com/* (accessed Jan. 25, 2011).

[2] (Kabler 2011).

[3] Brooks McCabe, "Maintaining Stability in the West Virginia Senate," posted Jan. 18, 2011, *http://www.brooks mccabewv.com/2011/01/18/maintaining-stability-in-the-west-virginia-senate/* (accessed March 17, 2011).

[4] (McCabe 2011).

[5] Chris Bishop, "If you're having a problem, call me, text me," phillyburbs.com, March 10, 2011, *http://www.philly burbs.com/news/local/business/article_8a151685-9bea-5b85-88a0-5a1411ec19ad.html* (accessed March 16, 2011).

[6] Lisa Fleisher, "Kim Guadagno to become New Jersey's first lieutenant governor," nj.com, Jan. 19, 2010, *http://www.nj.com/news/index.ssf/2010/01/new_jersey_gets_its_first_lieu.html* (accessed Feb. 15, 2011).

[7] (Fleisher 2011).

[8] Rutgers/Eagleton Institute of Politics, "New Jersey Lieutenant Governor," *http://www.njvoterinfo.org/lieutenantgov.php/* (accessed Feb. 15, 2011).

[9] National Governors Association, "New Jersey Governor Donald T. DiFrancesco," *http://www.nga.org/portal/site/nga/menuitem.29fab9fb4add37305ddcbeeb501010a0/?vgnextoid=47c6ae3effb81010VgnVCM1000001a01010aRCRD&vgnextchannel=e449a0ca9e3f1010VgnVCM1000001a01010aRCRD* (accessed March 18, 2011).

[10] National Governors Association, "New Jersey Governor Richard J. Codey," *http://www.nga.org/portal/site/nga/menuitem.29fab9fb4add37305ddcbeeb501010a0/?vgnextoid=0347ae3effb81010VgnVCM1000001a01010aRCRD&vgnextchannel=e449a0ca9e3f1010VgnVCM1000001a01010aRCRD* (accessed March 18, 2011).

[11] Marie DeNoia Aronsohn, "Lieutenant Governor Guadagno's One Year Anniversary," NJNNews.com, *http://njnnewspublictv.wordpress.com/2011/01/19/guadagnooneyearanniversary/* (accessed March 18, 2011).

[12] (Aronsohn 2011).

[13] Julia Nienaber Hurst, "Lieutenant Governors: Significant and Visible," in *The Book of the States 2006*, ed. Keon S. Chi, 181–183. Lexington: The Council of State Governments, 2006.

[14] (Hurst 2006).

[15] (Hurst 2006).

[16] Carol West, "Despite flaws in Proposition 111, Arizona could use a lieutenant governor," *Inside Tucson Business*, Sept. 17, 2010, *http://www.insidetucsonbusiness.com/opinion/columnists/carol_west/despite-flaws-in-proposition-arizona-could-use-a-lieutenant-governor/article_b8fb664e-09a3-5bf6-8262-01b9cc438b6c.html* (accessed March 18, 2011).

[17] "Lieutenant Governor Could Replace Secretary of State in Arizona," *The Tucson Citizen*, July 18, 2010, *http://tucsoncitizen.com/national-news/2010/07/18/lieutenant-governor-could-replace-secretary-of-state-in-arizona/* (accessed March 18, 2011).

[18] (*The Tucson Citizen*, 2010).

[19] Richard Ruelas, "Arizona secretary of state vs. lieutenant governor," *The Arizona Republic*, Oct. 14, 2010, *http://www.azcentral.com/travel/articles/2010/10/14/20101014arizona-secretary-state-lieutenant-governor.html* (accessed March 18, 2011).

[20] (Ruelas 2011).

[21] (Ruelas 2011).

[22] Julia Nienaber Hurst, "Executive Branch Successors and the Line of Succession," in *The Book of the States 2009*, ed. Audrey S. Wall, 214–217. Lexington: The Council of State Governments, 2009.

[23] Julia Nienaber Hurst, "Lieutenant Governors: Quantified as Risen Powers," in *The Book of the States 2007*, ed. Keon S. Chi, 193–195. Lexington: The Council of State Governments, 2007.

About the Author

Mary Branham is the managing editor for The Council of State Governments, including its bimonthly magazine, *Capitol Ideas*.

Table A
STATE SUCCESSION OF POWERS

State or other jurisdiction	Authority	1	2	3	4	5	6	7	8	9
Alabama	Article 5, Section 127	Governor	Lieut. Gov.	Senate Pres. Pro Tem	Speaker of House of Reps.	Atty. General	State Auditor	Sec. of State	State Treasurer	
Alaska	Chapter 3, Sections 3.9–3.14	Governor	Lieut. Gov.							
Arizona	Article 5, Section 6	Governor	Sec. of State	Atty. General	State Treasurer	Supt. of Public Ed.				
Arkansas	Article 6, Sections 12–13; Constitutional Amendment 6	Governor	Lieut. Gov.	Senate Pres.	Speaker of the Assembly					
California (a)	CAL. CONST. art. 5, § 10, CAL GOV CODE § 12058, CAL GOV CODE § 12061	Governor	Lieut. Gov.	Senate Pres. Pro Tem	Speaker of the Assembly	Sec. of State	Atty. General	Treasurer	Controller	Supt. of Public Instruction
Colorado	Article 4, Section 13	Governor	Lieut. Gov.	Senate Pres. (who is member of same party as Governor)	Spkr. of House (who is member of same party as Governor)	Minority Ldr. of House (who is member of same party as Governor)	Minority Ldr. of Senate (who is member of same party as Governor)			
Connecticut	Article 4, Sections 18–21	Governor	Lieut. Gov.	Senate Pres. Pro Tem						
Delaware	Article 3, Section 20	Governor	Lieut. Gov.	Sec. of State	Atty. General	Senate Pres. Pro Tem	Speaker of House of Reps.			
Florida	Article 4, Section 3	Governor	Lieut. Gov.	Atty. General	Chief Financial Officer	Commr. of Agriculture				
Georgia	Article 5, Section 1, Paragraph 5	Governor	Lieut. Gov.							
Hawaii	Article 4, Section 4: Statute § 26-2	Governor	Lieut. Gov.	Senate Pres.	Speaker of House of Reps.	Atty. General	Dir. of Finance	Comptroller	Dir. of Taxation	Dir. of Human Resources Dev.
Idaho	Article 4, Sections 12–14	Governor	Lieut. Gov.	Senate Pres. Pro Tem						
Illinois	Article 4, Sections 6–7 15 ILCS 5	Governor	Lieut. Gov.	Atty. General	Sec. of State					
Indiana	Article 5, Sections 10–11	Governor	Lieut. Gov.	Senate Pres. Pro Tem	Senate Pres. Pro Tem	Treasurer of the State	Auditor of the State	Sec. of State	State Supt. of Public Instruction	
Iowa	Article 4, Sections 17–19	Governor	Lieut. Gov.	Senate Pres.	Speaker of House of Reps.					
Kansas	Article 1, Section 11 & KSA Statute 75-125	Governor	Lieut. Gov.	Senate Pres.	Speaker of House of Reps.					

See footnotes at end of table.

STATE SUCCESSION OF POWERS — Continued

State or other jurisdiction	Authority	1	2	3	4	5	6	7	8	9
Kentucky	Sections 84, 85, and 87 & KRS 118.710	Governor	Lieut. Gov.	Senate Pres. (if Senate in session)	Atty. General (if Senate not in session)	State Auditor (if Senate not in session and Atty. General fails to qualify)				
Louisiana	Const. Article IV	Governor	Lieut. Gov.	Atty. General	Treasurer	Presiding Off. of Senate	Presiding Off. of House of Reps.			
Maine	Article 5, Part 1, Sections 14–15	Governor	Senate Pres.	Speaker of House of Reps.						
Maryland	Article 2, Section 6	Governor	Lieut. Gov.	Sec. of State						
Massachusetts	Constitution of Massachusetts, Part 2, c. 2, § 2, Art. III	Governor	Lieut. Gov.	Sec. of State	Atty. General	Treasurer and Receiver General	State Auditor			
Michigan	Article 5, Sections 26–27	Governor	Lieut. Gov.	Sec. of State	Atty. General					
Minnesota	Article 5, Section 5	Governor	Lieut. Gov.	Senate Pres. Pro Tem	Speaker of House of Reps.	Sec. of State	State Auditor	Atty. General		
Mississippi	Article 5, Section 131	Governor	Lieut. Gov.	Senate Pres. Pro Tem	Speaker of House of Reps.					
Missouri	Article 4, Sections 11(a)–11©	Governor	Lieut. Gov.	Senate Pres. Pro Tem	Spkr. of House	Sec. of State	State Auditor	State Treasurer	Atty. General	
Montana	Article 6, Sections 6 & 14 & 2009 Revised Statutes: 2-16-513-521.	Governor	Lieut. Gov.	Senate Pres.	Spkr. of House	Senior Member of Legislature (if tie, Eldest to Youngest of Senior Member of Legislature)				
Nebraska	Article 4, Section 16	Governor	Lieut. Gov.	Spkr. of the Legislature						
Nevada	Legislature under its authority of Article 4, Section 37 Section 223.080 of the Nevada Revised Statutes (NRS)	Governor	Lieut. Gov.	Senate Pres. Pro Tem	Speaker of the Assembly	Sec. of State				
New Hampshire	NH Const. Pt. 2 Art. 49	Governor	Senate Pres.	Spkr. of House	Sec. of State	State Treasurer				

See footnotes at end of table.

STATE SUCCESSION OF POWERS—Continued

State or other jurisdiction	Authority	1	2	3	4	5	6	7	8	9
New Jersey	Article 5, Section 1, Paragraphs 6-9 & Article IV, Section VI, Paragraph 7 the Legislature adopted the "Emergency Interim Executive Succession Act," N.J.S.A. 52:14A-1 et seq.	Governor	Lieut. Gov.	Senate Pres.	Speaker of Gen. Assembly	Atty. General	State Highway Commr. (Commr. of Transp.)			
New Mexico	Article 5, Section 7	Governor	Lieut. Gov.	Sec. of State	Senate Pres. Pro Tem	Spkr. of House				
New York (b)	Article 4, Sections 5–6 & the NYS Defense Emergency Act Article I-A (NYS DEA)	Governor	Lieut. Gov.	Senate Pres.	Speaker of the Assembly	Atty. General	Comptroller	Commr. of Transp.	Commr. of Health	Commr. of Commerce
North Carolina (c)	Article 3, Section 3 & Statutes § 147-11.1	Governor	Lieut. Gov.	Senate Pres. Pro Tem	Spkr. of House	Sec. of State	Auditor of the State	Treasurer	Supt. of Public Instruction	Atty. General
North Dakota	Article 5, Section 11	Governor	Lieut. Gov.	Sec. of State						
Ohio	Article 3, Section 15 & Ohio Revised Code, Section 161.03	Governor	Lieut. Gov.	Senate Pres.	Speaker of House of Reps.		State Treasurer	Auditor of the State	Atty. General	
Oklahoma	Article 6, Sections 15–16	Governor	Lieut. Gov.	Senate Pres. Pro Tem	Speaker of House of Reps.					
Oregon	Article 5, Section 8a	Governor	Sec. of State	State Treasurer	Senate Pres.	Speaker of House of Reps.				
Pennsylvania	PA Constitution Article 4, Sections 13 and 14	Governor	Lieut. Gov.	Senate Pres. Pro Tem						
Rhode Island	Article 9, Sections 9–10	Governor	Lieut. Gov.	Speaker of House of Reps.						
South Carolina	Article 3, Sections 1.3.110–1.3.150 & Article 4, Sections 6, 7, 9, 11–12	Governor	Lieut. Gov.	Senate Pres. Pro Tem	Speaker of House of Reps.					
South Dakota	Article 4, Section 6	Governor	Lieut. Gov.							

See footnotes at end of table.

STATE SUCCESSION OF POWERS—Continued

State or other jurisdiction	Authority	1	2	3	4	5	6	7	8	9
Tennessee............	Article 3, Section 12 & Acts 1941, ch. 99, § 1; C. Supp. 1950, § 187.1; T.C.A. (orig. ed.), § 8-105	Governor	Speaker of the Senate/ Lieut. Gov.	Spkr. of House	Sec. of State	Comptroller of Treasury				
Texas...............	Article 3, Section 9; Article 4, Sections 3a, 16–18 & Acts 1987, 70th Leg., ch. 147, Sec. 1, eff. Sept. 1, 1987	Governor	Lieut. Gov.	Senate Pres. Pro Tem	Speaker of House of Reps.	Atty. General	Chief justices of the courts of appeals, in the numerical order of the supreme judicial districts the courts serve			
Utah.................	Article 7, Sections 10–11 & Emergency Interim Succession Act found in Title 63K, Chapter 1	Governor	Lieut. Gov.	Senate Pres.	Speaker of House of Reps.	Atty. General	State Auditor	State Treasurer		
Vermont.............	VSA, Chapter 7, Section 183	Governor	Lieut. Gov.	Speaker of House of Reps.	Senate Pres. Pro Tem	Sec. of State	State Treasurer			
Virginia.............	Virginia Constitution, Article V, Executive, Section 16	Governor	Lieut. Gov.	Atty. General	Spkr. of House of Delegates	House of Delegates convenes to fill vacancy				
Washington.........	Washington State Constitution, Article III, Section 10	Governor	Lieut. Gov.	Sec. of State	Treasurer	Auditor	Atty. General	Supt. of Public Instruction	Commr. of Public Lands	
West Virginia.......	Article 7, Section 7-8	Governor	Acting Pres. of the Senate	Spkr. of House of Delegates						
Wisconsin	Article 5, Section 7-8	Governor	Lieut. Gov.	Sec. of State						
Wyoming	Article 4, Section 6	Governor	Sec. of State							
Dist. of Columbia ...	Title IV– District Charter, Section 421. Part B	Mayor	Chair of D.C. Council							
American Samoa ...	Article IV	Governor	Lieut. Gov.	Senate Pres.	Spkr. of House					
Commonwealth of No. Mariana Is.	Article 3, Section 7	Governor	Lieut. Gov.	Senate Pres.	Spkr. of House					

See footnotes at end of table.

STATE SUCCESSION OF POWERS—Continued

State or other jurisdiction	Authority	1	2	3	4	5	6	7	8	9
Guam................	48 U.S.C. Section 1422b Subsection (A)(C), Guam Code Annotated §§ 1101 and 1102	Governor	Lieut. Gov.	Speaker or Acting Speaker of Guam Legislature						
Puerto Rico (d).....	July 24, 1952, No. 7, p. 12, § 1, Jan. 10, 1998, No. 19, § 1; May 2, 2005, No. 7, § 1	Governor	Sec. of State	Sec. of Justice	Sec. of Treasury	Sec. of Ed.	Sec. of Labor and Human Resources	Sec. of Transp. and Public Works	Sec. of Ec. Dev. and Commerce	Sec. of Health
U.S. Virgin Islands...	July 27, 1972, No. 3280, Sess. L. 1972, p. 247; amended June 15, 1984, No. 4964, § 1(b), Sess. L. 1984	Governor	Lieut. Gov.	Commr. of Finance	Atty. General	Dir. of Office of Mgmt. and Budget	Commr. of Education	Commr. of Public Works	Commr. of Housing, Parks, and Recreation	Police Commr.

Sources: The National Emergency Management Association and The Council of State Governments, April 2011.
Additional Reference Material:
http://www.csg.org/policy/documents/TIA_FF_Succession_Law_000.pdf
http://www.nlga.us/web-content/LtGovernors/SuccessionLawGov&LG.html

Key:
(a) California's line of succession continues after the Superintendent of Public Instruction, with the Insurance Commissioner and then the Chair of the Board of Equalization.
(b) New York's line of succession continues after the Commissioner of Commerce, with the Industrial Commissioner, then the Chairman of the Public Service Commission and then the Secretary of State.
(c) North Carolina's line of succession continues after the Attorney General, with the Commissioner of Agriculture, then the Commissioner of Labor and then the Commissioner of Insurance.
(d) Puerto Rico's line of succession continues after the Secretary of Health, with the Secretary of Agriculture.

Table 4.12
THE LIEUTENANT GOVERNORS, 2011

State or other jurisdiction	Name and party	Method of selection	Length of regular term in years	Date of first service	Present term ends	Number of previous terms	Joint election of governor and lieutenant governor (a)
Alabama....................	Kay Ivey (R)	CE	4	1/2011	1/2015	...	No
Alaska........................	Mead Treadwell (R)	CE	4	12/2010	12/2014	...	Yes
Arizona......................	....(b)..
Arkansas...................	Mark Darr (R)	CE	4	1/2011	12/2015	...	No
California	Gavin Newson (D)	CE	4	1/2011	1/2015		No
Colorado....................	Joseph Garcia (D)	CE	4	1/2011	1/2015	...	Yes
Connecticut..............	Nancy Wyman (D)	CE	4	1/2011	1/2015	...	Yes
Delaware	Matthew Denn (D)	CE	4	1/2009	1/2013	...	No
Florida	Jennifer Carroll (R)	CE	4	1/2011	1/2015	...	Yes
Georgia......................	Casey Cagle (R)	CE	4	1/2007	1/2015	1	No
Hawaii........................	Brian Schatz (D)	CE	4	12/2010	12/2014	...	Yes
Idaho..........................	Brad Little (R)	CE	4	1/2009 (c)	1/2015	(c)	No
Illinois.......................	Sheila Simon (D)	CE	4	1/2011	1/2015	...	Yes
Indiana......................	Becky Skillman (R)	CE	4	1/2005	1/2013	1	Yes
Iowa	Kim Reynolds (R)	CE	4	1/2011	1/2015	...	Yes
Kansas	Jeff Colyer (R)	CE	4	1/2011	1/2015	...	Yes
Kentucky	Daniel Mongiardo (D)	CE	4	1/2007	1/2011	...	Yes
Louisiana...................	Jay Dardenne (R)	CE	4	11/2010 (d)	1/2012	...	No
Maine.........................	....(b)..
Maryland	Anthony Brown (D)	CE	4	1/2007	1/2015	1	Yes
Massachusetts	Tim Murray (D)	CE	4	1/2007	1/2015	1	Yes
Michigan....................	Brian Calley (R)	CE	4	1/2011	1/2015	...	Yes
Minnesota..................	Yvonne Prettner Solon (D)	CE	4	1/2011	1/2015	...	Yes
Mississippi.................	Phil Bryant (R)	CE	4	1/2008	1/2012	...	Yes
Missouri.....................	Peter Kinder (R)	CE	4	1/2005	1/2013	1	No
Montana	John Bohlinger (R)	CE	4	1/2005	1/2013	1	Yes (e)
Nebraska	Rick Sheehy (R)	CE	4	1/2005 (f)	1/2011	(f)	Yes
Nevada	Brian Krolicki (R)	CE	4	1/2007	1/2015	1	No
New Hampshire	....(b)..
New Jersey	Kim Guadagno (R)	CE	4	1/2010	1/2014	...	Yes
New Mexico	John Sanchez (R)	CE	4	1/2011	1/2015	...	Yes
New York...................	Robert Duffy (D)	CE	4	1/2011	1/2015	...	Yes
North Carolina..........	Walter Dalton (D)	CE	4	1/2009	1/2013	...	No
North Dakota.............	Drew Wrigley (R)	CE	4	12/2010 (g)	12/2014	...	Yes
Ohio..........................	Mary Taylor (R)	SE	4	1/2011	1/2015	...	Yes
Oklahoma..................	Todd Lamb (R)	CE	4	1/2011	1/2015	...	No
Oregon......................	....(b)..
Pennsylvania	Jim Cawley (R)	CE	4	1/2011	1/2015	...	Yes
Rhode Island..............	Elizabeth H. Roberts (D)	SE	4	1/2007	1/2015	1	No
South Carolina..........	Ken Ard (R)	CE	4	1/2011	1/2015	...	No
South Dakota.............	Matt Michels (R)	CE	4	1/2011	1/2015	...	Yes
Tennessee	Ron Ramsey (R)	(h)	2	1/2007	1/2013	2 (h)	No
Texas........................	David Dewhurst (R)	CE	4	1/2003	1/2015	2	No
Utah..........................	Greg Bell (R)	CE	4	8/2009	1/2013 (i)	...	Yes
Vermont.....................	Phil Scott (R)	CE	2	1/2011	1/2015	...	No
Virginia.....................	William T. Bolling (R)	CE	4	1/2006	1/2014	1	No
Washington................	Brad Owen (D)	CE	4	1/1997	1/2013	3	No
West Virginia.............	vacant (j)	(k)	2	...	...	...	No
Wisconsin	Rebecca Kleefisch (R)	CE	4	1/2011	1/2015	...	Yes
Wyoming....................	....(b)..
American Samoa	Ipulasi Aitofele Sunia (D)	CE	4	4/2003 (l)	1/2013	2 (l)	Yes
Guam	Michael W. Cruz (R)	CE	4	1/2007	1/2015	1	Yes
No. Mariana Islands...	Eloy Inos (D) (m)(n)	CE	4	4/2009 (n)	1/2015 (n)	(n)	Yes
Puerto Rico................	....(b)..
U.S. Virgin Islands	Gregory Francis (D)	SE	4	1/2007	1/2015	1	Yes

See footnotes at end of table.

THE LIEUTENANT GOVERNORS, 2011 — Continued

Source: The Council of State Governments, March 2011.
Key:

CE — Constitutional, elected by public.

SE — Statutory, elected by public.

. . . — Not applicable.

(a) The following also choose candidates for governor and lieutenant governor through a joint nomination process: Florida, Kansas, Maryland, Minnesota, Montana, North Dakota, Ohio, Utah, American Samoa, Guam, No. Mariana Islands, and U.S. Virgin Islands. For additional information see The National Lieutenant Governors Association website at *http://www.nlga.us.*

(b) No lieutenant governor.

(c) Brad Little was appointed by Governor Otter and confirmed by the state senate after Lieutenant Governor Ritsch won the U.S. Senate seat.

(d) Lieutenant Governor Dardenne won a special election in Nov. 2010 to replace Lieutenant Governor Mitch Landrieu after he left to become New Orleans mayor.

(e) Lieutenant Governor Bohlinger, a Republican, ran on a bipartisan ticket with Governor Brian Schweitzer, a Democrat, in 2004 and again in 2008.

(f) Lt. Governor Sheehy was appointed to the position of Lieutenant Governor January 24, 2005, by Governor Heineman.

(g) Lieutenant Governor Drew Wrigley was appointed by Gov. Jack Dalrymple, who moved from the office of lieutenant governor to governor when Gov. John Hoeven resigned to become a U.S. senator.

(h) In Tennessee, the President of the Senate and the Lieutenant Governor are one in the same. The legislature provided in statute the title of Lieutenant Governor upon the Senate President. The Senate President serves two-year terms, elected by the Senate on the first day of the first session of each two-year legislative term.

(i) Lieutenant Governor Gary Herbert was sworn in as Governor on August 10, 2009 after Governor Huntsman resigned to accept President Obama's appointment as Ambassador to China. Utah law states that a replacement Governor elevated in a term's first year will face a special election at the next regularly scheduled general election, November 2010, instead of serving the remainder of the term. Lt. Gov. Bell was named by Gov. Herbert in 2009 and together they won the 2010 special election to fill the regular term until 1/2013.

(j) The Lieutenant Governor position is currently open as President of the Senate Earl Ray Tomblin is currently serving as Governor following the 2010 resignation of Gov. Joe Manchin to become U.S. Senator. The West Virginia Supreme Court ruled that a special election for governor must be held in 2011. A May 14 primary and Oct. 4 general election have been set. The next regular election for governor is in 2014.

(k) In West Virginia, the President of the Senate and the Lieutenant Governor are one in the same. The legislature provided in statute the title of Lieutenant Governor upon the Senate President. The Senate President serves two-year terms, elected by the Senate on the first day of the first session of each two-year legislative term.

(l) Lt. Governor Sunia was appointed to the position of Lieutenant Governor in April 2003 by Governor Togiola Tulafono.

(m) Covenant Party.

(n) Lieutenant Governor Inos replaced Lieutenant Governor Villagomez after his resignation in 2009. Subsequently Governor Fitial and Lieutenant Governor Inos were elected to another term in the 2009 run-off election for the November 2009 general election. The current administration will serve a five-year term to change future CNMI elections to even-numbered years. The next election will occur in November 2014.

Secretaries of State Confront the Growing Problem of Business Identity Theft

By Kay Stimson

Secretaries of state are warning about the increasing risk of business identity theft as the problem spreads across the states. Criminals have been altering online business records housed by their offices and using them to open up phony lines of credit to illegally obtain valuable goods and services. Secretaries of state are working to establish new safeguards against such fraud, as they alert state legislators and other key stakeholders about the magnitude of the issue.

Secretaries of state are preparing to take on a new threat that has emerged during the nation's economic downturn. The officials who oversee corporate registrations and other business filing processes on behalf of the states say that business identity theft—a criminal mutation of classic identity theft—is on the rise and spreading across states. Computer-savvy thieves are literally hijacking business entities from their owners, leaving behind a digital vapor trail of fraudulent credit purchases and other damages. Several states have already adopted new or improved safeguards for protecting the state-held data that offers a potential gateway to this type of crime, and they are warning others to do the same.

"This can explode quickly and become a big problem," said Colorado Secretary of State Scott Gessler, who noted that his state has already registered 85 victim entities with total losses of approximately $3.4 million. "We are committed to making Colorado a hard target for identity thieves, and that means identifying new policies and protections for state-based businesses as well."

National numbers on business identity theft are virtually impossible to calculate; federal law enforcement agencies typically haven't kept such statistics. However, Dun & Bradstreet, a leading provider of business credit information in the United States, has reported documented cases of business identity theft in at least 22 states.

"What is particularly disturbing about this trend is the significant dollar amounts involved," said Robert Strezze, a senior risk analyst with Dun & Bradstreet. "It's not unusual for the losses to be in the mid-six figures by the time the criminal activity is detected, and it's a lot more lucrative than stealing individual identities."

That sentiment is echoed by Colorado's Gessler, who added that one business in his state suffered a loss of at least $250,000 at the hands of corporate identity thieves.

The cost to state and local governments is harder to determine, but just as with regular identity theft, costs add up for law enforcement and other government officials who investigate and help remediate damages from the crime. Plus, few dispute that a state with a reputation damaged by repeated or large-scale fraud of this type could see damage to its economic development plans.

Methods of Deception

According to the experts, the process of business identity theft is very similar to regular identity theft, only on a more complex scale. Criminals look for ways to steal a legitimate business identity, securing lines of credit with banks and retailers at the expense of the unsuspecting victim entity. Once the fraudsters get the money or goods involved, they leave the legitimate business owners steeped in debt and typically unaware that a crime has occurred until creditors come calling—giving the bad guys ample time to find new victims and evade detection.

Enterprising thieves are stealing business identities in a number of ways. In California, they have rented virtual office space, sometimes in the same building as the victim entity, ordering everything from corporate credit cards to electronics and hot tubs.[1] The crooks then sell the illegally obtained merchandise, shut down the virtual office and move on to the next victim as quickly as possible.

In other states, thieves have been able to carry out their scheme by gaining access to legitimate business records. This happened in Colorado, where criminals were able to exploit the state business registration website, altering the names of company officers and addresses for at least 85 victim entities.

Once the criminals were able to change the corporate registration information for each business that became a victim of the scam, they were able to use the business's corporate registration history—along with additional false documents—to establish lines of credit with banks or retailers. Identity thieves then purchased items that could be bought and exchanged for cash or sold with relative ease.

"Make no mistake about it, this is organized crime," warned Georgia Secretary of State Brian Kemp, who has implemented new protections in his state to curb business identity theft. "And there is more than one victim—it's actually much larger than some might think."

Kemp pointed to a whole chain of victims who must clean up in the wake of such fraud. Beyond the business which has its identity stolen, the crime affects the companies that have received the orders for stolen goods and services, the banks or lending companies that have issued any credit and entities like state governments that house business filings and related documents to provide confidence in commercial transactions.

Businesses of all sizes are being victimized by identity theft, but small and midsize companies are most often targeted.[2] Experts say this is mainly because they have extensive credit lines and cash reserves, but fewer legal and financial protections at their disposal than larger corporations.

In Georgia, Kemp noted he has also seen cases of such fraud related to churches and family-owned businesses at the center of divorces or disputes between relatives. Dun & Bradstreet's Strezze has also seen thieves taking on the identity of dormant or well-aged shelf companies whose owners are no longer doing business.

State Solutions

In order to make it more difficult to perpetrate corporate identity theft, secretaries of state are urging states to take action. For them, it often means ensuring that state safeguards keep pace with advances in online services for the business community.

Nevada, which is home to one of the largest numbers of corporate registrations in the nation, is unveiling its Nevada Business Portal this spring. The unique, new one-stop shop for business/government transactions will help guard against business identity theft by incorporating single sign-on and identity management elements in the online service. When fully launched, the portal will dramatically streamline the processes for establishing and maintaining corporate entities in the state.

Meanwhile, Colorado is establishing an optional password system for businesses on its corporate registration website, along with an e-mail alert system that will send electronic notice whenever a company's information is changed online. Georgia has already established a similar system for e-mail alerts.

The real challenge that lies ahead, secretaries of state said, is ensuring that business owners are aware of the relatively new risk of corporate identity theft, and getting them to sign up for e-mail alerts or password protections while checking their filings regularly.

"We are trying to protect businesses in every way that we can," said Nevada Secretary of State Ross Miller, "but this type of crime is relatively new and the methods of fraud are constantly changing. States need to engage multiple partners in their efforts, including the business community and registered agents, law enforcement, financial institutions and other industry stakeholders. Otherwise, the criminals will just figure out new ways to pull off this crime."

Miller pointed out that because catching the perpetrators of business identity theft can be difficult—and sometimes impossible if they are based overseas or moving from state to state—it is a wise investment strategy for states to focus on preventing such fraud.

Since nearly every state offers a searchable database that can tell users whether a company is in good standing and can identify the names and addresses of registered agents, Miller and his colleagues at the National Association of Secretaries of State are looking to form a business identity theft task force to focus on this issue.

"These business records are supposed to be used as a tool for commerce," says NASS Executive Director Leslie Reynolds. "While banks and other entities can use the information available on state websites for legitimate purposes in business transactions, the number of would-be criminals who are looking to exploit this information appears to be rapidly growing. It has raised some important policy implications for state officials."

Reynolds added states want to work together to combat corporate identity theft crimes, share strategies for communicating with the business community and others who deal with state business registrations and reporting, and discuss ideas for engaging law enforcement in helping to prevent or detect this type of fraud.

With an estimated 2 million corporate entities being formed in the U.S. each year, secretaries of state have a compelling reason to work together on this issue. They will also look to state legislators, governors, attorneys general and other state leaders for assistance in protecting businesses and conducting proactive outreach on the risks of business identity theft.

"No state wants to become known as an easy target for corporate identity fraud when they are already facing financial hardships. Having a thriving business climate is vital to their economic health," Reynolds said.

Notes

[1] Greg T. Spielberg, Bloomberg Businessweek, "Taking on Small-Business Identity Theft," July 9, 2009, available at *http://www.businessweek.com/bwdaily/dnflash/content/jul2009/db2009079_858536.htm*.
[2] Dun & Bradstreet White Paper, "Tackling Corporate Identity Theft with a Public-Private Partnership," submitted to the National Association of Secretaries of State, February 2011, available at *http://www.nass.org/index.php?option=com_docman&task=doc_download&gid=1097*.

About the Author

Kay Stimson is director of communications and special projects for the National Association of Secretaries of State in Washington, D.C. A former television news reporter who covered the state legislatures in Maryland and South Carolina, she frequently writes about state and federal policy issues for lawmakers.

Table 4.15
THE SECRETARIES OF STATE, 2011

State or other jurisdiction	Name and party	Method of selection	Length of regular term in years	Date of first service	Present term ends	Number of previous terms	Maximum consecutive terms allowed by constitution
Alabama	Beth Chapman (R)	E	4	1/2007	1/2015	1	2
Alaska				...(a)			
Arizona	Ken Bennett (R)	E (b)	4	1/2009 (b)	1/2015	(b)	2
Arkansas	Mark Martin (R)	E	4	12/2010	12/2014	...	2
California	Debra Bowen (D)	E	4	1/2007	1/2015	1	2
Colorado	Scott Gessler (R)	E	4	1/2011	1/2015	...	2
Connecticut	Denise Merrill (D)	E	4	1/2011	1/2015	...	...
Delaware	Jeffrey Bullock (D)	A (c)	...	1/2009	...	...	...
Florida	Kurt Browning (R)	A	...	12/2006	...	1	2
Georgia	Brian Kemp (R)	E (d)	4	1/2010 (d)	1/2015	(d)	...
Hawaii				...(a)			
Idaho	Ben Ysursa (R)	E	4	1/2003	1/2015	2	...
Illinois	Jesse White (D)	E	4	1/1999	1/2015	3	...
Indiana	Charlie White (R)	E	4	1/2011	1/2015	...	2
Iowa	Matt Schultz (R)	E	4	12/2010	12/2014	...	...
Kansas	Kris Kobach (R)	E	4	1/2011	1/2015	...	...
Kentucky	Elaine Walker (D)	E (e)	4	1/2011 (e)	12/2011	...	2
Louisiana	Tom Schedler (R)	E (f)	4	11/2010	1/2012	...	...
Maine	Charles Summers (R)	L	2	1/2011	1/2013	...	4 (g)
Maryland	John P. McDonough (D)	A	...	6/2008	...	...	...
Massachusetts	William Francis Galvin (D)	E	4	1/1995	1/2015	4	...
Michigan	Ruth Johnson (R)	E	4	1/2011	1/2015	...	2
Minnesota	Mark Ritchie (DFL)	E	4	1/2007	1/2015	1	...
Mississippi	C. Delbert Hosemann, Jr.(R)	E	4	1/2008	1/2012	...	...
Missouri	Robin Carnahan (D)	E	4	1/2005	1/2013	1	...
Montana	Linda McCulloch (D)	E	4	1/2009	1/2013	...	(i)
Nebraska	John Gale (R)	E	4	12/2000 (h)	1/2015	(h)	...
Nevada	Ross Miller (D)	E	4	1/2007	1/2015	1	2
New Hampshire	William Gardner (D)	L	2	12/1976	12/2012	17	...
New Jersey				...(a)(j)			
New Mexico	Dianna Duran (R)	E	4	12/2010	12/2014	...	2
New York	Ruth Noemí Colón (I) (m)	A	...	9/2010	...	...	...
North Carolina	Elaine Marshall (D)	E	4	1/1997	1/2013	2	...
North Dakota	Alvin A. Jaeger (R)	E	4 (k)	1/1993	12/2014	5	...
Ohio	Jon Husted (R)	E	4	1/2011	1/2015	...	2
Oklahoma	Glenn Coffee (R)	A	4	1/2011	1/2015	...	...
Oregon	Kate Brown (D)	E	4	1/2009	1/2013	...	2
Pennsylvania	Carol Aichele (R)	A	...	1/2011	...	...	...
Rhode Island	Ralph Mollis (D)	E	4	1/2007	1/2015	1	2
South Carolina	Mark Hammond (R)	E	4	1/2003	1/2015	2	...
South Dakota	Jason Gant (R)	E	4	1/2011	1/2015	...	2
Tennessee	Tre Hargett (R)	L	4	1/2009	1/2013	...	...
Texas	Esperanza Andrade (R)	A	...	7/2008	...	...	...
Utah				...(a)			
Vermont	Jim Condos (D)	E	2	1/2011	1/2013	...	...
Virginia	Janet Polarek (R)	A	...	1/2010	...	...	...
Washington	Sam Reed (R)	E	4	1/2001	1/2013	2	...
West Virginia	Natalie Tennant (D)	E	4	1/2009	1/2013	...	...
Wisconsin	Douglas La Follette (D)	E	4	1/1974 (l)	1/2015	8 (l)	...
Wyoming	Max Maxfield (R)	E	4	1/2007	1/2015	1	...
American Samoa				...(a)			
Guam				...(a)			
No. Mariana Islands				...(a)			
Puerto Rico	Kenneth McClintock (NPP)	A	...	1/2009	...	...	...
U.S. Virgin Islands				...(a)			

See footnotes at end of table.

THE SECRETARIES OF STATE, 2011 — Continued

Source: The Council of State Governments, April 2011.
Key:
E — Elected by voters.
A — Appointed by governor.
L — Elected by legislature.
... — No provision for.

(a) No secretary of state; lieutenant govenor performs functions of this office. See Tables 4.12 through 4.14.

(b) Ken Bennett was appointed by Gov. Brewer in January 2009 to fill her term after she was sworn in as governor; replacing Janet Napolitano who became the U.S. Secretary of Homeland Security. Bennett was elected to a full term in the 2010 general election.

(c) Appointed by the governor and confirmed by the Senate.

(d) Gov. Perdue appointed Brian Kemp on January 8, 2010, to replace Karen Handel after she resigned to run for the office of governor. Kemp was elected to a full term in the 2010 general election.

(e) Gov. Beshear appointed Elaine Walker on January 7, 2011, to replace Trey Grayson after he resigned to become Director of the Institute of Politics within Harvard's John F. Kennedy School of Government.

(f) Schedler was appointed and sworn in as secretary of state on November 22, 2010, after Jay Dardenne was elected to serve as lieutenant governor.

(g) Statutory term limit of four consecutive two-year terms.

(h) Secretary Gale was appointed by Gov. Mike Johanns in December 2000 upon the resignation of Scott Moore. He was elected to full four-year terms in November 2002, 2006 and 2010.

(i) Eligible for eight out of 16 years.

(j) The secretary of state of New Jersey is an appointed position. Gov. Christie appointed Lt. Governor Kim Guadagno to serve as secretary of state for this term of office.

(k) Because of a constitutional change approved by voters in 2000, the term for the secretary elected in 2004 was for two years. It reverted to a four-year term in 2007.

(l) Secretary La Follette was first elected in 1974 and served a 4-year term. He was elected again in 1982 and has been re-elected since. The present term ends in 2011.

(m) Currently serving as acting secretary of state.

State Attorneys General Fight Financial Fraud

By the National Association of Attorneys General

As the chief legal officers of the states, commonwealths and territories of the United States, attorneys general serve as counselors to state government agencies and legislatures, and as representatives of the public interest. A large group of new state attorneys general were sworn in at the beginning of 2011, following the November 2010 elections. This year will bring a continued effort to fight financial fraud but attorneys general now have expanded enforcement authority under a new federal law. The National Association of Attorneys General (NAAG) is also making a priority of providing the highest quality legal training for those in state government service.

New Attorneys General

Twenty new attorneys general began work in 2011. That is an approximate 35 percent change in membership for the National Association of Attorneys General (NAAG), with a total of 56 state and territorial attorneys general.

Fourteen attorneys general were elected in the November 2010 elections and five were newly appointed by a governor, state legislature or mayor (Alaska, Hawaii, Wyoming, Maine and District of Columbia). Additionally, Pennsylvania Attorney General Tom Corbett won in his bid for governor, so at press time, he was to appoint an attorney general to complete the term through 2012.

Two other attorneys general won in their bid for governor, California's Jerry Brown and New York's Andrew Cuomo. A former attorney general, Brian Sandoval, was elected Nevada governor. Connecticut Attorney General Richard Blumenthal won a U.S. Senate seat, as did former New Hampshire Attorney General Kelly Ayotte.

Also of note, voters in the District of Columbia approved a November 2010 ballot initiative to make the D.C. Attorney General an elected position, starting with the 2014 election. However, it is not a done deal, as there is a required congressional review by both the U.S. House of Representatives and Senate of amendments to D.C.'s Home Rule Charter. At press time there was no indication yet by the 112th Congress as to how or when the issue would be addressed.

New or incumbent, the attorneys general will work collectively and individually on a wide range of legal and law enforcement issues. Antitrust, bankruptcy, civil rights, consumer protection, cyberspace law, energy and environment, Medicaid fraud, tobacco and Supreme Court cases remain constant in the workload. However, fighting financial fraud is a primary focus this year.

Fighting Financial Fraud

State attorneys general have been in the forefront in protecting consumers from mortgage fraud, and fraud arising from the resulting economic downturn, including foreclosure rescue, mortgage modification, debt settlement, debt collection, and work-at-home schemes. In July 2010, state attorneys general gained expanded enforcement authority under the federal financial reform law [*Dodd-Frank Wall Street Reform and Consumer Protection Act*, P.L. 111-203]. Combine that with more substantive collaboration with other law enforcement agencies and attorneys general will continue to be leaders in protecting consumers from many types of financial fraud.

A Decade of Combating Predatory Lending Practices

State attorneys general have been one of few law enforcers actively investigating predatory lending practices, and fraud targeted at vulnerable consumers. In the past decade, state attorneys general, individually and collectively, have taken numerous enforcement actions against lenders that misrepresented the terms of their loans, made loans without regard to consumers' ability to repay, made loans with deceptive "teaser" rates, or packed loans with undisclosed charges and fees. For example, state attorneys general, along with state banking and financial regulators reached a $484 million settlement in 2002 with Household Finance that resolved allegations Household violated state laws by misrepresenting loan terms and failing to disclose material information to borrowers. Consumers had complained that Household charged far higher interest rates than promised, charged costly prepayment penalties, or deceived consumers about insurance policies. Four years later, state attorneys general reached a $325 million settlement with

Ameriquest, after investigations revealed Ameriquest employees deceived consumers as part of high-pressure tactics to sell mortgage refinances. Additionally, state attorneys general alleged that the high-pressure sales tactics were used to reach desired sales levels and high monthly individual sales quotas. In 2008, state attorneys general reached an $8.7 billion settlement with Countrywide, one of the nation's largest mortgage lenders and servicers. The settlement resolved allegations that Countrywide engaged in unfair and deceptive conduct by marketing and originating unnecessarily risky and costly mortgage loans to homeowners. Under the settlement, Countrywide must implement a mandatory loan modification program to provide immediate relief to homeowners who were put into the riskiest types of loans. Most recently, state attorneys general announced in October 2010 an investigation into banks' and servicers' foreclosure proceedings and whether faulty procedures were used to sign foreclosures.

In addition to these significant multistate actions, state attorneys general have been protecting their consumers from other types of financial fraud.[1] For example, the Illinois attorney general has brought lawsuits against more than 24 mortgage rescue fraud schemes and recovered more than $1.8 million in restitution for homeowners. Florida, Missouri, New York, Texas, and other states have taken action against debt settlement companies that use monies paid by consumers to settle their debts for company fees and profits. Other attorneys general, including those in Colorado, Pennsylvania, and West Virginia, continue to be active in their investigations of illegal debt collection practices. Lastly, state attorneys general have worked with the Federal Trade Commission to announce numerous enforcement actions against individuals and companies that offer bogus work-from-home business opportunities.

An Era of Preemption

Despite the successful enforcement efforts of the state attorneys general to address the deceptive and unfair practices by lenders and financial institutions, the Office of the Comptroller of the Currency (OCC) in 2003 invoked a clause from the National Bank Act to issue formal opinions preempting all state predatory lending laws. This bold move seemed to contradict the OCC's previous position, in accordance with the Supreme Court case of *Barnett Bank of Marion County, N.A. v. Nelson, Florida Insurance Commissioner, et al.* that

held that state laws can regulate national banks where doing so does not "prevent or significantly interfere with" a national bank's exercise of its powers. The OCC made another bold move by promulgating new rules that prevented states from enforcing any of their own consumer protection laws against national banks.

State attorneys general actively fought the OCC by issuing formal comments to the OCC opposing its preemptive rules; meeting with OCC representatives to discuss its preemption position; testifying before Congress on legislation aimed at restoring state authority against federally chartered national banks; and initiating various litigation strategies. Despite these efforts, the OCC's actions appeared to have a chilling effect on state predatory lending laws and state consumer protection efforts in this area. There was a reluctance to bring state action against national banks.

New Enforcement Authority

In July 2010, the largest overhaul of financial-industry regulation known as the Dodd-Frank Wall Street Reform and Consumer Protection Act (The Act) was signed into law in an effort to prevent another collapse of the financial system. In addition to creating oversight for systemic risk posed by large, complex financial companies, products, and activities, the Act enhances the role of the states in the regulation of federally chartered institutions and clarifies federal preemption of state laws. It establishes a new framework for federal preemption of state consumer financial laws by curtailing the OCC's preemption authority. Under the bill, the OCC may preempt a state law only in accordance with *Barnett Bank*, on a case-by-case basis and on the basis of "substantial evidence." Furthermore, preemption authority is not granted for subsidiaries, affiliates or agents of national banks that are not national banks themselves, contrary to the Supreme Court's ruling in *Watters v. Wachovia Bank, N.A.*

The Act expands the role of state attorneys general and clarifies the June 2009 Supreme Court holding in *Cuomo v. Clearing House Association, L.L.C.* by stating that no provision of the National Bank Act relating to state visitorial authority may be construed so as to limit the authority of state attorneys general to bring action to enforce any applicable law against a national bank.

State attorneys general enjoy dual enforcement authority with the newly created Consumer Financial Protection Bureau (CFPB) and other entities and may bring civil actions against national banks and federal thrifts to enforce the regulations prescribed by the CFPB under Title X, but not to enforce Title X itself. State attorneys general may bring civil actions to enforce Title X or CFPB regulations with respect to any state-chartered entity. Any actions brought by state attorneys general may be brought in a federal court or state court in the attorney general's own state.

Moving Forward

Many state attorneys general have already begun the process of developing relationships with the CFPB. NAAG President and North Carolina Attorney General Roy Cooper formed a Presidential Initiative Working Group to develop protocols and principles to formalize the working relationship between state attorneys general and the CFPB on its dual enforcement responsibilities. The working group is tasked with addressing data sharing, coordination of enforcement, and preemption. In addition, Attorney General Cooper will hold his NAAG Presidential Initiative Summit, titled "America's Financial Recovery: Protecting Consumers While We Rebuild" in April 2011. The summit will bring together representatives from the financial industry, academia, government, and consumer advocacy organizations to share perspectives on these issues and provide a forum for meaningful exchange.

State attorneys general will continue their vigorous enforcement efforts against many types of financial fraud that harm consumers, as well as our nation's economy. With the preservation of their roles in protecting consumers from financial fraud, enhanced enforcement authority, and active collaboration with other law enforcement agencies, state attorneys general will continue to lead and make significant contributions in this vitally important area.

Legal Training

NAAG is also making a priority of providing the highest quality legal training for those in state government service. State budget cuts mean funding for continuing legal education and training for lawyers working in attorneys general offices is extremely limited or nonexistent.

The National Attorneys General Training and Research Institute (NAGTRI) is NAAG's research and training arm. NAGTRI offers between 25–30 national programs annually providing high-quality, responsive and innovative legal training to assistant attorneys general across the country. In the

two years since it launched, NAGTRI has trained approximately 6,200 assistant attorneys general in important legal topics such as charities fraud, e-discovery, computer forensics for attorneys, predatory lending, ethics, bankruptcy, trial advocacy, depositions, negotiations and management, among others. NAGTRI provides full scholarships, including all travel and lodging costs, for all participants. The states have also recognized NAGTRI trainings as satisfying continuing legal education (CLE) credits.

NAGTRI also organizes, on request, "mobile training teams" to conduct training at attorneys general offices at no cost to individual states. These programs offer a cost effective and direct approach by providing training onsite. Approximately 25–30 mobile-based programs are offered each year. Faculty for these programs includes some of the nation's preeminent experts in various legal fields.

NAGTRI has also leveraged other approaches to maximize its reach. Intellectual property theft training is underway in partnership with the National White Collar Crime Center and funding from the Bureau of Justice Assistance (BJA). BJA is also funding a NAGTRI course this year for prosecutors and judges on human trafficking issues in cooperation with the Upper Midwest Community Policing Institute and the National Judicial College. NAGTRI offers "train the trainer" courses where assistant attorneys general are supplied with the expertise and materials necessary to return to their states and train others.

NAGTRI provides training through a number of different methods including the use of intensive, practical and hands-on "learning by doing" method and through seminar/lecture formats. NAGTRI sponsors the best, brightest and most experienced assistant attorneys general from around the country to serve as faculty.

Lastly, NAGTRI is further developing its website, *http://www.naag.org/nagtri-courses.php*, so that all training materials, and all videotaped courses are available online, eventually providing an extensive research library.

International Training

NAGTRI has an international component, started in 2009 but expanding in 2011. In April 2009, NAGTRI trained 26 Mexican prosecutors in oral trial advocacy as Mexico switches to an adversarial system similar to the U.S. courts. It was done in conjunction with the U.S.-Mexico State Alliance Partnership and funded by the U.S. Agency for International Development.

In June 2010, a memorandum of understanding (MOU) was signed between NAAG and the Iraq Jurists Union (IJU). The IJU is an organization that represents Iraqi government attorneys, including judges, prosecutors and attorney general equivalents. The goals of the MOU include the provision by NAAG of training and technical assistance to the IJU, as well as the exchange of personnel and ideas. It is the U.S. justice system that Iraq has chosen as a model as it rebuilds its legal system.

To begin the Iraqi training, as well as involve other international partners of NAAG, NAGTRI will hold an international fellowship program this year with representatives from at least nine different countries.

Conclusion

Virtually every issue in today's complex society has a legal component, and articulation of this perspective falls within the scope of the attorneys general responsibilities. Through their actions, and on a daily basis, they play a critical role in the preservation of the rule of law and in protecting the citizens they are sworn to serve. The attorneys general and the men and women who work in their offices are dedicated public servants making important contributions to state government.

Notes

[1] It would be nearly impossible to capture every state attorney general's initiative. The purpose of this section is to provide a sampling of state initiatives. It is neither exhaustive nor all-inclusive.

About the National Association of Attorneys General

The **National Association of Attorneys General** (NAAG), *www.naag.org*, was founded in 1907 to help attorneys general fulfill the responsibilities of their office and to assist in the delivery of high quality legal services to the states and territorial jurisdictions.

The association provides a forum for the exchange of views and experiences on priority issues, fosters interstate cooperation on legal and law enforcement issues, conducts policy research and analysis of issues, improves the quality of legal services provided to the states and territories, and facilitates communication between its members and all levels of government. The association's members are the attorneys general of the 50 states and Washington, D.C., and the chief legal officers of the commonwealths of Puerto Rico (secretary of justice) and the Northern Mariana Islands, and the territories of American Samoa, Guam and the U.S. Virgin Islands.

This article was written by NAAG Consumer Protection Counsel Dennis Cuevas, NAGTRI Program Coordinator Bill Malloy and NAAG Director of Communications Marjorie Tharp.

Table 4.19
THE ATTORNEYS GENERAL, 2011

State or other jurisdiction	Name and party	Method of selection	Length of regular term in years	Date of first service	Present term ends	Number of previous terms	Maximum consecutive terms allowed
Alabama	Luther Strange (R)	E	4	1/2011	1/2015	0	2
Alaska	John J. Burns (R)	A	...	12/2010	...	0	...
Arizona	Tom Horne (R)	E	4	1/2011	1/2015	0	2
Arkansas	Dustin McDaniel (D)	E	4	1/2007	1/2015	1	2
California	Kamala Harris (D)	E	4	1/2011	1/2015	0	2
Colorado	John W. Suthers (R)	E	4	1/2005 (a)	1/2015	1 (a)	2
Connecticut	George Jepsen (D)	E	4	1/2011	1/2015	0	★
Delaware	Joseph R. Biden III (D)	E	4	1/2007	1/2015	1	★
Florida	Pam Bondi (R)	E	4	1/2011	1/2015	0	2
Georgia	Sam Olens (R)	E	4	1/2011	1/2015	0	★
Hawaii	David Louie (D)	A	4 (b)	1/2011	1/2015	0	...
Idaho	Lawrence Wasden (R)	E	4	1/2003	1/2015	2	★
Illinois	Lisa Madigan (D)	E	4	1/2003	1/2015	2	★
Indiana	Greg Zoeller (R)	E	4	1/2009	1/2013	0	★
Iowa	Tom Miller (D)	E	4	1/1979 (c)	1/2015	7 (c)	★
Kansas	Derek Schmidt (R)	E	4	1/2011	1/2015	0	★
Kentucky	Jack Conway (D)	E	4	1/2008	1/2012	0	2
Louisiana	James D. Caldwell (D)	E	4	1/2008	1/2012	0	★
Maine	William J. Schneider (R)	L (d)	2	1/2011	1/2013	0	4
Maryland	Douglas F. Gansler (D)	E	4	1/2007	1/2015	1	★
Massachusetts	Martha Coakley (D)	E	4	1/2007	1/2015	1	2
Michigan	Bill Schuette (R)	E	4	1/2011	1/2015	0	2
Minnesota	Lori Swanson (D)	E	4	1/2007	1/2015	1	★
Mississippi	Jim Hood (D)	E	4	1/2004	1/2012	1	★
Missouri	Chris Koster (D)	E	4	1/2009	1/2013	0	★
Montana	Steve Bullock (D)	E	4	1/2009	1/2013	0	2
Nebraska	Jon Bruning (R)	E	4	1/2003	1/2015	2	★
Nevada	Catherine Cortez Masto (D)	E	4	1/2007	1/2015	1	2
New Hampshire	Michael Delaney (D)	A	4	8/2009	8/2013	0	...
New Jersey	Paula T. Dow (D)	A	4	1/2010	...	0	...
New Mexico	Gary King (D)	E	4	1/2007	1/2015	1	2 (e)
New York	Eric Schneiderman (D)	E	4	1/2011	1/2015	0	★
North Carolina	Roy Cooper (D)	E	4	1/2001	1/2013	2	★
North Dakota	Wayne Stenehjem (R)	E	4 (f)	1/2001	12/2014	3 (f)	★
Ohio	Mike Dewine (R)	E	4	1/2009 (i)	1/2015	0	2
Oklahoma	Scott Pruitt (R)	E	4	1/2011	1/2015	0	★
Oregon	John R. Kroger (D)	E	4	1/2009	1/2013	0	★
Pennsylvania	William H. Ryan Jr. (R) (g)	E	4	1/2011	1/2013 (g)	0	2
Rhode Island	Peter Kilmartin (D)	E	4	1/2011	1/2015	0	2
South Carolina	Alan Wilson (R)	E	4	1/2011	1/2015	0	★
South Dakota	Martin J. Jackley (R)	E	4	9/2009 (h)	1/2015	1	2 (e)
Tennessee	Robert E. Cooper Jr. (D)	(i)	8	10/2006	8/2014	0	...
Texas	Greg Abbott (R)	E	4	1/2003	1/2015	2	★
Utah	Mark Shurtleff (R)	E	4	1/2001	1/2013	2	★
Vermont	William H. Sorrell (D)	E	2	5/1997 (j)	1/2013	6 (j)	★
Virginia	Ken Cuccinelli (R)	E	4	1/2010	1/2014	0	(k)
Washington	Rob McKenna (R)	E	4	1/2005	1/2013	1	★
West Virginia	Darrell Vivian McGraw Jr. (D)	E	4	1/1993	1/2013	4	★
Wisconsin	J.B. Van Hollen (R)	E	4	1/2007	1/2015	1	★
Wyoming	Greg A. Phillips (D)	A (l)	...	3/2011	...	0	...
Dist. of Columbia	Irvin Nathan (D)	A	...	1/2011	...	0	...
American Samoa	Fepulea'i Afa Ripley Jr. (D)	A	4	1/2007	...	1	...
Guam	Lenny Rapadas	E	4	1/2011	1/2015	0	...
No. Mariana Islands	Edward T. Buckingham	A	4	8/2009	...	0	...
Puerto Rico	Guillermo Somoza-Colombani	A	4	12/2009	...	0	...
U.S. Virgin Islands	Vincent Frazer	A	4	1/2007	1/2011	0	...

See footnotes at end of table.

THE ATTORNEYS GENERAL, 2011 — Continued

Sources: National Association of Attorneys General and The Council of State Governments' survey of attorneys general, March 2011.

Key:

★ — No provision specifying number of terms allowed.

. . . — No formal provision, position is appointed or elected by governmental entity (not chosen by the electorate).

A — Appointed by the governor.

E — Elected by the voters.

L — Elected by the legislature.

N.A. — Not available.

(a) Appointed to fill unexpired term in January 2005 and elected to a full term in November 2006.

(b) Term runs concurrently with the governor.

(c) Attorney General Miller was elected in 1978, 1982, 1986, 1994, 1998, 2002, 2006 and 2010.

(d) Chosen biennially by joint ballot of state senators and representatives.

(e) After two consecutive terms, must wait four years and/or one full term before being eligible again.

(f) The term of the office of the elected official is four years, except that in 2004 the attorney general was elected for a term of two years.

(g) Appointed to fill Tom Corbett's unexpired term after he was elected to Pennsylvania governor's office in November 2010.

(h) Appointed September 4, 2009 to fill Larry Long's unexpired term. Attorney General Long resigned to accept a state judgeship.

(i) Appointed by judges of state Supreme Court.

(j) Appointed to fill unexpired term in May 1997. He was elected in 1998 to his first full term.

(k) Provision specifying individual may hold office for an unlimited number of terms.

(l) Must be confirmed by the Senate.

State Treasurers and Public Funds Management

By the National Association of State Treasurers

State treasurers provide professional financial management and accountability for a variety of public funds. These include general operating funds and special funds such as unclaimed property programs. They also borrow money through the municipal debt market to finance state projects.

State treasurers safeguard many types of public funds. These include the general funds that keep state governments operating and special funds such as employee pension programs. Treasurers also help finance capital projects by issuing municipal bonds and managing the repayment of debt. The duties of treasurers vary significantly across the states (see Table A).

One responsibility of almost every treasurer is cash management. In the time between revenue collection and expenditure, treasurers invest general funds to earn interest. This provides income for states rather than letting funds sit idle.

State investment policies typically require use of the principles of safety, liquidity and yield to govern cash management. Safety, the highest priority, means only investing cash in instruments that protect principle. These include U.S. government securities, securities of federally sponsored agencies and repurchase agreements. Liquidity, the second priority, means having funds available on the day they are needed to meet obligations. Yield, or the earnings on an investment, is sought only after the first two priorities are met. Using these broad guidelines, treasurers determine how much excess cash the state has and places it into appropriate investment instruments. When funds are needed to pay expenses, treasurers make sure money is available and distributed properly.

Beyond general funds, states manage a large number of special funds. Public employee retirement funds—pensions—are the largest in terms of dollar value. These retirement systems are managed differently in each state, with the state treasurer often overseeing them in whole or as part of a board of directors.

All of the states and the District of Columbia have college savings programs that help families save for higher education. Treasurers manage the day-to-day operations of these programs in 25 states. Like pension systems, the college savings plans make long-term investments.[1] In 2010, state college savings programs had more than $157 billion in assets under management.

Unclaimed Property Programs

Every state has an unclaimed property program, 35 of which are managed by state treasurers.[2] Unclaimed property is a financial asset a business holds that is owed to an individual or organization when the business has had no documented transactions or contact with the owners for a statutory period of time, usually between one and five years depending upon the type of property. When a business's efforts to locate the owner fail, it must turn over the funds to a state treasurer's office or other state agency, which then becomes responsible for safeguarding the funds, attempting to locate the owners, publicizing the names of apparent owners who cannot be located and returning the assets to the owners as they come forward. Unclaimed property is one of the original consumer protection programs dating back decades.

According to the National Association of Unclaimed Property Administrators, state treasurers and other agencies are safeguarding at least $32 billion in 117 million accounts. Claims can be made into perpetuity in most cases, even by heirs who are able to prove ownership.

Unclaimed property programs provide for a central repository where citizens can seek any lost property that might belong to them. Congress and the U.S. Supreme Court have determined those programs should send unclaimed property to the state of the last known address of the owner. If no address is available, the program should send the property to the responsible state agency in which the business holding the asset is incorporated. All businesses and organizations, except the federal government, must turn over any unclaimed property annually.

Table A
RESPONSIBILITIES OF THE TREASURER'S OFFICE

State or other jurisdiction	Cash management	Investment of retirement funds	Investment of trust funds	Deferred compensation	Management of bonded debt	Bond issuance	Debt service	Arbitrage rebate	Banking services	Unclaimed property	Archives for disbursement of documents	College savings	Collateral programs	Local government investment pool	Other
Alabama	★	...	...	...	★	...	★	...	★	★	...	★	★	...	...
Alaska	★	★	★	...	★	★	★	★	★	★	...	...	...	...	(a)
Arizona	★	...	★	...	...	...	...	★	★	...	...	...	...	★	...
Arkansas	★	...	★	...	...	...	...	...	★	...	...	...	...	★	...
California	★	...	★	...	★	★	★	★	★	...	...	...	★	★	...
Colorado	★	...	...	...	★	...	...	...	★	★	...	...	...	...	...
Connecticut	★	★	★	...	★	★	★	★	★	★	...	★	...	★	(b)
Delaware	★	...	...	★	...	★	★	★	★	...	...	★	★	★	(c)
Florida	★	...	★	★	...	...	...	...	★	...	...	★	★	...	(d)
Georgia	★	...	...	...	...	...	★	...	★	...	...	★	★	★	...
Hawaii	★	★	...	...	★	★	...	...	★	...	...	★	...	...	...
Idaho	★	...	...	...	...	...	...	...	★	...	...	★	...	★	...
Illinois	★	...	★	...	...	...	★	★	★	★	...	★	...	★	...
Indiana	★	...	★	...	★	...	...	...	★	...	★	★	...	★	...
Iowa	★	★	...	...	★	★	★	★	★	★	...	★	★	...	...
Kansas	★	...	...	...	...	...	...	...	★	★	...	★	...	...	(e)
Kentucky	★	...	...	...	...	...	...	...	★	★	★	...	...	...	...
Louisiana	★	...	★	...	★	★	★	★	★	★	...	...	★	...	(f)
Maine	★	...	...	★	★	★	★	★	★	★	...	★	...	...	(g)
Maryland	★	...	...	...	★	★	★	★	★	★	...	...	★	★	...
Massachusetts	★	★	★	★	★	★	★	★	★	★	...	★	...	★	(h)
Michigan	★	★	★	...	★	★	★	★	★	★	...	★	...	...	...
Minnesota	★	...	...	...	★	★	★	★	★	★	...	...	★	...	...
Mississippi	★	★	★	...	★	★	★	★	★	★	...	★	★	...	...
Missouri	★	...	★	...	...	...	...	...	★	★	...	★	...	...	(i)
Montana	★	...	...	...	★	★	★	★	★	...	...	...	...	...	...
Nebraska	★	...	...	...	...	...	...	...	★	★	...	★	...	...	(j)
Nevada	★	...	★	...	★	★	★	...	★	★	...	★	★	★	...
New Hampshire	★	...	...	...	★	★	★	★	★	★	...	★	...	...	...
New Jersey	★	★	...	★	★	★	★	...	★	...	...	...	...	★	...
New Mexico	★	...	...	...	★	...	...	...	★	★	...	★	...	★	...
New York	★	...	...	...	...	...	★	...	★	★	...	...	★	...	(k)
North Carolina	★	★	★	...	★	★	★	★	★	★	...	★	...	...	...
North Dakota	★	...	★	...	...	...	...	...	...	...	...	...	...	★	...
Ohio	★	...	★	...	★	★	★	...	★	★	...	...	...	★	...
Oklahoma	★	...	...	...	...	★	★	...	★	★	...	★	★	...	...
Oregon	★	★	★	★	★	★	★	★	★	...	...	★	★	★	(l)
Pennsylvania	★	★	★	...	...	★	★	★	★	★	...	★	...	★	...
Rhode Island	★	★	...	...	...	...	★	★	...	★	★	...	...	...	...
South Carolina	★	★	★	★	★	★	★	★	★	★	...	★	★	★	...
South Dakota	★	★	★	...	...	...	...	...	★	★	...	...	★	...	(m)
Tennessee	★	★	...	★	...	...	...	...	★	★	...	★	★	★	...
Texas	★	...	★	...	...	★	...	...	★	★	...	★	★	★	(n)
Utah	★	...	★	...	★	★	★	★	★	★	...	...	...	...	...
Vermont	★	★	★	★	★	★	★	★	★	★	...	...	...	...	...
Virginia	★	...	★	...	★	★	★	★	★	★	...	...	★	★	(o)
Washington	★	...	★	...	★	★	★	★	★	★	...	...	...	★	...
West Virginia	★	...	...	...	...	...	★	...	...	★	...	★	★	...	...
Wisconsin	...	...	...	...	...	...	...	...	...	★	...	★	...	★	...
Wyoming	★	...	★	...	★	★	★	★	★	★	...	★	★	★	...
Dist. of Columbia	★	★	★	★	★	★	★	★	★	★	...	★	★	...	...

Source: The National Association of State Treasurers, March 2008.
Key:
★ — Responsible for activity.
... — Not responsible for activity.
(a) Revenue collection including oil and gas royalties and corporate income taxes; child support enforcement; permanent fund dividend eligibility.
(b) Second Injury Fund.
(c) General Fund account reconcilement; disbursements.
(d) State Accounting Disbursement, Fire Marshall, Insurance and Banking Consumer Services, Insurance Rehabilitation and Liquidation, Risk Management, Workers' Compensation, Insurance Fraud, Insurance Agent and Agency Services.

(e) Municipal bond servicing.
(f) Social Security for Section 218 Agreements.
(g) Municipal Revenue Sharing.
(h) Massachusetts Municipal Depository Trust Funds for Cities and Towns.
(i) Investment of all state funds.
(j) Nebraska Child Support Payment Center.
(k) Linked Deposit Program.
(l) Legislation pending to move Unclaimed Property program to Treasurer's office.
(m) Treasurer is a member of the trust and retirement investment programs.
(n) Tax Administration/Collection.
(o) Risk Management.

Unclaimed property is generally a financial asset (real estate is not covered by unclaimed property statutes). Examples of unclaimed assets are outstanding payroll and vendor checks; matured certificates of deposit; savings and checking accounts; uncashed dividends; unclaimed securities; principal on debt; uncashed money orders, cashier's checks, traveler's checks and official checks; unreturned and unused security deposits; accounts receivable credit balances and discounts due; escrow balances; property held by courts and other governmental entities; and amounts due under terms of insurance policies. Some states also require reporting of the physical contents of abandoned safe deposit boxes.

Assets become unclaimed property for a variety of reasons. Among them: businesses can lose track of owners due to a change of address; an owner can forget about an asset; following the death of the owner, the decedent's family does not know about the asset; business dissolutions and mergers; customers can overpay accounts or send remittances with no indication as to which account the payment applies; or checks can simply be lost in the mail or misplaced.

Most state unclaimed property statutes require businesses to make a good faith effort to locate asset owners before reporting property to the state

as unclaimed. After the property is reported, state agencies utilize many methods to locate owners, including publishing the information on state-maintained websites and in newspapers, cross-checking public data, working with other officials such as legislators and county clerks, staging thousands of awareness events at state fairs and other public events, and making the names available on a national website database—MissingMoney.com. Currently, unclaimed property agencies return more than $2 billion to rightful owners annually.

State agencies continually improve the process by which unclaimed property is reported and returned. Many states now accept information via the Internet for increased convenience to businesses and the public.

State Debt

States borrow money to finance a variety of projects. Highways, schools, health care facilities and public utilities are among the undertakings commonly financed over a period of many years. Forty treasurers are involved in the issuance or maintenance of public debt, along with a host of other agencies dedicated to specific types of projects.[3]

Tax-exempt bonds are an important funding tool for states and municipalities. They allow governments to borrow at low rates because purchas-

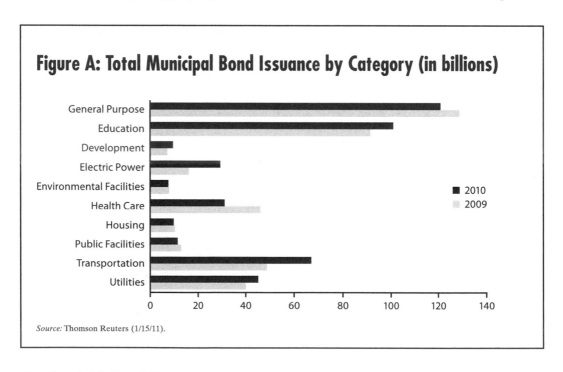

Figure A: Total Municipal Bond Issuance by Category (in billions)

Source: Thomson Reuters (1/15/11).

ers of the bonds do not have to pay federal—and sometimes state—income taxes on earnings. Governments sometimes issue taxable bonds as well. In 2010, states issued more than $175 billion in bonds. When cities, towns and governmental authorities are included, the total amount of municipal debt issued in 2010 comes to more than $430 billion.[4] (See Figure A for a breakdown of the categories of projects funded through bonds.)

State treasurers and other officials manage the process of selling bonds to investors in the municipal market. Since the sums involved are so large, the process is more complicated than taking out a bank loan.

Officials must assess market conditions, prepare disclosure documents for investors and regulators, market their bonds and ultimately sell them. Treasurers also manage repayment of bonds that are issued. To accomplish all these tasks, treasurers and other agencies engage a variety of financial and legal advisers to help finance projects at the lowest possible cost and to ensure compliance with state and federal laws. State treasurers play a key role in promoting sound financial management practices in order to maintain good credit ratings, thus preserving the ability to borrow at relatively low interest rates.

Tax-exempt bonds are the primary mechanism for governments to fund projects, but in the past two years taxable bonds became another important tool. The 2009 American Recovery and Reinvestment Act created the Build America Bonds program, through which the federal government subsidized the interest costs of taxable state and local bonds. This program helped lower borrowing costs and made new construction projects more affordable for states and municipalities. In 2010, 35 percent of all municipal bonds were taxable, mostly due to the $117 billion in Build America Bonds issued. The program was temporary, however, and expired at the end of 2010. The end of the program likely means taxable bonds will decrease as a share of the overall municipal market in 2011.

Treasurers play an important role in determining how much debt states can afford. Debt affordability reports explain how much debt states carry and what portion of states' budgets must be dedicated to interest payments. This information helps policymakers determine when and how to finance future projects through borrowing.[5]

When viewed collectively, state debt levels have remained fairly constant for the last two decades. In 1986, the states had approximately $250 billion in outstanding long-term (payable more than one year after date of issue) bonds.[6] This total was 65 percent of state general expenditures that year. In 2008, the states had $990 billion in long-term debt outstanding, or about 66 percent of general expenditures.[7]

Investors have historically viewed state governments' debt as very safe. In fact, no state has defaulted on its general obligation bonds since the Great Depression. Prudent financial management is critical to maintaining strong credit ratings and, by extension, the ability to borrow at affordable rates to finance public projects.

Notes

[1] For more information about state college savings programs, see *www.collegesavings.org*, which provides an overview of the programs and links to each state's plan.

[2] For links to every unclaimed property program and more information, see *www.unclaimed.org*.

[3] These include dormitory authorities, highway authorities, universities, water districts and school systems.

[4] "2010 in Statistics." *The Bond Buyer*. February 14, 2011.

[5] For examples, see California Treasurer Bill Lockyer's report: *http://www.treasurer.ca.gov/publications/2010dar. pdf* and the report of the Oregon Debt Policy Advisory Commission: *http://www.ost.state.or.us/About/SDPAC/Re port/SDPAC.Report.2011.pdf*.

[6] U.S. Bureau of the Census. *State Government Finances in 1986*.

[7] U.S. Census Bureau. *2008 Annual Survey of State Government Finances*.

About the Author

The National Association of State Treasurers is an organization of the state treasurers, or officials with comparable duties, of the United States, its commonwealths, territories, and the District of Columbia.

Table 4.24
THE TREASURERS, 2011

State or other jurisdiction	Name and party	Method of selection	Length of regular term in years	Date of first service	Present term ends	Maximum consecutive terms allowed by constitution
Alabama	Young Boozer III (R)	E	4	1/2011	1/2015	2
Alaska (a)..................	Jerry Burnett	A	Governor's Discretion	1/2009	...	...
Arizona......................	Doug Ducey (R)	E	4	1/2011	1/2015	2
Arkansas...................	Martha Shoffner (D)	E	4	1/2007	1/2015	2
California	Bill Lockyer (D)	E	4	1/2007	1/2015	2
Colorado....................	Walker Stapleton (R)	E	4	1/2011	1/2015	2
Connecticut...............	Denise L. Nappier (D)	E	4	1/1999	1/2015	★
Delaware	Chip Flowers (D)	E	4	1/2011	1/2015	★
Florida (b)	Jeff Atwater (R)	E	4	1/2011	1/2015	2
Georgia (c).................	Thomas Hills	A	Pleasure of the Board	9/2010	...	...
Hawaii (d)	Kalbert Young	A	Governor's Discretion	12/2010	...	...
Idaho........................	Ron G. Crane (R)	E	4	1/1999	1/2015	★
Illinois......................	Dan Rutherford (R)	E	4	1/2011	1/2015	★
Indiana.....................	Richard Mourdock (R)	E	4	2/2007	2/2015	(e)
Iowa.........................	Michael L. Fitzgerald (D)	E	4	1/1983	1/2015	★
Kansas	Ron Estes (R)	E	4	1/2011	1/2015	★
Kentucky	Todd Hollenbach (D)	E	4	12/2007	12/2011	2
Louisiana..................	John N. Kennedy (R)	E	4	1/2000	1/2012	★
Maine	Bruce Poliquin	L	2	1/2011	1/2013	4
Maryland	Nancy K. Kopp (D)	L	4	2/2002	2/2015	★
Massachusetts	Steve Grossman (D)	E	4	1/2011	1/2015	★
Michigan...................	Andy Dillon (D) (f)	A	Governor's Discretion	1/2011	...	...
Minnesota (g)............	James Schowalter	A	Governor's Discretion	1/2011	...	...
Mississippi	Tate Reeves (R)	E	4	1/2004	1/2012	★
Missouri....................	Clint Zweifel (D)	E	4	1/2009	1/2013	2
Montana	Janet Kelly	A	Governor's Discretion	1/2005	...	...
Nebraska	Don Stenberg (R)	E	4	1/2011	1/2015	2
Nevada......................	Kate Marshall (D)	E	4	1/2007	1/2015	2
New Hampshire	Catherine Provencher	L	2	1/2007	12/2010	★
New Jersey	Andrew P. Sidamon-Eristoff	A	Governor's Discretion	2/2010	...	...
New Mexico	James B. Lewis (D)	E	4	1/2007	1/2015	2
New York...................	Aida Brewer	A	Governor's Discretion	2/2002	...	...
North Carolina..........	Janet Cowell (D)	E	4	1/2009	1/2013	★
North Dakota............	Kelly L. Schmidt (R)	E	4	1/2005	1/2013	★
Ohio	Josh Mandel (R)	E	4	1/2011	1/2015	2
Oklahoma..................	Ken Miller (R)	E	4	1/2011	1/2015	★
Oregon......................	Ted Wheeler (D) (h)	E	4	3/2010	1/2015	2
Pennsylvania	Robert McCord (D)	E	4	1/2009	1/2013	2
Rhode Island.............	Gina Raimondo (D)	E	4	1/2011	1/2015	2
South Carolina..........	Curtis Loftis (R)	E	4	1/2011	1/2015	★
South Dakota............	Richard Sattgast (R)	E	4	1/2011	1/2015	2
Tennessee	David H. Lillard Jr.	L	2	1/2009	1/2013	...
Texas (i)...................	Susan Combs (R)	E	4	1/2007	1/2015	★
Utah.........................	Richard K. Ellis (R)	E	4	1/2009	1/2013	★
Vermont.....................	Elizabeth Pearce (D)	E	2	1/2011	1/2015	★
Virginia.....................	Manju Ganeriwala	A	Governor's Discretion	1/2009	...	...
Washington...............	James L. McIntire (D)	E	4	1/2009	1/2013	★
West Virginia............	John D. Perdue (D)	E	4	1/1997	1/2013	★
Wisconsin	Kurt Schuller (R)	E	4	1/2011	1/2015	★
Wyoming	Joseph B. Meyer (R)	E	4	1/2007	1/2015	2
American Samoa	Magalei Logovi'i	A	4	1/2009	...	...
Dist. of Columbia	Lasana Mack	A	Pleasure of CFO	8/2005	N.A.	...
Guam	Rose T. Fejeran	CS	...	N.A.	...	...
No. Mariana Islands...	Antoinette S. Calvo	A	4	N.A.	N.A.	...
Puerto Rico...............	Juan Carlos Puig	A	4	1/2009	N.A.	...
U.S. Virgin Islands	Laurel Payne	A	4	2007	N.A.	...

Sources: National Association of State Treasurers and The Council of State Governments, January 2011.

Key:

★ — No provision specifying number of terms allowed.

... — No formal provision, position is appointed or elected by governmental entity (not chosen by the electorate).

A — Appointed by the governor. (In the District of Columbia, the Treasurer is appointed by the Chief Financial Officer. In Georgia, position is appointed by the State Depository Board.)

E — Elected by the voters.

L — Elected by the legislature.

CS — Civil Service

N.A.— Not available.

(a) The Deputy Commissioner of Department of Revenue performs this function.

(b) The official title of the office of state treasurer is Chief Financial Officer.

(c) The title is Director of the Office of Treasury and Fiscal Services.

(d) The Director of Finance performs this function.

(e) Eligible for eight out of any period of twelve years.

(f) Andy Dillon, former Speaker of the House of Representatives and a Democrat, was appointed by Governor Rick Snyder, a Republican.

(g) The Commissioner of Management and Budget performs this function.

(h) Wheeler was appointed as State Treasurer in March 2010 and had served as an interim designee. He was elected by Oregon voters in November 2010 to a full four-year term.

(i) The Comptroller of Public Accounts performs this function.

Faster, Cheaper, Better:
Demands for Financial Reporting from State Governments

By Nancy Kopp

Financial reporting and auditing professionals ensure that the public has a clear view of the health and viability of state governments. They are keepers of the public trust. Today, however, these professionals face more demands than ever and have fewer resources than ever to support their important efforts. Cumbersome, and often burdensome, processes and financial limitations are now colliding with a multi-faceted push for financial reporting that is faster, cheaper and better. Can states sustain current efforts, and even go beyond, pushing the limits of their capacity to provide speed, economy and quality?

Setting the Stage

Faster comprehensive annual financial reports, faster annual single audits of federal grant funds, quarterly financial statements, quarterly grant reporting, more transparent reporting of state government pension plans, interim financial reporting—these items are just part of a growing list of reporting demands presenting real challenges to state government financial management and audit professionals.

One can hardly open a newspaper, go online or even watch the local evening news these days without confronting a headline about state government financial woes. The Great Recession has affected just about everyone, but it has been particularly hard on state governments. States are strapped for cash, and in most cases, tax revenues have decreased dramatically, exacerbating the problem. A recent study by the National Association of State Budget Officers reports that state sales tax, personal income tax and corporate income tax—which make up about 80 percent of state general fund revenue—all declined in the 2009 and 2010 fiscal years.[1] Even now, after economists have officially declared the recession over, state tax revenues have risen slowly, if at all.

The American Recovery and Reinvestment Act of 2009 helped, but the majority of its funding to state governments is set to expire in 2011 and 2012. Even though it provided much-needed aid to states, the Recovery Act came with significant accountability requirements. Among other things, states were required for the first time to report federal grant expenditures on a quarterly basis. Many said this feat could not be accomplished. However, through the efforts of dedicated government accountability professionals across the country, quar-terly grant reporting became a reality beginning in September 2009.

Satisfaction with this accomplishment, however, was short-lived, as the demands continued to increase.

Recent reports by the U.S. Government Accountability Office have concluded there is a need for faster reporting of single audits (the organization-wide audit of any entity expending $500,000 or more of federal assistance), particularly reporting of internal control deficiencies.[2] To accomplish faster single audits, states must complete comprehensive annual financial reports in a more timely fashion. While state governments historically have been vastly more transparent than the private sector, there also have been recent calls for increased transparency and greater control over the promulgation of state and local government accounting standards. As if these issues were not daunting enough, Congress recently showed unprecedented interest in the pension plans of state and local governments, demonstrating that the federal government desires to exert its influence in areas it perceives as weak.

The clamor for faster and more transparent financial reporting from state governments is louder than ever.

What's At Stake?

States have plenty at stake in this regard. First, citizens have a right to financial information from their governments. Citizens must be confident that government is being run in an efficient, effective and financially stable manner. A loss of confidence in government by its citizens is hard to regain.

Second, investors must have adequate and timely financial information upon which to base their investment decisions. If investor demands are not met, governments run the risk of not being able to sell bonds. Given the current financial stresses upon states, any decrease in bond sales would be devastating and would likely result in the stoppage of key infrastructure projects (e.g., road improvements, new school buildings, etc.).

Third, bond raters need timely, reliable and easily accessible financial information upon which to base their decisions. Without providing such information, governments run the risk that bond raters will downgrade their bonds. This is not a desirable outcome under any circumstance, but especially in the current economic environment.

The Government Financial Reporting Environment and Obstacles to Faster Reporting

Government is Different

Critics argue that state government year-end financial reporting is hardly timely. While comprehensive annual financial reports are audited and presumably accurate, critics say they are not very useful for making timely investment or management decisions. When compared to large, multi-national private sector corporations, where audited financial statements are available within 60 to 90 days, states lag far behind.

Generally, states strive to issue their comprehensive annual financial reports (CAFRs) within six months—or 180 days—after the end of the fiscal year. As Table A reveals, states have been very consistent in their completion dates. On average, states fall short of meeting the six-month target.

Time has passed and technology has evolved, yet improving the completion time for state comprehensive annual financial reports has remained

elusive. Perhaps the most significant reason is that government accounting and reporting requirements are fundamentally different from those for companies in the private sector. In fact, the differences are so profound that two separate accounting standards-setting boards are needed: the Financial Accounting Standards Board for the private sector and the Governmental Accounting Standards Board for state and local governments. Among the key differences are:

- *Collecting data from component units and agencies.* To complete the comprehensive annual financial reports, state finance officials are dependent upon data from a number of entities referred to as "component units" (e.g., public colleges and universities). Not only does each state have multiple component units, the component units in turn have their own component units (e.g., foundations at a public university). The flow of information from each of these levels to the preparers of the comprehensive annual financial report is not always as expedient as desired or as timely as may be technically required. In a recent survey, state comptrollers indicated that even if all other obstacles to completing a faster comprehensive annual financial report were addressed, difficulties with getting data from component units would preclude success. In addition, obtaining financial information from a myriad of state agencies also contributes to delays in completing the annual report. In many cases, state agencies operate in a decentralized environment that differs vastly from the private sector.

- *Dual perspective reporting model.* In its landmark Statement No. 34,[3] the Governmental Accounting Standards Board prescribed a dual

Table A: Comprehensive Annual Financial Report (CAFR) Completion Dates

	FY 05	FY 06	FY 07	FY 08	FY 09
Average number of days for states to complete the CAFR	208	204	205	204	206

Source: National Association of State Comptrollers, November 2010.

perspective reporting model for state and local government financial statements resulting in two different sets of financial statements. One set examines the government from a government-wide, or enterprise perspective. Here, activities are measured on a full accrual basis of accounting. The second set contains the fund statements, where activities are measured using a modified accrual basis of accounting. Differences between the two sets of financial statements must then be reconciled, adding further complexity to the overall process. Then, there is a statement that compares actual financial results to the approved budget. All told, preparers of state financial statements must use at least three different bases of accounting to compile the comprehensive annual financial reports. Of course, auditors similarly have to audit these different bases of accounting. The audit is further complicated by auditing standards that require opinion units, which results in the auditor having to issue multiple opinions. Simply stated, the rules in government accounting and auditing are much different than those in the private sector. These differences contribute significantly to the delays in preparing and auditing the comprehensive annual financial reports.

States are also faced with other obstacles to faster reporting. These include:

- *Funding/staffing for accounting and auditing.* According to a recent report from National Association of State Budget Officers,[4] in the 2010 fiscal year, 25 states used layoffs and 22 used furloughs to help reduce or eliminate budget gaps. The 2011 fiscal year looks similar, with 24 states using layoffs and 16 using furloughs. Some National Association of State Auditors, Comptrollers and Treasurers members recently reported 25 to 30 percent reductions of their professional staff at a time when the workload was increased dramatically during the implementation of the Recovery Act. Clearly, these resource reductions compound the problem and reduce the ability of states to produce faster financial information. Undoubtedly, reduced funding and staffing is having an impact on states. Some suggest the current workload in this environment is not sustainable. Unfortunately, reduced staff levels will likely remain an obstacle to faster financial reporting, at least in the near term, until the overall economy recovers and state tax revenue rates return to normal.

- *Outdated accounting systems that need to be upgraded or replaced.* The status of accounting systems in the states varies widely. While some states have purchased and implemented new, robust enterprise resource planning systems, others continue to operate on aging legacy systems. New, updated systems clearly will be needed at some point in the future for many states. However, funding constraints make major system purchases a long shot in the short-term.

Year-end reporting is not the only government financial reporting issue receiving attention.

The U.S. Securities and Exchange Commission is conducting field hearings to examine various issues pertaining to the municipal market. Not only is the SEC concerned about the lack of timely financial statements, it also would like to see more reporting of financial information on an interim basis. Publicly traded companies that must register with the SEC are required to file quarterly financial statements. While the SEC has indicated it does not believe the same requirement should be applied to municipal issuers, it is clear the SEC would like to see reporting of financial information on a more frequent basis than annual.

It is important to note the distinction between financial information and financial statements. Clearly, producing GAAP-based financial statements on a quarterly basis would be very problematic for states for the same reasons it is difficult for states to produce faster annual financial statements.

Are There Solutions?

There are no easy solutions, that is for sure. However, there may be some areas where progress can be achieved. The National Association of State Auditors, Comptrollers and Treasurers is examining how improvements can be made for both year-end annual financial reporting and interim reporting.

In the fall of 2010, the association developed a Faster Financial Reporting Work Group to examine the issue of timely financial reporting and to make recommendations on how to improve the timeliness. The work group conducted a survey to find the top barriers for states to faster financial reporting. Each identified barrier is being examined and evaluated. While the group is still in the midst of its work, no idea is being left off the table. Ideas such as changing fiscal year-ends of either the state or its component units, passing legislation to require faster comprehensive annual financial reports, using estimates to a much greater degree, interim auditing and re-examining materiality levels are all items receiving close scrutiny.

In 2003, NASACT convened a group of interested state government and bond market stakeholders to examine the issue of interim reporting. The goal was to develop a template of items governments could make available on an interim basis. The group identified the following four specific items as a recommended minimum set of financial information to be provided to investors and the general public at least quarterly:

1. Budget-to-actual operations, showing major categories of revenues and expenditures, for the general fund and major governmental and enterprise funds, year-to-date and an explanation of the major variances.

2. Cash receipts and cash disbursements in the general fund and major governmental and enterprise funds, year-to-date, compared to the previous fiscal year.

3. Balances and changes in long-term and short-term debt, year-to-date.

4. Significant events (e.g., loss of a major employer or taxpayer, a natural disaster, change in the tax laws that would have a substantial effect on its financial condition, etc.).

It seems these items, and perhaps others, are still relevant today and would address most major concerns about the lack of timely financial information. States generally do have a variety of financial information that could be of significant benefit to citizens and investors.

NASACT's Government Accounting Standards and Market Oversight Committee is re-examining the recommended disclosures and reaching out to relevant parties for input. Posting financial information of this nature on government websites in an easy-to-find "investor's section" appears to be one area where financially feasible improvements could be made.

Additionally, states are working to find innovative ways to fund underfunded pension systems, which have suddenly been thrust into the spotlight and fallen out of favor with the general public. While recently proposed federal legislation regarding reporting for public pensions may be well intentioned, it is misguided. The promulgation of generally accepted accounting principles for state and local governments is the responsibility of the states. The states have delegated this task to GASB and not to the federal government. States are addressing pension management and report-ing in meaningful ways. State and local pension systems collectively have pre-funded nearly four-fifths of their future pension liabilities, and have done so in an undeniably challenging economic environment. In fact, GAO has found that public pensions as a whole are financially secure and positioned to meet their long-term obligations, and public pension stakeholders and decision makers continue to seek meaningful ways to improve funding and reporting.

Conclusion

In its most recent *Fiscal Survey of the States*,[5] the National Association of State Budget Officers found the 2010 fiscal year presented "the most difficult challenge for states' financial management since The Great Depression." States will likely face these and other challenges in 2011. However, it is during the most challenging times that leaders rise to the occasion.

Citizens can be optimistic that in 2011 states will find a way to balance the challenges they face, including increased desires for faster financial reporting, with the limited resources available to them. As the top state fiscal officers, NASACT members will continue working to develop solutions to meet the increasing demands being placed upon them. Achieving faster, cheaper and better financial reporting will not be easy; however, states have faced, and overcome, so-called impossible challenges before.

Notes

[1] *Fiscal Survey of the States*, National Association of State Budget Officers, Fall 2010.

[2] *Recovery Act: As Initial Implementation Unfolds in States and Localities, Continued Attention to Accountability Issues Is Essential*, GAO-09-631T, U.S. Government Accountability Office, April 2009.

[3] *Basic Financial Statements—and Management's Discussion and Analysis—for State and Local Governments*, Governmental Accounting Standards Board, June 1999.

[4] *Fiscal Survey of the States*, National Association of State Budget Officers, Fall 2010.

[5] Ibid.

About the Author

Nancy Kopp is the state treasurer of Maryland and 2010–2011 president of the National Association of State Auditors, Comptrollers and Treasurers.

Table 4.27
THE STATE AUDITORS, 2011

State or other jurisdiction	State agency	Agency head	Title	Legal basis for office	Method of selection	Term of office	U.S. citizen	State resident	Maximum consecutive terms allowed
Alabama	Office of the Examiner of Public Accounts	Ronald L. Jones	Chief Examiner	S	LC	7 yrs.	★	...	None
Alaska	Division of Legislative Audit	Pat Davidson	Legislative Auditor	C,S	L	(a)	...	...	None
Arizona	Office of the Auditor General	Debra K. Davenport	Auditor General	S	LC	5 yrs.	★	★	None
Arkansas	Division of Legislative Audit	Roger A. Norman	Legislative Auditor	S	LC	Indefinite	★	★	None
California	Bureau of State Audits	Elaine Howle	State Auditor	C,S	G	4 yrs.	★	...	None
Colorado	Office of the State Auditor	Sally Symanski	Colorado State Auditor	C	LC	5 yrs.	★	★	None
Connecticut	Office of the Auditors of Public Accounts	John C. Geragosian and Robert M. Ward	State Auditors	C	L	4 yrs.	...	...	None
Delaware	Office of the Auditor of Accounts	R. Thomas Wagner, Jr.	Auditor of Accounts	C,S	E	4 yrs.	★	★	None
Florida	Office of the Auditor General	David W. Martin	Auditor General	S	L	(a)	...	...	None
Georgia	Department of Audits and Accounts	Russell W. Hinton	State Auditor	C	L	Indefinite	...	★	None
Hawaii	Office of the Auditor	Marion M. Higa	State Auditor	S	L	8 yrs.	...	★	None
Idaho	Legislative Services Office—Legislative Audits	Don Berg	Division Manager	C,S	LC	(b)	...	...	None
Illinois	Office of the Auditor General	William G. Holland	Auditor General	S	L	10 yrs.	...	...	None
Indiana	State Board of Accounts	Bruce Hartman	State Examiner	C,S	G	4 yrs.	...	★	None
Iowa	Office of the Auditor of State	David A. Vaudt	Auditor of State	S	E	4 yrs.	★	★	None
Kansas	Legislative Division of Post Audit	Scott E. Frank	Legislative Post Auditor	C,S	LC	(b)	...	★	2
Kentucky	Office of the Auditor of Public Accounts	Crit Luallen	Auditor of Public Accounts	S	E	4 yrs.	★	★	2
Louisiana	Office of the Legislative Auditor	Daryl G. Purpera	Temporary Legislative Auditor	S	L	(a)	...	...	None
Maine	Department of Audit	Neria R. Douglass	State Auditor	C,S	L	4	...	...	None
Maryland	Office of Legislative Audits	Bruce A. Myers	Legislative Auditor	C	ED	(a)	...	...	None
Massachusetts	Office of the Auditor of the Commonwealth	Suzanne Bump	Auditor of the Commonwealth	C	E	4 yrs.	★	★	None
Michigan	Office of the Auditor General	Thomas H. McTavish	Auditor General	C	L	8 yrs.	...	★	None
Minnesota	Office of the Legislative Auditor	James R. Nobles	Legislative Auditor	C,S	L	6 yrs.	...	...	None
	Office of the State Auditor	Rebecca Otto	State Auditor	C,S	E	4 yrs.	★	★	None
Mississippi	Office of the State Auditor	Stacey E. Pickering	State Auditor	C,S	E	4 yrs.	★	★	None
Missouri	Office of the State Auditor	Thomas A. Schweich	State Auditor	C	E	4 yrs.	★	★	None
Montana	Legislative Audit Division	Tori Hunthausen	Legislative Auditor	C,S	LC	2 yrs.	...	...	None
Nebraska	Office of the Auditor of Public Accounts	Mike Foley	Auditor of Public Accounts	C	E	4 yrs.	★	★	None
Nevada	Legislative Counsel Bureau, Audit Division	Paul Townsend	Legislative Auditor	S	LC	Indefinite	★	...	None
New Hampshire	Legislative Budget Office	Jeffry Pattison	Legislative Budget Assistant	S	LC	2 yrs.	...	...	None
New Jersey	Office of the State Auditor	Stephen Eells	State Auditor	C,S	L	5-yr. term and until successor is appointed	...	★	None
	Office of the State Comptroller	Matthew Boxer	State Comptroller	C	G	6 yrs.	...	...	2
New Mexico	Office of the State Auditor	Hector H. Balderas	State Auditor	C,S	E	4 yrs.	★	★	2
New York	Office of the State Comptroller, State Audit Bureau	Thomas P. DiNapoli	State Comptroller	C,S	E	4 yrs.	★	★	None
North Carolina	Office of the State Auditor	Beth A. Wood	State Auditor	C	E	4 yrs.	★	★	None
North Dakota	Office of the State Auditor	Robert R. Peterson	State Auditor	C,S	E	4 yrs.	...	★	None
Ohio	Office of the Auditor of State	Mark Yost	Auditor of State	C,S	E	4 yrs.	★	★	2

See footnotes at end of table.

THE STATE AUDITORS, 2011—Continued

State or other jurisdiction	State agency	Agency head	Title	Legal basis for office	Method of selection	Term of office	U.S. citizen	State resident	Maximum consecutive terms allowed
Oklahoma	Office of the State Auditor and Inspector	Gary Jones	State Auditor and Inspector	C,S	E	4 yrs.	★	★	None
Oregon	Secretary of State, Audits Division	Gary Blackmer	Director	C	SS	(c)	...	...	None
Pennsylvania	Department of the Auditor General	Jack Wagner	Auditor General	C,S	E	4 yrs.	...	...	2
Rhode Island	Legislative Finance and Budget Cmte.	Philip R. Durgin	Executive Director	S	LC	(b)	...	...	None
South Carolina	Office of the Auditor General	Dennis E. Hoyle	Acting Auditor General	S	LC	(b)	...	...	None
	Legislative Audit Council	Thomas J. Bardin, Jr.	Director	S	LC	4 yrs.	...	...	None
	Office of the State Auditor	Richard H. Gilbert, Jr.	Interim State Auditor	S	SB	Indefinite	...	...	None
South Dakota	Department of Legislative Audit	Martin L. Guindon	Auditor General	S	L	8 yrs.	...	...	None
Tennessee	Comptroller of the Treasury, Dept. of Audit	Justin P. Wilson	Comptroller of the Treasury	C,S	L	2 yrs.	...	...	None
Texas	Office of the State Auditor	John Keel	State Auditor	S	LC	(b)	...	...	None
Utah	Office of the State Auditor	Auston G. Johnson	State Auditor	C,S	E	4 yrs.	★	★	None
Vermont	Office of the State Auditor	Thomas M. Salmon	State Auditor	C	E	2 yrs.	...	★	None
Virginia	Office of the Auditor of Public Accounts	Walter J. Kucharski	Auditor of Public Accounts	C,S	L	4 yrs.	...	...	None
Washington	Office of the State Auditor	Brian Sonntag	State Auditor	C,S	E	4 yrs.	★	★	None
West Virginia	Office of the Legislative Auditor	Aaron Allred	Legislative Auditor	S	LC		★	★	None
Wisconsin	Legislative Audit Bureau	Janice Mueller	State Auditor	S	LC	(b)	...	...	None
Wyoming	Department of Audit	Michael Geesey	Director	S	GC	6 yrs.	...	...	None
Dist. Of Columbia	Office of the D.C. Auditor	Deborah Kay Nichols	District of Columbia Auditor				...	...	None
Guam	Office of the Public Auditor	Doris Flores Brooks	Public Auditor	S	E	4 yrs.	★	★	None
No. Mariana Islands	Office of the Public Auditor	Michael Pai	Public Auditor	C,S	GL	6 yrs.	N.A.	N.A.	2
Puerto Rico	Office of the Comptroller of Puerto Rico	Yesmin M. Valdivieso-Galib	Comptroller of Puerto Rico	C	GL	10 yrs.	★	★	1

Sources: Auditing in the States: A Summary, 2009 edition, The National Association of State Auditors, Comptrollers and Treasurers and state websites, April 2011.

Key:
★ – Provision for.
. . . – No provision for.
E – Elected by the public.
L – Appointed by the legislature.
G – Appointed by the governor.
SS – Appointed by the secretary of state.
LC – Selected by legislative committee, commission or council.

ED – Appointed by the executive director of legislative services.
GC – Appointed by governor, secretary of state and treasurer.
GL – Appointed by the governor and confirmed by both chambers of the legislature.
SB – Appointed by state budget and control board.
C – Constitutional
S – Statutory
N.A. – Not applicable.

(a) Serves at the pleasure of the legislature.
(b) Serves at the pleasure of a legislative committee.
(c) Serves at the pleasure of the secretary of state.

Table 4.30
THE STATE COMPTROLLERS, 2011

State	Agency or office	Name	Title	Legal basis for office	Method of selection	Approval or confirmation, if necessary	Date of first service	Present term ends	Consecutive time in office	Length of term	Elected comptroller's maximum consecutive terms	Civil service or merit system employee
Alabama	Office of the State Comptroller	Thomas L. White, Jr.	State Comptroller	S	(c)	AG	1/2010	(a)	1.5 yrs.	(b)	...	★
Alaska	Division of Finance	Kim J. Garnero	Director of Finance	S	(a)	AG	8/1999	...	11 yrs.	(b)	...	...
Arizona	General Accounting Office	D. Clark Partridge	State Comptroller	S	(d)	AG	4/2002	(a)	9 yrs.	(a)	...	...
Arkansas	Dept. of Finance and Administration	Richard A. Weiss	Chief Fiscal Officer, Director	C	G	...	5/2002	(a)	9 yrs.	4 yrs.	2 terms	...
California	Office of the State Controller	John Chiang (D)	State Controller	S	E	...	1/2007	(b)	4.5 yrs.	4 yrs.	2 terms	★
Colorado	Office of the State Controller	David J. McDermott	State Controller	C	(d)	AG	4/2008	(b)	3.5 yrs.	(g)	...	...
Connecticut	Office of the Comptroller	Kevin P. Lembo (D)	Comptroller	C	E	...	1/2011	1/2015	5 mos.	4 yrs.	unlimited	...
Delaware	Dept. of Finance	Thomas J. Cook	Secretary of Finance	S	G	AS	3/2010	(a)	1 yr.	(a)	...	...
Florida	Dept. of Financial Services	Jeff Atwater (R)	Chief Financial Officer	C,S	E	...	1/2011	1/2015	5 mos.	4 yrs.	2 terms	...
Georgia	State Accounting Office	Greg S. Griffin	State Accounting Officer	S	G	AS	8/2008	(a)	3 yrs.	(a)	...	...
Hawaii	Dept. of Accounting and General Services	Bruce Coppa	State Comptroller	S	G	AS	12/2010	12/2014	6 mos.	4 yrs.	...	...
Idaho	Office of State Controller	Donna Jones (R)	State Controller	C	E	...	1/2007	1/2015	4.5 yrs.	4 yrs.	2 terms	...
Illinois	Office of the State Comptroller	Judy Baar Topinka (R)	State Comptroller	C	E	...	1/2011	1/2015	5 mos.	4 yrs.	unlimited	...
Indiana	Office of the Auditor of State	Tim Berry (R)	Auditor of State	C	E	...	5/2004	1/2015	7 yrs.	4 yrs.	2 terms	...
Iowa	State Accounting Enterprise	Calvin McKelvogue	Chief Operating Officer	S	(g)	AS	6/2007	N.A.	4 yrs.	(b)	...	★
Kansas	Division of Accounts and Reports	Kent Olson	Director	S	(d)	AG	6/1975	N.A.	36 yrs.	(b)	...	...
Kentucky	Office of the Controller	Edgar C. Ross	Controller	S	(f)	...	6/2010	N.A.	1 yr.	(i)	...	Exempt
Louisiana	Division of Administration	Paul W. Rainwater	Commissioner	C	G	AG	5/2010	N.A.	1 yr.	(i)	...	...
Maine	Office of the State Controller	Terry Brann	State Controller	S	(f)	...	1/2007	N.A.	4.5 yrs.	(b)	...	...
Maryland	Office of the Comptroller of the Treasury	Peter Franchot (D)	State Comptroller	C	E	...	1/2007	1/2015	4.5 yrs.	4 yrs.	unlimited	...
Massachusetts	Office of the Comptroller	Martin J. Benison	State Comptroller	S	G	SBD	1/1999	N.A.	12.5 yrs.	(j)	...	★
Michigan	Office of Financial Management	Michael J. Moody	Director	S	SBD	AS	8/2002	N.A.	9 yrs.	(k)	...	...
Minnesota	Dept. of Finance and Administration	James Schowalter	Commissioner	S	G	AS	1/2011	(a)	5 mos.	(a)	unlimited	...
Mississippi	Dept. of Finance and Administration	Max Arinder	Executive Director	C,S	G	AS	1/2011	N.A.	5 mos.	(a)	unlimited	...
Missouri	Division of Accounting	Mark A. Kaiser	Director of Accounting	S	(d)	...	1/2009	N.A.	2.5 yrs.	(g)	...	...
Montana	State Accounting Division	Paul Christofferson	Administrator	S	(m)	...	6/2004	N.A.	7 yrs.	(b)	...	★
Nebraska	Accounting Division	Michael Keays	State Accounting Administrator	C	(d)	...	1/2010	N.A.	1.5 yrs.	(b)	2 terms	...
Nevada	Office of the State Controller	Kim Wallin (D)	State Controller	S	E	...	1/2007	1/2015	4.5 yrs.	4 yrs.	...	...
New Hampshire	Division of Accounting Services	Edgar R. Carter	Comptroller	S	G	...	1/2011	N.A.	5 mos.	4 yrs.	...	...
New Jersey	Office of Management and Budget	Matthew Boxer	Director	S	G	AS	1/2008	(b)	3.5 yrs.	(a)	...	...

See footnotes at end of table.

THE STATE COMPTROLLERS, 2011 — Continued

State	Agency or office	Name	Title	Legal basis for office	Method of selection	Approval or confirmation, if necessary	Date of first service	Present term ends	Consecutive time in office	Length of term	Elected comptroller's maximum consecutive terms	Civil service or merit system employee
New Mexico	Dept. of Finance and Administration, Financial Control Division	Anthony J. Armijo	State Controller and Director	S	G	...	1/1991	1/2015	20 yrs.	4 yrs.	unlimited	★
New York	Office of the State Comptroller	Thomas P. DiNapoli	State Comptroller	C,S	E	...	1/2007	1/2015	4.5 yrs.	4 yrs.	unlimited	...
North Carolina	Office of the State Controller	David McCoy	State Controller	S	G	GA	8/2008	7/2013	3 yrs.	7 yrs.	unlimited	...
North Dakota	Office of Management and Budget	Pam Sharp	Director	S	G	...	1/2003	(a)	8.5 yrs.	(a)	unlimited	...
Ohio	Office of Budget and Management	Timothy S. Keen	Director	S	G	AS	1/2011	1/2015	5 mos.	(a)	...	...
Oklahoma	Office of State Finance	Brenda Bolander	State Comptroller	S	(e)	...	10/2001	N.A.	10 yrs.	(h)	...	...
Oregon	State Controller's Division	John J. Radford	State Controller	S	(d)	AG	11/1989	(b)	22 yrs.	(g)	...	...
Pennsylvania	Comptroller Operations	Anna Maria Kiehl	Chief Accounting Officer	S	SBD	AG	12/2007	12/2011	4 yrs.	(a)	...	...
Rhode Island	Office of Accounts and Control	Marc Leonetti	State Controller	S	(d)	...	6/2008	N.A.	3 yrs.	(b)	...	...
South Carolina	Office of the Comptroller General	Richard Eckstrom (R)	Comptroller General	C,S	E	...	1/2003	1/2015	8 yrs.	4 yrs.	unlimited	★
South Dakota	Office of the State Auditor	Steve Barnett (R)	State Auditor	C	E	...	1/2011	1/2015	5 mos.	4 yrs.	2 terms	...
Tennessee	Division of Accounts	Jan I. Sylvis	Chief of Accounts	S	(f)	...	12/1995	N.A.	16 yrs.	(b)	...	...
Texas	Office of the Comptroller of Public Accounts	Susan Combs (R)	Comptroller of Public Accounts	C,S	E	...	1/2007	1/2015	4.5 yrs.	4 yrs.	unlimited	...
Utah	Division of Finance	John Reidhead	Director	S	(d)	AG	9/2005	N.A.	5.5 yrs.	(g)	...	...
Vermont	Dept. of Finance and Management	James Reardon	Commissioner	S	G	AS	2/2005	N.A.	6 yrs.	(a)	...	...
Virginia	Department of Accounts	David A. Von Moll	State Comptroller	S	G	GA	11/2001	(a)	9.5 yrs.	(a)	...	...
Washington	Office of Financial Management	Marty Brown	Director	C	G	...	1/1999	N.A.	5 yrs.	(a)	...	★
West Virginia	Office of the State Auditor	Glen B. Gainer III (D)	State Auditor	C	E	...	1/1993	1/2013	18 yrs.	4 yrs.	unlimited	...
West Virginia	Finance Division, Office of the State Comptroller	Ross Taylor	State Comptroller and Finance Director	S	(d)	AG	10/2005	N.A.	6 yrs.	(g)	...	...
Wisconsin	State Controller's Office	Steve Censky	State Controller	S	CS	...	8/2007	N.A.	4 yrs.	(g)	unlimited	★
Wyoming	Office of the State Auditor	Cynthia Cloud	State Auditor	C,S	E	...	1/2011	1/2015	5 mos.	4 yrs.	2 terms	...

Source: Comptrollers: Technical Activities and Functions, 2008 edition, National Association of State Auditors, Comptrollers and Treasurers. April 2011.

Key:

... — No provision for.
C — Constitutional.
S — Statutory.
N.A. — Not applicable.
E — Elected by the public.
G — Appointed by the Governor.
CS — Civil Service.
AG — Approved by the Governor.
AS — Approved/confirmed by the Senate.
SBD — Approved by State Budget Director.
GA — Confirmed by the General Assembly.
SDB — Confirmed by State Depository Board.

(a) Serves at the pleasure of the governor.
(b) Indefinite.
(c) Appointed by the Director of the Department of Finance (merit system position).
(d) Appointed by the head of the department of administration or administrative services.
(e) Appointed by the head of finance, department or agency.
(f) Appointed by the head of financial and administrative services.
(g) Serves at the pleasure of the head of the department of administration or administrative services.
(h) Serves at the pleasure of the head of the finance department or agency.
(i) Serves at the pleasure of the head of financial and administrative services.
(j) Appointed by the governor for a term coterminous with the governor.
(k) Two-year renewable contractual term; classified executive service.
(l) As of July 1, 2005, the responsibility for accounting and financial reporting in Georgia was transferred to the newly created State Accounting Office.
(m) Classified position.

Chapter Five

STATE JUDICIAL BRANCH

The Power of Fixing People
Rather than Filling Prisons

By Hon. Sue Bell Cobb

Like most states, Alabama is currently facing the crisis of an overcrowded prison population and a recidivism rate that significantly threatens public safety and exacerbates already bleak state and local government budget shortfalls. Rather than continue to spend vast sums of money on a system that is clearly broken, Alabama is beginning the process of interbranch cooperation to implement effective reforms in the areas of sentencing and corrections at the state and local levels. A number of efforts are currently underway. For the sake of public safety and stark financial reality, Alabama must continue to modify its laws and carry out reforms to lower the costly burden of corrections and stop the revolving door of recidivism.

I cannot begin to count the number of times during my thirteen years as a trial judge that I said to victims of crime, troubled youth, or dysfunctional families, "I wish I could snap my fingers and make things better. I wish I could snap my fingers and undo all the harm that has caused you to be in court today. Unfortunately, I do not have that kind of power."

No human being has that kind of power. However, judges can use their power in sentencing juvenile and adult offenders in a way that significantly reduces the likelihood that offenders will again cause harm. That ultimately makes life better for the offender, for his or her potential victims, and for the community.[1] This power—the power "to fix people rather than fill prisons"[2]—is growing in Alabama's criminal justice system.

Fulfilling the Power and Mission of a Unified Court System

As chief justice of a unified court system, I feel privileged to be given the opportunity to enhance that "positive coercive power"[3] possessed by every trial judge in our state. Because of the wisdom and political courage of former Chief Justice Howell Heflin, in 1973 Alabama became one of the first states to unify its judicial system.[4] The result was the placement of the administrative oversight of the trial courts with the chief justice[5] and the abolition of non-lawyer judges.[6] Adequate and reasonable funding of the court system became the responsibility of the state.[7] Consolidation such as this empowers state court leaders to promote policy changes that are in the best interest of the people. Thus, the courts can fulfill their ultimate mission to

fairly, impartially and swiftly resolve disputes, and to adjudicate criminal matters in order to make the public safer.

Making the Public Safer Under Increased Budgetary Constraint

The constitutional power or authority invested in every trial judge to detain or incarcerate offenders is momentous. As a judge, I did not have the ability to instantly improve people's lives or situations, but I did possess the power to lock them up. Taking away a person's freedom is an enormous responsibility and should never be taken lightly. We now know there has been an overreliance on incarceration of nonviolent offenders.[8] Unfortunately, research has demonstrated that it has not necessarily made us safer. As Chief Justice Ray Price of Missouri said:

"I could quote different statistics and relationships to you all morning, but the simple fact is, we are spending unbelievable sums of money to incarcerate nonviolent offenders, and our prison population of new offenders is going up, not down—with a recidivism rate that guarantees this cycle will continue to worsen at a faster and faster pace, eating tens of millions of dollars in the process."[9]

The Public Safety Performance Project of the Pew Center on the States has reported that we in the United States lock up more of our citizens than any other country in the world.[10] In the past, Alabama has certainly not been the exception to this trend. Alabama has the most overcrowded prison system in the United States, at 190 percent of institutional capacity,[11] and, unfortunately, the least funded.[12] Alabama ranks sixth in the country in the number of adults in prison or jail, with one in 75 behind bars, compared to one in 100 nationally.[13] Alabama's per diem per inmate could be doubled and not even meet the national average.[14] Alabamians are more at risk because of our failure to keep corrections funding at the same pace as our prison population. This has resulted in Alabama having one of the largest ratios of inmates to correctional officers in the country.[15]

Despite our failure to adequately fund corrections, corrections costs consume an ever larger portion of our state budget. Over the past 20 years, the annual cost of corrections in Alabama has more than quadrupled—growing from $105 million in 1988 to $577 million in 2008. Yet for all this spending, taxpayers are not seeing a solid return in terms of public safety. In fact, recidivism rates are on the rise.[16]

Let me be absolutely clear: We *must* lock up violent and serious offenders so they cannot continue to harm innocent people.[17] However, where nonviolent offenders are concerned, an alternative to the costly cycle of crime, incarceration and recidivism exists. As observed by Roger Warren, president emeritus of the National Center for State Courts: "Today, ... there is a voluminous body of solid research showing that certain 'evidence-based' sentencing and corrections practices do work and can reduce crime rates as effectively as prisons at much lower cost."[18]

The Alabama Sentencing Commission

As the administrative leader of the court system, I stated in my 2010 State of the Judiciary Address that, "[w]e pledge ourselves to the change necessary to stop the revolving door.[19] I see a day when someone breaks the law, that he or she will go before a judge committed to fixing people rather than filling prisons, a judge empowered by the legislature to do just that."[20]

In an effort to make that pledge a reality, court leaders and the Alabama Legislature have taken many steps. Of enormous significance was the creation of the Alabama Sentencing Commission in 2000.[21] The Sentencing Commission's mission is to review Alabama's criminal justice system and recommend changes that provide just and adequate punishment for crime, improve public safety, address prison overcrowding, and establish a fair and effective sentencing system while providing judges with flexibility in sentencing options and meaningful discretion in imposing sentences.[22]

The Sentencing Commission has determined public safety and crime prevention can best be improved in Alabama by encouraging the use of alternative sentencing options for nonviolent offenders.[23] To reach these goals, the commission adopted voluntary sentencing standards, which the legislature approved in 2006.[24] Since then, the Commission has continued providing recommendations, assistance, and training in implementing the new sentencing guidelines.[25]

Currently, "[o]ne of the most exciting initiatives of the Alabama Sentencing Commission is the Cooperative Community Alternative Sentencing Project,"[26] a project that began in 2007.[27] Funded by the Pew Center on the States, the Cooperative Community Alternative Sentencing Project ("CCASP") is a joint venture of the sentencing commission and the chief justice, with technical assistance provided by Vera Institute of Justice and the Crime and Justice Institute.[28]

Since its inception, the Sentencing Commission was aware that, although Alabama has a number of agencies and government entities involved in community supervision of felony offenders, it lacks an organized, continuous system of community punishment, intermediate criminal sanctioning alternatives, and community supervision.[29] Local district attorneys operate pre-trial diversion programs; circuit courts in the various counties handle the day-to-day operation of drug courts; the Alabama Administrative Office of Courts oversees the Court Referral program, which places criminal defendants in drug treatment programs; county governments operate localized community corrections programs; the Alabama Department of Corrections provides for work release programs; and the Alabama Board of Pardons and Paroles operates probation and parole services.[30] While each of these services is beneficial, the Sentencing Commission has questioned the effectiveness and efficiency of operating these programs as a diffracted system that sometimes duplicates services.[31] Further, Alabama currently has no comprehensive, consistent data collection system for these programs that would aid in determining and improving their effectiveness.[32] The need for proven solutions to Alabama's current lack of a cohesive community punishment system is exacerbated by the current financial crisis.[33] As the Sentencing Commission recognizes, "Alabama cannot afford to duplicate services or provide services to offenders the services will not benefit."[34]

For seven years, the Sentencing Commission attempted through various means to bring the parties together at the state and local levels to address the problems caused by lack of a cohesive system of community supervision of nonviolent felony offenders.[35] Until recently, state efforts on these issues largely failed to actively engage local jurisdictions or substantially correct these problems.[36]

CCASP, however, offers a new and promising approach by encouraging active community involvement at the local level and focusing on evidence-based practices, collaboration among agencies, and coordination of services.[37] Starting in 2010, CCASP has been working with four pilot sites in Alabama that are expected to become models and mentors for other community programs in the state.[38] Currently, the primary goal is for each of the four pilot jurisdictions to actively involve all major criminal justice stakeholders and, through self-examination and meaningful data analysis, collaboration, and cooperation, improve corrections services at the local level.[39] Although CCASP is guided by a state steering committee, a committee of local stakeholders determines the best options for each jurisdiction using evidence-based practices to accomplish proven changes in criminal behavior.[40] By forming local alliances among the agencies supervising offenders in the community, each jurisdiction can define a cohesive model system that establishes a continuum of graduated supervision for the fair, effective, and efficient delivery of services.[41]

Currently, each pilot jurisdiction is testing a comprehensive risk and needs assessment system that could greatly benefit the criminal justice system by (1) determining the risk of reoffending for each convicted offender and (2) suggesting the dynamic factors present for each offender that, if changed, can lower the risk.[42] As the Sentencing Commission notes, "[l]owering the risk of reoffending, of course, increases public safety. By identifying those whose behavior can be changed by addressing needs, and identifying those needs, the criminal justice system can target those offenders most likely to change and identify the services needed to accomplish those changes. The use of the risk and needs assessment system [will] thereby allow the State to more specifically target the best use of its scarce resources."[43]

The ongoing success of the Alabama Sentencing Commission in achieving its mission demonstrates the power of cooperation in providing Alabama with a safer, more cost-efficient criminal justice system. Alabama is moving away from anger- and fear-based "sentencing that ignores cost and effectiveness to evidence-based sentencing that focuses on results."[44]

The Importance and Expansion of Drug Courts and Community Corrections in Evidence-Based Sentencing

We must recognize that although judges possess the power to imprison or not to imprison, it is the legislature and county commissions that have the power to fund or not to fund local alternatives to locking up nonviolent adult or juvenile offenders. This clearly explains why interbranch cooperation is essential to making the public safer and reducing recidivism.

Following the recommendation of the Alabama Sentencing Commission, I made the statewide replication of model drug courts a top priority as chief justice.[45] With the assistance of the legislature and an earmark of $3.5 million for model drug courts, the expansion of this proven method of reducing recidivism has been gratifying. The program has grown from 17 drug courts operating in 23 counties in 2007, to 62 drug courts operating in 58 counties as of February 2011.[46] Alabama judges and district attorneys have chosen to use their power and dedicate time and effort each week in model drug courts. Consequently, they have witnessed firsthand how their "positive coercive power" can transform people's lives.

The expansion and implementation of community corrections programs is also imperative in order to "stop the revolving door."[47] Securing funding—which requires a voluntary partnership between county, state and criminal justice stakeholders—continues to be the most significant challenge. However, thanks to the assistance of Pew Center on the States, Vera Institute of Justice and the Crime and Justice Institute, and the participation of trial judges and local stakeholders, the success of the joint Cooperative Community Alternative Sentencing Project[48] demonstrates the progress that can be made with the cooperation of key parties.

A Mandatory Judicial Conference: Taking Evidence-Based Practices to Alabama's Judges

History was made in 2010. With funding provided by the U.S. Department of Justice's Bureau of Justice Assistance and the State Justice Institute, with support from the Pew Center on the States, I was able to use my power as administrative head of the trial courts to order all judges having jurisdiction over criminal felony offenders to attend a sentencing workshop at the Alabama Judicial College.[49]

The goal was clear. Fifty percent of those "behind the wire" are violent offenders and should be incarcerated for sufficiently long sentences to protect the public and deter others from committing similar crimes. The focus of the mandatory training session was appropriate sentencing for nonviolent offenders. Sentencing judges need to examine their practices, recognize the importance of their gate-keeping function and its impact on public safety, and understand the importance of risk and need factors in determining sentences. Judges also need to have an opportunity to express their concerns, frustrations and ideas concerning community corrections and sentencing matters. A bipartisan group of local and national experts presented Alabama's judges with evidence that sentencing certain lower-risk offenders to mandatory supervision rather than prison does improve public safety.

The success of this training event depended on two elements: an order mandating judges' attendance with a direction to reschedule all cases unless specifically excused, and mandatory tours of four Alabama prisons.[50] The presence of justices and judges from six other states who were themselves experts on the topic of evidence-based sentencing practices was also key to the overall effectiveness of the conference.[51]

During the training session, one question was repeatedly presented to Alabama jurists: Why are you putting criminal offenders behind bars? Is it because you are mad at them or because you are afraid of them?[52] The overwhelming majority of judges had confined hundreds of inmates, a large number of them nonviolent offenders imprisoned for technical violations of probation and repeat nonviolent offenders sentenced under Alabama's Habitual Felony Offender Act.[53] These sentencing decisions were and are made by well-intended judges who lack local sentencing options. Now they sentence having personally seen at least two of Alabama's massively overcrowded correctional institutions.

Although a number of judges initially took umbrage at my order of mandatory attendance—and many of them during training sessions stated quite fervently their opinions, which conflicted with the overall message of the expert presenters—the prison tours were sobering and certainly motivated many to re-evaluate their sentencing

policies. As the Vera Institute of Justice reported following the conference:

"On the second day of the conference, nearly 200 participants boarded buses, received box lunches, and saw for themselves the problems facing the Alabama prison system by touring medium- and maximum-level correctional facilities. For many, it was the first time they stepped inside the places where they send thousands of individuals every year.

"What they saw astonished them: 196 inmates in a bunk house monitored by a single correctional officer. Feeding schedules that require inmates to be served breakfast at 3:30 in the morning. Temperatures that soar over 100 degrees Fahrenheit in the summer, cooled only by fans. In the judges' own words, the visit was life-changing. One judge told Chief Justice Cobb that the tours had a 'tremendous impact' on him. As a result, the week after the conference this judge changed the sentences of two incarcerated individuals to mandatory community corrections supervision."[54]

As a result of the evidence presented at the conference, judges promised to not just consider the voluntary sentencing guidelines, but to apply them in all drug cases. Judges also offered their own recommendations for improvements to Alabama's sentencing laws. In addition, the judges committed to use their "positive coercive power" to establish community corrections programs and model drug courts.

Where Do We Go From Here?

In 2010, the Alabama Legislature enacted several important sentencing reforms. These included enactment of minimum standards for drug courts,[55] an amendment to the Community Punishment and Corrections Act to allow participation in Community Corrections programs of offenders convicted of selling controlled substances,[56] and enactment of the technical violator bill, which limits incarceration in the penitentiary for technical violations of probation.[57]

In addition, before the legislature adjourned, it enacted legislation establishing a bipartisan, interbranch Public Safety and Sentencing Coalition. Among its members are legislators, members of the judiciary, district attorneys, defense lawyers, the Board of Pardons and Paroles, the Sentencing Commission, law enforcement and victims' advocates.[58] The coalition has secured the services of John Speir of Applied Research Services Inc., who has performed a detailed analysis of Alabama's prison population. Speir's study showed the number of felony convictions in Alabama had increased 31 percent since 2001.[59] Similarly, the Alabama Department of Corrections' jurisdictional population has increased 27 percent since 2000, and its in-house population has increased 16 percent since 2000.[60] Although Alabama's overall in-house prison population is approximately 190 percent of designed capacity, three facilities are at 314 percent, 271 percent and 257 percent of designed capacity.[61]

Speir's study has shown that Alabama has a major problem with the revolving door of recidivism. Within the current jurisdictional population of the state Department of Corrections, 40.5 percent have had a previous sentence.[62] Even more staggering is the fact that 24.4 percent of the current prison population had returned to prison within three years of a previous release.[63]

Speir's study also revealed that a significant percentage of Department of Corrections' in-house population are not violent offenders. A ranking of the top 10 offenses for admissions during the 2009 fiscal year included four nonviolent offenses. The number one offense for admission was possession or receipt of a controlled substance.[64] The other nonviolent offenses included in the top 10 were distribution of a controlled substance at number three, third-degree burglary at number four, and first-degree possession of marijuana at number seven.[65]

After being educated as to the drivers of our burgeoning prison population, the coalition has endorsed the following concepts: (1) the creation of a new Class D felony classification and the reclassification of certain drug and property offenses as Class D felonies;[66] (2) revising the valuation threshold for property offenses;[67] (3) restructuring and reclassifying offenses involving marijuana and controlled substances;[68] (4) establishing an earned compliance credit for probationers who comply with the conditions of probation so officers may focus limited resources on those who need more intense supervision;[69] (5) mandatory re-entry supervision for offenders near the end of their sentence;[70] (6) codifying minimum standards for jurisdictions in Alabama, which are emulating Hawaii's Opportunity Probation with Enforcement Program;[71] and (7) amending Alabama's driver's license suspension law to remove certain drug-re-

lated offenses to assist participants in drug court and other rehabilitative programs in mobility.[72]

Currently, "the devil is in the details" as legal experts draft proposed legislation that implement the reforms. Change is never easy, but change is essential. We must modify our laws in a way that enhances public safety and focuses limited tax dollars on programs that reduce recidivism, thereby stopping the revolving door.

Conclusion

As chief justice, clearly I cannot snap my fingers and instantly improve life for the citizens of my state. I can, however, use whatever power or influence I have to encourage meaningful change that is proved to make communities safer. This is not a partisan issue or just a legislative and executive branch issue. It is an issue of enhancing public safety while saving desperately needed state and local funding. I want to encourage leaders of all three branches and of every political persuasion to do as we are doing in Alabama. All of us working together can use our power to transform the lives and communities of those we have taken an oath to protect—"to the best of [our] ability, so help [us] God."[73]

Author's Note

Chief Justice Cobb would like to thank her staff attorney, Elizabeth Bowles, for her invaluable assistance with researching and editing this article. Chief Justice Cobb would also like to thank her Chief of Staff, Scott Mitchell, for his invaluable editorial assistance.

Notes

[1] Roger K. Warren, *The Most Promising Way Forward: Incorporating Evidence-Based Practice Into State Sentencing and Corrections Policies*, 20 Fed. Sent'g Rep. 322, 324 (2008); See generally Hon. Michael A. Wolff, *Lock 'Em Up and Throw Away the Key: Cutting Recidivism by Analyzing Sentencing Outcomes*, 20 Fed. Sent'g Rep. 320, 321 (2008).

[2] Sue Bell Cobb, Chief Justice, Alabama Supreme Court, 2010 State of the Judiciary Address (Jan. 26, 2010), available at *http://216.226.178.196/cdm4/item_viewer.php?CISOROOT=/ADAH&CISOPTR=1733&CISOBOX=1&REC=3* ("I see a day when someone breaks the law—that he will go before a judge committed to fixing people rather than filling prisons, a judge empowered by the legislature to do just that."); Sue Bell Cobb, *Alabama Voices: Coalition Working on Better Strategies*, Anniston Star, Sept. 5, 2010 ("I believe that we need to be about the hard work of fixing people instead of the easy work of filling prisons."), *http://www.annistonstar.com/pages/full_story/push?article-Stopping+the+revolving+door%20&id=9382511*.

[3] J. David Bleich, *Contemporary Halakhic Problems* (1977), 180.

[4] John Hayman and Clara Ruth Hayman, *A Judge in the Senate: Howell Heflin's Career of Politics and Principle* 184 (2001); see also *Ex parte Collins*, [Ms. 1091310, Nov. 24, 2010], __ So. 3d __, __, 2010 WL 4777537, at *4 (Ala. 2010) (discussing the December 1973 ratification of a constitutional amendment revising the entire Judicial Article (Article VI of the Alabama Constitution) and mandating a unified judicial system).

[5] See Ala. Const. 1901 art. VI, § 149 ("The chief justice of the supreme court shall be the administrative head of the judicial system. He shall appoint an administrative director of courts and other needed personnel to assist him with his administrative tasks."); see also Ala. Code 1975 § 12-2-30(a) ("The Chief Justice shall see that the business of the several courts of the state is attended with proper dispatch and that cases, civil and criminal, are not permitted to become congested or delayed, and he shall take care that prisoners are not allowed to remain in the jails without a prompt trial."); Ala. Code 1975 § 12-5-3 ("There shall be a state department to be known as the Department of Court Management. This department shall be specifically charged with the duty of assisting the Chief Justice of the Supreme Court of Alabama in connection with his duties as the chief administrative officer of all the trial courts of this state, the Chief Justice's task of insuring that the business of said courts of the state is attended with proper dispatch and the Chief Justice's task of seeing that the dockets of such courts are not permitted to become congested and that trial of cases, civil and criminal, is not delayed unreasonably.").

[6] Ala. Const. 1901 art. VI, § 146 ("Judges of the supreme court, courts of appeals, circuit court and district court shall be licensed to practice law in this state.").

[7] Ala. Const. 1901 art. VI, § 149 ("Adequate and reasonable financing for the entire unified judicial system shall be provided. Adequate and reasonable appropriations shall be made by the legislature for the entire unified judicial system, exclusive of probate courts and municipal courts.").

[8] Roger K. Warren, *Evidence-Based Sentencing: the Application of Principles of Evidence-Based Practice to State Sentencing Practice and Policy*, 43 U.S.F. L. Rev. 585, 591 (2009); Hon. W.M. Ray Price, Jr., *Chief Justice Delivers 2010 State of the Judiciary Address*, 66 J. Mo. B. 68, 70 (2010) ("Nonviolent offenders need to learn their lesson. I'm not against punishment. ... Putting them in a very expensive concrete box with very expensive guards, feeding them, providing them with expensive medical care, surrounding them with hardened criminals for long periods of time, and separating them from their families who love them and could otherwise help them does not work. Proof is in the numbers: 41.6 percent are back within two years."). See generally Public Safety Performance Project, Pew Center on the States, *One in 31: The Long Reach of American Corrections* (2009); Public Safety Performance Project, Pew Center on the States, *One in 100: Behind Bars in America in 2008* (2008) (providing detailed statistics on the prison populations, recidivism rates, public safety, and financial costs caused by over-reliance on prisons).

[9] Price, see note 8, p. 70.

[10] Public Safety Performance Project, Pew Center on the States, *One in 100: Behind Bars in America in 2008* 5 (2008).

[11] See Press Release, State of Alabama Unified Judicial System, *Chief Justice Sue Bell Cobb Convened Judges from Around the State for Sentencing and Corrections Conference* 2 (Sept. 10, 2010), available at *http://www.alacourt.gov/publications.aspx.*

[12] Public Safety Performance Project, Pew Center on the States, *One in 100: Behind Bars in America in 2008* 14 (2008).

[13] Press Release, State of Alabama Unified Judicial System, *Chief Justice Sue Bell Cobb Convened Judges from Around the State for Sentencing and Corrections Conference* 2 (Sept. 10, 2010) available at *http://www.alacourt.gov/publications.aspx.*

[14] Information obtained from Richard Allen, former Commissioner, Alabama Department of Corrections (Feb. 1, 2011).

[15] Information obtained from Richard Allen, former Commissioner, Alabama Department of Corrections (Feb. 1, 2011).

[16] Press Release, State of Alabama Unified Judicial System, *Chief Justice Sue Bell Cobb Convened Judges from Around the State for Sentencing and Corrections Conference* 2 (Sept. 10, 2010), available at *http://www.alacourt.gov/publications.aspx.*

[17] Price, see note 8, p. 70.

[18] Roger K. Warren, Pew Center on the States, Public Policy Safety Brief No. 8, *Arming the Courts With Research: 10 Evidence-Based Sentencing Initiatives to Control Crime and Reduce Costs* 1 (2009). See generally Roger K. Warren, *Evidence-Based Sentencing: Are We Up to the Task?*, 23 Fed. Sent'g Rep. 153, 153 (2010):

[19] See Roger K. Warren, Pew Center on the States, Public Policy Safety Brief No. 8, *Arming the Courts With Research: 10 Evidence-Based Sentencing Initiatives to Control Crime and Reduce Costs* 1 (2009).

[20] Sue Bell Cobb, Chief Justice, Alabama Supreme Court, 2010 State of the Judiciary Address, 9 (Jan. 26, 2010).

[21] See Ala. Code 1975, § 12-25-1 (creating the Alabama Sentencing Commission).

[22] See Ala. Code 1975 § 12-25-2 (setting forth the purpose of the Alabama Sentencing Commission); see also Alabama Sentencing Commission, *Signs of Progress: 2010 Report* xiii (2010) (describing the mission of the sentencing commission). The Alabama Sentencing Commission 2010 report can be accessed at *http://sentencingcommission.alacourt.gov/publications.html.*

[23] Alabama Sentencing Commission, *Signs of Progress: 2010 Report* xiii (2010).

[24] Ibid; see also Ala. Code 1975 § 12-25-34.1 (approving the initial voluntary sentencing standards recommended by the Sentencing Commission).

[25] See note 23.

[26] Ibid. at 8 (2010).

[27] Ibid.

[28] Ibid at 13. "CCASP is funded by Pew Charitable Trusts and is facilitated through technical assistance provided by the Vera Institute of Justice (Vera) and the Crime and Justice Institute (CJI). The national experts from Vera and CJA helped design the CCASP project and have facilitated

meetings of the State Steering Committee and local steering committees, providing research assistance on various topics to help Alabama come to grips with the State's local supervision issues." Ibid at 13 n.5.

[29] Ibid at 13.

[30] Ibid.

[31] Ibid.

[32] Ibid.

[33] Ibid.

[34] Ibid.

[35] Ibid.

[36] Ibid.

[37] Ibid.

[38] Ibid.

[39] Ibid.

[40] Ibid.

[41] Ibid.

[42] Ibid.

[43] Ibid.

[44] Price, see note 9, at 71.

[45] See Susan Pace Hammill, *An Argument for Providing Drug Courts in All Alabama Counties Based on Judeo-Christian Ethics*, 59 Ala. L. Rev. 1305 (2008).

[46] Information obtained from the Alabama Administrative Office of Courts Court Referral Program (Feb. 1, 2011).

[47] "'We have two choices: we can continue the revolving door of recidivism or we can create policy to mandate evidence-based sentencing.'" Roger K. Warren, *Evidence-Based Sentencing: Are We Up to the Task?*, 23 Fed. Sent'g Rep. 153, 153 (2010) (quoting Bonnie M. Dumania, *One Size Does Not Fit All*, 1 Chapman J. Crim. Just. 21 (2009).

[48] The CCASP program is discussed in detail on the second and third pages of this article.

[49] See generally Press Release, State of Alabama Unified Judicial System, *Chief Justice Sue Bell Cobb Convened Judges from Around the State for Sentencing and Corrections Conference* (Sept. 10, 2010), available at *http://www.alacourt.gov/publications.aspx*; Press Release, State of Alabama Unified Judicial System, *Chief Justice Cobb Bringing Together Judges From Around the State for a Sentencing Workshop* (Sept. 9, 2010), available at *http://www.alacourt.gov/publications.aspx*.

[50] Each conferee visited two of four ADOC facilities located in Elmore County, Alabama: Tutwiler Correctional Facility, Draper Correctional Facility, Staton Correctional Facility, and Elmore Correctional Facility. In September 2010, Tutwiler's designed capacity was 417 beds and it had a population of 729, or an occupancy rate of 178.4 percent. Draper's designed capacity is 656, but in September 2010 it had a population of 1,249, or an occupancy rate of 190.4 percent. Staton has a designed capacity of 508, but in September 2010 it had a population of 1,376, or an occupancy rate of 270.9 percent. Elmore has a designed capacity of 600, but in September 2010 its population was 1,171, an occupancy rate of 195.2 percent. See Alabama Department of Corrections, *Monthly Statistical Report for September 2010* (2010).

[51] Appellate justices and judges, trial court judges, and court administrators from Alaska, Georgia, Idaho, Indiana, Kentucky, and Oklahoma attended the conference.

[52] "Prison, it hardly needs to be said, should be reserved for those whom we really are afraid of, not those we are mad at." Wolff, see note 1 at 321.

[53] See Ala.Code 1975 § 13A-5-9 (Alabama's Habitual Felony Offender Act). In January 2010, there were approximately 1,400 individuals incarcerated in the Alabama Department of Corrections for the technical violation of the conditions of probation (i.e., something other than a new offense).

[54] Alison Shames, Vera Institute of Justice, *In Alabama, a Hard Look at Sentencing Practices*, available at *http://www.vera.org/blog/alabama-hard-look-sentencing-practices*.

[55] See Ala. Code 1975 § 12-3A-1 et seq. (also known as the "Alabama Drug Offender Accountability Act").

[56] See Ala. Act No. 2010-734.

[57] See Ala. Act No. 2010-753.

[58] The Public Safety and Sentencing Coalition is supported with the assistance from the Vera Institute of Justice and the Public Safety Performance Project of the Pew Center on the States.

[59] Allison Shames and John Speir, *Alabama Public Safety and Sentencing Coalition: Policy Framework* (Alabama Interbranch Public Safety and Sentencing Coalition, Working Paper, Jan. 6, 2001) (on file with author).

[60] Ibid.

[61] Ibid.

[62] Ibid.

[63] Ibid.

[64] Ibid.

[65] Ibid.

[66] Ibid.

[67] Ibid.

[68] Ibid.

[69] Ibid.

[70] Ibid.

[71] Ibid.

[72] Ibid.

[73] Ala. Const. 1901, art. XVI, § 279 (setting forth the mandatory oath of office for "all members of the legislature, and all officers, executive and judicial").

About the Author

Hon. Sue Bell Cobb is the first female chief justice of the Alabama Supreme Court. A nationally recognized speaker on public safety and sentencing reform, Sue Bell Cobb became one of Alabama's youngest judges in 1981 when she was appointed to serve as a district judge in Conecuh County, Alabama. While serving as a district judge from 1981–1994, she was known for accepting trial court assignments in 40 Alabama counties. From 1994–2006, Cobb served two terms on the Alabama Court of Criminal Appeals before being elected to her current position as chief justice of the Alabama Supreme Court in 2006. Throughout her nearly 30 year judicial career, Chief Justice Cobb has devoted her time and talent to improving the justice system of Alabama, and has championed juvenile justice and sentencing reforms.

Do Americans Still Value an Independent Judiciary?

By Marsha Ternus
Former Chief Justice of the Iowa Supreme Court

In the November 2010 retention elections in Iowa, out-of-state special interest groups funded a vigorous campaign to oust three justices of the Iowa Supreme Court who had joined in the court's unanimous decision declaring Iowa's defense of marriage act a violation of the equality clause of the Iowa Constitution. The avowed purpose of these groups was to send a message across the country that judges ignore the will of the people at their peril. Intimidation of judges and retaliation against judges who make politically unpopular decisions undermine our Founding Fathers' vision of a society governed by the rule of law. "Judicial independence is the vital mechanism that empowers judges to make decisions that may be unpopular but nonetheless correct. ... And it gives life to the promise that the Rule of Law safeguards the minority from the tyranny of the majority."[1]

Alexander Hamilton said in The Federalist No. 78 that, "[t]he complete independence of the courts of justice" was "essential" in a constitution that limited legislative authority.[2] Without the power of the courts to declare acts of the legislature contrary to the constitution, he suggested, the "rights [and] privileges [reserved to the people] would amount to nothing."[3] Hamilton also recognized that an independent judiciary was necessary to guard the rights of individuals from the will of the majority, who may wish to oppress a minority group in a manner incompatible with a constitutional provision.[4] As he expressed in The Federalist No. 51: "It is of great importance in a republic, not only to guard the society against the oppression of its rulers; but to guard one part of the society against the injustice of the other part."[5] "[I]t is easy to see," Hamilton observed, "that it would require an uncommon portion of fortitude in the Judges to do their duty as faithful guardians of the Constitution, where Legislative invasions of it have been instigated by the major voice of the community."[6]

These underpinnings of judicial independence were recently tested in Iowa. In April 2009, the Iowa Supreme Court issued a decision in *Varnum v. Brien* unanimously declaring Iowa's defense of marriage act violated the equality rights of same-sex couples under the Iowa Constitution.[7] In the next general election, opponents of this decision convinced Iowa voters not to retain three justices of the Iowa Supreme Court based on the justices' role in this decision. Since the election, members of the Iowa legislature have called for the impeachment of the remaining four justices, citing the jus-

tices' participation in the *Varnum* decision as the basis for their removal from the court.[8] The events in Iowa suggest Americans may not value the role an independent judiciary plays in protecting the constitutional rights of all citizens.[9]

The Iowa experience presents the opportunity to reflect on whether Americans still share our Founding Fathers' commitment to the values that shaped our national and state constitutions: The civil rights reserved to all members of our nation, as set forth in the constitution, must be protected from infringement by the government and by the majority, and the most reliable way to ensure these rights are preserved is to create and support an independent judiciary. Before this issue is addressed, it is helpful first to discuss the role of courts in protecting constitutional rights, the scope of the *Varnum* decision and this decision's catalytic effect on the 2010 retention elections in Iowa.

Role of the Courts

America's system of justice is based on the rule of law. The rule of law is a process of governing by laws that are applied fairly and uniformly to all people. Because the same rules are applied in the same manner to everyone, the rule of law protects the civil, political, economic and social rights of all citizens, not just the rights of the most vociferous, the most organized, the most popular or the most powerful. Applying the rule of law is the sum and substance of the work of the courts.

The people of Iowa created a government under the rule of law when they adopted the Iowa Constitution, which sets forth the fundamental rules and principles that govern Iowans and their government. In fact, the Iowa Constitution expressly states: "This constitution shall be the supreme law of the land," and it goes on to say, "any law inconsistent therewith, shall be void."

When a person believes a law adopted by the legislature violates the person's constitutional rights, he or she may challenge the law in court. Upon being called upon to do so, the courts review the law and decide whether it complies with the constitution. Judicial review of the constitutionality of legislative acts is one of the checks and balances in our form of government and has existed in America for more than 200 years.[10]

The duty of courts to determine the constitutionality of statutes does not mean the judicial power is superior to legislative power. Rather, when the will of the legislature expressed in its statutes stands in opposition to the will of the people as expressed in their constitution, the courts must prefer the constitution over the statutes. Thus, regardless of whether a particular result will be popular, courts must, under all circumstances, protect the supremacy of the constitution by declaring an unconstitutional statute void. Only by protecting the supremacy of the constitution can the people be assured the freedoms and rights set out in the constitution will be preserved.

If the majority disagrees with a court ruling interpreting the constitution, there is a process for changing constitutional interpretations the people do not like. That process is to amend the constitution to override the court's decision. In this way, the people always have the last say about the content and meaning of the constitution. As Alexander Hamilton pointed out, however, until the people have amended the constitution, "it is binding upon themselves collectively, as well as individually; and no presumption or even knowledge of [the people's] sentiments, can warrant their representatives in a departure from it."[11]

The *Varnum* Decision

Courts exist to resolve disputes, including disputes between citizens and their government. In *Varnum*, the dispute was between six same-sex couples and a county recorder, the government official responsible for issuing licenses to marry. These couples applied for marriage licenses but were told by the county recorder that a state law prohibited him from issuing licenses to them. The state law upon which the county recorder relied provided that, "[o]nly a marriage between a male

and a female is valid."[12] After the county recorder denied the marriage license applications of these couples, they filed a lawsuit asking that the court order the county recorder to issue the requested licenses. The couples claimed the law upon which the county recorder relied was unconstitutional and unenforceable.

The law at issue in the *Varnum* decision placed limitations on who was eligible to enter into a civil contract created by the legislature. The statute creating this contract provided: "Marriage is a civil contract, requiring the consent of the parties capable of entering into other contracts, except as herein otherwise provided."[13] Thus, the Iowa Supreme Court was asked to consider a law governing a legal contract, not the religious institution of marriage. The court pointed out this distinction in its opinion:

> "Our constitution does not permit any branch of government to resolve ... religious debates and entrusts to courts the task of ensuring government avoids them. The statute at issue in this case does not prescribe a definition of marriage for religious institutions. Instead, the statute declares: 'Marriage is a civil contract' and then regulates that civil contract. Thus, in pursuing our task in this case, we proceed as civil judges, far removed from the theological debate of religious clerics, and focus only on the concept of civil marriage and the state licensing system that identifies a limited class of persons entitled to secular rights and benefits associated with civil marriage.
>
> . . . .
>
> As a result, civil marriage must be judged under our constitutional standards of equal protection and not under religious doctrines or the religious views of individuals."

The constitutional standard applied in *Varnum* was the equality clause Iowans included in their constitution when Iowa became a state. It provides in relevant part: "[T]he general assembly shall not grant to any citizen or class of citizens, privileges or immunities, which, upon the same terms shall not equally belong to all citizens."[14] When the court determined the legislature's restriction of the privileges[15] that flow from civil marriage to a limited class of citizens violated the plaintiffs' equality rights, the court performed its constitutional duty by declaring the statute void. Then, as is customary when a party proves its claim, the court granted the plaintiffs the relief they sought—an order that the county recorder could not rely on the unconstitutional restriction on the individuals who could obtain a marriage license and was, therefore, obligated to issue licenses to the six same-sex couples who brought the lawsuit.

The Retention Election

In the 2010 general election that followed the 2009 *Varnum* decision, three members of the Iowa Supreme Court were on the ballot for retention. In retention elections, a judge runs unopposed and voters simply choose whether to retain the judge for another term.[16] Politics had played no role in prior retention elections, and Iowa judges had not found it necessary to form campaign committees, to engage in fundraising or to campaign in any manner.

The 2010 retention elections were very different. Iowa For Freedom, a project of Mississippi-based AFA Action Inc., targeted the justices on the ballot. It claimed, "the Iowa Supreme Court clearly stepped out of its constitutional boundaries and imposed its will on the people of Iowa ... by declaring Iowa to be a 'same-sex' marriage state."[17] The avowed purpose of ousting the three justices was to send a message "in Iowa and across the country [that] [t]he ruling class ignores the people at its peril."[18] Iowa For Freedom and its campaign were heavily funded by out-of-state special interest groups, which together significantly outspent groups supporting the justices on the retention ballot.[19] In the end, the three justices were not retained because a majority of Iowans voting in the election were persuaded the court had exceeded its proper role.

Threat to an Independent Judiciary

An Iowa statute requires judges to take an oath before assuming their position. In this oath, judges promise to "support the Constitution of the United States and the Constitution of the State of Iowa," and, "without fear, favor, affection, or hope of reward, [and] to the best of their knowledge and ability, administer justice according to the law, equally to the rich and the poor."[20] Following this oath sometimes leads to unpopular decisions, as demonstrated by the *Varnum* decision and its aftermath.

Dealing with controversial issues has always been part of being a judge, and, certainly, public debate about the merits of court decisions is a healthy aspect of a democratic society. But what message is sent when a retention election is used as a referendum on a particular court decision?

Clearly, as noted above, the message intended in Iowa was that courts should rule in accordance with public opinion.[21] In fact, opponents of the *Varnum* decision justified their attack on the judiciary by arguing justices must be held accountable to the people when the court makes a decision the people do not like. A Minnesota judge responded to similar contentions with this observation:

> "It might sound good to have judges 'accountable to the people.' But which people? Should judges be accountable to those who shout the loudest or make the most threats? Should judges be accountable to the majority? If so, what happens to the rights of the minority? And what happens to a judge's responsibility to uphold the law and the Constitution? When a judge starts to worry about who [the judge] will please or displease with a ruling, then we cease to be a government based on law."[22]

In view of what happened in Iowa, we must ask ourselves whether we still believe in the rule of law and an impartial judiciary. We will have neither if we expect judges to rule on the basis of public opinion or the views of special interest groups. Of course, applying the rule of law in a fair and impartial manner does not mean everyone will agree with court decisions or that courts are immune from error. But it does mean courts are accountable to the law and, above all else, accountable to the people's constitution, and in this way, courts are always accountable to the people.

Conclusion

At the end of the day, the debate about controversial court decisions and the judges who make them boils down to a simple question: What kind of court system do Americans want? A court system that issues rulings based upon public opinion polls, campaign contributions and political intimidation, or a court system that issues impartial rulings based upon the rule of law?

If we as Americans value the rule of law and reject a society controlled by the tyranny of the majority, we must act as if we do. Efforts to intimidate the judiciary and to turn judges into politicians in robes undermine fair and impartial justice and will, over time, destroy the ability and willingness of judges "to do their duty as faithful guardians of the Constitution." Only through an unwavering commitment to an independent judiciary can we assure future generations that they too will enjoy a society governed by the rule of law.

Notes

[1] Sandra Day O'Connor, *Judicial Accountability Must Safeguard, Not Threaten, Judicial Independence: An Introduction*, 86 Denv. U. L. Rev. 1, 1 (2008), available at *http://law.du.edu/documents/denver-university-law-review/v86_i1_oconnor.pdf*.

[2] The Federalist No. 78, at 426 (Alexander Hamilton) (E.H. Scott ed., 2002).

[3] *Ibid*.

[4] *Ibid*. at 428–29.

[5] The Federalist No. 51 (Alexander Hamilton), *supra* note 2, at 288.

[6] The Federalist No. 78 (Alexander Hamilton), *supra* note 2, at 429.

[7] *Varnum v. Brien*, 763 N.W.2d 862, 906 (Iowa 2009) ("Iowa Code section 595.2 denies gay and lesbian people the equal protection of the law promised by the Iowa Constitution."), available at *http://www.iowacourts.gov/Supreme_Court/Recent_Opinions/20090403/07-1499.pdf*.

[8] Jason Clayworth, Blog, "Judges Did Commit Malfeasance and Should Be Impeached, Rep Says," *Des Moines Register*, Jan. 17, 2011, available at *http://blogs.desmoinesregister.com/dmr/index.php/2011/01/17/state-rep-judges-did-commit-malfeasance-and-should-be-impeached/*.

[9] This suggestion is not limited to the Iowans who voted in the 2010 retention election. As noted later in this article, nearly all the funding for the anti-retention effort came from outside of Iowa. In addition, several national politicians visited Iowa in the months leading up to the election and expressed their support for the campaign to oust the Iowa justices for the justices' role in the *Varnum* decision.

[10] "Checks and balances" is a "[s]ystem of overlapping the powers of the Legislative, Executive, and Judicial branches to permit each branch to check the actions of the others." Vocabulary for *Marbury v. Madison*, at 1, *http://www.uscourts.gov/EducationalResources/ConstitutionResources/LegalLandmarks/VocabularyForMarburyVMadison.aspx*. The United States Supreme Court's decision in *Marbury v. Madison*, 5 U.S. (1 Cranch) 137, 177, 2 L. Ed. 60, 73 (1803), established that the Supreme Court has the power to determine the constitutionality of the acts of the other two branches of government.

[11] The Federalist No. 78 (Alexander Hamilton), *supra* note 2, at 429.

[12] Iowa Code § 595.2(1) (2009).

[13] Iowa Code § 595.1A (2009).

[14] Iowa Const. art. I, § 6.

[15] See *Varnum*, 763 N.W.2d at 902-03 n.28 (noting the plaintiffs identified over two hundred Iowa statutes creating rights or privileges affected by civil-marriage status).

[16] Iowa Const. art. V, § 17 (adopted 1962). Depending on the year of appointment, there may be one or more justices on the ballot at any general election; some years there are none.

[17] Bob Vander Plaats, *All Power is Inherent in the People* (October 20, 2010), *http://iowaforfreedom.com/news/all_power_is_inherent_in_the_people-1/*. Mr. Vander Plaats was the state chair of Iowa For Freedom.

[18] Bob Vander Plaats, *Lawless Judges Deserve to Lose Jobs* (August 26, 2010), *http://iowaforfreedom.com/news/lawless_judges_deserve_to_lose_jobs_/*; see also Andy Kopsa, "Anti-Retention Leaders: Iowa Just the Start of National Gay Marriage Battle," *Iowa Independent* (Oct. 29, 2010), *http://iowaindependent.com/46519/anti-retention-leaders-iowa-just-the-start-of-gay-marriage-battle*.

[19] See Andy Kopsa, "National Anti-Gay Groups Unite to Target Iowa Judges," *Iowa Independent* (Oct. 21, 2010) (listing Mississippi-based American Family Association, Washington, D.C.-based Family Research Council, Arizona-based Alliance Defense Fund, Georgia-based Faith & Freedom Coalition and New Jersey-based National Organization for Marriage as providing "direct funding or in-kind legal and promotional support … to oust the justices"),*http://iowaindependent.com/45701/national-anti-gay-groups-unite-to-target-iowa-judges*; see also Iowa Ethics and Campaign Disclosure Board Web Reporting System, available at *https://webapp.iecdb.iowa.gov/PublicView/?d=IndepExpend%2f2010*.

[20] Iowa Code § 63.6 (2009). Similarly, Iowa's rules governing judges' conduct state: "A judge shall not be swayed by public clamor or fear of criticism." Iowa Code of Judicial Conduct r. 51:2.4(A).

[21] Of course, if public opinion were the standard by which judges should make decisions, the United States Supreme Court's 1954 decision in *Brown v. Board of Education* would probably have had a different outcome. See *Brown v. Board of Educ.*, 347 U.S. 483, 74 S. Ct. 686, 98 L. Ed. 873 (1954) (declaring segregation in public schools unconstitutional). Retired United States Supreme Court Justice Sandra Day O'Connor has observed that this "unpopular decision" "provoked a firestorm of criticism in much of the country." O'Connor, *supra* note 1, at 3. She has also called the *Brown* decision "an exercise of accountability to the Rule of Law over the popular will." *Id*.

[22] George Harrelson, *Marshall Independent* (July 8–9, 2006). Justice O'Connor has expressed a similar opinion: "The law sometimes demands unpopular outcomes, and a judge who is forced to weigh what is popular rather than focusing solely on what the law demands has lost some independence and impartiality." Elaine E. Bucklo and Jeffrey Cole, *Thoughts on Safeguarding Judicial Independence: An Interview with Justice Sandra Day O'Connor*, 35 Litig. 6, 7 (2009).

About the Author

Marsha K. Ternus was appointed from private law practice to the Iowa Supreme Court in 1993 and was selected by her peers to serve as the court's first woman chief justice in 2006. After serving more than seventeen years on the court, her term expired on December 31, 2010, after voters failed to retain her and two of her colleagues in the 2010 retention election. Chief Justice Ternus has returned to the private practice of law.

Table 5.1
STATE COURTS OF LAST RESORT

State or other jurisdiction	Name of court	Justices chosen (a) — At large	By district	No. of judges (b)	Term (in years) (c)	Chief justice — Method of selection	Chief justice — Term of office for chief justice
Alabama	S.C.	★		9	6	Non-partisan popular election	6 years
Alaska	S.C.	★		5	10	By court	3 years
Arizona	S.C.	★		5	6	By court	5 years
Arkansas	S.C.	★		7	8	Non-partisan popular election	8 years
California	S.C.	★		7	12	Appointed by governor	12 years
Colorado	S.C.	★		7	10	By court	Indefinite
Connecticut	S.C.	★		7	8	Gubernatorial appointment from judicial nominating commission with consent of legislature	8 years
Delaware	S.C.	★		5	12	Appointed by governor	12 years
Florida	S.C.	(d)		7	6	By court	2 years
Georgia	S.C.	★		7	6	By court	2 years
Hawaii	S.C.	★		5	10	Gubernatorial appointment from judicial nominating commission with consent of legislature	10 years
Idaho	S.C.	★		5	6	By court	4 years
Illinois	S.C.		★	7	10	By court	3 years
Indiana	S.C.	★		5	10 (e)	Judicial nominating commission appointment	5 years
Iowa	S.C.	★		7	8	By court	8 years
Kansas	S.C.	★		7	6	Rotation by seniority	Indefinite
Kentucky	S.C.		★	7	8	By court	4 years
Louisiana	S.C.		★	7	10	By seniority of service	Duration of service
Maine	S.J.C.	★		7	7	Appointed by governor	7 years
Maryland	C.A.		★	7	10	Appointed by governor	Indefinite
Massachusetts	S.J.C.	★		7	To age 70	Appointed by governor (f)	To age 70
Michigan	S.C.	★		7	8	By court	2 years
Minnesota	S.C.	★		7	6	Gubernatorial appointment	6 years
Mississippi	S.C.		★	9	8	By seniority of service	Duration of service
Missouri	S.C.	★		7	12	By court	2 years
Montana	S.C.	★		7	8	Non-partisan popular election	8 years
Nebraska	S.C.	★(g)	★(g)	7	6 (h)	Appointed by governor from Judicial Nominating Commission	Duration of service
Nevada	S.C.	★		7	6	Rotation	2 years (i)
New Hampshire	S.C.	★		5	5	Seniority	5 years
New Jersey	S.C.	★		7	7 (j)	Gubernatorial appointment with consent of the legislature	Duration of service
New Mexico	S.C.	★		5	8	By court	2 years
New York	C.A.	★		7	14	Appointed by governor from Judicial Nomination Commission	14 years
North Carolina	S.C.	★		7	8	Non-partisan popular election	8 years
North Dakota	S.C.	★		5	10	By Supreme and district court judges	5 years (k)
Ohio	S.C.	★		7	6	Popular election (l)	6 years
Oklahoma	S.C.		★	9	6	By court	Duration of service
Oklahoma	C.C.A.		★	5	6	By court	5 years
Oregon	S.C.	★		7	6	By court	6 years
Pennsylvania	S.C.	★		7	10	Seniority	6 years
Rhode Island	S.C.	★		5	Life	Appointed by governor from Judicial Nominating Commission	Duration of term
South Carolina	S.C.	★		5	10	Legislative appointment	Life

See footnotes at end of table.

STATE COURTS OF LAST RESORT — Continued

State or other jurisdiction	Name of court	Justices chosen (a)		No. of judges (b)	Term (in years) (c)	Chief justice	
		At large	By district			Method of selection	Term of office for chief justice
South Dakota	S.C.	★(m)	★(m)	5	8	By court	4 years
Tennessee	S.C.	★		5	8	By court	4 years
Texas	S.C.	★		9	6	Partisan election	6 years
Texas	C.C.A.	★		9	6	Partisan election	6 years (n)
Utah	S.C.	★		5	10 (o)	By court	4 years
Vermont	S.C.	★		5	6	Appointed by governor from Judicial Nomination Commission, with consent of the legislature	6 years
Virginia	S.C.	★		7	12	Seniority	4 years
Washington	S.C.	★		9	6	By court	4 years
West Virginia	S.C.A.	★		5	12	Seniority	1 year
Wisconsin	S.C.	★		7	10	Seniority	Until declined
Wyoming	S.C.	★		5	8	By court	4 years
Dist. of Columbia	C.A.	★		9	15	Judicial Nominating Commission appointment	4 years
Puerto Rico	S.C.	★		7	To age 70	Gubernatorial appointment with consent of the legislature	To age 70

Sources: *State Court Organization, 2004*, U.S. Department of Justice Statistics, National Center for State Courts, March 2011.

Key:
S.C. — Supreme Court
S.C.A. — Supreme Court of Appeals
S.J.C. — Supreme Judicial Court
C.A. — Court of Appeals
C.C.A. — Court of Criminal Appeals
H.C. — High Court
★ — Yes

(a) See Chapter 5 table entitled, "Selection and Retention of Appellate Court Judges," for details.
(b) Number includes chief justice.
(c) The initial term may be shorter. See Chapter 5 table entitled, "Selection and Retention of Appellate Court Judges," for details.
(d) Regional (5). Statewide (2). Regional based on District of Appeal.
(e) Initial term is two years; retention 10 years.

(f) Chief Justice, in the appellate courts, is a separate judicial office from that of an Associate Justice. Chief Justices are appointed, until age 70, by the Governor with the advice and consent of the Executive (Governor's) Council.
(g) Chief justice chosen statewide; associate judges chosen by district.
(h) More than three years for first election and every six years thereafter.
(i) The term may be split between eligible justices.
(j) Followed by tenure. All judges are subject to gubernatorial reappointment and consent by the Senate after and initial seven-year term; thereafter, they may serve until mandatory retirement at age 70.
(k) Or expiration of term, whichever is first.
(l) Party affiliation is not included on the ballot in the general election, but candidates are chosen through partisan primary nominations.
(m) Initially chosen by district; retention determined statewide.
(n) Presiding judge of Court of Criminal Appeals.
(o) The initial term of appointment is until the next general election immediately following the third year from the time of the initial appointment.

Table 5.2
STATE INTERMEDIATE APPELLATE COURTS AND GENERAL TRIAL COURTS: NUMBER OF JUDGES AND TERMS

State or other jurisdiction	Intermediate appellate court			General trial court		
	Name of court	No. of judges	Term (years)	Name of court	No. of judges	Term (years)
Alabama	Court of Criminal Appeals	5	6	Circuit Court	143	6
	Court of Civil Appeals	5	6			
Alaska	Court of Appeals	3	8	Superior Court	49	6 (a)
Arizona	Court of Appeals	22	6	Superior Court	174	4
Arkansas	Court of Appeals	12	8	Chancery/Probate Court and Circuit Court	118	6
California	Courts of Appeal	105	12	Superior Court	2,022	6
Colorado	Court of Appeals	22	8	District Court	153	6 (b)
Connecticut	Appellate Court	10	8	Superior Court	180	8
Delaware	...	...	...	Superior Court	19	12
				Court of Chancery	5	12
Florida	District Courts of Appeals	61	6	Circuit Court	599	6
Georgia	Court of Appeals	12	6	Superior Court	202	4
Hawaii	Intermediate Court of Appeals	6	10	Circuit Court	46	10
Idaho	Court of Appeals	4	6	District Court	43	4
Illinois	Appellate Court	54	10	Circuit Court	510	6
Indiana	Court of Appeals	15	12 (c)	Superior Court, Probate Court and Circuit Court	308	6
Iowa	Court of Appeals	9	6	District Court	348 (d)	6 (e)
Kansas	Court of Appeals	15	4	District Court	243 (f)	4
Kentucky	Court of Appeals	14	8	Circuit Court	95	8
Louisiana	Courts of Appeal	53 (g)	10	District Court	236	6
Maine	...	...	...	Superior Court	17	7
Maryland	Court of Special Appeals	13	10	Circuit Court	153	15
Massachusetts	Appeals Court	28 (h)	To age 70	Superior Court	82	To age 70
Michigan	Court of Appeals	28	6	Circuit Court	221	6
Minnesota	Court of Appeals	19	6	District Court	281	6
Mississippi	Court of Appeals	10	8	Circuit Court	51	4
Missouri	Court of Appeals	32	12	Circuit Court	369 (i)	6 (j)
Montana	...	...	...	District Court	43 (k)	6
Nebraska	Court of Appeals	6	3 (l)	District Court	55	6 (m)
Nevada	...	...	...	District Court	64	6
New Hampshire	...	...	...	Superior Court	24	To age 70
New Jersey	Appellate Division of Superior Court	35	7 (n)	Superior Court	411	7 (o)
New Mexico	Court of Appeals	10	8	District Court	89	6
New York	Appellate Division of Supreme Court	56	5 (p)	Supreme Court	385	14
	Appellate Terms of Supreme Court	(q)	...	County Court	129	10
North Carolina	Court of Appeals	15	8	Superior Court	111 (r)	8 (s)
North Dakota	Temporary Court of Appeals	3 (ff)	1 (gg)	District Court	42	6
Ohio	Courts of Appeal	68	6	Court of Common Pleas	391	6

See footnotes at end of table.

STATE INTERMEDIATE APPELLATE COURTS AND GENERAL TRIAL COURTS: NUMBER OF JUDGES AND TERMS—Continued

State or other jurisdiction	Intermediate appellate court			General trial court		
	Name of court	No. of judges	Term (years)	Name of court	No. of judges	Term (years)
Oklahoma	Court of Appeals	12	6	District Court	241 (t)	4 (u)
Oregon	Court of Appeals	10	6	Circuit Court	173	6
				Tax Court	7	6
Pennsylvania	Superior Court	23 (v)	10	Court of Common Pleas	521 (x)	10
	Commonwealth Court	9 (w)	10			
Rhode Island	…	…	…	Superior Court	27 (y)	Life
South Carolina	Court of Appeals	9	6	Circuit Court	46 (aa)	6
South Dakota	…	…	…	Circuit Court	39	8
Tennessee	Court of Appeals	12	8	Chancery Court	34	8
	Court of Criminal Appeals	12	8	Circuit Court	85	8
				Criminal Court	33	8
				Probate Court	2	8
Texas	Courts of Appeal	80	6	District Court	444	4
Utah	Court of Appeals	7	6 (aa)	District Court	103 (bb)	6 (cc)
Vermont	…	…	…	Superior Court and District Court	42 (cc)	6
Virginia	Court of Appeals	11	8	Circuit Court	157	8
Washington	Courts of Appeal	25	6	Superior Court	176	4
West Virginia	…	…	…	Circuit Court	65	8
Wisconsin	Court of Appeals	16	6	Circuit Court	246	6
Wyoming	…	…	…	District Court	21	6
Dist. of Columbia	…	…	…	Superior Court	62	15
Puerto Rico	Circuit Court of Appeals	39	16	Court of First Instance	326 (dd)	12 (ee)

Sources: State Court Organization, 2004, U.S. Department of Justice Statistics, update from the National Center for State Courts, March 2011.

Key:

… — Court does not exist in jurisdiction or not applicable.

(a) The initial term for Superior Court judges is three years.

(b) The initial term for District Court, Denver Probate Court, Denver Juvenile Court and County Court judges is two years.

(c) Two years initial; 10 years retention.

(d) The number of District Court judges includes associate judges and magistrates.

(e) The initial term for District judges is at least one year. Associate judges serve a term of four years with an initial term of at least one year, and magistrate judges serve a term of four years.

(f) The number of District Court judges includes magistrates.

(g) The Courts of Appeal have 55 authorized judicial positions.

(h) The Appeals Court has 25 authorized judicial positions. The judges of the Appeals Court are assisted by the services on recall of several retired judges.

(i) The number of Circuit Court judges includes associate judges.

(j) Associate Circuit judges serve a term of four terms.

(k) There are actually 43 District Court judges. Three of those judges serve the Water Court and are included in the data for that court.

(l) More than three years for first election and retention is every six years thereafter.

(m) The initial term is for three years but not more than five years.

(n) Followed by tenure. All judges are subject to gubernatorial reappointment and consent by the Senate after an initial seven-year term; thereafter, they may serve until mandatory retirement at age 70.

(o) After an initial seven-year term, the reapportionment term for Superior and Tax Court judges is open-ended until mandatory retirement at age 70.

(p) Or duration.

(q) Appellate Terms of the Supreme Court have been established within the First and Second Departments of the Appellate Division. Data for the Appellate Terms are not included in the information presented here.

(r) The number of Superior Court judges includes special judges.

(s) Special judges serve a term of four years.

(t) The number of District Court judges includes associate judges and special judges.

(u) District and associate judges serve four-year terms; special judges serve at pleasure.

(v) The Superior Court has 15 authorized judicial positions. The judges of the Superior Court are assisted by senior judges specially appointed by the Supreme Court.

(w) The judges of the Commonwealth Court are assisted by senior judges specially appointed by the Supreme Court. Also, senior Common Pleas Court judges occasionally serve on the Commonwealth Court.

(x) These numbers include both active and senior judges.

(y) The number of judges includes magistrates.

(aa) Four to five judges are currently working as active retired judges.

(bb) Effective 2011, the Family, District, and Probate Courts were combined into the Superior Court.

(cc) The initial term of appointment is until the next general election immediately following the third year from the time of the initial appointment.

(dd) The number of Court of First Instance judges includes Municipal Division judges.

(ee) Municipal judges serve a term of eight years.

(ff) The supreme court may provide for the assignment of active or retired district court judges, retired justices of the supreme court, and lawyers, to serve on three-judge panels.

(gg) Assignments are for a specified time, not to exceed one year or the completion of one or more cases on the docket of the supreme court.

Table 5.3
QUALIFICATIONS OF JUDGES OF STATE APPELLATE COURTS AND GENERAL TRIAL COURTS

State or other jurisdiction	Residency requirement				Minimum age		Legal credentials	
	State		Local					
	A	T	A	T	A	T	A	T
Alabama	1 yr.	1 yr.	...	1 yr.	...	...	10 years state bar	5 years state bar
Alaska	5 yrs.	5 yrs.	...	...	...	...	8 years practice	5 years practice
Arizona	10 yrs. (a)	5 yrs.	(b)	1 yr.	(e)	30	(c)	(d)
Arkansas	2 yrs.	2 yrs.	(b)	...	30	28	8 years practice	6 years licensed in state
California	...	...	...	...	...	...	10 years state bar	10 years state bar
Colorado	★	★	...	★	...	...	5 years state bar	5 years state bar
Connecticut	★	★	...	...	...	...	Licensed attorney	Member of the bar
Delaware	★	★	...	★	...	...	"Learned in law"	"Learned in law"
Florida	★(f)	★	★(f)	★(g)	...	...	10 years state bar	5 years state bar
Georgia	★	3 yrs.	...	...	...	30	7 years state bar	7 years state bar
Hawaii	★	★	...	...	...	...	10 years state bar	10 years state bar
Idaho	2 yrs.	1 yr.	...	...	30	...	10 years state bar	10 years state bar
Illinois	★	★	★	★	...	...	Licensed attorney	...
Indiana	★	1 yr.	...	★	...	...	10 years state bar (h)	...
Iowa	★	★	...	★	...	...	Licensed attorney	Admitted to state bar
Kansas	...	...	...	...	30	...	10 years active and continuous practice (i)	5 years state bar
Kentucky	2 yrs.	2 yrs.	2 yrs.	2 yrs.	...	...	8 years state bar and licensed attorney	8 years state bar
Louisiana	2 yrs.	2 yrs.	2 yrs.	2 yrs.	...	...	5 years state bar	5 years state bar
Maine	...	...	...	...	...	...	"Learned in law"	"Learned in law"
Maryland	5 yrs.	5 yrs.	6 mos.	6 mos.	30	30	State bar member	State bar member
Massachusetts	...	...	...	...	...	...	...	...
Michigan	★	★	...	...	...	...	State bar member and 5 years practice	State bar member
Minnesota	...	...	...	...	...	...	Licensed attorney	Licensed attorney
Mississippi	5 yrs.	5 yrs.	★(j)	...	30	26	5 years state bar	5 years practice
Missouri	9 yrs. (k)	3 yrs. (k)	...	★(k)	30	30	State bar member	State bar member
Montana	2 yrs.	2 yrs.	...	...	...	...	5 years state bar	5 years state bar
Nebraska	3 yrs.	★	★	★	30	30	5 years practice	5 years practice
Nevada	2 yrs.	2 yrs.	...	...	25	25	State bar member (l)	2 years state bar member and 10 years practice
New Hampshire	...	...	...	...	...	...	...	...
New Jersey	...	(m)	...	(m)	...	...	Admitted to practice in state for at least 10 years	10 years practice of law
New Mexico	3 yrs.	3 yrs.	...	★	35	35	10 years practice and/or current state judge	6 years active practice
New York	★	★	...	...	...	18	10 years state bar	10 years state bar
North Carolina	...	★	...	(n)	...	...	State bar member	State bar member
North Dakota	★	★	...	★	...	...	License to practice law	State bar member
Ohio	★	★	...	★	...	...	6 years practice	6 years practice
Oklahoma	★	(o)	1 yr.	★	30	...	5 years state bar	(p)
Oregon	3 yrs.	3 yrs.	...	1 yr.	...	...	State bar member	State bar member
Pennsylvania	1 yr.	★	...	1 yr.	...	...	State bar member	State bar member
Rhode Island	...	...	...	...	21	...	License to practice law	State bar member
South Carolina	5 yrs.	5 yrs.	...	(q)	32	32	8 years state bar	8 years state bar
South Dakota	★	★	★	★	...	...	State bar member	State bar member
Tennessee	5 yrs.	5 yrs.	★(r)	1 yr.	35	30	Qualified to practice law	Qualified to practice law
Texas	★	...	...	2 yrs.	35	25	(s)	(t)
Utah	5 yrs.	3 yrs.	...	★	30	25	Admitted to practice law	Admitted to practice law
Vermont	...	...	...	...	...	...	5 years state bar	5 years state bar
Virginia	...	★	...	★	...	...	5 years state bar	5 years state bar
Washington	1 yr.	1 yr.	1 yr.	1 yr.	...	...	State bar member	State bar member
West Virginia	5 yrs.	★	...	★	30	30	10 years state bar	5 years state bar
Wisconsin	10 days	10 days	10 days	10 days	...	...	5 years state bar	5 years state bar
Wyoming	3 yrs.	2 yrs.	...	...	30	28	9 years state bar	...
Dist. of Columbia	★	★	90 days	90 days	...	...	5 years state bar	5 years state bar (u)
Puerto Rico	5 yrs.	...	...	...	...	...	10 years state bar	7 years state bar

See footnotes at end of table.

QUALIFICATIONS OF JUDGES OF STATE APPELLATE COURTS
AND GENERAL TRIAL COURTS — Continued

Sources: State Court Organization, 2004, U.S. Department of Justice Statistics, update from the National Center for State Courts, March 2011.

Key:

A — Judges of courts of last resort and intermediate appellate courts.

T — Judges of general trial courts.

★ — Provision; length of time not specified.

... — No specific provision.

N.A.— Not applicable.

(a) For court of appeals, five years.

(b) No local residency requirement stated for Supreme Court. Local residency required for Court of Appeals.

(c) Supreme Court—ten years state bar, Court of Appeals—five years state bar.

(d) Admitted to the practice of law in Arizona for five years.

(e) Court of Appeals minimum age is 30.

(f) The candidate must be a resident of the district at the time of the original appointment.

(g) Circuit court judge must reside within the territorial jurisdiction of the court.

(h) In the Supreme Court and the Court of Appeals, five years service as a general jurisdiction judge may be substituted.

(i) Relevant legal experience, such as being a member of a law faculty or sitting as a judge, may qualify under the 10-year requirement.

(j) Must reside within the district.

(k) At the appellate level must have been a state voter for nine years. At the general trial court level must have been a state voter for three years and resident of the circuit for one year.

(l) Minimum of two years state bar member and at least 15 years of legal practice.

(m) For Superior court: out of a total of 441 authorized judgeships there are 283 restricted Superior court judgeships that require residence within the particular county of assignment at time of appointment and reappointment; there are 158 unrestricted judgeships for which assignment of county is made by the chief justice.

(n) Resident judges of the Superior Court are required to have local residency, but special judges are not.

(o) District and associate judges must be state residents for six months if elected, and associate judges must be county residents.

(p) District Court: judges must be a state bar member for four years or a judge of court record. Associate judges must be a state bar member for two years or a judge of a court of record.

(q) Circuit judges must be county electors and residents of the circuit.

(r) Supreme Court: One justice from each of three divisions and two seats at large; no more than two may be from any grand division. Court of Appeals and Court of Criminal Appeals: Must reside in the grand division served.

(s) Ten years practicing law and judge of a court of record at least 10 years.

(t) District Court: judges must have been a practicing lawyer or a judge of a court in this state, or both combined, for four years.

(u) Superior Court: Judge must also be an active member of the unified District of Columbia bar and have been engaged, during the five years immediately preceding the judicial nomination, in the active practice of law as an attorney in the District, been on the faculty of a law school in the District, or been employed by either the United States or District of Columbia government.

Table 5.4
COMPENSATION OF JUDGES OF APPELLATE COURTS AND GENERAL TRIAL COURTS

State or other jurisdiction	Appellate courts						General trial courts	
	Court of last resort	Chief Justice salaries	Associate Justice salaries	Intermediate appellate court	Chief/Presiding salaries	Judges salaries		Salary
Eastern Region								
Connecticut	Supreme Court	$175,645	$162,520	Appellate Court	$160,722	$152,637	Superior courts	$146,780
Delaware	Supreme Court	194,750	185,050	...	...	...	Superior courts	168,850
Maine	Supreme Judicial Court	138,138	119,476	...	...	...	Superior courts	111,969
Maryland	Court of Appeals	181,352	162,352	Court of Special Appeals	152,552	149,552	Circuit courts	140,352
Massachusetts	Supreme Judicial Court	151,239	145,984	Appellate Court	140,358	135,087	Superior courts	129,694
New Hampshire	Supreme Court	151,477	146,917	...	...	...	Superior courts	137,084
New Jersey	Supreme Court	192,795	185,482	Appellate division of	175,534	175,534	Superior courts	165,000
New York	Court of Appeals	156,000	151,200	Appellate divisions of	148,000	144,000	Supreme courts	136,700
Pennsylvania	Supreme Court	191,876	186,450	Superior Court	181,349	175,923	Courts of common pleas	161,850
Rhode Island	Supreme Court	171,835	156,213	...	...	...	Superior courts	140,642
Vermont	Supreme Court	135,421	129,245	...	...	...	Superior/District/Family	122,867
Regional averages		166,821	156,898		159,753	155,456		141,981
Midwestern Region								
Illinois	Supreme Court	207,066	207,066	Court of Appeals	194,888	194,888	Circuit courts	178,835
Indiana	Supreme Court	151,328	151,328	Court of Appeals	147,103	147,103	Circuit courts	125,647
Iowa	Supreme Court	170,850	163,200	Court of Appeals	153,000	147,900	District courts	137,700
Kansas	Supreme Court	139,310	135,905	Court of Appeals	134,750	131,518	District courts	120,037
Michigan	Supreme Court	164,610	164,610	Court of Appeals	151,441	151,441	Circuit courts	139,919
Minnesota	Supreme Court	160,579	145,981	Court of Appeals	144,429	137,552	District courts	129,124
Nebraska	Supreme Court	142,760	142,760	Court of Appeals	135,622	135,622	District courts	132,053
North Dakota	Supreme Court	133,968	130,228	...	...	...	District courts	119,330
Ohio	Supreme Court	150,850	141,600	Court of Appeals	132,000	132,000	Courts of common pleas	121,350
South Dakota	Supreme Court	120,173	118,173	...	...	...	Circuit courts	110,377
Wisconsin	Supreme Court	152,495	144,495	Court of Appeals	136,316	136,316	Circuit courts	128,600
Regional averages		153,999	149,577		147,728	146,038		131,179
Southern Region								
Alabama	Supreme Court	(a)	(b)	Court of Criminal Appeals	(c)	(d)	Circuit courts	(e)
Arkansas	Supreme Court	156,864	145,204	Court of Appeals	142,969	140,732	Circuit courts	136,257
Florida	Supreme Court	157,976	157,976	District Court of Appeals	150,077	150,077	Circuit courts	142,178
Georgia	Supreme Court	167,210	167,210	Court of Appeals	166,186	166,186	Superior courts	(f)
Kentucky	Supreme Court	140,504	135,504	Court of Appeals	133,044	130,044	Circuit courts	124,620
Louisiana	Supreme Court	157,050	149,572	Court of Appeals	149,570	142,477	District courts	136,544
Mississippi	Supreme Court	115,390	112,530	Court of Appeals	108,130	105,050	Chancery courts	104,170
Missouri	Supreme Court	139,534	137,034	Court of Appeals	128,207	128,207	Circuit courts	120,484
North Carolina	Supreme Court	140,932	137,249	Court of Appeals	135,061	131,531	Superior courts	124,382
Oklahoma	Supreme Court	147,000	137,655	Court of Appeals	132,825	130,410	District courts	124,373
South Carolina	Supreme Court	144,029	137,171	Court of Appeals	135,799	133,741	Circuit courts	130,312
Tennessee	Supreme Court	170,340	165,336	Court of Appeals	162,336	159,840	Chancery courts	154,320
Texas	Supreme Court	152,500	150,000	Court of Appeals	(e)	(g)	District courts	(h)
Virginia	Supreme Court (i)	183,839	178,043	Court of Appeals (j)	168,322	161,650	Circuit courts	158,134
West Virginia	Supreme Court	121,000	121,000	...	...	...	Circuit courts	116,000
Regional averages		149,583	145,106		141,955	138,484		129,770

See footnotes at end of table.

COMPENSATION OF JUDGES OF APPELLATE COURTS AND GENERAL TRIAL COURTS — Continued

State or other jurisdiction	Appellate courts						General trial courts	Salary
	Court of last resort	Chief Justice salaries	Associate Justice salaries	Intermediate appellate court	Chief/Presiding salaries	Judges salaries		
Western Region								
Alaska.............	Supreme Court	189,156	188,604	Court of Appeals	178,188	178,188	Superior courts	174,396
Arizona............	Supreme Court	160,000	155,000	Court of Appeals	150,000	150,000	Superior courts	145,000
California..........	Supreme Court	228,856	218,237	Court of Appeals		204,599	Superior court	178,789
Colorado..........	Supreme Court	142,708	139,660	Court of Appeals	137,201	134,128	District courts	128,598
Hawaii.............	Supreme Court	156,727	151,118	Intermediate Court	145,532	139,924	Circuit courts	136,127
Idaho..............	Supreme Court	121,006	119,506	Court of Appeals	118,506	118,506	District courts	112,043
Montana...........	Supreme Court	115,160	113,964	...	...	...	District courts	106,870
Nevada............	Supreme Court	170,000	170,000	...	...	...	District courts	160,000
New Mexico.......	Supreme Court	125,691	123,691	Court of Appeals	119,406	117,506	District courts	111,631
Oregon............	Supreme Court	128,556	125,688	Court of Appeals	125,688	122,820	Circuit courts	114,468
Utah...............	Supreme Court	147,350	145,350	Court of Appeals	140,750	138,750	District courts	132,150
Washington........	Supreme Court	164,221	164,221	Court of Appeals	156,328	156,328	Superior courts	148,832
Wyoming...........	Supreme Court	126,500	126,500	...			District courts	120,400
Regional averages........		150,494	147,628		107,769	105,923		126,769
Regional averages w/o California........		135,000	133,167		137,937	142,425		130,140
Dist. of Columbia........	Court of Appeals	180,000	179,500	...			Superior courts	169,300
American Samoa........	High Court	125,000	119,000	...			District courts	97,000
Guam.............	Supreme Court	133,000	131,000	...			Superior courts	112,486
No. Mariana Islands.........	Commonwealth Supreme Court	130,000	126,000	...			Superior courts	120,000
Puerto Rico........	Supreme Court	125,000	120,000	Appellate Court	105,000	105,000	Superior courts	90,000
U.S. Virgin Islands........	Territorial Court	186,300	181,300	...	...	...	...	...

Source: National Center for State Courts, July 1, 2010.

Note: Compensation is shown rounded to the nearest thousand, and is reported according to most recent legislation, even though laws may not yet have taken effect. There are other non-salary forms of judicial compensation that can be a significant part of a judge's compensation package. It should be noted that many of these can be important to judges or attorneys who might be interested in becoming judges or justices. These include retirement, disability, and death benefits, expense accounts, vacation, holiday, and sick leave and various forms of insurance coverage.

Key:
(a) Salary range is between $161,002–$201,252.
(b) Salary range is between $160,003–$200,007.
(c) Salary range is between $159,503–$199,378.
(d) Salary range is between $159,003–$198,753.
(e) Salary range is between $119,949–$149,936.
(f) Salary range is between $120,252–$187,352.
(g) Salary range is between $137,500–$145,000.
(h) Salary range is between $125,000–$140,000.
(i) Plus $13,500 in lieu of travel, lodging, and other expenses.
(j) Plus $6,500 in lieu of travel, lodging, and other expenses.

Table 5.5
SELECTED DATA ON COURT ADMINISTRATIVE OFFICES

State or other jurisdiction	Title	Established	Appointed by (a)	Salary
Alabama	Administrative Director of Courts	1971	CJ (b)	(g)
Alaska	Administrative Director	1959	CJ (b)	186,604
Arizona	Administrative Director of Courts	1960	SC	(h)
Arkansas	Director, Administrative Office of the Courts	1965	CJ (c)	108,230
California	Administrative Director of the Courts	1960	JC	(i)
Colorado	State Court Administrator	1959	SC	137,201
Connecticut	Chief Court Administrator (d)	1965	CJ	168,783
Delaware	Director, Administrative Office of the Courts	1971	CJ	126,550
Florida	State Courts Administrator	1972	SC	134,879
Georgia	Director, Administrative Office of the Courts	1973	JC	140,949
Hawaii	Administrative Director of the Courts	1959	CJ (b)	124,708
Idaho	Administrative Director of the Courts	1967	SC	118,506
Illinois	Administrative Director of the Courts	1959	SC	194,888
Indiana	Executive Director, Division of State Court Administration	1975	CJ	116,594
Iowa	Court Administrator	1971	SC	154,300
Kansas	Judicial Administrator	1965	CJ	120,037
Kentucky	Administrative Director of the Courts	1976	CJ	124,620
Louisiana	Judicial Administrator	1954	SC	142,447
Maine	Court Administrator	1975	CJ	111,969
Maryland	State Court Administrator	1955	CJ (b)	142,287
Massachusetts	Chief Justice for Administration & Management	1978	SC	140,358
Michigan	State Court Administrator	1952	SC	(j)
Minnesota	State Court Administrator	1963	SC	(k)
Mississippi	Court Administrator	1974	SC	76,500
Missouri	State Courts Administrator	1970	SC	118,450
Montana	State Court Administrator	1975	SC	99,840
Nebraska	State Court Administrator	1972	CJ	116,389
Nevada	Director, Office of Court Administration	1971	SC	123,783
New Hampshire	Director of the Administrative Office of the Court	1980	SC	117,820
New Jersey	Administrative Director of the Courts	1948	CJ	175,534
New Mexico	Director, Administrative Office of the Courts	1959	SC	120,752
New York	Chief Administrator of the Courts	1978	CJ	147,600
North Carolina	Director, Administrative Office of the Courts	1965	CJ	126,738
North Dakota	Court Administrator (h)	1971	CJ	111,756
Ohio	Administrative Director of the Courts	1955	SC	(l)
Oklahoma	Administrative Director of the Courts	1967	SC	130,410
Oregon	Court Administrator	1971	SC	(m)
Pennsylvania	Court Administrator	1968	SC	171,129
Rhode Island	State Court Administrator	1969	CJ	(n)
South Carolina	Director of Court Administration	1973	CJ	123,453
South Dakota	State Court Administrator	1974	SC	100,000
Tennessee	Director	1963	SC	147,000
Texas	Administrative Director of the Courts (i)	1977	SC	130,000
Utah	Court Administrator	1973	SC	132,150
Vermont	Court Administrator	1967	SC	122,867
Virginia	Executive Secretary to the Supreme Court	1952	SC	165,149
Washington	Administrator for the Courts	1957	SC (e)	142,800
West Virginia	Administrative Director of the Supreme Court of Appeals	1975	SC	122,004
Wisconsin	Director of State Courts	1978	SC	136,316
Wyoming	Court Coordinator	1974	SC	114,234
Dist. of Columbia	Executive Officer, Courts of D.C.	1971	(f)	174,000
American Samoa	Administrator/Comptroller	N.A.	N.A.	N.A.
Guam	Administrative Director of Superior Court	N.A.	CJ	120,000 (o)
No. Mariana Islands	Director of Courts	N.A.	N.A.	N.A.
Puerto Rico	Administrative Director of the Courts	1952	CJ	N.A.
U.S. Virgin Islands	Court/Administrative Clerk	N.A.	N.A.	118,500

Source: National Center for State Courts, July 1, 2010.

Note: Compensation shown is rounded to the nearest thousand, and is reported according to most recent legislation, even though laws may not yet have taken effect. Other information from State Court Administrator websites.

Key:
SC — State court of last resort.
CJ — Chief justice or chief judge of court of last resort.
JC — Judicial council.
N.A. — Not available.
(a) Term of office for all court administrators is at pleasure of appointing authority.
(b) With approval of Supreme Court.

(c) With approval of Judicial Council.
(d) Administrator is an associate judge of the Supreme Court.
(e) Appointed from list of five submitted by governor.
(f) Joint Committee on Judicial Administration.
(g) Salary range is between $100,197 and $152,618.
(h) Salary range is between $109,000 and $179,000.
(i) Salary range is between $192,000 and $211,000.
(j) Salary range is between $109,704 and $148,123.
(k) Salary range is between $97,322 and $150,816.
(l) Salary range is between $125,000 and $145,000.
(m) Salary range is between $96,672 and $157,380.
(n) Salary range is between $112,762 and $125,471.
(o) After supplements: $149,000.

Table 5.6
SELECTION AND RETENTION OF APPELLATE COURT JUDGES

State or other jurisdiction	Name of court	Type of court	Method of selection		Method of retention	Geographic basis for selection
			Unexpired term	*Full term*		
Alabama	Supreme Court	SC	GU	PE	PE	SW
	Court of Civil Appeals	IA	GU	PE	PE	SW
	Court of Criminal Appeals	IA	GU	PE	PE	SW
Alaska	Supreme Court	SC	GN	GN	RE (a)	SW
	Court of Appeals	IA	GN	GN	RE (a)	SW
Arizona	Supreme Court	SC	GN	GN	RE	SW
	Court of Appeals	IA	GN	GN	RE	DS
Arkansas	Supreme Court	SC	GU	NP	NP	SW
	Court of Appeals	IA	GU	NP	NP	DS
California	Supreme Court	SC	GU	GU	RE	SW
	Courts of Appeal	IA	GU	GU	RE	DS
Colorado	Supreme Court	SC	GN	GN	RE	SW
	Court of Appeals	IA	GN	GN	RE	SW
Connecticut	Supreme Court	SC	GNL	GNL	GNL	SW
	Appellate Court	IA	GNL	GNL	GNL	SW
Delaware	Supreme Court	SC	GNL	GNL	GNL	SW
Florida	Supreme Court	SC	GN	GN	RE	DS and SW (b)
	District Courts of Appeal	IA	GN	GN	RE	DS
Georgia	Supreme Court	SC	GN	NP	NP	SW
	Court of Appeals	IA	GN	NP	NP	SW
Hawaii	Supreme Court	SC	GNL	GNL	JN	SW
	Intermediate Court of Appeals	IA	GNL	GNL	JN	SW
Idaho	Supreme Court	SC	GN	NP	NP	SW
	Court of Appeals	IA	GN	NP	NP	SW
Illinois	Supreme Court	SC	CS	PE	RE	DS
	Appellate Court	IA	SC	PE	RE	DS
Indiana	Supreme Court	SC	GN	GN	RE	SW
	Court of Appeals	IA	GN	GN	RE	DS
	Tax Court	IA	GN	GN	RE	SW
Iowa	Supreme Court	SC	GN	GN	RE	SW
	Court of Appeals	IA	GN	GN	RE	SW
Kansas	Supreme Court	SC	GN	GN	RE	SW
	Court of Appeals	IA	GN	GN	RE	SW
Kentucky	Supreme Court	SC	GN	NP	NP	DS
	Court of Appeals	IA	GN	NP	NP	DS
Louisiana	Supreme Court	SC	CS (c)	PE (d)	PE (d)	DS
	Courts of Appeal	IA	SC (c)	PE (d)	PE (d)	DS
Maine	Supreme Judicial Court	SC	GL	GL	GL	SW
Maryland	Court of Appeals	SC	GNL	GNL	RE	DS
	Court of Special Appeals	IA	GNL	GNL	RE	DS
Massachusetts	Supreme Judicial Court	SC	(e)	GNE (f)	(g)	SW
	Appeals Court	IA	(e)	GNE (f)	(g)	SW
Michigan	Supreme Court	SC	GU	NP (h)	NP (h)	SW
	Court of Appeals	IA	GU	NP (h)	NP (h)	DS
Minnesota	Supreme Court	SC	GU	NP	NP	SW
	Court of Appeals	IA	GU	NP	NP	SW
Mississippi	Supreme Court	SC	GU	NP	NP	DS
	Court of Appeals	IA	GU	NP	NP	DS
Missouri	Supreme Court	SC	GN	GN	RE	SW
	Court of Appeals	IA	GN	GN	RE	DS
Montana	Supreme Court	SC	GNL	NP	NP (i)	SW
Nebraska	Supreme Court	SC	GN	GN	RE	SW and DS (j)
	Court of Appeals	IA	GN	GN	RE	DS
Nevada	Supreme Court	SC	GN	NP	NP	SW

See footnotes at end of table.

SELECTION AND RETENTION OF APPELLATE COURT JUDGES — Continued

State or other jurisdiction	Name of court	Type of court	Method of selection		Method of retention	Geographic basis for selection
			Unexpired term	Full term		
New Hampshire	Supreme Court	SC	GE	GE	(k)	SW
New Jersey	Supreme Court	SC	GL	GL	GL	SW
	Superior Court, Appellate Div.	IA	GL	GL (l)	GL (l)	SW
New Mexico	Supreme Court	SC	GN	PE	RE	SW
	Court of Appeals	IA	GN	PE	RE	SW
New York	Court of Appeals	SC	GNL	GNL	GNL	SW
	Supreme Ct., Appellate Div.	IA	GN	GN	GN	SW (m)
North Carolina	Supreme Court	SC	GU	NP	NP	SW
	Court of Appeals	IA	GU	NP	NP	SW
North Dakota	Supreme Court	SC	GN (n)	NP	NP	SW
	Temporary Court of Appeals	IA	(w)	SC (x)	(w)	SW
Ohio	Supreme Court	SC	GU	PE (o)	PE (o)	SW
	Courts of Appeals	IA	GU	PE (o)	PE (o)	DS
Oklahoma	Supreme Court	SC	GN	GN	RE	DS
	Court of Criminal Appeals	SC	GN	GN	RE	DS
	Court of Civil Appeals	IA	GN	GN	RE	DS
Oregon	Supreme Court	SC	GU	NP	NP	SW
	Court of Appeals	IA	GU	NP	NP	SW
Pennsylvania	Supreme Court	SC	GL	PE	RE	SW
	Superior Court	IA	GL	PE	RE	SW
	Commonwealth Court	IA	GL	PE	RE	SW
Rhode Island	Supreme Court	SC	GN	GN	(p)	SW
South Carolina	Supreme Court	SC	LA	LA	LA	SW
	Court of Appeals	IA	LA	LA	LA	SW
South Dakota	Supreme Court	SC	GN	GN	RE	DS and SW (q)
Tennessee	Supreme Court	SC	GN	GN	RE	SW
	Court of Appeals	SC	GN	GN	RE	SW
	Court of Criminal Appeals	IA	GN	GN	RE	SW
Texas	Supreme Court	SC	GU	PE	PE	SW
	Court of Criminal Appeals	SC	GU	PE	PE	SW
	Courts of Appeals	IA	GU	PE	PE	DS
Utah	Supreme Court	SC	GNL	GNL	RE	SW
	Court of Appeals	IA	GNL	GNL	RE	SW
Vermont	Supreme Court	SC	GNL	GNL	LA	SW
Virginia	Supreme Court	SC	GU (r)	LA	LA	SW
	Court of Appeals	IA	GU (r)	LA	LA	SW
Washington	Supreme Court	SC	GU	NP	NP	SW
	Courts of Appeals	IA	GU	NP	NP	DS
West Virginia	Supreme Court of Appeals	SC	GU (s)	PE	PE	SW
Wisconsin	Supreme Court	SC	GN	NP	NP	SW
	Court of Appeals	IA	GN	NP	NP	DS
Wyoming	Supreme Court	SC	GN	GN	RE	SW
District of Columbia	Court of Appeals	SC	(t)	(t)	(t)	SW (u)
Puerto Rico	Supreme Court	SC	GL	GL	(v)	SW
	Court of Appeals	IA	GL	GL	GL	SW

See footnotes at end of table.

SELECTION AND RETENTION OF APPELLATE COURT JUDGES — Continued

Source: Bureau of Justice Statistics, *State Court Organization, 2004* NCJ 212351, Update from the National Center for State Courts, March 2011.

Key:
SC — Court of last resort
IA — Intermediate appellate court
N/S — Not stated
N.A. — Not applicable
AP — At pleasure
CS — Court selection
DS — District
DU — Duration of service
GE — Gubernatorial appointment with approval of elected executive council
GL — Gubernatorial appointment with consent of the legislature
GN — Gubernatorial appointment from judicial nominating commission
GNE — Gubernatorial appointment from judicial nominating commission with approval of elected executive council
GNL — Gubernatorial appointment from judicial nominating commission with consent of the legislature
GU — Gubernatorial appointment
ID — Indefinite
JN — Judicial nominating commission appoints
LA — Legislative appointment
NP — Non-partisan election
PE — Partisan election
RE — Retention election
SC — Court of last resort appoints
SCJ — Chief justice/judge of the court of last resort appoints
SN — Seniority
SW — Statewide

(a) A judge must run for a retention election at the next election, immediately following the third year from the time of initial appointment.

(b) Five justices are selected by region (based on the District Courts of Appeal) and two justices are selected statewide.

(c) The person selected by the Supreme Court is prohibited from running for that judgeship; an election is held within one year to serve the remainder of the term.

(d) Louisiana uses a blanket primary, in which all candidates appear with party labels on the primary ballot. The two top vote-getters compete in the general election.

(e) There are no expired judicial terms. A judicial term expires upon the death, resignation, retirement, or removal of an incumbent.

(f) The Executive (Governor's) Council is made up of nine people elected by geographical area and presided over by the Lieutenant Governor.

(g) There is no retention process. Judges serve during good behavior to age 70.

(h) Candidates may be nominated by political parties and are elected on a nonpartisan ballot.

(i) If the justice/judge is unopposed, a retention election is held.

(j) Chief Justices are selected statewide while Associate Justices are selected by district.

(k) There is no retention process. Judges serve during good behavior to age 70.

(l) All Superior Court judges, including Appellate Division judges, are subject to gubernatorial reappointment and consent by the Senate after an initial seven-year term. Among all the judges, the Chief Justice designates the judges of the Appellate Division.

(m) The Presiding Judge of each Appellate Division must be a resident of the department.

(n) The Governor may appoint from a list of names or call a special election at his discretion.

(o) Party affiliation is not included on the ballot in the general election, but candidates are chosen through partisan primary nominations.

(p) There is no retention process. Judges serve during good behavior for a life tenure.

(q) Initial selection is by district, but retention selection is statewide.

(r) Gubernatorial appointment is for interim appointments.

(s) Appointment is effective only until the next election year; the appointee may run for election to any remaining portion of the unexpired term.

(t) Initial appointment is made by the President of the United States and confirmed by the Senate. Six months prior to the expiration of the term of office, the judge's performance is reviewed by the tenure commission. Those found "well qualified" are automatically reappointed. If a judge is found to be "qualified" the President may nominate the judge for an additional term (subject to Senate confirmation). If the President does not wish to reappoint the judge, the District of Columbia Nomination Commission compiles a new list of candidates.

(u) The geographic basis of selection is the District of Columbia.

(v) There is no retention process. Judges serve during good behavior to age 70.

(w) The supreme court may provide for the assignment of active or retired district court judges, retired justices of the supreme court, and lawyers, to serve on three-judge panels.

(x) There is neither a retention process nor unexpired terms. Assignments are for a specified time, not to exceed one year or the completion of one or more cases on the docket of the supreme court.

Table 5.7
SELECTION AND RETENTION OF TRIAL COURT JUDGES

State or other jurisdiction	Name of Court	Types of court	Method of selection		Method of retention	Geographic basis for selection
			Unexpired term	Full term		
Alabama......................	Circuit	GJ	GU (a)	PE	PE	Circuit
	District	LJ	GU (a)	PE	PE	County
	Municipal	LJ	MU	MU	RA	Municipality
	Probate	LJ	GU	PE	PE	County
Alaska	Superior	GJ	GN	GN	RE (b)	State (c)
	District	LG	GN	GN	RE (d)	District
	Magistrate's Division	N.A.	PJ	PJ	PJ	District
Arizona	Superior	GJ	GN or VA (e)	GN or NP (f)	NP or RE (f)	County
	Justice of the Peace	LJ	CO	PE	PE	Precinct
	Municipal	LJ	CC (g)	CC (g)	CC (g)	Municipality
Arkansas	Circuit	GJ	GU (h)	NP	NP	Circuit
	District	LJ	GU	NP	NP	District
	City	LJ	LD	LD	LD	City
California	Superior	GJ	GU	NP	NP (i)	County
Colorado	District	GJ	GN	GN	RE	District
	Denver Probate	GJ	GN	GN	RE	District
	Denver Juvenile	GJ	GN	GN	RE	District
	Water	GJ	SC (j)	SC (j)	RE	District
	County	LJ	GN	GN (k)	RE	County
	Municipal	LJ	MU	MU	RA	Municipality
Connecticut	Superior	GJ	GNL	GNL	GNL	State
	Probate	LJ	PE	PE	PE	District
Delaware......................	Superior	GJ	GNL	GNL	GNL	State
	Chancery	LJ	GNL	GNL	GNL	State
	Justice of the Peace	LJ	GNL (l)	GNL (l)	GU	County
	Family	LJ	GNL	GNL	GNL	County
	Common Pleas	LJ	GNL	GNL	GNL	County
	Alderman's	LJ	LD	CC	LD	Town
Florida........................	Circuit	GJ	GN	NP	NP	Circuit
	County	LJ	GN	NP	NP	County
Georgia	Superior	GJ	GN	NP	NP	Circuit
	Juvenile	LJ	CS (m)	CS (m)	CS (m)	County/Circuit
	Civil	LJ	GU	PE	PE	County
	State	LJ	GU	NP	NP	County
	Probate	LJ	GU	PE (n)	PE (n)	County
	Magistrate	LJ	LD	LD (o)	LD (o)	County
	Municipal/of Columbus	LJ	MA	Elected	Elected	Municipality
	County Recorder's	LJ	LD	LD	LD	County
	Municipal/City of Atlanta	LJ	MU	MU	LD	Municipality
Hawaii	Circuit	GJ	GNL	GNL	JN	State
	District	LJ	SCJ (p)	SCJ (p)	JN	Circuit
Idaho	District	GJ	GN	NP	NP	District
	Magistrate's Division	LJ	JN (q)	JN (q)	RE	County
Illinois........................	Circuit	GJ	SC	PE	RE	Circuit/County (r)
	Associate Division	N.A.	SC	PE	RE	Circuit/County (r)
Indiana	Superior	GJ	GU	PE (s)	PE (s)	County
	Circuit	GJ	GU	PE (t)	PE (t)	County
	Probate	GJ	GU	PE	PE	County
	County	LJ	GU	PE	PE	County
	City	LJ	GU	PE	PE	Municipality
	Town	LJ	GU	PE	PE	Municipality
	Small Claims/Marion County	LJ	GU	PE	PE	Township
Iowa............................	District	GJ	GN (u)	GN (u)	RE (u)	District
Kansas	District	GJ	GN and PE(v)	GN and PE (v)	RE and PE (v)	District
	Municipal	LJ	MU	MU	MU	City
Kentucky......................	Circuit	GJ	GN	NP	NP	Circuit
	District	LJ	GN	NP	NP	District
Louisiana	District	GJ	SC (w)	PE	PE	District
	Juvenile & Family	GJ	SC (w)	PE	PE	District
	Justice of the Peace	LJ	SC (w)	PE (x)	PE	Ward
	Mayor's	LJ	MA	LD	LD	City
	City & Parish	LJ	SC (w)	PE	PE	Ward

See footnotes at end of table.

SELECTION AND RETENTION OF TRIAL COURT JUDGES — Continued

State or other jurisdiction	Name of Court	Types of court	Method of selection		Method of retention	Geographic basis for selection
			Unexpired term	Full term		
Maine	Superior	GJ	GL	GL	GL	State
	District	GJ	GL	GL	GL	State and District (y)
	Probate	LJ	GU	PE	PE	County
Maryland	Circuit	GJ	GNL	GNL	NP	County
	District	LJ	GNL	GNL	RA	District
	Orphan's	LJ	GU	PE (z)	PE (z)	County
Massachusetts	Superior	GJ	(aa)	GNE (bb)	(cc)	State
	District	LJ	(aa)	GNE (bb)	(cc)	State
	Probate & Family	LJ	(aa)	GNE (bb)	(cc)	State
	Juvenile	LJ	(aa)	GNE (bb)	(cc)	State
	Housing	LJ	(aa)	GNE (bb)	(cc)	State
	Boston Municipal	LJ	(aa)	GNE (bb)	(cc)	State
	Land	LJ	(aa)	GNE (bb)	(cc)	State
Michigan	Circuit	GJ	GU	NP	NP	Circuit
	Claims	GJ	GU	NP	NP	Circuit
	District	LJ	GU	NP	NP	District
	Probate	LJ	GU	NP	NP	District and Circuit
	Municipal	LJ	LD	NP	NP	City
Minnesota	District	GJ	GN	NP	NP	District
Mississippi	Circuit	GJ	GU	NP	NP	District
	Chancery	LJ	GU	NP	NP	District
	County	LJ	GU	NP	NP	County
	Municipal	LJ	LD	LD	LD	Municipality
	Justice	LJ	LD	PE	PE	District in County
Missouri	Circuit	GJ	GU and GN (dd)	PE and GN (ee)	PE and RE (ff)	Circuit/County (gg)
	Municipal	LJ	LD	LD	LD	City
Montana	District	GJ	GN	NP	NP	District
	Workers' Compensation	GJ	GN	GN	RA	State
	Water	GJ	SCJ (hh)	SCJ (hh)	SCJ (ii)	State
	Justice of the Peace	LJ	CO	NP	NP	County
	Municipal	LJ	MU	NP	NP	City
	City	LJ	CC	NP	NP	City
Nebraska	District	GJ	GN	GN	RE	District
	Separate Juvenile	LJ	GN	GN	RE	District
	County	LJ	GN	GN	RE	District
	Workers' Compensation	LJ	GN	GN	RE	District
Nevada	District	GJ	GN	NP	NP	District
	Justice	LJ	CO	NP	NP	Township
	Municipal	LJ	CC	NP	NP	City
New Hampshire	Superior	GJ	GE	GE	(jj)	State
	District	LJ	GE	GE	(jj)	District
	Probate	LJ	GE	GE	(jj)	County
New Jersey	Superior	GJ	GL	GL	GL	County
	Tax	LJ	GL	GL	GL	State
	Municipal	LJ	MA or MU (kk)	MA or MU (kk)	MU	Municipality
New Mexico	District	GJ	GN	PE	RE	District
	Magistrate	LJ	GU	PE	PE	County
	Metropolitan/Bernalillo County	LJ	GN	PE	RE	County
	Municipal	LJ	MU	PE	PE	City
	Probate	LJ	CO	PE	PE	County
New York	Supreme	GJ	GL	PE	PE	District
	County	GJ	GL	PE	PE	County
	Claims	GJ	GNL	GNL	GU	State
	Surrogates'	LJ	GNL	PE	PE	County
	Family	LJ	GNL and MU (ll)	PE and MU (ll)	PE and MU (ll)	County and NYC
	District	LJ	(mm)	PE	PE	District
	City	LJ	Elected	Elected	LD	City
	NYC Civil	LJ	MA (nn)	PE	PE	City
	NYC Criminal	LJ	MA	MA	MA	City
	Town & Village Justice	LJ	LD	LD	LD	Town or Village
North Carolina	Superior	GJ	GU	NP	NP	District
	District	LJ	GU	NP	NP	District

See footnotes at end of table.

SELECTION AND RETENTION OF TRIAL COURT JUDGES — Continued

State or other jurisdiction	Name of Court	Types of court	Method of selection Unexpired term	Method of selection Full term	Method of retention	Geographic basis for selection
North Dakota	District	GJ	GN	NP	NP	District
	Municipal	LJ	MA	NP	NP	City
Ohio	Common Pleas	GJ	GU	PE (oo)	PE (oo)	County
	Municipal	LJ	GU	PE (oo)	PE (oo)	County/City
	County	LJ	GU	PE (oo)	PE (oo)	County
	Claims	LJ	SCJ	SCJ	SCJ	N.A.
	Mayor's	LJ	Elected	PE	PE	City/Village
Oklahoma	District	GJ	GN (pp)	NP (pp)	NP (pp)	District
	Municipal Not of Record	LJ	MM	MM	MM	Municipality
	Municipal of Record	LJ	MU	MU	MU	Municipality
	Workers' Compensation	LJ	GN	GN	GN	State
	Tax Review	LJ	SCJ	SCJ	SCJ	District
Oregon	Circuit	GJ	GU	NP	NP	District
	Tax	GJ	GU	NP	NP	State
	County	LJ	CO	NP	NP	County
	Justice	LJ	GU	NP	NP	County
	Municipal	LJ	CC	CC/Elected	CC/Elected	(qq)
Pennsylvania	Common Pleas	GJ	GL	PE	RE	District
	Philadelphia Municipal	LJ	GL	PE	RE	City/County
	Magisterial District Judges	LJ	GL	PE	PE	District
	Philadelphia Traffic	LJ	GL	PE	RE	City/County
Rhode Island	Superior	GJ	GN	GN	(rr)	State
	Workers' Compensation	LJ	GN	GN	(rr)	State
	District	LJ	GN	GN	(rr)	State
	Family	LJ	GN	GN	(rr)	State
	Probate	LJ	CC	CC or MA	RA	Town
	Municipal	LJ	CC	CC or MA	CC or MA	Town
	Traffic Tribunal	LJ	GN	GN	(rr)	State
South Carolina	Circuit	GJ	LA and GN (ss)(tt)	LA and GN (tt)	LA and GL (tt)	Circuit and State (tt)
	Family	LJ	LA	LA	LA	Circuit
	Magistrate	LJ	GL	GL	GL	County
	Probate	LJ	GU	PE	PE	County
	Municipal	LJ	CC	CC	CC	District
South Dakota	Circuit	GJ	GN	NP	NP	Circuit
	Magistrate	LJ	PJS	PJS	PJS	Circuit
Tennessee	Circuit	GJ	GU	PE (uu)	PE	District
	Chancery	GJ	GU	PE (uu)	PE	District
	Criminal	GJ	GU	PE (uu)	PE	District
	Probate	GJ	(vv)	PE (uu)	PE	District
	Juvenile	LJ	(vv)	PE (uu)	PE	County
	Municipal	LJ	LD	LD (uu)	LD	Municipality
	General Sessions	LJ	MU	PE (uu)	PE	County
Texas	District	GJ	GL	PE	PE	District
	Constitutional County	LJ	CO	PE	PE	County
	Probate	LJ	CO	PE	PE	County
	County at Law	LJ	CO	PE	PE	County
	Justice of the Peace	LJ	CO	PE	PE	Precinct
	Municipal	LJ	CC	LD	LD	Municipality
Utah	District	GJ	(ww)	GNL	RE	District
	Justice	LJ	MM (xx)	MM (xx)	RE and RA (yy)	County/Municipality
	Juvenile	LJ	(ww)	GNL	RE	District
Vermont	Superior (zz)	GJ	GNL	GNL	LA	State
	Judicial Bureau	LJ	PJ	PJ	AP	State
Virginia	Circuit	GJ	GU	LA	LA	Circuit
	District	LJ	CS (aaa)	LA	LA	District
Washington	Superior	GJ	GU	NP	NP	County
	District	LJ	CO	NP	NP	District
	Municipal	LJ	CC	MA/CC	MA/CC (bbb)	Municipality
West Virginia	Circuit	GJ	GU	PE	PE	Circuit
	Magistrate	LJ	PJ	PE	PE	County
	Municipal	LJ	LD	LD	LD	Municipality
	Family	LJ	GU	PE	PE	Circuit

See footnotes at end of table.

SELECTION AND RETENTION OF TRIAL COURT JUDGES — Continued

State or other jurisdiction	Name of Court	Types of court	Method of selection		Method of retention	Geographic basis for selection
			Unexpired term	Full term		
Wisconsin	Circuit	GJ	GU	NP	NP	District
	Municipal	LJ	MU (ccc)	NP	NP	Municipality
Wyoming	District	GJ	GN	GN	RE	District
	Circuit	LJ	GN	GN	RE	Circuit
	Municipal	LJ	MA	MA	LD	Municipality
Dist. of Columbia	Superior	GJ	(ddd)	(ddd)	(ddd)	State (eee)
Puerto Rico	First Instance	GJ	GL	GL	GL	State

Source: Bureau of Justice Statistics, *State Court Organization, 2004* NCJ 212351, Update from the National Center for State Courts, March 2011.

Key:
GJ — General jurisdiction court
LJ — Limited jurisdiction court
N/S — Not stated
N.A.— Not applicable
AP — At pleasure
CA — Court administrator appointment
CC — City or town council/commission appointment
CO — County board/commission appointment
CS — Court selection
DU — Duration of service
GE — Gubernatorial appointment with approval of elected executive council
GL — Gubernatorial appointment with consent of the legislature
GN — Gubernatorial appointment from judicial nominating commission
GNE — Gubernatorial appointment from judicial nominating commission with approval of elected executive council
GNL — Gubernatorial appointment from judicial nominating commission with consent of the legislature
GU — Gubernatorial appointment
JN — Judicial nominating commission appoints
LA — Legislative appointment
LD — Locally determined
MA — Mayoral appointment
MC — Mayoral appointment with consent of city council
MM — Mayoral appointment with consent of governing municipal body
MU — Governing municipal body appointment
NP — Non-partisan election
PE — Partisan election
PJ — Presiding judge of the general jurisdiction court appoints
PJS — Presiding judge of the general jurisdiction court appoints with approval of the court of last resort
RA — Reappointment
RE — Retention election
SC — Court of last resort appoints
SCJ — Chief justice/judge of the court of last resort appoints
(a) The counties of Baldwin, Jefferson, Lauderdale, Madison, Mobile, Shelby, Talladega, and Tuscaloosa use gubernatorial appointment from the recommendations of the Judicial Nominating Commission.
(b) A judge must run for retention at the next election immediately following the third year from the time of the initial appointment.
(c) Judges are selected on a statewide basis, but run for retention on a district-wide basis.
(d) Judges must run for retention at the first general election held more than one year after appointment.
(e) Maricopa and Pima counties use the gubernatorial appointment from the Judicial Nominating Commission process. The method for submitting names for the other 13 counties varies.
(f) Maricopa and Pima counties use the gubernatorial appointment from the Judicial Nominating Commission process. The other 13 counties hold non-partisan elections.
(g) Municipal court judges are usually appointed by the city or town council except in Yuma, where judges are elected.
(h) The office can be held until December 31 following the next general election and then the judge must run in a non-partisan election for the remainder of the term.
(i) If unopposed for reelection, incumbent's name does not appear on the ballot unless a petition was filed not less than 83 days before the election date indicating that a write-in campaign will be conducted for the office.

An unopposed incumbent is not declared elected until the election date. This is for the general election; different timing may apply for the primary election (see Elec. Code §8203).
(j) Judges are chosen by the Supreme Court from among District Court judges.
(k) The mayor appoints Denver County Court judges.
(l) The Magistrate Screening Commission recommends candidates.
(m) Juvenile Court judges are appointed by Superior Court judges in all but one county, in which juvenile judges are elected. Associate judges (formerly referees) must be a member of the state bar or law school graduates. They serve at the pleasure of the judge(s).
(n) Probate judges are selected in non-partisan elections in 66 of 159 counties.
(o) Magistrate judges are selected in nonpartisan elections in 41 of 159 counties.
(p) Selection occurs by means of Chief Justice appointment from the Judicial Nominating Commission with consent of the Senate.
(q) The Magistrate Commission consists of the administrative judge, three mayors and two electors appointed by the governor, and two attorneys (nominated by the district bar and appointed by the state bar). There is one commission in each district.
(r) There exists a unit less than county in Cook County.
(s) Non-partisan elections are used in the Superior Courts in Allen and Vanderburgh counties. Nominating commissions are used in St. Joseph County and in some courts in Lake County. In those courts that use the nominating commission process for selection; retention elections are used as the method of retention.
(t) Non-partisan elections are used in the Circuit Courts in Vanderburgh County.
(u) This applies to district judges only. Associate judges are selected by the district judges and retention is by a retention election. Magistrates are selected and retained by appointment from the County Judicial Magistrate Nominating Commission. The County Judicial Magistrate Nominating Commission consists of three members appointed by the county board and two elected by the county bar, presided over by a District Court judge.
(v) Seventeen districts use gubernatorial appointment from the Judicial Nominating Commission for selection and retention elections for retention. Fourteen districts use partisan elections for selection and retention.
(w) Depending on the amount of time remaining, selection may be by election following a Supreme Court appointment.
(x) Louisiana uses a blanket primary in which all candidates appear with party labels on the primary ballot. The top two vote-getters compete in the general election.
(y) At least one judge who is a resident of the county in which the district lies must be appointed from each of the 13 districts.
(z) Two exceptions are Hartford and Montgomery counties where Circuit Court judges are assigned.
(aa) There are no expired judicial terms. A judicial term expires upon the death, resignation, retirement, or removal of an incumbent.
(bb) The Executive (Governor's) Council is made up of eight people elected by geographical area and presided over by the lieutenant governor.
(cc) There is no retention process. Judges serve during good behavior to age 70.
(dd) Gubernatorial appointment occurs in partisan circuits; gubernatorial appointment from Judicial Nominating Commission takes place in non-partisan circuits.
(ee) Partisan elections occur in some circuits; gubernatorial appointment from the Judicial Nominating Commission with a non-partisan election takes place in others.
(ff) Partisan elections take place in some circuits; retention elections occur in other circuits.

SELECTION AND RETENTION OF TRIAL COURT JUDGES — Continued

(gg) Associate circuit judges are selected on a county basis.

(hh) Selection occurs through Chief Justice appointment from Judicial Nominating Commission.

(ii) Other judges are designated by the District Court judges.

(jj) There is no retention process. Judges serve during good behavior to age 70.

(kk) In multi-municipality, joint, or countywide municipal courts, selection is by gubernatorial appointment with consent of the senate.

(ll) Mayoral appointment occurs in New York City.

(mm) The appointment is made by the County Chief Executive Officer with confirmation by District Board of Supervisors.

(nn) Housing judges are appointed by the Chief Administrator of the courts.

(oo) Party affiliation is not included on the ballot in the general election, but candidates are chosen through partisan primary nominations.

(pp) This applies to district and associate judges; special judges are selected by the district judges.

(qq) The geographic basis for selection is the municipality for those judges that are elected. Judges that are either appointed or are under contract may be from other cities.

(rr) There is no retention process. Judges serve during good behavior for a life tenure.

(ss) The governor may appoint a candidate if the unexpired term is less than one year.

(tt) In addition to Circuit Court judges, the Circuit Court has masters-in-equity whose jurisdiction is in matters referred to them in the Circuit Court. Masters-in-equity are selected by gubernatorial appointment from the Judicial Merit Selection Commission, retained by gubernatorial appointment with the consent of the senate, and the geographic basis for selection is the state.

(uu) Each county legislative body has the discretion to require elections to be non-partisan.

(vv) The selection method used to fill an unexpired term is established by a special legislative act.

(ww) There are no expired terms; each new judge begins a new term.

(xx) Appointment is by the local government executive with confirmation by the local government legislative body (may be either county or municipal government).

(yy) County judges are retained by retention election; municipal judges are reappointed by the city executive.

(zz) Effective 2011, the Family, District, Environmental and Probate Courts were combined into the Superior Court.

(aaa) Circuit Court judges appoint.

(bbb) Full-time municipal judges must stand for non-partisan election.

(ccc) A permanent vacancy in the office of municipal judge may be filled by temporary appointment of the municipal governing body or jointly by the governing bodies of all municipalities served by the judge.

(ddd) The Judicial Nomination Commission nominates for Presidential appointment and Senate confirmation. Not less than six months prior to the expiration of the term of office, the judge's performance is reviewed by the Commission on Judicial Disabilities and Tenure. A judge found "well qualified" is automatically reappointed for a new term of 15 years; a judge found "qualified" may be renominated by the President (and subject to Senate confirmation). A judge found "unqualified" is ineligible for reappointment or if the President does not wish to reappoint a judge, the Nomination Commission compiles a new list of candidates.

(eee) The geographic basis for selection is the District of Columbia.

Table 5.8
JUDICIAL DISCIPLINE: INVESTIGATING AND ADJUDICATING BODIES

State or other jurisdiction	Investigating body	Adjudicating body	Appeals from adjudication are filed with:	Final disciplining body	Point at which reprimands are made public
Alabama	Judicial Inquiry Committee	Court of the Judiciary	Supreme Court	Court of the Judiciary	Filing of the complaint with the Court of the Judiciary
Alaska	Committee on Judicial Conduct	Supreme Court	N.A.	Supreme Court	Filing of recommendation with Supreme Court
Arizona	Commission on Judicial Conduct	Commission on Judicial Conduct	Discretionary with Supreme Court	Supreme Court	Commission on Judicial Conduct determines if there is probable cause to bring formal charges.
Arkansas	Judicial Discipline and Disability Committees	Commission	Supreme Court	Supreme Court	At disposition of case
California	Commission on Judicial Performance	Commission on Judicial Performance	Supreme Court has discretionary review	Commission on Judicial Performance	Upon commission determination (a)
Colorado	Committee on Judicial Discipline	Commission on Judicial Discipline	No appeal	Supreme Court	Adjudication
Connecticut	Judicial Review Council	Judicial Review Council; Supreme Court	Supreme Court	Supreme Court	Public censure is issued at between 10 and 30 days after notice to the judge, provided that if the judge appeals, there is an automatic stay of disclosure.
Delaware	Council on Probate Judicial Conduct; Preliminary Committee of the Court on the Judiciary; Investigatory Committee of the Court on the Judiciary	Council on Probate Judicial Conduct; Court on the Judiciary	Supreme Court; No appeal	Supreme Court; Court on the Judiciary	Upon issuance of opinion and imposition of sanction
Florida	Judicial Qualifications Commission	Judicial Qualifications Commission (b)	No appeal	Supreme Court (c)	Filing of formal charges by Committee with Supreme Court Clerk
Georgia	Judicial Qualifications Commission	Supreme Court	No appeal	Supreme Court	Formal Hearing
Hawaii	Commission on Judicial Conduct	Commission on Judicial Conduct	No appeal	Supreme Court	Imposition of public discipline by Supreme Court
Idaho	Judicial Council	Supreme Court	Supreme Court	Supreme Court	Filing with Supreme Court
Illinois	Judicial Inquiry Board	Courts Commission	No appeal	Courts Commission	Filing of complaint by Judicial Inquiry Board to Courts Commission
Indiana	Judicial Qualifications Committee	Supreme Court	N.A.	Supreme Court	Institution of Formal Proceedings
Iowa	Judicial Qualifications Commission	Judicial Qualifications Commission	Supreme Court	Supreme Court	Application by the commission to the Supreme Court
Kansas	Commission on Judicial Qualifications	Supreme Court	Supreme Court	Supreme Court	Reprimand is published by Supreme Court if approved by Supreme Court.
Kentucky	Judicial Conduct Committee	Judicial Conduct Committee	Supreme Court	Judicial Conduct Committee	Application of judge under investigation
Louisiana	Judiciary Commission	Supreme Court	No appeal	Supreme Court	Filing of formal complaint by commission with Supreme Court
Maine	Committee on Judicial Responsibility and Disability	Supreme Judicial Court	No appeal	Supreme Judicial Court	Filing of report to Supreme Judicial Court

See footnotes at end of table.

JUDICIAL DISCIPLINE: INVESTIGATING AND ADJUDICATING BODIES — Continued

State or other jurisdiction	Investigating body	Adjudicating body	Appeals from adjudication are filed with:	Final disciplining body	Point at which reprimands are made public
Maryland	Commission on Judicial Disabilities	Court of Appeals	N.A.	Court of Appeals	Filing of record by Committee to Court of Appeals
Massachusetts	Commission on Judicial Conduct	Supreme Judicial Court	N.A.	Supreme Judicial Court	After final of formal charges with the Supreme Judicial Court
Michigan	Judicial Tenure Commission	Supreme Court	Supreme Court	Supreme Court	Filing of formal complaint by commission with Supreme Court
Minnesota	Board of Judicial Standards	Supreme Court	No appeal	Supreme Court	Filing of formal charges by Committee with Supreme Court
Mississippi	Commission on Judicial Performance	Supreme Court	N.A.	Supreme Court	Recommendation of Commission to Supreme Court
Missouri	Commission on Retirement, Removal and Discipline	Commission on Retirement, Removal and Discipline	Supreme Court	Supreme Court	Filing of recommendation by Committee to Supreme Court
Montana	Judicial Standards Commission	Supreme Court	No appeal	Supreme Court	Filing of record by Committee with Supreme Court
Nebraska	Commission on Judicial Qualification	Supreme Court	No appeal	Supreme Court	Commission may issue a public reprimand
Nevada	Commission on Judicial Discipline	Commission on Judicial Discipline	Supreme Court	Commission on Judicial Discipline	Upon filing of report by Committee and service upon judge
New Hampshire	Supreme Court Committee on Judicial Conduct		Supreme Court	Supreme Court	On issuance of reprimand (d)
New Jersey	Advisory Committee on Judicial Conduct	Supreme Court	N.A.	Supreme Court	Filing of formal complaint
New Mexico	Judicial Standards Commission	Supreme Court	N.A.	Supreme Court	Filing of record by Commission with Supreme Court
New York	Commission on Judicial Conduct	Commission on Judicial Conduct	Court of Appeals	Commission on Judicial Conduct and Court of Appeals	Completion of service of record on respondent
North Carolina	Judicial Standards Commission	Supreme Court	No appeals	Supreme Court	Upon recommendation of Commission to Supreme Court
North Dakota	Commission on Judicial Conduct	Supreme Court	N.A.	Supreme Court	At formal hearing
Ohio	Board of Commissioners on Grievance and Discipline (e)	Board of Commissioners on Grievance and Discipline	Supreme Court	Supreme Court	Adjudication
Oklahoma	Court on the Judiciary Trial Division Council; Council on Judicial Complaints	Court on the Judiciary Trial Division; Council on Judicial Complaints	Court on the Judiciary Appellate Division; no appeal from Council on Judicial Complaints	Court on the Judiciary Appellate Division	Filing with clerk of the Appellate Court
Oregon	Commission on Judicial Fitness and Disability (f)	Supreme Court	No appeal	Supreme Court	(g)
Pennsylvania	Judicial Conduct Board	Court of Judicial Discipline	Supreme Court	Supreme Court	Once a final decision has been made
Rhode Island	Commission on Judicial Tenure and Discipline	Supreme Court	No appeals	Supreme Court	When Supreme Court affirms a recommendation for reprimand or removal

See footnotes at end of table.

JUDICIAL DISCIPLINE: INVESTIGATING AND ADJUDICATING BODIES—Continued

State or other jurisdiction	Investigating body	Adjudicating body	Appeals from adjudication are filed with:	Final disciplining body	Point at which reprimands are made public
South Carolina	Commissioners on Judicial Conduct	Supreme Court	N.A.	Supreme Court	Adjudication
South Dakota	Judicial Qualifications Commission	Supreme Court	No appeals	Supreme Court	Filing with the Supreme Court
Tennessee	Court of the Judiciary	Court of the Judiciary	Supreme Court, then General Assembly	Supreme Court or General Assembly	Filing of complaint in Appellate Court Clerk's office
Texas	State Commission on Judicial Conduct	Supreme Court, Commission on Judicial Conduct, or review tribunal consisting of Justices of the Courts of Appeals	Supreme Court	Supreme Court, Commission on Judicial Conduct, or review tribunal consisting of Justices of the Courts of Appeals	Convening of formal hearing by the Commission on Judicial Conduct
Utah	Judicial Conduct Commission	Judicial Conduct Commission	Supreme Court	Supreme Court	10 days after filing appeal
Vermont	Judicial Conduct Board	Supreme Court	Supreme Court	Supreme Court	Filing of formal charges by Board with Supreme Court
Virginia	Judicial Inquiry and Review Commission	Supreme Court	Supreme Court	Supreme Court	Filing of formal complaint by Committee with Supreme Court
Washington	Commission on Judicial Conduct	Supreme Court	No appeal	Committee on Judicial Conduct or Supreme Court	Beginning of fact finding hearing by Committee
West Virginia	Judicial Investigation Committee and Judicial Hearing Board	Judicial Hearing Board (JHB)	JHB recommends to SCA (i)	Supreme Court of Appeals (h)	Upon decision by Supreme Court of Appeals
Wisconsin	Judicial Commission	Supreme Court (i)	No appeal	Supreme Court	Filing of petitioner formal complaint by Judicial Commission w/Supreme Court
Wyoming	Commission on Judicial Conduct and Ethics	Supreme Court	N.A.	Supreme Court	Filing with Supreme Court
Dist. of Columbia	Commission on Judicial Disabilities and Tenure	Commission on Judicial Disabilities and Tenure	Federal judge panel: 3 appointments by Chief Justice of Supreme Court	Commission on Judicial Disabilities and Tenure	Filing of order with D.C. Court of Appeals (j)
Puerto Rico	Disciplinary and Removal from office for health reasons	Supreme Court	N.A.	Supreme Court	Filing of formal complaint to the Discipline Commission

Source: Bureau of Justice Statistics, *State Court Organization, 2004* NCJ 212351, update from the National Center for State Courts, March 2011.

Key:

N.A.— Not applicable

(a) In cases involving more serious misconduct, the commission may issue a public admonishment or public censure. The nature and impact of the misconduct generally determine the level of discipline. Both public admonishments and public censures are notices sent to the judge describing the improper conduct and stating the findings made by the commission. These notices are also made available to the press and the general public.

(b) The Judicial Qualifications Commission investigates and makes recommendations to the Supreme Court for discipline or removal.

(c) The Supreme Court power of removal is alternative and cumulative to the power of impeachment and suspension by the Governor and Senate.

(d) The Supreme Court Committee on Judicial Conduct may admonish, reprimand or order conditions, and the Supreme Court may impose formal discipline.

(e) Initial review is carried out by a panel of three commissioners.

(f) Technically, the Commission of Judicial Fitness and Disability does not adjudicate disciplinary matters. It hears the evidence and makes recommendations to the Supreme Court, which must review the records, or any stipulation for discipline and can hear additional evidence. Technically, then, there is no appeal. The Supreme Court orders any discipline, including any stipulated sanction.

(g) In Oregon, the allegations become public when the Commission issues a notice of public hearing, generally 14 days in advance of the hearing (although it can be less in the public interest). The actual complaint is not made public then, but the notice includes the general nature of the allegations. In a disciplinary case (but not a disability case), the Commission hearing, the evidence received there, and the Commission's decisions and recommendations are public. The Supreme Court decision is public when the Court files its opinion. There is no reprimand or other sanction until the Supreme Court decision.

(h) The final disciplining body is the same for both the Commission and Judicial Hearing Board.

(i) The Judicial Conduct and Disability Panel, through an ad hoc three-judge panel (two must be Court of Appeals judges, one can be a retired, reserve judge or Court of Appeals judge appointed as a hearing examiner) makes a report to the Supreme Court.

(j) This only applies in cases of removal or involuntary retirement wherein the Chief Justice appoints a three-member federal judge panel to review commission's order of removal.

Chapter Six

ELECTIONS

THE FOLLOWING TABLES ARE AN ONLINE-ONLY FEATURE FOR THE 2011 VOLUME OF *THE BOOK OF THE STATES.*

THESE TABLES CAN BE ACCESSED AT
http://knowledgecenter.csg.org/drupalview-content-type/1219

Elections At Risk in 2012 and Beyond?
Budget Reductions May Lead to New Election Problems

By R. Doug Lewis

States need to be aware that the budget crisis for state and local governments is likely to put the 2012 presidential election—and beyond—more at risk than at any time since the 2000 election. Despite the successes of each election cycle in 2004, 2006, 2008 and 2010, severe budget constraints have the potential to cause voting concerns in 2012. Actions, if taken soon, can lessen the strain on state and local governments. Changes in state election laws and practices can result in temporary and/or permanent savings for both state and local election offices. Some federal mandates will trigger greater expenses for both near-term and long-term future decisions.

Some states and local jurisdictions will likely have significant election administration problems in 2012. Clearly budget constraints will have an impact: States and local election jurisdictions are reporting 20 percent or higher budget reductions that began in 2009 and continue. Compounding of budget cuts is causing some election administrators to worry about the impact in a major election. Presidential elections tend to bring far more voters than any other election cycle, and the increased numbers of voters can overwhelm the election process when there are fewer resources.

The drying up of federal funds for elections is compounding the budget constraints of almost all state and local governments. The Help America Vote Act pumped more than $3 billion into state and local governments for election reforms, but the likelihood of any additional funds in the near-term is almost non-existent. Congress and the White House seem to have lost interest in continued federal funding for elections. States, of necessity, have begun to seek ways to reduce election costs.

Much coverage has been given to the idea of eliminating separate presidential primaries in many states or at least merging those primaries with primaries for other state elections. Alabama indicates it could save more than $4 million and California estimates as high as a $100 million savings from consolidating primary elections. Missouri is considering changing its primary to consolidation, and Kansas, Washington state and Massachusetts are thinking of political party caucuses rather than presidential primaries.

But presidential primaries are not the only places states can make changes to their election practices, procedures or laws to save considerable

funds. According to a survey conducted by The Election Center, a nonprofit organization representing city, county and state voter registrars and election administrators, other significant changes could save millions of dollars, depending on the particular practices of each state.

Higher Cost Factors Mandated by Federal Law

Legal factors affecting the 2012 election and beyond are new requirements for state and local jurisdictions to provide language assistance to voters for the first time. Many states have had bilingual or multilingual ballots for many years, but the explosive growth of Spanish and Asian language citizens is indicating the cost of elections will escalate significantly for many election jurisdictions. Since many of those will be encountering the language requirements for the first time (results of the Census Bureau's 2010 Census are now being reported to states), the extra costs of printing ballots and voting materials, translation costs, programming costs and poll worker training, among other things, will require more expenses in a time of declining budgets.

Added to this will be increased compliance enforcement by the U.S. Department of Justice for the National Voter Registration Act, the Help America Vote Act and the Military and Overseas Voter Empowerment Act. Leadership at the U.S. Department of Justice has indicated in meetings of state officials their intent to focus more on providing agency-based registration efforts in social service agencies. The Justice Department also began enforcement actions against states related to the Military and Overseas Voter Empowerment Act and indicates they will be reviewing state efforts again in the 2012 elections. For several years, the department has focused on increased enforcement of language minority efforts, including emphasis on having language minority poll workers at polling sites to serve voters with limited English proficiency.

Major Cost and Concern for Near Future

The Help America Vote Act mandates alone have dramatically increased the cost of elections in America. Prior to the passage of the act, the cost of voting equipment was rarely a major expenditure of governments at either state or local levels. The use of lever machines—first introduced in the 1890s—and punch card voting machines meant that local jurisdictions or state governments rarely replaced voting equipment. Such equipment was simple and relatively inexpensive to repair. The aftermath of the 2000 election forced state and local jurisdictions to eliminate those types of voting devices and replace them with either optical scan units or electronic voting machines, which dramatically increased the cost of elections.

Another impact of the Help America Vote Act has left states with a new major cost factor: The new voting equipment will not last as long as the old lever machines and punch card devices. Where it was not uncommon for election jurisdictions to use voting devices for 30 years or more—in some cases 50 years or more—the newer devices are likely to require replacements every 10 to 12 years. Many people believe those devices should be replaced even sooner with current technology realities. States and local governments are now seeing problems with older equipment due to the inability to update some devices since there are no replacement parts identical to those of the originally manufactured units.

The confluence of federal mandates, increased federal enforcement of multiple federal election laws greatly increased costs for election jurisdictions. Coupled with budget reductions, it means policymakers need to be aware that the 2012 election may be more at risk than any previous election in the last 10 years.

Determining Courses of Action

Election officials at state and local levels remain optimistic they will get through the budget crisis in 2012, but are concerned constraints beyond that may seriously affect future elections.

States can review and repeal mandates and requirements that are no longer as necessary in elections within their states. Total quality management studies in industry and government show that policymakers working with practitioners can develop better quality performance. Clearly, election administrators have had significant time to think through the myriad reforms implemented in the aftermath of the 2000 election and they are anxious to assist policymakers in making the right budget decisions that can reduce costs without threatening the viability of the democratic process.

The reality of budget constraints for the 2012 election and the ones immediately following is that the election process will be strained. Policymakers, advocacy groups and voters should be aware of the dangers to the process that such severe reductions are likely to mean in the near future. Among those consequences related to lack of resources: longer lines, more mistakes, less ability to recover from mistakes, less ability to add voters to rolls, less ability to serve voters at the polling sites and less ability to communicate with voters. Increased compliance efforts by the federal government will conflict with reduced ability to fund and manage federal mandates.

Cost Savings Recommendations

A minority of states (roughly 20 percent) require sample ballots be printed and mailed to each voter in the state. Local governments indicated, in the Election Center's national survey of election jurisdictions, this is one of their single largest costs and they could save significant sums of money if they could instead put the sample ballots on their websites. Some states require governments to prepare and distribute candidate or voters' guides, often running into 100 pages or more. The costs of preparation, printing, mailing and other distribution methods add significantly to the costs of elections in those states.

State and local election officials indicated some of the following as suggestions for saving significant sums of money so that other critical areas of the budget do not have to be cut:

- Kansas: Eliminate ballot rotation, which only a few states do. It saves significant ballot printing costs and considerable time in ballot counting.

- Ohio and Georgia: No longer require higher than necessary numbers of poll workers per polling place, especially in locations with multiple precincts at the same site.

- Ohio, California and others: Cut the number of elections by consolidating regularly scheduled elections and/or eliminating requirements for separate special elections, such as those required to fill vacancies.
- Wyoming, Colorado, California and Florida: Allow use of all-mail elections for any location less than 400 voters or in situations where overwhelming numbers of voters already are voting by mail and eliminate precinct-based voting in those cases.

Multiple states listed these additional cost-savings ideas:

- Eliminate political party offices, including precinct committee officers. Let the parties do those themselves or pay the jurisdictions for running their elections.
- Eliminate the requirements to post legal notices of impending elections and especially the requirements that they be in newspapers that fewer voters are reading. Let those notices be posted on state and county websites. Review all laws requiring voting information to be advertised.
- Reduce the number of days for early voting. Voters primarily use the last week of early voting, so restrict early voting to one week. Or, combine early voting with Election Day and just do four or five days of voting. (A change of this magnitude would likely need to be done in a nonpresidential election year.)
- Many voters are voting either absentee or early voting, so restrictions on number of voters per precinct on Election Day can rise to significantly higher numbers—meaning that states with early voting methods can look at increasing the numbers of voters allowed per precinct for Election Day, which will help reduce the numbers of precincts needed.
- Eliminate voter registration cards in states that require identification and simply use the allowed state ID.
- Allow online voter registration to eliminate the thousands of paper registrations that must be filed and maintained. And change state laws to allow electronic storage of records rather than paper records.
- Allow Vote Centers or consolidation of precincts to reduce the number of polling sites and poll workers required. Officials indicate it is easier for voters to find major sites—and the number one complaint of voters registered in national studies is not knowing where to go to vote.

State and local governments report the following as potential sources of concern related to their budget challenges:

- Reduced resources when the number of voters is likely to swell significantly.
- Budget reductions have meant:
  · Fewer replacement machines for voting equipment that has failed, needed spares or new machines for growth;
  · Lack of funds for maintenance of equipment;
  · Lack of funds for software upgrades to equipment;
  · Lack of funds for needed training of both permanent and temporary election workers;
  · Lack of funds to order sufficient ballots to cover the maximum number of voters;
  · Less ability to recover from election problems; i.e., rather than being able to insert resources as a problem develops, it escalates to a major problem unlikely to be resolved prior to an election;
  · Less technical support for key election functions by both government and vendors; and
  · Longer lines and/or other voter service issues become likely due to lack of resources.

Necessary Policy Decisions

State and local governments face not only financial decisions, but also policy decisions that will directly impact whether the states will be able to serve voters' interests in coming elections. In some cases, states may have to provide the overall policy leadership to ensure local governments maintain spending at an appropriate level to assure voters of services necessary for quality elections. While states need to take action to assure local governments appropriately fund the elections, states can also take actions to defer or eliminate some mandates that will protect local governments and allow for appropriate expenditures.

About the Author

Doug Lewis, a certified elections/registration administrator (CERA), is executive director of The Election Center, a nonpartisan, nonprofit organization representing the nation's election officials. He has been called on by Congress, federal agencies, state legislatures, and national and worldwide news media for solutions to voting issues.

Table 6.1
STATE EXECUTIVE BRANCH OFFICIALS TO BE ELECTED: 2011–2015

State or other jurisdiction	2011	2012	2013	2014	2015
Alabama				G,LG,AG,AR,A,SS,T	
Alaska				G,LG	
Arizona				G,AG,SS,SP,T (a)	
Arkansas				G,LG,AG,A,SS,T (b)	
California				G,LG,AG,C,CI,SS,SP,T (c)	
Colorado				G,LG,AG,SS,T	
Connecticut				G,LG,AG,C,SS,T	
Delaware		G,LG,CI		AG,A,T	
Florida				G,LG,AG,AR,CFO	
Georgia				G,LG,AG,AR,CI,SS,SP (d)	
Hawaii				G,LG	
Idaho				G,LG,AG,C,SS,SPT	
Illinois				G,LG,AG,C,SS,T	
Indiana		G,LG,AG,SP		A,SS,T	
Iowa (e)				G,LG,AG,AR,A,SS,T	
Kansas				G,LG,AG,CI,SS,T	
Kentucky	G,LG,AG,AR,A,SS,T				G,LG,AG,AR,A,SS,T
Louisiana	G,LG,AG,AR,CI,SS,T				G,LG,AG,AR,CI,SS,T
Maine (e)					
Maryland				G	
Massachusetts				G,LG,AG,C	
Michigan		(f)		G,LG,AG,A,SS,T	
Minnesota				G,LG,AG,SS (f)	
Mississippi	G,LG,AG,AR,A,CI,SS,T			G,LG,AG,A,SS	G,LG,AG,AR,A,CI,SS,T
Missouri		G,LG,AG,SS,T		A	
Montana		G,LG,AG,A,SS,SP		G,LG,AG,A,SS,T	
Nebraska				G,LG,AG,C,SS,T	
Nevada		G		G	
New Hampshire		G		G	
New Jersey			G,LG		
New Mexico				G,LG,AG,A,SS,T (g)	
New York				G,LG,AG,C	
North Carolina		G,LG,AG,AR,A,CI,SS,SP,T (h)		AG,AR,SS (i)(j)	
North Dakota		G,LG,A,CI,SP,T (i)		G,LG,AG,A,SS,T	
Ohio					
Oklahoma				G,LG,AG,A,CI,SP,T (k)	
Oregon		(k)		G,SP	
Pennsylvania		AG,SS,T (l)		G,LG	
Rhode Island				G,LG,AG,SS,T	
South Carolina		AG,A,T		G,LG,AG,AR,C,SS,SP,T (m)	
South Dakota				G,LG,AG,A,SS,SP,T (n)	
Tennessee		(n)		G	
Texas				G,LG,AG,AR,C (o)	
Utah		G,LG,AG,A,T			
Vermont		G,LG,AG,A,SS,T		G,LG,AG,A,SS,T	

See footnotes at end of table.

STATE EXECUTIVE BRANCH OFFICIALS TO BE ELECTED: 2011–2015—Continued

State or other jurisdiction	2011	2012	2013	2014	2015
Virginia	...	...	G,LG,AG	...	...
Washington	G(q)	G,LG,AG,A,CI,SS,SP,T (p)	...	...	...
West Virginia	...	G,AG,AR,A,SS,T	SP	G,LG,AG,SS,T	...
Wisconsin	...	...	...	G,A,SS,SP,T	...
Wyoming	...	...	...	...	...
American Samoa	...	G,LG	...	...	...
Guam	...	...	...	G,LG,AG,A	...
No. Mariana Islands	...	G	...	G,LG(r)	...
Puerto Rico	...	G	...	...	...
U.S. Virgin Islands	...	...	...	G,LG	...
Totals for year					
Governor	4	13	2	38	3
Lieutenant Governor	3	10	2	33	3
Attorney General	3	10	1	31	3
Agriculture	3	2	0	7	3
Auditor	2	8	0	16	2
Chief Financial Officer	0	0	0	1	0
Comptroller	0	0	0	9	0
Comm. of Insurance	2	4	0	4	2
Secretary of State	3	7	0	26	3
Supt. of Public Inst. or Comm. of Education	0	5	1	9	0
Treasurer	3	9	0	24	3

Sources: The Council of State Governments' survey and state election administration offices and websites, May 2011.

Note: This table shows the executive branch officials up for election in a given year. Footnotes indicate other offices (e.g., commissioners of labor, public service, etc.) also up for election in a given year. The data contained in this table reflect information available at press time.

Key:

... – No regularly scheduled elections of state executive officials.

G – Governor
LG – Lieutenant Governor
AG – Attorney General
AR – Agriculture
A – Auditor
C – Comptroller/Controller
CFO – Chief Financial Officer
CI – Commissioner of Insurance
SS – Secretary of State
SP – Superintendent of Public Instruction or Commissioner of Education
T – Treasurer

(a) Corporation commissioners (5)—4-year terms, 2012–2016—3 seats, 2014—2 seats. State Mine Inspector—4-year term, 2014 election.

(b) Commissioner of State Lands.

(c) Five (5) Board of Equalization members are elected to serve 4-year concurrent terms that will expire January 2014.

(d) Commissioner of Labor—4-year term, 2014.

(e) In Maine the legislature elects constitutional officers (AG, SS, T) in even-numbered years for 2-year terms; the auditor was elected by the legislature in 2008 and will serve a 4-year term.

(f) Michigan State University trustees (8)—8-year terms, 2012—2, 2014—2, 2016—2, 2018—2; University of Michigan regents (8)—8-year terms, 2012—2, 2014—2, 2016—2, 2018—2; Wayne State University governors (8)—8-year terms, 2012—2, 2014—2, 2016—2, 2018—2; State Board of Education (8)—8-year terms, 2012—2, 2014—2, 2016—2, 2018—2.

(g) Commissioner of Public Lands—4-year term, 2014.

(h) Commissioner of Labor elected in 2014.

(i) There are 3 Public Service Commissioners. One is up for election every two years. (3)—6-year terms, 2012—1, 2014—1, 2016—1.

(j) Tax Commissioner.

(k) Corporation Commissioners (3)—6-year terms, 2012—1, 2014—1, 2016—1; Commissioner of Labor—2014, 4-year term.

(l) Commissioner of the Bureau of Labor and Industries.

(m) Adjutant general—4-year term.

(n) The title is Commissioner of School and Public Lands; Public Utility Commissioners (3)—6-year terms, 2012—2, 2014—1. The terms are typically staggered, but one commissioner was appointed to fill a vacancy in 2011, and can only serve until the next general election at which time he may run for the remainder of the unexpired term.

(o) Commissioner of General Land Office—4-year term, 2014; railroad commissioners (3)—6-year terms, 2012—1, 2014—1, 2016—1.

(p) Commissioner of Public Lands.

(q) The West Virginia Supreme Court of Appeals ruled in January that the state must hold a special election for governor by November 15. The winner will complete the remaining one-year term of former Governor Joe Manchin, who is now a U.S. Senator. An election will be held as scheduled in 2012. the remainder of the term.

(r) The current governor and lieutenant governor are serving a 5-year term to change future CNMI elections to even-numbered years.

Table 6.2
STATE LEGISLATURE MEMBERS TO BE ELECTED: 2011–2015

State or other jurisdiction	Total legislators		2011		2012		2013		2014		2015	
	Senate	House/Assembly	Senate	House/Assembly	Senate	House/Assembly	Senate	House/Assembly	Senate	House/Assembly	Senate	House/Assembly
Alabama	35	105	…	…	…	…	…	…	35	105	…	…
Alaska	20	40	…	…	10	40	…	…	10	40	…	…
Arizona	30	60	…	…	30	60	…	…	30	60	…	…
Arkansas	35	100	…	…	35	100	…	…	(a)	100	…	…
California	40	80	…	…	20	80	…	…	20	80	…	…
Colorado	35	65	…	…	17	65	…	…	18	65	…	…
Connecticut	36	151	…	…	36	151	…	…	36	151	…	…
Delaware	21	41	…	…	21	41	…	…	11	41	…	…
Florida	40	120	…	…	40 (h)	120	…	…	20	120	…	…
Georgia	56	180	…	…	56	180	…	…	56	180	…	…
Hawaii	25	51	…	…	12	51	…	…	13	51	…	…
Idaho	35	70	…	…	35	70	…	…	35	70	…	…
Illinois	59 (b)	118	…	…	59	118	…	…	20	118	…	…
Indiana	50	100	…	…	25	100	…	…	25	100	…	…
Iowa	50	100	…	…	25 (c)	100	…	…	25 (d)	100	…	…
Kansas	40	125	…	…	40	125	…	…	…	125	…	…
Kentucky	38	100	…	…	19 (d)	100	…	…	19 (c)	100	…	…
Louisiana	39	105	39	105	…	…	…	…	…	…	…	…
Maine	35	151	…	…	35	151	…	…	35	151	…	…
Maryland	47	141	…	…	…	…	…	…	47	141	…	…
Massachusetts	40	160	…	…	40	160	…	…	40	160	…	…
Michigan	38	110	…	…	…	110	…	…	38	110	…	…
Minnesota	67	134	…	…	…	134	…	…	67	134	…	…
Mississippi	52	122	52	122	…	…	…	…	…	…	52	122
Missouri	34	163	…	…	17 (d)	163	…	…	17 (c)	163	…	…
Montana	50	100	…	…	25	100	…	…	25	100	…	…
Nebraska	49	U	…	…	25 (d)	U	…	…	24 (c)	U	…	…
Nevada	21	42	…	…	10	42	…	…	11	42	…	…
New Hampshire	24	400	…	…	24	400	…	…	24	400	…	…
New Jersey	40	80	40	80	…	…	40	80	…	…	…	80
New Mexico	42	70	…	…	42	70	…	…	…	70	…	…
New York	62	150	…	…	62	150	…	…	62	150	…	…
North Carolina	50	120	…	…	50	120	…	…	50	120	…	…
North Dakota	47	94	…	…	23 (c)	47	…	…	24 (d)	47	…	…
Ohio	33	99	…	…	16 (c)	99	…	…	17 (d)	99	…	…
Oklahoma	48	101	…	…	24 (d)	101	…	…	24 (c)	101	…	…
Oregon	30	60	…	…	15	60	…	…	15	60	…	…
Pennsylvania	50	203	…	…	25 (d)	203	…	…	25 (c)	203	…	…
Rhode Island	38	75	…	…	38	75	…	…	38	75	…	…
South Carolina	46	124	…	…	46	124	…	…	…	124	…	…

See footnotes at end of table.

STATE LEGISLATURE MEMBERS TO BE ELECTED: 2011-2015—Continued

State or other jurisdiction	Total legislators Senate	Total legislators House/Assembly	2011 Senate	2011 House/Assembly	2012 Senate	2012 House/Assembly	2013 Senate	2013 House/Assembly	2014 Senate	2014 House/Assembly	2015 Senate	2015 House/Assembly
South Dakota	35	70	…	…	35	70	…	…	35	70	…	…
Tennessee	33	99	…	…	16	99	…	…	17	99	…	…
Texas	31	150	…	…	15 (g)	150	…	…	16	150	…	…
Utah	29	75	…	…	15	75	…	…	14	75	…	…
Vermont	30	150	…	…	30	150	…	…	30	150	…	…
Virginia	40	100	40	100				100			40	100
Washington	49	98	…	…	25 (c)	98	…	…	24 (d)	98	…	…
West Virginia	34	100	…	…	17	100	…	…	17	100	…	…
Wisconsin	33	99	…	…	16 (c)	99	…	…	17 (d)	99	…	…
Wyoming	30	60	…	…	15 (c)	60	…	…	15 (d)	60	…	…
Dist. of Columbia	13	U	…	…	6	U	…	…	7	U	…	…
American Samoa	18	20	…	…	(e)	20	…	…	(e)	20	…	…
Guam	15	U	…	…	15	…	…	…	15	…	…	…
No. Mariana Islands	9	18	3	18	…	…	6	18	…	…	3	18
Puerto Rico (f)	31	54	…	…	28	51	…	…	…	…	…	…
U.S. Virgin Islands	15	U	…	…	15	U	…	…	15	U	…	…
State Totals	1,971	5,411	171	407	1,113	4,711	0	180	1,158	4,957	92	302
Totals	2,072	5,505	174	425	1,177	4,782	6	198	1,195	4,977	92	302

Source: The Council of State Governments' survey, April 2011.
Note: This table shows the number of elections in a given year. As a result of redistricting, states may adjust some elections. The data compiled in this table reflect information available at press time. See the Chapter 3 table entitled, "The Legislators: Numbers, Terms, and Party Affiliations," for specific information on legislative terms.

Key:
… – No regularly scheduled elections
U – Unicameral legislature
(a) As of printing, the Arkansas Senate had not determined whether half the Senate seats will be up for election in 2014, or whether no Senate election will be held in 2014.
(b) The Illinois Senate operates on a 10-year election cycle. All 59 senators are elected in each year ended in a "2" (following the redistricting based upon the decennial census). Senate districts are then divided into three groups. One group of senators is elected for terms of four years, four years and two years; two years, four years and four years; four years, two years and four years.
(c) Even-numbered Senate districts.
(d) Odd-numbered Senate districts.

(e) In American Samoa, Senators are not elected by popular vote. They are selected by county councils of chiefs.
(f) If in the general election more than 2/3 of the members of either house are elected from one party or from a single ticket, as both are defined by law, the numbers shall be increased in accordance with Article III Section 7 of the Puerto Rico Constitution.
(g) After reapportionment, every Texas senator will potentially have to be up for re-election. Only half will actually be up for re-election in 2012.
(h) According to Florida's Department of Reapportionment, all 40 Senate seats will be up for election in 2012. For years ending in "2," all Senate seats are up for election to reflect reapportionment/redistricting that occurs at the start of each decade. Senators serve four-year terms. Senators from odd-numbered districts run in presidential election years; for example, 2000, 2004, 2008, 2012. Senators from even-numbered districts run in even-numbered "off" years; for example, 2002, 2006, 2010, 2014. However, because all Senate seats will be elected in 2012, senators from even-numbered districts will serve truncated two-year terms, returning them to their regular election cycle in 2014. Thus, 20 Senate seats from even-numbered districts will be up for election in 2014, and the elected senators will serve regular four-year terms through 2018.

Table 6.4

ELECTION DATES FOR NATIONAL AND STATE ELECTIONS
(Formulas and dates of state elections)

State or other jurisdiction	Type of primary	National (a) Primary	National (a) Runoff	National (a) General	State (b) Primary	State (b) Runoff	State (b) General
Alabama	Open	Feb., 1st T / Feb. 7, 2012	… / …	Nov., ★ / Nov. 6, 2012	June, 1st T / June 5, 2012	July, 1st T after 2nd M (even years) / July 10, 2012	Nov., ★ / Nov. 6, 2012
Alaska	Closed	Aug., 4th T / Aug. 28, 2012	… / …	Nov., ★ / Nov. 6, 2012	Aug., 4th T / Aug. 28, 2012	… / …	Nov., ★ / Nov. 6, 2012
Arizona	Closed	(c) / Feb. 28, 2012	… / …	Nov., ★ / Nov. 6, 2012	8th T Prior / Aug. 28, 2012	… / …	Nov., ★ / Nov. 6, 2012
Arkansas	Open	T 3 wks. Prior to runoff / May 22, 2012	… / …	Nov., ★ / Nov. 6, 2012	T 3 wks. prior to runoff / May 22, 2012	June, 2nd T / June 12, 2012	Nov., ★ / Nov. 6, 2012
California	Semi-Closed	Feb., 1st T / Feb. 7, 2012	… / …	Nov., ★ / Nov. 6, 2012	June, ★ / June 5, 2012 (d)	… / …	Nov., ★ / Nov. 6, 2012
Colorado	Closed	Caucus / March 20, 2012	… / …	Nov., ★ / Nov. 6, 2012	Aug., 2nd T / Aug. 14, 2012	… / …	Nov., ★ / Nov. 6, 2012
Connecticut	Closed	Feb., 1st T / Feb. 7, 2012	… / …	Nov., ★ / Nov. 6, 2012	Aug., 2nd T / Aug. 14, 2012	… / …	Nov., ★ / Nov. 6, 2012
Delaware	Closed	Feb., 1st T / Feb. 7, 2012	… / …	Nov., ★ / Nov. 6, 2012	Sept., 1st S after 1st M / Sept. 8, 2012	… / …	Nov., ★ / Nov. 6, 2012
Florida	Closed	(e) / Jan. 31, 2012	… / …	Nov., ★ / Nov. 6, 2012	9th T prior to General / Aug. 28, 2012	… / …	Nov., ★ / Nov. 6, 2012
Georgia	Open	(f) / Feb. 7, 2012	… / …	Nov., ★ / Nov. 6, 2012	July, last T / July 31, 2012	3rd T AP / Aug. 21, 2012	Nov., ★ / Nov. 6, 2012
Hawaii	Closed	Caucus / Feb. 21, 2012	… / …	Nov., ★ / Nov. 6, 2012	Aug., 2nd S / Aug. 11, 2012	… / …	Nov., ★ / Nov. 6, 2012
Idaho	Open	(e) / May 15, 2012	… / …	Nov., ★ / Nov. 6, 2012	(e) / May 15, 2012	… / …	Nov., ★ / Nov. 6, 2012
Illinois	Semi-Open	Feb., 1st T / Feb. 7, 2012	… / …	Nov., ★ / Nov. 6, 2012	March, 3rd T / March 20, 2012	… / …	Nov., ★ / Nov. 6, 2012
Indiana	Open	May, ★ / May 8, 2012	… / …	Nov., ★ / Nov. 6, 2012	May, ★ / May 8, 2012	… / …	Nov., ★ / Nov. 6, 2012
Iowa	Closed	Caucus (g) (h) / Feb. 6, 2012	… / …	Nov., ★ / Nov. 6, 2012	June, / June 5, 2012	… / …	Nov., ★ / Nov. 6, 2012
Kansas	Closed	April, 1st T / April 3, 2012	… / …	Nov., ★ / Nov. 6, 2012	Aug., 1st T / Aug. 7, 2012	… / …	Nov., ★ / Nov. 6, 2012
Kentucky	Closed	May, 1st T after 3rd M / May 22, 2012	… / …	Nov., ★ / Nov. 6, 2012	May, 1st T after 3rd M / May 17, 2012	…	Nov., ★ / Nov. 8, 2011
Louisiana	Open (i)	(e) / Feb. 11, 2012	… / …	Nov., ★ / Nov. 6, 2012	(i) / Oct. 22, 2011	(i)	(i) / Nov. 19, 2011
Maine	Closed	Caucus / (j)	… / …	Nov., ★ / Nov. 6, 2012	June, 2nd T / June 12, 2012	… / …	Nov., ★ / Nov. 6, 2012
Maryland	Closed	April, 1st T / April 3, 2012	… / …	Nov., ★ / Nov. 6, 2012	June, last T / June 26, 2012	… / …	Nov., ★ / Nov. 6, 2012
Massachusetts	Semi-Closed	(e) / March 6, 2012	… / …	Nov., ★ / Nov. 6, 2012	7th T Prior / Sept. 18, 2012	… / …	Nov., ★ / Nov. 6, 2012
Michigan	Open	(e) / Feb. 28, 2012	… / …	Nov., ★ / Nov. 6, 2012	Aug., ★ / Aug. 7, 2012	… / …	Nov., ★ / Nov. 6, 2012

See footnotes at end of table.

ELECTION DATES FOR NATIONAL AND STATE ELECTIONS
(Formulas and dates of state elections)

State or other jurisdiction	Type of primary	National (a) Primary	National (a) Runoff	National (a) General	State (b) Primary	State (b) Runoff	State (b) General
Minnesota	Open	(k) Feb. 7, 2012	...	Nov., ★ Nov. 6, 2012	(k) Aug. 14, 2012	...	Nov., ★ Nov. 6, 2012
Mississippi	Open	March, 2nd T March 13, 2012	3 wks. after 1st Primary April 3, 2012	Nov., ★ Nov. 6, 2012	(e) Aug. 2, 2011	3rd T AP Aug. 23, 2011	Nov., ★ Nov. 8, 2011
Missouri	Open	Feb., ★ Feb. 7, 2012	...	Nov., ★ Nov. 6, 2012	Aug., ★ Aug. 7, 2012	...	Nov., ★ Nov. 6, 2012
Montana	Open	June, ★ June 5, 2012	...	Nov., ★ Nov. 6, 2012	June, ★ June 5, 2012	...	Nov., ★ Nov. 6, 2012
Nebraska	Closed	May, 1st T after 2nd M May 15, 2012	...	Nov., ★ Nov. 6, 2012	May, 1st T after 2nd M May 15, 2012	...	Nov., ★ Nov. 6, 2012
Nevada	Closed	Caucus (h) Feb. 18, 2012	...	Nov., ★ Nov. 6, 2012	Aug., 3rd T Aug. 21, 2012	...	Nov., ★ Nov. 6, 2012
New Hampshire	Semi-Closed (l)	Set by SS (h) Feb. 15, 2012	...	Nov., ★ Nov. 6, 2012	Sept., 2nd T Sept. 11, 2012	...	Nov., ★ Nov. 6, 2012
New Jersey	Semi-Closed	Feb., ★ Feb. 7, 2012	...	Nov., ★ Nov. 6, 2012	June, ★ June 4, 2013	...	Nov., ★ Nov. 5, 2013
New Mexico	Closed	June, 1st T June 5, 2012	...	Nov., ★ Nov. 6, 2012	June, 1st T June 5, 2012	...	Nov., ★ Nov. 6, 2012
New York	Closed	Feb., ★ Feb. 7, 2012	...	Nov., ★ Nov. 6, 2012	Sept., ★ Sept. 11, 2012	...	Nov., ★ Nov. 6, 2012
North Carolina	Semi-Closed (l)	May, ★ May 8, 2012	7 wks. AP June 26, 2012	Nov., ★ Nov. 6, 2012	May, ★ May 8, 2012	7 wks. AP June 26, 2012	Nov., ★ Nov. 6, 2012
North Dakota	Open	(m)	...	Nov., ★ Nov. 6, 2012	June, 2nd T June 12, 2012	...	Nov., ★ Nov. 6, 2012
Ohio	Semi-Closed	(j)	...	Nov., ★ Nov. 6, 2012	March, ★ March 6, 2012	...	Nov., ★ Nov. 6, 2012
Oklahoma	Closed	March, 1st T March 6, 2012	...	Nov., ★ Nov. 6, 2012	July, last T July 31, 2012	Aug., 4th T Aug. 28, 2012	Nov., ★ Nov. 6, 2012
Oregon	Closed	May, 3rd T May 15, 2012	...	Nov., ★ Nov. 6, 2012	May, 3rd T May 15, 2012	...	Nov., ★ Nov. 6, 2012
Pennsylvania	Closed	April, 4th T April 24, 2012	...	Nov., ★ Nov. 6, 2012	April, 4th T April 24, 2012	...	Nov., ★ Nov. 6, 2012
Rhode Island	Semi-Closed	(e) March 6, 2012	...	Nov., ★ Nov. 6, 2012	Sept., 2nd T after 1st M Sept. 11, 2012	...	Nov., ★ Nov. 6, 2012
South Carolina	Open	(e) Feb. 28, 2012 (h)	...	Nov., ★ Nov. 6, 2012	June, 2nd T June 12, 2012	2nd T AP June 26, 2012	Nov., ★ Nov. 6, 2012
South Dakota	Closed	June, ★ June 5, 2012	2nd T AP June 19, 2012	Nov., ★ Nov. 6, 2012	June, ★ June 5, 2012	2nd T AP June 19, 2012	Nov., ★ Nov. 6, 2012
Tennessee	Open	March, 1st T March 6, 2012	...	Nov., ★ Nov. 6, 2012	Aug., 1st TH Aug. 2, 2012	...	Nov., ★ Nov. 6, 2012
Texas	Open	March, 1st T March 6, 2012	...	Nov., ★ Nov. 6, 2012	March, 1st T March 6, 2012	April, 2nd T April 10, 2012	Nov., ★ Nov. 6, 2012
Utah	Closed	(e) (j)	...	Nov., ★ Nov. 6, 2012	June, 4th T June 26, 2012	...	Nov., ★ Nov. 6, 2012

See footnotes at end of table.

ELECTION DATES FOR NATIONAL AND STATE ELECTIONS
(Formulas and dates of state elections)

State or other jurisdiction	Type of primary	National (a) Primary	National Runoff	National General	State (b) Primary	State Runoff	State General
Vermont	Open	March, 1st T	...	Nov., ★	Sept., 2nd T	...	Nov., ★
		March 6, 2012	...	Nov. 6, 2012	Aug. 28, 2012	...	Nov. 6, 2012
Virginia	Open	(e)	...	Nov., ★	June, 2nd T	...	Nov., ★
		March 6, 2012	...	Nov. 6, 2012	June 11, 2013	...	Nov. 5, 2013
Washington	Private Choice	Caucus (n)	...	Nov., ★	Aug., 1st T	...	Nov., ★
		(j)	...	Nov. 6, 2012	Aug. 7, 2012	...	Nov. 6, 2012
West Virginia	Closed	May, 2nd T	...	Nov., ★	May, 2nd T	...	Nov., ★
		May 8, 2012	...	Nov. 6, 2012	May 8, 2012	...	Nov. 6, 2012
Wisconsin	Open	(e)	...	Nov., ★	Sept., 2nd T	...	Nov., ★
		Feb. 21, 2012	...	Nov. 6, 2012	Sept. 11, 2012	...	Nov. 6, 2012
Wyoming	Closed	Caucus	...	Nov., ★	Aug., 1st T after 3rd M	...	Nov., ★
		(j)	...	Nov. 6, 2012	Aug. 21, 2012	...	Nov. 6, 2012
Dist. of Columbia	Closed	(e)	...	Nov., ★	(e)	...	Nov., ★
		Feb. 14, 2012	...	Nov. 6, 2012	(j)	...	Nov. 6, 2012
American Samoa	N.A.	(e)	14 days after general	Nov., ★	(o)	14 days after general	Nov., ★
		(j)	...	Nov. 6, 2012		Nov. 20, 2012	Nov. 6, 2012
Puerto Rico	N.A.	...	...	...	(e)	...	...
		(j)	...	Nov. 6, 2012	(j)	...	Nov. 6, 2012
U.S. Virgin Islands	N.A.	...	...	...	Sept., 2nd S	14 days AP	Nov., ★
		(j)	...	Nov. 6, 2012	Sept. 8, 2012	Sept. 22, 2012	Nov. 6, 2012

Sources: The Council of State Governments, April 2011.

Note: This table describes the basic formulas for determining when national and state will be held. For specific information on a particular state, the reader is advised to contact the state election administration office. All dates provided are based on the state election formula and dates are subject to change.

Key:
★ — First Tuesday after first Monday.
... — No provision.
M — Monday.
T — Tuesday.
TH — Thursday.
S — Saturday.

AP — After primary.
V — Varies.
N.A. — Not applicable.
Nat. — Same date as national elections.
State — Same date as state elections.
Prior — Prior to general election.

(a) National refers to presidential elections.
(b) State refers to election in which a state executive official or U.S. senator is to be elected. See Table 6.2, State Officials to be Elected.
(c) The Arizona governor can use his or her proclamation powers to move the state's primary to a date on which the event would have an impact on the nomination.
(d) In June 2010, California voters approved Proposition 410. State primary elections will now be open to all registered voters and the top two vote getters in every race—no matter their party affiliations—will advance to the November general election.
(e) Formula not available at press time.
(f) The Secretary of State has the authority to set the date of the presidential primary election. Currently held in February, the presidential primary could be held as late as June 14.
(g) Iowa does not have a presidential primary. The Iowa Caucuses mark the beginning of the presidential candidate selection process by choosing delegates to the next level of political party conventions.
(h) Under new rules established by the two national parties, only Iowa, New Hampshire, South Carolina and Nevada can have presidential primaries in February. At press time, Florida has scheduled

its primary for January 31. If it is not moved back, it is likely that these four states will select a new date for their primaries/caucuses earlier in January.
(i) Louisiana has an open primary which requires all candidates, regardless of party affiliation, to appear on a single ballot. If a candidate receives over 50 percent of the vote in the primary, that candidate is elected to the office. If no candidate receives a majority vote, then a single election is held between the two candidates receiving the most votes. For national elections, the first vote is held on the first Saturday in October of even-numbered years with the general election held on the first Tuesday after the first Monday in November. For state elections, the election is held on the second to last Saturday in October with the runoff being held on the fourth Saturday after first election. Local elections vary depending on the location and the year.
(j) Date not available at press time.
(k) Parties must notify the Secretary of State's Office in writing prior to Dec. 1st the year preceding the date of the election of their intentions to hold a preference primary election.
(l) Unaffiliated voters, by state statute and with permission of a party, may vote in a party primary. Currently both the Democratic and Republican parties allow this.
(m) On one designated day, following presidential nominating contests in the states of Iowa and New Hampshire and prior to the first Wednesday in March in every presidential election year, every political party entitled to a separate column may conduct a presidential preference caucus. Before August 15 of the odd-numbered year immediately preceding the presidential election year, the secretary of state shall designate the day after consulting with and taking recommendations from the two political parties casting the greatest vote for president of the United States at the most recent general elections when the office of president appeared on the ballot.
(n) The Washington Legislature voted to suspend the 2012 presidential primary for budgetary reasons, replacing it with caucuses. The primary is expected to return in 2016.
(o) American Samoa does not conduct primary elections.

Table 6.5
POLLING HOURS: GENERAL ELECTIONS

State or other jurisdiction	Polls open	Polls close	Notes on hours (a)
Alabama	7 a.m.	7 p.m.	
Alaska	7 a.m.	8 p.m.	
Arizona	6 a.m.	7 p.m.	
Arkansas	7:30 a.m.	7:30 p.m.	
California	7 a.m.	8 p.m.	
Colorado	7 a.m.	7 p.m.	
Connecticut	6 a.m.	8 p.m.	
Delaware	7 a.m.	8 p.m.	
Florida	7 a.m.	7 p.m.	
Georgia	7 a.m.	7 p.m.	
Hawaii	7 a.m.	6 p.m.	
Idaho	8 a.m.	8 p.m.	Clerk has the option of opening all polls at 7 a.m. Idaho is in two time zones—MST and PST.
Illinois	6 a.m.	7 p.m.	
Indiana	6 a.m.	6 p.m.	
Iowa	7 a.m.	9 p.m.	Hours for school and city elections: polls open at 7 a.m. or noon (depending upon choice of county auditor, with legal limitations on opening the polls at noon). Polls close at 8 p.m.
Kansas	7 a.m.	7 p.m.	Counties may choose to open polls as early as 6 a.m. and close as late as 8 p.m. Several western counties are on Mountain time.
Kentucky	6 a.m.	6 p.m.	Counties may be either in Eastern or Central time zones.
Louisiana	6 a.m.	8 p.m.	
Maine	Between 6 and 10 a.m.	8 p.m.	Applicable opening time depends on variables related to the size of the precinct.
Maryland	7 a.m.	8 p.m.	Anyone in line at 8 p.m. will be allowed to vote.
Massachusetts	7 a.m.	8 p.m.	
Michigan	7 a.m.	8 p.m.	Eastern time zone and Central time zone.
Minnesota	7 a.m.	8 p.m.	Towns outside of the Twin Cities metro area with less than 500 inhabitants may have a later time for the polls to open as long as it is not later than 10 a.m.
Mississippi	7 a.m.	7 p.m.	
Missouri	6 a.m.	7 p.m.	Those individuals in line at 7 p.m. will be allowed to vote.
Montana	7 a.m.	8 p.m.	Polling places with fewer than 400 registered electors must open no later than noon and until 8 p.m. or until all registered electors in any precinct have voted.
Nebraska	7 a.m MST/8 a.m. CST	7 p.m. MST/8 p.m. CST	
Nevada	7 a.m.	7 p.m.	
New Hampshire	No later than 11 a.m.	No earlier than 7 p.m.	Polling hours vary from town to town. The hours of 11 a.m. to 7 p.m. are by statute.
New Jersey	6 a.m.	8 p.m.	
New Mexico	7 a.m.	7 p.m.	
New York	6 a.m.	9 p.m.	
North Carolina	6:30 a.m.	7:30 p.m.	
North Dakota	Between 7 and 9 a.m.	Between 7 and 9 p.m.	Counties must have polls open by 9 a.m., but can choose to open as early as 7 a.m. Polls must remain open until 7 p.m., but can be open as late as 9 p.m. The majority of polls in the state are open from 8 a.m. to 7 p.m. in their respective time zones (CST and MST).
Ohio	6:30 a.m.	7:30 p.m.	
Oklahoma	7 a.m.	7 p.m.	
Oregon	7 a.m.	8 p.m.	Oregon's polls (County Clerk's office and dropsites) are open from 7 a.m. to 8 p.m.
Pennsylvania	7 a.m.	8 p.m.	
Rhode Island	Between 7 and 9 a.m.	9 p.m.	
South Carolina	7 a.m.	7 p.m.	
South Dakota	7 a.m.	7 p.m.	Local time.
Tennessee	7 a.m. (as early as 6 a.m.)	7 p.m. CST/8 p.m. EST	Poll hours are set by each county election commission. Polling places shall be open a minimum of 10 hours but no more than 13 hours. All polling locations in the Eastern time zone shall close at 8 p.m. and those in the Central time zone shall close at 7 p.m. Polls may open as early as 6 a.m.
Texas	7 a.m.	7 p.m.	
Utah	7 a.m.	8 p.m.	
Vermont	Between 5 and 10 a.m.	7 p.m.	The opening time for polls is set by local boards of civil authority.

See footnotes at end of table.

POLLING HOURS: GENERAL ELECTIONS — Continued

State or other jurisdiction	Polls open	Polls close	Notes on hours (a)
Virginia	6 a.m.	7 p.m.	
Washington............................	7 a.m.	8 p.m.	
West Virginia.........................	6:30 a.m.	7:30 p.m.	
Wisconsin	Between 7 and 9 a.m.	8 p.m.	In cities with a population of 10,000 or more, the polls must open at 7:00 a.m. In cities, towns and villages with populations of 10,000, the polls may open any time between 7:00 a.m. and 9:00 a.m.
Wyoming	7 a.m.	7 p.m.	
Dist. of Columbia	7 a.m.	8 p.m.	
American Samoa	6 a.m	6 p.m.	Election proclamation issued by Chief Election Officer contains a statement of time and place for each territorial election.
Guam.....................................	7 a.m.	8 p.m.	
No. Mariana Islands	7 a.m.	7 p.m.	Elections are held on six separate islands. At the close of the polls, ballots are flown to Saipan where they are tabulated at election headquarters.
Puerto Rico..........................	8 a.m.	3 p.m.	
U.S. Virgin Islands..............	7 a.m.	7 p.m.	

Sources: The Council of State Governments' survey, January 2007 and state election websites, March 2011.

Note: Hours for primary, municipal and special elections may differ from those noted.

Key:
(a) In all states, voters standing in line when the polls close are allowed to vote; however, provisions for handling those voters vary across jurisdictions.

Table 6.7
VOTING STATISTICS FOR GUBERNATORIAL ELECTIONS BY REGION

State or other jurisdiction	Date of last election	Primary election					General election								
		Republican	Democrat	Independent and third party	Other	Total votes	Republican	Percent	Democrat	Percent	Independent and third party	Percent	Other	Percent	Total votes
Eastern Region															
Connecticut	2010			(a)			560,874	49.0	567,278 (b)	49.5	17,629	1.5	18	0.0	1,145,799
Delaware	2008	28,972	73,961	0	0	102,933	126,662	32.0	266,861	67.5	0	0.0	1,681	0.4	395,204
Maine	2010	131,407	122,936	0	0	254,343	218,065	38.1	109,387	19.1	242,690	42.4	2,624	0.5	572,766
Maryland	2010	278,792	480,523	0	0	759,315	776,319	41.8	1,044,961	56.2	34,574	1.9	2,026	0.1	1,857,880
Massachusetts	2010	218,656	358,145	0	0	576,801	964,866	42.0	1,112,283	48.4	217,290	9.5	2,600	0.1	2,297,039
New Hampshire	2010	128,091	57,558	0	0	185,649	205,616	45.0	240,346	52.6	10,089	2.2	537	0.1	456,588
New Jersey	2009	334,215	209,304	0	0	543,519	1,174,445	48.5	1,087,731	44.9	161,508	6.7	0	0.0	2,423,684
New York	2010	479,684	(c)	19,051	0	498,735	1,548,184 (d)	33.3	2,911,721 (d)	62.6	194,447	4.2	0	0.0	4,654,352
Pennsylvania	2010	852,416	1,021,068	0	0	1,873,484	2,172,763	54.5	1,814,788	45.5	0	0.0	0	0.0	3,987,551
Rhode Island	2010	18,182	73,142 (c)	0	0	91,324	114,911	33.6	78,896	23.0	148,483	43.4	0	0.0	342,290
Vermont	2010	28,868	73,576	369	0	102,813	115,212	47.7	119,543	49.5	6,190	2.6	660	0.3	241,605
Regional total		2,499,283	2,470,213	19,420	0	4,988,916	7,977,917	43.4	9,353,795	50.9	1,032,900	5.6	10,146	0.1	18,374,758
Midwestern Region															
Illinois	2010	767,485	915,726	5,086	0	1,688,297	1,713,385	45.9	1,745,219	46.8	271,142	7.3	243	0.0	3,729,989
Indiana	2008	350,390	1,151,951	0	0	1,502,341	1,563,885	57.8	1,082,463	40.0	28	0.0	57,376	2.1	2,703,752
Iowa	2010	227,525	58,827	0	0	286,352	592,494	52.8	484,798	43.2	38,014	3.4	6,707	0.6	1,122,013
Kansas	2010	321,080	74,754 (c)	0	0	395,834	530,760	63.3	270,166	32.2	37,857	4.5	7	0.0	838,790
Michigan	2010	1,048,384	528,822	0	0	1,577,206	1,874,834	58.1	1,287,320	39.9	63,907	2.0	27	0.0	3,226,088
Minnesota	2010	130,408	442,137	17,714	0	590,259	910,462	43.2	919,232	43.6	275,463	13.1	1,864	0.1	2,107,021
Nebraska	2010	170,090	57,463 (c)	0	0	227,553	360,645	73.9	127,343	26.1	0	0.0	0	0.0	487,988
North Dakota	2008	50,226	38,784	0	18	89,028	235,009	74.4	74,279	23.5	6,404	2.0	0	0.0	315,692
Ohio	2010	746,719 (c)	630,785 (c)	5,331	0	1,382,835	1,889,186	49.0	1,812,059	47.0	150,591	3.9	633	0.0	3,852,469
South Dakota	2010	83,817	(c)	0	0	83,817	195,046	61.5	122,037	38.5	0	0.0	0	0.0	317,083
Wisconsin	2010	618,828	235,762	2,437	0	857,027	1,128,941	9.9	1,004,303	87.9	25,671	2.2	59	0.0	1,142,927
Regional total		4,514,952	4,135,011	30,568	18	8,680,549	9,978,600	50.3	8,929,219	45.0	869,077	4.4	66,916	0.3	19,843,812
Southern Region															
Alabama	2010	492,897 (e)	318,330	0	0	811,227	860,272	57.9	625,052	42.1	0	0.0	0	0.0	1,485,324
Arkansas	2010	(c)	(c)	0	0		262,784	33.6	503,336	64.4	14,513	1.9	700	0.1	781,333
Florida	2010	1,294,438	871,335	0	0	2,165,773	2,619,335	48.9	2,557,785	47.7	123,831	2.3	58,784	1.1	5,359,735
Georgia	2010	680,499	395,467	0	0	1,075,966	1,365,832	53.0	1,107,011	43.0	103,194	4.0	124	0.0	2,576,161
Kentucky	2007	202,339	348,238	0	0	550,577	435,773	41.3	619,552	58.7	0	0.0	0	0.0	1,055,325
Louisiana (f)	2007	699,275	397,755	200,810	0	1,297,840	699,275 (f)	53.9	397,755	30.6	200,810	15.5	0	0.0	1,297,840
Mississippi	2007	197,647	446,722	0	0	644,369	430,807	57.9	313,232	42.1	0	0.0	0	0.0	744,039
Missouri	2008	395,885	358,016	0	1,729	755,630	1,136,364	39.5	1,680,611	58.4	0	0.0	60,803	2.1	2,877,778
North Carolina	2008	504,973	1,494,998	0	0	1,999,971	2,001,168	46.9	2,146,189	50.3	0	0.0	121,584	2.8	4,268,941
Oklahoma	2010	249,069	263,688	0	0	512,757	625,506	60.4	409,261	39.6	0	0.0	0	0.0	1,034,767
South Carolina	2010	422,251 (g)	189,348	0	0	611,599	690,525	51.4	630,534	46.9	20,114	1.5	3,025	0.2	1,344,198
Tennessee	2010	725,408	284,894 (c)	0	0	1,010,302	1,041,545	65.0	529,851	33.1	30,092	1.9	61	0.0	1,601,549
Texas	2010	1,484,542	680,548	0	0	2,165,090	2,737,481	55.0	2,106,395	42.3	128,727	2.6	7,267	0.1	4,979,870
Virginia	2009	(a)	319,168	0	0	319,168	1,163,523	58.7	818,901	41.3	0	0.0	0	0.0	1,982,424
West Virginia	2008	81,019	354,849	0	0	435,868	181,612	25.7	492,697	69.8	31,486	4.5	0	0.0	705,795
Regional total		7,430,242	6,723,356	200,810	1,729	14,356,137	16,251,802	50.6	14,938,162	46.5	652,767	2.0	252,348	0.8	32,095,079

See footnotes at end of table.

VOTING STATISTICS FOR GUBERNATORIAL ELECTIONS BY REGION—Continued

State or other jurisdiction	Date of last election	Primary election					General election								
		Republican	Democrat	Independent and third party	Other	Total votes	Republican	Percent	Democrat	Percent	Independent and third party	Percent	Other	Percent	Total votes
Western Region															
Alaska (h)	2010	107,982	46,427	0	0	154,409	151,318	59.1	96,519	37.7	7,457	2.9	898	0.4	256,192
Arizona	2010	585,851	286,565	4,485	0	876,901	938,934	54.3	733,935	42.5	54,850	3.2	362	0.0	1,728,081
California (i)	2010	2,377,079	2,395,287	85,097	0	4,857,463	4,127,391	40.9	5,428,149	53.8	539,282	5.3	363	0.0	10,095,185
Colorado	2010	390,108	303,245 (c)	2,246	0	695,599	199,034	11.1	912,005	51.0	676,605	37.8	86	0.0	1,787,730
Hawaii	2010	44,599	236,607	679	0	281,885	157,311	41.1	222,724	58.2	2,548	0.7	0	0.0	382,583
Idaho	2010	167,617	27,412	0	0	195,029	267,483	59.1	148,680	32.9	36,372	8.0	0	0.0	452,535
Montana	2008	81,526	175,043	0	0	256,569	158,268	32.5	318,670	65.5	0	0.0	9,796	2.0	486,734
Nevada	2010	175,040	114,391	0	0	289,431	382,350	53.4	298,171	41.6	23,777	3.3	12,231	1.7	716,529
New Mexico	2010	122,269	109,318	0	0	231,587	321,219	53.3	280,614	46.5	0	0.0	994	0.2	602,827
Oregon	2010	314,087	374,404	0	0	688,491	694,287	47.8	716,525	49.3	39,523	2.7	3,213	0.2	1,453,548
Utah	2010			(a)			412,151	64.1	205,246	31.9	25,909	4.0	1	0.0	643,307
Washington	2008	695,116	712,952	10,884	23,505	1,442,457	1,404,124	46.8	1,598,738	53.2	0	0.0	0	0.0	3,002,862
Wyoming	2010	105,760	22,851	0	0	128,611	123,780	65.7	43,240	22.9	5,362	2.8	16,081	8.5	188,463
Regional total		5,167,034	4,804,502	103,391	23,505	10,098,432	9,337,650	42.8	11,003,216	50.5	1,411,685	6.5	44,025	0.2	21,796,576
Regional total without California		2,789,955	2,409,215	18,294	23,505	5,240,969	5,210,259	44.5	5,575,067	47.6	872,403	7.5	43,662	0.4	11,701,391
American Samoa (j)	2008	N.A.	N.A.	N.A.	N.A.		0	0.0	6,590	56.5	5,084	43.5	0	0.0	11,674
U.S. Virgin Islands	2010	N.A.	14,046	0	0	14,046	0	0.0	17,535	56.3	13,580	43.6	45	0.1	31,160
Puerto Rico	2008	N.A.	N.A.	N.A.	N.A.		1,025,945	52.8	801,053	41.3	53,690	2.8	60,975	3.1	1,941,663

Sources: The Council of State Governments' survey of election administration offices, November 2009 and state elections websites, March 2011.

Key:

N.A.— Not applicable

(a) Candidate nominated by convention.

(b) Democratic vote includes 26,308 from the Working Families Party.

(c) Candidate ran unopposed.

(d) Democratic vote includes 146,648 from the Independent Party and 154,843 from the Working Families Party. The Republican vote includes 232,281 from the Conservative Party and 25,821 from the Taxpayers Party.

(e) In the Republican primary in Alabama, a runoff was held because no candidate received more than 50% of the vote. The vote total in the runoff election was 465,736.

(f) Louisiana has an open primary which requires all candidates, regardless of party affiliation, to appear on a single ballot. If a candidate receives over 50 percent of the vote in the primary, he is elected to the office. If no candidate receives a majority vote, then a single election is held between the two candidates receiving the most votes. In the October 20, 2007 primary election Bobby Jindahl (R) received 54 percent of the vote, the five Democrats received 30.6 percent of the vote and the other candidates received the remaining 15.6 percent of the vote. No run-off election was required.

(g) In the Republican primary in South Carolina, a runoff was held because no candidate received more than 50% of the vote. The vote total in the runoff election was 359,334.

(h) The Democratic Primary combines the candidates from the Democratic Party, the Libertarian Party, and the Alaskan Independence Party.

(i) California became an open primary state after passage of Proposition 14 in the June 2010 election. The top two vote-getters in primary races for congressional, state legislative and statewide offices, regardless of political party, will be in a face-off in the general election.

(j) The results displayed in the table are from the Nov. 18, 2008 run-off election.

2010 Ballot Propositions

By John G. Matsusaka

Voters decided 184 ballot propositions in 38 states in 2010, approving two-thirds of them. No single issue emerged as a common theme across the country, but individual states featured high-profile battles over marijuana legalization, taxes on millionaires, secret voting in union elections and health care systems. The number of initiatives—new laws brought to the ballot by citizen petition—was only 46 for the year, the lowest annual total for an even-numbered year in a quarter century.

Overview

Fueled by the tea party movement, conservative groups won big in elections across the country in November 2010. The conservative surge spilled over to ballot propositions, as progressive measures went down to defeat and many conservative measures were approved. Voters in 37 states decided 184 propositions in 2010 (see Table A). The overall number was up from 174 in 2008, but below the 226 decided in 2006. The number of citizen-initiated proposals was at its lowest level since 1986. Voters approved 65 percent of the measures in 2010, roughly consistent with historical averages.

The 2010 propositions reached the ballot in several different ways. Forty-six were *initiatives*, new laws proposed by citizen groups and qualified for the ballot by petition. Four *referendums*, proposals to repeal existing laws, also qualified by petition.[1] Initiatives and referendums come to the ballot when citizen groups become dissatisfied with the status quo and seek to change existing laws by a direct appeal to voters. Voters approved 43 percent of initiatives, roughly the historical average, and three of the four referendums.

Four propositions gave voters the option to call a constitutional convention, as required by state constitutions, all of which were rejected. The other 130 propositions were *legislative measures*, placed on the ballot by a state's legislature. As usual, most of the measures that went before the voters originated in the legislature, and as usual, most were approved (75 percent for the year). Most legislative measures were constitutional amendments—every state but Delaware requires voter approval to amend the constitution—while 17 were bond measures and a few concerned statutory matters.

Initiative Trends

One of the more intriguing stories this year was the relative scarcity of initiatives. Citizen-initiated laws usually attract the most money and the most attention, and propose the boldest policies. Initiatives are the poster child for direct democracy, and in the eyes of advocates and opponents, encapsulate all of the promises and perils of popular lawmaking. South Dakota in 1898 was the first state to adopt the process. Mississippi was the latest adopter in 1992, bringing the total number of states that allow initiatives to 24.[2]

The 46 initiatives in 2010 is the lowest since 1986, when 42 initiatives were on ballots nationwide. The 2010 total is well below the annual average of 60 since the modern initiative movement began in 1978 with California's tax-cutting Proposition 13, and less than half of the record 93 on the ballot in 1996.

The reason for the waning of the initiative process is unclear. Initiatives may have been a casualty of the economic and financial crisis, as citizens found they had more pressing concerns to deal with than enact new laws. However, initiative activity did not decline during other troubled economic times, such as the 2001 or the 1990–91 recessions, and initiative activity exploded during the Great Depression (with 69 on the ballot in 1932). A fair amount of recent activity has been in response to court rulings, such as initiatives banning same-sex marriage or restricting the use of eminent domain. One reason for the decline in initiative activity may be the absence of similar catalyzing court rulings in the last few years.

It remains to be seen if the decline in initiative activity in 2010 signals an end to the epic wave of initiatives that began in the late 1970s. Figure A shows the number of initiatives by decade, beginning in 1904 when the first initiatives appeared in Oregon. Initiatives were used extensively in the 1920s, 1930s and 1940s. Much of that activity arose from tensions between the new urban majorities in many states and the rural interests that controlled the legislatures.[3] Initiative activity trailed off in the middle decades of the century, with only

Table A: State-by-State Totals for 2010

State	Initiatives	Referendums	Legislative measures	Constitutional convention	Total	Notable issues
Alabama (a)	...	...	5 (0)	...	5 (0)	Diversion of Alabama Trust Fund
Alaska (b)	2 (1)	...	3 (2)	...	5 (3)	Sales tax surtax, parental notification for abortion
Arizona (c)	1 (1)	...	10 (4)	...	11 (5)	Health care system, union elections, medical marijuana
Arkansas.................	...	...	3 (3)	...	3 (3)	Maximum interest rates
California (d)	11 (4)	...	3 (2)	...	14 (6)	Marijuana legalization, budget rules, redistricting
Colorado..................	6 (0)	...	3 (1)	...	9 (1)	Health care system, property taxes, vehicle taxes
Florida	3 (2)	...	4 (2)	...	7 (4)	Land use plans, class sizes, redistricting
Georgia....................	...	...	6 (4)	...	6 (4)	Vehicle registration fees, property taxes
Hawaii......................	...	...	2 (2)	...	2 (2)	Appointment to state board of education
Idaho.......................	...	...	4 (4)	...	4 (4)	Debt issues without voter approval
Illinois....................	...	...	1 (1)	...	1 (1)	Recall of governor
Indiana....................	...	...	1 (1)	...	1 (1)	Property tax limits
Iowa	...	...	1 (1)	1 (0)	2 (1)	Sales tax for conservation
Kansas	...	...	2 (2)	...	2 (2)	Right to own guns
Louisiana (e)...........	...	...	12 (10)	...	12 (10)	Property taxes, public retirement system
Maine (f)	1 (1)	1 (0)	6 (6)	...	8 (7)	Casino, income versus sales tax
Maryland.................	...	...	2 (2)	1 (0)	3 (2)	Constitutional convention, jury trials
Massachusetts	3 (1)	...	...	...	3 (1)	Sales taxes, low income housing approval
Michigan..................	...	...	1 (1)	1 (0)	2 (1)	Officeholding by felons, constitutional convention
Missouri (g)	3 (3)	...	3 (3)	...	6 (6)	Health care system, living space for dogs
Montana	3 (3)	...	...	1 (0)	4 (3)	Payday loans, hunting fees
Nebraska (h)	...	...	3 (2)	...	3 (2)	Economic development
Nevada.....................	...	...	4 (0)	...	4 (0)	Courts, eminent domain
New Jersey	...	...	1 (1)	...	1 (1)	Public employee funds
New Mexico	...	...	9 (6)	...	9 (6)	Bonds
North Carolina........	...	...	1 (1)	...	1 (1)	Felons holding office of sheriff
North Dakota...........	1 (0)	...	1 (1)	...	2 (1)	State legacy fund, hunting in game preserves
Ohio (i)....................	...	...	2 (2)	...	2 (2)	Development bonds
Oklahoma.................	1 (0)	...	10 (9)	...	11 (9)	School spending, term limits, healh care system
Oregon (j)	4 (2)	2 (2)	5 (5)	...	11 (9)	Income and corporate tax increases
Rhode Island...........	...	...	4 (3)	...	4 (3)	State name, bonds
South Carolina........	...	...	4 (4)	...	4 (4)	Union elections, right to hunt and fish
South Dakota	1 (0)	1 (1)	2 (1)	...	4 (2)	Union elections, medical marijuana, smoking ban
Tennessee	...	...	1 (1)	...	1 (1)	Right to hunt and fish
Utah	...	...	4 (4)	...	4 (4)	Public and union elections
Vermont...................	...	...	1 (1)	...	1 (1)	Voting by 17-year-olds
Virginia...................	...	...	3 (3)	...	3 (3)	Property taxes, rainy day fund
Washington..............	6 (2)	...	3 (2)	...	9 (4)	Tax on millionaires, candy tax, state liquor stores
Total........................	46 (20)	4 (3)	130 (97)	4 (0)	184 (120)	

Source: Initiative & Referendum Institute (*www.iandrinstitute.org*).

Note: The table reports the total number of propositions during 2010. Except as noted below, all propositions appeared on the ballot on November 2. The main entry is the number of propositions appearing, and the number approved is in parentheses. A referendum in which the original law is *retained* is considered to have been "approved" (Maine reports in the opposite way on its website).

Key:

(a) Alabama includes one legislative measure from June 1.

(b) Alaska includes two initiatives from August 24, one of which was approved.

(c) Arizona includes one legislative measure from May 18 that was approved.

(d) California includes two initiatives (both failed) and three legislative measures (two passed) from June 8.

(e) Louisiana includes two legislative measures from October 2, both of which passed.

(f) Maine includes one referendum (law was repealed) and four legislative measures (all approved) from June 8.

(g) Missouri includes one legislative measure from August 3 that was approved.

(h) Nebraska includes one legislative measure from May 11 that was approved.

(i) Ohio includes two legislative measures from May 4 that were approved.

(j) Oregon includes two referendums (both laws sustained) from January 26, and two legislative measures (both approved) from May 18.

Figure A: Number of Initiatives by Decade

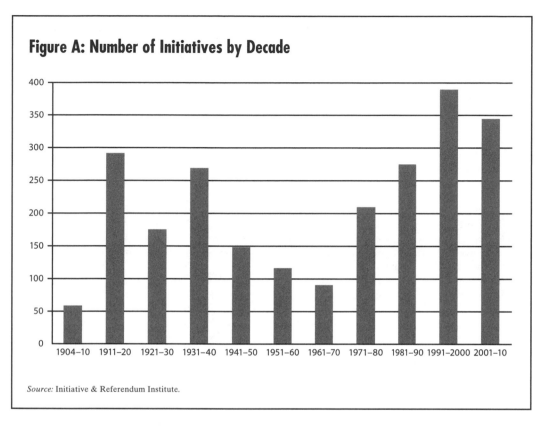

Source: Initiative & Referendum Institute.

89 measures from 1961 to 1970. Beginning in the late 1970s, initiative use picked up again, following California's Proposition 13 in 1978 that set off a national tax revolt. Each successive decade set a new record for the number of initiatives, peaking with 389 in 1991 to 2000. The 344 initiatives for the decade of 2001 to 2010 is high by historical standards, but down 12 percent from the previous decade. The numbers hint that we may be at the start of a down period for citizen lawmaking.

Conservative Victories

In contrast to previous election years, 2010 did not see the emergence of a national issue that spread across the states, such as same-sex marriage and eminent domain that dominated ballots in 2004 to 2008. Instead, an array of state-specific issues appeared that addressed real or perceived needs in individual states. Although the issues were promoted by groups across the ideological spectrum, the energized conservative base that flocked to the polls in November gave many of the ballot proposition results a conservative cast. The propositions included such topics as:

Marijuana legalization. Marijuana opponents were victorious in three of four contests across the country. California's Proposition 19, which would have legalized marijuana, was one of the highest profile initiatives in 2010. It led in early polls, but ended up failing 53 to 47 percent. The silver lining for marijuana proponents is that support for legalization appears to be growing over time, albeit slowly. The last attempt to legalize marijuana in the Golden State in 1972 failed by a much larger margin, 65 to 35 percent. According to a post-election survey by Greenberg-Quinlan-Rosner, voters favored the idea of legalization 49 to 41 percent, but they appeared to dislike the details of Prop 19—placing regulation in the hands of local government rather than the state, and preventing employers from prohibiting marijuana use by employees unless it "actually impairs" job performance.

South Dakota voters rejected Initiated Measure 13, which would have authorized the use of marijuana for medical purposes. Oregon voters rejected Measure 74, which would have expanded the scope of the state's existing medical marijuana law. The only victory for marijuana proponents came in

Arizona, where voters narrowly approved—by 5,000 votes out of 1.6 million cast—Proposition 203, which legalized medical marijuana. Before 2010, voters across the country generally had supported medical marijuana at the ballot box, with 12 of 15 medical marijuana measures passing.

"Soaking the rich." Two of the year's most discussed measures concerned surtaxes on the wealthy. Washington's I-1098 would have established a state income tax on individuals earning more than $200,000, with revenue dedicated to supporting public education. Despite prominent support from Bill Gates Sr., (who filmed a "soak the rich" commercial in which he was dunked in a pool of water) and Microsoft founder Bill Gates Jr., the state's voters rejected the measure 64 to 36 percent. An interesting aspect of the campaign was that prominent business leaders associated with Microsoft took opposing sides, as the initiative's opponents included Microsoft CEO Steve Ballmer and co-founder Paul Allen. Voters apparently were persuaded by arguments that the tax would drive high-skill workers out of the state, and that once imposed, the income threshold would gradually fall, extending the tax to lower-income individuals.

The debate over I-1098 had overtones of the national discussion over whether the Bush tax cuts should be allowed to expire for high-income individuals. Some of the issues surrounding I-1098 are specific to Washington and may not apply to the Bush tax cuts, but the election results suggest that one should not assume voters are eager to raise revenue by targeting the rich. In January 2010, well before the tea party storm hit, Oregon voters rejected an attempt to repeal an income surtax on individuals earning more than $250,000.

Government health care. Voters in Arizona (Proposition 106), Missouri (Proposition C), and Oklahoma (Question 756) approved ballot measures declaring that individuals and business cannot be required to participate in a government health care system, and that individuals and businesses have a right to privately contract for medical services. These votes were a symbolic rejection of President Obama's health care plan adopted earlier in the year. Bucking the trend, Colorado (Amendment 63) voters rejected a similar measure.

Secret votes in union elections. Voters approved several measures that were targeted at labor unions. Voters in Arizona (Proposition 103), South Carolina (Amendment 2) and Utah (Amendment A) approved propositions requiring secret ballots for union elections. These measures were intended to block the "card check" system that allows workers to unionize without a secret ballot by signing cards stating support for unionization. It represented another refutation of President Obama, who made approval of a federal card check law a prominent part of his campaign in 2008, although the rejections took place in three states that Obama lost in 2008.

Affirmative action. By a 60 to 40 percent margin, Arizona voters approved Proposition 107, which prohibits the state from "giving preferential treatment to or discriminating against any person or group" on the basis of race and ethnicity, effectively banning many forms of affirmative action. The state joins California, Michigan, Nebraska and Washington, which previously approved such measures.

Other Issues across the Political Spectrum

Animals. Propositions relating to animals have been increasingly common, with 13 animal-related initiatives appearing over the past decade. Many of these measures have been promoted by animal rights groups in order to improve the living conditions of farm animals and limit hunting practices. Voters this year approved "pro-animal" Proposition B in Missouri—which established minimum space requirements for dog breeders—but rejected North Dakota's Initiated Statutory Measure 2, which would have banned hunting in fenced game preserves. Partly in response to the growing success of animal rights activists, hunting and fishing advocates have been seeking to amend their state constitutions to guarantee residents the right to hunt and fish. Voters in Arkansas (Amendment 1), South Carolina (Amendment 1), and Tennessee (Amendment 1) approved such constitutional amendments in 2010, but voters rejected a similar measure in Arizona (Proposition 109).

Election reform. Dissatisfaction with the performance of American democracy continued to fuel election reform proposals. With redistricting looming nationwide following the census, California (Proposition 20) created a citizen commission to draw the lines for Congressional districts, Florida (Amendments 5 and 6) prohibited redistricting plans that favored incumbents or particular political parties, and Oklahoma (Question 748) made the state's redistricting commission bipartisan. California (Proposition 27) declined to abolish its new citizen commission for redistricting the state legislature. Voters were not attracted to the idea of publicly funding campaigns, repealing a public funding law in Florida (Amendment 1) and rejecting a California initiative (Proposition 15) that would have established a public funding system for secretary of state. Oklahoma (Question 747) approved term limits for state officers and New Mexico (Amendment 2) rejected a proposal to weaken term limits for county officials. Oklahoma voters approved a law requiring proof of identity to vote (Question 746). Illinois voters approved a constitutional amendment allowing recall of the governor in response to the Rod Blagojevich scandal. And in June, California voters approved a nonpartisan top-two primary system (Proposition 13).

Big spending by big businesses. The most expensive campaign of the year involved California's Proposition 16 on the June ballot, which would have required approval from two-thirds of voters before public funds could be used to enter the electricity business. The initiative was sponsored by Pacific Gas and Electric Company, the main private electricity supplier for North and Central California, which contributed $43 million in support. Despite only $130,000 in formal campaign spending, opponents of Proposition 16 received extensive support from media outlets throughout the state and managed to defeat the initiative 53 to 47 percent.

Another expensive campaign involved California's Proposition 17, which would have allowed car insurance companies to base premiums on a driver's history of insurance coverage, presumably raising rates for drivers that were periodically uninsured and lowering rates for drivers with continuous coverage. Insurance giant Mercury Insurance sponsored the initiative and contributed $13 million to the campaign in favor. Opponents spent only $2 million against Proposition 17, but voters rejected the initiative 52 to 48 percent. The outcomes of the Proposition 16 and 17 campaigns support the conventional view that spending against a measure is more potent than spending in favor of a measure, and the uneven spending ratios in the campaigns undercut the claim that special interests can use their deep pockets to buy favorable legislation by outspending opponents.

Bonds. Voters decided 17 state-level bond measures in six states in 2010, approving 15 of them that authorized a total of $2 billion, and rejecting two that would have borrowed $660 million. In comparison, in 2008 voters approved 14 of 15 bond propositions, authorizing more than $13 billion. Sponsors pulled a huge water bond measure in California from the ballot before the election

out of concern it would fail. Overall, legislatures seem to have become hesitant about borrowing, perhaps due to huge federal and state deficits that have begun worrying citizens across the country.

Rhode Island name change. Voters in Rhode Island rejected by more than a 3-to-1 margin a proposal to change the name of the state from "Rhode Island and the Providence Plantations" to simply "Rhode Island." Proponents of the measure argued the reference to plantations in the name evokes the state's slaveholding past.

California budget process. California is one of a small number of states that require a two-thirds vote of the legislature to approve the annual budget. Desperate for a solution to the recurrent nightmare of projected deficits, overdue budgets and state-issued IOUs, voters approved Proposition 25. It repealed the two-thirds rule in the hope that majority rule will restore fiscal sanity. Whether or not it will have that effect is not clear; the state still has in place a two-thirds requirement for tax increases. Voters approved a similar rule for fee increases, creating the possibility the legislature could approve a budget that authorizes spending but not be able to raise the revenue to pay for it.

Washington liquor stores. Washington voters rejected two initiatives that would have privatized its state-run retail liquor stores. Both initiatives proposed to replace lost state revenue by imposing a tax on liquor sales, but differed in how they regulated the distribution channel. I-1100, the more "free market" of the two, allowed retailers to purchase alcohol directly from manufacturers, while I-1105 required retailers to purchase through distributors. I-1100 was backed by retailer Costco, while I-1105 was backed by distributors, including Odom Corporation, a partner of the nation's largest liquor distributor.

Louisiana retirement systems. Louisiana voters approved a constitutional amendment requiring a supermajority for the legislature to increase benefits in public retirement systems.

California greenhouse gases. Proposition 23, an initiative sponsored by two Texas oil companies, proposed to suspend (until the economy improves) a state law passed in 2006 that requires reductions in greenhouse gas emissions, as well as to abandon a number of renewable and clean fuel requirements. The proposition was ahead in early polls, but a flood of money against it—as well as opposition from the current governor and both gubernatorial candidates—turned the tide, leading to a decisive 62 to 38 percent rejection.

Table B
COMPLETE LIST OF STATEWIDE BALLOT PROPOSITIONS IN 2010

State	Type	Result	Short description
Alabama			
Amendment (June 1)	L/CA	Failed 40-60	Assessments on propane gas industry to fund promotion programs.
Amendment 1	L/CA	Failed 45-55	Allows fees for assessment and collection of special property taxes.
Amendment 2	L/CA	Failed 48-52	Allows approval of county school taxes with majority versus 3/5 vote.
Amendment 3	L/CA	Failed 43-57	Allows state trust fund to be used for transportation purposes.
Amendment 4	L/CA	Failed 49.6-50.4	Regulates taxes in Blount County.
Alaska			
Ballot Measure 1 (August 24)	I/ST	Failed 39-61	Prohibits use of public funds and public union funds for campaigns.
Ballot Measure 2 (August 24)	I/ST	Approved 56-44	Requires parental notification before a minor has an abortion.
Ballot Measure 1	L/CA	Failed 40-60	Increases number of state senators and house members.
Bonding Proposition A	L/ST	Approved 62-38	$600 million bond issue for veterans mortgages.
Bonding Proposition B	L/ST	Approved 59-41	$397 million bond issue for libraries and education facilities.
Arizona			
Prop 100 (May 18)	L/CA	Approved 64-36	Imposes 3-year 1% sales tax surtax for schools and public health.
Prop 106	L/CA	Approved 55-45	Bans mandatory government health insurance plans.
Prop 107	L/CA	Approved 60-40	Bans racial preferences in government.
Prop 109	L/CA	Failed 43-57	Declares a right to hunt and fish.
Prop 110	L/CA	Failed 49.7-50.3	Allows state to dispose of lands in order to protect military facilities.
Prop 111	L/CA	Failed 41-59	Creates office of Lieutenant Governor, eliminates Secretary of State.
Prop 112	L/CA	Failed 49.99-50.01	Requires initiative petitions to be filed longer before election.
Prop 113	L/CA	Approved 60-40	Requires secret ballot for union elections.
Prop 203	I/ST	Approved 50.1-49.9	Allows medical use of marijuana.
Prop 301	L/ST	Failed 26-74	Transfers funds in land conservation fund to state general fund.
Prop 302	L/ST	Failed 30-70	Transfers childhood development funds to state general fund.
Arkansas			
CA 1	L/CA	Approved 83-17	Declares a right to hunt and fish.
CA 2	L/CA	Approved 64-36	Removes maximum rates of interest on government bonds.
CA 3	L/CA	Approved 62-38	Removes limitation on economic development bonds.
California			
Prop 13 (June 8)	L/CA	Approved 85-15	Property tax exemption for seismic retrofitting.
Prop 14 (June 8)	L/CA	Approved 54-46	Establishes top-two primary systems.
Prop 15 (June 8)	L/ST	Failed 43-57	Provides public funding for Secretary of State elections.
Prop 16 (June 8)	I/CA	Failed 47-53	Requires 2/3 vote for local government electricity provision.
Prop 17 (June 8)	I/ST	Failed 48-52	Permits auto insurance premiums based on history of coverage.
Prop 19	I/ST	Failed 47-53	Legalizes marijuana.
Prop 20	I/CA	Approved 61-39	Creates citizen commission for Congressional redistricting.
Prop 21	I/ST	Failed 43-57	Establishes $18 car tax for state parks.
Prop 22	I/CA	Approved 61-39	Prohibits state from diverted revenue intended for local governments.
Prop 23	I/ST	Failed 38-62	Suspends state greenhouse gas emission laws.
Prop 24	I/ST	Failed 42-58	Repeals recent laws concerning business tax exemptions.
Prop 25	I/CA	Approved 55-45	Allows legislature to pass budget with majority rather than 2/3 vote.
Prop 26	I/CA	Approved 52-48	Requires 2/3 legislative vote for charges, voter approval of local taxes.
Prop 27	I/CA+ST	Failed 41-59	Repeals citizen commission to redistrict state legislature.
Colorado			
Amendment 60	I/CA	Failed 25-75	Allows voters to vote on property taxes where they own property.
Amendment 61	I/CA	Failed 27-73	Prohibits borrowing by state, required voter approval for local debt.
Amendment 62	I/CA	Failed 29-71	Defines a "person" as human from start of biological development.
Amendment 63	I/CA	Failed 47-53	Bans mandatory government health insurance plans.
Amendment P	L/CA	Failed 38-62	Allows General Assembly to regulate gaming.
Amendment Q	L/CA	Approved 58-42	Allows move of capital to Denver in emergency.
Amendment R	L/CA	Failed 38-62	Exempts possessory interest in property from property tax.
Prop 101	I/ST	Failed 32-68	Reduces vehicle fees, cuts income tax.
Prop 102	I/ST	Failed 38-62	Limits eligibility of defendants for pretrial release.
Florida			
Amendment 1	L/CA	Failed 52-481	Repeals public funding of campaigns.
Amendment 2	L/CA	Approved 78-22	Property tax credit for deployed military personnel.
Amendment 4	I/CA	Failed 33-67	Voters must approve land use plans.
Amendment 5	I/CA	Approved 62-38	Sets standards for state redistricting.
Amendment 6	I/CA	Approved 63-37	Sets standards for Congressional redistricting.
Amendment 8	L/CA	Failed 54-461	Increases maximum allowable class sizes.
Referendum 1	L/ST	Approved 72-28	Calls for federal balanced budget amendment.
Georgia			
Amendment 1	L/CA	Approved 68-32	Allows enforcement of contracts with non-compete clauses.
Amendment 2	L/CA	Failed 47-53	$10 vehicle registration fee for state trauma centers.
Amendment 3	L/CA	Failed 49.9-50.1	Allows multiyear construction agreements by state.
Amendment 4	L/CA	Approved 61-39	Allows multiyear energy efficiency agreements by state.
Amendment 5	L/CA	Approved 64-36	Permits land owners to remove their property from an industrial area.
Referendum A	L/ST	Approved 54-46	Exempts business inventory from property taxes.

See footnotes at end of table.

COMPLETE LIST OF STATEWIDE BALLOT PROPOSITIONS IN 2010—Continued

State	Type	Result	Short description
Hawaii			
(HB 2376)	L/CA	Approved 60-40	Replaces elected with appointed state board of education.
NA	L/CA	Approved 65-35	Removes requirement that state rebate surplus tax revenue.
Idaho			
HJR 4	L/CA	Approved 64-36	Allows public hospitals to incur debt.
HJR 5	L/CA	Approved 53-47	Allows local airports to issue revenue bonds.
HJR 7	L/CA	Approved 57-43	Allows municipal electric utilities to issue revenue bonds.
SJR 101	L/CA	Approved 64-36	Allows University of Idaho to charge tuition, not just fees.
Illinois			
(HJCA 31)	L/CA	Approved 66-34	Allows voters to recall governor.
Indiana			
Public Question 1	L/CA	Approved 72-28	Limits property taxes on homes and other property.
Iowa			
Amendment 1	L/CA	Approved 63-37	Creates conservation program with revenue from new sales taxes.
Constitutional Conv Question	X	Failed 33-67	Calls a constitutional convention.
Kansas			
Amendment 1	L/CA	Approved 88-12	Provides a right to own guns.
Amendment 2	L/CA	Approved 62-38	Prohibits legislature from removing voting rights for mentally ill.
Louisiana			
Amendment 1 (October 2)	L/CA	Approved 63-37	Changes the day the legislature convenes.
Amendment 2 (October 2)	L/CA	Approved 52-48	Civil service for state homeland security office.
Amendment 1	L/CA	Approved 73-27	Limits salary increases for state elected officials.
Amendment 10	L/CA	Approved 55-45	Limits ability of criminal defendants to waive their right to jury trial.
Amendment 2	L/CA	Approved 58-42	Dedicates severance taxes to local governments and conservation.
Amendment 3	L/CA	Approved 65-35	Property tax exemption for veterans and surviving spouses.
Amendment 4	L/CA	Failed 48-52	Limits property tax increases by non-elected governments.
Amendment 5	L/CA	Approved 62-38	Property tax exemption for property damaged in disasters.
Amendment 6	L/CA	Approved 65-35	Requires 2/3 legislative vote to increase public retirement benefits.
Amendment 7	L/CA	Failed 45-55	Authorizes bidder at tax sale to bid down existing 5% tax penalty.
Amendment 8	L/CA	Approved 51-49	Property expropriated as threat to public safety.
Amendment 9	L/CA	Approved 57-43	Workers' compensation and court of appeals.
Maine			
Question 1 (June 8)	R/ST	Approved 61-39	Asks voters to repeal law cutting income tax and increasing sales tax.
Question 2 (June 8)	L/ST	Approved 59-41	$26.5 million bond issue for energy projects.
Question 3 (June 8)	L/ST	Approved 58-42	$47.8 million bond issue for highways, railroads, and marine facilities.
Question 4 (June 8)	L/ST	Approved 51-49	$23.75 million bond issue for R&D.
Question 5 (June 8)	L/ST	Approved 56-44	$10.25 million bond issue for water projects.
Question 1	I/ST	Approved 50.4-49.6	Authorizes a casino in Oxford County.
Question 2	L/ST	Approved 51-49	$5 M bond issue for dental care.
Question 3	L/ST	Approved 59-41	$9.75 M bond issue for land and waterfront conservation.
Maryland			
Question 1	X	Failed 54-462	Calls a constitutional convention.
Question 2	L/CA	Approved 66-34	Allows limits on jury trials for civil trials with small stakes.
Question 3	L/CA	Approved 83-17	Requires certain judges to be practicing lawyers.
Massachusetts			
Question 1	I/ST	Approved 52-48	Removes certain sales taxes on alcohol.
Question 2	I/ST	Failed 42-58	Repeals law that eases zoning rules for low income housing.
Question 3	I/ST	Failed 43-57	Reduces state sales tax from 6.25% to 3%.
Michigan			
Proposal 10-1	X	Failed 33-67	Calls a constitutional convention.
Proposal 10-2	L/CA	Approved 75-25	Bans certain felons from holding elective office.
Missouri			
Proposition C (August 3)	L/ST	Approved 71-29	Prohibits mandatory health insurance.
CA 1	L/CA	Approved 74-26	Requires county assessor to be an elected office.
CA 2	L/CA	Approved 66-34	Property tax exemption for disabled veterans.
CA 3	I/CA	Approved 84-16	Prohibits new taxes on home sales.
Prop A	I/ST	Approved 68-32	Requires voter approval of municipal earnings taxes.
Prop B	I/ST	Approved 52-48	Minimum space requirements for dog breeders.
Montana			
CC-2	X	Failed 41-59	Calls a constitutional convention.
CI-105	I/CA	Approved 73-27	Prohibits new taxes on property sales.
I-161	I/ST	Approved 54-46	Increases nonresident fees for big game and deer hunting.
I-164	I/ST	Approved 72-28	Reduces the maximum interest rate on loans to 36%.

See footnotes at end of table.

COMPLETE LIST OF STATEWIDE BALLOT PROPOSITIONS IN 2010 — Continued

State	Type	Result	Short description
Nebraska			
Amendment 1 (May 11)	L/CA	Approved 53-47	Allows nonprofits to use revenue bonds.
Amendment 1	L/CA	Approved 51-49	Allows cities to tax for economic development.
Amendment 2	L/CA	Failed 33-67	Abolishes position of state treasurer.
Nevada			
Ballot Question 1	L/CA	Failed 42-58	Allows governor to appoint appellate and supreme court judges.
Ballot Question 2	L/CA	Failed 47-53	Creates an intermediate appellate court.
Ballot Question 3	L/ST	Failed 32-68	Legislature can adjust sales tax without voter approval.
Ballot Question 4	L/CA	Failed 33-67	Allows more uses of eminent domain.
New Jersey			
Public Question	L/CA	Approved 80-20	Prohibits diversion of money for public employee benefits.
New Mexico			
Amendment 1	L/CA	Approved 77-23	Veterans pay resident tuition rates at state colleges.
Amendment 2	L/CA	Failed 17-83	Eases term limits for county officials.
Amendment 3	L/CA	Approved 57-43	Extends eligibility to vote.
Amendment 4	L/CA	Approved 58-42	Property tax exemption for veterans organizations.
Amendment 5	L/CA	Failed 23-77	Allows former legislators to hold civil offices.
Bond Question A	L/ST	Approved 54-46	$7.8 million bond issue for senior citizen facilities.
Bond Question B	L/ST	Approved 52-48	$7 million bond issue for libraries.
Bond Question C	L/ST	Approved 61-39	$5.1 million bond issue for schools.
Bond Question D	L/ST	Failed 49.9-50.1	$156 million bond issue for higher education.
North Carolina			
Constitutional Amendment	L/CA	Approved 85-15	Prohibits felons from running for county sheriff.
North Dakota			
Constitutional Measure 1	L/CA	Approved 64-36	Creates state fund from oil and gas extraction revenue.
Initiated Statutory Measure 2	I/ST	Failed 43-57	Bans hunting in fenced game preserves.
Ohio			
Issue 1 (May 4)	L/CA	Approved 62-38	$700 M bond issue for R&D.
Issue 2 (May 4)	L/CA	Approved 68-32	Changes location of Columbus casino.
Oklahoma			
State Question 744	I/CA	Failed 19-81	Increases required education spending.
State Question 746	L/ST	Approved 74-26	Proof of identity required to vote.
State Question 747	L/CA	Approved 70-30	Term limits on statewide officers.
State Question 748	L/CA	Approved 58-42	Makes redistricting commission bipartisan.
State Question 750	L/CA	Approved 50.4-49.6	Lowers initiative signature requirement.
State Question 751	L/CA	Approved 76-24	English declared official language.
State Question 752	L/CA	Approved 63-37	Membership on Judicial Nominating Commission.
State Question 754	L/CA	Failed 37-63	Prohibits mandatory spending amendments.
State Question 755	L/CA	Approved 70-30	Prohibits courts from using international law or Sharia.
State Question 756	L/CA	Approved 65-35	Prohibits mandatory health insurance.
State Question 757	L/CA	Approved 51-49	Increases state reserve fund.
Oregon			
Measure 66 (January 26)	R/ST	Approved 54-46	Asks if voters want to keep tax on wealthy.
Measure 67 (January 26)	R/ST	Approved 54-46	Asks if voters want to keep high corporate taxes.
Measure 68 (May 18)	L/CA	Approved 65-35	Allows state to issue bond for school buildings.
Measure 69 (May 18)	L/CA	Approved 72-28	Allows state to borrow for higher education projects.
Measure 70	L/CA	Approved 84-16	Expands access to veterans' home loan program.
Measure 71	L/CA	Approved 68-32	Requires annual legislative sessions, limits session length.
Measure 72	L/CA	Approved 59-41	Exception from state borrowing limit.
Measure 73	I/ST	Approved 57-43	Increases sentences for sex crimes.
Measure 74	I/ST	Failed 44-56	Establishes medical marijuana supply system.
Measure 75	I/ST	Failed 32-68	Authorizes casino in Multnomah County.
Measure 76	I/CA	Approved 69-31	Continues lottery funding (15%) for parks.
Rhode Island			
Question 1	L/CA	Failed 22-78	Deletes "and Providence Plantations" from state name.
Question 2	L/ST	Approved 55-45	$61 million bond issue for college buildings.
Question 3	L/ST	Approved 73-27	$84.7 million bond issue transportation.
Question 4	L/ST	Approved 65-35	$10 million bond issue for state parks.
South Carolina			
Amendment 1	L/CA	Approved 89-11	Declares a right to hunt and fish.
Amendment 2	L/CA	Approved 86-14	Right to secret ballot in union elections.
Amendment 3	L/CA	Approved 71-29	Increases size of rainy day fund.
Amendment 4	L/CA	Approved 73-27	Requires maintenance of rainy day fund.

See footnotes at end of table.

COMPLETE LIST OF STATEWIDE BALLOT PROPOSITIONS IN 2010—Continued

State	Type	Result	Short description
South Dakota			
Constitutional Amendment K	L/CA	Approved 79-21	Right to secret ballot in government/union elections.
Constitutional Amendment L	L/CA	Failed 41-59	Transfers from cement plant trust fund.
Initiated Measure 13	I/ST	Failed 37-63	Allows medical marijuana.
Referred Law 12	R/ST	Approved 64-36	Asks voters to approve smoking ban.
Tennessee			
Constitutional Amendment 1	L/CA	Approved 90-10	Declares a right to hunt and fish.
Utah			
Constitutional Amendment A	L/CA	Approved 60-40	Right to secret ballot in government/union elections.
Constitutional Amendment B	L/CA	Approved 85-15	Residency requirements to hold office.
Constitutional Amendment C	L/CA	Approved 60-40	Creates property tax exemption for nonprofit water suppliers.
Constitutional Amendment D	L/CA	Approved 67-33	Creates a legislative ethics commission to review complaints
Vermont			
Proposal 5	L/CA	Approved 81-19	Allows certain 17-year-olds to vote in primaries.
Virginia			
Ballot Question 1	L/CA	Approved 76-24	Property tax exemption for senior citizens.
Ballot Question 2	L/CA	Approved 82-18	Property tax exemption for disabled veterans.
Ballot Question 3	L/CA	Approved 51-49	Increases size of rainy day fund.
Washington			
HJR 4220	L/CA	Approved 85-15	Allows courts to deny bail.
I-1053	I/ST	Approved 64-36	Reinstates 2/3 requirement for legislative tax increases.
I-1082	I/ST	Failed 41-59	Allows employers to opt out of workers' compensation program.
I-1098	I/ST	Failed 36-64	Establishes a state income tax on wealthy.
I-1100	I/ST	Failed 47-53	Closes state liquor stores.
I-1105	I/ST	Failed 35-65	Closes state liquor stores, regulates distribution.
I-1107	I/ST	Approved 60-40	Ends sales tax on candy.
Referendum Bill 52	L/ST	Failed 46-54	$505 million bond issue for schools, sales tax on bottled water.
SJR 8225	L/CA	Approved 52-48	Allows state to borrow more.

Source: Initiative & Referendum Institute (*www.iandrinstitute.org*).

Note: Unless another date is given, a proposition appeared on the November __ ballot. For referendums, "appproved" means that the challenged law was upheld by the voters; "failed" means it was repealed.

Key:
CA — Constitutional amendment
I — Initiative

L — Legislative measure
R — Referendum
ST — Statute
X — Vote on whether to call constitutional convention, required by constitution
Z — Commission

Notes

[1] This article uses referend*ums* instead of referend*a* as the plural, following the *Oxford English Dictionary* and common practice.

[2] For detailed information on initiative adoption and provisions, see the appendixes of John G. Matsusaka, *For the Many or the Few: The Initiative, Public Policy, and American Democracy* (University of Chicago Press, 2004) and M. Dane Waters, *Initiative and Referendum Almanac* (Carolina Academic Press, 2003).

[3] See Chapter 7 in Matsusaka, *For the Many or the Few* (2004).

About the Author

John G. Matsusaka is the Charles F. Sexton chair in American Enterprise in the Marshall School of Business, Gould School of Law, and Department of Political Science, and president of the Initiative & Referendum Institute, all at the University of Southern California. He is the author of *For the Many or the Few: The Initiative, Public Policy, and American Democracy* (University of Chicago Press, 2004).

Chapter Seven

STATE FINANCE

State Budgets in 2010 and 2011:

Difficult Decisions Remain for States as Slow Growth Follows Unprecedented Declines

By Brian Sigritz

The 2010 fiscal year was another difficult year for states. State revenue collections continued to fall, while general fund spending declined for the second year in a row, marking the first time state spending has declined in back-to-back years. Additionally, 39 states were forced to make midyear budget cuts. Fiscal conditions have improved somewhat for states thus far in the 2011 fiscal year. The number of states making budget cuts has declined and both revenue collections and spending have grown. However, states remain well below pre-recession levels even with the recent increases. States will have to continue to make difficult decisions in the 2012 fiscal year and beyond as Recovery Act funds wind down, spending demands remain high and revenues are slow to recover.

Introduction

The 2010 fiscal year was one of the most challenging for state budgets since the Great Depression. After a revenue decline of 8 percent in the 2009 fiscal year, revenues declined an additional 2.5 percent in 2010.[1] State general fund spending also remained negative, with spending declining an unprecedented 7.3 percent. This followed a 3.8 percent decline in general fund spending in 2009, marking the first time in the 33 year history of the National Association of State Budget Officers' Fiscal Survey of States that general fund spending declined two years in a row.[2] Perhaps not surprisingly, the number of states making midyear budget cuts also remained high, with 39 states making cuts totaling $18.3 billion in the 2010 fiscal year.[3]

Fiscal conditions for states have improved somewhat in 2011. Following two straight years of revenue declines, state revenues are expected to increase 4.4 percent in the 2011 fiscal year according to governors' enacted budgets. Likewise, general fund expenditures are expected to increase by 5.3 percent according to appropriated budgets. For the 2010 fiscal year, 45 states had general fund expenditures below the 2009 levels. In the 2011 fiscal year, 35 states enacted a budget with general fund spending levels above those of 2010.[4]

States will still face a difficult budgetary environment for several years to come even with the recent improvements in fiscal conditions. Revenues, spending and balances all remain well below prerecession levels. Total state general fund revenues in the 2011 fiscal year are forecast to be $44 billion, or 6.5 percent below general fund revenue collections in 2008. Similarly, state general fund spending remains nearly $42 billion, or 6.2 percent below its 2008 level. Total state balance levels have declined from a high of $69 billion in the 2006 fiscal year to $36 billion in 2011. Furthermore, in the 2012 fiscal year, states will have to contend with the $66 billion dropoff of temporary federal aid provided through the American Recovery and Reinvestment Act of 2009.[5] States are also facing increased spending demands in areas such as Medicaid and public assistance due to the recession and are being asked to maintain adequate funding levels in areas such as education. As a result of all these factors, states will be forced to make painful budgetary decisions in 2012 and beyond.

The Current State Fiscal Condition

Revenues in the 2010 Fiscal Year

The 2010 fiscal year marked a continuation of the revenue declines that began in 2009. After growing 4 percent in the 2008 fiscal year,[6] revenues declined sharply by 8 percent in 2009 and an additional 2.5 percent in 2010.[7] To put it another way, over a two-year period between the 2008 and 2010 fiscal years, state revenues declined more than 10 percent. Sales, personal income and corporate income tax revenues all continued to decline in the 2010 fiscal year. Individually, sales tax collections decreased 0.6 percent, personal income tax collections declined 3.8 percent, and corporate income tax collections were 6.9 percent lower than their 2009 fiscal year levels. In actual dollar terms, sales tax revenues declined by $1.1 billion, personal income tax revenues shrank by $9.2 billion, and corporate income tax collections decreased by $2.9 billion.[8]

Another indication of the severity of the revenue strain states faced in 2010 is that revenue collections from all sources[9] were lower than anticipated in 36 states, on target in another two states, and were higher than budgeted amounts in only 12 states. These totals would have been even worse had state revenues not seen a slight uptick at the end of 2010. As recently as the spring of 2010, 46 states were reporting their revenue collections were below their original forecast.[10]

Revenues in the 2011 Fiscal Year

The revenue outlook for states has brightened somewhat in the 2011 fiscal year. Following two straight years of revenue declines, state revenues are expected to increase 4.4 percent in 2011 according to governors' enacted budgets.[11] Sales, personal income and corporate income taxes are all projected to increase by 4.5 percent, 4.8 percent and 8.5 percent respectively.[12] The latest data from the Nelson A. Rockefeller Institute of Government indicates state revenues are growing as expected. According to the Rockefeller Institute, state tax revenues grew by 4.5 percent in the first quarter of the 2011 fiscal year (third quarter of calendar year 2010) compared to the same quarter of the 2010 fiscal year. Additionally, preliminary figures for the second quarter of the 2011 fiscal year show state revenues growing by 6.9 percent compared to 2010.[13]

While encouraging, the revenue growth figures do not tell the entire story. Even if revenues grow 4.4 percent in the 2011 fiscal year as projected, state revenues will still be 6.5 percent below 2008. In actual dollar terms, revenues are projected to be $636.3 billion in the 2011 fiscal year, compared to $680.2 billion in 2008, a decline of nearly $44 billion. Revenues in the 2011 fiscal year will even be nearly $19 billion less than 2007 levels.[14] To find revenue totals similar to the 2011 fiscal year, you have to go back five years to 2006.

Tax and Fee Changes in the 2011 Fiscal Year

In reaction to significant reductions in revenue, states enacted $23.9 billion in tax and fee changes in the 2010 fiscal year. This marked the highest dollar amount since NASBO's Fiscal Survey of the States began tracking tax and fee changes in 1979. In total, 29 states enacted net increases, while nine states enacted net decreases. States continued to enact tax and fee increases in the 2011 fiscal year, although at a lower level. Through December 2010, states had enacted $6.2 billion in tax and fee increases, with 23 states enacting net increases and six states enacting net decreases.[15]

Although sales, personal income and corporate income tax collections comprise approximately 80 percent of state revenue, a large share of the tax increases in the 2011 fiscal year came from outside these three major sources. For example, 17 states enacted fee increases in their 2011 budgets for a net increase of $1.1 billion. Additionally, seven states enacted cigarette tax increases for a net increase of $472 million, and 10 states enacted tax increases in other, smaller tax sources for an increase of $1.1 billion.

States also enacted $2.5 billion in motor fuel taxes, but this was due almost entirely to a tax shift in California in which motor fuel taxes were increased while at the same time sales taxes were decreased. The shift in California also led to states enacting a net decrease in sales tax revenue of $613 million. Personal income taxes experienced a net increase of $424 million, with eight states enacting increases. Corporate taxes increased by $1.1 billion, with seven states enacting increases.[16]

State Spending in the 2010 Fiscal Year

The recent economic downturn has created a unique and, in some ways, unprecedented situation for state expenditures. Spending from state funds (general funds and other state funds combined) declined in both the 2009 fiscal year and estimated 2010 fiscal year, marking the first occurrence in the 23-year history of NASBO's State Expenditure Report. The decline in spending from state funds was precipitated by a rapid reduction in state revenue. However, not all components of state expenditures declined during this period. Federal funds increased sharply in both the 2009 and 2010 fiscal years due to the Recovery Act. This large increase in temporary federal aid, targeted to help states weather the recession, caused total state expenditures to grow modestly in both 2009 and 2010.[17]

Looking in greater detail at the 2010 fiscal year, general fund spending is estimated to be $618.2 billion, a 5.9 percent decline from 2009. General funds typically receive their revenue from broad-based state taxes—such as sales and personal income taxes—and serve as the primary source for financing state operations. All areas of general fund spending, with the exception of transportation, experienced a decline in the 2010 fiscal year.[18] Elementary and secondary education remained the largest category of general fund expenditures in the 2010 fiscal year, accounting for 35.7 percent of all general fund expenditures. Medicaid represented 15.4 percent, and higher education accounted for 12.1 percent. Combined, Medicaid and education comprised more than 63 percent of total state general fund spending. Other categories of general fund spending included corrections at 7.2 percent, public assistance at 1.9 percent, transportation at 0.8 percent, and all other spending[19] at 27 percent.[20]

While general fund spending was declining by nearly 6 percent in the 2010 fiscal year, federal funds increased by 23.4 percent due to the Recovery Act. Federal fund spending went from $457 billion in the 2009 fiscal year to an estimated $563.7 billion in 2010.[21] In contrast to general funds, all spending categories of federal funds increased in the 2010 fiscal year. Medicaid accounted for the largest share of state spending from federal funds at 39.5 percent. Elementary and secondary education at 13.1 percent and transportation at 8 percent represented the next largest shares.[22]

The drastic increase in federal funds from the Recovery Act led to an overall increase in total state expenditures, even after accounting for the aforementioned sharp dropoff in general fund spending. Total state expenditures grew by an estimated 5 percent in the 2010 fiscal year to $1.62 trillion.[23] Additionally, Medicaid surpassed elementary and secondary education as the largest component of total state spending for the first time since 2006, based on estimated 2010 fiscal year spending data. Medicaid expenditures increased sharply due both to Recovery Act funds and a significant increase in Medicaid enrollment brought on by the national recession. In the 2010 fiscal year, Medicaid is estimated to represent 21.8 percent of total state expenditures, with elementary and secondary education close behind at 20.8 percent. Other categories of total state expenditures include higher education at 10.1 percent, transportation at 8.1 percent, corrections at 3.1 percent, public assistance at 1.7 percent, and all other spending at 34.4 percent.[24]

Finally, the Recovery Act, passed in February 2009, produced a shift in the funding sources for state expenditures. Federal funds grew from 26.3 percent of total state expenditures in the 2008 fiscal year to 34.7 percent in the estimated 2010 fiscal year, while general funds shrank from representing 45.9 percent of total state spending in 2008 to 38.1 percent in 2010.[25]

State Spending in the 2011 Fiscal Year

According to appropriated budgets, general fund expenditures are expected to increase by 5.3 percent in the 2011 fiscal year. This would mark the first year that general fund spending has increased since 2008.[26] General fund spending is estimated to be $645.1 billion in the 2011 fiscal year, a $32.5 billion increase from 2010. Not surprisingly, the number of states assuming general fund spending growth greatly increased in the 2011 fiscal year. Thirty-five states enacted a 2011 fiscal year budget with general fund spending levels greater than 2010. By comparison, 45 states in the 2010 fiscal year had general fund expenditures less than 2009 levels.[27]

It should be noted that the 2011 fiscal year general fund spending is expected to remain well below prerecession levels, even after assuming 5.3 percent growth. General fund spending remains nearly $42 billion, or 6.2 percent, below its 2008 fiscal year level. Furthermore, 2011 spending is roughly $10 billion less than even 2007 levels.[28]

Budget Cuts

The number of states forced to make midyear budget cuts remained high in the 2010 fiscal year, with 39 states making cuts totaling $18.3 billion. This was only slightly lower than the 2009 fiscal year, when 41 states made midyear budget cuts.[29] States made budget cuts in a wide range of areas in the 2010 fiscal year. Thirty-five states made cuts in K–12, 32 cut higher education, 31 reduced corrections spending and 28 made cuts to Medicaid. Twenty states also made cuts in public assistance, while 15 cut transportation spending and 37 made cuts in other areas of the budget.[30]

So far in the 2011 fiscal year, the number of states making budget cuts has decreased. Fourteen states have made $4 billion in cuts through December 2010.[31] The reason the number of budget cuts has decreased can likely be traced to the fact that a number of states are meeting or exceeding their revenue projections. Through December, 14 states were exceeding revenue projections, while 20 were on target and 13 were seeing revenues coming in lower than projected.[32] However, states will likely face an additional round of budget cuts in the 2012 fiscal year as Recovery Act funding winds down and state revenues remain below prerecession levels.

Balances

Total balances include both ending balances as well as the amounts in states' budget stabilization funds, which are funds states may use to respond to unforeseen circumstances such as revenues coming in below projections. Forty-eight states have either a budget stabilization fund or a rainy day fund, with about three-fifths of the states having limits on the size of these funds.[33]

Balances have fallen since the start of the recession as states have turned to them in response to declining revenue levels. In the 2010 fiscal year, balances were 6.4 percent of expenditures ($39.2 billion), considerably less than 2008 when balances were 8.6 percent of expenditures ($59.1 billion). As recently as the 2006 fiscal year, balances were at record high levels of 11.5 percent of expenditures ($69 billion). The informal rule-of-thumb is that balances should be at least 5 percent of expenditures.

While the 2010 50-state average balance level of 6.4 percent may seem like a significant cushion, two states—Alaska and Texas—represent 65 percent of the total balance. When those two states are removed, total balance levels drop to 2.4 percent of expenditures. In the 2011 fiscal year, balance levels are projected to fall even further to 5.6 percent of expenditures ($36.2 billion) from 6.4 percent in 2010. Over the last 33 years, balances have averaged 5.8 percent of general fund expenditures.[34]

Looking Ahead

States are likely to continue to face tight fiscal conditions for a number of years to come. While revenues have begun to rise for many states in the 2011 fiscal year, overall state revenues remain $44 billion, or 6.5 percent, less than prerecession levels. Typically, state tax revenues remain weak for several years after a recession ends. For example, it took state revenues at least five years to fully recover after the last two recessions.[35]

Similar to revenue, state general fund spending remains nearly $42 billion, or 6.2 percent, less than the 2008 fiscal year. This is even after factoring in the 5.3 percent growth of fiscal year 2011. At the same time that state spending remains below prerecession levels, states are facing increased spending demands in areas such as Medicaid and public assistance due to the recession and are being asked to maintain adequate funding levels in areas such as education. States also will have to soon contend with the rapid winding down of Recovery Act

funds. They are projected to receive roughly $66 billion less in temporary federal aid in the 2012 fiscal year than they received in 2011.[36]

Looking forward, states will be forced to contend with a number of issues, such as the uncertain impact of federal health care legislation, the continued rise in Medicaid costs and enrollment, the need for additional funds for infrastructure maintenance and the desire to reform pension and retiree health benefits. These factors mean states will have to continue to make difficult decisions regarding funding levels, priorities, and the roles and responsibilities of state government. Although states face a challenging road ahead, they will continue to balance their budgets and meet their obligations as they historically have done in the past.

Notes

[1] National Association of State Budget Officers, *The Fiscal Survey of States*, (December 2010), 4, 5.

[2] *The Fiscal Survey of States*, (December 2010), 2.

[3] *The Fiscal Survey of States*, (December 2010), 8.

[4] *The Fiscal Survey of States*, (December 2010), 8.

[5] National Association of State Budget Officers, *Preliminary Summary NGA/NASBO Fall 2010 Fiscal Survey of States*, (November 2010), 1–4.

[6] *The Fiscal Survey of States*, (December 2009), 31.

[7] See note 1 above.

[8] *The Fiscal Survey of States*, (December 2010), 42.

[9] "All Sources" includes revenues from sales, personal income, corporate income, gaming taxes, and all other taxes and fees.

[10] *The Fiscal Survey of States*, (December 2010), 39.

[11] Ibid.

[12] *The Fiscal Survey of States*, (December 2010), 43.

[13] Nelson A. Rockefeller Institute of Government, *State Revenue Report*, (February 2011), 1.

[14] See note 5 above.

[15] Ibid.

[16] *The Fiscal Survey of States*, (December 2010), 44–46.

[17] National Association of State Budget Officers, *2009 State Expenditure Report*, (Fall 2010), 2.

[18] Ibid.

[19] "All Other" spending in states includes the State Children's Health Insurance Program (SCHIP), institutional and community care for the mentally ill and developmentally disabled, public health programs, employer contributions to pensions and health benefits, economic development, environmental projects, state police, parks and recreation, housing, and general aid to local governments.

[20] *2009 State Expenditure Report*, (Fall 2010), 8.

[21] *2009 State Expenditure Report*, (Fall 2010), 6.

[22] See note 20 above.

[23] See note 21 above.

[24] See note 20 above.

[25] See note 17 above.

[26] See note 2 above.

[27] *The Fiscal Survey of States*, (December 2010), 1.

[28] *Preliminary Summary NGA/NASBO Fall 2010 Fiscal Survey of States*, (November 2010), 1.

[29] See note 3 above.

[30] *The Fiscal Survey of States*, (December 2010), 11.

[31] See note 3 above.

[32] *The Fiscal Survey of States*, (December 2010), 40.

[33] National Association of State Budget Officers, *Budget Processes in the States*, (Summer 2008), 67–69.

[34] *The Fiscal Survey of States*, (December 2010), 50.

[35] Nelson A. Rockefeller Institute of Government, *Fiscal Features: What Will Happen to State Budgets When the Money Runs Out?*, (February 2009), 2.

[36] See note 5 above.

About the Author

Brian Sigritz is the director of state fiscal studies at the National Association of State Budget Officers. He received his master's degree from the George Washington University and his bachelor's degree from St. Bonaventure University. Sigritz previously worked for the Ohio Senate and the Ohio House of Representatives.

Table 7.1
FISCAL 2009 STATE GENERAL FUND, ACTUAL, BY REGION
(In millions of dollars)

State	Beginning balance	Revenues	Adjustments	Total resources	Expenditures	Adjustments	Ending balance	Budget stabilization fund
U.S. totals*	$34,260	$625,514	...	$670,301	$660,946	...	$4,682	$29,006
Eastern Region								
Connecticut (a)	0	15,701	179	15,880	16,806	0	-926	1,382
Delaware*	526	3,148	0	3,674	3,296	0	379	186
Maine (b)......................	1	2,855	244	3,100	3,018	30	52	0
Maryland (c)	487	12,901	1,008	14,396	14,309	0	87	692
Massachusetts (d)	2,406	31,181	0	33,587	32,570	0	1,017	841
New Hampshire	17	1,375	0	1,393	1,418	-25	0	9
New Jersey* (e)	1,304	29,061	562	30,926	30,312	0	614	0
New York* (f)	2,754	53,801	0	56,555	54,607	0	1,948	1,206
Pennsylvania (g)	583	24,305	166	25,054	27,084	0	-2,030	755
Rhode Island (h).........	-41	3,025	-45	2,939	3,001	0	-61	80
Vermont (i)	0	1,103	66	1,168	1,146	22	0	60
Regional totals............	8,037	178,456	2,180	188,672	187,567	27	1,080	5,211
Midwestern Region								
Illinois (j).....................	141	27,551	1,593	29,285	26,797	2,208	280	276
Indiana (k)	1,050	13,063	0	14,113	13,019	130	964	365
Iowa (l)	0	5,889	45	5,934	5,934	0	0	519
Kansas	527	5,587	0	6,114	6,064	0	50	0
Michigan (m)...............	458	7,161	1,014	8,633	8,456	0	177	2
Minnesota (n)	1,920	15,388	0	17,308	16,861	0	447	0
Nebraska (o)	584	3,351	-182	3,752	3,329	0	424	576
North Dakota (p)........	453	1,354	0	1,807	1,237	208	362	325
Ohio (q).......................	1,682	26,685	0	28,367	27,632	0	735	0
South Dakota (r)	0	1,141	13	1,154	1,153	0	0	107
Wisconsin (s)...............	131	12,113	573	12,817	12,744	-17	90	0
Regional totals............	6,946	119,283	3,056	129,284	123,226	2,529	3,529	2,170
Southern Region								
Alabama (t).................	219	6,753	529	7,501	7,735	-340	105	179
Arkansas......................	0	4,435	0	4,435	4,435	0	0	0
Florida	321	23,971	0	24,292	23,661	0	631	274
Georgia* (u)................	2,217	16,767	251	19,235	17,497	0	1,738	217
Kentucky (v)	86	8,553	625	9,263	9,158	66	40	7
Louisiana (w)	866	9,388	119	10,370	9,382	912	76	854
Mississippi	36	4,955	0	4,991	4,984	0	7	334
Missouri (x).................	836	7,451	425	8,712	8,449	0	263	260
North Carolina............	599	19,146	0	19,745	19,653	0	92	150
Oklahoma (y)..............	291	6,147	131	6,568	6,542	0	26	597
South Carolina*..........	324	5,544	0	5,869	5,748	0	121	0
Tennessee (z)	348	9,881	612	10,841	10,675	89	77	557
Texas (aa)	6,815	38,817	-870	44,763	42,411	-75	2,427	6,276
Virginia........................	313	15,791	0	16,104	15,943	0	161	575
West Virginia (bb)	550	3,902	27	4,479	3,980	18	481	473
Regional totals............	13,821	181,501	1,849	197,168	190,253	670	6,245	10,753
Western Region								
Alaska (cc)	0	5,858	-401	5,457	5,732	1,175	1,451	8,898
Arizona (dd)	1	6,966	1,307	8,274	8,754	0	-481	3
California*	2,314	82,772	0	85,086	90,940	0	-5,855	0
Colorado* (ee).............	284	6,743	803	7,830	7,386	0	444	444
Hawaii	330	5,008	0	5,338	5,375	0	-37	60
Idaho (ff).....................	240	2,466	15	2,721	2,959	-239	0	128
Montana (gg)	434	1,808	8	2,250	1,858	-1	393	0
Nevada.........................	316	3,673	0	3,989	3,777	0	212	1
New Mexico* (hh)	735	5,748	264	6,747	6,046	313	389	389
Oregon (ii)	5	5,836	48	5,889	5,889	0	0	113
Utah (jj).......................	0	4,567	470	5,037	4,817	200	21	419
Washington (kk)	790	13,089	928	14,807	14,617	0	189	21
Wyoming (ll)	10	1,745	0	1,755	1,750	0	5	398
Regional totals............	5,459	146,279	3,442	155,180	159,900	1,448	(3,269)	10,874
Regional totals without California....	3,145	63,507	3,442	70,094	68,960	1,448	2,586	10,874
Puerto Rico (jj)...........	0	7,761	3,490	11,250	11,250	0	0	0

See footnotes at end of table.

FISCAL 2009 STATE GENERAL FUND, ACTUAL, BY REGION—Continued
(In millions of dollars)

Source: National Association of State Budget Officers, *The Fiscal Survey of the States* (December 2010).

Note: For all states, unless otherwise noted, transfers into budget stabilization funds are counted as expenditures, and transfers from budget stabilization funds are counted as revenues.

Key:

*In these states, the ending balance includes the balance in the budget stabilization fund.

NA — Indicates data are not available.

... — Not applicable.

(a) Statutory transfer from restricted accounts.

(b) Revenue and Expenditure adjustments reflect legislatively authorized transfers.

(c) Revenue adjustments reflect a $13.2 million reimbursement from the reserve for Heritage Tax Credits, $6 million reimbursement from the reserve for Biotechnology Tax Credits, transfer of $170 million from the State Reserve Fund, transfer of $380.2 million from Accounting Reserves, and transfers of $439.0 million from other special funds.

(d) Includes Budgeted Fund balances.

(e) Transfers from other funds and budget vs. GAAP adjustments.

(f) The ending balance includes $1.2 billion in rainy day reserve funds, $503 million reserved for timing-related changes and other risks, $145 million in a community projects fund, $73 million reserved for debt reduction and $21 million in a reserve for litigation risks.

(g) Revenue adjustment includes a $2.5 million adjustment to the beginning balance and $163.8 million in prior year lapses.

(h) Opening balance includes a deficit of $43.0 million and re-appropriations of $1.7 million from the prior year. Adjustments to revenues represent (net) transfers to the Budget Stabilization (Rainy Day) Fund, including a transfer-in of $66.1 million and an appropriation from the fund of $22.0 million.

(i) FY 2009 adjustments (revenues) include $39.0 million direct applications and transfers in, $6.5 other bills/other revenue, $1.3 additional property transfer tax to GF, and $19.1 from the General Fund Surplus Reserve. Adjustments (expenditures) include ($1.0) from the Human Services Caseload Reserve, ($3.7) from the Tobacco Settlement Fund, ($2.0) from the General Bond Fund, $0.7 to the Education Fund, $3.3 to the unreserved/undesignated balance, $3.1 to Internal Service Funds, $7.3 to the Next Generation Fund, ($3.9) from other assorted funds, $2.2 to the Budget Stabilization Reserve, $1.2 reserved in the GF for bond issuance premium, and $14.9 reserved in the Revenue Shortfall/other reserves.

(j) If our proposed pension borrowing passes ($4.157B), then our GRF spending will increase by 10 percent and an anticipated $6.6B backlog in bills will be paid off. If you take a/p out of the calculation, the passing of our pension borrowing proposal will reflect a decrease in GRF spending by 2 percent. Revenue adjustments are accounted for by statutory transfers in. Expenditure adjustments are accounted for by the sum of (legislatively required transfers plus pension obligation bond debt service plus debt service transfers for capital projects) subtracting the sum of (short term borrowing proceeds minus repayment short-term borrowing).

(k) Expenditure adjustments: Local Option Income Tax Distributions, Reversal of Payment Delays, PTRF Adjust for Abstracts.

(l) Revenue adjustments are for the $45.3 million transfer from the Economic Emergency Fund to the General Fund per Executive Order 18. An additional $56 million was appropriated from the Economic Emergency Fund to pay for disaster related expenses relating to the 2008 flood/storm disaster.

(m) FY 2009 revenue adjustments include the impact of federal and state law changes ($205.3 million); revenue sharing law changes ($530.7 million); and deposits from state restricted revenues (278.0 million).

(n) Ending balance includes cash flow account of $350 million and appropriations carried forward of $44.8 million.

(o) Revenue adjustments are transfers between the General Fund and other funds. This includes a $115 million transfer from the General Fund to the Property Tax Credit Cash Fund. Also includes, per Nebraska law, a transfer of $117.0 million to the Cash Reserve Fund (Rainy Day Fund) of the amount the prior year's net General Fund receipts exceeded the official certified forecast.

(p) Expenditure adjustments are $77.0 million of expenditure authority carried over to the 2009–2011 biennium, obligating an equal amount of the general fund balance. The balance shown is the unobligated balance after subtracting all expenditures and obligations. Also included in the adjustments are a $125.0 million transfer to the budget stabilization fund and $6.0 million of other transfers from the general fund.

(q) FY 2009 required the use of state budget stabilization (rainy day) fund. At the end of the year the balance of the fund was exhausted.

(r) Adjustments in Revenues: $12.8 million was from one-time receipts and $0.2 million was obligated cash carried forward from FY 2008. Adjustments in Expenditures: $0.2 million was transferred to the Budget Reserve Fund from the prior year's unobligated cash.

(s) Adjustments to Revenues include Tribal Gaming ($93.9 million), transfers-in, general fund ($151.7 million), and other departmental revenues ($327.6 million). Adjustments to Expenditures include designation for continuing balances ($10.6 million) and unreserved designated balance (-$27.4 million).

(t) Revenue adjustments include Privilege Tax Escrow, Education Proration Prevention Account, and Education Rainy Day Fund Transfers. Expenditure adjustments include reversions, savings due to the Governor's Deficit Prevention Plan, and FMAP savings.

(u) Agency surplus returned.

(v) Revenue includes $126.5 million in Tobacco Settlement funds. Adjustment for Revenues includes $280.2 million that represents appropriation balances carried over from the prior fiscal year, and $344.5 million from fund transfers into the General Fund. Adjustment to Expenditures represents appropriation balances forwarded to the next fiscal year.

(w) Actuals (FY 2008–2009) reflect the Legislative Auditors reviewed revenues and expenditures made per the fiscal status summary presented to the Joint Legislative Committee on the Budget (JLCB) on January 15, 2010, as required by Louisiana Revised Statue 39:75 A.(3)(a)—REVENUE—$88.9 and $3.3 million carry-forward of mid-year adjustments; $24.4 million transfer of statutory dedication funds to the State General Fund approved by JLCB on January 9, 2009; $1.9 million carry-forward of capitol outlay re-appropriated. EXPENDITURES—$15 million of FY 2007–2008 ending balance for debt service per Act 122 of the 2009 Regular Legislative Session (RLS); $67.4 million of FY 2007–2008 ending balance transferred to the Budget Stabilization Fund; $782.3 million of FY 2007–2008 ending balance to be utilized for FY 2009–2010 expenditures per Act 20 of the 2009 RLS; $3.5, $9.7, and $34.4 million of carry-forward expenditures—$76 million Ending Balance was recognized as surplus, transferred to the Coastal Fund, and therefore not usable as SGF.

(x) Revenue adjustments are transfers from other funds into the general revenue fund, including $250 million from the enhanced FMAP authorized in the American Recovery and Reinvestment Act of 2009.

(y) Adjusted revenues for FY 2009 represents the difference in cash flow amounts.

(z) Adjustments (Revenues) include $127.2 million transfer from debt service fund unexpended appropriations, $81.5 million transfer from TennCare reserve, $190.2 million transfer from capital outlay projects fund, $20.0 million transfer from other agency reserves, and $193.5 million transfer from Rainy Day Fund. Adjustments (Expenditures) include $70.5 million transfer to capital outlay projects fund and $18.3 million transfer to reserves for dedicated revenue appropriations.

(aa) Revenue Adjustments represent transfers to the Economic Stabilization Fund (Rainy Day Fund) pursuant to Texas Constitution, Article III, Section 49-g. Expenditure Adjustments are related to adjustments to dedicated account balances.

(bb) Rainy Day Fund data as of 6/30/2009. Fiscal Year 2009 Beginning balance includes $409.6 million in Reappropriations, Unappropriated Surplus Balance of $35.3 million, and FY 2008 13th month expenditures of $105.5 million. Expenditures include Regular, Surplus and Reappropriated and $105.5 million of 31 days prior year expenditures. Revenue adjustment is from prior year redeposit and expirations from Rainy Day Fund for Flood Relief. Expenditure adjustment represents the amount transferred to the Rainy Day Fund.

(cc) Revenue adjustments: 14.0 million reappropriate and carry forward, (450.0) million + 35.0 million oil & gas tax credit fund. Expenditure adjustments: 1,000.0 million CBR savings deposit, 175.3 million PEF savings.

(dd) Revenue adjustments include $150 million transfer from the Rainy Day Fund, $813 million agency fund transfers, and $344 million proceed from prior-year school lease purchase financing.

(ee) Revenue adjustments in this year are significant as it includes $458.1 million in transfers that were fully restored on the first day of the following fiscal year.

(ff) Specific transfers include: $20 million to the Water Resources Aquifer Study; $1 million to Health and Welfare Community Health Center Grant; $10 million to Opportunity Scholarship Fund, and $1.8 million to the Water Resource Board Revolving Development Fund. Transfers from include: $12 million from the Water Resources aquifer study, $5 million from Capitol Commission, $12.4 million from the Budget Stabilization Fund, $11,950,00 from the Permanent Building Fund, and $11.7 million from the Public School Stabilization Fund. Deficiency warrants include: $58,300 for Military Division Hazardous Materials and $511,500 for Potato Cyst Nematode in the Dept. of Agriculture.

(gg) Adjustments to revenues reflects prior year revenues which were collected in FY 2009. Adjustments to expenditures reflect CAFR adjustments.

(hh) All adjustments are transfers between reserve accounts, except for $48.9 million transferred out from Tobacco Settlement Permanent Fund, a reserve account to the Tobacco Settlement Program Fund, a nonreserve account.

(ii) Revenue adjustment transfers prior biennium ending GF balance to Rainy Day Fund (which can be up to 1 percent of total budgeted appropriation) plus other administrative actions. Rainy Day Fund balance includes normal RDF plus an Education Stability Fund. Balances in RDF & ESF may include donations and Lottery Funds.

(jj) Includes transfers from previous year balance, to/from Rainy Day Fund, and special revenue funds.

(kk) Fund transfers between General Fund and other accounts, and balancing to the final audited ending balance.

(ll) Wyoming budgets on a biennial basis to arrive at annual figures assumptions and estimates were required.

Table 7.2
FISCAL 2010 STATE GENERAL FUND, PRELIMINARY ACTUAL, BY REGION
(In millions of dollars)

State	Beginning balance	Revenues	Adjustments	Resources	Expenditures	Adjustments	Ending balance	Budget stabilization fund
U.S. totals	$7,437	$609,723	...	$628,901	$612,600	...	$13,936	$27,589
Eastern Region								
Connecticut.................	0	17,687	0	17,687	17,238	0	449	103
Delaware*	379	3,235	0	3,614	3,077	0	537	186
Maine (a).....................	26	2,693	202	2,921	2,849	71	0	0
Maryland (b)...............	87	12,891	795	13,773	13,429	0	344	612
Massachusetts (c).........	1,017	31,428	0	32,444	31,693	0	752	657
New Hampshire..........	0	1,410	25	1,435	1,408	-43	70	9
New Jersey* (d)	614	27,382	871	28,867	28,362	0	505	0
New York* (e).............	1,948	52,556	0	54,504	54,262	-2,060	2,302	1,206
Pennsylvania (f)..........	-2,030	26,523	155	24,648	25,138	-196	-294	1
Rhode Island (g).........	-61	3,016	-71	2,883	2,862	0	21	112
Vermont (h)	0	1,038	52	1,090	1,088	2	0	57
Regional totals............	1,980	179,859	2,029	183,866	181,406	-2,226	4,686	2,943
Midwestern Region								
Illinois (i)...................	280	25,254	1,836	27,370	22,675	4,565	130	276
Indiana (j)	964	12,321	371	13,656	12,877	-52	831	0
Iowa (k).......................	0	5,634	0	5,634	5,298	0	336	419
Kansas.........................	50	5,291	0	5,341	5,408	0	-67	0
Michigan (l).................	177	6,740	855	7,772	7,772	0	0	2
Minnesota (m)	447	14,694	0	15,141	14,799	0	342	0
Nebraska (n)................	424	3,207	-21	3,610	3,313	0	297	467
North Dakota..............	362	1,538	0	1,898	1,316	0	582	325
Ohio............................	735	24,950	0	25,685	25,174	0	510	0
South Dakota (o).........	0	1,110	22	1,132	1,132	0	0	107
Wisconsin (p)	90	12,132	742	12,963	12,824	68	71	0
Regional totals............	3,529	112,871	3,805	120,202	112,588	4,581	3,032	1,596
Southern Region								
Alabama (q).................	105	6,513	124	6,742	7,275	-533	0	55
Arkansas......................	0	4,323	0	4,323	4,323	0	0	0
Florida	631	22,133	0	22,765	21,581	0	1,183	275
Georgia* (r)	1,738	15,216	156	17,110	15,971	0	1,138	193
Kentucky (s)................	40	8,331	234	8,604	8,452	72	80	0
Louisiana* (t)..............	0	7,175	1,401	8,576	7,951	732	-107	644
Mississippi (u).............	7	4,432	0	4,439	4,899	-467	7	250
Missouri (v).................	263	6,774	670	7,707	7,522	0	185	252
North Carolina............	92	18,657	0	18,750	18,513	0	237	150
Oklahoma (w)..............	26	5,166	-30	5,163	5,119	2	42	373
South Carolina*..........	121	5,242	0	5,363	5,117	0	245	111
Tennessee (x)	77	9,784	210	10,071	9,738	58	276	453
Texas (y)	2,427	36,668	-256	38,838	32,734	-118	6,223	7,736
Virginia.......................	161	14,758	0	14,919	14,787	0	132	295
West Virginia (z).........	481	3,758	1	4,240	3,677	11	552	556
Regional totals............	6,169	168,930	2,510	177,610	167,659	-243	10,193	11,343
Western Region								
Alaska (aa)..................	0	5,597	18	5,615	4,606	60	950	10,497
Arizona (bb)	-481	6,316	2,009	7,844	7,852	0	-7	0
California*	-5,375	86,920	0	81,545	86,349	0	-4,804	0
Colorado* (cc)	444	6,455	-48	6,851	6,705	0	146	146
Hawaii	-37	4,854	0	4,817	4,838	0	-21	63
Idaho* (dd)	0	2,286	156	2,442	2,507	-65	1	31
Montana (ee)	393	1,627	6	2,026	1,716	0	310	0
Nevada........................	212	3,206	0	3,418	3,250	0	167	0
New Mexico* (ff)........	389	5,312	260	5,960	5,471	236	253	253
Oregon (gg).................	0	5,956	49	6,004	6,431	0	-427	16
Utah (hh)....................	22	4,220	221	4,462	4,441	22	0	209
Washington (ii)	189	13,575	730	14,494	15,036	0	-542	95
Wyoming (jj)	5	1,745	0	1,750	1,750	0	0	398
Regional totals............	-4,239	148,069	3,401	147,228	150,952	253	-3,974	11,708
Regional totals without California....	1,136	61,149	3,401	65,683	64,603	253	830	11,708
Puerto Rico (kk)..........	0	7,670	2,500	10,170	10,170	0	0	0

See footnotes at end of table.

FISCAL 2010 STATE GENERAL FUND, PRELIMINARY ACTUAL, BY REGION — Continued
(In millions of dollars)

Source: National Association of State Budget Officers, *The Fiscal Survey of the States* (December 2010).

Note: For all states unless otherwise noted, transfers into budget stabilization funds are counted as expenditures and transfers from budget stabilization funds are counted as revenues.

Key:

*In these states, the ending balance includes the balance in the budget stabilization fund.

NA — Indicates data are not available.

... — Not applicable.

(a) Revenue and Expenditure adjustments reflect legislatively authorized transfers.

(b) Revenue adjustments reflect a $13.0 million reimbursement from the reserve for Heritage Tax Credits, $6 million reimbursement from the reserve for Biotechnology Tax Credits, and transfers of $775.6 million from other special funds.

(c) Includes Budgeted Fund balances.

(d) Balances targeted to be lapsed.

(e) Total expenditures are adjusted to reflect the impact of delaying the end-of-year school aid payment ($2.06 billion) from March 2010 to the statutory deadline of June 1, 2010, which was done to carry forward the 2009–2010 budget shortfall into 2010–2011. The ending balance includes $1.2 billion in rainy day reserve funds, $85 million in a community projects fund, $73 million reserved for debt reduction and $21 million reserved for litigation risks. The ending balance also includes a reserve of $906 million for deferred payments, a result of deferring more payments than were needed to carry forward the 2009–2010 budget shortfall, which was used when the deferred payments were made during the first quarter of 2010–2011.

(f) Revenues include $755 million transferred from the Rainy Day fund. Revenue adjustment includes a $5 million adjustment to the beginning balance and $150.4 million in prior year lapses. Expenditure adjustment includes $195.5 million in current year lapses.

(g) Opening balance includes a deficit of $62.3 million and re-appropriations of $1.0 million from the prior year. Adjustments to revenues reflect a transfer to the Budget Stabilization Fund.

(h) FY 2010 adjustments (revenues) include $20.5 direct applications and transfers in, $9.8 other bills/other revenue, $6.5 additional property transfer tax to GF, and $14.8 from the Revenue Shortfall Reserve. Adjustments (expenditures) include ($16.2) from the Human Services Caseload Reserve, ($1.7) from the Transportation Fund, ($2.6) from the General Bond Fund, $6.9 to the Education Fund, ($3.3) from the unreserved/undesignated balance, $3.3 to the Next Generation Fund, $2.0 to other assorted funds, ($2.7) from the Budget Stabilization Reserve, $1.5 reserved in the GF for bond issuance premium, and $15.2 reserved in the Revenue Shortfall/other reserves.

(i) Revenue adjustments are accounted for by statutory transfers in. Expenditure adjustments are accounted for by the sum of (legislatively required transfers plus pension obligation bond debt service plus debt service transfers for capital projects) adding the sum of (short-term borrowing proceeds minus repayment short-term borrowing).

(j) Revenue adjustments: Transfer from Rainy Day Fund to General Fund; Expenditure adjustments: Local Option Income Tax Distributions, PTRF Adjust for Abstracts.

(k) FY 2010 preliminary actual figures are as reported by Governor Culver on September 30, 2010.

(l) FY 2010 revenue adjustments include the impact of federal and state law changes (-$84.6 million); revenue sharing law changes ($520.8 million); and deposits from state restricted revenues ($419.1 million).

(m) Ending balance includes cash flow account of $266 million.

(n) Revenue adjustments are transfers between the General Fund and other funds. Among others, this includes a $112 million transfer from the General Fund to the Property Tax Credit Cash Fund as well as a $105 million transfer to the General Fund from the Cash Reserve Fund (Rainy Day Fund).

(o) Adjustments in Revenues: $21.8 million was from one-time receipts.

(p) Adjustment to Revenues include Tribal Gaming ($25.1 million); transfers-in, general fund ($418.8 million); and other departmental revenues ($297.8 million). Adjustments to Expenditures include designation for continuing balances ($78.5 million) and unreserved designated balance (-$10.6 million).

(q) Revenue adjustments include a General Fund Rainy Day Transfer. Expenditure adjustments include reversions and appropriation reductions (proration).

(r) Agency surplus returned.

(s) Revenue includes $105.5 million in Tobacco Settlement funds. Adjustment for Revenues includes $66.2 million that represents appropriation balances carried over from the prior fiscal year, and $167.4 million from fund transfers into the General Fund. Adjustment to Expenditures represents appropriation balances forwarded to the next fiscal year.

(t) Revenue–State General Fund (SGF) revenues estimated to be $7,174.8 million; Act 122 of 2009 allowed the use of $86.2 million of Budget Stabilization Fund (BSF); Act 51 of 2010 used $198.4 million of BSF; Act 20 used $782.3 million of the Fiscal Year 2007–2008 surplus; Act 633 of 2010 transferred $83.4 million from various funds to the SGF; Act 226 of 2009 transferred $13.5 million from the Rapid Response Fund, $75.6 million from the Insure Louisiana Program Fund, and $3.9 million from the Incentive Fund to the SGF; $42.8 million was carried forward from prior years SGF appropriations to FY 2010–11; and Act 51 of 2010 appropriated $115 million from the Amnesty Fund.

(u) Expenditures adjustment reflects FY 2010 budget cuts.

(v) Revenue adjustments are transfers from other funds into the general revenue fund, including $371 million from the enhanced FMAP authorized in the American Recovery and Reinvestment Act of 2009.

(w) Adjusted revenues for FY 2010 represents the difference in cash flow amounts. The FY 2010 Adjusted expenditure amount of $1.6 million is interest paid on funds borrowed for cash management until action was taken by the legislature on the budget shortfall.

(x) Adjustments (Revenues) include $107.0 million transfer from debt service fund unexpended appropriations and $103.4 million transfer from Rainy Day Fund. Adjustments (Expenditures): include $40.1 million transfer to capital outlay projects fund and $17.7 million transfer to reserves for dedicated revenue appropriations.

(y) Revenue Adjustments represent transfers to the Economic Stabilization Fund (Rainy Day Fund) pursuant to Texas Constitution, Article III, Section 49-g. Expenditure Adjustments are related to adjustments to dedicated account balances.

(z) Rainy Day Fund data as of 6/30/2010. Fiscal Year 2010 Beginning balance includes $432.6 million in Reappropriations, Unappropriated Surplus Balance of $22.2 million, and FY 2009 13th month expenditures of $26.0 million. Expenditures include Regular, Surplus and Reappropriated and $26.0 million of 31 day prior year expenditures. Revenue adjustment is for prior year redeposits. Expenditure adjustment represents the amount transferred to the Rainy Day Fund. The ending balance is mostly the historically carried forward reappropriation amounts that will remain and be reappropriated to the next fiscal year.

(aa) Revenue adjustment: 17.8 million reappropriate and carry forward. Expenditure adjustments: net of (1,057.4) million PEF draw and 1,117.0 million PEF forward funding = 59.6 million.

(bb) FY 2010 ending balance is preliminary and subject to change. Revenue adjustments include $359 million fund transfers, $123 million from revenue measures, $22 million transfer from local government, $19 million from lottery redirect, $1,035 million asset lease purchase financing, and $450 lottery revenue bond.

(cc) Revenue adjustments in this year included the repayment of the $458.1 million in transfers from the previous fiscal year, resulting in a net negative transfer to the GF of $47.6 million.

(dd) Specific transfers include: $54,993,300 from the Budget Stabilization Fund; $1,680,000 from Div. of Human Resources cash on hand; $1,000,000 from the Dept. of Agriculture; $446,900 from Dept. of Labor — Rural Broadband; $661,900 from dedicated agencies for Attorney General; $10 million from Permanent Building Fund; $7,782,400 from the Eli Lily and Co. lawsuit; $781,600 Public Utilities Civil Penalties Fund; and $20 million from Economic Recovery; $33,505,000 from the Budget Stabilization Fund; and $1,105,000 from dedicated funds.

(ee) Adjustments to revenues reflects prior year revenues which were collected in FY 2010.

(ff) All adjustments are transfers between reserve accounts, except for (1) $40.9 million transferred out from Tobacco Settlement Permanent Fund, a reserve account to the Tobacco Settlement Program Fund, a nonreserve account; (2) $25 million transferred from the appropriation account to the Appropriation Contingency Fund; and (3) $40 million

FISCAL 2010 STATE GENERAL FUND, PRELIMINARY ACTUAL, BY REGION — Continued
(In millions of dollars)

transferred from the appropriation account to the separate account of the Appropriation Contingency Fund for the purpose of implementing and maintaining educational reforms.

(gg) Oregon budgets on a biennial basis. The constitution requires the state to be balanced at the end of each biennium (June 30, 2011), so a negative balance at the end of the first fiscal year does not necessarily translate into a budget gap. Revenue adjustments from legislative action to sweep other funds into GF plus other administrative actions.

(hh) Includes transfers from previous year balance, to/from Rainy Day Fund, and special revenue funds.

(ii) Fund transfers between General Fund and other accounts.

(jj) Wyoming budgets on a biennial basis to arrive at annual figures assumptions and estimates were required.

(kk) The General Fund Budget includes an allocation of $1 billion to facilitate the orderly implementation of certain expense reduction measures adopted by the Government of Puerto Rico pursuant to Act 7 of March 8, 2009. This allocation will cover the cost of transitioning public employees to non-governmental sectors by providing re-training vouchers, self employment opportunities, relocation and salary subsidies alternatives. On the other hand, the General Fund Budget also includes an allocation from the State Stabilization Fund of $1.5 billion to cover payroll and operating expenses that are expected to be reduced through fiscal year 2010, but whose savings will not be realized in such fiscal year. The State Stabilization Fund is funded with proceeds from the bonds issued by the Sales Tax Financing Corporation.

Table 7.3
FISCAL 2011 STATE GENERAL FUND, APPROPRIATED, BY REGION
(In millions of dollars)

State or other jurisdiction	Beginning balance	Revenues	Adjustments	Resources	Expenditures	Adjustments	Ending balance	Budget stabilization fund
U.S. totals	$12,255	$636,299	. . .	$656,155	$645,104	. . .	$10,831	$28,037
Eastern Region								
Connecticut.................	0	17,667	0	17,667	17,667	0	0	0
Delaware*................	537	3,338	0	3,875	3,316	0	464	186
Maine (a).....................	0	2,774	26	2,801	2,705	95	1	25
Maryland (b)...............	344	13,128	153	13,625	13,094	0	531	631
Massachusetts (c)........	780	31,086	0	31,866	31,329	0	537	657
New Hampshire..........	70	1,434	60	1,564	1,344	219	0	97
New Jersey*	505	27,826	0	28,330	28,028	0	302	0
New York*(d)	2,302	54,676	0	56,978	53,533	2,060	1,385	1,206
Pennsylvania (e)	-294	25,587	0	25,293	25,289	1	3	1
Rhode Island (f)	21	3,020	-79	2,962	2,942	-3	24	127
Vermont (g).................	0	1,088	54	1,142	1,081	61	0	54
Regional totals............	4,265	181,624	. . .	186,103	180,328	. . .	3,247	2,984
Midwestern Region								
Illinois (h)....................	130	25,939	1,716	27,785	29,097	-1,441	130	276
Indiana (i)	831	12,911	0	13,741	13,599	1	182	7
Iowa (j).......................	0	5,758	0	5,758	5,277	0	480	434
Kansas	-67	5,767	0	5,700	5,627	0	73	0
Michigan (k)................	0	7,163	1,088	8,251	8,251	0	0	2
Minnesota (l)	342	15,844	0	16,186	15,914	0	272	0
Nebraska (m)..............	297	3,422	33	3,752	3,405	213	134	322
North Dakota..............	582	1,394	0	1,976	1,933	0	43	325
Ohio............................	510	26,834	0	27,345	27,191	0	154	0
South Dakota (n)........	0	1,155	10	1,165	1,165	0	0	107
Wisconsin (o).............	71	12,787	837	13,695	14,109	-471	57	0
Regional totals............	2,696	188,974	. . .	125,354	125,568	. . .	1,525	1,473
Southern Region								
Alabama (p)................	0	6,943	79	7,022	7,022	0	0	0
Arkansas......................	0	4,479	0	4,479	4,479	0	0	0
Florida	1,183	23,416	0	24,599	24,137	0	462	276
Georgia*......................	1,138	16,535	0	17,673	16,535	0	1,138	193
Kentucky (q)...............	50	8,682	148	8,880	8,554	326	0	0
Louisiana (r)	-107	7,719	4	7,616	7,723	0	-107	644
Mississippi...................	7	4,484	0	4,491	4,491	0	0	156
Missouri (s).................	185	6,932	732	7,849	7,751	0	99	257
North Carolina............	237	18,978	0	19,215	18,959	0	256	150
Oklahoma....................	42	5,442	0	5,484	5,309	0	175	0
South Carolina* (t)......	245	5,171	0	5,416	5,033	0	383	277
Tennessee (u)..............	276	10,324	376	10,976	10,598	153	225	257
Texas (v)	6,223	39,552	-922	44,852	44,891	-122	84	8,156
Virginia.......................	132	15,251	0	15,384	15,377	0	7	298
West Virginia (w)........	552	3,742	0	4,294	3,773	51	469	631
Regional totals............	10,163	177,650	. . .	188,230	184,632	. . .	3,191	11,295
Western Region								
Alaska (x)....................	0	5,292	180	5,472	5,722	17	-267	11,334
Arizona (y)..................	48	6,790	1,720	8,559	8,495	0	63	0
California	-4,804	94,230	0	89,426	86,552	0	2,874	0
Colorado* (z)...............	146	6,810	90	7,046	7,168	-257	136	136
Hawaii	-21	5,075	0	5,054	5,016	0	38	46
Idaho (aa)...................	1	2,305	80	2,385	2,384	0	2	0
Montana	310	1,829	0	2,139	1,860	-30	309	0
Nevada........................	167	3,379	0	3,547	3,372	0	174	0
New Mexico* (bb)	253	5,256	154	5,663	5,424	194	45	45
Oregon (cc)	-427	6,352	116	6,040	6,995	-955	0	110
Utah (dd).....................	0	4,361	432	4,793	4,769	14	0	209
Washington (ee)..........	-542	14,937	514	14,910	15,430	0	-520	4
Wyoming (ff)...............	0	1,438	0	1,438	1,433	0	5	402
Regional totals............	-4,869	158,054	. . .	156,472	154,620	-1,017	. . .	12,286
Regional totals without California....	-65	63,824	. . .	67,046	68,068	-1,017	. . .	12,286
Puerto Rico (gg)	0	8,134	$1,000	9,134	9,134	0	. . .	0

See footnotes at end of table.

FISCAL 2011 STATE GENERAL FUND, APPROPRIATED, BY REGION — Continued
(In millions of dollars)

Source: National Association of State Budget Officers, *The Fiscal Survey of the States* (December 2010).

Note: For all states, unless otherwise noted, transfers into budget stabilization funds are counted as expenditures, and transfers from budget stabilization funds are counted as revenues.

Key:

*In these states, the ending balance includes the balance in the budget stabilization fund.

NA — Indicates data are not available.

. . . — Not applicable.

(a) Revenue and Expenditure adjustments reflect legislatively authorized transfers.

(b) Revenue adjustments reflect a $12.9 million reimbursement from the reserve for Heritage Tax Credits, $6 million reimbursement from the reserve for Biotechnology Tax Credits, and transfers of $134.0 million from other special funds.

(c) Includes Budgeted Fund balances.

(d) Total expenditures are adjusted to reflect the impact of delaying the end-of-year school aid payment ($2.06 billion) from March 2010 to the statutory deadline of June 1, 2010, which was done to carry forward the 2009–2010 budget shortfall into 2010–11. The ending balance includes $1.2 billion in rainy day reserve funds, $85 million in a community projects fund, $73 million reserved for debt reduction and $21 million reserved for litigation risks.

(e) Revenues include $1 million transferred from the Rainy Day fund. Expenditure adjustment includes transfer of 25 percent of the ending balance to the Budget Stabilization Reserve (Rainy Day) fund.

(f) Opening balance includes a surplus of $17.7 million and re-appropriations of $3.4 million from the prior year. Adjustments to revenues reflect a transfer to the Budget Stabilization Fund and the adjustments to expenditures are the appropriations from FY 2010.

(g) FY 2011 adjustments (revenues) include $25.8 direct applications and transfers in, $6.8 other bills/other revenue, $5.9 additional property transfer tax to GF, and $15.2 from the Revenue Shortfall Reserve. Adjustments (expenditures) include $62.3 to the Human Services Caseload Reserve, ($1.5) from the General Bond Fund, $0.3 to Internal Service Funds, $4.8 to the Next Generation Fund, ($3.3) from the Budget Stabilization Reserve, and ($1.5) from the Revenue Shortfall/other reserves.

(h) Revenue adjustments are accounted for by statutory transfers in. Expenditure adjustments are accounted for by the sum of (legislatively required transfers plus pension obligation bond debt service plus debt service transfers for capital projects minus reduced transfer to local government distributive fund) subtracting the sum of voucher payments notes.

(i) Expenditure adjustments: PTRF Adjust for Abstracts.

(j) FY 2011 General Fund revenues are updated for the October 10, 2010 Revenue Estimating Conference.

(k) FY 2011 revenue adjustments include the impact of federal and state law changes (-$66.3 million); revenue sharing law changes ($477.8 million); deposits from state restricted revenues ($413.4 million); and pending revenue options ($263.0 million).

(l) Ending balance includes cash flow account of $266 million.

(m) Revenue adjustments are transfers between the General Fund and other funds. Among others, this includes a $112 million transfer from the General Fund to the Property Tax Credit Cash Fund as well as a $154 million transfer to the General Fund from the Cash Reserve Fund (Rainy Day Fund). Expenditure adjustments are reappropriations ($207.9 million) of the unexpended balance of appropriations from the prior fiscal year and a small amount ($5 million) reserved for supplemental/deficit appropriations.

(n) Adjustments in Revenues: $9.9 million was from one-time receipts.

(o) The figures for revenues and expenditures are updated projections completed by the Legislative Fiscal Bureau on July 6, 2010, after completion of the 2009 Legislative Session. The revenue adjustments include departmental revenue ($815 million) and tribal gaming ($22.3 million). Adjustments to expenditures include compensation reserves ($96 million), lapses (-$323.8 million) and FY 2010 biennial adjustments (-$242.7 million).

(p) Revenue adjustments include estimated unrealized capital gains.

(q) Revenue includes $111.3 million in Tobacco Settlement funds Adjustment for Revenues includes $44.7 million that represents appropriation balances carried over from the prior fiscal year, and $102.8 million from fund transfers into the General Fund. Adjustment to Expenditures represents appropriation balances forwarded and to the next fiscal year and budgeted balances to be expended in the next fiscal year.

(r) State General Fund beginning balance deficit recognized by the Joint Legislative Committee on the Budget on October 22, 2010. Executive Order issued to reduce state general fund expenditures accordingly.

(s) Revenue adjustments are transfers from other funds into the general revenue fund, including $572 million from the enhanced FMAP authorized in the American Recovery and Reinvestment Act of 2009. In addition, $8.7 million due to administrative efficiencies related to collection efforts.

(t) Rainy day fund balance includes General Reserve and Capital Reserve Funds.

(u) Adjustments (Revenues) include $195.7 million transfer from Rainy Day Fund, $170.0 million transfer from TennCare reserve, and $10.3 million transfer from other agency reserves. Adjustments (Expenditures) include $135.4 million transfer to capital outlay projects fund, and $17.7 million transfer to reserves for dedicated revenue appropriations.

(v) Revenue Adjustments represent transfers to the Economic Stabilization Fund (Rainy Day Fund) pursuant to Texas Constitution, Article III, Section 49-g. Expenditure Adjustments are related to adjustments to dedicated account balances.

(w) Rainy Day Fund data as of 10/22/2010. Fiscal Year 2011 Beginning balance includes $418.7 million in Reappropriations, Unappropriated Surplus Balance of $102.6 million, and FY 2010 13th month expenditures of $30.6 million. Expenditures include Regular appropriations $3,740.3 million and surplus appropriations of $2.5 million and $30.6 million of 31 day prior year expenditures. Ending Balance includes the amount that is available for appropriation (From FY 2011 revenue estimate ~$1.4~ and from surplus ~$48.9~ {previous year} general revenue) and anticipated reappropriations (estimated at $418.7) carried forward from FY 2012. Historically carried forward reappropriation amounts will remain consistent and be reappropriated to the next fiscal year.

(x) Revenue adjustments: $180.0 million oil and gas tax credits. Expenditure adjustments: net of (1,114.3) million PEF draw and 1,131.0 million PEF forward funding = 16.7 million.

(y) The estimated balance forward for FY 11 from the enacted budget was $48 million. However, the preliminary ending balance for FY 2010 right now stands at -$7 million. Revenue adjustments include $195 million agency fund transfers, $509 million fund transfer subject to voters approval, $98.2 million from revenue generation plan and from lottery, $34.6 million transfer from local governments and $918 million from temporary 1 cent sale tax increase.

(z) All entries include the August 23, 2010 budget balancing proposals by the Governor, addressing a June 2010 projected GF shortfall. Based on an updated revenue forecast released September 20, 2010, an additional $256.9M shortfall is anticipated, but has not yet been addressed.

(aa) Specific transfers include: $30,134,600 from the Budget Stabilization Fund and $48,846,700 from the Economic Recovery Reserve Fund.

(bb) All adjustments are transfers between reserve accounts, except for $40.0 million transferred out from Tobacco Settlement Permanent Fund, a reserve account to the Tobacco Settlement Program Fund, a nonreserve account.

(cc) Revenue adjustment is a transfer from the Education Stability Fund to General Fund. Expenditure adjustment is Executive allotment reductions to end biennium with $0 GF ending balance. Legislative action may be required to fully implement (or avoid) some allotment reductions.

(dd) Includes transfers from previous year balance, to/from Rainy Day Fund, and special revenue funds.

(ee) Fund transfers between General Fund and other accounts.

(ff) Wyoming budgets on a biennial basis to arrive at annual figures assumptions and estimates were required.

(gg) Includes $1.0 billion from the State Stabilization Fund to cover payroll expenses expected to be reduced through the fiscal year 2011.

Table 7.4
FISCAL 2010 STATE TAX COLLECTIONS COMPARED WITH PROJECTIONS
USED IN ADOPTING FISCAL 2010 BUDGETS, BY REGION
(In millions of dollars)

State or other jurisdiction	Sales tax Original estimate	Sales tax Current estimate	Personal income tax Original estimate	Personal income tax Current estimate	Corporate income tax Original estimate	Corporate income tax Current estimate	Revenue collection (a)
U.S. totals	$206,808	$200,546	$250,886	$236,073	$39,183	$39,310	-
Eastern Region							
Connecticut..................	3,167	3,204	6,631	6,585	722	667	H
Delaware	NA	NA	936	853	47	88	H
Maine...........................	939	954	1,291	1,298	148	175	H
Maryland	3,605	3,523	6,602	6,178	556	689	H
Massachusetts	4,501	4,612	10,241	10,110	1,501	1,600	H
New Hampshire	NA	NA	NA	NA	321	328	L
New Jersey	8,579	7,871	10,393	10,243	2,440	2,289	L
New York.....................	10,389	9,872	37,238	34,751	5,495	5,371	L
Pennsylvania	8,391	8,029	10,277	9,969	1,878	1,791	L
Rhode Island (c)..........	815	803	963	898	113	144	L
Vermont.......................	211	207	502	498	48	63	H
Regional totals (b).......	40,597	39,075	85,074	81,383	13,269	13,205	-
Midwestern Region							
Illinois.........................	6,394	6,308	9,206	8,510	1,133	1,360	L
Indiana.........................	6,132	5,915	4,289	3,876	800	592	L
Iowa	2,398	2,293	3,309	3,236	376	389	H
Kansas	1,845	1,858	2,510	2,418	250	225	L
Michigan......................	6,067	6,167	5,354	5,381	2,214	1,861	H
Minnesota....................	4,157	4,197	7,043	6,548	448	672	L
Nebraska......................	1,320	1,290	1,585	1,515	165	154	L
North Dakota...............	598	610	321	302	120	88	L
Ohio............................	7,077	6,995	7,247	7,479	142	100	L
South Dakota...............	659	643	NA	NA	NA	NA	L
Wisconsin....................	4,089	3,944	6,231	6,089	717	835	T
Regional totals (b).......	40,736	40,220	47,095	45,354	6,365	6,276	-
Southern Region							
Alabama......................	1,959	1,851	2,883	2,609	347	402	L
Arkansas......................	2,139	1,966	2,189	2,091	233	362	L
Florida	15,902	16,015	NA	NA	1,508	1,790	H
Georgia........................	5,213	4,865	8,338	7,017	543	685	L
Kentucky......................	3,067	2,794	3,630	3,154	506	238	L
Louisiana.....................	2,866	2,612	2,557	2,281	517	208	L
Mississippi	1,924	1,781	1,535	1,340	379	403	L
Missouri.......................	1,861	1,732	5,122	4,434	410	288	L
North Carolina.............	5,629	5,565	9,514	9,048	990	1,198	L
Oklahoma....................	1,754	1,516	2,044	1,709	307	168	L
South Carolina.............	2,192	2,191	2,469	2,171	129	110	H
Tennessee (d)..............	6,414	6,189	188	172	1,340	1,424	L
Texas (e)......................	21,100	21,100	NA	NA	NA	NA	L
Virginia........................	3,022	3,043	8,947	8,960	705	731	H
West Virginia...............	1,194	1,143	1,617	1,542	235	237	L
Regional totals (b).......	76,236	74,363	51,033	46,528	8,149	8,244	-
Western Region							
Alaska..........................	NA	NA	NA	NA	650	557	H
Arizona (f)	3,481	3,382	2,306	2,416	426	413	L
California	27,609	26,218	48,868	44,820	8,799	9,275	L
Colorado......................	2,020	1,825	4,341	4,084	319	372	L
Hawaii (g)	2,279	2,316	1,352	1,528	60	59	L
Idaho...........................	1,026	950	1,212	1,125	162	131	L
Montana	58	66	867	718	160	88	L
Nevada.........................	831	758	NA	NA	NA	NA	L
New Mexico	2,428	2,081	1,237	945	273	120	L
Oregon.........................	NA	NA	5,242	4,943	279	354	L
Utah.............................	1,473	1,430	2,260	2,229	274	217	L
Washington..................	7,551	7,031	NA	NA	NA	NA	L
Wyoming.....................	485	433	NA	NA	NA	NA	T
Regional totals (b).......	49,241	46,490	676,685	62,808	11,402	11,586	-
Regional totals w/o California (b)	21,632	20,272	18,817	17,988	2,603	2,311	-
Puerto Rico	606	545	2,614	2,614	1,541	1,556	T

See footnotes at end of table.

FISCAL 2010 STATE TAX COLLECTIONS COMPARED WITH PROJECTIONS USED IN ADOPTING FISCAL 2010 BUDGETS, BY REGION — Continued
(In millions of dollars)

Source: National Association of State Budget Officers, *The Fiscal Survey* of the States (December 2010).

Note: Unless otherwise noted, original estimates reflect the figures used when the fiscal 2010 budget was adopted, and current estimates reflect preliminary actual tax collections.

Key:

H — Revenues higher than estimates.

L — Revenues lower than estimates.

T — Revenues on target.

NA — Indicates data are not available because, in most cases, these states do not have that type of tax.

(a) Refers to whether actual fiscal 2010 collections of Sales, Personal Income and Corporate taxes were higher than, lower than, or on target with original estimates.

(b) Totals include only those states with data for both original and current estimates for fiscal 2010.

(c) Final total FY 2010 General Fund Revenues are not available yet. Designation is based on preliminary Final Total General Fund Revenues which are subject to further revisions.

(d) FY 2010 revenues "Lower than projected" estimates used when budget adopted FY 2010. FY 2010 revenues "lower than projected" with revised estimates made when budget adopted FY 2011. FY 2011 revenues "more than projected" for two months.

(e) Preliminary actual data for 2010 is based off data submitted in the spring of 2010. An updated estimate is expected in January 2011.

(f) None of the estimated Disproportionate Share amount was deposited in the General Fund by the end of FY 2010. If it were, we would have made our forecast.

(g) Dollar values represent totals from June 2010 Fiscal Survey. Total collections were lower due to delayed processing of tax refunds for tax year 2009.

Table 7.5
COMPARISON OF TAX COLLECTIONS IN FISCAL 2009, FISCAL 2010, AND ENACTED FISCAL 2011, BY REGION
(In millions of dollars)

State or other jurisdiction	Sales tax			Personal income tax			Corporate income tax		
	Fiscal 2009	Fiscal 2010	Fiscal 2011	Fiscal 2009	Fiscal 2010	Fiscal 2011	Fiscal 2009	Fiscal 2010	Fiscal 2011
U.S. totals (a)	$201,627	$200,546	$209,513	$245,297	$236,073	$247,258	$42,244	$39,310	$42,739
Eastern Region									
Connecticut	$3,319	$3,204	$3,165	$6,386	$6,586	$6,683	$616	$667	$663
Delaware	NA	NA	NA	911	853	849	127	88	79
Maine (b).....................	975	954	963	1,243	1,298	1,316	143	175	156
Maryland (c)	3,620	3,523	3,667	6,477	6,178	6,292	551	689	514
Massachusetts	3,869	4,612	4,897	10,584	10,110	10,704	1,549	1,600	1,397
New Hampshire	NA	NA	NA	NA	NA	NA	252	328	325
New Jersey	8,264	7,871	8,353	10,476	10,243	9,855	2,810	2,289	2,455
New York.....................	10,274	9,872	10,775	36,840	34,751	36,897	5,556	5,371	5,714
Pennsylvania	8,136	8,029	8,337	10,199	9,969	10,125	1,980	1,791	1,847
Rhode Island...............	808	803	787	941	898	938	104	144	119
Vermont.......................	214	207	214	530	498	527	66	63	66
Regional totals (a).......	39,479	39,075	41,158	84,586	81,384	84,186	13,755	13,205	13,355
Midwestern Region									
Illinois..........................	6,773	6,308	6,290	9,223	8,510	8,686	1,710	1,360	1,570
Indiana.........................	6,153	5,915	6,438	4,314	3,876	4,547	839	592	819
Iowa	2,327	2,293	2,228	3,331	3,236	3,226	417	398	341
Kansas	1,925	1,858	2,242	2,682	2,418	2,577	240	225	255
Michigan (d)................	6,089	6,167	6,261	5,856	5,381	5,538	2,285	1,861	2,191
Minnesota.....................	4,344	4,197	4,492	6,988	6,548	7,342	708	672	799
Nebraska (e)	1,326	610	1,365	1,600	1,515	1,630	199	154	185
North Dakota..............	622	6,995	599	375	302	334	99	88	119
Ohio..............................	7,113	943	7,267	7,628	7,479	7,568	521	100	132
South Dakota..............	659	3,944	671	NA	NA	NA	NA	NA	NA
Wisconsin (f)...............	4,084	4,089	4,321	6,223	6,089	6,432	630	835	808
Regional totals (a).......	41,415	43,319	42,174	48,220	45,354	47,880	7,647	6,265	7,219
Southern Region									
Alabama	1,823	1,851	1,869	2,681	2,609	2,691	447	402	531
Arkansas......................	2,081	1,966	2,087	2,239	2,091	2,203	323	362	344
Florida	16,531	16,015	16,824	NA	NA	NA	1,833	1,790	2,180
Georgia.........................	5,307	4,865	5,254	7,815	7,017	7,282	695	685	602
Kentucky......................	2,858	2,794	2,919	3,315	3,154	3,300	268	238	235
Louisiana.....................	3,071	2,612	2,669	2,966	2,281	2,466	825	208	372
Mississippi	1,922	1,781	1,765	1,475	1,340	1,353	422	403	393
Missouri.......................	1,813	1,732	1,746	4,876	4,434	4,522	358	288	310
North Carolina............	4,678	5,565	5,695	9,470	9,048	9,588	836	1,198	1,003
Oklahoma....................	1,647	1,516	1,584	1,960	1,709	1,703	266	168	172
South Carolina............	2,248	2,191	2,137	2,327	2,171	2,046	207	110	120
Tennessee	6,321	6,189	6,249	220	172	186	1,362	1,424	1,476
Texas (g)	20,900	21,100	22,500	NA	NA	NA	NA	NA	NA
Virginia........................	2,903	3,043	2,881	9,481	8,960	9,588	685	731	793
West Virginia...............	1,159	1,143	1,173	1,653	1,542	1,586	285	235	214
Regional totals (a).......	75,261	74,363	77,352	50,477	46,528	48,514	8,811	8,242	8,745
Western Region									
Alaska...........................	NA	NA	NA	NA	NA	NA	613	557	669
Arizona........................	3,756	3,382	3,601	2,568	2,416	2,470	592	413	446
California	23,753	26,618	27,044	43,376	44,820	47,127	9,536	9,275	10,897
Colorado......................	1,931	1,825	2,010	433	4,084	4,609	293	372	342
Hawaii (h)	2,418	2,316	2,496	1,339	1,528	1,349	54	59	37
Idaho............................	1,022	950	989	1,168	1,125	1,171	141	131	133
Montana	57	66	59	815	718	853	166	88	121
Nevada.........................	860	758	733	NA	NA	NA	NA	NA	NA
New Mexico	2,307	2,081	2,234	959	945	1,057	163	120	200
Oregon.........................	NA	NA	NA	5,117	4,943	5,781	244	354	331
Utah.............................	1,547	1,430	1,462	2,339	2,229	2,264	269	217	265
Washington..................	7,330	7,031	7,768	NA	NA	NA	NA	NA	NA
Wyoming......................	492	433	433	NA	NA	NA	NA	NA	NA
Regional totals (a).......	45,473	46,890	48,829	58,114	62,808	66,681	12,071	11,586	13,441
Regional totals w/o California (a).....	21,720	20,272	21,785	14,738	17,988	19,554	2,535	2,311	2,544
Puerto Rico (i).............	895	545	604	2,614	2,614	2,812	1,364	1,556	1,667

See footnotes at end of table.

COMPARISON OF TAX COLLECTIONS IN FISCAL 2009, FISCAL 2010, AND ENACTED FISCAL 2011, BY REGION—Continued
(In millions of dollars)

Source: National Association of State Budget Officers, *The Fiscal Survey of the States* (December 2010).

Note: Unless otherwise noted, fiscal 2009 figures reflect actual tax collections, 2010 figures reflect preliminary actual tax collections estimates, and fiscal 2011 figures reflect the estimates used in enacted budgets.

Key:

NA — Indicates data are not available because, in most cases, these states do not have that type of tax.

(a) Totals include only those states with data for all years.

(b) FY 2010 and 2011 estimate amounts come from the RFC on 3/10/10.

(c) Corporate Income Tax totals include $129.0 million of extraordinary income from the sale of Constellation Energy. Excluding extraordinary income, corporate income taxes increased 1.7 percent in FY 2010 and fell 8.3 percent in FY 2011.

(d) The fiscal 2011 enacted budget is based on the May 2010 consensus estimates and is net of all enacted tax changes. Tax estimates represent total tax collections. Sales tax collections are for the Michigan sales tax only and do not include collections from Michigan use tax. Michigan does not have a Corporate Income tax; estimates are for the Michigan Business Tax that replaced Michigan's Single Business Tax effective December 2007. The fiscal 2010 revenues appear to be higher than May 2010 consensus revenue estimates which may translate into higher fiscal 2011 revenues; updated fiscal 2011 revenue figures will be released at the next regularly scheduled consensus revenue conference in January 2011.

(e) Fiscal 2011 amounts represent revenue estimates at the conclusion of the most recent legislative session.

(f) FY 2009 Actuals from Exhibit A-1 of Wisconsin's Annual Fiscal Report. Preliminary FY 2010 Actuals from September 3, 2010 Legislative Fiscal Bureau Memo, Preliminary 2009–10 General Fund Tax Collections. Tax collection estimates used to budget for FY 2010 and FY 2011 from Legislative Fiscal Bureau, Comparative Summary of Budget Recommendations, 2009 Act 28.

(g) Preliminary actual data for 2010 is based off data submitted in the spring of 2010. An updated estimate is expected in January 2011.

(h) Dollar values represent totals from June 2010 Fiscal Survey.

(i) For FY 2010 the amount of sales tax collections going into the General Fund was reduced by 0.75 percent to provide funding for the Sales Tax Financing Corporation debt service requirements, as mandated by law.

Table 7.6
TOTAL STATE EXPENDITURES: CAPITAL INCLUSIVE, BY REGION
(In millions of dollars)

State	Actual fiscal 2008					Actual fiscal 2009					Estimated fiscal 2010				
	General fund	Federal funds	Other state funds	Bonds	Total	General fund	Federal funds	Other state funds	Bonds	Total	General fund	Federal funds	Other state funds	Bonds	Total
U.S. total	$678,911	$388,184	$376,894	$34,793	$1,478,782	$656,722	$456,968	$396,755	$36,359	$1,546,804	$618,191	$563,692	$398,607	$44,176	$1,624,666
Eastern Region															
Connecticut (a)	16,627	2,117	3,494	2,032	24,270	17,235	2,327	4,385	1,852	25,799	17,251	3,099	3,918	1,794	26,062
Delaware	3,422	1,113	3,811	275	8,621	3,296	1,256	3,908	281	8,741	3,077	1,607	3,783	253	8,720
Maine	3,084	2,182	2,053	108	7,427	3,020	2,778	2,184	110	8,092	2,866	3,151	2,159	81	8,257
Maryland	14,488	6,561	8,520	839	30,408	14,353	7,759	8,759	926	31,797	13,428	9,795	9,058	1,128	33,409
Massachusetts	28,934	2,525	10,928	1,420	43,807	30,016	3,405	14,004	1,568	48,993	28,912	5,722	16,889	1,887	53,410
New Hampshire	1,515	1,498	1,680	114	4,807	1,438	1,682	1,687	171	4,978	1,401	2,073	1,853	138	5,465
New Jersey (b)	33,112	8,851	5,233	1,508	48,704	30,825	10,788	3,437	1,627	46,677	29,862	14,045	3,411	1,657	48,975
New York (c)	53,385	34,680	26,122	1,869	116,056	54,607	38,425	25,386	3,153	121,571	54,262	44,843	28,569	3,263	130,937
Pennsylvania	26,969	18,037	12,952	738	58,696	27,085	20,825	13,735	999	62,644	25,177	29,363	14,181	1,655	70,376
Rhode Island (d)	3,405	1,939	1,589	185	7,118	3,001	2,271	1,680	149	7,101	2,887	3,096	2,085	94	8,162
Vermont	1,225	1,312	2,734	37	5,308	1,159	1,468	2,934	56	5,617	1,109	1,845	2,796	72	5,822
Regional totals	186,166	80,815	79,116	9,125	355,222	186,035	92,984	82,099	10,892	371,810	180,232	118,639	88,702	12,022	399,595
Midwestern Region															
Illinois	22,140	11,073	11,047	306	44,566	19,831	13,253	13,224	161	46,469	17,244	14,686	14,657	839	47,426
Indiana (e)	12,880	7,818	3,380	161	24,239	13,036	9,060	3,525	98	25,719	12,915	10,333	3,245	169	26,662
Iowa	5,867	4,565	5,668	29	16,129	5,904	6,031	5,499	43	17,477	5,302	6,642	6,143	459	18,546
Kansas	6,102	3,522	2,787	278	12,689	6,064	3,795	3,800	301	13,960	5,451	4,544	4,178	324	14,497
Michigan (f)	9,822	12,660	21,081	419	43,982	8,506	16,510	20,502	241	45,759	8,110	19,238	18,183	192	45,723
Minnesota	17,600	6,264	3,891	691	28,446	17,555	7,563	4,180	599	29,897	15,567	10,400	4,792	743	31,502
Nebraska (g)	3,247	2,411	3,053	0	8,711	3,329	2,566	3,244	0	9,139	3,313	2,973	3,305	0	9,591
North Dakota	1,204	1,241	1,125	27	3,597	1,240	1,362	1,329	10	3,941	1,551	1,767	1,370	22	4,710
Ohio	25,722	9,655	20,633	753	56,763	26,783	10,342	19,819	850	57,794	24,141	13,029	19,827	643	57,640
South Dakota	1,176	1,182	842	17	3,217	1,153	1,396	920	77	3,546	1,129	1,718	855	67	3,769
Wisconsin	13,527	7,534	15,028	0	36,089	12,744	9,709	15,989	0	38,442	12,824	11,531	15,730	0	40,085
Regional totals	119,287	67,925	88,535	2,681	278,428	116,145	81,587	92,031	2,380	292,143	107,547	96,861	92,285	3,458	300,151
Southern Region															
Alabama (h)	8,460	6,291	4,537	552	19,840	7,284	6,831	5,052	593	19,760	6,847	10,181	7,024	406	24,458
Arkansas	4,274	4,806	7,756	63	16,899	4,380	5,425	8,337	51	18,193	4,207	7,091	8,862	89	20,249
Florida	27,513	18,754	14,916	3,196	64,379	23,662	19,825	15,088	2,099	60,674	21,195	22,744	20,733	1,833	66,505
Georgia	17,934	10,268	8,773	1,519	38,494	16,750	11,477	9,376	1,367	38,970	14,870	13,066	9,594	1,091	38,621
Kentucky	9,334	6,720	6,941	0	22,995	9,031	8,233	6,793	0	24,057	8,348	10,477	7,012	0	25,837
Louisiana	10,372	12,883	5,342	291	28,888	9,444	10,951	4,667	592	25,654	9,011	14,798	5,177	626	29,612
Mississippi	4,842	6,434	4,029	234	15,539	4,692	6,712	4,557	367	16,328	4,597	8,832	5,536	419	19,384
Missouri (i)	8,084	5,632	7,165	551	21,432	8,402	6,265	8,318	89	23,094	7,565	8,743	7,791	712	24,811
North Carolina (j)	20,376	10,914	10,098	200	41,588	19,653	11,856	10,981	600	43,090	13,765	10,492	7,046	489	31,792
Oklahoma	6,793	9,030	4,803	104	20,730	6,732	9,852	4,742	104	21,430	6,036	10,899	4,480	144	21,559
South Carolina (k)	7,149	6,654	6,866	118	20,787	5,812	7,378	7,702	182	21,074	5,275	10,117	7,175	0	22,567
Tennessee (l)	11,570	9,343	4,969	151	26,033	11,921	11,032	5,587	578	29,118	10,671	12,903	5,291	271	29,136
Texas	41,184	25,023	12,634	2,256	81,097	44,214	31,102	13,358	1,291	89,965	44,156	38,001	13,412	2,298	97,867
Virginia	15,099	6,342	13,040	849	35,330	16,065	7,078	15,134	1,747	40,024	14,989	9,327	15,001	1,456	40,773
West Virginia	3,824	3,287	11,422	177	18,710	3,901	3,824	12,592	130	20,447	3,779	4,418	11,919	131	20,247
Regional totals	196,808	142,381	123,291	10,261	472,741	191,943	157,861	132,284	9,790	491,878	175,311	192,089	136,053	9,965	513,418

See footnotes at end of table.

TOTAL STATE EXPENDITURES: CAPITAL INCLUSIVE, BY REGION — Continued
(In millions of dollars)

State	Actual fiscal 2008					Actual fiscal 2009					Estimated fiscal 2010				
	General fund	Federal funds	Other state funds	Bonds	Total	General fund	Federal funds	Other state funds	Bonds	Total	General fund	Federal funds	Other state funds	Bonds	Total
Western Region															
Alaska	5,090	2,314	4,226	26	11,656	5,407	3,042	4,730	345	13,524	5,375	3,178	1,193	0	9,746
Arizona	10,368	7,820	6,405	654	25,247	9,239	10,240	6,768	833	27,080	9,079	10,655	6,891	886	27,511
California (m)	102,986	56,211	26,674	8,405	194,276	90,940	73,090	23,844	7,602	195,476	86,465	95,398	23,326	12,653	217,842
Colorado (n)	7,908	4,739	12,482	-	25,129	7,722	6,447	14,637	-	28,806	7,326	8,920	12,757	0	29,003
Hawaii	5,407	1,760	3,376	617	11,160	5,375	1,919	3,958	570	11,822	4,838	2,391	3,045	674	10,948
Idaho	2,799	2,005	1,097	31	5,932	2,724	2,304	1,257	29	6,314	2,349	2,952	1,808	21	7,130
Montana (o)	1,901	1,646	1,810	-	5,357	1,753	1,827	1,946	-	5,526	1,628	2,285	2,136	-	6,049
Nevada	4,031	1,780	3,028	401	9,240	4,202	2,272	1,963	602	9,039	3,291	2,705	1,702	177	7,875
New Mexico	6,027	4,506	3,091	583	14,207	6,080	4,946	3,873	606	15,505	5,468	5,580	2,711	592	14,351
Oregon	6,601	4,625	10,763	185	22,174	5,889	5,914	12,466	255	24,524	5,969	8,275	13,203	473	27,920
Utah (p)	5,784	2,503	3,033	3	11,323	4,817	2,963	3,736	279	11,795	4,441	3,672	3,555	1,259	12,927
Washington	14,616	6,678	8,617	1,821	31,732	14,617	8,146	8,775	2,176	33,714	15,036	8,662	6,849	1,996	32,543
Wyoming	3,132	476	1,350	0	4,958	3,834	1,426	2,388	0	7,648	3,836	1,430	2,391	0	7,657
Regional totals	176,650	97,063	85,952	12,726	372,391	162,599	124,536	90,341	13,297	390,773	155,101	156,103	81,567	18,731	411,502
Regional totals without California	73,664	40,852	59,278	4,321	178,115	71,659	51,446	66,497	5,695	195,297	68,636	60,705	58,241	6,078	193,660

Source: National Association of State Budget Officers, *State Expenditure Report 2009* (December 2010).

Note: State funds refers to general funds plus other state fund spending. State spending from bonds is excluded. Total funds refers to funding from all sources—general fund, federal funds, other state funds and bonds. Small dollar amounts, when rounded, cause an aberration in the percentage increase. In these instances, the actual dollar amounts should be consulted to determine the exact percentage increase.

Key:

(a) Bonds data is based on bond allocations by the State Bond Commission.

(b) Totals include pension, post retirement medical, debt service on pension bonds, payroll taxes, and health benefits expenditures which total $1.18 billion in State General Fund in fiscal 2009 and $1.32 billion in fiscal 2010 spread across Education, Corrections, Transportation and All Other.

(c) New York budgets most employer contributions to employees' benefits and pensions centrally. The portion of employer contributions to employees' benefits are not distributed to an expenditure category has been included in the All Other Expenditures category. Fiscal 2009–10 spending is adjusted to exclude the impact of paying the end-of-year school aid payment from 2009–10 in the first quarter of 2010–11, as authorized in statute.

(d) Fiscal 2010 estimated bond payments are based on year-to-date expenditures.

(e) Expenditure figures for "2008 Actual—General Funds" include $149.7 million of Homestead Credits distributed as part of HEA 1001 (2008), the Governor's property tax reform legislation. The revenue for these expenditures was provided by the 1% increase in the sales tax from 6% to 7%, effective April 1, 2008, which generated $151.6 million during fiscal 2008. Excluding these expenditures, total General Fund expenditures for fiscal 2008 would have been $12,730 million (instead of $12,880 million). Expenditure figures for "2009 Actual—General Funds" include $1,122.4 million of appropriations made in HEA 1001 (2008), the Governor's property tax reform legislation. The revenue for these expenditures was provided by the 1% increase in the sales tax from 6% to 7% ($879.0 million), the riverboat admissions tax ($12.8 million), and the motor vehicle excise tax and FIT ($13.0 million). Excluding these appropriations, total General Fund expenditures for fiscal 2009 would have been $11,915 million (instead of $13,037 million). Expenditure figures for "2010 Estimated—General Funds" include $1,085.3 million of appropriations made in HEA 1001 (2008), the Governor's property tax reform legislation. Excluding these appropriations, total General Fund expenditures for fiscal 2010 would have been $11,830 million (instead of $12,915 million). As requested, expenditure figures for "2009 Actual and 2010 Estimated—Federal Funds" include American Recovery and Reinvestment Act (ARRA) expenditures.

(f) Fiscal 2008 general funding spending is artificially high, distorting year-to-year comparisons, due to the deferral of partial fiscal 2007 payments to higher education institutions. Adjusting for this one-time action results in nominal expenditure changes of 4.4% (Total Funds) and -9.1% (General Fund) from fiscal 2008 to fiscal 2009.

(g) Fiscal 2008, fiscal 2009, and fiscal 2010 totals reflect actual expenditures for each of the spending categories.

(h) Amounts shown in fiscal years 2008 and 2009 are based on actual expenditures during these years, regardless of the year appropriated. Fiscal 2010 amounts shown are equal to appropriations for the year, except for bond proceeds, which are estimated. It is assumed that some level of appropriations will not be expended this fiscal year.

(i) Total expenditures exclude refunds. Fiscal 2008 expenditures exclude refunds of $1,307 million, including $1,258 million general revenue. Fiscal 2009 expenditures exclude refunds of $1,488 million, including $1,441 million general revenue. Fiscal 2010 estimates exclude refunds of $1,548 million, including $1,469 million general revenue. Other funds include federal reimbursements received by the Department of Highways and Transportation and the Department of Conservation which have constitutionally created funds.

(j) North Carolina was unable to provide complete expenditure figures for estimated fiscal 2010 in both the Public Assistance and All Other categories.

(k) Estimated capital expenditures are no longer collected. Therefore, no capital expenditure data is included for estimated fiscal 2010.

(l) Tennessee collects personal income tax on income from dividends on stocks and interest on certain bonds. Tax revenue estimates do not include federal funds and other departmental revenues. However, federal funds and other departmental revenues are included in the budget as funding sources for the general fund, along with state tax revenues.

(m) Data are based on May 2010 Revision.

(n) All actual expenditures reflected conform to state accounting records as reported in the Colorado financial reports.

(o) Fiscal 2008 total expenditures reflect over $220 million in various one-time-only general fund expenditures including nearly $96 million for a $400 tax rebate and $50 million general fund for fire fighting. Fiscal 2009 total expenditures reflect $46 million in various one-time-only general fund expenditures. Principal and interest payments on bonds are included in total expenditures. Capital expenditures are not reported separately but are included in total expenditures.

(p) All numerical information presented represents bond "expenditures". All bond information included in the report is for General Obligation bonds. Not included in the report is State Building Ownership Authority (SBOA) Revenue Bonds or Board of Regents Revenue Bonds.

Table 7.7
ELEMENTARY AND SECONDARY EDUCATION EXPENDITURES, BY STATE AND REGION
(In millions of dollars)

State	Actual fiscal 2008					Actual fiscal 2009					Estimated fiscal 2010				
	General fund	Federal funds	Other state funds	Bonds	Total	General fund	Federal funds	Other state funds	Bonds	Total	General fund	Federal funds	Other state funds	Bonds	Total
U.S. totals	$237,624	$45,401	$38,526	$3,347	$324,898	$235,191	$54,828	$39,684	$5,591	$335,294	$220,708	$74,104	$39,220	$3,356	$337,388
Eastern Region															
Connecticut	2,569	422	5	736	3,732	2,672	441	4	642	3,759	2,393	860	4	700	3,057
Delaware	1,133	141	496	225	1,995	1,163	150	524	234	2,071	1,117	242	531	188	2,078
Maine	1,211	179	3	2	1,395	1,201	218	3	0	1,422	1,171	276	10	0	1,457
Maryland	5,317	901	10	0	6,228	5,548	904	13	0	6,465	5,339	1,643	25	0	7,007
Massachusetts	4,672	844	658	0	6,174	4,454	1,279	636	0	6,369	4,304	1,230	731	0	6,265
New Hampshire	0	161	898	8	1,067	0	168	898	48	1,114	0	193	797	50	1,040
New Jersey	10,973	786	18	0	11,777	10,416	832	18	0	11,266	10,167	1,968	19	0	12,154
New York	17,946	3,655	2,910	17	24,277	19,435	3,579	3,098	7	26,110	19,119	4,275	2,949	20	26,363
Pennsylvania	9,361	2,015	17	0	11,393	9,629	2,101	632	0	12,362	9,132	4,520	629	0	14,281
Rhode Island	909	176	8	5	1,098	826	213	16	6	1,061	807	311	21	20	1,159
Vermont	46	109	1,236	9	1,400	48	119	1,294	11	1,472	52	181	1,284	10	1,527
Regional totals	54,137	9,389	6,259	1,002	70,536	55,392	10,004	7,136	948	73,471	53,601	15,699	7,000	988	76,388
Midwestern Region															
Illinois	8,180	1,983	28	30	10,221	8,959	2,130	26	3	11,118	8,087	2,330	20	18	10,455
Indiana (a)	4,801	870	36	0	5,707	5,695	1,476	51	0	7,222	7,155	1,377	104	0	8,636
Iowa	2,523	380	13	0	2,916	2,598	425	56	0	3,079	2,235	507	285	0	3,027
Kansas	3,076	399	101	0	3,576	3,147	420	115	0	3,682	2,848	768	134	0	3,750
Michigan (b)	44	1,550	11,394	0	12,988	85	2,179	10,968	0	13,232	42	2,532	10,632	0	13,206
Minnesota	6,819	624	43	20	7,506	6,938	642	41	7	7,628	5,352	1,801	42	1	7,197
Nebraska	980	273	34	0	1,287	1,064	270	45	0	1,379	1,071	380	42	0	1,493
North Dakota	363	121	39	0	523	388	124	39	0	551	543	232	44	0	819
Ohio	6,933	1,647	2,251	56	10,887	8,125	1,700	2,702	0	12,527	7,927	2,109	2,958	4	12,998
South Dakota	378	150	127	0	655	381	198	12	0	591	388	196	3	0	587
Wisconsin	5,974	688	214	0	6,876	5,623	1,327	204	0	7,154	5,946	1,131	198	0	7,275
Regional totals	40,071	8,685	14,280	106	63,142	43,003	10,891	14,259	10	68,163	41,594	13,363	14,463	23	69,443
Southern Region															
Alabama (c)	4,497	824	169	0	5,490	3,910	859	171	0	4,940	3,661	1,575	204	0	5,440
Arkansas	1,911	453	789	0	3,153	1,949	494	774	0	3,217	1,852	699	876	0	3,427
Florida (d)	9,943	2,422	632	0	12,997	8,698	2,561	586	0	11,845	8,133	4,968	540	0	13,641
Georgia	7,795	1,548	0	454	9,797	7,348	1,776	0	305	9,429	6,606	2,247	0	298	9,151
Kentucky	4,016	707	17	0	4,740	4,017	707	15	0	4,739	3,840	1,169	11	0	5,020
Louisiana	3,344	1,106	363	0	4,813	3,410	1,058	387	0	4,855	3,235	1,464	329	0	5,028
Mississippi	2,180	652	332	7	3,171	2,147	645	311	4	3,107	2,115	797	504	0	3,416
Missouri	2,864	848	1,404	0	5,116	3,019	888	1,321	0	5,228	2,559	1,578	1,289	0	5,426
North Carolina	7,977	1,199	144	0	9,320	8,142	1,450	120	0	9,712	7,487	1,503	429	0	9,419
Oklahoma	1,723	606	860	0	3,189	1,740	731	833	0	3,304	1,432	951	860	0	3,243
South Carolina	2,443	682	792	0	3,917	2,150	765	678	0	3,593	1,928	901	564	0	3,393
Tennessee	3,757	842	63	0	4,662	3,967	929	46	0	4,942	3,708	1,485	62	0	5,255
Texas	16,767	4,189	4,586	6	25,548	19,332	4,538	3,981	43	27,894	15,349	8,705	4,191	53	28,298
Virginia	5,375	826	618	0	6,819	5,678	844	665	0	7,187	4,853	1,335	641	0	6,829
West Virginia	1,767	320	13	23	2,123	1,795	345	13	23	2,176	1,790	415	13	23	2,241
Regional totals	76,359	17,224	10,782	490	104,855	77,302	18,590	9,901	375	106,168	68,548	29,792	10,513	374	109,227

See footnotes at end of table.

ELEMENTARY AND SECONDARY EDUCATION EXPENDITURES, BY STATE AND REGION—Continued
(In millions of dollars)

State	Actual fiscal 2008					Actual fiscal 2009					Estimated fiscal 2010				
	General fund	Federal funds	Other state funds	Bonds	Total	General fund	Federal funds	Other state funds	Bonds	Total	General fund	Federal funds	Other state funds	Bonds	Total
Western Region															
Alaska	1,027	189	112	0	1,328	1,037	196	117	0	1,350	1,104	291	122	0	1,517
Arizona	4,547	913	1,231	102	6,793	3,954	971	1,457	96	6,478	3,275	1,664	1,067	90	6,096
California	39,038	5,840	414	1,647	46,939	31,476	9,982	737	3,977	46,172	31,344	8,480	85	1,634	41,543
Colorado (e)	3,024	519	3,328	0	6,871	3,215	535	3,653	0	7,403	3,240	629	3,801	0	7,670
Hawaii	2,172	226	44	0	2,442	2,272	207	44	0	2,523	1,349	317	44	0	1,710
Idaho	1,392	234	69	0	1,695	1,360	218	151	0	1,729	1,166	303	298	0	1,767
Montana (f)	691	140	57	0	888	661	145	66	0	872	568	207	137	0	912
Nevada	1,303	230	0	0	1,533	1,616	243	0	0	1,859	1,395	242	0	0	1,637
New Mexico	2,513	402	11	0	2,926	2,524	504	17	0	3,045	2,326	627	1	0	2,954
Oregon	2,916	511	444	0	3,871	2,745	631	484	0	3,860	2,435	737	604	0	3,776
Utah (g)	2,519	379	-14	0	2,884	2,293	552	165	0	3,010	2,271	556	59	0	2,886
Washington	5,903	697	716	0	7,316	6,334	1,067	712	185	8,298	6,485	1,104	231	247	8,067
Wyoming	12	74	793	0	879	7	92	794	0	893	7	93	795	0	895
Regional totals	67,057	10,354	7,205	1,749	86,365	59,494	15,343	8,397	4,258	87,492	56,965	15,250	7,244	1,971	81,430
Regional totals without California	28,019	4,514	6,791	102	39,426	28,018	5,361	7,660	281	41,320	25,621	6,770	7,159	337	39,887

Source: National Association of State Budget Officers, *State Expenditure Report 2009* (December 2010).

Key:

(a) Expenditure figures for "2009 Actual and 2010 Estimated—Elementary and Secondary Education (General Funds)" increased in part due to HEA 1001 (2008), the Governor's property tax reform legislation whereby the state assumed the responsibility for funding 100% of the K–12 tuition support formula.

(b) Figures reflect K–12 education, the Michigan Department of Education, adult education and pre-school. Employer contributions to current employees' pensions and health benefits are reported for Department of Education employees but excluded for employees of K–12 schools. General fund revenue support increased for fiscal 2009 as support from other revenue sources in the State School Aid Fund declined. Federal revenue support increases in fiscal 2009 and fiscal 2010 are largely due to federal ARRA funding for K–12 and other education programs. Actual ARRA expenditures will be recorded with the fiscal 2010 annual financial report.

(c) Federal funds received directly by local school systems are not reported at the state budget level.

(d) State appropriations to school districts for operational costs include funding intended to be expended by school districts for contributions to current employees' pensions, employee health benefits, and for the operational cost of libraries.

(e) Elementary and Secondary education totals include capital expenditures.

(f) For fiscal 2010, general funds decreased and other state funds increased as a result of Otter Creek Coal Tract Bonus Payment (approximately $81 million offset to general fund). Additionally, for fiscal 2010 and to a lesser extent fiscal 2009, federal funds increased and general funds decreased due to ARRA SFSF.

(g) Included with the General Fund is the Education Fund (income tax revenue) which in Utah is restricted by the Utah state constitution for the sole use of public and higher education. Public education in Utah is organized to include the Utah State Office of Rehabilitation (USOR). The numbers reflected in this report for public education include USOR. The USOR amounts are as follows: fiscal 2008—$23 million general fund/education fund, $40 million federal funds, $1 million other state funds for a total of $64 million; fiscal 2009—does not include USOR; fiscal 2010—does not include USOR.

Table 7.8
MEDICAID EXPENDITURES BY STATE AND REGION
(In millions of dollars)

State	Actual fiscal 2008				Actual fiscal 2009				Estimated fiscal 2010			
	General fund	Federal funds	Other state funds	Total	General fund	Federal funds	Other state funds	Total	General fund	Federal funds	Other state funds	Total
U.S. totals	$111,711	$172,290	$26,884	$310,885	$107,524	$199,625	$28,028	$335,177	$94,942	$222,646	$36,249	$353,837
Eastern Region												
Connecticut (a)	3,471	0	794	4,265	3,851	0	820	4,671	3,855	$0	$1,125	$4,980
Delaware	494	497	0	991	538	539	0	1,077	481	777	0	1,258
Maine	594	1,319	178	2,091	544	1,735	183	2,462	418	1,802	175	2,395
Maryland (b)	2,580	2,821	217	5,618	2,400	3,629	324	6,353	2,005	4,098	558	6,661
Massachusetts	8,247	0	0	8,247	8,688	0	0	8,688	9,465	0	0	9,465
New Hampshire	468	615	167	1,250	406	644	266	1,316	392	802	180	1,374
New Jersey	4,734	4,640	134	9,508	4,230	5,485	136	9,851	4,111	6,007	136	10,254
New York	8,568	19,102	3,370	31,040	7,689	21,310	3,429	32,428	6,296	26,060	4,669	37,025
Pennsylvania	6,488	9,596	1,701	17,785	6,029	11,096	1,625	18,750	5,523	12,188	1,716	19,427
Rhode Island (c)	899	933	5	1,837	731	1,029	6	1,766	724	1,227	7	1,958
Vermont	199	595	209	1,003	153	714	221	1,088	149	837	227	1,213
Regional totals	36,742	40,118	6,775	83,635	35,259	46,181	7,010	88,450	33,419	53,798	8,793	96,010
Midwestern Region												
Illinois	4,491	6,496	2,837	13,824	4,367	7,837	2,284	14,488	3,793	9,292	2,466	15,551
Indiana (d)	1,537	3,335	380	5,252	1,225	3,986	384	5,595	1,186	4,554	432	6,172
Iowa	661	1,641	590	2,892	602	1,865	643	3,110	590	2,148	632	3,370
Kansas	871	1,395	106	2,372	801	1,705	87	2,593	727	1,686	96	2,509
Michigan (e)	2,308	5,680	1,762	9,750	1,625	7,471	1,455	10,551	1,425	8,586	1,518	11,529
Minnesota	3,188	3,252	0	6,440	3,002	3,656	0	6,658	2,822	3,891	61	6,774
Nebraska	634	890	20	1,544	613	993	23	1,629	532	1,095	22	1,649
North Dakota	189	352	2	543	162	380	7	549	190	469	6	665
Ohio	9,346	2,480	1,338	13,164	10,237	2,886	928	14,051	8,613	2,992	1,049	12,654
South Dakota	261	440	0	701	229	547	0	776	219	631	0	850
Wisconsin	1,627	2,986	264	4,877	1,250	3,953	995	6,198	1,220	4,665	701	6,586
Regional totals	25,113	28,947	7,299	61,359	24,113	35,279	6,806	66,198	21,317	40,009	6,983	68,309
Southern Region												
Alabama (f)	572	2,899	929	4,400	552	3,351	968	4,871	701	3,250	906	4,857
Arkansas	615	2,494	322	3,431	654	2,725	387	3,766	609	3,302	250	4,161
Florida	4,454	8,114	2,354	14,922	4,614	8,522	2,983	16,119	3,018	11,993	3,799	18,810
Georgia	2,370	4,448	393	7,211	1,818	5,353	444	7,615	1,753	5,600	321	7,674
Kentucky	1,133	3,362	410	4,905	1,020	4,152	337	5,509	811	4,499	383	5,693
Louisiana	871	4,278	631	5,780	1,151	5,111	326	6,588	900	5,246	480	6,626
Mississippi	317	2,629	547	3,493	300	3,176	727	4,203	166	3,210	879	4,255
Missouri (g)	1,175	4,288	1,848	7,311	1,257	4,920	2,442	8,619	1,422	4,020	2,629	8,071
North Carolina	2,915	6,395	1,684	10,994	2,766	6,672	1,283	10,721	2,319	8,113	1,364	11,796
Oklahoma	1,009	2,419	291	3,719	1,006	2,498	464	3,968	681	3,105	417	4,203
South Carolina	906	3,006	471	4,383	587	3,340	635	4,562	521	3,929	555	5,005
Tennessee (h)	2,525	4,675	297	7,497	2,588	4,514	287	7,389	1,917	5,536	231	7,684
Texas	5,539	7,813	108	13,460	6,098	8,248	125	14,471	2,379	4,885	58	7,322
Virginia	2,756	2,587	0	5,343	2,903	3,176	0	6,079	2,590	3,963	1	6,554
West Virginia	389	1,633	239	2,261	301	1,921	245	2,467	217	2,090	244	2,551
Regional totals	27,546	61,040	10,524	99,110	27,615	67,679	11,653	108,947	20,004	72,741	12,517	105,262

See footnotes at end of table.

MEDICAID EXPENDITURES BY STATE AND REGION—Continued
(In millions of dollars)

	Actual fiscal 2008				Actual fiscal 2009				Estimated fiscal 2010			
State	General fund	Federal funds	Other state funds	Total	General fund	Federal funds	Other state funds	Total	General fund	Federal funds	Other state funds	Total
Western Region												
Alaska	408	612	11	1,031	402	770	29	1,201	314	789	17	1,120
Arizona	1,285	3,815	546	5,646	1,239	5,971	762	7,972	1,187	5,608	868	7,663
California	12,708	24,857	726	38,291	10,910	28,371	622	39,903	11,170	32,147	5,009	48,326
Colorado	1,309	1,398	79	2,786	1,223	1,756	135	3,114	1,116	2,539	1,115	4,770
Hawaii	505	740	0	1,245	447	884	0	1,331	499	957	0	1,456
Idaho	369	848	84	1,301	331	1,015	91	1,437	288	1,116	102	1,506
Montana (i)	165	531	57	753	142	642	57	841	137	728	65	930
Nevada	455	684	0	1,139	475	857	0	1,332	403	961	0	1,364
New Mexico	699	2,199	172	3,070	604	2,604	193	3,401	567	2,683	113	3,363
Oregon	873	1,902	322	3,097	711	2,452	369	3,532	681	2,880	387	3,948
Utah	333	1,123	239	1,695	270	1,211	239	1,720	229	1,377	205	1,811
Washington	2,954	3,219	50	6,223	3,528	3,633	62	7,223	3,415	3,950	75	7,440
Wyoming	247	257	0	504	255	320	0	575	196	363	0	559
Regional totals	22,310	42,185	2,286	66,781	20,537	50,486	2,559	73,582	20,202	56,098	7,956	84,256
Regional totals without California	9,602	17,328	1,560	28,490	9,627	22,115	1,937	33,679	9,032	23,951	2,947	35,930

Source: National Association of State Budget Officers, *State Expenditure Report 2009* (December 2010).

Note: States were asked to report Medicaid expenditures as follows: General funds: all general funds appropriated to the Medicaid agency and any other agency which are used for direct Medicaid matching purposes under Title XIX. Other state funds: other funds and revenue sources used as Medicaid match, such as local funds and provider taxes, fees, donations, assessments (as defined by the Health Care Finance Administration). Federal Funds: all federal matching funds provided pursuant to Title XIX. As noted above, the figures reported as Other State Funds reflect the amounts reported as provider taxes, fees, donations, assessments and local funds by states. State Medicaid agencies report these amounts to the Health Care Financing Administration (HCFA) on form 37, as defined by the Medicaid Voluntary Contribution and Provider-specific Tax Amendments of 1991 (PL. 102-234). However, some state budget offices are unable to align their financial reporting to separate these costs for the NASBO State Expenditure Report. Thus, this report does not capture 100 percent of state provider taxes, fees, donations, assessments and local funds. Small dollar amounts, when rounded, cause an aberration in the percentage increase. In these instances, the actual dollar amounts should be consulted to determine the exact percentage increase. The states were asked to separately detail the amount of provider taxes, fees, donations, assessments and local funds reported as Other State Funds.

Key:

(a) Medicaid appropriation is "gross funded"—Federal funds are deposited directly to the State Treasury. Connecticut's FMAP is currently at 50 percent, excluding enhanced FMAP available under ARRA ($403 million in fiscal 2009 and $539 million in fiscal 2010). Excludes state portion of Qualified Medicare Beneficiaries and School Based Child Health as those expenditures are netted out of federal Medicaid reimbursement. Other: State Funds in fiscal 2009 and fiscal 2010 includes retroactive adjustments for facilities at the Department of Developmental Services, which were claimed under the Medicaid program.

(b) Fiscal 2008 Other Funds include: $106.7 million in tobacco settlement funds, $65.0 million in HMO/MCO tax, $25.8 million in nursing facility assessments, $13.6 million in provider repayments of audit disallowance, $7.0 million in local funds, and $0.9 million in interest from trust fund. Fiscal 2009 Other Funds include: $125.4 million in tobacco settlement funds, $102.3 million in HMO/MCO tax, $44.0 million in nursing facility assessments, $83.8 million in Medicaid expansion fund, $10.8 million in lottery over-attainment, $7.7 million in local funds, and $0.9 million in interest from trust fund. Fiscal 2010 Other Funds include: $214.6 million in Medicaid expansion fund, $117.5 million in tobacco settlement funds, $115.7 million in HMO/MCO tax, $45.8 million in hospital assessments, $42.3 million in nursing facility

assessments, $12.1 million redirected from contributions from non-profit health plan, $8.0 million in local funds, and $1.5 million in interest from trust fund.

(c) Commencing in fiscal 2009, federal expenditures for Medicaid are inclusive of "pass-through" financing for qualifying LEA-administered special education expenditures.

(d) As requested, expenditure figures for "2009 Actual and 2010 Estimated—Federal Funds" include American Recovery and Reinvestment Act (ARRA) expenditures. For "Medicaid," these increased federal expenditures are partially offset by lower state general fund expenditures.

(e) Other state funds include local funds of $101.0 million, and provider taxes of $1,022.0 million for fiscal 2008; local funds of $102.0 million and provider taxes of $888.0 million for fiscal 2009; and local funds of $78.0 million and provider taxes of $743.0 million for fiscal 2010. The decline in provider assessment funds is due to federal ARRA FMAP increase and the elimination of the provider assessment program for HMOs as of April 1, 2009. Increases in federal revenue support are due to increases in federal ARRA/FMAP funding ($1,042.0 million for fiscal 2009 and $1,157.0 for fiscal 2010). Actual ARRA expenditures will be recorded with the fiscal 2010 annual financial report. Public health and community and institutional care for mentally and developmentally disabled persons are partially reported in the Medicaid totals.

(f) Fiscal 2008 through fiscal 2010 Other State Funds includes provider taxes in the amounts of $59 million, $59 million, and $66 million, respectively.

(g) Medicaid data is based on total state Medicaid report. Other Funds include an estimated $601 million in fiscal 2008, $829 million in fiscal 2009 and $708 million in fiscal 2010 of local funds used to match Title XIX. The Missouri Medicaid program was budgeted in fiscal years 2009 and 2010 based on the regular FMAP. Enhanced FMAP earned and claimed under ARRA provisions was deposited into a designated fund, Fund 2000, to comply with state law.

(h) Regarding premium revenue: fiscal 2008 totals $70 million, fiscal 2009 totals $77 million, and fiscal 2010 totals $221 million. Regarding Certified Public Expenditures—Local fund from Hospitals: fiscal 2008 totals $325 million, fiscal 2009 totals $248 million, and fiscal 2010 totals $198 million. Regarding Nursing Home Tax: fiscal 2008 totals $85 million, fiscal 2009 totals $84 million, and fiscal 2010 totals $83 million. Regarding the ICF/MR 6 percent Gross Receipts Tax: fiscal 2008 totals $12 million, fiscal 2009 totals $21 million, and fiscal 2010 totals $14 million. Regarding Intergovernmental Transfers: fiscal 2008 totals $0 million, fiscal 2009 totals $0 million, and fiscal 2010 totals $0 million.

(i) For fiscal 2009 and fiscal 2010, general fund decreased and federal funds increased due to ARRA enhanced FMAP rate.

Tax Revenue is Recovering, but Fiscal Stress Continues
By William F. Fox

The state fiscal environment remains very weak despite the turnaround in revenue growth. It will be at least several years before many states see revenues return to their previous peak levels and several years more before revenues reach similar proportions of the economy. Though states may be less inclined to seek the tax rate increases that occurred after previous recessions, many are examining ways to tax cross-border activity more effectively.

Fiscal Conditions in the States

Almost every state experienced a dramatic drop in tax revenues during the Great Recession of 2008–09. State tax revenues declined more rapidly than the gross domestic product and other broad measures of economic activity resulting in taxes being historically low relative to the economy (see Figure A). State taxes fell from 5.5 percent of GDP in 2008 to 4.8 percent in 2010.[1] Taxpayers, government officials and service providers should not anticipate a quick return of service levels and expenditures (should these be goals) to their pre-recession peaks.

Taxes returned close to their pre-recession share of GDP through a combination of natural growth and policy changes—such as tax rate increases— after previous recessions. This can be seen by the 2007 peak in revenues being a little higher than in 1995 taxes. But, the rebound took approximately three years once revenues began growing again, meaning the overall cycle from one revenue peak to the next can easily be seven to eight years.

Most States Are Seeing a Rebound in Revenues

Tax revenues have begun to grow again in many states after the sharp contraction in 2009 and 2010. The average state saw tax revenues decline by 11.1 percent between 2008 and 2010, including the effects of any tax policy changes. Personal income taxes were off 17.3 percent across the two years, compared to a 7.3 percent decline in the sales tax. Tax revenues have now risen three consecutive

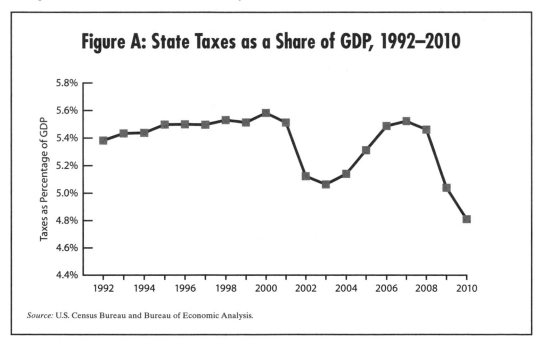

Figure A: State Taxes as a Share of GDP, 1992–2010

Source: U.S. Census Bureau and Bureau of Economic Analysis.

quarters following five quarters of decline. On average, revenues were 3.9 percent higher in the third quarter of 2010 compared to the same period a year earlier, but were still 7 percent lower than 2008.[2] Revenues increased in 42 of the 48 reporting states during the third quarter, and fell in only six. Personal income taxes rose the fastest at 4.7 percent, followed by sales taxes at 4.1 percent. Corporate income taxes, which have fallen 12 of the past 13 quarters, continued to decline and were down 2.5 percent.

The role that policy changes will play in raising or lowering taxes during the current expansion is difficult to anticipate given the significant turnover in state legislatures and governor's offices. The focus on limiting or reducing taxes during the recent election cycle could mean states are less willing to use policy increases to return taxes to previous levels. However, voters sent mixed messages on direct ballot initiatives. For example, Colorado and Massachusetts rejected significant tax cuts, while Washington voters opposed introduction of a personal income tax. Also, voters approved property tax caps and exemptions in a number of states. No effort is made here to anticipate how these various political forces will influence tax patterns in coming years, but instead the discussion is placed in the context of current trends in tax policy and revenue growth.

Fiscal Problems Remain as the Economy Rebounds

Many state budgets will remain under pressure during the 2012 fiscal year as the end of the American Recovery and Reinvestment Act funds offsets much of the growth in tax revenues. In fact, aggregate tax revenues will only return to 2008 peaks in 2013, meaning taxes will remain well below previous peaks relative to GDP for several more years. Taxes will grow rapidly relative to the economy in many states as the expansion improves because of the rapid increase of the non-labor income component of the personal income tax, such as dividends and interest, and significant increases in housing and vehicle sales, even though the levels of housing and vehicles purchased will be much lower than the peaks achieved in the 2005–06 time period.

The opportunity to right-size government is an obvious silver lining of the tight fiscal conditions, particularly the chance to readjust the distribution of spending across programs. But the severity of ongoing fiscal problems differs across states depending on such factors as the degree to which recurring expenditure cuts were enacted over the past several years, the extent to which tax revenues have fallen, and the revenue rebound that will occur this year and next. States with large structural economic changes, such as long-term reductions in housing and other construction, will continue to have significant fiscal difficulties over the next several years. States that made significant cuts in recurring spending and did not see the greatest revenue losses will be best able to accommodate the loss of federal dollars. Forty-five states reported to the National Association of State Budget Officers that they had cut their budgets in the 2010 fiscal year, though the amount cut varied widely.[3] Texas reported reducing its general fund budget by 22.8 percent, while New Hampshire lowered spending by only 0.7 percent.

Even the states least affected by the recession will continue experiencing fiscal difficulties in the sense that tax revenues declined relative to the economy and will not return to the pre-recession share for several more years, depending on the state. This can mean lower service levels compared with pre-recession levels, though the specific areas where cuts are made differ by state. Public service expenditures could return to their earlier levels as revenues continue to rise through the expansion.

State Policy Actions

Rate Changes

States appear to have relied less frequently on tax rate increases to moderate budget problems during this economic downturn than earlier ones. Ten states increased their sales tax rate and nine raised their personal income tax rate during 2009 and 2010. At the same time, five states lowered their income tax rate. In addition, 12 states raised their tobacco tax rate.

Sales tax rate increases were more common during the recessions of the 1980s and 1990s, with more than 30 increases in the first half of the 1980s and about 25 in the first half of the 1990s. More than 20 states increased their tobacco tax rates in 2001 and 2002, during and around the recession. More rate changes may occur over the next several years, but they seem less likely during the next several years than in the years following the previous recessions. Nonetheless, the dollar value of tax revenues generated by rate increases in 2010 was the highest in history; of course, this is, in part, the result of inflation.

Sales Taxes

Many states are focusing on ways to better tax cross-state or multi-state economic activity. Fiscal pressure is only one of the reasons for these policy initiatives. Expanding globalization emphasizes the imperative for tax policies that support rising cross-border trade and factor flows. Tax systems should support better and more consistent economic growth while protecting state revenue bases. Solutions to cross-border taxation are complicated, so the intent here is to provide a thumbnail sketch of some recent actions. We discuss two taxes here, the sales and corporate income taxes, but similar issues are being addressed for other taxes, such as the individual income tax.

Many efforts are underway to allow states to collect the sales tax more effectively on in-state purchases from out-of-state vendors. The U.S. economy is hampered when taxes are not collected evenly on in-state and cross-state transactions, because vendors have an incentive to arrange their affairs to avoid establishing a taxable presence, thereby giving consumers a tax incentive to purchase from out-of-state vendors. The economy suffers as firms incur higher costs to avoid creating taxable presence and states lose tax revenues. For example, Bruce, Fox and Luna estimate that state and local governments will lose about $12 billion in 2012 due to the inability to collect sales taxes due on e-commerce.[4]

Among state efforts to improve their ability to collect the tax, the Streamlined Sales Tax Governing Board continues to move forward, with Georgia becoming the 24th member. More states have recently been found out of compliance with the Streamlined Agreement, as states are being required to comply more stringently with every detail of the agreement. The Governing Board is seeking agreement on a number of remaining elements in a simplified sales tax structure. Vendor compensation for collecting the sales tax has proved one of the most difficult issues, perhaps because vendor compensation can significantly reduce net state revenues obtained from establishing a collection responsibility for remote vendors. The Governing Board also has discussed seeking to overturn the *Quill v. North Dakota* Supreme Court decision, which limits states to only requiring firms with a physical presence to collect sales tax.

Other state efforts to tax remote sales also appear to be increasing, perhaps reflecting frustration with slow congressional movement in areas such as the Main Street Fairness Act. Twenty-three states include a line on their personal income tax return allowing taxpayers to report use tax obligations. Most states report modest collections as a result, but the approach represents a step in the right direction.

Disagreement exists regarding whether some of the other new state approaches are helpful in enhancing states' ability to require remote vendors to collect sales and use taxes. Several states have enacted so-called "Amazon Laws." For example, New York enacted legislation asserting that a vendor must collect taxes on behalf of the state if in-state affiliates solicit sales and direct customers to the site.[5] Several other states passed similar legislation, which in some cases has been vetoed or cancelled. Amazon is challenging New York's authority to require collection of the sales tax and lost the first round in New York courts.

Colorado enacted reporting requirements for firms that do not collect state sales taxes. Firms with more than $100,000 in sales to Colorado buyers are required to report the buyer and the dollar amount to the state Department of Revenue. The vendors are also required to send letters to buyers of more than $500 in purchases to alert them that use tax may be due to Colorado. The Direct Marketers' Association is challenging the legislation in court. Oklahoma also has enacted legislation requiring firms to say that tax may be due on their purchases. Further, North Carolina has asked online vendors who are affiliates of sites such as Amazon and that operate in North Carolina to collect and report sales taxes. Amazon has gone to court questioning North Carolina's ability to require the information, with some initial success. Finally, Texas is auditing Amazon and arguing that the firm owes four years worth of back sales taxes because it operates a distribution center in the state.

Corporate Income Taxes

States continue to focus on the best means to tax corporations and businesses. State business tax policy goals seem somewhat schizophrenic as states are torn between economic development and tax revenues. One issue is how to determine the taxable income of related corporations. The options include separate reporting, elective consolidated reporting and mandatory combined reporting. Combined reporting requires certain related companies to file a single return as if related entities were collapsed into one entity. Six additional states have adopted required combined reporting in recent years, including Vermont (2006), New York (2007), West

Virginia (2009), Michigan (2009), Wisconsin (2009) and Massachusetts (2009), raising the number of states with combined reporting to 22. Combined reporting is intended to reduce tax planning, increase corporate tax revenues and develop a more accurate measure of profits earned in a state. Combined reporting may help achieve some of these goals, but does not measure up to the expectations that many have placed on it.[6] It can close some tax planning opportunities, but will not close them all since the combined group normally excludes some affiliates.[7]

Our research suggests that combined reporting likely raises a small amount of revenue, but should not be counted on for significant new revenue. Thus far, statutes requiring addbacks of related company deductions appear to be more effective at generating revenues. Further, our research and that conducted by others over the years suggests any increase in the effective tax rate, including increases resulting from combined reporting and addbacks, could have a small negative effect on the state's economy. It should also be noted that states have a series of options besides combined reporting, such as addbacks, to reduce tax planning. States should also consider these other options in efforts to reduce abusive tax planning.

States also continue to increase the weight on the sales factor in the corporate income tax formula with the apparent goals of lessening the tax implicit on production without significant tax revenue losses. A single weighted sales factor apportionment formula distributes the tax burden much like a gross receipts or sales tax because the receipts are sitused at the destination of goods. Effectively, a single factor sales apportioned corporate income tax operates like a sales tax on profitable corporations. At the same time, the tax on capital or labor used in a state is lessened. But, most states have not recognized that this logic only works for goods. The sales factor in most state formulas locates sales of services where production takes place. The result is that moving to 100 percent weight on the sales factor may actually increase the tax imposed on production of services in a state. In recent years 11 states have moved the sales factor for services so that both goods and services are sitused where the purchase is to be enjoyed and attributes the service where the customer is located.

This remains an important issue for other states to consider. As a general rule, moving to destination situsing of sales of services is good policy, though this issue has not been widely researched to date.

Notes

[1] Local taxes, on the other hand, rose from 3.6 percent to 4 percent of GDP in the same time period, so that the overall decline in state and local taxes is modest.

[2] See Lucy Dadayan and Donald Boyd, "State Tax Revenues Rebound Further, Growing for the Third Straight Quarter," *State Revenue Flash Report*, Nelson A. Rockefeller Institute of Government, SUNY Albany November 30, 2010.

[3] See NGA/NASBO Fall 2010 Fiscal Survey of States at *http://nasbo.org/LinkClick.aspx?fileticket=wJKroFj6QDA%3d&tabid=38*.

[4] See Bruce, Fox and Luna, "State and Local Government Sales Tax Revenue Losses from E-commerce," *State Tax Notes*, May 18, 2009.

[5] The term affiliates is used in a different context in the discussion of Amazon Laws than with the corporate income tax. These affiliates are normally not owned or controlled by the vendor.

[6] See William F. Fox and LeAnn Luna, "Combined Reporting with the Corporate Income Tax: Issues for State Legislators," *State Tax Notes*, January, 17, 2011.

[7] States may exclude certain affiliates, such as insurance or banking firms, and often some foreign businesses.

About the Author

Bill Fox is the William B. Stokely Distinguished Professor of Business and the director of the Center for Business and Economic Research at the University of Tennessee. He is a past president and recipient of the Steven D. Gold Award from the National Tax Association and former chairman of the Economics Department at the University of Tennessee. He has held visiting appointments as professor at the University of Hawaii, scholar at the Federal Reserve Bank of Kansas City, and Distinguished Fulbright Chair at the University of Frankfurt, Germany. Fox has served as a consultant in more than 25 countries and 10 U.S. states on a wide range of public policy issues.

Table 7.9
STATE TAX AMNESTY PROGRAMS, 1982–Present

State or other jurisdiction	Amnesty period	Legislative authorization	Major taxes covered	Accounts receivable included	Collections ($ millions) (a)	Installment arrangements permitted (b)
Alabama	1/20/84–4/1/84	No (c)	All	No	3.2	No
	2/1/09–5/15/09	Yes	Ind. Income, Corp. Income, Business, Sales & Use	N.A.	8.1	N.A.
Arizona	11/22/82–1/20/83	No (c)	All	No	6.0	Yes
	1/1/02–2/28/02	Yes	Individual income	No	N.A.	No
	9/1/03–10/31/03	Yes	All (t)	N.A.	73.0	Yes
	5/1/09–6/1/09	N.A.	All	N.A.	32.0	N.A.
Arkansas	9/1/87–11/30/87	Yes	All	No	1.7	Yes
	7/1/04–12/31/04	Yes	All	N.A.	N.A.	No
California	12/10/84–3/15/85	Yes	Individual income	Yes	154.0	Yes
		Yes	Sales	No	43.0	Yes
	2/1/05–3/31/05	Yes	Income, Franchise, Sales	N.A.	N.A.	Yes
Colorado	9/16/85–11/15/85	Yes	All	No	6.4	Yes
	6/1/03–6/30/03	N.A.	All	N.A.	18.4	Yes
Connecticut	9/1/90–11/30/90	Yes	All	Yes	54.0	Yes
	9/1/95–11/30/95	Yes	All	Yes	46.2	Yes
	9/1/02–12/2/02	N.A.	All	N.A.	109.0	N.A.
	5/1/09–6/25/09	Yes	All	No	40.0	No
Delaware	9/1/09–10/30/09	Yes	All	Yes	N.A.	Yes
Florida	1/1/87–6/30/87	Yes	Intangibles	No	13.0	No
	1/1/88–6/30/88	Yes (d)	All	No	8.4 (d)	No
	7/1/03–10/31/03	Yes	All	N.A.	80.0	N.A.
	7/1/10–9/30/10	Yes	All	Yes		Yes
Georgia	10/1/92–12/5/92	Yes	All	Yes	51.3	No
Hawaii	5/27/09–6/26/09	N.A.	All	No	14.0	No
Idaho	5/20/83–8/30/83	No (c)	Individual income	No	0.3	No
Illinois	10/1/84–11/30/84	Yes	All (u)	Yes	160.5	No
	10/1/03–11/17/03	Yes	All	N.A.	532.0	N.A.
	10/1/10–11/8/10	Yes	All	Yes		No
Indiana	9/15/05–11/15/05	N.A.	All	N.A.	255.0	Yes
Iowa	9/2/86–10/31/86	Yes	All	Yes	35.1	N.A.
	9/4/07–10/31/07	Yes	All	Yes	N.A.	N.A.
Kansas	7/1/84–9/30/84	Yes	All	No	0.6	No
	10/1/03–11/30/03	Yes	All	Yes	53.7	N.A.
	9/1/10–10/15/10	Yes	All	Yes		No
Kentucky	9/15/88–9/30/88	Yes (c)	All	No	100.0	No
	8/1/02–9/30/02	Yes (c)	All	No	100.0	No
Louisiana	10/1/85–12/31/85	Yes	All	No	1.2	Yes (f)
	10/1/87–12/15/87	Yes	All	No	0.3	Yes (f)
	10/1/98–12/31/98	Yes	All	No (q)	1.3	No
	9/1/01–10/30/01	Yes	All	Yes	192.9	No
	9/1/09–10/31/09	Yes	All		303.7	
Maine	11/1/90–12/31/90	Yes	All	Yes	29.0	Yes
	9/1/03–11/30/03	Yes	All	N.A.	37.6	N.A.
	9/1/09–11/30/09	Yes	All	Yes	16.2	No
	9/1/10–11/30/10	Yes	Tax Receivables Reduction Initiative	Yes	16.2	No
Maryland	9/1/87–11/2/87	Yes	All	Yes	34.6 (g)	No
	9/1/01–10/31/01	Yes	All	Yes	39.2	No
	9/1/09–10/31/09	Yes	Income, Withholding, Sales & Use	Yes	9.6	Yes
Massachusetts	10/17/83–1/17/84	Yes	All	Yes	86.5	Yes (h)
	10/1/02–11/30/02	Yes	All	Yes	96.1	Yes
	1/1/03–2/28/03	Yes	All	Yes	11.2	N.A.
	4/1/10–6/1/10	Yes	All	Yes	32.6	No
Michigan	5/12/86–6/30/86	Yes	All	Yes	109.8	No
	5/15/02–6/30/02	Yes	All	Yes	N.A.	N.A.
Minnesota	8/1/84–10/31/84	Yes	All	Yes	12.1	No
Mississippi	9/1/86–11/30/86	Yes	All	No	1.0	No
	9/1/04–12/31/04	Yes	All	No	7.9	No

See footnotes at end of table.

STATE TAX AMNESTY PROGRAMS, 1982–Present — Continued

State or other jurisdiction	Amnesty period	Legislative authorization	Major taxes covered	Accounts receivable included	Collections ($ millions) (a)	Installment arrangements permitted (b)
Missouri	9/1/83 – 10/31/83	No (c)	All	No	0.9	No
	8/1/02 – 10/31/02	Yes	All	Yes	76.4	N.A.
	8/1/03 – 10/31/03	Yes	All	Yes	20.0	N.A.
Nebraska	8/1/04 – 10/31/04	Yes	All	No	7.5	No
Nevada..........................	2/1/02 – 6/30/02	N.A.	All	N.A.	7.3	N.A.
	7/1/08 – 10/28/08	No	Sales, business, license	Yes		No
	7/1/10 – 10/1/10	Yes	All	Yes		No
New Hampshire	12/1/97 – 2/17/98	Yes	All	Yes	13.5	No
	12/1/01 – 2/15/02	Yes	All	Yes	13.5	N.A.
New Jersey	9/10/87 – 12/8/87	Yes	All	Yes	186.5	Yes
	3/15/96 – 6/1/96	Yes	All	Yes	359.0	No
	4/15/02 – 6/10/02	Yes	All	Yes	276.9	N.A.
	5/4/09 – 6/15/09	Yes	All	N.A.	725.0	N.A.
New Mexico	8/15/85 – 11/13/85	Yes	All (i)	No	13.6	Yes
	8/16/99 – 11/12/99	Yes	All	Yes	45.0	Yes
	6/7/10 – 9/30/10	Yes	All	No		Yes
New York......................	11/1/85 – 1/31/86	Yes	All (j)	Yes	401.3	Yes
	11/1/96 – 1/31/97	Yes	All	Yes	253.4	Yes (o)
	11/18/02 – 1/31/03	Yes	All	Yes	582.7	Yes (s)
	10/1/05 – 3/1/06	N.A.	Income, corporate	N.A.	349.0	N.A.
	1/15/10 – 3/15/10	Yes		Yes	56.5	No
North Carolina............	9/1/89 – 12/1/89	Yes	All (k)	Yes	37.6	No
North Dakota...............	9/1/83 – 11/30/83	No (c)	All	No	0.2	Yes
	10/1/03 – 1/31/04	Yes	N.A.	N.A.	6.9	N.A.
Ohio.............................	10/15/01 – 1/15/02	Yes	All	No	48.5	No
	1/1/06 – 2/15/06	Yes	All	No	63.0	No
Oklahoma....................	7/1/84 – 12/31/84	Yes	Income, Sales	Yes	13.9	No (l)
	8/15/02 – 11/15/02	N.A.	All (r)	Yes	N.A.	N.A.
	9/15/08 – 11/14/08	Yes	All	Yes	81.0	Yes
Oregon.........................	10/1/09 – 11/19/09	Yes	Personal, Corporate, Inheritance	N.A.	N.A.	N.A.
Pennsylvania	10/13/95 – 1/10/96	Yes	All	Yes	N.A.	No
	4/26/10 – 6/18/10	Yes	All	Yes	261.0	No
Rhode Island...............	10/15/86 – 1/12/87	Yes	All	No	0.7	Yes
	4/15/96 – 6/28/96	Yes	All	Yes	7.9	Yes
	7/15/06 – 9/30/06	N.A.	All	Yes	6.5	Yes
South Carolina............	9/1/85 – 11/30/85	Yes	All	Yes	7.1	Yes
	10/15/02 – 12/2/02	Yes	All	Yes	66.2	N.A.
South Dakota...............	4/1/99 – 5/15/99	Yes	All	Yes	0.5	N.A.
Texas............................	2/1/84 – 2/29/84	No (c)	All (m)	No	0.5	No
	3/11/04 – 3/31/04	No (c)	All (m)	No	N.A.	No
	6/15/07 – 8/15/07	No (c)	All (m)	No	N.A.	No
Vermont........................	5/15/90 – 6/25/90	Yes	All	Yes	1 (e)	No
	7/20/09 – 8/31/09	Yes	All	N.A.	2.2	N.A.
Virginia........................	2/1/90 – 3/31/90	Yes	All	Yes	32.2	No
	9/2/03 – 11/3/03	Yes	All	Yes	98.3	N.A.
	10/7/09 – 12/5/09	Yes	All	Yes	102.1	No
Washington..................	2/1/11 – 4/30/11	N.A.	N.A.	N.A.		N.A.
West Virginia...............	10/1/86 – 12/31/86	Yes	All	Yes	15.9	Yes
	9/1/04 – 10/31/04	Yes	All	N.A.	10.4	Yes
Wisconsin	9/15/85 – 11/22/85	Yes	All	Yes (n)	27.3	Yes
	6/15/98 – 8/14/98	Yes	All	Yes	30.9	N.A.
Dist. of Columbia	7/1/87 – 9/30/87	Yes	All	Yes	24.3	Yes
	7/10/95 – 8/31/95	Yes	All (p)	Yes	19.5	Yes (p)
	8/2/10 – 9/30/10	Yes	All (p)	Yes	20.8	No
No. Mariana Islands	9/30/05 – 3/30/06	Yes	All	N.A.	N.A.	N.A.

See footnotes at end of table.

STATE TAX AMNESTY PROGRAMS, 1982–Present — Continued

Source: The Federation of Tax Administrators, March 2011.
Key:
N.A.— Not available.

(a) Where applicable, figure includes local portions of certain taxes collected under the state tax amnesty program.

(b) "No" indicates requirement of full payment by the expiration of the amnesty period. "Yes" indicates allowance of full payment after the expiration of the amnesty period.

(c) Authority for amnesty derived from pre-existing statutory powers permitting the waiver of tax penalties.

(d) Does not include intangibles tax and drug taxes. Gross collections totaled $22.1 million, with $13.7 million in penalties withdrawn.

(e) Preliminary figure.

(f) Amnesty taxpayers were billed for the interest owed, with payment due within 30 days of notification.

(g) Figure includes $1.1 million for the separate program conducted by the Department of Natural Resources for the boat excise tax.

(h) The amnesty statute was construed to extend the amnesty to those who applied to the department before the end of the amnesty period, and permitted them to file overdue returns and pay back taxes and interest at a later date.

(i) The severance taxes, including the six oil and gas severance taxes, the resources excise tax, the corporate franchise tax, and the special fuels tax were not subject to amnesty.

(j) Availability of amnesty for the corporation tax, the oil company taxes, the transportation and transmissions companies tax, the gross receipts oil tax and the unincorporated business tax restricted to entities with 500 or fewer employees in the United States on the date of application. In addition, a taxpayer principally engaged in aviation, or a utility subject to the supervision of the State Department of Public Service was also ineligible.

(k) Local taxes and real property taxes were not included.

(l) Full payment of tax liability required before the end of the amnesty period to avoid civil penalties.

(m) Texas does not impose a corporate or individual income tax. In practical effect, the amnesty was limited to the sales tax and other excises.

(n) Waiver terms varied depending upon the date the tax liability was assessed.

(o) Installment arrangements were permitted if applicant demonstrated that payment would present a severe financial hardship.

(p) Does not include real property taxes. All interest was waived on tax payments made before July 31, 1995. After this date, only 50% of the interest was waived.

(q) Exception for individuals who owed $500 or less.

(r) Except for property and motor fuel taxes.

(s) Multiple payments could be made so long as the required balance was paid in full no later than March 15, 2003.

(t) All taxes except property, estate and unclaimed property.

(u) Does not include the motor fuel use tax.

(v) The Massachusetts Department of Revenue was required to hold an amnesty to end before June 30, 2010.

Table 7.10
STATE EXCISE TAX RATES
(As of January 1, 2011)

State or other jurisdiction	General sales and gross receipts tax (percent)	Cigarettes (cents per pack of 20)	Distilled spirits		Motor fuel excise tax rates (cents per gallon) (a)		
			Excise tax rate ($ per gallon)	Sales taxes applied	Gasoline	Diesel	Gasohol
Alabama	4.0	42.5 (b)	(c)	Yes	18.0 (e)(g)	19.0 (e)(g)	18.0 (e)(g)
Alaska	0.0	200	12.80 (d)	...	8.0	8.0	8.0
Arizona	6.6	200	3.00	Yes	19.0 (f)(g)	19.0 (f)(g)	19.0 (f)(g)
Arkansas	6.0	115	2.50 (d)	Yes	21.8 (g)	22.8 (g)	21.8 (g)
California	8.25 (h)	87	3.30 (d)	Yes	35.3 (g)(i)(u)	18.0 (g)(i)(u)	18.0 (g)(i)(u)
Colorado	2.9	84	2.28	Yes	22.0	20.5	22.0
Connecticut	6.0	300	4.50 (d)	Yes	25.0	39.6	25.0
Delaware	0.0	160	5.46 (d)	...	23.0 (g)	22.0 (g)	23.0 (g)
Florida	6.0	133.9 (j)	6.50 (k)	Yes	16.2 (g)(l)	30.0 (g)(l)	16.2 (g)(l)
Georgia	4.0	37	3.79 (d)	Yes	17.6 (g)	18.8 (g)	17.6 (g)
Hawaii	4.0	300 (m)	5.98	Yes	17.0 (e)(g)	17.0 (e)(g)	17.0 (e)(g)
Idaho	6.0	57	(c)	Yes	26.0 (g)(n)	26.0 (g)(n)	26.0 (g)(n)
Illinois	6.25	98 (b)	8.55 (d)	Yes	20.1 (e)(f)(g)	22.6 (e)(f)(g)	20.1 (e)(f)(g)
Indiana	7.0	99.5	2.68 (d)	Yes	18.0 (f)(g)	16.0 (f)(g)	18.0 (f)(g)
Iowa	6.0	136	(c)	Yes	22.0 (g)	23.5 (g)	20.0 (g)
Kansas	6.3	79	2.50 (d)	...	24.0	26.0	24.0
Kentucky	6.0	60 (o)	1.92 (d)	Yes (k)	25.9 (f)(g)(p)	22.9 (f)(g)(p)	25.9 (f)(g)(p)
Louisiana	4.0	36	2.50 (d)	Yes	20.0	20.0	20.0
Maine	5.0	200	(c)	Yes	29.5 (q)	30.7 (q)	29.5 (q)
Maryland	6.0	200	1.50	Yes	23.5	24.25	23.5
Massachusetts	6.25	251	4.05 (d)	Yes	21.0	21.0	21.0
Michigan	6.0	200	(c)	Yes	19.0 (g)	15.0 (g)	19.0 (g)
Minnesota	6.875	123 (r)	5.03 (d)	Yes	29.6 (g)(q)	29.6 (g)(q)	29.6 (g)(q)
Mississippi	7.0	68	(c)	Yes	18.4 (g)	18.4 (g)	18.4 (g)
Missouri	4.225	17 (b)	2.00	Yes	17.3 (g)	17.3 (g)	17.3 (g)
Montana	0.0	170	(c)	...	27.0	27.75	27.0
Nebraska	5.5	64	3.75	Yes	27.3 (g)(q)	26.7 (g)(q)	27.3 (g)(q)
Nevada	6.85	80	3.60 (d)	Yes	24.805 (e)(g)	27.75 (e)(g)	24.805 (e)(g)
New Hampshire	0.0	178	(c)	...	19.625 (g)	19.625 (g)	19.625 (g)
New Jersey	7.0	270	5.50	Yes	14.5 (g)	17.5 (g)	14.5 (g)
New Mexico	5.125	166	6.06	Yes	18.875 (g)	22.875 (g)	18.875 (g)
New York	4.0	435 (b)	6.44 (d)	Yes	25.0 (g)	23.25 (g)	25.0 (g)
North Carolina	5.75	45	(c)	Yes (k)	32.75 (g)(p)	32.75 (g)(p)	32.75 (g)(p)
North Dakota	5.0	44	2.50 (d)	...	23.0	23.0	23.0
Ohio	5.5	125	(c)	Yes	28.0 (g)	28.0 (g)	28.0 (g)
Oklahoma	4.5	103	5.56 (d)	Yes	17.0 (g)	14.0 (g)	17.0 (g)
Oregon	0.0	118	(c)	...	30.0 (e)	30.0 (e)	30.0 (e)
Pennsylvania	6.0	160	(c)	Yes	31.2 (g)	38.1 (g)	31.2 (g)
Rhode Island	7.0	346	3.75	Yes	33.0 (g)	33.0 (g)	33.0 (g)
South Carolina	6.0	57	2.72 (d)	Yes	16.75 (g)	16.75 (g)	16.75 (g)
South Dakota	4.0	153	3.93 (d)	Yes	24.0 (e)(g)	24.0 (e)(g)	22.0 (e)(g)
Tennessee	7.0	62 (b)(o)	4.40 (d)	Yes	21.4 (e)(g)	18.4 (e)(g)	21.4 (e)(g)
Texas	6.25	141	2.40 (d)	Yes	20.0	20.0	20.0
Utah	5.95	170	(c)	Yes	24.5	24.5	24.5
Vermont	6.0	224	(c)(d)	...	24.98 (g)	29.0 (g)	24.98 (g)
Virginia	5.0 (t)	30 (b)	(c)	Yes	17.5 (e)(s)	17.5 (e)(s)	17.5 (e)(s)
Washington	6.5	302.5	(c)	Yes (k)	37.5 (g)	37.5 (g)	37.5 (g)
West Virginia	6.0	55	(c)	Yes	32.2 (g)	32.2 (g)	32.2 (g)
Wisconsin	5.0	252	3.25	Yes	32.9 (g)	32.9 (g)	32.9 (g)
Wyoming	4.0	60	(c)	Yes	14.0 (g)	14.0 (g)	14.0 (g)
Dist. of Columbia	6.0	250	1.50 (d)	Yes	20.0	20.0	20.0

See footnotes at end of table.

STATE EXCISE TAX RATES — Continued
(As of January 1, 2011)

Source: Compiled by The Federation of Tax Administrators from various sources, January 2011.

Key:

... — Tax is not applicable.

(a) The tax rates listed are fuel excise taxes collected by distributor/supplier/retailers in each state. Additional taxes may apply to motor carriers. Carrier taxes are coordinated by the International Fuel Tax Association.

(b) Counties and cities may impose an additional tax on a pack of cigarettes in Alabama 1¢ to 6¢; Illinois, 10¢ to 15¢; Missouri, 4¢ to 7¢; New York City, $1.50; Tennessee, 1¢; and Virginia, 2¢ to 15¢.

(c) In 18 states, the government directly controls the sales of distilled spirits. Revenue in these states is generated from various taxes, fees and net liquor profits.

(d) Other taxes in addition to excise taxes for the following states: Alaska, under 21 percent — $2.50/gallon; Arkansas, under 5 percent — $0.50/gallon, under 21 percent — $1.00/gallon, $0.20/case and 3 percent off- 14 percent on-premise retail taxes; California, over 50 percent — $6.60/gallon; Connecticut, under 7 percent — $2.05/gallon; Delaware, under 25 percent — $3.64/gallon; Florida, under 17.259 percent — $2.25/gallon, over 55.780 percent — $9.53/gallon and $0.0667/ounce on-premise retail tax; Georgia, $0.83/gallon local tax; Illinois, under 20 percent — $1.39/gallon, $2.68/gallon in Chicago and $2.00/gallon in Cook County; Indiana, under 15 percent — $0.47/gallon; Kansas, 8 percent off- and 10 percent on-premise retail tax; Kentucky, under 6 percent — $0.25/gallon, $0.05/case and 11 percent wholesale tax; Louisiana, under 6 percent — $0.32/gallon; Massachusetts, under 15 percent — $1.10/gallon, over 50 percent alcohol — $4.05/proof gallon, 0.57 percent on private club sales; Minnesota, $0.01/bottle (except miniatures) and 9 percent sales tax; Nevada, under 14 percent — $0.70/gallon and under 21 percent — $1.30/gallon; New York, under 24 percent — $2.54/gallon, $1.00/gallon New York City; North Dakota, 7 percent state sales tax; Oklahoma, 13.5 percent on-premise; South Carolina, $5.36/case and 9 percent surtax additional 5 percent on-premise tax; South Dakota, under 14 percent — $0.93/gallon, 2 percent wholesale tax; Tennessee, $0.15/case and 15 percent on-premise, under 7 percent — $1.10/gallon; Texas, 14 percent on-premise and $0.05/drink on airline sales; Vermont, 10 percent on-premise sales tax; and District of Columbia, 8 percent off- and 10 percent on-premise sales tax.

(e) Tax rates do not include local option taxes. In Alabama, 1 to 3 cents; Hawaii, 8.8 to 18.0 cents; Illinois, 5 cents in Chicago and 6 cents in Cook County (gasoline only); Nevada, 4 to 9 cents; Oregon, 1 to 3 cents; South Dakota and Tennessee, 1 cent; and Virginia, 2 percent.

(f) Carriers pay an additional surcharge: Arizona, 8 cents; Illinois, 12.3 cents (gasoline), 13.5 cents (diesel); Indiana, 11 cents; Kentucky, 2 percent (gasoline), 4.7 percent (diesel).

(g) Other taxes and fees: Alabama — inspection fee; Arizona — leaking underground storage tax (LUST); Arkansas — environmental fee; California — sales tax additional; 2.2; Delaware — plus 0.9 percent GRT; Florida — sales tax added to excise; Georgia — sales tax added to excise; Hawaii — sales tax applicable; Idaho — clean water tax; Illinois — sales tax applicable, environmental fee and leaking underground storage tax (LUST); Indiana — sales tax additional; Iowa — environmental fee; Kentucky — environmental fee; Michigan — sales tax additional; Minnesota — environmental and inspection fee; Mississippi — environmental fee; Missouri — inspection fee; Nebraska — petroleum fee; Nevada — inspection fee and cleanup fee; New Hampshire — oil discharge cleanup fee; New Jersey — petroleum fee; New Mexico — petroleum loading fee; New York — sales tax applicable and petroleum tax; North Carolina — inspection tax; Ohio — plus 3 cents commercial; Oklahoma — environmental fee; Pennsylvania — oil franchise tax; Rhode Island — leaking underground storage tank tax (LUST); South Carolina — inspection fee and leaking underground storage tank tax (LUST); South Dakota — inspection fee; Tennessee — petroleum tax and environmental fee; Vermont — petroleum cleanup fee and transportation fee; Washington — 0.5 percent privilege tax; West Virginia — sales tax added to excise; Wisconsin — petroleum inspection fee; Wyoming — license tax.

(h) Tax rate may be adjusted annually according to a formula based on balances in the unappropriated general fund and the school foundation fund.

(i) California gasoline subject to 2.25 percent sales tax. Diesel tax rate will decrease to 13.6 cents and sales tax rate will decrease to 9 percent. Sales tax prepayment rates are not included above.

(j) Includes a $1 per pack surcharge.

(k) Sales tax is applied to on-premise sales only.

(l) Local taxes for gasoline and gasahol vary from 12.6 cents to 18.6 cents. Plus a 2.2 cent per gallon pollution tax.

(m) Tax rate is scheduled to increase to $3.20 per pack effective July 1, 2011.

(n) Tax rate is reduced by the percentage of ethanol used in blending (reported rate assumes the maximum 10 percent ethanol).

(o) Dealers pay an additional enforcement and administrative fee of 0.1 cent per pack in Kentucky and .05 cent in Tennessee.

(p) Tax rate is based on the average wholesale price and is adjusted quarterly. The actual rates are: Kentucky, 9 percent and North Carolina, 17.5 cents plus 7 percent.

(q) Portion of the rate is adjustable based on maintenance costs, sales volume, cost of fuel to state government, or inflation.

(r) In addition, Minnesota imposes an in lieu cigarette sales tax determined annually by the Department of Revenue. The current rate is 34.6 cents through July 31, 2011.

(s) Large trucks pay an additional 3.5 cents.

(t) Includes statewide tax of 1.0 percent levied by local governments in Virginia.

Table 7.11
FOOD AND DRUG SALES TAX EXEMPTIONS
(As of January 2011)

State or other jurisdiction	Tax rate (percentage)	Exemptions		
		Food (a)	Prescription drugs	Nonprescription drugs
Alabama	4.0	...	★	...
Alaska	0.0	...	...	...
Arizona	6.6	★	★	...
Arkansas	6.0	2% (b)	★	...
California (c)	8.25	★	★	...
Colorado	2.9	★	★	...
Connecticut	6.0	★	★	...
Delaware	0.0	...	...	...
Florida	6.0	★	★	★
Georgia	4.0	★(b)	★	...
Hawaii	4.0	...	★	...
Idaho	6.0	...	★	...
Illinois	6.25	1%	1%	1%
Indiana	7.0	★	★	...
Iowa	6.0	★	★	...
Kansas	6.3	...	★	...
Kentucky	6.0	★	★	...
Louisiana	4.0	★(b)	★	...
Maine	5.0	★	★	...
Maryland	6.0	★	★	★
Massachusetts	6.25	★	★	...
Michigan	6.0	★	★	...
Minnesota	6.875	★	★	★
Mississippi	7.0	...	★	...
Missouri	4.225	1.225%	★	...
Montana	0.0	...	★	...
Nebraska	5.5	★	★	...
Nevada	6.85	★	★	...
New Hampshire	0.0	...	...	...
New Jersey	7.0	★	★	★
New Mexico	5.125	★	★	...
New York	4.0	★	★	★
North Carolina	5.75	★(b)	★	...
North Dakota	5.0	★	★	...
Ohio	5.5	★	★	...
Oklahoma	4.5	...	★	...
Oregon	0.0	...	...	...
Pennsylvania	6.0	★	★	★
Rhode Island	7.0	★	★	★
South Carolina	6.0	★	★	...
South Dakota	4.0	...	★	...
Tennessee	7.0	5.5%	★	...
Texas	6.25	★	★	★
Utah	5.95	1.75 (b)(e)	★	...
Vermont	6.0	★	★	★
Virginia	5.0 (d)	2.5% (d)	★	★
Washington	6.5	★	★	...
West Virginia	6.0	3% (b)	★	...
Wisconsin	5.0	★	★	...
Wyoming	4.0	★	★	...
Dist. of Columbia	6.0	★	★	★

Source: The Federation of Tax Administrators, January 2011.
Key:
★ — Yes, exempt from tax.
... — Subject to general sales tax.
N.A. — Not applicable.
(a) Some states tax food, but allow a rebate or income tax credit to compensate poor households. They are: Hawaii, Idaho, Kansas, Oklahoma and South Dakota.

(b) Food sales are subject to local sales tax.
(c) The tax rate may be adjusted annually according to a formula based on balances in the unappropriated general fund and the school foundation fund. Rate scheduled to fall to 7.25 percent on July 1, 2011.
(d) Includes statewide tax of 1.0 percent levied by local governments in Virginia.
(e) Includes a 1.25 percent tax levied by local governments in Utah.

Table 7.12
STATE INDIVIDUAL INCOME TAXES
(Tax rates for tax year 2011—as of January 1, 2011)

State or other jurisdiction	Tax rate range (in percents) Low	High	Number of brackets	Income brackets Lowest	Highest	Personal exemptions Single	Married	Dependents	Federal income tax deductible
Alabama	2.0 –	5.0	3	500(b) –	3,001(b)	1,500	3,000	500(e)	★
Alaska				——————— (No state income tax) ———————					...
Arizona	2.59 –	4.54	5	10,000(b) –	150,001(b)	2,100	4,200	2,300	...
Arkansas (a)	1.0 –	7	6	3,899 –	32,700	23(c)	46(c)	23(c)	...
California (a)	1.00 –	9.3(f)	6	7,124(b) –	46,767(b)	99(c)	198(c)	99(c)	...
Colorado	4.63		1	——————— Flat rate ———————		3,650(d)	7,300(d)	3,650(d)	...
Connecticut	3.0 –	6.5	3	10,000(b) –	500,001(b)	13,000(g)	26,000(g)	0	...
Delaware	2.2 –	6.95	6	5,000 –	60,001	110(c)	220(c)	110(c)	...
Florida				——————— (No state income tax) ———————					...
Georgia	1.0 –	6.0	6	750(h) –	7,001(h)	2,700	5,400	3,000	...
Hawaii	1.4 –	11.0	12	2,400(b) –	200,001(b)	1,040	2,080	1,040	...
Idaho (a)	1.6 –	7.8	8	1,315(b) –	26,320(h)	3,650(d)	7,300(d)	3,650(d)	...
Illinois	5.0(i)		1	——————— Flat rate ———————		2,000	4,000	2,000	...
Indiana	3.4		1	——————— Flat rate ———————		1,000	2,000	2,500(j)	...
Iowa (a)	0.36 –	8.98	9	1,439(k) –	64,756(k)	40(c)	80(c)	40(c)	★
Kansas	3.5 –	6.45	3	15,000(b) –	30,001(b)	2,250	4,500	2,250	...
Kentucky	2.0 –	6.0	6	3,000 –	75,001	20(c)	40(c)	20(c)	...
Louisiana	2.0 –	6.0	3	12,500(b) –	50,001(b)	4,500(l)	9,000(l)	1,000	★
Maine (a)	2.0 –	8.5	4	4,949(b) –	19,750(b)	2,850	5,700	2,850	...
Maryland	2.0 –	5.50	7	1,000 –	500,001	3,200	6,400	3,200	...
Massachusetts (a)	5.3		1	——————— Flat rate ———————		4,400	8,800	1,000	...
Michigan (a)	4.35		1	——————— Flat rate ———————		3,600	7,200	4,200(m)	...
Minnesota (a)	5.35 –	7.85	3	22,770(n) –	74,781(n)	3,650(d)	7,300(d)	3,650(d)	...
Mississippi	3.0 –	5.0	3	5,000 –	10,001	6,000	12,000	1,500	...
Missouri	1.5 –	6.0	10	1,000 –	9,001	2,100	4,200	1,200	★(o)
Montana (a)	1.0 –	6.9	7	2,600 –	15,601	2,130	4,260	2,130	★(o)
Nebraska (a)	2.56 –	6.84	4	2,400(b) –	27,001(b)	118(c)	236(c)	118(c)	...
Nevada				——————— (No state income tax) ———————					...
New Hampshire				——— (State income tax of 5% on dividends and interest income only.) ———					...
New Jersey	1.4 –	8.97	6	20,000(p) –	500,000(p)	1,000	2,000	1,500	...
New Mexico	1.7 –	4.9	4	5,500(q) –	16,001(q)	3,650(d)	7,300(d)	3,650(d)	...
New York	4.0 –	8.97	7	8,000(r) –	500,001(r)	0	0	1,000	...
North Carolina	6.0 –	7.75	3	12,750(s) –	60,000(s)	1,150	2,300	1,150	...
North Dakota (a)	1.84 –	4.86	5	34,000(t) –	373,651(t)	3,650(d)	7,300(d)	3,650(d)	...
Ohio (a)	0.587(u)–5.925(u)		9	5,050 –	200,001	1,600(u)	3,200(u)	1,600(u)	...
Oklahoma	0.5 –	5.5	7	1,000(v) –	8,701(y)	1,000	2,000	1,000	...
Oregon (a)	5.0 –	11.0	5	2,000(b) –	250,001(b)	177(c)	354(c)	177(c)	★(o)
Pennsylvania	3.07		1	——————— Flat rate ———————		None			...
Rhode Island (a)	3.75 –	5.9	3	55,000 –	125,001	3,500(d)	7,000(d)	3,500(d)	...
South Carolina (a)	0.0 –	7.0	6	2,740 –	13,701	3,650(d)	7,300(d)	3,650(d)	...
South Dakota				——————— (No state income tax) ———————					...
Tennessee				– (State income tax 6% on dividends and interest income only.) –		1,250	2,500	0	...
Texas				——————— (No state income tax) ———————					...
Utah	5.0		1	——————— Flat rate ———————		(w)	(w)	(w)	...
Vermont (a)	3.55 –	8.95	5	34,000(x) –	373,651(x)	3,650(d)	7,300(d)	3,650(d)	...
Virginia	2.0 –	5.75	4	3,000 –	17,001	930	1,860	930	...
Washington				——————— (No state income tax) ———————					...
West Virginia	3.0 –	6.5	5	9,999 –	60,000	2,000	4,000	2,000	...
Wisconsin (a)	4.6 –	7.75	5	10,070(y) –	221,661(y)	700	1,400	700	...
Wyoming				——————— (No state income tax) ———————					...
Dist. of Columbia	4.0 –	8.5	3	10,000 –	40,001	1,675	3,350	1,675	...

See footnotes at end of table.

STATE INDIVIDUAL INCOME TAXES—Continued
(Tax rates for tax year 2011—as of January 1, 2011)

Source: The Federation of Tax Administrators from various sources, January 2011.

Key:

★ — Yes

... — No

(a) Seventeen states have statutory provision for automatically adjusting to the rate of inflation the dollar values of the income tax brackets, standard deductions, and/or personal exemptions. Massachusetts, Michigan, and Nebraska index the personal exemption only. Oregon does not index the income brackets for $125,000 and over. Because the inflation adjustments for 2011 are not yet available in most cases, the table reports the 2010 amounts, unless 2011 is specified in a footnote.

(b) For joint returns, taxes are twice the tax on half the couple's income.

(c) The personal exemption takes the form of a tax credit instead of a deduction.

(d) These states use the personal exemption amounts provided in the federal Internal Revenue Code.

(e) In Alabama, the per-dependent exemption is $1,000 for taxpayers with state AGI of $20,000 or less, $500 with AGI from $20,001 to $100,000, and $300 with AGI over $100,000.

(f) California imposes an additional 1% tax on taxable income over $1 million, making the maximum rate 10.3% over $1 million.

(g) Connecticut's personal exemption incorporates a standard deduction. An additional tax credit is allowed ranging from 75% to 0% based on state adjusted gross income. Exemption amounts are phased out for higher income taxpayers until they are eliminated for households earning over $71,000.

(h) The Georgia income brackets reported are for single individuals. For married couples filing jointly, the same tax rates apply to income brackets ranging from $1,000, to $10,000.

(i) Illinois's flat tax rate increased from 3% to 5%, effective January 1, 2011.

(j) In Indiana, includes an additional exemption of $1,500 for each dependent child.

(k) 2011 income brackets for Iowa.

(l) The amounts reported for Louisiana are a combined personal exemption-standard deduction.

(m) In Michigan, includes an additional exemption of $600 for children age 18 and under. Tax rate scheduled to decrease to 4.25% on 10/1/11.

(n) The income brackets reported for Minnesota are for single individuals. For married couples filing jointly, the same tax rates apply to income brackets ranging from $33,280, to $132,220.

(o) The deduction for federal income tax is limited to $5,000 for individuals and $10,000 for joint returns in Missouri and Montana, and to $5,850 for all filers in Oregon.

(p) The New Jersey rates reported are for single individuals. For married couples filing jointly, the tax rates also range from 1.4% to 8.97%, with seven brackets and the same high and low income ranges.

(q) The income brackets reported for New Mexico are for single individuals. For married couples filing jointly, the same tax rates apply to income brackets ranging from $8,000, to $24,000.

(r) The tax brackets reported are for single individuals. For married taxpayers filing jointly, the same tax rates apply to income brackets ranging from $16,000 to $500,000.

(s) The income brackets reported for North Carolina are for single individuals. For married taxpayers filing jointly, the same tax rates apply to income brackets ranging from $21,250, to $100,000.

(t) The income brackets reported for North Dakota are for single individuals. For married couples filing jointly, the same tax rates apply to income brackets ranging from $56,850, to $373,650.

(u) Ohio provides an additional tax credit of $20 per exemption. 2011 tax rates and brackets reported.

(v) The income brackets reported for Oklahoma are for single persons. For married persons filing jointly, the same tax rates apply to income brackets ranging from $2,000, to $15,000.

(w) Utah provides a tax credit equal to 6% of the federal personal exemption amounts (an applicable standard deduction).

(x) Vermont's income brackets reported are for single individuals. For married taxpayers filing jointly, the same tax rates apply to income brackets ranging from $56,800, to $373,650.

(y) The Wisconsin income brackets reported are for single individuals. For married taxpayers filing jointly, the same tax rates apply to income brackets ranging from $13,420, to $295,550.

Table 7.13
STATE PERSONAL INCOME TAXES: FEDERAL STARTING POINTS
(As of January 1, 2011)

State or other jurisdiction	Relation to Internal Revenue Code	Federal tax base used as a starting point to calculate state taxable income
Alabama	...	...
Alaska		————No state income tax ————
Arizona	1/1/2010	Adjusted gross income
Arkansas	...	...
California	1/1/2009	Adjusted gross income
Colorado	Current	Taxable income
Connecticut	Current	Adjusted gross income
Delaware	Current	Adjusted gross income
Florida		————No state income tax ————
Georgia	1/1/2010	Adjusted gross income
Hawaii	12/31/2009	Adjusted gross income
Idaho	1/1/2011	Taxable income
Illinois	Current	Adjusted gross income
Indiana	1/1/2010	Adjusted gross income
Iowa	1/1/2008	Adjusted gross income
Kansas	Current	Adjusted gross income
Kentucky	12/31/2006	Adjusted gross income
Louisiana	Current	Adjusted gross income
Maine	12/31/2010	Adjusted gross income
Maryland	Current	Adjusted gross income
Massachusetts	1/1/2005	Adjusted gross income
Michigan	Current (a)	Adjusted gross income
Minnesota	3/18/2010	Taxable income
Mississippi	...	...
Missouri	Current	Adjusted gross income
Montana	Current	Adjusted gross income
Nebraska	Current	Adjusted gross income
Nevada		————No state income tax ————
New Hampshire		————On interest and dividends only————
New Jersey	...	...
New Mexico	Current	Adjusted gross income
New York	Current	Adjusted gross income
North Carolina	5/1/2010	Taxable income
North Dakota	Current	Taxable income
Ohio	12/15/2010	Adjusted gross income
Oklahoma	Current	Adjusted gross income
Oregon	12/31/2009	Taxable income
Pennsylvania	...	...
Rhode Island	Current	Adjusted gross income
South Carolina	12/31/2009	Taxable income
South Dakota		————No state income tax ————
Tennessee		————On interest and dividends only————
Texas		————No state income tax ————
Utah	Current	Adjusted gross income
Vermont	1/1/2009	Taxable income
Virginia	1/22/2010	Adjusted gross income
Washington		————No state income tax ————
West Virginia	1/1/2010	Adjusted gross income
Wisconsin	12/31/2008	Adjusted gross income
Wyoming		————No state income tax ————
Dist. of Columbia	Current	Adjusted gross income

Source: Compiled by the Federation of Tax Administrators from various sources, January 2011.

Key:
... — State does not employ a federal starting point.
Current — Indicates state has adopted the Internal Revenue Code as currently in effect. Dates indicate state has adopted IRC as amended to that date.
(a) Michigan's taxpayers can choose to use either current or 1/1/1996 federal law.

Table 7.14
RANGE OF STATE CORPORATE INCOME TAX RATES
(For tax year 2011, as of January 1, 2011)

State or other jurisdiction	Tax rate (percent)	Tax brackets		Number of brackets	Financial institution tax rates (percent) (a)	Federal income tax deductible
		Lowest	Highest			
Alabama	6.5	--------- Flat Rate ---------		1	6.5	★
Alaska	1.0–9.4	9,999	90,000	10	1.0–9.4	...
Arizona	6.968 (b)	--------- Flat Rate ---------		1	6.968 (b)	...
Arkansas	1.0–6.5	3,000	100,001	6	1.0–6.5	...
California	8.84 (c)	--------- Flat Rate ---------		1	10.84 (c)	...
Colorado	4.63	--------- Flat Rate ---------		1	4.63	...
Connecticut	7.5 (d)	--------- Flat Rate ---------		1	7.5 (d)	...
Delaware	8.7	--------- Flat Rate ---------		1	8.7–1.7 (e)	...
Florida	5.5 (f)	--------- Flat Rate ---------		1	5.5 (f)	...
Georgia	6.0	--------- Flat Rate ---------		1	6.0	...
Hawaii	4.4–6.4 (g)	25,000	100,001	3	7.92 (g)	...
Idaho	7.6 (h)	--------- Flat Rate ---------		1	7.6 (h)	...
Illinois	9.5 (i)	--------- Flat Rate ---------		1	9.5 (i)	...
Indiana	8.5	--------- Flat Rate ---------		1	8.5	...
Iowa	6.0–12.0	25,000	250,001	4	5.0	★(j)
Kansas	4.0 (k)	--------- Flat Rate ---------		1	2.25 (k)	...
Kentucky	4.0–6.0	50,000	100,001	3	(a)	...
Louisiana	4.0–8.0	25,000	200,001	5	4.0–8.0	★
Maine	3.5–8.93 (n)	25,000	250,000	4	1.0 (l)	...
Maryland	8.25	--------- Flat Rate ---------		1	8.3	...
Massachusetts	8.75 (m)	--------- Flat Rate ---------		1	9.5 (m)	...
Michigan	4.95 (n)	--------- Flat Rate ---------		1	(a)	...
Minnesota	9.8 (o)	--------- Flat Rate ---------		1	9.8 (o)	...
Mississippi	3.0–5.0	5,000	10,001	3	3.0–5.0	...
Missouri	6.25	--------- Flat Rate ---------		1	7.0	★(j)
Montana	6.75 (p)	--------- Flat Rate ---------		1	6.75 (p)	...
Nebraska	5.58–7.81	100,000		2	(a)	...
Nevada	-------------------------------------- No corporate income tax ------------------------------------					
New Hampshire	8.5 (q)	--------- Flat Rate ---------		1	8.5 (q)	...
New Jersey	9.0 (r)	--------- Flat Rate ---------		1	9.0 (r)	...
New Mexico	4.8–7.6	500,000	1 million	3	4.8–7.6	...
New York	7.1 (s)	--------- Flat Rate ---------		1	7.1 (s)	...
North Carolina	6.9	--------- Flat Rate ---------		1	6.9 (t)	...
North Dakota	2.1–6.4	25,000	50,001	3	7.0 (b)	★
Ohio	-------------------------------------- (u) ------------------------------------					...
Oklahoma	6.0	--------- Flat Rate ---------		1	6.0	...
Oregon	6.6–7.6 (v)	250,000		2	6.6–7.6 (v)	...
Pennsylvania	9.99	--------- Flat Rate ---------		1	(a)	...
Rhode Island	9.0 (w)	--------- Flat Rate ---------		1	9.0 (w)	...
South Carolina	5.0	--------- Flat Rate ---------		1	4.5 (x)	...
South Dakota	...	...		...	6.0–0.25% (b)	...
Tennessee	6.5	--------- Flat Rate ---------		1	6.5	...
Texas	-------------------------------------- (y) ------------------------------------					...
Utah	5.0 (b)	--------- Flat Rate ---------		...	5.0 (b)	...
Vermont (b)	6.0–8.5 (b)	10,000	250,000	3	(a)	...
Virginia	6.0	--------- Flat Rate ---------		1	6.0	...
Washington	-------------------------------------- No corporate income tax ------------------------------------					
West Virginia	8.5 (z)	--------- Flat Rate ---------		1	8.5 (z)	...
Wisconsin	7.9	--------- Flat Rate ---------		1	7.9	...
Wyoming	-------------------------------------- No corporate income tax ------------------------------------					
Dist. of Columbia	9.975 (b)	--------- Flat Rate ---------		1	9.975 (b)	...

See footnotes at end of table.

RANGE OF STATE CORPORATE INCOME TAX RATES — Continued
(For tax year 2011, as of January 1, 2011)

Source: Compiled by the Federation of Tax Administrators from various sources January 2011.

Key:

★ — Yes

... — No

(a) Rates listed are the corporate income tax rate applied to financial institutions or excise taxes based on income. Some states have other taxes based upon the value of deposits or shares.

(b) Minimum tax is $50 in Arizona, $100 in District of Columbia, $50 in North Dakota (banks), $500 in Rhode Island, $200 per location in South Dakota (banks), $100 in Utah, $250 in Vermont.

(c) The minimum corporation franchise tax in California is $800. The additional alternative minimum tax is levied at a 6.65% rate.

(d) Connecticut's tax is the greater of the 7.5% tax on net income, a 0.31% tax on capital stock and surplus (maximum tax of $1 million), or $250 (the minimum tax).

(e) The Delaware Bank marginal rate decreases over four brackets ranging from $20 to $650 million in taxable income. Building and loan associations are taxed at a flat 8.7%.

(f) An exemption of $5,000 is allowed. Florida's Alternative Minimum Tax rate is 3.3%.

(g) Hawaii taxes capital gains at 4%. Financial institutions pay a franchise tax of 7.92% of taxable income (in lieu of the corporate income tax and general excise taxes).

(h) Idaho's minimum tax on a corporation is $20. The $10 Permanent Building Fund Tax must be paid by each corporation in a unitary group filing a combined return. Taxpayers with gross sales in Idaho under $100,000, and with no property or payroll in Idaho, may elect to pay 1% on such sales (instead of the tax on net income).

(i) The Illinois rate of 9.5% is the sum of a corporate income tax rate of 7.0% plus a replacement tax of 2.5%. Tax rate increased from 7.3% on 1/1/11.

(j) 50% of the federal income tax is deductible.

(k) In addition to the flat 4% corporate income tax, Kansas levies a 3.0% surtax on taxable income over $50,000. Banks pay a privilege tax of 2.25% of net income, plus a surtax of 2.125% (2.25% for savings and loans, trust companies, and federally chartered savings banks) on net income in excess of $25,000.

(l) The state franchise tax on financial institutions is either (1) the sum of 1% of the Maine net income of the financial institution for the taxable year, plus 8¢ per $1,000 of the institution's Maine assets as of the end of its taxable year, or (2) 39¢ per $1,000 of the institution's Maine assets as of the end of its taxable year.

(m) In 2012, the Massachusetts tax rate on business and manufacturing corporations is scheduled to fall to 8.0% and the rate on financial institutions to 9.0%. Business and manufacturing corporations pay an additional tax of $2.60 per $1,000 on either taxable Massachusetts tangible property or taxable net worth allocable to the state (for intangible property corporations). The minimum tax for both corporations and financial institutions is $456.

(n) The Michigan Business Tax is levied at rate of 4.95% on income plus 0.8% on modified gross receipts; there is a 21.99% surcharge, capped at $6 million per year. The tax applies to businesses with gross receipts of $350,000 or more.

(o) In addition, Minnesota levies a 5.8% tentative minimum tax on Alternative Minimum Taxable Income.

(p) Montana levies a 7% tax on taxpayers using water's edge combination. The minimum tax per corporation is $50; the $50 minimum applies to each corporation included on a combined tax return. Taxpayers with gross sales in Montana of $100,000 or less may pay an alternative tax of 0.5% on such sales, instead of the net income tax.

(q) New Hampshire's 8.5% Business Profits Tax is imposed on both corporations and unincorporated associations with gross income over $50,000. In addition, New Hampshire levies a Business Enterprise Tax of 0.75% on the enterprise base (total compensation, interest and dividends paid) for businesses with gross income over $150,000 or base over $75,000.

(r) In New Jersey small businesses with annual entire net income under $100,000 pay a tax rate of 7.5%; businesses with income under $50,000 pay 6.5%. The minimum Corporation Business Tax is based on New Jersey gross receipts. It ranges from $500 for a corporation with gross receipts less than $100,000, to $2,000 for a corporation with gross receipts of $1 million or more.

(s) New York's General business corporate rate shown. Corporations may also be subject to AMT tax at 1.5% (3% banks), or a capital stocks tax. A minimum tax ranges from $25 to $5,000, depending on receipts ($250 minimum for banks). Certain qualified New York manufacturers pay 6.5%. Small business taxpayers in New York pay rates of 6.5%, 7.1%, and 4.35% on three brackets of entire net income up to $390,000.

(t) In North Carolina financial institutions are also subject to a tax equal to $30 per one million in assets.

(u) Ohio no longer levies a tax based on income (except for a particular subset of corporations), but instead imposes a Commercial Activity Tax (CAT) equal to $150 for gross receipts sitused to Ohio of between $150,000 and $1 million, plus 0.26% of gross receipts over $1 million. Banks continue to pay a franchise tax of 1.3% of net worth. For those few corporations for whom the franchise tax on net worth or net income still applies, a litter tax also applies.

(v) Oregon's minimum tax for C corporations depends on the Oregon sales of the filing group. The minimum tax ranges from $150 for corporations with sales under $500,000, up to $100,000 for companies with sales of $100 million or above.

(w) Rhode Island's tax is the greater of 9% of net income or an alternative annual franchise tax at the rate of $2.50 per $10,000 of authorized capital stock (valued at a minimum of $100/share) with a minimum tax of $500.

(x) South Carolina taxes savings and loans at a 6% rate.

(y) Texas imposes a Franchise Tax, otherwise known as margin tax, imposed on entities with more than $1,000,000 total revenues at rate of 1%, or 0.5% for entities primarily engaged in retail or wholesale trade, on lesser of 70% of total revenues or 100% of gross receipts after deductions for either compensation or cost of goods sold.

(z) West Virginia's corporate rate is scheduled for reduction as follows: 7.75% after 2011, 7.0% after 2012, 6.5% after 2013.

Table 7.15
STATE SEVERANCE TAXES: 2011

State	Title and application of tax (a)	Rate
Alabama	Iron Ore Mining Tax	$.03/ton
	Forest Products Severance Tax	Varies by species and ultimate use.
	Oil and Gas Conservation & Regulation of Production Tax	2% of gross value at point of production, of all oil and gas produced. 1% of the gross value (for a 5-year period from the date production begins) for well, for which the initial permit issued by the Oil and Gas Board is dated on or after July 1, 1996 and before July 1, 2002, except a replacement well for which the initial permit was dated before July 1, 1996.
	Oil and Gas Privilege Tax on Production	8% of gross value at point of production; 4% of gross value at point of incremental production resulting from a qualified enhanced recovery project; 4% if wells produce 25 bbl. or less oil per day or 200,000 cu. ft. or less gas per day; 6% of gross value at point of production for certain on-shore and off-shore wells. A 50% rate reduction for wells permitted by the oil and gas board on or after July 1, 1996 and before July 1, 2002 for 5 years from initial production, except for replacement wells for which the initial permit was dated before July 1, 1996.
	Coal Severance Tax	$.135/ton
	Coal and Lignite Severance Tax	$.20/ton in addition to coal severance tax.
	Local Solid Minerals Tax	Varies by county.
	Uniform Natural Minerals Tax	$.10/ton
Alaska	Cost Recovery Fisheries Assessment (b)	Elective; currently no assessments in place.
	Dive Fishery Management Assessment (b)	Elective; currently 7% of value for select dive fishery species in select management regions.
	Fisheries Business Tax	Tax based on unprocessed value of fishery resources processed in or exported from the state. 1% of value for shore-based processing in developing fisheries; 3% of value for floating processing in developing fisheries or shore-based processing in established fisheries; 4.5% of value for salmon cannery processing in established fisheries; 5% of value for floating processing in established fisheries.
	Fishery Resource Landing Tax	Tax based on unprocessed value of fishery resources processed outside and first landed in the state. 1% of value for developing fisheries; 3% of value for established fisheries.
	Mining License Tax	Up to 7% of net income and royalties received in connection with mining properties and activities in Alaska. New mining operations other than sand and gravel exempt for 3½ years after production begins.
	Petroleum Profits Tax (PPT)	22.5% net value at wellhead (excludes capital costs, operating costs and other qualified expenditures) minus credits. Additional 0.25% surcharge for each dollar that net value exceeds $40 per barrel; surcharge cannot exceed 25% of the monthly production tax value of taxable oil and gas. Conservation surcharge of 4 cents per barrel; plus another 1 cent per barrel surcharge if there is less than $50 million in the Hazardous Release Fund.
	Salmon Enhancement Tax (b)	Elective; 2% or 3% of value for salmon sold in or exported from select aquaculture regions.
	Seafood Development Tax (b)	Elective; currently 1% of value for select commercial fish species in select seafood development regions.
	Seafood Marketing Assessment (b)	Elective; currently 0.3% of value for all commercial fish species.
Arizona	Severance Tax	2.5% of net severance base for mining (metalliferous minerals); $1.51/1000 board ft. ($2.13 for ponderosa pine) for timbering.
Arkansas	Natural Resources Severance Tax	Separate rate for each substance.
	Oil and Gas Conservation Tax	Natural gas 0.3 of $.01 cent per MCF; crude oil 4% to 5% depending on production levels.
	Oil and Gas Conservation Assessment	Maximum 43 mills/bbl. of oil and 9 mills per MCF produced of gas.
California	Oil and Gas Production Assessment	Rate determined annually by Department of Conservation.
Colorado	Severance Tax (c)	Taxable years commencing prior to July 1, 1999, 2.25% of gross income exceeding $11 million for metallic minerals and taxable years commencing after July 1, 1999, 2.25% of gross income exceeding $19 million for metallic minerals; on or after July 1, 1999, $.05/ton for each ton exceeding 625,000 tons each quarter for molybdenum ore; 2% to 5% based on gross income for oil, gas, CO_2, and coalbed methane; after July 1, 1999, $.36/ton adjusted by the producers' prices index for each ton exceeding 300,000 tons each quarter for coal; and 4% of gross proceeds on production exceeding 15,000 tons per day for oil shale.
	Oil and Gas Conservation Levy	Maximum 1.5 mills/$1 of market value at wellhead. (d)

See footnotes at end of table.

STATE SEVERANCE TAXES: 2011 — Continued

State	Title and application of tax (a)	Rate
Florida	Oil, Gas and Sulfur Production Tax	5% of gross value for small well oil, and 8% of gross value for all other, and an additional 12.5% for escaped oil; the gas base rate ($0.171) times the gas base adjustment rate each fiscal year for gas; and the sulfur base rate ($2.43) times the sulfur base rate adjustment each fiscal year for sulfur.
	Solid Minerals Tax (e)	8% of the value of the minerals severed, except phosphate rock (rate computed annually at $1.95/ton plus year 2010 surcharge rate of $1.38/ton) and heavy minerals (rate computed annually at a base rate of $1.34/ton times the base rate adjustment). Yet solid minerals, except phosphate rock and heavy minerals, upon which the sales tax is ultimately paid to the state are exempt from severance tax.
Idaho	Ore Severance Tax	1% of net value
	Oil and Gas Production Tax	Maximum of 5 mills/bbl. of oil and 5 mills/50,000 cu. ft. of gas. (f)
	Additional Oil and Gas Production Tax	2% of market value at site of production.
Illinois	Timber Fee	4% of purchase price (g)
Indiana	Petroleum Production Tax (h)	1% of value or $.24 per barrel for oil or $.03 per 1000 cu. ft. of gas, whichever is greater.
Kansas	Severance Tax (i)	8% of gross value of oil and gas, less property tax credit of 3.67%; $1/ton of coal.
	Oil and Gas Conservation Tax	91.00 mills/bbl. crude oil or petroleum marketed or used each month; 12.9 mills/1,000 cu. ft. of gas sold or marketed each month.
	Mined-Land Conservation & Reclamation Tax	$50, plus per ton fee of between $.03 and $.10.
Kentucky	Oil Production Tax	4.5% of market value
	Coal Severance Tax	4.5% of gross value, less transportation expenses
	Natural Resource Severance Tax (j)	4.5% of gross value, less transportation expenses
Louisiana	Natural Resources Severance Tax	Rate varies according to substance.
	Oil Field Site Restoration Fee	Rate varies according to type of well and production.
	Freshwater Mussel Tax	5% of revenues from the sale of whole freshwater mussels, at the point of first sale.
Maine	Mining Excise Tax	The greater of a tax on facilities and equipment or a tax on gross proceeds.
Maryland	Mine Reclamation Surcharge	$.17/ton of coal removed by open-pit, strip or deep mine methods. Of the $.15, $.06 is remitted to the county from which the coal was removed.
Michigan	Gas and Oil Severance Tax	5% (gas), 6.6% (oil) and 4% (oil from stripper wells and marginal properties) of gross cash market value of the total production. Maximum additional fee of 1% of gross cash market value on all oil and gas produced in state in previous year.
Minnesota	Taconite and Iron Sulfides	$2.38 per ton of concentrates or pellets
	Direct Reduced Iron (k)	$2.38 per ton of concentrates plus an additional $.03 per ton for each 1% that the iron content exceeds 72%.
Mississippi	Oil and Gas Severance Tax	6% of value at point of gas production; 3% of gross value of occluded natural gas from coal seams at point of production for well's first five years; also, maximum 35 mills/bbl. oil or 4 mills/1,000 cu. ft. gas (Oil and Gas Board maintenance tax). 6% of value at point of oil production; 3% of value at production when enhanced oil recovery method used.
	Timber Severance Tax	Varies depending on type of wood and ultimate use.
	Salt Severance Tax	3% of value of entire production in state.
Montana	Coal Severance Tax	Varies from 3% to 15% depending on quality of coal and type of mine.
	Metalliferous Mines License Tax (l)	Progressive rate, taxed on amounts in excess of $250,000. For concentrate shipped to smelter, mill or reduction work, 1.81%. Gold, silver or any platinum group metal shipped to refinery, 1.6%.
	Oil or Gas Conservation Tax	Maximum 0.3% on the market value of each barrel of crude petroleum oil or 10,000 cu. ft. of natural gas produced, saved and marketed or stored within or exported from the state. (m)
	Oil and Natural Gas Production Tax	Varies from 0.5% to 14.8% according to the type of well and type of production.
	Micaceous Minerals License Tax	$.05/ton
	Cement License Tax (n)	$.22/ton of cement, $.05/ton of cement, plaster, gypsum or gypsum products.
	Resource Indemnity Trust Tax	$25 plus 0.5% of gross value greater than $5,000. For talc, $25 plus 4% of gross value greater than $625. For coal, $25 plus 0.40% of gross value greater than $6,250. For vermiculite, $25 plus 2% of gross value greater than $1,250. For limestone, $25 plus 10% of gross value greater than $250. For industrial garnets, $25 plus 1% of gross value greater than $2,500.00.

See footnotes at end of table.

STATE SEVERANCE TAXES: 2011 — Continued

State	Title and application of tax (a)	Rate
Nebraska	Oil and Gas Severance Tax	3% of value of nonstripper oil and natural gas; 2% of value of stripper oil.
	Oil and Gas Conservation Tax	Maximum 15 mills/$1 of value at wellhead, as of January 1, 2000. (f)
	Uranium Tax	2% of gross value over $5 million. The value of the uranium severed subject to tax is the gross value less transportation and processing costs.
Nevada	Minerals Extraction Tax	Between 2% and 5% of net proceeds of each geographically separate extractive operation, based on ratio of net proceeds to gross proceeds of whole operation.
	Oil and Gas Conservation Tax	$50/mills/bbl. of oil and 50 mills/50,000 cu. ft. of gas.
New Hampshire	Refined Petroleum Products Tax	0.1% of fair market value
	Excavation Tax	$.02 per cubic yard of earth excavated.
	Timber Tax	10% of stumpage value at the time of cutting.
New Mexico	Resources Excise Tax (o)	Potash .5%, molybdenum .125%, all others .75% of value.
	Severance Tax (o)	Copper .5%, timber .125% of value. Pumice, gypsum, sand, gravel, clay, fluorspar and other non-metallic minerals, .125% of value. Gold, silver .20%. Lead, zinc, thorium, molybdenum, manganese, rare earth and other .125% of value.
	Oil and Gas Severance Tax	3.75% of value of oil, other liquid hydrocarbons, natural gas and carbon dioxide.
	Oil and Gas Emergency School Tax	3.15% of value of oil, other liquid hydrocarbons and carbon dioxide. 4% of value of natural gas.
	Natural Gas Processor's Tax	$0.0220/Mmbtu tax on volume.
	Oil and Gas Ad Valorem Production Tax	Varies, based on property tax in district of production.
	Oil and Gas Conservation Tax (p)	0.19% of value.
North Carolina	Oil and Gas Conservation Tax	Maximum 5 mills/barrel of oil and 0.5 mill/1,000 cu. ft. of gas.
	Primary Forest Product Assessment Tax	$.50/1,000 board ft. for softwood sawtimber, $.40/1,000 board ft. for hardwood sawtimber, $.20/cord for softwood pulpwood, $.12/cord hardwood pulpwood.
North Dakota	Oil Gross Production Tax	5% of gross value at well.
	Gas Gross Production Tax	$.04/1000 cu.ft. of gas produced (the rate is subject to a gas rate adjustment each fiscal year). For FY05, the rate was 10.37 cents per mcf.
	Coal Severance Tax	$.375/ton plus $.02/ton. (q)
	Oil Extraction Tax	6.5% of gross value at well (with exceptions due to production volumes and and production incentives for enhanced recovery projects).
Ohio	Resource Severance Tax	$.10/bbl. of oil; $.025/1,000 cu. ft. of natural gas; $.04/ton of salt; $.02/ton of sand, gravel, limestone and dolomite; $.10/ton of coal; and $0.01/ton of clay, sandstone or conglomerate, shale, gypsum or quartzite.
Oklahoma	Oil, Gas and Mineral Gross Production Tax and Petroleum Excise Tax (r)	Rate: 0.75% levied on asphalt and metals. 7% (if greater than $2.10 mcf) 4% (if greater than $1.75 mcf, but less than $2.10 mcf) 1% (if less than $1.75 mcf) casinghead gas and natural gas as well as 0.95% being levied on crude oil, casinghead gas and natural gas. Oil Gross Production Tax is now a variable rate tax, beginning with January 1999 production, at the following rates based on the average price of Oklahoma oil: a) If the average price equals or exceeds $17/bbl, the tax shall be 7%; b) If the average price is less than $17/bbl, but is equal to or exceeds $14/bbl, the tax shall be 4%; c) If the average price is less than $14/bbl, the tax shall be 1%.
Oregon	Forest Products Harvest Tax	$3.5750/1000 board ft. harvested from public and private land. (rate is for 2009 harvests).
	Oil and Gas Production Tax	6% of gross value at well.
	STF Severance Tax — Eastern Oregon Forestland Option	$3.60/1000 board ft. harvested from land under the Small Tract Forestland Option.
	STF Severance Tax — Western Oregon Forestland Option	$4.61/1000 board ft. harvested from land under the Small Tract Forestland Option.
South Carolina	Forest Renewal Tax	Softwood products: 50 cents per 1,000 board feet or 25 cents per cord. Hardwood products: 25 cents per 1,000 board feet or 7 cents per cord.
South Dakota	Precious Metals Severance Tax	$4 per ounce of gold severed plus additional tax depending on price of gold; 10% on net profits or royalties from sale of precious metals, and 8% of royalty value.
	Energy Minerals Severance Tax (s)	4.5% of taxable value of any energy minerals.
	Conservation Tax	2.4 mills of taxable value of any energy minerals.
Tennessee	Oil and Gas Severance Tax	3% of sales price.
	Coal Severance Tax (t)	$.50/ton (effective 7/1/09)
	Mineral Tax	Up to $0.15 per ton, rate set by county legislative body.

See footnotes at end of table.

STATE SEVERANCE TAXES: 2011 — Continued

State	Title and application of tax (a)	Rate
Texas............................	Natural Gas Production Tax	7.5% of market value of gas. Condensate Production Tax: 4.6% of market value of gas.
	Crude Oil Production Tax	4.6% of market value or $.046/bbl.
	Sulphur Production Tax	$1.03/long ton or fraction thereof.
	Cement Production Tax	$0.55 per ton or $.0275/100 lbs. or fraction of 100 pounds of taxable cement.
	Oil-Field Cleanup Regulatory Fees	5/8 of $.01/barrel; 1/15 of $.01/1000 cubic feet of gas. (u)
	Oyster Sales Fee	$1 per 300 lb. barrel of oysters taken from Texas waters.
Utah..............................	Mining Severance Tax	2.6% of taxable value for metals or metalliferous minerals sold or otherwise disposed of.
	Oil and Gas Severance Tax	3% of value for the first $13 per barrel of oil, 5% from $13.01 and above; 3% of value for first $1.50/mcf, 5% from $1.51 and above; and 4% of taxable value of natural gas liquids.
	Oil and Gas Conservation Fee	.002% of market value at wellhead.
Virginia........................	Forest Products Tax	$1.15 per 1000 feet B.M. of pine lumber and 1000 board feet of pine logs. $0.475 collected per cord of pine pulpwood.
	Coal Surface Mining Reclamation Tax	Varies depending on balance of Coal Surface Mining Reclamation Fund.
Washington...................	Uranium and Thorium Milling Tax (tax reported as inactive)	$0.05/per pound.
	Enhanced Food Fish Tax	0.09% to 5.62% of value (depending on species) at point of landing.
	Timber Excise Tax	5% of stumpage value for harvests on public and private lands.
West Virginia................	Natural Resource Severance Taxes	Coal: State rate is greater of 5% or $.75 per ton (4.65% for state purposes and .35% for distribution to local governments). Special state rates for coal from new low seam mines. For seams between 37" and 45" the rate is greater of 2% or $.75/ton (1.65% for state purposes and .35% for distribution to local governments). For seams less than 37" the rate is greater of 1% or $.75/ton (.65% for state purposes and .35% for distribution to local governments). For coal from gob, refuse piles, or other sources of waste coal, the rate is 2.5% (distributed to local governments). Additional tax for workers' compensation debt reduction is $.56/ton. Two special reclamation taxes at $.07/clean ton and $.02/clean ton. Limestone or sandstone, quarried or mined, and other natural resources: 5% of gross value. Natural gas: 5% of gross value (10% of net tax distributed to local governments), additional tax for workers' compensation debt reduction is $.047/mcf of natural gas produced. Oil: 5% of gross value (10% of net tax distributed to local governments). Sand, gravel or other mineral products not quarried or mined: 5% of gross value. Timber: 1.22%, additional tax for workers' compensation debt reduction is 2.78%.
Wisconsin	Mining Net Proceeds Tax	Progressive net proceeds tax ranging from 3% to 15% is imposed on the net proceeds from mining metalliferous minerals. The tax brackets are annually adjusted for inflation based on the change in the GNP deflator.
	Oil and Gas Severance Tax	7% of market value of oil or gas at the mouth of the well.
	Forest Crop Law Severance Tax	10% of stumpage.
	Managed Forest Law Yield Tax	5% yield tax. This tax will be waived for the first five years of most MFL land.
Wyoming	Severance Taxes	Severance Tax is defined as an excise tax imposed on the present and continuing privilege of removing, extracting, severing or producing any mineral in this state. Except as otherwise provided by W.S. 39-14-205. The total Severance Tax on crude oil, lease condensate or natural gas shall be six percent (6%). Stripper oil is taxed at four percent (4%). Surface coal is taxed at seven percent (7%). Underground coal is taxed at three and three-fourths percent (3.75%). Trona is taxed at four percent (4%). Bentonite, sand and gravel, and all other minerals are taxed at two percent (2%). Uranium is taxed at four percent (4%).

See footnotes at end of table.

STATE SEVERANCE TAXES: 2011 — Continued

Source: The Council of State Governments, 2011.

Note: Severance tax collection totals may be found in the Chapter Seven table entitled "State Government Revenue, By Type of Tax: 2008."

Key:

(a) Application of tax is same as that of title unless otherwise indicated by a footnote.

(b) Tax rates and applicability for these severance taxes determined by a vote of the appropriate association within the seafood industry, by the Alaska Seafood Marketing Institute, or by the Department of Revenue. Proceeds from these elective assessments are customarily appropriated for benefit of the seafood industry.

(c) Metallic minerals, molybdenum ore, coal, oil shale, oil, gas, CO_2, and coalbed methane.

(d) As of July 1, 2004, set at .0005 mill/\$1.

(e) Clay, gravel, phosphate rock, lime, shells, stone, sand, heavy minerals and rare earths.

(f) Actual rate set by administrative actions. Idaho—Current conservation rate is 5 mills (.005); Nebraska—Current conservation rate is 3 mills (.003).

(g) Buyer deducts amount from payment to grower; amount forwarded to Department of Natural Resources.

(h) Petroleum, oil, gas and other hydrocarbons.

(i) Coal, oil and gas.

(j) Coal and oil excepted.

(k) Production is considered commercial when it exceeds 50,000 tons annually. There is a six-year phase-in of the tax. In years one and two, the rate is zero. In year three, it is 25% of the statutory rate and 50% and 75% in years four and five respectively. An Aggregate Materials Tax is imposed by resolution of of county boards. It is not required that any county impose the tax, which is \$.10/cubic yard or \$.07/ton on materials produced in the county.

(l) Metals, precious and semi-precious stones and gems.

(m) The maximum rate of 0.3% is split between the Oil or Gas Conservation Tax and the Oil, Gas and Coal Natural Resource Account Fund. Currently the Oil or Gas Conservation Tax is .18% and the Oil, Gas and Coal Natural Resource Account fund tax rate is .08%.

(n) Cement and gypsum or allied products.

(o) Natural resources except oil, natural gas, liquid hydrocarbons or carbon dioxide.

(p) Oil, coal, gas, liquid hydrocarbons, geothermal energy, carbon dioxide and uranium.

(q) Rate reduced by 50 percent if burned in cogeneration facility using renewable resources as fuel to generate at least 10 percent of its energy output. Coal shipped out of state is subject to the \$.02/ton tax and 30% of the \$.375/ton tax. The coal may be subject to up to the \$.375/ton tax at the option of the county in which the coal is mined.

(r) Asphalt and ores bearing lead, zinc, jack, gold, silver, copper or petroleum or other crude oil or other mineral oil, natural gas or casing-head gas and uranium ore.

(s) Any mineral fuel used in the production of energy, including coal, lignite, petroleum, oil, natural gas, uranium and thorium.

(t) Counties and municipalities also authorized to levy severance taxes on sand, gravel, sandstone, chert and limestone at a rate up to \$.15/ton.

(u) Fees will not be collected when Oil-Field Cleanup Fund reaches \$20 million, but will again be collected when fund falls below \$10 million.

Table 7.16
STATE GOVERNMENT TAX REVENUE, BY SELECTED TYPES OF TAX: 2009
(In thousands of dollars)

State	Total taxes	Sales and gross receipts	Licenses	Individual income	Corporation net income	Severance	Property taxes	Death and gift	Documentary and stock transfer	Other
United States	$715,086,270	$342,247,049	$49,756,825	$245,930,476	$40,477,747	$13,440,072	$12,963,472	$4,682,966	$4,926,780	$660,883
Alabama	8,306,446	4,203,283	478,927	2,662,759	493,972	115,374	315,784	0	36,347	0
Alaska	4,953,342	244,282	135,947	0	632,123	3,829,564	111,251	175	0	0
Arizona	11,864,046	7,390,022	404,101	2,575,753	592,187	19,481	835,240	210	25,954	21,098
Arkansas	7,467,679	3,750,943	328,393	2,238,958	346,215	33,547	733,035	224	24,613	11,751
California	101,007,459	36,381,343	8,371,914	44,355,959	9,535,679	27,105	2,335,214	245	0	0
Colorado	8,682,822	3,299,250	365,544	4,403,446	329,545	285,015	0	22	0	0
Connecticut	12,927,619	5,425,933	363,502	6,376,921	444,061	0	0	230,503	86,699	0
Delaware	2,806,031	474,278	1,154,915	910,693	208,677	0	0	0	56,586	882
Florida	31,956,841	26,874,027	1,818,414	0	1,836,800	81,300	800	4,800	1,328,300	12,400
Georgia	16,077,948	7,001,141	481,555	7,801,185	694,717	0	82,764	83	16,503	0
Hawaii	4,712,651	3,125,035	146,270	1,338,702	78,597	0	0	274	23,773	0
Idaho	3,171,863	1,574,348	268,208	1,175,604	142,240	4,952	0	264	0	6,247
Illinois	29,268,349	14,482,811	2,445,281	9,183,002	2,752,353	0	63,853	300,408	40,641	0
Indiana	14,900,123	8,856,580	697,487	4,313,759	838,974	162	7,499	185,662	0	0
Iowa	6,984,279	3,272,176	658,128	2,703,190	264,365	0	0	72,562	13,858	0
Kansas	6,694,630	3,044,904	301,953	2,731,559	370,889	142,658	80,137	22,530	0	0
Kentucky	9,755,544	4,663,830	473,206	3,315,368	389,634	355,985	513,121	41,234	3,166	0
Louisiana	10,014,637	5,015,610	464,971	2,940,633	612,545	911,433	64,377	5,068	0	0
Maine	3,489,105	1,640,671	243,313	1,370,710	143,086	0	41,719	31,819	17,787	0
Maryland	15,126,893	6,136,613	690,914	6,478,236	749,001	0	688,535	205,627	115,670	62,297
Massachusetts	19,699,494	6,112,981	753,807	10,599,085	1,789,553	0	4,180	259,734	135,595	44,559
Michigan	22,757,818	12,504,160	1,351,556	5,856,751	703,250	53,233	2,163,428	147	125,293	0
Minnesota	17,161,299	7,362,340	1,022,182	6,948,119	779,055	45,820	713,019	129,811	160,953	277,516
Mississippi	6,470,593	4,138,039	403,120	1,485,592	324,301	113,762	5,779	0	0	0
Missouri	10,345,250	4,598,920	642,305	4,771,576	278,661	18	30,031	3,030	8,576	12,133
Montana	2,407,400	529,392	297,986	827,196	164,255	349,714	235,150	213	0	3,494
Nebraska	4,000,939	2,015,283	167,014	1,602,091	198,442	4,718	1,964	493	10,934	0
Nevada	5,564,170	4,341,127	525,565	0	0	145,450	203,469	0	71,043	277,516
New Hampshire	2,125,722	829,654	227,589	98,191	493,431	0	392,652	77	84,128	0
New Jersey	27,074,472	11,652,984	1,413,730	10,476,267	2,528,913	0	33,009	653,440	316,129	0
New Mexico	4,851,689	2,493,029	214,014	932,442	203,584	931,832	65,075	32	0	11,681
New York	65,029,871	20,238,418	1,528,785	36,840,019	4,427,675	0	0	1,165,247	829,727	0
North Carolina	20,496,106	8,430,223	1,449,683	9,560,353	901,445	1,740	0	116,624	36,038	0
North Dakota	2,414,010	943,614	141,290	370,165	129,542	827,417	1,942	40	0	0
Ohio	23,952,422	12,149,489	2,880,397	8,323,352	521,363	11,052	0	66,769	0	0
Oklahoma	8,160,670	3,158,336	993,304	2,544,576	342,762	1,067,182	0	39,562	12,822	2,126
Oregon	7,419,494	744,458	847,716	5,434,777	258,778	13,038	22,121	87,211	11,395	0
Pennsylvania	30,071,179	15,096,410	2,503,297	9,550,238	1,740,532	0	55,536	748,648	349,181	27,337
Rhode Island	2,586,184	1,383,764	96,880	960,885	108,497	0	1,617	27,262	7,149	130
South Carolina	7,146,034	4,078,360	452,195	2,351,324	219,484	0	9,994	153	34,524	0

See footnotes at end of table.

STATE GOVERNMENT TAX REVENUE, BY SELECTED TYPES OF TAX: 2009
(In thousands of dollars) — Continued

State	Total taxes	Sales and gross receipts	Licenses	Individual income	Corporation net income	Severance	Property taxes	Death and gift	Documentary and stock transfer	Other
South Dakota..............	1,333,835	1,083,611	192,685	0	48,772	7,668	0	16	163	920
Tennessee	10,442,552	8,000,471	1,138,070	221,685	816,261	2,413	0	91,490	138,055	34,107
Texas.........................	40,786,857	31,540,978	6,905,394	0	0	2,338,481	0	2,004	0	0
Utah...........................	5,422,858	2,398,162	356,742	2,319,632	245,880	102,121	0	321	0	0
Vermont.....................	2,505,665	822,006	98,324	532,911	86,759	0	911,811	23,397	26,472	3,985
Virginia......................	16,331,388	5,638,353	670,999	8,918,232	633,490	1,997	31,375	6,005	313,594	117,343
Washington................	16,408,838	13,110,784	929,358	0	0	29,681	1,785,065	138,535	415,415	0
West Virginia.............	4,788,157	2,226,921	193,192	1,557,403	420,530	376,677	4,868	29	8,537	0
Wisconsin	14,402,506	6,647,399	914,493	5,971,177	656,872	5,669	134,006	20,853	41,160	10,877
Wyoming	2,760,491	1,120,303	152,210	0	0	1,203,813	284,052	113	0	0

Source: U.S. Census Bureau, 2009 Annual Survey of State Government Finances. For information on sampling and nonsampling errors and definitions, see *http://www.census.gov/govs/state/how_data_collected.html.* Data users who create their own estimates from this table should cite the U.S. Census Bureau as the source of the original data only.

Table 7.17
STATE GOVERNMENT SALES AND GROSS RECEIPTS TAX REVENUE: 2009
(In thousands of dollars)

State	Total	General sales or gross receipts	Total	Motor fuels	Insurance premiums	Public utilities	Tobacco products	Alcoholic beverages	Amusements	Pari-mutuels	Other
							Selective sales taxes				
United States	$342,247,049	$227,702,510	$114,544,539	$35,368,850	$14,803,990	$14,840,404	$16,677,835	$5,348,822	$6,267,579	$190,682	$21,046,377
Alabama	4,203,283	2,069,535	2,133,748	546,467	269,808	801,096	141,176	167,830	87	2,427	204,857
Alaska	244,282	0	244,282	10,064	52,286	4,127	73,079	39,626	9,161	0	55,939
Arizona	7,390,022	5,675,531	1,714,491	813,794	439,132	24,049	373,882	62,799	542	293	0
Arkansas	3,750,943	2,765,996	984,947	462,221	149,457	0	171,038	45,623	7,076	5,334	144,198
California	36,381,343	28,972,302	7,409,041	3,180,128	2,053,850	782,368	1,000,456	323,934	0	30,737	37,568
Colorado	3,299,250	2,123,671	1,175,579	616,589	197,414	12,168	217,165	35,972	95,650	621	0
Connecticut	5,425,933	3,290,050	2,135,883	490,804	159,588	277,337	316,246	47,064	445,272	7,583	391,989
Delaware	474,278	0	474,278	114,579	88,849	57,592	125,505	15,519	0	121	72,113
Florida	26,874,027	19,228,000	7,646,027	2,229,827	651,300	3,170,100	447,061	590,400	0	24,348	532,991
Georgia	7,001,141	5,306,491	1,694,650	861,153	314,583	0	229,673	166,618	0	0	122,623
Hawaii	3,125,035	2,461,618	663,417	91,712	98,038	126,069	88,145	47,242	0	0	212,211
Idaho	1,574,348	1,206,137	368,211	218,180	78,886	2,018	52,918	8,122	0	1,325	6,762
Illinois	14,482,811	7,470,532	7,012,279	1,467,402	334,126	1,914,327	582,323	157,622	558,471	6,865	1,991,143
Indiana	8,856,580	6,205,638	2,650,942	798,739	187,410	215,659	510,585	43,498	880,988	3,975	10,088
Iowa	3,272,176	2,201,396	1,070,780	434,243	90,035	0	238,153	14,704	289,867	3,778	0
Kansas	3,044,904	2,227,183	817,721	422,865	136,544	512	112,943	111,589	515	265	32,488
Kentucky	4,663,830	2,857,665	1,806,165	632,655	125,168	61,229	214,597	111,596	231	4,388	656,301
Louisiana	5,015,610	2,963,758	2,051,852	600,786	484,858	12,788	145,578	56,881	715,458	5,973	29,530
Maine	1,640,671	1,012,357	628,314	220,772	89,528	26,763	144,425	17,438	26,161	2,918	100,309
Maryland	6,136,613	3,851,341	2,285,272	734,836	390,848	124,914	405,558	29,168	19,909	1,609	578,430
Massachusetts	6,112,981	3,880,087	2,232,894	654,022	335,646	23,504	587,331	72,598	3,366	2,773	553,654
Michigan	12,504,160	8,998,942	3,505,218	969,959	261,003	28,913	1,043,532	140,488	121,364	7,488	932,471
Minnesota	7,362,340	4,375,200	2,987,140	750,308	330,206	49	422,780	75,225	37,750	705	1,370,117
Mississippi	4,138,039	3,026,497	1,111,542	425,020	188,256	1,961	83,589	42,464	172,429	0	197,823
Missouri	4,598,920	3,030,477	1,568,443	707,331	292,412	0	107,864	31,990	370,447	0	58,399
Montana	529,392	0	529,392	191,188	66,755	50,968	89,776	28,095	62,487	96	40,027
Nebraska	2,015,283	1,504,174	511,109	292,857	51,040	59,116	70,438	26,925	6,225	216	4,292
Nevada	4,341,127	2,684,029	1,657,098	298,135	238,622	12,283	119,566	37,867	905,656	0	44,969
New Hampshire	829,654	0	829,654	132,122	81,543	87,002	195,034	12,451	256	1,967	319,279
New Jersey	11,652,984	8,264,162	3,388,822	538,166	456,810	936,429	747,777	105,488	351,039	0	253,113
New Mexico	2,493,029	1,887,343	605,686	188,943	128,731	33,323	48,270	39,251	62,233	614	104,321
New York	20,238,418	11,073,898	9,164,520	506,741	1,111,852	799,294	1,337,665	206,453	773	27,939	5,173,803
North Carolina	8,430,223	4,963,434	3,466,789	1,515,944	506,452	393,923	243,370	264,067	14,748	0	528,285
North Dakota	943,614	607,171	336,443	143,796	34,583	36,822	24,114	7,161	9,398	304	80,265
Ohio	12,149,489	7,328,388	4,821,101	1,726,742	425,089	1,172,100	924,764	93,782	0	9,544	469,080
Oklahoma	3,158,336	2,162,693	995,643	420,109	157,894	32,729	257,812	90,064	13,972	1,648	21,415
Oregon	744,458	0	744,458	397,609	57,050	23,509	248,205	15,852	84	2,149	0
Pennsylvania	15,096,410	8,496,182	6,600,228	2,025,778	731,865	1,382,977	989,716	294,334	1,006,612	13,943	155,003
Rhode Island	1,383,764	814,511	569,253	122,833	48,771	125,385	130,503	10,819	0	2,490	128,452
South Carolina	4,078,360	2,910,183	1,168,177	514,667	125,797	26,961	30,573	150,146	33,508	0	286,525

See footnotes at end of table.

STATE GOVERNMENT SALES AND GROSS RECEIPTS TAX REVENUE: 2009—Continued
(In thousands of dollars)

State	Total	General sales or gross receipts	Selective sales taxes								
			Total	Motor fuels	Insurance premiums	Public utilities	Tobacco products	Alcoholic beverages	Amusements	Pari-mutuels	Other
South Dakota..............	1,083,611	756,598	327,013	117,489	63,165	3,322	68,323	14,232	8,044	276	52,162
Tennessee	8,000,471	6,356,962	1,643,509	815,611	299,006	8,071	301,219	116,056	0	0	103,546
Texas........................	31,540,978	21,034,946	10,506,032	3,036,068	1,140,217	854,708	1,556,795	796,949	37,277	9,234	3,074,784
Utah..........................	2,398,162	1,744,035	654,127	350,469	132,214	26,117	59,821	40,762	0	0	44,744
Vermont....................	822,006	321,162	500,844	84,044	56,111	12,022	63,796	20,682	0	0	264,189
Virginia.....................	5,638,353	3,372,974	2,265,379	891,401	387,305	151,278	167,579	180,096	96	0	487,624
Washington...............	13,110,784	10,035,359	3,075,425	1,181,837	408,464	467,235	431,998	276,082	98	2,858	306,853
West Virginia.............	2,226,921	1,110,017	1,116,904	384,538	113,528	163,291	115,095	9,479	0	3,008	327,965
Wisconsin	6,647,399	4,084,147	2,563,252	970,173	152,050	309,838	593,575	54,047	329	678	482,562
Wyoming	1,120,303	989,738	130,565	67,134	29,845	4,158	26,449	1,672	0	192	1,115

Source: U.S. Census Bureau, 2009 Annual Survey of State Government Finances. For information on sampling and nonsampling errors and definitions, see *http://www.census.gov/govs/state/how_data_collected.html.*

Data users who create their own estimates from this table should cite the U.S. Census Bureau as the source of the original data only.

Table 7.18
STATE GOVERNMENT LICENSE TAX REVENUE: 2009
(In thousands of dollars)

State	Total license tax revenue	Motor vehicle license revenue	Occupation and business license, NEC	Corporation license	Motor vehicle operator's license	Hunting and fishing license	Public utility license	Alcoholic beverage license	Amusement license	Other license taxes
United States	$49,756,825	$2,185,321	$13,115,927	$10,064,406	$19,984,760	$1,449,870	$979,344	$436,893	$694,339	$845,965
Alabama	478,927	15,625	118,668	109,384	195,459	21,549	14,360	3,881	0	1
Alaska	135,947	0	38,791	2	55,267	30,036	169	1,819	1	9,862
Arizona	404,101	24,529	113,839	29,640	196,054	28,997	0	7,928	0	3,114
Arkansas	328,393	16,782	113,098	23,967	141,524	21,591	8,520	1,619	441	851
California	8,371,914	258,998	4,438,221	59,297	2,978,475	95,426	476,323	49,448	11,860	3,866
Colorado	365,544	14,171	33,003	14,674	211,319	71,796	12,739	5,939	830	1,073
Connecticut	363,502	40,773	94,568	16,731	193,402	6,195	0	6,571	38	5,224
Delaware	1,154,915	4,362	245,161	705,618	48,236	2,701	6,928	1,187	440	140,282
Florida	1,818,414	181,209	215,104	239,887	1,119,332	15,509	30,500	8,629	4,177	4,067
Georgia	481,555	64,162	72,851	30,241	283,406	19,390	16	2,053	220	9,216
Hawaii	146,270	291	26,390	1,402	100,413	397	16,171	0	0	1,206
Idaho	268,208	7,773	62,404	1,927	122,231	35,562	32,416	1,486	325	4,084
Illinois	2,445,281	63,893	637,188	209,869	1,481,125	32,805	0	11,729	1,187	7,485
Indiana	697,487	203,899	40,733	3,629	207,710	18,674	0	11,244	204,763	6,835
Iowa	658,128	18,345	108,813	30,855	426,321	28,259	10,136	11,004	24,016	379
Kansas	301,953	15,537	29,038	50,352	171,588	23,140	6,840	2,745	29	2,684
Kentucky	473,206	16,100	115,300	82,531	206,782	26,724	14,658	6,272	350	4,489
Louisiana	464,971	10,967	103,551	232,660	78,172	27,844	8,416	0	0	3,361
Maine	243,313	10,841	103,278	7,459	91,030	16,006	0	4,704	727	9,268
Maryland	690,914	29,932	126,940	76,463	438,868	15,595	0	1,014	27	2,075
Massachusetts	753,807	93,471	219,336	24,429	293,845	5,620	0	2,941	427	113,738
Michigan	1,351,556	58,595	154,244	19,585	874,833	51,020	25,328	14,078	0	153,873
Minnesota	1,022,182	47,977	329,440	8,871	526,032	58,586	872	1,724	1,143	47,537
Mississippi	403,120	32,510	88,486	111,892	125,497	15,771	8,215	2,828	5,004	12,917
Missouri	642,305	17,114	148,837	88,136	268,599	31,749	20,573	5,086	694	61,517
Montana	297,986	7,428	92,600	2,768	139,012	45,849	9	2,087	923	7,310
Nebraska	167,014	9,820	47,309	2,269	74,723	14,727	0	542	735	16,889
Nevada	525,565	15,964	172,176	64,913	163,707	8,591	0	0	95,096	5,118
New Hampshire	227,589	12,893	53,814	38,589	98,938	10,324	9,406	3,245	174	206
New Jersey	1,413,730	43,876	485,748	280,990	504,575	13,287	6,277	9,485	67,182	2,310
New Mexico	214,014	3,873	21,737	13,012	145,963	23,538	851	3,583	420	1,037
New York	1,528,785	138,239	253,650	62,981	951,855	47,059	29,180	43,701	69	2,051
North Carolina	1,449,683	130,377	180,922	527,598	572,968	16,877	0	15,261	756	5,680
North Dakota	141,290	4,116	42,660	0	78,599	14,903	6	250		0
Ohio	2,880,397	80,216	635,544	1,222,426	806,294	40,651	31,018	33,302	8,551	22,395
Oklahoma	993,304	15,257	78,264	63,327	582,683	19,824	9	9,831	221,533	2,576
Oregon	847,716	29,011	301,517	10,372	437,866	40,241	16,556	3,423	2,631	6,099
Pennsylvania	2,503,297	61,861	813,026	620,004	824,678	68,642	62,546	16,224	18,342	17,974
Rhode Island	96,880	658	36,317	4,289	52,317	1,795	0	121	429	954
South Carolina	452,195	46,989	138,676	78,570	152,287	15,907	0	8,306	2,600	8,860

See footnotes at end of table.

STATE GOVERNMENT LICENSE TAX REVENUE: 2009—Continued
(In thousands of dollars)

State	Total license tax revenue	Motor vehicle license revenue	Occupation and business license, NEC	Corporation license	Motor vehicle operator's license	Hunting and fishing license	Public utility license	Alcoholic beverage license	Amusement license	Other license taxes
South Dakota............	192,685	2,062	100,759	3,033	48,655	28,081	0	320	29	9,746
Tennessee...............	1,138,070	41,180	274,401	524,685	251,335	23,464	4,402	12,445	353	5,805
Texas....................	6,905,394	103,181	811,726	4,250,332	1,500,323	98,867	24,337	64,976	8,365	43,287
Utah.....................	356,742	14,301	45,734	3,249	256,863	28,752	0	1,890	0	5,953
Vermont.................	98,324	5,989	16,253	2,053	62,890	6,401	0	371	0	4,367
Virginia.................	670,999	57,979	170,158	53,675	350,852	22,421	0	11,514	118	4,282
Washington..............	929,358	63,330	254,931	24,652	455,901	32,936	19,202	11,336	8,542	58,528
West Virginia...........	193,192	3,972	43,100	2,463	89,837	17,060	18,910	17,483	151	216
Wisconsin...............	914,493	42,715	246,773	17,122	465,014	72,187	63,455	1,268	641	5,318
Wyoming.................	152,210	2,178	20,850	11,533	81,105	36,544	0	0	0	0

Source: U.S. Census Bureau, 2009 Annual Survey of State Government Finances. For information on sampling and nonsampling errors and definitions, see *http://www.census.gov/govs/state/how_data_collected.html*.

Data users who create their own estimates from this table should cite the U.S. Census Bureau as the source of the original data only.

A Picture of State Governments in 2009

By Christopher Pece

State governments play an important role in national and regional economic conditions and are subject to prevailing economic conditions. The Census Bureau's official statistics provide a full picture of the early impact of the most recent recession from tax revenues to expenditures to employment.

Introduction

State governments play an important role in national and regional economic conditions and are subject to prevailing economic conditions. The most recent economic recession that began in the fourth quarter of 2007 and lasted through the second quarter of 2009 created great fiscal stress for the states. As many state governments are dependent on either a sales tax or income tax, or both, revenues declined in every state. Even those that are dependent on revenues from oil and gas and other forms of natural resource extraction were impacted. As "own source" revenues declined, state revenues from the federal government rose.

At the same time, expenditures associated with basic services also increased despite modest changes in state government employment. The combination of these factors paint an informative picture of where state governments have been and how they were individually and collectively impacted. This chapter examines state tax revenues and intergovernmental revenues, expenditures by characteristic, object and function, as well as the nature of state employment—both the functional distribution of workers and corresponding payroll. It further describes the environment in 2009[1] in terms of the debt and assets of state governments.

The Census Bureau's statistics on government are divided into four sectors (general, utility, liquor store and insurance trust). This chapter focuses on the general sector of state government, as most traditional governmental services, such as education, police, highways and welfare, are accounted for there. Although some states may have substantial utility or insurance trust sector activities, these activities may distort the picture of what is traditionally considered to be the core state government activities. Additionally, due to the changing economic and demographic climate in the country, this chapter will discuss some aspects of the insurance trust sector. This sector is particularly

important to understand due to the public pension systems and their impact on the fiscal welfare of state governments.

The General Picture—Revenues[2]

State government general revenue totaled $1.495 trillion at the end of fiscal year 2009, a decrease of 1.2 percent from fiscal year 2008. Recent year-to-year percent changes in general revenue have shown slower increases in growth since 2006. General revenue increased 7.7 percent from 2005 to 2006; 4.8 percent from 2006 to 2007; and 3.9 percent from 2007 to 2008. The major revenue sources and share of general revenue in 2009 were taxes (47.8 percent), federal grants (32.0 percent)—compared to 28.0 percent in 2008 and 27.1 percent in 2007—current, charges (10.6 percent) and miscellaneous revenues (9.6 percent).[3] Consequently, for the first time in several years, states' ability to fund their own reserves has weakened while their dependence on federal revenues has increased.

State governments acquire the majority of their revenues through taxes and intergovernmental exchanges of funds; therefore, in order to best understand the "state" of the states, these categories are the most critical to understand. The Census Bureau defines taxes as compulsory contributions exacted by governments for public purposes, including general revenue and/or regulation.[4] 2009 data from the Census Bureau demonstrate that taxes are the single largest source of general revenues for state governments. In 2009, taxes comprised 47.8 percent of general revenues, compared with the previous year when they accounted for 51.6 percent of general revenues. Tax revenues in 2009 for the 50 state governments amounted to $715 billion, a decline of 8.5 percent from 2008.[5]

The type of tax a state imposes helps to identify the ability of state governments to raise revenues. Some types of taxes are more responsive to economic conditions than others. To illustrate, in 2008 corporation net income and documentary and stock transfer taxes declined by 7.3 percent from 2007 levels. These declines continued in 2009, showing a 22.4 percentage point decline to a new level of 36.4 percent in these tax categories.[6] These declines demonstrate that these two tax categories are responsive to changes in the economy. This finding is consistent with trends seen in previous time periods.[7] Understanding the responsiveness of certain tax categories to trends in the economy illustrates differences in state fiscal policy and provides a sense of how states may weather the economic climate.

Historically, sales and gross receipt taxes are among the predominant tax sources for state governments,[8] totaling $342 billion and representing 47.9 percent of total taxes in 2009. These same taxes totaled $359 billion in 2008, $353 billion in 2007, $338 billion in 2006 and $314 billion in 2005. 2009 marked the first decline in these taxes in the last five years. Declines were also seen in taxes on specific commodities, a 2.5 percent decline from 2008, and motor vehicle fuel sales taxes, a 3.0 percent decline from 2008. Tobacco product sales taxes increased 3.8 percent from 2008 in 2009.

Forty-six state governments depend on an income tax—either personal and corporate income taxes, or both—as a method of generating revenue.[9] Income tax revenues for states that collect such taxes totaled $286 billion in fiscal year 2009, a decrease of 13 percent from 2008. This was the first decline in the past five years. State government receipts from income taxes totaled $329 billion in 2008, $319 billion in 2007, $293 billion in 2006, and $262 billion in 2005.[10]

The responsiveness of certain tax categories to the economy illustrates states' abilities to generate revenues from different sources. For example, while documentary and stock transfer taxes constitute only 0.7 percent of total state government tax revenues, their importance among the states varies widely. In 2009, documentary and stock transfer taxes were prevalent in Florida, where such a tax constituted 4.2 percent of the state's total revenue, but for Kentucky, it represented only 0.03 percent of total revenues.

Just as some states have used the documentary and stock transfer tax to supplement their reliance on sales and/or income taxes, other states—including Alaska, Texas, Oklahoma and Wyoming—have relied on severance taxes from their supply of natural resources. Wyoming and North Dakota benefited from severance tax receipts in 2009, with increases in receipts of 36.2 percent and 4.5 percent respectively. Alaska and Texas saw declines in severance taxes revenues by 44.8 percent and 43.4 percent respectively in 2009. Overall, with the drop in energy prices and other commodities, severance taxes for all states declined 26.5 percent to $13 billion.

Although state tax revenues declined—some more severe than others—federal funding increased over previous years because of the American Recovery and Reinvestment Act of 2009. Although Congress passed the Recovery Act in February 2009, states began receiving the funds in the second quarter of 2009. Total federal grants to states were up 13 percent from 2008, and, combined with the declines in tax revenues, the overall share of intergovernmental revenues increased in 2009 as well. The sum of all federal grants accounted for 32.0 percent of all state government general revenues in 2009, compared with 28 percent of state government general revenues in 2008.

The primary source of direct revenue from the federal government to the states in 2009 was in the public welfare category, which increased 16.3 percent compared with its 2008 levels. The total revenues from the federal government for all states in 2009 was $283 billion, up from $244 billion in 2008, $233 billion in 2007, $224 billion in 2006 and $223 billion in 2005. Although the Census Bureau does not identify specific funds or programmatic data, this category does include the two most prominent public assistance programs, Temporary Assistance to Needy Families, known as TANF, and Medicaid, among other programs. Without the federal money associated with public welfare programs, federal grants rose only 8.5 percent from 2008.

Separating the welfare-related programs from total federal grants to states in 2008, the next largest category of intergovernmental transfers is in education. Federal grants to state governments for education increased 11 percent from the previous year to a total of $82 billion, compared with $74 billion in 2008, $73 billion in 2007, $72 billion in 2006 and $69 billion in 2005. Federal education grants amounted to 17.2 percent of total federal grants to state governments in 2009.

State Government Expenditures— A Rich Canvas of Activities

Census Bureau data paint a picture of state government expenditures by three criteria: characteristic, object and function. Expenditure character defines the nature of the expenditure payment and refers to the broad group of related expenditure types, such as direct expenditures and intergovernmental expenditures. Expenditure object, on the other hand, refers to the specific type of financial transaction, such as current operation, capital outlay, interest on debt, grants and subsidies, or payments to other governments. The functional classification is the arrangement of expenditure data according to purpose or type of service rendered, such as health, hospitals, education, airports, parks, police protection, etc.

State government general expenditures in 2009 totaled $1.554 trillion. The 3.3 percent increase in general expenditures from 2008 to 2009 was in contrast to the 1.2 percent decline in general revenues. Compare this with 2007 and 2008, when general revenues rose 3.9 percent and general expenditures rose 5.6 percent. In 2009, state government general expenditures in the form of grants and aid to local governments were 31.3 percent of total general expenditures (including public schools). State expenditures on capital outlay accounted for 7.5 percent of general expenditures, a much smaller amount than the dependency on grants and aid. Expenditures for education and public welfare, together, comprised 64.6 percent of all state government general expenditures, accounting for 36.5 percent and 28.2 percent, respectively in 2009. Expenditures on health and hospitals amounted to 7.7 percent of general expenditures.

Expenditures associated with current operations, including salaries and wages, increased 3.5 percent in 2009 from 2008 to $895 billion. This compares with a 7.7 percent increase in 2008 and a 3.7 percent increase in 2007. Spending on capital outlay, including construction, as well as land and equipment purchases, increased 3.1 percent from 2008 to $117 billion. This increase was fairly consistent with the previous year.

Expenditures for assistance and subsidies for 2009 totaled $36 billion, an increase of 9.6 percent over 2008. At the same time total intergovernmental expenditures—payments and grants to local governments—totaled $487 billion in 2009, up 2.8 percent from 2008 spending of $473 billion.[11] Spending for education is the single largest functional activity of state governments, totaling $567 billion in 2009. The largest characteristic of education spending is found in transfers to local governments and school districts, which totaled $324 billion in 2009, compared with $315 billion in 2008, an increase of 3.1 percent; while assistance and subsidies to individuals for education totaled $23 billion in 2009, a 6.5 percent increase over 2008 levels.

Other functions with substantial contributions to general expenditures for state governments are public welfare, health, hospitals, highways and interest on debt. Combined, these activities account for an additional 45.6 percent—expenditures for public welfare (28.2 percent), health and hospitals (7.7 percent), highways (6.9 percent), and interest on general debt (2.9 percent).

Total public welfare expenditures rose 6.1 percent in 2009 to $437 billion, from $412 billion in 2008. From that amount, approximately $365 billion was for current operations, including payments to vendors, and $13 billion was for assistance and subsidies to individuals. Health and hospital-related spending rose 7.7 percent in 2009 to $119 billion, up from $115 billion in 2008. Although spending on education, health and welfare activities increased from the previous year, expenditures on highways remained relatively unchanged from the previous year at $107 billion. Highways accounted for 53 percent of total state government spending on all capital outlay—$162 billion in 2009. Interest payments on long-term debt also increased just 1.5 percent from the previous year to $47 billion.

Not surprisingly, state government unemployment compensation expenditures increased 86 percent from $35 billion in 2008 to $66 billion in 2009.

A Snapshot of State Government Employment

When it comes to state governments, employment is a reflection of their overall finances. The challenges states are facing as a result of decreasing revenues with increasing cost to provide services can also be seen in the employment statistics. Nationally, state governments added 17,967 full-time employees from 2008 to 2009. State governments employed 3.8 million full-time workers as of March 2009,[12] with total full-time equivalent[13] of 4.4 million people.[14] While this was a marginal increase from 2008, the functions state workers are involved in changed. For example, while the number of full-time employees in higher education was relatively constant at about 1.2 million and public hospitals increased slightly from 377,749 to 380,993, full-time employment declined in natural resources operations (129,698 in 2009 compared with 131,051 in 2008), government financial administration (162,839 in 2009 compared with 165,576 in 2008), and highways (229,873 in 2009 compared with 231,896 in 2008). At the same time, mixed growth occurred in the police protection services function, an increase in full-time police officers from 67,219 in 2008 to 67,389 in 2009, but a decline in non-police officer employees from 39,587 in 2008 to 37,507 in 2009. Part-time employment for non-police officer employees also declined from 2,522 to 1,987 during this period. The data suggest that states are maintaining the workforce in some categories, while making cuts in others to account for declines in revenues across all functions.

Among state-level employees, 1.3 million, or 47.9 percent, worked in education, and the majority of those, some 1.2 million, worked in the higher education systems. The majority of those in higher education (837,135) worked as non-instructional personnel. State-administered colleges and universities employed 401,040 instructional personnel; an increase from 389,610 in 2008 employment levels. But in cases where elementary and secondary education is directly provided by state governments, the number of instructional personnel declined from 36,460 in 2008 to 34,730 in 2009.[15] An additional 13,314 state employees worked as non-instructional personnel in elementary and secondary education as of 2009. After education, corrections and hospitals were the most common activities for state employees, constituting 479,024 (9.2 percent) and 380,993 (8.4 percent) of all state employees respectively. State governments employed 72 percent of their workers on a full-time basis in 2009.

The dynamics of state government employees and their activities show a combination of slight declines and increases across categories. The same movement occurred in total payroll, which totaled $19.4 billion in 2009, compared to $18.7 billion in 2008.

Public-Employee Retirement Systems — A Complex Picture

Membership in the 222 state-administered pension systems remained fairly constant from 2008 to 2009 at 17,215,183 and 17,428,583 respectively.[16] However, revenues for these systems faced substantial changes that may be directly related to overall market conditions. Revenues for these public pension systems come from three main sources: contributions from employees, contributions from the employer — generally the state government in this case, and earnings on investment.

Although contributions from employees and employer amount to $33.3 billion and $64.1 billion respectively, an increase of 5.4 percent and 0.4 percent from the previous fiscal year, the largest piece of the puzzle that illustrates the challenges facing state pension systems, based on the Census Bureau's data, are the trends in the earnings on

investment. In 2009, the earning on investment declined approximately $487 billion. This decline was offset somewhat by the contributions from employees and employers to bring total revenues up to a negative $426.4 billion. The impact of these losses on investments captured through the market valuation of these revenues shows how closely the finances of these pension systems are related to the overall market conditions, and how the recent economic recession has hit financial earnings hard.

Assets

State government cash and investments amounted to $3.1 trillion in 2009, including $1.9 trillion in employee retirement trust funds; $488 billion in funds held as offsets to long-term debt; and $674 billion in miscellaneous insurance trust funds, bond funds, other cash and securities.

Of the total cash and investments, 16.5 percent of these funds remained available for financing general government activities. The remaining funds were reserved for public employee retirement systems, unemployment compensation, workers' compensation and payments on existing debt. States dedicated 62.4 percent of their assets for public employee retirement systems; 15.8 percent for the redemption of long-term debt; and 3.7 percent for insurance trust purposes, such as unemployment or workers' compensation; while 1.7 percent was unspent proceeds of bond issues. Total cash and investment decreased by 19.2 percent between 2008 and 2009.

Indebtedness

State government long-term debt at the end of fiscal year 2009 totaled $1.038 trillion, up 4.8 percent over 2008. When examining the state and local government sectors together, total long-term debt was $2.5 trillion in fiscal year 2008; 39.5 percent belonged to state governments and 60.5 percent to local governments.

The Census Bureau identifies two main types of long-term debt for state and local governments: general government debt and public debt for private purposes, also known as conduit debt. The distinction between these two types of indebtedness shows the distribution of debt issuance for government-related activities compared with those used for economic development-related activities in partnership with private sector initiatives. During 2009, state governments' public debt for private purposes was $393 billion, an increase of 3.8 percent from 2008. Debt for general purpose was $645 billion in the same year, an increase of 5.5 percent. Debt issues in 2009 totaled $152 billion, with $58 billion in issues of public debt for private purposes and $94 billion in issues for general-purpose debt. Although the total debt issues in 2009 were virtually unchanged from 2008, the distribution of the issues changed. In 2008, $66 billion in new issues was for public debt for private purposes and $86 billion was for general-purpose debt.

The 2009 fiscal year also posted a 16.7 percent increase in the amount of debt retired. Total debt retirements in 2009 were $109 billion, with $46 billion in retirements of public debt for private purposes, and $62 billion in retirements of general-purpose debt. This compared with 2008 total debt retirements of $93 billion, with $41 billion in the retirement of public debt for private purposes and $53 billion in the retirement of general-purpose debt.

A Look Ahead

The Census Bureau is in the process of collecting statistics for the fiscal year 2010 period, but early indications on tax revenues help to identify the direction and trend of revenues and assets. For example, data from the FY '10 Survey of State Government Tax Collections[17] show a 1.9 percent decrease in general sales tax revenues for all states. Individual income taxes decreased 4.5 percent for the same period for all states. But these declines are not as steep as we saw in FY 2009. In addition, FY '10 shows 11 states with positive growth from the previous year compared to 2009 when only five states had positive year-over-year growth in total taxes. This suggests that the recovery has begun, but it will take some time before receipts for state and local governments return to levels prior to the recession.

Author's Note

This paper is released to inform interested parties of research and to encourage discussion of works in progress. The views expressed in this paper are those of the author and not necessarily those of the U.S. Census Bureau.

Notes

[1] Throughout this chapter, 2009 and fiscal year 2009 will be used interchangeably. Both terms, for the purpose of this chapter, refer to a fiscal year.

[2] In 2009, most state governments ended their fiscal years on June 30. However, four states had alternate fiscal year end dates. Those states (and their fiscal year end dates) are: New York (March 31), Texas (Aug. 31), and Alabama and Michigan (both Sept. 30).

[3] U.S. Census Bureau, 2009 Annual Survey of State Government Finances, *http://www.census.gov/govs/state/*.

[4] U.S. Census Bureau, *Government Finance and Employment Classification Manual*, 2006, Section 4.3.1, page 4-4.

[5] U.S. Census Bureau, 2009 Annual Survey of State Tax Collections, *http://www.census.gov/govs/statetax/*.

[6] U.S. Census Bureau, 2009 Annual Survey of State Tax Collections, *http://www.census.gov/govs/statetax/*.

[7] For historical data on these and other tax categories see *http://www.census.gov/govs/statetax/historical_data.html*.

[8] All states except Alaska, Delaware, Montana, New Hampshire and Oregon had some form of general sales and gross receipts tax. The Census Bureau defines sales taxes as, "Taxes applicable with only specified exceptions (e.g., food and prescribed medicines) to sales of all types of goods and services or to all gross receipts, whether at a single rate or at classified rates; and sales use taxes." U.S. Census Bureau, *Government Finance and Employment Classification Manual*, 2006, Section 4.9, page 4-10.

[9] The following states do not have an individual income tax: Alaska, Florida, Nevada, South Dakota, Texas, Washington and Wyoming; while the following states do not have a corporation net income tax: Nevada, Texas, Washington and Wyoming.

[10] Although some of these intergovernmental expenditures may include both state-originated grants as well as federal pass-throughs, the Census Bureau statistics do not provide additional detail to determine the proportion of federal pass-throughs to state-originated grants.

[11] U.S. Census Bureau, 2009 Annual Survey of State Government Finances, *http://www.census.gov/govs/state/*.

[12] Data for state government employment is not measured by fiscal year, but rather statistics are collected from each government for its pay period that includes March 12, regardless of the length of the pay period.

[13] Full-time equivalent is a computed statistic representing the number of full-time employees that could have been employed if the reported number of hours worked by part-time employees had been worked by full-time employees. This statistic is calculated separately for each function of a government by dividing the "part-time hours paid" by the standard number of hours for full-time employees in the particular government and then adding the resulting quotient to the number of full-time employees.

[14] U.S. Census Bureau, 2009 Annual Survey of Public Employment and Payroll, *http://www.census.gov/govs/apes/*.

[15] Although most elementary and secondary education is performed by local governments, state governments in some instances manage elementary and secondary education. For

example, in Hawaii, state government, not local governments, operates all elementary and secondary schools.

[16] U.S. Census Bureau, 2009 Annual Survey of State and Local Public-Employee Retirement Systems, *http://www.census.gov/govs/retire/*.

[17] U.S. Census Bureau, 2010 Annual Survey of State Government Tax Collections, *http://www.census.gov/govs/statetax/*.

About the Author

Christopher Pece is the senior technical advisor for the U.S. Census Bureau's Governments Division. He previously managed both the Census of Governments and many of its related annual and quarterly programs, specifically the Annual Survey of State Government Finances, the Annual Survey of State Government Tax Collections and the Quarterly Summary of State and Local Government Revenues. He has worked at the Census Bureau since 1998 on several important economic indicators before moving to Governments Division in 2004. He holds a master's in philosophy from Bowling Green State University and a bachelor's in economics from St. John's University.

Table 7.19
SUMMARY OF FINANCIAL AGGREGATES, BY STATE: 2009
(In millions of dollars)

State	Revenue				Expenditure				Total debt outstanding at end of fiscal year	Total cash and security holdings at end of fiscal year
	Total	General	Utilities & liquor store	Insurance trust (a)	Total	General	Utilities & liquor store	Insurance trust		
United States	$1,123,776	$1,495,253	$22,848	-$394,325	$1,826,666	$1,554,074	$31,714	$240,878	$1,045,167	$3,090,423
Alabama..................	21,400	21,998	252	-851	26,422	23,335	240	2,847	8,156	33,878
Alaska....................	8,868	11,529	18	-2,679	11,338	9,896	135	1,307	6,590	60,168
Arizona..................	23,962	26,278	30	-2,345	31,517	27,819	32	3,666	12,325	42,878
Arkansas................	12,880	15,211	0	-2,331	16,169	14,553	0	1,616	4,135	20,892
California...............	113,389	186,315	4,652	-77,578	254,334	211,083	4,673	38,578	134,572	432,286
Colorado................	10,337	19,303	0	-8,966	24,886	20,818	23	4,046	17,202	55,701
Connecticut............	21,700	21,847	29	-176	25,684	21,377	513	3,794	28,394	34,027
Delaware	5,787	6,700	13	-926	7,361	6,634	135	592	5,985	12,386
Florida..................	45,495	64,241	18	-18,764	75,688	66,057	108	9,524	38,885	146,604
Georgia..................	33,614	34,366	7	-759	41,452	35,956	37	5,460	13,455	65,325
Hawaii...................	6,751	9,164	0	-2,413	11,200	10,051	2	1,147	6,880	13,164
Idaho....................	5,537	6,410	101	-973	8,217	7,119	89	1,010	3,509	14,643
Illinois..................	40,318	55,580	0	-15,261	68,450	57,160	0	11,290	56,962	102,215
Indiana..................	27,947	29,944	0	-1,997	32,719	28,856	65	3,798	23,712	53,141
Iowa	13,207	16,246	208	-3,247	18,304	16,172	142	1,990	6,353	27,429
Kansas	11,655	13,576	0	-1,921	15,832	14,156	0	1,676	5,857	14,909
Kentucky	19,008	21,487	0	-2,479	26,853	23,019	30	3,804	13,364	36,442
Louisiana...............	22,913	27,024	7	-4,117	31,099	27,649	6	3,444	17,505	51,118
Maine....................	6,462	8,138	0	-1,676	8,781	7,891	1	888	5,397	14,790
Maryland	23,913	29,518	117	-5,722	36,023	31,665	821	3,538	23,473	49,434
Massachusetts	36,942	41,255	212	-4,524	47,911	40,909	235	6,767	74,598	91,988
Michigan................	46,252	49,587	782	-4,117	59,191	50,584	634	7,973	29,591	75,720
Minnesota..............	22,781	29,043	0	-6,262	36,309	31,550	144	4,615	10,524	47,854
Mississippi	14,374	16,819	257	-2,702	19,246	17,162	207	1,877	6,209	24,819
Missouri	17,981	24,453	0	-6,472	28,651	24,819	0	3,831	19,217	57,583
Montana	4,827	5,711	67	-951	6,268	5,419	73	775	4,764	14,828
Nebraska	7,381	8,403	0	-1,022	9,034	8,548	0	486	2,517	12,372
Nevada	7,484	9,383	86	-1,985	12,056	9,870	88	2,099	4,445	22,532
New Hampshire	5,640	5,721	492	-573	6,956	5,847	425	684	8,412	11,348
New Jersey	43,346	49,063	868	-6,585	62,044	48,208	2,807	11,029	56,898	99,693
New Mexico	9,666	13,512	0	-3,846	17,112	15,512	26	1,574	8,002	38,317
New York	92,386	135,224	8,304	-51,142	163,706	133,941	12,586	17,180	122,652	274,762
North Carolina........	31,576	43,398	0	-11,822	48,585	42,306	35	6,244	19,911	80,395
North Dakota..........	4,372	4,913	0	-541	4,487	4,069	0	417	1,753	11,717
Ohio......................	24,964	54,443	766	-30,246	71,600	56,355	472	14,774	27,949	157,209
Oklahoma...............	17,444	18,664	501	-1,721	21,356	18,159	932	2,265	9,855	31,154
Oregon...................	7,812	18,057	414	-10,660	24,381	19,388	225	4,767	12,495	56,991
Pennsylvania	38,795	60,726	1,492	-23,422	77,564	64,612	1,439	11,513	41,924	111,349
Rhode Island..........	4,711	6,527	34	-1,851	7,347	5,964	149	1,234	9,181	13,801
South Carolina........	19,407	21,141	1,574	-3,308	28,664	22,932	2,654	3,078	15,313	31,131
South Dakota.........	2,446	3,746	0	-1,300	4,109	3,732	0	377	3,626	10,502
Tennessee	18,760	23,665	0	-4,905	27,815	25,870	0	1,946	4,848	32,334
Texas.....................	81,144	95,252	0	-14,109	110,726	98,107	96	12,524	30,438	228,482
Utah......................	8,783	12,837	227	-4,281	15,568	13,961	167	1,440	6,268	24,733
Vermont.................	4,559	4,978	44	-463	5,449	5,035	74	340	3,427	6,034
Virginia.................	25,949	34,748	552	-9,351	42,053	37,871	474	3,707	24,301	65,217
Washington............	24,478	32,521	561	-8,604	43,443	36,537	564	6,342	24,603	65,478
West Virginia..........	11,113	11,114	81	-82	11,482	10,398	77	1,006	6,502	16,208
Wisconsin	8,474	29,437	0	-20,964	35,646	30,177	9	5,461	20,913	77,112
Wyoming	4,785	6,037	83	-1,335	5,578	4,963	72	543	1,321	17,328

Source: U.S. Census Bureau, 2009 Annual Survey of State Government Finances. For information on sampling and nonsampling errors and definitions, see *http://www.census.gov/govs/state/how_data_collected.html.* Data users who create their own estimates from this table should cite the U.S. Census Bureau as the source of the original data only.

Note: Detail may not add to total due to rounding. Data presented are statistical in nature and do not represent an accounting statement. Therefore, a difference between an individual government's total revenue and expenditure does not necessarily indicate a budget surplus or deficit.

Key:
(a) Within insurance trust revenue, net earnings of state retirement systems is a calculated statistic (the item code in the data file is X08), and thus can be positive or negative. Net earnings is the sum of earnings on investments plus gains on investments minus losses on investments. The change made in 2002 for asset valuation from book to market value in accordance with Statement 34 of the Governmental Accounting Standards Board is reflected in the calculated statistics.

Table 7.20
NATIONAL TOTALS OF STATE GOVERNMENT FINANCES FOR SELECTED YEARS: 2005–2009

Item	2009	2008	2007	2006	2005
Revenue total	$1,123,775,985	$1,619,198,444	$2,000,377,812	$1,774,648,692	$1,642,469,224
General revenue	1,495,253,448	1,513,974,657	1,457,814,343	1,391,133,672	1,286,900,580
Taxes	715,086,270	781,647,244	757,470,540	715,973,170	650,611,855
Intergovernmental revenue	498,278,914	446,136,746	430,278,239	419,640,660	407,791,786
From Federal Government	478,241,224	423,178,152	410,184,409	398,200,459	386,313,543
Public welfare	283,319,087	243,512,900	233,478,692	224,406,166	223,248,268
Education	82,425,828	74,232,848	73,411,218	72,376,901	68,882,228
Highways	36,529,755	35,689,545	35,172,738	34,187,690	32,676,739
Employment security administration	4,455,882	3,952,385	3,932,896	4,380,567	4,412,445
Other	71,510,672	65,790,474	64,188,865	62,849,135	57,093,863
From local government	20,037,690	22,958,594	20,093,830	21,440,201	21,478,243
Charges and miscellaneous revenue	281,888,264	286,190,667	270,065,564	255,519,842	228,496,939
Liquor stores revenue	6,376,562	6,128,282	5,799,273	5,475,237	5,118,462
Utility revenue	16,471,341	16,521,947	16,735,684	15,816,555	14,628,425
Insurance trust revenue (a)	-394,325,366	82,573,558	520,028,512	362,223,228	335,821,757
Employee retirement	-462,279,790	20,664,213	456,789,127	295,602,816	269,617,472
Unemployment compensation	41,976,470	34,359,648	34,063,242	36,863,504	35,242,919
Worker compensation	16,458,766	18,695,989	19,798,108	21,906,234	23,352,729
Other	9,519,188	8,853,708	9,378,035	7,850,674	7,608,637
Expenditure and debt redemption	1,931,655,484	1,813,957,020	1,710,220,557	1,631,438,503	1,556,924,635
Debt redemption	104,989,120	77,621,222	74,473,633	76,905,629	84,382,231
Expenditure total	1,826,666,364	1,736,335,798	1,635,746,924	1,554,532,874	1,472,542,404
General expenditure	1,554,074,163	1,504,224,481	1,424,194,906	1,349,968,143	1,278,433,682
Education	567,107,433	546,825,678	514,147,211	483,476,753	454,348,376
Intergovernmental expenditure	324,495,673	314,612,137	300,279,257	280,090,982	263,625,820
State institutions of higher education	206,794,634	197,573,148	180,816,751	169,883,923	160,884,249
Other education	360,312,799	349,252,530	333,330,460	313,592,830	293,464,127
Public welfare	437,468,368	412,141,472	393,690,330	376,675,058	368,764,661
Intergovernmental expenditure	59,183,863	58,093,847	57,180,236	54,858,307	52,935,802
Cash assistance, categorical program	27,142,499	26,750,011	28,925,166	30,310,961	32,738,159
Cash assistance, other	10,111,336	9,307,894	7,579,673	4,516,397	3,265,312
Other public welfare	400,214,533	376,083,567	357,185,491	341,847,700	332,761,190
Highways	107,097,616	107,190,485	103,201,172	100,841,813	92,816,461
Intergovernmental expenditure	16,453,767	16,545,920	14,868,267	15,495,306	14,500,232
Regular state highway facilities	98,862,414	99,013,779	95,863,536	93,964,195	86,571,074
State toll highways/facilities	8,235,202	8,176,706	7,337,636	6,877,618	6,245,387
Health and hospitals	119,141,570	114,639,378	106,304,509	96,663,369	92,256,859
Hospitals	56,957,190	53,682,058	48,916,252	45,960,293	43,623,308
Health	62,184,380	60,957,320	57,388,257	50,703,076	48,633,551
Natural resources	22,585,813	22,522,407	22,038,266	20,036,460	18,822,456
Corrections	50,398,928	49,897,531	46,498,162	42,793,514	40,562,217
Financial administration	22,856,414	23,638,591	22,431,017	21,676,940	21,224,584
Employment security administration	4,552,973	4,071,956	3,973,946	4,551,037	4,259,347
Police protection	13,657,151	13,594,279	12,875,855	12,220,732	11,395,489
Interest on general debt	45,384,838	44,719,371	41,593,827	38,231,722	34,242,019
Veterans' services	933,222	1,083,098	1,030,506	992,146	1,188,935
Utility expenditure	26,539,464	26,072,981	24,530,299	24,922,440	21,827,440
Insurance trust expenditure	240,878,086	201,093,686	182,357,609	175,304,033	168,199,527
Employee retirement	155,629,540	146,664,804	135,759,777	127,501,115	118,332,771
Unemployment compensation	65,974,092	35,470,883	28,854,007	28,008,860	29,776,222
Other	19,274,454	18,957,999	17,743,825	19,794,058	20,090,534
Total expenditure by character and object	1,826,666,364	1,736,335,798	1,635,746,924	1,554,532,874	1,472,542,404
Direct expenditure	1,335,344,493	1,026,000,719	1,176,142,138	1,122,267,668	1,066,617,117
Current operation	894,758,578	864,649,739	809,535,238	774,002,589	738,885,771
Capital outlay	116,577,726	113,078,527	110,043,921	103,253,138	95,155,295
Construction	97,526,425	92,081,784	90,788,297	85,712,794	78,049,253
Other capital outlay	19,051,301	20,996,743	19,255,624	17,540,344	17,106,042
Assistance and subsidies	35,702,856	32,572,852	30,620,935	29,564,773	28,403,006
Interest on debt	47,427,247	46,717,232	43,584,435	40,143,135	35,973,518
Insurance benefits and repayments	240,878,086	201,093,686	182,357,609	175,304,033	168,199,527
Intergovernmental expenditure	491,321,871	478,223,762	459,604,786	432,265,206	405,925,287
Cash and security holdings at end of fiscal year	3,090,422,982	3,826,448,037	3,922,371,315	3,443,236,625	3,153,795,074
Insurance trust	2,042,210,313	2,732,775,260	2,870,082,818	2,495,133,155	2,306,208,483
Unemployment fund balance	9,820,731	38,489,823	39,795,912	35,053,864	27,595,746
Debt offsets	488,429,982	459,687,881	430,238,320	390,865,042	363,955,939

Source: U.S. Census Bureau, 2009 Annual Survey of State Government Finances. For information on sampling and nonsampling errors and definitions, see http://www.census.gov/govs/state/how_data_collected.html. Data users who create their own estimates from this table should cite the U.S. Census Bureau as the source of the original data only.

Key:
(a) Within insurance trust revenue, net earnings of state retirement systems is a calculated statistic (the item code in the data file is X08), and thus can be positive or negative. Net earnings is the sum of earnings on investments plus gains on investments minus losses on investments. The change made in 2002 for asset valuation from book to market value in accordance with Statement 34 of the Governmental Accounting Standards Board is reflected in the calculated statistics.

Table 7.21
STATE GENERAL REVENUE, BY SOURCE AND BY STATE: 2009 (In thousands of dollars)

State	Total general revenue (a)	Total	Taxes								Intergovernmental revenue	Charges and miscellaneous general revenue
			Sales and gross receipts			Licenses		Individual income	Corporation net income			
			Total (b)	General	Motor fuels	Total (b)	Motor vehicle					
United States	$1,495,253,448	$715,086,270	$342,247,049	$227,702,510	$35,368,850	$49,756,825	$19,934,760	$245,930,476	$40,477,747	$498,278,914	$281,888,264
Alabama	21,998,366	8,306,446	4,203,283	2,069,535	546,467	478,927	195,459	2,662,759	493,972	8,622,220	5,069,700
Alaska	11,529,146	4,953,342	244,282	0	10,064	135,947	55,267	0	632,123	2,391,445	4,184,359
Arizona	26,277,519	11,864,046	7,390,022	5,675,531	813,794	404,101	196,054	2,575,753	592,187	10,402,074	4,011,399
Arkansas	15,210,774	7,467,679	3,750,943	2,765,996	462,221	328,393	141,524	2,238,958	346,215	4,949,582	2,793,513
California	186,314,745	101,007,459	36,381,343	28,972,302	3,180,128	8,371,914	2,978,475	44,355,959	9,535,679	60,516,817	24,790,469
Colorado	19,302,583	8,682,822	3,299,250	2,123,671	616,589	365,544	211,319	4,403,446	329,545	5,576,955	5,042,806
Connecticut	21,846,755	12,927,619	5,425,933	3,290,050	490,804	363,502	193,402	6,376,921	444,061	5,518,398	3,400,738
Delaware	6,700,350	2,806,031	474,278	0	114,579	1,154,915	48,236	910,693	208,677	1,575,270	2,319,049
Florida	64,241,428	31,956,841	26,874,027	19,228,000	2,229,827	1,818,414	1,119,332	0	1,836,800	21,083,791	11,200,796
Georgia	34,365,954	16,077,948	7,001,141	5,306,491	861,153	481,555	283,406	7,801,185	694,717	12,830,886	5,457,120
Hawaii	9,163,828	4,712,651	3,125,035	2,461,618	91,712	146,270	100,413	1,338,702	78,597	2,225,268	2,225,909
Idaho	6,409,721	3,171,863	1,574,348	1,206,137	218,180	268,208	122,231	1,175,604	142,240	2,153,027	1,084,831
Illinois	55,579,661	29,268,349	14,482,811	7,470,532	1,467,402	2,445,281	1,481,125	9,183,002	2,752,353	17,409,027	8,902,285
Indiana	29,944,355	14,900,123	8,856,580	6,205,638	798,739	697,487	207,710	4,313,759	838,974	9,383,442	5,660,790
Iowa	16,245,544	6,984,279	3,272,176	2,201,396	434,243	658,128	426,321	2,703,190	264,365	5,670,077	3,591,188
Kansas	13,575,933	6,694,630	3,044,904	2,227,183	422,865	301,953	171,588	2,731,559	370,889	3,815,931	3,065,372
Kentucky	21,486,569	9,755,544	4,663,830	2,857,665	632,655	473,206	206,782	3,315,368	389,634	7,487,283	4,243,742
Louisiana	27,023,538	10,014,637	5,015,610	2,963,758	600,786	464,971	78,172	2,940,633	612,545	12,521,094	4,487,807
Maine	8,138,033	3,489,105	1,640,671	1,012,357	220,772	243,313	91,030	1,370,710	143,086	3,101,082	1,547,846
Maryland	29,517,988	15,126,893	6,136,613	3,851,341	734,836	690,914	438,868	6,478,236	749,001	8,775,964	5,615,131
Massachusetts	41,254,783	19,699,494	6,112,981	3,880,087	654,022	753,807	293,845	10,599,085	1,789,553	12,178,164	9,377,125
Michigan	49,587,193	22,757,818	12,504,160	8,998,942	969,959	1,351,556	874,833	5,856,751	703,250	16,475,729	10,353,646
Minnesota	29,042,836	17,161,299	7,362,340	4,375,200	750,308	1,022,182	525,032	6,948,119	779,055	8,006,629	3,874,908
Mississippi	16,819,004	6,470,593	4,138,039	3,026,497	425,020	403,120	125,497	1,485,592	324,301	8,209,225	2,139,186
Missouri	24,452,996	10,345,250	4,598,920	3,030,477	707,331	642,305	268,599	4,771,576	278,661	9,581,085	4,526,661
Montana	5,710,939	2,407,400	529,392	0	191,188	297,986	139,012	827,196	164,255	2,097,188	1,206,351
Nebraska	8,403,141	4,000,939	2,015,283	1,504,174	292,857	167,014	74,723	1,602,091	198,442	2,770,131	1,632,071
Nevada	9,383,361	5,564,170	4,341,127	2,684,029	298,135	525,565	163,707	0	0	2,510,358	1,308,833
New Hampshire	5,721,403	2,125,722	829,654	0	132,122	227,589	98,938	98,191	493,431	1,952,361	1,643,320
New Jersey	49,062,985	27,074,472	11,652,984	8,264,162	538,166	1,413,730	504,575	10,476,267	2,528,911	12,424,668	9,563,645
New Mexico	13,512,204	4,851,689	2,493,029	1,887,343	188,943	214,014	145,963	932,442	203,584	5,072,725	3,587,790
New York	135,223,957	65,029,871	20,238,418	11,073,898	506,741	1,528,785	955,855	36,840,019	4,427,675	49,089,065	21,105,021
North Carolina	43,398,303	20,496,106	8,430,223	4,963,434	1,515,944	1,449,683	572,968	9,560,353	901,445	16,092,266	6,809,931
North Dakota	4,913,104	2,414,010	943,614	607,171	143,796	141,290	78,599	370,165	129,542	1,349,857	1,149,282
Ohio	54,443,346	23,952,422	12,149,489	7,328,388	1,726,742	2,880,397	806,294	8,323,352	521,363	19,265,922	11,225,002
Oklahoma	18,664,169	8,160,670	3,158,336	2,162,693	420,109	993,304	582,683	2,544,576	342,762	6,553,620	3,949,879
Oregon	18,056,866	7,419,494	744,458	0	397,609	847,716	437,866	5,434,777	258,778	5,867,264	4,770,108
Pennsylvania	60,725,555	30,071,179	15,096,410	8,496,182	2,025,778	2,503,297	824,678	9,550,238	1,740,532	18,314,112	12,340,264
Rhode Island	6,527,473	2,586,184	1,383,764	814,511	122,833	96,880	52,317	960,885	108,497	2,420,320	1,520,969
South Carolina	21,141,141	7,146,034	4,078,360	2,910,183	514,667	452,195	152,287	2,351,324	219,484	8,195,615	5,799,492

See footnotes at end of table.

STATE GENERAL REVENUE, BY SOURCE AND BY STATE: 2009 (In thousands of dollars)—Continued

State	Total general revenue (a)	Taxes Total	Sales and gross receipts Total (b)	Sales and gross receipts General	Sales and gross receipts Motor fuels	Licenses Total (b)	Licenses Motor vehicle	Individual income	Corporation net income	Intergovernmental revenue	Charges and miscellaneous general revenue
South Dakota	3,745,652	1,333,835	1,083,611	756,598	117,489	192,685	48,655	0	48,772	1,542,361	869,456
Tennessee	23,665,207	10,442,552	8,000,471	6,356,962	815,611	1,138,070	251,335	221,685	816,261	8,507,222	4,715,433
Texas	95,252,084	40,786,857	31,540,978	21,034,946	3,036,068	6,905,394	1,500,323	0	0	35,574,008	18,891,219
Utah	12,837,189	5,422,858	2,398,162	1,744,035	350,469	356,742	256,863	2,319,632	245,880	3,853,815	3,560,516
Vermont	4,977,974	2,505,665	822,006	321,162	84,044	98,324	62,890	532,911	86,759	1,573,825	898,484
Virginia	34,747,884	16,331,388	5,638,353	3,372,974	891,401	670,999	350,852	8,918,232	633,490	8,058,669	10,357,827
Washington	32,521,403	16,408,838	13,110,784	10,035,359	1,181,837	929,358	455,901	0	0	9,829,012	6,283,553
West Virginia	11,113,930	4,788,157	2,226,921	1,110,017	384,538	193,192	89,837	1,557,403	420,530	3,775,786	2,549,987
Wisconsin	29,437,323	14,402,506	6,647,399	4,084,147	970,173	914,493	465,014	5,971,177	656,872	8,796,443	6,238,374
Wyoming	6,037,408	2,760,491	1,120,303	989,738	67,134	152,210	81,105	0	0	2,331,836	945,081

Source: U.S. Census Bureau, 2009 Annual Survey of State Government Finances. For information on sampling and nonsampling errors and definitions, see http://www.census.gov/govs/state/how_data_collected.html. Data users who create their own estimates from this table should cite the U.S. Census Bureau as the source of the original data only.

Note: Detail may not add to total due to rounding.
Key:
(a) Total general revenue equals total taxes plus intergovernmental revenue plus charges and miscellaneous revenue.
(b) Total includes other taxes not shown separately in this table.

Table 7.22
STATE EXPENDITURE, BY CHARACTER AND OBJECT AND BY STATE: 2009 (In thousands of dollars)

State	Intergovernmental expenditures	Total	Direct expenditures Current operation	Capital outlay Total	Capital outlay Construction	Other	Assistance and subsidies	Interest on debt	Insurance benefits and repayments	Exhibit: Total salaries and wages
United States	$491,321,871	$1,335,344,493	$894,758,578	$116,577,726	$97,526,425	$19,051,301	$35,702,856	$47,427,247	$240,878,086	$237,785,167
Alabama	6,535,634	19,886,481	13,906,375	2,319,427	1,960,754	358,673	473,380	340,732	2,846,567	4,424,475
Alaska	1,616,689	9,721,120	6,672,521	1,245,331	1,019,729	225,602	186,426	310,326	1,306,516	1,600,451
Arizona	9,618,970	21,897,848	15,450,621	1,700,592	1,437,153	263,439	572,839	508,006	3,665,790	3,286,804
Arkansas	4,698,889	11,469,828	8,500,184	919,939	805,852	114,087	273,041	161,048	1,615,616	1,529,945
California	94,909,240	159,424,822	103,604,985	8,965,869	7,159,994	1,805,875	2,055,490	6,220,851	38,577,627	28,307,687
Colorado	6,845,674	18,040,727	11,527,879	1,392,365	1,173,618	218,747	269,232	805,668	4,045,583	3,830,753
Connecticut	4,351,337	21,332,351	14,290,387	1,332,174	1,117,010	215,164	482,596	1,432,900	3,794,294	4,459,197
Delaware	1,205,247	6,155,706	4,472,028	678,810	521,082	157,728	128,945	284,055	591,868	2,278,043
Florida	17,677,928	58,010,112	38,867,846	5,950,721	5,138,321	812,400	2,007,346	1,660,593	9,523,606	8,706,829
Georgia	10,816,572	30,635,855	20,928,676	2,634,311	2,361,229	273,082	952,900	660,288	5,459,680	5,483,243
Hawaii	159,452	11,040,316	8,503,593	832,058	643,008	189,050	125,042	432,964	1,146,659	2,806,515
Idaho	2,077,028	6,140,450	3,938,096	849,555	749,701	99,854	162,219	180,803	1,009,777	1,080,463
Illinois	15,235,221	53,214,500	33,872,837	3,960,571	3,618,537	342,034	1,127,203	2,963,785	11,290,104	8,719,444
Indiana	8,204,196	24,514,365	16,629,136	2,383,372	1,902,747	480,625	804,475	899,488	3,797,894	3,899,747
Iowa	4,660,802	13,643,184	9,280,109	1,614,519	1,375,547	238,972	505,797	252,713	1,990,046	2,442,092
Kansas	4,314,940	11,517,282	8,163,777	1,135,684	965,480	170,204	194,699	346,754	1,676,368	3,189,772
Kentucky	4,769,871	22,083,260	15,067,628	1,941,550	1,629,863	311,687	744,925	525,344	3,803,813	3,747,841
Louisiana	6,505,389	24,593,370	16,386,323	3,158,557	2,684,609	473,948	650,613	954,107	3,443,770	4,569,340
Maine	1,325,723	7,454,783	5,761,183	311,203	262,414	48,789	220,864	273,497	888,036	786,019
Maryland	8,654,935	27,368,349	18,927,879	2,492,962	1,863,273	629,689	1,365,033	1,044,928	3,537,547	4,889,162
Massachusetts	8,890,500	39,020,038	25,324,484	2,471,221	2,170,370	300,851	721,052	3,736,377	6,766,904	5,024,519
Michigan	19,629,569	39,561,607	27,425,212	1,713,391	1,363,412	349,979	1,302,438	1,147,573	7,972,993	6,228,656
Minnesota	11,199,230	25,109,659	17,327,259	1,778,742	1,434,952	343,790	862,045	526,994	4,614,619	5,180,278
Mississippi	5,156,650	14,089,426	10,581,014	1,213,912	904,889	309,023	199,186	218,614	1,876,700	2,291,866
Missouri	5,888,392	22,762,428	15,692,584	1,843,989	1,565,715	278,274	546,686	847,712	3,831,457	3,820,020
Montana	1,276,112	4,991,641	3,241,813	707,903	629,145	78,758	99,478	167,139	775,308	912,618
Nebraska	2,064,173	6,970,013	5,298,318	926,936	840,088	86,848	151,017	108,050	485,692	2,177,828
Nevada	3,864,223	8,191,985	4,776,583	907,637	812,867	94,770	197,014	212,010	2,098,741	1,716,603
New Hampshire	1,278,589	5,677,585	4,011,931	446,981	398,700	48,281	142,678	391,573	684,422	921,285
New Jersey	11,135,809	50,908,314	32,028,780	4,525,536	3,731,929	793,607	1,185,041	2,139,595	11,029,362	10,097,140
New Mexico	4,740,669	12,371,032	9,210,748	1,028,133	918,071	110,062	233,969	324,507	1,573,675	2,406,539
New York	55,107,082	108,599,110	74,106,427	10,361,149	8,267,538	2,093,611	1,446,900	5,505,131	17,179,503	17,398,991
North Carolina	13,562,079	35,023,273	24,950,944	2,816,076	2,122,163	693,913	374,478	637,401	6,244,374	7,968,755
North Dakota	933,974	3,552,639	2,433,709	423,839	374,233	49,606	131,341	146,457	417,293	931,072
Ohio	18,988,114	52,612,032	30,535,701	3,533,058	3,191,174	341,884	2,323,844	1,445,927	14,773,502	8,210,805

See footnotes at end of table.

STATE EXPENDITURE, BY CHARACTER AND OBJECT AND BY STATE: 2009 (In thousands of dollars) — Continued

State	Intergovernmental expenditures	Direct expenditures		Capital outlay			Assistance and subsidies	Interest on debt	Insurance benefits and repayments	Exhibit: Total salaries and wages
		Total	Current operation	Total	Construction	Other				
Oklahoma...........	4,506,456	16,849,484	11,323,040	2,401,615	2,025,764	375,851	369,344	490,185	2,265,300	3,091,929
Oregon...............	5,703,775	18,677,287	11,581,072	1,447,670	1,125,728	321,942	425,254	456,106	4,767,185	4,229,330
Pennsylvania......	19,110,552	58,453,695	36,302,898	6,798,987	5,885,182	913,805	2,015,399	1,823,759	11,512,652	7,976,822
Rhode Island......	963,902	6,382,760	4,257,066	327,375	272,259	55,116	126,794	437,293	1,234,232	1,056,400
South Carolina....	5,520,979	23,142,687	15,550,152	2,490,785	2,180,056	310,729	1,243,287	780,304	3,078,159	3,623,919
South Dakota......	707,862	3,401,631	2,277,851	541,123	493,419	47,704	70,350	135,135	377,172	883,257
Tennessee...........	6,797,935	21,017,539	15,447,191	2,098,027	1,732,024	366,003	1,290,657	236,118	1,945,546	3,781,185
Texas..................	29,252,364	81,473,416	58,003,667	7,671,578	6,151,352	1,520,226	2,031,549	1,242,925	12,523,697	15,118,481
Utah...................	3,120,527	12,447,935	8,467,249	1,809,748	1,610,236	199,512	486,914	243,708	1,440,316	2,667,813
Vermont..............	1,532,766	3,916,471	3,034,712	218,279	188,683	29,596	159,534	164,354	339,592	749,271
Virginia..............	11,810,753	30,241,942	21,381,057	2,868,699	2,303,968	564,731	1,365,669	919,732	3,706,785	6,348,555
Washington.........	10,043,789	33,399,641	20,887,192	3,599,861	3,044,613	555,248	1,459,966	1,110,674	6,341,948	6,528,415
West Virginia......	2,232,558	9,249,003	6,718,670	1,094,253	948,673	145,580	183,911	246,458	1,005,711	1,574,456
Wisconsin...........	10,199,520	25,446,752	15,406,009	2,129,786	1,900,807	228,979	1,187,778	1,262,365	5,460,814	4,150,383
Wyoming	1,919,231	3,658,759	2,423,182	561,867	548,494	13,373	66,218	64,221	543,271	680,154

Source: U.S. Census Bureau, 2009 Annual Survey of State Government Finances. For information on sampling and nonsampling errors and definitions, see *http://www.census.gov/govs/state/how_data_collected. html.* Data users who create their own estimates from this table should cite the U.S. Census Bureau as the source of the original data only.
Note: Detail may not add to total due to rounding.

Table 7.23
STATE GENERAL EXPENDITURE, BY FUNCTION AND BY STATE: 2009 (In thousands of dollars)

State	Total general expenditures (a)	Education	Public welfare	Highways	Hospitals	Natural Resources	Health	Corrections	Financial administration	Employment security administration	Police
United States	$1,554,074,163	$567,107,433	$437,468,368	$107,097,616	$56,957,190	$22,585,813	$62,184,380	$50,398,928	$22,856,414	$4,552,973	$13,657,151
Alabama............	23,335,185	10,562,134	5,452,015	1,630,041	1,781,709	296,527	586,529	541,049	223,425	89,763	188,250
Alaska..............	9,896,330	2,200,202	1,582,972	1,338,876	35,668	308,909	321,686	259,889	234,889	37,985	88,285
Arizona............	27,819,006	8,859,323	8,770,335	2,309,492	62,173	273,817	1,728,249	1,135,021	368,821	67,289	268,685
Arkansas...........	14,553,101	6,524,569	3,831,405	912,721	837,945	231,121	208,984	305,250	331,044	43,221	64,360
California..........	211,083,320	73,248,498	63,579,401	10,731,047	7,276,117	4,590,592	10,932,467	9,110,775	3,656,490	426,581	1,683,827
Colorado..........	20,817,538	8,634,021	4,777,952	1,224,706	514,114	463,570	1,063,230	1,084,368	512,741	67,550	130,808
Connecticut	21,376,500	6,118,111	6,094,081	950,797	1,455,247	126,134	972,080	735,438	399,257	94,731	209,541
Delaware	6,634,392	2,302,154	1,515,666	529,442	59,063	88,653	393,254	272,763	210,309	16,316	106,079
Florida	66,056,700	22,131,046	18,569,342	6,228,758	892,655	1,588,917	3,651,980	2,670,803	1,175,418	107,258	424,007
Georgia	35,956,143	16,570,989	9,892,972	1,778,524	636,995	469,241	1,162,192	1,429,373	453,001	114,891	267,760
Hawaii	10,051,242	3,556,817	1,688,167	455,985	568,768	118,376	668,180	230,656	123,137	52,705	28,394
Idaho...............	7,118,726	2,864,001	1,760,304	729,798	50,337	188,889	154,581	257,810	166,191	31,022	54,254
Illinois.............	57,159,617	16,732,763	18,636,498	5,270,169	1,116,377	254,267	2,298,444	1,292,008	639,782	126,771	431,348
Indiana.............	28,855,900	12,646,914	7,509,909	2,072,949	205,453	309,901	645,042	674,337	316,913	127,110	252,094
Iowa................	16,172,418	6,147,569	4,263,942	1,613,728	1,193,593	323,176	262,034	292,609	204,610	37,526	97,987
Kansas	14,155,854	6,013,798	3,282,069	1,244,991	1,002,199	230,085	249,872	358,672	180,953	23,107	110,155
Kentucky..........	23,019,129	8,866,268	6,842,092	1,906,011	1,262,836	322,654	669,338	505,941	247,126	95,115	183,117
Louisiana..........	27,649,319	9,239,286	4,867,135	2,666,699	1,049,897	639,880	672,118	832,499	355,331	111,192	343,922
Maine	7,891,060	2,067,434	2,847,046	520,967	59,199	193,702	489,231	148,446	145,469	15,853	75,535
Maryland	31,665,036	11,190,257	8,131,885	2,513,661	556,339	645,965	2,077,774	1,412,584	562,807	55,952	471,575
Massachusetts	40,908,513	11,275,401	13,189,704	1,911,792	489,859	401,929	1,050,574	1,329,086	647,830	58,593	579,052
Michigan...........	50,584,008	21,926,048	14,416,340	2,730,831	2,366,161	340,598	1,225,891	1,797,152	417,734	214,457	334,927
Minnesota	31,550,435	12,889,957	9,926,096	2,110,697	366,903	554,166	662,491	554,952	287,446	74,558	349,589
Mississippi........	17,162,353	5,442,830	5,130,483	1,204,070	1,042,491	256,402	399,109	367,878	95,391	88,412	115,494
Missouri............	24,819,363	8,742,798	7,045,430	2,230,978	1,351,676	383,460	1,300,238	765,995	196,283	26,683	211,349
Montana	5,419,049	1,786,990	1,235,984	640,962	47,418	229,264	139,165	180,160	221,856	23,744	45,213
Nebraska...........	8,548,494	3,130,952	2,171,990	706,424	248,014	205,476	407,012	228,871	109,399	34,302	89,722
Nevada.............	9,869,734	4,100,694	1,865,609	792,451	256,894	133,926	238,918	398,522	116,908	57,956	110,772
New Hampshire ...	5,846,814	1,998,981	1,778,194	477,085	55,452	65,723	102,740	107,683	75,235	33,151	56,063
New Jersey........	48,208,101	16,423,092	13,170,854	2,662,684	2,131,413	646,124	1,327,419	1,473,703	781,318	180,074	469,289
New Mexico	15,512,488	5,223,404	3,860,365	1,057,458	832,952	232,723	508,665	379,599	209,813	9,836	144,802
New York	133,940,570	42,373,865	45,235,958	4,533,585	5,898,259	546,375	8,584,306	3,083,344	2,110,204	311,001	967,673
North Carolina....	42,305,938	18,029,629	11,213,283	2,885,414	1,501,079	778,046	1,653,556	1,353,509	374,217	177,702	484,271
North Dakota......	4,069,320	1,371,414	820,797	544,043	15,432	176,663	69,146	66,027	71,013	7,951	30,173
Ohio................	56,354,660	21,396,588	16,493,561	3,265,756	2,451,790	374,480	2,278,192	1,732,289	860,866	274,549	284,908

See footnotes at end of table.

STATE GENERAL EXPENDITURE, BY FUNCTION AND BY STATE: 2009 (In thousands of dollars)—Continued

State	Total general expenditures (a)	Education	Public welfare	Highways	Hospitals	Natural Resources	Health	Corrections	Financial administration	Employment security administration	Police
Oklahoma	18,158,546	7,390,486	5,116,159	1,648,001	230,161	243,031	828,620	629,731	241,224	48,057	165,575
Oregon	19,388,496	7,133,379	4,925,374	1,565,818	1,220,844	454,327	447,523	713,821	567,172	54,888	166,662
Pennsylvania	64,612,112	21,050,374	20,207,292	7,347,576	3,023,026	637,931	1,918,740	1,702,602	1,080,503	109,900	849,120
Rhode Island	5,963,618	1,670,031	2,175,941	220,513	64,742	40,416	181,653	179,649	164,500	18,662	67,514
South Carolina	22,931,853	7,834,782	6,170,057	1,070,776	1,398,273	239,503	1,056,196	486,737	724,765	65,867	187,735
South Dakota	3,732,321	1,211,838	894,392	480,144	60,465	129,866	134,191	114,507	111,945	21,088	31,338
Tennessee	25,869,928	8,957,181	8,749,889	2,204,291	466,221	381,408	1,279,444	810,953	382,832	116,108	183,422
Texas	98,106,540	44,354,519	26,582,564	6,776,659	3,763,065	863,925	2,519,399	3,689,841	618,885	290,340	747,902
Utah	13,961,499	6,370,956	2,458,093	1,325,376	927,095	183,443	393,241	333,720	268,327	22,837	125,867
Vermont	5,035,486	2,269,224	1,359,222	335,679	20,175	73,121	164,536	120,183	58,080	19,642	74,996
Virginia	37,871,467	14,755,276	7,888,513	2,987,783	2,991,710	226,464	1,128,702	1,547,595	566,550	115,737	671,407
Washington	36,537,414	15,295,072	8,189,020	2,896,426	1,859,169	926,500	1,802,465	1,158,924	421,821	199,399	322,286
West Virginia	10,398,477	3,892,978	2,860,952	1,209,882	114,021	187,066	290,263	256,169	192,656	27,910	101,691
Wisconsin	30,176,862	10,717,030	7,736,417	2,162,554	1,142,446	628,189	588,734	1,136,178	282,781	96,607	135,843
Wyoming	4,963,188	1,715,510	704,647	482,546	3,300	380,892	295,986	149,257	91,146	31,024	72,513

Source: U.S. Census Bureau, 2009 Annual Survey of State Government Finances. For information on sampling and nonsampling errors and definitions, see *http://www.census.gov/govs/state/how_data_collected. html.* Data users who create their own estimates from this table should cite the U.S. Census Bureau as the source of the original data only.

Note: Detail may not add to total due to rounding.
Key:
(a) Does not represent sum of state figures because total includes miscellaneous expenditures not shown.

Table 7.24
STATE DEBT OUTSTANDING AT END OF FISCAL YEAR, BY STATE: 2009
(In thousands of dollars)

State	Total	Long-term total	Short-term	Net long-term total (a)
United States	$1,045,166,873	$1,037,998,190	$7,168,683	$549,568,208
Alabama	8,155,943	8,127,979	27,964	5,989,237
Alaska..	6,589,698	6,439,974	149,724	2,497,530
Arizona......................................	12,324,879	12,282,443	42,436	7,562,391
Arkansas....................................	4,135,051	4,135,051	0	2,034,213
California	134,571,934	134,537,934	34,000	102,956,033
Colorado....................................	17,202,374	16,660,983	541,391	3,087,797
Connecticut	28,394,151	28,390,255	3,896	15,585,203
Delaware	5,984,645	5,984,645	0	2,857,918
Florida	38,885,422	38,850,695	34,727	28,603,423
Georgia.....................................	13,455,164	13,373,256	81,908	10,706,484
Hawaii.......................................	6,880,242	6,880,242	0	5,836,330
Idaho...	3,508,973	3,499,980	8,993	452,728
Illinois.......................................	56,962,364	56,947,518	14,846	27,527,652
Indiana......................................	23,711,889	22,607,133	1,104,756	1,811,285
Iowa..	6,353,306	6,353,306	0	1,717,718
Kansas	5,857,295	5,852,295	5,000	3,545,241
Kentucky	13,364,138	13,347,039	17,099	6,456,200
Louisiana	17,504,772	17,487,439	17,333	8,325,994
Maine	5,396,983	5,396,983	0	1,127,942
Maryland	23,472,579	23,399,760	72,819	10,741,462
Massachusetts	74,597,901	74,554,996	42,905	34,393,444
Michigan...................................	29,591,278	29,317,041	274,237	12,766,575
Minnesota..................................	10,524,424	10,518,900	5,524	5,950,963
Mississippi	6,208,639	6,169,824	38,815	4,441,223
Missouri	19,217,206	19,183,968	33,238	4,846,396
Montana	4,763,503	4,762,623	880	950,513
Nebraska	2,516,775	2,515,085	1,690	370,135
Nevada	4,444,804	4,444,804	0	3,211,872
New Hampshire	8,411,660	8,342,213	69,447	2,050,360
New Jersey	56,897,866	56,872,606	25,260	35,674,908
New Mexico	8,001,721	7,979,318	22,403	3,194,175
New York....................................	122,651,630	122,175,644	475,986	64,216,752
North Carolina...........................	19,910,714	19,735,723	174,991	7,425,866
North Dakota.............................	1,752,558	1,751,460	1,098	535,570
Ohio..	27,949,184	27,204,472	744,712	15,199,590
Oklahoma..................................	9,855,393	9,842,485	12,908	5,267,442
Oregon......................................	12,494,686	12,434,686	60,000	9,368,685
Pennsylvania	41,924,042	41,072,705	851,337	18,077,369
Rhode Island.............................	9,180,938	9,139,652	41,286	2,853,766
South Carolina	15,313,021	15,077,114	235,907	10,714,721
South Dakota	3,626,024	3,625,344	680	724,138
Tennessee	4,847,786	4,565,164	282,622	2,451,712
Texas...	30,438,160	29,053,108	1,385,052	16,082,764
Utah..	6,267,888	6,232,261	35,627	2,004,865
Vermont.....................................	3,426,670	3,341,214	85,456	980,609
Virginia.....................................	24,301,179	24,191,449	109,730	10,503,588
Washington................................	24,603,219	24,603,219	0	15,225,026
West Virginia.............................	6,501,995	6,501,995	0	3,101,151
Wisconsin	20,913,355	20,913,355	0	7,484,632
Wyoming	1,320,852	1,320,852	0	76,617

Source: U.S. Census Bureau, 2009 Annual Survey of State Government Finances. For information on sampling and nonsampling errors and definitions, see *http://www.census.gov/govs/state/how_data_collected.html.* Data users who create their own estimates from this table should cite the U.S. Census Bureau as the source of the original data only.

Note: Detail may not add to total due to rounding.
Key:
(a) Long-term debt outstanding minus long-term debt offsets.

Table 7.25
NUMBER AND MEMBERSHIP OF STATE PUBLIC EMPLOYEE-RETIREMENT SYSTEMS
BY STATE: FISCAL YEAR 2009

State	Number of systems	Membership Total	Active members	Inactive members	Total beneficiaries receiving periodic benefit payments
United States..........................	222	17,436,114	13,087,349	4,348,765	6,808,000
Alabama................................	4	261,339	232,966	28,373	106,361
Alaska...................................	4	52,372	43,719	8,653	34,714
Arizona	4	490,263	258,627	231,636	116,082
Arkansas	6	160,848	132,329	28,519	66,097
California	5	1,920,900	1,396,440	524,460	779,637
Colorado	2	360,728	201,524	159,204	87,174
Connecticut	6	125,188	112,835	12,353	83,002
Delaware................................	1	44,795	42,878	1,917	23,286
Florida...................................	1	651,824	572,887	78,937	304,610
Georgia	9	581,211	365,274	215,937	140,046
Hawaii	1	72,436	66,589	5,847	36,271
Idaho	2	77,937	67,862	10,075	32,268
Illinois..................................	6	801,683	491,283	310,400	292,907
Indiana	8	290,992	229,330	61,662	109,175
Iowa......................................	4	205,115	172,465	32,650	94,226
Kansas	1	197,822	156,073	41,749	71,268
Kentucky...............................	6	326,728	221,130	105,598	135,907
Louisiana	14	301,930	213,187	88,743	139,493
Maine	1	58,249	50,477	7,772	35,368
Maryland...............................	2	254,931	202,537	52,394	117,331
Massachusetts........................	13	248,252	207,224	41,028	119,011
Michigan	6	371,760	344,094	27,666	243,675
Minnesota	8	505,070	286,153	218,917	155,159
Mississippi............................	4	294,541	167,901	126,640	79,085
Missouri	10	280,721	229,472	51,249	123,832
Montana	9	74,371	53,350	21,021	32,687
Nebraska...............................	5	86,903	63,069	23,834	15,970
Nevada	2	117,069	105,462	11,607	42,207
New Hampshire	2	57,831	51,087	6,744	24,549
New Jersey.............................	7	595,443	524,107	71,336	247,461
New Mexico...........................	5	155,286	122,026	33,260	57,782
New York...............................	2	960,402	841,361	119,041	500,134
North Carolina	6	626,847	491,608	135,239	210,030
North Dakota	2	34,702	29,650	5,052	13,606
Ohio......................................	5	1,260,690	696,160	564,530	396,276
Oklahoma	6	166,549	152,429	14,120	87,698
Oregon	1	214,465	171,068	43,397	108,222
Pennsylvania..........................	3	512,134	392,889	119,245	285,831
Rhode Island	1	29,897	24,933	4,964	20,905
South Carolina	4	386,230	219,582	166,648	116,327
South Dakota	2	52,582	38,596	13,986	20,075
Tennessee..............................	1	244,040	213,276	30,764	107,702
Texas.....................................	7	1,559,639	1,351,195	208,444	457,736
Utah......................................	6	139,856	106,261	33,595	42,138
Vermont	3	33,109	25,427	7,682	12,244
Virginia	1	380,194	346,929	33,265	141,746
Washington............................	6	277,094	238,867	38,227	124,076
West Virginia	1	73,787	56,506	17,281	52,077
Wisconsin..............................	1	413,029	265,721	147,308	144,033
Wyoming................................	6	46,330	40,534	5,796	20,503

Source: 2009 Survey of State and Local Public Employee Retirement Systems. Data users who create their own estimates using data from this report should cite the U.S. Census Bureau as the source of the original data only. The data in this table are based on information from public records and contain no confidential data. Although the data in this table come from a census of retirement systems and are not subject to sampling error, the census results do contain nonsampling error. Additional information on nonsampling error, and response rates may be found at *http://www.census. gov/govs/retire/how_data_collected.html.*

Data Created: April 14, 2011
Data Last Revised: April 22, 2011

Table 7.26
FINANCES OF STATE-ADMINISTERED EMPLOYEE RETIREMENT SYSTEMS, BY STATE: FISCAL YEAR 2009
(In thousands of dollars)

State and level of government	Total receipts	Employee contributions	Government contributions			Earnings on investments (a)	Total payments	Benefits	Withdrawals	Other payments
			Total	From state government	From local government					
United States.........	-$425,782,081	$33,335,871	$64,836,246	$29,618,588	$35,217,658	-$523,954,198	$161,686,475	$151,850,339	$3,282,212	$6,553,924
Alabama.................	-611,382	532,899	1,218,255	745,123	473,132	-2,362,536	2,345,244	2,235,727	75,122	34,395
Alaska	-2,059,283	173,593	1,040,480	406,974	633,506	-3,273,356	1,211,596	1,140,122	16,120	55,354
Arizona	-3,067,641	1,011,813	1,141,998	941,586	200,412	-5,221,452	2,536,348	2,336,076	143,343	56,929
Arkansas	-2,518,813	159,528	630,374	452,123	178,251	-3,308,715	1,151,919	1,064,651	11,157	76,111
California	-88,070,593	6,392,953	10,707,966	6,296,479	4,411,487	-105,171,512	23,615,500	22,212,331	371,689	1,031,480
Colorado	-9,724,258	594,258	909,159	596,109	313,050	-11,227,675	3,168,263	2,792,002	147,629	228,632
Connecticut	414,746	366,352	1,289,220	35,937	1,253,283	-1,240,826	2,579,716	2,554,940	23,895	881
Delaware................	-864,909	54,374	181,485	15,408	166,077	-1,100,768	431,957	405,291	3,450	23,216
Florida...................	-21,277,473	138,264	3,235,407	2,556,630	678,777	-24,651,144	5,669,558	5,669,558	0	0
Georgia	-389,323	623,812	1,378,860	318,533	1,060,327	-2,391,995	3,894,515	3,771,435	56,843	66,237
Hawaii	-2,117,520	169,394	513,209	129,166	384,043	-2,800,123	838,438	792,313	3,669	42,456
Idaho	-1,203,070	180,389	284,991	182,145	102,846	-1,668,450	568,407	522,133	0	46,274
Illinois..................	-14,265,491	1,723,182	3,530,434	783,485	2,746,949	-19,519,107	7,940,064	7,450,969	143,667	345,428
Indiana	-2,415,920	335,654	1,342,195	343,610	998,585	-4,093,769	1,693,360	1,572,261	49,030	72,069
Iowa......................	-3,561,630	297,803	475,736	394,390	81,346	-4,335,169	1,385,185	1,318,363	35,230	31,592
Kansas	-1,823,412	271,600	485,570	140,223	345,347	-2,580,582	1,142,708	1,065,317	42,929	34,462
Kentucky...............	-2,683,214	592,373	852,522	287,668	564,854	-4,128,109	2,864,756	2,753,502	38,836	72,418
Louisiana	-3,283,799	758,703	1,695,175	250,812	1,444,363	-5,737,677	3,015,331	2,812,469	100,690	102,172
Maine	-1,478,376	154,546	332,102	14,711	317,391	-1,965,024	701,309	622,605	45,612	33,092
Maryland................	-5,588,921	532,101	1,136,818	108,800	1,028,018	-7,257,840	2,347,061	2,324,174	22,324	563
Massachusetts........	-4,863,709	1,122,144	1,540,161	147,764	1,392,397	-7,526,014	3,455,142	3,434,872	7,754	12,516
Michigan	-5,524,419	470,726	1,729,334	1,310,135	419,199	-7,724,479	4,979,693	4,518,683	39,883	421,127
Minnesota	-6,986,925	710,464	816,872	635,002	181,870	-8,514,261	3,261,922	3,102,164	56,778	102,980
Mississippi............	-2,572,370	436,608	740,508	469,986	270,522	-3,749,486	1,667,123	1,525,234	70,143	71,746
Missouri	-6,815,393	712,965	1,268,347	782,361	485,986	-8,796,705	2,990,827	2,810,513	62,081	118,233
Montana................	-1,201,723	150,722	201,191	108,333	92,858	-1,553,636	502,748	456,560	19,290	26,898
Nebraska...............	-1,081,953	137,584	170,098	114,720	55,378	-1,389,635	309,280	308,445	155	680
Nevada..................	-2,160,662	121,795	1,213,269	1,030,827	182,442	-3,495,726	1,266,879	1,190,033	18,586	58,260
New Hampshire	-573,752	143,185	236,209	157,993	78,216	-953,146	490,828	456,588	24,204	10,036
New Jersey.............	-7,849,261	1,726,545	2,346,807	54,184	2,292,623	-11,922,613	7,014,775	6,818,568	143,753	52,454
New Mexico...........	3,542,737	422,392	640,575	212,777	427,790	-4,605,704	1,305,314	1,224,190	61,369	19,733
New York	-55,362,479	411,601	3,953,806	1,846,771	2,107,035	-59,727,886	11,518,754	11,022,304	17,080	479,370
North Carolina	-12,903,549	1,175,167	798,247	266,000	532,247	-14,876,963	4,004,061	3,862,811	121,022	20,228
North Dakota	-785,264	48,057	78,059	62,291	15,768	-911,380	202,561	185,136	7,779	9,646
Ohio......................	-33,430,236	2,799,886	3,062,681	1,239,341	1,823,340	-39,292,803	11,126,107	10,076,775	397,164	652,168
Oklahoma..............	-1,699,587	391,027	957,146	448,618	508,528	-3,047,760	1,744,659	1,569,153	88,612	86,894
Oregon	-11,875,407	8,452	658,159	502,280	155,879	-12,542,018	3,222,318	2,790,218	36,549	395,551
Pennsylvania.........	-25,739,993	1,265,855	1,030,888	401,946	628,942	-28,036,696	7,291,173	6,880,677	36,236	374,260
Rhode Island	-2,037,133	184,688	399,413	141,770	257,643	-2,621,234	687,704	687,704	0	0
South Carolina	-3,742,754	645,116	962,559	659,067	303,492	-5,350,429	2,186,231	2,001,313	87,668	97,250
South Dakota	-1,292,568	95,458	94,245	59,008	35,237	-1,482,271	334,423	306,769	24,225	3,429
Tennessee..............	-4,757,311	253,558	844,371	235,754	608,617	-5,855,240	1,010,467	1,010,467	0	0
Texas.....................	-14,264,782	3,094,575	3,393,997	1,451,182	1,942,815	-20,753,354	9,630,849	8,993,245	460,600	177,004
Utah......................	-4,152,103	36,245	641,690	0	641,690	-4,830,038	894,275	863,530	5,177	25,568
Vermont	-488,464	55,630	50,840	1,421	49,419	-594,934	185,693	170,097	2,627	12,969
Virginia	-9,136,639	20,543	2,076,860	1,504,430	572,430	-11,234,042	3,091,535	2,733,223	91,348	266,964
Washington	-10,931,846	615,456	1,301,913	144,368	1,157,545	-12,849,215	2,909,111	2,568,727	42,589	297,795
West Virginia	142,151	181,504	516,181	89,387	426,794	-555,534	774,140	749,156	16,565	8,419
Wisconsin..............	-21,897,842	736,149	630,840	461,965	168,875	-23,264,831	4,217,330	3,822,544	0	394,786
Wyoming................	-1,663,129	98,183	99,024	78,995	20,029	-1,860,336	309,318	294,401	11,740	3,177

Source: 2009 Survey of State and Local Public Employee Retirement Systems. Data users who create their own estimates using data from this report should cite the U.S. Census Bureau as the source of the original data only. The data in this table are based on information from public records and contain no confidential data. Although the data in this table come from a census of retirement systems and are not subject to sampling error, the census results do contain nonsampling error. Additional information on nonsampling error, and response rates may be found at *http://www.census. gov/govs/retire/how_data_collected.html*.

Key:
(a) The total of "net earnings" is a calculated statistic (the item code in the data file is X08), and thus can be positive or negative. Net earnings is the sum of earnings on investments plus gains on investments minus losses on investments. The change made in 2002 for asset valuation from book to market value in accordance with Statement 34 of the Governmental Accounting Standards Board is reflected in the calculated statistics.
Data Created: April 14, 2011
Data Last Revised: April 22, 2011

Table 7.27
NATIONAL SUMMARY OF STATE PUBLIC EMPLOYEE RETIREMENT SYSTEM FINANCES: SELECTED YEARS, 2007–2009

	Amount (in thousands of dollars)			Percentage distribution		
	2008–2009	2007–2008	2006–2007	2008–2009	2007–2008	2006–2007
Total Receipts	-425,782,081	56,645,613	488,102,626	100.0	100.0	100.0
Employee contributions	33,335,871	31,639,290	29,789,803	-7.8	55.9	6.1
Government contributions	64,836,246	64,095,752	57,645,659	-15.2	113.2	11.8
From State Government	29,618,588	28,340,230	26,058,758	-7.0	50.0	5.3
From Local Government	35,217,658	35,755,522	31,586,901	-8.3	63.1	6.5
Earnings on investments (a)	-523,954,198	-39,089,429	400,667,164	123.1	-69.0	82.1
Total Payments	161,686,475	157,459,093	149,093,838	100.0	100.0	100.0
Benefits paid	151,850,339	143,453,487	131,639,204	93.9	91.1	88.3
Withdrawals	3,282,212	3,260,178	4,562,127	2.0	2.1	3.1
Other payments	6,553,924	10,745,428	12,892,507	4.1	6.8	8.6
Total cash and investment holdings at end of fiscal year	2,029,201,192	2,670,483,906	2,822,660,076	100.0	100.0	100.0
Cash and short-term investments	84,254,144	66,321,984	93,440,645	4.2	2.5	3.3
Total Securities	1,616,544,698	2,237,097,553	2,431,581,706	79.7	83.8	86.1
Government securities	163,891,577	197,554,688	226,911,170	8.1	7.4	8.0
Federal government	163,220,670	196,302,107	225,457,403	8.0	7.4	8.0
United States Treasury	112,446,110	119,174,614	134,835,661	5.5	4.5	4.8
Federal agency	50,774,560	77,127,493	90,621,742	2.5	2.9	3.2
State and local government	670,907	1,252,581	1,453,767	0.0	0.0	0.1
Nongovernment securities	1,452,653,121	2,039,542,865	2,204,670,536	71.6	76.4	78.1
Corporate bonds	336,130,557	431,406,612	364,378,880	16.6	16.2	12.9
Corporate stocks	658,838,580	951,034,623	1,033,710,822	32.5	35.6	36.6
Mortgages	14,113,984	9,476,389	12,715,529	0.7	0.4	0.5
Funds held in trust	62,800,512	58,585,393	68,544,899	3.1	2.2	2.4
Foreign and international	316,141,175	396,971,226	443,007,121	15.6	14.9	15.7
Other nongovernmental	64,628,313	192,068,622	282,313,285	3.2	7.2	10.0
Other investments	328,402,350	367,064,369	297,637,725	16.2	13.7	10.5
Real property	92,729,218	79,794,658	87,675,532	4.6	3.0	3.1
Miscellaneous investments	235,673,132	287,269,711	209,962,193	11.6	10.8	7.4

Source: 2009 Survey of State and Local Public Employee Retirement Systems. Data users who create their own estimates using data from this report should cite the U.S. Census Bureau as the source of the original data only. The data in this table are based on information from public records and contain no confidential data. Although the data in this table come from a census of retirement systems and are not subject to sampling error, the census results do contain nonsampling error. Additional information on nonsampling error, and response rates may be found at *http://www.census.gov/govs/retire/how_data_collected.html.*

Key:
(a) The total of "net earnings" is a calculated statistic (the item code in the data file is X08), and thus can be positive or negative. Net earnings is the sum of earnings on investments plus gains on investments minus losses on investments. The change made in 2002 for asset valuation from book to market value in accordance with Statement 34 of the Governmental Accounting Standards Board is reflected in the calculated statistics.
 Data Created: April 14, 2011
 Data Last Revised: April 22, 2011

Chapter Eight

STATE MANAGEMENT, ADMINISTRATION AND DEMOGRAPHICS

The Citizens Jury Process

By Ned Crosby and John C. Hottinger

The Citizens Jury process was one of the first, and yet most thorough, democratic processes created in the 20th century. It gathers a microcosm of the public to study an issue for at least five days, drawing upon witnesses from a number of points of view. It was used extensively in the 1990s and early 2000s on topics as diverse as the size of hog feedlots in a Minnesota county to global climate change, conducted in 2002 for the EPA. Its most recent major use has been to evaluate ballot initiatives in Oregon and to recommend changes to the election recount law in Minnesota. This article lays out some of the history of the process and how the Jefferson Center, its originator, hopes to use it in the future. Details about how the process is conducted can be learned at www.jefferson-center.org.

"At a time when our discourse has become so sharply polarized, at a time when we are far too eager to lay the blame for all that ails the world at the feet of those who think differently than we do, it's important for us to pause for a moment and make sure that we are talking with each other in a way that heals, not a way that wounds."

—President Obama, speaking in Arizona on Jan. 12, 2011

How do we talk with each other in a way that heals? Many methods to do this were created in the past 40 years, as any visitor to the National Coalition for Dialogue and Deliberation website will discover.[1] The Citizens Jury process, which was invented by the Jefferson Center for New Democratic Processes, a Minneapolis non-partisan non-profit organization focused on citizen participation, was one of the first of such methods created.[2] It is distinguished from other methods by the length of time people are brought together and the selection process for participants. The typical Citizens Jury project lasts five full days. The goal is to make sure that a group of people—randomly selected and demographically balanced—have enough time to learn about the issue from witnesses and to be able to talk among themselves about what they are learning.

During the 1980s, the Citizens Jury process grew in use and the sophistication of its methods. By the 1990s it was attracting considerable attention, as noted in following sections. Other methods were also attracting national media attention.[3]

Ironically, the 1990s were also the time when the American political system became increasingly subject to criticism that it was becoming more rigid and partisan. By the turn of the 21st century, the rising complaints of legislative gridlock, festering problems and inflexible policy positions led to a broad range of attacks on legislative and executive leaders at the state and national level. A growing chorus of critics have labeled government decision-making dysfunctional and flagrantly disconnected from the general public.

Thus in the 1990s, as the need for something like the Citizens Jury process grew, it was not seen by those in power as a solution to their problems. Candidates and policymakers frequently turned to divisive tactics to win elections and gain electoral advantage, rather than turning to methods to improve civil discourse, engage the public and overcome gridlock. By 2002 the Jefferson Center saw that it was fighting an uphill battle and cut back on the attempt to conduct Citizens Juries unless they were likely to have more impact on the political system.

It was only in 2008 that the fortunes of the Citizens Jury process began to turn significantly. As the result of a successful demonstration project in Oregon in that year, the Oregon legislature took steps to see if Citizens Juries (for Oregon the term used was "Citizen Initiative Reviews" due to their focus on the initiative process) should be made a standard way of informing voters about ballot initiatives. In 2009 a Citizens Jury was conducted in Minnesota to review how recounts should be conducted on close elections. This led to legislation improving the way recounts are conducted. These are discussed later in the article. First, it is important to give more background on the process itself and its early history.

Citizens Juries on Issues

Citizens Juries often are used to examine specific issues. Around the world, most of these appear to be on local topics. The Jefferson Center in Minneapolis has conducted a variety on issues over the years. Besides the Citizens Juries on local issues, some were on statewide issues in Minnesota and three were on national issues.

The Jefferson Center conducted these issue Citizens Juries from 1974 to 2002, always with the hope they would have enough impact so there would be "return business." Many of the projects did have some impact and the method gained considerable respect from editorial writers. For example, William Raspberry, commenting on the Citizens Jury on the Clinton health care plan in 1993, said in *The Washington Post*[4] "The Citizens Jury ... is a paragon of representative democracy."

Despite this editorial support and generally positive response, the Jefferson Center finally had to conclude that the more likely the recommendations of a Citizens Jury would have an impact on public policy, the less likely the process was to be used. It became clear to us that even a small project could be very sensitive politically. By the mid-2000s, however, the growing citizen frustration and yearning for meaningful impact sparked a renewed interest in methods that would elevate the public discourse and influence in government decisions.

Why then the Citizens Jury process on government issues? The position taken by the Jefferson Center is that it is not enough for small groups to talk respectfully with each other, even when considerable publicity is given to the event. What is needed is to conduct a deliberative method that helps the public take strong and well-informed actions that can have a significant political impact.

Citizens Juries to Inform Voters

The Jefferson Center always had an interest in seeing whether it would be valuable to ask a Citizens Jury to evaluate candidates in an election. The first test of this came when two advocates argued the virtues of Ford vs. Carter in the 1976 election. The jurors were asked to evaluate the candidates on their stands on issues. It was only an experiment, but it worked well, although it was not widely publicized.

In 1988, many voters around the country expressed discontent about the quality of the debate in the presidential election that year. This led the Jefferson Center to team up with the League of Women Voters in St. Paul, Minn., to conduct a Citizens Jury to evaluate the candidates in the St. Paul mayoral race. The goal was not to have the jurors recommend which candidate to vote for, but simply to evaluate the candidates on three major issues. The Center and the League went to considerable lengths to be sure none of their views would influence the jurors in any way.

The success of that project led the Center and the League to cooperate on a Citizens Jury project to evaluate candidates in the 1990 Minnesota gubernatorial race. The project was very successful. We were able to determine that half the reporting on issues in newspapers around the state was directly stimulated by the six Citizens Juries we conducted around the state. That project provided the basis for David Broder's comments in *The Washington Post*[5] that it was "one of the two most interesting voter reform projects in the nation." Research conducted by the center led us to believe that if the project had been widely publicized, it could have influenced between 5 and 10 percent of the vote.

The Jefferson Center also teamed up with the League of Women Voters of Pennsylvania to conduct a Citizens Jury on the U.S. Senate race in 1992 between Sen. Arlen Specter and Lynn Yeakel. This high-profile project was very successful. *The Philadelphia Inquirer* called it "a portrait of democracy the way democracy was supposed to be."[6]

In 1993, the Internal Revenue Service informed the Center it would take away its tax-deductible status and issue a fine in six figures for having "influenced" the outcome of an election. Despite evidence to the contrary, the IRS persisted and the Center settled the case in 1996 by promising to not conduct these events again as long as the IRS would not take away our tax-deductible status and not issue a fine.

Citizens Initiative Review

As the Jefferson Center continued its work through the 1990s, it became clear that using the Citizens Jury projects to inform voters was the best thing we could do. Citizens as voters clearly valued what a microcosm of the public had to say about candidates after examining them closely. Because of this, efforts were made by supporters of the Center's methods to explore if these projects could be conducted in a way that would avoid problems with the IRS.

This led to an exploration of some new ways to link up the Citizens Jury process with voters.

In 1999, former Washington Gov. Mike Lowry brought together a group of bipartisan leaders. He suggested the Citizens Jury process should not be used to evaluate candidates, but rather ballot initiatives, with the recommendations placed in the official voters' pamphlet sent to all voters at election time. As a result, the Citizens Initiative Review was born. Citizen Jury inventor Ned Crosby and his wife Pat Benn pursued the effort legislatively in Washington, but by 2007, it was clear success was unlikely in that state.

In 2006, Oregon residents Tyrone Reitman and Elliot Shuford asked if they could attempt to get the Citizens Initiative Review adopted in their state. With support from Crosby and Benn, they established Healthy Democracy Oregon, a nonpartisan, nonprofit organization committed to strengthening the integrity of the ballot initiative process. This led to a demonstration project in 2008. The Oregon legislature in 2009 passed a bill authorizing up to three Citizens Initiative Review projects to be conducted, with the results to be published in the voters' pamphlet.

The purpose of the Citizens Initiative Review (CIR) is to provide voters with clear, useful and trustworthy information about ballot measures. It does so by giving a microcosm of the public the unique opportunity to fairly examine ballot initiatives closely during five days of public hearings. At the conclusion of the evaluation, the panel drafts a statement for inclusion in the official statewide voters' pamphlet, sent out to all voters by the secretary of state, describing the panel's key findings and assessment of the measure.

In 2010, Healthy Democracy Oregon raised sufficient funds from foundations and donors to conduct two sets of hearings. These CIR projects were held in August 2010. One reviewed Measure 73, proposing mandatory sentences on certain sex crimes and drunken driving; the other reviewed Measure 74, proposing dispensaries for medical marijuana.

A $218,000 National Science Foundation grant funded evaluation of the two Citizens Initiative Reviews. A survey measured voters' awareness of the report and their vote. On Measure 73, 60 percent were unaware of the report and voted 66 percent in favor of the measure. Twenty percent of voters were somewhat aware of the project, with 50 percent of them supporting the measure. But among the 20 percent who had read the statement thoroughly, only 35 percent voted in favor of the measure. In November, Oregon voters gave

57 percent approval to Measure 73. From this, it seems reasonable to conclude that the findings of the Citizens Initiative Review dropped support for the bill by 9 percent, even though only 40 percent of the voters were aware of them.

A Changing Political Climate

Recent events have provided new momentum in efforts to give citizens valued input into policy discussions and have raised the necessity—and respect—for listening to the ideas, opinions and judgments of ordinary citizens. The Citizen Jury process provides a unique method for obtaining the kind of deliberative representation of public views. The history of citizen juries reflects the strong capability of citizens to arrive at sound decisions when given the opportunity to hear from witnesses who represent different viewpoints.

This climate change triggered increased activity by the Jefferson Center to publicize and demonstrate the value of its method. A recent example was in Minnesota during the 2008 recount of the extremely close election for the U.S. Senate between Norm Coleman and Al Franken. With the support and leadership of state Rep. Laura Brod, a Republican leader on election issues, and Democratic Secretary of State Mark Ritchie, a Citizen Jury on Elections Recounts was convened before the recount was even finished to examine changes in Minnesota election law to make future recounts less controversial. This project was not a five-day project, but rather borrowed from the Citizens' Assembly method by holding three, three-day weekends, held over a six-week period.

When the jurors presented their findings at the 2009 summer meeting of the National Association of Secretaries of State in Minnesota, the report was met with a standing ovation from the 20 plus secretaries of state in attendance. The Citizen Jury attracted favorable media attention across Minnesota and elsewhere. For instance, the *Grand Forks Herald* in North Dakota editorialized, "Just when Minnesota politics seems ready to reach a new low, along comes the Citizens Jury on Election Recounts to offer a reminder of the state at its best."[7]

In 2009, the Minnesota legislature passed many of the recommendations into law. Those changes smoothed the way for a less controversial recount process in the extremely close 2010 governor's race. That outcome reinforced the Jefferson Center view that an informed microcosm of the public can lead to the informed political will that will give guidance and necessary support to our elected officials when they make the tough decisions they face on major issues.

Looking to the Future

The basic methods of the Jefferson Center are transferable to other states, as shown by the recent success in both Minnesota and Oregon. Given the ongoing budgetary challenges arising from the national and world economic downturn, we also are looking at new and expanded methods to empower citizens to work effectively with their legislators to find solid solutions for long-term budget challenges.

We believe a new community consensus is needed, a spirit that enables us to deal intelligently and respectfully with the major challenges we face. Our long-term budget challenges will be resolved effectively only if citizens can agree on workable solutions. So long as the voices of disunity and short-term self-interest dominate our political discourse, our elected leaders will not receive the support they need to make the tough choices ahead of us.

But a new community consensus is not easy to build. It must emerge as part of a trend that encourages citizens to trust each other and see that they can create a future for themselves and their families. Steps can be taken, however, to build an informed and stable public opinion with a majority of voters. Such an informed political will can provide the support our elected leaders need to find solid solutions to our long-term budget challenges.

For many years, the only method that came close to the Citizens Jury process in length of time it takes was the Deliberative Poll. But in 2004, the government of British Columbia sponsored a Citizens' Assembly, which used 160 randomly selected citizens, meeting for 10 weekends, spread out over the better part of the year. Like the Citizens Jury process, the citizens were paid $150 a day for their participation. The method was very successful in terms of the enthusiasm of the participants and the quality of their recommendations. The recommendations were put before the people of British Columbia in a referendum and gathered 58 percent of the vote, just short of the 60 percent required for passage.

In light of this, the Jefferson Center is proposing a Minnesota Citizens' Assembly to be held in 2013 to create the informed political will needed. This project will be built on the model of the Citizens Jury process, developed in Minnesota and

now used worldwide, and the Citizens' Assembly method, developed in Canada. The key aspects of the Minnesota Citizens' Assembly are:

- There will be 100 randomly selected participants, a microcosm of Minnesota, who will review key aspects of the state's budget and make recommendations to elected officials. They will meet in a series of three-day weekends, with three or four weeks between each meeting.

- The panelists will work carefully with elected officials to ensure they pay close attention to their recommendations.

The first step will be a demonstration project in 2012, which will introduce the Minnesota Citizens' Assembly and do research on some key aspects of the project. The demonstration will likely focus on health care because the costs of health care, broadly defined, are the most significant factor driving the long-term budget challenge. Dealing with these costs presents some of the toughest choices our society faces. If the Minnesota Citizens' Assembly approach can do a solid job of examining health care, this will show it is a method that deserves serious consideration as a way to deal with our long-term budget challenges.

The goals of the demonstration project include:

- Introducing to Minnesotans the way the Minnesota Citizens' Assembly will work. We propose in this project to have a group of about 24 randomly selected citizens meet for four three-day weekends.

- Demonstrating the clarity with which a topic as complex as health care can be presented. This will entail laying out the pros and cons for different positions on health care in a clear way that is seldom publicly done today.

- Using a carefully designed research strategy to learn how it will be possible to get the broader public to trust the Minnesota Citizens' Assembly. Focus groups are being used to learn what people who are not directly involved with the project think of it.

- Asking some current and/or former state legislators to observe the demonstration closely and come up with recommendations about how the legislature could work with the Minnesota Citizens' Assembly when the full project is run. This is an important step in designing how the full citizens' assembly will interact with the legislature.

Assuming these goals are met, it will set the stage for the Jefferson Center to gather the support needed to conduct a Minnesota Citizens' Assembly in 2013. It is not our goal to have an immediate impact on health policy. Instead, we aim to make clear to civic leaders in Minnesota how it will be possible to involve citizens intelligently in a discussion of health policy and how this can lead to the creation of an informed political will. It will also properly set the stage for the larger effort to build informed public support for the budget strategies required to deal with the changes necessary for Minnesota—and potentially other states—to adapt to the rapidly changing economies and demographics of today's national trends.

Notes

[1] See *www.thataway.org*. Best known are the Study Circles as conducted by Everyday Democracy which bring people together in small discussion groups for a couple of hours to discuss a specific issue; and the 21st Century Town Meeting of America Speaks. This meeting gathers several thousand people for a day, sometimes in one large meeting or in large interactive meetings around the nation. Also well known is the Deliberative Poll, created by James Fishkin in the late 1980s, which typically convened several hundred people for three-day meetings. For many years it was the only method that came close to the Citizens Jury process in the length of time it takes. These and other methods gather a cross section of the public to talk about a social or political issue in facilitated discussions. The people attending are respectful of each other and the large majority is enthusiastic about the experience.

[2] The Citizens Jury process is one of the longest-in-use new democratic processes introduced in the 20th century. It, along with its twin the German *Planungszelle*, were the first significant democratic processes to engage randomly selected citizens. The *Planungszelle* was invented by Prof. Peter Dienel of Germany in January 1971, and first used the following year. The Citizens Jury process was invented by Ned Crosby in March 1971 and was first used in 1974. Crosby and Dienel did not learn of each other's work until 1985. By that time the *Planungszelle* was being used in a nationwide project in Germany, with 23 four-day events around the country. Meanwhile, the Citizens Jury process was being used on a statewide basis in Minnesota with five four-day events around the state and a statewide follow-up drawing from the five separate Citizens Juries. The Citizens Jury process took off in Britain in the 1990s and over 300 have now been run. The method continues to be used in Germany and has spread to many other countries, mainly Australia, Spain and Canada. One-day "citizens juries" are being run in Japan. In this article, the term Citizens Jury is capitalized when referring to the process as conducted by the Jefferson Center, but throughout the world the process is referred to in lower case.

[3] Joe Klein commented on James Fishkin's extensive use of the deliberative poll in an article published in *TIME* magazine on Sept. 9, 2010 entitled, "How Can a Democracy Solve Tough Problems?" *http://www.time.com/time/politics/article/0,8599,2015481,00.html#ixzz1GawQdNYV*. In 2002, the deliberative poll was incorporated into a production by MacNeil/Lehrer Productions called "By the People" which "… has supported well over 200 Citizen Deliberations around the country and more than 100 national and local PBS broadcasts, on issues ranging from national security to healthcare." *http://cdd.stanford.edu/polls/btp/index.html*.

"In 2010, America*Speaks* designed and facilitated AmericaSpeaks: Our Budget, Our Economy, a national discussion that gave ordinary people the opportunity to make tough decisions about our nation's looming deficit and debt crisis. Over 3,500 people joined the discussion from 19 primary sites, and still more participated in locally organized Community Conversations and online. The results of the discussion were presented to President Obama's Commission on Fiscal Responsibility and Reform, leading Members of Congress, and the Bipartisan Policy Center's Debt Reduction Task Force." *http://americaspeaks.org/about/history*.

[4] *Washington Post*, October 19, 1993.
[5] *Washington Post*, December 27, 1990.
[6] *Washington Post*, September 30, 1992.
[7] *Grand Forks Herald*, July 21, 2009.

About the Authors

Ned Crosby invented the Citizens Jury process while getting a Ph.D. in political science from the University of Minnesota (1973). In 1974 he set up the Jefferson Center to explore new democratic processes, primarily the Citizens Jury. This led to the development of the Citizens Jury process into one of the world's most frequently used new democratic processes, now found principally in Australia, Britain and Germany. Crosby has worked in recent years to get the Citizens Jury process used to evaluate ballot initiatives. He also taught briefly at the University of Minnesota and Yale.

John C. Hottinger was the 2004 chair of The Council of State Governments and the 2000 chair of the Midwest Legislative Conference. He served in the Minnesota Senate from 1991 through 2006 and was the majority leader in 2003. An attorney, he is the lead program consultant for the Jefferson Center and a principal in Hottinger and Gillette, LLC, which provides services in legal mediation, citizen engagement and public policy development. He also is a member of the Board of Directors of the Northeast-Midwest Institute in Washington, D.C.

States in Crisis:
Unemployment Insurance Trust Fund Solvency

By Jennifer Burnett

As state leaders came together to hammer out their 2012 fiscal year budgets, they faced a challenging task: Find a way to close huge budget gaps while facing an increased demand for services like unemployment benefits. Sustained high unemployment rates, long-term unemployment and unsustainable funding models have exhausted state unemployment trust funds, requiring states to borrow large sums from the federal government. As of March 2011, 31 states had borrowed more than $42.5 billion from the federal government to continue paying unemployment benefits, and sizable interest payments on those loans come due in the fall of 2011. Paying back those loans with interest will be a struggle and could have an impact on both economic recovery and future fiscal stability.

Unemployment Rates Remain High and People are Unemployed Longer

In 2010, the national average unemployment rate was 9.6 percent and forecasters predict that rate will hover around 9 percent throughout the rest of 2011, with moderate improvement in 2012—around 8 percent. While the national unemployment rate is elevated, rates in the states and regions vary significantly. North Dakota (3.9) and Nebraska (4.7) had

the lowest rates in 2010, while Michigan (12.5) and Nevada (14.9) had the highest. The Midwest had the lowest average annual unemployment rate in 2010 at 7.7, followed by the East at 8.4. The Western and Southern regions both had annual rates of 9.3.

In addition to elevated unemployment rates, people are receiving benefits longer. Based on U.S. Department of Labor reports, the average amount of time individuals received unemployment bene-

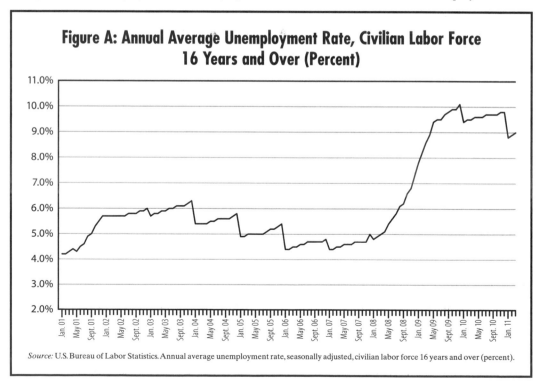

Figure A: Annual Average Unemployment Rate, Civilian Labor Force 16 Years and Over (Percent)

Source: U.S. Bureau of Labor Statistics. Annual average unemployment rate, seasonally adjusted, civilian labor force 16 years and over (percent).

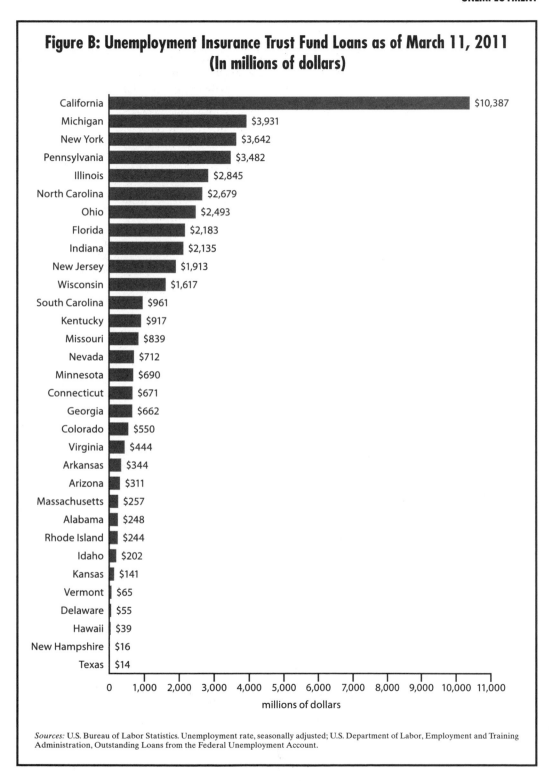

Figure B: Unemployment Insurance Trust Fund Loans as of March 11, 2011 (In millions of dollars)

California	$10,387
Michigan	$3,931
New York	$3,642
Pennsylvania	$3,482
Illinois	$2,845
North Carolina	$2,679
Ohio	$2,493
Florida	$2,183
Indiana	$2,135
New Jersey	$1,913
Wisconsin	$1,617
South Carolina	$961
Kentucky	$917
Missouri	$839
Nevada	$712
Minnesota	$690
Connecticut	$671
Georgia	$662
Colorado	$550
Virginia	$444
Arkansas	$344
Arizona	$311
Massachusetts	$257
Alabama	$248
Rhode Island	$244
Idaho	$202
Kansas	$141
Vermont	$65
Delaware	$55
Hawaii	$39
New Hampshire	$16
Texas	$14

millions of dollars

Sources: U.S. Bureau of Labor Statistics. Unemployment rate, seasonally adjusted; U.S. Department of Labor, Employment and Training Administration, Outstanding Loans from the Federal Unemployment Account.

fits was 37.1 weeks in February 2011—more than double the average duration of unemployment when the recession began in December 2007 and up from 29.3 weeks a year before. Those workers considered to be "long term unemployed"—jobless for 27 weeks or more—made up 43.9 percent of the unemployed in February, essentially unchanged from January but up from 39.3 percent a year before.

State Unemployment Trust Fund Loans Have Been Exhausted

Since the beginning of the Great Recession in 2007, states have struggled to continue paying unemployment benefits to thousands of citizens month after month. Eventually, many states ran out of money to pay those benefits and were forced to turn to the federal government for help. The Federal Unemployment Account allows states to obtain loans to make sure the flow of unemployment benefit dollars remains uninterrupted even if states are fiscally struggling.

According to the Department of Labor, at the end of January 2010, 26 states were borrowing money from the Federal Unemployment Account to help pay increasing claims for unemployment insurance benefits, with outstanding loans then totaling more than $30 billion. By March 18, 2011, 32 states plus the Virgin Islands were borrowing nearly $45.7 billion. By the end of 2010, Maryland, New Hampshire, South Dakota, Tennessee and Texas had repaid their loans in full, but New Hampshire and Texas have borrowed more since the beginning of 2011.

The Labor Department estimates by the fourth quarter of 2013, as many as 40 states may need to borrow more than $90 billion to fund their unemployment programs and those loans may take a decade or more to pay off. California and Michigan are the top borrowers of federal funds, with a combined total of more than $14.3 billion in loans.

Sustained high unemployment affects unemployment insurance trust funds in two primary ways—decreased supply and increased demand. More people need unemployment benefits for longer, increasing the money going out, while fewer people are paying into the reserves through payroll tax collections, draining the supply of funds coming in.

The Bill Comes Due

Until the end of 2010, a provision in the American Recovery and Reinvestment Act delayed interest from accruing on state unemployment loans.

Now, that provision has expired and interest payments will become due in September 2011 at a rate of nearly 4.1 percent. When President Obama unveiled his 2012 budget in February, it included a provision that would give states a two-year respite from automatic tax increases and interest payments on unemployment insurance loans. The status of that proposal remains unclear amid heated Congressional debates over the federal budget.

Failure to extend an interest or tax-increase moratorium could jeopardize or stall economic recovery—states have and will continue to raise state taxes on employers to regain trust fund solvency and to avoid automatic federal tax increases. States also must find nearly $1.7 billion for interest repayment in their already stressed budgets: The Center on Budget and Policy Priorities is projecting shortfalls totaling $112 billion for fiscal year 2012.

To start paying down their debt before an interest payment comes due, states are evaluating their current tax rates and making changes. In Delaware, that means the state's employers will find a new bill in the mail this year. The state has borrowed less than $41 million so far—less than 1 percent of what larger states like California have borrowed—but Tom MacPherson, director of the unemployment insurance division at the state Department of Labor, estimates that number will eventually grow to around $76 million. When the state's unemployment trust fund became insolvent, it triggered an automatic "temporary emergency employer assessment," which means the state's employers will be billed up to $11.50 per employee this year.

"Although this provision has been a part of Delaware unemployment law for over 20 years, this is the first time that we have actually had to use it," said MacPherson. According to him, that equals an interest payment that is a little more than $3.1 million for his state, which would come due Sept. 30, 2011. In 2008, Delaware increased the taxable wage base for the first time in 20 years—from $8,500 to $10,500—but it is likely no new changes are on the horizon.

In August 2011, Connecticut will begin charging businesses a special assessment equal to about $40 million—or around $40 per employee. The state could eventually borrow more than $1 billion to keep its unemployment program afloat, bringing total interest costs to a projected $100 million.

Florida has borrowed more than $2 billion so far and continues to borrow more each month. Florida's unemployment taxes have nearly tripled this year and the minimum tax employers pay will more than double again in 2012. The state will have to pay out up to $61 million in interest charges in September.

In Indiana, state legislators are trying to get borrowing under control by both cutting unemployment benefits and raising employer insurance premiums. Under House Bill 1450, which was signed into law earlier this year, average weekly payouts for unemployment benefits were cut by more than 20 percent, down from the previous average of $283, and reduces eligibility for seasonal employees. Employer premiums will also increase under the bill, but will not be as high as previously scheduled under a law passed two years ago. At the end of March, the state had borrowed nearly $2.2 billion.

Gov. Earl Ray Tomblin of West Virginia—one of the few states that have not yet had to borrow money—has proposed the state use rainy day funds to replenish the state's unemployment account so that it won't face a big interest bill later.

Texas has also taken a pre-emptive approach: The state sold $2 billion in bonds that it used to pay down the state's debt at the end of 2010. The interest rate on the bond is about half the rate it would be paying the federal government. According to Ann Hatchitt, director of communications for the Texas Workforce Commission, bond sales allow Texas to have more control over the interest rate and the payback period for any debt necessary to replenish the trust fund and may limit the need for tax increases. "By issuing bonds over a seven-year period, we can minimize the impact of rising tax rates for Texas employers," said Hatchitt. Although the state paid off its previous debt in 2010, the state has since borrowed more, owing $14.3 million at the end of March 2011.

Paying interest to the federal government is a difficult pill to swallow for states as they struggle to balance their budgets in one of the most challenging fiscal situations in memory. During The Council of State Governments' 2010 National Conference in Providence, R.I., the Executive Committee passed a resolution in support of extending interest relief on unemployment loans. The resolution urges Congress to delay interest accrual on state loans from the Federal Unemployment Account until states have recovered from the impact of the recent recession.

In addition to CSG's resolution, governors from 14 states wrote a letter to Congress at the end of 2010, also urging the federal government to extend the interest moratorium for another two years.

"Extending the interest-free loans would allow states to avoid increasing payroll taxes, reducing benefits, or both, while the economic recovery continues," the letter said.

As state leaders work to regain solvency in their unemployment programs while addressing the myriad other fiscal concerns in their states, it is uncertain whether Congress will take action to extend the interest moratorium or offer states other relief. It is certain, however, that states face a long road ahead to recovery.

About the Author

Jennifer Burnett, senior research analyst, joined The Council of State Governments in 2006. She coordinates the research efforts at CSG, including requests for information from members, analysis and presentation of data—particularly public access to interactive online databases—and reports on emerging state policy trends. Burnett manages *States Perform*, a website that provides users with access to customizable and up-to-date comparative performance measurement data for 50 states in six key areas.

Prior to joining CSG, Burnett was a research associate at the University of Kentucky Center for Business and Economic Research and a legislative aide for a member of Canadian Parliament.

She holds bachelor's degrees in economics and finance from the University of Kentucky, a master's degree from the Patterson School of Diplomacy and International Commerce at the University of Kentucky and a juris doctor from the Salmon P. Chase College of Law. Her areas of expertise include: tracking fiscal and economic trends, performance management and measurement, tax policy, state budgets, income trends, unemployment insurance, surveys, evaluations and data collection and analysis.

State Chief Administrators:
The Lynchpins in State Government Reform

By Paul Campbell and Michael E. Snyder

State governments are facing a fiscal crisis, the worst since the Great Depression. Unprecedented challenges seem overwhelming when change requires working with state bureaucracies so large and entrenched that state administrators are unable to affect meaningful improvements. State administrators are, in fact, an integral part of state reform.

Introduction

Does management matter in the public sector? Norma Riccucci, a professor of public administration at Rutgers University, writes in her award-winning book that, "Although there is abundant evidence that management makes a difference in the operations and productivity of public sector bureaucracies, there is another body of literature purporting that management does not matter. This research paints a very pessimistic picture of the ability of administrators and managers to redirect the juggernaut of modern society—large, entrenched bureaucracies."[1]

If better management can help states restore fiscal stability, can it also help convince the public that tax dollars are being spent wisely? Recent studies, including several from the Pew Center on the States, show the general public is losing faith in the state and federal governments' ability to manage itself effectively.[2]

The National Association of State Chief Administrators, known as NASCA, believes management does matter and state chief administrators can play a significant role in reforming and restoring the public's faith in government. Eggers and Campbell add that the "... issue of trust transcends the mere balancing of budgets ... and the public seems skeptical of the competence and integrity of their public leaders."[3] NASCA believes effective management of the core business functions for any organization, public or private, will determine the overall performance and efficiency of the entire organization.

Former Georgia Gov. Sonny Perdue set out in 2002 to reform several state administrative functions with the goal of making Georgia one of the best managed states within five years.[4] Perdue was named as one of the "2010 Public Officials of the Year" by *Governing* magazine because of his business-like management of state operations and his approach to running some functions of

government like a business.[5] State chief administrators across the country can use their business expertise to support major reform initiatives that can dramatically improve the operations of state government.

Defining State Chief Administrators and their Role in Government

Responsibilities of a chief administrator vary greatly from state to state. The most commonly held view of the position's responsibilities is the management and delivery of a state's administrative or business functions on behalf of other state agencies. In other words, the chief administrator runs the back office business functions of state government. These functions include roughly 60 different services across all 50 states.[6] As a result, chief administrators have been at the center of a move in state government toward shared services and consolidation over the past decade.[7]

Throughout the past 10 years, many states have looked to the shared-services model when organizing the core business functions of state government. According to a survey on shared services in state and local government conducted by Government Technology, the most common reason for shared services is saving money.[8] The model has no doubt played, and continues to play, a significant role in the management philosophy of state government. Moreover, whether part of a shared services strategy or not, agency consolidations have been used to save money and shrink government. Since 2009 alone, at least 17 states have consolidated or eliminated agencies that have been identified as duplicative or nonessential.[9]

Throughout all the consolidations and reorganizations, however, the old axiom remains true: To know one state is to know one state. This holds especially true when trying to describe the various responsibilities of state chief administrators.

The type of functions that fall under the jurisdiction of chief administrators are diverse and numerous. NASCA identifies roughly 60 different functions, not counting miscellaneous programs and boards that are often relegated to a chief administrator's department. Yet, despite such a large number of functions, the average number of functions a state chief administrator is responsible for is only 15, which illustrates the diversity of responsibilities among the position in the states. Administrative agencies in Florida (25 functions), New Jersey (23 functions), Alaska (22 functions), Kentucky (21 functions) and Louisiana (21 functions) are responsible for the most functions. Conversely, agencies in Maryland and Texas, both with six functions, have the fewest number of responsibilities.

Despite this diversity in responsibilities, there are some common trends. Of the more than 60 functions state chief administrators face, many share a predominant set of common responsibilities; the most common functions are procurement services (44), building and facility maintenance (43), and construction (40). More than 30 chief administrators are responsible for managing the state's vehicle fleet (36), auctioning state and federal surplus property (36 and 30 states, respectively), leasing agreements (33), printing (31) and risk management/state liability insurance (30).

At least half the state chief administrators are responsible for human resources (28), health insurance benefits (25), statewide accounting services (25) and information technology (26). Additional major functions managed by less than half the chief administrators, but by more than 10, include supplies purchasing (20), state budget services (18), nature conservation (13), and telecommunications (12). Chief administrators are required to manage roughly 40 additional responsibilities, such as the state audit (12), archives and record keeping (9), or wireless communications (8).

The role of a state chief administrator can be broken down into four categories based on their common primary functions—infrastructure, personnel, finance management and general services.

The infrastructure category includes those chief administrators whose primary responsibilities are maintaining state infrastructure, including construction, maintenance, telecommunications and information technology, and building and grounds management. The personnel category includes chiefs with primary responsibilities around human resources, health care benefits, professional development and insurance. The finance management category includes departments that primarily focus on services related to accounting, budget, debt, audit and other similar financial services. Finally, the general services category is for all other services, such as printing, mail, fleet, archiving, storage, travel assistance and procurement.

Table A:
Common Responsibilities of State Chief Administrators

Area	Percentage of members that have the responsibility
General Services	
Procurement	88%
Fleet	72
Mail	70
Printing	62
Supplies	40
Infrastructure	
Facilities	86
Construction	80
Information Technology	52
Telecommunications	24
Finance Management	
Risk Management	60
Accounting	50
State Insurance	50
State Budget	36
Audit	24
Personnel	
Human Resources	56
Benefits (Health)	50
Professional Development	36

Source: Compiled from "Areas of Responsibility for NASCA MEMBERS 2010" database.

The data also show some interesting regional patterns in the responsibilities of state chief administrators.[10]

Tables A and B show that general services are significant responsibilities compared to the other categories. Infrastructure is a close second, but

Table B:
Common Responsibilities, by Region, of State Chief Administrators

Region	General Services	Infrastructure	Finance Management	Personnel
West (13 states)	85%	54%	38%	54%
Midwest (12 states)	92	50	42	67
Northeast (9 states)	78	33	44	67
South (16 states)	69	31	25	56

Source: Compiled from "Primary Functions of NASCA MEMBERS 2010" database.

only general services manage to beat out all other categories for every region of the country in terms of the number of state chief administrative offices with this responsibility. Personnel is the next most common category—it's the second most common responsibility in all regions except the West, where the percentage is tied with infrastructure. Financial management responsibilities are the least common, with less than 50 percent of the chief administrators having those responsibilities in all regions.

This information is helpful to understand who is accountable within each state for many key business functions. The more important role of a state chief administrator, however, is the way they manage these core business functions to support major statewide reforms.

Primary Responsibilities and How They Impact Overall State Functionality

The chief administrator's greatest impact on the operations of state government will not come from simply reducing the cost of administrative functions. For example, administrative functions typically represent about 10 percent of the total state budget.[11] If a savings initiative targeted at the administrative functions saved 10 percent, that 10 percent equals 1 percent of the overall budget.[12] Cuts in a state chief administrator's budget, therefore, are simply not large enough to have an appreciable effect on a state deficit. While savings anywhere are helpful these days, states will not dig themselves out of their budget holes by expanding video conferencing and sourcing commodities alone.

Massive budget cuts alone are also not likely to restore public faith in state government. A Pew Center on the States study found citizens "... are more likely to say their elected leaders ... could deliver services more efficiently than to complain that state government is too big."[13] Therefore, to restore fiscal stability as well as public trust in state government, states will need to find innovative ways to reinvent government.

The chief administrator's most important role is to support and at times lead, major change management initiatives that reinvent government. If any state wants to tackle real game changers—such as privatization, true shared services or public-private partnerships—all paths lead through the state chief administrator's office. For example, any public-private partnerships will require a much more sophisticated approach to procurement, where 44 of the chief administrators have primary responsibility.[14] Innovative new approaches will require a more highly trained and skilled work force and 27 state chief administrators manage human resources. Any successful new program or initiative must have strong information technology support involving 25 of the administrator's offices. In 15 states,[15] the state chiefs are responsible for all three functions. In the end, the ability of the state chief administrator and his team to support major management initiatives will determine the overall success of any state reforms.

Moreover, the state chief administrator, through effective execution of reforms, can act as an example and help restore the public's faith in government. The Pew study on public trust confirms a growing frustration with government.[16] This frustration will not be curtailed by political rhetoric coupled with a token trimming of state budgets. If people are to have faith in government again, government needs new solutions to old problems and the public needs

Table C:
Primary Functions of State Chief Administrators

State	State Chief Administrative Office	General Services					Infrastructure			
		Procurement	Fleet	Mail	Printing	Supplies	Facilities	Construction	Information Technology	Telecommunications
Alabama	Dept. of Finance	★	★	★.	...	...	★	★	★	★
Alaska	Dept. of Administration	★	...	...	...	★	...	...	★	★
Arizona	Dept. of Administration	★	★	...	★	★	★	★	★	★
Arkansas	Dept. of Finance and Administration	★	...	...	...	...	...	...	★	...
California	Dept. of General Services	★	★	★	★	...	★	★	★	...
Colorado	Dept. of Personnel and Administration	★	★	★	★	...	★	...	...	...
Connecticut	Dept. of Administrative Services	★	★	★	★	★	...	★	...	...
Delaware	Office of Management and Budget	...	★	★	★	★	★	★	...	...
Florida	Dept. of Management Services	★	★	...	...	★	★	★	★	★
Georgia	Dept. of Administrative Services	★	★	★	★	★	...	...	...	...
Hawaii	Dept. of Accounting and General Services	...(c)	★	★	...	...	★	★	★	★
Idaho	Dept. of Administration	...	...	★	★	★	★	★	★	...
Illinois	Dept. of Central Management Services	★	★(d)	★	★	★	...	...	...	★
Indiana	Dept. of Administration	★(e)	★	★	★	...	★	★	...	...
Iowa	Dept. of Administrative Services	★	★	★	...	...	★	★	★	...
Kansas	Dept. of Administration	★	★(f)	...	★	...	★	★	...	★
Kentucky	Finance and Administration Cabinet	★	★	★	★	...	★	★	★	★
Louisiana	Division of Administration	★	...	★	★	...	★	...	★	★
Maine	Bureau of General Services	★	★	★	★	★	★	★	...	...
Maryland	Dept. of General Services	★	...	...	...	...	★	★	...	...
Massachusetts	Office for Administration and Finance	★	...	★	★	★	★	★	★	...
Michigan	Dept. of Technology, Management and Budget	★	★	★	★	★	★	★	★	...
Minnesota	Dept. of Administration	★	★	★	...	★	★	★	...	...
Mississippi	Dept. of Finance and Administration	★	★	...	...	...	★	★	...	...
Missouri	Office of Administration	★	★	...	★	...	★	★	...	★
Montana	Dept. of Administration	...	...	★	★	...	★	★	★	...
Nebraska	Dept. of Administrative Services	★	★	★	★	★	★	★	★	...
Nevada	Dept. of Administration	...	★	★	...	★	★	...	...	...
New Hampshire	Dept. of Administrative Services	★	★	★	★	...	★	★	...	...
New Jersey	Dept. of the Treasury	★	★	★	★	★	★	★	★	★
New Mexico	General Services Dept.	★	★	...	★	...	★	★	...	...
New York	Office of General Services	★	★	★	★	...	★	★	...	...
North Carolina	Dept. of Administration	★	★	★	...	...	★	★	...	...
North Dakota	Office of Management and Budget	★	...	...	★	★	★(i)	★(i)	...	...
Ohio	Dept. of Administrative Services	★	★	★	★	...	★	★	★	...
Oklahoma	Dept. of Central Services	★	★	★	★	...	★	★	...	...
Oregon	Dept. of Administrative Services	★	★	...	★	...	★	★	★	...
Pennsylvania	Office of Administration	...	...	...	...	...	...	...	★	★
Rhode Island	Dept. of Administration	★	...	★	...	...	★	★	★	★
South Carolina	Budget and Control Board	★	...	★	...	...	★	★	★	...
South Dakota	South Dakota Bureau of Administration	★	★	★	★	★	★	★	...	...
Tennessee	Dept. of General Services	★	★	★	★	...	★	...	...	...
Texas	Facilities Commission	★	...	...	...	...	★	★	...	...
Utah	Dept. of Administrative Services	★	★	★	★	...	★	★	...	...
Vermont	Agency of Administration	★	★	★	★	...	★	★	...	...
Virginia	Dept. of General Services	★	★	★	...	★	★	★	...	...
Washington	Dept. of General Administration	★	★	★	...	...	★	★	...	...
West Virginia	Dept. of Administration	★	...	...	...	...	★	★	★	...
Wisconsin	Dept. of Administration	★	★	★	★	...	★	★	★	...
Wyoming	Dept. of Administration and Information	★	★	★	...	...	★	★	★	...
Total Number of Functions		44	36	35	31	20	43	40	26	12

See footnotes at end of table.

Primary Functions of State Chief Administrators — Continued

State	State Chief Administrative Office	Finance Management					Personnel	
		Risk Management	Accounting	State Budget	State Insurance	Audit	Human Resources	Professional Dev. Training
Alabama	Dept. of Finance	★	...	★	...	...	★	★
Alaska	Dept. of Administration	★	★	...	...	...	★	★
Arizona	Dept. of Administration	★	★	...	...	...	★	★
Arkansas	Dept. of Finance and Administration	...	...	★	...	...	★(a)	...
California	Dept. of General Services	★	...	...	★	...	...	...
Colorado	Dept. of Personnel and Administration	★	★	...	...	...	★	★
Connecticut	Dept. of Administrative Services	...	★	...	★(b)	...	★	...
Delaware	Office of Management and Budget	...	...	★	★	...	★	★
Florida	Dept. of Management Services	...	...	...	...	★	★	★
Georgia	Dept. of Administrative Services	★	...	...	★	...	...	...
Hawaii	Dept. of Accounting and General Services	...	★	...	...	★	...	...
Idaho	Dept. of Administration	★	...	...	★	...	...	...
Illinois	Dept. of Central Management Services	★	...	...	...	...	★	...
Indiana	Dept. of Administration	...	...	...	...	...	...	...
Iowa	Dept. of Administrative Services	★	★	...	...	...	★	★
Kansas	Dept. of Administration	...	★	★	...	...	★	...
Kentucky	Finance and Administration Cabinet	★	★	...	★	★	...	...
Louisiana	Division of Administration	★	★(g)	★	...	...	★(g)	★
Maine	Bureau of General Services	★	...	...	★	...	...	...
Maryland	Dept. of General Services	...	...	...	...	...	...	...
Massachusetts	Office for Administration and Finance	...	...	★	...	...	★	...
Michigan	Dept. of Technology, Management and Budget	...	★	★	...	★	...	...
Minnesota	Dept. of Administration	★	★	...	★	...	★	...
Mississippi	Dept. of Finance and Administration	...	★	★	★	...	★	...
Missouri	Office of Administration	★	★	★	★	...	★	★
Montana	Dept. of Administration	★	★	...	★	★	★	★
Nebraska	Dept. of Administrative Services	★	★	★	★	...	★	...
Nevada	Dept. of Administration	★	...	★	★	★	...	★(h)
New Hampshire	Dept. of Administration Services	★	★	★	★	...	★	...
New Jersey	Dept. of the Treasury	★	★	★	...	★	...	★
New Mexico	General Services Dept.	★	...	...	...	...	...	...
New York	Office of General Services	...	...	...	★	...	...	...
North Carolina	Dept. of Administration	...	...	...	...	...	★	...
North Dakota	Office of Management and Budget	★	★	★	★(b)	...	★	★
Ohio	Dept. of Administrative Services	★	...	...	★	...	★	★
Oklahoma	Dept. of Central Services	★	...	...	...	...	...	...
Oregon	Dept. of Administrative Services	★	★	★	★	★(j)	...	★
Pennsylvania	Office of Administration	...	...	...	...	...	★	★
Rhode Island	Dept. of Administration	★	★	★	★(b)	★	★	...
South Carolina	Budget and Control Board	...	...	...	★	...	★	...
South Dakota	South Dakota Bureau of Administration	★	...	...	★	...	...	...
Tennessee	Dept. of General Services	...	...	...	...	...	...	...
Texas	Facilities Commission	...	...	...	...	...	...	...
Utah	Dept. of Administrative Services	★	★	...	★	...	...	...
Vermont	Agency of Administration	★	★	...	★	★	★	...
Virginia	Dept. of General Services	...	...	...	...	...	...	...
Washington	Dept. of General Administration	...	...	...	...	...	...	...
West Virginia	Dept. of Administration	★	★	...	★	★	★	★
Wisconsin	Dept. of Administration	...	★	★	...	...	...	...
Wyoming	Dept. of Administration and Information	★	...	★	★	...	★	...
Total Number of Functions		30	25	18	25	12	28	17

See footnotes at end of table.

Primary Functions of State Chief Administrators — Continued

Source: Compiled from "Areas of Responsibility for NASCA MEMBERS 2010" database.

Note: Total Number of Functions is by definition the total number of each area of responsibility. It does not include attached boards and commissions that may peform some of these functions.

Key:

★ — Responsible for function.
... — Not responsible for function.
(a) Employment only.
(b) Workers' compensation only.
(c) This function is performed by the Procurement Policy Board, which is attached to the Department of Accounting and General Services.
(d) Repairs and maintenance only.
(e) Except the Indiana Department of Transportation.
(f) Through Enterprise.
(g) Limited agency coverage.
(h) In the area of budgeting.
(i) Capitol building only.
(j) Currently unstaffed and being revised.

Procurement — Aid or management of other state agencies in purchasing a wide variety of goods or services.

Fleet — Department that covers management of fleet services including both state-owned vehicles and fleet services provided by private vehicle rental companies.

Mail — Provision of interagency general mail services, and sometimes managing the distribution of mail from other mail services so that they reach the proper agency.

Printing — Responsibility to provide general printing and copying needs for state agencies.

Supplies — The provision or aid in purchasing general supplies, general of that nature of office supplies, for other state agencies.

Facilities — General maintenance and upkeep of state property, such as providing groundskeeping, general maintenance, and utilities.

Construction — Provides review and management of construction contracts for the construction of state facilities and infrastructure.

Information Technology — Provision and administration of information technology infrastructure and services. Includes elements related to provision of computer networking, Internet, and computer software support.

Telecommunications — Provision and management of the state's communications infrastructure.

Risk Management — Office that aids other state agencies by reducing risk to state assets and finances, and often includes state insurance against liability claims and workers' compensation.

Accounting — General accounting process such as preparing and maintaining financial reports.

State Budget — Responsible for the state budget, and providing budget proposals for the Governor's office.

State Insurance — Administration of state liability insurance for state property and personnel, including state liability for workers' compensation claims.

Audit — Oversight over other state agency accounting, budget, or other functions as an attempt to eliminate government waste and prevent fraud.

Human Resources — A resource agency for state employees to get information and assistance with a wide range of topics, but generally include payroll, hiring, retirement benefits, and insurance.

Professional Development — Agencies provide periodic training sessions to help state employees develop job-related skills, often related to management skills.

to see managers in government can successfully execute these new strategies. As Thomas Edison said, "vision without execution is hallucination." This is the area where the management skills of chief administrators will play a critical role in substantially improving the functionality of state operations.

Georgia's approach is again worth noting. Gov. Perdue created the Commission for a New Georgia and included senior business executives that were influential leaders in the state.[17] He added a chief operating officer to the state, a role that many chief administrators already play within state government. Georgia's administrator was recruited based on his "extensive expertise in purchasing and supply chain management."[18] "It's an approach to government that allowed Perdue to keep the state's fiscal house in order in the midst of the worst financial crisis to hit the nation — and Georgia — in generations."[19]

"What are the skills necessary for an SCA to play such a transformative role? Is the job more operations or politics?" One could argue the state chief administrator is the least political job in the governor's cabinet because it's a pure operations role. On the other hand, when managing large contracts, hiring and budgeting, a chief administrator should understand the political landscape if he or she plans to help change the view. This is the primary reason the role can be so difficult to fill. Governors must find someone with an understanding of both the business and political world. As Eggers and Campbell point out, "Our nation's new governors take office at a difficult time. These newcomers have to balance their budgets, but they also need to reform how state government operates."[20] In 2011, with dozens of new chief administrators entering state government, and nearly every state headed toward a fiscal cliff,[21] the administrators must be effective managers with a track record of successful innovation.

Conclusion

The critical business functions state chief administrators manage places them squarely at the center of state operations. The question is whether they will use their role to push for real reforms in state government. As state government wrestles with the worst fiscal climate since World War II, officials will have real opportunities to challenge the status quo and execute real change. State chief administrators can play a central role in that transformation.

Notes

[1] Norma M. Riccucci, *How Management Matters: Street Level Bureaucrats and Welfare Reform*. (Washington, D.C.: Georgetown University, 2005).

(Norma M. Riccucci is a professor in the Graduate Department of Public Administration at Rutgers University, Newark; and author of "Managing Diversity in Public Sector Workforces" and "Unsung Heroes: Federal Executives Making a Difference." "How Management Matters" draws upon two years of personal interviews and national surveys to examine how public management matters in government organizations.)

[2] Pew Research Center for the People and the Press, "Distrust, Discontent, Anger, and Partisan Rancor: The People and Their Government," (2010). *http://pewre search.org/pubs/1569/trust-in-government-distrust-discon tent-anger-partisan-rancor*.

Pew Center on the States, "Facing facts: Public Attitudes and Fiscal Realities in Five Stressed States," (2010). *http://www.pewcenteronthestates.org/report_detail.aspx?id=60803*.

[3] William D. Eggers and Robert N. Campbell III, (2010). "How New Governors Can Renew Public Trust," *Governing*. *http://www.governing.com/columns/mgmt-insights/new-governors-renew-public-trust.html*.

[4] Michael D. Keats and Jason L. Owens. "Procurement in the State of Georgia." Presented at the National Association of State Chief Administrator's Institute on Management and Leadership, Atlanta, (2010).

[5] "Top Officials of the Year Named by *Governing* Magazine," *Governing*. (2010) *http://media.navigatored.com/documents/POY+2010+Press+Release.pdf*.

[6] "Areas of Responsibilities for NASCA Members," *National Association of State Chief Administrators*. (Available soon) at *http://www.nasca.org/Pages/resources.aspx*.

[7] National Governors Association, NGA Center for Best Practices, *State Government Redesign Efforts 2009 and 2010*, (2010). *http://www.nga.org/Files/pdf/1010STATE GOVTREDESIGN.PDF*.

[8] Survey on Shared Services in State and Local Government, (2007). *http://www.oracle.com/us/industries/046114.pdf*.

[9] National Governors Association, NGA Center for Best Practices, *State Government Redesign Efforts 2009 and 2010*, (2010), 14-6. *http://www.nga.org/Files/pdf/1010 STATEGOVTREDESIGN.PDF*. Consolidations do not always accomplish the stated goal of creating efficiencies. As Petronius noted in 210 B.C., "we trained hard, but it seemed that every time we were beginning to form up into teams we would be reorganized. ... I was to learn later in life that we tend to meet any new situation by reorganizing and what a wonderful method it can be for creating the illusion of progress while producing confusion, inefficiency and demoralization." As found in a recent McKinsey Study, "the tactics used most by the most successful organizations suggest that all organizations implementing a redesign would benefit from explaining to employees how the new design works, ensuring that systems and processes support it, and winning hearts and minds." See: Giancarlo Ghislanzoni, Stephen Heidari-Robinson, and Martin Jermiin, "Taking Organizational Redesigns From Plan to Practice: McKinsey Global Survey Results," *McKinsey Quarterly: The Online Journal of McKinsey & Company*, (2010). *http://www.mckin seyquarterly.com/Taking_organizational_redesigns_from_ plan_to_practice_McKinsey_Global_Survey_results_2721*.

[10] State chief administrators might not be counted as having a significant emphasis for a category if that administrator only covered a minimum number of the responsibilities that constitute that category. Each state chief administrator was ranked according to the level of focus in a category by counting the number of functions under that category that the state has responsibility for. If a state chief administrator was responsible for about half of the functions of that category it was counted as having a significant emphasis on that category. Please contact the National Association of State Chief Administrators at *http://www.nasca.org/Pages/resources.aspx* for the most updated comprehensive list of each SCA's responsibilities.

[11] Bill Bott and Ken Miller, "Worse, Slower, Cheaper, But ..." *Governing*, (2010). *http://www.governing.com/blogs/public-great/The-False-Promises-of-Consolidation-But.html*.

[12] Ibid.

[13] Pew Center on the States. "Facing facts: Public Attitudes and Fiscal Realities in Five Stressed States," (2010). *http://www.pewcenteronthestates.org/report_detail.aspx?id=60803*.

[14] Stephen Goldsmith and William D. Eggers, *Governing by Network: The New Shape of the Public Sector*. (Washington, D.C.: Brookings Institution, 2004).

[15] AK, AL, AZ, FL, IA, KS, MA, MO, NE, OH, RI, SC, VT, WV and WY.

[16] Pew Research Center for the People and the Press, "Distrust, Discontent, Anger, and Partisan Rancor: The People and Their Government," (2010). *http://pewre search.org/pubs/1569/trust-in-government-distrust-discon tent-anger-partisan-rancor*.

[17] "The Businessman: Sonny Perdue," (2010) *Governing*. *http://www.governing.com/poy/sonny-perdue.html*.

[18] See note 4.

[19] See note 15.

[20] See note 3.

[21] National Association of State Budget Officers, *The Fiscal Survey of the States: An Update of State Fiscal Conditions*, (2010), *http://www.nasbo.org/LinkClick.aspx?fileti cket=C6q1M3kxaEY%3d&tabid=38*.

About the Authors

Paul Campbell is a member of the Board of Directors for NASCA. He served as chief administrator in Illinois and previously as a federal agent and prosecutor. His private sector experience includes serving as partner with the law firm DLA Piper and national head of business development for Unitedhealthcare's Public Sector Group state market. Campbell has his M.B.A. from Northwestern University.

Michael E. Snyder is a researcher for NASCA. He has also worked for the University of Illinois at Springfield's Department of Political Science as a research assistant and assistant editor. Snyder holds an M.A. in political science from the University of Illinois at Springfield.

Table 8.1
SUMMARY OF STATE GOVERNMENT EMPLOYMENT: 1953–2009

| | Employment (in thousands) | | | | | | Monthly payrolls (in millions of dollars) | | | Average monthly earnings of full-time employees | | |
| | Total, full-time and part-time | | | Full-time equivalent | | | | | | | | |
Year (October)	All	Education	Other	All	Education	Other	All	Education	Other	All	Education	Other
1953	1,082	294	788	966	211	755	$278.6	$73.5	$205.1	$289	$320	$278
1954	1,149	310	839	1,024	222	802	300.7	78.9	221.8	294	325	283
1955	1,199	333	866	1,081	244	837	325.9	88.5	237.4	302	334	290
1956	1,268	353	915	1,136	250	886	366.5	108.8	257.7	321	358	309
1957 (April)	1,300	375	925	1,153	257	896	372.5	106.1	266.4	320	355	309
1958	1,408	406	1,002	1,259	284	975	446.5	123.4	323.1	355	416	333
1959	1,454	443	1,011	1,302	318	984	485.4	136.0	349.4	373	427	352
1960	1,527	474	1,053	1,353	332	1,021	524.1	167.7	356.4	386	439	365
1961	1,625	518	1,107	1,435	367	1,068	586.2	192.4	393.8	409	482	383
1962	1,680	555	1,126	1,478	389	1,088	634.6	201.8	432.8	429	518	397
1963	1,775	602	1,173	1,558	422	1,136	696.4	230.1	466.3	447	545	410
1964	1,873	656	1,217	1,639	460	1,179	761.1	257.5	503.6	464	560	427
1965	2,028	739	1,289	1,751	508	1,243	849.2	290.1	559.1	484	571	450
1966	2,211	866	1,344	1,864	575	1,289	975.2	353.0	622.2	522	614	483
1967	2,335	940	1,395	1,946	620	1,326	1,105.5	406.3	699.3	567	666	526
1968	2,495	1,037	1,458	2,085	694	1,391	1,256.7	477.1	779.6	602	687	544
1969	2,614	1,112	1,501	2,179	746	1,433	1,430.5	554.5	876.1	655	743	597
1970	2,755	1,182	1,573	2,302	803	1,499	1,612.2	630.3	981.9	700	797	605
1971	2,832	1,223	1,609	2,384	841	1,544	1,741.7	681.5	1,060.2	731	826	686
1972	2,957	1,267	1,690	2,487	867	1,619	1,936.6	746.9	1,189.7	778	871	734
1973	3,013	1,280	1,733	2,547	887	1,660	2,158.2	822.2	1,336.0	843	952	805
1974	3,155	1,357	1,798	2,653	929	1,725	2,409.5	932.7	1,476.9	906	1,023	855
1975	3,271	1,400	1,870	2,744	952	1,792	2,652.7	1,021.7	1,631.1	964	1,080	909
1976	3,343	1,434	1,910	2,799	973	1,827	2,893.7	1,111.5	1,782.1	1,031	1,163	975
1977	3,491	1,484	2,007	2,903	1,005	1,898	3,194.6	1,234.4	1,960.1	1,096	1,237	1,031
1978	3,539	1,508	2,032	2,966	1,016	1,950	3,483.0	1,332.9	2,150.2	1,167	1,311	1,102
1979	3,699	1,577	2,122	3,072	1,046	2,026	3,869.3	1,451.4	2,417.9	1,257	1,399	1,193
1980	3,753	1,599	2,154	3,106	1,063	2,044	4,284.7	1,608.0	2,676.6	1,373	1,523	1,305
1981	3,726	1,603	2,123	3,087	1,063	2,024	4,667.5	1,768.0	2,899.5	1,507	1,671	1,432
1982	3,747	1,616	2,131	3,083	1,051	2,032	5,027.7	1,874.0	3,153.7	1,625	1,789	1,551
1983	3,816	1,666	2,150	3,116	1,072	2,044	5,345.5	1,989.0	3,357.0	1,711	1,850	1,640
1984	3,898	1,708	2,190	3,177	1,091	2,086	5,814.9	2,178.0	3,637.0	1,825	1,991	1,740
1985	3,984	1,764	2,220	2,990	945	2,046	6,328.6	2,433.7	3,884.9	1,935	2,155	1,834
1986	4,068	1,800	2,267	3,437	1,256	2,181	6,801.4	2,583.4	4,226.9	2,052	2,263	1,956
1987	4,115	1,804	2,310	3,491	1,264	2,227	7,297.8	2,758.3	4,539.5	2,161	2,396	2,056
1988	4,236	1,854	2,381	3,606	1,309	2,297	7,842.3	2,928.6	4,913.7	2,260	2,490	2,158
1989	4,365	1,925	2,440	3,709	1,360	2,349	8,443.1	3,175.0	5,268.1	2,372	2,627	2,259
1990	4,503	1,984	2,519	3,840	1,418	2,432	9,083.0	3,426.0	5,657.0	2,472	2,732	2,359
1991	4,521	1,999	2,522	3,829	1,375	2,454	9,437.0	3,550.0	5,887.0	2,479	2,530	2,433
1992	4,595	2,050	2,545	3,856	1,384	2,472	9,828.0	3,774.0	6,054.0	2,562	2,607	2,521
1993	4,673	2,112	2,562	3,891	1,436	2,455	10,288.2	3,999.3	6,288.9	2,722	3,034	2,578
1994	4,694	2,115	2,579	3,917	1,442	2,475	10,666.3	4,176.8	6,489.3	2,776	3,073	2,640
1995	4,719	2,120	2,598	3,971	1,469	2,502	10,926.5	4,173.3	6,753.2	2,854	3,138	2,725
1996	(a)	(a)	(a)	(a)	(a)	(a)	(a)	(a)	(a)	(a)	(a)	(a)
1997 (March)	4,733	2,114	2,619	3,987	1,484	2,503	11,413.1	4,372.0	7,041.1	2,968	3,251	2,838
1998 (March)	4,758	2,173	2,585	3,985	1,511	2,474	11,845.2	4,632.1	7,213.1	3,088	3,382	2,947
1999 (March)	4,818	2,229	2,588	4,034	1,541	2,493	12,564.1	4,957.0	7,607.7	3,236	3,544	3,087
2000 (March)	4,877	2,259	2,618	4,083	1,563	2,520	13,279.1	5,255.3	8,023.8	3,374	3,692	3,219
2001 (March)	4,985	2,329	2,656	4,173	1,615	2,559	14,136.3	5,620.7	8,515.6	3,521	3,842	3,362
2002 (March)	5,072	2,414	2,658	4,223	1,659	2,564	14,837.8	5,996.6	8,841.2	3,657	4,007	3,479
2003 (March)	5,043	2,413	2,630	4,191	1,656	2,534	15,116.4	6,154.4	8,962.0	3,751	4,115	3,566
2004 (March)	5,041	2,432	2,609	4,188	1,673	2,515	15,477.5	6,411.8	9,065.7	3,845	4,256	3,631
2005 (March)	5,078	2,459	2,620	4,209	1,684	2,525	16,061.6	6,668.9	9,392.6	3,966	4,390	3,745
2006 (March)	5,128	2,493	2,635	4,251	1,708	2,542	16,769.4	6,960.9	9,808.6	4,098	4,505	3,883
2007 (March)	5,200	2,538	2,663	4,307	1,740	2,566	17,788.7	7,418.9	10,369.9	4,276	4,670	4,063
2008 (March)	5,270	2,593	2,677	4,363	1,780	2,582	18,725.9	7,883.2	10,842.7	4,445	4,853	4,222
2009 (March)	5,329	2,648	2,681	4,399	1,814	2,585	19,388.1	8,277.1	11,110.9	4,565	5,007	4,320

Source: U.S. Census Bureau, 2009 Annual Survey of Public Employment and Payroll. For information on sampling and nonsampling errors and definitions, see http://www.census.gov/govs/apes/how_data_collected.html. Data users who create their own estimates from this table should cite the U.S. Census Bureau as the source of the original data only.
Note: Detail may not add to totals due to rounding.

Key:
(a) Due to a change in the reference period, from October to March, the October 1996 Annual Survey of Government Employment and Payroll was not concluded. This change in collection period was effective beginning with the March 1997 survey.

Table 8.2
EMPLOYMENT AND PAYROLLS OF STATE AND LOCAL GOVERNMENTS BY FUNCTION: MARCH 2009

Functions	All employees, full-time and part-time (in thousands)			March payrolls (in millions of dollars)			Average March earnings of full-time employees
	Total	State government	Local government	Total	State government	Local government	
All functions...	19,809	5,329	14,480	$70,108,428	$19,388,085	$50,720,343	$4,319
Education:							
Higher education	3,093	2,487	606	9,225,649	7,654,755	1,570,894	5,031
Instructional personnel only..........	1,104	811	293	4,320,444	3,485,145	835,299	6,869
Elementary/secondary schools..........	8,037	67	7,970	26,725,330	243,352	26,481,978	3,986
Instructional personnel only..........	5,431	47	5,383	21,018,414	198,389	20,820,025	4,483
Libraries...	194	1	193	433,039	1,886	431,153	3,611
Other education	95	95	0	379,041	379,041	0	4,393
Selected functions:							
Streets and highways...........................	560	240	320	2,205,974	1,016,003	1,189,971	4,106
Public welfare.....................................	549	247	303	1,946,356	886,704	1,059,652	3,752
Hospitals...	1,090	446	644	4,408,234	1,827,022	2,581,211	4,431
Police protection	1,017	107	909	4,797,253	542,689	4,254,564	5,136
Police officers.................................	732	68	665	3,881,652	395,404	3,486,247	5,517
Fire protection...................................	429	0	429	1,928,504	0	1,928,504	5,717
Firefighters only.............................	396	0	396	1,800,208	0	1,800,208	5,787
Natural resources	208	159	49	756,480	591,433	165,047	4,189
Correction...	763	489	274	3,061,453	1,970,057	1,091,396	4,085
Social insurance.................................	83	83	0	330,173	327,679	2,494	4,111
Financial admin.................................	432	173	258	1,699,966	720,565	979,401	4,300
Judicial and legal...............................	456	183	273	2,054,678	897,578	1,157,100	4,810
Other government admin.	429	62	366	1,234,182	256,352	977,830	4,429
Utilities	525	38	487	2,484,047	223,712	2,260,336	4,983
State liquor stores	10	10	0	24,338	24,338	0	3,263
Other and unallocable	1,839	443	1,396	6,413,732	1,824,919	4,588,813	4,199

Source: U.S. Census Bureau, 2009 Annual Survey of Public Employment and Payroll. For information on sampling and nonsampling errors and definitions, see *http://www.census.gov/govs/apes/how_data_collected.html.*

Data users who create their own estimates from this table should cite the U.S. Census Bureau as the source of the original data only.

Table 8.3
STATE AND LOCAL GOVERNMENT EMPLOYMENT, BY STATE: MARCH 2009

State or other jurisdiction	All employees (full-time and part-time)			Full-time equivalent employment		
	Total	State	Local	Total	State	Local
United States	19,808,604	5,329,022	14,479,582	16,807,109	4,399,190	12,407,919
Alabama	324,549	107,362	217,187	289,900	89,467	200,433
Alaska	62,721	29,372	33,349	53,861	26,183	27,678
Arizona	358,519	83,707	274,812	309,963	68,972	240,991
Arkansas	194,018	71,832	122,186	169,243	61,337	107,906
California	2,259,501	501,172	1,758,329	1,845,472	411,142	1,434,330
Colorado	330,520	95,677	234,843	275,823	72,778	203,045
Connecticut	231,997	81,256	150,741	195,917	66,498	129,419
Delaware	57,479	31,831	25,648	49,625	26,510	23,115
Florida	1,024,089	216,958	807,131	888,882	185,630	703,252
Georgia	597,690	150,212	447,478	533,992	122,582	411,410
Hawaii	91,822	75,482	16,340	75,478	60,041	15,437
Idaho	100,296	28,913	71,383	78,950	23,179	55,771
Illinois	805,580	162,135	643,445	661,922	136,542	525,380
Indiana	414,238	117,499	296,739	350,309	92,484	257,825
Iowa	231,968	68,814	163,154	182,385	52,288	130,097
Kansas	252,361	55,781	196,580	204,018	45,163	158,855
Kentucky	285,923	97,501	188,422	244,063	81,117	162,946
Louisiana	315,985	107,588	208,397	277,459	91,809	185,650
Maine	96,376	28,592	67,784	74,063	21,497	52,566
Maryland	340,908	94,789	246,119	303,630	89,511	214,119
Massachusetts	400,064	117,163	282,901	344,158	96,865	247,293
Michigan	601,223	183,131	418,092	482,579	142,924	339,655
Minnesota	356,926	96,282	260,644	284,579	80,536	204,043
Mississippi	218,327	65,102	153,225	194,738	57,773	136,965
Missouri	389,129	106,070	283,059	328,828	90,092	238,736
Montana	71,749	26,360	45,389	56,857	20,590	36,267
Nebraska	144,226	37,663	106,563	119,271	32,333	86,938
Nevada	136,228	35,958	100,270	116,651	29,517	87,134
New Hampshire	87,440	25,577	61,863	74,029	19,591	54,438
New Jersey	598,100	180,066	418,034	514,041	154,106	359,935
New Mexico	147,427	56,764	90,663	130,494	48,680	81,814
New York	1,422,282	293,424	1,128,858	1,251,498	257,490	994,008
North Carolina	654,349	174,624	479,725	562,657	147,895	414,762
North Dakota	55,605	23,699	31,906	42,281	17,667	24,614
Ohio	739,860	188,676	551,184	619,568	142,945	476,623
Oklahoma	256,276	90,242	166,034	221,134	72,198	148,936
Oregon	250,428	80,774	169,654	199,298	63,086	136,212
Pennsylvania	708,152	195,197	512,955	605,927	163,903	442,024
Rhode Island	62,001	24,483	37,518	53,033	19,669	33,364
South Carolina	287,223	89,816	197,407	257,243	77,261	179,982
South Dakota	61,842	18,406	43,436	47,074	14,053	33,021
Tennessee	369,075	100,377	268,698	329,715	84,387	245,328
Texas	1,584,754	347,601	1,237,153	1,430,094	300,112	1,129,982
Utah	187,350	65,334	122,016	141,615	51,606	90,009
Vermont	48,802	17,036	31,766	39,653	14,598	25,055
Virginia	531,403	161,472	369,931	449,701	125,570	324,131
Washington	452,248	157,555	294,693	360,532	125,423	235,109
West Virginia	118,248	46,657	71,591	102,579	39,505	63,074
Wisconsin	382,781	101,130	281,651	284,963	70,457	214,506
Wyoming	61,748	15,910	45,838	51,828	13,628	38,200
District of Columbia	46,798	0	46,798	45,536	0	45,536

Source: U.S. Census Bureau, 2009 Annual Survey of Public Employment and Payroll. For information on sampling and nonsampling errors and definitions, see *http://www.census.gov/govs/apes/how_data_collected.html.*

Data users who create their own estimates from this table should cite the U.S. Census Bureau as the source of the original data only.

Note: Statistics for local governments are estimates subject to sampling variation.

Table 8.4
STATE AND LOCAL GOVERNMENT PAYROLLS AND AVERAGE EARNINGS
OF FULL-TIME EMPLOYEES, BY STATE: MARCH 2009

State or other jurisdiction	Amount of payroll (in thousands of dollars)			Percentage of March payroll		Average earnings of full-time state and local government employees (dollars)		
	Total	State government	Local governments	State government	Local government	All	Education employees	Other
United States	$64,575,770	$17,513,133	$47,062,638	27%	73%	$4,319	$4,189	$4,459
Alabama	928,193	325,586	602,608	35	65	3,459	3,447	3,472
Alaska..................	240,671	122,809	117,862	51	49	4,948	4,586	5,256
Arizona................	1,135,563	254,003	881,559	22	78	4,125	3,757	4,550
Arkansas..............	516,031	206,612	309,419	40	60	3,266	3,413	3,074
California	9,085,109	2,014,955	7,070,154	22	78	5,767	5,547	5,949
Colorado..............	1,020,521	271,087	749,434	27	73	4,327	4,040	4,623
Connecticut..........	884,121	332,706	551,415	38	62	5,118	4,833	5,492
Delaware	189,344	99,772	89,572	53	47	4,353	4,780	4,031
Florida	3,311,074	655,001	2,656,074	20	80	4,062	3,772	4,300
Georgia................	1,753,995	423,015	1,330,980	24	76	3,550	3,631	3,440
Hawaii..................	306,435	233,046	73,389	76	24	4,387	4,135	4,613
Idaho...................	246,959	81,862	165,097	33	67	3,563	3,270	3,879
Illinois..................	2,609,375	552,982	2,056,393	21	79	4,570	4,374	4,808
Indiana................	1,122,228	320,573	801,656	29	71	3,672	3,731	3,593
Iowa....................	638,581	232,178	406,403	36	64	4,200	4,067	4,365
Kansas	625,043	163,147	461,896	26	74	3,519	3,463	3,596
Kentucky	739,306	279,625	459,682	38	62	3,316	3,216	3,475
Louisiana.............	923,315	348,328	574,987	38	62	3,605	3,519	3,687
Maine..................	231,587	76,170	155,417	33	67	3,618	3,419	3,924
Maryland	1,337,916	375,308	962,608	28	72	4,970	5,198	4,723
Massachusetts	1,470,117	420,488	1,049,630	29	71	4,815	4,641	5,005
Michigan..............	1,867,815	587,657	1,280,158	31	69	4,663	4,758	4,536
Minnesota............	1,089,903	352,770	737,133	32	68	4,583	4,481	4,710
Mississippi	562,086	179,868	382,218	32	68	3,117	3,113	3,122
Missouri...............	1,018,858	271,796	747,062	27	73	3,429	3,443	3,413
Montana	175,763	67,720	108,043	39	61	3,653	3,588	3,717
Nebraska	395,694	104,651	291,043	26	74	3,792	3,611	3,984
Nevada................	507,922	128,023	379,899	25	75	5,024	4,310	5,625
New Hampshire ...	248,178	71,946	176,232	29	71	3,924	3,760	4,161
New Jersey	2,511,637	797,521	1,714,116	32	68	5,333	5,381	5,277
New Mexico	433,228	168,478	264,750	39	61	3,627	3,534	3,737
New York.............	5,862,152	1,271,751	4,590,402	22	78	5,101	4,978	5,199
North Carolina.....	1,873,573	522,596	1,350,977	28	72	3,705	3,639	3,778
North Dakota.......	131,287	60,458	70,829	46	54	3,682	3,813	3,523
Ohio	2,261,436	572,246	1,689,190	25	75	4,204	4,219	4,188
Oklahoma............	675,457	239,873	435,584	36	64	3,331	3,245	3,441
Oregon................	737,759	252,978	484,781	34	66	4,321	4,070	4,557
Pennsylvania	2,239,194	622,297	1,616,897	28	72	4,150	4,288	3,991
Rhode Island........	236,774	91,758	145,015	39	61	4,859	4,969	4,749
South Carolina.....	832,680	252,862	579,818	30	70	3,512	3,573	3,446
South Dakota.......	137,705	46,155	91,550	34	66	3,311	3,261	3,378
Tennessee	1,057,280	289,494	767,786	27	73	3,468	3,353	3,583
Texas...................	4,866,764	1,116,475	3,750,290	23	77	3,678	3,579	3,821
Utah....................	470,442	190,601	279,841	41	59	3,984	4,016	3,947
Vermont...............	137,626	60,162	77,464	44	56	3,914	3,755	4,169
Virginia................	1,619,734	460,546	1,159,188	28	72	3,992	3,940	4,061
Washington..........	1,558,289	492,449	1,065,841	32	68	5,165	5,180	5,154
West Virginia........	306,101	123,570	182,531	40	60	3,262	3,534	2,929
Wisconsin	1,046,358	277,834	768,525	27	73	4,387	4,422	4,341
Wyoming..............	183,297	49,346	133,951	27	73	4,046	4,140	3,964
Dist. of Columbia	215,292	0	215,292	0	100	5,025	5,708	4,893

Source: U.S. Census Bureau, 2009 Annual Survey of Public Employment and Payroll. For information on sampling and nonsampling errors and definitions, see *http://www.census.gov/govs/apes/how_data_collected.html.*

Data users who create their own estimates from this table should cite the U.S. Census Bureau as the source of the original data only.

Note: Statistics for local governments are estimates subject to sampling variation.

Table 8.5
STATE GOVERNMENT EMPLOYMENT (FULL-TIME EQUIVALENT) FOR SELECTED FUNCTIONS, BY STATE: 2009

| | | Education | | | | | Selected functions | | | | | |
State	All functions	Higher education (a)	Other education (b)	Highways	Public welfare	Hospitals	Corrections	Police protection	Natural resources	Financial and other governmental administration	Judicial and legal administration
United States	4,399,190	1,673,771	140,256	235,496	241,999	417,553	484,426	106,017	145,342	225,805	178,602
Alabama	89,467	38,412	3,089	4,685	4,246	11,954	5,298	1,693	2,303	3,396	3,030
Alaska	26,183	5,234	3,530	3,043	1,879	235	1,903	459	2,413	1,875	1,419
Arizona	68,972	28,075	3,032	2,797	4,899	754	10,509	2,146	2,074	4,028	2,084
Arkansas	61,337	24,531	1,482	3,612	3,809	5,768	5,154	1,236	2,007	2,795	1,514
California	411,142	154,753	4,383	21,680	3,829	43,129	64,496	12,094	15,237	27,494	6,777
Colorado	72,778	39,378	1,296	3,168	2,215	5,353	7,434	1,264	1,459	2,547	4,313
Connecticut	66,498	18,226	2,614	3,113	6,304	7,310	7,931	2,081	1,136	4,299	5,006
Delaware	26,510	7,791	372	1,625	1,795	1,821	2,954	1,022	531	1,191	1,715
Florida	185,630	55,623	3,171	7,791	9,747	3,749	29,962	4,356	9,823	9,100	19,815
Georgia	122,582	52,392	3,061	5,591	8,396	6,979	18,203	2,077	4,391	5,053	3,582
Hawaii	60,041	9,268	28,361	886	652	4,387	2,453	0	1,246	1,512	2,536
Idaho	23,179	8,320	515	1,698	1,879	852	2,026	504	2,050	1,582	489
Illinois	136,542	64,369	2,065	6,837	9,888	11,509	12,062	3,791	3,695	7,671	2,596
Indiana	92,484	56,784	1,124	4,246	4,988	2,597	7,358	2,112	3,158	3,048	1,430
Iowa	52,288	22,522	1,180	2,400	3,232	8,368	3,415	1,042	1,748	1,720	2,382
Kansas	45,163	20,003	600	3,374	2,537	3,096	3,604	1,148	860	2,587	2,166
Kentucky	81,117	36,385	2,546	4,214	5,976	5,628	4,088	2,357	3,268	3,322	5,365
Louisiana	91,809	30,327	5,673	4,839	6,018	14,872	7,733	1,744	4,675	5,105	1,663
Maine	21,497	7,366	244	2,351	3,099	584	1,297	408	1,015	1,490	730
Maryland	89,511	26,907	2,243	4,850	6,722	4,591	12,769	2,355	2,151	5,076	5,140
Massachusetts	96,865	30,686	1,184	3,638	7,111	7,189	6,209	6,239	1,109	5,904	10,038
Michigan	142,924	70,557	507	2,973	10,807	18,820	16,097	2,695	4,075	5,585	1,493
Minnesota	80,536	37,398	3,893	4,618	2,901	5,115	4,214	1,032	3,117	3,843	3,467
Mississippi	57,773	19,375	1,618	3,389	2,695	12,038	3,669	1,218	3,180	1,959	732
Missouri	90,092	28,564	1,755	6,272	8,054	11,631	12,782	2,434	2,888	4,233	3,381
Montana	20,590	7,183	388	2,158	1,721	583	1,292	484	1,525	1,662	704
Nebraska	32,333	12,397	560	2,128	2,576	3,908	2,967	770	2,170	1,073	728
Nevada	29,517	11,436	135	1,779	1,553	1,411	3,677	808	958	2,679	688
New Hampshire ...	19,591	6,568	314	1,777	1,623	771	1,335	512	370	1,294	992
New Jersey	154,106	33,521	21,856	6,871	9,036	18,398	9,943	4,471	2,191	7,339	13,984
New Mexico	48,680	19,385	1,030	2,571	1,897	7,428	4,133	734	1,216	1,562	3,322
New York	257,490	53,162	4,669	12,686	5,331	46,056	33,739	6,741	3,498	16,980	22,290
North Carolina	147,895	58,578	1,567	10,976	1,646	20,001	22,410	3,327	4,431	4,182	7,262
North Dakota	17,667	8,481	299	1,111	493	898	738	188	586	1,010	541
Ohio	142,945	71,110	2,484	6,958	2,777	15,538	16,045	2,609	2,817	8,732	2,928
Oklahoma	72,198	30,405	1,984	3,069	7,127	2,968	5,842	1,997	1,997	2,552	2,962
Oregon	63,086	22,966	736	3,802	6,442	5,073	5,509	1,374	2,497	5,472	3,285
Pennsylvania	163,903	60,458	4,046	13,119	11,835	11,699	17,683	6,403	6,645	11,326	3,063
Rhode Island	19,669	5,683	1,048	695	1,265	1,047	1,620	384	418	1,480	1,172
South Carolina	77,261	29,767	2,659	4,952	4,584	7,282	7,814	1,882	2,132	4,051	766
South Dakota	14,053	5,159	389	1,004	1,089	970	883	301	953	793	610
Tennessee	84,387	33,358	2,156	4,149	8,769	5,670	7,086	2,211	3,905	4,338	2,499
Texas	300,112	121,917	4,887	14,730	25,133	30,554	44,093	4,358	10,922	12,359	5,685
Utah	51,606	23,635	1,208	1,664	3,167	6,950	3,288	808	1,315	2,957	1,629
Vermont	14,598	4,914	577	1,023	1,364	294	1,104	610	597	1,266	631
Virginia	125,570	53,249	2,987	8,545	2,786	15,154	14,460	3,047	3,325	4,868	3,685
Washington	125,423	55,623	2,071	7,568	10,001	10,440	9,962	2,305	5,396	4,655	1,934
West Virginia	39,505	13,193	1,323	5,149	3,322	1,647	3,362	998	2,326	2,367	1,476
Wisconsin	70,457	34,557	1,086	1,410	1,967	3,590	10,772	886	2,575	3,559	2,344
Wyoming	13,628	3,820	259	1,912	817	894	1,049	302	968	834	559

Source: U.S. Census Bureau, 2009 Annual Survey of Public Employment and Payroll. For information on sampling and nonsampling errors and definitions, see *http://www.census.gov/govs/apes/how_data_collected.html.* Data users who create their own estimates from this table should cite the U.S. Census Bureau as the source of the original data only.

Key:
(a) Includes instructional and other personnel.
(b) Includes instructional and other personnel in elementary and secondary schools.

Table 8.6
STATE GOVERNMENT PAYROLLS FOR SELECTED FUNCTIONS, BY STATE: MARCH 2009
(In thousands of dollars)

State	All functions	Education Higher education (a)	Education Other education (b)	Highways	Public welfare	Hospitals	Corrections	Police protection	Natural resources	Financial and other governmental administration	Judicial and legal administration
United States	$19,388,085	$7,654,755	$622,393	$1,016,003	$886,704	$1,827,022	$1,970,057	$542,689	$591,433	$976,917	$897,578
Alabama	353,235	164,060	11,377	16,230	15,232	46,695	17,341	6,505	8,616	14,765	11,008
Alaska..................	129,449	26,569	13,466	17,233	7,559	1,121	10,536	2,649	11,664	9,336	7,730
Arizona................	278,908	126,461	10,049	10,234	14,157	3,077	40,085	11,534	8,081	15,163	9,119
Arkansas.............	219,299	98,752	5,049	12,903	11,326	20,166	14,445	4,411	6,250	9,707	5,059
California	2,249,832	818,025	20,423	140,000	16,551	273,313	390,409	77,640	71,586	119,980	42,281
Colorado..............	344,631	189,099	6,175	15,036	10,294	21,436	32,001	6,601	7,747	12,027	21,790
Connecticut.........	371,750	99,428	15,040	18,054	34,421	44,391	47,863	11,427	5,814	21,899	28,555
Delaware	110,567	37,087	2,028	6,046	6,170	6,167	11,105	6,032	1,981	4,490	7,731
Florida	709,474	269,877	10,519	31,484	29,132	11,384	91,700	16,764	31,819	32,760	78,638
Georgia................	466,076	238,680	12,745	17,791	23,673	18,777	50,314	8,040	14,650	19,722	16,347
Hawaii..................	253,441	46,863	107,517	4,140	2,557	21,332	10,985	0	5,552	6,184	11,611
Idaho...................	92,183	33,167	2,178	5,870	6,366	2,661	7,805	2,257	8,208	6,586	3,467
Illinois.................	634,744	262,230	10,674	36,551	50,175	55,973	62,034	22,782	14,671	37,052	21,643
Indiana................	357,158	226,794	4,394	14,557	16,525	8,137	24,137	8,624	10,247	12,977	9,542
Iowa....................	264,792	118,251	5,849	11,106	13,843	44,367	15,043	5,932	9,442	8,047	12,241
Kansas	179,022	91,381	2,447	11,328	7,812	9,625	10,946	4,927	3,316	8,983	8,982
Kentucky	310,257	155,290	10,200	14,855	18,575	22,072	11,153	9,340	10,581	13,961	18,587
Louisiana............	370,585	127,983	23,447	18,377	21,385	55,786	29,520	9,003	18,823	20,908	7,229
Maine..................	87,268	29,249	949	9,119	11,347	2,472	5,585	1,962	4,375	6,285	3,421
Maryland	411,315	135,601	10,530	22,254	26,031	18,361	53,229	12,309	10,167	23,905	26,781
Massachusetts	468,637	139,178	6,621	19,718	34,778	29,883	30,954	36,429	6,088	28,773	50,095
Michigan..............	666,911	326,083	2,651	14,680	48,559	85,138	77,280	11,410	19,175	28,045	9,704
Minnesota............	398,757	195,226	20,417	22,181	11,270	22,001	18,230	4,874	14,484	18,573	18,272
Mississippi	192,905	76,149	5,224	9,885	7,211	35,023	9,591	3,900	9,605	7,223	4,171
Missouri...............	295,984	111,918	5,651	21,851	20,818	34,620	32,991	9,278	9,150	14,625	10,158
Montana	77,090	25,713	1,512	9,304	5,964	1,979	4,436	1,579	5,875	6,000	3,060
Nebraska	115,486	46,146	2,302	7,810	7,418	13,390	9,154	3,397	6,962	3,970	3,394
Nevada................	139,439	50,861	722	8,607	6,417	7,282	18,072	4,625	4,527	12,465	4,647
New Hampshire.....	82,783	31,235	1,242	6,948	5,835	2,899	6,010	2,548	1,722	5,459	3,976
New Jersey	850,601	202,084	129,058	36,304	45,296	79,795	55,058	30,266	12,088	35,670	78,991
New Mexico	183,298	68,145	4,042	9,151	6,451	29,116	14,986	4,154	5,021	6,879	13,827
New York.............	1,341,741	262,798	22,343	61,302	23,976	218,963	167,603	47,458	18,068	80,718	136,424
North Carolina....	580,511	249,159	7,900	35,132	6,551	77,261	71,175	14,146	16,572	18,261	31,171
North Dakota......	67,733	34,149	1,001	4,445	1,486	2,489	2,322	877	2,266	3,895	2,336
Ohio	644,887	304,039	12,388	30,954	15,172	72,823	68,546	13,171	11,549	44,156	17,047
Oklahoma............	264,770	121,523	7,289	10,133	20,345	8,869	18,849	8,348	6,753	9,415	12,918
Oregon................	282,288	109,045	3,194	17,097	25,679	23,193	22,874	6,534	10,145	23,090	14,245
Pennsylvania	704,079	290,143	16,709	47,779	43,956	39,205	70,647	34,870	28,566	46,510	16,002
Rhode Island.......	98,331	25,503	5,433	3,601	6,393	4,966	9,133	2,308	2,151	7,093	6,234
South Carolina....	269,970	116,983	9,906	15,196	12,614	17,673	22,255	6,626	6,728	14,066	3,737
South Dakota......	50,707	20,587	1,317	3,372	3,291	2,882	2,508	1,132	3,555	2,958	2,412
Tennessee	311,320	127,673	7,629	13,456	27,690	25,352	20,193	7,028	14,381	17,370	12,696
Texas...................	1,225,534	563,448	21,634	58,807	75,163	144,578	121,644	17,177	47,355	50,326	28,306
Utah....................	212,334	105,989	4,778	6,949	11,084	25,101	11,613	3,227	4,854	13,151	7,323
Vermont...............	64,168	23,088	2,503	4,167	5,585	1,238	4,552	3,244	2,839	4,885	2,822
Virginia...............	523,438	247,149	12,936	35,236	10,936	56,616	44,572	13,789	12,337	20,115	17,332
Washington..........	572,428	257,895	9,298	39,632	33,803	56,120	41,574	12,072	22,788	21,334	11,169
West Virginia.......	133,801	53,514	5,218	14,801	8,619	4,148	8,718	3,867	7,832	7,380	6,216
Wisconsin	322,316	160,122	5,292	7,125	8,248	14,651	44,649	4,341	10,731	15,950	14,367
Wyoming	51,850	14,368	1,126	7,213	2,966	2,454	3,633	1,272	3,678	3,827	2,766

Source: U.S. Census Bureau, 2009 Annual Survey of Public Employment and Payroll. For information on sampling and nonsampling errors and definitions, see http://www.census.gov/govs/apes/how_data_collected.html. Data users who create their own estimates from this table should cite the U.S. Census Bureau as the source of the original data only.

Key:
(a) Includes instructional and other personnel.
(b) Includes instructional and other personnel in elementary and secondary schools.

Women in State Government:
Past, Present, Future

By Susan J. Carroll

In recent years, the movement of women into state-level offices has slowed following several decades of gains. Following the 2010 elections, the number of women in both state legislative and statewide elective office declined. Efforts to actively recruit women for elective and appointive positions will be critical in determining what the future holds for women in state government.

In the history of our nation, women are relative newcomers among state elected and appointed officials. Women first entered state-level offices in the 1920s following passage and ratification of the 19th Amendment to the U.S. Constitution, which granted women suffrage. Significant growth in the numbers of women in office, however, occurred only after the emergence of the contemporary women's movement during the late 1960s and early 1970s. Since the mid-1970s, as data collected by the Center for American Women and Politics show,[1] women have greatly increased their numbers among elected and appointed officials in state government. Nevertheless, in recent years progress has slowed and nationwide statistics show a leveling off in the number of women serving in state-level offices since the turn of the century.

Women suffered major setbacks in the 2010 elections. The number of women serving in state legislatures actually decreased following the elections for the first time in more than four decades, and the number of women serving in statewide office continued a downward slide that has been evident since 2000.

Governors

Since the founding of our country, only 34 women (19 Democrats, 15 Republicans) have served as state governors (Table A), and only one woman has served as governor of a U.S. territory (Puerto Rico).[2] Almost half the states, 23, have never had a female chief executive. Arizona is the only state to have had four women governors as well as the only state where a woman succeeded another as governor. Connecticut, Texas, Kansas, Washington and New Hampshire each have had two women governors, although one of the governors of New Hampshire, Vesta Roy, served for only seven days following the death of an incumbent.

The first woman governor, Nellie Tayloe Ross of Wyoming, was selected in a special election to succeed her deceased husband in 1925. Fifteen days later, a second woman, Miriam "Ma" Ferguson, was inaugurated as governor of Texas. Having been elected as a surrogate for her husband, a former governor who had been impeached and consequently was barred constitutionally from running again, Ferguson's campaign slogan was "Two governors for the price of one."[3] The third woman to serve as a governor, Lurleen Wallace of Alabama, campaigned on the slogan, "Let George do it," and was similarly elected to replace a husband who was prohibited by term limits from seeking an additional term in office.[4]

The first woman elected in her own right (i.e., without following her husband) into the governorship was Ella Grasso, who presided over the state of Connecticut from 1975 to 1980. Twenty-three of the women governors (including Grasso) who have served since the mid-1970s were elected in their own right. The other eight became governor through constitutional succession; only three of these eight were subsequently elected to full terms.

Six women (two Democrat, four Republican) serve as governors in 2011, falling short of the record nine women who served simultaneously in 2004 and again in 2007. With three women governors leaving office—two as a result of term limits and one by choice—the number of women governors did not change following the 2010 elections despite the election of three new women governors: Mary Fallin (R-Oklahoma), Nikki Haley (R-South Carolina), and Susana Martinez (R-New Mexico). These three join one woman—Jan Brewer (R-Arizona)—who sought and won re-election; and two women—Christine Gregoire (D-Washington) and Beverly Perdue (D-North Carolina)—whose seats were not up in 2010. Susana Martinez, a Latina, and

Table A: Women Governors Throughout History

Name (Party-State)	Dates served	Special Circumstances
Nellie Tayloe Ross (D-WY)	1925–1927	Won special election to replace deceased husband.
Miriam "Ma" Ferguson (D-TX)	1925–1927, 1933–1935	Inaugurated 15 days after Ross; elected as surrogate for husband who could not succeed himself.
Lurleen Wallace (D-AL)	1967–1968	Elected as surrogate for husband who could not succeed himself.
Ella Grasso (D-CT)	1975–1980	First woman elected governor in her own right; resigned for health reasons.
Dixy Lee Ray (D-WA)	1977–1981	
Vesta Roy (R-NH)	1982–1983	Elected to state senate and chosen as senate president; served as governor for seven days when incumbent died.
Martha Layne Collins (D-KY)	1984–1987	
Madeleine Kunin (D-VT)	1985–1991	First woman to serve three terms as governor.
Kay Orr (R-NE)	1987–1991	First Republican woman governor and first woman to defeat another woman in a gubernatorial race.
Rose Mofford (D-AZ)	1988–1991	Elected as secretary of state, succeeded governor who was impeached and convicted.
Joan Finney (D-KS)	1991–1995	First woman to defeat an incumbent governor.
Ann Richards (D-TX)	1991–1995	
Barbara Roberts (D-OR)	1991–1995	
Christine Todd Whitman (R-NJ)	1994–2001	Resigned to take presidential appointment as commissioner of the Environmental Protection Agency.
Jeanne Shaheen (D-NH)	1997–2003	
Jane Dee Hull (R-AZ)	1997–2003	Elected as secretary of state, succeeded governor who resigned; later elected to a full term.
Nancy Hollister (R-OH)	1998–1999	Elected lieutenant governor; served as governor for 11 days when predecessor took U.S. Senate seat and successor had not yet been sworn in.
Jane Swift (R-MA)	2001–2003	Elected as lieutenant governor, succeeded governor who resigned for an ambassadorial appointment.
Judy Martz (R-MT)	2001–2005	
Olene Walker (R-UT)	2003–2005	Elected as lieutenant governor, succeeded governor who resigned to take a federal appointment.
Ruth Ann Minner (D-DE)	2001–2009	
Jennifer M. Granholm (D-MI)	2003–2011	
Linda Lingle (R-HI)	2003–2011	
Janet Napolitano (D-AZ)	2003–2009	First woman to succeed another woman as governor. Resigned to become U.S. Secretary of Homeland Security.
Kathleen Sebelius (D-KS)	2003–2009	Father was governor of Ohio. Resigned to become U.S. Secretary of Health and Human Services.
Kathleen Blanco (D-LA)	2004–2008	
M. Jodi Rell (R-CT)	2004–2011	Elected as lieutenant governor, succeeded governor who resigned.
Christine Gregoire (D-WA)	2005–present	
Sarah Palin (R-AK)	2007–2009	Resigned.
Beverly Perdue (D-NC)	2009–present	
Jan Brewer (R-AZ)	2009–present	Elected as secretary of state, succeeded governor who resigned.
Mary Fallin (R-OK)	2011–present	
Nikki Haley (R-SC)	2011–present	First Asian (Indian) American woman to be elected governor.
Susana Martinez (R-NM)	2011–present	First Latina to be elected governor.

Source: Center for American Women and Politics, Eagleton Institute of Politics, Rutgers University.

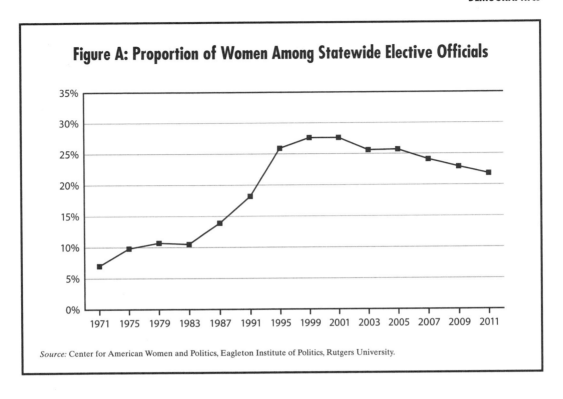

Figure A: Proportion of Women Among Statewide Elective Officials

Source: Center for American Women and Politics, Eagleton Institute of Politics, Rutgers University.

Nikki Haley, an Indian-American, are the first two women of color ever to serve as governor of a state.

Other Statewide Elected and Appointed Officials in the Executive Branch

The states vary greatly in their numbers of statewide elected and appointed officials. For example, Maine and New Hampshire have only one statewide elected official, the governor, while North Dakota, at the other extreme, has 12.

The first woman to ever hold a major statewide office was Soledad C. Chacon (D-New Mexico) who was secretary of state in New Mexico from 1923 to 1926;[5] Delaware, Kentucky, New York, South Dakota and Texas also had women secretaries of state in the 1920s. The first woman treasurer, Grace B. Urbahns (R-Indiana), also served during this time period, from 1926 to 1932.

Several more years passed before a woman became lieutenant governor. Matilda R. Wilson (R-Michigan) served briefly as lieutenant governor of Michigan in 1940 when she was appointed to fill an expiring term. However, the first woman elected as a lieutenant governor was Consuelo N. Bailey (R-Vermont) who served from 1955 to 1956. An additional three decades passed before a

woman became attorney general of a state; the first was Arlene Violet (R-Rhode Island) who served from 1985 to 1987.

As evident from Figure A, the proportion of women among statewide elective officials has grown substantially since the early 1970s. From 1971 to 1983 the increases were small and incremental. Then, between 1983 and 2000, a period of significant growth, the number and proportion of women serving statewide almost tripled, reaching a record of 92 women, constituting 28.5 percent of all statewide elected officials, in 2000. Since 2000, the numbers and proportions have dropped notably.

The decline in women statewide elected officials continued following the 2010 elections. Despite the election of three new women governors, the number of women serving in statewide elective offices actually decreased by two, and fewer women, 69,[6] hold statewide offices in 2011 than in 1995 when there were 84 women.

In early 2011, women hold 21.8 percent of the 317 statewide elective positions. In addition to the six women governors, 11 women (four Democrat, seven Republican) serve as lieutenant governors in the 44 states that elect lieutenant governors in statewide elections. This is considerably fewer than

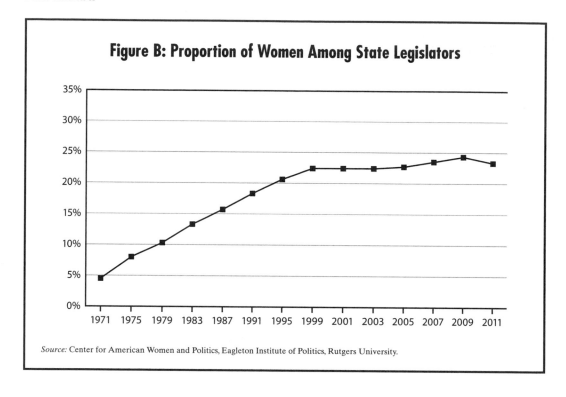

Figure B: Proportion of Women Among State Legislators

Source: Center for American Women and Politics, Eagleton Institute of Politics, Rutgers University.

the record number of 19 women who served as lieutenant governors in 1995.

Other women statewide elected officials include: 11 secretaries of state (eight Democrats, three Republicans), seven state auditors (five Democrats, two Republicans), six state treasurers (five Democrats, one Republican), seven attorneys general (five Democrats, two Republicans), five chief education officials (two Democrats, two Republicans, one nonpartisan), four public service commissioners (three Democrats, one Republican), four state comptroller/controllers (one Democrat, three Republicans), two commissioners of insurance (one Democrat, one Republican), three corporation commissioners (one Democrat, two Republicans), one commissioner of labor (Republican), one railroad commissioner (Republican), and one public regulatory commissioner (Democrat). In addition to the two women of color who serve as governors, the women serving in statewide elective office include four African-Americans (the lieutenant governor of Florida, the attorney general of California, the state treasurer of Connecticut and the corporation commissioner of Arizona); three Latinas (the secretary of state of New Mexico, the attorney general of Nevada and the

superintendent of public instruction for Oregon); and one Native American (the public regulatory commissioner of New Mexico).

Women may be slightly better represented among top appointed officials in state government than among statewide elected officials, although it is not possible to know for certain since the most recent data available are from 2007. According to nationwide data collected by the Center on Women in Government and Civil Society at SUNY-Albany, in 2007 women constituted 32.2 percent of department heads with major policy-making responsibilities (including heads of departments, agencies, offices, boards, commissions and authorities) who were appointed by governors. This proportion represented a substantial increase over 1997, when women constituted just 23.2 percent of department heads. Women were even better represented in 2007 among top appointed advisers in governors' offices, with women holding 41.9 percent of these positions—a just slightly higher proportion than the 39.5 percent of these positions they held in 1997. Women of color are still a rarity among appointed officials, constituting just 6.3 percent of all department heads and top advisers in governors' offices in 2007.

Justices on Courts of Last Resort

The first woman to win election to a state court of last resort was Florence E. Allen, who was elected to the Ohio Supreme Court in 1922 and re-elected in 1928. Nevertheless, it was not until 1960 that a second woman, Lorna Lockwood of Arizona, was elected to a state supreme court. In 1965, Lockwood's colleagues on the Arizona Supreme Court selected her to be chief justice, thereby also making her the first woman in history to preside over a state court of last resort.[7] She was followed by Susie Sharp of North Carolina, who in 1974 became the first woman to be elected by popular vote to be chief justice of a state court of last resort.[8]

In 2003, Petra Jimenez Maes of New Mexico, who currently serves as an associate justice, became the first Latina chief justice of a state supreme court. Similarly, in 2005, Leah Ward Sears of Georgia became the first African-American woman to preside over a state court of last resort.[9]

According to the National Center for State Courts, 111, or 32.6 percent, of the 341 justices on state courts of last resort in early 2011 are women.[10] Of the 53 chief justices of these courts, 19, or 35.8 percent, are women. Women comprise a majority of justices on the courts of last resort in California, Michigan, Tennessee, Wisconsin and the District of Columbia. Women constitute at least 40 percent of the justices but less than a majority on an additional 17 courts of last resort.

Legislators

Even before 1920 when women won the right to vote across the country, a few women had been elected to legislatures in states that had granted the franchise to women. By 1971, the proportion of women serving in state legislatures across the country had grown to 4.5 percent, and over the years this proportion has increased more than fivefold. As Figure B illustrates, the proportion of women among legislators grew steadily throughout the 1970s and 1980s. However, the rate of growth slowed in the 1990s, and similar to the pattern for statewide elected officials, the numbers and proportions of women legislators nationally have leveled off since the late 1990s. Following the 2010 elections, the number of women legislators actually decreased quite dramatically from 1,811 in late 2010 to 1,718 in early 2011.

The proportion of women among legislators declined from 24.5 percent in 2010 to 23.3 percent in January 2011. Women now hold 415, or 21.1 percent, of all state senate seats and 1,303, or 24.1 percent, of all state house seats across the country. The number of women who serve in state legislatures at the beginning of 2011 is only slightly greater than the number of women who served in 1999!

Great variation exists across the states in the proportion of legislators who are women. (See Table B) Colorado ranks first among the states with 40 percent women in its legislature, followed by Vermont (37.8 percent), Arizona (34.4 percent), Hawaii (32.9 percent), Minnesota (31.8 percent) and Washington (31.3 percent). With the exception of Minnesota and Illinois, all the states ranked in the top 10 in the proportion of women in their legislatures are located in the West or the Northeast. However, despite this geographic concentration, no easy explanation exists for why these states have risen to the top, and, indeed, scholars who have statistically examined the variation among the states in the representation of women in their legislatures have found no simple patterns.[11]

At the other extreme, South Carolina with only 9.4 percent ranks last among the 50 states in the representation of women among its legislators. Accompanying South Carolina in the bottom five states are Oklahoma (12.8 percent), Alabama (13.6 percent), Mississippi (14.4 percent) and North Dakota (14.9 percent). Eight of the 10 states with the lowest proportions of women are Southern or border states. Only one Southern state—Florida ranked 20th with 24.4 percent women—is above the national average. As these rankings make clear, the South as a region lags the rest of the country in the representation of women within its legislatures.

Following gains in the 2010 elections, Republicans outnumber Democrats among state legislators nationwide, with 53.4 percent of all legislators Republican.[12] The opposite is true among women, however, where Democrats outnumber Republicans by a sizeable margin. Among women state senators nationwide, 62.5 percent are Democrats; among women state representatives, 60.9 percent are Democrats.

About one-fifth of women state legislators, 20.3 percent, are women of color. Of the 96 senators and 253 representatives serving in legislatures in early 2011, all but 18 are Democrats. African-American women hold 64 seats in state senates and 175 seats in state houses across 40 states. Latinas are concentrated in 21 states; they hold 21 senate and 47 house seats. Asian-American women count among their numbers eight senators and 27 representatives in 10 states, while Native American women hold three senate and four house seats in six states.

Table B: Women in State Legislatures

State	Senate Democrats	Senate Republicans	Senate % Women	House Democrats	House Republicans	House % Women	Legislature (both houses) % Women	Legislature (both houses) State rank (a)
Alabama	4	0	14.3(b)	9	5	13.3	13.6	48
Alaska	1	3	20.0	4	6	25.0	23.3	25
Arizona	5	6	36.7	7	13	33.3	34.4	3
Arkansas	5	3	22.9	11	10	21.0	21.5	31
California	9	2	27.5	16	5	26.3	26.7	16
Colorado	14	2	45.7	17	7	36.9	40.0	1
Connecticut	7	1	22.2	32	14	30.5	28.9	8
Delaware	4	3	33.3	7	2	22.0	25.8	18
Florida	6	7	32.5	11	15	21.7	24.4	20
Georgia	7	1	14.3	32	15	26.1	23.3	25
Hawaii	7	0	28.0	14	4	35.3	32.9	4
Idaho	3	6	25.7	8	11	27.1	26.7	16
Illinois	9	5	23.7	27	11	32.2	28.8	9
Indiana	4	6	20.0	11	10	21.0	20.7	36
Iowa	4	4	16.0	16	8	24.0	21.3	32
Kansas	5	9	35.0	14	18	25.6	27.9	13
Kentucky	3	3	15.8	11	8	19.0	18.1	41
Louisiana	6	2	20.5	11	4	14.3	16.0	43
Maine	4	3	20.0	27	18	29.8	28.0	12
Maryland	10	1	23.4	35	12	33.3	30.9	7
Massachusetts	11	0	27.5	31	5	22.5	23.5	22
Michigan	2	2	10.5	16	11	24.5	20.9	35
Minnesota	11	10	31.3	25	18	32.1	31.8	5
Mississippi	3	1	7.7	17	4	17.2	14.4	47
Missouri	3	2	14.1	23	18	25.2	23.4	24
Montana	6	1	14.0	19	9	28.0	23.3	25
Nebraska (c)	Nonpartisan		22.4	Unicameral			22.4	29
Nevada	4	2	28.6	11	1	28.6	28.6	10
New Hampshire	3	3	25.0	38	56	23.5	23.6	21
New Jersey	7	3	25.0	16	8	30.0	28.3	11
New Mexico	8	2	23.8	12	9	30.0	27.7	15
New York	8	3	17.7	30	7	24.7	22.6	28
North Carolina	3	3	12.0	22	10	26.7	22.4	29
North Dakota	3	3	12.8	3	12	16.0	14.9	46
Ohio	5	3	24.2	12	8	20.2	21.2	33
Oklahoma	3	1	8.3	4	11	14.9	12.8	49
Oregon	7	2	30.0	11	5	26.7	27.8	14
Pennsylvania	4	6	20.0	13	19	15.8	16.6	42
Rhode Island	9	1	26.3	17	2	25.3	25.7	19
South Carolina	0	0	0.0	8	8	12.9	9.4	50
South Dakota	1	6	20.0	4	9	20.0(b)	20.0	37
Tennessee	4	3	21.2	11	6	17.2	18.2	40
Texas	3	3	19.4	14	18	21.3	21.0	34
Utah	4	1	17.2	9	5	18.7	18.3	39
Vermont	9	2	36.7	42	11	38.0(d)	37.8	2
Virginia	7	1	20.0	13	6	19.0	19.3	38
Washington	11	6	34.7	19	10	30.0	31.3	6
West Virginia	0	2	5.9	13	6	19.0	15.7	44
Wisconsin	3	5	24.2	16	7	23.2	23.5	22
Wyoming	0	1	3.3	3	10	21.7	15.6	45

Source: Center for American Women and Politics, Eagleton Institute of Politics, Rutgers University. Figures are as of January 2011.

Key:

(a) States share the same rank if their proportions of women legislators are exactly equal or round off to be equal (CA, ID; MA, WI; AK, GA, MT; NE, NC).

(b) Includes one Independent.

(c) Nebraska has a unicameral legislature with nonpartisan elections.

(d) Includes two members of the Progressive Party.

Looking Toward the Future

Although women have made substantial progress over time in increasing their presence in state government, the leveling off in the decade of the 2000s and the decline following the 2010 elections in women's numbers among statewide elective officials and state legislators are troubling developments. At a minimum, these developments provide evidence that increases over time are not inevitable; there is no invisible hand at work to ensure that more

Table C: Women Statewide Elected Officials 2011

State	Governor	Lieutenant Governor	Attorney General	Secretary of State	Treasurer
Alabama	★	W	★	W	★
Alaska	★	★	★	...	...
Arizona	W	...	★	★	★
Arkansas	★	★	★	★	W
California	★	★	W	W	★
Colorado	★	★	★	★	★
Connecticut	★	W	★	W	W
Delaware	★	★	★	...	★
Florida	★	W	W	...	★
Georgia	★	★	★	★	...
Hawaii	★	★	...	...	...
Idaho	★	★	★	★	★
Illinois	★	W	W	★	★
Indiana	★	W	★	★	★
Iowa	★	W	★	★	★
Kansas	★	★	★	★	★
Kentucky	★	★	★	W	★
Louisiana	★	★	★	★	★
Maine	★	...	...	...	...
Maryland	★	★	★	...	...
Massachusetts	★	★	W	★	★
Michigan	★	★	★	W	...
Minnesota	★	W	W	★	...
Mississippi	★	★	★	★	★
Missouri	★	★	★	W	★
Montana	★	★	★	W	...
Nebraska	★	★	★	★	...
Nevada	★	★	W	★	W
New Hampshire	★	...	...	...	...
New Jersey	★	W	...	...	...
New Mexico	W	★	★	W	★
New York	★	★	★	...	...
North Carolina	W	★	★	W	W
North Dakota	★	★	★	★	W
Ohio	★	W	★	★	★
Oklahoma	W	★	★	...	★
Oregon	★	...	★	W	★
Pennsylvania	★	★	W	...	★
Rhode Island	★	W	★	★	W
South Carolina	W	★	★	★	★
South Dakota	★	★	★	★	★
Tennessee	★	...	...	...	...
Texas	★	★	★	...	...
Utah	★	★	★	...	★
Vermont	★	★	★	★	★
Virginia	★	★	★	...	...
Washington	W	★	★	★	★
West Virginia	★	...	★	W	★
Wisconsin	★	W	★	★	★
Wyoming	★	...	...	★	★

Source: Data for elected officials are current as of January 2011 and have been provided by the Center for American Women and Politics, Eagleton Institute of Politics, Rutgers University.
Key:
★ — Denotes that this position is filled through a statewide election.

W — Denotes that this position is filled through a statewide election and is held by a woman.
... — Denotes that this position is not filled through a statewide election.

women will seek and be elected to office with each subsequent election.

The leveling off and recent decline has implications for women's representation not only among state legislators and nongubernatorial statewide officeholders, but also among governors and members of Congress. Probably the most striking positive development for women in state government in recent years has been the increase in women governors. Of the 34 women governors across the entire history of our country, a majority—20—have served all or part of their terms during the first few years of the 21st century. Of the six sitting governors, four held statewide elective office before running for governor; two were lieutenant governors, one served as an attorney general and one was a secretary of state. Four of the current women governors also served in their state legislatures. Similarly, many of the women who have run for Congress gained experience and visibility in state government before seeking federal office. Of the 71 women members of the U.S. House, 35 served in their state houses, 20 in their state senates, and six in statewide elective offices. Of the 17 women U.S. senators, seven served in their state legislatures, three in statewide elective offices, and two in an appointed state cabinet post.

Activists who are interested in increasing the numbers of women serving in office often refer to a political "pipeline" through which potential women candidates for higher level office come forward from among the pool of women who have gained experience at lower levels of office. Clearly, the pipeline has worked well in the case of the current women governors and members of Congress. But what if the pool of candidates in statewide and state legislative offices continues to stagnate or decline? Then, the number of politically experienced women with the visibility and contacts necessary to run for governor or a seat in the U.S. House or Senate is also likely to stagnate or decline.

While several different factors may be responsible for the recent leveling off in the numbers of women in statewide elective and state legislative office, a lack of effective recruitment certainly is one of the most important. Statistics on the number of women candidates over time seem clearly to point to a problem with recruitment. For example, even though a record 2,537 women were general election candidates for the 6,115 seats up for election in state legislatures in 2010, this was only 162 more women than in 1992.[13] Clearly, then, a major factor contributing to the leveling off in the number of women officeholders is a lack of greater numbers of women candidates.

Research has found that women who run for office are less likely than their male counterparts to be "self-starters." Women more often than men seek office only after receiving encouragement from others. In a 2008 nationwide study of state legislators, scholars at the Center for American Women and Politics found only 26 percent of women state

representatives, compared with 43 percent of their male counterparts, said it was entirely their own idea to run for their first elective office. In contrast, 53 percent of women state representatives, compared with 28 percent of men, said they had not thought seriously about running for office until someone else suggested it.[14] Similarly, a study of major party candidates in state legislative races conducted a few years earlier found only 11 percent of women, compared with 37 percent of men, were self-starters who said it was entirely their own idea to run for the legislature; in contrast, 37 percent of women, compared with 18 percent of men, reported they had not seriously thought about running until someone else suggested it.[15] Another recent study of people in the professions from which political candidates are most likely to emerge (i.e., law, business, education and politics) found notably fewer women (43 percent) than men (59 percent) had ever considered running for office.[16]

Findings such as these suggest the future for women in state government will depend, at least in part, upon the strength of efforts to actively recruit women for both elected and appointed positions. Legislative leaders, public officials, party leaders and advocacy organizations can help by renewing their commitment and augmenting their efforts to identify and support potential women candidates, especially in winnable races with open seats or vulnerable incumbents. Recruitment efforts may well be key to determining whether the numbers of women officials continue to stagnate or again begin to move steadily upward as they did in earlier decades.

Notes

[1] All statistical information in this essay, unless otherwise noted, has been provided by the Center for American Women and Politics, Eagleton Institute of Politics, Rutgers University. Additional information is available at *www. cawp.rutgers.edu*. This essay would not be possible without the tireless efforts of Gilda Morales, who oversees the collection of data on women officeholders for the Center for American Women and Politics. In addition to Gilda, I would like to thank Linda Phillips from the Center for American Women and Politics and Joan Cochet from the National Center for State Courts for their assistance with the data for this essay.

[2] Sila Calderon (Popular Democratic Party) served as governor of Puerto Rico from 2001 to 2004.

[3] Martin Gruberg, *Women in American Politics* (Oshkosh, WI: Academia Press, 1968), 189.

[4] Gruberg, 190.

[5] Women did serve as superintendents of public instruction in a few states earlier than this.

[6]These 68 women serving in statewide elective office include 38 Democrats, 29 Republicans, and one nonpartisan.

[7]Gruberg, 190, 192.

[8]Susie Sharp (1906–1996), North Carolina History Project. *http://www.northcarolinahistory.org/encyclopedia/40/entry*.

[9]Information provided by the National Center for State Courts.

[10]Unlike all the other statistics in this essay, these numbers from the National Center for State Courts include the District of Columbia as well as the 50 states.

[11]See, for example, Barbara Norrander and Clyde Wilcox, "The Geography of Gender Power: Women in State Legislatures," in Sue Thomas and Clyde Wilcox, ed., *Women and Elective Office: Past, Present, and Future* (New York: Oxford University Press, 1998).

[12]This proportion is calculated from data in a table entitled "State and Legislative Partisan Composition Following the 2010 Elections," dated Dec. 23, 2010, on the website of the National Conference of State Legislatures. *http://www.ncsl.org/documents/statevote/2010_Legis_and_State_post.pdf*.

[13]There were 2,302 women candidates for state legislative seats in 1992; 2,222 in 1994; 2,215 in 1996; 2,213 in 1998; 2,228 in 2000; 2,348 in 2002; 2,220 in 2004; 2,429 in 2006; and 2,337 in 2008.

[14]Kira Sanbonmatsu, Susan J. Carroll and Debbie Walsh, *Poised to Run: Women's Pathways to the State Legislatures* (New Brunswick, NJ: Center for American Women and Politics, 2009), 8. *http://www.cawp.rutgers.edu/research/reports/PoisedtoRun.pdf*.

[15]Gary Moncrief, Peverill Squire, and Malcolm Jewell, *Who Runs for the Legislature?* (New York: Prentice-Hall, 2001), Table 5.5, 102.

[16]Jennifer L. Lawless and Richard L. Fox, *It Takes a Candidate: Why Women Don't Run for Office* (New York: Cambridge University Press, 2005), 44.

About the Author

Susan J. Carroll is professor of Political Science and Women's and Gender Studies at Rutgers University and Senior Scholar at the Center for American Women and Politics of the Eagleton Institute of Politics. She has published numerous works on women public officials, candidates and voters.

SELECTED STATE POLICIES AND PROGRAMS

THE FOLLOWING TABLE IS AN ONLINE-ONLY FEATURE FOR THE 2011 VOLUME OF *THE BOOK OF THE STATES.*

THIS TABLE CAN BE ACCESSED AT
http://knowledgecenter.csg.org/drupalview-content-type/1219

Chapter 9   SELECTED STATE POLICIES AND PROGRAMS

Table 9.15   PUBLIC ROAD LENGTH MILES BY OWNERSHIP:2008

An Impossible Choice: Reconciling State Budget Cuts and Disasters That Demand Adequate Management

By Beverly Bell

Faced with severe budget deficits across the nation, state governments are making difficult, if not impossible, choices when it comes to cutting services for their residents. Like most functions within state government, emergency management is feeling the brunt of this brutal environment. On one side are the economic constraints. On the other is the reality of disasters, which don't care about budgets and whether resources are available or not. Only one constant remains—if a disaster occurs, citizens expect an adequate level of public resources to manage the disaster. Every well-managed disaster teaches the benefits of a comprehensive capability. Effective and exercised evacuation plans remove people from harm's way. A fully functioning tsunami warning system saves lives. Rigorous building codes mean fewer deaths and lower costs for expensive reconstruction and debris removal after a devastating event. For the foreseeable future, the challenge for emergency management is balancing these conflicting realities while meeting the responsibility of saving lives and protecting property.

Impacts of the Past Year

2010 was a devastating year in the annals of disasters. It began with a 7.0 magnitude earthquake in Haiti that claimed more than 200,000 lives. Although this didn't occur on American soil, several federal agencies—including the Federal Emergency Management Agency—provided significant assistance and expertise in terms of logistics, communications, and urban search and rescue. Only a few months later, the BP Deepwater Horizon oil drilling rig exploded, killing 11 people and resulting in a massive, three-month-long oil spill of more than 200 million gallons into the Gulf Coast. This presented unique challenges because of the involvement of the private sector, multiple federal agencies and several states. That same month, an explosion at a West Virginia coal mine resulted in the deaths of 29 miners. In addition to these events, there were record-breaking snowstorms along the East Coast, flooding in the South and Great Plains, and tornadoes in the Midwest. For the year, there were 81 presidentially declared disasters, the most since FEMA started keeping records in 1953.

As all of this was taking place, the country continued to face the worst economic conditions since the Great Depression. State revenues plummeted while demand for government assistance was higher than ever. After the 2008 financial meltdown, the federal government provided monetary assistance to state and local government through the American Recovery and Reinvestment Act. Many states used these funds over the past two years to plug holes in their budgets. Now, however, the money is no longer available, so states must find other fixes to address their serious budget dilemmas. These include tax increases and drastic cuts. The latter is particularly worrisome to state emergency management, where eliminated positions can endanger a population.

New Faces, Old Problems

In 2010, 37 states and two U.S. territories held gubernatorial races. While 12 incumbent governors were re-elected, 27 were new to the office. Since a disaster can be the first true test of an administration, not only did many of them need to learn quickly how the emergency management system works, but they also were at the same time appointing new state emergency management directors.

Budget struggles continue to plague the far majority of these governors and their directors. State budgets usually take longer to rebound from economic downturns because sales, income and property taxes—which are used to fund vital state functions such as emergency management and homeland security—don't increase until the economic picture has improved. As a result, agencies are dealing with budget cuts and hiring moratoriums.

Because of all-time-high deficits, Congress and the Washington administration are scrutinizing federal grants. These include two that are critical to state emergency management and homeland security, the Homeland Security Grant Program

(HSGP) and the Emergency Management Performance Grant (EMPG). HSGP consists of five grants and its central element provides funds to build capabilities at the state and local levels. Money also can be used to implement the goals and objectives included in state homeland security strategies and initiatives in each State Preparedness Report. EMPG is a core state emergency management funding mechanism and the only source of federal money directed to state and local governments for planning, training, exercises and personnel for all-hazards emergency preparedness. The role it plays cannot be overstated because it serves as the lifeblood to emergency management throughout the United States.

Any kind of reduction to these grants will impact not only the grant amount itself, but the match as well. Since its inception, EMPG has required a 50 percent federal and at least a 50 percent non-federal match. Even as the economic picture has worsened and some have suggested requesting a higher match from the federal government, state government has stood fast, believing that every level of government has a responsibility in building emergency management capacity nationwide. In many cases, state and local governments continue to demonstrate a commitment to building that capacity by contributing more than the required 50 percent contribution.

However, if states aren't able to provide the match, they lose out on irreplaceable dollars. Investments made thus far in terrorism-preparedness programs, response equipment, planning efforts and training are jeopardized without adequate money to sustain them. States are already seeing the ramifications at the local emergency management level. Because local emergency management programs can't provide their EMPG cost share, they're turning down grant funding, which puts local agencies across the country at risk and seriously compromises that vital first rung of response capability.

The importance of EMPG and a strong local component is obvious in the fact that there were more than 44,637 actual local and tribal emergency response incidents in the 2010 fiscal year, including 19,571 state response incidents, which were supported utilizing EMPG funds.[1] In addition, in 2009, 59 disasters occurred requiring a presidential declaration and federal assistance. At the state level, however, 180 disasters required a gubernatorial declaration but no federal assistance, and another 122 events required state resources, but no decla-

ration. Without solid capabilities at the state and local level afforded through EMPG, events normally not requiring federal action could end up at the federal government's footsteps, requiring more costly expenditures.

As part of its budget examination process, the Obama administration is also actively pursuing a performance metrics approach—asking that both federal agencies and federal grants substantiate specific outcomes based on the investment and programmatic goals. State and local emergency management have already taken a significant step in this area with a report to Congress on EMPG that quantifies the full reach of the program, from enhanced interoperable communications and public education campaigns to emergency response plans and personnel training.

Another concern for emergency management is emergency operation centers (EOCs) funding. During emergencies and disasters, these facilities serve as the nerve center for state and local coordination, and are necessary to ensure continuity of operations and government in major disasters caused by any hazard. Federal agencies also use these EOCs as a central point for communication during response and recovery phases. Congress did appropriate some funding to states to update their centers after September 2001. However, it only allowed for limited planning and a needs assessment.

It's estimated that $398 million would be needed to build, retrofit and upgrade state primary and alternate EOCs. In addition, when considering the needs to build, retrofit and upgrade local primary and alternate EOCs as well, the overall requirement is approximately $1.3 billion.[2] The current Emergency Operation Centers Grant Program is intended to improve emergency management and preparedness capabilities by supporting flexible, sustainable, secure and interoperable EOCs with a focus on addressing identified deficiencies. This program has become markedly less effective, however, because of Congressional earmarks that prevent funds from reaching the most pressing projects as determined by state officials. It's hoped that Congress will recommit to tackling the EOC problem and acknowledge its critical role by allotting funds based on true need.

Finally, there's the issue of communications. After the 2001 terrorist attacks, communication challenges and failures were examined and debated. A current example of these is referred to as the D-Block. The Federal Communications Commission has licensed 10 MHz of radio spectrum in the 700 MHz band to

Table A: State Emergency Management: Agency Structure, Budget and Staffing

State or other jurisdiction	Position appointed	Appointed/ selected by	Organizational structure	Agency operating budget FY 2011	Full-time employee positions
Alabama	★	G	Stand-Alone Agency	$5,170,000	96
Alaska	★	G	Adjutant General/Military Affairs	$2,389,000	58 (c)
Arizona	★	ADJ	Adjutant General/Military Affairs	$1,337,205	60
Arkansas	★	G	Governor's Office	$2,394,335	100 (c)
California	★	G	Governor's Office	$48,229,000	598 (c)
Colorado	…	ED	Department of Local Affairs	$637,624	29
Connecticut	…	HSEMC	Governor's Office	$5,400,000	34 (c)
Delaware	....(a)..				
Florida	★	G	Governor's Office	$43,163,922	136
Georgia	★	G	Governor's Office	$3,115,577	107 (c)
Hawaii	★	ADJ/DCD	Adjutant General/Military Affairs	$1,500,000	92 (c)
Idaho	★	ADJ	Adjutant General/Military Affairs	$1,500,000	66 (c)
Illinois	★	G	Governor's Office	$33,481,400	228 (c)
Indiana	★	G	Combined Homeland Security/Emerg. Mgt.	$12,150,000	248 (b)
Iowa	★	G	Adjutant General/Military Affairs	$2,987,819	120 (c)
Kansas	★	G	Adjutant General/Military Affairs	$1,025,147	37.5
Kentucky	★	G	Adjutant General/Military Affairs	$1,741,100	97
Louisiana	★	G	Governor's Office	$19,068,341	164 (c)
Maine	★	G	Adjutant General/Military Affairs	$970,000	21
Maryland	★	G	Governor's Office	$2,500,000	65
Massachusetts	★	G	Public Safety	$4,324,135	71
Michigan	★	G	State Police	$4,638,700	221 (c)
Minnesota	★	PSS	Public Safety	$5,433,000	73 (c)
Mississippi	★	G	Stand-Alone Agency	$6,822,493	116
Missouri	★	PSS	Public Safety	$3,378,000	65
Montana	…	ADJ	Adjutant General/Military Affairs	$775,000	23 (c)
Nebraska	★	ADJ	Adjutant General/Military Affairs	$1,410,112	36
Nevada	★	PSS	Public Safety	$593,043	35 (c)
New Hampshire	★	G	Public Safety	$3,703,064	43 (c)
New Jersey	★	G	State Police	$6,243,118	353 (d)
New Mexico	★	G	Stand-Alone Agency	$3,100,000	68 (c)
New York	★	G	Governor's Office	$6,600,000	386 (c)
North Carolina	★	G	Public Safety	$8,800,246	178
North Dakota	★	ADJ	Adjutant General/Military Affairs	$6,200,000	12
Ohio	★	PSS	Public Safety	$5,168,480	94
Oklahoma	★	G	Governor's Office	$700,000	32
Oregon	★	ADJ	Adjutant General/Military Affairs	$1,700,000	45
Pennsylvania	★	G	Governor's Office	$11,882,000	150
Rhode Island	★	G	Adjutant General/Military Affairs	$1,335,731	28 (c)
South Carolina	★	ADJ	Adjutant General/Military Affairs	$2,224,987	64
South Dakota	★	PSS	Public Safety	$615,466	19
Tennessee	★	G	Adjutant General/Military Affairs	$2,500,000	100
Texas	…	G	Public Safety	$5,403,000	185
Utah	★	G	Public Safety	$951,100	52
Vermont	★	PSS	Public Safety	$2,380,000	18.5
Virginia	★	G	Public Safety	$7,500,000	141
Washington	★	ADJ	Adjutant General/Military Affairs	$4,066,276	89 (c)
West Virginia	★	G	Adjutant General/Public Safety	$5,296,187	53
Wisconsin	★	G	Adjutant General/Military Affairs	$9,207,600	52
Wyoming	....(a)..				
Dist. of Columbia	★	M	Combined Homeland Security/Emerg. Mgt.	$1,994,000	56 (c)
American Samoa	★	G	Combined Homeland Security/Emerg. Mgt.	$111,500	6 (c)
Guam	★	G	Governor's Office	$0	10 (c)
Puerto Rico	★	G	Combined Homeland Security/Emerg. Mgt.	$6,401,000	200 (c)
U.S. Virgin Islands	★	G	Governor's Office	$5,441,382	93 (c)

Source: The National Emergency Management Association, February 2011
Key:
★ — Yes
… — No
G — Governor
ADJ — Adjutant General
ADJ/DCD — Adjutant General/Director of Civil Defense
ED — Executive Director, Dept. of Local Affairs
M — Mayor

HSEMC — Homeland Security/Emergency Management Commissioner
PSS — Public Safety Secretary/Commissioner/Director
(a) Not a member of NEMA, and is not represented in the survey data.
(b) Includes homeland security, emergency management and other positions.
(c) Includes both homeland security and emergency management positions.
(d) Includes telecommunications personnel.

public safety for broadband services. Many national organizations agree this 10 MHz is insufficient to meet public safety's bandwidth needs and public safety must have more spectrum.

Such spectrum exists and is available through the D-Block, which is located directly adjacent to the spectrum currently licensed to public safety for broadband services. The D-Block is also the only substantial contiguous spectrum remaining in the 700 MHz band yet to be licensed. However, under current statute, the FCC is required to auction the D-Block spectrum for commercial services. Once auctioned, the D-Block would be encumbered and public safety could be forced to build an interoperable network in two separate bands. This would mean additional expense to bridge the disparate systems. Congress is being asked to support legislation allocating the D-Block to public safety and to provide a funding mechanism to build-out the network so that essential communications systems are available during an emergency situation.

State Emergency Management and Homeland Security Structures

When a disaster strikes, emergency management becomes one of the most crucial functions of state government. It is the central coordination point for all resources and assistance provided during disasters and emergencies, including acts of terrorism. It also has the overarching responsibility of saving lives, protecting property and helping citizens recover once a disaster has occurred. Typically, emergency management comes to the forefront once an event has taken place. In reality, much of the work comes before—in the form of disaster drills and exercises, hazard mitigation programs, public warning tests and preparedness education.

Emergency management includes four main parts, referred to as the "Four Pillars":

- Mitigation—Activities that reduce or eliminate the degree of risk to human life and property;

- Preparedness—Pre-disaster activities to develop and maintain a capability to respond rapidly and effectively to emergencies and disasters;

- Response—Activities to assess and contain the immediate effects of disasters, provide life support to victims and deliver emergency services; and

- Recovery—Activities to restore damaged facilities and equipment, and support the economic and social revitalization of affected areas to their pre-emergency status.

On the state level, these four elements encompass many different aspects, from planning and implementation to training and exercising. A state emergency manager will interact with all sectors of the population, including other state agencies, elected officials, local jurisdictions, all public safety personnel, the private sector and the general public.

Emergency Management-Homeland Security Organizations/Budgets

In 12 states, the emergency management agency is currently located within the department of public safety; in 18 states it is located within the military department under the auspices of the adjutant general; and in 13 states, it is in the governor's office.[3] In five of the six states with the most disaster declarations since 1953, the emergency management director reports directly to the governor.[4]

Regardless of agencies' organizational structure for daily operations, emergency management ranks high among governors' priorities. In 35 states, the governor appoints the emergency management director, an increase from 32 in the 2010 fiscal year. In eight other states, the adjutant general appoints the position, while the secretary of public safety appoints the position in six states.

For the homeland security function, only three states house the day-to-day operations in a stand-alone homeland security agency or office. In 17 states, either emergency management or a combined emergency management/homeland security office oversees daily operations. Eight states run it out of the governor's office while another eight have it in the adjutant general/military affairs department. Fourteen states keep the homeland security function in their public safety department.

Every state has a designated homeland security point of contact. Who takes on this responsibility varies from state to state. Currently, 14 states assign the homeland security advisor role to their homeland security director. In another 19 states, either the emergency management director or a combined emergency management/homeland security director is the primary point of contact. Seven states have the adjutant general serving in this capacity. Six public safety secretaries/commissioners are in this role. The remaining states have other options in place.

Emergency management agency operating budgets for the 2011 fiscal year range up to about $48 million. Twenty-six states saw their emergency management funds shrink. This trend is expected to continue until the economic recovery is realized

Table B: Homeland Security Structures

State or other jurisdiction	State homeland security advisor — Designated homeland security advisor	Homeland security organizations — Day-to-day operations under	Full-time employee positions
Alabama	Homeland Security Director	Homeland Security (stand-alone office)	7
Alaska	Combined Emerg. Mgt./Homeland Security Director	Adjutant General/Military Affairs	58 (c)
Arizona	Homeland Security Director	Homeland Security (stand-alone office)	17
Arkansas	Emergency Management Director	Emergency Management	100 (c)
California	Combined Emerg. Mgt./Homeland Security Director	Combined Emerg. Mgt./Homeland Security Office	598 (c)
Colorado	Homeland Security Director	Governor's Office	14
Connecticut	Commissioner of Emerg. Mgt./Homeland Security	Governor's Office	34 (c)
Delaware	....	(a)	
Florida	Florida Dept. of Law Enforcement	Governor's Office	58
Georgia	Combined Emerg. Mgt./Homeland Security Director	Emergency Management	107 (c)
Hawaii	Adj. General/Director of Civil Defense	Adjutant General/Military Affairs	92 (c)
Idaho	Adjutant General	Adjutant General/Military Affairs	66 (c)
Illinois	Combined Emerg. Mgt./Homeland Security Director	Combined Emerg. Mgt./Homeland Security Office	228 (c)
Indiana	Combined Emerg. Mgt./Homeland Security Director	Combined Emerg. Mgt./Homeland Security Office	248 (b)
Iowa	Emergency Management Director	Combined Emerg. Mgt./Homeland Security Office	120 (c)
Kansas	Adjutant General	Adjutant General/Military Affairs	5
Kentucky	Homeland Security Director	Governor's Office	16
Louisiana	Combined Emerg. Mgt./Homeland Security Director	Governor's Office	164 (c)
Maine	Adjutant General	Emergency Management	3
Maryland	Homeland Security Advisor	Governor's Office	3
Massachusetts	Public Safety Secretary/Commissioner	Public Safety	8
Michigan	State Police Lieutenant	State Police	221 (c)
Minnesota	Emergency Management Director	Public Safety	73 (c)
Mississippi	Homeland Security Director	Public Safety	15
Missouri	Public Safety Secretary/Commissioner	Public Safety	19
Montana	Combined Emerg. Mgt./Homeland Security Director	Emergency Management	23 (c)
Nebraska	Lieutenant Governor	Emergency Management	10 (d)
Nevada	Combined Emerg. Mgt./Homeland Security Director	Emergency Management	35 (c)
New Hampshire	Combined Emerg. Mgt./Homeland Security Director	Public Safety	43 (c)
New Jersey	Homeland Security Director	Homeland Security (stand-alone office)	105
New Mexico	Combined Emerg. Mgt./Homeland Security Director	Stand Alone Cabinet Agency	68 (c)
New York	Public Safety Secretary/Commissioner	Combined Emerg. Mgt./Homeland Security Office	386 (c)
North Carolina	Public Safety Secretary/Commissioner	Emergency Management	11 (d)
North Dakota	Homeland Security Director	Adjutant General/Military Affairs	6
Ohio	Homeland Security Director	Public Safety	35
Oklahoma	Homeland Security Director	Public Safety	19
Oregon	Adjutant General	Adjutant General/Military Affairs	2
Pennsylvania	Emergency Management Director	Emergency Management	2
Rhode Island	Adjutant General	Emergency Management	28 (c)
South Carolina	State Police Superintendent/Director/Commissioner	State Police	26
South Dakota	Homeland Security Director	Public Safety	3
Tennessee	Public Safety Commissioner	Public Safety	28
Texas	Public Safety Secretary/Commissioner	Public Safety	36
Utah	Combined Emerg. Mgt./Homeland Security Director	Public Safety	65
Vermont	Homeland Security Director	Public Safety	8
Virginia	Special Assistant to Governor	Governor's Office	9
Washington	Adjutant General	Adjutant General/Military Affairs	89 (c)
West Virginia	Public Safety Secretary/Commissioner	Public Safety	8
Wisconsin	Adjutant General	Adjutant General/Military Affairs	0
Wyoming	....	(a)	
Dist. of Columbia	Combined Emerg. Mgt./Homeland Security Director	Combined Emerg. Mgt./Homeland Security Office	56 (c)
American Samoa	Homeland Security Director	Combined Emerg. Mgt./Homeland Security Office	6 (c)
Guam	Homeland Security Director	Governor's Office	10 (c)
Puerto Rico	Combined Emerg. Mgt./Homeland Security Director	Public Safety	200 (c)
U.S. Virgin Islands	Combined Emerg. Mgt./Homeland Security Advisor	Combined Emerg. Mgt./Homeland Security Office	93 (c)

Source: The National Emergency Management Association, February 2011.

(a) Not a member of NEMA and is not represented in the survey data.

(b) Includes homeland security, emergency management and other positions.

(c) Includes homeland security and emergency management positions.

(d) Part of emergency management personnel.

in state coffers. The median for the 2011 fiscal year state emergency management budgets is $3,115,577, down for the second year in a row. Last year, it was $3,300,000 and in the 2009 fiscal year, it stood at $3,406,500.

What's Ahead

In the current disaster assistance system, Congress appropriates money every year to the Disaster Relief Fund, which is designed to assist individuals and communities that have been struck by disasters. Despite regular funding, the amount in the DRF is rarely sufficient, particularly if there's a devastating event such as the 2008 Iowa floods or a catastrophic disaster such as Hurricane Katrina. In these situations, Congress adds money to the DRF fund in the form of emergency supplemental appropriations. Between 1990 and 2010, Congress provided additional DRF funding in 16 years. In fact, over the 21-year span, the total funding averaged nearly six times the original appropriated amount.[5]

This means Congress must intervene almost 75 percent of the time. Sometimes, these additional appropriations are delayed, which hurts jurisdictions that have experienced a disaster and need help. It also wreaks havoc on the federal budgeting process as well as federal budget deficits. As a result, states have begun discussing alternative ways to provide federal financial assistance. They're exploring options that save money while delivering financial aid in a faster, more efficient manner. These proposals are expected to be presented in 2011.

From the federal perspective, FEMA has initiated a comprehensive review of its Public Assistance Program. After a presidentially declared disaster or emergency, this program gives grants to state, tribal and local governments for certain work that protects life and property, and for damaged infrastructure. FEMA has indicated that it's open to a total revamping of the Public Assistance Program, with the express goal of improving the effectiveness and efficiency of the program.

States are also waiting to see how this project will complement another federal initiative, the development of the National Disaster Recovery Framework. Mandated by Congress, this document will culminate in a review of the entire disaster recovery process, with a focus on long-term recovery. Every aspect of disaster recovery assistance—roles, programs and responsibilities—is being studied, and FEMA indicates this will result

in modifications, though the degree is unknown. The release of the framework was delayed from 2010 until sometime in 2011.

Even before the 2011 Japan earthquake and the ensuing nuclear events, state emergency management had worked closely for years with its respective nuclear facilities on radiological emergency procedures, notifications and evacuations. Last year, state emergency management across the country weighed in on key documents involving radiological emergency preparedness programs, and will follow it up in 2011 with comments on NUREG 0654, which provides guidance for response to nuclear power facility emergencies. The tragic occurrences in Japan illustrate that so much of effective emergency management must take place in the preparation phase with plans that are tried and tested, and procedures that cover all facets of an incident.

Finally, the National Level Exercise takes place in 2011 and will simulate a major catastrophic earthquake of the New Madrid Seismic Zone, which cuts across the central United States. 2011 is the bicentennial anniversary of the 1811 New Madrid earthquake. Congress mandates these national exercises, which include all appropriate federal agencies and state counterparts. Participating states are Alabama, Arkansas, Illinois, Indiana, Kentucky, Mississippi, Missouri and Tennessee. The overall goal of the exercise is to push response and recovery mechanisms to the breaking point, so that officials can determine the gaps in the systems and address those before an earthquake, or any catastrophic event, actually occurs.

The exercise and related activities also will reveal more about the concept of interdependencies, how one disaster can cause a series of cascading failures, thereby multiplying the consequences of the original event. The National Level Exercise could assist in determining how these relationships can be integrated into the planning process, including building in resilient approaches. An instance of interdependencies occurred after the BP oil spill when fish/seafood markets throughout the United States that relied on the Gulf Coast experienced price increases and reduced inventory. The country has also witnessed larger examples of this with the political upheaval in the Middle East, which elevated oil prices. A New Madrid earthquake that takes out major transportation corridors could not only affect the heating oil supply to the Northeast, but also disrupt commerce across the nation.

Notes

[1] *Emergency Management Performance Grants Providing Returns on a Nation's Investment*, National Emergency Management Association and International Association of Emergency Managers, March 2011.

[2] *NEMA 2010 Biennial Report*, National Emergency Management Association, July 2010.

[3] This data is based on an annual NEMA survey of state emergency management directors. NEMA received 53 responses, which included 48 states, the District of Columbia, American Samoa, Guam, Puerto Rico and the U.S. Virgin Islands. The term "state" throughout the text refers to all respondents.

[4] *Declared Disasters by Year or State*, Federal Emergency Management Agency.

[5] *Disaster Relief Funding and Emergency Supplemental Appropriations*, Congressional Research Service, July 2009.

About the Author

Beverly Bell is the senior policy analyst for the National Emergency Management Association, an affiliate of The Council of State Governments. In her position, she coordinates and conducts research, interacts with the states on changing federal policy and acts as an information clearinghouse for emergency management and homeland security issues.

Reducing Class Size:
Is it Worth the Investment?

By Tim Weldon

It has been a widely held belief for many years that the number of students in a class can impact student learning through the amount of individualized instruction students receive and the level of disruptive behavior, which can be worse in classrooms with too many students. However, despite those popularly held views, empirical evidence does not show a clear-cut connection between class size and student achievement, particularly at the secondary school level. This lack of evidence showing favorable outcomes associated with reduced class size, combined with restrictive state budgets, has resulted in bigger class sizes in recent years. This article examines conflicting research regarding class size and student learning, as well as state policies governing the number of students per class.

Florida voters sent state leaders a conflicting message during the 2010 election. On one hand, they elected a conservative Republican legislature and governor running on a platform of controlling government spending. At the same time, they rejected Amendment 8, which would have eased class size restrictions put in place by a ballot initiative in 2002. The defeat of Amendment 8 will cost taxpayers $40 billion over the next decade, according to the Florida Education Finance Program.

Clearly, Florida voters believe the investment in smaller class sizes is worth the expense. Questions linger, however, among education researchers over the value of smaller class sizes.

Consider the following conclusions reached in two policy studies. In a report published in the *American Education Research Journal*, Jeremy Finn and Charles Achilles wrote, "This research leaves no doubt that small classes have an advantage over larger classes in reading and math in the early primary grades."[1] Another study by Chester Finn and Michael Petrilli, however, stated, "There is no credible evidence that across-the-board reductions in class size boost pupil achievement."[2]

Those conflicting research findings pose a dilemma for legislators and other state policymakers in making critical decisions regarding class sizes. Without clear-cut evidence demonstrating students in smaller classes achieve at a higher rate than those in larger classes, some policymakers might wonder whether investing in smaller classes is worth the cost, particularly during a time of increasingly tight budgets.

The Case for Smaller Classes

According to the National Center for Education Statistics, the national ratio of students to teachers declined from 17.6 in 1990 to 15.8 in 2008.[3] That number is artificially low because it includes special education and other specialized teachers who typically have much smaller classes than most teachers. The U.S. Department of Education estimates the current average class size in departmental instruction—such as English, science, mathematics and social studies—is closer to 25 students per teacher.[4] The pupil-teacher ratio is determined by dividing the number of students at a given period of time by the full-time equivalent number of classroom teachers serving those students.

Despite the expense of employing more teachers to reduce pupil-teacher ratio, one study concludes reducing class sizes from 22 to 15 in grades K–3 actually results in a $2 return on every $1 spent. That calculation is based on the assumption that the smaller classes will result in increased student achievement and increased earnings later in life.[5]

One study found that when compared to average-sized classes, students in smaller classes in the early years take more advanced courses in high school and are more likely to graduate in the top 10 percent of their class.[6] Another study found that African-American students who attended small classes in the early elementary years were more likely to take the SAT and ACT in high school. This study estimated that smaller elementary class sizes alone could reduce the black/white gap in SAT and ACT participation by 60 percent.[7]

The National Education Association also argues reducing the pupil-teacher ratio helps in the early identification of learning disabilities and leads to fewer special education placements in later grades, improves high school graduation rates, and results in fewer incarcerations and improved student behavior.[8]

The most highly regarded study of the relationship between pupil-teacher ratio and achievement is the four-year Student/Teacher Achievement Ratio, known as Project STAR, which began in 1984 and tracked more than 7,000 students in 79 schools in Tennessee. The students were randomly assigned to one of three groups: small class (13 to 17 students per teacher), regular class (22 to 25 students per teacher), and regular-with-aide class (22 to 25 students with a teacher and full-time teacher's aide).

The interventions began when students entered kindergarten and continued through third grade. Project STAR demonstrated that students in smaller classes scored higher than students in larger classes on standardized and curriculum-based tests. This was true for white and minority students and for students from inner-city, urban, suburban and rural schools. In each grade, minorities and disadvantaged students enjoyed greater small-class advantages than whites on some or all measures. In addition, the schools retained a smaller proportion of students in the smaller classes and identified more students with special needs early.[9] In 1999, more than a decade after the study began, researchers reported the students who had been placed in small classes in grades K–3 had better high school graduation rates, higher grade point averages and were more likely to pursue postsecondary education.[10]

Likewise, a 2001 study by researchers at the Education Policy Studies Laboratory at Arizona State University and the University of Wisconsin-Milwaukee found a class size reduction program known as the Student Achievement Guarantee in Education in Wisconsin, known as Project SAGE, had resulted in higher achievement for children living in poverty.[11]

Project SAGE was enacted by state law in 1995 as a five-year pilot program to determine whether smaller class sizes in elementary school raise academic achievement for disadvantaged students. SAGE classrooms had a student-teacher ratio of 12 to 15 students per teacher, compared to 21 to 25 students per teacher in comparison classes. Though they started first grade with the same academic

profiles, African-American students made greater gains in the small SAGE classes than African-Americans in larger classes.[12]

A report by the California Senate Office of Research concluded a partial list of positive outcomes associated with class size reductions includes:

- For students
  - More individual attention;
  - Increased time on task;
  - Increased opportunities to participate;
  - Improved self-image; and
  - Improved attendance.
- For teachers
  - More job satisfaction;
  - More activities initiated by the teacher, especially enrichment activities;
  - Less time spent on discipline; and
  - Better ability to assess and monitor student performance.[13]

The National Education Association recommends an optimum class size of 15 students in regular programs, especially in the early grades, and a proportionately lower number in programs for students with exceptional needs, including children with disabilities and English language learners.[14]

Class Size Does Not Matter

Not all research has come to the same conclusion as the STAR study. One conducted by Matthew Chingos, a research fellow at Harvard University's Program on Educational Policy and Governance, analyzed reading and math test scores for all Florida students in grades four through eight between 2001 and 2007.

In 2002, Florida voters approved an amendment mandating that by the beginning of the 2010–11 school year, class sizes were to be reduced to no more than 18 students in prekindergarten through third grade, 22 students in fourth through eighth grade, and 25 students in ninth through 12th grade.

According to the Florida Department of Education, the amendment resulted in a drop in pupil-teacher ratio in grades four through eight from 24.3 in 2003 to 18.6 in 2009 at a cost to taxpayers of approximately $4 billion per year.

In his study, Chingos evaluated the impact Florida's statewide class size reduction policy had on student achievement. He found students attending schools in districts that were required to reduce class size did no better on state assessments than students in schools with higher pupil-teacher ratios. His study also showed no significant impact on student absenteeism and behavior.[15]

Other research analysts have concluded class size reduction does not have a significant effect on achievement. One such study examined trend data from the 1950s to 1986 and did not find any consistent relationship between class size and standardized test scores. In the U.S. Department of Education report, "Class size and public policy: Politics and panacea," author Tom Tomlinson concluded existing research did not justify a policy to reduce class size in view of the costs involved.[16]

Similarly, a review of research published in *Educational Evaluation and Policy Analysis* concluded, "... A system-wide class reduction policy would produce only modest gains in student achievement and incur an unjustifiably high cost."[17]

One Policymaker's Perspective

Illinois State Rep. Roger Eddy has an unusual perspective on state policies that address class size. Not only is he a veteran legislator, but he also serves as superintendent of Hutsonville School District in southern Illinois. Thus, he not only is a voice on educational issues in the state legislature, but as a local school district superintendent he must implement policies enacted in Springfield.

Eddy believes smaller class sizes are generally beneficial for students through grade eight, as well as those with special needs.

"I think it makes the most difference for the students who need it the most. If a student has some sort of developmental delay or any type of need for special attention, they're the ones who are going to be affected," he explained.

For students whose academic abilities are average or above average, however, Eddy says he does not believe smaller class sizes are necessarily helpful in secondary grades. In fact, he believes for some advanced students, the opposite might be true.

"Sometimes the above-average student benefits from being in a class with more interaction and more opportunities for teamwork and cooperative learning," he said. "Perhaps in some cases (with small class size), it may actually inhibit (learning). So, I don't think for the average or above-average student, the size of the class makes all that much difference."

Like many states, recent budget constraints have resulted in teacher reductions in many school districts in Illinois. The effect has been larger class sizes, a trend that Eddy foresees continuing for the foreseeable future.

What States are Doing

According to the Education Commission of the States, 25 states have policies addressing class-size reductions to a level below 22 students per classroom. (State-by-state data of pupil-teacher ratios can be found at the end of this report.) The vast majority of these policies target students in elementary grades, particularly K–3.

For example, an Illinois statute created a voluntary program that provides grants to reduce class size to no more than 20 students per teacher in grades K–3. Eligibility is limited to districts with schools serving grades K–3 that are on the State Board of Education academic warning or academic watch lists.[18]

Nevada's economic woes led legislators to enact Assembly Bill 4, which was signed into law in February 2010. It gave school districts a temporary reprieve from class size caps in grades 1–3 by allowing them to increase maximum class sizes by up to two students above the caps enacted by the legislature in 1989. The new law contains the following provisions for the 2010–11 school year:

- School districts may increase class sizes in grades 1–2 from a maximum of 16 to a maximum of 18.

- The maximum class size in third grade increased from 19 to 21.

- Any funds a district would have used to achieve the lower class sizes in grades 1–3 must be used to minimize the impact of budget cuts on class sizes in grades 4–12.

Texas, which faces a potential budget shortfall of more than $20 billion over the next biennium, is considering increasing its cap on pupil-teacher ratio in the 2011 legislative session. Texas currently limits the number of students in grades K–4 to 22 unless a school obtains a waiver. The Senate Education Committee has recommended easing class size limits as a cost-saving measure.

In a speech in November 2010, U.S. Education Secretary Arne Duncan called for class size flexibility. "In our blueprint for reauthorizing the Elementary and Secondary Education Act, we support shifting away from class-size based reduction that is not evidence-based. It might be that districts would vary class sizes by the subject matter or the skill of the teacher, or that part-time staff could be leveraged to lower class size during critical reading blocks," he said.[19]

Table A: Student/Teacher Ratio, by State (2007–08)

State or other jurisdiction	Students	Staff	Total student/teacher ratio	Elementary student/teacher ratio	Secondary student/teacher ratio
Alabama	744,865	111,656	14.8	20.1	10.2
Alaska	131,029	16,593	17.2	22.9	11.3
Arizona	1,087,447	104,670	20.1	18.9	20.8
Arkansas	479,016	70,331	14.1	19.9	10.3
California	6,343,471	583,625	20.8	20.7	23.4
Colorado	801,867	99,326	16.8	20.8	11.3
Connecticut	570,626	86,762	14.5	14.1	14.4
Delaware	122,574	15,524	15	20.4	9.2
Florida	2,666,811	329,726	15.8	25.3	12.1
Georgia	1,649,589	235,083	14.1	16.6	10.3
Hawaii	179,897	21,657	15.8	21.2	10.3
Idaho	272,119	27,149	18.1	23.5	11.3
Illinois	2,112,805	214,459	15.5	25.1	10.9
Indiana	1,046,766	139,460	16.8	21.8	11.3
Iowa	485,115	71,794	13.4	17.3	9.4
Kansas	468,295	54,232	13.2	19.5	7.6
Kentucky	666,225	100,362	15.3	20.4	19.4
Louisiana	681,038	99,625	14	13.8	12.5
Maine	196,245	39,918	11.9	11	12.6
Maryland	845,700	116,857	14.3	15.9	10.8
Massachusetts	962,958	123,114	13.6	13.4	12.5
Michigan	1,692,739	208,987	17.6	29.3	14.3
Minnesota	837,578	108,432	15.8	21.1	11.4
Mississippi	494,122	71,144	14.7	22.2	10.5
Missouri	917,188	133,607	13.4	18	8.6
Montana	142,823	19,179	13.6	13.8	13.5
Nebraska	291,244	43,672	13.3	13.7	11.6
Nevada	494,122	71,144	18.3	24.8	15.1
New Hampshire	200,772	32,573	13	12.1	13.5
New Jersey	1,382,348	201,552	12.4	18.8	8.9
New Mexico	329,040	46,699	14.8	14.3	15
New York	2,765,435	374,080	13.1	18.1	12
North Carolina	1,489,492	203,287	14	19.4	8.6
North Dakota	95,059	15,385	11.8	12.6	10.2
Ohio	1,827,184	243,579	16.6	23.8	11.2
Oklahoma	642,065	86,758	13.7	20	8.9
Oregon	565,586	64,619	18.8	18.4	19.9
Pennsylvania	1,801,971	254,476	13.3	18.9	9.4
Rhode Island	147,629	17,559	13.1	18	8.2
South Carolina	712,317	66,087	15	38.6	6.8
South Dakota	121,606	17,019	12.9	14.1	15.1
Tennessee	964,259	126,646	14.9	14.7	15.2
Texas	4,674,832	635,715	14.5	21.1	10.5
Utah	576,244	48,515	23.7	32.9	17.1
Vermont	94,038	19,184	10.7	17.8	8.6
Virginia	1,230,857	204,384	17.1	25.3	10.3
Washington	1,030,247	103,714	19.1	25.6	14.9
West Virginia	282,535	38,309	13.9	20.5	7.8
Wisconsin	874,633	104,981	14.8	21	9.4
Wyoming	86,422	15,464	12.5	16.4	8.1
Dist. of Columbia	78,422	12,532	12.4	15.4	7.7
Dept. of Defense (excludes overseas schools)	27,548	3,994	12.3	24.4	6.3
Puerto Rico	526,565	71,847	12.9	15.5	10.7
U.S. Virgin Islands	15,903	3,137	10.5	16.6	8.7

Source: National Center for Education Statistics. *Public Elementary and Secondary School Student Enrollment and Staff Counts from the Common Core of Data: School Year 2007–08.*
Accessed at *http://nces.ed.gov/pubs2010/2010309/tables/table_04.asp.*

Duncan predicted some school districts in coming years will be forced to weigh class size increases against the loss of music, arts and after-school programs. He also pointed out that, "Many high-performing education systems, especially in Asia, have substantially larger classes than the United States." For example, he said the average class size is 36 students per teacher in South Korea and 33 students per teacher in Japan.

Conclusion

Reducing class size is widely considered one of the most expensive education reform measures a state can take. As state policymakers look for ways to cut costs and respond to budget deficits, many will undoubtedly insist on spending money only on proven policies they can reasonably expect to produce results.

While conventional wisdom would seem to indicate that smaller class sizes have benefits over larger ones, legislators and other policymakers will likely need to be convinced that the additional funds they spend to hire thousands more teachers and build thousands of new classrooms will be worth the cost. At this time, the evidence is murky at best, contradictory at worst, making it difficult for policymakers to make well-informed decisions whether to spend money to continue strict caps on pupil-teacher ratios.

Notes

[1] J.D. Finn, et al., "Answers and questions about class size." *American Educational Research Journal*, (1990), 557–77.

[2] C. Finn, et al., *The elixir of class size*, Thomas B. Fordham Foundation.

[3] National Education Association Policy Brief, *Class size reduction: A proven reform strategy*. Accessed at http://www.nea.org/assets/docs/mf_PB08_ClassSize.pdf on Dec. 14, 2011.

[4] National Center for Education Statistics. *Schools and staffing survey*. (2007–08) Accessed at http://nces.ed.gov/surveys/sass/tables/sass0708_2009324_t1s_08.asp on January 18, 2011.

[5] Alan Krueger, "Economic Considerations and Class Size," *The Economic Journal*, (2003) 113:485, 34–63.

[6] HEROS study, at www.heros-inc.org.

[7] A. Krueger, A. and D. Whitmore, *Would smaller classes help close the black/white achievement gap?* In J. Chubb and T. Loveless (Eds.), *Bridging the achievement gap*, (Washington, D.C.: Brookings Institute Press, 2002). Quoted in The Professional Learning Exchange. Accessed at https://psea.org/uploadedFiles/Publications/Professional_Publications/Advisories/ClassSizeReduction.pdf on Jan. 18, 2011.

[8] See note 3.

[9] Health and Education Research Operative Services. *Project STAR*. Accessed at http://www.heros-inc.org/star.htm on Dec. 14, 2010.

[10] See note 7.

[11] Phil Smith, et al., Class size reduction in Wisconsin: A fresh look at the data. Education Policy Research Unit. (September 2003). Accessed at http://epsl.asu.edu/epru/documents/EPRU-0309-29-RW.pdf on Dec. 14, 2010.

[12] American Youth Policy Forum. Raising Minority Academic Achievement. *Class size: Project SAGE*. Accessed at http://www.aypf.org/publications/rmaa/pdfs/ClassSizeSAGE.pdf on Jan. 18, 2011.

[13] Kim Connor, et al., "Class size: When less is more," Senate Office of Research, California Legislature, (1989).

[14] National Education Association. Class Size. Accessed at http://www.nea.org/home/13120.htm on Dec. 14, 2010.

[15] Matthew Chingos, *The impact of a universal class-size reduction policy: Evidence from Florida's statewide mandate*, Harvard University Program on Educational Policy and Governance, (August 2010) Accessed at http://www.hks.harvard.edu/pepg/PDF/Papers/PEPG10-03_Chingos.pdf on Dec. 14, 2010.

[16] Tom Tomlinson, "Class size and public policy: Politics and panaceas," U.S. Department of Education Office of Educational Research and Improvement (1988).

[17] Allen Odden, "Class Size and Student Achievement: Research-based policy alternatives," Educational Evaluation and Policy Analysis 12 (2): 213–227 (1990).

[18] Education Commission of the States, *Class Size Policies*, (April 2010). Accessed at http://www.ecs.org/clearinghouse/85/21/8521.pdf on Dec. 14, 2010.

[19] United States Department of Education, *The new normal: Doing more with less—Secretary Arne Duncan's remarks at the American Enterprise Institute* (November 2010). Accessed at http://www.ed.gov/news/speeches/new-normal-doing-more-less-secretary-arne-duncans-remarks-american-enterprise-instituton Jan. 18, 2011.

About the Author

Tim Weldon is an education policy analyst at The Council of State Governments. He is a former television and newspaper journalist and high school social studies teacher. He holds an M.A. degree in secondary education curriculum.

Table 9.1
NUMBER AND TYPES OF PUBLIC ELEMENTARY AND SECONDARY SCHOOLS, BY STATE OR JURISDICTION: SCHOOL YEAR 2008–09

State or other jurisdiction	Total number of schools	Type of school				Charter	Magnet (a)	Title I (b)	Title I schoolwide
		Regular	Special education	Vocational education	Alternative education				
Reporting states (c)	98,706	88,801	2,289	1,409	6,207	4,694	3,021	62,305	40,984
Alabama	1,605	1,375	41	73	116	n/a	27	855	768
Alaska...........................	507	451	2	3	51	24	13	358	312
Arizona..........................	2,186	1,908	20	172	86	477	N.A.	1,188	774
Arkansas.......................	1,129	1,089	4	24	12	32	39	818	692
California	10,029	8,451	145	76	1,357	751	438	6,032	4,556
Colorado......................	1,779	1,672	10	5	92	148	24	615	372
Connecticut..................	1,150	1,037	48	17	48	18	56	529	158
Delaware	240	182	19	6	33	18	3	111	101
Florida	3,985	3,328	173	53	431	399	357	2,538	2,323
Georgia.........................	2,472	2,230	73	1	168	63	N.R.	1,320	1,166
Hawaii..........................	290	286	3	0	1	31	n/a	182	172
Idaho............................	735	629	11	11	84	31	n/a	508	415
Illinois..........................	4,402	4,010	150	53	189	39	337	3,037	1,275
Indiana.........................	1,973	1,885	37	29	22	51	26	1,353	889
Iowa	1,490	1,423	8	0	59	9	n/a	940	482
Kansas	1,428	1,416	10	1	1	35	33	1,180	712
Kentucky	1,531	1,235	11	126	159	n/a	41	1,062	964
Louisiana......................	1,643	1,262	202	6	173	88	81	1,222	1,123
Maine...........................	663	633	1	27	2	n/a	1	N.A.	N.A.
Maryland......................	1,457	1,328	39	24	66	34	87	359	315
Massachusetts	1,855	1,771	26	39	19	61	N.A.	1,019	479
Michigan......................	4,078	3,365	317	62	334	283	479	3,514	1,426
Minnesota....................	2,263	1,654	271	12	326	174	75	868	277
Mississippi...................	1,077	921	4	90	62	1	6	709	682
Missouri.......................	2,423	2,193	66	63	101	41	37	1,133	523
Montana	830	823	2	0	5	n/a	n/a	662	370
Nebraska	1,122	1,081	36	0	5	n/a	n/a	485	262
Nevada	617	579	7	1	30	30	1	319	270
New Hampshire	492	492	0	0	0	15	n/a	238	37
New Jersey	2,588	2,351	74	55	108	62	N.A.	1,367	379
New Mexico	853	808	6	1	38	67	2	713	678
New York	4,690	4,587	47	28	28	115	318	4,410	2,197
North Carolina.............	2,548	2,417	33	10	88	96	127	1,135	982
North Dakota...............	525	484	34	7	0	n/a	n/a	310	77
Ohio.............................	3,852	3,710	61	72	9	326	n/a	2,837	1,830
Oklahoma....................	1,796	1,787	4	0	5	16	n/a	1,123	926
Oregon.........................	1,304	1,261	3	0	40	87	N.A.	579	399
Pennsylvania	3,248	3,136	12	87	13	127	57	2,425	704
Rhode Island................	327	299	3	10	15	11	n/a	231	121
South Carolina.............	1,211	1,129	10	39	23	36	57	928	869
South Dakota...............	721	687	7	0	27	n/a	n/a	621	331
Tennessee	1,755	1,689	19	21	26	14	34	1,355	1,275
Texas............................	8,530	7,434	20	0	1,076	499	n/a	6,411	6,044
Utah.............................	1,029	849	81	6	93	67	20	245	193
Vermont........................	328	312	0	15	1	n/a	n/a	223	142
Virginia........................	2,009	1,865	5	32	107	4	158	713	378
Washington..................	2,321	1,883	106	12	320	n/a	n/a	1,249	547
West Virginia...............	762	697	6	31	28	n/a	n/a	357	351
Wisconsin	2,268	2,159	9	8	92	221	5	1,517	380
Wyoming	360	332	3	0	25	3	n/a	186	80
Dist. of Columbia	230	206	10	1	13	90	4	216	206
DoDDS: DoDs Overseas (d)	125	125	0	0	0	n/a	n/a	n/a	n/a
DDESS: DoDs Domestic (d) ...	67	67	0	0	0	n/a	n/a	n/a	n/a
Bureau of Indian Ed.	173	173	0	0	0	n/a	n/a	173	173
American Samoa	31	29	1	1	0	n/a	n/a	N.A.	N.A.
Guam	36	36	0	0	0	n/a	n/a	N.A.	N.A.
No. Mariana Islands	31	30	0	0	1	n/a	n/a	N.A.	N.A.
Puerto Rico..................	1,511	1,446	27	29	9	n/a	n/a	1,489	1,402
U.S. Virgin Islands	33	32	0	1	0	n/a	1	N.A.	N.A.

See footnotes at end of table.

NUMBER AND TYPES OF PUBLIC ELEMENTARY AND SECONDARY SCHOOLS, BY STATE OR JURISDICTION: SCHOOL YEAR 2008–09 — Continued

Source: U.S. Department of Education, National Center for Education Statistics, Common Core of Data (CCD), "Public Elementary/Secondary School Universe Survey," 2008–09, Version 1a.

Note: Every school is assigned a school type. A school may also be included under the Charter, Magnet, and/or Title I statuses, which are independent of one another and of school type.

Key:

N.A. — Not available.

n/a — Not applicable. Some states do not have charter school authorization and some states do not designate magnet schools.

N.R. — Reporting standards not met. Information about whether or not a school was a magnet school was missing for more than 80 percent of schools in the state.

(a) Arizona, Georgia, Massachusetts, New Jersey and Oregon have magnet schools but were not able to provide data that indicate school's magnet status. The list of magnet schools for Georgia was taken from a public website. Total includes suppressed data due to unmet reporting standards.

(b) Schools eligible for Title I schoolwide programs are also included in the count of all Title I eligible schools.

(c) A reporting state's total is shown if data for any item in the table were not available to some, but not for more than 15 percent of all schools in the United States.

(d) DoDDS and DDESS are the Department of Defense dependent schools (overseas) and the Department of Defense dependent schools (domestic) respectively.

Table 9.2
TOTAL NUMBER OF STUDENTS IN MEMBERSHIP IN OPERATING PUBLIC AND SECONDARY SCHOOLS, BY SCHOOL TYPE, AND STATE OR JURISDICTION: SCHOOL YEAR 2008–09

State or other jurisdiction	Total number of students (a)	Type of school				Charter	Magnet (b)	Title I (c)	Title I schoolwide (c)
		Regular	Special education	Vocational education	Alernative education				
Reporting states (d)......	49,053,786	48,168,727	164,874	156,390	563,795	1,433,116	2,307,712	30,329,962	20,291,993
Alabama	742,997	739,820	941	54	2,182	n/a	13,322	396,489	346,655
Alaska...........................	130,662	116,603	82	715	13,262	4,847	4,283	69,863	54,214
Arizona.........................	1,085,822	1,070,598	774	2,281	12,169	105,209	N.A.	627,124	445,522
Arkansas.......................	478,965	476,911	217	346	1,491	6,989	23,156	316,481	259,898
California	6,240,184	6,030,248	27,377	568	181,991	284,986	508,863	3,726,436	2,892,720
Colorado.......................	817,605	801,988	1,073	769	13,775	61,460	9,272	215,705	146,133
Connecticut	561,766	545,421	3,052	10,257	3,036	4,536	20,334	253,764	73,904
Delaware	123,968	113,741	2,206	6,763	1,258	8,626	1,865	59,184	52,865
Florida	2,631,020	2,571,745	17,204	3,619	38,452	117,640	378,761	1,775,463	1,573,121
Georgia........................	1,655,792	1,653,059	1,700	0	1,033	33,894	N.R.	821,395	729,998
Hawaii..........................	179,406	179,186	81	0	139	7,328	n/a	102,985	96,008
Idaho...........................	274,672	269,076	104	62	5,430	11,898	n/a	187,859	151,066
Illinois.........................	2,119,707	2,117,175	860	0	1,672	30,789	229,120	1,516,571	707,564
Indiana........................	1,046,147	1,042,472	1,232	0	2,443	16,442	13,165	695,198	443,573
Iowa............................	482,735	478,532	621	0	3,582	655	n/a	285,436	150,523
Kansas	471,060	470,679	333	0	48	4,344	13,542	352,122	223,889
Kentucky	670,030	661,662	599	0	7,769	n/a	38,426	542,135	482,043
Louisiana......................	684,745	650,881	1,269	0	32,595	26,012	44,875	561,360	510,328
Maine	187,484	187,422	13	0	49	n/a	118	N.A.	N.A.
Maryland	843,781	823,675	3,655	7,915	8,536	9,829	75,682	153,155	132,810
Massachusetts	958,910	915,101	5,250	35,089	3,470	26,384	N.A.	482,153	219,133
Michigan.......................	1,629,880	1,554,685	37,957	2,527	34,711	103,606	217,237	1,596,371	572,035
Minnesota.....................	828,943	800,881	14,853	5	13,204	29,501	36,092	315,287	88,403
Mississippi	491,924	491,780	144	0	0	371	2,351	343,457	329,750
Missouri........................	917,871	908,040	4,601	3,125	2,105	17,165	15,980	372,246	170,395
Montana	141,899	141,786	41	0	72	n/a	n/a	113,923	54,050
Nebraska	292,590	291,297	1,293	0	0	n/a	n/a	108,391	65,255
Nevada.........................	433,371	427,626	544	74	5,127	8,915	188	205,441	180,481
New Hampshire	197,934	197,934	0	0	0	585	n/a	83,215	10,699
New Jersey....................	1,379,873	1,346,946	8,579	21,811	2,537	19,271	N.A.	709,831	203,892
New Mexico	328,420	323,292	619	327	4,182	11,735	9	268,367	246,971
New York.......................	2,740,592	2,694,896	1,000	37,270	7,426	34,683	240,351	2,626,345	1,225,434
North Carolina...............	1,457,835	1,447,416	2,247	550	7,622	35,677	91,004	516,477	437,969
North Dakota.................	94,728	94,706	22	0	0	n/a	n/a	49,302	13,280
Ohio............................	1,813,999	1,806,935	5,268	1,058	738	86,824	n/a	1,244,127	751,294
Oklahoma......................	645,108	643,830	254	0	1,024	5,418	n/a	383,272	300,981
Oregon.........................	556,380	551,019	170	0	5,191	14,366	N.A.	207,649	149,577
Pennsylvania	1,769,784	1,750,071	1,807	16,520	1,388	73,051	27,883	1,255,030	377,045
Rhode Island.................	143,591	139,814	156	1,600	2,021	3,128	n/a	115,385	53,537
South Carolina...............	718,113	716,207	822	0	1,084	8,638	42,165	536,250	483,712
South Dakota.................	126,425	125,063	43	0	1,319	n/a	n/a	98,805	41,590
Tennessee	971,950	966,687	2,037	1,733	1,493	3,103	17,683	710,746	656,280
Texas...........................	4,751,003	4,673,212	1,816	0	75,975	127,637	n/a	3,573,283	3,343,153
Utah............................	559,687	548,532	5,602	0	5,553	27,117	7,651	112,220	88,266
Vermont........................	90,106	90,088	0	0	18	n/a	n/a	53,931	33,031
Virginia........................	1,235,143	1,232,294	410	0	2,439	250	155,313	316,249	166,037
Washington....................	1,037,018	986,310	4,201	455	46,052	n/a	n/a	526,205	227,760
West Virginia.................	282,718	281,625	266	7	820	n/a	n/a	101,923	99,851
Wisconsin......................	873,607	867,409	126	771	5,301	35,624	1,777	537,586	147,531
Wyoming	87,153	85,888	11	0	1,254	304	n/a	39,089	17,519
Dist. of Columbia	68,681	66,463	1,342	119	757	24,279	2,159	68,681	64,248
DoDDS:									
DoDs Overseas (e)	56,279	56,279	0	0	0	n/a	n/a	n/a	n/a
DDESS:									
DoDs Domestic (e)	27,384	27,384	0	0	0	n/a	n/a	n/a	n/a
Bureau of Indian Ed. ...	40,830	40,830	0	0	0	n/a	n/a	40,830	40,830
American Samoa	N.A.	N.A.	N.A.	N.A.	N.A.	n/a	n/a	N.A.	N.A.
Guam..........................	N.A.	N.A.	0	0	0	n/a	n/a	N.A.	N.A.
No. Mariana Islands	10,913	10,892	0	0	21	n/a	n/a	N.A.	N.A.
Puerto Rico...................	503,635	484,446	2,596	16,221	372	n/a	n/a	499,965	467,760
U.S. Virgin Islands	15,768	15,768	0	0	0	n/a	1,382	N.A.	N.A.

See footnotes at end of table.

TOTAL NUMBER OF STUDENTS IN MEMBERSHIP IN OPERATING PUBLIC AND SECONDARY SCHOOLS, BY SCHOOL TYPE, AND STATE OR JURISDICTION: SCHOOL YEAR 2008–09—Continued

Source: U.S. Department of Education, National Center for Education Statistics, Common Core of Data (CCD), "Public Elementary/Secondary School Universe Survey," 2008–09, Version 1a.

Key:

N.A. — Not available.

n/a — Not applicable. Membership reported as not applicable or some states do not have charter school authorization and some states do not designate magnet schools.

N.R. — Reporting standards not met. Data missing for more than 80 percent of schools in state.

(a) Individual state total number of students are included only if the state reports data for regular, special education, vocational education, and alternative school types.

(b) Total includes suppressed data due to unmet reporting standards.

(c) Schools eligible for Title I schoolwide programs are also included in the count of all Title I eligible schools.

(d) A reporting state's total is shown if data for any item in the table were not available for some, but not more than 15 percent, of all schools in the United States.

(e) DoDDS and DDESS are the Department of Defense dependents schools (overseas) and the Department of Defense dependents schools (domestic), respectively.

Table 9.3
PUBLIC SCHOOL GRADUATION AND DROPOUT RATES: SCHOOL YEAR 2007–08

State or other jurisdiction	Averaged freshman graduation rate (b)	2007–08 graduates	Number of graduates (a)		Number of of dropouts (c)	Dropout rate (c)(d)(e)
			Males	Females		
United States (f)	74.9 (g)	2,965,286 (g)	1,426,949	1,489,987	613,379	4.1
Alabama	69.0	41,346	19,782	21,531	4,654	2.2
Alaska	69.1	7,855	3,670	3,821	3,040	7.3
Arizona	70.7	61,667	30,124	31,543	21,034	6.7
Arkansas	76.4	28,725	13,892	14,833	6,492	4.7
California	71.2	374,561	176,744	189,754	98,230	5.0
Colorado	75.4	46,082	22,595	23,487	15,119	6.4
Connecticut	82.2	38,419	19,135	19,284	4,906	2.8
Delaware	72.1	7,388	N.A.	N.A.	2,212	6.0
Florida	66.9	149,046	70,331	75,923	26,635	3.3
Georgia	65.4	83,505	39,036	42,997	20,135	4.3
Hawaii	76.0	11,613	5,813	5,800	2,922	5.4
Idaho	80.1	16,567	8,221	8,346	1,589	2.0
Illinois	80.4	135,143	65,506	68,048	32,638	5.2
Indiana	74.1	61,901	29,606	31,186	5,417	1.7
Iowa	86.4	34,573	17,384	17,189	4,437	2.9
Kansas	79.1	30,737	15,141	14,991	3,497	2.5
Kentucky	74.4	39,339	19,181	19,798	5,516	2.8
Louisiana	63.5	34,401	15,698	18,703	13,580	7.5
Maine	79.1 (g)	14,350 (g)	N.A.	N.A.	2,642	4.4
Maryland	80.4	59,171	28,730	30,441	9,816	3.6
Massachusetts	81.5	65,197	31,864	32,473	9,957	3.4
Michigan	76.3	115,183	55,985	58,672	34,702	6.2
Minnesota	86.4	60,409	30,025	30,384	7,826	2.8
Mississippi	63.9	24,795	11,097	13,644	6,399	4.6
Missouri	82.4	61,717	30,709	31,008	13,931	4.9
Montana	82.0	10,396	5,158	5,238	2,435	5.2
Nebraska	83.8	20,035	9,958	10,077	2,244	2.5
Nevada	51.3	17,149	8,106	8,903	6,170	5.1
New Hampshire	83.4	14,982	7,515	7,467	1,987	3.0
New Jersey	84.6	94,994	47,487	47,312	6,320	1.7
New Mexico	66.8	18,264	8,776	9,488	5,132	5.2
New York	70.8	176,310	85,887	90,163	34,069	3.9
North Carolina	72.8	83,307	39,616	42,150	21,477	5.2
North Dakota	83.8	6,999	3,498	3,501	754	2.4
Ohio	79.0	120,758	59,397	59,450	24,980	4.3
Oklahoma	78.0	37,630	18,550	19,080	5,598	3.1
Oregon	76.7	34,949	16,838	17,223	6,676	3.8
Pennsylvania	82.7	130,298	64,725	65,304	15,288	2.6
Rhode Island	76.4	10,347	5,065	5,282	2,559	5.3
South Carolina	N.A.	N.A.	N.A.	N.A.	8,013	3.9
South Dakota	84.4	8,582	4,288	4,291	871	2.3
Tennessee	74.9	57,486	28,109	29,376	11,200	3.9
Texas	73.1	252,121	125,157	126,964	51,369	4.0
Utah	74.3	28,167	13,846	14,245	6,920	4.2
Vermont	89.3	7,392	3,277	3,131	N.A.	N.A.
Virginia	77.0	77,369	36,716	39,682	10,135	2.7
Washington	71.9	61,625	29,579	31,418	18,976	5.7
West Virginia	77.3	17,489	8,714	8,775	3,680	4.4
Wisconsin	89.6	65,183	32,261	32,922	6,659	2.3
Wyoming	76.0	5,494	2,754	2,740	1,366	5.0
Dist. of Columbia	N.A.	N.A.	1,403	1,949	1,175	5.5
DoDDS: DoDs Overseas (h)	N.A.	N.A.	N.A.	N.A.	N.A.	N.A.
DDESS: DoDs Domestic (h)	N.A.	N.A.	N.A.	N.A.	N.A.	N.A.
Bureau of Indian Education	N.A.	N.A.	N.A.	N.A.	N.A.	N.A.
American Samoa	N.A.	N.A.	N.A.	N.A.	N.A.	N.A.
Guam	N.A.	N.A.	N.A.	N.A.	N.A.	N.A.
No. Mariana Islands	N.A.	N.A.	N.A.	N.A.	N.A.	N.A.
Puerto Rico	64.5	30,016	N.A.	N.A.	N.A.	N.A.
U.S. Virgin Islands	58.2	820	338	482	400	7.8

See footnotes at end of table.

PUBLIC SCHOOL GRADUATION AND DROPOUT RATES: SCHOOL YEAR 2007–08 — Continued

Sources: Columns 1 and 2: U.S. Department of Education, National Center for Education Statistics, Common Core of Data (CCD), "NCES Common Core of Data State Dropout and Completion Data File," School Year 2007–08, Version 1b; "State Nonfiscal Survey of Public Elementary/Secondary Education," 2003–04, Version 1b; 2004–05, Version 1f; 2005–06, Version 1b. Columns 3 and 4: U.S. Department of Education, National Center for Education Statistics, Common Core of Data (CCD), "NCES Common Core of Data State Dropout and Completion Data File," School Year 2007–08, Version 1a; and "NCES Common Core of Data Local Education Agency Universe Survey Dropout and Completion Restricted-Use Data File," School Year 2007–08, Version 1a. Columns 5 and 6: U.S. Department of Education, National Center for Education Statistics, Common Core of Data (CCD), "NCES Common Core of Data State Dropout and Completion Data File," School Year 2007–08, Version 1a.

Key:

N.A.— Not available. State or jurisdiction did not report.

(a) Graduate counts were calculated using district-level data. Totals may differ from graduate counts on other columns/tables due to different reporting levels.

(b) Averaged Freshman Graduation Rate (AFGR) is an estimate of the percentage of an entering freshman class graduating in 4 years. For 2007–08, it equals the total number of diploma recipients in 2007–08 divided by the average membership of the 8th-grade class in 2003–04, the 9th-grade class in 2004–05, and the 10th-grade class in 2005–06.

(c) Ungraded dropouts are prorated by NCES into grades based on the graded dropout counts to calculate numerators for dropout rates.

(d) Ungraded student enrollments are prorated by NCES into grades based on graded enrollments to calculate denominators for dropout rates.

(e) The event dropout rate is defined as the count of dropouts from a given school year divided by the count of student enrollments within the same grade span at the beginning of the same school year.

(f) Reporting states totals include any of the 50 states and the District of Columbia that reported all data elements.

(g) Maine reported 1,161 diplomas that were awarded to students attending private high schools that received a majority of their funding from public sources. These 1,161 diplomas were included in Maine and the Reporting States counts but were not included in the AFGR calculations for the state and for the reporting states totals. The diploma counts used to calculate the AFGR for Maine and for the reporting states were 13,189 and 2,964,125, respectively.

(h) DoDDS and DDESS are the Department of Defense Overseas Dependent Elementary and Secondary Schools and the Department of Defense Domestic Dependent Elementary and Secondary Schools, respectively.

Table 9.4
TOTAL REVENUES, PERCENTAGE DISTRIBUTION, AND REVENUES PER PUPIL FOR PUBLIC ELEMENTARY AND SECONDARY SCHOOLS, BY SOURCE AND STATE OR JURISDICTION: FISCAL YEAR 2008

State or other jurisdiction	Revenues (in thousands of dollars)				Percentage distribution		
	Total	Local (a)	State	Federal	Local (a)	State	Federal
United States (b)	$584,728,896	$254,358,830	$282,662,805	$47,707,260	43.5	48.3	8.2
Alabama.............................	7,693,742	2,290,506	4,658,854	744,382	29.8	60.6	9.7
Alaska................................	2,289,219	465,859	1,517,297	306,063	20.4	66.3	13.4
Arizona..............................	10,283,842	3,872,761	5,318,991	1,092,090	37.7	51.7	10.6
Arkansas............................	4,674,053	1,518,518	2,649,411	506,124	32.5	56.7	10.8
California	71,224,024	20,880,862	43,660,964	6,682,198	29.3	61.3	9.4
Colorado............................	8,113,611	4,130,447	3,423,454	559,710	50.9	42.2	6.9
Connecticut.......................	9,459,433	5,295,735	3,743,350	420,348	56.0	39.6	4.4
Delaware	1,690,557	508,795	1,048,771	132,991	30.1	62.0	7.9
Florida	29,321,189	15,403,664	11,389,951	2,527,574	52.5	38.8	8.6
Georgia..............................	18,671,345	8,699,180	8,476,711	1,495,453	46.6	45.4	8.0
Hawaii (c)..........................	2,541,703	76,658	2,154,312	310,732	3.0	84.8	12.2
Idaho.................................	2,167,455	499,820	1,454,112	213,522	23.1	67.1	9.9
Illinois...............................	25,426,959	15,497,303	7,929,343	2,000,312	60.9	31.2	7.9
Indiana..............................	12,295,901	4,840,831	6,578,455	876,615	39.4	53.5	7.1
Iowa	5,297,527	2,429,015	2,465,113	403,399	45.9	46.5	7.6
Kansas...............................	5,528,071	1,915,792	3,176,570	435,710	34.7	57.5	7.9
Kentucky	6,561,268	2,091,168	3,759,235	710,865	31.9	57.3	10.8
Louisiana...........................	7,861,130	3,020,548	3,523,670	1,316,912	38.4	44.8	16.8
Maine................................	2,601,563	1,199,195	1,168,949	233,419	46.1	44.9	9.0
Maryland...........................	13,060,333	6,849,098	5,499,098	712,141	52.4	42.1	5.5
Massachusetts	14,632,845	7,752,915	6,127,024	752,906	53.0	41.9	5.1
Michigan............................	19,620,055	6,799,938	11,287,553	1,532,564	34.7	57.5	7.8
Minnesota..........................	10,293,655	2,902,518	6,783,079	608,058	28.2	65.9	5.9
Mississippi.........................	4,388,016	1,290,291	2,389,464	708,262	29.4	54.5	16.1
Missouri.............................	9,876,930	5,784,488	3,292,456	799,986	58.6	33.3	8.1
Montana.............................	1,559,091	595,154	774,708	189,229	38.2	49.7	12.1
Nebraska............................	3,286,862	1,899,176	1,089,026	298,660	57.8	33.1	9.1
Nevada...............................	4,364,266	2,730,522	1,344,111	289,633	62.6	30.8	6.6
New Hampshire	2,613,798	1,467,992	1,009,291	136,516	56.2	38.6	5.2
New Jersey	24,892,358	13,430,129	10,472,031	990,198	54.0	42.1	4.0
New Mexico........................	3,655,607	571,035	2,587,683	496,889	15.6	70.8	13.6
New York............................	52,766,249	25,961,248	23,641,251	3,163,749	49.2	44.8	6.0
North Carolina...................	12,426,731 (d)	3,021,338 (d)	8,158,251	1,247,143	24.3	65.7	10.0
North Dakota......................	1,056,726	527,728	383,231	145,767	49.9	36.3	13.8
Ohio..................................	22,796,037	10,745,329	10,392,395	1,658,314	47.1	45.6	7.3
Oklahoma..........................	5,482,414	1,862,240	2,973,757	646,417	34.0	54.2	11.8
Oregon...............................	6,118,492	2,364,047	32,000,001	554,444	38.6	52.3	9.1
Pennsylvania	24,973,392	14,055,263	9,122,496	1,795,633	56.3	36.5	7.2
Rhode Island......................	2,223,575	1,162,770	887,762	173,043	52.3	39.9	7.8
South Carolina...................	7,773,773	3,108,367	3,949,713	715,692	40.0	50.8	9.2
South Dakota.....................	1,206,955	612,726	409,680	184,549	50.8	33.9	15.3
Tennessee	8,230,341	3,614,048	3,752,493	863,801	43.9	45.6	10.5
Texas.................................	45,574,722	20,602,720	20,400,120	4,571,881	45.2	44.8	10.0
Utah..................................	4,396,364	1,563,374	2,490,823	342,166	35.6	56.7	7.8
Vermont.............................	1,504,572	118,258	1,291,690	94,624	7.9	85.9	6.3
Virginia..............................	14,527,472	7,678,728	5,951,317	897,427	52.9	41.0	6.2
Washington........................	11,107,344	3,270,611	6,941,092	895,641	29.4	62.5	8.1
West Virginia......................	3,166,494	947,243	1,872,918	346,332	29.9	59.1	10.9
Wisconsin	10,485,161	4,570,797	5,244,730	669,635	43.6	50.0	6.4
Wyoming	1,601,628	653,305	846,053	102,270	40.8	52.8	6.4
Dist. of Columbia (c).........	1,364,048	1,208,775	n/a	155,273	88.6	n/a	11.4
American Samoa	65,624	297	15,529 (e)	49,798	0.5	23.7	75.9
Guam................................	243,990	190,437	n/a	53,553	78.1	n/a	21.9
No. Marianas Islands.........	63,012	403	35,847 (e)	26,762	0.6	56.9	42.5
Puerto Rico........................	3,365,390	1,135	2,424,243 (e)	940,011	(f)	72.0	27.9
U.S. Virgin Islands.............	233,195	193,777	n/a	39,418	83.1	n/a	16.9

Source: U.S. Department of Education, National Center for Education Statistics, Common Core of Data (CCD), "National Public Education Financial Survey (NPEFS)," fiscal year 2008, Version 1a.

Note: Detail may not sum to totals because of rounding.

Key:

n/a. — Not applicable.

(a) Local revenues include intermediate revenues.

(b) U.S. totals include the 50 states and the District of Columbia.

(c) Both the District of Columbia and Hawaii have only one school district each; therefore, neither is comparable to other states. Local revenues in Hawaii consist almost entirely of student fees and charges for services, such as food services, summer school, and student activities.

(d) Value affected by redistribution of reported values to correct for missing data items.

(e) Reported state revenue data are revenues received from the central government.

(f) Rounds to zero.

Table 9.5
TOTAL EXPENDITURES FOR PUBLIC ELEMENTARY AND SECONDARY EDUCATION: FISCAL YEAR 2008

State or other jurisdiction	Expenditures (in thousands of dollars)					
	Total	Current for elementary/ secondary education (a)	Facilities acquisitions and construction	Replacement equipment	Other programs (b)	Interest on debt
United States (c)..........	$596,610,358 (d)	$506,827,246 (d)	$58,698,867 (d)	$7,080,995 (d)	$8,307,762 (d)(e)	$15,695,488
Alabama.......................	7,908,316	6,832,439	712,932	106,099	121,772	135,074
Alaska.........................	2,274,715	1,918,375	281,986	25,674	7,986	40,694
Arizona........................	10,538,886 (d)	8,403,221	1,266,202	347,508 (d)	53,845 (e)	468,110
Arkansas......................	4,800,320	4,156,368	436,676	70,811	26,041	110,424
California.....................	73,868,616 (d)	61,570,555 (d)	9,083,314	251,143	1,185,793	1,777,810
Colorado......................	8,927,548	7,338,766	1,003,467	160,891	57,109	367,315
Connecticut..................	9,576,944 (d)	8,336,789 (d)	833,692	102,877 (d)	143,574 (e)	160,011
Delaware	1,795,613	1,489,594	237,940	12,288 (d)	20,614 (d)	35,178
Florida	31,518,715 (d)	24,224,114 (d)	5,813,991	158,505	499,419	822,687
Georgia........................	19,007,701	16,030,039	2,521,259	186,601	40,297	229,506
Hawaii (f)	2,342,493	2,122,779	82,496	13,233	25,381	98,604
Idaho...........................	2,324,360 (d)	1,891,505 (d)	334,935	32,110	4,474	61,337
Illinois.........................	25,246,942 (d)	21,874,484 (d)	1,981,763	578,098 (d)	157,308	655,289
Indiana........................	10,638,810 (d)	9,281,709 (d)	712,083	286,005 (d)	126,989	232,024
Iowa	5,286,896	4,499,236	576,241	100,853	28,028	82,538
Kansas	5,161,192	4,627,994	180,910	190,815	5,517	155,956
Kentucky	6,803,420	5,822,550	610,713	135,892	88,436	145,829
Louisiana.....................	7,771,248 (d)	6,814,455 (d)	644,704	154,751	54,429	102,910
Maine..........................	2,516,597	2,308,071	105,520	32,407	24,887	45,713
Maryland......................	12,740,155 (d)	11,192,623 (d)	1,279,055	107,945	27,439	133,094
Massachusetts	13,776,420	13,160,383	279,056	4,622 (d)	64,156	268,203
Michigan......................	19,729,953	17,053,521	1,287,924	215,187 (d)	353,457	819,865
Minnesota....................	10,402,154 (d)	8,415,969 (d)	1,012,472	151,271 (d)	395,046	427,395
Mississippi	4,273,451 (d)	3,898,401 (d)	147,561	127,387 (d)	29,779	70,322
Missouri.......................	10,093,669	8,526,641	821,942	257,786 (d)	189,834	297,465
Montana	1,564,569	1,392,449	120,116	28,363	7,479	16,161
Nebraska	3,457,340	2,970,323	325,029	89,560 (d)	2,912	69,515
Nevada........................	4,477,823	3,515,004	655,739	38,986	22,095	245,999
New Hampshire	2,618,360	2,399,330	134,173	29,705 (d)	6,795	48,358
New Jersey	26,478,109 (d)	24,357,079 (d)	1,416,357	98,705 (d)	252,989 (d)	352,979
New Mexico	3,556,459	3,057,061	478,154	17,545 (d)	3,537 (d)	163
New York......................	51,991,666 (d)	46,443,426 (d)	2,072,747	386,895	2,002,817	1,085,781
North Carolina..............	13,382,049	11,482,912 (d)	1,702,548	127,208 (d)	61,905	7,476
North Dakota................	993,651	886,317	55,454	32,255	7,014	12,610
Ohio	22,362,887	18,892,374	2,148,066	398,053	441,528	482,867
Oklahoma....................	5,400,091	4,932,913	324,700	67,989	24,557	49,933
Oregon........................	6,331,026	5,409,630	575,387	46,126	21,205	278,678
Pennsylvania	25,346,538	21,157,430	2,227,538	364,767	634,096	962,707
Rhode Island................	2,252,275	2,134,609	16,625	12,057	52,909	36,075
South Carolina.............	8,003,122	6,453,817	986,023	129,459	75,791	358,032
South Dakota...............	1,180,854	1,037,875	81,762	34,520 (d)	3,247	23,449
Tennessee	8,494,430 (d)	7,540,306 (d)	561,127	149,287	59,633	184,077
Texas...........................	49,841,926 (d)	39,033,235 (d)	7,697,179	433,871	305,952	2,371,689
Utah............................	4,571,248	3,444,936	814,234	104,970	99,930	107,179
Vermont.......................	1,462,893	1,356,165	59,255	24,873	8,481	14,119
Virginia........................	14,885,599	13,125,666	1,243,519	285,239 (d)	78,139	153,035
Washington..................	11,597,118 (d)	9,331,539 (d)	1,704,412	96,070	58,034	407,063
West Virginia................	2,962,122 (d)	2,841,962 (d)	19,670	52,236	39,663	8,591
Wisconsin	10,972,162	9,366,134	503,263	147,274	282,554	672,937
Wyoming	1,511,335	1,191,736	266,835	43,062	7,038	2,663
Dist. of Columbia (f) ...	1,589,568 (d)	1,282,437 (d)	260,120 (d)	31,158 (d)	15,853	0
American Samoa	67,373	63,105	1,105	1,279	1,885	0
Guam..........................	233,448 (d)	229,243 (d)	N.A.	4,205	0	0
No. Mariana Islands	53,615	51,241	1,088	810	477	0
Puerto Rico..................	3,584,905	3,413,884	4,093	78,441	83,390	5,096
U.S. Virgin Islands	220,496 (d)	196,533 (d)	20,995	1,752 (d)	1,216	0

See footnotes at end of table.

TOTAL EXPENDITURES FOR PUBLIC ELEMENTARY AND SECONDARY EDUCATION: FISCAL YEAR 2008 — Continued

Source: U.S. Department of Education, National Center for Education Statistics, Common Core of Data (CCD), "National Public Education Financial Survey (NPEFS)," fiscal year 2008, Version 1a.

Note: Detail may not sum to totals because of rounding.

Key:

N.A. — Not available. Data are reported in other expenditure data items and included in the total.

(a) Include instruction, instruction-related, support services, and other elementary/secondary current expenditures, but exclude expenditures on capital outlay, other programs, and interest on long-term debt.

(b) Includes expenditures for community services, adult education, community colleges, private schools, and other programs that are not part of public elementary and secondary education.

(c) U.S. totals include the 50 states and the District of Columbia.

(d) Value affected by redistribution of reported values to correct for missing data items and/or to distribute state direct support expenditures.

(e) Value contains imputation for missing data.

(f) Both the District of Columbia and Hawaii have only one school district each; therefore, neither is comparable to other states.

Table 9.6
CURRENT EXPENDITURES AND PERCENTAGE DISTRIBUTION FOR PUBLIC ELEMENTARY AND SECONDARY EDUCATION, BY FUNCTION AND STATE OR JURISDICTION: FISCAL YEAR 2008

State or other jurisdiction	Current expenditures (in thousands of dollars) (a)					Percentage distribution			
	Total	Instruction and instruction related (b)	Student support (c)	Administration (d)	Operations (e)	Instruction and instruction related (b)	Student support (c)	Admin. (d)	Ops. (e)
United States (f)	$506,827,246 (g)	$333,598,810 (g)	$27,385,688 (g)	$54,571,056 (g)	$91,271,692 (g)	65.8	5.4	10.8	18.0
Alabama	6,832,439	4,336,775	369,939	727,897	1,397,827	63.5	5.4	10.7	20.5
Alaska	1,918,375	1,217,916	137,986	211,401	351,072	63.5	7.2	11.0	18.3
Arizona	8,403,221	4,971,462 (g)	901,085 (g)	863,409 (g)	1,667,265 (g)	59.2	10.7	10.3	19.8
Arkansas	4,156,368	2,744,622 (g)	204,167 (g)	429,615 (g)	777,964 (g)	66.0	4.9	10.3	18.7
California	61,570,555 (g)	41,221,735 (g)	3,062,280 (g)	7,235,517 (g)	10,051,023 (g)	67.0	5.0	11.8	16.3
Colorado	7,338,766	4,646,517	343,099	1,153,086	1,196,065	63.3	4.7	15.7	16.3
Connecticut	8,336,789 (g)	5,494,291 (g)	506,672 (g)	845,212 (g)	1,490,614 (g)	65.9	6.1	10.1	17.9
Delaware	1,489,594	916,082	76,411	184,631	312,470	61.5	5.1	12.4	21.0
Florida	24,224,114 (g)	16,218,702 (g)	1,107,958 (g)	2,240,879 (g)	4,656,575 (g)	67.0	4.6	9.3	19.2
Georgia	16,030,039	10,947,252	743,695	1,724,996	2,614,096	68.3	4.6	10.8	16.3
Hawaii (h)	2,122,779	1,359,347	239,459	216,125	307,848	64.0	11.3	10.2	14.5
Idaho	1,891,505 (g)	1,230,970 (g)	107,754 (g)	190,314 (g)	362,467 (g)	65.1	5.7	10.1	19.2
Illinois	21,874,484 (g)	13,878,223 (g)	1,421,224 (g)	2,602,559 (g)	3,972,479 (g)	63.4	6.5	11.9	18.2
Indiana	9,281,709 (g)	6,025,607 (g)	388,487 (g)	958,429 (g)	1,909,186 (g)	64.9	4.2	10.3	20.6
Iowa	4,499,236	2,927,176	257,575	530,109	784,376	65.1	5.7	11.8	17.4
Kansas	4,627,994	3,000,653	262,588	526,292	838,462	64.8	5.7	11.4	18.1
Kentucky	5,822,550	3,768,146	251,346	576,758	1,226,300	64.7	4.3	9.9	21.1
Louisiana	6,814,455 (g)	4,364,322 (g)	297,598 (g)	720,162 (g)	1,432,372 (g)	64.0	4.4	10.6	21.0
Maine	2,308,071	1,576,821 (g)	104,008 (g)	206,884 (g)	420,357	68.3	4.5	9.0	18.2
Maryland	11,192,623 (g)	7,469,581 (g)	498,920 (g)	1,136,692 (g)	2,087,431	66.7	4.5	10.2	18.7
Massachusetts	13,160,383	9,168,460 (g)	736,133 (g)	1,126,219	2,129,571	69.7	5.6	8.6	16.2
Michigan	17,053,521	10,477,065	1,276,683	2,162,825	3,136,948	61.4	7.5	12.7	18.4
Minnesota	8,415,969 (g)	5,822,654 (g)	228,804 (g)	851,355 (g)	1,513,155 (g)	69.2	2.7	10.1	18.0
Mississippi	3,898,401 (g)	2,478,077 (g)	181,505 (g)	420,501 (g)	818,319 (g)	63.6	4.7	10.8	21.0
Missouri	8,526,641	5,509,910	400,600	942,872	1,673,259	64.6	4.7	11.1	19.6
Montana	1,392,449	891,913	77,242	148,575	274,720	64.1	5.5	10.7	19.7
Nebraska	2,970,323	2,009,116	115,328	308,272	537,607	67.6	3.9	10.4	18.1
Nevada	3,515,004	2,270,090	164,350	432,782	647,782	64.6	4.7	12.3	18.4
New Hampshire	2,399,330	1,621,275	164,418	233,288	380,349	67.6	6.9	9.7	15.9
New Jersey	24,357,079 (g)	15,271,767 (g)	2,303,520 (g)	2,322,227 (g)	4,459,565 (g)	62.7	9.5	9.5	18.3
New Mexico	3,057,061	1,860,370	314,843	336,372	545,476	60.9	10.3	11.0	17.8
New York	46,443,426 (g)	33,305,098 (g)	1,536,857 (g)	4,051,984 (g)	7,549,487 (g)	71.7	3.3	8.7	16.3
North Carolina	11,482,912 (g)	7,539,482 (g)	564,546 (g)	1,405,457 (g)	1,973,427 (g)	65.7	4.9	12.2	17.2
North Dakota	886,317	543,680	36,992	106,351	199,293	61.3	4.2	12.0	22.5
Ohio	18,892,374	12,002,759	1,131,996	2,469,521	3,288,098	63.5	6.0	13.1	17.4
Oklahoma	4,932,913	3,023,423	331,037	544,559	1,033,893	61.3	6.7	11.0	21.0
Oregon	5,409,630	3,382,515	374,495	766,235	886,384	62.5	6.9	14.2	16.4
Pennsylvania	21,157,430	13,668,997	1,051,775	2,332,731	4,103,927	64.6	5.0	11.0	19.4
Rhode Island	2,134,609	1,394,592 (g)	252,541 (g)	173,421 (g)	314,055 (g)	65.3	11.8	8.1	14.7
South Carolina	6,453,817	4,124,810	469,949	662,865	1,196,193	63.9	7.3	10.3	18.5
South Dakota	1,037,875	646,115	56,942	125,726	209,092	62.3	5.5	12.1	20.1
Tennessee	7,540,306 (g)	5,192,953 (g)	298,693	713,896	1,334,764	68.9	4.0	9.5	17.7
Texas	39,033,235 (g)	25,442,790 (g)	1,893,545 (g)	4,128,351 (g)	7,568,549 (g)	65.2	4.9	10.6	19.4
Utah	3,444,936	2,386,355	126,893	317,787	613,900	69.3	3.7	9.2	17.8
Vermont	1,356,165	905,735	99,426	155,773	195,231	66.8	7.3	11.5	14.4
Virginia	13,125,666	8,879,325	627,358	1,191,811	2,427,172	67.6	4.8	9.1	18.5
Washington	9,331,539 (g)	5,975,610 (g)	612,168	1,069,852	1,673,909	64.0	6.6	11.5	17.9
West Virginia	2,841,962 (g)	1,198,224 (g)	103,735 (g)	266,270 (g)	673,733 (g)	63.3	3.7	9.4	23.7
Wisconsin	9,366,134	6,151,439	428,833	1,219,547	1,566,315	65.7	4.6	13.0	16.7
Wyoming	1,191,736	780,511	69,303	132,575	209,347	65.5	5.8	11.1	17.6
Dist. of Columbia (h)	1,282,437 (g)	757,501 (g)	72,931 (g)	170,086 (g)	281,920 (g)	59.1	5.7	13.3	22.0
American Samoa	63,105	35,180	1,732	8,566	17,627	55.7	2.7	13.6	27.9
Guam	229,243 (g)	137,201 (g)	24,976 (g)	19,350 (g)	47,716 (g)	59.8	10.9	8.4	20.8
No. Mariana Islands	51,241 (g)	40,904 (g)	450 (g)	2,278 (g)	7,609 (g)	79.8	0.9	4.4	14.8
Puerto Rico	3,413,884	2,382,930	219,663	116,215	695,076	69.8	6.4	3.4	20.4
U.S. Virgin Islands	196,533 (g)	117,715	12,600	21,146 (g)	45,071 (g)	59.9	6.4	10.8	22.9

See footnotes at end of table.

CURRENT EXPENDITURES AND PERCENTAGE DISTRIBUTION FOR PUBLIC ELEMENTARY AND SECONDARY EDUCATION, BY FUNCTION AND STATE OR JURISDICTION: FISCAL YEAR 2008 — Continued

Source: U.S. Department of Education, National Center for Education Statistics, Common Core of Data (CCD), "National Public Education Financial Survey (NPEFS)," fiscal year 2008, Version 1a.

Note: Detail may not sum to totals because of rounding.

Key:

(a) Include instruction, instruction-related, support services, and other elementary/secondary current expenditures, but exclude expenditures on capital outlay, other programs, and interest on long-term debt.

(b) Include current expenditures for classroom instruction (including teachers and teaching assistants), libraries, in-service teacher training, curriculum development, student assessment and instruction technology.

(c) Include attendance and social work, guidance, health, psychological services, speech pathology, audiology, and other student support services.

(d) Include general administration, school administration, and other support services.

(e) Include operations and maintenance, student transportation, food services, and enterprise operations.

(f) U.S. totals include the 50 states and the District of Columbia.

(g) Value affected by redistribution of reported values to correct for missing data items, and/or to distribute state direct support expenditures.

(h) Both the District of Columbia and Hawaii have only one school district each; therefore, neither is comparable to other states.

Table 9.7

CURRENT INSTRUCTION AND INSTRUCTION-RELATED EXPENDITURES FOR PUBLIC ELEMENTARY AND SECONDARY EDUCATION, BY OBJECT AND STATE OR JURISDICTION: FISCAL YEAR 2008

State or other jurisdiction	Current instruction and instruction-related expenditures (in thousands of dollars)(a)						
	Total	Salaries	Employee benefits	Purchased services	Tuition to out-of-state and private schools	Instructional supplies	Other
United States (b)	$333,598,810 (c)	$221,892,162 (c)	$73,972,233 (c)	$15,542,775 (c)	$4,577,028 (c)	$16,097,805 (c)	$1,516,808 (c)
Alabama	4,336,775	2,746,581	1,084,650	138,830	2,587	345,460	18,668
Alaska	1,217,916	623,045	441,636	77,013	254	65,455	10,514
Arizona	4,971,462 (c)	3,546,146 (c)	836,664 (c)	251,228 (c)	5,585	191,756 (c)	140,082 (c)
Arkansas	2,744,622 (c)	1,872,871 (c)	486,665 (c)	126,701 (c)	10,372	227,970 (c)	20,041 (c)
California	41,221,735 (c)	26,823,297 (c)	8,657,786 (c)	2,525,171 (c)	768,743	2,439,946 (c)	6,792 (c)
Colorado	4,646,517	3,052,387	1,007,222	160,054	53,048	308,815	64,990
Connecticut	5,494,291 (c)	3,488,187 (c)	1,318,145 (c)	191,725 (c)	338,337	149,025 (c)	8,873 (c)
Delaware	916,082	590,445	263,219	12,862	5,896	34,497	9,165
Florida	16,218,702 (c)	10,233,984 (c)	3,001,136 (c)	2,166,068 (c)	1,581	685,072 (c)	130,862 (c)
Georgia	10,947,252	7,385,703	2,564,523	280,804	5,740	647,335	63,146
Hawaii (d)	1,359,347	872,265	302,944	70,860	4,531	99,307	9,441
Idaho	1,230,970 (c)	835,069 (c)	268,988 (c)	56,300 (c)	1,070	68,924 (c)	618 (c)
Illinois	13,878,223 (c)	9,359,692 (c)	2,994,528 (c)	539,978 (c)	383,310	572,390 (c)	28,325 (c)
Indiana	6,025,607 (c)	4,464,238 (c)	1,113,195 (c)	170,813 (c)	119,486	124,691 (c)	33,184 (c)
Iowa	2,927,176	2,076,073	625,883	77,249	23,272	120,517	4,181
Kansas	3,000,653	2,172,806	529,874	102,039	2,581	173,605	19,747
Kentucky	3,768,146	2,689,264	816,603	82,616	200	156,596	22,868
Louisiana	4,364,322 (c)	2,953,099 (c)	996,561 (c)	108,399 (c)	1,336	292,443 (c)	12,484 (c)
Maine	1,576,821 (c)	979,269	399,166 (c)	63,246	82,634	46,098	6,409
Maryland	7,469,581 (c)	4,932,452	1,804,298 (c)	224,156	255,876	238,792	14,007
Massachusetts	9,168,460 (c)	5,718,880	2,570,772 (c)	54,400	615,513	189,487	19,407
Michigan	10,477,065	6,440,156	2,949,947	719,866	126	343,818	23,152
Minnesota	5,822,654 (c)	3,991,567 (c)	1,237,216 (c)	300,113 (c)	58,335	218,606 (c)	16,817 (c)
Mississippi	2,478,077 (c)	1,706,233 (c)	516,990 (c)	85,990 (c)	5,383	151,522 (c)	12,073 (c)
Missouri	5,509,910	3,841,388	979,806	215,676 (c)	9,289	438,355	25,396 (c)
Montana	891,913	584,938	164,520	61,427	750	76,050	4,228
Nebraska	2,009,116	1,374,792	449,345	78,927	13,340	76,035	16,678
Nevada	2,270,090	1,470,620	524,508	72,100	1,801	188,699	12,363
New Hampshire	1,621,275	1,003,385	387,249	50,684	125,828	50,726	3,401
New Jersey	15,271,767 (c)	9,161,452	4,486,869 (c)	402,908	611,551	480,428	128,560
New Mexico	1,860,370	1,275,660	382,709	77,769	0	123,892	340
New York	33,305,098 (c)	21,609,774 (c)	8,827,346 (c)	1,603,148 (c)	271,762	988,307 (c)	4,762 (c)
North Carolina	7,539,482 (c)	5,635,958	1,358,420	205,750 (c)	0	339,307	48
North Dakota	543,680	385,570	109,485	18,083	1,013	26,753	2,777
Ohio	12,002,759	7,834,999	2,643,415	679,955	197,052	482,676	164,662
Oklahoma	3,023,423	2,137,313	581,273	64,786	0	225,925	14,125
Oregon	3,382,515	2,015,106	944,928	168,009	22,649	213,670	18,153
Pennsylvania	13,668,997	8,805,742	3,214,910	790,501	227,049	603,948	26,848
Rhode Island	1,394,592 (c)	886,048 (c)	378,867 (c)	24,539 (c)	75,224	26,975 (c)	2,940 (c)
South Carolina	4,124,810	2,883,624	837,374	174,792	993	198,379	29,648
South Dakota	646,115	430,564	119,853	33,155	7,724	52,899	1,920
Tennessee	5,192,953 (c)	3,555,494	993,899	139,957	332 (c)	478,033	25,239
Texas	25,442,790 (c)	19,322,448 (c)	2,976,448 (c)	1,071,646 (c)	44,589	1,774,130 (c)	253,534 (c)
Utah	2,386,355	1,496,947	618,499	71,791	445	190,147	8,527
Vermont	905,735	560,460	201,834	53,204	60,838	27,160	2,239
Virginia	8,879,325	6,062,348	2,149,922	262,565	5,852	393,524	5,114
Washington	5,975,610 (c)	4,102,633	1,239,216	316,011	11,016 (c)	262,644	44,089
West Virginia	1,798,224 (c)	1,112,741 (c)	533,444 (c)	49,008 (c)	663	102,103 (c)	264 (c)
Wisconsin	6,151,439	3,807,138	1,829,710	141,018	105,917	253,342	14,314
Wyoming	780,511	521,054	181,458	36,897	1,018	38,872	1,212
Dist. of Columbia (d)	757,501 (c)	460,258 (c)	68,319 (c)	92,102 (c)	34,540 (c)	92,700 (c)	9,582 (c)
American Samoa	35,180	20,861	3,255	4,138	0	3,030	3,897
Guam	137,201 (c)	102,560	28,982	2,572	0	2,782	304
No. Mariana Islands	40,904 (c)	30,365 (c)	5,782 (c)	2,550 (c)	0	2,159 (c)	47 (c)
Puerto Rico	2,382,930	1,814,028	279,664	102,267	0	100,496	86,475
U.S. Virgin Islands	117,715	86,300	29,432	246	0	1,663	74

See footnotes at end of table.

CURRENT INSTRUCTION AND INSTRUCTION-RELATED EXPENDITURES FOR PUBLIC ELEMENTARY AND SECONDARY EDUCATION, BY OBJECT AND STATE OR JURISDICTION: FISCAL YEAR 2008 — Continued

Source: U.S. Department of Education, National Center for Education Statistics, Common Core of Data (CCD), "National Public Education Financial Survey (NPEFS)," fiscal year 2008, Version 1a.

Note: Detail may not sum to totals due to rounding.

Key:

(a) Includes salaries and benefits for teachers, teaching assistants, librarians and library aides, in-service teacher trainers, curriculum development, student assessment, technology, and supplies and purchased services related to these activities.

(b) U.S. totals include the 50 states and the District of Columbia.

(c) Value affected by redistribution of reported values to correct for missing data items, and/or to distribute state direct support expenditures.

(d) Both the District of Columbia and Hawaii have only one school district each; therefore, neither is comparable to other states.

Table 9.8
AVERAGE UNDERGRADUATE TUITION AND FEES AND ROOM AND BOARD RATES IN INSTITUTIONS OF HIGHER EDUCATION, BY CONTROL OF INSTITUTION AND STATE: 2007–2008 AND 2008–2009

State or other jurisdiction	Public 4-year 2007–2008 Total	Public 4-year 2007–2008 Tuition and required fees (in-state)	Public 4-year 2008–2009 (a) Total	Public 4-year 2008–2009 (a) Tuition and required fees (in-state)	Public 4-year 2008–2009 (a) Room	Public 4-year 2008–2009 (a) Board	Private 4-year 2007–2008 Total	Private 4-year 2007–2008 Tuition and required fees	Private 4-year 2008–2009 (a) Total	Private 4-year 2008–2009 (a) Tuition and required fees	Private 4-year 2008–2009 (a) Room	Private 4-year 2008–2009 (a) Board	Public 2-year tuition and required fees (in-state) 2007–08	Public 2-year tuition and required fees (in-state) 2008–09 (a)
United States	$13,429	$5,943	$14,256	$6,319	$4,322	$3,616	$30,778	$21,979	$31,704	$22,449	$5,041	$4,214	$2,061	$2,137
Alabama	11,031	4,916	12,166	5,538	3,288	3,340	21,383	14,428	22,444	15,358	3,538	3,548	2,823	2,823
Alaska	11,725	4,747	12,970	5,008	4,367	3,595	26,380	18,401	28,837	19,517	4,284	5,036	2,920	3,119
Arizona	12,275	4,951	13,995	5,580	4,915	3,500	22,858	14,188	21,813	13,124	4,962	3,727	1,475	1,612
Arkansas	10,615	5,425	11,669	5,762	3,234	2,673	19,967	14,025	21,053	14,860	3,105	3,089	1,921	2,128
California	14,885	4,870	15,683	5,254	5,425	5,004	35,182	24,616	37,017	26,032	5,958	5,026	588	586
Colorado	13,342	5,262	14,240	5,683	4,352	4,205	30,126	19,587	29,331	19,293	5,698	4,340	2,077	2,197
Connecticut	16,253	7,459	17,364	7,891	5,075	4,399	40,209	29,321	42,268	30,911	6,295	5,063	2,829	2,982
Delaware	16,162	7,819	17,185	8,288	5,261	3,636	20,251	12,523	21,454	13,005	4,345	4,105	2,490	2,684
Florida	10,698	2,967	11,506	3,309	4,592	3,605	27,996	19,645	28,185	19,325	4,809	4,051	1,864	2,099
Georgia	10,962	3,988	11,540	4,270	4,360	2,911	28,988	20,074	30,594	21,283	5,323	3,988	1,873	1,890
Hawaii	12,178	4,630	13,434	5,391	3,936	4,107	21,465	11,344	22,957	12,297	4,588	6,071	1,567	1,757
Idaho	9,861	4,380	10,408	4,612	2,626	3,170	10,886	6,015	11,724	6,335	1,794	3,596	2,110	2,242
Illinois	16,782	8,968	18,213	9,847	4,366	4,001	30,853	21,504	32,359	22,599	5,370	4,390	2,375	2,519
Indiana	14,084	6,590	14,973	6,923	3,898	4,152	29,639	22,101	31,310	23,350	4,021	3,938	2,819	2,930
Iowa	13,189	6,219	13,831	6,435	3,593	3,804	24,122	17,680	25,280	18,643	3,079	3,558	3,264	3,415
Kansas	11,335	5,402	12,012	5,746	3,075	3,191	22,642	16,589	23,842	17,522	2,880	3,439	2,029	2,091
Kentucky	12,611	6,330	13,190	6,828	3,328	3,034	22,407	15,817	23,691	16,779	3,424	3,488	2,772	2,929
Louisiana	9,462	3,826	10,384	4,085	3,598	2,700	30,320	22,157	32,013	23,454	4,839	3,720	1,634	1,713
Maine	14,818	7,275	16,112	8,018	4,028	4,066	32,495	23,651	34,784	25,059	4,672	5,053	3,287	3,272
Maryland	15,661	7,155	16,111	7,249	4,963	3,899	36,213	26,883	38,453	28,483	5,886	4,083	3,014	3,071
Massachusetts	16,167	7,928	17,112	8,201	5,212	3,699	41,396	30,408	43,522	32,086	6,453	4,984	3,070	3,255
Michigan	16,014	8,479	17,039	9,078	4,236	3,725	21,890	14,828	22,862	15,552	3,684	3,626	2,186	2,255
Minnesota	14,173	7,696	15,105	8,292	3,474	3,338	30,076	22,595	31,706	23,860	4,101	3,745	4,532	4,614
Mississippi	10,794	4,764	11,047	4,942	3,419	2,686	18,372	12,659	19,358	13,276	2,942	3,140	1,725	1,770
Missouri	13,383	6,641	14,009	6,904	4,258	2,847	25,091	17,529	26,509	18,576	4,022	3,911	2,384	2,456
Montana	11,606	5,418	11,970	5,462	2,986	3,522	21,355	14,982	22,884	16,054	3,107	3,723	2,993	3,092
Nebraska	11,857	5,446	12,641	5,878	3,320	3,443	22,642	16,189	23,722	17,079	3,416	3,228	2,129	2,220
Nevada	12,152	3,034	12,869	3,348	5,469	4,052	25,764	15,025	25,897	15,998	5,583	4,316	1,763	1,920
New Hampshire	18,266	9,601	19,242	10,193	5,405	3,644	34,859	25,483	36,786	26,817	5,714	4,255	5,975	6,001
New Jersey	19,479	9,636	20,735	10,375	6,597	3,763	35,073	24,804	37,156	26,305	5,849	5,002	3,057	3,193
New Mexico	10,619	4,147	11,266	4,413	3,666	3,186	24,441	16,057	25,458	16,720	4,371	4,367	1,267	1,272
New York	14,143	5,060	14,865	5,103	5,818	3,943	36,394	26,044	38,488	27,527	6,486	4,475	3,422	3,525
North Carolina	10,894	4,300	11,333	4,373	3,848	3,112	29,143	21,492	30,963	22,904	4,185	3,874	1,376	1,404
North Dakota	11,137	5,757	11,418	5,780	2,479	3,159	14,804	10,108	15,614	10,666	2,159	2,790	3,599	4,104
Ohio	16,353	8,083	16,582	8,067	4,697	3,817	30,119	22,360	31,611	23,542	4,085	3,985	3,200	3,150

See footnotes at end of table.

AVERAGE UNDERGRADUATE TUITION AND FEES AND ROOM AND BOARD RATES IN INSTITUTIONS OF HIGHER EDUCATION, BY CONTROL OF INSTITUTION AND STATE: 2007–2008 AND 2008–2009—Continued

State or other jurisdiction	Public 4-year 2007–2008 Total	Tuition and required fees (in-state)	Public 4-year 2008–2009 (a) Total	Tuition and required fees (in-state)	Room	Board	Private 4-year 2007–2008 Total	Tuition and required fees	Private 4-year 2008–2009 (a) Total	Tuition and required fees	Room	Board	Public 2-year, tuition and required fees (in-state) 2007–08	2008–09 (a)
Oklahoma	10,607	4,470	12,333	5,011	3,441	3,881	22,898	16,221	24,762	17,420	3,612	3,730	2,360	2,531
Oregon	13,852	5,926	15,179	6,286	4,611	4,282	31,765	23,906	33,763	25,254	4,435	4,074	2,893	2,937
Pennsylvania	17,218	9,608	18,124	10,132	4,557	3,435	35,939	26,559	37,964	28,057	5,395	4,512	3,185	3,308
Rhode Island	15,809	7,147	17,266	7,648	5,776	3,842	36,586	26,782	39,072	28,409	5,870	4,792	2,846	3,090
South Carolina	15,091	8,375	16,136	8,976	4,587	2,574	24,944	18,307	25,336	18,553	3,315	3,468	3,231	3,361
South Dakota	10,530	5,393	11,373	5,755	2,543	3,074	20,559	15,242	21,697	15,774	2,757	3,167	3,707	3,931
Tennessee	11,343	5,361	12,026	5,680	3,431	2,915	25,810	18,510	27,364	19,659	4,122	3,583	2,631	2,778
Texas	12,337	5,535	13,222	6,030	3,778	3,414	27,241	19,735	29,228	21,124	4,423	3,681	1,430	1,471
Utah	9,685	4,025	10,352	4,262	2,579	3,510	12,817	6,144	13,482	6,598	3,400	3,484	2,439	2,553
Vermont	18,295	10,443	19,661	11,316	5,302	3,043	33,883	25,148	36,101	26,788	5,121	4,192	4,420	4,684
Virginia	13,926	6,890	14,868	7,448	4,084	3,336	25,684	18,551	27,280	19,673	3,937	3,669	2,486	2,666
Washington	13,512	5,378	14,165	5,704	4,188	4,273	31,408	23,442	33,455	24,955	4,489	4,010	2,768	2,850
West Virginia	11,425	4,383	12,131	4,703	3,935	3,493	21,950	15,221	19,859	12,625	3,463	3,770	2,704	2,790
Wisconsin	11,750	6,182	12,406	6,554	3,531	2,322	28,410	21,329	30,001	22,520	3,839	3,642	3,375	3,536
Wyoming	10,068	2,990	10,556	3,057	3,346	4,153	N.A.	10,890	N.A.	11,325	N.A.	N.A.	1,920	2,007
Dist. of Columbia	N.A.	3,140	N.A.	3,140	N.A.	N.A.	35,592	24,826	37,554	26,152	7,424	3,978	N.A.	N.A.

Source: U.S. Department of Education, National Center for Education Statistics, 2007–08 and 2008–09 Integrated Postsecondary Education Data System (IPEDS), Fall 2007, Fall 2008, Spring 2008. (This table was prepared August 2009.)

Note: Data are for the entire academic year and are average charges. Tuition and fees were weighted by the number of full-time equivalent undergraduates, but are not adjusted to reflect student residency. Room and board are based on full-time students. Degree-granting institutions grant associate's or higher degrees and participate in Title IV federal financial aid programs. Some data have been revised from previously published figures. Detail may not sum to totals because of rounding.

Key:
N.A. – Not applicable
(a) Preliminary data based on fall 2007 enrollment weights.

Table 9.9
DEGREE GRANTING INSTITUTIONS AND BRANCHES, BY TYPE AND CONTROL OF INSTITUTION, 2008–2009

State or other jurisdiction	Total	All public institutions	Public 4-year institutions Total	Doctoral (a)	Master's (b)	Baccalaureate (c)	Special focus (d)	Public 2-year	All not-for-profit institutions	Not-for-profit 4-year institutions Total	Doctoral (a)	Master's (b)	Baccalaureate (c)	Special focus (d)	Not-for-profit 2-year	For profit institutions Total	For profit 4-year	For profit 2-year
United States (e)	4,409	1,676	652	165	261	181	45	1,024	1,629	1,537	105	344	532	556	92	1,104	530	574
Alabama	72	39	14	4	9	1	0	25	19	19	1	2	10	6	0	14	10	4
Alaska	7	5	3	1	2	0	0	2	1	1	0	1	0	0	0	1	1	0
Arizona	75	24	3	3	0	0	0	21	10	10	0	2	2	6	0	41	28	13
Arkansas	50	33	11	2	5	3	1	22	12	12	0	1	9	2	0	5	3	2
California	426	147	35	9	19	5	2	112	146	138	15	26	22	75	8	133	60	73
Colorado	80	27	12	5	2	5	0	15	12	11	1	3	3	4	1	41	23	18
Connecticut	46	22	10	1	4	4	1	12	18	16	3	6	5	2	2	6	4	2
Delaware	10	5	2	1	1	0	0	3	5	4	1	1	1	1	1	0	0	0
Florida	188	40	20	8	2	9	1	20	56	55	4	11	21	19	1	92	51	41
Georgia	135	73	25	4	13	7	1	48	35	32	2	4	17	9	3	27	18	9
Hawaii	21	10	4	1	0	3	0	6	5	5	0	2	1	2	0	6	4	2
Idaho	14	7	4	2	1	1	0	3	4	4	1	1	1	1	0	3	2	1
Illinois	180	60	12	5	7	0	0	48	84	80	6	16	22	36	4	36	21	15
Indiana	107	29	15	2	6	4	3	14	43	42	1	9	21	11	1	35	19	16
Iowa	66	19	3	2	1	0	0	16	36	35	0	5	20	10	1	11	10	1
Kansas	66	32	8	3	4	0	1	24	24	22	1	6	13	2	2	10	5	5
Kentucky	73	24	8	2	5	1	0	16	27	27	1	3	14	9	0	22	8	14
Louisiana	85	51	17	4	9	3	1	34	10	10	1	2	4	3	0	24	4	20
Maine	30	15	8	1	1	6	0	7	13	12	0	3	6	3	1	2	0	2
Maryland	57	29	13	3	8	1	1	16	21	21	4	4	7	6	0	7	4	3
Massachusetts	124	30	14	3	7	2	2	16	84	80	9	14	25	32	4	10	4	6
Michigan	106	45	15	7	7	1	0	30	52	52	1	9	23	19	0	9	6	3
Minnesota	114	42	11	1	8	2	0	31	37	36	3	6	11	16	1	35	29	6
Mississippi	40	24	9	4	4	0	1	15	11	11	0	3	4	4	0	5	0	5
Missouri	131	34	13	4	6	3	0	21	56	52	2	12	12	26	4	41	20	21
Montana	23	18	6	2	1	3	0	12	5	4	0	1	2	1	1	0	0	0
Nebraska	42	15	7	1	3	1	2	8	19	17	0	3	9	5	2	8	5	3
Nevada	21	7	6	2	0	4	0	1	2	2	0	0	1	1	0	12	7	5
New Hampshire	28	12	5	1	2	2	0	7	14	13	2	2	6	3	1	2	1	1
New Jersey	63	33	14	3	9	2	0	19	25	25	3	9	3	10	0	5	3	2
New Mexico	42	28	8	2	4	1	1	20	5	5	0	1	1	3	0	9	8	1
New York	307	78	43	6	20	13	4	35	186	166	17	39	30	80	20	43	18	25
North Carolina	133	75	16	6	6	3	1	59	45	44	2	5	28	9	1	13	10	3
North Dakota	22	14	8	2	1	4	1	6	6	5	0	1	1	3	1	2	2	0
Ohio	209	60	30	10	1	16	3	30	77	71	3	18	25	25	6	72	10	62
Oklahoma	59	29	17	2	6	7	2	12	14	14	2	3	5	4	0	16	7	9
Oregon	60	26	9	3	3	2	1	17	25	25	2	3	9	11	0	9	5	4
Pennsylvania	262	65	44	4	16	22	2	21	114	101	7	30	36	28	13	83	9	74
Rhode Island	13	3	2	1	1	0	0	1	9	9	1	4	1	3	0	1	0	1
South Carolina	69	33	13	3	4	5	1	20	25	23	0	5	14	4	2	11	7	4

See footnotes at end of table.

DEGREE GRANTING INSTITUTIONS AND BRANCHES, BY TYPE AND CONTROL OF INSTITUTION, 2008–2009 — Continued

State or other jurisdiction	Total	All public institutions (Total)	Public 4-year institutions Total	Doctoral (a)	Master's (b)	Baccalaureate (c)	Special focus (d)	Public 2-year	All not-for-profit institutions	Not-for-profit 4-year institutions Total	Doctoral (a)	Master's (b)	Baccalaureate (c)	Special focus (d)	Not-for-profit 2-year	For profit institutions Total	4-year	2-year
South Dakota	24	12	7	2	0	3	2	5	8	7	0	1	3	3	1	4	4	0
Tennessee	105	22	9	4	5	0	0	13	48	46	2	10	17	17	2	35	16	19
Texas	218	109	45	11	21	5	8	64	57	53	4	16	17	16	4	52	15	37
Utah	38	14	7	2	2	3	0	7	4	3	1	1	1	0	1	20	17	3
Vermont	25	6	5	1	2	2	0	1	17	16	0	5	9	2	1	2	2	0
Virginia	114	39	15	6	6	3	0	24	35	35	1	7	20	7	0	40	21	19
Washington	78	43	13	2	6	4	1	30	18	18	0	10	3	5	0	17	12	5
West Virginia	44	23	12	1	1	9	1	11	9	9	0	2	6	1	0	12	2	10
Wisconsin	75	31	14	2	9	3	0	17	30	28	1	10	10	7	2	14	10	4
Wyoming	11	8	1	1	0	0	0	7	0	0	0	0	0	0	0	3	2	1
Dist. of Columbia	16	2	2	0	1	0	1	0	11	11	4	3	0	3	0	3	3	0
U.S. Service Academies	5	5	5	0	0	5	0	0	n/a	n/a	n/a	n/a	n/a	n/a	n/a	n/a	n/a	n/a
American Samoa	1	1	1	0	0	1	0	0	0	0	0	0	0	0	0	0	0	0
Federated States of Micronesia	1	1	0	0	0	0	0	1	0	0	0	0	0	0	0	0	0	0
Guam	3	2	1	0	1	0	0	1	1	1	0	0	0	1	0	0	0	0
Marshall Islands	1	1	0	0	0	0	0	1	0	0	0	0	0	0	0	0	0	0
No. Mariana Islands	1	1	1	0	0	1	0	0	0	0	0	0	0	0	0	0	0	0
Palau	1	1	0	0	0	0	0	1	0	0	0	0	0	0	0	0	0	0
Puerto Rico	77	17	14	1	1	9	3	3	43	37	0	5	19	11	6	17	8	9
U.S. Virgin Islands	1	1	1	0	0	1	0	0	0	0	0	0	0	0	0	0	0	0

Source: U.S. Department of Education, National Center for Education Statistics, 2008–09 Integrated Postsecondary Education Data System (IPEDS), Fall 2008.

Key:
n/a — Not applicable
(a) Institutions that award at least 20 doctor's degrees per year.
(b) Institutions that award at least 50 master's degrees per year.
(c) Institutions that primarily emphasize undergraduate education.
(d) Four-year institutions that award degrees primarily in single fields of study, such as medicine, business, fine arts, theology, and engineering. Includes some institutions that have 4-year programs, but have not reported sufficient data to identify program category. Also, includes institutions classified as 4-year under the IPEDS system, which had been classified as 2-year in the Carneigie Classification system because they primarily award an associate's degree.
(e) U.S. totals include the District of Columbia and U.S. Service Schools.

Table 9.10
AVERAGE SALARY OF FULL-TIME FACULTY ON 9-MONTH CONTRACTS: 2008–2009

State or other jurisdiction	Total	Public institutions						Not-for-profit institutions						For-profit institutions
		All public institutions	4-year Total	4-year Doctoral (a)	4-year Master's (b)	4-year Other	Public 2-year	All not-for-profit	Total	Doctoral (a)	Master's (b)	Other	Not-for-profit 2-year	
United States	$73,570	$71,237	$75,245	$81,485	$66,700	$62,475	$61,433	$79,358	$79,554	$97,702	$67,324	$65,522	$44,302	$52,557
Alabama	63,086	64,645	69,198	72,769	59,032	68,352	53,220	54,675	54,675	68,717	54,022	47,876	N/A	N/A
Alaska	68,104	68,659	68,603	70,151	67,492	N/A	75,472	54,209	54,209	N/A	54,209	N/A	N/A	N/A
Arizona	75,466	76,007	80,469	80,469	N/A	N/A	67,921	55,739	55,739	N/A	40,237	64,448	N/A	63,912
Arkansas	54,600	54,828	59,677	66,021	51,993	55,010	43,128	53,319	53,319	N/A	55,943	51,399	N/A	N/A
California	87,736	86,049	89,809	102,078	77,680	71,245	81,765	94,773	94,909	105,468	79,040	88,890	62,991	68,821
Colorado	68,753	67,636	71,528	78,352	57,697	55,539	49,338	76,485	76,485	78,473	75,991	51,824	N/A	51,390
Connecticut	90,314	83,590	87,922	99,894	76,374	N/A	70,449	98,126	98,126	118,151	84,013	77,179	N/A	45,490
Delaware	85,476	85,941	90,935	94,470	65,480	N/A	63,686	81,080	81,080	61,582	100,835	N/A	N/A	N/A
Florida	68,068	67,215	71,664	76,734	63,243	60,518	52,738	70,522	70,522	83,157	66,826	53,037	N/A	88,304
Georgia	67,190	66,001	68,128	81,422	57,028	50,282	46,760	70,456	70,666	93,680	62,981	55,540	55,528	42,000
Hawaii............	78,957	81,325	86,586	91,265	71,505	70,071	69,049	68,855	68,855	N/A	63,240	86,087	N/A	N/A
Idaho............	57,786	58,458	60,118	61,869	59,757	49,141	49,160	50,935	50,935	N/A	49,020	52,415	N/A	N/A
Illinois............	75,346	70,507	73,756	79,571	61,667	N/A	64,566	82,725	82,901	105,247	64,206	62,201	38,004	33,192
Indiana............	69,408	69,076	72,799	78,145	59,200	54,592	45,219	70,111	70,259	95,408	60,436	59,845	43,093	39,985
Iowa............	67,526	71,915	82,343	86,921	65,847	N/A	51,400	59,879	59,879	58,024	59,357	60,444	N/A	N/A
Kansas	62,666	65,322	72,275	78,223	58,819	60,351	48,888	46,137	46,390	N/A	49,453	41,076	39,941	40,000
Kentucky	60,003	61,384	66,203	78,108	59,534	54,918	49,103	54,474	54,474	61,304	48,837	56,889	N/A	N/A
Louisiana	63,098	61,824	63,980	72,432	55,885	57,807	50,573	69,400	69,400	82,084	63,366	52,693	N/A	45,000
Maine	70,138	67,178	70,224	76,500	73,173	56,479	54,586	75,373	75,565	N/A	54,660	86,301	58,264	N/A
Maryland	73,023	72,457	76,057	88,029	65,484	N/A	65,426	75,103	75,103	91,836	68,430	72,324	N/A	N/A
Massachusetts	91,612	74,391	79,992	90,300	69,726	N/A	60,200	99,351	99,494	114,790	81,855	80,206	52,515	53,878
Michigan............	77,147	79,589	80,787	84,356	68,284	54,918	74,237	63,349	63,349	45,630	61,108	65,375	N/A	N/A
Minnesota	70,044	71,351	77,573	94,300	68,319	59,220	61,523	67,425	67,433	67,223	63,823	69,581	41,256	40,126
Mississippi	55,302	55,667	60,225	62,602	50,465	N/A	49,495	52,073	52,073	N/A	56,707	39,662	N/A	N/A
Missouri............	66,082	63,537	66,698	73,326	58,098	57,068	53,540	71,233	71,612	88,555	55,798	50,605	48,030	52,745
Montana	56,689	58,350	61,125	64,168	55,677	48,435	41,786	43,354	44,769	N/A	40,822	45,848	34,077	N/A
Nebraska	64,340	66,923	72,146	78,026	58,195	N/A	49,373	57,693	57,732	71,232	52,888	50,095	45,240	N/A
Nevada	79,794	80,216	81,709	89,145	†	67,202	63,195	62,802	62,802	N/A	62,802	N/A	N/A	53,580
New Hampshire	80,335	76,729	84,608	93,396	71,060	79,127	49,874	86,103	86,103	112,768	66,806	60,516	41,256	47,364
New Jersey	89,013	86,968	94,427	98,116	90,170	N/A	68,821	93,781	93,781	111,787	72,640	62,959	48,030	58,640
New Mexico	51,853	61,500	67,632	73,274	55,896	45,087	47,062	70,995	70,995	N/A	76,805	64,217	N/A	N/A
New York............	32,642	76,180	80,096	92,583	77,077	70,554	67,773	89,041	89,288	99,952	72,568	79,701	47,620	41,892
North Carolina	57,498	64,880	77,643	83,046	68,898	67,639	47,331	76,300	76,416	101,230	55,743	55,496	36,389	N/A
North Dakota.........	54,551	56,877	58,822	64,538	52,085	45,853	44,119	40,935	46,552	49,011	†	44,381	20,339	N/A
Ohio	59,235	70,766	74,227	76,439	69,724	57,588	58,185	65,988	66,046	79,927	59,383	66,066	56,651	37,780
Oklahoma............	61,106	61,223	64,758	74,679	55,535	47,723	47,932	60,590	60,590	N/A	63,477	42,909	N/A	N/A
Oregon............	64,928	63,880	66,497	70,070	54,578	56,705	50,211	68,151	68,151	59,234	71,672	67,562	67,562	N/A
Pennsylvania............	77,822	75,247	78,274	85,872	74,055	63,882	58,666	80,862	81,101	98,297	69,413	71,990	41,565	36,960
Rhode Island............	82,332	71,330	75,110	81,830	62,994	N/A	59,617	89,110	89,110	93,215	83,485	114,596	N/A	N/A
South Carolina	59,920	61,508	68,918	77,755	62,230	53,103	46,492	52,851	53,182	N/A	53,650	52,491	38,577	125,743

See footnotes at end of table.

AVERAGE SALARY OF FULL-TIME FACULTY ON 9-MONTH CONTRACTS, 2008–2009—Continued

State or other jurisdiction	Total	Public institutions							Not-for-profit institutions						For-profit institutions
		All public institutions	4-year				Public 2-year	All not-for-profit	4-year				Not-for-profit 2-year	
			Total	Doctoral (a)	Master's (b)	Other			Total	Doctoral (a)	Master's (b)	Other		
South Dakota	55,667	57,484	59,903	60,589	61,041	41,736	44,556	48,579	48,579	N/A	47,598	49,155	N/A	36,775
Tennessee	63,167	60,962	65,308	68,345	59,946	N/A	46,984	67,685	67,685	92,784	51,874	54,094	N/A	27,532
Texas	69,131	68,029	74,035	79,941	60,852	51,206	54,510	74,682	74,908	87,080	64,911	59,610	33,137	21,430
Utah	71,309	64,770	67,810	77,045	58,361	57,961	49,790	89,305	89,658	92,672	65,180	N/A	56,641	N/A
Vermont	69,851	69,505	69,505	75,162	58,219	55,326	N/A	70,193	73,487	N/A	76,985	52,172	43,065	N/A
Virginia	71,924	74,242	78,740	85,851	64,873	66,540	57,742	64,539	64,539	63,943	66,522	63,239	N/A	N/A
Washington	67,287	67,215	74,658	81,718	66,315	54,137	55,328	67,637	67,637	71,754	66,582	66,715	N/A	58,968
West Virginia	57,440	59,333	61,764	73,454	57,638	51,321	45,352	45,924	45,924	49,092	45,745	44,552	N/A	N/A
Wisconsin	68,531	70,148	69,973	79,971	58,249	86,476	70,493	62,286	62,384	72,233	58,235	55,381	49,631	N/A
Wyoming	68,020	68,020	76,719	76,719	N/A	N/A	58,089	N/A	N/A	N/A	N/A	N/A	N/A	52,283
Dist. of Columbia	88,635	78,932	78,932	N/A	78,454	85,278	N/A	91,487	91,487	92,640	78,241	N/A	N/A	N/A
U.S. Service Academies	113,473	113,473	113,473	N/A	N/A	113,473	N/A	N/A	N/A	N/A	N/A	N/A	N/A	N/A
American Samoa	28,336	28,336	28,336	N/A	N/A	28,336	N/A	N/A	N/A	N/A	N/A	N/A	N/A	N/A
Federated States of Micronesia	20,727	20,727	N/A	N/A	N/A	N/A	20,727	N/A	N/A	N/A	N/A	N/A	N/A	N/A
Guam	56,815	56,815	63,389	N/A	63,389	N/A	47,327	N/A	N/A	N/A	N/A	N/A	N/A	N/A
Marshall Islands	26,335	26,335	N/A	N/A	N/A	N/A	26,335	N/A	N/A	N/A	N/A	N/A	N/A	N/A
No. Marianas Islands	41,592	41,592	41,592	N/A	N/A	41,592	N/A	N/A	N/A	N/A	N/A	N/A	N/A	N/A
Palau	17,321	17,321	N/A	N/A	N/A	N/A	17,321	N/A	N/A	N/A	N/A	N/A	N/A	N/A
Puerto Rico	64,208	64,772	64,772	N/A	72,836	58,603	N/A	33,971	33,971	N/A	33,971	N/A	N/A	N/A
U.S. Virgin Islands	59,906	59,906	59,906	N/A	59,906	59,906	N/A	N/A	N/A	N/A	N/A	N/A	N/A	N/A

Source: U.S. Department of Education, National Center for Education Statistics, 2008–09 Integrated Postsecondary Education Data System (IPEDS), Winter 2008–2009.

n/a—Not applicable

(a) Institutions that awarded 20 or more doctor's degrees during the previous academic year.

(b) Institutions that awarded 20 or more master's degrees, but fewer than 20 doctor's degrees, during the previous academic year.

Note: Degree-granting institutions grant associate's or higher degrees and participate in Title IV federal financial aid programs. Data include imputations for nonrespondent institutions.

States Face Medicaid Match Loss After Recovery Act Expires

By Debra Miller

Medicaid, the largest health insurance program in the nation, is jointly financed by state and federal governments. The federal government establishes matching rates for each state each year, setting the percentage of overall costs paid by the federal government—between 50 and 83 percent—based on a state's per capita income compared to the nation's per capita income. The American Recovery and Reinvestment Act of 2009 provided all states with enhanced matching rates for their Medicaid programs in recognition of the fiscal issues states faced in the Great Recession.

In this report, CSG analyzes the value of the Medicaid matching rate to states before, during and after Recovery Act funding. CSG interprets Medicaid matching rates in a straightforward way: For every dollar a state spends for Medicaid, we calculate how many federal dollars flow to the state through the federal match. On average, states gained $1.07 additional match for each state dollar spent under the Recovery Act enhanced rates, as the average federal return on a state dollar rose from $1.61 in 2008 to $2.68 in late 2010. The additional match for states ranged from 56 cents in Alaska to $2.39 in Mississippi.

States lost any additional federal stimulus match June 30, 2011, and reverted back to the pre-recession calculation of Medicaid matching rates. For 20 states, the Medicaid match rate in the 2012 fiscal year is lower than the pre-recession rate in the 2008 fiscal year, ranging from 52 cents less per state dollar expended in North Dakota to 2 cents in Rhode Island. The rate increased for 17 states, ranging from 57 cents more per state dollar expended in Michigan to 4 cents in Idaho. It remained the same for 13 states and the District of Columbia.

Medicaid Match Basics

Introduction

The Medicaid program is the biggest health insurance program in the country. As of December 2009, the program covered nearly 49 million low-income adults and children. The federal and state governments jointly administer the program. In many states, Medicaid spending exceeds elementary and secondary education as the largest state government expenditure.

The Medicaid program is important not only to the millions of low-income Americans who receive benefits, but also to the economy of each state. Medicaid funds support thousands of health-related jobs and facilities, as well as medical education and work force development programs.

Medicaid Match Calculation

Since the beginning of the Medicaid program in the 1960s, the federal and state governments have shared the program costs. Each state's share of costs is set by a formula that compares a state's per capita income to the U.S. per capita income. This calculation is called the federal medical assistance percentage, commonly referred to as either FMAP or simply Medicaid match. Poorer states receive a higher match, but no more than the statutory maximum of 83 percent, and relatively wealthier states receive a lower match, but no less than 50 percent.

The U.S. Department of Health and Human Services publishes the FMAPs for states in the Federal Register, generally in November for the federal fiscal year beginning the following October so states can use the rates in their budget deliberations. The formula uses three years of data; for instance, the FMAPs set in November 2010 for the year October 2011 to September 2012 used per capita income data for 2007, 2008 and 2009.

American Recovery and Reinvestment Act Enhanced Match

When Congress passed the American Recovery and Reinvestment Act in 2009, it provided financial relief for the states during the recession through an enhanced matching rate for Medicaid. The Recovery Act provided nine quarters of increased federal funding with the assumption that enrollments in Medicaid would increase given the unemployment increases during the recession, and that states' revenues would decrease as incomes fell. The calculation of states' enhanced FMAP included an across-the-board increase as well as an adjustment based on the state's unemployment increase. The Congressional Budget Office originally estimated the value of the enhanced match to states at $91 billion and later reduced it to $89 billion.

The original enhanced match was slated to expire Dec. 31, 2010, yet CSG found in a survey of states' 2011 fiscal year budgets that 24 states had assumed the enhanced FMAPs would be extended by Congress until at least June 30, 2011.

In response to states' pressure for continued relief in the face of extended unemployment, Congress did extend the enhanced matching provisions for Medicaid in late 2010, albeit at a lesser level than the original stimulus provisions. CSG calculated the additional aid to states is an estimated $1.74 billion short of the amount the 24 states included in their official 2011 fiscal year budgets. After the two-step phase-down, Medicaid match rates returned to pre-recession calculation rates on July 1, 2011. The 2012 fiscal year rates begin Oct. 1, 2011.

CSG Analysis of States' Medicaid Match, 2008–2012

For the purposes of this analysis of states' Medicaid matching rates from 2008 to 2012, CSG has calculated matching rates in a straightforward way: For every state dollar a state spends for Medicaid, we determine how many federal dollars are provided through federal match. This investment calculation is familiar to state policymakers who, for instance, ask about the dollar-for-dollar return on state economic development incentive programs. When Congress passed the Recovery Act in 2009, all states received a jump in their Medicaid matching rates. The increased match was made retroactive to the first two quarters of 2009, but only reflected the across-the-board increase. In the third quarter of 2009—April, May and June—the enhanced match rate calculations also factored in state unemployment rates, so states' rates of increase differed accordingly. After the first quarter of 2011—October, November and December 2010—matching funds decline in accordance with the phaseout of the enhanced match and then level out as the regularly calculated 2011 and 2012 fiscal year match rates take effect.

On average, the increased match for states amounted to an additional $1.07 in federal funds for every state dollar when the 2008 fiscal year FMAP is compared to the enhanced match provided in the first quarter of 2011—October, November and December 2010. The federal match, although continued for two more quarters in 2011, decreases in value to states, before it reverted to the prerecession calculation methodology.

One state dollar invested in Medicaid in the 2008 fiscal year yielded, on average, $1.61 in federal funding. Under the Recovery Act provisions, that same dollar yielded $2.68 on average in the first quarter of the 2011 fiscal year, yielding an additional $1.07. The average state spending one dollar of its general fund for Medicaid purchased $2.61 worth of Medicaid services in 2008. With the enhanced match, one state dollar bought $3.68 worth of Medicaid services, a 41 percent increase in the average state's purchasing power.

At the low end of additional match for states was Alaska at 56 cents, North Dakota at 57 cents, and California, Colorado, Connecticut, Maryland, Massachusetts, Minnesota, New Hampshire, New Jersey, New York, Virginia and Wyoming at 60 cents. The largest gains were $1.85 for Kentucky, $2.02 for West Virginia and $2.39 for Mississippi.

FMAP Declines in 2012 Compared to 2008 for 20 States

Twenty states are experiencing a decline in FMAP rates in 2012 compared to the prerecession calculation in 2008. These are the states whose per capita income is relatively better than the national average both in the three years used in the 2012 calculation (2007, 2008 and 2009 data) and compared to the earlier calculation for the 2008 FMAP.

The loss of federal matching funds ranges 52 cents less per state dollar expended in North Dakota to 22 cents less in Rhode Island. For instance, Mississippi received $3.22 in federal funds for each $1 it spent in 2008, but will receive just $2.87 in the 2012 fiscal year, a difference of 35 cents. That difference alone presents obvious budget issues for Mississippi, but the dilemma is likely to be compounded by the fact that during 2010, one Mississippi dollar generated $5.61 in federal matching funds.

Another 17 states are receiving a larger FMAP in 2012 than they did in 2008, although their 2012 rates are below the enhanced rates provided by federal stimulus funds. The range for the 17 states is from 57 cents more per state dollar expended in Michigan to 4 cents more in Idaho. For instance,

Table A: State Medicaid Matching Rates, FY 2008 to FY 2012
(Matching rates expressed as federal dollars returned for each state dollar.)

State or other jurisdiction	2008 FMAP	Q1 2009	Q2 2009	Q3 2009	Q4 2009	Q1 2010	Q2 2010	Q3 2010	Q4 2010	Q1 2011	Q2 2011	Q3 2011	Q4 2011 FMAP	2012 FMAP
Alabama	$2.09	$3.28	$3.28	$3.45	$3.45	$3.45	$3.45	$3.45	$3.45	$3.55	$3.03	$2.74	$2.18	$2.19
Alaska	1.10	1.42	1.42	1.57	1.57	1.57	1.66	1.66	1.66	1.66	1.47	1.36	1.00	1.00
Arizona	1.96	3.00	3.00	3.15	3.15	3.15	3.15	3.15	3.15	3.15	2.72	2.47	1.93	2.06
Arkansas	2.70	3.79	3.79	4.12	4.12	4.12	4.31	4.31	4.31	4.31	3.61	3.24	2.49	2.41
California	1.00	1.60	1.60	1.60	1.60	1.60	1.60	1.60	1.60	1.60	1.43	1.32	1.00	1.00
Colorado	1.00	1.43	1.43	1.60	1.60	1.60	1.60	1.60	1.60	1.60	1.43	1.32	1.00	1.00
Connecticut	1.00	1.51	1.51	1.51	1.60	1.60	1.60	1.60	1.60	1.60	1.43	1.32	1.00	1.00
Delaware	1.00	1.51	1.51	1.60	1.60	1.62	1.62	1.62	1.62	1.81	1.60	1.48	1.13	1.18
Florida	1.32	2.09	2.09	2.09	2.09	2.09	2.09	2.09	2.09	2.09	1.84	1.70	1.24	1.27
Georgia	1.71	2.77	2.77	2.91	2.91	2.99	2.99	2.99	2.99	3.03	2.61	2.38	1.88	1.96
Hawaii	1.30	1.95	1.95	2.06	2.06	2.06	2.06	2.06	2.06	2.06	1.82	1.68	1.07	1.02
Idaho	2.32	3.62	3.62	3.80	3.80	3.80	3.80	3.80	3.80	3.80	3.23	2.92	2.21	2.36
Illinois	1.00	1.53	1.53	1.62	1.62	1.62	1.62	1.62	1.62	1.62	1.44	1.33	1.01	1.00
Indiana	1.68	2.74	2.74	2.88	2.88	3.11	3.11	3.11	3.11	3.20	2.76	2.51	1.99	2.03
Iowa	1.61	2.21	2.21	2.21	2.41	2.64	2.64	2.64	2.64	2.64	2.30	2.10	1.68	1.55
Kansas	1.46	1.97	1.97	2.16	2.27	2.30	2.30	2.30	2.30	2.30	2.01	1.85	1.44	1.32
Kentucky	2.31	3.50	3.50	3.86	3.86	4.04	4.04	4.04	4.04	4.16	3.50	3.15	2.51	2.47
Louisiana	2.63	4.00	4.00	4.00	4.19	4.40	4.40	4.40	4.40	4.40	3.68	3.30	2.13	2.31
Maine	1.73	2.62	2.62	2.90	2.90	2.98	2.98	2.98	2.98	2.98	2.58	2.35	1.76	1.72
Maryland	1.00	1.43	1.43	1.51	1.60	1.60	1.60	1.60	1.60	1.60	1.43	1.32	1.00	1.00
Massachusetts	1.00	1.43	1.43	1.51	1.60	1.60	1.60	1.60	1.60	1.60	1.43	1.32	1.00	1.00
Michigan	1.39	2.29	2.29	2.41	2.41	2.74	2.74	2.74	2.74	3.09	2.67	2.43	1.92	1.95
Minnesota	1.00	1.51	1.51	1.60	1.60	1.60	1.60	1.60	1.60	1.60	1.34	1.24	1.00	1.00
Mississippi	3.22	5.11	5.11	5.35	5.35	5.61	5.61	5.61	5.61	5.61	4.56	4.04	2.96	2.87
Missouri	1.66	2.48	2.48	2.74	2.74	2.91	2.91	2.91	2.91	2.91	2.52	2.30	1.72	1.74
Montana	2.18	3.22	3.22	3.37	3.37	3.54	3.54	3.54	3.54	3.54	3.03	2.74	2.01	1.95
Nebraska	1.38	1.92	1.92	2.10	2.10	2.20	2.20	2.20	2.20	2.20	1.93	1.77	1.41	1.31
Nevada	1.11	1.77	1.77	1.77	1.77	1.77	1.77	1.77	1.77	1.77	1.57	1.45	1.07	1.28
New Hampshire	1.00	1.28	1.28	1.43	1.51	1.60	1.60	1.60	1.60	1.60	1.43	1.32	1.00	1.00
New Jersey	1.00	1.43	1.43	1.60	1.60	1.60	1.60	1.60	1.60	1.60	1.43	1.32	1.00	1.00
New Mexico	2.45	3.39	3.39	3.69	3.86	4.13	4.13	4.13	4.13	4.13	3.48	3.13	2.31	2.26
New York	1.00	1.43	1.43	1.51	1.60	1.60	1.60	1.60	1.60	1.60	1.43	1.32	1.00	1.00
North Carolina	1.78	2.78	2.78	2.92	2.92	3.00	3.00	3.00	3.00	3.00	2.59	2.36	1.83	1.88
North Dakota	1.76	2.33	2.33	2.33	2.33	2.33	2.33	2.33	2.33	2.33	2.03	1.85	1.52	1.24
Ohio	1.55	2.36	2.36	2.62	2.62	2.77	2.77	2.77	2.77	2.80	2.43	2.23	1.75	1.79
Oklahoma	2.04	2.99	2.99	2.99	3.14	3.14	3.30	3.30	3.30	3.30	2.83	2.57	1.85	1.77
Oregon	1.55	2.52	2.52	2.65	2.65	2.69	2.69	2.69	2.69	2.70	2.35	2.15	1.69	1.70
Pennsylvania	1.18	1.71	1.71	1.80	1.91	1.93	1.93	1.93	1.93	1.99	1.76	1.62	1.25	1.23
Rhode Island	1.11	1.77	1.77	1.77	1.77	1.77	1.77	1.77	1.77	1.79	1.59	1.47	1.13	1.09
South Carolina	2.31	3.66	3.66	3.84	3.84	3.90	3.90	3.90	3.90	3.90	3.30	2.98	2.34	2.36
South Dakota	1.50	2.20	2.20	2.41	2.41	2.42	2.42	2.42	2.42	2.42	2.11	1.94	1.58	1.45
Tennessee	1.76	2.74	2.74	2.88	2.88	3.06	3.06	3.06	3.06	3.10	2.68	2.44	1.93	1.97
Texas	1.54	2.20	2.20	2.20	2.32	2.44	2.44	2.44	2.44	2.44	2.14	1.96	1.54	1.39
Utah	2.52	3.51	3.51	4.00	4.00	4.20	4.20	4.20	4.20	4.20	3.54	3.18	2.46	2.45
Vermont	1.44	2.10	2.10	2.33	2.33	2.33	2.33	2.33	2.33	2.33	1.94	1.78	1.42	1.36
Virginia	1.00	1.43	1.43	1.60	1.60	1.60	1.60	1.60	1.60	1.60	1.43	1.32	1.00	1.00
Washington	1.06	1.51	1.51	1.70	1.70	1.70	1.70	1.70	1.70	1.70	1.51	1.39	1.00	1.00
West Virginia	2.88	4.12	4.12	4.46	4.90	4.90	4.90	4.90	4.90	4.90	4.06	3.62	2.74	2.65
Wisconsin	1.36	1.91	1.91	2.20	2.32	2.40	2.40	2.40	2.40	2.40	2.11	1.93	1.51	1.53
Wyoming	1.00	1.28	1.28	1.28	1.43	1.60	1.60	1.60	1.60	1.60	1.43	1.32	1.00	1.00
Dist. of Columbia	2.33	3.48	3.48	3.83	3.83	3.83	3.83	3.83	3.83	3.83	3.25	2.93	2.33	2.33

Sources:
FY 2008 FMAP rates, Nov. 30, 2006, *http://aspe.hhs.gov/health/fmap08.pdf.*
FY 2011 FMAP rates, Nov. 27, 2009, *http://aspe.hhs.gov/health/fmap11.pdf.*
FY 2012 FMAP rates, Nov. 10, 2010 Federal Register, *http://www.federalregister.gov/articles/2010/11/10/2010-28319/federal-financial-participation-in-state-assistance-expenditures-federal-matching-shares-for.*
FY 2012, Disaster Recovery State Adjustment for Louisiana, December 22, 2010 *http://www.federalregister.gov/articles/2010/12/22/2010-32054/adjustments-for-disaster-recovery-states-to-the-fourth-quarter-of-fiscal-year-2011-and-fiscal-year.*
FY 2009–2011 FMAP rates, FFIS Issue Brief 10-44, October 25, 2010, Preliminary FY 2011 First Quarter ARRA FMAPs.
Calculations by The Council of State Governments.

Table B: State Medicaid Matching Rates, FY 2008 to FY 2012
(Federal Matching Percentage)

State or other jurisdiction	2008 FMAP	Q1 2009	Q2 2009	Q3 2009	Q4 2009	Q1 2010	Q2 2010	Q3 2010	Q4 2010	Q1 2011	Q2 2011	Q3 2011	Q4 2011 FMAP	2012 FMAP
Alabama	67.62%	76.64%	76.64%	77.51%	77.51%	77.53%	77.53%	77.53%	77.53%	78.00%	75.17%	73.29%	68.54%	68.62%
Alaska	52.48	58.68	58.68	61.12	61.12	61.12	62.46	62.46	62.46	62.46	59.58	57.67	50.00	50.00
Arizona	66.20	75.01	75.01	75.93	75.93	75.93	75.93	75.93	75.93	75.93	73.1	71.22	65.85	67.30
Arkansas	72.94	79.14	79.14	80.46	80.46	80.46	81.18	81.18	81.18	81.18	78.3	76.39	71.37	70.71
California	50.00	61.59	61.59	61.59	61.59	61.59	61.59	61.59	61.59	61.59	58.77	56.88	50.00	50.00
Colorado	50.00	58.78	58.78	61.59	61.59	61.59	61.59	61.59	61.59	61.59	58.77	56.88	50.00	50.00
Connecticut	50.00	60.19	60.19	61.59	61.59	61.59	61.59	61.59	61.59	61.59	58.77	56.88	50.00	50.00
Delaware	50.00	60.19	60.19	61.59	61.59	61.78	61.78	61.78	61.78	64.38	61.55	59.67	53.15	54.17
Florida	56.83	67.64	67.64	67.64	67.64	67.64	67.64	67.64	67.64	67.64	64.81	62.93	55.45	56.04
Georgia	63.10	73.44	73.44	74.42	74.42	74.96	74.96	74.96	74.96	75.16	72.33	70.45	65.33	66.16
Hawaii	56.50	66.13	66.13	67.35	67.35	67.35	67.35	67.35	67.35	67.35	64.52	62.63	51.79	50.48
Idaho	69.87	78.37	78.37	79.18	79.18	79.18	79.18	79.18	79.18	79.18	76.35	74.47	68.85	70.23
Illinois	50.00	60.48	60.48	61.88	61.88	61.88	61.88	61.88	61.88	61.88	59.05	57.16	50.20	50.00
Indiana	62.69	73.23	73.23	74.21	74.21	75.69	75.69	75.69	75.69	76.21	73.39	71.5	66.52	66.96
Iowa	61.73	68.82	68.82	68.82	70.71	72.55	72.55	72.55	72.55	72.55	69.68	67.76	62.63	60.71
Kansas	59.43	66.28	66.28	68.31	69.41	69.68	69.68	69.68	69.68	69.68	66.81	64.9	59.05	56.91
Kentucky	69.78	77.8	77.8	79.41	79.41	80.14	80.14	80.14	80.14	80.61	77.78	75.9	71.49	71.18
Louisiana	72.47	80.01	80.01	80.01	80.75	81.48	81.48	81.48	81.48	81.48	78.65	76.77	68.04	69.78
Maine	63.31	72.4	72.4	74.35	74.35	74.86	74.86	74.86	74.86	74.86	72.03	70.15	63.80	63.27
Maryland	50.00	58.78	58.78	60.19	61.59	61.59	61.59	61.59	61.59	61.59	58.77	56.88	50.00	50.00
Massachusetts	50.00	58.78	58.78	60.19	61.59	61.59	61.59	61.59	61.59	61.59	58.77	56.88	50.00	50.00
Michigan	58.10	69.58	69.58	70.68	70.68	73.27	73.27	73.27	73.27	75.57	72.74	70.86	65.79	66.14
Minnesota	50.00	60.19	60.19	61.59	61.59	61.59	61.59	61.59	61.59	61.59	57.31	55.4	50.00	50.00
Mississippi	76.29	83.62	83.62	84.24	84.24	84.86	84.86	84.86	84.86	84.86	82.03	80.15	74.73	74.18
Missouri	62.42	71.24	71.24	73.27	73.27	74.43	74.43	74.43	74.43	74.43	71.61	69.72	63.29	63.45
Montana	68.53	76.29	76.29	77.14	77.14	77.99	77.99	77.99	77.99	77.99	75.17	73.28	66.81	66.11
Nebraska	58.02	65.74	65.74	67.79	67.79	68.76	68.76	68.76	68.76	68.76	65.84	63.9	58.44	56.64
Nevada	52.64	63.93	63.93	63.93	63.93	63.93	63.93	63.93	63.93	63.93	61.1	59.22	51.61	56.20
New Hampshire	50.00	56.2	56.2	58.78	60.19	61.59	61.59	61.59	61.59	61.59	58.77	56.88	50.00	50.00
New Jersey	50.00	58.78	58.78	61.59	61.59	61.59	61.59	61.59	61.59	61.59	58.77	56.88	50.00	50.00
New Mexico	71.04	77.24	77.24	78.66	79.44	80.49	80.49	80.49	80.49	80.49	77.66	75.78	69.78	69.36
New York	50.00	58.78	58.78	60.19	61.59	61.59	61.59	61.59	61.59	61.59	58.77	56.88	50.00	50.00
North Carolina	64.05	73.55	73.55	74.51	74.51	74.98	74.98	74.98	74.98	74.98	72.16	70.27	64.71	65.28
North Dakota	63.75	69.95	69.95	69.95	69.95	69.95	69.95	69.95	69.95	69.95	66.95	64.95	60.35	55.40
Ohio	60.79	70.25	70.25	72.34	72.34	73.47	73.47	73.47	73.47	73.71	70.88	69	63.69	64.15
Oklahoma	67.10	74.94	74.94	74.94	75.83	75.83	76.73	76.73	76.73	76.73	73.9	72.01	64.94	63.88
Oregon	60.86	71.58	71.58	72.61	72.61	72.87	72.87	72.87	72.87	72.97	70.14	68.25	62.85	62.91
Pennsylvania	54.08	63.05	63.05	64.32	65.59	65.85	65.85	65.85	65.85	66.58	63.76	61.87	55.64	55.07
Rhode Island	52.51	63.89	63.89	63.89	63.89	63.92	63.92	63.92	63.92	64.22	61.39	59.51	52.97	52.12
South Carolina	69.79	78.55	78.55	79.36	79.36	79.58	79.58	79.58	79.58	79.58	76.75	74.86	70.04	70.24
South Dakota	60.03	68.75	68.75	70.64	70.64	70.8	70.8	70.8	70.8	70.8	67.88	65.94	61.25	59.13
Tennessee	63.71	73.25	73.25	74.23	74.23	75.37	75.37	75.37	75.37	75.62	72.79	70.91	65.85	66.36
Texas	60.56	68.76	68.76	68.76	69.85	70.94	70.94	70.94	70.94	70.94	68.11	66.23	60.56	58.22
Utah	71.63	77.83	77.83	79.98	79.98	80.78	80.78	80.78	80.78	80.78	77.95	76.07	71.13	70.99
Vermont	59.03	67.71	67.71	69.96	69.96	69.96	69.96	69.96	69.96	69.96	65.96	64.05	58.71	57.58
Virginia	50.00	58.78	58.78	61.59	61.59	61.59	61.59	61.59	61.59	61.59	58.77	56.88	50.00	50.00
Washington	51.52	60.22	60.22	62.94	62.94	62.94	62.94	62.94	62.94	62.94	60.11	58.23	50.00	50.00
West Virginia	74.25	80.45	80.45	81.7	83.05	83.05	83.05	83.05	83.05	83.05	80.23	78.34	73.24	72.62
Wisconsin	57.62	65.58	65.58	68.77	69.89	70.63	70.63	70.63	70.63	70.63	67.8	65.92	60.16	60.53
Wyoming	50.00	56.2	56.2	56.2	58.78	61.59	61.59	61.59	61.59	61.59	58.77	56.88	50.00	50.00
Dist. of Columbia	70.00	77.68	77.68	79.29	79.29	79.29	79.29	79.29	79.29	79.29	76.47	74.58	70.00	70.00

Sources:
FY 2008 FMAP rates, Nov. 30, 2006, http://aspe.hhs.gov/health/fmap08.pdf.
FY 2011 FMAP rates, Nov. 27, 2009, http://aspe.hhs.gov/health/fmap11.pdf.
FY 2012 FMAP rates, Nov. 10, 2010 Federal Register, http://www.federalregister.gov/articles/2010/11/10/2010-28319/federal-financial-participation-in-state-assistance-expenditures-federal-matching-shares-for.
FY 2012, Disaster Recovery State Adjustment for Louisiana, December 22, 2010 http://www.federalregister.gov/articles/2010/12/22/2010-32054/adjustments-for-disaster-recovery-states-to-the-fourth-quarter-of-fiscal-year-2011-and-fiscal-year.
FY 2009–2011 FMAP rates, FFIS Issue Brief 10-44, October 25, 2010, Preliminary FY 2011 First Quarter ARRA FMAPs.

in Michigan one state dollar will be matched with $1.95 in federal funds in the 2012 fiscal year, compared to $1.39 in the 2008 fiscal year, an increase of 57 cents, without rounding, each significantly below the highest Recovery Act match of $3.09. These states' recovery from the recession—relative to the nation—is slower, as the FMAP calculation is based on state per capita income relative to national per capita income. These states likely are experiencing higher unemployment and increased Medicaid enrollment.

The remaining 13 states and the District of Columbia have the same match rates in 2012 as they did in 2008. Except for the District of Columbia and Maine, the remaining states are those that receive one federal dollar for each state dollar spent, doubling their state investment. Even these states, whose per capita income is relatively better than other states, benefited from the Recovery Act match bump. Rather than matching a state dollar with one additional federal dollar, these states received anywhere from $1.60 to $1.81 under the Recovery Act.

Regional Analysis

All states received significantly more FMAP funding under the Recovery Act. However, the value of the increased match does differ by region. When the prerecession 2008 match is compared to the highest Recovery Act match, the Southern states saw their state dollar yield a larger amount of federal funding. On average, at the height of the Recovery Act funding, the average state in the South collected an additional $1.42 for each state dollar spent on Medicaid. Western states collected $1 more, Midwestern states 99 cents more, and Eastern states 73 cents more.

The differences in the overall economic conditions of the four regions are reflected in the matching amounts in the regions. In the South, even before the enhanced match of the Recovery Act, states' dollar-for-dollar investment in Medicaid yields ranged from $1 to almost $3 in federal funding. During the Recovery Act, the poorest states in the South had federal returns of $4 to $5 for each dollar invested by the state. By contrast, in the East and Midwest where states are relatively better off, the enhanced match did not return as much per state dollar. Even under the Recovery Act, only Indiana and Michigan dollar investments yielded more than $3 in federal return. In the West, several states' investment yielded $3, but only two states (Utah and New Mexico) exceeded $4.

Conclusion

All states' return on Medicaid funding dropped severely beginning July 1, 2011, even while the effects of the Great Recession continue for states. The dramatic enrollment increases that occurred in 2009 may have moderated for many states, but very few, if any, are experiencing declines in Medicaid enrollment. While state revenues are beginning to grow again year-over-year, many states' revenues are not back to their prerecession levels

About the Author

Debra Miller is the director of health policy at The Council of State Governments' headquarters office in Lexington, KY. Before coming to CSG in 2007, Ms. Miller was a state-level lobbyist and policy analyst on issues relating to children and families, especially those of low and moderate incomes. She holds a master's degree in social work from the University of Kentucky and a bachelor's degree from Duke University.

The Resurgence of Crystal Meth:
Trends and State Responses

By Jeremy L. Williams

Crystal methamphetamine, perhaps one of the most addictive and dangerous drugs in existence, has continuously plagued rural and urban regions of the country for the last three decades. States have attempted to address the growing production and distribution of the drug, along with the destructive repercussions it has wrought in the lives of those who have become addicted to it, largely through tougher laws that restrict the sale of precursor drugs used in meth production. While these measures have been as a whole effective in temporarily reducing the production of crystal meth, producers have found new ways of circumventing existing laws. For this reason, states are examining new and innovative ways to combat this terrible drug.

Introduction

Methamphetamine is a highly addictive, synthetically produced, central nervous system stimulant. According to the U.S. Drug Enforcement Administration (DEA), it is the most common synthetic drug manufactured in the United States and is second only to marijuana in overall production and use.[1] According to the National Survey on Drug Use and Health, the percentage of primary substance abuse treatment admissions for methamphetamine abuse in the United States more than doubled from 1995 (4 percent) to 2005 (9 percent).[2] In addition, while only two states—Hawaii and California—reported more than 5 percent in meth-related treatment admissions in 1992, by 2003 that number had risen to 26. Eight states reported more than 20 percent and two states—Hawaii and Idaho—reported more than 40 percent of all drug treatment admissions related to methamphetamine use.[3] According to the National Institute on Drug Abuse, approximately 10 million people in the United States ages 12 and older have abused methamphetamine and in 2005 about 500,000 people were current users.[4]

Methamphetamine has dozens of common nicknames, usually derived from the form the drug is in when it is consumed. These include "speed," "crank," "ice," "crystal," "glass," "chalk" and "meth."[5] It can be snorted, injected, smoked or swallowed. The term "crystal meth" refers to the most common form methamphetamine takes—a crystallized formation. When consumed, methamphetamine creates a sense of euphoria by increasing the release of dopamine in the brain. The drug has profound effects on the user's mood, metabolism, ability to concentrate and sex drive. The euphoric high is followed by a crash, which often leads to increased use of the drug. Eventually, meth abuse may lead to difficulty feeling any pleasure at all, except that which can be derived from the drug itself, which enhances the potential for addiction and continued abuse.[6]

History of Methamphetamine Use in the United States

Amphetamine was first synthesized in the late 1800s, and methamphetamine[7] was first synthesized in Japan in 1919. Both drugs have been used throughout the last century to treat a variety of ailments, from narcolepsy to depression to obesity. Both were widely used as a stimulant during World War II. Following the war, the United States saw a slight rise in legal, prescribed use of amphetamine and methamphetamine, the dangerous effects of which were not fully known. It was not until the 1960s that the clandestine manufacturing of methamphetamine for recreational use was first discovered.[8]

The steady growth of methamphetamine use in the United States during the past 50 years largely is due to the ability to produce it using conventional, easily accessible chemicals and supplies. While other major illegal drugs—such as cocaine or heroin—are imported from South American or Asian countries, most methamphetamine consumed in the United States is produced locally with recipes that can be accessed through the Internet and readily available products like pseudoephedrine and ephedrine,[9] iodine, rock salt, battery acid, anhydrous ammonia and many basic kitchen items like plastic bags, glass cookware, funnels and soda bottles. Other than marijuana, methamphetamine is the first major drug to have vast quantities produced in rural regions of the country. This is attributable to the fact that meth production requires discreet locations, such as abandoned farms, fields, vehicles, barns or old hotel rooms. According to the DEA, meth labs are, by far, the most common clandestine laboratories in the United States.[10]

The United States also has large amounts of methamphetamine, as well as precursor drugs, trafficked into the country from or through Mexico. In 2005, the Mexican federal government began implementing restrictions on imports of pseudoephedrine, ephedrine and other chemicals used in methamphetamine production. In 2007, Mexico prohibited ephedrine imports into the country and banned the use of the chemical by 2009. These restrictions have contributed to a significant decrease in methamphetamine production in Mexico and a corresponding decrease in the amount of meth trafficked into the United States. For instance, the amount of methamphetamine seized along the U.S.-Mexico border fell 38 percent between 2006 and 2007. According to the DEA, 80 percent of the methamphetamine produced in the United States is made in large production operations, or "super labs," in Mexico or California. In most cases, these labs are operated or owned by organized crime syndicates.[11] Estimates of the amount of methamphetamine smuggled from Canada into the United States are limited. The available data do not indicate increases in seizures along the border or increases in the amount of methamphetamine entering the United States from Canada.

Effects of Methamphetamine Use

Methamphetamine has serious physical and psychological implications for users, such as tooth decay, also referred to as "meth mouth." Contrary to the popular belief that this condition is a result of the harsh chemicals contained in the drug, meth mouth is the result of the drying of saliva glands and grinding of teeth that occur during methamphetamine use, as well as lapses in personal hygiene and the consumption of sugary foods, which methamphetamine users typically desire. Methamphetamine also causes structural damage to regions of the brain that control motor skills and memory. Methamphetamine can produce euphoric effects from eight to 24 hours, depending on the amount consumed. In comparison to cocaine, which only produces a 20- to 30-minute "high" and after only

one hour 50 percent has left the body, methamphetamine remains in the brain for long periods of time and can cause much more serious damage to blood vessels and dopamine transporters than other major drugs. Correspondingly, methamphetamine can cause significant visual hallucinations, violent behavior, paranoia and confusion that far exceed the degrees of negative side effects from other common illegal drugs. The long-term effects of methamphetamine, even after use has ceased, also are more severe, leading to profound anxiety, confusion, insomnia, cardiovascular problems and psychotic episodes, such as delusions.[12]

Although the euphoric effects of the drug are similar to those produced by cocaine and heroin, the rate of recovery from methamphetamine use is much lower than any other drug. According to the National Center on Substance Abuse and Child Welfare, approximately 50 percent of methamphetamine users relapse, 36 percent of those within the first six months of treatment. The center also indicates that the rates of treatment completion for methamphetamine users in the country are similar, if not lower, to treatment completion rates for drugs like heroin and cocaine.[13] This is due, in part, to the fact that treatment options for methamphetamine, unlike those for heroin and cocaine, are largely behavioral therapies. Medical treatments similar to a methadone regimen to treat heroin addiction essentially are nonexistent for methamphetamine users.[14] Also, unlike other drugs where greater tolerance comes with more frequent use, the addictive properties of methamphetamine mean the more individuals consume, the more they crave it. In addition, many rural areas where methamphetamine use is more prevalent do not have the health facilities necessary for treating addicts, leaving numerous users with no treatment options.[15]

Extended methamphetamine use also can lead to brain damage, with symptoms similar to those of Parkinson's disease or Alzheimer's disease. Methamphetamine damages nerve terminals in the brain that contain dopamine and serotonin, two chemicals essential for the central nervous system to function properly. Methamphetamine alters essential brain functions by impairing decision-making, memory and motor skills. It also can cause structural and functional deficits in brain areas associated with depression and anxiety. Studies have indicated that, in some tests, extended abstinence from the drug may allow some recovery from deficits in dopamine function in various regions of the brain. Other tests, however, have shown little or no recovery in brain function even in cases involving up to two years of abstinence, suggesting that long-term and even permanent brain damage may result from methamphetamine abuse.[16] In addition, methamphetamine use can cause death through the collapse of the cardiovascular system or hemorrhaging in the brain.[17]

In addition to the immediate physical toll the drug can have on the body, methamphetamine is associated with higher rates of riskier sexual behavior and violence than other drugs. Methamphetamine simultaneously heightens the libido and lowers inhibition, therefore linking it to higher rates of domestic violence, including sexual abuse. For this reason as well, methamphetamine is inextricably linked to the spread of hepatitis C, HIV and other sexually transmitted diseases. Along with riskier sexual behavior, the use of contaminated injection equipment plays a role in the spread of these diseases among intravenous methamphetamine users. Some studies indicate that physiological changes in meth users, such as compromised immune systems, may make them more vulnerable to developing HIV if exposed. HIV-positive meth users also may develop AIDS sooner than other patients due to poor medication adherence or interactions between methamphetamine and HIV medications.[18]

Moreover, the production of methamphetamine results in a host of environmental and health hazards, including airborne and persistent toxins and frequent explosions. The regular presence of children near meth labs compounds the risks of production by placing more vulnerable populations in danger.

The economic impact of crystal meth can be significant. A 2005 study issued by the Sam Walton College of Business at the University of Arkansas indicates that in Benton County alone, the home of Wal-Mart Stores Inc., absenteeism and loss in productivity related to methamphetamine addiction costs employers more than $21 million annually. The Centers for Disease Control and Prevention reports that the average age for first use is 22.1 years old and the highest rate of methamphetamine use is found in young adults, ages 18–25, followed by youth, ages 12–17. This shows the high potential for lifelong addiction and a large loss of productivity for communities.[19] Overall, according to a study by the RAND Corporation, methamphetamine addiction costs reached $23.4 billion in 2005, including law enforcement, environmental cleanup and drug treatment expenditures.[20]

Federal Legislation

The first federal law targeting the use of methamphetamine in the United States—passed in 1983—addressed the possession of cooking equipment and precursor drugs. Canada passed similar legislation the same year. In 1986, the U.S. Congress passed the Federal Controlled Substance Analogue Enforcement Act with the goal of curbing the rapidly growing designer drug market. The Anti-Drug Abuse Act of 1988 was the first piece of legislation to attempt to control the sale of precursor drugs used in methamphetamine production, but it did not regulate the over-the-counter sale of ephedrine and pseudoephedrine products.[21]

The Crime Control Act of 1990, the Domestic Chemical Diversion and Control Act of 1993 and the Comprehensive Methamphetamine Control Act of 1996 all increased penalties for production and use of methamphetamine and established various provisions for tracking and prosecuting the buying or selling of large amounts of precursor products. However, these laws did not address exemptions in regulations pertaining to the retail sale of precursor drugs. These exemptions collectively became known as the "blister pack exemption," referring to the unregulated sale of small amounts of ephedrine and pseudoephedrine products ostensibly for individual consumption.[22] Despite these federal efforts, methamphetamine production, distribution and use continued to increase in various parts of the American West and Midwest, eventually spreading east and taking root in the South.[23] Until recently, products containing precursor drugs, such as Sudafed and Claritin-D, continued to be sold as over-the-counter drugs.

In 2005, the U.S. Congress passed the Combat Methamphetamine Epidemic Act, which mandates all products containing precursor compounds be kept behind the counter or locked in a cabinet. President George W. Bush signed the act into law in March 2006. The act restricts individuals from purchasing more than 3.6 grams of precursor products in a single day, more than nine grams in any 30-day period, or more than 7.5 grams in a 30-day period from a mail-order pharmacy or "mobile vendor." In addition, the Combat Methamphetamine Epidemic Act requires individuals to present a state or federal government issued photo identification card at the time of each purchase. Also, beginning in September 2006, pharmacies were required to keep written or electronic logbooks of all ephedrine and pseudoephedrine transactions, including the customer's name and address; date of purchase; product name; and the quantity purchased, for at least two years from the date of purchase.[24] According to the Act, the customer must provide a signature and confirm that the information provided is true and accurate.[25]

The Resurgence of Methamphetamine Use

Methamphetamine laboratory seizures steadily decreased both nationally and in individual states from 2004 to 2007, due largely to restrictions on ephedrine and pseudoephedrine sales. However, according to the U.S. Department of Justice's National Drug Intelligence Center, the United States saw an increase in lab seizures from 2007 to 2008. By midyear 2008, in many states, methamphetamine laboratory seizures significantly outpaced or exceeded seizures reported for all of 2007. For example, Alabama saw more laboratories seized from January through July 2008 (125 labs) than in all of 2007 (81 labs).[26]

In addition to the increase of ephedrine and pseudoephedrine products being trafficked between states, increases in meth production most likely are attributable to several factors. First, the ability of customers to circumnavigate existing ephedrine and pseudoephedrine purchasing restrictions has continued to increase. Individuals and criminal groups have learned to get around these restrictions by making numerous, small quantity purchases of products containing precursor drugs, a strategy often referred to as "smurfing." Often, smurfing operations are organized to sell the precursor chemical to methamphetamine producers or trade it for the drug.[27]

The second major reason for the abrupt increase in methamphetamine use is the development of new ways to produce meth, namely the "shake-and-bake" method. Methamphetamine laboratories increasingly are shifting away from large production facilities to more portable ones. Shake-and-bake is a new method of production that replaces cooking the substances required to make methamphetamine by simply shaking the chemicals in a bottle to initiate the necessary chemical reaction. The method produces smaller amounts of meth, usually around 8 grams, but is easier to carry out and less likely to be detected by law enforcement personnel. Since this new process requires neither a large space nor as many materials as traditional cooking methods—producing meth with the shake-and-bake method only requires a few pills, a 2-liter bottle and some common household chemicals—this new method is quick, cheap and mobile, reducing the likelihood that producers will be apprehended.

This method of production requires far less ephedrine or pseudoephedrine than traditional cooking methods, making laws that restrict purchasing large amounts of precursor drugs obsolete. Smaller, low-capacity labs have been growing in popularity since the advent of illegal methamphetamine production, accounting for approximately 20 percent of all meth consumed in the U.S., according to the DEA.[28] Correspondingly, the shake-and-bake method appeals to addicts, since their interest predominantly is producing small amounts for personal use, while minimizing risk, as opposed to producing large amounts required by dealers or distributors.[29]

The shake-and-bake method allows producers to easily dispose of leftover materials once the substance is produced, often involving throwing the residue out of a vehicle in a plastic bag, which has given rise to the term "trash labs." Trash labs come with serious environmental consequences since they contain noxious chemicals. Animals as large as deer have been found dead near disposal sites. They also can cause complications for law enforcement, since each trash lab becomes a crime scene. Evidence must be collected and the area must be cleared as quickly as possible to avoid explosions and other environmental damage that could further harm humans or wildlife. Cleanup of labs can cost thousands of dollars and can put personnel in danger. Also, when law enforcement personnel find remnants of a trash lab, the illegal product confiscated often is too small for state or federal prosecutors to initiate legal action.[30]

Beyond the environmental complications produced by trash labs, their sheer prevalence indicates an alarming trend: Methamphetamine is becoming easier to make and existing meth laws are becoming easier to circumvent. Officials in many states have indicated the majority of meth lab seizures are now shake-and-bake operations. For instance, approximately 65 percent of all meth laboratory seizures in Tennessee are of the shake-and-bake variety. The state is among those that saw a decrease in lab seizures from 2005 to 2007, but are now seeing an increase. Similarly, the number of lab seizures in Oklahoma—which dropped from 1,200 in 2003 to 148 in 2006—rose to 743 in 2009 due in part to the pervasiveness of shake-and-bake labs.[31] The DEA has stated the number of meth labs, which includes trash labs and remnants of production operations, rose nationally from

5,910 in 2007 to 6,783 in 2008, nearly a 15 percent increase. This followed nearly a 58 percent drop from 2003 to 2006, from 17,356 to 7,347 labs.[32]

State Laws

In addition to federal laws, at least 40 states have passed methamphetamine laws in recent years, such as restrictions on the sale of ephedrine or pseudoephedrine. Two states—Oregon and Mississippi—require a prescription for their purchases. Electronic monitoring of precursor drug purchases is growing in popularity, as it is an extremely useful surveillance device for both pharmacies and law enforcement personnel. States that have instituted electronic reporting systems have seen dramatic reductions in the rate of illicit manufacturing of methamphetamine. Most systems simply require pharmacists or police personnel to have Internet access, along with a username and password, to log onto secure Web portals that house the information. At least 10 states use databases to track ephedrine and pseudoephedrine sales.

States are experimenting with other avenues to combat this epidemic. Although some states restrict the number of packages of precursor drugs that may be purchased, others limit only the quantity based on weight. Some states are examining not only the sale of methamphetamine precursors but also the possession of precursor drugs. Some states have explored creating methamphetamine conviction registries, similar to those used to track sex offenders, and logs for tracking real estate that has been damaged by methamphetamine production.

While ephedrine and pseudoephedrine are the primary precursor drugs used in the production of methamphetamine, other harsh chemicals—such as hydrogen peroxide, iodine crystals and red phosphorous—are required as well. Many states have begun examining the benefits of restricting the sale of these compounds. For instance, Iowa has attempted to limit access to anhydrous ammonia, a primary ingredient in methamphetamine production in agricultural states where the chemical is routinely used as a fertilizer. In Iowa, more than 90 percent of all meth laboratories use the chemical in the production process. A $1.2 million national research project at Iowa State University, and confirmed by the DEA's forensics lab, found that meth operations attempting to use anhydrous ammonia that has a calcium nitrate inhibitor added to it generally extract only 2 percent of ephedrine for conversion to methamphetamine,

as opposed to an approximate 42 percent yield for production methods without the inhibitor. The inhibitor also reduces the purity of any amount of the drug produced from the ephedrine extraction. The chemical reaction between calcium nitrate and anhydrous ammonia that causes the decrease in ephedrine production actually continues even if more ammonia is added. In other words, if producers add more treated ammonia to the recipe to defeat the inhibitor, even less meth will be produced. The inhibitor is used on a voluntary basis in Iowa, but agriculture retailers who participate in the program receive the formula, along with signage for placement on their tanks, which could help dissuade potential users. Additionally, calcium nitrate is a common fertilizer compound used primarily for horticulture. It is nontoxic, safe for food supplies and has no adverse impact on the environment or farm equipment.[33]

Oregon and Mississippi

In 2006, Oregon became the first state to require a doctor's prescription to purchase an ephedrine or pseudoephedrine product, essentially eliminating a once thriving meth industry in the state. In 2004, police seized 472 meth labs; by 2007, that number had decreased to 20. According to the Oregon Narcotics Enforcement Association, by 2010 the number of meth lab seizures in the state had dropped to 13, a 97 percent decrease from 2004.[34] In addition, the state's property crime rate, which has a direct correlation to methamphetamine use, declined by approximately 17 percent in 2006, the largest decrease in the country.[35]

In 2009, Mississippi became the second state to pass a law restricting access to ephedrine and pseudoephedrine products to patients possessing a prescription from a physician. The legislation states that medicine containing precursor drugs only can be dispensed after the buyer produces a doctor's prescription to the pharmacy. According to the DEA, methamphetamine is the fastest-growing drug threat in the state. Although Mississippi experienced an 89 percent increase in lab seizures from 2007 to 2009, in six months following the implementation of this new law, many counties have reported 70 to 80 percent decreases in methamphetamine-related crimes.[36]

Like Oregon, the passage of Mississippi's prescription bill was fairly contentious. Opponents argued the law would create undue additional costs for individuals paying for doctor's visits and co-pays at the pharmacy in order to obtain these medications. Opponents also argue it would simply drive methamphetamine producers and users, as well as innocent individuals who are ill, across state lines to purchase the medication. Proponents of the measure argued alternatives to decongestants and cold medications that contain ephedrine and pseudoephedrine are available for minor illnesses.[37]

Conclusion

Overall, the United States experienced a significant decrease in methamphetamine lab seizures from 2004 (17,170) to 2007 (5,910), a drop of 66 percent, but has seen a steady resurgence since then. The same is true for many states that have continuously fought this epidemic. The dynamic is likely due to the ability of methamphetamine producers to circumvent existing federal and state precursor laws. An independent study in 2003 concluded that while federal laws aimed at the sale or possession of large amounts of ephedrine and pseudoephedrine products used in the production of methamphetamine in "super labs" dramatically affected rates of meth-related hospital and treatment admissions, similar federal regulations aimed at the sale of individual purchases of these products had little or no impact on such admissions.[38]

For this reason, states are taking action to address this trend and have a variety of options to consider. The promising results seen in both Oregon and Mississippi are incentive for states to consider requiring a doctor's prescription to purchase drugs containing ephedrine and pseudoephedrine. However, this drastic step comes with certain consequences, including increased medical costs associated with doctor visits and the general inconvenience to common cold sufferers.

States can further explore the benefits of implementing stricter ephedrine and pseudoephedrine purchasing laws, the use of electronic monitoring systems, as well as databases that provide information about offenders and other dangers associated with meth production and use. In addition, state governments can assess the impact of passing laws that restrict access to other precursor chemicals and materials, such as those implemented in Iowa.

Perhaps most importantly, states can work together to reduce the ability of traffickers to capitalize on looser methamphetamine laws in one state, thereby negating the efforts of surrounding states. A regional approach for coordinating information pertaining to ephedrine and pseudoephedrine sales is an effective technique for combating the rise of meth production and distribution. For instance, although Tennessee maintains a statewide monitoring computer database, no such system exists in Georgia. While ephedrine and pseudoephedrine products can be sold only as behind-the-counter products in pharmacies in Tennessee, gas stations and other stores in Georgia can sell these restricted products. Like Tennessee, Georgia collects buyer information, but the customer provides it and there is no guarantee the information is accurate. In Tennessee, a photo identification card is required. The restrictions on the allowable amount of ephedrine or pseudoephedrine purchased in Georgia easily can be circumvented, which means Georgia counties that border Tennessee are ideal hubs for smurfers to gather precursor drugs, returning to Tennessee to produce and/or distribute the product. Tennessee's Methamphetamine Task Force is working with Georgia officials to produce a system to link the two states' computer databases.

The methamphetamine epidemic does not appear to be slowing, and states must be poised to make critical decisions regarding prevention, education, enforcement, treatment and rehabilitation. A "one-size-fits-all" approach is not necessarily prudent, but states can learn from one another and work across jurisdictional lines in new ways, so together they might begin to address this disturbing trend.

States and local entities are in a unique position to play a pivotal role in addressing the myriad public safety and health needs associated with methamphetamine production and use, since states and local regulations, especially those aimed at practices that historically have circumvented existing federal laws, can be tailored to address the specific meth problems facing their pharmacies, doctors, law enforcement personnel and addicted population.

Notes

[1] Dana Hunt, Sarah Kuck and Linda Truitt, *Methamphetamine Use: Lessons Learned* (Washington: U.S. Department of Justice, 2006), iii–iv.

[2] Substance Abuse and Mental Health Services Administration, Office of Applied Studies, *The DASIS Report: Primary Methamphetamine/Amphetamine Admissions to Substance Abuse Treatment*, (Rockville, MD: U.S. Department of Health and Human Services, 2005), 1.

[3] Hunt, iv.

[4] National Institute on Drug Abuse, *Methamphetamine Addiction: Cause for Concern* (Washington: National Institutes of Health, 2007), 1.

[5] For the purposes of this article, all the names for methamphetamine will be considered interchangeable under the umbrella terms "methamphetamine" or "meth."

[6] National Institute on Drug Abuse, *NIDA InfoFacts: Methamphetamine* (Washington: National Institutes of Health, 2007).

[7] Methamphetamine, dextroamphetamine and amphetamine, as well as their various salts, are collectively referred to as "amphetamines." Their chemical properties and effects are very similar. Methamphetamine is the most commonly abused of these substances.

[8] Methamphetamine Addiction.com, *History of Methamphetamine*, available at:

http://www.methamphetamineaddiction.com/metham phetamine_hist.html

[9] Pseudoephedrine and ephedrine both have the same molecular formula and the same sequence of molecular bonds, but different three-dimensional spatial arrangements. They both, along with related compounds like phenylpropanolamine, or other salts, optical isomers, or salts of optical isomers, serve the same function in the production of methamphetamine. Pseudoephedrine is more widely used in sinus and allergy medications and ephedrine typically is used in asthma medications.

[10] Hunt, 12.

[11] National Drug Intelligence Center, *2009 National Drug Threat Assessment* (Washington: U.S. Department of Justice), 9.

[12] National Institute on Drug Abuse, *NIDA InfoFacts: Methamphetamine*.

[13] Cathleen Otero, et al., *Methamphetamine Addiction, Treatment and Outcomes: Implications for Child Welfare Workers* (Irvine, California: National Center on Substance Abuse and Child Welfare, 2006), 7.

[14] National Institute on Drug Abuse, *Methamphetamine Addiction: Cause for Concern*, 2.

[15] Otero, 7.

[15] National Institute on Drug Abuse, *Methamphetamine Addiction: Cause for Concern*, 2.

[16] Ibid.

[17] National Institute on Drug Abuse, *NIDA InfoFacts: Methamphetamine*.

[18] Ibid.

[19] The Centers for Disease Control and Prevention, *Methamphetamine Use and Risk for HIV/AIDS* (Atlanta: January 2007), 3.

[20] Nancy Nicosia, et al., *The Economic Cost of Methamphetamine Use in the United States*, (Santa Monica, CA: RAND Corporation, 2009), iii.

[21] Jean C. O'Connor, Jamie F. Chriqui and Duane C. McBride, *Developing Lasting Legal Solutions to the Dual Epidemics of Methamphetamine Production and Use*, (82 North Dakota Law Review, 2006), 1176.

[22] Ibid, 1178.

[23] Hunt, 12.

[24] Products packaged for individual sale that contain less than 60 milligrams of ephedrine or pseudoephedrine are exempt from the logbook requirements, but must be kept behind the counter or in a locked cabinet.

[25] Combat Methamphetamine Epidemic Act, H.R. 3199, (109th Congress § 711, 2006).

[26] Hunt, 12.

[27] Ibid.

[28] *International Meth Trafficking: Hearing Before the Subcommittee on International Economic Policy, Export and Trade Promotion and the Subcommittee on Western Hemisphere, Peace Corps and Narcotics Affairs, S. Foreign Relations Committee*, 109th Congress (statement of Karen P. Tandy, Administrator, Drug Enforcement Administration).

[29] Susan Saulny, "With Cars as Meth Labs, Evidence Litters Roads," *The New York Times*, April 14, 2010.

[30] Ibid.

[31] Ibid.

[32] *International Meth Trafficking*.

[33] Office of Drug Control Policy, "Iowa Unveils 'Chemical Lock' to Clamp Down on U.S. Meth Labs" (State of Iowa, October 2006), 1–2.

[34] Oregon Narcotics Enforcement Association, *Oregon Meth Lab Incident Statistics*, available at: *http://www.oregon dec.or/OregonMethLabStats.pdf*.

[35] "Follow Oregon's Meth Lead: Bill Would Require Prescriptions for Pseudoephedrines," *The Register-Guard*, April 2010.

[36] Steve Rogers, "Meth Law Called a Success," *WCBI News*, January 2011.

[37] Phil West, "Mississippi House Complicates Meth Recipe," *Commercial Appeal*, January 2010.

[38] James K. Cunningham, Lon-Mu Liu, "Impacts of Federal Ephedrine and Pseudoephedrine Regulations on Methamphetamine-related Hospital Admissions," in *Addiction* (Irvine, CA: Public Statistics Institute and The University of Illinois at Chicago, 2003), 1231–5.

About the Author

Jeremy L. Williams is a policy analyst at The Council of State Governments' Southern office in Atlanta, Georgia, where he researches, analyzes and writes on issues related to health, human services, public safety, energy and environment, as they apply to Southern states. In addition, he tracks legislative issues and policy developments in Georgia, Louisiana, Texas and West Virginia. Williams has focused a great deal of attention on emerging issues, such as the resurgence of HIV/AIDS in Southern states and the continued fight against human trafficking.

Table 9.11
HEALTH INSURANCE COVERAGE STATUS BY STATE FOR ALL PEOPLE, BY REGION: 2009
(In thousands)

State or other jurisdiction	Total	Covered and not covered by health insurance during the year			
		Covered	Percent	Not covered	Percent
United States	304,280	253,606	83.3	50,674	16.7
Eastern Region					
Connecticut.................................	3,480	3,062	88	418	12
Delaware.....................................	884	766	86.6	118	13.4
Maine..	1,300	1,167	89.8	133	10.2
Maryland.....................................	5,667	4,874	86	793	14
Massachusetts.............................	6,631	6,337	95.6	295	4.4
New Hampshire	1,314	1,176	89.5	138	10.5
New Jersey	8,680	7,309	84.2	1,371	15.8
New York.....................................	19,184	16,347	85.2	2,837	14.8
Pennsylvania	12,414	11,004	88.6	1,409	11.4
Rhode Island................................	1,033	906	87.7	127	12.3
Vermont.......................................	618	557	90.1	61	9.9
Regional total	61,205	53,505	87.4	7,700	12.6
Midwestern Region					
Illinois...	12,767	10,875	85.2	1,891	14.8
Indiana..	6,364	5,462	85.8	902	14.2
Iowa	2,995	2,654	88.6	342	11.4
Kansas	2,745	2,380	86.7	365	13.3
Michigan......................................	9,815	8,465	86.2	1,350	13.8
Minnesota....................................	5,203	4,747	91.2	456	8.8
Nebraska.....................................	1,780	1,574	88.5	205	11.5
North Dakota...............................	632	565	89.3	67	10.7
Ohio..	11,462	9,819	85.7	1,643	14.3
South Dakota...............................	800	693	86.5	108	13.5
Wisconsin....................................	5,565	5,037	90.5	527	9.5
Regional total	60,128	52,271	86.9	7,856	13.1
Southern Region					
Alabama	4,669	3,880	83.1	789	16.9
Arkansas......................................	2,852	2,304	80.8	548	19.2
Florida...	18,405	14,287	77.6	4,118	22.4
Georgia..	9,671	7,687	79.5	1,985	20.5
Kentucky......................................	4,282	3,588	83.8	694	16.2
Louisiana.....................................	4,453	3,741	84	711	16
Mississippi	2,850	2,349	82.4	502	17.6
Missouri.......................................	5,969	5,055	84.7	914	15.3
North Carolina.............................	9,348	7,663	82	1,685	18
Oklahoma....................................	3,636	2,977	81.9	659	18.1
South Carolina.............................	4,507	3,740	83	766	17
Tennessee	6,253	5,290	84.6	963	15.4
Texas	24,657	18,224	73.9	6,433	26.1
Virginia	7,778	6,764	87	1,014	13
West Virginia...............................	1,805	1,552	86	253	14
Regional total	111,135	89,101	80.2	22,034	19.8
Western Region					
Alaska..	691	568	82.3	122	17.7
Arizona..	6,513	5,239	80.4	1,273	19.6
California	36,794	29,449	80	7,345	20
Colorado......................................	4,971	4,209	84.7	762	15.3
Hawaii	1,251	1,149	91.8	102	8.2
Idaho...	1,526	1,294	84.8	232	15.2
Montana.......................................	972	823	84.6	149	15.4
Nevada...	2,632	2,086	79.2	546	20.8
New Mexico	1,978	1,548	78.3	430	21.7
Oregon...	3,835	3,156	82.3	678	17.7
Utah	2,800	2,385	85.2	415	14.8
Washington..................................	6,714	5,845	87.1	869	12.9
Wyoming	541	455	84.2	86	15.8
Regional total	71,218	58,206	81.7	13,009	18.3
Regional total without California	34,424	28,757	83.5	5,664	16.5
Dist. of Columbia.........................	596	522	87.6	74	12.4

Source: U.S. Census Bureau, Current Population Survey, 2010 Annual Social and Economic Supplement. URL: *http://www.census.gov/hhes/ www/cpstables/032010/health/h06_000.htm.* A joint effort between the Bureau of Labor Statistics and the Census Bureau.

Note: Unrelated individuals under 15 are included.

Table 9.12
NUMBER AND PERCENT OF CHILDREN UNDER 19 YEARS OF AGE, AT OR BELOW 200 PERCENT OF POVERTY, BY HEALTH INSURANCE COVERAGE, STATE AND REGION: 2009
(In thousands)

State or other jurisdiction	Total children under 19 years, all income levels	At or below 200 percent of poverty					
		Number	Percent	Health insurance coverage			
				With		Without	
				Number	Percent	Number	Percent
United States	78,857	33,150	42	27,942	35.4	5,207	6.6
Eastern Region							
Connecticut........................	852	196	23	164	19.2	33	3.8
Delaware	223	79	35.7	67	29.9	13	5.7
Maine..................................	287	107	37.1	101	35.2	5	1.8
Maryland	1,409	416	29.5	353	25	63	4.5
Massachusetts	1,545	514	33.3	484	31.3	30	1.9
New Hampshire	303	69	22.9	66	21.7	4	1.2
New Jersey	2,191	637	29.1	529	24.1	109	5
New York............................	4,700	2,086	44.4	1,854	39.4	233	4.9
Pennsylvania	2,990	1,077	36	958	32	119	4
Rhode Island......................	240	100	41.5	89	37	11	4.5
Vermont..............................	130	46	35.6	41	31.7	5	3.9
Regional total	14,870	5,327	35.8	4,706	31.6	625	4.2
Midwestern Region							
Illinois................................	3,384	1,423	42	1,206	35.6	217	6.4
Indiana...............................	1,723	760	44.1	665	38.6	95	5.5
Iowa	754	282	37.4	251	33.2	31	4.1
Kansas	743	302	40.6	260	35	41	5.5
Michigan............................	2,503	976	39	893	35.7	83	3.3
Minnesota..........................	1,306	447	34.3	402	30.8	45	3.5
Nebraska	477	168	35.2	147	30.7	21	4.4
North Dakota	153	51	33.1	46	30.4	4	2.7
Ohio....................................	2,843	1,164	41	987	34.7	177	6.2
South Dakota.....................	209	90	43.1	77	36.9	13	6.2
Wisconsin	1,369	447	32.7	412	30.1	35	2.6
Regional total	15,464	6,110	39.5	5,346	34.6	762	4.9
Southern Region							
Alabama	1,165	649	55.7	576	49.5	73	6.2
Arkansas............................	742	373	50.2	319	43	53	7.2
Florida...............................	4,197	1,891	45.1	1,369	32.6	522	12.4
Georgia..............................	2,717	1,217	44.8	1,000	36.8	217	8
Kentucky............................	1,066	464	43.5	411	38.5	53	5
Louisiana...........................	1,225	538	43.9	466	38.1	72	5.8
Mississippi.........................	825	477	57.8	423	51.3	54	6.5
Missouri.............................	1,517	647	42.7	544	35.9	103	6.8
North Carolina...................	2,425	1,064	43.9	837	34.5	226	9.3
Oklahoma...........................	976	431	44.2	369	37.9	62	6.4
South Carolina...................	1,154	464	40.2	384	33.3	80	6.9
Tennessee..........................	1,565	709	45.3	623	39.8	86	5.5
Texas..................................	7,293	3,676	50.4	2,875	39.4	801	11
Virginia..............................	2,016	665	33	580	28.8	85	4.2
West Virginia......................	410	168	40.9	155	37.7	13	3.2
Regional total	29,293	13,433	45.9	10,931	37.3	2,500	8.5
Western Region							
Alaska................................	194	66	34	56	29	10	5
Arizona..............................	1,811	919	50.7	727	40.1	192	10.6
California	9,964	4,392	44.1	3,728	37.4	664	6.7
Colorado............................	1,312	477	36.4	389	29.6	88	6.7
Hawaii	312	129	41.2	123	39.5	5	1.7
Idaho..................................	441	197	44.7	166	37.6	31	7.1
Montana	229	102	44.4	86	37.5	16	7
Nevada...............................	706	306	43.4	245	34.6	62	8.8
New Mexico	545	289	53.1	229	42.1	60	11
Oregon...............................	906	386	42.6	320	35.3	66	7.3
Utah...................................	921	305	33.1	236	25.7	68	7.4
Washington........................	1,629	599	36.8	555	34.1	44	2.7
Wyoming............................	143	50	34.9	43	30	7	4.9
Regional total	19,113	8,217	43.0	6,903	36.1	1,313	6.9
Regional total without California	9,149	3,825	41.8	3,175	34.7	649	7.1
Dist. of Columbia	119	63	53.3	56	47.2	7	6.1

Source: U.S. Census Bureau, Current Population Survey, 2010 Annual Social and Economic Supplement. URL: *http://www.census.gov/hhes/www/* *cpstables/032010/health/h10_000.htm*. A joint effort between the Bureau of Labor Statistics and the Census Bureau.

A State Wildlife Agency Adapts

By Corky Pugh

State fish and wildlife agencies across the U.S. are faced with an uncertain future. As the economy impacts both revenues and costs of operations, these user-funded agencies must adapt to the new realities. One innovative employee-based initiative is well underway in the state of Alabama. Substantive cost-savings and increased cost-effectiveness are already being realized.

We are truly fortunate in this country that fish and wildlife belong to the public. Because the public owns these natural resources, the government is given the privilege and responsibility for managing fish and wildlife for the benefit of everyone. This public trust doctrine—along with dedicated funding sources established in 1937, 1950 and 1984—is at the core of wildlife and fisheries restoration and management in the United States.

State fish and wildlife agencies across the country are responsible for managing and protecting fish and wildlife resources for the sustainable benefit of the people. Agencies fulfill this public trust responsibility through fisheries biologists, wildlife biologists and conservation enforcement officers.

Management throughout most of the 20th century focused on restoring populations decimated by loss of habitat, environmental contamination and over-harvest due to unregulated year-round hunting. The early 21st century brings new management challenges. Although Americans continue to care deeply about wildlife and our natural resources, many are less connected to the natural world. Urbanization, our time-intense society and competing activities have affected hunting and fishing participation. Changes in technology and the economy have led to altered land use patterns, increased rural development and new agricultural practices. Changes in the distribution and abundance of some species have led to increased conflicts between humans and wildlife. Declines in the number of anglers, hunters and trappers, and increases in the numbers of nonconsumptive users of wildlife, present both challenges and opportunities.

Funding issues provide other challenges. State fish and wildlife agency funding comes primarily from those who participate in fishing, hunting and trapping, yet the public trust mandate covers all wildlife and the demand to broaden emphasis is growing. At the same time, dedicated funding sources for wildlife management have not been growing at the pace of costs and expenditures necessary to maintain traditional programs. Demands from different user groups are increasingly conflicting.

Early in 2009, in response to the shifting economic climate, leadership at the Alabama Wildlife and Freshwater Fisheries Division began aggressively working toward increased cost-effectiveness. Regardless of how the state's general fund issues were to be dealt with, the financial challenges facing the Wildlife and Freshwater Fisheries Division would not be solved, because the division is funded through hunting and fishing license revenue and matching federal aid funds.

Key staff learned the adaptive leadership traits set out in a series of articles published in *The Harvard Business Review* by Ronald Heifitz, et al. as a common set of change principles. Work sessions resulted in a heightened awareness of the need to adapt division programs to the new realities.

Giving Employees Ownership of the Problems and Solutions

When revenue/expenditure estimates were clearer, leadership conducted extensive briefings for all 325 division employees. These briefings were held to transparently communicate with employees about the financial situation and to solicit employee input. Utilizing the Wildlife and Freshwater Fisheries Division's mission, vision and values, as well as guiding principles, staff were asked to answer the following question: "What are the things we can do to operate more effectively in order to meet public demands for service within available funding?" In the ensuing weeks, employees offered more than 500 items of input, which were assimilated along with recommendations from specially commissioned work groups.

As the leadership team began assimilating the input from employees and the work groups, meaningful themes emerged as promising avenues to pursue for increased cost-effectiveness.

A readily apparent theme concerned lack of effective lateral communication and coordination at the district level. While this problem varied from district to district, improvement was needed throughout the state. This area was addressed early in the process because the capability to implement other improvements hinged largely on effective communication and coordination to achieve synergistic solutions to cost-effectiveness problems.

Acting on the Input

Several items of employee input dealt with restructuring. Some suggested reducing from six districts to three. While this was seriously considered by leadership, it was deemed unworkable due to the resulting excessively large districts and extreme span of control. Also, without attrition of higher-paid supervisory personnel, little cost savings would be realized. Some suggested closure of all "store-front" offices. Simply closing district offices, most of which the division owns, would not be cost-effective, nor would it maintain an acceptable level of service to the public insofar as local points of contact.

Division leadership decided, however, to reduce the number of districts from six to five. Anticipated retirements of supervisory level personnel and the terms of the lease on a district office presented a unique opportunity. Ultimately, this action will save more than $650,000 annually.

The Hunter Education Program is a major responsibility of the division, with a seasonal high-demand period that coincides with the onset of hunting season. Use of volunteers to achieve program purposes has historically been a tremendous asset. With the need to become more cost-effective, volunteerism is of even greater benefit. Several modifications have been made to better utilize volunteers and Hunter Education coordinators.

Many other improvements have been implemented or begun.

Guiding Principles and Strategies

The *Guiding Principles and Strategies* document is a result of this comprehensive review. Involvement from staff was crucial for its development. Naming the document *Guiding Principles and Strategies* is intentional, as it points toward Wildlife and Freshwater Fisheries Division's destination. It establishes waypoints and provides our itinerary; it guides how the division will allocate limited time and resources to priority issues and management needs. The document details the process, estab-

lishes priority recommendations (several already implemented), and sets forth goals and objectives. The Wildlife and Freshwater Fisheries Division commits to an ongoing process of continual improvement in order to remain responsive and relevant as manager and protector of Alabama's natural resources.

The Division may encounter unforeseen detours and roadblocks, so the *Guiding Principles and Strategies* document is designed to be flexible and to account for change along the way. Because this journey has no real end, it also is adaptable and revisions are expected as we confront future challenges.

Alabama's fish and wildlife is a resource that belongs to all the people and provides recreation, enjoyment and reflection. It shaped how our state was settled; it impacts our state's economy, attracts tourists and is critical to our future. The Wildlife and Freshwater Fisheries Division of the Alabama Department of Conservation and Natural Resources is responsible for this public resource to be enjoyed today and managed for tomorrow. We are on a journey to ensure that wildlife and aquatic resources continue to play a defining role in Alabama. This document, *Guiding Principles and Strategies*, sets strategic direction for the next leg of this journey.

The Wildlife and Freshwater Fisheries Division staff rises to the challenge to ensure the plan is implemented and the responsibility of managing and protecting Alabama's wildlife and aquatic resources is fulfilled. This same level of involvement will be critical as the *Guiding Principles and Strategies* document is used to navigate into an uncertain future. Alabama residents, stakeholders and our partners will be important in moving toward our destinations by ground-truthing, providing input, assisting with projects and holding the division accountable to the direction set by *Guiding Principles and Strategies*. We will need to work together to fulfill this vision.

As this plan is implemented by managing adaptively, the Wildlife and Freshwater Fisheries Division will strive to become a learning organization with improved performance and accountability. Adaptive management requires that management activities are designed as experiments with expectations described in advance. We will monitor and evaluate progress to understand how planned actions met expectations. We also will compare expected and actual outcomes and adjust activities as needed to improve our work.

The *Guiding Principles and Strategies* document contains the routes and destinations of our trip, and we will detail the itinerary of each annual leg through annual work plans and budgets to properly allocate our staff and resources. We will develop an annual report to allow the public, stakeholders and our partners to monitor our progress.

The Wildlife and Freshwater Fisheries Division commits to planning, monitoring and evaluating annual progress of the *Guiding Principles and Strategies*. Changes will occur based on new information or circumstances and we will take the necessary detours to continue to follow our routes and reach our destinations. These reviews and evaluations, along with continued engagement with our partners, will ensure the document remains active and relevant in a changing environment as it directs us toward our common vision for wildlife conservation.

Editor's Note

For additional information on the Alabama Wildlife and Freshwater Fisheries' *Guiding Principles and Strategies*, see: *http://www.outdooralabama.com/hunting/WFFGPS.pdf.*

About the Author

Corky Pugh is Director of the Alabama Wildlife and Freshwater Fisheries Division. He has served in a wide range of leadership roles in Alabama state government since the mid-1970's. Pugh has a Master's Degree in Public Administration from Auburn University in Montgomery.

Recovery Act Transportation Spending: 'Summer of Recovery' Becomes Fall of Discontent

By Sean Slone

The American Recovery and Reinvestment Act of 2009 provided $48 billion to states for transportation infrastructure projects. States achieved significant successes in 2010 in meeting deadlines associated with the legislation, starting and completing projects on time and under budget, creating jobs and doing it all with little fraud or waste. Still, some questions have been raised about whether the stimulus could have had a greater impact, which types of projects were funded and which states received the most funding. Despite its political unpopularity in 2010, the Recovery Act proved its worth to state transportation officials around the country.

2010's 'Summer of Recovery'

The Obama administration dubbed the summer of 2010 the "Summer of Recovery" because it expected to see many of the infrastructure projects funded by 2009's American Recovery and Reinvestment Act finally come to fruition. As the summer got under way, President Obama and U.S. Secretary of Transportation Ray LaHood traveled to Columbus, Ohio, to celebrate the groundbreaking of the 10,000th Recovery Act road project[1] and work was completed on the nation's first Recovery Act-funded project, a bridge near Tuscumbia, Mo.[2] A Jacksonville, Fla., road project stalled for 30 years was among the projects finally able to move forward with Recovery Act funding as well.[3]

But despite all the orange barrels and Recovery Act project signs visible on the nation's roads in 2010 and despite the many administrative successes achieved by state government officials and others around the country in getting those projects up and running, the Recovery Act did not prove to be a politically popular program in midterm elections and in the post-election environment of Washington, D.C., and state capitals. That lack of popularity can be traced to the depth of the nation's economic funk as well as to how the legislation was structured and the choices states made along the way.

The Successes of Recovery Act Transportation Spending

By many measures and according to many different Recovery Act watchdogs, the implementation of transportation spending has been a success.

- **Deadlines Met**—In March, Vice President Joe Biden and LaHood announced that every state and the District of Columbia had met the deadline to obligate 100 percent of their Recovery highway funds.[4] The Federal Highway Administration met a Sept. 30 deadline for awarding $27.5 billion for highway and bridge projects and the Federal Transit Administration met the deadline for awarding $8.8 billion for transit projects.[5] The U.S. House Transportation and Infrastructure Committee reported in December that 44 states had begun work on at least 90 percent of their Recovery Act highway projects. Of the $38 billion available for highway, transit and wastewater infrastructure formula program projects, $35.6 billion—or 94 percent—had been put out to bid on 20,132 projects as of the end of October. Within that total, 92 percent were under contract.[6]

- **Savings**—The U.S. Department of Transportation was able to fund an additional 2,500 projects because contract bids on funded projects came in $7.5 billion less than expected.[7]

- **Speed of Completion**—In addition to coming in under budget, a slight majority of projects were completed earlier than estimated, producing additional savings. The investigative website ProPublica reported in November that of the 12,932 projects listed in a Federal Highway Administration database, 5,752—or 45 percent—were marked as completed. Of those, 51 percent were completed earlier than the estimated date.[8]

- **Management**—Despite the speed with which the money has been allocated and spent, government watchdogs reported that stimulus contracts and grants have been relatively free of fraud and waste compared to many government programs.[9]

- **Job Creation**—The President's Council of Economic Advisers estimated that construction of transportation infrastructure helped save or create 321,900 jobs during the first three quarters of 2010.[10]

Obstacles to Success

But some believe there were a number of factors that may have limited the impact of Recovery Act transportation spending in 2010. Among them:

- The Government Accountability Office reported in September that state departments of transportation were slower in obligating regular federal-aid highway funds during the last fiscal year because they've been so busy trying to spend Recovery Act dollars. That raises questions about whether the Recovery Act money is having the full economic stimulative effect intended because it was supposed to be in addition to and on top of the highway money states already had available to spend. GAO said staffing shortages in states dealing with budget challenges may have been partially to blame for some of the slowness in obligating regular funding. But uncertainty about future program funding levels and federal inaction on the next long-term authorization of federal programs clearly prompted many states to spend more cautiously as well. At the end of June, states had $19.7 billion in regular funds remaining to be obligated, 63 percent more funds than they did at the same time for the three previous years.[11]

- An analysis of federal data by McClatchy Newspapers showed that a number of states suffering from some of the nation's highest unemployment rates were among those slowest to spend stimulus money intended for highway projects. California, with the nation's third worst unemployment rate, had yet to start on 41 percent of its highway projects in September. The state had spent just 26 percent of its highway money, one of the lowest rates of those states monitored by the GAO. The delay in spending there was blamed on the involvement of more levels of government in planning processes. Virginia had an even higher percentage of projects it hadn't started—52 percent. Transportation officials in Virginia blamed an emphasis on more projects expected to have a long-term impact and the collaborative process of choosing projects for causing the delay.[12]

- The Recovery Act's focus on funding "shovel-ready projects" also came in for a fair amount

of criticism. That focus meant many of the projects were short-term fixes, like repaving roads and painting bridges, rather than major transformative projects that might have produced a greater impact both economically and in terms of investing in a transportation system for the 21st century. Some shovel-ready projects took longer than anticipated to get going, providing more evidence to Recovery Act detractors.[13] In October, as President Obama prepared for what turned out to be a bruising election for his party, even he sounded disappointed when he told *The New York Times Magazine*, despite significant evidence to the contrary, "there's no such thing as shovel-ready projects."[14]

- But Recovery Act funding for more transformational transportation projects was heavily scrutinized as well. Fifty-one projects around the country were awarded Recovery Act funding as part of the TIGER (Transportation Investment Generating Economic Recovery) discretionary grants program. The program was intended to provide funding for innovative freight rail, highway, transit and port projects expected to produce significant economic and environmental benefits. Many of them were multimodal, regional projects that have proved difficult to fund and build under other programs.[15] At a hearing in February marking the one year anniversary of the Recovery Act, U.S. Rep. John Mica, then the ranking member on the House Transportation and Infrastructure Committee, questioned why more of the TIGER funds did not go to states with higher unemployment. About 60 percent of the funding went to economically distressed areas.[16] Mica also complained that his own state of Florida received no TIGER funds. He said the project selection process lacked transparency and the program represented, in effect, an executive earmarks program.[17] By year's end, Mica was the incoming chairman of the committee and the TIGER program, which was once seen as a potential model for future federal transportation funding, appeared likely to fall out of favor as earmarks of any kind were scorned by the new Republican Congress.

- Year's end also brought a power struggle over Recovery Act funds intended for the intercity passenger rail program. Ohio and Wisconsin, two states hit hard by the economic downturn, were among states that were awarded a portion of $8 billion in Recovery Act funding to build new high-speed rail lines. But both states elected

Table A: Recovery Act Funds for Highway Infrastructure Investment (Data Reported as of October 31, 2010)

State	Funds allocated	Funds obligated	Funds outlayed	Projects put out to bid	Projects under contract	Completed projects	Direct jobs created or sustained during July 2010	Direct jobs created or sustained during October 2010
Alabama	$511,924,313	$513,692,083	$339,136,034	251	250	125	727	1,680
Alaska	175,461,487	178,520,994	147,479,134	28	28	8	571	265
Arizona	520,884,655	521,394,538	275,179,127	184	184	95	1,503	1,305
Arkansas	351,544,468	351,894,468	174,533,417	123	123	55	715	916
California	2,537,626,450	2,540,826,450	940,700,736	912	825	619	8,023	3,319
Colorado	385,324,130	385,324,130	275,222,170	109	108	51	1,029	782
Connecticut	298,903,956	302,053,956	114,243,851	151	136	63	469	505
Delaware	121,828,650	121,828,650	60,122,259	40	38	3	514	192
Florida	1,344,471,413	1,349,735,003	551,621,045	641	615	268	3,073	3,017
Georgia	901,585,680	903,008,364	369,421,375	390	376	193	1,398	unavailable
Hawaii	125,746,380	125,746,380	29,500,647	22	20	3	85	84
Idaho	178,878,631	178,878,631	131,157,795	83	80	23	705	372
Illinois	935,592,704	935,590,765	713,760,878	972	946	453	1,288	1,315
Indiana	657,967,707	672,625,386	538,521,683	1,105	1,105	906	0	990
Iowa	357,623,007	357,623,007	323,123,401	244	242	130	780	507
Kansas	347,817,167	347,817,167	180,455,012	150	145	82	1,338	967
Kentucky	419,899,347	420,139,347	283,325,473	106	106	17	1,548	873
Louisiana	429,859,427	429,859,427	148,830,992	117	116	19	708	1,010
Maine	130,752,032	130,752,032	120,274,022	72	72	59	319	172
Maryland	413,934,777	413,934,777	230,100,987	170	170	36	842	511
Massachusetts	378,205,755	378,205,755	179,227,960	94	90	21	596	432
Michigan	846,598,715	855,873,754	669,422,076	744	735	634	3,037	1,858
Minnesota	502,284,177	506,463,421	423,113,315	223	220	155	1,364	996
Mississippi	354,564,343	354,564,343	288,702,292	173	172	98	1,050	14
Missouri	637,121,984	637,121,984	420,275,806	329	327	246	999	1,310
Montana	211,793,391	212,835,558	174,917,017	86	85	43	639	593
Nebraska	231,926,771	231,016,489	176,256,448	129	124	46	676	624
Nevada	201,352,460	201,352,460	108,386,168	71	69	35	470	403
New Hampshire	129,440,556	129,440,556	97,693,283	34	34	27	365	171
New Jersey	651,774,480	651,774,480	320,150,776	173	163	22	950	975
New Mexico	252,644,377	252,644,377	167,788,812	96	92	1	826	1,110
New York	945,218,723	943,468,723	518,732,379	426	413	180	1,928	1,610
North Carolina	730,409,684	730,409,684	461,235,450	461	459	66	2,021	2,410
North Dakota	170,126,497	170,126,497	149,641,232	164	164	93	617	81
Ohio	935,677,030	919,945,446	427,190,394	426	400	208	5,022	2,062
Oklahoma	464,655,225	464,655,225	422,889,280	274	274	176	195	734
Oregon	280,088,100	275,293,522	212,280,209	319	318	177	797	395
Pennsylvania	1,026,429,012	1,026,429,012	718,602,931	354	354	179	2,714	2,077
Rhode Island	137,095,725	137,095,725	93,547,883	62	62	37	310	295
South Carolina	463,081,483	463,519,259	275,749,159	187	185	107	774	23
South Dakota	186,689,867	186,689,867	168,421,517	52	52	17	605	450
Tennessee	569,511,063	569,511,063	375,494,523	421	404	214	1,262	1,372
Texas	2,233,015,146	2,240,957,908	1,036,709,084	848	847	317	3,225	204
Utah	213,545,653	213,545,653	180,120,389	127	122	103	0	106
Vermont	125,791,291	125,791,291	112,638,788	73	73	61	257	77
Virginia	678,670,823	632,910,364	131,205,755	123	124	39	551	735
Washington	490,542,853	490,542,853	367,350,916	218	214	169	3,214	1,016
West Virginia	210,852,204	211,342,557	170,465,509	154	147	104	88	178
Wisconsin	529,111,915	529,111,422	439,003,147	418	416	341	1,498	845
Wyoming	157,616,058	157,616,058	147,228,506	69	69	56	590	60
Dist. of Columbia	123,507,842	123,507,842	50,603,407	18	18	1	319	460
American Samoa	4,500,000	4,500,000	0	1	1	0	0	6
Guam	18,000,000	19,560,000	0	7	6	0	0	101
No. Mariana Islands	4,500,000	4,500,000	115,413	1	1	0	1	20
Puerto Rico	105,000,000	105,000,000	30,110,787	23	23	5	218	559
U.S. Virgin Islands	18,000,000	10,729,584	450,561	3	3	0	0	0

Source: U.S. House Transportation and Infrastructure Committee. "State by State Formula Program Table." Accessed from: *http://trans portation.house.gov/Media/file/ARRA/20101202/Recovery%20Act%20* *Funds%20by%20State%20and%20Program%20as%20of%20October %2031%202010.pdf.*

new Republican governors who campaigned on pledges to kill rail projects, arguing they would become a financial burden their states could not afford.[18] Both governors-elect sought to hold onto the money and divert it to road projects. But in December, LaHood announced that the $1.2 billion of rail funds originally designated for those states would be redirected to 13 other states for their high-speed rail projects.[19]

In the fall Congressional campaigns, many challengers were able to tar incumbents with having voted for "the failed stimulus" in campaign ads. After all, when President Obama signed the Recovery Act into law in February 2009, the unemployment rate was 8.1 percent and 12.5 million people were unemployed. In November 2010, the rate was 9.8 percent and more than 14 million were unemployed.[20]

But many state officials said the impact of the infrastructure projects funded with Recovery Act dollars shouldn't be dismissed or taken lightly. Things could have been much worse without them.

"I've heard naysayers talk about how the federal stimulus program didn't do what it was supposed to do here and there," said Kentucky Transportation Secretary Mike Hancock. "We would have had an incredibly weak year in terms of our ability to put projects on the street without that stimulus program. ... I feel very good about the projects that we were able to do. The only regret that I have is that we couldn't do more."

Notes

[1] U.S. Department of Transportation. "President Obama breaks ground on 10,000th Recovery Act road project; let the Summer of Recovery begin!" Fast Lane: The Official Blog of the U.S. Secretary of Transportation. June 18, 2010. Accessed from: *http://fastlane.dot.gov/2010/06/welcome-every one-to-the-summer-of-recovery-and-what-better-way-to-kick-off-a-season-of-renewed-american-infrastructure-and.html #more.*

[2] Kathie Sutin. "Nation's First ARRA Funded Projects Nears Completion." Construction Equipment Guide.com May 1, 2010. Accessed from: *http://www.constructionequip mentguide.com/Nations-First-ARRA-Funded-Project-Nears-Completion/14343/.*

[3] American Association of State Highway and Transportation Officials (AASHTO). "Florida 9B Construction Underway in Jacksonville." *AASHTO Journal.* July 9, 2010. Accessed from: *http://www.aashtojournal.org/Pages/070910 florida.aspx.*

[4] AASHTO. "All States Meet Deadline for 100% Obligation of Recovery Funds." *AASHTO Journal.* March 5, 2010. Accessed from: *http://www.aashtojournal.org/Pages/ 030510deadline.aspx.*

[5] U.S. Department of Transportation. "DOT meets Recovery Act deadlines; more good jobs, more good projects." Fast Lane: The Official Blog of the U.S. Secretary of Transportation. September 30, 2010. Accessed from: *http://fastlane. dot.gov/2010/09/dot-meets-recovery-act-deadlines-more-good-jobs-more-good-projects-.html#more.*

[6] U.S. House Committee on Transportation and Infrastructure. "The American Recovery and Reinvestment Act of 2009 Transportation and Infrastructure Provisions Implementation Status as of November 12, 2010." Accessed from: *http://transportation.house.gov/Media/file/ARRA/2010 1202/Recovery%20Act%2012-2-10%20Report.pdf.*

[7] Recovery.gov. "2010 Fiscal Year End Report to the President on Progress Implementing the American Recovery and Reinvestment Act of 2009." September 2010. Accessed from: *http://www.whitehouse.gov/sites/default/files/ recovery_act_report_9-30-2010.PDF.*

[8] Rob Farley and Michael Grabell. "ProPublica and PolitiFact Test Obama Claims on Stimulus." ProPublica/ PolitiFact November 10, 2010. Accessed from: *http://www. propublica.org/article/propublica-and-politifact-test-obama-claims-on-stimulus.*

[9] Recovery.gov.

[10] Executive Office of the President. Council of Economic Advisers. "The Economic Impact of the American Recovery and Reinvestment Act of 2009: Fifth Quarterly Report." November 18, 2010. Accessed from: *http://www. whitehouse.gov/sites/default/files/cea_5th_arra_report.pdf.*

[11] Government Accountability Office. "Recovery Act: Opportunities to Improve Management and Strengthen Accountability over States' and Localities' Uses of Funds." September 2010. Accessed from: *http://www.gao. gov/new.items/d10999.pdf.*

[12] Chris Adams. "Stimulus spending on highways isn't delivering on job promises." McClatchy. September 26, 2010. Accessed from: *http://www.mcclatchydc.com/2010/ 09/26/101055/stimulus-spending-on-highways.html.*

[13] Blair Kamin. "Obama's stimulus package, one year later: Too much quick fix; too little long-term infrastructure." *Chicago Tribune.* February 18, 2010. Accessed from: *http://featuresblogs.chicagotribune.com/theskyline/2010/ 02/heres-something-you-probably-havent-heard-lately-a-stimulus-story-where-democrats-and-republicans-arent-hurling-ac.html.*

[14] Peter Baker. "Education of a President." *The New York Times Magazine.* October 12, 2010. Accessed from: *http:// www.nytimes.com/2010/10/17/magazine/17obama-t.html? _r=4&ref=magazine&pagewanted=all%22.*

[15] Kent Hoover. "Washington Recovery Report: Stimulus to fund 23,500 projects this year." *Phoenix Business Journal.* February 26, 2010. Accessed from: *http://www.bizjour nals.com/phoenix/stories/2010/02/22/daily45.html?t= printable.*

[16] AASHTO. "House T&I Committee Reviews One Year of Recovery Act Spending." *AASHTO Journal.* February 26, 2010. Accessed from: *http://www.aashtojournal.org/Pages /022610oneyear.aspx.*

[17] Josh Voorhees. "TRANSPORTATION: Boxer wants TIGER to roar in next highway bill." *Environment & Energy Daily.* March 25, 2010.

[18] Michael Cooper. "More U.S. Rail Funds for 13 States as 2 Reject Aid." *The New York Times*. December 9, 2010. Accessed from: *http://www.nytimes.com/2010/12/10/us/10 rail.html?_r=2*.

[19] AASHTO. "USDOT Redirects $1.2 Billion from Ohio and Wisconsin to 13 Other States." December 10, 2010. Accessed from: *http://www.aashtojournal.org/Pages/121010re directed.aspx*.

[20] Bureau of Labor Statistics. "Labor Force Statistics from the Current Population." Accessed from: *http://www. bls.gov/cps/*.

About the Author

Sean Slone is a transportation policy analyst at the Council of State Governments. He staffs CSG's Transportation Policy Task Force and writes about transportation policy for CSG publications, such as *Capitol Ideas* magazine, the Capitol Comments blog and Capitol Research policy materials. He is the author of two CSG national reports: *Transportation and Infrastructure Finance* (2009) and *Shovel-Ready or Not? State Stimulus Successes on the Road to Recovery* (2010).

Table 9.13
REVENUES USED BY STATES FOR HIGHWAYS, BY REGION: 2009

State or other jurisdiction	Beginning balance total (a)	Highway-user revenues (b)				Appropriations from general funds (c)	Other state imposts	Miscellaneous	Bond proceeds (d)	Payments from other governments			Total receipts
		Motor-fuel taxes	Motor-vehicle and motor-carrier taxes	Road and crossing tolls	Total					Federal funds		From local government	
										Federal Hwy. Administration	Other agencies		
United States	64,609,388	30,696,156	22,146,885	7,704,701	60,547,742	7,308,616	5,113,180	8,393,216	21,119,139	34,553,020	1,869,305	3,658,387	142,562,602
Eastern Region													
Connecticut...........	330,928	253,744	128,590	161	382,495	0	57,134	76,421	855,838	481,421	11,498	24,376	1,889,183
Delaware...............	450,402	65,927	67,674	254,158	387,759	57,427	0	24,861	237,261	174,991	7,347	0	889,646
Maine....................	58,374	231,369	54,849	132,842	419,060	0	0	32,961	88,695	149,719	5,774	0	696,209
Maryland................	1,243,969	564,787	577,737	275,715	1,418,239	78,578	0	72,097	847,599	480,481	8,594	0	2,905,587
Massachusetts........	1,356,303	588,395	317,559	380,423	1,286,377	115,401	0	232,764	440,199	670,745	6,312	0	2,751,798
New Hampshire......	1,457,529	131,461	121,482	104,788	357,731	0	0	137,108	30,000	158,874	15,981	5,889	705,583
New Jersey.............	1,913,221	281,555	462,054	1,152,093	1,895,702	0	0	329,361	2,741,519	595,762	19,208	0	5,581,552
New York...............	226,694	1,204,390	896,954	1,187,354	3,288,698	588,465	0	680,519	1,856,058	1,614,690	26,247	38,051	8,072,728
Pennsylvania..........	3,634,656	1,256,277	446,579	793,886	2,496,742	844,963	0	650,843	1,203,050	1,467,701	30,564	30,364	6,724,227
Rhode Island..........	92,471	47,993	21,974	10,630	80,597	0	0	56,011	52,985	183,538	6,062	0	379,193
Vermont................	9,455	53,004	100,560	0	153,564	13,439	0	17,765	15,200	145,265	20,594	1,104	366,391
Regional total.........	10,774,002	4,678,902	3,196,012	4,292,050	12,166,964	1,698,273	57,134	2,310,711	8,368,404	6,123,187	158,181	99,784	30,962,097
Midwestern Region													
Illinois..................	2,002,261	844,383	857,823	665,687	2,367,893	540,802	280	39,799	780,000	1,232,205	27,020	829	4,988,828
Indiana (e).............	394,256	793,884	214,744	149,246	1,157,874	496	82,900	285,138	415,850	1,084,642	8,813	32,503	3,068,214
Iowa.....................	253,268	411,494	443,471	0	854,965	51,074	219,101	25,743	0	429,706	93,095	0	1,673,684
Kansas..................	727,574	331,620	92,967	79,589	504,176	29,032	276,305	38,251	77,425	425,981	8,610	48,780	1,408,560
Michigan...............	896,710	803,857	732,352	33,660	1,569,869	91,718	71,767	115,145	326,513	1,037,570	23,476	17,096	3,253,154
Minnesota..............	948,757	533,873	392,029	0	925,902	0	205,425	102,022	174,500	614,941	42,337	204,630	2,269,757
Nebraska...............	135,931	305,979	61,157	0	367,136	49,439	151,801	37,018	0	261,746	9,935	474,428	1,351,503
North Dakota..........	93,732	130,590	75,306	0	205,896	6,064	0	674	0	238,923	8,148	28,678	488,383
Ohio.....................	1,500,300	1,600,371	713,338	186,824	2,500,533	21,433	0	427,729	528,450	1,138,720	36,122	99,985	4,752,972
South Dakota..........	110,826	106,644	2,974	0	109,618	0	53,153	39,293	0	221,603	10,978	11,414	446,059
Wisconsin..............	471,646	771,167	479,059	0	1,250,226	58,507	0	81,401	281,118	792,103	88,355	96,881	2,648,591
Regional total.........	7,535,261	6,633,862	4,065,220	1,115,006	11,814,088	848,565	1,060,732	1,192,213	2,583,856	7,478,140	356,889	1,015,224	26,349,705
Southern Region													
Alabama................	363,835	697,010	167,725	0	864,735	98,825	47,670	8,930	0	735,944	39,704	3,460	1,799,268
Arkansas...............	273,216	392,517	148,689	0	541,206	54,662	5,198	21,628	0	390,773	46,256	14,074	1,073,797
Florida..................	2,762,547	1,535,672	783,253	1,001,075	3,320,000	251,573	111,955	257,381	12,570	1,802,075	185,733	257,663	6,198,950
Georgia.................	1,368,660	836,561	184,748	19,491	1,040,800	232,193	0	100,201	988,863	1,166,196	51,778	35,043	3,615,074
Kentucky...............	411,644	534,759	493,689	0	1,028,448	4,875	0	306,884	361,152	533,913	12,131	0	2,247,403
Louisiana...............	2,664,683	596,301	181,504	38,730	816,535	306,341	53,131	39,590	435,928	893,001	93,041	0	2,637,567
Mississippi............	260,905	368,623	144,108	0	512,731	0	41,755	6,341	0	528,559	22,084	104,405	1,215,875
Missouri................	1,052,560	677,287	287,087	0	964,374	6,875	266,774	181,437	145,570	844,571	33,184	53,965	2,496,750
North Carolina........	1,059,348	1,384,845	599,849	2,106	1,986,800	0	454,122	51,469	0	1,031,606	16,197	33,611	3,573,805
Oklahoma..............	516,115	68,218	90,710	206,431	365,359	223,333	294,181	135,670	35,000	752,190	13,851	29,343	1,848,927
South Carolina........	426,229	501,363	172,839	12,374	686,576	141	2,726	29,958	0	412,014	12,689	34,720	1,178,824
Tennessee..............	1,580,878	703,203	316,467	36	1,019,706	25,737	57,667	47,480	0	690,779	44,525	0	1,860,157
Texas....................	6,622,599	1,113,441	1,824,260	413,599	3,351,300	25,737	39,631	1,498,760	2,046,412	2,511,426	43,641	154,993	9,671,400
Virginia.................	2,104,707	630,807	574,348	20,545	1,225,700	235,119	689,244	178,454	0	660,702	29,452	80,772	3,099,443
West Virginia..........	293,543	381,091	242,378	53,673	677,142	17,889	3,494	42,283	134,108	475,433	20,356	439	1,371,144
Regional total.........	21,761,469	10,421,698	6,211,654	1,768,060	18,401,412	1,457,563	2,067,548	2,906,466	4,159,603	13,429,182	664,622	802,488	43,888,384

See footnotes at end of table.

REVENUES USED BY STATES FOR HIGHWAYS, BY REGION: 2009 — Continued

State or other jurisdiction	Beginning balance total (a)	Highway-user revenues (b)				Appropriations from general funds (c)	Other state imposts	Miscellaneous	Bond proceeds (d)	Payments from other governments			Total receipts
										Federal funds			
		Motor-fuel taxes	Motor-vehicle and motor-carrier taxes	Road and crossing tolls	Total					Federal Hwy. Administration	Other agencies	From local government	
Western Region													
Alaska	0	7,331	36,190	21,409	64,930	337,300	0	26,205	162,160	335,810	9,070	0	935,475
Arizona	1,618,788	459,283	236,636	0	695,919	0	692,836	136,338	734,593	569,708	39,436	10,587	2,879,417
California	15,294,246	5,239,858	5,937,943	344,450	11,522,251	2,328,686	786,048	940,005	3,547,924	2,604,757	106,112	1,545,518	23,381,301
Colorado	2,981,290	460,840	808,979	0	1,269,819	0	0	34,028	0	800,380	23,452	34,668	2,162,347
Hawaii	313,164	78,223	87,917	0	166,140	0	0	20,110	126,033	217,025	3,107	0	532,415
Idaho	133,042	196,529	142,531	0	339,060	0	0	16,131	179,086	289,894	38,751	6,248	869,170
Montana	54,652	92,861	105,845	0	198,706	3,468	6,488	58,037	0	359,321	34,951	2,559	663,530
Nevada	471,261	436,131	205,863	649	642,643	46	0	114,097	0	323,713	11,347	0	1,091,846
New Mexico	658,553	175,942	215,268	0	391,210	53,781	11,619	80,082	0	303,617	63,532	0	903,841
Oregon	1,625,367	266,419	262,278	0	528,697	53,364	13,718	96,800	352,204	392,394	129,758	5,015	1,571,950
Utah	719,820	329,243	111,175	1,221	441,639	178,367	276,001	24,635	398,000	313,124	86,338	96,701	1,814,805
Washington	1,038,818	1,163,235	411,664	161,856	1,736,755	0	49,002	311,443	507,276	741,909	100,807	39,595	3,486,787
Wyoming	58,840	32,415	37,221	0	69,636	112,759	73,705	45,613	0	270,189	39,567	0	611,469
Regional total	24,967,841	8,938,310	8,599,510	529,585	18,067,405	3,067,771	1,909,417	1,903,524	6,007,276	7,521,841	686,228	1,740,891	40,904,353
Regional total without California	9,673,595	3,698,452	2,661,567	185,135	6,545,154	739,085	1,123,369	963,519	2,459,352	4,917,084	580,116	195,373	17,523,052
Dist. of Columbia	24,203	23,384	74,489	0	97,873	236,944	18,349	100,302	0	670	3,385	0	457,523

Source: U.S. Department of Transportation, Federal Highway Administration, *Highway Statistics,* 2009,(March 2011).

Note: Detail may not add to totals due to rounding. This table was compiled from reports of state authorities.

Key:

(a) Any differences between beginning balances and the closing balances on last year's table are the result of accounting adjustments, inclusion of funds not previously reported, etc.

(b) Amounts shown represent only those highway user revenues that were expended on state or local roads.

(c) Amounts shown represent gross general fund appropriations for highways reduced by the amount of highway-user revenues placed in the State General Fund.

(d) Amount shown represents original and refunding issues.

Table 9.14
STATE DISBURSEMENTS FOR HIGHWAYS, BY REGION: 2009

State or other jurisdiction	Capital outlay total (a)	Maintenance and services total (a)	Administration research and planning	Highway law enforcement and safety	Interest	Bond retirement		Grants in-aid to local governments	Total disbursements	Total end-of-year balances (b)
						Current revenues or sinking funds	Refunding bonds			
United States	$71,158,739	$21,722,397	$9,487,572	$8,272,690	$6,304,759	$5,979,441	$2,129,304	$18,711,683	$143,766,587	$63,405,403
Eastern Region										
Connecticut............	659,277	112,391	330,181	14,724	240,989	279,493	506,285	32,117	2,175,457	44,654
Delaware................	334,746	108,347	93,621	78,641	13,884	81,887	-	-	711,126	628,922
Maine....................	299,913	220,807	24,331	34,678	24,388	23,310	-	24,807	652,234	102,349
Maryland................	1,474,659	386,165	94,376	120,696	127,452	131,493	-	465,079	2,799,920	1,349,636
Massachusetts.........	1,046,031	397,205	252,735	180,837	463,792	292,395	-	177,297	2,810,292	1,297,809
New Hampshire.......	230,115	208,415	63,564	68,464	18,200	21,210	-	31,137	641,105	1,522,007
New Jersey.............	1,594,245	616,875	166,289	398,271	819,041	475,764	-	151,726	4,222,211	3,272,562
New York...............	3,229,953	1,396,630	325,818	410,993	572,659	642,616	2,430	396,264	6,977,364	868,670
Pennsylvania	3,638,187	1,730,356	455,090	574,136	203,885	110,962	-	266,148	6,978,764	3,380,119
Rhode Island..........	153,323	109,307	31,651	27,347	31,126	23,461	12,485	-	388,700	82,964
Vermont.................	191,853	86,297	33,892	57,939	4,281	1,494	-	24,551	400,307	23,921
Regional total........	12,852,302	5,372,795	1,871,548	1,966,726	2,519,697	2,084,085	521,200	1,569,126	28,757,480	12,573,613
Midwestern Region										
Illinois..................	3,000,966	799,994	250,695	257,528	265,281	237,633	-	572,420	5,384,517	1,606,572
Indiana (e).............	2,266,370	220,604	382,857	9,901	268,440	130,658	-	1,544	3,280,374	182,096
Iowa.....................	680,583	188,138	69,381	122,057	-	-	-	661,339	1,721,498	205,454
Kansas	904,092	166,668	69,844	79,841	87,614	9,950	-	145,866	1,463,875	672,259
Michigan................	2,260,625	295,922	122,088	253,184	110,073	55,900	42,920	37,111	3,177,823	972,041
Minnesota..............	848,952	437,633	134,999	155,139	28,171	45,057	12,849	702,518	2,365,318	853,196
Nebraska................	606,510	347,492	131,332	78,146	-	-	-	234,891	1,398,371	89,063
North Dakota..........	313,349	37,687	21,690	24,002	2,063	3,255	-	74,592	477,638	104,477
Ohio......................	2,068,001	610,980	310,377	280,582	70,859	266,435	147,450	1,097,774	4,852,458	1,400,814
South Dakota..........	349,865	70,820	41,389	35,078	-	-	-	2,697	499,849	57,036
Wisconsin	1,369,599	224,807	183,026	106,177	111,546	136,834	-	417,105	2,549,094	571,143
Regional total........	14,668,912	3,400,745	1,717,678	1,401,635	944,047	885,722	203,219	3,947,857	27,170,815	6,714,151
Southern Region										
Alabama.................	1,182,119	160,406	184,536	147,659	-	12,450	-	281,432	1,968,602	194,501
Arkansas................	561,904	276,746	56,327	98,227	20,803	52,685	-	5,526	1,072,218	274,795
Florida..................	4,589,386	925,110	238,818	420,253	399,962	231,180	-	389,090	7,193,799	1,767,698
Georgia..................	2,198,897	213,370	441,169	196,855	181,076	259,793	12,758	1,669	3,505,587	1,478,147
Kentucky................	1,735,079	427,558	20,568	84,310	118,863	133,390	-	2,439	2,522,207	136,840
Louisiana...............	2,973,935	327,469	52,723	80,226	3,542	34,182	3,799	3,754	3,479,630	1,822,620
Mississippi.............	867,005	127,600	76,143	36,874	27,462	65,044	-	100,906	1,301,034	175,746
Missouri.................	1,595,920	526,300	71,924	204,395	114,698	84,890	-	248,175	2,846,302	703,008
North Carolina........	1,989,813	693,956	324,030	359,568	44,955	99,835	-	147,069	3,659,226	973,927
Oklahoma...............	1,040,529	179,039	130,291	107,307	99,221	66,555	-	141,931	1,764,873	600,169
South Carolina........	645,602	404,342	90,710	94,268	31,862	84,027	-	2,266	1,353,077	251,976
Tennessee..............	1,035,883	321,511	262,296	36,560	-	-	-	280,137	1,936,387	1,504,648
Texas....................	5,364,789	1,285,943	288,814	777,356	713,907	310,555	678,626	463,221	9,883,211	6,410,788
Virginia.................	1,091,029	1,240,877	366,911	191,353	95,775	231,204	-	355,134	3,572,283	1,631,867
West Virginia..........	841,764	289,994	95,672	38,549	31,684	48,661	52,602	10,683	1,409,609	255,078
Regional total........	27,713,654	7,400,221	2,700,932	2,873,760	1,883,810	1,714,451	747,785	2,433,432	47,468,045	18,181,808

See footnotes at end of table.

STATE DISBURSEMENTS FOR HIGHWAYS, BY REGION: 2009—Continued

State or other jurisdiction	Capital outlay total (a)	Maintenance and services total (a)	Administration research and planning	Highway law enforcement and safety	Interest	Bond retirement Current revenues or sinking funds	Bond retirement Refunding bonds	Grants in-aid to local governments	Total disbursements	Total end-of-year balances (b)
Western Region										
Alaska	578,918	240,030	56,202	37,597	6,832	14,123	0	1,774	935,476	1
Arizona	1,273,127	142,088	267,325	196,566	134,422	212,065	0	762,650	2,988,243	1,509,962
California	6,198,986	3,153,472	1,440,968	1,039,052	311,202	400,300	657,100	8,606,525	21,807,605	16,867,942
Colorado	925,307	227,847	220,400	136,748	57,460	108,040	0	230,297	1,906,099	3,237,538
Hawaii	276,618	55,781	80,042	9,390	17,610	27,445	0	37,297	504,183	341,396
Idaho	537,617	104,496	29,477	37,988	-	22,852	0	157,717	890,147	112,065
Montana	435,888	107,326	56,018	49,888	6,910	9,070	0	42,787	707,887	10,295
Nevada	738,746	137,254	134,787	115,459	37,578	51,420	0	5,409	1,220,654	342,453
New Mexico	528,548	152,547	235,146	23,535	96,213	74,500	0	161,948	1,272,437	289,957
Oregon	820,255	222,826	132,380	94,779	60,282	34,365	0	29,634	1,394,521	1,802,796
Utah	911,965	241,536	247,548	55,702	46,058	112,491	0	239,933	1,855,233	679,392
Washington	1,981,924	627,698	215,427	190,781	182,638	128,190	0	480,759	3,807,417	718,188
Wyoming	429,025	83,146	51,443	43,084	0	0	0	4,538	611,236	59,073
Regional total	15,636,924	5,496,047	3,167,163	2,030,569	957,205	1,194,861	657,100	10,761,268	39,901,138	25,971,058
Regional total without California	9,437,938	2,342,575	1,726,195	991,517	646,003	794,561	0	2,154,743	18,093,533	9,103,116
Dist. of Columbia	285,947	52,589	30,251	-	-	100,322	-	-	469,109	12,617

Source: U.S. Department of Transportation, Federal Highway Administration, Highway Statistics, 2009, (March 2011).

Note: Detail may not add to totals due to rounding. This table was compiled from reports of state authorities.

Key:
(a) Includes state administered and local roads and streets.
(b) Amounts shown represent both reserves for current highway work and reserves for debt service.

Table 9.16

APPORTIONMENT OF FEDERAL FUNDS ADMINISTERED BY THE FEDERAL HIGHWAY ADMINISTRATION BY REGION: FISCAL YEAR 2010 (In thousands of dollars)

State or other jurisdiction	Interstate maintenance	National highway system	Surface transportation program	Bridge program	Congestion mitigation & air quality improvement	Highway safety improvement program	Appalachian development highway system
Total............................	$7,040,519	$8,704,980	$9,010,263	$5,726,448	$2,372,787	$1,502,675	$470,000
United States Total...	7,040,519	8,549,974	9,010,263	5,726,448	2,372,787	1,502,675	470,000
Eastern Region							
Connecticut..............	70,173	64,704	82,578	177,451	45,739	12,460	0
Delaware..................	10,589	63,680	43,003	14,340	11,702	7,175	0
Maine.......................	32,511	35,634	38,399	34,056	10,287	6,307	0
Maryland..................	102,006	115,036	125,507	128,095	55,487	19,363	13,696
Massachusetts...........	89,098	90,290	112,758	205,603	65,711	15,268	0
New Hampshire........	23,005	45,784	39,830	26,303	10,797	6,620	0
New Jersey...............	134,269	194,985	196,995	235,880	107,653	27,244	0
New York..................	219,727	249,362	296,405	522,834	189,706	44,987	9,399
Pennsylvania............	228,758	241,422	272,982	532,787	109,255	42,701	111,768
Rhode Island............	12,193	52,765	37,611	83,232	10,245	6,251	0
Vermont...................	21,545	50,744	41,856	37,862	11,349	6,958	0
Regional average......	85,807	109,491	117,084	181,677	57,085	17,758	12,260
Midwestern Region							
Illinois.....................	306,813	261,610	338,729	169,267	111,127	52,727	0
Indiana.....................	211,206	213,613	242,223	91,274	49,685	33,020	0
Iowa........................	87,348	126,963	121,787	71,427	11,171	20,333	0
Kansas	70,530	98,458	110,402	48,416	9,827	21,089	0
Michigan...................	177,500	222,131	282,047	132,034	77,305	45,384	0
Minnesota.................	122,756	151,811	190,205	43,747	32,646	29,990	0
Nebraska	51,198	88,946	76,246	27,902	10,559	13,502	0
North Dakota............	35,954	99,817	48,616	13,236	10,801	9,254	0
Ohio.........................	281,303	246,549	308,456	208,863	99,864	45,563	22,703
South Dakota............	49,852	96,331	62,810	15,143	12,357	12,771	0
Wisconsin	128,223	218,572	209,186	29,129	28,202	35,404	0
Regional average......	138,426	165,891	180,973	77,313	41,231	29,003	2,064
Southern Region							
Alabama...................	131,657	148,409	171,792	86,252	12,023	33,785	117,500
Arkansas...................	97,382	121,568	125,680	79,890	12,518	23,440	0
Florida	352,758	504,803	539,351	149,575	14,344	92,297	0
Georgia	293,814	270,085	345,553	89,386	71,483	59,007	11,849
Kentucky	136,321	155,284	146,401	85,465	14,250	24,444	39,081
Louisiana..................	121,325	113,260	137,216	228,236	11,637	24,458	0
Mississippi................	85,629	125,209	121,839	66,514	11,431	25,535	5,019
Missouri...................	184,968	207,283	223,455	158,699	23,981	39,929	0
North Carolina..........	188,798	221,564	253,020	156,065	53,912	39,868	32,922
Oklahoma.................	115,769	150,073	165,888	94,405	11,860	30,694	4
South Carolina.........	131,951	132,536	173,403	69,171	12,840	35,143	7,174
Tennessee	188,204	191,807	206,055	70,539	38,423	36,967	24,658
Texas	630,130	794,503	843,434	206,626	159,567	132,142	0
Virginia....................	203,571	199,071	243,839	137,829	57,160	38,069	38,091
West Virginia............	74,230	74,821	80,964	83,953	14,806	16,253	36,139
Regional average......	195,767	227,352	251,859	117,507	34,682	43,469	20,829
Western Region							
Alaska......................	90,106	106,251	91,612	37,605	25,448	15,603	0
Arizona.....................	157,595	190,727	181,335	28,676	55,162	35,950	0
California	583,434	738,463	811,930	558,734	475,106	136,379	0
Colorado...................	106,037	142,205	133,659	41,594	43,446	21,581	0
Hawaii	11,204	55,225	38,463	34,184	10,426	6,393	0
Idaho........................	58,499	78,061	61,213	27,654	13,316	11,746	0
Montana	91,664	121,937	68,790	20,721	14,732	13,947	0
Nevada.....................	77,442	86,032	79,756	17,322	31,855	14,327	0
New Mexico	94,711	113,914	81,068	16,839	11,857	15,245	0
Oregon.....................	88,019	111,957	109,996	100,737	19,218	18,995	0
Utah.........................	101,882	70,192	75,708	14,901	12,159	11,028	0
Washington...............	111,642	127,683	143,203	172,532	37,385	22,168	0
Wyoming	62,398	106,337	39,763	13,325	10,873	6,724	0
Regional average......	125,741	157,614	147,423	83,448	58,537	25,391	0
Regional average without California .	87,600	109,210	92,047	43,841	23,823	16,142	0
Dist. of Columbia......	2,823	61,505	37,247	30,141	10,097	6,190	0
American Samoa	0	5,283	0	0	0	0	0
Guam	0	13,670	0	0	0	0	0
No. Mariana Islands..	0	4,914	0	0	0	0	0
Puerto Rico (b).........	0	117,721	0	0	0	0	0
U.S. Virgin Islands.....	0	13,418	0	0	0	0	0

Source: U.S. Department of Transportation, Federal Highway Administration, Highway Statistics, 2009 (October 2010).

Note: Apportioned pursuant to the Safe, Accountable, Flexible, Efficient Transportation Act: A Legacy for Users (SAFETEA-LU). Does not include funds from the Mass Transit Account of the Highway Trust Fund.

(a) Does not include funds from the following programs: emergency relief,

APPORTIONMENT OF FEDERAL FUNDS ADMINISTERED BY THE FEDERAL HIGHWAY ADMINISTRATION BY REGION: FISCAL YEAR 2010 (In thousands of dollars)

State or other jurisdiction	Recreation trails	Metropolitan planning	Railroad highway crossings	Coordinated border infrastructure	Safe routes to school	Equity bonus (a)	Total (b)
Total...........................	$84,160	$303,967	$220,000	$210,000	$180,000	$2,692,857	$38,518,656
United States	84,160	303,967	220,000	210,000	180,000	2,692,857	38,363,650
Eastern Region							
Connecticut	1,037	4,300	1,301	0	2,017	36,592	498,352
Delaware	885	1,520	1,100	0	1,000	7,361	162,355
Maine	1,817	1,520	1,206	12,677	1,000	0	175,412
Maryland	1,159	6,492	2,262	0	3,148	24,101	596,354
Massachusetts	1,238	8,507	2,347	0	3,456	11,991	606,268
New Hampshire	1,460	1,520	1,100	333	1,000	8,200	165,951
New Jersey	1,280	11,706	3,644	0	5,066	72,578	991,301
New York..................	2,888	23,408	6,342	27,536	10,322	66,361	1,669,277
Pennsylvania	2,211	12,396	7,068	0	6,720	76,037	1,644,105
Rhode Island.............	875	1,520	1,100	0	1,000	0	206,791
Vermont....................	1,166	1,520	1,100	8,485	1,000	513	184,096
Regional average	1,456	6,764	2,597	4,457	3,248	27,612	627,297
Midwestern Region							
Illinois......................	1,769	14,701	10,157	0	7,554	94,568	1,369,022
Indiana......................	1,409	5,150	7,264	0	3,806	107,261	965,912
Iowa	1,308	1,683	5,045	0	1,694	17,232	465,991
Kansas	1,148	1,823	6,159	0	1,647	6,135	375,633
Michigan...................	3,908	9,932	7,522	28,298	5,992	64,447	1,056,502
Minnesota	3,151	4,094	6,000	4,181	2,907	41,516	633,005
Nebraska	1,051	1,520	3,452	0	1,024	9,646	285,045
North Dakota............	1,120	1,520	3,479	10,495	1,000	8,338	243,629
Ohio..........................	1,880	11,038	8,566	0	6,577	100,313	1,341,675
South Dakota	1,056	1,520	2,306	0	1,000	16,351	271,497
Wisconsin	2,792	4,291	5,437	0	3,072	78,409	742,717
Regional average	1,872	5,207	5,944	3,907	3,298	49,474	704,603
Southern Region							
Alabama	1,490	2,931	4,369	0	2,739	46,544	759,490
Arkansas...................	1,399	1,520	3,788	0	1,622	34,866	503,673
Florida	2,041	20,336	8,632	0	9,725	225,478	1,919,342
Georgia.....................	1,698	7,564	8,024	0	5,631	139,735	1,303,829
Kentucky...................	1,452	2,365	3,600	0	2,356	48,800	659,819
Louisiana..................	1,447	3,828	4,252	0	2,588	36,210	684,458
Mississippi................	1,311	1,520	3,409	0	1,848	23,065	472,328
Missouri....................	1,545	4,666	5,807	0	3,318	68,476	922,396
North Carolina..........	1,719	5,678	6,200	0	5,034	88,794	1,053,573
Oklahoma.................	1,362	2,240	5,121	0	2,097	32,682	612,191
South Carolina..........	1,222	2,829	4,160	0	2,434	56,858	629,722
Tennessee	1,516	4,476	4,615	0	3,405	67,789	838,455
Texas........................	2,997	22,337	16,975	55,859	15,219	337,934	3,217,725
Virginia.....................	1,415	7,116	4,487	0	4,291	78,752	1,013,690
West Virginia............	1,280	1,520	1,975	0	1,000	39,682	426,625
Regional average	1,593	6,062	5,694	3,724	4,220	88,378	1,001,154
Western Region							
Alaska.......................	1,931	1,520	1,100	1,421	1,000	55,892	429,490
Arizona.....................	1,615	5,900	2,671	10,157	3,612	75,660	749,060
California	4,680	45,321	15,618	26,560	22,580	182,640	3,601,446
Colorado...................	1,710	4,851	3,126	0	2,660	26,506	527,375
Hawaii	853	1,520	1,100	0	1,000	3,077	163,445
Idaho........................	1,707	1,520	1,690	1,481	1,000	26,738	284,624
Montana....................	1,521	1,520	1,787	7,763	1,000	37,363	382,744
Nevada......................	1,308	2,531	1,100	0	1,456	23,120	336,248
New Mexico	1,167	1,520	1,589	1,880	1,122	25,359	366,271
Oregon......................	1,548	2,983	3,091	0	1,963	15,711	474,219
Utah..........................	1,591	2,639	1,533	0	1,718	19,161	312,512
Washington...............	1,824	6,498	4,023	12,973	3,577	13,924	657,331
Wyoming...................	1,377	1,520	1,100	0	1,000	12,904	257,319
Regional average	1,756	6,142	3,041	4,787	3,361	39,850	657,083
Regional average without California .	1,513	2,877	1,993	2,973	1,759	27,951	411,720
Dist. of Columbia......	825	1,520	1,100	0	1,000	915	153,363
American Samoa	0	0	0	0	0	0	5,283
Guam	0	0	0	0	0	0	13,670
No. Mariana Islands..	0	0	0	0	0	0	4,914
Puerto Rico (b).........	0	0	0	0	0	0	117,721
U.S. Virgin Islands.....	0	0	0	0	0	0	13,418

federal lands highway programs, Commonwealth of Puerto Rico highway programs, high priority projects, Woodrow Wilson Bridge, National Byways, construction of ferry terminal facilities, and intelligent vehicle-system, among others. These funds are distributed from the Highway Trust Fund.

(b) Under SAFETEA-LU, Puerto Rico received a stand-alone authorization of $217,665,552.

States Promote Public Safety through Effective Prisoner Re-entry:

The Second Chance Act and the National Reentry Resource Center

By Le'Ann Duran

The number of people being released from prisons and jails is growing steadily in the United States. In 2000, about 600,000 people were released from prison; that number grew to more than 680,000 people in 2008.[1] Between 1990 and 2004, the jail population increased from approximately 400,000 people to slightly more than 700,000.[2] Unfortunately, there has not been a corresponding increase in the rate of successful reintegration into the community for people released from prison. A study of 15 states found more than two-thirds of state prisoners released in 1994 were rearrested and more than half returned to prison within three years of their release.[3]

Current State of the Re-entry Field

In the past decade, innumerable government officials and community leaders have sought to reduce the number of crimes committed by the record number of people released from prisons, jails and juvenile facilities. What was once the goal of a relatively small number of corrections managers, jail administrators and scattered service providers has recently become a national priority. It resulted in the exponential growth of people, organizations and governmental agencies interested in helping people who have been incarcerated become law-abiding and contributing members of families and communities. The Second Chance Act has played a significant role in this growth in re-entry programs and priorities nationwide.

Government officials and community leaders recognize that people released into the community have significant and diverse needs. Halting the cycle of criminal behavior in youth, which is often the antecedent to adult criminal behavior, for example, requires strategies and programs distinct from those designed for adults. At the same time, the level of sophistication in the re-entry field varies considerably. Some organizations understand effective practices and have retooled staff development and training efforts, modified policies and invested in community-based interventions; however, most are still in the early stages of understanding and implementing effective re-entry strategies. Some specialize in narrow focus areas, such as literacy or services for HIV, while others try to provide a comprehensive range of services.

Some have received local, state and/or federal funding; others operate solely on a shoestring budget of contributions and volunteer resources.

Yet these policymakers and practitioners share a common struggle: They must meet the needs of people returning from prisons, jails and juvenile detention facilities often without immediate access to data-driven strategies, evidence-based practices, models for oversight and accountability, and other methods for efficiently and effectively carrying out their efforts.

Introduction to the National Reentry Resource Center

The National Reentry Resource Center provides education, training and technical assistance to states, tribes, territories, local governments, service providers, nonprofit organizations and corrections institutions working on prisoner re-entry. The Resource Center is operated by The Council of State Governments' Justice Center, with support from the Bureau of Justice Assistance, U.S. Department of Justice, the Annie E. Casey Foundation, the Public Welfare Foundation and the Open Society Institute.

Background

Signed into law on April 9, 2008, the Second Chance Act (Public Law 110-199) was designed to improve outcomes for people returning to communities from prisons and jails. This first-of-its-kind legislation authorizes federal grants to government agencies and nonprofit organizations to provide employment assistance, substance abuse treatment, housing, family programming, mentoring, victims support and other services that can help reduce recidivism.

By establishing a national re-entry resource center, Congress and the Bureau of Justice Assistance have ensured the needs of anyone working in the area of re-entry are met. They are effectively buttressing the government agencies and community-based organizations receiving federal funds to ensure the most effective use of those investments. They are also ensuring the rest of the re-entry field is progressing and maturing.

Before the enactment of the Second Chance Act and the subsequent launch of the National Reentry Resource Center in October 2009, government officials and community leaders, under pressure to launch and administer a re-entry program, sought help wherever they could find it. Surfing the Web, they downloaded stacks of tools and guides, but were unsure which ones were credible or most relevant.[4] Research was similarly mystifying. Nothing succinctly reviewed what the evidence said are the essential elements of any re-entry initiative, and it was similarly unclear who was setting a research agenda to address gaps in the knowledge base. The field was missing one place to go where reliable information was compiled, developed and easily accessible, as well as a single place to connect with an expert to navigate this sea of information and be linked to a peer who could share valuable experiences.

National Reentry Resource Center Goals

The Resource Center was created as a one-stop resource for the field. Since opening its doors in October 2009, the Resource Center has helped many individuals, agencies and organizations that have typically struggled to implement effective practices with scarce funding in order to better address community safety.

Re-entry efforts must start with a strong program design that clearly describes who will be targeted for intervention and outlines the services and supervision appropriate for the target population. In order to create an effective program design, those involved in re-entry must first knit together a joint venture among state, county and city justice and human services agencies that often have distinct missions—with varying levels of commitment to serving people involved in the justice system. Second, they must agree on how the re-entry effort

will target resources precisely and scientifically by collecting and analyzing data to identify a subset of people released from prison or jail most likely to reoffend. Third, they must determine the specific service packages and supervision strategies that are tailored to this target population and most likely to change those behaviors that can lead to reincarceration. Fourth, to sustain the initiative, re-entry program administrators must demonstrate how many people they served, what those program participants received and what difference it made.

Guided by these challenges, the National Reentry Resource Center has brought together the most experienced re-entry practitioners and researchers to inform the tools and assistance provided by the center. Available assistance includes collected resource materials—including a "what works" library, distance learning tools, individualized assistance and peer-to-peer learning opportunities.

For more information about National Reentry Resource Center, please visit:
www.nationalreentryresourcecenter.org

Notes

[1] William J. Sabol, Heather C. West, and Matthew Cooper, *Prisoners in 2008*, NCJ 221944 (Washington, D.C.: U.S. Department of Justice, Bureau of Justice Statistics, 2009).

[2] Paige M. Harrison and Allen J. Beck, *Prison and Jail Inmates at Midyear 2004*, NCJ 208801, (Washington, D.C.: U.S. Department of Justice, Bureau of Justice Statistics, 2005).

[3] Patrick A. Langan and David J. Levin, *Recidivism of Prisoners Released in 1994*, NCJ 193427, (Washington, D.C.: U.S. Department of Justice, Bureau of Justice Statistics, 2002).

[4] Even the *Report of the Reentry Policy Council*—a seminal publication with hundreds recommendations from more than 75 national experts—can be overwhelming, especially to someone just starting a program. The full *Report of the Reentry Policy Council* can be found at *http://reentrypolicy. org/Report/About.*

About the Author

Le'Ann Duran is the Reentry Project director at The Council of State Governments Justice Center. Before joining CSG, Le'Ann was the administrator of the Office of Offender Reentry for the Michigan Department of Corrections, where she managed Michigan's Prisoner Reentry Initiative. She also has served as a senior research associate with Public Policy Associates in Lansing, Mich., where she worked as a consultant to the Michigan Department of Corrections. Le'Ann received her bachelor's degree from Texas Tech University, where she graduated Summa Cum Laude, and her master's from Colorado State University.

Table 9.17
TRENDS IN STATE PRISON POPULATION BY REGION, 2000, 2008 and 2009

State or other jurisdiction	Total state prison population			Average annual change 2000–2008	Percent change 2008–2009
	December 31, 2009	December 31, 2008	December 31, 2000		
United States	1,613,740	1,609,759	1,391,261	1.8%	0.2%
Federal...........................	208,118	201,280	145,416	4.1	3.4
State................................	1,405,622	1,408,479	1,245,845	1.5	-0.2
Eastern Region					
Connecticut (a).................	19,716	20,661	18,355	1.5	-4.6
Delaware (a)......................	6,794	7,075	6,921	0.3	-4.0
Maine................................	2,206	2,195	1,679	3.4	0.5
Maryland...........................	22,255	23,324	23,538	-0.1	-4.6
Massachusetts	11,316	11,408	10,722	0.8	-0.8
New Hampshire (b)..........	2,731	2,702	2,257	2.3	1.1
New Jersey	25,382	25,953	29,784	-1.7	-2.2
New York..........................	58,687	60,347	70,199	-1.9	-2.8
Pennsylvania	51,429	49,215	36,847	3.7	4.5
Rhode Island (a)...............	3,674	4,045	3,286	2.6	-9.2
Vermont (a).......................	2,220	2,116	1,697	2.8	4.9
Regional total	206,410	209,041	205,285	2.3	-1.3
Midwestern Region					
Illinois...............................	45,161	45,474	45,281	0.1	-0.7
Indiana..............................	28,808	28,322	20,125	4.4	1.7
Iowa	8,813	8,766	7,955	1.2	0.5
Kansas	8,641	8,539	8,344	0.3	1.2
Michigan...........................	45,478	48,738	47,718	0.3	-6.7
Minnesota.........................	9,986	9,910	6,238	6.0	0.8
Nebraska...........................	4,474	4,520	3,895	1.9	-1.0
North Dakota....................	1,486	1,452	1,076	3.8	2.3
Ohio..................................	51,606	51,686	45,833	1.5	-0.2
South Dakota....................	3,434	3,342	2,616	3.1	2.8
Wisconsin	23,153	23,379	20,754	1.5	-1
Regional total	231,040	234,128	209,835	1.3	-1.3
Southern Region					
Alabama	31,874	30,508	26,332	1.9	4.5
Arkansas............................	15,208	14,716	11,915	2.7	3.3
Florida	103,915	102,388	71,319	4.6	1.5
Georgia (c)........................	53,371	52,719	44,232	2.2	1.2
Kentucky	21,638	21,706	14,919	4.8	-0.3
Louisiana..........................	39,780	38,381	35,207	1.1	3.6
Mississippi	21,482	22,754	20,241	1.5	-5.6
Missouri............................	30,563	30,186	27,543	1.2	1.2
North Carolina..................	39,860	39,482	31,266	3.0	1.0
Oklahoma..........................	26,397	25,864	23,181	1.4	2.1
South Carolina..................	24,288	24,326	21,778	1.4	-0.2
Tennessee	26,965	27,228	22,166	2.6	-1.0
Texas	171,249	172,506	166,719	0.4	-0.7
Virginia.............................	38,092	38,276	30,168	3.0	-0.5
West Virginia....................	6,367	6,059	3,856	5.8	5.1
Regional total	651,049	647,099	550,842	1.9	0.6
Western Region					
Alaska (a)..........................	5,285	5,014	4,173	2.3	5.4
Arizona (c)........................	40,627	39,589	26,510	5.1	2.6
California	171,275	173,670	163,001	0.8	-1.4
Colorado...........................	22,795	23,274	16,833	4.1	-2.1
Hawaii (a)	5,891	5,955	5,053	2.1	-1.1
Idaho................................	7,400	7,290	5,535	3.5	1.5
Montana............................	3,605	3,545	3,105	1.7	1.7
Nevada..............................	12,482	12,743	10,063	3.0	-2.0
New Mexico	6,519	6,402	5,342	2.3	1.8
Oregon..............................	14,403	14,167	10,580	3.7	1.7
Utah..................................	6,533	6,552	5,637	1.9	-0.3
Washington.......................	18,233	17,926	14,915	2.3	1.7
Wyoming	2,075	2,084	1,680	2.7	-0.4
Regional total	317,123	318,211	272,427	1.9	-0.3
Regional total without California	145,848	144,541	109,426	3.6	0.9

Source: U.S. Department of Justice, Bureau of Justice Statistics, Prisoners in 2009—NCJ 231675 (December 21, 2010).

Note: Sentenced prisoner is defined as a prisoner sentenced to more than one year.

Key:
(a) Prisons and jails form one integrated system. Data include total jail and prison populations.
(b) Prison population for year end 2008 is as of January 2, 2009.
(c) Prison population based on custody counts.

Table 9.18
NUMBER OF SENTENCED PRISONERS ADMITTED AND RELEASED FROM STATE AND FEDERAL JURISDICTION, BY REGION: 2000, 2008 and 2009

State or other jurisdiction	Admissions					Releases				
	2009	2008	2000	Average annual change 2000–2008	Percent change 2008–2009	2009	2008	2000	Average annual change 2000–2008	Percent change 2008–2009
United States...................	730,860	744,616	625,219	2.2%	-1.8%	729,295	735,454	604,858	2.5%	-0.8%
Federal.........................	56,153	53,662	43,732	2.6	4.6	50,720	52,348	35,259	5.1	-3.1
State	674,707	690,954	581,487	2.2	-2.4	678,575	683,106	569,599	2.3	-0.7
Eastern Region										
Connecticut	6,293	6,503	6,185	0.6	-3.2	6,850	6,404	5,918	1.0	7.0
Delaware	1,550	1,494	2,709	-7.2	3.7	1,697	1,617	2,260	-4.1	4.9
Maine	856	756	751	0.1	13.2	1,141	720	677	0.8	58.5
Maryland	9,959	10,396	10,327	0.1	-4.2	10,807	10,383	10,004	0.5	4.1
Massachusetts	2,789	2,998	2,062	4.7	-6.7	2,850	2,667	2,889	-1.0	6.9
New Hampshire.............	1,416	1,258	1,051	2.3	12.6	1,564	1,507	1,044	2.9	19.4
New Jersey.....................	12,251	12,984	13,653	-0.6	-5.6	12,860	13,885	15,362	-1.3	-7.4
New York.......................	24,058	25,302	27,601	-1.1	-4.9	25,481	27,482	28,828	-0.6	-7.3
Pennsylvania	16,914	17,493	11,777	5.1	-3.3	14,630	15,618	11,759	3.6	-6.3
Rhode Island.................	959	1,090	3,701	:	-12.0	1,246	1,086	3,223	:	14.7
Vermont	2,106	2,273	984	:	-7.3	1,973	2,241	946	:	-12.0
Regional total................	79,151	82,547	80,801	0.2	-4.1	81,099	83,610	82,910	0.8	-3.0
Midwestern Region										
Illinois	37,718	36,125	29,344	2.6	4.4	38,034	35,780	28,876	2.7	6.3
Indiana	19,689	18,363	11,876	5.6	7.2	19,699	18,308	11,053	6.5	7.6
Iowa..............................	4,376	5,592	4,656	2.3	-21.7	4,648	5,557	4,379	3.0	-16.4
Kansas..........................	4,816	4,506	5,002	-1.3	6.9	4,721	4,655	5,231	-1.4	1.4
Michigan.......................	14,955	12,071	12,169	-0.1	23.9	18,197	13,621	10,874	2.9	33.6
Minnesota.....................	7,361	7,555	4,406	7.0	-2.6	7,777	7,936	4,244	8.1	-2.0
Nebraska.......................	2,101	2,059	1,688	2.5	2.0	2,107	1,963	1,503	3.4	7.3
North Dakota................	1,042	1,085	605	7.6	-4.0	1,003	1,051	598	7.3	-4.6
Ohio..............................	26,864	29,510	23,780	2.7	-9.0	26,949	28,552	24,793	1.8	-5.6
South Dakota...............	3,170	3,116	1,400	10.5	1.7	3,079	3,102	1,327	11.2	-0.7
Wisconsin......................	7,245	7,571	8,396	-1.3	-4.3	8,771	9,391	8,158	1.8	-6.6
Regional total................	129,337	127,553	103,322	2.6	1.4	134,985	129,916	101,036	3.2	3.4
Southern Region										
Alabama	13,093	11,037	6,296	7.3	18.6	12,231	11,556	7,136	6.2	5.8
Arkansas........................	7,383	7,017	6,941	0.01	5.2	6,990	6,610	6,308	0.6	5.7
Florida...........................	38,050	40,860	35,683	1.7	-6.9	37,167	37,277	33,994	1.2	-0.3
Georgia.........................	17,600	18,625	17,373	0.9	-5.5	16,161	19,463	14,797	3.5	-17.0
Kentucky........................	14,033	14,273	8,116	7.3	-1.7	14,138	15,413	7,733	9.0	-8.3
Louisiana	14,940	15,854	15,735	0.1	-5.8	14,924	14,991	14,536	0.4	-0.4
Mississippi.....................	8,239	7,908	5,796	4.0	4.2	9,270	7,817	4,940	5.9	18.6
Missouri.........................	18,216	18,611	14,454	3.2	-2.1	18,097	18,864	13,346	4.4	-4.1
North Carolina...............	11,693	11,825	9,848	2.3	-1.1	11,056	10,615	9,687	1.2	4.2
Oklahoma......................	8,120	7,935	7,426	0.8	2.3	8,004	7,915	6,628	2.2	1.1
South Carolina	9,352	9,650	8,460	1.7	-3.1	9,321	9,506	8,676	1.1	-1.9
Tennessee......................	13,783	14,196	13,675	0.5	-2.9	15,762	15,414	13,893	1.3	2.3
Texas.............................	71,489	73,490	58,197	3.0	-2.7	72,320	72,168	59,776	2.4	0.2
Virginia	12,631	13,625	9,791	4.2	-7.3	13,168	13,194	9,148	4.7	-0.2
West Virginia.................	3,204	3,127	1,577	8.9	2.5	2,943	3,126	1,261	12.0	-5.9
Regional total................	261,826	268,033	219,368	2.5	-2.3	261,552	263,929	211,859	2.7	-0.9
Western Region										
Alaska	2,761	4,857	2,427	9.1	-43.2	3,196	3,741	2,599	4.7	-14.6
Arizona	14,526	14,867	9,560	5.7	-2.3	13,854	13,192	9,100	4.8	5.0
California.......................	129,705	140,827	129,640	1.0	-7.9	128,869	136,925	129,621	0.7	-5.9
Colorado........................	11,054	11,089	7,036	5.9	-0.3	10,858	10,616	5,881	7.7	2.3
Hawaii...........................	1,714	1,731	1,594	1.0	-1.0	1,915	1,795	1,379	3.4	6.7
Idaho	3,857	3,867	3,386	1.7	-0.3	3,743	3,891	2,697	4.7	-3.8
Montana........................	2,295	2,253	1,202	8.2	1.9	2,212	2,117	1,031	9.4	4.5
Nevada..........................	5,409	4,610	4,929	-0.8	17.3	5,967	5,278	4,374	2.4	13.1
New Mexico	5,650	4,092	3,161	3.3	38.1	3,650	4,013	3,383	2.2	-9.0
Oregon..........................	5,950	5,395	4,059	3.6	10.3	5,422	5,055	3,371	5.2	7.3
Utah..............................	3,583	3,394	3,270	0.5	5.6	3,498	3,400	2,897	2.0	2.9
Washington....................	17,074	15,070	7,094	9.9	13.3	17,035	15,061	6,764	10.5	13.1
Wyoming.......................	815	779	638	2.5	4.6	824	764	697	1.2	7.9
Regional total................	204,393	212,831	177,996	2.3	-4.0	201,043	205,848	173,794	2.1	-2.3
Regional total without California	74,688	72,004	48,356	5.4	3.7	72,174	68,923	44,173	6.2	4.7

Source: U.S. Department of Justice, Bureau of Justice Statistics, *Prisoners in 2009*—NCJ 231675 (December 21, 2010).

Note: Totals based on prisoners with a sentence of more than 1 year. Totals exclude escapees, AWOLS, and transfers to and from other jurisdictions.

Key:
:—Not calculated.

Table 9.19
STATE PRISON CAPACITIES, BY REGION: 2009

State	Type of capacity measure			Population as a percent of capacity	
	Rated capacity	Operational capacity	Design capacity	Highest capacity (a)	Lowest capacity (a)
Federal..............................	125,811	...	...	136%	136%
Eastern Region					
Connecticut (b).................	...	...	...	...	...
Delaware	5,446	5,250	4,161	121	158
Maine..................................	2,339	2,133	2,339	89	97
Maryland	...	23,240	...	95	95
Massachusetts	...	...	7,979	140	140
New Hampshire	...	...	2,199	133	133
New Jersey	...	22,233	16,152	95	131
New York............................	57,838	58,986	56,868	99	103
Pennsylvania	43,584	43,584	43,584	114	114
Rhode Island......................	4,004	4,004	4,265	80	85
Vermont..............................	1,613	1,613	1,322	96	117
Midwestern Region					
Illinois................................	34,473	34,473	30,564	131	148
Indiana...............................	...	29,078	...	83	83
Iowa....................................	...	...	7,414	120	120
Kansas	8,880	...	...	97	97
Michigan.............................	...	50,435	...	90	90
Minnesota...........................	...	9,099	...	102	102
Nebraska	...	3,969	3,175	113	141
North Dakota.....................	1,044	991	1,044	138	145
Ohio....................................	38,665	...	...	126	126
South Dakota......................	...	3,562	...	95	95
Wisconsin (c)......................	...	...	17,561	127	127
Southern Region					
Alabama (d)........................	...	25,341	13,403	104	197
Arkansas.............................	13,263	13,912	13,163	96	101
Florida (d)..........................	...	106,433	...	86	86
Georgia (e).........................	...	58,231	...	100	100
Kentucky	13,722	13,722	14,057	89	91
Louisiana (e)......................	19,889	20,720	...	110	115
Mississippi (e)	...	23,795	23,795	50	50
Missouri..............................	...	31,159	...	98	98
North Carolina (d).............	34,229	11,710	10,167	118	397
Oklahoma (e)......................	25,250	25,250	25,250	95	95
South Carolina....................	...	24,172	...	98	98
Tennessee	20,946	20,498	...	71	72
Texas (c)	163,306	159,322	163,306	85	87
Virginia...............................	32,178	...	32,178	91	91
West Virginia......................	4,135	5,113	4,135	99	122
Western Region					
Alaska.................................	3,058	3,206	...	120	126
Arizona...............................	35,939	41,426	35,939	76	88
California	...	157,427	84,056	109	204
Colorado.............................	...	15,056	13,055	118	136
Hawaii.................................	...	3,327	2,291	96	140
Idaho (e).............................	7,071	6,717	7,071	102	107
Montana (c)	0	1,679	...	98	98
Nevada................................	12,715	9,364	10,715	99	134
New Mexico (e)	6,001	6,984	6,619	54	63
Oregon................................	...	...	...	...	...
Utah....................................	...	6,661	6,901	76	79
Washington.........................	17,137	18,051	18,051	95	100
Wyoming	1,713	1,603	1,598	88	95

Source: U.S. Department of Justice, Bureau of Justice Statistics, Prisoners in 2009—NCJ 231675 (December 21, 2010).

Key:

... — Not available.

(a) Population counts are based on the number of inmates held in facilities operated by the jurisdiction. Excludes inmates held in local jails, in other states, or in private facilities.

(b) Connecticut no longer reports capacity because of a law passed in 1995.

(c) Excludes capacity of county facilities and inmates housed in them.

(d) Capacity definition differs from BJS definition, see NPS jurisdiction notes.

(e) Includes capacity of private and contract facilities and inmates housed in them.

Table 9.20
ADULTS ON PROBATION BY REGION: 2009

State or other jurisdiction	Probation population				Percent change during 2009	Number on probation on 12/31/09 per 100,000 adult residents
	1/1/09	2009		12/31/09		
		Entries (a)	Exits (a)			
United States	4,244,046	2,143,734	2,180,721	4,203,967	-0.9%	1,799
Federal	22,483	11,322	11,022	22,783	1.3	10
State	4,221,563	2,132,412	2,169,699	4,181,184	-1.0	1,789
Eastern Region						
Connecticut (b)(d)............	56,155	28,026	27,845	56,336	0.3	2,070
Delaware (b).....................	17,216	14,512	14,897	16,831	-2.2	2,469
Maine (b).........................	7,504	3,648	3,836	7,316	-2.5	698
Maryland	100,958	50,190	46,607	104,541	3.5	2,393
Massachusetts (c)..............	184,079	88,341	91,743	180,677	-1.8	3,481
New Hampshire (c)	4,549	2,581	2,621	4,509	-0.9	434
New Jersey	127,560	41,934	45,318	124,176	-2.7	1,856
New York	118,814	36,340	35,497	119,657	0.7	788
Pennsylvania (d)(e)..........	186,973	3,064	2,756	192,231	2.8	1,947
Rhode Island (b)..............	26,137	6,484	5,867	26,754	2.4	3,251
Vermont (b)(c)..................	26,754	5,223	4,954	25,924	-3.1	3,129
Regional total	856,699	280,343	281,941	858,952	-0.3	:
Midwestern Region						
Illinois (b)(d)	144,904	58,788	59,000	144,692	-0.1	1,480
Indiana (c)(d)...................	130,178	98,619	98,590	130,207	0.0	2,683
Iowa (c)(d)	22,958	18,325	18,082	23,201	1.1	1,007
Kansas (b)	16,263	21,317	20,344	17,236	6.0	811
Michigan (c)(d)(e)............	175,421	125,217	122,422	175,131	-0.2	2,296
Minnesota (b)	127,963	70,504	77,021	121,446	-5.1	3,018
Nebraska	18,910	14,719	14,023	19,606	3.7	1,460
North Dakota....................	4,266	2,806	2,899	4,173	-2.2	825
Ohio (c)(d)(e)..................	260,577	142,773	143,870	254,949	-2.2	2,880
South Dakota	6,146	3,869	3,413	6,602	7.4	1,071
Wisconsin (d)	49,093	23,051	24,723	47,421	-3.4	1,087
Regional total	956,679	579,988	584,387	944,644	0.5	:
Southern Region (a)						
Alabama (b)	53,250	23,520	26,815	49,955	-6.2	1,389
Arkansas..........................	30,939	9,059	9,868	30,130	-2.6	1,376
Florida (b)(d)(e)..............	279,057	218,729	230,612	267,738	-4.1	1,841
Georgia (d)(f)	389,901	228,318	225,531	392,688	0.7	5,385
Kentucky (b)(d)................	51,424	33,719	30,938	54,205	5.4	1,636
Louisiana (b).....................	40,025	16,311	14,077	42,259	5.6	1,247
Mississippi	22,267	10,637	8,628	24,276	9.0	1,108
Missouri (b)(d)(e)	57,360	22,932	22,260	57,665	0.5	1,260
North Carolina (d)............	109,678	65,725	68,822	106,581	-2.8	1,490
Oklahoma (b)(d)	27,940	12,363	13,236	27,067	-3.1	972
South Carolina.................	40,621	14,034	14,967	39,688	-2.3	1,133
Tennessee (b)	57,605	24,619	23,907	59,558	3.4	1,234
Texas (b).........................	428,014	172,666	174,349	426,331	-0.4	2,361
Virginia (b)(d)	53,614	27,572	25,541	55,645	3.8	917
West Virginia (b)(d)	8,283	1,558	1,447	8,409	1.5	585
Regional total	1,649,978	881,762	890,998	1,642,195	0.6	:
Western Region						
Alaska (c)..........................	6,689	1,171	1,113	6,747	0.9	1,301
Arizona (b)(d)	82,212	18,273	22,242	78,243	-4.8	1,597
California (d)	325,069	168,610	181,633	312,046	-4.0	1,126
Colorado (c)(d)(e)............	74,123	51,705	47,878	78,114	5.4	2,040
Hawaii (b)(d)	19,097	5,849	5,477	19,469	1.9	1,932
Idaho (d)(g)	49,513	47,195	39,733	56,975	15.1	5,029
Montana (b)(d).................	10,422	3,493	3,830	10,085	-3.2	1,329
Nevada	13,337	6,231	7,268	12,300	-7.8	624
New Mexico (b)(e)	20,883	4,354	5,391	20,086	-3.8	1,332
Oregon	40,921	15,169	15,366	40,724	-0.5	1,371
Utah................................	11,030	5,915	5,417	11,528	4.5	596
Washington (c)(d)(e).........	110,268	55,529	68,812	96,369	-12.6	1,877
Wyoming (b)	5,438	3,169	3,371	4,668	-14.2	1,121
Regional total	769,002	386,663	407,531	747,354	-1.8	:
Regional total without California	443,933	218,053	225,898	435,308	-1.6	:
Dist. of Columbia (b)	7,706	7,405	6,156	8,955	16.2	1,825

See footnotes at end of table.

ADULTS ON PROBATION BY REGION: 2009 — Continued

Source: U.S. Department of Justice, Bureau of Justice Statistics, Probation and Parole in the United States, 2009, Statistical Tables NCJ 231674 (December 21, 2010).

Note: Because of nonresponse or incomplete data, the probation population for some jurisdictions on December 31, 2009, does not equal the population on January 1, plus entries, minus exits. Rates were computed using the estimated adult resident population in each state on January 1, 2009. See Methodology for more detail.

: — Not calculated.

(a) Reflects reported data except for jurisdictions in which data were not available. Details may not sum to totals because of rounding.

(b) See Explanatory notes for more detail.

(c) Population excludes probationers in one of the following categories: inactive, warrant, supervised out of jurisdiction, or probationers who had their location tracked by GPS. See Explanatory notes for more detail.

(d) Some or all detailed data are estimated.

(e) Data for entries and exits were estimated for nonreporting agencies. See Methodology for more detail.

(f) Counts include private agency cases and may overstate the number of persons under supervision. See Explanatory notes for more detail.

(g) Counts include estimates for misdemeanors based on entries during the year. See Explanatory notes for more detail.

Table 9.21
ADULTS ON PAROLE BY REGION: 2009

State or other jurisdiction	Parole population				Percent change during 2009	Number on parole on 12/31/09 per 100,000 adult residents
	1/1/09	2009		12/31/09		
		Entries (a)	Exits (a)			
United States	824,834	573,900	579,100	819,308	-0.70%	351
Federal...........................	97,010	46,348	41,116	102,242	5.4	44
State..............................	727,824	527,500	538,000	717,066	-1.5	307
Eastern Region						
Connecticut (b).................	2,328	3,354	2,809	2,873	23.4	106
Delaware (b).....................	551	426	458	519	-5.8	76
Maine................................	31	1	1	31	0	3
Maryland	13,220	7,463	6,941	13,742	3.9	315
Massachusetts (b)..............	3,113	4,716	4,464	3,365	8.1	65
New Hampshire (b)..........	1,661	1,107	948	1,820	9.6	175
New Jersey	15,532	8,497	8,673	15,356	-1.1	229
New York..........................	52,225	24,224	26,499	49,950	-4.4	329
Pennsylvania (d)	72,951	39,700	37,600	75,112	3.0	761
Rhode Island (d)...............	469	626	510	585	24.7	71
Vermont (b)(c)...................	1,081	606	600	1,087	0.6	219
Regional total	163,162	90,720	89,503	164,440	0.8	:
Midwestern Region (a)						
Illinois..............................	33,683	34,693	35,214	33,162	-1.5	339
Indiana (d)	10,653	11,280	11,406	10,527	-1.2	217
Iowa (d)	3,159	2,506	2,400	3,265	3.4	142
Kansas (d)	4,958	4,803	4,751	5,010	1.0	236
Michigan (b)......................	22,523	13,618	11,767	24,374	8.2	320
Minnesota.........................	5,093	5,642	5,300	5,435	6.7	135
Nebraska	846	1,044	1,067	823	-2.7	61
North Dakota....................	386	727	756	357	-7.5	71
Ohio (b)............................	19,119	8,711	13,255	14,575	-23.8	165
South Dakota....................	2,720	1,767	1,739	2,748	1.0	446
Wisconsin (c).....................	19,063	7,698	7,427	19,334	1.4	443
Regional total	122,203	92,489	95,082	119,610	-2.1	:
Southern Region						
Alabama (b).......................	8,042	3,181	2,794	8,429	4.8	234
Arkansas (b)......................	1,714	616	454	1,939	13.1	374
Florida (b)(c)	4,528	6,993	7,198	4,323	-4.5	30
Georgia..............................	23,448	13,008	12,427	24,029	2.5	329
Kentucky (b)	12,377	6,632	6,472	12,537	1.3	378
Louisiana...........................	24,636	13,660	12,613	25,683	4.2	758
Mississippi (b)....................	2,922	4,078	1,574	5,426	85.7	248
Missouri............................	19,212	11,934	11,473	19,673	2.4	430
North Carolina (b)(c)........	3,409	3,677	3,542	3,544	4.0	50
Oklahoma (c).....................	3,073	894	997	2,970	-3.4	107
South Carolina..................	1,857	376	621	1,612	-13.2	46
Tennessee (b)	10,464	5,080	3,616	11,627	11.1	241
Texas (c)	102,921	34,702	32,680	104,943	2.0	581
Virginia (b)(c)...................	4,471	876	742	4,605	3.0	76
West Virginia.....................	2,005	1,341	1,457	1,889	-5.8	131
Regional total	225,079	107,048	98,660	233,229	3.6	:
Western Region						
Alaska (b)	1,714	616	454	1,939	13.1	374
Arizona (c)........................	7,537	14,143	13,471	8,209	8.9	168
California (d)	120,753	175,840	190,558	106,035	-12.2	383
Colorado (b)	11,654	9,981	9,980	11,655	0	304
Hawaii (b)	1,904	733	806	1,831	-3.8	182
Idaho................................	3,361	1,756	1,670	3,447	2.6	304
Montana (b)......................	1,062	548	603	1,007	-5.2	133
Nevada..............................	3,908	4,202	3,924	4,186	7.1	212
New Mexico (b)	3,724	276	843	3,157	-15.2	209
Oregon..............................	21,962	8,987	8,555	22,394	2.0	754
Utah..................................	3,566	2,144	2,506	3,204	-10.2	166
Washington (b)	11,768	6,111	11,316	6,563	-44.2	128
Wyoming	727	296	373	614	-15.5	147
Regional total	193,640	225,633	245,059	174,241	-10.0	:
Regional total without California	72,887	49,793	54,501	68,206	-6.4	:
Dist. of Columbia..............	5,767	2,326	1,774	6,319	9.6	1,288

See footnotes at end of table.

ADULTS ON PAROLE BY REGION: 2009 — Continued

Source: U.S. Department of Justice, Bureau of Justice Statistics, Probation and Parole in the United States, 2009, Statistical Tables NCJ 231674 (December 21, 2010).

Note: Because of nonresponse or incomplete data, the parole population for some jurisdictions on December 31, 2009, does not equal the population on January 1, plus entries, minus exits. Rates were computed using the estimated adult resident population in each state on January 1, 2009.

Key:
:—Not calculated.

(a) Reflects reported data except for jurisdictions in which data were not available. Details may not sum to totals because of rounding.

(b) See Explanatory notes for more detail.

(c) Some or all data were estimated.

(d) Population excludes parolees in one of the following categories: absconder or supervised out of state. See Explanatory notes for more detail.

(e) Some or all data were estimated.

Table 9.22
ADULTS LEAVING PAROLE BY TYPE OF EXIT, BY REGION: 2009

State or other jurisdiction	Total reported exits	Completion	Returned to prison or jail				Absconder	Other unsatisfactory (a)	Death	Other (b)	Unknown or not reported
			With new sentence	With revocation	To receive treatment	Other Unknown					
United States	552,611	277,276	47,882	131,734	1,482	4,452	48,608	10,707	5,099	19,345	6,026
Federal	41,116	22,739	2,102	8,926	0	64	1,425	1,094	545	540	3,681
State	511,495	254,537	45,780	122,808	1,482	4,388	47,183	9,613	4,554	18,805	2,345
Eastern Region											
Connecticut	2,809	1,514	0	0	0	1,157	138	0	**	0	0
Delaware	458	262	**	**	**	8	**	83	7	98	0
Maine	1	0	0	0	0	0	0	0	1	0	0
Maryland	6,941	5,360	**	**	**	**	**	1,474	107	**	0
Massachusetts	4,464	3,566	231	642	0	4	0	0	21	0	0
New Hampshire	948	408	**	**	**	540	0	0	**	**	0
New Jersey	8,673	6,663	189	1,734	**	**	**	**	87	**	0
New York (d)	26,499	15,248	1,558	7,967	1,378	136	~	**	212	0	0
Pennsylvania (e)	11,039	4,880	2,216	3,202	0	0	0	134	182	425	0
Rhode Island	510	362	34	113	**	0	0	0	1	**	0
Vermont (c)	600	366	97	69	~	28	0	~	10	30	0
Regional total	62,942	38,629	4,325	13,727	1,378	1,873	138	1,691	628	553	0
Midwestern Region											
Illinois	35,214	20,017	3,357	9,493	~	~	1,066	0	40	808	433
Indiana	11,406	5,775	844	1,724	0	0	1,098	0	48	1,917	0
Iowa (c)	2,400	1,525	**	605	**	0	1	6	20	58	185
Kansas	4,751	2,144	141	1,124	~	3	1,203	**	40	96	0
Michigan	11,767	7,537	1,967	2,105	0	~	~	~	0	158	0
Minnesota	5,300	2,778	256	1,854	0	0	395	0	17	0	0
Nebraska	1,067	771	15	277	~	0	~	0	4	0	0
North Dakota	756	564	33	139	**	**	19	**	1	**	0
Ohio	13,255	8,180	1,045	194	0	0	222	0	141	3,473	0
South Dakota	1,739	821	101	787	0	19	~	**	11	**	0
Wisconsin (c)	7,427	3,761	965	2,572	**	**	**	31	98	**	0
Regional total	95,082	53,873	8,724	20,874	0	22	4,004	37	420	6,510	618
Southern Region											
Alabama	2,794	1,387	606	339	100	3	0	0	91	268	0
Arkansas	454	132	14	138	**	143	**	**	**	**	27
Florida	7,198	5,152	420	775	**	**	**	**	51	525	275
Georgia	12,427	8,401	395	2,534	0	962	45	0	82	0	8
Kentucky	6,472	3,254	463	2,076	~	~	435	~	90	154	0
Louisiana	12,613	7,352	1,204	643	~	212	~	2,974	130	98	0
Mississippi	1,574	1,167	0	0	0	255	115	0	19	18	0
Missouri	11,473	5,007	548	5,762	**	**	**	**	156	**	0
North Carolina	3,542	2,791	115	194	~	0	185	23	32	0	202
Oklahoma (c)	997	804	112	44	0	0	**	0	37	**	0
South Carolina	621	488	16	90	0	0	0	0	19	8	0
Tennessee	3,616	2,214	651	652	0	0	0	0	99	0	0
Texas	32,680	24,132	5,844	1,564	~	33	~	~	1,140	~	0
Virginia (c)	742	664	0	0	0	0	0	0	36	9	0
West Virginia	1,457	896	8	507	0	0	34	0	12	0	0
Regional total	98,660	63841	10,396	15,318	100	1,608	814	2,997	1,994	1,080	512

Number of adults exiting parole, 2009

See footnotes at end of table.

ADULTS LEAVING PAROLE BY TYPE OF EXIT, BY REGION: 2009 — Continued

State or other jurisdiction	Number of adults exiting parole, 2009										
	Total reported exits	Completion	Returned to prison or jail				Absconder	Other unsatisfactory (a)	Death	Other (b)	Unknown or not reported
			With new sentence	With revocation	To receive treatment	Other Unknown					
Western Region											
Alaska	454	132	14	138	**	143	**	**	**	**	27
Arizona (c)	13,471	6,819	266	3,152	0	0	0	3,228	6	**	0
California	190,558	61,227	18,286	58,958	**	**	41,958	2	764	9,363	0
Colorado	9,980	4,641	1,051	3,979	0	0	0	0	93	216	0
Hawaii	806	316	2	256	0	0	0	0	12	0	220
Idaho	1,670	674	173	553	~	0	~	254	16	~	0
Montana	603	320	9	265	0	0	0	0	9	0	0
Nevada (c)	3,924	3,198	290	168	~	164	66	0	38	0	0
New Mexico (d)	843	**	**	**	**	**	**	**	**	**	843
Oregon	8,555	5,084	881	1,564	4	**	7	762	120	10	123
Utah	2,506	585	285	1,333	0	20	0	174	19	90	0
Washington	11,316	10,740	**	**	**	0	0	374	202	0	0
Wyoming	373	284	13	47	0	0	**	0	0	**	29
Regional total	245,059	94,020	21,270	70,413	4	327	42,031	4,794	1,279	9,679	1,242
Regional total without California	54,501	32,793	2,984	11,455	4	327	73	4,792	515	316	1,242
District of Columbia	1,774	581	**	**	**	601	0	94	77	421	0

Source: U.S. Department of Justice, Bureau of Justice Statistics, Probation and Parole in the United States, 2009, Statistical Tables NCJ 231674 (December 21, 2010).

Key:
** – Not known.
~ – Not applicable.

(a) Includes parolees discharged from supervision who failed to meet all conditions of supervision, had their parole sentence rescinded, or had their parole sentence revoked but were not returned to incarceration because their sentence was immediately reinstated, and other types of unsatisfactory exits; includes some early terminations and expirations of sentence.

(b) Includes 4,967 parolees who were transferred to another state and 14,378 parolees who exited for other reasons. Other reasons include parolees who were deported or transferred to the jurisdiction of Immigration and Customs Enforcement (ICE), had their sentence terminated by the court through an appeal, were transferred to another state through an interstate compact agreement or discharged to probation supervision, and other types of exits.

(c) Some or all detailed data are estimated type of exit.
(d) See Explanatory notes for more detail.
(e) Data represent state parolees only. Data are not available for county parolees.

Table 9.23
CAPITAL PUNISHMENT

State or other jurisdiction	Capital offenses by state (a)	Prisoners under sentence of death (b)	Method of execution (a)
Alabama	Intentional murder with 18 aggravating factors (Ala. Stat. Ann. 13A-5-40(a)(1)-(18)).	204	Electrocution or lethal injection
Alaska	...	...	...
Arizona	First-degree murder accompanied by at least 1 of 14 aggravating factors (A.R.S. § 13-703(F)).	135	Lethal gas or lethal injection (c)
Arkansas	Capital murder (Ark. Code Ann. 5-10-101) with a finding of at least 1 of 10 aggravating circumstances; treason.	42	Lethal injection or electrocution (d)
California	First-degree murder with special circumstances; sabotage; train wrecking causing death; treason; perjury causing execution of an innocent person; fatal assault by a prisoner serving a life sentence.	702	Lethal gas or lethal injection
Colorado	First-degree murder with at least 1 of 17 aggravating factors; first-degree kidnapping resulting in death; treason.	3	Lethal injection
Connecticut	Capital felony with 8 forms of aggravated homicide (C.G.S. § 53a-54b).	10	Lethal injection
Delaware	First-degree murder with at least 1 statutory aggravating circumstance. (11Del. C. §4209).	20	Lethal injection (e)
Florida (f)	First-degree murder; felony murder; capital drug trafficking; capital sexual battery.	398	Electrocution or lethal injection
Georgia	Murder; kidnapping with bodily injury or ransom when the victim dies; aircraft hijacking; treason.	105	Lethal injection
Hawaii	...	...	...
Idaho	First-degree murder with aggravating factors; first-degree kidnapping; perjury resulting in death.	17	Lethal injection (g)
Illinois	... (h)		
Indiana	Murder with 16 aggravating circumstances (IC 35-50-2-9).	15	Lethal injection
Iowa	...	...	...
Kansas	Capital murder with 8 aggravating circumstances (KSA 21-3439, KSA 21-4625, KSA 21-4636).	9	Lethal injection
Kentucky	Murder with aggravating factors; kidnapping with aggravating factors (KRS 32.025).	35	Electrocution or lethal injection (i)
Louisiana (f)	First-degree murder; aggravated rape of victim under age 13; treason (La. R.S. 14:30, 14:42, and 14:113).	85	Lethal injection
Maine	...	...	...
Maryland	First-degree murder, either premeditated or during the commission of a felony, provided that certain death eligibility requirements are satisfied.	5	Lethal injection or lethal gas (j)
Massachusetts	...	...	...
Michigan	...	...	...
Minnesota	...	...	...
Mississippi	Capital murder (Miss Code Ann. § 97-3-19(2)); aircraft piracy (Miss Code Ann. § 97-25-55(1)).	61	Lethal injection
Missouri	First-degree murder (565.020 RSMO 2000).	51	Lethal injection or lethal gas
Montana (f)	Capital murder with 1 of 9 aggravating circumstances (Mont. Code Ann. § 46-18-303); aggravated sexual intercourse without consent (Mont. Code Ann. § 45-5-503).	2	Lethal injection
Nebraska (k)	First-degree murder with a finding of at least 1 statutorily defined aggravating circumstance.	12	Lethal injection (k)
Nevada	First-degree murder with at least 1 of 15 aggravating circumstances (NRS 200.030, 200.033, 200.035).	77	Lethal injection
New Hampshire	Murder committed in the course of rape, kidnapping, or drug crimes; killing of a law enforcement officer; murder for hire; murder by an inmate while serving a sentence of life without parole (RSA 630:1, RSA 630:5).	1	Lethal injection or hanging (l)
New Jersey	...		
New Mexico (m)	First-degree murder with at least 1 of 7 statutorily defined aggravating circumstances (Section 30-2-1 A, NMSA). New Mexico no longer has a death penalty statute. (m)	2	Lethal injection (m)
New York (n)	First-degree murder with 1 of 13 aggravating factors (NY Penal Law §125.27).	0	Lethal injection

See footnotes at end of table.

CAPITAL PUNISHMENT — Continued

State or other jurisdiction	Capital offenses by state (a)	Prisoners under sentence of death (b)	Method of execution (a)
North Carolina..............	First-degree murder (NCGS §14-17).	167	Lethal injection
North Dakota................	...	...	...
Ohio.............................	Aggravated murder with at least 1 of 10 aggravating circumstances (O.R.C. secs. 2903.01, 2929.02, and 2929.04).	165	Lethal injection
Oklahoma (f)	First-degree murder in conjunction with a finding of at least 1 of 8 statutorily defined aggravating circumstances; sex crimes against a child under 14 years of age.	84	Electrocution, lethal injection or firing squad (o)
Oregon..........................	Aggravated murder (ORS 163.095).	33	Lethal injection
Pennsylvania	First-degree murder with 18 aggravating circumstances.	222	Lethal injection
Rhode Island................	...	...	...
South Carolina (f)........	Murder with 1 of 12 aggravating circumstances (§ 16-3-20(C)(a)); criminal sexual conduct with a minor with 1 of 9 aggravators (§ 16-3-655).	64	Electrocution or lethal injection
South Dakota	First-degree murder with 1 of 10 aggravating circumstances. Revision: Revised the code ~of criminal procedure. Changes included establishing procedures to be used by circuit judges in determining whether to stop an execution because the inmate is mentally incompetent (SDCL § 23A-27A-22) and clarifying that persons carrying out executions are immune from civil and/or criminal liability (SDCL § 23A-27A-31.2), effective July 1, 2008.	3	Lethal injection
Tennessee	First-degree murder with 1 of 16 aggravating circumstances (Tenn. Code Ann. § 39-13-204).	89	Lethal injection or electrocution (p)
Texas (f).......................	Criminal homicide with 1 of 9 aggravating circumstances (TX Penal Code § 19.03).	333	Lethal injection
Utah.............................	Aggravated murder (76-5-202, Utah Code Annotated). Revision: Amended the criminal code to allow aggravating circumstances to be treated as separate acts from the capital offense which can be prosecuted as a separate offense (Utah Code Ann. § 76-5-202), effective February 26, 2008.	10	Lethal injection or firing squad (q)
Vermont........................	...	...	...
Virginia........................	First-degree murder with 1 of 15 aggravating circumstances (VA Code § 18.2-31).	14	Electrocution or lethal injection
Washington...................	Aggravated first-degree murder.	9	Lethal injection or hanging
West Virginia................	...	...	...
Wisconsin	...	...	...
Wyoming	First-degree murder; murder during the commission of sexual assault, sexual abuse of a minor, arson, robbery, escape, resisting arrest, kidnapping, or abuse of a minor under 16.	1	Lethal injection or lethal gas (r)
Dist. of Columbia	...	...	...

Note: At press time, a severe shortage of barbiturate sodium thiopental—one of the three drugs used in most lethal injections—has delayed or suspended executions in many states. When the sole U.S. supplier of the drug stopped producing it, many states were forced to seek new sources, including overseas suppliers. In recent weeks, the U.S. Drug Enforcement Administration has seized many states' stock of the imported drug because of allegations that it may have been illegally obtained from an unregulated overseas supplier. Other states have since changed their method of lethal injection to use a different cocktail of drugs.

The United States Supreme Court ruling in *Roper v. Simmons*, 543 U.S. 551 (2005) declared unconstitutional the imposition of the death penalty on persons under the age of 18.

The United States Supreme Court ruling in *Atkins v. Virginia*, 536 U.S. 304 (2002) declared unconstitutional the imposition of the death penalty on mentally handicapped persons.

The method of execution of Federal prisoners is lethal injection, pursuant to 28 CFR, Part 26. For offenses under the Violent Crime Control and Law Enforcement Act of 1994, the execution method is that of the State in which the conviction took place (18 U.S.C. 3596).

Key:

... — No capital punishment statute.

(a) *Source:* U.S. Department of Justice, Bureau of Statistics, Capital Punishment, 2008—Statistical Tables, NCJ 2286662 (December 2009).

(b) *Source:* NAACP Legal Defense Fund, Death Row U.S.A.: As of April 1, 2010 (Spring 2010).

(c) Arizona authorizes lethal injection for persons sentenced after November 15, 1992; inmates sentenced before that date may select lethal injection or gas.

(d) Arkansas authorizes lethal injection for those whose offense occurred on or after July 4, 1983; inmates whose offense occurred before that date may select lethal injection or electrocution.

(e) Delaware authorizes lethal injection for those whose capital offense occurred on or after June 13, 1986; those who committed the offense before that date may select lethal injection or hanging. However, as of July 2002, no inmates on death row were eligible to choose this alternative and Delaware dismantled its gallows.

(f) The United States Supreme Court struck a portion of the Louisiana capital statute on June 25, 2008 (*Kennedy v. Louisiana*, U.S. 128 S.Ct. 2641). The statute (La. Rev. Stat. Ann. § 14:42(D)(2)) allowing execution as a punishment for the rape of a minor when no murder had been committed had been ruled constitutionally permissible by the Louisiana Supreme Court. The U.S. Supreme Court found that since no national consensus existed for application of the death penalty in cases of rape where no murder had been committed, such laws constitute cruel and unusual punishment under the Eighth and Fourteenth Amendments. The ruling affects laws passed in Florida, Oklahoma, South Carolina, Texas, and Montana.

(g) On April 1, 2009, Governor C.L. "Butch" Otter signed legislation (HB 107) that eliminates death by firing squad as an alternative method of execution.

CAPITAL PUNISHMENT — Continued

(h) Governor Pat Quinn signed a bill (SB 3539) on March 9, 2011, that abolishes the death penalty effective July 1, 2011. He commuted all death sentences to life without parole and said he would commute any other death sentences prior to the effective date.

(i) Kentucky authorizes lethal injection for persons sentenced on or after March 31, 1998; inmates sentenced before that date may select lethal injection or electrocution.

(j) Maryland authorizes lethal injection for persons sentenced on or after March 24, 1994; those sentenced before that date can select lethal injection or lethal gas.

(k) The Nebraska Supreme Court struck a portion of the state's capital statute on February 8, 2008 (*State v. Mata*, 745 N.W.2d 229, 278 (2008)). The court found that Nebraska's electrocution procedure violated the state constitution's prohibition of cruel and unusual punishment. In May 2009, the Nebraska Legislature approved lethal injection.

(l) New Hampshire authorizes hanging only if lethal injection cannot be given.

(m) Governor Bill Richardson signed a bill in March of 2009 abolishing the death penalty. The law is not retroactive and leaves two inmates on death row.

(n) The New York Court of Appeals has held that a portion of New York's death penalty sentencing statute (CPL 400.27) was unconstitutional (*People v. Taylor*, 9 N.Y.3d 129 (2007)). As a result, no defendants can be sentenced to death until the legislature corrects the errors in this statute.

(o) Oklahoma authorizes electrocution if lethal injection is held to be unconstitutional, and firing squad if both lethal injection and electrocution are held to be unconstitutional.

(p) Tennessee authorizes lethal injection for those whose capital offense occurred after December 31, 1998; those who committed the offense before that date may select electrocution by written waiver.

(q) Authorizes firing squad if lethal injection is held unconstitutional. Inmates who selected execution by firing squad prior to May 3, 2004, may still be entitled to execution by that method.

(r) Wyoming authorizes lethal gas if lethal injection is ever held to be unconstitutional.

Chapter Ten

STATE PAGES

THE FOLLOWING TABLES ARE AN ONLINE-ONLY FEATURE FOR THE 2011 VOLUME OF *THE BOOK OF THE STATES.*

THESE TABLES CAN BE ACCESSED AT
http://knowledgecenter.csg.org/drupalview-content-type/1219

Table 10.3
STATE STATISTICS

State or other jurisdiction	Land area		Population (a)		Percentage change 2000 to 2010	Density per square mile	Rank in nation	Number of Representatives in Congress	Capital	Population (a)	Rank in state	Largest city	Rank in state	Population (a)
	In square miles	Rank in nation	Size	Rank in nation										
Alabama	50,645	28	4,779,736	23	7.5	94.4	27	7	Montgomery	202,696	2	Birmingham	1	228,798
Alaska	570,641	1	710,231	47	13.3	1.2	50	1	Juneau	30,988	2	Anchorage (b)	1	279,243
Arizona	113,594	6	6,392,017	16	24.6	56.3	33	9	Phoenix	1,567,924	1	Phoenix	1	1,567,924
Arkansas	52,035	27	2,915,918	32	9.1	56.0	34	4	Little Rock	189,515	1	Little Rock	1	189,515
California	155,779	3	37,253,956	1	10.0	239.1	11	53	Sacramento	463,794	7	Los Angeles	1	3,833,995
Colorado	103,642	8	5,029,196	22	16.9	48.5	37	7	Denver	598,707	1	Denver	1	598,707
Connecticut	4,842	48	3,574,097	29	4.9	738.1	4	5	Hartford	124,062	3	Bridgeport	1	136,405
Delaware	1,949	49	897,934	45	14.6	460.8	6	1	Dover	36,107	2	Wilmington	1	72,592
Florida	53,625	26	18,801,310	4	17.6	350.6	8	27	Tallahassee	171,922	8	Jacksonville	1	807,815
Georgia	57,513	21	9,687,653	9	18.3	168.4	18	14	Atlanta	537,958	1	Atlanta	1	537,958
Hawaii	6,423	47	1,360,301	40	12.3	211.8	13	2	Honolulu	374,676	1	Honolulu	1	374,676
Idaho	82,643	11	1,567,582	39	21.1	19.0	44	2	Boise	205,314	1	Boise	1	205,314
Illinois	55,519	24	12,830,632	5	3.3	231.1	12	18	Springfield	117,352	6	Chicago	1	2,853,114
Indiana	35,826	38	6,483,802	15	6.6	181.0	16	9	Indianapolis	798,382	1	Indianapolis	1	798,382
Iowa	55,857	23	3,046,355	30	4.1	54.5	36	4	Des Moines	197,052	1	Des Moines	1	197,052
Kansas	81,759	13	2,853,118	33	6.1	34.9	40	4	Topeka	123,446	4	Wichita	1	366,046
Kentucky	39,486	37	4,339,367	26	7.4	109.9	22	6	Frankfort	27,322	7	Louisville (c)	1	557,224
Louisiana	43,204	33	4,533,372	25	1.4	104.9	24	6	Baton Rouge	223,689	6	New Orleans	1	311,853
Maine	30,843	39	1,328,361	41	4.2	43.1	38	2	Augusta	18,282	9	Portland	1	62,561
Maryland	9,707	42	5,773,552	19	9.0	594.8	5	8	Annapolis	36,524	7	Baltimore	1	636,919
Massachusetts	7,800	45	6,547,629	14	3.1	839.4	3	9	Boston	609,023	1	Boston	1	609,023
Michigan	56,539	22	9,883,640	8	-0.6	174.8	17	14	Lansing	113,968	6	Detroit	1	912,062
Minnesota	79,627	14	5,303,925	21	7.8	66.6	31	8	St. Paul	279,590	2	Minneapolis	1	382,605
Mississippi	46,923	31	2,967,297	31	4.3	63.2	32	4	Jackson	173,861	1	Jackson	1	173,861
Missouri	68,742	18	5,988,927	18	7.0	87.1	28	8	Jefferson City	40,771	15	Kansas City	1	451,572
Montana	145,546	4	989,415	44	9.7	6.8	48	1	Helena	29,351	6	Billings	1	103,994
Nebraska	76,824	15	1,826,341	38	6.7	23.8	43	3	Lincoln	251,624	2	Omaha	1	438,646
Nevada	109,781	7	2,700,551	35	35.1	24.6	42	4	Carson City	54,867	6	Las Vegas	1	558,383
New Hampshire	8,953	44	1,316,470	42	6.5	147.0	21	2	Concord	42,255	3	Manchester	1	108,586
New Jersey	7,354	46	8,791,894	11	4.5	1,195.5	1	12	Trenton	82,883	9	Newark	1	278,980
New Mexico	121,298	5	2,059,179	36	13.2	17.0	45	3	Santa Fe	71,831	3	Albuquerque	1	521,999
New York	47,126	30	19,378,102	3	2.1	411.2	7	27	Albany	93,539	6	New York City	1	8,363,710
North Carolina	48,618	29	9,535,483	10	18.5	196.1	15	13	Raleigh	392,552	2	Charlotte	1	687,456
North Dakota	69,001	17	672,591	48	4.7	9.7	47	1	Bismarck	60,389	2	Fargo	1	93,531
Ohio	40,861	35	11,536,504	7	1.6	282.3	10	16	Columbus	754,885	1	Columbus	1	754,885
Oklahoma	68,595	19	3,751,351	28	8.7	54.7	35	5	Oklahoma City	551,789	1	Oklahoma City	1	551,789
Oregon	95,988	10	3,831,074	27	12.0	39.9	39	5	Salem	153,435	3	Portland	1	557,706
Pennsylvania	44,743	32	12,702,379	6	3.4	283.9	9	18	Harrisburg	47,148	13	Philadelphia	1	1,447,395
Rhode Island	1,034	50	1,052,567	43	0.4	1,018.1	2	2	Providence	171,557	1	Providence	1	171,557
South Carolina	30,061	40	4,625,364	24	15.3	153.9	20	7	Columbia	127,029	1	Columbia	1	127,029

See footnotes at end of table.

STATE STATISTICS—Continued

State or other jurisdiction	Land area		Population (a)		Percentage change 2000 to 2010	Density per square mile	Rank in nation	Number of Representatives in Congress	Capital	Population (a)	Rank in state	Largest city	Population (a)
	In square miles	Rank in nation	Size	Rank in nation									
South Dakota............	75,811	16	814,180	46	7.9	10.7	46	1	Pierre	13,899	7	Sioux Falls	154,997
Tennessee..............	41,235	34	6,346,105	17	11.5	153.9	19	9	Nashville (d)	596,462	2	Memphis	669,651
Texas..................	261,232	2	25,145,561	2	20.6	96.3	26	36	Austin	757,688	4	Houston	2,242,193
Utah...................	82,170	12	2,763,885	34	23.8	33.6	41	4	Salt Lake City	181,698	1	Salt Lake City	181,698
Vermont................	9,217	43	625,741	49	2.8	67.9	30	1	Montpelier	7,760	13	Burlington	38,897
Virginia...............	39,490	36	8,001,024	12	13.0	202.6	14	11	Richmond	202,002	4	Virginia Beach	433,746
Washington.............	66,456	20	6,724,540	13	14.1	101.2	25	10	Olympia	45,322	18	Seattle	598,541
West Virginia..........	24,038	41	1,852,994	37	2.5	77.1	29	3	Charleston	50,302	1	Charleston	50,302
Wisconsin	54,158	25	5,686,986	20	6.0	105.0	23	8	Madison	231,916	2	Milwaukee	604,477
Wyoming	97,093	9	563,626	50	14.1	5.8	49	1	Cheyenne	56,915	1	Cheyenne	56,915
Dist. of Columbia	61	...	601,723	...	4.9	9,856.5	...	1 (e)	...	...	...	...	...
American Samoa	77	...	65,628	...	12.7	852.3	...	1 (e)	Pago Pago (g)	4,278	3	Tafuna (g)	8,409
Guam	210	...	178,430	...	13.2	849.7	...	1 (e)	Hagatna (g)	1,122	13	Tamuning (g)	10,833
No. Mariana Islands	179	...	88,662	...	21.9	495.3	...	1 (e)	Saipan (b)(g)	62,392	1	Saipan (b)(g)	62,392
Puerto Rico............	3,424	...	3,725,789	...	-2.2	1,088.2	...	1 (f)	San Juan	434,919	1	San Juan	434,919
U.S. Virgin Islands.......	134	...	109,825	...	1.1	819.6	...	1 (e)	Charlotte Amalie, St. Thomas	18,914	1	Charlotte Amalie, St. Thomas	18,914

Source: U.S. Census Bureau, March 2011.
Key:
... — Not applicable
(a) 2008 Census Bureau estimates
(b) Municipality.

(c) This city is part of a consolidated city-county government and is coextensive with Jefferson County.
(d) This city is part of a consolidated city-county government and is coextensive with Davidson County.
(e) Represented by one non-voting House Delegate.
(f) Represented by one non-voting House Resident Commissioner.
(g) 2000 Census figures.

Table 10.4
PER CAPITA PERSONAL INCOME, PERSONAL INCOME, AND POPULATION, BY STATE AND REGION, 2009–2010

State or other jurisdiction	Per capita personal income (dollars) 2009r	2010p	Rank in the U.S. 2009r	Rank in the U.S. 2010p	Percent of the U.S. 2009r	Percent of the U.S. 2010p	Percent change 2009–10	Rank of percent change 2009–10	Personal income (millions of dollars) 2009r	2010p	Percent change 2009–10	Rank of percent change 2009–10	Population (thousands of persons) 2009r	2010p	Percent change 2009–10	Rank of percent change 2009–10
United States	$39,635	$40,584	—	—	100	100	2.3	—	$12,168,161	$12,530,101	3.0	—	307,007	308,746	0.56	—
Alabama	33,411	33,945	41	42	84	84	1.6	38	157,324	162,249	3.1	17	4,709	4,780	1.49	12
Alaska	43,211	44,174	8	8	109	109	2.2	22	30,182	31,374	3.9	4	698	710	1.66	8
Arizona	33,207	34,999	43	40	84	86	5.1	1	219,027	223,716	2.1	48	6,596	6,392	-3.19	50
Arkansas	32,315	33,150	45	46	82	82	2.5	17	93,374	96,663	3.5	10	2,889	2,916	0.91	26
California	42,395	43,104	11	12	107	106	1.6	32	1,566,999	1,605,790	2.5	39	36,962	37,254	0.78	29
Colorado	41,895	42,802	13	14	106	105	2.1	26	210,513	215,259	2.3	43	5,025	5,029	0.09	39
Connecticut	55,296	56,001	1	1	140	138	1.3	42	194,547	200,154	2.9	26	3,518	3,574	1.56	11
Delaware	39,597	39,962	19	20	100	98	0.9	44	35,048	35,883	2.4	42	885	898	1.43	16
Florida	38,965	39,272	23	24	98	97	0.8	45	722,328	738,373	2.2	46	18,538	18,801	1.40	17
Georgia	34,129	35,490	39	37	86	87	3.8	3	335,466	343,817	2.5	38	9,829	9,688	-1.46	49
Hawaii	42,152	41,021	12	17	106	101	-2.8	50	54,594	55,801	2.2	47	1,295	1,360	4.79	1
Idaho	31,857	32,257	48	49	80	79	1.2	43	49,245	50,565	2.7	32	1,546	1,568	1.39	18
Illinois	41,856	43,159	14	11	106	106	3.0	9	540,380	553,753	2.5	40	12,910	12,831	-0.62	44
Indiana	34,022	34,943	40	41	86	86	2.6	15	218,527	226,562	3.7	8	6,423	6,484	0.94	24
Iowa	37,647	38,281	27	28	95	94	1.7	31	113,236	116,616	3.0	23	3,008	3,046	1.26	21
Kansas	39,173	39,737	22	21	99	98	1.4	39	110,418	113,375	2.7	33	2,819	2,853	1.20	22
Kentucky	32,258	33,348	46	44	81	82	3.3	6	139,166	144,711	4.0	3	4,314	4,339	0.58	34
Louisiana	37,632	38,446	28	26	95	95	2.1	25	169,046	174,292	3.1	20	4,492	4,533	0.91	25
Maine	36,547	37,300	30	29	92	92	2.0	27	48,180	49,548	2.8	28	1,318	1,328	0.76	31
Maryland	48,247	49,025	5	4	122	121	1.6	35	274,980	283,049	2.9	24	5,699	5,774	1.28	20
Massachusetts	49,654	51,552	3	2	125	127	3.7	4	327,395	337,542	3.1	21	6,594	6,548	-0.70	45
Michigan	34,315	35,597	37	36	87	88	3.6	5	342,114	351,830	2.8	27	9,970	9,884	-0.87	48
Minnesota	41,854	42,843	15	13	106	106	2.3	20	220,413	227,234	3.1	22	5,266	5,304	0.71	32
Mississippi	30,401	31,186	50	50	77	77	2.5	16	89,743	92,539	3.1	19	2,952	2,967	0.52	36
Missouri	36,181	36,979	32	32	91	91	2.2	23	216,637	221,465	2.2	45	5,988	5,989	0.02	40
Montana	34,828	35,317	36	38	88	87	1.4	40	33,957	34,943	2.9	25	975	989	1.46	14
Nebraska	39,332	39,557	20	22	99	97	0.6	46	70,665	72,244	2.2	44	1,797	1,826	1.63	9
Nevada	37,670	36,997	26	31	95	91	-1.8	49	99,566	99,913	0.3	50	2,643	2,701	2.13	5
New Hampshire	42,646	44,085	10	9	108	109	3.3	7	56,488	58,036	2.7	30	1,325	1,316	-0.62	43
New Jersey	49,980	50,781	2	3	126	125	1.6	36	435,216	446,464	2.6	36	8,708	8,792	0.96	23
New Mexico	33,267	33,837	42	43	84	83	1.7	30	66,856	69,676	4.2	1	2,010	2,059	2.40	4
New York	46,516	48,821	6	5	117	120	4.7	2	908,997	946,054	4.1	2	19,541	19,378	-0.84	47
North Carolina	34,879	35,638	35	35	88	88	2.1	24	327,199	339,828	3.9	5	9,381	9,535	1.62	10
North Dakota	40,803	40,597	17	18	103	100	-0.5	47	26,393	27,305	3.5	12	647	673	3.83	2
Ohio	35,408	36,395	34	34	89	90	2.7	13	408,707	419,871	2.7	31	11,543	11,537	-0.05	41
Oklahoma	35,837	36,421	33	33	90	90	1.6	33	132,132	136,627	3.4	15	3,687	3,751	1.71	7
Oregon	36,191	37,095	31	30	91	91	2.4	18	138,453	142,113	2.6	34	3,826	3,831	0.14	38
Pennsylvania	40,175	41,152	18	16	101	101	2.4	19	506,397	522,731	3.2	16	12,605	12,702	0.77	30
Rhode Island	41,392	42,579	16	15	104	105	2.8	11	43,594	44,817	2.8	29	1,053	1,053	-0.06	42
South Carolina	32,505	33,163	44	45	82	82	2.0	28	148,265	153,392	3.5	11	4,561	4,625	1.39	19

See footnotes at end of table.

PER CAPITA PERSONAL INCOME, PERSONAL INCOME, AND POPULATION, BY STATE AND REGION, 2009–2010 — Continued

State or other jurisdiction	Per capita personal income (dollars)								Personal income (millions of dollars)				Population (thousands of persons)			
			Rank in the U.S.		Percent of the U.S.			Rank of				Rank of				Rank of
							Percent change	percent change			Percent change	percent change			Percent change	percent change
	2009r	2010p	2009r	2010p	2009r	2010p	2009–10	2009–10	2009r	2010p	2009–10	2009–10	2009r	2010p	2009–10	2009–10
South Dakota.........	38,374	38,865	25	25	97	96	1.3	41	31,174	31,643	1.5	49	812	814	0.22	37
Tennessee	34,277	35,307	38	39	86	87	2.9	10	215,819	224,064	3.8	6	6,296	6,346	0.79	28
Texas......................	38,609	39,493	24	23	97	97	2.2	21	956,808	993,063	3.8	7	24,782	25,146	1.44	15
Utah........................	31,584	32,595	49	48	80	80	3.1	8	87,947	90,090	2.4	41	2,785	2,764	-0.75	46
Vermont..................	39,205	40,283	21	19	99	99	2.7	14	24,376	25,207	3.4	14	622	626	0.64	33
Virginia..................	44,057	44,762	7	7	111	110	1.6	37	347,284	358,140	3.1	18	7,883	8,001	1.48	13
Washington.............	42,870	43,564	9	10	108	107	1.6	34	285,696	292,950	2.5	37	6,664	6,725	0.90	27
West Virginia...........	32,080	32,641	47	47	81	80	1.7	29	58,378	60,484	3.6	9	1,820	1,853	1.79	6
Wisconsin................	37,373	38,432	29	27	94	95	2.8	12	211,337	218,564	3.4	13	5,655	5,687	0.57	35
Wyoming	48,301	47,851	4	6	122	118	-0.9	48	26,289	26,970	2.6	35	544	564	3.43	3
Dist. of Columbia ...	68,843	71,044	—	—	174	175	3.1	—	41,282	42,749	3.6	—	600	602	0.34	—

Source: U.S. Bureau of Economic Analysis and Bureau of the Census, released March 23 and March 25, 2011.

Key:

r — revised

p — preliminary

Alabama

Nickname	The Heart of Dixie
Motto	*Aldemus Jura Nostra Defendere*
	(We Dare Defend Our Rights)
Flower	Camellia
Bird	Yellowhammer
Tree	Southern (Longleaf) Pine
Song	*Alabama*
Entered the Union	December 14, 1819
Capital	Montgomery

STATISTICS

Land Area (square miles)	50,645
Rank in Nation	28th
Population	4,779,736
Rank in Nation	23rd
Density per square mile	94.4
Capital City	Montgomery
Population	202,696
Rank in State	2nd
Largest City	Birmingham
Population	228,798
Number of Representatives in Congress	7
Number of 2012 Electoral Votes	9
Number of County Governments	67
Number of Municipal Governments	458
Number of School Districts	131
Number of Special Districts	529

LEGISLATIVE BRANCH

Legislative Body	Legislature
President of the Senate	Lt. Gov. Kay Ivey
President Pro Tem of the Senate	Del Marsh
Secretary of the Senate	D. Patrick Harris
Speaker of the House	Mike Hubbard
Speaker Pro Tem of the House	Victor Gaston
Clerk of the House	Greg Pappas
2011 Regular Session	March 1 – mid-June, 2011
Number of Senatorial Districts	35
Number of Representative Districts	105

EXECUTIVE BRANCH

Governor	Robert J. Bentley
Lieutenant Governor	Kay Ivey
Secretary of State	Beth Chapman
Attorney General	Luther Strange
Treasurer	Young Boozer
Auditor	Samantha Shaw
State Comptroller	Tom White
Governor's Present Term	1/2011 – 1/2015
Number of Elected Officials in the Executive Branch	7
Number of Members in the Cabinet	25

JUDICIAL BRANCH

Highest Court	Supreme Court
Supreme Court Chief Justice	Sue Bell Cobb
Number of Supreme Court Judges	9
Number of Intermediate Appellate Court Judges	10
Number of U.S. Court Districts	3
U.S. Circuit Court	11th Circuit

STATE INTERNET ADDRESSES

Official State Website	http://www.alabama.gov
Governor's Website	http://www.governor.state.al.us
State Legislative Website	http://www.legislature.state.al.us
State Judicial Website	http://www.judicial.state.al.us

Alaska

Nickname	The Last Frontier
Motto	*North to the Future*
Flower	Forget-Me-Not
Bird	Willow Ptarmigan
Tree	Sitka Spruce
Song	*Alaska's Flag*
Entered the Union	January 3, 1959
Capital	Juneau

STATISTICS

Land Area (square miles)	570,641
Rank in Nation	1st
Population	710,231
Rank in Nation	47th
Density per square mile	1.2
Capital City	Juneau
Population	30,988
Rank in State	2nd
Largest City	Anchorage
Population	279,243
Number of Representatives in Congress	1
Number of 2012 Electoral Votes	3
Number of Geographic Boroughs	16
Number of County Governments	11
Number of Consolidated Governments	5
Number of Municipal Governments	148
Number of School Districts	0
Number of Special Districts	15

LEGISLATIVE BRANCH

Legislative Body	Legislature
President of the Senate	Gary Stevens
Secretary of the Senate	Kirsten Waid
Speaker of the House	Mike Chenault
Chief Clerk of the House	Suzanne Lowell
2011 Regular Session	Jan. 18 – April 17, 2011
Number of Senatorial Districts	20
Number of Representative Districts	40

EXECUTIVE BRANCH

Governor	Sean Parnell
Lieutenant Governor	Mead Treadwell
Attorney General	John J. Burns
Treasurer	Jerry Burnett
Auditor	Pat Davidson
Comptroller	Kim Garnero
Governor's Present Term	7/2009 – 12/2014
Number of Elected Officials in the Executive Branch	2
Number of Members in the Cabinet	19

JUDICIAL BRANCH

Highest Court	Supreme Court
Supreme Court Chief Justice	Walter Carpeneti
Number of Supreme Court Judges	5
Number of Intermediate Appellate Court Judges	3
Number of U.S. Court Districts	1
U.S. Circuit Court	9th Circuit

STATE INTERNET ADDRESSES

Official State Website	http://www.alaska.gov
Governor's Website	http://www.gov.state.ak.us
State Legislative Website	http://www.legis.state.ak.us
State Judicial Website	http://www.state.ak.us/courts

Arizona

Nickname...The Grand Canyon State
Motto...*Ditat Deus* (God Enriches)
Flower ....Blossom of the Saguaro Cactus
Bird.. Cactus Wren
Tree .... Palo Verde
Songs ....*Arizona March Song* and *Arizona*
Entered the Union..February 14, 1912
Capital .... Phoenix

STATISTICS

Land Area (square miles)...113,594
Rank in Nation...6th
Population..6,392,017
Rank in Nation...16th
Density per square mile 56.3
Capital City.. Phoenix
Population...1,567,924
Rank in State...1st
Largest City .... Phoenix
Number Representatives in Congress...................................9
Number of 2012 Electoral Votes......................................11
Number of County Governments....................................15
Number of Municipal Governments 90
Number of School Districts..239
Number of Special Districts 301

LEGISLATIVE BRANCH

Legislative Body ....Legislature

President of the Senate .... Russell K. Pearce
President Pro Tem of the Senate..........................Sylvia Allen
Secretary of the Senate ....Charmion Billington

Speaker of the House.. Kirk Adams
Speaker Pro Tem of the House .... Steve Montenegro
Chief Clerk of the House...Cheryl Laube

2011 Regular Session..........................Jan. 10 – April 20, 2011
Number of Senatorial Districts 30
Number of Representative Districts 30

EXECUTIVE BRANCH

Governor ....Jan Brewer
Secretary of State... Ken Bennett
Attorney General .... Tom Horne
Treasurer.. Doug Ducey
Auditor..Debra K. Davenport
Comptroller...D. Clark Partridge

Governor's Present Term................................ 1/2009 – 1/2015
Number of Elected Officials in the Executive Branch.......................11
Number of Members in the Cabinet 38

JUDICIAL BRANCH

Highest Court..Supreme Court
Supreme Court Chief Justice...............................Rebecca White Berch
Number of Supreme Court Judges 5
Number of Intermediate Appellate Court Judges..............................22
Number of U.S. Court Districts..1
U.S. Circuit Court... 9th Circuit

STATE INTERNET ADDRESSES

Official State Website ....http://www.az.gov
Governor's Website ....http://www.azgovernor.gov/
State Legislative Website .... http://www.azleg.state.az.us
State Judicial Website .... http://www.supreme.state.az.us

Arkansas

Nickname...The Natural State
Motto...*Regnat Populus* (The People Rule)
Flower ....Apple Blossom
Bird.. Mockingbird
Tree ....Pine
Song ....*Arkansas*
Entered the Union...June 15, 1836
Capital ....Little Rock

STATISTICS

Land Area (square miles)...52,035
Rank in Nation...27th
Population..2,915,918
Rank in Nation...32nd
Density per square mile 56
Capital City..Little Rock
Population...189,515
Rank in State...1st
Largest City ....Little Rock
Number of Representatives in Congress..............................4
Number of 2012 Electoral Votes..6
Number of County Governments....................................75
Number of Municipal Governments 502
Number of School Districts..247
Number of Special Districts 724

LEGISLATIVE BRANCH

Legislative Body .... General Assembly

President of the Senate ....Lt. Gov. Mark Darr
President Pro Tem of the Senate......................Paul Bookout
Secretary of the Senate ....Ann Cornwell

Speaker of the House.. Robert Moore
Speaker Pro Tem of the House ....Bobby Pierce
Chief Clerk of the House..Sherri Stacks

2011 Regular Session..........................Jan. 10 – April 27, 2011
Number of Senatorial Districts 35
Number of Representative Districts 100

EXECUTIVE BRANCH

Governor .... Mike Beebe
Lieutenant Governor ....Mark Darr
Secretary of State..Mark Martin
Attorney General .... Dustin McDaniel
Treasurer...Martha A. Shoffner
Auditor .... Charlie Daniels
Comptroller ....Richard Weiss

Governor's Present Term................................ 1/2007 – 1/2015
Number of Elected Officials in the Executive Branch.........................7
Number of Members in the Cabinet 47

JUDICIAL BRANCH

Highest Court..Supreme Court
Supreme Court Chief Justice................................. Jim Hannah
Number of Supreme Court Judges 7
Number of Intermediate Appellate Court Judges.............................12
Number of U.S. Court Districts...2
U.S. Circuit Court... 8th Circuit

STATE INTERNET ADDRESSES

Official State Website ....http://www.state.ar.us
Governor's Website ....http://www.governor.arkansas.gov/
State Legislative Website ....http://www.arkleg.state.ar.us
State Judicial Website .... http://courts.state.ar.us

California

Nickname..The Golden State
Motto...*Eureka* (I Have Found It)
Flower ....California Poppy
Bird.......................................California Valley Quail
Tree ....California Redwood
Song...*I Love You, California*
Entered the Union....................................September 9, 1850
Capital...Sacramento

STATISTICS

Land Area (square miles)..155,779
Rank in Nation...3rd
Population...37,253,956
Rank in Nation..1st
Density per Square Mile 239.1
Capital City...Sacramento
Population...463,794
Rank in State...7th
Largest City ....Los Angeles
Population..3,833,995
Number of Representatives in Congress 53
Number of 2012 Electoral Votes.....................................55
Number of Geographic Counties....................................58
Number of County Governments....................................57
Number of Consolidated Governments..............................1
Number of Municipal Governments 478
Number of School Districts 1,044
Number of Special Districts 2,765

LEGISLATIVE BRANCH

Legislative Body ....Legislature

President of the Senate ....Lt. Gov. Gavin Newsom
President Pro Tem of the Senate.............................Darrell Steinberg
Secretary of the Senate ....Gregory Schmidt

Speaker of the Assembly ....John A. Perez
Speaker Pro Tem of the Assembly.............................Fiona Ma
Chief Clerk of the Assembly ....E. Dotson Wilson

2011 Regular Session....................Dec. 6, 2010 – Sept. 9, 2011
Number of Senatorial Districts 40
Number of Representative Districts 80

EXECUTIVE BRANCH

Governor ....Edmund G. Brown Jr.
Lieutenant Governor ....Gavin Newsom
Secretary of State... Debra Bowen
Attorney General ....Kamala Harris
Treasurer...Bill Lockyer
Auditor ....Elaine M. Howle
Controller ....John Chiang

Governor's Present Term............................... 1/2011 – 1/2015
Number of Elected Officials in the Executive Branch.........................8
Number of Members in the Cabinet 11

JUDICIAL BRANCH

Highest Court...Supreme Court
Supreme Court Chief Justice................................ Tani Cantil-Sakauye
Number of Supreme Court Judges 7
Number of Intermediate Appellate Court Judges.............................88
Number of U.S. Court Districts..4
U.S. Circuit Court... 9th Circuit

STATE INTERNET ADDRESSES

Official State Website ....http://www.ca.gov
Governor's Website .... http://gov.ca.gov/
State Legislative Website ....http://www.leginfo.ca.gov
State Judicial Website...................................http://www.courtinfo.ca.gov

Colorado

Nickname..The Centennial State
Motto...*Nil Sine Numine*
(Nothing Without Providence)
Flower ....Rocky Mountain Columbine
Bird...Lark Bunting
Tree ....Blue Spruce
Song...*Where the Columbines Grow*
Entered the Union.................................... August 1, 1876
Capital... Denver

STATISTICS

Land Area (square miles)..103,642
Rank in Nation...8th
Population...5,029,196
Rank in Nation..22nd
Density per square mile 48.5
Capital City... Denver
Population...598,707
Rank in State...1st
Largest City ....Denver
Number of Representatives in Congress 7
Number of 2012 Electoral Votes.....................................9
Number of Geographic Counties....................................64
Number of County Governments....................................62
Number of Consolidated Governments..............................2
Number of Municipal Governments 270
Number of School Districts 180
Number of Special Districts 1,904

LEGISLATIVE BRANCH

Legislative Body .... General Assembly

President of the Senate ....Brandon Shaffer
President Pro Tem of the Senate.............................Betty Boyd
Secretary of the Senate ....Cindy Markwell

Speaker of the House......................................Frank McNulty
Speaker Pro Tem of the House ....Kevin Priola
Chief Clerk of the House.......................Marilyn Eddins

2011 Regular Session....................Jan. 12 – May 11, 2011
Number of Senatorial Districts 35
Number of Representative Districts 65

EXECUTIVE BRANCH

Governor ....John Hickenlooper
Lieutenant Governor ....Joe Garcia
Secretary of State...Scott Gessler
Attorney General ....John W. Suthers
Treasurer... Walter Stapleton
Auditor .... Sally Symanski
Controller .... David McDermott

Governor's Present Term............................... 1/2011 – 1/2015
Number of Elected Officials in the Executive Branch.........................5
Number of Members in the Cabinet 21

JUDICIAL BRANCH

Highest Court...Supreme Court
Supreme Court Chief Justice................................ Michael L. Bender
Number of Supreme Court Judges 7
Number of Intermediate Appellate Court Judges.............................16
Number of U.S. Court Districts..1
U.S. Circuit Court... 10th Circuit

STATE INTERNET ADDRESSES

Official State Website ....http://www.state.co.us
Gov's Website.......http://www.state.co.us/gov_dir/governor_office.html
State Legislative Website ....http://www.leg.state.co.us
State Judicial Website...................................http://www.courts.state.co.us

Connecticut

Nickname	The Constitution State
Motto	*Qui Transtulit Sustinet*
	(He Who Transplanted Still Sustains)
Flower	Mountain Laurel
Bird	American Robin
Tree	White Oak
Song	*Yankee Doodle*
Entered the Union	January 9, 1788
Capital	Hartford

STATISTICS

Land Area (square miles)	4,842
Rank in Nation	48th
Population	3,574,097
Rank in Nation	29th
Density per square mile	738.1
Capital City	Hartford
Population	124,062
Rank in State	3rd
Largest City	Bridgeport
Population	136,405
Number of Representatives in Congress	5
Number of 2012 Electoral Votes	7
Number of Geographic Counties	8
Number of County Governments	0
Number of Municipal Governments	30
Number of School Districts	17
Number of Special Districts	453

LEGISLATIVE BRANCH

Legislative Body	General Assembly
President of the Senate	Lt. Gov. Nancy Wyman
President Pro Tem of the Senate	Donald E. Williams
Clerk of the Senate	Thomas P. Sheridan
Speaker of the House	Christopher G. Donovan
Deputy Speakers of the House	Emil Altobello, Bob Godfrey, Marie Kirkley-Bey, Joe Aresimowicz, Linda Orange, Kevin Ryan
Clerk of the House	Garey E. Coleman
2011 Regular Session	Jan. 5 – June 8, 2011
Number of Senatorial Districts	36
Number of Representative Districts	151

EXECUTIVE BRANCH

Governor	Dan Malloy
Lieutenant Governor	Nancy Wyman
Secretary of State	Denise W. Merrill
Attorney General	George C. Jepsen
Treasurer	Denise L. Nappier
Auditors	John C. Geragosian and Robert M. Ward
Comptroller	Kevin P. Lembo
Governor's Present Term	1/2011 – 1/2015
Number of Elected Officials in the Executive Branch	6
Number of Members in the Cabinet	27

JUDICIAL BRANCH

Highest Court	Supreme Court
Supreme Court Chief Justice	Chase T. Rogers
Number of Supreme Court Judges	7
Number of Intermediate Appellate Court Judges	10
Number of U.S. Court Districts	1
U.S. Circuit Court	2nd Circuit

STATE INTERNET ADDRESSES

Official State Website	http://www.ct.gov/
Governor's Website	http://www.state.ct.us/governor
State Legislative Website	http://www.cga.ct.gov/
State Judicial Website	http://www.jud.state.ct.us

Delaware

Nickname	The First State
Motto	*Liberty and Independence*
Flower	Peach Blossom
Bird	Blue Hen Chicken
Tree	American Holly
Song	*Our Delaware*
Entered the Union	December 7, 1787
Capital	Dover

STATISTICS

Land Area (square miles)	1,949
Rank in Nation	49th
Population	897,934
Rank in Nation	45th
Density per square mile	460.8
Capital City	Dover
Population	36,107
Rank in State	2nd
Largest City	Wilmington
Population	72,592
Number of Representatives in Congress	1
Number of 2012 Electoral Votes	3
Number of County Governments	3
Number of Municipal Governments	57
Number of School Districts	19
Number of Special Districts	259

LEGISLATIVE BRANCH

Legislative Body	General Assembly
President of the Senate	Lt. Gov. Matthew Denn
President Pro Tem of the Senate	Anthony J. DeLuca
Secretary of the Senate	Bernard J. Brady
Speaker of the House	Robert F. Gilligan
Clerk of the House	Richard Puffer
2011 Regular Session	Jan. 11 – June 30, 2011
Number of Senatorial Districts	21
Number of Representative Districts	41

EXECUTIVE BRANCH

Governor	Jack Markell
Lieutenant Governor	Matthew Denn
Secretary of State	Jeffrey Bullock
Attorney General	Joseph R. Biden III
Treasurer	Chip Flowers Jr.
Auditor	R. Thomas Wagner
Comptroller	Thomas J. Cooke
Governor's Present Term	1/2009 – 1/2013
Number of Elected Officials in the Executive Branch	5
Number of Members in the Cabinet	16

JUDICIAL BRANCH

Highest Court	Supreme Court
Supreme Court Chief Justice	Myron T. Steele
Number of Supreme Court Judges	5
Number of Intermediate Appellate Court Judges	0
Number of U.S. Court Districts	1
U.S. Circuit Court	3rd Circuit

STATE INTERNET ADDRESSES

Official State Website	http://www.delaware.gov
Governor's Website	http://www.state.de.us/governor
State Legislative Website	http://legis.delaware.gov/
State Judicial Website	http://courts.state.de.us

Florida

Nickname..The Sunshine State
Motto..*In God We Trust*
Flower..Orange Blossom
Bird..Mockingbird
Tree.. Sabal Palmetto Palm
Song........................ *The Swannee River* (Old Folks at Home)
Entered the Union.. March 3, 1845
Capital...Tallahassee

STATISTICS

Land Area (square miles)...53,625
Rank in Nation...26th
Population..18,801,310
Rank in Nation...4th
Density per square mile 350.6
Capital City...Tallahassee
Population...171,922
Rank in State...8th
Largest City ....Jacksonville
Population...807,815
Number of Representatives in Congress 27
Number of 2012 Electoral Votes.......................................29
Number of Geographic Counties...............................67
Number of County Governments....................................66
Number of Consolidated Governments.............................1
Number of Municipal Governments 411
Number of School Districts 95
Number of Special Districts 1,051

LEGISLATIVE BRANCH

Legislative Body ....Legislature

President of the Senate ....Mike Haridopolos
President Pro Tem of the Senate.............................Michael S. Bennett
Secretary of the Senate ....Philip Twogood

Speaker of the House...Dean Cannon
Speaker Pro Tem of the House ....John Legg
Clerk of the House ....Bob Ward

2011 Regular Session.................................March 8 – May 6, 2011
Number of Senatorial Districts 40
Number of Representative Districts 120

EXECUTIVE BRANCH

Governor .... Rick Scott
Lieutenant Governor ....Jennifer Carroll
Secretary of State...Kurt S. Browning
Attorney General .... Pam Bondi
Chief Financial Officer .... Jeffrey H. Atwater
Auditor...David Martin

Governor's Present Term................................... 1/2011 – 1/2015
Number of Elected Officials in the Executive Branch........................5
Number of Members in the Cabinet 4

JUDICIAL BRANCH

Highest Court..Supreme Court
Supreme Court Chief Justice....................................Charles T. Canady
Number of Supreme Court Judges 7
Number of Intermediate Appellate Court Judges............................62
Number of U.S. Court Districts...3
U.S. Circuit Court..11th Circuit

STATE INTERNET ADDRESSES

Official State Website ....http://www.myflorida.com
Governor's Website .... http://www.flgov.com/
State Legislative Website ....http://www.leg.state.fl.us
State Judicial Website................................. http://www.flcourts.org

Georgia

Nickname.. The Empire State of the South
Motto...*Wisdom, Justice and Moderation*
Flower ....Cherokee Rose
Bird.. Brown Thrasher
Tree .... Live Oak
Song...*Georgia on My Mind*
Entered the Union.. January 2, 1788
Capital.. Atlanta

STATISTICS

Land Area (square miles)..57,513
Rank in Nation..21st
Population...9,687,653
Rank in Nation..9th
Density per square mile 168.4
Capital City.. Atlanta
Population...537,958
Rank in State...1st
Largest City ....Atlanta
Number of Representatives in Congress 14
Number of 2012 Electoral Votes......................................16
Number of Geographic Counties.......................................159
Number of County Governments 154
Number of Consolidated Governments.....................................5
Number of Municipal Governments 535
Number of School Districts 180
Number of Special Districts 570

LEGISLATIVE BRANCH

Legislative Body .... General Assembly

President of the Senate .... Lt. Gov. Casey Cagle
President Pro Tem of the Senate................................ Tommie Williams
Secretary of the Senate .... Bob Ewing

Speaker of the House.. David Ralston
Speaker Pro Tem of the House .... Jan Jones
Clerk of the House .... Robert E. Rivers Jr.

2011 Regular Session...................................... Jan. 10 – April 20, 2011
Number of Senatorial Districts 56
Number of Representative Districts 180

EXECUTIVE BRANCH

Governor .... Nathan Deal
Lieutenant Governor .... Casey Cagle
Secretary of State... Brian Kemp
Attorney General ....Sam Olens
Treasurer.. Tommy Hills
Auditor.. Russell W. Hinton

Governor's Present Term................................ 1/2011 – 1/2015
Number of Elected Officials in the Executive Branch.......................13
Number of Members in the Cabinet .... No formal cabinet system

JUDICIAL BRANCH

Highest Court...Supreme Court
Supreme Court Chief Justice....................................Carol W. Hunstein
Number of Supreme Court Judges 7
Number of Intermediate Appellate Court Judges...........................12
Number of U.S. Court Districts...3
U.S. Circuit Court.. 11th Circuit

STATE INTERNET ADDRESSES

Official State Website ....www.georgia.gov/
Governor's Website .... http://gov.georgia.gov/
State Legislative Website .... http://www.legis.state.ga.us
State Judicial Website.............................http://www.georgiacourts.org

Hawaii

Nickname..The Aloha State
Motto...*Ua Mau Ke Ea O Ka Aina I Ka Pono*
(The Life of the Land Is Perpetuated in Righteousness)
Flower ....Native Yellow Hibiscus
Bird...Hawaiian Goose (Nene)
Tree...Kukue Tree (Candlenut)
Song..*Hawaii Ponoi*
Entered the Union..August 21, 1959
Capital...Honolulu

STATISTICS

Land Area (square miles)...6,423
Rank in Nation...47th
Population...1,360,301
Rank in Nation...40th
Density per square mile 211.8
Capital City...Honolulu
Population..374,676
Rank in State...1st
Largest City...Honolulu
Number of Representatives in Congress 2
Number of 2012 Electoral Votes 4
Number of Geographic Counties..4
Number of County Governments..3
Number of Consolidated Governments...................................1
Number of Municipal Governments 1
Number of School Districts 0
Number of Special Districts 15

LEGISLATIVE BRANCH

Legislative Body ....Legislature

President of the Senate ....Shan S. Tsutsui
President Pro Tempore of the Senate.................Donna Mercado Kim
Chief Clerk of the Senate ....Carol Taniguchi

Speaker of the House ....Calvin K.Y. Say
Speaker Pro Tempore of the House ....Joey Manahan
Chief Clerk of the House................................Patricia A. Mau-Shimizu

2011 Regular Session.............................Jan. 19 – May 5, 2011
Number of Senatorial Districts 25
Number of Representative Districts 51

EXECUTIVE BRANCH

Governor ....Neil Abercrombie
Lieutenant Governor ....Brian Schatz
Attorney General ....David Louie
Treasurer...Kalbert Young
Auditor...Marion M. Higa
Comptroller...Bruce Coppa

Governor's Present Term........................... 12/2010 – 12/2014
Number of Elected Officials in the Executive Branch.........2
Number of Members in the Cabinet 22

JUDICIAL BRANCH

Highest Court...Supreme Court
Supreme Court Chief Justice............................ Mark E. Recktenwald
Number of Supreme Court Judges 5
Number of Intermediate Appellate Court Judges..................6
Number of U.S. Court Districts...1
U.S. Circuit Court...9th Circuit

STATE INTERNET ADDRESSES

Official State Website .... http://www.ehawaii.gov
Governor's Website .... http://hawaii.gov/gov
State Legislative Website ....http://www.capitol.hawaii.gov
State Judicial Website................................ http://www.courts.state.hi.us/

Idaho

Nickname..The Gem State
Motto....................................*Esto Perpetua* (Let It Be Perpetual)
Flower ....Syringa
Bird..Mountain Bluebird
Tree..Western White Pine
Song...*Here We Have Idaho*
Entered the Union...July 3, 1890
Capital..Boise

STATISTICS

Land Area (square miles)...82,643
Rank in Nation...11th
Population...1,567,582
Rank in Nation...39th
Density per square mile 19
Capital City..Boise
Population..205,314
Rank in State...1st
Largest City...Boise
Number of Representatives in Congress 2
Number of 2012 Electoral Votes 4
Number of County Governments..44
Number of Municipal Governments 200
Number of School Districts 116
Number of Special Districts 880

LEGISLATIVE BRANCH

Legislative Body ....Legislature

President of the Senate ....Lt. Gov. Brad Little
President Pro Tem of the Senate...........................Brent Hill
Secretary of the Senate ....Jeannine Wood

Speaker of the House..............................Lawerence Denney
Chief Clerk of the House...........................Bonnie Alexander

2011 Regular Session...............................Jan. 10 – April 7, 2011
Number of Senatorial Districts 35
Number of Representative Districts 35

EXECUTIVE BRANCH

Governor ....C.L. "Butch" Otter
Lieutenant Governor ....Brad Little
Secretary of State..Ben Ysursa
Attorney General ....Lawrence Wasden
Treasurer ....Ron Crane
Controller ....Donna Jones

Governor's Present Term............................... 1/2007 – 1/2015
Number of Elected Officials in the Executive Branch.........7
Number of Members in the Cabinet 43

JUDICIAL BRANCH

Highest Court...Supreme Court
Supreme Court Chief Justice............................ Daniel Eismann
Number of Supreme Court Judges 5
Number of Intermediate Appellate Court Judges..................3
Number of U.S. Court Districts...1
U.S. Circuit Court...9th Circuit

STATE INTERNET ADDRESSES

Official State Website..............................http://www.state.id.us
Governor's Website http://www2.state.id.us/gov
State Legislative Website http://www2.state.id.us/legislat
State Judicial Website.......................http://www2.state.id.us/judicial

Illinois

Nickname	The Prairie State
Motto	*State Sovereignty — National Union*
Flower	Native Violet
Bird	Cardinal
Tree	White Oak
Song	*Illinois*
Entered the Union	December 3, 1818
Capital	Springfield

STATISTICS

Land Area (square miles)	55,519
Rank in Nation	24th
Population	12,830,632
Rank in Nation	5th
Density per square mile	231.1
Capital City	Springfield
Population	117,352
Rank in State	6th
Largest City	Chicago
Population	2,853,114
Number of Representatives in Congress	18
Number of 2012 Electoral Votes	20
Number of County Governments	102
Number of Municipal Governments	1,299
Number of School Districts	912
Number of Special Districts	3,249

LEGISLATIVE BRANCH

Legislative Body	General Assembly
President of the Senate	John J. Cullerton
President Pro Tem of the Senate	Don Harmon
Secretary of the Senate	Jillayne Rock
Speaker of the House	Michael J. Madigan
House Chief Clerk	Mark Mahoney
2011 Regular Session	Jan. 12, 2011 – Meets year-round
Number of Senatorial Districts	59
Number of Representative Districts	118

EXECUTIVE BRANCH

Governor	Patrick Quinn
Lieutenant Governor	Sheila Simon
Secretary of State	Jesse White
Attorney General	Lisa Madigan
Treasurer	Don Rutherford
Auditor	William G. Holland
Comptroller	Judy Baar Topinka
Governor's Present Term	1/2009 – 1/2015
Number of Elected Officials in the Executive Branch	6
Number of Members in the Cabinet	18

JUDICIAL BRANCH

Highest Court	Supreme Court
Supreme Court Chief Justice	Thomas L. Kilbride
Number of Supreme Court Judges	7
Number of Intermediate Appellate Court Judges	53
Number of U.S. Court Districts	3
U.S. Circuit Court	7th Circuit

STATE INTERNET ADDRESSES

Official State Website	http://www.state.il.us
Governor's Website	http://www.state.il.us/gov
State Legislative Website	http://www.illinois.gov/government/gov_legislature.cfm
State Judicial Website	http://www.illinois.gov/government/judiciary.cfm

Indiana

Nickname	The Hoosier State
Motto	*Crossroads of America*
Flower	Peony
Bird	Cardinal
Tree	Tulip Poplar
Song	*On the Banks of the Wabash, Far Away*
Entered the Union	December 11, 1816
Capital	Indianapolis

STATISTICS

Land Area (square miles)	35,826
Rank in Nation	38th
Population	6,483,802
Rank in Nation	15th
Density per square mile	181
Capital City	Indianapolis
Population	798,382
Rank in State	1st
Largest City	Indianapolis
Number of Representatives in Congress	9
Number of 2012 Electoral Votes	11
Number of Geographic Counties	92
Number of County Governments	91
Number of Consolidated Governments	1
Number of Municipal Governments	567
Number of School Districts	293
Number of Special Districts	1,272

LEGISLATIVE BRANCH

Legislative Body	General Assembly
President of the Senate	Lt. Gov. Becky Skillman
President Pro Tem of the Senate	David C. Long
Secretary of the Senate	Jennifer Mertz
Speaker of the House	Brian C. Bosma
Clerk of the House	M. Carolyn Spotts
2011 Regular Session	Jan. 5 – April 29, 2011
Number of Senatorial Districts	50
Number of Representative Districts	100

EXECUTIVE BRANCH

Governor	Mitch Daniels
Lieutenant Governor	Becky Skillman
Secretary of State	Charlie White
Attorney General	Greg Zoeller
Treasurer	Richard E. Mourdock
Auditor	Tim Berry
Governor's Present Term	1/2005 – 1/2013
Number of Elected Officials in the Executive Branch	7
Number of Members in the Cabinet	16

JUDICIAL BRANCH

Highest Court	Supreme Court
Supreme Court Chief Justice	Randall T. Shepard
Number of Supreme Court Judges	5
Number of Intermediate Appellate Court Judges	15
Number of U.S. Court Districts	2
U.S. Circuit Court	7th Circuit

STATE INTERNET ADDRESSES

Official State Website	http://www.state.in.us
Governor's Website	http://www.in.gov/gov
State Legislative Website	http://www.in.gov/legislative
State Judicial Website	http://www.in.gov/judiciary

Iowa

Nickname..The Hawkeye State
Motto..*Our Liberties We Prize and*
Our Rights We Will Maintain
Flower .... Wild Rose
Bird...Eastern Goldfinch
Tree..Oak
Song..*The Song of Iowa*
Entered the Union..December 28, 1846
Capital..Des Moines

STATISTICS

Land Area (square miles)..55,857
Rank in Nation..23rd
Population...3,046,355
Rank in Nation...30th
Density per square mile 54.5
Capital City...Des Moines
Population...197,052
Rank in State...1st
Largest City...Des Moines
Number of Representatives in Congress 4
Number of 2012 Electoral Votes..6
Number of County Governments..99
Number of Municipal Governments 947
Number of School Districts 380
Number of Special Districts 528

LEGISLATIVE BRANCH

Legislative Body .... General Assembly

President of the Senate ....John P. Kibbie
President Pro Tem of the Senate......................Jeff Danielson
Secretary of the Senate ....Michael E. Marshall

Speaker of the House...Kraig Paulsen
Speaker Pro Tem of the House ....Jeff Kaufmann
Chief Clerk of the House...........................Mark Brandsgard

2011 Regular Session.......................Jan.10 – Late April, 2011
Number of Senatorial Districts 50
Number of Representative Districts 100

EXECUTIVE BRANCH

Governor ....Terry Branstad
Lieutenant Governor ....Kim Reynolds
Secretary of State.. Matt Schultz
Attorney General ....Thomas Miller
Treasurer.. Michael Fitzgerald
Auditor...David A. Vaudt
Chief Operating Officer........................... Calvin McKelvogue

Governor's Present Term................................. 1/2011 – 1/2015
Number of Elected Officials in the Executive Branch.........................7
Number of Members in the Cabinet 30

JUDICIAL BRANCH

Highest Court..Supreme Court
Supreme Court Chief Justice................................Mark S. Cady
Number of Supreme Court Judges 7
Number of Intermediate Appellate Court Judges...............................9
Number of U.S. Court Districts...2
U.S. Circuit Court..8th Circuit

STATE INTERNET ADDRESSES

Official State Website ....http://www.iowa.gov/
Governor's Website ....http://www.governor.state.ia.us/
State Legislative Website .... http://www.legis.state.ia.us
State Judicial Website....................................http://www.iowacourts.gov/

Kansas

Nickname.. The Sunflower State
Motto..*Ad Astra per Aspera*
(To the Stars through Difficulties)
Flower .... Wild Native Sunflower
Bird.. Western Meadowlark
Tree...Cottonwood
Song ....*Home on the Range*
Entered the Union.. January 29, 1861
Capital...Topeka

STATISTICS

Land Area (square miles)...81,759
Rank in Nation.. 13th
Population...2,853,118
Rank in Nation...33rd
Density per square mile 34.9
Capital City...Topeka
Population...123,446
Rank in State..4th
Largest City...Wichita
Population...366,046
Number of Representatives in Congress 4
Number of 2012 Electoral Votes..6
Number of Geographic Counties...105
Number of County Governments..103
Number of Consolidated Governments 2
Number of Municipal Governments 627
Number of School Districts 316
Number of Special Districts 1,531

LEGISLATIVE BRANCH

Legislative Body ....Legislature

President of the Senate ....Stephen Morris
President Pro Tem of Senate .... John Vratil
Secretary of the Senate .... Pat Saville

Speaker of the House..Michael O'Neal
Chief Clerk of the House...........................Susan W. Kannarr

2011 Regular Session.....................Jan. 10 – Late May, 2011
Number of Senatorial Districts 40
Number of Representative Districts 125

EXECUTIVE BRANCH

Governor ....Sam Brownback
Lieutenant Governor ....Jeff Colyer
Secretary of State...Kris Kobach
Attorney General .... Derek Schmidt
Treasurer...Ron Estes
Auditor.. Scott Frank
Director, Division of Accounts & Reports .... Kent Olson

Governor's Present Term................................. 1/2011 – 1/2015
Number of Elected Officials in the Executive Branch.........................6
Number of Members in the Cabinet 14

JUDICIAL BRANCH

Highest Court..Supreme Court
Supreme Court Chief Justice......................................Lawton R. Nuss
Number of Supreme Court Judges 7
Number of Intermediate Appellate Court Judges...........................12
Number of U.S. Court Districts...1
U.S. Circuit Court..10th Circuit

STATE INTERNET ADDRESSES

Official State Website ....http://www.accesskansas.org
Governor's Website ....http://www.ksgovernor.org
State Legislative Website .... http://www.kslegislature.org
State Judicial Website....................................http://www.kscourts.org

Kentucky

Nickname .... The Bluegrass State
Motto .... *United We Stand, Divided We Fall*
Flower .... Goldenrod
Bird .... Cardinal
Tree .... Tulip Poplar
Song .... *My Old Kentucky Home*
Entered the Union .... June 1, 1792
Capital .... Frankfort

STATISTICS

Land Area (square miles) 39,486
Rank in Nation 37th
Population 4,339,367
Rank in Nation 26th
Density per square mile 109.9
Capital City .... Frankfort
Population 27,322
Rank in State 7th
Largest City .... Louisville
Population 557,224
Number of Representatives in Congress 6
Number of 2012 Electoral Votes 8
Number of Geographic Counties 120
Number of County Governments 118
Number of Consolidated Governments 2
Number of Municipal Governments 419
Number of School Districts 175
Number of Special Districts 634

LEGISLATIVE BRANCH

Legislative Body .... General Assembly

President of the Senate .... David L. Williams
President Pro Tem of the Senate .... Katie Stine
Secretary of the Senate .... Donna Holiday

Speaker of the House .... Gregory Stumbo
Speaker Pro Tem of the House .... Larry Clark
Chief Clerk of the House .... Jean Burgin

2011 Regular Session .... Jan. 4 – March 9, 2011
Number of Senatorial Districts 38
Number of Representative Districts 100

EXECUTIVE BRANCH

Governor .... Steve Beshear
Lieutenant Governor .... Daniel Mongiardo
Secretary of State .... Elaine Walker
Attorney General .... Jack Conway
Treasurer .... Todd Hollenbach
Auditor .... Crit Luallen
Controller .... Edgar C. Ross

Governor's Present Term .... 12/2007 – 12/2011
Number of Elected Officials in the Executive Branch 7
Number of Members in the Cabinet 15

JUDICIAL BRANCH

Highest Court .... Supreme Court
Supreme Court Chief Justice .... John D. Minton
Number of Supreme Court Judges 7
Number of Intermediate Appellate Court Judges 14
Number of U.S. Court Districts 2
U.S. Circuit Court .... 6th Circuit

STATE INTERNET ADDRESSES

Official State Website .... http://kentucky.gov
Governor's Website .... http://governor.ky.gov/
Legislative Website .... http://www.lrc.state.ky.us
Judicial Website .... http://www.kycourts.net

Louisiana

Nickname .... The Pelican State
Motto .... *Union, Justice and Confidence*
Flower .... Magnolia
Bird .... Eastern Brown Pelican
Tree .... Bald Cypress
Songs .... *Give Me Louisiana* and
You Are My Sunshine
Entered the Union .... April 30, 1812
Capital .... Baton Rouge

STATISTICS

Land Area (square miles) 43,204
Rank in Nation 33rd
Population 4,533,372
Rank in Nation 25th
Density per square mile 104.9
Capital City .... Baton Rouge
Population 223,689
Rank in State 2nd
Largest City .... New Orleans
Population 311,853
Number of Representatives in Congress 6
Number of 2012 Electoral Votes 8
Number of Geographic Parishes 64
Number of Parish Governments 60
Number of Consolidated Governments 1
Number of Municipal Governments 303
Number of School Districts 68
Number of Special Districts 95

LEGISLATIVE BRANCH

Legislative Body .... Legislature

President of the Senate .... Joel T. Chaisson II
President Pro Tem of the Senate .... Sharon Weston Broome
Secretary of the Senate .... Glenn Koepp

Speaker of the House .... Jim Tucker
Speaker Pro Tem of the House .... Joel C. Robideaux
Clerk of the House and Chief of Staff .... Alfred W. Speer

2011 Regular Session .... April 25 – June 23, 2011
Number of Senatorial Districts 39
Number of Representative Districts 105

EXECUTIVE BRANCH

Governor .... Bobby Jindal
Lieutenant Governor .... Jay Dardenne
Secretary of State .... Tom Schedler
Attorney General .... James D. Caldwell
Treasurer .... John Neely Kennedy

Governor's Present Term .... 1/2008 – 1/2012
Number of Elected Officials in the Executive Branch 8
Number of Members in the Cabinet 16

JUDICIAL BRANCH

Highest Court .... Supreme Court
Supreme Court Chief Justice .... Catherine D. Kimball
Number of Supreme Court Judges 7
Number of Intermediate Appellate Court Judges 53
Number of U.S. Court Districts 3
U.S. Circuit Court .... 5th Circuit

STATE INTERNET ADDRESSES

Official State Website .... http://www.state.la.us
Governor's Website .... http://www.gov.state.la.us
Legislative Website .... http://www.legis.state.la.us
Judicial Website .... http://www.louisiana.gov/Government/
Judicial_Branch/

Maine

Nickname	The Pine Tree State
Motto	*Dirigo* (I Direct or I Lead)
Flower	White Pine Cone and Tassel
Bird	Chickadee
Tree	White Pine
Song	*State of Maine Song*
Entered the Union	March 15, 1820
Capital	Augusta

STATISTICS

Land Area (square miles)	30,843
Rank in Nation	39th
Population	1,328,361
Rank in Nation	41st
Density per square mile	43.1
Capital City	Augusta
Population	18,282
Rank in State	9th
Largest City	Portland
Population	62,561
Number of Representatives in Congress	2
Number of 2012 Electoral Votes	4
Number of County Governments	16
Number of Municipal Governments	22
Number of School Districts	98
Number of Special Districts	248

LEGISLATIVE BRANCH

Legislative Body	Legislature
President of the Senate	Kevin L. Raye
Secretary of the Senate	Joseph Carleton Jr.
Speaker of the House	Robert W. Nutting
Clerk of the House	Heather J.R. Priest
2011 Regular Session	Dec. 1, 2010 – June 15, 2011
Number of Senatorial Districts	35
Number of Representative Districts	151

EXECUTIVE BRANCH

Governor	Paul LePage
Secretary of State	Charlie Summers
Attorney General	William Schneider
Treasurer	Bruce Poliquin
Auditor	Neria R. Douglass
Controller	Terry Brann
Governor's Present Term	1/2011 – 1/2015
Number of Elected Officials in the Executive Branch	1
Number of Members in the Cabinet	16

JUDICIAL BRANCH

Highest Court	Supreme Judicial Court
Supreme Court Chief Justice	Leigh Ingalls Saufley
Number of Supreme Court Judges	7
Number of Intermediate Appellate Court Judges	0
Number of U.S. Court Districts	1
U.S. Circuit Court	1st Circuit

STATE INTERNET ADDRESSES

Official State Website	http://www.state.me.us
Governor's Website	http://www.maine.gov/governor/baldacci/index.shtml
Legislative Website	http://janus.state.me.us/legis
Judicial Website	http://www.courts.state.me.us

Maryland

Nicknames	The Old Line State and Free State
Motto	*Fatti Maschii, Parole Femine* (Manly Deeds, Womanly Words)
Flower	Black-eyed Susan
Bird	Baltimore Oriole
Tree	White Oak
Song	*Maryland, My Maryland*
Entered the Union	April 28, 1788
Capital	Annapolis

STATISTICS

Land Area (square miles)	9,707
Rank in Nation	42nd
Population	5,773,552
Rank in Nation	19th
Density per square mile	594.8
Capital City	Annapolis
Population	36,524
Rank in State	7th
Largest City	Baltimore
Population	636,919
Number of Representatives in Congress	8
Number of 2012 Electoral Votes	10
Number of Geographic Counties	24
Number of County Governments	23
Number of County Equivalents	1*
Number of Municipal Governments	157
Number of School Districts	0
Number of Special Districts	76

LEGISLATIVE BRANCH

Legislative Body	General Assembly
President of the Senate	Thomas V. Mike Miller Jr.
President Pro Tem of the Senate	Nathaniel J. McFadden
Secretary of the Senate	William B.C. Addison Jr.
Speaker of the House	Michael Erin Busch
Speaker Pro Tem of the House	Adrienne A. Jones
Clerk of the House	Mary Monahan
2011 Regular Session	Jan. 12 – April 11, 2011
Number of Senatorial Districts	47
Number of Representative Districts	47

EXECUTIVE BRANCH

Governor	Martin O'Malley
Lieutenant Governor	Anthony Brown
Secretary of State	John McDonough
Attorney General	Douglas Gansler
Treasurer	Nancy K. Kopp
Auditor	Bruce A. Myers
Comptroller	Peter Franchot
Governor's Present Term	1/2007 – 1/2015
Number of Elected Officials in the Executive Branch	4
Number of Members in the Cabinet	25

JUDICIAL BRANCH

Highest Court	Court of Appeals
Court of Appeals Chief Judge	Robert M. Bell
Number of Court of Appeals Judges	7
Number of Intermediate Appellate Court Judges	13
Number of U.S. Court Districts	1
U.S. Circuit Court	4th Circuit

STATE INTERNET ADDRESSES

Official State Website	http://www.maryland.gov/Pages/default.aspx
Governor's Website	http://www.gov.state.md.us
Legislative Website	http://www.mlis.state.md.us
Judicial Website	http://www.courts.state.md.us/

*The city of Baltimore is an Independent City and considered a county equivalent.

Massachusetts

Nickname..The Bay State
Motto................................ *Ense Petit Placidam Sub Libertate Quietem*
(By the Sword We Seek Peace, but Peace Only under Liberty)
Flower ....Mayflower
Bird..Chickadee
Tree...American Elm
Song..*All Hail to Massachusetts*
Entered the Union...February 6, 1788
Capital... Boston

STATISTICS

Land Area (square miles)..7,800
Rank in Nation...45th
Population..6,547,629
Rank in Nation..14th
Density per square mile 839.4
Capital City..Boston
Population..609,023
Rank in State...1st
Largest City..Boston
Number of Representatives in Congress 9
Number of 2012 Electoral Votes......................................11
Number of Geographic Counties..14*
Number of County Governments...5
Number of Consolidated Governments..................................2
Number of Municipal Governments 45
Number of School Districts 82
Number of Special Districts 423

LEGISLATIVE BRANCH

Legislative Body .... General Court

President of the Senate ....Therese Murray
President Pro Tem of the Senate.......................Stanley C. Rosenberg
Clerk of the Senate ....William F. Welch

Speaker of the House............................Robert A. DeLeo
Speaker Pro Tempore ....Patricia A. Haddad
Clerk of the House ....Steven T. James

2011 Regular Session...........................Jan. 5, 2011 – Meets year-round
Number of Senatorial Districts 40
Number of Representative Districts 160

EXECUTIVE BRANCH

Governor ....Deval Patrick
Lieutenant Governor ....Tim Murray
Secretary of the Commonwealth .... William F. Galvin
Attorney General .... Martha Coakley
Treasurer & Receiver General.....................Steven Grossman
Auditor... Suzanne Bump
Comptroller.. Martin J. Benison

Governor's Present Term........................... 1/2007 – 1/2015
Number of Elected Officials in the Executive Branch.........6
Number of Members in the Cabinet 10

JUDICIAL BRANCH

Highest Court....................................Supreme Judicial Court
Supreme Judicial Court Chief Justice................... Roderick L. Ireland
Number of Supreme Judicial Court Judges.............................7
Number of Intermediate Appellate Court Judges.................28
Number of U.S. Court Districts...1
U.S. Circuit Court...1st Circuit

STATE INTERNET ADDRESSES

Official State Website .... http://www.mass.gov
Governor's Website .... http://www.state.ma.us/gov
Legislative Website ....http://www.state.ma.us/legis
Judicial Website......................http://www.state.ma.us/courts

*Seven counties have been abolished and are only geographic in nature.

Michigan

Nickname.. The Wolverine State
Motto..........................*Si Quaeris Peninsulam Amoenam Circumspice*
(If You Seek a Pleasant Peninsula, Look About You)
Flower ....Apple Blossom
Bird..Robin
Tree.. White Pine
Song...*Michigan, My Michigan*
Entered the Union................................... January 26, 1837
Capital..Lansing

STATISTICS

Land Area (square miles)..56,539
Rank in Nation..22nd
Population..9,883,640
Rank in Nation..8th
Density per square mile 174.8
Capital City..Lansing
Population..113,968
Rank in State...6th
Largest City..Detroit
Population..912,062
Number of Representatives in Congress 14
Number of 2012 Electoral Votes......................................16
Number of County Governments..83
Number of Municipal Governments 533
Number of School Districts 579
Number of Special Districts 456

LEGISLATIVE BRANCH

Legislative Body ....Legislature

President of the Senate ....Brian Calley
President Pro Tem of the Senate...........................Tonya Schuitmaker
Secretary of the Senate ....Carol Morey Viventi

Speaker of the House.......................................Jase Bolger
Speaker Pro Tem of the House ....John J. Walsh
Clerk of the House .... Gary Randall

2011 Regular Session.......................Jan. 12, 2011 – Meets year-round
Number of Senatorial Districts 38
Number of Representative Districts 110

EXECUTIVE BRANCH

Governor .... Rick Snyder
Lieutenant Governor ....Brian Calley
Secretary of State... Ruth Johnson
Attorney General .... Bill Schuette
Treasurer...Andy Dillon
Auditor..Thomas McTavish
Director, Office of Financial Management ....Michael J. Moody

Governor's Present Term........................... 1/2011 – 1/2015
Number of Elected Officials in the Executive Branch.........4
Number of Members in the Cabinet 18

JUDICIAL BRANCH

Highest Court..Supreme Court
Supreme Court Chief Justice.................... Robert P. Young Jr.
Number of Supreme Court Judges 7
Number of Intermediate Appellate Court Judges.................28
Number of U.S. Court Districts...2
U.S. Circuit Court... 6th Circuit

STATE INTERNET ADDRESSES

Official State Website ....http://www.michigan.gov
Governor's Website ....http://www.michigan.gov/gov
Legislative Website .... http://www.michiganlegislature.org
Judicial Website..................................... http://www.courts.michigan.gov

Minnesota

Nickname.. The North Star State
Motto..*L'Etoile du Nord* (The North Star)
Flower ....Pink and White Lady-Slipper
Bird...Common Loon
Tree.. Red Pine
Song..*Hail! Minnesota*
Entered the Union..May 11, 1858
Capital... St. Paul

STATISTICS

Land Area (square miles)..79,627
Rank in Nation..14th
Population..5,303,925
Rank in Nation..21st
Density per square mile 66.6
Capital City..St. Paul
Population...279,590
Rank in State 2nd
Largest City ....Minneapolis
Population...382,605
Number of Representatives in Congress 8
Number of 2012 Electoral Votes......................................10
Number of County Governments.....................................87
Number of Municipal Governments 854
Number of School Districts 341
Number of Special Districts 456

LEGISLATIVE BRANCH

Legislative Body ....Legislature

President of the Senate ....Michelle Fischbach
President Pro Tem of the Senate..........................Gen Olson
Secretary of the Senate ....Cal Ludeman

Speaker of the House...Kurt Zellers
Chief Clerk of the House................................. Al Mathiowetz

2011 Regular Session......................Jan. 4 – May 23, 2011
Number of Senatorial Districts 67
Number of Representative Districts 67

EXECUTIVE BRANCH

Governor ....Mark Dayton
Lieutenant Governor .... Yvonne Prettner Solon
Secretary of State... Mark Ritchie
Attorney General ....Lori Swanson
Commissioner of Finance ....Jim Schowalter
Auditor.. Rebecca Otto

Governor's Present Term.............................. 1/2011 – 1/2015
Number of Elected Officials in the Executive Branch........5
Number of Members in the Cabinet 24

JUDICIAL BRANCH

Highest Court...Supreme Court
Supreme Court Chief Justice..................... David R. Stras
Number of Supreme Court Judges 7
Number of Intermediate Appellate Court Judges..............16
Number of U.S. Court Districts.......................................1
U.S. Circuit Court... 8th Circuit

STATE INTERNET ADDRESSES

Official State Website .... http://www.state.mn.us
Governor's Website ....http://www.governor.state.mn.us
Legislative Website .... http://www.leg.state.mn.us
Judicial Website...http://www.mncourts.gov/
default.aspx?fontsize=up2 /

Mississippi

Nickname.. The Magnolia State
Motto................................*Virtute et Armis* (By Valor and Arms)
Flower ....Magnolia
Bird...Mockingbird
Tree...Magnolia
Song...*Go, Mississippi*
Entered the Union...................................December 10, 1817
Capital...Jackson

STATISTICS

Land Area (square miles)..46,923
Rank in Nation..31st
Population..2,967,297
Rank in Nation..31st
Density per square mile 63.2
Capital City..Jackson
Population...173,861
Rank in State 1st
Largest City ....Jackson
Number of Representatives in Congress 4
Number of 2012 Electoral Votes......................................6
Number of County Governments.....................................82
Number of Municipal Governments 296
Number of School Districts 164
Number of Special Districts 458

LEGISLATIVE BRANCH

Legislative Body ....Legislature

President of the Senate ....Lt. Gov. Phil Bryant
President Pro Tem of the Senate.........................Billy Hewes
Secretary of the Senate ....Tressa W. Guynes

Speaker of the House..William J. McCoy
Speaker Pro Tem of the House .......................J.P. Compretta
Clerk of the House ....Don Richardson

2011 Regular Session......................Jan. 4 – April 7, 2011
Number of Senatorial Districts 52
Number of Representative Districts 122

EXECUTIVE BRANCH

Governor .... Haley Barbour
Lieutenant Governor ....Phil Bryant
Secretary of State.............................Delbert Hosemann Jr.
Attorney General ....Jim Hood
Treasurer...Tate Reeves
Auditor..Stacey Pickering

Governor's Present Term.............................. 1/2004 – 1/2012
Number of Elected Officials in the Executive Branch........8
Number of Members in the Cabinet .... No formal cabinet system

JUDICIAL BRANCH

Highest Court...Supreme Court
Supreme Court Chief Justice................................ William L. Waller Jr.
Number of Supreme Court Judges 9
Number of Intermediate Appellate Court Judges..............10
Number of U.S. Court Districts.......................................2
U.S. Circuit Court... 5th Circuit

STATE INTERNET ADDRESSES

Official State Website .... http://www.ms.gov
Governor's Website ....http://www.governor.state.ms.us
Legislative Website ....http://billstatus.ls.state.ms.us/
Judicial Website... http://www.mssc.state.ms.us

Missouri

Nickname	The Show Me State
Motto	*Salus Populi Suprema Lex Esto*
	(The Welfare of the People Shall Be the Supreme Law)
Flower	White Hawthorn Blossom
Bird	Bluebird
Tree	Flowering Dogwood
Song	*Missouri Waltz*
Entered the Union	August 10, 1821
Capital	Jefferson City

STATISTICS

Land Area (square miles)	68,742
Rank in Nation	18th
Population	5,988,927
Rank in Nation	18th
Density per square mile	87.1
Capital City	Jefferson City
Population	40,771
Rank in State	15th
Largest City	Kansas City
Population	451,572
Number of Representatives in Congress	8
Number of 2012 Electoral Votes	10
Number of Geographic Counties	115
Number of County Governments	114
Number of County Equivalents	1*
Number of Municipal Governments	952
Number of School Districts	536
Number of Special Districts	1,809

LEGISLATIVE BRANCH

Legislative Body	General Assembly
President of the Senate	Lt. Gov. Peter Kinder
President Pro Tem of the Senate	Robert N. Mayer
Secretary of the Senate	Terry L. Spieler
Speaker of the House	Steven Tilley
Speaker Pro Tem of the House	Shane Schoeller
Clerk of the House	D. Adam Crumbliss
2011 Regular Session	Jan. 5 – May 30, 2011
Number of Senatorial Districts	34
Number of Representative Districts	163

EXECUTIVE BRANCH

Governor	Jay Nixon
Lieutenant Governor	Peter Kinder
Secretary of State	Robin Carnahan
Attorney General	Chris Koster
Treasurer	Clint Zweifel
Auditor	Tom Schweich
Director, Division of Accounting	Mark A. Kaiser
Governor's Present Term	1/2009 – 1/2013
Number of Elected Officials in the Executive Branch	6
Number of Members in the Cabinet	17

JUDICIAL BRANCH

Highest Court	Supreme Court
Supreme Court Chief Justice	William Ray Price Jr.
Number of Supreme Court Judges	7
Number of Intermediate Appellate Court Judges	32
Number of U.S. Court Districts	2
U.S. Circuit Court	8th Circuit

STATE INTERNET ADDRESSES

Official State Website	http://www.mo.gov/
Governor's Website	http://governor.mo.gov/
Legislative Website	http://www.moga.mo.gov/
Judicial Website	http://www.courts.mo.gov/

*The city of St. Louis is an Independent City and considered a county equivalent.

Montana

Nickname	The Treasure State
Motto	*Oro y Plata* (Gold and Silver)
Flower	Bitterroot
Bird	Western Meadowlark
Tree	Ponderosa Pine
Song	*Montana*
Entered the Union	November 8, 1889
Capital	Helena

STATISTICS

Land Area (square miles)	145,546
Rank in Nation	4th
Population	989,415
Rank in Nation	44th
Density per square mile	6.8
Capital City	Helena
Population	29,351
Rank in State	6th
Largest City	Billings
Population	103,994
Number of Representatives in Congress	1
Number of 2012 Electoral Votes	3
Number of Geographic Counties	56
Number of County Governments	54
Number of Consolidated Governments	2
Number of Municipal Governments	129
Number of School Districts	332
Number of Special Districts	758

LEGISLATIVE BRANCH

Legislative Body	Legislature
President of the Senate	Jim Peterson
President Pro Tem of the Senate	Bruce Tutvedt
Secretary of the Senate	Marilyn Miller
Speaker of the House	Mike Milburn
Speaker Pro Tem of the House	Janna Taylor
Chief Clerk of the House	Beth Cargo
2011 Regular Session	Jan. 3 – April 28, 2011
Number of Senatorial Districts	50
Number of Representative Districts	100

EXECUTIVE BRANCH

Governor	Brian Schweitzer
Lieutenant Governor	John Bohlinger
Secretary of State	Linda McCulloch
Attorney General	Steve Bullock
Treasurer	Janet Kelly
Auditor	Monica Lindeen
Administrator, State Accounting	Paul Christofferson
Governor's Present Term	1/2005 – 1/2013
Number of Elected Officials in the Executive Branch	6
Number of Members in the Cabinet	21

JUDICIAL BRANCH

Highest Court	Supreme Court
Supreme Court Chief Justice	Mike McGrath
Number of Supreme Court Judges	7
Number of Intermediate Appellate Court Judges	0
Number of U.S. Court Districts	1
U.S. Circuit Court	9th Circuit

STATE INTERNET ADDRESSES

Official State Website	http://mt.gov/
Governor's Website	http://governor.mt.gov/
Legislative Website	http://leg.mt.gov/css/default.asp
Judicial Website	www.montanacourts.org

Nebraska

Nickname...The Cornhusker State
Motto.. *Equality Before the Law*
Flower .... Goldenrod
Bird .... Western Meadowlark
Tree.. Western Cottonwood
Song .... *Beautiful Nebraska*
Entered the Union.. March 1, 1867
Capital... Lincoln

STATISTICS

Land Area (square miles)...76,824
Rank in Nation..15th
Population..1,826,341
Rank in Nation..38th
Density per square mile 23.8
Capital City...Lincoln
Population..251,624
Rank in State 2nd
Largest City ....Omaha
Population..438,646
Number of Representatives in Congress 3
Number of 2012 Electoral Votes..5
Number of County Governments...93
Number of Municipal Governments 530
Number of School Districts 288
Number of Special Districts 1,294

LEGISLATIVE BRANCH

Legislative Body ....Unicameral Legislature

President of the Legislature ....Lt. Gov. Rick Sheehy
Speaker of the Legislature.. Mike Flood
Chairperson of the Executive Board.......................... John Wightman
Clerk of the Legislature .... Patrick J. O'Donnell

2011 Regular Session.......................................Jan. 5 – Early June, 2011
Number of Legislative Districts 49

EXECUTIVE BRANCH

Governor ....David Heineman
Lieutenant Governor ....Rick Sheehy
Secretary of State...John Gale
Attorney General ....Jon Bruning
Treasurer...Don B. Stenberg
Auditor..Mike Foley
State Accounting Administrator ....Michael Keays

Governor's Present Term... 1/2005 – 1/2015
Number of Elected Officials in the Executive Branch.........................6
Number of Members in the Cabinet 30

JUDICIAL BRANCH

Highest Court...Supreme Court
Supreme Court Chief Justice................................ Michael G. Heavican
Number of Supreme Court Judges 7
Number of Intermediate Appellate Court Judges................................6
Number of U.S. Court Districts 1
U.S. Circuit Court...8th Circuit

STATE INTERNET ADDRESSES

Official State Website ....http://www.state.ne.us
Governor's Website ....http://www.governor.nebraska.gov/
Legislative Website .... http://nebraskalegislature.gov/
Judicial Website................................ http://www.supremecourt.ne.gov/
supreme-court/index.shtml?sub1

Nevada

Nickname...The Silver State
Motto..*All for Our Country*
Flower ....Sagebrush
Bird .... Mountain Bluebird
Tree...Bristlecone Pine and Single-leaf Piñon
Song .... *Home Means Nevada*
Entered the Union.. October 31, 1864
Capital...Carson City

STATISTICS

Land Area (square miles)...109,781
Rank in Nation..7th
Population..2,700,551
Rank in Nation..35th
Density per square mile 24.6
Capital City..Carson City
Population..54,867
Rank in State 6th
Largest City .... Las Vegas
Population..558,383
Number of Representatives in Congress 4
Number of 2012 Electoral Votes..6
Number of Geographic Counties..17
Number of County Governments...16
Number of County Equivalents...1*
Number of Municipal Governments 19
Number of School Districts 17
Number of Special Districts 146

LEGISLATIVE BRANCH

Legislative Body ....Legislature

President of the Senate ....Lt. Gov. Brian K. Krolicki
President Pro Tem of the Senate...................... Michael A. Schneider
Secretary of the Senate ....David A. Byerman

Speaker of the Assembly ....John Oceguera
Speaker Pro Tem of the Assembly.......................Deborah June Smith
Chief Clerk of the Assembly .... Susan Furlong Reil

2011 Regular Session.............................Feb. 7 – June 6, 2011
Number of Senatorial Districts 21
Number of Representative Districts 42

EXECUTIVE BRANCH

Governor ....Brian Sandoval
Lieutenant Governor ....Brian Krolicki
Secretary of State.. Ross Miller
Attorney General ....Catherine Cortez Masto
Treasurer...Kate Marshall
Auditor.. Paul V. Townsend
Controller ....Kim Wallin

Governor's Present Term.. 1/2011 – 1/2015
Number of Elected Officials in the Executive Branch.........................6
Number of Members in the Cabinet 23

JUDICIAL BRANCH

Highest Court...Supreme Court
Supreme Court Chief Justice..................................Michael L. Douglas
Number of Supreme Court Judges 7
Number of Intermediate Appellate Court Judges................................0
Number of U.S. Court Districts 1
U.S. Circuit Court...9th Circuit

STATE INTERNET ADDRESSES

Official State Website ....http://www.nv.gov
Governor's Website .... http://www.gov.state.nv.us
Legislative Website .... http://www.leg.state.nv.us
Judicial Website.................... http://www.nevadajudiciary.us/index.php/
supnews/349-welcome-to-the-new-nevada-judiciary-website.html

*Carson City is an Independent City and considered a county equivalent.

New Hampshire

Nickname... The Granite State
Motto.. *Live Free or Die*
Flower .... Purple Lilac
Bird .... Purple Finch
Tree.. White Birch
Song.. *Old New Hampshire*
Entered the Union...June 21, 1788
Capital.. Concord

STATISTICS

Land Area (square miles)...8,953
Rank in Nation.. 44th
Population.. 1,316,470
Rank in Nation... 42nd
Density per square mile 147
Capital City.. Concord
Population... 42,255
Rank in State.. 3rd
Largest City .... Manchester
Population.. 108,586
Number of Representatives in Congress 2
Number of 2012 Electoral Votes 4
Number of County Governments... 10
Number of Municipal Governments 13
Number of School Districts 164
Number of Special Districts 137

LEGISLATIVE BRANCH

Legislative Body .... General Court

President of the Senate .... Peter E. Bragdon
President Pro Tem of the Senate............................. John S. Barnes Jr.
Clerk of the Senate .... Tammy L. Wright

Speaker of the House.. William L. O'Brien
Clerk of the House .... Karen O. Wadsworth

2011 Regular Session...................................... Jan. 5 – July 1, 2011
Number of Senatorial Districts 24
Number of Representative Districts 103

EXECUTIVE BRANCH

Governor ....John Lynch
Secretary of State..................................... William M. Gardner
Attorney General .... Michael A. Delaney
Treasurer.. Catherine Provencher
Auditor..Jeffrey A. Pattison
Comptroller..Edgar R. Carter

Governor's Present Term........................... 1/2005 – 1/2013
Number of Elected Officials in the Executive Branch........................1
Number of Members in the Cabinet .... No formal cabinet system

JUDICIAL BRANCH

Highest Court..Supreme Court
Supreme Court Chief Justice..................................... Linda S. Dalianis
Number of Supreme Court Judges 5
Number of Intermediate Appellate Court Judges 0
Number of U.S. Court Districts 1
U.S. Circuit Court...1st Circuit

STATE INTERNET ADDRESSES

Official State Website ....http://www.state.nh.us
Governor's Website .... http://www.nh.gov/governor/
Legislative Website .... http://www.gencourt.state.nh.us
Judicial Website...http://www.courts.state.nh.us/

New Jersey

Nickname...The Garden State
Motto..*Liberty and Prosperity*
Flower ....Violet
Bird..Eastern Goldfinch
Tree...Red Oak
Song..*I'm From New Jersey*
Entered the Union...December 18, 1787
Capital..Trenton

STATISTICS

Land Area (square miles)..7,354
Rank in Nation..46th
Population...8,791,894
Rank in Nation...11th
Density per square mile 1,195.5
Capital City..Trenton
Population...82,883
Rank in State...9th
Largest City ....Newark
Population..278,980
Number of Representatives in Congress 12
Number of 2012 Electoral Votes 14
Number of County Governments..21
Number of Municipal Governments 324
Number of School Districts 549
Number of Special Districts 247

LEGISLATIVE BRANCH

Legislative Body ....Legislature

President of the Senate ....Stephen Sweeney
President Pro Tem of the Senate............................Nia H. Gil
Secretary of the Senate ....Kent Hicks

Speaker of the Assembly ....Sheila Y. Oliver
Speaker Pro Tem of the Assembly........................Jerry Green
Clerk of the General Assembly....................................Dana M. Burley

2011 Regular Session.........................Jan. 12, 2011 – Meets year-round
Number of Senatorial Districts 40
Number of Representative Districts 40

EXECUTIVE BRANCH

Governor .... Chris Christie
Lieutenant Governor ....Kim Guadagno
Attorney General .... Paula Dow
Treasurer......................................Andrew P. Sidamon-Eristoff
Auditor..Stephen Eells
Controller .... Matthew Boxer

Governor's Present Term.............................. 1/2010 – 1/2014
Number of Elected Officials in the Executive Branch.......................2
Number of Members in the Cabinet 24

JUDICIAL BRANCH

Highest Court...Supreme Court
Supreme Court Chief Justice..Stuart Rabner
Number of Supreme Court Judges 7
Number of Intermediate Appellate Court Judges............................35
Number of U.S. Court Districts 1
U.S. Circuit Court...3rd Circuit

STATE INTERNET ADDRESSES

Official State Website ....http://www.state.nj.us
Governor's Website ....http://www.state.nj.us/governor
Legislative Website ....http://www.njleg.state.nj.us
Judicial Website.................................http://www.judiciary.state.nj.us

New Mexico

Nickname...The Land of Enchantment
Motto...*Crescit Eundo* (It Grows As It Goes)
Flower .... Yucca (Our Lord's Candles)
Bird...Chaparral Bird
Tree.. Piñon
Songs ....*Asi es Nuevo Mexico* and
O, Fair New Mexico
Entered the Union... January 6, 1912
Capital .... Santa Fe

STATISTICS

Land Area (square miles).......................................121,298
Rank in Nation..5th
Population..2,059,179
Rank in Nation...36th
Density per square mile 13.2
Capital City... Santa Fe
Population..71,831
Rank in State..3rd
Largest City .... Albuquerque
Population..521,999
Number of Representatives in Congress 3
Number of 2012 Electoral Votes 5
Number of County Governments..33
Number of Municipal Governments 101
Number of School Districts 96
Number of Special Districts 633

LEGISLATIVE BRANCH

Legislative Body .... Legislature

President of the Senate .... Lt. Gov. John A. Sanchez
President Pro Tem of the Senate.......................... Timothy Z. Jennings
Chief Clerk of the Senate ....Lenore Naranjo

Speaker of the House... Ben Lujan
Chief Clerk of the House...Stephen R. Arias

2011 Regular Session..Jan. 18 – March 19, 2011
Number of Senatorial Districts 42
Number of Representative Districts 70

EXECUTIVE BRANCH

Governor ....Susana Martinez
Lieutenant Governor .... John A. Sanchez
Secretary of State .... Dianna J. Duran
Attorney General .... Gary King
Treasurer...James Lewis
Auditor..Hector Balderas
Controller ....Anthony Armijo

Governor's Present Term... 1/2011 – 1/2015
Number of Elected Officials in the Executive Branch.........................5
Number of Members in the Cabinet 25

JUDICIAL BRANCH

Highest Court..Supreme Court
Supreme Court Chief Justice....................................Charles W. Daniels
Number of Supreme Court Judges 5
Number of Intermediate Appellate Court Judges.............................10
Number of U.S. Court Districts 1
U.S. Circuit Court... 10th Circuit

STATE INTERNET ADDRESSES

Official State Website .... http://www.state.nm.us
Governor's Website ....http://www.governor.state.nm.us
Legislative Website .... http://legis.state.nm.us
Judicial Website...http://www.nmcourts.com

New York

Nickname...The Empire State
Motto...*Excelsior* (Ever Upward)
Flower ....Rose
Bird.. Bluebird
Tree .... Sugar Maple
Song...*I Love New York*
Entered the Union..July 26, 1788
Capital ....Albany

STATISTICS

Land Area (square miles)..47,126
Rank in Nation...30th
Population...19,378,102
Rank in Nation..3rd
Density per square mile 411.2
Capital City..Albany
Population..93,539
Rank in State...6th
Largest City ....New York City
Population...8,363,710
Number of Representatives in Congress 27
Number of 2012 Electoral Votes 29
Number of Geographic Counties...62*
Number of County Governments..57
Number of Consolidated Governments...................................1*
Number of Municipal Governments 618
Number of School Districts 680
Number of Special Districts 1,119

LEGISLATIVE BRANCH

Legislative Body .... Legislature

President of the Senate .... Lt. Gov. Robert Duffy
Majority Leader of the Senate...................................Dean G. Skelos
Secretary of the Senate .... Frank Patience

Speaker of the Assembly .... Sheldon Silver
Clerk of the Assembly......................................Laurene R. Kretzler

2011 Regular Session...........................Jan. 5, 2011 – Meets year-round
Number of Senatorial Districts 62
Number of Representative Districts 150

EXECUTIVE BRANCH

Governor ....Andrew M. Cuomo
Lieutenant Governor ....Robert Duffy
Secretary of State...Ruth Noemi-Colon
Attorney General .... Eric T. Schneiderman
Treasurer.. Aida Brewer
Comptroller ....Thomas P. DiNapoli

Governor's Present Term... 1/2011 – 1/2015
Number of Elected Officials in the Executive Branch.........................4
Number of Members in the Cabinet 75

JUDICIAL BRANCH

Highest Court..Court of Appeals
Court of Appeals Chief Justice ....Jonathan Lippman
Number of Court of Appeals Judges 7
Number of Intermediate Appellate Court Judges...........................57
Number of U.S. Court Districts 4
U.S. Circuit Court... 2nd Circuit

STATE INTERNET ADDRESSES

Official State Website .... http://www.state.ny.us
Governor's Website ....http://www.state.ny.us/governor
Senate Website ....http://www.senate.state.ny.us
Assembly Website...http://assembly.state.ny.us
Judicial Website..http://www.courts.state.ny.us

*New York City is coextensive with the five boroughs (counties).

North Carolina

Nickname .... The Tar Heel State and Old North State
Motto .... *Esse Quam Videri*
(To Be Rather Than to Seem)
Flower .... Dogwood
Bird .... Cardinal
Tree .... Long Leaf Pine
Song .... *The Old North State*
Entered the United States .... November 21, 1789
Capital .... Raleigh

STATISTICS

Land Area (square miles) 48,618
Rank in Nation 29th
Population 9,535,483
Rank in Nation 10th
Density per square mile 196.1
Capital City .... Raleigh
Population 392,552
Rank in State 2nd
Largest City .... Charlotte
Population 687,456
Number of Representatives in Congress 13
Number of 2012 Electoral Votes 15
Number of County Governments 100
Number of Municipal Governments 548
Number of School Districts 0
Number of Special Districts 315

LEGISLATIVE BRANCH

Legislative Body .... General Assembly

President of the Senate .... Lt. Gov. Walter Dalton
President Pro Tem of the Senate .... Phil Berger
Principal Clerk of the Senate .... Janet Pruitt

Speaker of the House .... Thom Tillis
Principal Clerk of the House .... Denise Weeks

2011 Regular Session .... Jan. 26 – Early July, 2011
Number of Senatorial Districts 50
Number of Representative Districts 120

EXECUTIVE BRANCH

Governor .... Beverly Perdue
Lieutenant Governor .... Walter Dalton
Secretary of State .... Elaine Marshall
Attorney General .... Roy A. Cooper III
Treasurer .... Jane Cowell
Auditor .... Beth Wood
Controller .... David McCoy

Governor's Present Term .... 1/2009 – 1/2013
Number of Elected Officials in the Executive Branch 10
Number of Members in the Cabinet 10

JUDICIAL BRANCH

Highest Court .... Supreme Court
Supreme Court Chief Justice .... Sarah Parker
Number of Supreme Court Judges 7
Number of Intermediate Appellate Court Judges 15
Number of U.S. Court Districts 3
U.S. Circuit Court .... 4th Circuit

STATE INTERNET ADDRESSES

Official State Website .... http://www.ncgov.com
Governor's Website .... http://www.governor.state.nc.us
Legislative Website .... http://www.ncleg.net
Judicial Website .... http://www.nccourts.org

North Dakota

Nickname .... Peace Garden State
Motto .... *Liberty and Union, Now and Forever,*
One and Inseparable
Flower .... Wild Prairie Rose
Bird .... Western Meadowlark
Tree .... American Elm
Song .... *North Dakota Hymn*
Entered the Union .... November 2, 1889
Capital .... Bismarck

STATISTICS

Land Area (square miles) 69,001
Rank in Nation 17th
Population 672,591
Rank in Nation 48th
Density per square mile 4.7
Capital City .... Bismarck
Population 60,389
Rank in State 2nd
Largest City .... Fargo
Population 93,531
Number of Representatives in Congress 1
Number of 2012 Electoral Votes 3
Number of County Governments 53
Number of Municipal Governments 357
Number of School Districts 198
Number of Special Districts 771

LEGISLATIVE BRANCH

Legislative Body .... Legislative Assembly

President of the Senate .... Lt. Gov. Drew Wrigley
President Pro Tem of the Senate .... Richard Wardner
Secretary of the Senate .... Fran Gronberg

Speaker of the House .... David Drovdal
Clerk of the House .... Buell Reich

2011 Regular Session .... Jan. 4 – April 28, 2011
Number of Senatorial Districts 47
Number of Representative Districts 47

EXECUTIVE BRANCH

Governor .... Jack Dalrymple
Lieutenant Governor .... Drew Wrigley
Secretary of State .... Alvin Jaeger
Attorney General .... Wayne Stenehjem
Treasurer .... Kelly Schmidt
Auditor .... Robert R. Peterson

Governor's Present Term .... 12/2010 – 12/2012
Number of Elected Officials in the Executive Branch 10
Number of Members in the Cabinet 18

JUDICIAL BRANCH

Highest Court .... Supreme Court
Supreme Court Chief Justice .... Jerry W. VandeWalle
Number of Supreme Court Judges 5
Number of Intermediate Appellate Court Judges 0
Number of U.S. Court Districts 1
U.S. Circuit Court .... 8th Circuit

STATE INTERNET ADDRESSES

Official State Website .... http://discovernd.com
Governor's Website .... http://www.governor.state.nd.us
Legislative Website .... http://www.legis.nd.gov/
Judicial Website .... http://www.court.state.nd.us

Ohio

Nickname..The Buckeye State
Motto...*With God, All Things Are Possible*
Flower ....Scarlet Carnation
Bird ....Cardinal
Tree.. Buckeye
Song...*Beautiful Ohio*
Entered the Union.. March 1, 1803
Capital...Columbus

STATISTICS

Land Area (square miles)..40,861
Rank in Nation..35th
Population..11,536,504
Rank in Nation...7th
Density per square mile 282.3
Capital City...Columbus
Population...754,885
Rank in State...1st
Largest City...Columbus
Number of Representatives in Congress 16
Number of 2012 Electoral Votes...................................18
Number of County Governments.....................................88
Number of Municipal Governments...............................938
Number of School Districts 668
Number of Special Districts 700

LEGISLATIVE BRANCH

Legislative Body .... General Assembly

President of the Senate ....Thomas E. Niehaus
President Pro Tem of the Senate...........................Keith Faber
Clerk of the Senate.. Vincent Keeran

Speaker of the House......................................William G. Batchelder
Speaker Pro Tem of the House .... Louis W. Blessing Jr.
Legislative Clerk of the House .... Laura P. Clemens

2011 Regular Session............................Jan. 3, 2011 – Meets year-round
Number of Senatorial Districts 33
Number of Representative Districts 99

EXECUTIVE BRANCH

Governor ....John Kasich
Lieutenant Governor .... Mary Taylor
Secretary of State...Jon Husted
Attorney General ....Mike DeWine
Treasurer..Josh Mandel
Auditor.. David A. Yost

Governor's Present Term.. 1/2011 – 1/2015
Number of Elected Officials in the Executive Branch........................6
Number of Members in the Cabinet 24

JUDICIAL BRANCH

Highest Court...Supreme Court
Supreme Court Chief Justice................................. Maureen O'Connor
Number of Supreme Court Judges...7
Number of Intermediate Appellate Court Judges...............................68
Number of U.S. Court Districts...2
U.S. Circuit Court... 6th Circuit

STATE INTERNET ADDRESSES

Official State Website ....http://www.state.oh.us
Governor's Website ....http://governor.ohio.gov/
Legislative Website ....http://www.legislature.state.oh.us
Judicial Website.................................. http://www.sconet.state.oh.us

Oklahoma

Nickname.. The Sooner State
Motto.................... *Labor Omnia Vincit* (Labor Conquers All Things)
Flower .... Mistletoe
Bird .... Scissor-tailed Flycatcher
Tree..Redbud
Song...*Oklahoma*
Entered the Union..................................... November 16, 1907
Capital..Oklahoma City

STATISTICS

Land Area (square miles)..68,595
Rank in Nation..19th
Population...3,751,351
Rank in Nation...28th
Density per square mile 54.7
Capital City..Oklahoma City
Population...551,789
Rank in State...1st
Largest City..Oklahoma City
Number of Representatives in Congress 5
Number of 2012 Electoral Votes......................................7
Number of County Governments.....................................77
Number of Municipal Governments...............................594
Number of School Districts 567
Number of Special Districts 642

LEGISLATIVE BRANCH

Legislative Body ....Legislature

President of the Senate ....Lt. Gov. Todd Lamb
President Pro Tem of the Senate...................Brian Bingman
Secretary of the Senate .... Paul Ziriax

Speaker of the House...Kris Steele
Speaker Pro Tem of the House ....Jeffrey W. Hickman
Chief Clerk/Administrator of the House...........................Joel Kintsel

2011 Regular Session.......................Feb. 7 – May 27, 2011
Number of Senatorial Districts 50
Number of Representative Districts 101

EXECUTIVE BRANCH

Governor ....Mary Fallin
Lieutenant Governor .... Todd Lamb
Secretary of State...Glenn Coffee
Attorney General ....Scott Pruitt
Treasurer..Ken Miller
Auditor.. Gary Jones
Comptroller... Brenda Bolander

Governor's Present Term.. 1/2011 – 1/2015
Number of Elected Officials in the Executive Branch........................8
Number of Members in the Cabinet 16

JUDICIAL BRANCH

Highest Court...Supreme Court
Supreme Court Chief Justice.................................Steven W. Taylor
Number of Supreme Court Judges...9
Number of Intermediate Appellate Court Judges...............................10
Number of U.S. Court Districts...3
U.S. Circuit Court... 10th Circuit

STATE INTERNET ADDRESSES

Official State Website ....http://www.state.ok.us
Governor's Website ....http://www.governor.state.ok.us/
Legislative Website ....http://www.lsb.state.ok.us
Judicial Website...http://www.oscn.net

Oregon

Nickname..The Beaver State
Motto...*She Flies with Her Own Wings*
Flower .... Oregon Grape
Bird.. Western Meadowlark
Tree .... Douglas Fir
Song..*Oregon, My Oregon*
Entered the Union...February 14, 1859
Capital...Salem

STATISTICS

Land Area (square miles)..95,988
Rank in Nation...10th
Population..3,831,074
Rank in Nation...27th
Density per square mile...39.9
Capital City...Salem
Population..153,435
Rank in State..3rd
Largest City...Portland
Population..557,706
Number of Representatives in Congress 5
Number of 2012 Electoral Votes 7
Number of County Governments 36
Number of Municipal Governments 242
Number of School Districts 234
Number of Special Districts 1,034

LEGISLATIVE BRANCH

Legislative Body ....Legislative Assembly

President of the Senate ....Peter Courtney
President Pro Tem of the Senate....................Ginny Burdick
Secretary of the Senate .... Robert Taylor

Speaker of the House...............................Bruce Hanna; Arnie Roblan
Chief Clerk of the House.............................. Ramona Kenady

2011 Regular Session.....................................Feb. 1 – June 30, 2011
Number of Senatorial Districts 30
Number of Representative Districts 60

EXECUTIVE BRANCH

Governor ....John A. Kitzhaber
Secretary of State... Kate Brown
Attorney General ....John Kroger
Treasurer..Ted Wheeler
Auditor...Gary Blackmer
Controller...John Radford

Governor's Present Term......................... 1/2011 – 1/2015
Number of Elected Officials in the Executive Branch.........................6
Number of Members in the Cabinet .... No formal cabinet system

JUDICIAL BRANCH

Highest Court...Supreme Court
Supreme Court Chief Justice....................... Paul J. De Muniz
Number of Supreme Court Judges....................................7
Number of Intermediate Appellate Court Judges.............................10
Number of U.S. Court Districts...1
U.S. Circuit Court.. 9th Circuit

STATE INTERNET ADDRESSES

Official State Website .... http://www.oregon.gov
Governor's Website ....http://governor.oregon.gov/
Legislative Website .... http://www.leg.state.or.us
Judicial Website..................................... https://www.ojd.state.or.us

Pennsylvania

Nickname..The Keystone State
Motto...*Virtue, Liberty and Independence*
Bird.. Ruffed Grouse
Flower ....Mountain Laurel
Tree ....Hemlock
Song..*Pennsylvania*
Entered the Union...December 12, 1787
Capital... Harrisburg

STATISTICS

Land Area (square miles)..44,743
Rank in Nation...32nd
Population..12,702,379
Rank in Nation...6th
Density per square mile...283.9
Capital City... Harrisburg
Population..47,148
Rank in State..13th
Largest City ....Philadelphia
Population..1,447,395
Number of Representatives in Congress 18
Number of 2012 Electoral Votes 20
Number of Geographic Counties.......................................67
Number of County Governments.......................................66
Number of Consolidated Governments............................1
Number of Municipal Governments 1,016
Number of School Districts 515
Number of Special Districts 1,728

LEGISLATIVE BRANCH

Legislative Body .... General Assembly

President of the Senate ....Lt. Gov. Jim Cawley
President Pro Tem of the Senate...............Joseph B. Scarnati
Secretary-Parliamentarian of the Senate.................Mark R. Corrigan

Speaker of the House.. Samuel H. Smith
Chief Clerk of the House............................... Anthony Frank Barbush

2011 Regular Session...........................Jan. 4, 2011 – Meets year-round
Number of Senatorial Districts 50
Number of Representative Districts 203

EXECUTIVE BRANCH

Governor .... Tom Corbett
Lieutenant Governor .... Jim Cawley
Secretary of State.. Carol Aichele
Attorney General .... William H. Ryan Jr.
Treasurer..Robert McCord
Comptroller..Anna Marie Kiehl

Governor's Present Term........................... 1/2011 – 1/2015
Number of Elected Officials in the Executive Branch.........................5
Number of Members in the Cabinet 28

JUDICIAL BRANCH

Highest Court...Supreme Court
Supreme Court Chief Justice....................Ronald D. Castille
Number of Supreme Court Judges 7
Number of Intermediate Appellate Court Judges.............................23
Number of U.S. Court Districts...3
U.S. Circuit Court..3rd Circuit

STATE INTERNET ADDRESSES

Official State Website ....http://www.state.pa.us
Governor's Website ....http://www.governor.state.pa.us/
Legislative Website ....http://www.legis.state.pa.us
Judicial Website..................................... http://www.courts.state.pa.us

Rhode Island

Nicknames ....Little Rhody and Ocean State
Motto...*Hope*
Flower ....Violet
Bird...Rhode Island Red
Tree.. Red Maple
Song...*Rhode Island*
Entered the Union...May 29, 1790
Capital ....Providence

STATISTICS

Land Area (square miles) 1,034
Rank in Nation..50th
Population..1,052,567
Rank in Nation...43rd
Density per square mile 1,018.1
Capital City...Providence
Population...171,557
Rank in State..1st
Largest City..Providence
Number of Representatives in Congress 2
Number of 2012 Electoral Votes 4
Number of Geographic Counties...5
Number of County Governments..0
Number of Municipal Governments 8
Number of School Districts 4
Number of Special Districts 91

LEGISLATIVE BRANCH

Legislative Body .... General Assembly

President of the Senate .... M. Teresa Paiva-Weed
President Pro Tem of the Senate...............................Juan M. Pichardo
Secretary of the Senate ....Joseph Brady

Speaker of the House ....Gordon Fox
Speaker Pro Tem of the House ....Elaine A. Coderre
Clerk of the House ....Frank McCabe

2011 Regular Session.......................... Jan. 4 – Late June, 2011
Number of Senatorial Districts 38
Number of Representative Districts 75

EXECUTIVE BRANCH

Governor ....Lincoln D. Chafee
Lieutenant Governor ....Elizabeth H. Roberts
Secretary of State...Ralph Mollis
Attorney General.......................................Peter F. Kilmartin
Treasurer...Gina M. Raimondo
Auditor .... Dennis Hoyle
Controller ....Marc Leonetti

Governor's Present Term............................. 1/2011 – 1/2015
Number of Elected Officials in the Executive Branch........................5
Number of Members in the Cabinet 20

JUDICIAL BRANCH

Highest Court..Supreme Court
Supreme Court Chief Justice..........................Paul A. Suttell
Number of Supreme Court Judges 5
Number of Intermediate Appellate Court Judges 0
Number of U.S. Court Districts 1
U.S. Circuit Court..1st Circuit

STATE INTERNET ADDRESSES

Official State Website .... http://www.state.ri.us
Governor's Website ....http://www.governor.state.ri.us
Legislative Website .... http://www.rilin.state.ri.us
Judicial Website.................................http://www.courts.state.ri.us

South Carolina

Nickname.. The Palmetto State
Motto...*Animis Opibusque Parati*
(Prepared in Mind and Resources) and
Dum Spiro Spero (While I breathe, I Hope)
Flower .... Yellow Jessamine
Bird...Carolina Wren
Tree...Palmetto
Songs .... *Carolina* and *South Carolina on My Mind*
Entered the Union..May 23, 1788
Capital .... Columbia

STATISTICS

Land Area (square miles) 30,061
Rank in Nation..40th
Population..4,625,364
Rank in Nation...24th
Density per square mile 153.9
Capital City... Columbia
Population...127,029
Rank in State..1st
Largest City.. Columbia
Number of Representatives in Congress 7
Number of 2012 Electoral Votes 9
Number of County Governments..46
Number of Municipal Governments 268
Number of School Districts 85
Number of Special Districts 299

LEGISLATIVE BRANCH

Legislative Body .... General Assembly

President of the Senate ....Lt. Gov. Ken Ard
President Pro Tem of the Senate...........................Glenn F. McConnell
Clerk of the Senate................................Jeffrey S. Gossett

Speaker of the House............................ Robert W. Harrell Jr.
Speaker Pro Tem of the House ....James H. Lucas
Clerk of the House ....Charles F. Reid

2011 Regular Session...........................Jan. 11 – June 2, 2011
Number of Senatorial Districts 46
Number of Representative Districts 124

EXECUTIVE BRANCH

Governor .... Nikki Haley
Lieutenant Governor .... Ken Ard
Secretary of State.. Mark Hammond
Attorney General..Alan Wilson
Treasurer...Curtis Loftis
Auditor...Richard H. Gilbert Jr.
Comptroller..Richard Eckstrom

Governor's Present Term............................. 1/2011 – 1/2015
Number of Elected Officials in the Executive Branch........................9
Number of Members in the Cabinet 16

JUDICIAL BRANCH

Highest Court..Supreme Court
Supreme Court Chief Justice......................Jean Hoefer Toal
Number of Supreme Court Judges 5
Number of Intermediate Appellate Court Judges 10
Number of U.S. Court Districts 1
U.S. Circuit Court..4th Circuit

STATE INTERNET ADDRESSES

Official State Website .... http://www.sc.gov/
Governor's Website .... http://www.scgovernor.com
Legislative Website ....http://www.scstatehouse.net
Judicial Website...http://www.judicial.state.sc.us

South Dakota

Nickname..The Mt. Rushmore State
Motto.. *Under God the People Rule*
Flower ....American Pasque
Bird...Ring-necked Pheasant
Tree...Black Hills Spruce
Song.. *Hail, South Dakota*
Entered the Union...................................... November 2, 1889
Capital ....Pierre

STATISTICS

Land Area (square miles)...75,811
Rank in Nation 16th
Population...814,180
Rank in Nation 46th
Density per square mile 10.7
Capital City...Pierre
Population...13,899
Rank in State 7th
Largest City ....Sioux Falls
Population...154,997
Number of Representatives in Congress 1
Number of 2012 Electoral Votes..3
Number of County Governments..66
Number of Municipal Governments 309
Number of School Districts 166
Number of Special Districts 526

LEGISLATIVE BRANCH

Legislative Body ....Legislature

President of the Senate ....Lt. Gov. Matthew Michels
President Pro Tem of the Senate.. Bob Gray
Secretary of the Senate .... Trudy Evenstad

Speaker of the House...Val Rausch
Speaker Pro Tem of the House ....Brian G. Gosch
Chief Clerk of the House...Karen Gerdes

2011 Regular Session....................................Jan. 11 – March 28, 2011
Number of Senatorial Districts 35
Number of Representative Districts 35

EXECUTIVE BRANCH

Governor ....Dennis Daugaard
Lieutenant Governor ....Matthew Michels
Secretary of State...Jason M. Gant
Attorney General ....Martin Jackley
Treasurer...Rich Sattgast
Auditor...Steve Barnett

Governor's Present Term................................... 1/2011 – 1/2015
Number of Elected Officials in the Executive Branch........................7
Number of Members in the Cabinet 19

JUDICIAL BRANCH

Highest Court...Supreme Court
Supreme Court Chief Justice...................................David E. Gilbertson
Number of Supreme Court Judges 5
Number of Intermediate Appellate Court Judges................................0
Number of U.S. Court Districts...1
U.S. Circuit Court ....8th Circuit

STATE INTERNET ADDRESSES

Official State Website ....http://www.state.sd.us
Governor's Website .... http://www.state.sd.us/governor
Legislative Website ....http://legis.state.sd.us
Judicial Website..http://www.sdjudicial.com

Tennessee

Nickname..The Volunteer State
Motto...*Agriculture and Commerce*
Flower ....Iris
Bird...Mockingbird
Tree...Tulip Poplar
Songs .... *When It's Iris Time in Tennessee*;
The Tennessee Waltz; *My Homeland, Tennessee*;
My Tennessee; and *Rocky Top*;
Entered the Union..June 1, 1796
Capital .... Nashville

STATISTICS

Land Area (square miles)..41,235
Rank in Nation 34th
Population...6,346,105
Rank in Nation 17th
Density per square mile 153.9
Capital City...Nashville
Population...596,462
Rank in State 2nd
Largest City .... Memphis
Population...669,651
Number of Representatives in Congress 9
Number of 2012 Electoral Votes......................................11
Number of Geographic Counties..95
Number of County Governments....................................92
Number of Consolidated Governments....................................3
Number of Municipal Governments 347
Number of School Districts 14
Number of Special Districts 475

LEGISLATIVE BRANCH

Legislative Body .... General Assembly

Senate President .... Lt. Gov. Ron Ramsey
Speaker Pro Tem of the Senate..................................... Jamie Woodson
Chief Clerk of the Senate .... Russell Humphrey

Speaker of the House.. Beth Harwell
Speaker Pro Tem of the House ....Judd Matheny
Chief Clerk of the House.. Joe McCord

2011 Regular Session......................................Jan. 11 – mid-May, 2011
Number of Senatorial Districts 33
Number of Representative Districts 99

EXECUTIVE BRANCH

Governor .... Bill Haslam
Lieutenant Governor .... Ron Ramsey
Secretary of State... Tre Hargett
Attorney General .... Robert Cooper
Treasurer...David H. Lillard Jr.
Auditor.. Arthur A. Hayes Jr.
Comptroller ....Jan I. Sylvis

Governor's Present Term.................................... 1/2011 – 1/2015
Number of Elected Officials in the Executive Branch........................1
Number of Members in the Cabinet 28

JUDICIAL BRANCH

Highest Court...Supreme Court
Supreme Court Chief Justice...Cornelia Clark
Number of Supreme Court Judges 5
Number of Intermediate Appellate Court Judges..............................24
Number of U.S. Court Districts...3
U.S. Circuit Court...6th Circuit

STATE INTERNET ADDRESSES

Official State Website .... http://www.state.tn.us
Governor's Website ....http://www.state.tn.us/governor
Legislative Website ....http://www.legislature.state.tn.us
Judicial Website..http://www.tsc.state.tn.us

Texas

Nickname	The Lone Star State
Motto	*Friendship*
Flower	Bluebonnet (Buffalo Clover, Wolf Flower)
Bird	Mockingbird
Tree	Pecan
Song	*Texas, Our Texas*
Entered the Union	December 29, 1845
Capital	Austin

STATISTICS

Land Area (square miles)	261,232
Rank in Nation	2nd
Population	25,145,561
Rank in Nation	2nd
Density per square mile	96.3
Capital City	Austin
Population	757,688
Rank in State	4th
Largest City	Houston
Population	2,242,193
Number of Representatives in Congress	36
Number of 2012 Electoral Votes	38
Number of County Governments	254
Number of Municipal Governments	1,209
Number of School Districts	1,081
Number of Special Districts	2,291

LEGISLATIVE BRANCH

Legislative Body	Legislature
President of the Senate	Lt. Gov. David Dewhurst
President Pro Tem of the Senate	Steve Ogden
Secretary of the Senate	Patsy Spaw
Speaker of the House	Joe Straus
Speaker Pro Tem of the House	Craig Eiland
Chief Clerk of the House	Robert Haney
2011 Regular Session	Jan. 11 – May 30, 2011
Number of Senatorial Districts	31
Number of Representative Districts	150

EXECUTIVE BRANCH

Governor	Rick Perry
Lieutenant Governor	David Dewhurst
Secretary of State	Esperanza Andrade
Attorney General	Greg Abbott
Comptroller of Public Accounts	Susan Combs
Auditor	John Keel
Governor's Present Term	12/2000 – 1/2015
Number of Elected Officials in the Executive Branch	9
Number of Members in the Cabinet	No formal cabinet system

JUDICIAL BRANCH

Highest Court	Supreme Court
Supreme Court Chief Justice	Wallace B. Jefferson
Number of Supreme Court Judges	9
Number of Intermediate Appellate Court Judges	80
Number of U.S. Court Districts	4
U.S. Circuit Court	5th Circuit

STATE INTERNET ADDRESSES

Official State Website	http://www.state.tx.us
Governor's Website	http://www.governor.state.tx.us
Legislative Website	http://www.capitol.state.tx.us
Judicial Website	http://www.courts.state.tx.us

Utah

Nickname	The Beehive State
Motto	*Industry*
Flower	Sego Lily
Bird	California Seagull
Tree	Blue Spruce
Song	*Utah, We Love Thee*
Entered the Union	January 4, 1896
Capital	Salt Lake City

STATISTICS

Land Area (square miles)	82,170
Rank in Nation	12th
Population	2,763,885
Rank in Nation	34th
Density per square mile	33.6
Capital City	Salt Lake City
Population	181,698
Rank in State	1st
Largest City	Salt Lake City
Number of Representatives in Congress	4
Number of 2012 Electoral Votes	6
Number of County Governments	29
Number of Municipal Governments	242
Number of School Districts	40
Number of Special Districts	288

LEGISLATIVE BRANCH

Legislative Body	Legislature
President of the Senate	Michael G. Waddoups
Secretary of the Senate	Annette B. Moore
Speaker of the House	Rebecca D. Lockhart
Chief Clerk of the House	Sandy Tenney
2011 Regular Session	Jan. 24 – March 10, 2011
Number of Senatorial Districts	29
Number of Representative Districts	75

EXECUTIVE BRANCH

Governor	Gary R. Herbert
Lieutenant Governor	Gregory Bell
Attorney General	Mark L. Shurtleff
Treasurer	Richard Ellis
Auditor	Auston G. Johnson
Governor's Present Term	8/2009 – 1/2013
Number of Elected Officials in the Executive Branch	5
Number of Members in the Cabinet	21

JUDICIAL BRANCH

Highest Court	Supreme Court
Supreme Court Chief Justice	Christine M. Durham
Number of Supreme Court Judges	5
Number of Intermediate Appellate Court Judges	7
Number of U.S. Court Districts	1
U.S. Circuit Court	10th Circuit

STATE INTERNET ADDRESSES

Official State Website	http://www.utah.gov
Governor's Website	http://www.utah.gov/governor/
Legislative Website	http://www.le.state.ut.us
Judicial Website	http://www.utcourts.gov/

Vermont

Nickname..The Green Mountain State
Motto..*Freedom and Unity*
Flower .... Red Clover
Bird...Hermit Thrush
Tree.. Sugar Maple
Song..*Hail, Vermont!*
Entered the Union.. March 4, 1791
Capital..Montpelier

STATISTICS

Land Area (square miles)..9,217
Rank in Nation...43rd
Population...625,741
Rank in Nation..49th
Density per square mile 67.9
Capital City..Montpelier
Population..7,760
Rank in State...13th
Largest City...Burlington
Population..38,897
Number of Representatives in Congress 1
Number of 2012 Electoral Votes..3
Number of County Governments.......................................14
Number of Municipal Governments..................................45
Number of School Districts...293
Number of Special Districts 144

LEGISLATIVE BRANCH

Legislative Body .... General Assembly

President of the Senate ....Lt. Gov. Phil Scott
President Pro Tem of the Senate....................John F. Campbell
Secretary of the Senate ....John H. Bloomer Jr.

Speaker of the House.......................................Shap Smith
Clerk of the House .... Donald G. Milne

2011 Regular Session....................................Jan. 5 – May 6, 2011
Number of Senatorial Districts 13
Number of Representative Districts 106

EXECUTIVE BRANCH

Governor ....Peter E. Shumlin
Lieutenant Governor ....Phil Scott
Secretary of State ....Jim Condos
Attorney General ....William H. Sorrell
Treasurer...Elizabeth Pearce
Auditor...Thomas M. Salmon

Governor's Present Term.....................................1/2011 – 1/2013
Number of Elected Officials in the Executive Branch.......................6
Number of Members in the Cabinet 7

JUDICIAL BRANCH

Highest Court...Supreme Court
Supreme Court Chief Justice............................. Paul L. Reiber
Number of Supreme Court Judges 5
Total Number of Appellant Court Judges 0
Number of U.S. Court Districts...1
U.S. Circuit Court... 2nd Circuit

STATE INTERNET ADDRESSES

Official State Website .... http://vermont.gov
Governor's Website ....http://www.vermont.gov/governor/
Legislative Website......................................http://www.leg.state.vt.us
Judicial Website...................................http://www.vermontjudiciary.org

Virginia

Nickname.. The Old Dominion
Motto..........................*Sic Semper Tyrannis* (Thus Always to Tyrants)
Flower .... Dogwood
Bird... Cardinal
Tree.. Dogwood
Song, emeritus........................*Carry Me Back to Old Virginia*
Entered the Union...June 25, 1788
Capital .... Richmond

STATISTICS

Land Area (square miles)...39,490
Rank in Nation..36th
Population..8,001,024
Rank in Nation..12th
Density per square miles..202.6
Capital City... Richmond
Population...202,002
Rank in State...4th
Largest City ....Virginia Beach
Population...433,746
Number of Representatives in Congress 11
Number of 2012 Electoral Votes......................................13
Number of Geographic Counties.....................................95
Number of County Governments....................................95*
Number of Consolidated Governments...........................5*
Number of Municipal Governments 229
Number of School Districts...1
Number of Special Districts...186

LEGISLATIVE BRANCH

Legislative Body .... General Assembly

President of the Senate ....Lt. Gov. Bill Bolling
President Pro Tem of the Senate.................Charles J. Colgan
Clerk of the Senate.....................................Susan Clarke Schaar

Speaker of the House...............................William J. Howell
Clerk of the House ....Bruce F. Jamerson

2011 Regular Session.................... Jan. 12 – Feb. 27, 2011
Number of Senatorial Districts 40
Number of Representative Districts 100

EXECUTIVE BRANCH

Governor .... Bob McDonnell
Lieutenant Governor ....Bill Bolling
Secretary of the Commonwealth ....Janet Polarek
Attorney General ....Ken Cuccinelli
Treasurer...Manju Ganeriwala
Auditor.. Walter J. Kucharski
Comptroller ....David Von Moll

Governor's Present Term............................... 1/2010 – 1/2014
Number of Elected Officials in the Executive Branch.........................3
Number of Members in the Cabinet 14

JUDICIAL BRANCH

Highest Court...Supreme Court
Supreme Court Chief Justice.................... Cynthia D. Kinser
Number of Supreme Court Judges 7
Total Number of Appellant Court Judges 11
Number of U.S. Court Districts...2
U.S. Circuit Court... 4th Circuit

STATE INTERNET ADDRESSES

Official State Website ....http://www.virginia.gov
Governor's Website ....http://www.governor.virginia.gov/
Legislative Website ....http://legis.state.va.us
Judicial Website...http://www.courts.state.va.us

*In addition to 95 counties, Virginia has 39 Independent Cities,
considered county equivalents. Five cities in the Hampton Roads
area were formed of entire counties and function at the county
level of government. They are listed with the Independent Cities but
counted as consolidated governments in Virginia.

Washington

Nickname...The Evergreen State
Motto......................*Alki* (Chinook Indian word meaning *By and By*)
Flower ....Coast Rhododendron
Bird..Willow Goldfinch
Tree.. Western Hemlock
Song...*Washington, My Home*
Entered the Union...November 11, 1889
Capital.. Olympia

STATISTICS

Land Area (square miles)...66,456
Rank in Nation...20th
Population...6,724,540
Rank in Nation...13th
Density per square mile 101.2
Capital City.. Olympia
Population...45,322
Rank in State...18th
Largest City ....Seattle
Population...598,541
Number of Representatives in Congress 10
Number of 2012 Electoral Votes..12
Number of County Governments...39
Number of Municipal Governments...................................281
Number of School Districts...296
Number of Special Districts 1,229

LEGISLATIVE BRANCH

Legislative Body .... Legislature

President of the Senate ....Lt. Gov. Brad Owen
President Pro Tem of the Senate............................Margarita Prentice
Secretary of the Senate .... Tom Hoemann

Speaker of the House .... Frank Chopp
Speaker Pro Tem of the House ....Jim Mueller
Chief Clerk of the House...Barbara Baker

2011 Regular Session........................Jan. 10 – April 22, 2011
Number of Senatorial Districts 49
Number of Representative Districts 49

EXECUTIVE BRANCH

Governor ....Christine O. Gregoire
Lieutenant Governor .... Brad Owen
Secretary of State..Sam Reed
Attorney General ....Rob McKenna
Treasurer...James McIntire
Auditor..Brian Sonntag
Director of Office of Financial Management .... Marty Brown

Governor's Present Term.............................. 1/2005 – 1/2013
Number of Elected Officials in the Executive Branch.........................9
Number of Members in the Cabinet 28

JUDICIAL BRANCH

Highest Court...Supreme Court
Supreme Court Chief Justice.....................Barbara A. Madsen
Number of Supreme Court Judges 9
Total Number of Appellant Court Judges 22
Number of U.S. Court Districts...2
U.S. Circuit Court... 9th Circuit

STATE INTERNET ADDRESSES

Official State Website ....http://access.wa.gov
Governor's Website .... http://www.governor.wa.gov
Legislative Website ....http://www.leg.wa.gov
Judicial Website.. http://www.courts.wa.gov

West Virginia

Nickname..The Mountain State
Motto..*Montani Semper Liberi*
(Mountaineers Are Always Free)
Flower ....Rhododendron
Bird .... Cardinal
Tree .... Sugar Maple
Songs ....*West Virginia, My Home Sweet Home*;
The West Virginia Hills; and
This is My West Virginia
Entered the Union...June 20, 1863
Capital.. Charleston

STATISTICS

Land Area (square miles)...24,038
Rank in Nation...41st
Population...1,852,994
Rank in Nation...37th
Density per square mile 77.1
Capital City... Charleston
Population...50,302
Rank in State...1st
Largest City .... Charleston
Number of Representatives in Congress 3
Number of 2012 Electoral Votes..5
Number of County Governments...55
Number of Municipal Governments...................................232
Number of School Districts...55
Number of Special Districts 321

LEGISLATIVE BRANCH

Legislative Body .... Legislature

Acting President of the Senate ....Jeffrey V. Kessler
President Pro Tem of the Senate...................................Brooks McCabe
Clerk of the Senate..Darrell E. Holmes

Speaker of the House of Delegates .... Richard Thompson
Speaker Pro Tem of the House of Delegates ....Ron Fragale
Clerk of the House of Delegates .... Gregory M. Gray

2011 Regular Session.......................Jan. 12 – March 18, 2011
Number of Senatorial Districts 17
Number of Representative Districts 58

EXECUTIVE BRANCH

Governor ....Earl Ray Tomblin
Lieutenant Governor ....Jeffrey V. Kessler
Secretary of State..Natalie Tennant
Attorney General .... Darrell V. McGraw Jr.
Treasurer...John D. Perdue
Auditor...Glen B. Ganier III

Governor's Present Term.............................. 11/2010 – 1/2013
Number of Elected Officials in the Executive Branch.........................6
Number of Members in the Cabinet 9

JUDICIAL BRANCH

Highest Court..Supreme Court of Appeals
Supreme Court of Appeals Chief Justice ....Margaret L. Workman
Number of Supreme Court of Appeals Judges 5
Total Number of Appellant Court Judges 0
Number of U.S. Court Districts...2
U.S. Circuit Court.. 4th Circuit

STATE INTERNET ADDRESSES

Official State Website ....http://www.wv.gov/
Governor's Website .... http://www.wvgov.org/
Legislative Website ....http://www.legis.state.wv.us/
Judicial Website.......................................http://www.state.wv.us/wvsca/

Wisconsin

Nickname*... The Badger State
Motto... *Forward*
Flower...Wood Violet
Bird...Robin
Tree... Sugar Maple
Song...*On, Wisconsin!*
Entered the Union... May 29, 1848
Capitol... Madison

*unofficial

STATISTICS

Land Area (square miles)..54,158
Rank in Nation...25th
Population..5,686,986
Rank in Nation...20th
Density per square mile...105
Capital City... Madison
Population..231,916
Rank in State..2nd
Largest City.. Milwaukee
Population..604,477
Number of Representatives in Congress 8
Number of 2012 Electoral Votes...10
Number of County Governments..72
Number of Municipal Governments 592
Number of School Districts 441
Number of Special Districts 756

LEGISLATIVE BRANCH

Legislative Body ....Legislature

President of the Senate ....Michael G. Ellis
President Pro Tem of the Senate...........................Joseph K. Leibham
Chief Clerk of the Senate ....Robert J. Marchant

Speaker of the Assembly ....Jeff Fitzgerald
Speaker Pro Tem of the Assembly.........................Bill Kramer
Chief Clerk of the Assembly ....Patrick Fuller

2011 Regular Session...........................Jan. 11, 2011 – Meets year-round
Number of Senatorial Districts 33
Number of Representative Districts 99

EXECUTIVE BRANCH

Governor .... Scott K. Walker
Lieutenant Governor ....Rebecca Kleefisch
Secretary of State.....................................Douglas LaFollette
Attorney General .... J.B. Van Hollen
Treasurer... Kurt W. Schuller
Auditor..Janice L. Mueller
Controller .... Steve Censky

Governor's Present Term...................................... 1/2011 – 1/2015
Number of Elected Officials in the Executive Branch.........................6
Number of Members in the Cabinet 16

JUDICIAL BRANCH

Highest Court...Supreme Court
Supreme Court Chief Justice............................ Shirley S. Abrahamson
Number of Supreme Court Judges 7
Total Number of Appellant Court Judges 16
Number of U.S. Court Districts..2
U.S. Circuit Court.. 7th Circuit

STATE INTERNET ADDRESSES

Official State Website ....http://www.wisconsin.gov
Governor's Website ....http://www.wisgov.state.wi.us
Legislative Website ....http://www.legis.state.wi.us
Judicial Website..http://www.courts.state.wi.us

Wyoming

Nicknames ....The Equality State and The Cowboy State
Motto... *Equal Rights*
Flower... Indian Paintbrush
Bird.. Western Meadowlark
Tree..Cottonwood
Song.. *Wyoming*
Entered the Union..July 10, 1890
Capital ....Cheyenne

STATISTICS

Land Area (square miles)..97,093
Rank in Nation...9th
Population..563,626
Rank in Nation...50th
Density per square mile..14.1
Capital City...Cheyenne
Population..56,915
Rank in State..1st
Largest City...Cheyenne
Number of Representatives in Congress 1
Number of 2012 Electoral Votes...3
Number of County Governments..23
Number of Municipal Governments 99
Number of School Districts 55
Number of Special Districts 549

LEGISLATIVE BRANCH

Legislative Body ....Legislature

President of the Senate ....Jim Anderson
Vice President of the Senate .... Philip A. Nicholas
Chief Clerk of the Senate ....Diane Harvey

Speaker of the House.............................. Edward Buchanan
Speaker Pro Tem of the House ....Keith Gingery
Chief Clerk of the House..............................Patricia Benskin

2011 Regular Session.......................................Jan. 11 – March 3, 2011
Number of Senatorial Districts 30
Number of Representative Districts 60

EXECUTIVE BRANCH

Governor ....Matthew Mead
Secretary of State.. Max Maxfield
Attorney General .... Bruce A. Salzburg
Treasurer..Joseph B. Meyer
Auditor .... Cynthia Cloud

Governor's Present Term...................................... 1/2011 – 1/2015
Number of Elected Officials in the Executive Branch.........................5
Number of Members in the Cabinet 20

JUDICIAL BRANCH

Highest Court...Supreme Court
Supreme Court Chief Justice.......................... Marilyn S. Kite
Number of Supreme Court Judges 5
Total Number of Appellant Court Judges 0
Number of U.S. Court Districts..1
U.S. Circuit Court.. 10th Circuit

STATE INTERNET ADDRESSES

Official State Website .... http://www.state.wy.us
Governor'sWebsite...http://governor.wy.gov/
Legislative Website .... http://legisweb.state.wy.us
Judicial Website...http://www.courts.state.wy.us

District of Columbia

Motto..*Justitia Omnibus* (Justice to All)
Flower .... American Beauty Rose
Bird... Wood Thrush
Tree.. Scarlet Oak
Became U.S. Capital ....December 1, 1800

STATISTICS

Land Area (square miles)...61
Population...601,723
Density per square mile 9,856.5
Delegate to Congress* 1
Number of 2012 Electoral Votes..3
Number of Municipal Governments 1
Number of School Districts 1
Number of Special Districts 0

*Committee voting privileges only.

LEGISLATIVE BRANCH

Legislative Body .... Council of the District of Columbia

Chair..Kwame R. Brown
Chair Pro Tem .... Mary M. Cheh
Secretary to the Council .... Nyasha Smith
2011 Regular Session.............................Jan. 3, 2011 – Meets year-round

EXECUTIVE BRANCH

Mayor.. Vincent C. Gray
Secretary of the District of Columbia ....Cynthia Brock-Smith
Attorney General .... Irvin Nathan
Chief Financial Officer....................................Natwar Gandhi
Auditor..Deborah Nichols

Mayor's Present Term .... 1/2011 – 1/2015
Number of Elected Officials in the Executive Branch.......................10
Number of Members in the Cabinet 10

JUDICIAL BRANCH

Highest Court... D.C. Court of Appeals
Court of Appeals Chief Justice .... Eric Washington
Number of Court of Appeals Judges.....................................9
Number of U.S. Court Districts 1

INTERNET ADDRESSES

Official Website ....http://www.dc.gov/
Mayor's Website....................................http://dc.gov/mayor/index.shtm
Legislative Website ....http://www.dccouncil.washington.dc.us
Judicial Website.................http://www.dccourts.gov/dccourts/index.jsp

American Samoa

Motto........................*Samoa-Maumua le Atua* (In Samoa, God Is First)
Flower .... Paogo (Ula-fala)
Plant ....Ava
Song..*Amerika Samoa*
Became a Territory of the United States 1900
Capital.. Pago Pago

STATISTICS

Land Area (square miles) 77
Population...65,628
Density per square mile 852.3
Capital City.. Pago Pago
Population...4,278
Rank in Territory 3rd
Largest City ....Tafuna
Population...8,409
Delegate to Congress* 1
Number of School Districts 1

*Committee voting privileges only.

LEGISLATIVE BRANCH

Legislative Body ....Legislature

President of the Senate ....Gaoteote P.T. Gaoteote
President Pro Tem of the Senate.......................Tulifua Tini Lam Yuen
Secretary of the Senate ....Leo'o V. Ma'o

Speaker of the House.. Savali Talavou Ale
Chief Clerk of the House...Fialupe Lutu

2011 Regular Session...Jan. 10, 2011 – TBD
Number of Senatorial Districts..12
Number of Representative Districts 17

EXECUTIVE BRANCH

Governor ....Togiola T.A. Tulafono
Lieutenant Governor .... Ipulasi Aito Sunia
Attorney General .... Fepulea'i Afa Ripley Jr.
Treasurer .... Magalei Logovi'i

Governor's Present Term... 4/2003 – 1/2013
Number of Members in the Cabinet 16

JUDICIAL BRANCH

Highest Court...High Court
High Court Chief Justice.. F. Michael Kruse
Number of High Court Judges 6

INTERNET ADDRESSES

Official Website ....http://americansamoa.gov/
Governor's Website .... http://www.asg-gov.net/
Legislative Website .... http://www.government.as/legislative.htm
Judicial Website...http://www.asbar.org/

Guam

Nickname	Hub of the Pacific
Flower	Puti Tai Nobio (Bougainvillea)
Bird	Totot (Fruit Dove)
Tree	Ifit (Intsiabijuga)
Song	*Stand Ye Guamanians*
Stone	Latte
Animal	Iguana
Ceded to the United States by Spain	December 10, 1898
Became a Territory	August 1, 1950
Request to become a Commonwealth Plebiscite	November 1987
Capital	Hagatna

STATISTICS

Land Area (square miles)	210
Population	178,430
Density per square mile	849.7
Capital	Hagatna
Population	1,122
Rank in Territory	13th
Largest City	Tamuning
Population	10,833
Delegate to Congress*	1
Number of School Districts	1

*Committee voting privileges only.

LEGISLATIVE BRANCH

Legislative Body	Legislature
Speaker	Judith T. Won Pat
Vice Speaker	Benjamin J.F. Cruz
Clerk of the Legislature	Patricia C. Santos
2011 Regular Session	Jan. 10, 2011 – Meets year-round
Number of Senatorial Districts	15

EXECUTIVE BRANCH

Governor	Edward J.B. Calvo
Lieutenant Governor	Ray Tenorio
Attorney General	Leonardo Rapadas
Treasurer	Rose T. Fejeran
Auditor	Doris Flores Brooks
Governor's Present Term	1/2011 – 1/2015
Number of Elected Officials in the Executive Branch	10
Number of Members in the Cabinet	55

JUDICIAL BRANCH

Highest Court	Supreme Court
Supreme Court Chief Justice	F. Phillip Carbullido
Number of Supreme Court Judges	3

INTERNET ADDRESSES

Official Website	http://ns.gov.gu
Governor's Website	http://www.guamgovernor.net/
Legislative Website	http://www.guamlegislature.com/#
Judicial Website	http://www.justice.gov.gu

Northern Mariana Islands

Flower	Plumeria
Bird	Marianas Fruit Dove
Tree	Flame Tree
Song	*Gi Talo Gi Halom Tasi*
Administered by the United States a trusteeship for the United Nations	July 18, 1947
Voters approved a proposed constitution	June 1975
U.S. president signed covenant agreeing to commonwealth status for the islands	March 24, 1976
Became a self-governing Commonwealth	January 9, 1978
Capital	Saipan

STATISTICS

Land Area (square miles)	179
Population	88,662
Density per square mile	495.3
Capital City	Saipan
Population	62,392
Largest City	Saipan
Delegate to Congress*	1
Number of School Districts	1

*Committee voting privileges only.

LEGISLATIVE BRANCH

Legislative Body	Legislature
President of the Senate	Paul A. Manglona
Vice President of the Senate	Jude Hofschneider
Clerk of the Senate	Doris Bermudes
Speaker of the House	Eliceo D. Cabrera
Vice Speaker of the House	Felicidad T. Ogumoro
Clerk of the House	Linda B. Muna
2011 Regular Session	Jan. 10, 2011 – TBD
Number of Senatorial Districts	9
Number of Representative Districts	18

EXECUTIVE BRANCH

Governor	Benigno R. Fitial
Lieutenant Governor	Eloy S. Inos
Attorney General	Edward T. Buckingham
Treasurer	Antoinette S. Calvo
Governor's Present Term	1/2006 – 1/2015
Number of Elected Officials in the Executive Branch	10
Number of Members in the Cabinet	16

JUDICIAL BRANCH

Highest Court	Commonwealth Supreme Court
Commonwealth Supreme Court Chief Justice	Miguel S. Demapan
Number of Commonwealth Supreme Court Judges	3

INTERNET ADDRESSES

Official Website	www.gksoft.com/govt/en/mp.html
Governor's Website	http://www.gov.mp/
Legislative Website	http://www.cnmileg.gov.mp
Judicial Website	http://cnmilaw.org/htmlpage/hpg34.htm

Puerto Rico

Nickname...Island of Enchantment
Motto...*Joannes Est Nomen Ejus*
(John is His Name)
Flower ....Maga
Bird...Reinita
Tree... Ceiba
Song...*La Borinqueña*
Became a Territory of the United States ....December 10, 1898
Became a self-governing Commonwealth ....July 25, 1952
Capital.. San Juan

STATISTICS

Land Area (square miles)..3,424
Population...3,725,789
Density per square mile 1,088.2
Capital City... San Juan
Population...434,919
Largest City .... San Juan
Resident Commissioner in Congress*..1
Number of School Districts 1

*Committee voting privileges only.

LEGISLATIVE BRANCH

Legislative Body ....Legislative Assembly

President of the Senate ....Thomas Rivera Schatz
Vice President of the Senate .... Margarita Nolasco Santiago
Secretary of the Senate ....Manuel A. Torres Nieves

Speaker of the House ....Jenniffer González-Colón
Speaker Pro Tem ....Gabriel Rodriguez Aguilo
Clerk of the House ....Brunilda Ortiz-Rodriguez

2011 Regular Session............................. Jan. 10 – June 30, 2011

EXECUTIVE BRANCH

Governor ....Luis Fortuño
Secretary of State.. Kenneth McClintock
Attorney General .... Guillermo Somoza Colombani
Treasurer.. Juan Carlos Puig

Governor's Present Term.. 1/2009 – 1/2013
Number of Elected Officials in the Executive Branch.......................10
Number of Members in the Cabinet 10

JUDICIAL BRANCH

Highest Court...Supreme Court
Supreme Court Chief Justice.................Frederico Hernandez-Denton
Number of Supreme Court Judges 7

INTERNET ADDRESSES

Official State Website ....http://www.gobierno.pr/gprportal/inicio
Governor's Website .... http://www.fortaleza.gobierno.pr
Senate Website ....http://www.senadopr.us/Pages/default.aspx
House Website.....................http://www.camaraderepresentantes.org/
Judicial Website...http://www.tribunalpr.org

U.S. Virgin Islands

Nickname...The American Paradise
Motto.. *United in Pride and Hope*
Flower .... The Yellow Cedar
Bird...Yellow Breast or Banana Quit
Song... *Virgin Islands March*
Purchased from Denmark .... March 31, 1917
Capital...Charlotte Amalie, St. Thomas

STATISTICS

Land Area (square miles)*...134
Population...109,825
Density per square mile 819.6
Capital City..Charlotte Amalie, St. Thomas
Population...18,914
Largest City ....Charlotte Amalie, St. Thomas
Delegate to Congress** 1
Number of School Districts 1

*The U.S. Virgin Islands is comprised of three large islands (St. Croix, St. John, and St. Thomas) and 50 smaller islands and cays.

**Committee voting privileges only.

LEGISLATIVE BRANCH

Legislative Body ....Legislature

President .... Ronald E. Russell
Vice President ....Louis Patrick Hill
Legislative Secretary of the Senate .... Sammuel Sanes

2011 Regular Session......................... Jan.10, 2011 – Meets year-round

EXECUTIVE BRANCH

Governor ....John De Jongh Jr.
Lieutenant Governor .... Gregory Francis
Attorney General ....Vincent Frazer
Commissioner of Finance .... Laurel Payne

Governor's Present Term....................................... 1/2007 – 1/2015
Number of Elected Officials in the Executive Branch......................10
Number of Members in the Cabinet 21

JUDICIAL BRANCH

Highest Court..Territorial Court
Territorial Court Chief Justice ....Rhys S. Hodge
Number of Territorial Court Judges 3
U.S. Circuit Court...3rd

INTERNET ADDRESSES

Official Website .... http://www.statelocalgov.net/other-vi.CFM
Governor's Website .... www.governordejongh.com/
Legislative Website ....http://www.legvi.org/
Judicial Website..http://www.vid.uscourts.gov

Index

—G—